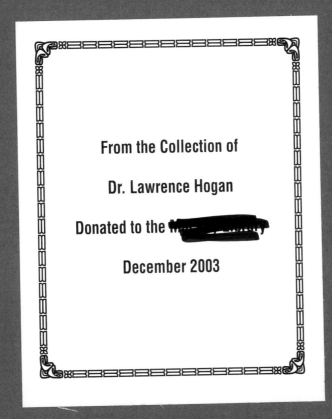

WESTERN CIVILIZATION

The Struggle for Empire to
Europe in the Modern World

WESTERN

Michael Ayrton: *Daedalus I*, 1960, bronze.

WILLIAM L. LANGER   General Editor

COOLIDGE PROFESSOR OF HISTORY, EMERITUS   HARVARD UNIVERSITY

PAUL MacKENDRICK   UNIVERSITY OF WISCONSIN
DENO J. GEANAKOPLOS   YALE UNIVERSITY
J. H. HEXTER   YALE UNIVERSITY
RICHARD PIPES   HARVARD UNIVERSITY

CIVILIZATION

THE STRUGGLE FOR EMPIRE
TO EUROPE IN THE MODERN WORLD

A HARPER-AMERICAN HERITAGE TEXTBOOK
American Heritage Publishing Co., Inc.   New York
Harper & Row, Publishers, Incorporated   New York and London

This book was prepared under the joint direction of
Alfred E. Prettyman of Harper & Row and Stephen W. Sears of American Heritage.
The text was edited by Jere Grant and Firth Fabend of Harper & Row.
American Heritage staff as follows:
Design and layout, Jean Brock and Harriet Cole, assisted by Karen G. Bowen.
Portfolio text, John Terry Chase and Dennis A. Dinan.
Copy editing and scheduling, Annette Welles.
Picture research, Mary Sherman Parsons (Chief) and Margaretta Barton.
Map research, Lucia Scala.
Editorial assistants, Sally Tyson and Nancy Richardson.

Maps by Francis & Shaw

In addition to the sources listed in the credits accompanying
the illustrations, special acknowledgment is made to the
Service Photographique of the Bibliothèque Nationale, to the
Trustees of the British Museum, and to the European bureau
of American Heritage, Gertrudis Feliu, Chief.

The map on page 310 and those on page 438 were adapted from *Atlas of World History*,
R.R. Palmer ed., © 1957 by Rand McNally & Company

The authors make grateful acknowledgment to:
Chatto & Windus Ltd., London, England: for the poems "Dulce et Decorum Est"
(pages 599–600) and "The End" (page 609) from *The Poems of Wilfred Owen*, edited by
Edmund Blunden (London: Chatto & Windus Ltd., 1921); also reprinted by permission
of New Directions Publishing Corporation, New York, N.Y. Thomas Nelson & Sons Ltd.,
London, England: the poem "1914" (pages 598–599) from *Poems of Rupert Brooke*
(London: Nelson, 1952). Reprinted by permission of Thomas Nelson & Sons Ltd.
Siegfried Sassoon: the poem "Attack" (page 599) and a selection from
Collected Poems, 1908–1956, by Siegfried Sassoon (London: Faber & Faber Ltd., 1961).
Reprinted by permission of the author.

Preface

The body of historical knowledge is now so great and is increasing at such a tempo that it has become all but impossible for any single human mind to encompass it. However desirable a survey of Western civilization written by one hand and reflecting one over-all interpretation might be, the demands of competent scholarship dictate that the assignment should be divided among at least several scholars conversant with the various major phases of historical development.

The present work is the product of four outstanding authorities in the various sectors. Professor Paul MacKendrick of the University of Wisconsin, who has published several books on classical archaeology, is responsible for the entire ancient section—the early cultures of the Middle East, of Egypt, and of Greece and Rome. Only a few short passages of his section, dealing chiefly with religion, science, philosophy, and literature, are from manuscript material by Professor J. H. Hexter, the author of a later division of the work.

The medieval section, reaching from the fall of Rome through the Renaissance, is the work of Professor Deno J. Geanakoplos of Yale University, an authority on Byzantine history, who has written and published books and articles on the impact of Eastern culture on the West.

Professor J. H. Hexter, also of Yale University, is a well-known expert on Tudor and Stuart history and on the early modern history of Europe in general. He carries the story from the point where Professor Geanakoplos leaves off to about the year 1800, when Napoleon took over the heritage of the French Revolution.

The longest section, covering the nineteenth and twentieth centuries, is the work of Professor Richard Pipes of Harvard University, whose specialty is Russian history. Eastern Europe is given rather more attention in this survey than is customary. Furthermore, Professor Pipes, in his concluding chapters, has made a valiant attempt to establish a synthesis of the trends and problems of the contemporary world.

The present book is distinguished not only by the high quality of the text but by the exceptionally voluminous and beautiful illustrative material. It is based squarely on the proposition that pictures can be as eloquent as words and can often convey more of the atmosphere of the past than can any amount of text. This is particularly true if the pictures are contemporary and authentic. The portfolios in this survey represent a pioneer effort to cover certain topics of major interest and importance in a coherent and convincing way.

WILLIAM L. LANGER

Table of Contents

The Problem of Reform; Enlightened Despotism; Frederick the Great and Prussia; Catherine the Great and Russia; Joseph II and the Hapsburg Empire; Enlightened Despotism in Ideal and Actuality; The Ambiguities of the Enlightenment

Similarities in Government and Society; Diversities in Government and Society; The Collapse of Poland; The Ancien Régime in France; The Inimitable English; Power Conflicts of European States in the Eighteenth Century; Revolution in North America, 1763–1788

The Era of Revolution; The Fiscal Crisis and the Revolt of the Privileged; The Estates General and the Bourgeois Revolt; Revolution by Consent of the Bourgeoisie; The Organization of Villainy; The Thermidorean Reaction; The Fruit of the Revolution

Napoleon's Rise to Power; From Consulate to Empire; Mastery of Europe; The Rise of Modern Nationalism; Disaster in Russia; The Achievement and Reputation of Napoleon

Ideological Controversies; The Peace Settlement; The Conflict of Liberal and Conservative Forces; Reaction and Reform in Britain; The Decline of the French Monarchy; The West Against the East

The Meaning of Industrialization; Technological Progress; The Spread of Industrialism to the Continent; Economic Liberalism; The Social Consequences of Early Industrialization

The Romantic Ideal; Literature and the Theater; Music, Painting, and Architecture; Philosophic Idealism; Historicism; Religion; The Historic Significance of Romanticism

The Revolutions of 1848; The Causes of Liberal Ascendancy; Mid-Victorian England; The Second Empire in France; The Risorgimento; The Papacy; The Unification of Germany; The Austro-Hungarian Empire; The Great Reforms in Russia; The Ottoman Empire

The Decline of Romanticism; Atoms, Cells, and Energy; The Theory of "Natural Selection"; Science and Philosophy; Social Science; Science and Religion; Realism in Literature; Voices of Opposition

How History is Written

Students entering college often resent historical study. Some actively dislike the subject and submit to the required history course as a necessary evil. Yet many of them soon become converted. They enroll in further courses, even when they are overcrowded, and frequently choose history as their major. Obviously there is a situation here which calls for explanation.

The common complaint, especially among students, is that the history work of the high school is a stultifying business of memorizing unrelated and meaningless facts and more particularly dates, dates, dates. Where this is so it is often a reflection of incompetent teaching, of inadequate training, and of a truly pathetic lack of understanding. It is tragic indeed when the study of the past, so much of it exciting and fascinating, is reduced to learning by rote.

Fortunately most college teachers of the subject are professionals who give much of their time and a good deal of their thought to the problems of history and to the methods of presenting them in speech or in writing. When the student discovers that mere facts and dates are only minor features of historical study, when he is introduced to some of the basic forces and obstacles in human development and comes to realize the endless complexities of the past and their bearing on the present, his eyes are opened and his attitude changed. Even those who do not choose history as their field of concentration frequently retain throughout their lives a genuine interest in historical literature and in the background of contemporary issues. In the United States, for example, there are thousands of people who can be counted on to buy new books on the Civil War and who have, in fact, an impressive, intimate knowledge of the subject.

Most men and women appear to have an innate interest in the past, just as they have a profound concern for the future. They abhor the notion of human life as a fleeting episode in the never-ending flux of time, much as they dread isolation from others of their kind. If family history is a subject of perennial interest, the past experiences of the community also have a deep and abiding significance for the individual. Even the most primitive tribes have bards or medicine men who uphold the traditions of the tribe and recite the exploits of its ancestors, in some cases over a period of centuries. Stories of the creation and of the descent of mankind from the gods are characteristic of most cultures. These are chiefly legends, not history, but they do reveal man's insatiable craving to extend the range of his experience and to find for himself a place in the course of time.

It is certainly true that we live in a historical age, that is, in a period when history is rated high and when much time and effort are devoted to the furtherance of historical knowledge. Yet, strange though it may seem, this habit of thinking in historical terms, this "historical-mindedness" and this systematic pursuit of knowledge of the past, is relatively recent, dating back less than two centuries. Early ages appear to have been quite content with myth and legend as explanations of their past. Neither the Babylonians nor the Egyptians had any real knowledge of their history. The same might be said of the Greeks and the Romans; the first great historians, Herodotus and Thucydides, who did so much to record the doings of men rather than of gods, treated of their own time in a critical way but had little interest and no competence in reviewing the past.

It is quite possible that the almost insuperable difficulty in the way of finding a reference point in time, to which the events of the past could be related, had something to do with what seems like a strange lack of historical-mindedness. The solar year is of awkward length, being not 365 1/4 days, but 365 days, 5 hours, 48 minutes, and 46 seconds and corresponding in no way with the lunar year of 354 days. It was only in the mid-fourth century B.C. that Timaeus of Sicily managed to correlate the numerous local chronologies and establish the first Olympiad (747 B.C.) as the point of departure. The Romans chose the legendary date of the founding of their city (753 B.C.) as their basic date and in 46 B.C. Caesar, with the help of Greek astronomers, was able to improve the Egyptian year of 365 days by providing for the addition of one day every fourth year (leap year of the Julian Calendar). The Christian practice of dating events before and after the birth of Christ (B.C. and A.D.) was established only in the early fourth century A.D. by Saint Eusebius. Ultimately, in 1582, Pope Gregory made the final improvement on Caesar's reform by omitting the extra day whenever leap year came on the century. The "new style" (Gregorian Calendar) was rejected by Protestant Britain until the eighteenth century, when Britain had fallen eleven days behind other countries, and was adopted by Orthodox Russia only after the Revolution of 1917. Since that time it has been adopted widely even in the non-Christian world.

This brief excursus will serve not only to illustrate the great difficulties in the way of measuring time, but also to point out the confusion of dates which is one of the plagues afflicting the historian. Many historical dates, even some of those marking the reigns of monarchs, are still uncertain and, it may be added, not very important. It is obviously desirable to fix the dates of specific events accurately, but since this is at times impossible, it is worth recalling that the sequence of events is generally the more significant. The relative dates of Hus, Wycliffe, and Luther are far more important than the specific dates for any one of them.

With the emergence of historical-mindedness and the professional study of history ("historicism") in the Western world there came in the nineteenth century a vast expansion of the scope and time span of history. In classical and medieval times and well into the modern period the chronicles of the past dealt primarily with the activities of the upmost social stratum: the ruler and his court, the palace struggles for influence and power, the disputed successions, the dynastic marriages, and, above all, the prince's conquests of territory and enslavement of peoples. Only with the rise of the middle classes and the emergence of the lower classes as a political force did the field of history expand. Economic and social forces were brought within its purview. Attention was given increasingly to the movement of ideas and their impact, whether political, religious, social, or scientific.

Present-day interests and problems invariably react upon historical attitudes, and new techniques open up new avenues of research. In an age of science much more attention is being devoted to the history of science than ever before. Current concern with the problem of overpopulation has greatly stimulated historical demography, which in turn has created interest in the history of famine and disease. Aerial photography has revealed, everywhere in Europe, the traces of numerous villages abandoned in the Middle Ages, throwing additional light not only on the organization of rural society but also on the movement of population. These are merely random examples of the strikingly rapid extension of the scope of history. Ever greater efforts are being made to see human activities and social organization in all their aspects, to integrate the history of thought and literature and art with the more traditional political, military, religious approach and, most recently, to bring the findings of psychology to bear on the explanation of individual action and collective behavior.

The time span of history has been correspondingly enlarged through the achievements of biblical scholarship and the discoveries of geologists, biologists, archaeologists, and anthropologists. Hardly more than a century ago it was still generally believed, on the basis of biblical chronology, that the world was created in the year 4004 B.C., and that the last day was probably not far off. The historian, therefore, had only the developments of about 6,000 years to concern himself with. Since then science has demonstrated that the earth is probably some billions of years old, that it was not created by one supreme divine act, and that modern man (*homo sapiens*) is the product of age-long evolution over a period of perhaps some two million years.

The evidence for the early history of the race is, to be sure, scanty indeed, consisting mainly of skeletal fragments and crude artifacts. No doubt there will be further important finds, as there have been in Africa in recent years. But it is unlikely that the record will ever be anything but meager—too meager to enable the historian to construct even an outline story of human development. It is a sad but inescapable conclusion that by far the larger part of man's past will remain closed to the historian and continue to be the domain of the anthropologist and paleontologist.

History, it has often been said, can deal only with such events as have left remains or records of some kind. This being so, it must be admitted that the time span of historical knowledge does not reach back much farther than 10,000 years, for several thousand of which the evidence is sketchy, to say the least. The famous cave paintings of France and Spain reveal the fact that European man of 10,000 or 12,000 B.C. had already reached a stage of astonishingly advanced artistic achievement. He obviously lived in caves and hunted. Beyond that the paintings tell us nothing—nothing of his social organization, his language, his religion, his experiences. Only the discovery and deciphering of tens of thousands of inscribed clay tablets in the Tigris-Euphrates Valley, together with somewhat later papyri records in Egypt have, within the last century and a half, given us real insight into the life of Near Eastern man in times as remote as 4000 B.C. These tablets, for the most part everyday business records, were preserved merely through chance, that is, through the extreme dryness of the climate. They were never intended for the historian of the future, yet they reveal to us the existence of well-organized cities and states with highly developed religion and literature, great artistic competence, sophisticated economic life, and elaborate legal systems. In short, for the historian human society springs fully developed out of the darkness of prehistoric time. The transition from the hunting to the settled agricultural society is still shrouded in obscurity, though the frontier of knowledge is constantly being advanced through new researches and discoveries.

Within the modest time span susceptible of systematic study the constant enrichment of the subject matter has made the historian's task more fascinating and rewarding, but also more difficult. He is being increasingly swamped with data of all kinds, even for the earliest period, where the mountains of cuneiform tablets demand long and arduous effort in deciphering and collating. More and more and in many ways the historian is having to accept limitations on his work. Ideally he should personally command all pertinent knowledge. Actually he is obliged to accept the work of many specialists such as archaeologists, linguists, epigraphers, numismatists, and, in the more modern periods, theologians, economists, statisticians, demographers, and so on.

Within the last generation or two many of the less developed peoples have learned the methods of historical work from the West. They have done much to assemble their records, to organize historical societies, and to publish the results of research. In almost every case national pride dictates that all this historical work be reported in the native language. This alone confronts the historians of other countries with insuperable language problems and entails more and more limitations on the field of their interest and activity. To be sure, we all live in an age of specialization. Scholars in all fields suffer from the same disabilities. The point to be made here is that in the case of the historian, where breadth of view and understanding are particularly desirable if not essential, the increasingly necessary breakup of the field is particularly regrettable. In many disciplines the problems of specialization have been solved by teamwork. This has been tried also in the historical field, but the results thus far have not been impressive. In history the products of teamwork lack a unified viewpoint and are therefore apt to be colorless and unconvincing.

The historian's first task is to collect his data, then sift and analyze them. Where the records are voluminous he must determine what is of historical importance, must test the selected data as to their nature and reliability, must arrange them in sequence, and must finally interpret them. Prior to the nineteenth century historians were pretty casual in their procedures. They tended to select from their sources what was picturesque or dramatic, or what suited their own interest or, more importantly, the interest of their patron. The great Roman historian Livy, who was one of the first to attempt to reach far back in time and tell the story of the state from the beginning, accepted legends and traditions quite uncritically. Similarly the chroniclers of the Middle Ages, mostly clerics with a predominantly religious interest, had a great penchant for the miraculous and frequently allowed their imagination free rein. The innumerable lives of the saints serve well as illustrations, but mention might also be made of the exaggerations so prevalent at that time. Medieval chroniclers attribute huge populations to their famous cities and speak commonly of armies of hundreds of thousands of men. Modern research leaves little doubt that even important cities of the Middle Ages rarely had populations of more than 50,000 (many far less), and that an army of 25,000 was about as large a one as could be supplied and transported under medieval conditions. The chroniclers were certainly not liars. Their use of bloated figures was simply their way of suggesting the vastness of cities and military hosts.

The scholars of the Renaissance and Reformation became more critical of documents and texts, especially those of religious import. By the eighteenth century—the Age of Reason—skepticism had become widespread and the analytic approach was being applied in many disciplines. Eventually, in the early years of the nineteenth century, the German historian B. G. Niebuhr undertook the critical study of early Roman history by sifting and testing the legends and traditions that Livy had so readily accepted. Thereby he established the principles of text criticism which have become the basis for all later historical training and research. Thenceforth the historian became more and more a professional and history a discipline cultivated in the universities rather than a pursuit of gentlemen scholars, retired statesmen, and professional writers. In university seminars students were trained in the general methods of criticism and in the particular techniques required for specific fields of research. As the volume of documentary and other sources grew, historical study became more intensive. The days when historians would, singlehanded, embark on vast projects such as the history of Greece or Rome, or of the Papacy, or of any major country were rapidly fading. The days of the exhaustive, comprehensive study of a limited period or subject were breaking. The monograph meant more accurate and reliable history, but it meant also the loss of the larger treatment, the broader interpretation. By the mid-twentieth century the point had been reached where most general treatments were textbook accounts, in some of which, as in the present volume, different sections are written by different authors in order to bring specialized knowledge to bear.

Since the days of Niebuhr and his successors among the German professors of history the methods of the profession have been constantly refined. Many books have been written on the subject and on the disciplines auxiliary to it. Naturally the requirements vary greatly according to the volume and nature of the data. Where the sources are so scanty that cross-checking is impossible, it may be necessary, through external and internal criticism, to establish authorship and authenticity. Forgery of important documents was common in ages past and in some cases, such as the Donation of Constantine, on which the Papal claims to temporal power rested, had far-reaching repercussions. In modern times, where there is so much evidence that any one item can be easily checked against others, successful forgery is more difficult. But it is by no means entirely a thing of the past, nor can it be ignored by the historian. To give but one recent example: on the outbreak of the First World War in 1914 the major participants each issued so-called color books, collections of documents in variously colored bindings purporting to demonstrate the efforts of the government in question to prevent the outbreak of conflict and to prove the responsibility of its opponents. Years later, when these documents could be critically examined, it turned out that in every case the governments had omitted important, possibly incriminating, passages and in some cases had rearranged the text and had even added material that was not contained in the original. In short, these documents, issued by leading European governments, were in varying degrees forged, and these forgeries had more than a little to do with determining the opinions of historians until their true character was revealed.

A related problem is that arising from errors in copying, whether unintentional, as they mostly were, or intentional, in which case they amounted to forgery. Prior to the introduction of printing, important documents were often copied and recopied from each other. In the process misunderstandings would arise and slips would be made, and these would be compounded as more and more copies were prepared. This means that the historian, before using any such manuscript, must collate it with others, attempt to establish their interrelationship and determine, if possible, the parent document. This is an arduous task calling not only for the most sophisticated critical techniques but also for competence in paleography (the science of deciphering ancient writings), philology, heraldry, and similar disciplines.

For the larger part of the historical time span the historian, far from suffering from lack of data, is apt to be confronted with a plethora of sources, including everything from government documents of all sorts (from relations with other states through parliamentary proceedings and reports, to tax records and other economic data, to population censuses, and even to cultural matters) to the records of religious and other private organizations, the periodical and newspaper press, and family, business, and other accounts. In general the historian gives the preference to documents because, with some exceptions, they belong to the class of unconscious sources, that is, they are records drawn for practical purposes and not with an eye to the future historian. Because they are essentially business records they aim at accuracy which, indeed, is of their essence.

As against such materials other data are apt to be biased or purposely slanted. The memoirs of statesmen and soldiers are a case in point. These men are apt to realize, belatedly, that in the long run their reputations will depend less on what they did than on what historians report them as having done. They hasten, therefore, to set down their recollections and explain their actions, revealing in the process how faulty the human memory can be and demonstrating clearly how the facts can be shaded or distorted to meet the requirements of an apology. It is certainly true that memoirs make good reading and it is equally true that they often reveal more about the personality of the author than about the events in which he played a role. But they obviously, from the standpoint of the historian, call for skepticism and critical analysis, for, as Goethe, one of the greatest of memoir writers, confessed, they are a compound of truth and fantasy.

The methods of historical criticism can be learned by any intelligent person, but the further task of determining the relative importance of data and arranging them so as to form an intelligible pattern calls not only for knowledge and skill but also for constructive imagination. Unfortunately the facts do not speak for themselves. Taken alone they constitute a jumble of miscellaneous data which, without selection, arrangement, and interpretation, remain meaningless. It would be a comfort to know that in the course of human events there is some structure, however obscure, that might be discovered through diligence and perseverance and that eventually might provide guidance for the historian. According to the Bible, history is the working out of God's plan for mankind. The same notion underlies St. Augustine's famous *City of God* and recurs even in the work of the great historian Leopold von Ranke when he speaks of the historian as working on God's tracks and enjoying the ineffable sweetness of sharing in the divine knowledge.

But these are matters of faith. They imply a readiness to believe that whatever happens, whether good or bad, is foreordained and serves a higher purpose. On a somewhat lower level repeated attempts have been made to demonstrate the "inevitability" of historical events and to establish the "laws" of history. None of these efforts have been successful. One cannot escape the fact that history does not repeat itself. In any given situation the conditions are different and the actors, though they may bear a resemblance to some forerunner, are individuals with their own traits and their own motives. No doubt history is checkered with wars and scarred with the brutalities and oppressions of conquerors. But attempts to generalize the causes of wars or to establish a conqueror-type have proved utterly futile. More recently the great political and social upheavals have inspired efforts to pattern revolutions and totalitarianism. The results, though stimulating, have generally left as many problems as they have resolved.

It is up to the historian, then, to interpret the facts, to devise a pattern of developments, to "make sense of what is essentially senseless."° The past without particularization is, according to one eminent historian, Johan Huizinga, merely chaos, and it is up to the historian to impose form upon it. And, to quote an equally outstanding practitioner, the late Sir Lewis Namier, the historian must avoid at all costs "the deadly morass of irrelevant narrative." His task is akin to that of the painter, not that of the photographer: "to discover and set forth, to single out and stress that which is of the nature of the thing, and not to reproduce indiscriminately all that meets the eye."†

Under these circumstances there can, of course, be no absolute historical truth. History is and will always be "an argument without end,"§ for no two historians will ever have the same viewpoint or make the same judgments. Indeed, one and the same historian is apt to see things in one way at the age of thirty and in quite another way at sixty. Historical writing is bound to be subjective, but it need not therefore be frivolous. The history most apt to find acceptance is the history that accounts for most of the established facts, and through the never-ending argument between those competent to judge there is gradually built up a body of agreed historical doctrine. To cite but one example: with regard to great and disastrous events such as the French Revolution there is always a strong

°*Geschichte als Sinngebung des Sinnlosen,* the title of a well-known treatise by the German philosopher Theodor Lessing (1919).

†Johan Huizinga, "A Definition of the Concept of History" in *Essays Presented to Ernst Cassirer* (1936); Sir Lewis Namier, "History" in *Avenues of History* (no date).

§Pieter Geyl, *The Use and Abuse of History* (1955).

human tendency to seek a villain. The Black Death of the fourteenth century, perhaps the greatest affliction to have ever stricken mankind, was attributed to the Jews, who suffered persecution in consequence. Similarly efforts have repeatedly been made to explain the French Revolution as the product of a conspiracy. But these explanations do not find acceptance. We know that great events are more complicated, and we favor interpretations which take account of all the cross-currents and conflicts of purpose as well as of interest. The arguments about the origins and significance of the French Revolution go on as actively as ever, but in the process the area of agreement is constantly enlarged and our understanding improved.

Good historical writing depends to a large extent on the integrity of the historian, that is, on his honesty in dealing with the evidence and his ability and willingness to do justice to forces or opinions that run counter to his own. Do what he will, he cannot escape the facts of his birth and family, of his education and social status, to say nothing of his national allegiance. One would hardly expect a historian born of well-to-do parents, educated in the best schools and living in comfort, to write of a labor movement in the same terms as a historian of workingman background, more or less self-educated through extension or correspondence courses. It is impossible to conjure up attitudes and insights at will, and it is therefore impossible for even the best-trained and best-intentioned historian to be completely objective and to do justice equally to all sides of a question. This does not mean, of course, that he cannot and should not strive for the utmost possible objectivity. He can make conscious, systematic efforts to counteract his known predilections, to discover and comprehend the motives, opinions, and acts that are uncongenial to him. In a word, objectivity is not something that the historian has or has not. It is something that is held before him as an ideal from the days of his professional training, something to be constantly kept in mind, something to be consciously worked toward.

On the student's or reader's side the relative objectivity of the historian is something to be alert to. He should note the author's sympathies, purposes, and prejudices. He should also recognize the fact that a certain measure of partiality is inescapable. It would be hardly reasonable to expect complete unanimity in the treatment of major issues or the interpretation of prominent personalities. One understands that the religious conflicts of the sixteenth century appear somewhat different to Catholic and Protestant writers and one is constantly reminded, in these days of the ecumenical movement, how difficult it is, even with great good will, to arrive at mutual understanding and a meeting of minds.

Related to the problem of objectivity is the problem of perspective. We all recognize that the outlook and attitudes of the present day are deeply affected by the developments of the past, and that the better we understand history the more intelligently we shall be able to deal with current problems. Our age is, in fact, so historically minded that all fields of knowledge rely to a large extent on the historical approach. But the reverse is also true. The opinions and problems of the present have a decisive effect on our interpretation of the past. Recall the disdain with which the men of the Renaissance looked back on the "Dark Ages," or the negative attitude of the Enlightenment toward all past institutions and traditions, or finally, the complete reversal of the Romantic period with its love and idealization of the Middle Ages, the ages of faith and of chivalry. Or take another example: until relatively recent times it was generally assumed that rulers were divinely appointed, that the aristocratic classes were chosen by God to enjoy the good things of the earth, while the vast lower classes—the "dumb herd," the "black masses"—were by higher decree condemned to suffer and to serve. In a later day it requires a real effort to recapture something of past viewpoints, to understand the ever-present specter of death and the prevalence of grief in times of recurrent epidemics, to appreciate the preoccupation of men with religious issues during the sixteenth and seventeenth centuries, or to reconcile oneself to the callous brutality that characterized past ages and that, unhappily, broke again on a horrified world in the days of Hitler and the Nazis.

The heavy bearing of the present on the historian's interpretation of the past is perhaps most vividly illustrated by the constantly changing treatment of the French Revolution, the principal facts of which are no longer in dispute. But an equally striking though less familiar phenomenon is the drastic change of view on the history of the Ottoman Turks. This is not a marginal matter, for the Turks ruled all of southeastern Europe for over five hundred years and exercised a direct and potent influence on the evolution of European history over several centuries. In the earlier years of their domination they were respected and feared but, at the same time, despised and hated as "infidels" and therefore the brood of Satan. This attitude was entirely natural in the days when Europe itself was torn by religious strife. It changed as religious passions cooled and as Turkish power diminished in relation to that of the European states. In recent years it has changed even more drastically as a result of the breakup of the Ottoman Empire and, more particularly, of the opening of the voluminous archival treasures of Istanbul to historical research and study. Much of Ottoman history is now to be rewritten in the light of fuller knowledge and deeper understanding.

The revolution of attitude with respect to modern imperialism is even more instructive. Less than a century ago the European powers embarked upon the conquest or control of the less developed regions of Africa, Asia, and the Pacific. The motives behind this world-shaking phenomenon are still in dispute and need not concern us here. The point is that prior to the First World War the expansion of European or American control was generally regarded as a meritorious development. Kipling was reflecting popular sentiment when he wrote of "the white man's burden" generously assumed in the interest of "lesser breeds." Yet now imperialism is hated and denounced not only by the former victims of European rule, not only by the Communist powers for propaganda purposes, but also by large segments of the public of the formerly imperialist states. For a long time it is going to be difficult for the historian to arrive at a judicious interpretation of one of the major events of recent centuries.

The impact of the present on the historian's views of the past raises the problem of historical perspective. In dealing with early periods or remote areas the historian may suffer for lack of sufficient data, but he can at least view his period in the context of long-term development. For later periods there may be far more material, but the time span between the subject of study and the present is correspondingly reduced and the historical setting therefore more restricted. Because this is so, it was long thought that the study of history should be closed out with the events of perhaps a century before, on the theory that more recent happenings could not be seen in proper perspective and should be regarded as politics, not history.

This position has now been generally abandoned. The modern world is so fast-moving and the need for historical background is so keenly felt by students and general public alike that historians devote a substantial part of their time and effort to the study and interpretation of the events of the most recent generation or two. Similarly, more attention is given to the history of the non-European American countries in the effort to understand the conditions and outlook which determine their attitudes and policies. Obviously it is impossible to attain proper perspective in these cases, but this weakness is in part compensated for by more direct and personal empathy with the developments of the immediate past. Even though it was hopeless to attempt, ten years after the Second World War, to evaluate that great conflict in terms of long-range history, the student could certainly gain a keener and more direct comprehension of the clash of ideologies and the hopes and fears of all parties than the historian of a few centuries hence can possibly recover. Whatever the difficulties and shortcomings, "contemporary history" has become well established and is bound to prosper. In most countries of the Western world professional journals have been founded to deal exclusively with matters of the recent past.

Since new facts are being constantly discovered about former times and former events, and since the never-ending changes in human outlook require reconsideration of earlier interpretations, we must accept the fact that there will never be absolute or definitive historical knowledge or understanding. Carl Becker, one of the most stimulating American historians of the past generation, made an address to the American Historical Association in 1931 which he entitled "Everyman His Own Historian." In this he stressed the inescapable relativity of historical knowledge and the personal stamp which each scholar is bound to put upon his work. Others have argued that each generation must and will rewrite history to suit its own predilections and requirements. But there is really nothing remarkable about this. All human study and thought is, in varying degrees, relative. In most disciplines the scholar starts with a problem which his work with the sources has forced on his attention and then seeks, successfully or unsuccessfully, to assemble sufficient evidence to support his hypothesis. Since accepted ideas are constantly being challenged by new data or novel ideas, knowledge is in a perpetual state of flux. In literature and art standards of taste oscillate with alarming rapidity, while in the natural sciences no one is in the least amazed or disquieted to see doctrines of a few years ago reversed or discarded. Viewpoints and interpretations in history are no more fluctuating and certainly no more capricious than in other areas of human thought.

The establishment of historical study as a rigorous and for the most part academic discipline has opened something of a rift between the professional and the general reading public. Much of the historical effort goes into specialized monographic studies, fortified with extensive references to the evidence on which the argument is based. It is natural that many readers, interested in some larger topic and partial to lively, colorful narrative, should find such detailed analyses uninspiring if not tiresome. Even a century ago history was for the most part written and read as literature. Historians allowed themselves ample elbow-room, in many instances twelve or more volumes, written with passion and conviction as well as with colorful detail. Great historians such as Macaulay and Michelet, who worked long and arduously with the sources, avoided whatever seemed uninteresting and dry and omitted from their narrative data that would not fit their purposes. Such histories were widely read by the relatively small literate public of the day and exercised an important influence.

The same could not be said of more than a very few modern historical works, for the reasons that have been discussed above. The result has been that popular writers have undertaken to supply the popular demand. A steady stream of historical narratives issues from our presses, and at the same time historical material is presented in periodicals and on television. This popular history is not all bad, for some of these writers do take the trouble to read serious history and so serve to make more generally available the knowledge arrived at by professionals. In this sense they serve a useful social purpose. But this can hardly be said of the majority, who have not even the competence to discriminate between historical treatises. The student should therefore be on his guard and avoid as much as possible the lively, dramatic, and often saucy story that purports to tell of past events.

When all is said and done, we will no longer look upon history merely as literature, nor will we scan it for evidence of the effects of good and evil. Specific lessons to be derived from history are few and imperfect and it is vain to look for the repetition of particular situations. It is even more futile for the historian, whose business is with the past, to undertake the forecast of the future. Mankind is understandably concerned with what may be in store for it and has been fascinated by the rise and fall of empires and the flowering and decay of civilizations. Numerous efforts have been made to discover the key to past development in the hope of solving the riddle of the future. Karl Marx, whose materialist interpretation of history has gained wider acceptance, even by professional historians, than any other, confined himself chiefly to the analysis of the past and had relatively little to say of the "classless society" which he foresaw as the organization of the future. But more recent philosophers of history, such as Oswald Spengler in his *Decline of the West* and Arnold Toynbee in his voluminous *Study of History*, have attempted to construct the bridge from the past to the future. They have aroused a great deal of attention and have no doubt influenced modern thought, whether for good or ill. But they have found very few adherents among professional historians, who in general have felt that such elaborate structures have been imposed on the historical data rather than derived from them. The late Dutch historian Pieter Geyl, who was one of the most persistent and effective critics of Toynbee, found little difficulty in demonstrating that some of the latter's interpretations, while plausible, were no more convincing than three or four others that might be drawn for the same subject. Search as we may, there seems to be little hope of ever discovering any plan or law of historical development. Human destiny appears to be determined by countless, varied factors working in multifarious combinations, to say nothing of the element of chance, which cannot be discounted entirely. There is still something alluring in the venerable proposition that if Cleopatra's nose had been a little smaller, Mark Antony might not have fallen in love with her and the whole history of Rome might have taken a different turn.

To say that history is full of uncertainties and in constant flux is not to disparage it. As aforesaid, the entire thought of the modern world rests on the idea of evolution, that is, on historical (or prehistorical) change. Non-European nations have adopted the methods of historical study devised in the West, and in all countries there is a proliferation of historical societies and journals. Every institution of higher learning offers a variety of history courses, and in the United States most state governments demand that students fulfill at least minimum history requirements in order to matriculate. But whatever the practical values of historical study, it should be thought of as one of the great cultural disciplines. History makes men wise, remarked Jacob Burckhardt, the great Swiss historian whose *Civilization of the Renaissance in Italy* is still one of the most read classics of historical literature. History provides an extension of the individual's experience, it furthers self-knowledge and understanding, it means a greatly enriched life and wider horizons. It may well be that human nature has not changed over the millennia, that men are as selfish, as brutal, as courageous, as generous as they ever were. But even though the basic drives may remain unaltered, the attitudes have changed and are constantly changing. The depth of religious faith is gone; slavery and class subordination have become abhorrent; sexual relations have been revolutionized. To study human nature and attitudes as they are revealed in the past is to find the road to real education, the road to a broader and deeper humanism.

Suggestions for Further Reading

Bloch, Marc, *The Historian's Craft* (1953). One of the best discussions of fundamental problems of historical work.

Carr, Edward H., *What Is History?* (1962). Thought-provoking lectures on many aspects of history and historical study.

Collingwood, R. G., *The Idea of History* (1946). An admirable survey of the evolution of historical thought.

Mazlish, Bruce, *The Riddle of History: The Great Speculators from Vico to Freud* (1966). A competent discussion of modern philosophies of history.

Among useful handbooks of historical study and writing are:

Jones, Tom B., *Paths to the Ancient Past* (1967).

Kent, Sherman, *Writing History*. 2nd rev. ed. (1966).

Nevins, Allan, *The Gateway to History* (1938).

Nugent, Walter T. K., *Creative History* (1967).

For stimulating essays on various aspects of historical work see, among many collections, the following:

Barraclough, Geoffrey, *History in a Changing World* (1955).

Butterfield, Herbert, *Man on His Past* (1955).

Geyl, Pieter, *The Use and Abuse of History* (1955).

Hexter, J. H., *Reappraisals in History* (1961).

Hughes, H. Stuart, *History as Art and as Science* (1964).

Namier, Sir Lewis, *Avenues of History* (no date).

1

---◆◆◆---

The Struggle for Empire

From the late fifteenth century on, Western civilization, in a series of explosive transformations, broke its bounds time and time again. The ultimate result was a drastic alteration in the Western world itself and in all the societies in contact with the Western world. So drastic was this alteration that in many areas of human activity the new society had no parallel in any society in all the preceding years of human history; it was incommensurate with anything man had ever seen or experienced before. The explosive transformations that so changed the conditions of human existence occurred in science, in religion, in political and social organization, in technology, and in methods of warfare. But the earliest transformation was the extension of Western man's knowledge of other areas of the earth and, more important, the intensification of his dealings with those areas and the assertion of his power over them and their inhabitants.

During the Middle Ages and up to the end of the fifteenth century, the world, as Western men knew it, was a narrow place. They knew that there was a vast continent to the east of which Europe was but a peninsula, and periodic nomadic invasions from Asia constantly reminded them of it. At intervals throughout the Middle Ages waves of Magyars, Mongols, Tartars, and Turks left their dry Eurasian plain and swept into Russia, the Balkans, the Levant, and North Africa and threatened to pour the Catholic Christian world to the west.

At the end of the thirteenth century, Western knowledge of the Far East was much augmented by the account that Marco Polo (1254–1324) gave of his remarkable adventures in the Orient. Polo was an accurate, observant, and intelligent Venetian merchant. On a trading trip his father and uncle had penetrated to China, known in the Middle Ages as Cathay. At that time China was ruled by the great Mongol conqueror Kublai Khan. On their second journey to the Far East the Polo brothers took Marco with them. After reaching the court of the Great Khan, Marco entered his service for several years. As a result, he enjoyed the opportunity to travel widely through the Khan's vast empire. Marco finally returned to Europe by way of India. Captured some years later by the Genoese, he whiled away his time in prison in 1298 by dictating to a fellow prisoner an account of the Far East that was superior in fullness and accuracy to any that the West was to see for the next two hundred years.

Despite the wondrous tales that Marco Polo told, he inspired only a dwindling trickle of emulators, and none after 1340. The West had less direct contact with the East during the century 1350–1450 than it had in the previous hundred years. The Arab merchants who had organized the Oriental trade brought the spices, fine textiles, and metal wares of the Far East, the Middle East, and India up the Red Sea to Egypt or overland to the ports of the Syrian coast of the Mediterranean. There, Venetian and Genoese traders bought them and carried them into Europe. Extensive European contact with the Orient took place only at Smyrna, Alexandria, Constantinople, and a few other eastern Mediterranean towns.

A fire-damaged drawing from a 1541 Portuguese manuscript, once owned by the American colonizer Sir Walter Raleigh, shows the ships of Portugal off the island of Socotra in the Indian Ocean. The vessels at right are lateen-rigged native craft.

A mariner takes a sun sighting to determine latitude in an illustration from a French work entitled Cosmographie (1583). *This instrument was superseded within a decade by the backstaff, in its turn replaced by the quadrant c. 1750.*

European knowledge of Africa was even more scanty, being confined to the Mediterranean littoral of the Dark Continent and a few hundred miles of its coastline southwest of Gibraltar. With one geographical part of Europe—the backward Slavic principalities of the Russian plain—Western Europeans had even less contact than they had with Asia and Africa. Merchants and travelers had ceased to penetrate these Slavic lands since the Tartar conquests in southern Russia had closed the old Varangian route to the Orient and Constantinople. Finally, Europeans knew nothing at all about Australia and the two great continents of the Western Hemisphere, North and South America. The Atlantic stretched away from the coast of Europe to the west, but, save for a few hardy Vikings, no European had ever seen what lay on the other shore or known where that shore was, and the tales of the deeds of such as Leif Ericson had not passed from Scandinavia to the rest of Europe.

Although Western civilization remained within geographical bounds far narrower than those of the Roman Empire, it was nevertheless slowly accumulating two indispensable aids to its future expansion. The merchants of Italy and Catalonia who sailed the Mediterranean gradually learned to draw the contours of its coast on parchment with remarkable precision. The maps they produced as early as 1300 were immeasurably superior to any that the medieval world or antiquity had known. The *portolani*, as the maps were called, give us our best insight into the geographical knowledge of those great seafaring people. The maps of their usual trade routes—the Mediterranean and Black seas, the west coast of Africa almost to Cape Bojador, the coast of the Atlantic, the English Channel, and the North Sea to Flanders—are superb, but the *portolani* also showed parts of the world unfamiliar to the traders and known to them only by hearsay. As the knowledge of traders, and later of explorers, improved, so did the accuracy of the maps, for each returning ship passed on to the next venturers a fuller and more precise knowledge of the shape, and some notion of the whereabouts, of the shores they reached.

For explorers on the open sea to know the whereabouts of their own ships was

24   THE STRUGGLE FOR EMPIRE

more difficult. Men had long known how to determine their latitude—that is, how far north or south they were—by measuring the angle of their position to the sun. Their ability accurately to determine longitude (east-west location), however, had to wait until clocks could keep time accurately at sea, and such clocks were not developed until the eighteenth century. The third problem was determining direction. In clear weather helmsmen steered by the sun in daylight and by the North Star at night. But it was not until the end of the twelfth century, with the discovery of the properties of the magnetic needle, that they could steer with accuracy in bad weather as well as in good. It was observed that in the Northern Hemisphere the point of a magnetic needle always inclines toward the north, regardless of the weather. Placing the needle on a pivot in the center of a card bearing directions gave mariners a compass by which to set their heading.

During the fifteenth and early sixteenth centuries, further improvements in technical knowledge and skills gave Europeans advantages that were at once indispensable and decisive in the early days of overseas expansion. For one thing, they greatly improved the sailing qualities of their ships by observing and adapting to their own purposes the rigging used by the Arab seamen of the Indian Ocean. After a period of experiment, they came up with a combination that enabled them to enjoy the advantages of the large sail area of the traditional European square rig along with the Arabian lateen rig's ability to sail into the wind. The result was a more versatile craft than the world had ever seen before, combining speed, maneuverability, weatherliness, and cargo capacity. Gradually, too, the European maritime states improved the armament of their ships. Naval artillery became at once more effective and more important. Ships' cannon were built more sturdily, increased in number, and improved in placement and ability to aim. Slowly, the cannonade as simply a preliminary to boarding gave place to broadside fire intended to disable the enemy vessel.

Had European expansion, especially in the Orient, depended initially on the superior mercantile skill of the European traders, it would not have gotten far against the Arabs and the Chinese. From about 1500 on, however, the Europeans liberally laced commercial enterprise with naval superiority, military organization, and brute force. In these matters they were technically well ahead of their competitors.

Portugal's Empire in the Orient

The powers that controlled the great trading and shipping centers of the medieval West—the Italian and Hanseatic ports—were not the first to employ the new aids to navigation to expand the horizons of the Western world. That achievement fell to two realms of the Iberian peninsula: first Portugal, the small, poor, backward kingdom on the Atlantic coast, and then Portugal's neighbor, Castile.

Portugal began to open new worlds to Western civilization for very old-fashioned reasons. When the flaming ardor for crusades against the Muslims had turned to ashes in the rest of Europe, it suddenly flared up again in the little Iberian kingdom. Muslim territory stretched along the entire African and almost the whole Asiatic shore of the Mediterranean. Western men had no way of knowing in the fifteenth century how far it extended east and south into Asia nor how far south into Africa, since they had only a vague notion of the contours of Asia and no idea whatever of the contours of Africa south of Cape Bojador.

Sixteenth-century West African artists depicted their Portuguese exploiters in ivory (above) and cast bronze (below).

In 1415 the Portuguese crossed the Strait of Gibraltar to conquer Ceuta on the African shore. Their victory had a vastly important consequence. It revived in Prince Henry, third son of the Portuguese king, an old idea. At the end of the thirteenth century a Genoese expedition had sailed through the Strait of Gibraltar and set a course down the then-unknown coast of Africa. The purpose of the expedition was to find a southward route around Africa and seek out the land of Prester John (that is, Presbyter or Priest John), of which rumor in the West had often spoken. This fabled land was supposed to be a Christian kingdom lying somewhere on the east flank of the Muslim world. It was hoped that, by making contact with Prester John, the Christians could secure the Muslim infidels in a vise.

The Genoese ships that went to look for Prester John were never heard from again, but the dream of the Genoese had been reborn in the mind of Prince Henry. He, however, did not intend to win a way to the soft underside of the Muslim world by a wild dash into the unknown. By patient, methodical exploration, each Portuguese expedition that Henry sent out returned home with information to make the work of the ones that followed easier and enable them to press further. Back in Portugal, Prince Henry and his aides put together the new information, worked out charts, trained and prepared new expeditions. Called the Navigator, Prince Henry was in fact the director of a great school of geography, discovery, and exploration.

Portuguese mariners, subsidized out of Henry's private fortune, conducted a twofold operation—exploring the middle Atlantic and pushing down the west coast of Africa. In the Atlantic they rediscovered and settled three clusters of islands—the Canaries, the Madeiras, and the Azores—and began to cultivate on them wine grapes and that sugar cane which later played so important a role in the imperial aims and policies of the Western European monarchies. Progress on the African coast was slower and more painful. Here the mariners were retarded by the natural obstacle of shallows and bad sailing around Cape Bojador and by the psychic obstacle of nameless fears of dreadful things—serpent rocks and boiling rivers—that they had been told they might encounter in the Southern Sea. Finally, however, an expedition rounded Cape Bojador. Year after year further stretches of West African coast—hitherto unknown to Christian or Muslim—yielded their secrets to the intrepid mariners of Portugal. Finally, the Portuguese got past the great bulge of Africa and turned east. Any hopes that the way to the Orient now lay open to them were dashed when the coast turned south again for hundreds of weary miles. Only in 1486—a quarter of a century after Prince Henry's death—did Bartholemew Diaz bring his ships past the storm-racked cape, later called Good Hope, to become the first mariner of the West to sail the Indian Ocean. It was to be more than a decade before another Portuguese, Vasco da Gama, actually reached the Orient along the seaway that the discovery of Diaz had so clearly pointed out.

Long before that, before Henry died, his pious aspiration had been transformed in other minds into a dream of an overseas empire, the first of its kind in European history. By the 1440s Henry no longer had to bear all the costs of his strange crusading effort, for by that time a prospect more attractive to mariners than that of trapping Islam in a vise had opened up—the prospect of gain. Along the African coast the Portuguese had discovered the two kinds of gold, the lust for which was to be at once the spur and the curse of European imperial ventures for centuries to come. They found yellow gold and hoped to find more, and they found "black gold," the African Negro, and learned that he could be bought cheap in Africa and sold dear at home.

Thus almost from the start, chattel slavery, which had nearly vanished from Christian Europe, became one of the economic piers on which were erected the overseas empires of Christian states. Attracted by the hope of profits, merchants sought and received trade licenses from Henry. They had to have such licenses because the Portuguese king had conferred upon him a monopoly of all enterprises along the African coast. Up and down West Africa traders established settlements where they pursued their trade with the natives. Soon the coast was dotted with the busy outposts of vigorous, violent, bold, and greedy trader-adventurers. The terrifying indifference of these pioneers to human suffering and to the laws of God and man were to be the despair of humane administrators in the mother country, but without their ruthless energy there would have been no European overseas empires for stay-at-homes to administer.

In 1497 Vasco da Gama set out on the voyage that was to shrink Portugal's new African empire into relative insignificance, to make it primarily important as a chain of way stations to the greater empire to the east. Following the indications of Diaz and of two Portuguese explorers who had set out overland from Egypt, da Gama led his little fleet around the Cape of Good Hope and up the east African coast. There he found a guide who directed him across the Indian Ocean to the Malabar Coast, the western shore of India. It was here that the Arabs gathered their cargoes for shipment westward. The cargoes came there by land from the interior of India across the mountain chain of the Western Ghats. They also came by water from eastern India, China, southeast Asia, and the East Indies—the fabled "Spice Islands." From the Malabar Coast the Arab merchants carried their goods up the Persian Gulf to the Middle East or up the Red Sea and over a short land haul to Alexandria, where the Venetians and Genoese bought them for the European trade.

Despite the efforts of the Arabs to drive him away, da Gama managed to get a full cargo for his ships. Two and a half years after his departure, his fleet again dropped anchor at Lisbon with less than two-thirds of the men who had set out for the East, but with a cargo worth enough to pay the costs of the great adventure sixty times over. The precious spices of the East had found a new way of entry to Europe.

The Portuguese were quick to exploit the sea road to riches that da Gama had opened up to them. And not to them alone. Portugal was short of capital, short of ships and men, and far from the great European marts. The merchants, shippers, and bankers from Genoa, Florence, and the Netherlands hastened to supply the needs of the little kingdom, to carry the products of the East from Lisbon to the commercial metropolis of Antwerp, and there to sell them to the traders of all Europe. With the European distribution of their new-found treasure in the ablest of hands, the Portuguese gave their full attention to the problems of the East.

The Arabs did not intend to give up without a fight the trade advantages they had so long enjoyed. Thus the Portuguese had the pleasant opportunity of

D. VASCO DA GAMA. VI.

In 1524, about the time this portrait appeared in a Portuguese manuscript, da Gama was made viceroy of India.

engaging in a struggle in which each victory was at once a triumph for the faith over the infidel and a gain for Portuguese traders over their rivals—a veritable spice merchant's crusade. They crushed Arab fleets at sea and drove them off the Malabar Coast. They attacked the town of Aden commanding the entrance to the Red Sea and seized Ormuz, which controlled the entrance to the Persian Gulf, severing the chief water arteries that carried the East-West trade of the Arabs. They set up firm bases for their own fleets on the east coast of Africa and organized a pilot service to take those fleets through the Indian Ocean to their trading bases in India.

The looting, ravaging, and burning that the Portuguese engaged in in the name of Christianity and their obliteration of the trade from which Persians and Turks had drawn great profit raised a coalition, surreptitiously backed by the Venetians, to drive them out of the eastern seas. In this crisis the Portuguese viceroy to the Indies, Afonso de Albuquerque, defended the newly won position of his native land by pushing its aggression yet further. In his ruthless haste to fasten down the trade empire Portugal had won, he shook all political relations from the Persian Gulf to the Moluccas, the Spice Islands.

Albuquerque rejected the solid, cautious policy of his predecessor, which had been based on the premise that so small a state as Portugal could only keep a secure hold on the trade of the East by concentrating all its energy on the command of the sea from Lisbon to Malabar. Instead, he set about erecting a chain of garrisons that would assure the flow of trade by dominating the whole route from its sources to its outlet at Lisbon. Under his driving force, the Portuguese settled themselves firmly at Ormuz and at Goa on the Malabar Coast.

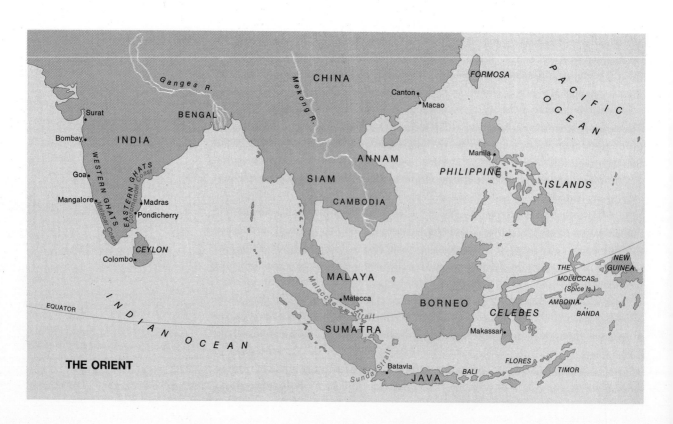

THE ORIENT

Then they pushed on and seized Malacca, the key emporium of Far Eastern commerce. The town, commanding the strait between Sumatra and Malaya, controlled the main routes to Indochina, China proper, and the further Indies. His successors continued Albuquerque's aggressive policy. By the middle of the sixteenth century, the Portuguese had garrisoned stations and trading posts all the way from Macao in China to the Moluccas to Ceylon to the mouth of the Tagus in Portugal. In less than half a century the sea-borne trade of the rich and ancient lands of the East lay in the hands of the rulers of a petty Western kingdom of scarcely a million and a half people, lying a year's journey from the furthest outpost of its trading empire.

While Portugal was expanding the power of the Western world into the Orient, its neighbor, Castile, was crusading against the Moors in Granada and fighting in Italy, in North Africa, and even in Germany. At the same time, Castile accidentally opened to Europe two continents that no European of that time had ever seen or even imagined. Indeed, the very discoverer of the new lands to the west, the Genoese sailor Christopher Columbus, insisted that he had not discovered new continents at all but rather a cheaper and shorter route to the Spice Islands—one that could be sailed in a couple of months as against the year the Portuguese might have to spend, supposing that they ever made their way east by the Cape of Good Hope route.

Spain's Empire in the New World

Castile became the beneficiary of an enormous error, an error that Columbus came by honestly. Of course, everyone in the Middle Ages who gave thought to such matters believed that the earth was a sphere, although the legend that before the voyages of Columbus men thought the earth was flat has died hard. One of the best traditions of medieval geographical speculation, however, was wildly wrong about the distance one would have to travel west from Europe to reach Eastern Asia. This tradition compounded a vast overestimate of the extent of the Eurasian continent with a gross underestimate of the circumference of the earth. Consequently, writers in this tradition held that the short route from Western Europe to the Far East lay not eastward, but westward across the Atlantic. They did not dream that between Cádiz and Cathay lay an almost unbroken continental barrier and *two* vast oceans, one of which covered almost half the face of the earth.

Columbus knew and accepted the tradition about the proximity of Eastern Asia to Western Europe. He believed he could open the short route to the Indies by sailing west across the Atlantic. He tried to peddle his idea to the great rulers of the Western European monarchies. The wager after all was small; the returns to a winner would be great. But at the time, the rulers of France and England were not making that kind of bet, and the ruler of Portugal had already staked a large fortune on seeking an eastward passage around Africa.

Columbus took his scheme to Isabella, queen of Castile, at a happy moment. A few years earlier she had been busy reducing her strife-ridden kingdom to order. A few years later the resources of Castile were heavily engaged in the Italian enterprises of Isabella's husband, Ferdinand of Aragon. At the moment Columbus made his successful appeal, however, Castile had just driven the Moors from Granada, the last foothold of the Muslims in Iberia. The crusading spirit was

At one point in his conquest of Mexico, Cortes had to evacuate the Aztec capital. Above, accompanied by a rear guard of Indian allies, the Spaniards begin to withdraw secretly. Below, an Aztec woman obtaining water from a canal sounds the alarm.

high, and Castilians were better aware than other Europeans of the solid gains Portugal had won in Africa and the high hopes Portugal entertained for a more resounding success. But Africa was out of bounds for Castile. The Pope had conferred a monopoly of African exploration and commerce on Portugal. The only way Castile could hope to rival its little neighboring kingdom was to strike out in the direction Columbus wanted to go.

Columbus set sail from Palos with three ships in August, 1492. Less than a year later he had returned to present Isabella with, he firmly believed, the lordship of the Indies. Two months out from Spain he had discovered a cluster of islands roughly within the latitude where the Spice Islands were supposed to be. He cruised among them and found nothing that looked like an insuperable barrier to further ventures westward. Columbus's return awakened hopes for riches in Castile, and on his second voyage he was provided with livestock, seed, sugarcane cuttings, and more than a thousand men in a fleet of seventeen ships. They set down on Santo Domingo, one of the larger islands. In their new world the Spanish were following the same pattern—that of colonial settlement—that the Portuguese had established in the Canaries, the Madeiras, and the Azores. Columbus made two more voyages from Spain to the new world he had found. Though he sailed as far south as Venezuela without encountering an east-west passage, he still firmly believed that he was within easy reach of Cathay and Cipango (Japan).

Columbus died in that faith in 1506, but some were coming to doubt it. Other mariners in the pay of Spain had gone far down the Atlantic coast of South America and found no way through. Nor had any passage to the Spice Islands been found due west or northwest of Spain's Caribbean settlements. In these rather miserable frontier outposts the Spaniards had to grow their own food, and though they grubbed for gold, they found little of it. The natives of the newly discovered lands were a few pitiful savages who made nothing worth buying and could buy nothing worth selling. In the quarter-century after Columbus's first voyage, the Spanish settlements made a sad comparison with the magnificent commercial empire that Prince Henry, Diaz, da Gama, and Albuquerque had founded for Portugal.

The Spanish were, therefore, still determined to gain the Orient by the western route and find a road to riches that would rival that of the Portuguese. Spanish explorers continued to push north and south along the eastern coast of the Americas, seeking the passage that would take them to the true Indies. Finally they found it. In 1513 a Spanish explorer named Vasco Núñez de Balboa crossed Central America at its narrowest point, the Isthmus of Panama, and became the first European to set eyes on the American shore of the Pacific. Seven years later, a Portuguese navigator in the employ of Spain painfully felt his way with his tiny fleet down the shores of South America. Just a little short of land's end he turned his ships into the perilous narrows that still bear his name—the Strait of Magellan. After six terrible weeks, Ferdinand Magellan left behind the terrors of the strait for the calm waters of the Pacific. Over its enormous breadth he sailed, making landfall in a cluster of islands later known as the Philippines, after Philip II of Spain, the son and successor of Magellan's master, Charles V. In the Philippines Magellan was killed in a fracas with the natives. After reaching the Spice Islands, his lieutenant brought his last ship, the *Victoria*, with eighteen survivors around the Cape of Good Hope to Spain—the first circumnavigation of the earth in history.

When in 1527 a Spanish ship set its course westward for the Spice Islands, its home port was not Cádiz but Acapulco in Mexico. It did not sail from old Spain but from New Spain, Spain in the Americas. In their quest for the Indies the Spanish had stumbled into control of the greatest of the early modern empires—an empire that at the end of the sixteenth century stretched over the whole of South America° and Central America and a sizable part of North America.

The Spanish crown owed the lordship of the New World to a mere handful of men, a few thousand adventurers and about a tenth of the number of soldiers it arrayed in battle against the French at Pavia in 1525 in the war for control of Lombardy. In the process of overrunning the Western Hemisphere, these men—the conquistadors, or conquerors—became masters of hundreds of thousands of native peoples and crushed the vast military empires of the Aztecs and the Incas and the civilizations that maintained them. The man who began the conquest was a minor Spanish military officer in Cuba, Hernando Cortes.

Rumors picked up from the natives by Spanish explorers told of a great empire, flowing with gold, in the interior of Mexico, and Cortes went to find it. He set out from Cuba in 1519 with six hundred men and a few horses to extend Spanish power to the mainland. When he landed on the coast of Mexico he burned his ships, thus ensuring himself against any timid desire of his men to return to the safety of the islands. Montezuma, the ruler of the Aztec empire, heard of the landing and sent Cortes word to depart. He also sent him gold as a present and thus destroyed the effect of his command, for gold was just what Cortes and his followers had come after. The Spanish band made alliances with and got aid from Indian tribes subjugated by the Aztecs and glad of an opportunity to throw off their yoke. Aided by his Indian allies, Cortes had the incredible good fortune, after several close calls, to take the capital of the great Aztec empire. He killed the war leader who tried to rally the Aztec forces, slaughtered the ruling group, and replaced it with his Spanish followers. In the treasures of the Aztec palaces and temples the conqueror's avaricious dream came true.

Before he had set out for the interior of Mexico, Cortes had established on the coast a town he called Villa Rica de Vera Cruz, literally Rich Town of the True Cross. The name symbolizes the forces that drove the conquistadors to their fantastic adventures. They advanced with sword in the right hand and cross in the left in quest of gold and to convert or destroy unbelievers. Their passion to bring glory to God in no way diminished their insatiable thirst for riches. That thirst was whetted by the triumph of Cortes over the Aztecs. The news of the astounding success of his venture triggered an explosion of new enterprises, all seeking to duplicate his happy experiment and conquer an empire with a handful of swashbucklers. In many of the places to which their adventures took them, the conquistadors found no empires to conquer, but wherever they went they established the supremacy of the Spanish king.

°Eastern Brazil, which was conquered and settled by the Portuguese, became part of the Spanish Empire when Philip II became ruler of Portugal in 1580. Spain lost Brazil along with Portugal when the latter regained its independence after 1640.

Above, Aztecs in canoes attack the conquistadors as they cross a causeway. Below, the grim aftermath of the battle. These drawings by native artists illustrated a late-sixteenth-century history of New Spain by the monk Bernardino de Sahagún.

SPAIN'S EMPIRE
IN THE AMERICAS
c. 1700

They fanned out from the mountain capital of the Aztecs, where Cortes had erected the new City of Mexico to replace the town he destroyed, and made themselves lords of northern Mexico and of all Central America. Before 1550, through the efforts of Juan Ponce de León, Hernando de Soto, and others, they had pushed around the Gulf of Mexico, up the Atlantic coast as far as Nova Scotia, and up the Mississippi as far as present-day Memphis. Despite all their efforts, however, they found little to their liking. What they saw was, they felt, too much like Spain. What later became the center of wealth of the world's richest nation was set down on the Spanish maps as *Tierras de Ningun Provecho*, Good-for-Nothing Lands. Further west, Francisco Coronado chased the mirage of a legendary city of gold up the Colorado River and eastward into the great prairie as far as Kansas. He returned to Mexico empty-handed. The Spanish for many years consigned America north of the Rio Grande to the special oblivion reserved for lands where they found no plunder.

The land south of the Isthmus of Panama presented a happier hunting ground. In the two decades after the exploit of Cortes, conquistadors spread their trail of victory, slaughter, and looting all along the northern and western coasts of South

America. They even penetrated the towering Andes. There they overthrew the powerful Indian dominion of the Incas and themselves became the rulers of the peoples the Incas had subjected. This last feat—the conquest of Peru—turned the territory now occupied by Bolivia, Ecuador, the northern half of Chile, and Peru itself into the hands of Spain. It was achieved by men who had all the demoniac violence of Cortes and none of his constructive abilities. Their leader was Francisco Pizarro, the bastard son of a soldier of fortune. For ten years Pizarro dreamed of conquering the empire of the Incas, of whose existence rumor had spread among the Spanish adventurers. Finally, having wheedled from Charles V a commission to conquer the greatest, richest, and most skillfully organized military state in the Western Hemisphere, Pizarro set out in 1530 with three little ships, thirty horses, and two hundred men, about a third of the force Cortes had used against the Aztecs. He achieved the miracle of bringing the Andean region under Spanish sway with this minuscule force—roughly the size of a present-day infantry company and not nearly so well armed—by taking advantage of a dispute over the succession to the kingship among the Incas. Compounding craft with treachery, murder, and massacre, he liberated the peoples of the central Andes from the yoke of the Incas and turned them over to the scarcely more tender mercies of his band of Christian brigands. Pizarro soon fell out with his lieutenant Diego de Almagro, whom he had sent to take Chile. When Almagro was killed in the ensuing hostilities, his son avenged him by assassinating Pizarro. At last an emissary of the crown managed to dampen the violence of the conquerors, and most of South America, like all of Mexico, thus came directly under the control of the Spanish monarchy.

The spoils of two empires vastly enhanced the private fortunes of the conquistadors. The Spanish crown, too, enjoyed the windfall that its one-fifth share of the loot provided, but gutting native American empires reached the point of diminishing returns when there were no important empires left to gut. In the 1540s, however, just as this source of plunder was drying up, the Spaniards came upon silver outcroppings in both Mexico and Peru, a seemingly inexhaustible hoard of treasure. Before the end of the decade, they were working the incredibly rich silver lodes at Zacatecas in Mexico and at Potosí in Peru, and the flood of precious metal pouring from the New World mines to old Spain was producing that gradual currency inflation which, because of its impact on the economy of Europe, has been called the Price Revolution.

Fifty years after Columbus sailed, then, the Spanish had laid hands on an abundant and continuous supply of the precious metals that had been one of the main objects of the explorers' quest. They had also carried Christianity to the pagan peoples of the New World. The patient missionary work of the Catholic priests undermined the beliefs of the natives, and the conquistadors destroyed the ancient temples and altars of their faith. Between the two forces, the Indians south of the Rio Grande had little choice but to submit to the religion of their conquerors.

In discovering the silver mines and in converting the Indians in America, the Spaniards achieved two of the ends that had impelled them to sail into unknown waters and claim dominion over strange lands—the propagation of the faith and the acquisition of treasure. The third end—the winning of access to the land of spices—they attained more easily when Philip II became ruler of Portugal in 1580. The united Iberian realms became the only European power with overseas possessions, the first monarchy in modern Western history to possess both a tribute empire, the East Indies, and a colonial empire, the New World.

Overseas Expansion of the Northwestern Powers

Philip II's peaceful enjoyment of his unique overseas dominion was brief. He had scarcely united the Spanish and Portuguese heritages when he was violently attacked by states that were destined to destroy the Portuguese tribute empire, weaken the grip of Spain on its colonial empire, and establish great empires of their own. About to enter the field of empire-building on their own, the English, the Dutch, and the French were making ready to repudiate the Papal proclamations of 1493 and 1494 that blandly divided the non-European world between Spain and Portugal.

They entered late into the scramble for overseas empire, partly because Portugal and Spain had pre-empted many of the choicest areas. Partly, however, their tardiness was due to the fact that a good deal of the capital available for maritime trading ventures in the Netherlands, England, and France went into older forms of commerce, less exciting, less portentous for the future, but in the short run probably more lucrative than the spices of the Indian islands or the silver of the American mines. In the later sixteenth century the increasing prosperity of the merchants of the northwestern states of Europe allowed them to invest in exploration. At the same time, the hostilities between their rulers and Philip prepared them for aggression against the Portuguese and Spanish empires.

The subsequent geographical expansion of Western civilization was almost entirely the result of the efforts of the Dutch, the English, and the French. During the next two hundred years men from these three states discovered and mapped the contours of every considerable remaining land mass habitable by man. Except for some minute island clusters and the Arctic regions, an outline map of the known world made in 1780 is little different from one made today. Exploration inland, which depended in the main on the presence of navigable rivers, trade prospects, and feeble native societies, was necessarily slower work.

The three principal areas of exploration were North America, South America, and—except for the East Indies—the islands of the Pacific. Maritime exploration falls into two distinct periods: one before 1650 in the New World in which France, England, and the Netherlands took part, the other in the Pacific between 1760 and 1780, when the Frenchman Bougainville and the Englishman James Cook ascertained the essential geographical facts about New Zealand and Australia, the existence of which had long been known to the Spanish and Dutch.

In the Atlantic region settlement and inland exploration went hand in hand. As early as 1550, Europeans were familiar with the whole eastern shore of North America from the St. Lawrence southward, for John Cabot for the English, Giovanni da Verrazano and Jacques Cartier for the French, and hosts of Spaniards had made it possible to map accurately the Atlantic coastline, including the great Gulf of the St. Lawrence. After 1559 the quest for the so-called Northwest Passage to the Indies attracted many sailors of Elizabethan England, and it was while engaged on such a quest that Henry Hudson passed through the strait and into the bay that both now bear his name.

Thereafter the major exploratory work in North America followed inland waterways, and in this kind of exploration the French led. In the St. Lawrence France held the eastern watergate to the magnificent waterway networks of North America's central plain—the Great Lakes and the Mississippi River system. Beginning in the early 1600s with Samuel de Champlain, the French pushed down the St. Lawrence to the Great Lakes. Well before the seventeenth century ran out they had explored the whole Great Lakes region, found the Mississippi, found its junction with the Ohio, and traversed much of its length. Finally, in 1682, Cavelier de la Salle journeyed down the great river to its mouth. Eighteenth-century explorers, in quest of an overland route that would connect France's American possessions with a seaway to the Orient, pushed into the wilderness west of the Mississippi and discovered the great American West as far as the Rocky Mountains.

Thus were the "good-for-nothing lands" of the conquistadors opened to the eyes of the three northwest European states. As latecomers, they found much of the Western Hemisphere occupied by the Spanish and Portuguese. The entire coastline from Argentina to the east coast of Florida was already in the hands of the Iberian states and to dislodge them called for more force and a greater expenditure than the rulers of France, England, and the Netherlands felt they could afford. It was only because they had no choice in the matter that so many colonists from the northwest of Europe made their new homes in the lands along the Atlantic coast of North America. It was an area most unattractive to the statesmen of the mother country, producing at first little that the mother country

In 1562 a French party led by a Huguenot sea captain named Jean Ribaut made a number of landfalls along the Atlantic coast, including one shown here in northern Florida, and then planted an abortive colony in South Carolina; it was destroyed two years later by the Spanish. Theodore de Bry engraved this view from a now-lost painting done in 1564 by the Frenchman Jacques le Moyne.

could use or profit from. The French, after failing to establish themselves in the Carolinas, settled along the shores of the Gulf of St. Lawrence and along the broad course of that river. In 1608, after a number of ill-planned and unsuccessful efforts by others, Samuel de Champlain at last planted at Quebec the first permanent French colony anywhere in the world. Thereafter, French settlement spread slowly westward along the St. Lawrence and southward into the area of Nova Scotia and New Brunswick known as Acadia.

What the St. Lawrence was to the French, the Hudson was to the Dutch. At first, taking its broad lower course to be the strait that separated the Atlantic from the Pacific oceans, Henry Hudson had explored the river while in the employ of the Netherlands. In the 1620s the Dutch began to colonize the Hudson Valley. Controlling the entrance to the stream was the fortress town of New Amsterdam on Manhattan Island.

The Dutch were thus firmly planted in North America while the first English settlement of Jamestown in Virginia, founded in 1607, wavered between survival and extermination. The Virginia colony finally survived, but not before a great new wave of English immigration, the most concentrated and rapid in the entire colonial period, had reached the rocky shores around Massachusetts Bay in the 1620s and 1630s. The English settlements pressed out from their places of origin, pushing into the hinterlands and up and down the coast; some decades later other settlers direct from England founded new colonies in Maryland and Pennsylvania.

What the seventeenth-century rulers of France, the Netherlands, and England most wanted to get out of their overseas expansion could not be gotten from their mainland settlements in North America. They wanted precious metals, they wanted spices, and they wanted sugar; of these their North American colonies produced little or none. Indeed, the Spanish and Portuguese had possession of or sole access to the lands where spices, precious metals, and sugar were to be found. If the other states wanted these things, they had either to buy them from the Spanish and Portuguese or take them by force of arms. They had no objection at all to fighting, and the Spanish seizure of Portugal in 1580 made the prospect all the more attractive, since to the Protestant English sailors, the Calvinist Dutch sailors, and the Huguenot sailors and merchants of western France, Philip of Spain was the Devil incarnate.

Although neither France nor England was openly at war with Philip before 1587, French and English sailors had not waited for their rulers to become officially embroiled with Spain. In the 1570s they had joined the Dutch rebels in preying on the commerce of Philip's subjects in the English Channel, in the Atlantic, and on the eastern and western coasts of the Americas. The outbreak of open war intensified the predatory activities of the northern mariners, but although such raiding could reduce the profitability of Spain's empire, it could not wrest it away. The Spanish-American coasts were ravaged intermittently for almost a hundred years. Dutch, French, and English privateers and naval forces in the early days pillaged and burned the great ports in the colonies and even Cádiz itself.

In the seventeenth century, however, despite the profound decline of its power, Spain learned the trick of defending its continental American empire. Except for a few points, Spain did not seriously attempt to protect the enormously lengthy American coastline; the Spanish Empire in America became an inland empire with most of its chief centers in such mountain towns as Bogotá, Quito, and Mexico City. The coastal points the Spanish did defend were Cartagena, Portobelo, and Vera Cruz, the only points where European goods could legally enter Spain's continental colonies. These they fortified so heavily as to discourage assault from the sea. After several setbacks, the marauding squadrons of Spain's European enemies stopped the futile and costly business of trying to seize these impregnable bastions.

Only the Dutch ever succeeded in making an important dent in the Iberian empire in America. The Portuguese, not the Spanish, were their victims, and their success was only temporary. At the end of the twelve-year truce with Spain in 1621, the Dutch, then in the midst of their meteoric rise to maritime ascendancy, diverted some of their energy from the East Indies to America. In 1630, operating from bases in the Caribbean, they seized the coastal towns of northern Brazil. Seven years later, under the leadership of a prince of the House of Nassau, they established a Dutch colony in that area. In their customary businesslike manner, the Dutch introduced the cultivation of sugar cane and prospered mightily, especially when compared to the Portuguese farther down the coast. When Portugal at last succeeded in breaking loose from Spanish rule, the Portuguese in Brazil took heart and turned on the Dutch. Aided by the diversion of Dutch energies to the Republic's first war against England, the Brazilians methodically pushed the northern intruders out of the hinterlands and into the ports. These they systematically reduced, and by 1654 the Dutch dominion of northern Brazil had come to an end. With it ended the only major effort of the new imperialist states of northwestern Europe to carve out a large plantation colony on the American mainland south of the Rio Grande.

It was a different story in the East. There the Portuguese were faring ill even before powerful European rivals appeared to challenge their position. Albuquerque's grandiose dream of conducting a holy war and a commercial empire simultaneously was turning into a nightmare. Christian missionaries attacked the religious faith of Islam and established the Inquisition at Portugal's Indian port of Goa. They added religious heat to the smouldering resentment of Muslim traders, whose commerce the Portuguese preyed on, and of Muslim princes in the Spice Islands, whom the Portuguese laid under tribute from their great fortress at Malacca. In 1557 the little kingdom, which needed all its energy to maintain its imperial holdings along the African coast and its long lifeline to the East, fell into the hands of a king burning with crusading zeal. King Sebastian wasted Portugal's slim military and economic resources on a disastrous crusade against the Moroccan Moors. Meantime, the pressure of native Islamic princes against the Portuguese in the Indies was increasing. The latter maintained themselves in key positions at Goa and Malacca, but they had not established any strong position in Java on which the Malacca post depended for rice. In the Spice Islands they had lost ground before the end of the sixteenth century to some of the native sultans who continued to trade with their Arab co-religionists. It was against this decaying empire of the Portuguese in the East that the English and Dutch launched their attack in about 1600.

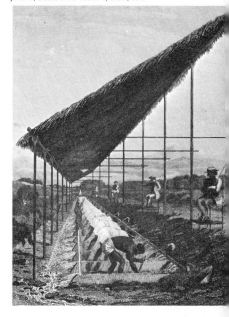

J. MAWE, *Travels in the Interior of Brazil*, 1812

Enslaved Negroes search for diamonds in the bed of a dammed-up Brazilian river under the watchful eyes of Portuguese overseers.

The Wars of Empire   The English and Dutch ventures in the East raised the curtain on almost two centuries of bloody imperial rivalry. Between 1600 and 1763, wars for empire were fought in the Spice Islands of the East Indies, the sugar islands of the West Indies, and the tea and cinnamon island of Ceylon; they were fought among the trading posts of Africa, in the colonial settlements of North America, on the Malay peninsula, and on the subcontinent of India; and most of all, they were fought on the old battlegrounds of Europe and on the high seas. What decided these battles in the end were shipping and sea power.

In maritime affairs the Dutch enjoyed a marked superiority over their European neighbors at the beginning of the seventeenth century. During the next fifty years, while Richelieu concentrated France's power on a showdown with the Hapsburgs and England invested most of its capital in domestic industry and most of its energies in a political crisis, the Dutch concentrated on overseas expansion. Following the instructions of voyagers who had learned the secrets of the passage east while in Portuguese employ, a small Dutch fleet made the round trip to Java between 1595 and 1597. The success of this voyage released a flood of Dutch commercial energies. Companies sprang up all over to try their luck in the Far East. They avoided the Strait of Malacca, which the Portuguese held by means of the fortress at Malacca, set up trading posts in Java, and found their way to the Spice Islands through the Sunda Strait between Java and Sumatra.

The Dutch soon learned by experience what the Portuguese already knew: that vigorous free trade in spices carried heavy penalties. The competition for cloves, nutmeg, and mace in the Moluccas drove up the buying price, while the sudden increase in supply depressed the selling price in the European market. The Dutch met the problem in 1602 by amalgamating all their existing enterprises into a single company. Commercially, the Dutch East India Company received a monopoly on Dutch trade in the East. Politically, the Estates General granted it power to arrange treaties, wage wars, and rule its own holdings.

The monopoly on Dutch trade in the Spice Islands only partially solved the company's problem. It eliminated competition among the Dutch for the goods of the East and the market in Europe, but it did not eliminate the competition of traders from England or Portugal. As long as that competition was intense, the price of spices in Europe would be depressed by an oversupply. Only the political powers that the Estates General granted the company could alter this situation, if the company decided to use those powers. It used them very vigorously indeed. It set out to drive all competitors from the Molucca trade by force. By 1615 the naval superiority of the Dutch had broken the grip of the Iberian powers on the Spice Islands. But the victorious Netherlanders then found themselves threatened by another competitor, the English East India Company, chartered by Queen Elizabeth in 1600. The futile efforts of far-off governments to negotiate a treaty dividing the Spice Island trade equitably between the two Protestant maritime states could not control the aggressive actions of company men on the scene in the East. The result was a foregone conclusion. The Dutch had invested the blood and money that drove out the Portuguese. Moreover, the Dutch company was far richer, more vigorous, and better organized than the English, and it had more ships. After squeezing the English from one position after another, the Dutch ended by massacring the English agents on the island of

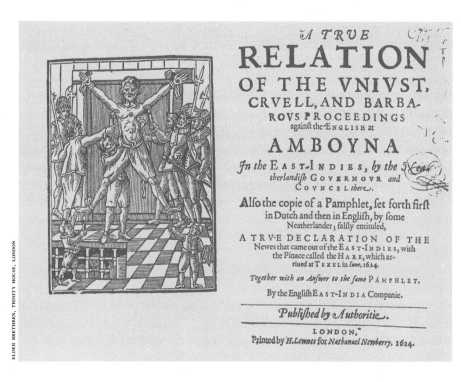

A pamphlet published in London in 1624 detailed the "cruell and barbarous" Dutch attack on the English outpost of Amboina that included, if the frontispiece is to be believed, the flaying of one of the victims.

Amboina in 1623. Though the incident embittered relations between the two Protestant powers in Europe, it did not result in war, and it gave the Dutch an undisputed monopoly of the spice trade from the Moluccas.

To press the attack further on the Portuguese position in the Orient, the Dutch needed a firmer base than that provided by the small trading posts they had established in the first years of the company's enterprise. Such a base they acquired on Java, by far the richest and most populous of the islands of the East Indies. Batavia (now Djakarta) became the center of Dutch power in the Indies, as Malacca was of Portuguese power, and Jan Pieterszoon Coen, the Dutch counterpart of Albuquerque, initiated a remorseless war of attrition in the East.

Eventually, the Dutch displaced the Portuguese from every strategic point the latter held in the East between Goa on the Malabar Coast and Macao in China. The capture of Malacca in 1641 gave the Dutch the key to the Chinese and Japanese trade. They drove the Portuguese from Formosa, and when the Japanese closed their empire to the West, the Dutch alone maintained a footing there. Finally, Ceylon engaged their vigorous attention. Here the Portuguese were strongly entrenched at Colombo and claimed a monopoly thereby on cinnamon, the world supply of which is still grown mainly on Ceylon. In a long campaign of almost twenty years, in which assaults on the Portuguese posts and forts were combined with attacks on Portuguese ships, the Dutch finally got rid of their rival in 1655, and thereafter the trade of the island remained in Dutch hands. Sixty years after their first Eastern venture the Dutch had battled their way into control of the greatest trading empire in the Orient. They were beyond dispute the paramount European power everywhere in the East—except on the coasts of India.

On those coasts, in the Caribbean Islands, and on the shores of Africa, the

Dutch, the French, and the English had also moved against the Iberian monopoly, but up to almost the middle of the eighteenth century none of the three powers had achieved the dominant position in those places that the Dutch had won east of India. Shortly after their respective East India companies were chartered, Dutch and English trading posts dotted the west (Malabar) and east (Coromandel) coasts of India and extended to the Ganges River country of Bengal. The Portuguese challenged the position of the newcomers both with their own arms and ships and by intriguing with the native rulers of the Indian states. But Portugal's power did not match its pretensions, and the combination of religious fanaticism and corruption that had marked its period of ascendancy ensured a welcome in India for its European enemies. The Portuguese were driven out of some of their positions and had to share others with rival European merchants; and their trade with Goa, their greatest Indian base, was strangled by a persistent Dutch blockade.

Although private companies of Frenchmen had made their way east earlier, it was 1664 before the French East India Company was launched. While the English company prospered greatly off the Indian trade and the Dutch company became in fact a great island empire, the French company teetered along feebly between life and death, its survival dependent less on its solvency than on the political purposes, fiscal needs, and whim of the royal government on which it leaned for support. Nevertheless, the French did secure and maintain a foothold at Pondicherry and a few other places. As we shall see in the following chapter, the decline of Dutch power in the eighteenth century and the collapse of the Mogul dynasty—Turkish in origin, Muslim in religion, Persian in culture—which had maintained order in India in the seventeenth century, left the French and the English to play for the high imperial stakes offered by a subcontinent in the throes of anarchy.

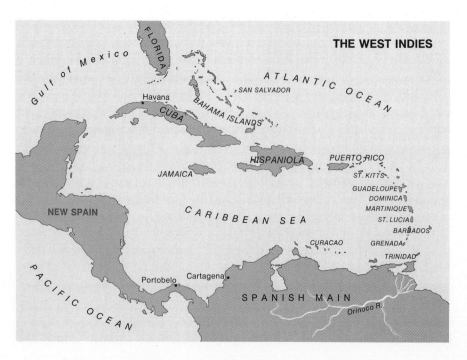

On the African coast, too, the three northern powers grasped the prize from the failing Portuguese. In this area the prize was black gold, the Negro slaves on whose labor depended the economic survival of the plantation colonies in the Caribbean and on the American mainland from Chesapeake Bay to the Río de la Plata. The English and the French established their slaving stations on sections of the coast not already occupied by the Portuguese. The Dutch arrived late, but characteristically seized the best stations by shooting the Portuguese out of them between 1617 and 1642.

The slave trade was of more than commercial interest to the three new imperial states, since in the course of the seventeenth century all of them acquired plantation colonies in America. Aside from the brief period when the Dutch held northern Brazil, only the English developed important plantation colonies on the mainland—Virginia, the Carolinas, and Maryland—by the large-scale cultivation of tobacco, but English, French, and Dutch alike seized Caribbean islands from the Spaniards. Since the Spanish had lost control of the American seas, they could not defend more than a few of the major spots in the West Indies. They clung to the greater islands, Cuba and Puerto Rico, fought a losing battle with the French in which they lost half of Hispaniola, or Santo Domingo, and another with the English in which they lost Jamaica. For lack of men to garrison them, Spain lost several smaller islands by default—Guadaloupe and Martinique to the French, Curaçao to the Dutch, and Barbados to the English.

By 1700, then, there were five important European empires instead of the dual Spanish-Portuguese empire of a century earlier. The French, the English, and the Dutch, as we have seen, acquired their overseas dominion by means varying all the way from peaceful occupation in North America through rapid and violent seizure in the Moluccas to long wars of attrition by sea and land in the Caribbean, Ceylon, and Malacca. While these colonial struggles were going on, the home countries were engaged intermittently in wars with one another on the European Continent.

We have said nothing so far of the relationship between the European and the overseas conflicts. The relationship in fact was tenuous through most of the seventeenth century. The Dutch were on terms of amity with the English in Europe while officials of the Dutch East India Company were slaughtering officials of the English East India Company on Amboina. Peace treaties in Europe did not necessarily make for peace overseas: there was, as the phrase went, "no peace beyond the line." Even treaties that were supposed to settle overseas conflicts were regarded by the hard-bitten men on the scene of the struggle as nuisances to be evaded or as nonsense to be disregarded. In Europe the Dutch passed from war to truce to war to peace with Portugal between 1600 and 1650, but through that same half-century not a year passed that the Dutch were not engaged in open military or naval operations against the Portuguese somewhere in the world.

By the same token, wars in Europe did not necessarily involve the imperial areas in the seventeenth century. Between 1652 and 1654 the Dutch and the English almost blew each other out of the seas around Britain in a great naval war, but the struggle in European waters produced no significant repercussions in the Indian Ocean or the western Atlantic, and the Dutch in New Amsterdam got along no worse than they had before with the English in Flushing scarcely ten miles away. When war threatened between their mother countries, the French and English colonists, who had amicably divided up the West Indian island of St. Kitts in 1625, covenanted to remain at peace with each other, whether their home countries came to blows or not.

The fact of the matter was that negotiating and treaty-making could not radically change a power situation built up overseas; they could only ratify it. If they failed to do so, the people involved simply evaded the agreements of their home governments and reversed decisions that they could not prevent. Consequently, the settlements that endured were those that accurately reflected the power position in the overseas areas to which they referred, regardless of the relative power of the European states involved. Thus, for example, no treaty for two hundred and fifty years attempted to transfer any substantial portion of the Spanish Empire on the American continent to any other European power, despite the fact that after 1660 Spain was practically impotent in Europe.

The only major transfers of territory on the American continents during the seventeenth century illustrate the same point. The revolt of the Portuguese against Spanish rule in 1641 in theory left Brazil divided between Spain and the Netherlands. Portugal was too heavily burdened with its fight for independence in Europe to intervene in Brazil. Yet the Brazilians not only adhered to Portugal, they also restored Portuguese rule in northern Brazil by driving out the Dutch. Moreover, in succeeding decades, they expanded up the Amazon and Paraná

The East Indies was the scene of shifting alliances. In 1602 an Anglo-Dutch squadron (the English ships are at top) took a huge Portuguese carrack in the Strait of Malacca. Within a year the Dutch and English were fierce trade rivals in the area.

rivers into territory assigned to Spain by the Pope in 1494. In 1750 the facts of power in the New World were recognized by the states of the Old in a treaty designed to shift the boundary of Brazil westward to conform to the actuality of Portuguese occupation. In return, Portugal acknowledged Spanish rule in the Philippines, although the Pope had assigned those islands to Portugal. Here again, European public law adjusted to the facts of overseas development, since Spanish settlers had long ruled and dominated in the Philippines.

Another major transfer of dominion in the New World was the Dutch cession of the extensive New Netherlands colony to England after the fall of New Amsterdam to the English in 1664. The fortress had fallen to an English force augmented by Connecticut settlers. Not a shot was fired. The Dutch colony was itself cosmopolitan rather than national. Few Dutchmen had chosen to emigrate from the Netherlands, since, as one of them remarked, anybody who cared to work for a living could make one at home. The treaty that ceded New Amsterdam to England ceded the English posts on the Surinam River in Guiana to the Dutch. Thus the Dutch, whose sole interest in America was the acquisition of exotic products for trading purposes, got what they wanted, and the English colonists, who had shown a capacity for large-scale settlement, won a continuous chain of holdings on the North American coast from the Carolinas to Maine.

The relative independence of the struggle for empire overseas from the struggle for power in Europe diminished toward the end of the seventeenth century. The conflicts among the trading posts and coastal fortresses in the East and among the colonial settlements in America increasingly blend with the conflicts on the battlegrounds of Europe into world wars of empire.

Meantime, in the midst of the fierce heat of religious wars, internal upheavals, and European power struggles, the colonizing and imperial states of the West had to work out terms for trading with and exploiting economically the lands they had seized or settled. They also had to develop powers of government and political controls over colonists and natives in territories a far journey from the European center, territories which their supreme rulers knew little about and never visited. And all the time that men in the mother countries of the new empires were working out the arrangement and rules that they conceived to be sound to regulate the relations of rulers to their overseas empires, the Europeans on the imperial frontier were making the terms that they deemed would best suit the varied and wholly new situations that faced them. All of this uncoordinated activity inaugurated the transformation of the many and varied civilizations of the earth into the interdependent world community of today. It also literally changed the face of the earth, since it set moving the greatest and most rapid displacements of vegetable and animal life that the world had ever known. It is these matters that will concern us in the next chapters.

2

The Imperial West

T he size of the trading area in which European merchants carried on business grew enormously between 1450 and 1750. Before 1450 Western merchants traded with those of other civilizations only in a few Levantine towns—Constantinople, Smyrna, Aleppo, Alexandria. By 1650 European merchants or their European agents were still doing business in these ports, but the Levant trade had been overshadowed by the new trade with India and the Far East. Trading stations were manned by Western merchants from Basra in the Persian Gulf to Japan—at Surat and Goa and Madras and a score of other towns of the Indian subcontinent; at Colombo on Ceylon; at Malacca on the strait that commanded the short route to the Spice Islands, China, and Japan; at Batavia on Java; at Amboina in the Spice Islands; and at Macao and Canton on the China coast. South of Europe, Western traders no longer confined themselves to the Mediterranean shore of Africa but ranged down its Atlantic coast picking up and dropping cargo all the way to the Cape of Good Hope. Westward across the Atlantic European ships entered ports that had not existed two hundred years before—Port Royal, Boston, New Amsterdam, Jamestown, Havana, Vera Cruz, Portobelo, Cartagena, Pernambuco, Belém.

As the area in which Europe traded grew, an equally significant transformation took place in the make up of the Western commercial community. At the beginning of the modern era this community was dominated by the Catalans, Venetians, and Genoese. By 1650 these merchants were being pushed aside by French, English, and Dutch merchants in all the ports of the Near East. In the new overseas areas of European trade the passing of Italian commercial primacy was even more evident. Nor were the Germans, formerly masters of northern European waters, able to keep up with the times. It was a rare sight to find a ship or a merchant of Venice or Genoa or any German city in the myriad ports of Africa, Persia, India, Southeast Asia, China, Japan, the Americas, or the East or West Indies. In the seventeenth century the seas were plied by the ships of Spain, Portugal, France, England, and above all Holland.

The struggle for commercial supremacy in transoceanic trade ran almost parallel to the struggle for overseas empire. For about a century after the earliest discoveries, Spain and Portugal, the states that pioneered in these adventures, monopolized the trade. Then, as the sixteenth century drew to a close, England and the Dutch Republic entered the competition; a few decades later the French made their debut. The heyday of the Dutch traders was the fifty-year period between the end of the truce with Spain in 1621 and Louis XIV's onslaught against Holland (1672–1678).

As for the English, the promise of trader-pirates like Hawkins and Drake to challenge the control of the Iberian merchants in the New World was long in being fulfilled. Balked by Spanish America's firm resistance in the West, crushed by the superior power of the Dutch in the East Indies, deprived of the steady

The Expansion of Europe's Trading Area

Aelbert Cuyp's sturdy Dutch merchant holding the hand of his equally sturdy wife and pointing with pride at the big East Indiamen that carried his goods seems to belong on an Amsterdam wharf; the setting is in fact the harbor of Batavia in Java.

support of the state by the civil dissension between 1603 and 1660, English merchants did not begin to catch up with the Dutch until the restoration of Charles II in 1660. Backed by a navy that had won mastery of the sea by 1715, they gradually gained a dominant position in overseas commerce, though not to the exclusion of the other nations. Portugal and Spain still traded with Latin America, the Dutch clung to their monopoly in the East Indies, the French, the Dutch, and the Spaniards continued to trade in the West Indies, and Portuguese, Dutch, and French merchants competed with the English on the coasts of Africa and India.

For the century after 1530 the bullion of America and the spices of the Indies remained the leading overseas imports of Europe. Europe's earliest exports to America were the necessities of life for the new settlers. As Spaniards and Portuguese in America organized the exploitation of nature and of Negro labor for production of the necessities, they turned to Europe for fine goods, which the skills of their enthralled labor force did not provide, and for the recruitment of that force by a steady flow of slaves from Africa. During most of the period Europe made little that the Orient cared to buy. The Dutch got around this difficulty in the Spice Islands by taking as tribute what they could not get by trade. Elsewhere in Eastern Asia they solved the problem much as they did in Europe. They became the major carrier of intra-Asiatic trade, and the profits of their shipping services paid for much that they sent to Europe from the East. Merchants of other lands, less fortunate than the Dutch, had to pay hard cash brought from Europe for Asiatic goods.

The cargoes carried from Asia west around the Cape included Japanese copper and silk, Chinese silk, porcelain, and tea, cloves and nutmegs from the Moluccas, pepper and coffee from Java, cinnamon from Ceylon, Indian silk, pepper, tea, and all kinds of cotton goods from the coarsest to the finest weaves, and rugs from Persia, along with some indigo, drugs, and fine oriental craftwork in metals and jewelry.

Because the trip from much of the American coast to the ports of Europe was far shorter than the passage from India and the Indies—four to six weeks as against six to nine months—lower shipping costs made it profitable to send products that were bulky in proportion to their price. The inexhaustible cod of the Newfoundland Grand Bank joined the North Sea herring to eke out the scanty ration of animal food in the European diet. Also from the north came a heavy harvest of furs that moved down the St. Lawrence and the Hudson. Farther south lay the tobacco plantations of Virginia and the rice fields and a few cotton fields in the Carolinas. From the islands of the West Indies and from tropical South American tobacco, cocoa, coffee, indigo, and above all vast quantities of sugar went to Europe; and late in the period the region of the Río de la Plata began to send cattle and grain to relieve the constant food deficit of Spain.

Mercantilism as Imperial Policy   The overseas expansion of the Western world and the elaboration of the economic policy of the various states along mercantilist lines took place concurrently. The men who looked for profit in the Indies trade and the men who sought gold, homes, land, or a religious refuge in the New World were simply seeking the things in life they valued most. But the statesmen of the lands from which they came acted with mercantilist principles in mind, and they could never be disinterested spectators in the drama of European expansion. The overseas settlements of European peoples had come into being either by permission of the state or with its active support and assistance. As the struggle for empire developed, trading outposts and settlement colonies alike called on their mother countries to help in defending them against the onslaught of hostile states. In that struggle, each country had to decide what overseas areas to protect and how much of its resources to allocate to such protection. In the myriad decisions involving the colonies that statesmen had to make after 1648, they were guided largely by their notion of what colonies in general, and each colony in particular, were worth to the mother country. They drew their conclusions from the common stock of economic ideas of the day, that is, from mercantilist ideas. We shall examine mercantilism in detail in Chapter 4; here we are interested in its application to the problems of empire.

The herring fisheries of the North Sea played an important role in the Dutch economy. Scenes painted on Delft plates depict net repairing (above) and packing the salted catch.

The imperial powers of Europe all wanted the same kind of empire—one that would give them the materials that the mother country did not produce. This way of regarding possessions outside Europe was very durable. Evaluation of overseas areas in terms less narrowly commercial and less naïvely mercantilist had scarcely begun before the great upheavals of the late eighteenth century took place in the colonies and trading empires, starting with the American Revolution.

The items of first importance in the eyes of the mother countries were gold and silver. From the time that Columbus, returning from his first voyage, speculated on the precious metals to be found in the lands he had discovered, European statesmen entertained hopes that great stores of such riches were to be had for the taking in whatever place colonists happened to be settling at the moment. Spices were also attractive to the empire-building states, for no European land produced them, all European peoples used them, and they brought a high price on the European market. Any state that could get them to that market seemed to have the next best thing to a gold mine. Disillusion with spices came slowly, though their value from a mercantilist point of view declined fairly rapidly. The total quantity that could be disposed of in Europe was small, and any sharp increase in supply sent prices tumbling toward the abyss where bankruptcies are made. By the eighteenth century, those spices that had first drawn men to brave the perils of the Indies voyage had become a secondary item of trade even for the Dutch, who had won a monopoly of the supply.

Indeed, if we regard the whole of overseas commerce, the same may be said of gold and silver. New exotic products that the Western world seemed ready to utilize in indefinite amounts—coffee, tea, furs, sugar, tobacco, and Negroes—took the place of precious metals and spices on the preferred list of European statesmen. To obtain and keep control of commerce in the relatively limited areas where these products grew or could be raised in profitable quantity became one of the prime objectives of mercantilist statesmen.

This led to a paradoxical situation. Excepting the area where Spain found some of its mines in America, it would be true to say that the value European statesmen set on an overseas possession was likely to be inversely proportional to its suitability for colonization. The products those statesmen most wanted generally came from areas that, for reasons of climate, conditions of living, and the density of the native population, were least suitable for European settlement. On the other hand, the statesmen tended to regard the areas most attractive to European settlers as mere nuisances, or even liabilities. From the mercantilist point of view, the East Indies, India itself, and the West Indies were the most precious parts of any overseas empire, yet the European populations in those regions were so small that they could not defend themselves against the assaults of other European powers. In the "bread colonies" or "provision colonies," the settlers from the Old World thrived and multiplied. Their products, however, did little to supplement those of the mother country, and so they were likely to receive little consideration—and that unfavorable—in the formation of mercantilist policy.

The policy pursued by all imperial states with respect to their empires was monopolistic. The so-called old colonial system was a system of control of the colonies by the mother country in which the means were political and the ends economic. Some European states wielded indirect control, as was the case when direct rule was held by one of the various trading companies. Whether control was direct or indirect, it was absolute—that is, there was no authority to whom the colonists could appeal against a law or decree of the ruler of the mother country. Moreover, except in the English colonies, the authority of European governments over their empires was despotic; they could (and did) legislate with finality on all matters concerning the colonies.

The despotic authority of the mother country was exercised to further the two related purposes of mercantilist policy: to maintain a favorable balance of trade for the mother country, and to increase the mother country's relative power among the states of Europe. Although there were a few minor and five major imperial states in the Western world—Portugal, France, the Dutch Republic, Spain, and England—we will deal with the imperial policy of only the last two, since, in their dealings with their empires, Spain and England tried almost all the mercantilist devices and exhibited all the mercantilist attitudes that characterized the policy of all the imperial states during the period.

In 1628 a fleet of massive Spanish treasure galleons ran aground near Havana and, as shown here, was plundered by a Dutch squadron. His poor seamanship cost the Spanish admiral his head and the Spanish king some 12 million guilders, mostly in silver.

The Spanish set the pace by framing a mercantilist policy for their American empire in the early days of its development and establishing a government bureau—the *Casa de Contratación*—to supervise all trade relations between Spain and the Spanish American colonies. To close out all other states from trading with its colonies, Spain established rules that drastically simplified, and distorted, the natural course of commerce. No goods could go from any non-Spanish port to the Spanish colonies. No goods could go from any Spanish port except Seville or Cádiz. No merchants could handle American-bound merchandise except members of the Sevillian merchant guild. The merchants of Seville could send goods only to three continental American ports—Cartagena, Vera Cruz, and Portobelo. Furthermore, they could not send their ships at their convenience, because for protection the ships had to sail in flotillas—two each year on the outward passage, one for South America and one for Mexico, one a year homeward bound making rendezvous at Havana. The concentration in one flotilla for the return voyage permitted the fullest possible protection for the bullion-laden treasure ships.

Theoretically, these regulations ensured the monopoly of the colonial market to Spanish manufacturers and, theoretically, they thus improved the general Spanish balance of trade. They made Seville and Cádiz the universal market or storehouse for all the products of the Spanish colonies, thus increasing Spain's independence from the products of its European rivals in the struggle for power. By confining colonial trade to Spanish ships, they encouraged the Spanish shipping industry and provided a mercantile foundation for Spanish sea power.

If in theory Spain's old colonial system was in every respect the answer to a mercantilist's dream, in actual operation it was a mercantilist's nightmare. Spain did not and could not supply demands of its colonies for manufactured goods. For reasons of a very complex sort, Spanish manufacturing declined from the sixteenth to the eighteenth centuries. The Seville merchants became in effect mere agents for French, Dutch, and English merchants, who found an outlet for the manufactures of their native lands in the colonies of Spain. And since neither Spain nor its colonies produced enough goods to offset their imports, the foreign merchants, by hook or by crook and despite the Spanish prohibition, had to be paid in gold and silver.

Thus, Spanish mercantilist regulations notwithstanding, the actual course of Spanish colonial commerce operated to secure a favorable balance of trade for its rivals. It did so through the foreign merchants who traded in Seville. It did so to an even greater extent through the larger number of foreign merchants who completely disregarded the whole apparatus of regulations to trade directly with the Spanish colonies. Here Buenos Aires, the "wrong" kind of colony from a mercantilist point of view, got its revenge on a neglectful mother country—as Massachusetts, another wrong kind of colony, was to do later to another mother country. Buenos Aires became the favored port of the contraband trade of all the great mercantile states. It had a good route up the Río de la Plata and across the Andes to the Spanish colonies on the west coast of South America, and goods came to it at a competitive free-market price instead of at the monopoly price at which goods came to the legal ports in Spanish America. Consequently, foreign goods smuggled through Buenos Aires frequently drove off the Peruvian and Chilean markets the legal goods that came through the Seville monopoly. Spain

The Colonial Systems of Spain and England

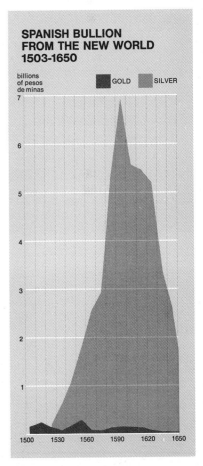

SPANISH BULLION
FROM THE NEW WORLD
1503-1650

billions of pesos de minas

GOLD   SILVER

The wealth of the New World, charted here in annual averages by decades, as it was received in Seville. Silver production skyrocketed with the discoveries of incredibly rich lodes at Potosí in Peru (1545) and at Zacatecas north of Mexico City (1548).

thus offers an example of a state with a formally perfect mercantilist policy that broke down completely because Spain could not hold up its end of the imperial compact—to supply finished goods in return for raw materials.

In contrast with Spain, England entered rather late into the race for empire and during the first half-century of its imperial history did not get around to formulating a coherent colonial policy with appropriate means of enforcement. It is perhaps an exaggeration to say, as some have said, that England acquired its first empire in a fit of absence of mind. It might better be suggested that the empire burgeoned almost unnoticed while Englishmen were attending to their country's internal ailments. Certainly no far-sighted mercantilist statesman would ever have planned such a queer empire or wished it on his successors. It had a bit of everything—trading posts in India, slave stations in Africa, a small wedge of the Caribbean coast of South America, West Indian islands, a frozen slab of fur country around Hudson Bay, plantation colonies in the Carolinas and Virginia, and farming, fishing, and trading colonies farther up the Atlantic coast of North America.

It was not until the second half of the seventeenth century that the rulers of England got around to developing a coherent policy for their empire. That policy represents the purest example of the application of mercantilist principles to the problems of empire. It was formulated between 1660 and 1696, coinciding with the ascendency of Colbert in France, when mercantilist notions had arrived at full maturity in Europe. Its basic framework was provided by the Navigation Act of 1660, the Staple Act of 1663, the Plantations Duties of 1673, and the codification of previous legislation in 1696. In 1696, too, King William III established the Board of Trade and Plantations, a permanent official body authorized to concern itself with the problems of imperial trade on mercantilist principles and to recommend appropriate policies to the government.

The Staple Act of 1663 makes explicit the mercantilist purpose of the whole body of English legislation and regulation. That purpose, the act stated, was to keep the colonies "in firmer dependence upon" England, to make them "more beneficial and advantageous unto it in the further employment and increase of English shipping, and vent [i.e., sale] of English manufactures and commodities," to render "the navigation from the same more safe and cheap," to make "the kingdom a staple, not only of the commodities of those Plantations but also of the commodities of other countries" trading with English colonies, and, in short, to follow "the usage of other nations" of keeping "their plantation trade to themselves."

The basic means to these ends were as follows: (1) Goods shipped from England to the colonies, or from the colonies to England, or among the colonies, had to be transported in English or colonial ships. (2) All goods consigned to the English colonies from other countries had to be disembarked in England and reshipped from there. (3) Certain articles produced by the colonies—sugar, rice, tobacco, indigo, and cotton, among others—could be shipped only to England. Foreign buyers could purchase them in England alone, not in the English colonies. On entry the enumerated products were subject to the regular English tariff. If they were reshipped to a foreign land, a part of that duty was refunded. (4) Goods could be shipped from one English colony to another on payment of a

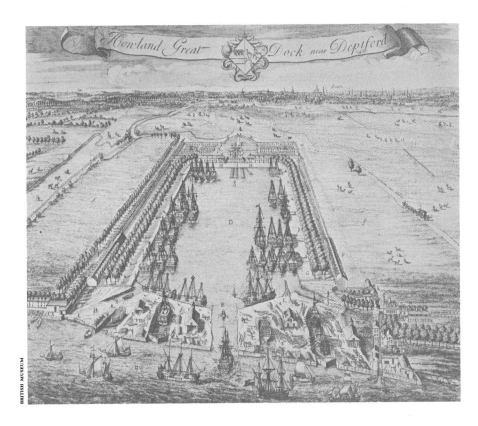

Britain's colonial policy led to the doubling of tonnage in its merchant marine between 1660 and 1688. An engraving of a dockyard at Deptford on the Thames shows five vessels under construction (foreground).

duty called the Plantation Duty and deposit of a bond to guarantee that any part of the cargo reshipped would go through the English staple.

The old colonial system embodied in the legislation enacted between 1660 and 1696 was clearly designed to apply mercantilist principles to the relations between the English colonies and the mother country. England was to benefit from the increase in ships and sailors that resulted from the exclusion of foreign shipping in the colonial trade. It was also to benefit from a first claim on the products of its colonies most in demand in Europe and from a near monopoly of the colonial market for manufactured goods. These benefits, if attained, would realize the mercantilist rationale: colonies existed to enrich the mother country by providing it with raw material it would otherwise have to purchase from other states, and with a market for its manufactures.

Although the mercantilists believed that profit to the mother country alone justified empire, they also believed that the colonists should derive benefits from the system. For one thing, the English navy and, during wartime, contingents of the English army helped protect the colonies from their enemies, the French and the Spanish; and it was England, not the colonies, that supported the army and navy. Moreover, England provided the colonies with a market for their principal exports, and in that market afforded them a considerable tariff preference to protect them from competition. In England, British West Indian sugar paid only half the duties paid by the sugar of foreign nations, and colonial tobacco was protected against competition by the actual destruction of tobacco crops grown by English farmers. This balance of privileges and restrictions constituted what

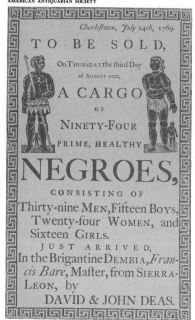

Charlestown, July 24th, 1769.

TO BE SOLD,

On THURSDAY the third Day
of AUGUST next,

A CARGO

OF

NINETY-FOUR

PRIME, HEALTHY

NEGROES,

CONSISTING OF

Thirty-nine MEN, Fifteen BOYS,
Twenty-four WOMEN, and
Sixteen GIRLS.

JUST ARRIVED,

In the Brigantine DEMBIA, *Francis Bare*, Master, from SIERRA-
LEON, by

DAVID & JOHN DEAS.

Notice of a slave auction in Charleston, South Carolina, in 1769. The slave trade was carried largely in colonial vessels; in 1770 Rhode Island alone dispatched 150 slavers.

the French, who copied the English system in the edicts of 1727 and 1737, called the Colonial Pact.

In the early eighteenth century the narrowest mercantilist ideas began to recede before the broader concept, still mercantilist, of an interdependent, self-sustaining Atlantic empire, an empire in which each part, even the hitherto unprepossessing northern colonies, had an indispensable function. English manufactures found an outlet in Africa in exchange for slaves, in the West Indies and the American southern colonies in exchange for sugar, cotton, rice, tobacco, and other exotic products, and in the northern colonies for cash. The Negroes bought in Africa by slavers of England and New England provided the labor force in the plantation colonies, and those colonies offered to the northern provision and mercantile colonies—the so-called bread colonies—a market for their food surpluses and for Negro slaves. Gains from this trade enabled the provision colonies to buy manufactures in England and Negroes in Africa with cash. The raw materials of the plantation colonies made the mother country independent of foreign supplies and provided it with surpluses to sell for cash on the European market. And, of course, this intricate circulation of goods and services throughout the Atlantic empire stimulated the growth of British maritime power.

This integrated mercantilist empire presented a number of problems. For one thing, it was sometimes difficult to find suitable colonial products for shipment to the English staple. It was also difficult to prevent the colonies from manufacturing products that competed with English exports to them. A third problem was that the colonial areas were hard pressed to come up with enough of either cash or supplies to enable them to buy their manufactures from Britain. In the first respect, the Carolinas were a problem; the colonies north of Maryland were a problem in all three respects.

The function of the Board of Trade and Plantations was to discover means for meeting these and other difficulties of imperial policy as they occurred. The proposed expedient of encouraging the Carolinas to produce silks, wines, currants, raisins, capers, wax, almonds, and olives by exempting them from duties was a veritable mercantilist's dream, since England had to buy those commodities from foreign states. The only trouble with the idea was that the Carolinas were wholly unsuitable for producing any of the proposed items. When the Carolinas at last hit upon rice as a plantation crop, it had to be exempted from the English staple in order to compete successfully in the southern European market, but at least it provided the plantation owners with the wherewithal to buy English manufactures and Negro slaves. The Board of Trade also offered a bounty to the northern colonies to produce ship supplies, a pressing need in England.

The northern colonies proved to be a somewhat disappointing market and compounded this defect by showing an inclination to manufacture products for their own consumption. Parliament sought to discourage such mercantilist heresies by prohibiting the colonial manufacture of ironware, beaver hats, and certain kinds of woolens. The problem of how the heavily populated northern colonies were to buy English manufactures without goods to exchange for them or cash to pay for them remained unsolved.

Once the subjects of European rulers had established themselves in lands separated by thousands of miles of ocean from their mother countries, those rulers faced the problem of contriving means to govern them. Unlike the ancient Greeks, the European states did not permit their colonists to establish independent regimes where they settled, for to do so would have frustrated the commercial aims that led these states to invest in expansion in the first place.

The oldest of the great overseas empires was Spain's. Except for the Philippine Islands, it was concentrated in the Western Hemisphere. It comprised practically all of South America except Brazil and the Guianas; all of Central America except British Honduras; Mexico, including most of what is now the western United States; Florida, extending north into a no man's land disputed between the Spanish and the English in Carolina, and west along the Gulf of Mexico into a no man's land disputed between the Spanish and the French in Louisiana; Cuba; Puerto Rico; and Santo Domingo, the eastern half of Hispaniola.

This vast empire received its basic institutions in the sixteenth century. Discovered, explored, and conquered by Castilians, its government bore the impress of the institutions of Castile in the age of the new monarchy. The most marked trait of Castilian administration was the concentration of supreme governing and policy-making powers not in ministers of the crown or in viceroys but in councils that followed the king on his travels. The supreme authority over the Spanish Empire was concentrated in 1524 in the Council of the Indies. The American empire belonged not to Castile but to the *crown* of Castile. Mexico and Peru were kingdoms independent of and coordinate with Castile under a common sovereign, and therefore the Council of the Indies was coordinate with, not subordinate to, the Council of Castile, and it performed parallel functions. It made all the laws for the administration, taxing, and policing of the empire. It nominated men to all the important offices in the imperial service, and all officials were accountable to it. It also supervised all ecclesiastical matters and nominated the American bishops. It exercised supreme judicial powers with final appellate jurisdiction over all other courts in Spain and America in matters concerning the colonies. It even decided what books might be introduced into the Indies.

The chief agents of the Council of the Indies in America were the viceroys of New Spain and Peru and the *audiencias*. The position of viceroy was a curious mixture of impotence and omnipotence. As supreme representatives of the king in America, viceroys had enormous responsibilities. Yet they were hampered at every turn by the Council of the Indies, which insisted that all major decisions be left in its hands, although few of the councilors had ever been to America. The Council's notion of a major decision was inclusive, extending even to the directions in which streets should be laid down and the size of city blocks.

On the other hand, the viceroys acted on a principle of Spanish law that permitted them to "obey but not execute" when a law or regulation seemed to them foolish or inconvenient in view of the particular circumstances of their viceroyalty. Such laws they sent back to the Council in Spain for amelioration. Since communication was slow, and several exchanges might be necessary, and since the Council was extremely deliberate in acting on viceregal requests for new legislation, the two institutions—Council and viceroyalty—tended to cancel out each other and prevent either from being able to do much harm—or good.

REAL BIBLIOTECA DE EL ESCORIAL

A manuscript illustration depicts a Franciscan monk presenting a census report he had prepared for the Mexican province of Mechoacan to the viceroy of New Spain in 1543.

A manuscript prepared by Mexican Indians in 1565 included these drawings of Viceroy Luis de Velasco (opposite page) in conversation with an Indian he had appointed judge.

Confusion was increased by the absence of any orderly collection of the Council's decrees. The Council itself had only a vague notion of the body of law it had created. In the 1630s a Spanish jurist reduced 400,000 orders under the king's seal to 11,000, but the final work of codification was not completed and in the hands of the administration in America until 1681.

The *audiencias* were the supreme courts for the viceroyalties. They were modeled on the Castilian court of the same name, and they functioned as the chief administrative council for the viceroyalty. Since the officers of the *audiencia* were appointed in Spain rather than by the viceroy in America, they often assumed an independent position with respect to the viceroy and hampered his freedom of action.

The rest of the imperial administration was also derived from Castilian models. As in Spain, the main local officer of the crown was the *corregidor*. This local governor usually ruled with the help of town officials. The latter were elective in the earliest days of Spanish settlement, but, strapped for cash, the crown soon took to selling the town offices. Thus, during most of the history of the Spanish Empire, the posts were the private property of the original purchasers, of their offspring, or of persons who had bought the office from its former owner. Of self-government in Spanish America there was scarcely a trace.

At the very outset the Spanish government in America ran into the problem of all imperial governments—the native non-Christian population. In most of the empire the American Indians were numerous, given to sedentary occupations, especially farming, and disciplined to a fairly highly organized economic life and political order. The Spanish government early made a series of crucial decisions: the American natives were not to be exterminated by direct violence; they were not to be enslaved or deprived of all means of livelihood; they were to be Christianized; they were to come directly under the protection of Spanish law; and they were to be required to pay tribute in labor and in kind to the colonizers.

These decisions found economic embodiment in the institutions of the *encomienda* and the *mita*. The *encomienda*, the earliest attempt to rescue the Indian population from extinction or enslavement at the hands of the insatiable Spanish settlers, obliged the natives to pay the settlers tribute from their lands. In return, the Spaniards were expected to allow the Indians to work their lands for their own subsistence for part of the year. The *mita*, intended as an alternative to chattel slavery, exacted periods of forced labor, but did not permanently assign particular native work gangs to particular Spanish-owned estates.

Nevertheless, despite a struggle on behalf of the Indian that became more and more feeble as it moved from the Council in Madrid to the fields and mines of America, permanent institutions of native bondage were established. For one thing, the impoverished Indians had to seek from the *encomienda* a commutation of tribute in money to tribute in labor. Secondly, loans to the natives laid the basis for debt peonage, since the loans were collectable in labor. Generations of work failed to free the Indians from their ever recurring obligations. Neither the *encomienda* nor the *mita* depopulated the mainland; they simply subjected the Indians to Spanish rather than to Aztec or Inca exploitation. But on the Caribbean islands the more backward natives were disastrously affected by forced labor and rapidly died off. To replace the exterminated native labor supply, black slaves were brought from Africa, and soon chattel slavery was extended to the mainland.

The social structure of the Spanish Empire paralleled its racial composition. The heights were occupied by the governing class, directly recruited in Spain. The Spanish settlers comprised an aristocracy living off the forced labor of those below them. Between the Spaniards and the natives were the mestizos, born of the union, usually illicit, of Spanish men and native women. Legally free, mestizos suffered social disabilities and occupied the lower-middle-class jobs. The native Indians and the Negroes, who provided the labor that maintained the colonial economy, were at the bottom of the social ladder.

This whole mass was ruled in the secular sphere by the Spanish government and in the spiritual sphere by the Catholic Church under Spanish ecclesiastics. The Church, which was the main agent of European culture, also participated in the exploitation of the Indians whom it baptized. The results of Spanish colonial policy were unique. In no other European empire (with the possible exception of the Portuguese in Brazil) was a large native population at least superficially Westernized and Christianized. Only in Latin America (and the Philippines) was a predominantly non-European population conquered not merely for Western exploitation but for Western civilization.

Portuguese imperial rule in Brazil was stamped with the effects of the sixty years (1580–1641) of Spanish rule in Portugal. The Spanish kings reorganized the administration along Castilian lines, so that, except for the somewhat slacker rein held by the governing council in Europe, Portuguese rule in Brazil was essentially very similar to Spain's rule in its own American empire.

The Dutch Empire in the Indies

The Dutch Empire comprised the small holding of Surinam, or Dutch Guiana, on the northern coast of South America, a few West Indian islands, some slave stations on Africa's west coast, a few way stations along the route to India (including one at the Cape of Good Hope), trading stations along the coast of India, on Formosa, and in Japan, and, above all, Ceylon and the East Indies.

The Dutch Empire in the East Indies was in every important respect different from the Spanish Empire. Spain's empire was primarily continental and colonial, based on the settlement of a considerable Spanish population in the imperial area. These Spanish colonists along with a few Spaniards in Europe formed the exclusive economic and political ruling class of the empire. They derived their income from directly exploiting the large native population, and they introduced this population to Western culture; the laws, language, institutions, and religion of European Spain became the laws, language, institutions, and religion of the subjected natives. By 1700 Spain's hold on its empire depended on the loyalty of the colonial Spaniards to the mother country and on their capacity to defend their land, rather than on the military or maritime power of the mother country itself—a power that was in fact quite feeble at the end of the seventeenth century.

The Dutch Empire in the East Indies was primarily insular, maritime, and commercial. Dutch settlers in the East were numerically insignificant in the vast sea of Oriental humanity. In the Indies the Dutch were the paramount military power, but they were by no means the only power. Native kingdoms abounded, and the Dutch were far too few to attempt to rule them. They left this task to the

A 1682 Dutch engraving of the Javanese port of Batavia—known as the "Queen of the Eastern Seas"—reveals a distinctive Dutch architecture amidst an Oriental setting.

native princes, who oppressed their own subjects and waged incessant war on one another. The Dutch intervened only when they judged that the oppression or wars endangered their access to and control of the products they wanted for the European market. They constituted an exclusive economic and political ruling class only in small areas of the East. The extent of these areas was determined not by an appetite for conquest and rule but by purely commercial considerations. The Dutch had gone east to trade, and they sought only so much political power there as they deemed necessary for trading purposes.

From beginning to end, the amount of power they felt impelled to acquire for commercial reasons was not inconsiderable, and it tended to increase rather than to decrease, but it was worlds away from the absolute sovereignty of the Spanish in America. The Dutch, as traders first and last, undertook no civilizing mission among the native population. They waged no religious wars against Islamism, Buddhism, or the primitive religions still practiced in parts of the Indies, and they made no serious effort to make converts to Christianity. Nor did they impose their language, laws, or customs on the peoples with whom they had dealings. If the Spanish colonial empire in America represented the maximum penetration of Western civilization among non-European peoples, the Dutch commercial empire in the Indies represented the minimum penetration. The hold of the Dutch on their empire depended entirely on their naval supremacy in the Indies.

Supreme control over the Dutch Empire in the East lay theoretically in the hands of seventeen merchants in the Netherlands, the directors of the Dutch East India Company. In actuality, however, the empire was controlled by the managers who ran the company from day to day, since the directors met only three times a year. The managers found that from Amsterdam they could exercise only the sketchiest authority over the company's agents in the East, thousands of miles away, yet the Amsterdam headquarters was the only formal link among those agents. When one of them applied to Amsterdam for a policy decision, communications were such that it was often two years before the decision was relayed to him.

This was an impossible situation, especially since the actions of one agent were likely to have important repercussions in the field of operations of another. In 1609, therefore, the company created the office of governor general. The governor general and his advisory council were to reside in the East Indies. A permanent fortified station to serve as headquarters for the governor and as a rendezvous for the company's ships was needed, and in 1619, after a sharp conflict with the English, Governor General Jan Coen secured Batavia (now Djakarta) in Java. Batavia was the first territorial base of the Dutch Empire in the Indies and its capital for more than three hundred years. The company established fortified posts on several other islands and entered into treaties for trade monopoly with the native rulers. From these posts the Dutch policed the seaways against pirates and smugglers.

When and where the company did assume sovereign authority, it did so in the interests of trade. For example, it restricted clove and nutmeg production in the Moluccas to Amboina and Banda, over which it exercised direct rule. It collected the spices as tribute and destroyed in the fields any surpluses that might disturb the monopoly by entering the channels of trade through smuggling. Company government in the Spice Islands was simply an efficient organization of extortion in the service of monopoly.

An unbending Calvinist, Jan Coen ruthlessly carved out a Dutch empire in the East Indies between 1618 and his death in 1629. His portrait was painted in about 1626.

WESTFRIESCH MUSEUM, HOORN

On Java the company was initially impelled to take political power in order to secure a food supply, since the company's officials, sailors, slaves, and the natives who raised its spices were dependent on a steady supply of Javanese rice. Later, the company used this power to maintain a monopoly of trade to and from Java and to control the production of coffee, which eventually became more profitable than spices in the European market. It held its political obligations in Java to a minimum, however, and directly ruled only the vicinity of Batavia. The other parts of the island under Dutch sovereignty were governed by "regents," native princes who had to obey all the orders of the local company agents. Since those agents rarely ordered anything but produce, however, the regents practically had a free hand. An even freer position was enjoyed by the rulers of the large remainder of Java, who were bound only to recognize a vague Dutch superiority and to live up to certain treaty obligations, largely commercial.

Thus the native peoples were completely untouched by the spirit of Western civilization, knowing the West through the Dutch only as a source of efficient violence, capable of exacting from them whatever goods it demanded. All the European states that participated in the early expansion of Western civilization were motivated to some extent by avarice, but in none of them was avarice so perfectly unalloyed as in the Dutch. Company government in the Dutch East Indies faithfully reflected the spirit of Dutch imperialism. It was devoid of any sense of a cultural or religious mission; "its pole star [was] profit, and its lodestone greed."

The French Colonial Empire Toward the end of the seventeenth century the French colonial empire comprised a few feeble trading posts in India, a slaving station in Senegal, several small Caribbean islands, and the vast North American territories of Canada and Louisiana. The latter included claims to the whole valley of the Mississippi and its tributaries.

The French colonial regime, like that of Spain and the Netherlands, reflected the character and practices of the home government. It breathed the absolutist spirit of Louis XIV and his adviser Colbert, who was responsible for determining its form. It was rigidly orthodox in its Catholicism, highly centralized in administration, vigorously paternalistic, and militarily efficient. Canada was treated as a province of the mother country. It had its governor, its *intendant*, and, in the so-called Supreme Council, a high court combining the traits of the French provincial *parlement* and the Grand Council. It did not have, however, that right to remonstrate against royal decrees so dear to the *parlements* of France and so hateful to Louis XIV.

As in France, the *intendant* was the center of governmental activity. He corresponded with Paris, planned internal improvements, pressed the home government to encourage settlement in New France, and rearranged land grants to protect the settlers and speed the clearing of the forests. The area suitable for settlement in Canada was rigidly determined by conditions of economic geography. Productive land with ready access to the sole effective channel of trade and line of communication lay along the banks of the St. Lawrence; that great valley thus became a sort of one-street village of farms, several hundred miles long and surrounded by wilderness.

In New France the problem posed by the natives was quite different from the problems faced by either the Spanish or the Dutch, for there was no great indigenous population of cultivators for the French settler to exploit. The Indians of eastern North America were few and culturally backward, hunters rather than farmers. The most powerful tribal confederation, the Iroquois, had been hostile to the French since the days of Champlain. Other tribes were friendly, and trade with them provided the French with furs, the major export of New France. But whether friendly or unfriendly, the Indians could not be transformed into the kind of native labor gangs who provided the economic foundation for the Spanish American and the Dutch East Indian empires. New France thus became a colony of French peasants and fur traders. The peasants were Catholic, since the home government, under pressure from the Church, prohibited the migration of Huguenots to New France. The extension of French control in the colonial area went hand in hand with an increase in the number of French settlers, and so Western culture in its seventeenth-century French Catholic form became rooted in Canada.

The date span in which the English achieved their most important overseas expansion is of crucial consequence. They established themselves in the New World during a period of great constitutional conflict at home. Two overthrows of the Stuart dynasty (in 1649 and 1688), civil war, and an interregnum of almost two decades (1642–1660) kept the rulers of England so preoccupied that they could not develop and pursue any colonial policy at all, much less a consistent and uniform one. When the dust settled and the policy makers in England got a chance to think about colonial policy, certain traits of the colonies were so fixed as to be irreversible or reversible only at a higher cost than the English were ready to pay.

The English Colonial Empire

For one thing, the West Indian and southern continental colonies had become economically dependent on Negro slaves. For another, there was no over-all colonial administration in America. Instead, there were more than a dozen separate colonies, each going its own way with little concern for any other colony and even less for the mother country. All were more or less resistant to merging their particular interests and to submitting those interests to a common colonial government. Moreover, the colonies had come into being in an age of religious ferment and conflict in England, and some of them—Massachusetts for Puritans, Maryland for Catholics, Pennsylvania for Quakers, and Rhode Island for radical sectaries—had their beginning as, and continued to be, refuges for men at odds with the dominant orthodoxy in England. The enforcement of over-all religious uniformity, a keystone of colonial policy in Spanish and French America, was therefore out of the question in English America.

So, for that matter, was the enforcement of "Englishness." Dutchmen and Swedes were already there when the English took over New York and New Jersey. Huguenots arrived in several colonies following the repeal of the Edict of Nantes, and William Penn welcomed and encouraged people of various nationalities to settle in his territory. By 1700 English America was already a melting pot of both the religions and the peoples of Europe. Finally, the haphazard pattern of English overseas expansion was reflected in the varied legal

Colonial artist Gustavus Hesselius painted an Indian chief with whom William Penn signed a treaty to acquire land in his Pennsylvania colony.

statuses of the colonies. Several, notably Massachusetts, Virginia, and Barbados, had started as joint-stock companies, but all of them had forfeited their charters and come directly under the power of the crown, as had most of the colonies begun by men with land grants from Charles II. Connecticut and Rhode Island, offshoots of the great Puritan settlement on Massachusetts Bay, acquired charters of their own, which they retained throughout the colonial period.

Two significant uniformities, as well as the above-mentioned diversities, marked the English colonies in America. First, the English did not have to deal with the problem, so acute in Spanish America, of a large indigenous population. The North American Indians were sparsely settled in the areas to which Englishmen migrated, and, as the colonial frontier moved slowly west, the Indians, despite occasional fierce resistance, either moved west with it or stayed on as small and diminishing population clusters amid an engulfing flood of immigrant settlers. The issue of "native policy," which preoccupied so many Spaniards in both the Old World and the New, got little high-level attention in either world from the English. Matters were settled locally with rum, trinkets, guns, massacres, and expropriations, and the Indians were almost always the losers.

The English colonists brought the other major uniformity with them from the mother country. In the seventeenth century Englishmen were better educated and more politically conscious than ever before in their history. The political tensions and crises that followed one another in such rapid succession during the age of the Stuarts created in all strata of society an awareness of the crucial importance of a few well-defined fundamental principles of law and politics. By the time of the first large migrations to America in the late 1620s, these principles—that property must be secure against arbitrary confiscation or taxation; that the ruled should participate, through elected representatives, in the making of the laws by which they were ruled; that the law should not be subject to the unrestrained whim of the ruler; and that no man should be imprisoned unless charged with a violation of the law and that, when held on charges, he must receive an early trial—were held by almost all Englishmen with even a vestigial political consciousness.

Because the American colonists of English origin held these deep-rooted political assumptions, expectations, and habits, a set of common institutional patterns emerged whenever and wherever Englishmen settled in America, regardless of the immediate wishes of the English government or the company or proprietor in charge of the settlement. Puritan Massachusetts, Quaker Pennsylvania, Anglican Virginia, and all the other colonies, even little Barbados in the West Indies, had elected representative assemblies. The franchise varied widely from one colony to another, but in all of them taxation required the consent of the assembly. The assembly also legislated for the internal affairs of the colony, although its enactments were subject to veto by the crown. Several of the colonies had a bill of rights or its equivalent, and some, like Connecticut, were governed under the terms of a written constitution.

Substantively, the law of the colonies was English common law, and due process established that administrative authority was subject to the limitations of that law and the protections it afforded to life, liberty, and property. These common limitations on the home government and on whatever agents, direct or indirect, it employed in ruling the colonies restricted everywhere the discretionary power of that government. The need to win the consent of about a dozen mutually independent assemblies meant that in many areas of policy-making, in which a single rule imposed from above was taken for granted in French and Spanish America, the English government could not establish a common policy at all. During the eighteenth century most of the English colonies had governors appointed by the crown acting with the advice of counselors who were also crown appointees, but the sphere of effective action of English imperial government in America was so sharply restricted that it could not even provide for the common defense. The Board of Trade and Plantations, which undertook direction of colonial policy in England, had to concentrate on the regulation of commerce among the colonies, between the colonies and the mother country, and between the colonies and foreign powers. If in governing its colonial empire in America England exhibited an almost exclusive preoccupation with trade and the construction of a viable mercantilist system, it was not because in contrast to the French and Spanish the English were a nation of shopkeepers; it was because the institutional mold into which the colonies fell as a result of historical circumstances made preoccupation with anything else futile.

One of the most dramatic and fundamental transformations that the European traders and settlers brought about as they spread to the four corners of the earth was an ecological revolution. Ecology deals with the distribution of living things on the face of the earth. The movement to far continents of vast numbers of Europeans, who wanted to eat and dress and live the way they had in the mother country, and the shuttling all over the earth of European traders on the lookout for produce to sell at home, resulted in the most rapid and radical change in the distribution of vegetable and animal life that the world has ever known. That process is not yet at an end, and some of its major episodes fall beyond the period we are here considering. The rubber plant, for example, migrated from Brazil to the South Seas as recently as the nineteenth century, and today most of the world's natural rubber comes from Malaya and Indonesia, where the plant that yields it is a naturalized foreigner from halfway around the world. Australia and New Zealand now produce almost half the world's wool; yet, before the nineteenth century, there were no sheep in those lands. In the eighteenth century America's greatest gift to the European table, the potato, had just begun its fabulous career in the Old World. Today, Europe's potato production is ten times that of America's. Nor had the native American tomato, string bean, and Indian corn yet become important European crops.

By 1700, however, great shifts in the earth's vegetable and animal life were well under way. The coffee bean had long been cultivated in the Near East, and the Dutch, seeking a supplement and then a substitute for the declining spice trade of the East Indies, brought coffee to Java in the late seventeenth century, where it—and Dutch trade—took a new lease on life. Coffee was also established in South America, which now produces more than four-fifths of the world crop.

The Western Hemisphere was the chief beneficiary of the ecological revolution. North America, South America, and the Caribbean islands had been singularly poor in their varieties of domesticated grains. Indian corn was the only important

The Ecological Revolution

An engraving from a 1667 volume on the West Indies shows a French sugar refinery operated by slave labor. The cane was harvested (left) and crushed in a mill (upper right). The heating and crystallization took place in the refinery shed at center.

grain crop. There were none of the cereals that had sustained the peoples of Eurasia for thousands of years—wheat and rye and oats and rice. All these the Europeans brought with them to the new-found lands, and all readily took root there and flourished. In domesticated animals the Western Hemisphere was even worse off. The only one of any account—and he was pretty well localized in the Andean region—was the llama. Elsewhere, the American native had no beasts of burden, no draft animals, no dairy stock, no herds of sheep, no domesticated meat animals, not even any domesticated fowl. To the New World the Europeans brought not only grains, but the horse, the donkey, and the mule to carry the loads borne hitherto on men's backs. They brought the ox to pull the plow, milk- and meat-giving cattle, the pig, and the goat. They brought the wool-bearing sheep and the barnyard chicken.

All these new plants and animals gradually changed the whole ecological make up of the Americas, and changed it to such an extent that only four of the indigenous domesticated plants of pre-Columbian times are still of first importance in the Americas today—tobacco, corn, cotton, and potatoes. Yet, important though they are, less than half of the Western Hemisphere's agricultural acreage is planted in them today, and they represent in dollars far less than half of the total annual yield of the hemisphere's fields and pastures.

Of the many cereals and animals that Europeans brought to the Americas, one, in the eyes of the early modern European merchant, threw all the rest into the shade: sugar cane. Indigenous to Asia, sugar cane was carried by Spaniards and Portuguese to the Canary Islands and Madeira, but it was many years before its cultivation was introduced on a considerable scale in Brazil and thence into the islands of the Caribbean. Once there, however, it thrived enormously and became the apple of the European merchant's and statesman's eye. It was the ideal colonial product. It could not be produced in Europe, native labor could produce it cheaply in the New World, and there was a vast market for it in Europe.

Historians have tended to overestimate the importance of overseas trade for the growth of mercantile capitalism, to exaggerate its relative magnitude, and to attribute an earlier date to its major influence than the evidence warrants. The rapid advance of the European merchant's influence after the late fifteenth century is potent, and it happens to coincide with the early age of expansion. The tendency, therefore, to attribute the influence of the merchant to overseas expansion is natural enough, but a consideration of the facts throws a good deal of doubt on such an explanation.

The Impact of Overseas Expansion

In the first place, it was only in the latter half of the period from 1450 to 1750—that is, after 1600—that a really considerable volume of overseas produce began to reach the markets of Europe, and only in the last third that the volume of the overseas trade of any major European state surpassed that of its trade with any one of a number of its neighboring states. Only then did the cotton and tea of India, the sugar of the Caribbean, the tobacco of Virginia and the Caribbean, and the coffee of Java flow with great force into the marts of Europe, and only then did the settlers in the New World attain numbers and acquire wealth sufficient to create in America markets for European goods comparable in importance to those of Europe itself.

Throughout the first half of the three centuries under consideration, Europe's two main imports from overseas were spices and precious metals, and the volume of the spice trade was far too insignificant to contribute in a major way to the growing importance of the European merchant class. A few annual shiploads of pepper could not, after all, sustain the rapid expansion of trade of a whole continent.

Bullion did arrive from overseas in sufficient volume to disturb seriously the European market. It had an inflationary effect and widespread social and economic repercussions—usually termed the "Price Revolution"—but it does not seem to have markedly affected the general European economy until the middle decades of the sixteenth century. By that time the commercial revival in Europe was already eighty to a hundred years old. Furthermore, there is no evidence that an increase in the supply of bullion automatically produces one and only one ultimate economic effect, and that a beneficial one. The dreary destiny of Spain, the land that had the first use of the whole of the American treasure, points up the fact that sharp increases in the money supply do not necessarily stimulate economic growth; Spain rode not to prosperity but to poverty and disaster on the flood of precious metal that poured into its ports from America. Common sense suggests that the potency of bullion, as of any other instrument, depends on the use to which it is put, and that the independent influence of American treasure, of the Price Revolution, and of the overseas expansion prior to 1600 on the economic growth of Europe has been somewhat exaggerated at the expense of other historical changes.

Spain: The Wages of Empire

In the early autumn of 1700 Charles II of Spain lay in a room in the Alcazar in Madrid, dying. Placed beside him, in hopes of divine intervention, were the withered remains of two Spanish saints; and to ease the pain in his tormented mind, pigeons had been killed and set upon his head. Yet on the first of November Charles, who during all his thirty-nine years had suffered fits of idiocy and epilepsy, breathed his last. With him the dynasty of Spanish Hapsburgs, which had led the realm to such heights and such depths, passed into extinction. And Spain, reduced to a pawn on the field of international power struggles, passed into the hands of the French House of Bourbon. The nation that a few generations earlier had controlled half the world's destiny now was incapable of controlling its own destiny.

In was in 1492, only slightly more than two centuries before, that two almost simultaneous events had set Spain on its rapid, spectacular climb to glory. Columbus' voyage added a vast overseas empire to what had been a poor, rock-bound land in a forgotten far corner of Europe. The reconquest of Granada from the Moors finally cleared the country of an enemy that had been there for nearly 800 years and opened up the Mediterranean as well. Coming within a few months of each other, these achievements were deemed miracles by contemporary Spaniards and affirmed Spain's sense of divine mission and limitless opportunity.

With 1492 a new age dawned in Spain, when intoxicating dreams of conquest and holy crusade, of booty and riches filled the land, when the God-given instruments of Faith and Sword seemed ready to carry the nation to the pinnacle of world power. This feeling was reflected in a great flood of chivalric tales and in such larger-than-life heroes as Cortes the Conqueror whose image (left)—with sword and cross—was recorded by a conquered Aztec. The purest expression of the Spanish mood, however, was found in its patron saint, Santiago Matamoros— St. James the Killer of Moors—depicted opposite in a scene *c.* 1500.

In 1556 Charles I (as Holy Roman Emperor, Charles V), son of the first Hapsburg king of Spain, willed his son Philip II an empire—to be ruled from Castile—whose European components were Franche-Comté, the Netherlands, most of Italy in the form of the kingdoms of Naples and Milan, Sardinia, Sicily, and the Balearic Isles. Across the Atlantic were the Indies, just then beginning to disgorge their wealth in truly fabulous amounts. In the Pacific were the Philippines. To these Philip later added Portugal and its possessions in Africa and Asia. But this colossal structure bore the seeds of its own destruction. Even in Philip's time it became evident that the commitments of empire were too much. Beset by war and revolt on all sides, experiencing decay and disillusion within, Spain was traveling a golden road to ruin.

El Dorado

The heaps of gold ornaments that Cortes received in tribute from Montezuma and the ransom, estimated at 13,000 pounds of gold, that Pizarro gathered up Cuzco in Peru served merely to whet the Spanish ap-tite for treasure. Full scale mining operations were gun in Mexico in the 1530s and in the next decade me the monumental strike at Potosí in Peru. One hun-ed and fifty-four ships arrived from the New World in 44, carrying 2 million ducats worth of gold and silver llion. In the peak years of the 1590s the average an-al imports reached a value of 8 million ducats, which d not include enormous sums sent westward across the cific in payment for Chinese silks. In all, some 500 mil-n ducats worth of bullion was unloaded at Seville be-een 1540 and 1640—raising Europe's silver supply by 0 percent and its gold supply by 20 percent.

Charles V, in whose reign the galleon convoys were ganized, is said to have cried with joy on receiving ws that the treasure fleets had arrived safely. Well he ight. Fully a fifth (the royal *quinto*) of the wealth g out of the mines of the New World belonged to the own outright. A considerable portion of the remainder nt into the king's treasury by way of taxes levied in th Spain and the Indies.

But in many respects El Dorado proved more of a curse an a blessing. It encouraged the crown into an exalted nse of its international responsibilities, with the result at military and bureaucratic expenses far exceeded in-me. By the middle of his reign Charles V was annually ending twice the amount being taken in, and under his n the national debt rose to the astronomical sum of 0 million ducats. As the flow of wealth quickened, in-tion began to run rampant, and the combination of gh prices and heavy taxation nearly wrecked Spain's dustries and agriculture. The tendency, born of visions quick money, to hold all manual labor in contempt had e same effect. Finally, much of the wealth found its ay to foreign banking houses, or was channeled into the onomically unproductive Church.

ost of the objects plundered by the conquistadors were elted down by native goldsmiths, who thus were forced to undo e work of their own hands. One of the few pieces to survive the gold figure from Colombia at lower right. The emerald-udded cross (top right) of native workmanship and the cap-in's whistle, suspended from an eleven-foot gold chain, were cently recovered from Spanish shipwrecks. In Spain the treas-e spurred production of ornate ecclesiastical art such as the ld and silver monstrance—a vessel for displaying the Host— own opposite, created for the New Cathedral of Salamanca.

A New Culture

Once the work of conquest was finished, the Spanish found themselves masters of a native population seemingly tractable and limitless in numbers. Quickly and often ruthlessly enveloped by the system of *encomienda*, the Indians became a source of virtually free labor that was as vital to colonial interests as gold and silver to the mother country.

Unlike the English colonies to the north, Spanish America saw the rise of close ties between conqueror and conquered. Almost at once an amalgam of Spanish-Indian culture began to emerge, the first sign being the mestizo, the offspring (usually illegitimate) of European and native parents. Since barely 10 percent of the Spaniards who migrated to the New World were women, such unions were inevitable; indeed, they received encouragement from the crown. Because of the Spaniards' aversion to manual labor, the artisan class consisted almost entirely of mestizos. They turned out products ranging from saddles to portraits, often superior to those from Spain.

In religion too, the trend was toward a synthesis of pagan and Christian forms. Led by such men as Vasco de Quiroga and Bartolomé de Las Casas, the missionary friars spread the gospel, translated catechisms, opened schools to train a native clergy, and even created jungle communities modeled after Thomas More's *Utopia*. But the result was often a lingering veneration of a "stag-god" or the cult of the Virgin Mary, based on the Indians' concept of the mother goddess.

Of greater concern to Las Casas and his companions was the tragic depletion of the Indian population. Brutality, harsh labor in the mines, and especially the white man's diseases reduced the pure-blooded native stock in some places by as much as 90 percent within a century after Cortes.

Mestizo art matured earliest in Peru, where native painters, using Old World woodcuts and icons as models, created a style distinctly New World in flavor. In their religious works the artists freely mixed Spanish and pre-conquest symbols. In the mid-seventeenth-century painting at left an Inca prince leads a Corpus Christi procession down a Cuzco thoroughfare. Also from the seventeenth century, the stone crucifix above exhibits stylistic traces of Mexico's Toltec culture in Teotihuacán. Though a descendant of a Peruvian Indian and an African, young Don Domingo de Arobe (opposite) remained one of Nature's Noblemen and as such was worthy of a portrait specifically commissioned for Philip III in 1599. The painting, of which this is a detail, is presumed to be by a Quito artist and is the earliest dated work from South America.

56.A

DÓDOMÍNGO. IƆ.A

† PHILIPPO.3.CATHOLICO
REGI.HISPANIARᵤ
INDIARᵤ Q̃ƷDÑO.SVO
DOCTOR.IOÁNES.DEL.BARRÍO
A SEPVLVEDA.AVDITOR.SVᴱ
CANCELLARÍÆ.DEL.QVITO
SVÍS EXPENSÍS. FIERÍ.
CVRAVIT
ANNO.1599

New Spain's Capital

Built upon the ruins of the Aztec's Tenochtitlán, Mexico City, the capital of New Spain, rapidly became a burgeoning center of culture and commerce. Although architecturally it bore traces of the Old World, the city itself was a creole city, a place born of the New World. It had a vitality and promise of growth completely lacking in Seville or Madrid, and by the 1550s some 100,000 people—Indian and European—lived here, more than in any other Spanish city.

Under the administration of Cortes, the capital was laid out in a neoclassic plan of broad, straight avenues and intersecting canals leading away from the Plaza Mayor. Depicted here on the occasion of the arrival of a new viceroy in 1695, the Plaza is dotted with gilded carriages of the nobility which, along with the constant peal of church bells, had become an early feature of the city. In the background— on the east side of the square— is the long, two-story viceregal palace, extensively damaged by fire in 1692, while on the north side stands the imposing Baroque façade of Mexico City Cathedral, completed in 1667 after slightly more than a century of construction. Large shopping arcades front on the remaining sides of the square.

71

EL ESCORIAL; BRADLEY SMITH

Ponte di Turgone

BIBLIOTECA NACIONAL, MADRID

Under covering artillery fire, Spanish infantry and cavalry launch their decisive attack against the walled city of St. Quentin during the campaign in northeastern France. The victory occurred in August of 1557 and followed nearly forty years of intermittent war with the French; soon afterward a thankful Philip made good his vow to build the Escorial.

With their infantry supreme on the open battlefield, the Spanish mastered siege warfare by using heavy artillery and novel assault pieces such as this mobile drawbridge.

Spanish Arms

Floating gun platforms helped the Spanish out-maneuver the water barriers of the Netherlands.

When Charles V inherited the Spanish throne in 1517 his patrimony included an army possessed of such qualities as to make it the master of Europe's battle-fields for 150 years. It was an infantry army, created at a time when cavalry could no longer stand up against the firepower of well-trained foot formations. The Spanish *tercio*, employing 3,000 musketeers and pikemen in roughly equal numbers, had no peer as a field unit. It struck a perfect balance between mobility on offense and near impenetrability on defense.

Though hardly a standing soldiery by modern terms, Spain's army was kept filled by a steady stream of volunteers, among them numerous sons of the lower nobility, the *hidalgos*. Like their brothers-in-arms the conquistadors, these men were inured to hunger, thirst, and heat, and feckless in their value of human life. They were superbly equipped as well, for under Charles V's patronage the latest weapons developments in Germany and Italy were quickly routed to Spain.

In 1525 this fighting machine was blooded in a stunning victory over the French at the Italian fortress-town of Pavia. Thenceforth until the middle of the seventeenth century, the Spanish army was to experience only about 20 widely separated years of peace. Drawn into war by religious, territorial, or dynastic disputes, or by its own zeal, Spain was to expend blood and fortune in amounts no nation could afford.

Before abdicating in 1556 Charles V joined battle with Moors and Turks in the Mediterranean, Lutheran princes in Germany, French and Papal forces in Italy, and savages in the New World. Philip II, who inherited his father's vision of empire as well as a debt of some 20 million ducats, started his reign auspiciously by defeating the French on French soil at the Battle of St. Quentin. But by some perverse twist victory in one quarter seemed always to be followed by grave crisis in another. In 1566 began the revolt of the Netherlands, which settled into a forty-year siege at an annual cost of 2 million ducats. The treasury was drained at such a rate that in 1576 the king could no longer pay his troops in the Lowlands; they responded with what has become known as the Spanish Fury, a brutal sacking of Antwerp.

At the same time, Philip was attempting to clear the Mediterranean of infidels, and his efforts were rewarded by the great naval victory over the Turks at Lepanto in 1571. Yet even this proved indecisive, for he lacked the means for holding the North African coast. At the end of his reign Philip found himself once more embroiled with France and goaded into an unwanted war with Elizabeth of England. The cost, reckoned simply in terms of the defeat of the Invincible Armada, was 63 ships, 9,000 men, and 10 million ducats.

Three decades later came the Thirty Years' War, crippling Spain's economy and destroying—virtually in one blow at the Battle of Rocroi in 1643—its magnificent army.

Spain's siege arsenal included a giant cross-bow (above) for launching bombs over fortress walls and a heavy mortar (below) designed by one of Charles V's German gunsmiths in 1556.

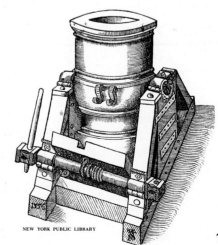

The Economics of Orthodoxy

With the crusading ardor of the late fifteenth century there developed an equally fervent quest for religious orthodoxy and purity of blood. Changed from a state of mind to official policy when the Office of Inquisition was established in 1478, these passions soon wrought great changes in the culture and economy of Spain. Within the course of a century they were to smother the country's middle class, encourage the flow of its assets into foreign banking houses, and help cripple its agricultural base.

Although joyously acclaimed throughout all Christendom, the reconquest of Granada nevertheless opened up deep and perplexing troubles in Spain: namely, what to do with a population of some 100,000 infidels. For a brief time the Moors, who were mostly farmers and artisans, were permitted to retain their customs and religion in hopes that they would be gradually absorbed into the mainstream of Spanish life. But in 1502 Ferdinand and Isabella decreed the forcible conversion of the Moors. The event was commemorated by the wooden altar piece at right, which was carved for the Royal Chapel in Granada and shows a crowd of men and women submitting to mass baptism.

Similar methods had already been used to deal with Spain's other non-believers. The zeal of 1492 found further outlet that same year in the expulsion of all unconverted Jews. More than 120,000 persons left the country, their places in trade and banking taken over by Germans and Italians whose profits found their way over the border instead of into the Spanish economy. The pressure for purity of blood— *limpieza de sangre*—continued to swell, and in 1556 Philip II ordered persons with the slightest trace of Jewish ancestry barred from high office.

Now the Moors came under increasing attack from the Inquisition. Like the Jews, a majority of the Moriscos (those who ostensibly had been converted) clung surreptitiously to Islam and to such disturbing customs as regular bathing. In the face of persecution and extortionate taxes the Moriscos of Granada rebelled in 1568 and for two years, while the Netherlands was going up in flames, a major civil war raged within Spain itself. The revolt was crushed, but the Moors continued their harassment by means of aid to the Turks and the French. Faced with an implacable enemy in its midst, Spain had only one alternative —expulsion of the Moors—which was begun in 1609.

CATEDRAL, GRANADA; YAN

In the spring of 1563, amid the bleak foothills of the Guadarrama mountains near Madrid, construction began on what was to be Philip II's one personal indulgence, the Escorial (right). For the next twenty-one years workers strove to build him an edifice that would proclaim his devotion to the Faith and at the same time provide a royal retreat and a pantheon for the House of Hapsburg. The result, combining palace, monastery, and mausoleum in a somber mass of gray granite, perfectly expressed the nature of its first occupant. Philip IV often removed himself to the gayer palace at Aranjuez to escape the disagreeable chore of ruling. There in 1665 Juan Bautista Martinez del Mazo painted the "hunt" scene below in which ladies of the court watch stags driven down a chute and slaughtered at their feet.

Society of the Bewitched

As viewed from Westminster or Paris, Spain in 1600 still seemed the formidable ruler of half the globe. Yet within the country itself there was a feeling of things gone sour, a fear of approaching doom. Those who dared probe beneath the façade found Spain's economic timbers rotted to the point of collapse. Groaning under the weight of Philip's extravagant foreign policy, the structure now was regularly beset by bankruptcy. Taxes stood at unbearable levels. Prices had undergone an increase of 400 percent since 1500. Spanish agriculture was withering and Castile was experiencing the pains of depopulation.

To González de Cellorigo, one of a group of outspoken reformers known as *arbitristas*, decay was the result of a great void between the "poor who beg" and the "rich who loll at ease." With no middle class to engage in trade and investment, Spain's wealth was being "dissipated on thin air—on papers, contracts, *censos*, and letters of exchange, on cash, and silver, and gold—instead of being expended on things that yield profits and attract riches from outside to augment riches within." Consequently, said Cellorigo, "there is no money, gold, or silver in Spain because there is so much; and it is not rich because of all its riches. . . ." The result was "a society of the bewitched, living outside the natural order of things."

Instead of retrenchment as the *arbitristas* urged, the country seemed bent on self-destruction. In contrast to Philip II, his successors and namesakes found the exercise of power less rewarding than theatricals, fiestas, and hunting trips. Under kings who did not rule, the court became a seat of bribery and corruption, where a member of Philip III's Council of Finance could pocket close to one and a half million ducats. Long held in check, the nobility now bestirred itself in extravagant display. Estates were maintained on a colossal scale with as many as 700 household servants; vast sums were expended on the accumulation of books and paintings. Even the Church joined the parade of opulence, building new cathedrals and abbeys and filling them with art treasures. By a final irony it was the largesse of the Church and nobility, spent in a time of economic crisis, that helped bring about Spain's golden age of art and literature.

77

Spanish Baroque

For his picture collection in the Escorial Philip II exhibited a strong taste for works by Italian masters, especially Titian, whose luxurious Venuses and Dianas dominated the galleries of the palace. Except for El Greco, who did not arrive in Spain until the late 1570s, the few Spanish artists represented in the royal collection were mainly pallid imitators of Italian or Flemish models.

Spain's imperial vision died with Philip in 1598. But at about the same time a new age dawned in Spanish art—the Baroque—when native genius blazed forth in the works of José de Ribera, Francisco de Zurbarán, Diego Velázquez, Bartolomé Murillo, and Alonso Cano. Born in the decade of Philip's death, Ribera, Zurbarán, and Velázquez had by the early 1620s established themselves under the eager patronage of Church and crown. At the age of twenty-three, Velázquez was appointed painter to the court of Philip IV where he joined a flourishing community of talent that included playwrights Lope de Vega and Calderón de la Barca and the lyrical poet Luis de Góngora y Argote.

At its core the Baroque in Spain was an epic of society tormented by doubt and disillusionment. Success somehow had become entangled with defeat. Reality and illusion stood indistinguishable. The mood induced a deep sense of mysticism and other-worldliness reflected in the haunting canvases of Zurbarán and in the portraits by Velázquez, whose seemingly cool realism often opens up to reveal intense personal vision.

No longer did the verities and harmony of the Renaissance express the nature of things. All was illusion, including life itself. "There are many things here that seem to exist and have their being," wrote the picaresque novelist Francisco de Quevedo, "yet they are nothing more than a name and an appearance." In Calderón's play *La Vida Es Sueño* ("Life is a Dream") even the dreams become dreams. The supreme literary work of the age, *Don Quixote* (published in two parts in 1605 and 1615), is at once a satire on the old chivalric romances, a commentary on Spain's decline, and an interplay between reality and make believe. Who is to be taken seriously, Cervantes asks: Don Quixote, whose world consists of inns that are castles and windmills that are giants; Sancho Panza, the earth-bound peasant who reluctantly joins his master's crusade and is taken up in it; or the rest of Spain, which claims them mad?

In Velázquez the dramatic lighting and realism-turned-illusion of the Spanish Baroque matured early. Shortly before his twenty-first birthday he rendered the heightened naturalism of the Water Carrier of Seville *(opposite). The portraits of the poet Góngora y Argote (upper left), whose ascetic features belied the florid qualities of his verse, and Count-Duke Gaspar de Guzmán Olivares (left), to whom Philip IV entrusted his government, were painted in the early 1620s.*

UFFIZI

An End to Glory

This year," read the unhappy report to Philip IV, "can undoubtedly be considered the most unfortunate that this Monarchy has ever experienced." The year was 1640, when the revolts of Portugal—a fief of the Spanish crown since 1580—and Catalonia threatened to disintegrate the empire. The writer was Count-Duke Olivares, who now recognized the failure of his frenzied efforts to shore up the Hapsburg monarchy and who would soon be banished from his position as court favorite.

Rebellion in Catalonia and Portugal came just as the Thirty Years' War and related tragedies were wearing Spain to the point of collapse. In 1638 the "Spanish Road" from Milan to the Netherlands was cut, forcing Olivares to supply his troops by way of the English Channel, a task his decrepit galleons (above) were hardly able to perform. So too, the treasure fleets were no longer an annual certainty. The New World mines were being exhausted, a whole year's supply of bullion had been seized by the Dutch Sea Beggars, and in at least one instance the fleet safely reached Seville carrying not silver but copper for debasing the currency. Finally, as if to symbolize the pall of disillusionment settling over the nation, Santiago, the warrior saint, had been displaced as Spain's patron.

By the middle of the century the crown had become so mired in debt it was said that "on many days the household of the King and the Queen lack everything, including bread." Still, there was the semblance of order and harmony represented in Velázquez' *Maids of Honor* (left), painted in 1656. The artist has portrayed himself painting a double portrait of Philip IV and his queen, who appear only as dim reflections in a mirror at the rear of the studio. In the foreground, as if paying a chance visit, are the Infanta Margarita and her retinue—maids, *guardasdamas*, dog, and dwarfs.

Philip died in 1665, having seen all pretensions to glory shattered by the peace treaties ending the Thirty Years' War. The fate of the nation passed to his four-year-old son, Charles II, who would soon be known to contemporaries as Charles the Bewitched.

81

3

Population, Industry, and Agriculture

In the early modern era Europe found that it had to produce more food and clothing than it had in the late Middle Ages, simply because there were more people to feed and clothe. Although it is not possible to measure the population increase that occurred in early modern Europe with anywhere near the accuracy with which present-day demographers measure trends, it is known that the general pattern was one of gradual and relatively steady growth for about two hundred years after 1450. The rate of growth would have been more striking were it not that periods of turmoil—civil wars, foreign invasion, and famines caused by bad weather and ravaging armies—reduced the populations of several countries at various times. Germany during the Thirty Years' War, France during the Wars of Religion and the War of the Spanish Succession, and Russia during the Time of Troubles after the death of Ivan the Terrible all suffered major declines in population. In the 1600s population growth appears to have become irregular all over Europe, and until well after 1700 it was spotty and subject to local reverses. England continued a slow growth, and Spain underwent a steady decline throughout the sixteenth century. Nowhere, however, did population fall back to the low levels of the early fifteenth century.

Sometime after 1700 a general upswing in population began. By 1750 almost all Europe was more thickly settled than ever before in its history. From the Urals to the Atlantic, Europe was on the verge of a population explosion that was to continue with increasing force for more than a hundred years. At the beginning of the eighteenth century, it is doubtful that there were 20 percent more Frenchmen than there had been four hundred years before, but during that century, up to the outbreak of the Revolution in 1789, the population of France increased almost 45 percent. More significant than the gross increase was the rate of growth. In France the population was growing ten times as rapidly in the eighteenth century as it had grown in the previous four centuries. Give or take a little, the same pattern of a steeply rising rate of population growth held true for the whole Western world.

The population of Europe was also undergoing significant shifts in its areas of concentration. Toward the end of the fifteenth century, many of the older industrial and commercial towns decayed. The areas that suffered most were the great centers of medieval economic life in northern Italy and in Flanders. To escape the rigidity of guild regulation, industrial producers moved to the countryside. On the other hand, certain commercial ports greatly expanded to handle an enlarged intra-European and overseas trade—Antwerp, Lisbon, and Seville in the early days; Marseilles, Cádiz, Nantes, Rouen, Bristol, Liverpool, Hamburg, Bremen, and Danzig later. An amalgam of industrial, commercial, and political activities created great metropolises in Paris, London, and Amsterdam, and the problem of supplying these large urban centers acted as a spur to marketing organization, to specialization in agricultural production, and to commercialized farming. At

The life of the Western European peasant was a frequent theme in the work of the Flemish painter Pieter Brueghel, and no artist left a more accurate or candid record of the common man of his time. This landscape, The Harvesters, *is dated 1565.*

the end of the period, a significant population shift heralded the coming of a new economic era. A rapid rise in population in the neighborhood of coal seams, ore deposits, and fast-falling rivers was prophetic of the transformation of the West from a predominantly agricultural to an industrial society—the first of its kind in human history.

The increased population of Europe had, naturally, to be fed, but the increase in demand does not seem to have led to any general improvement in farming methods up to the beginning of the eighteenth century. Except in a few areas, the three-field system and three-crop rotation—spring crop and winter crop of grain for human consumption followed by a year when the fields lay fallow— persisted in Europe's richest farm lands, so that each year a third of the best soil produced nothing but scanty pasturage for cattle.

The overseas expansion of Europe added somewhat to the available food supply. Three of the most important overseas products that the European learned to enjoy—coffee, tea, and tobacco—did not, however, add to his stock of nourishment, though they undoubtedly increased his pleasures in life. America's most revolutionary contribution to European diet and agriculture, the potato, was long considered by many a decorative but inedible plant. As late as 1700, only two American products contributed much to the nourishment of Europe—cane from the Caribbean islands, and cod from the Grand Bank of Newfoundland and the New England coast. The products of the cane benefited the European in three ways. Sugar sweetened his tea and coffee, rum warmed his stomach and lightened his head, and molasses mixed with sulphur supposedly cured him of many ills. The North Atlantic cod, dried or salted, served a double purpose. The better part of the catch supplemented the North Sea salt herring and helped provide Europeans with fish when the supply of salt meat gave out in Lent. The worse part—the refuse—helped to keep the Negro slaves of the Caribbean alive and thus ensured the production of sugar.

The Netherlanders waged a constant struggle to hold on to the farmland they had reclaimed from the sea. Jan de Bray sketched the repair of a breached dike at Haarlem in 1675.

At the beginning of the 1700s, the main source of Europe's expanded food supply was Europe itself. When market conditions warranted, pasture land was transformed into arable land, and lowland marshes were recaptured from the sea. In this, the Dutch, veterans of centuries of experience in stealing farmland from the waters, led the way. From projects at home they went on to manage projects abroad in England, France, and Prussia. The most important single new source of food, however, was surpluses of the grain-producing Baltic lands, Poland, and Prussia. They were transported to Western Europe to supplement grain deficits in the Netherlands, the realms of the Atlantic coast, and Italy. Yet all the new sources of food taken together were not enough to sustain a drastic increase in population.

The growth of Europe's population was limited not only by the slow increase of the food supply, but by high infant mortality, high childbearing mortality for mothers, and low adult resistance to the ravages of diseases. Drastic population growth waited on radical improvement in farming methods to raise yields per acre and per farm worker and on the adoption of elementary sanitary measures in midwifery and infant care.

Woolen cloth remained Europe's chief manufactured product, while other products that Europe had never before made commercially, or made only in insignificant quantities, slowly rose to an important place in commerce.

Industries Old and New

TEXTILES

In the mid-eighteenth century Europe's major industry was the textile industry, as it had been for more than half a millennium. European sheep produced adequate quantities of fibers warm enough and sturdy enough to clothe the people of the North Temperate Zone in winter. Wool was worked up into cloth all over Europe. Much of this cloth did not enter commerce at all, but went on the backs of the people who made it. Nevertheless, woolen cloth remained the principal product in interregional trade within Europe and Europe's main export through the period from 1450 to the eighteenth century.

Several significant changes in the textile industry took place after 1450. For one, the main areas of production shifted, with England becoming a major new producer. In the sixteenth century woolen cloth constituted about four-fifths of the value of all exports from England's greatest port, London; by the eighteenth century a statistician estimated the total value of English cloth as slightly higher than the total rent on agricultural land. The older Flemish towns saw their business decline in the face of competition not only from England but from the textile villages in the Flemish countryside that found an outlet for their produce in the market port of Antwerp. A second change took place in the sixteenth century, when cheaper and cheaper grades of cloth entered the channels of trade. Lighter goods, the "new drapery," began to drive out the older, heavier cloth, and by 1750 rough cheap Yorkshire woolens had come to the fore.

THE PRINTING INDUSTRY

The very beginning of economic revival in fifteenth-century Europe saw the birth of the printing industry, which had an impact on Western civilization extending far beyond the economic sphere.

The printing industry was a constellation of greater and lesser trades all created or vastly stimulated by the invention of movable metallic type. The impression of the inked surface of type on to paper reproduced books in any desired number of copies at an additional labor cost per copy that was insignificant in comparison to the costs of reproducing manuscripts by hand. Besides the older business of paper making, the sub-industries in the printing trade included book-binding, type-cutting and type-founding, press-building, ink-making, the manufacture of lamp black and linseed oil for ink, and printing itself, including type-setting and operating the presses. The most popular writings of Erasmus went through dozens of editions before the end of the sixteenth century. At the beginning of that century, a Nuremburg printer was employing more than a hundred hands in his plant, and an English publisher of the seventeenth century marketed 10,000 copies of a rather dreary work called the *Practice of Godliness.*

The invention of printing was the most important change in the technology of communication since the invention of alphabetic writing, perhaps the only one of first-rate importance until the revolution that began with the electric communication of signals (telegraph) and went on through the electric communication of sounds (telephone) to the wireless communication of sounds and sights (radio and television) and their permanent recording on sound track, film, and tape. For a brief period of about half a century, when its technology was being worked out and mastered, printing had to compete for the market with the manuscript book. Fifty years later, the printed book had almost completely displaced the manuscript book throughout the Western world. It is doubtful if there had ever before in history been a major technical innovation that so rapidly replaced its older alternative over so great a geographical area.

The invention of printing revolutionized the very process and dissemination of education. For the first time in history, the recorded word became a more important and universal vehicle of education than the spoken word. Reading rather than listening came to be the chief means of learning; and writers living and dead thenceforth communicated through print with those who sought their instruction, rather than indirectly through a lecture by a third party. The production of relatively cheap books meant that for the first time continuing self-education was attainable for any literate man of moderate means and moderate leisure. It no longer required access to the great manuscript collections of Europe, which were owned mainly by monasteries, cathedrals, universities, and a few princes and magnates. The consequence was that the intellectual traditions of the West, which had hitherto been known by few outside the ecclesiastical establishment, suddenly became available to laymen. Prior to the proliferation of printed matter, complex intellectual and theological squabbles among clerics might slowly be made known to the lay populace, and might even affect them, but such episodes were rare. When Luther posted his ninety-five theses on indulgences in 1517, Pope Leo X characterized the ferment it stirred up as a monk's quarrel, but by 1520 thousands of literate German laymen had read Luther's *Address to the German Nobility,* and Leo had discovered to his sorrow how wrong he was.

Learning was not only laicized; it was, so to speak, ruralized, at least from the mid-sixteenth century on. Inexpensive editions of Europe's rare collections of fine manuscripts found their way into dozens of manor houses. Latin and Greek

This 1642 engraving may well be the work of the French print shop specializing in engraved illustrations which it depicts.

classics, books on law and surveying, travelers' tales, romances of chivalry, and very often, and most dangerous for the rulers of Europe, treatises on theology and politics were read in villages all over Europe. It is surely no accident that about a century after the invention of printing the rebellions of rural aristocrats, pandemic in Europe throughout the Middle Ages, were for the first time in the history of the Western world inextricably intertwined with the ideological conflicts of the religious war. If it was hard to manage the landed classes when they had swords in their hands, it was even harder when they had ideas in their heads.

It was not a mere coincidence that the extension of printing went hand in hand with the religious ferment of the Reformation. The invention of printing gave the rulers of Europe the opportunity to publicize their commands and to propagandize their policies more extensively and effectively than ever before. But it also gave men who opposed those commands and policies more effective means for expressing and explaining their opposition. All over Europe men resorted to the printing press to appeal over the heads of their rightful rulers to the subjects of those rulers.

In the eyes of the rulers, both spiritual and temporal, such appeals were a menace and a subversive outrage. The only criticism that rulers hitherto had regarded as tolerable was criticism that they intentionally invited either from duly constituted advisers and councilors or from citizens petitioning for redress of grievances. The very essence of such advice and petitioning was that it should be directed solely to the ruler and be for his consideration only. The notion that men should be directing propaganda not to the prince but to the people at large with a view to creating opposition to the prince was intolerable, for no idea was more alien to the rulers than the idea of freedom of the press. One of the latest rights invented by Western man, freedom of the press has remained one of the most precarious.

All the rulers of sixteenth-century Europe believed it was their right and duty to suppress seditious opinions (that is, opinions markedly different from their own) simply by outlawing them—by enacting censorship and licensing laws. The trouble lay in enforcing these laws. The theoretical authority of European princes and potentates far outstripped their effective power, and none could muster a police force large enough to thwart determined men who would break the law. What is more, many rulers winked at those who pamphleteered against the policies of rival rulers. Thus, from places of refuge, dissident groups of exiles were able to direct barrages of printed propaganda in their native tongue against the religious policies of their natural rulers. English Catholic exiles in France and the southern Netherlands, and French and Dutch Protestant exiles in Geneva and on the Upper Rhine smuggled their heretical works through the ports and across the borders of their homelands with only occasional impediments. The permanent relaxation of government censorship and control had to wait until the fervor and fury generated by the religious conflict had cooled. It was not until the American Revolution that freedom of the press as a principle of public law was formally enunciated.

ARMAMENTS

The armament industry, one of the most ancient of all industries, underwent revolutionary changes in the early modern era. As with the textile industry, new forces imposed radical alterations on armaments manufacture. One was the development of artillery, another, the development of standing armies. These developments impelled the industry toward precision and standardization in the production of weapons, characteristics that were later to stand the English ironmasters in good stead when they were required to supply cylinders and pistons for the steam engines that provided the power for the Industrial Revolution. Moreover, although the armor of the medieval soldier proved vulnerable to the new firearms and was gradually discarded, the new armaments and the new big armies proved to be much heavier consumers of iron than the medieval host. The weapons industry thus stimulated the search for an inexpensive method of smelting iron ore that was as indispensable as the early steam engine itself.

COAL

The coal industry in the Middle Ages was an infant one. Coal from outcroppings was used locally as fuel in various parts of England and around Liège. Some diggings had gone fairly deep into the ground, but technical and economic circumstances kept coal mining within narrow bounds. Coal was so bulky that any considerable overland transport raised its price to a point where it could not compete with other fuels. Moreover, the deeper the diggings the greater the hazards and the higher the cost of fighting them. In any case, the industrial uses of coal were few. Its impurities left iron so brittle that it could not be used in smelting, and no device existed for transforming its concentrated heating capacity into usable industrial power.

The problems of converting coal to major industrial uses were not solved until well into the eighteenth century, but circumstances caused coal mining to become a major industry in England before that time. These circumstances were the invention of relatively efficient steam pumps for draining the mines, the growth of London, and the depletion of the forests of southeastern England by the iron industry, which used wood to stoke the smelting furnaces. The concurrence of these factors around the end of the 1600s enabled coal, water-borne all the way from collieries in northeastern England to the London docks, to undersell wood in the London market. The coal-mining industry mushroomed, its market extending to all the eastern coastal areas of England and, with the depletion of the timberlands across the Channel, to the Netherlands.

The actual labor in medieval craft industries was done in the main by men who owned the raw materials as well as the tools to process them. It was only rarely that men worked for wages on someone else's raw materials and with someone else's tools. In a few industries, especially textiles, a single entrepreneur (or a partnership) tended to own the raw materials and either processed them in a shop or mill that he also owned or else let them out to be processed by workers who provided the tools and the shop, but were paid for their work at pre-established piece rates and not by a share in the final product. This latter way of organizing production is called the putting-out system, and it has its nearest present-day parallel in the sweatshop.

Many of the industries that came into being or into new prominence after 1500 developed along capitalist rather than craft lines. A variety of circumstances pressed toward this result. The deeper the coal mines, the more capital had to be sunk into maintaining them—into timbering the galleries, pumping out the water, and sinking new shafts when old seams petered out. These costly and risky operations could be financed only by men with access to more capital than a craftsman would see in a lifetime. Some of the metallurgical industries also demanded a considerable initial investment in equipment—smelters, blast furnaces, rolling mills, boring machines. Producers of the various kinds of unfinished iron were craftsmen secondarily, if at all. Primarily, they were employers of wage labor, of industrial workers who owned neither the instruments of production nor the product of their own efforts and whose earnings were wages. The sugar-refining industry also took on a capitalist cast, for a sugar refinery employing scarcely a score of hands might require a plant costing from $25,000 to $125,000.

Industry, Capitalism, and the Labor Force

A 1690 engraved view of Magdalene College at Cambridge, north of London, includes a string of coal barges being poled down the Cam River (right).

D. LOGGAN, *Cantabrigia Illustrata*, 1690

The growth of capitalism in the newer manufacturing and mining enterprises was paralleled by its growth in Europe's great staple industry—the textile industry. Capitalism in the cloth trade was not an innovation of the new era, for the great textile centers of the Middle Ages—Flanders and northern Italy—had used the putting-out system since the twelfth or thirteenth century. In the early modern era the system spread to other areas, notably to England. From acting primarily as a supplier of raw wool to Continental textile centers, England became early in modern times the greatest cloth exporter in Europe.

The necessity of organizing production to meet the demands of a distant market tended in England, as it had earlier in Italy and Flanders, to put industrial control in the hands of the capitalist managers of the putting-out system. From the fifteenth century on, we catch an occasional glimpse in the English and French textile industries of what looks like the vanguard of a new age, the age of factory industry. But the occasional appearance of a factory—of an assembly of weavers gathered beneath one roof weaving wool that belonged to the owner of the establishment on his looms and under his supervision—is not a sign of the growth of the factory system. From the beginning of the period to the end, factory-weaving seems to have occupied an insignificant sector of the textile industry; in woolen textiles, factory industry had no decisive economic advantage over household production organized on a putting-out basis. This was because there were no major large-scale innovations in methods of manufacturing woolen cloth until the second half of the eighteen century. The main tools—the spinning wheel and the loom—were the tools of an earlier day; in the first factories the textile workers used the same apparatus of production they would otherwise have used at home, and the increase in efficiency gained through supervision scarcely paid the factory operator for the increased cost of maintaining a large plant.

Thus Europe's greatest processing industry became increasingly capitalistic without becoming organized into large factory units. In Western industrial society as a whole, the trend toward concentration of production and concentration of control was slight prior to 1750. Alongside the capitalist clothier—and his kind must have numbered in the thousands—tens of thousands of master weavers, who themselves worked up the wool they bought and then sold the cloth in the open market, not only survived but in a small way thrived. Large-scale operation with a heavy investment of capital for equipment would remain a rarity as long as the main tools of industry were hammer and chisel and file, shears and awl and wool comb, spinning wheel and hand loom, and as long as the power to move the tools was most effectively supplied by the muscles of men and beasts, helped out here and there by the force of wind and water.

The phenomenal expansion of towns that accompanied the industrial transformations of the late 1700s tends to make us equate the growth of industry with the growth of towns, but no such equation is valid for the period between 1450 and 1750. During those centuries, many of the new industries were developed in the country and in small villages, and a considerable sector of the older industries moved from long-established industrial towns to the suburbs, the villages, and the open country. Although there are no statistics to enable us to measure the *absolute* quantities of rural against urban industry, it seems fairly certain that the relative growth of rural industry outstripped that of the towns in this era.

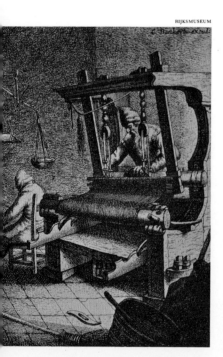

RIJKSMUSEUM

A Dutch weaver, one of a series of etchings of tradesmen done in the early 1630s by Jan van Vliet, a student of Rembrandt.

Several circumstances seem to have encouraged the migration of industry from the cities to the countryside. For one thing, the raw materials of the mining, metal-processing, and textile industries were found in the countryside. For another, most rural industry escaped the intricate network of guild regulation. This regulation had grown increasingly complex in many towns during the long period of economic decline before 1450. One of its prime purposes was to restrict production by reducing the labor force. Unnecessarily long terms of apprenticeship, sharp restrictions on the number of apprentices a master might have, requirements that those seeking the status of master craftsman produce a costly masterpiece—all such rules operated as deterrents to entry into a number of trades and made possible the fixing of monopoly prices. These protective regulations, though favorable to the industrial section of a guild, became particularly burdensome to the mercantile section, and merchants, especially when good times brought a potentially expanding market, began to look for a less costly way to stock their shops. They found this was by employing suburban and rural craftsmen who were not restricted by the guilds.

The major factor in the migration of industry from the cities, however, was the favorable differential in the cost of rural as against town production. Before the middle of the fifteenth century, the incentive to set up shop outside the town walls was counterbalanced by the disorder and violence of the period. Life within the confines of the town was far safer than life in the open countryside. The restoration of order achieved by the new monarchs increased the security of life in the country, removed the check that fear of violence had imposed on the migration of industry, and brought three purely economic considerations into operation.

First, rural industry was not subject to town taxes. Although the costs for urban services were small, what costs there were often fell on urban industry. Second, the costs of moving food for the labor force from the countryside into the city were prohibitive. The bulkiest item in most industrial processes was neither the raw material nor the finished product but the food consumed by the work force, and it was cheaper to maintain the work force near the food supply than to haul food to a work force situated many miles away. Third, an earlier technological change in the woolen industry had its full impact when the attraction of the towns as havens of security diminished. This was the development of a water-driven mill to perform the beating, cleaning, and nap-raising process known as "fulling." Streams had to be dammed to operate the water wheel, and, when the fulling mills moved out of the towns to be near the wheel sites, so did the master weavers and clothiers.

The movement of industry from cities to the country affected the capacity of the European industrial workers to protect themselves from the exploitive actions of their bosses. In the Middle Ages town authorities were forced to forfeit their charters if they were unable to maintain peace within the town walls; thus they often had to come to terms with the work force, whether that force consisted of guilds primarily industrial in character or of guilds of a mixed industrial and commercial character. When industry migrated to the country, the workers lost the advantage of proximity to each other that the town had provided. In the town, where they had lived in the same quarter and rubbed shoulders in off-hours, often taking their beer at the same tavern, the apprentices and journeymen had the chance to air their grievances and to band together to seek remedies. In the country the workers were dispersed among the partially industrialized inhabitants of thousands of still largely agricultural villages. In this situation, the awareness and unity of common grievances were hard to achieve. In the rare instances when men widely separated from one another did act together, their action was too sporadic to be effective. The infrequent exceptions to the general rule occurred where a special trade clustered very thickly in a particular area— the weavers in England's western counties, for example, or the cutlers around Sheffield.

It is noteworthy that the opposition of the state to combinations of workmen seeking to improve their terms of employment was by and large unnecessary when the craftsmen were scattered through the countryside and ineffectual when they were concentrated in towns. Despite suppressive measures by the state and employers, the silk workers of Lyons and the skilled laborers in half a dozen London trades managed to stick together.

Agrarian Economy and Social Structure

In the century prior to 1450, the plague decimated the population of Europe and caused urban markets to decline. As a result, commercial farming of foodstuffs declined, and many turned to subsistence farming. The rise in population, the restoration of order by the princes of the new monarchies, and the expansion of industry in the later fifteenth century increased demand for products of the soil, and farming for the market again became profitable.

The effort of every economic group with a stake in the land to keep its share in those profits or to increase its share at the expense of other agrarian groups became the driving force in a quiet but harsh social and economic conflict that, with only a few spectacular episodes, went on for centuries. The landlords were driven not only by greed but by the threat of ruin. During the bad times of the fourteenth and early fifteenth centuries, they had had to settle for a fixed money income from their estates. After 1450 the purchasing power of that income was curbed by two sharp blows: currency debasement and the influx of precious metals from the New World. After they had got all the credit they could to finance their wars, the rulers of the great European states debased the currency to repay their debts. By the simple expedient of reducing the precious-metal content of their coins, they scaled down their obligations, but they also brought about an inflationary rise in prices. The landlord, receiving his rents in depreciated money, found he could buy less. In the middle of the sixteenth century the second blow struck. From the rich mines of the New World a flood of precious metals poured into Europe. The value of money declined as its quantity increased, prices steadily rose, and many landlords again found themselves with their backs to the wall. Their income, bound to fixed rents, was sinking, their cost of living was rising, and they themselves were torn between the opposite economic pulls to which they were subjected.

Thus trapped, many aristocratic landed families went to ruin. They forfeited their estates to pay their debts, some sinking into the peasant mass, others vanishing into the urban middle class. The survivors were the careful, the calculating, and the alert. The landlords who weathered the economic storm did so by beating the peasantry to the profits that agriculture enjoyed during a century of rising food and wool prices.

The struggle ran a different course in different areas of Europe, and the outcome profoundly affected the later economic, social, and political history of each area. The most important geographical boundary for the peasantry was the Elbe River. Roughly speaking, to the east of that river the victory of the landlords brought with it the almost universal enserfment of the peasantry of Prussia, Russia, Poland, and the Hapsburg lands. West of the Elbe, serfdom was the exception rather than the rule. In the New World, on the tobacco plantations of Virginia, in the Carolina rice fields, on the sugar plantations of the West Indies, in the mines, fields, and workshops of New Spain, Peru, and Brazil, forced labor of one kind or another was the lot of many, in some places nearly all, of the tillers of the soil. The number of white Europeans subjected to personal servitude in the Americas was small: the overwhelming mass were African Negroes and, south of the Rio Grande, American Indians. The proportion of servile to free populations varied greatly, being in general smaller in the temperate zone than in the tropical and semitropical zones. The conditions of bondage also varied considerably. Only Negroes were outright chattel slaves, and even among them there were some differences of condition, at least on paper, since the Spanish government undertook to enforce on the masters a code of treatment for Negro slaves that was far more humane than the English code.

The process, almost continuous in Europe from the twelfth century onward, of public encroachment on the judicial powers of the landlords did not take place east of the Elbe. To their landlordship the Prussian and Polish squires added manlordship, judicial authority over those who owed them rents. The squires used their power in various ways, but for a single and simple set of connected purposes: to transform rents in cash or kind into labor dues and to supplant peasant holdings with domain land. The figures on landholding in the Pulany district of Poland show how well they succeeded in their second purpose. The percentage of estates in which the lord's reserve comprised 500 plots went from 13 percent in the mid-fifteenth century to 31 percent in the mid-seventeenth and to 42 percent in the late eighteenth century. Peasant holdings shrank proportionally. On one royal estate in Poland, peasant holdings of the kind that at an earlier time had customarily been farmed by a single family had shrunk to less than an eighth of the estate's arable land by the latter part of the sixteenth century. Furthermore, 50 percent of these peasant holdings were but half the usual single-family size. From such half-holdings the lords ordinarily extorted three days a week of labor on their domain land. The peasant also had to cut the lord's grain and provide the animals and farm equipment for his work. In 1566, 74 percent of the peasantry was enserfed in the freest provinces of Poland; in other areas, the proportion rose to 99 percent.

The impulse toward the enserfment of the peasantry on the eastern fringe of the Western world seems to have come from the West. The general economic revival of the Western world a little before the beginning of the sixteenth century involved an increasing segment of the population of the lands west of the Rhine in mining, sheepherding, maritime trade, shipbuilding, and manufacturing. There was, however, no major increase in Western agricultural yields until the eight-

eenth century was well under way. Part of the food supply for Western Europe thus had to be imported from the Baltic region and Central Europe.

During the seventeenth century, Dutch ships carried Prussian and Polish grain into the ports of every European state bordering on the Atlantic and even through the Mediterranean to Italy. Whichever class in the Baltic region could get its hands on grain surpluses for export could therefore increase its income and raise its standard of living. In sixteenth-century Brandenburg we find the landlords exacting from the prince a monopoly right to trade in grain, an economic activity usually reserved to merchants. The same motive that impelled the landlords east of the Elbe to drive merchants out of the grain trade impelled them to increase their domain lands and to force the peasantry to cultivate those lands: they wanted to have grain surpluses to sell. Economically, the lands east of the Elbe were dependent on Western Europe in the same sense that the West Indies were. Both the West Indies and the Baltic lands were agricultural areas that produced for the same center of industrial and commercial activity. In both areas, the drive toward producing surpluses was supplied by the larger landowners, who reaped the profits; and, in both areas, these landowners used a combination of legal sanction and force in order to impose the burden of labor on cultivators held in bondage.

Agricultural profits were not so easily acquired in the great states of the West, simply because, in France, England, the Netherlands, and western Germany, forced labor as a major trait of agricultural life was gone for good by the end of the fifteenth century. Although a few small islands of serfdom survived in France and in other Western European countries until the armies of the French Revolution forced a change, nowhere in the more advanced countries of Europe was serfdom of much consequence after 1500, and nowhere was a restoration of forced labor achieved or even attempted. To such a restoration in Western Europe there were two insuperable obstacles: a fairly firm legal structure of status

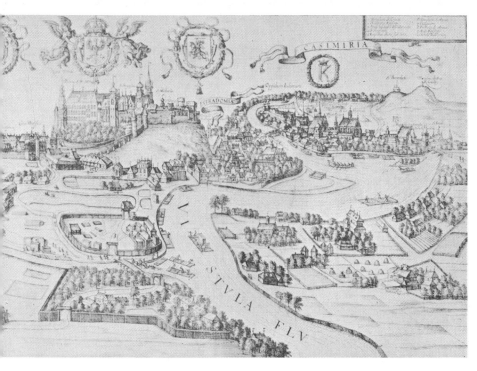

rights enforced by public courts, and numerous towns where refugees from overly oppressive lords might find means of livelihood.

If the habit of looking to land as a means of cash income and profit rather than solely as a means of subsistence is taken as a measure of the development of a modern capitalistic attitude in the farming population, the contrast between Eastern and Western Europe is clear. In the East that attitude was held only by the *Junkers*, the landed aristocracy in the Prussian class structure, but it found firm lodgment among members of all rural classes, except the very poorest peasants, in England and France. The struggle for agricultural profits in the West consequently did not follow a simple path to a uniform outcome as it did in the East. The course the struggle took in the West differed both from country to country and from time to time, and the outcome varied from place to place, even from one village community to the next, so that most generalizations are of dubious value.

Two generalizations, however, hold true of most of Western Europe in the beginning of our period. In the first place, the rural aristocracy entered this period with a relatively rigid income structure, with income receivable in money rents, to which they had bound themselves during the economic disasters of the waning Middle Ages. Second, up to 1600 the cost of living rose more precipitously than at any previous time for which records exist and at any subsequent time up to World War I. In England, for example, money prices of a dozen staple foodstuffs that had climbed little more than one-fourth over the previous two centuries jumped two-thirds in the forty years after 1500 and went up two-thirds again by the 1590s. In a little more than a century, these prices had nearly sextupled.

Although the drastic rise in prices spelled disaster for many of England's landlords, it did not ruin the landed aristocracy as a class. Quite the contrary. Despite individual casualties, the English squires—the social equivalent of the

The Tichborne Dole *(1670) records the annual ceremony in which Sir Henry Tichborne distributed his hereditary dole—apparently bread—to his tenants. Sir Henry is at left center, surrounded by his family. The Tichbornes are one of the oldest Roman Catholic families in England.*

Prussian *Junkers*—prospered during the seventeenth century. They held vast lands, and their lands provided them with a nice income. With as much enterprise as their mercantile contemporaries showed in trade, resolute squires contrived to avoid the squeeze of fixed rents and rising prices. Some did so by enclosing the open fields on their land and turning them into pasture for sheep—a profitable course, for with the burgeoning of the textile industry wool was in great demand. Many of the gentry re-established their position by less drastic but no less effective means. They held on to their lands until the long leases granted by their predecessors expired, and then in the new leases charged a rent in line with the day's prices. They also drastically shortened the length of leases, so they could better keep the rents abreast of prices.

When Henry VIII confiscated the estates of the monasteries, the gentry ended up with the lion's share of the estates he sold, and for the next hundred years they were the most avid purchasers of the royal lands that hard-pressed monarchs threw on the market. Although many tenants held land at fixed rents, most of them had to pay an "entry fine" to inherit land. By raising the entry fine, shrewd landlords made up for what they lost because of the fixed rents. Some landlords set out to reverse the process of 1350–1450 by reconstituting the demesne, or home farm as the English called it. Some pressed their legal advantage to the full to harass tenants into surrendering their holdings; others purchased tenant claims outright. In either case, they regained some of their former status as gentlemen farmers, rather than remaining simply rent collectors. They differed markedly from the *Junkers*, however, in that they held less land in demesne and farmed it with free agricultural wage labor rather than with forced labor.

The success of the English squire in re-establishing his old position did not bring disaster to the group just below him in country society—the yeomen. Middle-sized farms survived the resurgence of the gentry, and their holders throve on the rising prices. Like the gentleman with a home farm, the yeoman raised food and grazed and sheared sheep for the market, and although there were differences in their style of living, both squires and yeomen, given energy and shrewdness, found in farming a way of prospering.

The French landlords, in the same squeeze as those in England, resorted to similar measures but with less success, mainly because they only belatedly grasped some of the methods by which their English counterparts had enriched themselves. By the time the English ideas had taken hold, the period of rapid price rises had come to an end, and the French nobility had missed the boom. Moreover, the laws under which the French operated appear to have offered them less scope for economic maneuvering, and they had to cope with a religious civil war in the late sixteenth century at the very time that prices were rising fastest. Many of the ablest members of the aristocracy were attracted to military careers (as but few of the English gentry were) by the land wars, foreign and civil, that raged with only occasional brief intermissions from 1494 to 1714. In the long run, the French nobles improved their economic situation by building up their demesnes and replacing rent in money by rent in kind on a sharecropping basis.

It is ironic that although the French noble ended up in a less satisfactory economic position than the English squire, his efforts seem to have generated a greater legacy of hatred among the peasantry. This was probably due in part to the means he used. Many of the devices used by the English, like enclosure or buying out lease holders, were final. In contrast, a good number of the French devices were frequently recurring harassments of the peasantry. Such, for example, was the yearly squabble between sharecropper and lord over the division of the yield; such, too, was the enforcement of the rule requiring the peasant to use the lord's wine press, his flour mill, and his oven, or, worse, to pay for the privilege of not using them. To these persistent grievances of the French peasant was added another: the king's tax collector, who squeezed the peasants for all they were worth, laid not a hand on the revenues of their noble exploiter. By the eighteenth century, the French peasantry, but not the English peasantry, was ripening for a mass rising against the aristocracy.

4

The Age of the Merchants

In the past, economic historians writing of what we have called the early modern period labeled it either the commercial revolution, the period of mercantile capitalism, or the age of mercantilism. All of these terms are misleading, however. The term *commercial revolution* suggests and was suggested by the term *Industrial Revolution*. In the Industrial Revolution the interrelated discoveries of new sources of power and new, highly productive mechanical substitutes for the human hand resulted in a series of massive, irresistible, and continuing breakthroughs in production that had equally massive social repercussions. The miscellaneous and ill-related items that historians collected under the rubric *commercial revolution*, however, did not have an equivalent impact either on society or on commerce itself in the early modern era.

The phrase *mercantile capitalism* was coined by economic historians who thought in terms of a law of economic development that required universal fixed stages of economic change, which in turn determined the other traits of a society. The phrase overestimates the role of wholesale trade, wholesale traders, money, and credit in the early modern era, and underestimates their importance in the Middle Ages. It also underestimates the social, economic, and political power of the landed aristocracy in the early modern age. The term *age of mercantilism*, on the other hand, was somewhat too constrictive, since it concerned itself only with that rather limited area where trade entered the consciousness and consideration of the makers of state policy and their advisers.

Though each of these labels has defects, they also have something in common: they all indicate that merchants and their doings were of central interest in the economic history of the early modern era. It was the merchants—especially the wholesale merchants who bought in quantity in one market and sold in quantity in another market or in the same market at a later time—whose activities provided the leaven that made the economic life of the Western world bubble and rise after 1450. It was they who organized spectacular trading companies that sent great fleets to the Orient to bring back to the markets of Europe strange and precious products. In more modest partnerships they developed Europe's substantial trade with the settlements in America. It was the merchants who established and operated the woolen cloth markets in Halifax, London, Antwerp, and Hamburg, and it was they who ran the Amsterdam bourse, the great emporium of the Western world where all year round a buyer could purchase in quantity almost every commodity used in Europe and where he could speculate in precious metals and in the stocks of several Dutch and foreign companies. And it was the merchants whose credit kept goods moving by financing the producer at one end of the business chain and the distributor at the other—the country clothiers in southwest England and the local drapers and mercers in Mainz or Lisbon or St. Petersburg. To focus attention on their doings and the activities their doings generated in the early modern era, this chapter is entitled "The Age of the Merchants."

The commissioning of portraits is one index of the growing affluence and status of merchants in the early modern period. Here is one Georg Gisze, a merchant from the Hanseatic port of Danzig, painted in his London office by Hans Holbein in 1532.

The size and location of the producing units and the retail business units in the age of the merchants assured wholesale traders of the key position in economic life. For many products today, all manufacturing and distributive functions are divided between enormous processing concerns and enormous chain retail outlets. Often every necessary operation from the acquisition of the raw materials to the sale of the finished product is performed by two or three business concerns. Such a division of economic functions was altogether out of the question in the early modern era with its small undercapitalized producing and retailing organizations. The largest manufacturing and mining units were small by present-day standards; the ordinary unit in many lines of production was tiny: the family shop staffed by the master, an apprentice, and a journeyman or two. The ordinary retail outlet was no bigger; its stock was small, its owner of moderate circumstances.

Under such conditions it was impossible to dispense with the middleman or merchant, except for those goods sold in the locality where they were processed. Merchants were essential, for they sought out producers, gathered a sufficient quantity of their goods for shipment, warehoused the goods pending shipment, found shipping for them, located markets, and held the goods in the final market pending purchase by retailers. Middlemen function today in much the same way in those sections of the economy where many of the business units in the line of production from raw material to finished goods are small, notably in the textile and clothing industry and in the agricultural, food-processing, and food-vending industry.

In the second half of the fifteenth century several developments stimulated a period of economic growth that created new challenges and new opportunities for European merchants. These developments were interrelated and interdependent. First, the population of Western Europe, which for a century or more had declined and then reached a plateau, slowly but steadily began to increase. Second, the new monarchs created a situation of security conducive to commercial activity. During the disorders of the later Middle Ages, any merchant who embarked on an enterprise risked losing his goods as a result of the political violence that prevailed. The suppression of local disorders and anarchy from the late fifteenth century on largely removed this impediment to commercial enterprise. Third, the English woolen textile industry expanded enormously from the last decade of the fifteenth century to the middle of the sixteenth. Fourth, the Spanish monarchs Ferdinand and Isabella supported large-scale commercial sheep-raising, thus providing the cloth manufacturers of the Netherlands with wool to take the place of the English wool that was being increasingly absorbed by English manufacturers. Finally, great metropolises grew at an unprecedented rate after 1450. The supplies necessary to feed, clothe, and house the inhabitants of these cities had to be drawn from sources ever more distant, and the organization of supply to the new metropolitan markets provided a fertile field for the activity of the merchant.

The Merchant and His Firm The most spectacular development in the organization of business enterprise in the early modern era was the establishment of a number of so-called joint-stock companies that in form and law were similar to the modern corporation. Of these, the most important were the Dutch East India Company (1602), the British East

India Company (chartered in 1600, reorganized on a permanent joint-stock basis in 1657), and the Bank of England (1694).

These companies, which operated under government charters, had a legal permanence not available to partnerships, which terminated on the death or withdrawal of one of the members. They were unions of capital rather than of men. An investment of capital entitled the subscriber to a proportional share in the profits of the company. These shares were transferable, so that by selling his share a man could withdraw from participation in the company without withdrawing capital from the company. The shareholders of joint-stock companies also acquired the privilege of limited liability. In other words, if a company needed more capital to extend operations or even to avoid bankruptcy, it could not demand that its shareholders contribute that capital. If the company did fall into bankruptcy, the shareholders were not liable for all its debts; they lost only whatever they had paid for their shares. The ordinary shareholder had little part in determining the day-to-day policies of the joint-stock companies. A small group of directors, chosen by a method prescribed in the company's charter, formulated general policies, hired personnel, and conducted ordinary affairs.

The joint-stock company had several apparent advantages over other forms of business organization. For the business firm it provided access to a continuous capital fund for which payment was never due and it gave continuity of management and policy. To the investor it offered a holding that he could liquidate on very short notice, since there was always a market for shares; it also limited his liability for the debts of the concern. Yet, despite these apparent advantages, organization on a permanent joint-stock basis remained a rarity among business concerns in the early modern era. The joint-stock company enjoyed a brief period of favor from 1660 to 1715, and the year 1700 saw a great increase in the number of joint-stock corporations in England and France. In fact, promotion and speculation in company stocks boomed. The boom ended in the inevitable crash, however, with the collapse of two highly speculative joint-stock ventures, the so-called English South Sea Bubble and the French Mississippi Bubble (both in 1720). Legislation that followed on these financial disasters sharply restricted the privileges of incorporation and hampered the subsequent growth of corporate enterprise.

In point of fact, joint-stock enterprise had already compiled a dreary record of failure in the seventeenth century, whereas the older well-tried forms of business organization—the family firm and the partnership—had proved adequate to all but the most extraordinary economic demands of the age and continued to dominate trade and industry well into the nineteenth century. The very features of corporate organization that appear, to our eyes, as an advance over the simpler forms were a disadvantage, however, in the early modern era. The ordinary industrial unit was obviously much too small and operated on far too little capital to warrant the apparatus of incorporation with the attendant boards of directors. There was no regular market for shares in half a dozen hand looms or a couple of fulling mills. Incorporation with limited liability was a positive disadvantage for the purely mercantile firm. Merchants might own a warehouse or two but their investment in ships declined throughout the period as they increasingly rented shipping space instead of purchasing vessels. Thus merchant firms had little fixed capital. More and more their trade was on a credit basis. The full financial responsibility of each partner for the entire debt of the firm provided an inducement to lenders. But this responsibility, characteristic of partnerships, disappeared in limited liability companies. Indeed, the early history of the joint-stock companies indicates that their most important asset, the one enabling them to raise capital by sale of shares, was government support rather than corporate form. Among the English joint-stock companies, for example, the Levant Company received a monopoly in the Near East trade, the African Company in the slave trade, the Mines Royal in the mining of nonferrous metals, the Mineral and Battery Works in refining them, the South Sea Company in the Orient trade, the Hudson's Bay and East India companies in northern Canada and the Far East respectively, and the Bank of England in the management of a large share of the public debt. As many of these monopolistic ventures, some of which were cumbersome and unprofitable, disappeared, the volume of trade in the areas previously under monopoly control markedly increased. The greatest branch of English overseas trade, the commerce to British America, was conducted not by corporate monopolies but by private trading firms—partnerships and especially family firms.

In all the great commercial states family firms were the backbone of mercantile capitalism. Indeed, the geographical expansion and shifting centers of commercial capitalism in Europe can be traced by following the successive emergence of great family firms. The house of the Medici, the last and greatest of the major Florentine merchant bankers, rose in the first quarter of the fifteenth century and declined as a commercial house in the last quarter. The successors to the Medicis were a number of south German family firms—among them the Fuggers, Welsers, and Hochstetters—that dominated the commercial stage during the

In 1717 the Mississippi Company was founded to exploit the resources of French Louisiana. After wild speculation in the company's stock, especially in Paris, the "Mississippi Bubble" burst, ruining most of the investors. In a 1720 Dutch satire Folly's chariot crushes True Commerce while a seductive Chance distributes prospectuses. The crowd is driven to the almshouse, hospital, and madhouse in the left background.

Het Groote Tafereel der Dwaasheid, 1720

first half of the sixteenth century. The greatest of them was the House of Fugger.

The Fuggers first appeared in Augsburg late in the fourteenth century. By the third quarter of the fifteenth century they had built up a considerable but unspectacular fortune in the cloth industry. The third generation branched out into trade in silk, spice, fruit, and saffron; established commercial connections in the Netherlands, Silesia, Poland, and Hungary; engaged in financial dealings for the Papacy; and began a business in loans and bills of exchange. The last of that generation, Jakob the Rich, got control of large mining interests in the Tyrol and Hungary, built up the deposit and loan business, dealt in commercial paper (that is, in instruments of commercial credit), speculated in a variety of commodities on the Antwerp bourse, and helped finance the largest and most important political federation of the first half of the sixteenth century, the empire of Charles V. In the thirty years prior to Jakob's death in 1525, the Fugger firm increased its capital from about 54,000 gulden to 2 million gulden, which has been estimated as the largest sum under the control of a single business firm up to that time. In 1546 the Fugger capital was more than 5 million gulden, but by that time loans to the Hapsburgs represented an unduly large portion of the Fuggers' assets. The last half of the sixteenth century was a bad time for men, and especially bankers, who put their faith in princes, and the Hapsburg loans ultimately swamped the Fuggers. The first of a series of financial crises set in in the late 1550s. Though the Fugger firm kept its head above water longer than some of the lesser German family firms, in the early seventeenth century it too sank, overloaded by the bad debts of the Spanish Hapsburgs.

Jakob the Rich (standing), head of the Fugger banking house, with his bookkeeper, from a 1516 manuscript. Behind them are listed their banks.

From the 1530s on the merchants of Genoa had gathered into their hands the management of the trade of Spain, which the Spanish were incompetent to cope with and which the German bankers were too busy to handle. As the Germans declined in importance, Genoese families famous in trade for centuries dominated the economic life of Spain under Philip II.

Antwerp, the great goods emporium and trading center of the north during most of the sixteenth century, did not produce a crop of great merchants. Rather, it created a market in which merchants from the sprawling domains of the Hapsburgs and lands at peace with them could trade in loans, in currency, and in commodities. The commercial supremacy of Antwerp was destroyed during the religious civil wars of the later sixteenth century, partly by the violence of the Spanish, but far more effectively by the Zeelanders, who blockaded the mouth of the Scheldt, Antwerp's access to the sea. The beneficiary of the decline of Antwerp was Amsterdam, which for nearly the whole of the seventeenth century remained the mercantile metropolis not merely of northern Europe but of the entire Western world. During the period of Amsterdam's ascendancy the Dutch merchants stood in the forefront of the economic scene. Even in the eighteenth century, when Amsterdam sank toward a commercial twilight, it could still boast of the greatest mercantile firms in Europe—the deSmettes, the Cliffords, the Hopes, the Barings.

In the eighteenth century the Baring family transferred its main activities to London, the new mercantile center of the Western world. No one great merchant house dominated the rapidly growing trade of Britain. The varied activities that had made the Fuggers pre-eminent in Europe two hundred years earlier—

Das Burg Thor.

A woodcut dating from 1552 pictures the Baltic port of Lübeck, its harbor filled with ships, its highway crowded with the carts of merchants. At center is one of the city's forts.

accepting deposits, issuing loans, dealing in bills of exchange, and financing the world's greatest empire—were carried on in London by a joint-stock company, the Bank of England. Banking, which had been merely a sideline of the great merchant families, became a specialized business.

The path we have followed from the late fifteenth to the early eighteenth century—from Florence through Antwerp, Augsburg, and Genoa to Amsterdam and London, from the House of the Medici on the banks of the Arno to several hundred trading houses on the banks of the Thames, has a social as well as an economic significance. The Medici merchant princes soon became princes indeed —the dukes of Tuscany. Before the firm collapsed, the Fuggers were on the way to becoming considerable territorial nobles. But few of the merchants of eighteenth-century London cherished dreams of princely splendor; instead, in the arena of politics they pressed hard their group interests as merchants. Herein lies one of the great changes of the age. Without princely aspirations or oligarchic power, the English merchant of the eighteenth century was the member of a large and powerful interest group in a great territorial state. This group sought and got for itself an important role in setting the policy of the world's greatest empire.

The organization and mode of operation of the mercantile firm did not change much between 1450 and 1750. The head of the firm ordinarily remained at the home office, which consisted of a counting house and a warehouse, occasionally journeying to his chief markets to cement old trade connections and seek new ones. Junior partners were either in the hinterland buying up the goods the firm dealt in or in the markets deciding, with whatever degree of independence the head of the firm might grant them, on the terms and time for selling. In distant and lesser markets the merchant often disposed of his goods through a supercargo or by consignment. A supercargo acted as agent for a whole shipload of wares, ordinarily the shipments of several merchants. Acting on rather broad instructions from the merchants, he often exercised wide discretion in hunting out the best market in a particular area for the goods he had in charge. Consignees, on the other hand, usually were given very little discretion in the disposal of goods sent them, for the exporting merchant sent along with the goods binding instructions on the selling price he would accept. The consignee acted as a salesman working for a commission. What he could not sell at the quoted price he put in storage pending further instructions. When importing goods the mercantile firm reversed the procedures. On instruction from the head of the firm, its agents purchased goods in foreign markets or sent them to the home office on consignment. The home office sold to retailers both the goods it purchased outright and the goods it received on consignment.

The Medicis in the fifteenth century and hundreds of English firms in the eighteenth century carried on their business in this same manner, with one significant change in the direction of increasing the specialization of the activities of the firm into purely mercantile operations. In the earlier periods the firm itself was likely to be owner, in part at least, of the warehouses in which it stored its goods and of the ships that carried them. This was less frequently the case by the end of the eighteenth century. Instead of owning ships and warehouses, eighteenth-century trading firms preferred to rent space in both. In the greater ports even the business of finding space for a merchant's cargo became a specialized trade. One consequence of increasing specialization was that the working capital of the firm was not tied up in fixed assets but could be devoted wholly to the business of buying and selling goods. Another was that the efforts of the firm were not diverted to the problems of making its shipping and warehousing interests profitable and could concentrate on seeking gain by buying and selling goods. It was a sounder way to do business.

It is in ways of doing business rather than in the organization of the mercantile firm that the most significant changes took place after 1450. These very miscellaneous changes were linked together by one common bond: in one way or another they enabled merchants to carry on their affairs more efficiently or with more security.

As early as the twelfth century traveling Italian buyers found it advantageous, when away from their home towns, to obtain goods not with money but with a paper commitment to pay. The commitment took one of two forms: it was either a promise of the buyer to pay, or an instruction to some third party to pay. The former was very similar to a modern promissory note; the latter was like a postdated modern bank check and was called a bill of exchange. The bill of exchange was ordinarily drawn on a merchant of high repute in the buyer's town and was made to fall due on a set date, usually three months to a year after the

Improvements in Business Efficiency

transaction. The paper commitment relieved merchants of the risk of carrying their cash assets about with them and thus provided a secure means of exchange. Also, because the paper commitment usually postponed payment to a time when the buyer had disposed of and received payment for his purchase, it enabled him to pay for the merchandise he had bought with the proceeds of its sale. Promissory notes and bills of exchange thus provided the trading community with instruments of credit. When payment was due, the man who accepted such a commitment in exchange for goods could go to the place where it was to be paid, say, Genoa, and either buy merchandise there with the money he received or carry the money away with him. If business did not take him to Genoa when payment was due, he could assign—in effect, sell—the bill or note to a merchant who did have business to do in Genoa.

The merchants of the early modern age developed two devices that vastly increased the commercial utility of notes and especially of bills of exchange—endorsement and discounting. By simply endorsing the reverse side of a bill or note, a merchant could transfer it, that is, use it as a means of payment. There was no limit to the number of endorsements a particular bill or note might receive and therefore no limit to the number of times it could be used as a substitute for cash payment. Indeed, the more endorsements it carried, the more secure it became, because each endorser in turn was responsible for the payment of the face value of the note to the final holder. If the holder of a bill due in six months wanted cash, he could turn to a bill broker and sell his bill for somewhat less than its face value, taking £960, say, for a £1,000 bill. If he anticipated a deal demanding cash payment of £960 that would yield him £1,020 during the next half year, he would have gained £20 or 2 percent per half year (or 4 percent per year) by having sold his bill for cash at a discount. The buyer or discounter of the bill could hold it for payment at its face value of £1,000 and thus earn 8 percent per year on his purchase. Or he could sell it again, perhaps at a small premium, to a merchant with business to do in the town in which the bill was to be paid. The bill brokers were private bankers who provided the merchants with an important banking service.

During the seventeenth century the structure of trade in northern Europe was buttressed by the establishment of several great public banks, institutions operating under charters from public bodies. Of these the most important were the Bank of Amsterdam (1609), the Hamburg Bank (1619), the Bank of Stockholm (1656), reorganized as the Bank of Sweden (1668), and the Bank of England (1694). These banks did not all perform the same functions. The Bank of Amsterdam, for example, did not lend money to businessmen or issue paper money or discount bills. It accepted deposits in its regular accounts and transferred them from one account to another, but it did not give interest or even permit withdrawals. Yet so secure was the bank, and so convenient as a place of payment, that a record of a deposit there sold for cash at a premium—that is, for a little more than its face value. In the diversity of its operations, the Bank of England stood in complete contrast to the Bank of Amsterdam. It did about everything that a bank could do in connection with private business and in addition acted as banker to and financial agent of the English government.

Together, the public and private banks served the trading community in the

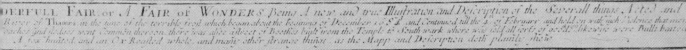

great commercial towns in a variety of ways. They provided a safe place of deposit for the merchant's cash. They made the payment of debts simple, speedy, and secure for depositors, reducing it to a bookkeeping transaction by simply subtracting the sum owed from the debtor's account and adding it to the creditor's. They loaned money to merchants on all sorts of securities—government obligations, joint-stock company shares, mortgages, jewelry and plate, warehouse receipts, bills of exchange, and even on promissory notes if they were endorsed by a responsible member of the trading community. Some bankers issued receipts for cash deposits that entitled the bearer to payment on demand. Except in periods of economic crisis, these receipts or banknotes circulated almost as freely as and a great deal more conveniently than hard cash.

In the latter half of the seventeenth century the London goldsmiths discovered that they could issue such demand notes in sums considerably in excess of the cash reserves on deposit with them. Since only a small fraction of what they had

Surely one of the more unique of Europe's trading fairs was the one held on the frozen Thames in London in "the time of the terrible frost" in 1684. The goods were displayed in the booths at center. Bull-baiting (right), a fox hunt (far right), and an ox roast (left) drew the crowds.

issued was likely to be presented for payment at any one time, they kept on hand only enough to meet the ordinary demand for cash payment. Thus the goldsmiths hit upon a basic principle of note issue: that notes can safely be issued considerably in excess of precious metal reserves. In the eighteenth century the bankers adopted this principle and thus were able to provide merchants with a workable paper currency that greatly increased the money supply and served to lubricate the wheels of commerce.

Another new economic institution of the early modern era was the bourse or merchants' exchange. The great bourse of the sixteenth century was in Antwerp, that of the seventeenth century in Amsterdam, and that of the eighteenth century in London. A bourse was simply a meeting place of buyers and sellers. It differed from the fairs, which were the main medieval meeting places of buyers and sellers, in three ways. First, fairs were of but a few weeks' duration, whereas bourses operated continuously. Second, merchants had to follow the fairs from place to place, while the location of the bourse was fixed in one town. And, third, the goods bought and sold at fairs were physically present at the fair and were delivered to their purchasers there. Goods exchanged at bourses might be in warehouses in the town, in ships at sea, in warehouses abroad, or they might not even be harvested or manufactured at the time they were sold. That is to say, on the bourse men could buy and sell for immediate delivery, and they could also buy and sell for future delivery.

A 1644 engraving of London's Royal Exchange shows investors crowded in the inner court. Writing of the Exchange, the essayist Joseph Addison marveled at the "private men . . . negotiating like princes for greater sums of money than were formerly to be met with in the royal treasury!"

For certain kinds of goods and for securities, the existence of a bourse created a market price. This was true of goods that were homogeneous or that could be made so by grading—that is, goods such as sugar, tobacco, English white cloth, raw wool, and wheat whose quality differed so little from one lot to the next that they could be marketed by weight or measure. Shares in a joint-stock company, municipal bonds, state bonds, and precious metals could be sold in the same way. As long as goods were exchanged by private bargaining between a buyer and a seller, one and the same commodity might sell for different prices at the same time in the same town. But in an open public market there was no reason for buyers to offer much more or sellers to accept much less than the price offered and accepted in the transaction most recently consummated.

Despite occasional manias of speculation and frequent attempts to corner or rig the market in one commodity or another, the bourses lent a greater measure of orderliness to buying and selling than those activities had possessed at any previous time. A further significant development occurred when, during the seventeenth century, weekly lists of "prices current" for the things regularly traded in the Amsterdam bourse began to be issued. The lists, sent to various other commercial centers in Europe, encouraged arbitrage operations. When the price of a commodity was markedly higher in Amsterdam than, say, in London, London merchants would buy at home to sell in Amsterdam. When the prices lay the opposite way, they would send orders to Amsterdam to have the commodity shipped to London. Thus, for many kinds of goods, the patchwork of isolated local markets, characteristic of the Middle Ages, gradually began to give way to a general European market kept in balance by the market prices of the bourses.

A well-known economic historian, who for many years kept the full sweep of the economic history of the Western world within the scope of his panoramic vision, once noted a peculiarity of that history. Of the medieval period there exists an orderly and effective account, beginning with the emergence in the eleventh century of new forms of economic organization and an unprecedented volume of economic activity and ending with the partial collapse of the medieval economy in the late Middle Ages. Of economic change in the West from the late eighteenth century on, historians also offered an intelligible, organized account by focusing attention on several interrelated phenomena: the explosion of productivity, the concentration of economic control in management, labor organizations and the state, the enhanced role and crucial importance of capital accumulation, scientific technology and machines, and the succession of new kinds of power—steam, gasoline and oil, electricity, atomic fission.

But for the early modern period, roughly from the late fifteenth to the late eighteenth century, economic historians failed to provide a satisfactory framework. Historians used to structure the data of early modern history by assigning the rise of capitalism to that era. This framework collapsed ignominiously when it appeared that none of the economic traits ascribed to capitalism had penetrated certain areas of the West even by the end of the early modern era and that nearly all the traits ascribed to capitalism had been operative in certain economically advanced areas in the West—especially at the Champagne fairs and in Italy—since the twelfth century.

Risk in the Early Modern Economy

An Indian artist painted this minia-
ture of an elegantly turned-out for-
eigner, probably a merchant of the
British East India Company, c. 1600.

Under these circumstances historians have tended to take one of four courses. Some have pretended that the disaster to the association of capitalism with the early modern era never took place, and have gone on associating "capitalist" and "modern." Others, giving up that hopeless pretense, have continued to separate the early modern era in economic matters from the medieval era without seeking any justification for the separation. A third group, denying that any adequate grounds for separation exist, have argued that the economy of the West, like many of its other modes of activity, underwent no fundamental transformation from the twelfth century to well into the eighteenth, and that, at least as a period in economic history, "early modern" makes no sense. Finally, some historians have tried to hang early modern economic history on a framework composed of overseas expansion, the westward and northward shift in the centers of economic power in Europe, and the replacement of the town by the crown as the effective external regulator of economic life.

We will discuss state economic policy later in this chapter, and we have already dealt with European overseas expansion and the growth of power of the states of northern and western Europe. These phenomena, however, do not fall within a very strict definition of the term *economic*, but there is one trait of the early modern era that is economic in the strictest sense. It has to do with a gradual but major change in the way the economy dealt with risk.

Risk is a necessary concomitant of investment, and investment is the indispensable condition of all economic activity. If a man puts time or capital or land to a particular use in the hope that his investment will bring him an economic return, he must always take the chance that his hopes will be disappointed, that his investment will not bring the expected return, or that it will bring no return at all. Investors may suffer loss through a variety of causes: the ravages of nature, damage of goods in transit, war, robbery, piracy, theft, fraud, default, and, finally, through underestimating cost and supply or overestimating demand. In one way or another, men have long sought for ways to reduce, to limit, to spread, or to counterbalance the risks that their economic activities have entailed. Although generalizations like this one must always encounter exceptions, it does seem that between the Middle Ages and the end of the early modern period there was a difference in the ways that men, and especially merchants, coped with risk.

The tendency in the Middle Ages was to distribute the risk among the whole group—the community or corporative unit—engaged in a particular kind of economic activity. Merchants obliged to transport their goods long distances over lonely routes banded together in caravans, forfeiting freedom of movement for the sake of mutual protection. Venetian merchants shipped their goods under limitations imposed by the Venetian state in order to have the protection of the state-supplied convoy of armed vessels. Guilds protected themselves, among other ways, by limiting admission to various trades and by establishing the price of the finished goods. The staplers and hanses established rules for entry into their enterprises, decreed where members could trade, and set up standards for the conduct of trade. And leagues of merchants or merchant towns diminished the risk that their members incurred from hostile towns and greedy princes by meeting acts of hostility with countermeasures, usually economic, sometimes political, and occasionally military. With undeniable exceptions, these methods of dealing with risk did diminish it, but at the cost of freedom of decision and action of each particular member of the merchant community or merchant corporation.

In the early modern era the medieval methods of dealing with risk were gradually replaced by methods that altered the conditions under which men engaged in the more complex kinds of economic activity. One of the most striking traits of the London business community in the early eighteenth century was, for example, the myriad outlets where a man could put his capital. Trading partnerships, commercial banking, bill-discounting, joint-stock companies, insurance underwriting, loans on mortgages, shares in shipping, commodity speculations, bank deposits, and government loans all offered attractive possibilities. Moreover, the risks involved among these various enterprises ranged from infinitesimal to enormous. At one extreme was a loan to the British government. Into such a loan one could put capital with almost complete security, but the yield (the interest on the loan) was low. At the other extreme was the partnership or lone venture into "interloping" in India, that is, trespassing on the monopoly of the East India Company. Here, with luck, the return on one's investment would be magnificent, but the risk was so great as to be practically uninsurable.

Though the total span of risk was great, the gap between any particular level of risk and the next higher or lower level was very small. This was the consequence of the number and variety of enterprises ready, willing, and able to sponge up capital. And, finally, the transfer of capital from one kind of investment to another was in most instances easy, because in large towns like London there were public markets for almost every kind of investment, places where potential buyers and potential sellers could meet and bargain. There were also many kinds of brokers—commodity brokers, mortgage brokers, insurance brokers, bill brokers, brokers of shares in ships—whose business it was to bring together those who wanted to get their capital out of a particular kind of enterprise or operation and those who wanted to get their money into it.

It was this combination of economic arrangements—the enormous total span of risks among possible investments, the narrow gaps in the degree of risk between investment opportunities, and the ease with which capital could move from one kind of investment to another—that fundamentally altered the way businessmen coped with risk in the early modern era. The effect of the combination was to deprive of attractions for many businessmen the kind of community or corporate risk-sharing with restrictions on the individual's employment of his capital which was so prevalent in the Middle Ages. The new combination of economic arrangements enabled the businessman to select the particular combination of levels of risk that he wished to impose on his capital at a particular time. It also enabled him to alter many of those levels at will and to do so within a few weeks, a few days, a few hours, occasionally even within a few minutes, of the time of his decision.

Within this framework we can thus speak with a reasonable degree of precision about an economic trend that has often been ascribed to early modern times—a trend toward economic individualism and economic freedom. By economic individualism we mean a state in which the risks of enterprise fall directly on the individual with only such buffers as he himself provides in the form of insurance, "hedging," and so on. From the sixteenth to the eighteenth centuries, the businessman enjoyed a growing freedom to deploy his capital as he saw fit, subject only to the laws of contract and property.

The various economic institutions that created the conditions fostering economic individualism and freedom in the early modern period were almost certainly favorable to economic growth. The geographical discoveries of the age were also favorable. And so, possibly, although this has never been proved, were the political measures taken by the statesmen of the age to expand the markets and encourage the trade of the lands whose rulers they served. These political measures and the ideas that prompted them have since been given the name mercantilism.

Among the European states in the early modern era there was wide diversity in level and kind of economic development, in social structure, in political organization, in size and wealth. Despite local differences, however, there remained in the three hundred years before the French Revolution similarities among all the states of Europe in economic policy—both in the purposes of state regulation and in the measures taken to achieve those purposes. Moreover, there was a convergence both in theories and practices of state action in the economic sphere, so that the policies of the European countries were more nearly alike and the common economic notions behind them were more distinctly articulated in 1700 than they had been in 1500. It is this discernible common pattern that has made it possible for historians to give a single name—mercantilism—to the economic policy of all the important states of Europe and to the theories connected with that policy.

Mercantilism and the Balance of Trade

The term *mercantilism* focuses attention on what during the early modern period became the main economic preoccupation both of statesmen and of writers on economic affairs. These men were primarily concerned with the activities of the merchant, with commerce, and especially commerce among the various states. We have seen that the period itself was one during which important economic developments took place in the area of the large-scale wholesale exchange of goods. Mercantilism was not, however, a policy simply dictated to the state by the merchant class in the interest of that class. The merchant whose company had received from the state a grant of the monopoly of trade to some foreign lands gratefully accepted that monopoly; but the merchants excluded from the monopoly were likely to be vigorous advocates of open trading. Measures that at first sight seemed most favorable to the merchants encountered the hostility of one sector or another of the trading community. The result of chronic division among the merchants in most lands was that statesmen could win support from some merchants for almost any policy they chose to pursue, and therefore their policy often reflected more than merchant-class pressures; it reflected the statesmen's conception of the economic policy favorable to the interests of the state. Moreover, there were few times and few places in early modern Europe where merchants had enough power to dictate policy to statesmen.

The dependence of the merchants on the state was reinforced by the very nature of trade in the medieval and early modern era. Competition in prices and services was only one of the means of finding a market or a source of supply. Another means, perhaps a more important one, was to get a trading monopoly in a foreign area and to defend it through force or threat of force. Trade wars often laid the basis for trade monopolies. Merchants were, therefore, dependent on those who would fight wars for them. Few medieval rulers of states had had enough power to spare from other kinds of warfare to deploy much of it on behalf of the merchants. With the emergence of powerful consolidated monarchies in Western Europe, however, merchants in those lands were able to enlist the support of the sovereign for their bellicose monopolistic ventures. They thus became partners with the princes in a national trading enterprise. But they were, after all, junior partners. The last word in trade was still trade-war; and the rulers of the states, who alone could speak that word, were the senior partners.

During the medieval period economic policy had been primarily fiscal—that is, it was concerned with expedients for squeezing money out of the economy and into the hands of the rulers. During the mercantilist era, however, statesmen were interested in how to get money into the economy. (This, of course, did not diminish their interest in getting the money into their own hands once they had got it into the economy—quite the contrary.) In a rough analogy, the difference between fiscal policy and mercantilist policy is that between the dairy maid trying to get as much milk as she can out of each cow every time, and the dairy farmer trying to enlarge and improve the whole herd so that it will have as much milk as possible to give. The dairy maid's policy is "fiscal"; the dairy farmer's is "mercantilist."

From the beginning, one of the main obstacles to fulfilling the long-term aims of mercantilist policy were the short-term fiscal needs of the state, and a good deal of the confusion in state economic policies after 1500 stems from the hasty measures taken in every land in Europe to get hard cash for the government whenever a crisis occurred. Carefully thought-out schemes for drawing money into the economy would be postponed, distorted, or abandoned in order to raise the cash to pay an army, which, if it went unpaid, might simply melt away in the midst of a campaign. To meet such emergencies, Philip II of Spain exported great masses of precious metals, although on mercantilist grounds he had forbidden such export. A century later, Colbert, the organizer of French mercantilist policy under Louis XIV, sold hundreds of posts in the economic administration of the state not because the offices he sold were useful to that administration, but merely because Louis was pressed for money to pay for his costly war with the Dutch.

Mercantilist statesmen were obsessed with precious metals—gold and silver. If there was any matter on which all European merchants agreed with all European statesmen, it was on the desirability of having an abundant supply of gold and silver coin in circulation in their respective countries. The common concern of merchants and statesmen with the supply of hard money was the consequence of the large number of transactions that both traders and rulers had to carry on in which hard money alone was an acceptable means of payment. A decrease in the hard-money supply seriously snarled economic arrangements by creating pressing demands for an amount of cash simply not available within the economy. A sudden shortage of money resulted in a calling of loans within the mercantile community and in a decline of available credit, and "tight" money drove traders to bankruptcy and forced merchants to curtail their activities. Naturally, it also increased the state's difficulty in collecting taxes. Since metallic money was so essential both in affairs of state and in business, much of the ingenuity of the statesmen who made economic policy was expended in contriving ways to obtain the precious metals their countries lacked or to keep what precious metals they had.

There were only three ways for a country to get precious metals: to have possession of the mines, to seize the metals of other countries by force, or to sell goods abroad that would bring precious metals into the country in return. Almost all the major known mines were in the hands of the rulers of Spain and Austria. Though the other states had no moral scruple about seizing these mines, they did not have enough power to do so. Nor did they have the power to seize much bullion in transit. Despite a few successes in capturing Spanish treasure ships, the risks and costs of robbery on the seas soon became so high as to discourage capital from investing in that kind of piratical enterprise. No land could consistently rely on maritime depredations for its supply of precious metals.

Since most European states found it impossible to discover precious metals

A panoramic view of Potosí, painted by an unknown artist late in the sixteenth century, shows the great Peruvian "mountain of silver" exploited by the Spanish. Llamas brought the ore to the processing plant in the foreground, where it was crushed in the water-driven stamping mill at the left center and then refined.

and impractical to steal them, their statesmen focused attention on ways and means to attract precious metals into their countries by trade and to keep them in once they got there. The simplest and most forthright expedient for keeping money in a country was to prohibit its export. This expedient is called bullionism, from the word *bullion*, meaning precious metals in the mass. The trouble with bullionism was that it did not work particularly well. The very trait of precious metals that made them a desirable form of money—their high value in proportion to their bulk and weight—made them the easiest of all things to smuggle. They could easily be hidden among the cargo of any outbound ships or hustled across land borders where the guard was inadequate or bribable. Moreover, statesmen themselves often had to relax their own prohibition when their rulers' armies were fighting in foreign lands, since soldiers' pay had to go out of the country in cash and would ordinarily be spent on the spot.

The impossibility of altogether damming the outward flow of bullion turned the attention of European statesmen to ways and means of directing that flow, so that in international trade more came into their country than went out. If the money paid out by a country's merchants for imports was less than the money they received for what they sold abroad, then the balance of trade was favorable, just as a merchant's books showed a favorable balance if, at the end of the year, his income was greater than his disbursement. The balance-of-trade idea was a natural one in an era in which merchants did most of the orderly thinking about economic matters.

In the crudest version of the mercantilist theory the statesman considered the commerce of his country with each foreign country separately, struck the balance, and took measures to discourage trade with countries with which there was an adverse balance and to encourage it with those with which there was a favorable balance. This highly fragmented way of looking at commerce broke down as more and more states established trade relations in Eastern Asia. As we have seen, until the end of the eighteenth century Europe simply did not produce much that the inhabitants of India and the Spice Islands wanted to buy. Every European state trading in Eastern Asia had an unfavorable balance of trade with the East. Yet everyone knew that the Eastern trade brought money into a country. States with a large Eastern trade often enjoyed a favorable balance of trade with other European countries only because they re-exported to them for precious metals the spices they had bought for precious metals in the Indies. Merchants with interests in the East believed that the bullion they paid out in the Indies was like seed planted by the farmer. Thomas Mun, an English writer on economics, voiced this belief in his *Discourse on England's Treasure by Forraign Trade* (1664): "If we only behold the actions of the husbandman in the seed-time when he casteth away much good corn into the ground, we will rather account him a mad man than a husbandman; but when we consider his labors in the harvest which is the end of his endeavors, we find the worth and plentiful increase of his actions."

Mercantilist statesmen had in their hands a powerful instrument for affecting the balance of trade—legislative and administrative authority to encourage, regulate, or prohibit imports and exports of all kinds of goods. From the vast imperial realms of the British and the Spanish to the tiny petty principalities of Germany, every state with any pretensions at all to an economic policy tinkered with foreign trade. In all countries similar devices for regulating the flow of goods were employed—import and export duties, export bounties, import and export embargoes; the common aim of most regulation was to maintain or to increase the domestic supply of precious metals.

The Balance of Trade in Practice Mercantilist trade regulation is well illustrated by England's policy with respect to the two principal products of its fields and farms—grain and wool. In the Middle Ages the English government prohibited grain export on the grounds that the country should be well supplied with the staple article of diet. For the same reason it levied no duty on the importation of grain. At the same time it imposed charges on the export of wool only for fiscal purposes. Since wool constituted England's main export, the king drew a sizable revenue from charges on its shipment abroad. The purpose of the policy was not to prevent the export of England's most valuable raw material but rather to profit from it.

In the early modern era, English mercantilist statesmen drastically modified the laws regulating the trade in wool and grain. In 1617 James I abolished the ancient staple at Bruges, which was the sole outlet for English wool on the Continent, and the sale abroad of what had been England's only major export in the Middle Ages ceased. Then during the seventeenth century almost all English cloth was freed of export duties in a gradual process culminating about 1700. Between 1663 and 1673 the medieval policy on grain was also completely reversed. Imported grain was subjected to a heavy duty, while a bounty was granted for exporting wheat when it fell below forty-eight shillings a quarter (eight bushels) in order "that the nation may have her stock [of capital] increased by the returns thereof." The pattern applied to grain was soon extended to the whole commercial complex. After the Revolution of 1688, Parliament took the export tariffs off such foodstuffs as beer, pork, butter, and cheese and later removed those on coal and flour, while at the same time levying higher and higher import duties on foreign manufactures.

The aim and the effect of this reversal of the medieval pattern of English trade regulation was to ban the export of raw wool, which could be worked up in England into a far more valuable finished product for sale abroad, and to encourage the export of food and fuel, raw materials that other countries could not work up into manufactures for re-export. Conversely, tariffs discouraged entry into England of goods manufactured abroad, but low customs duties or none at all encouraged the importation of those raw materials that could be worked up into expensive and exportable products. Thus medieval fiscal policy, which used customs duties directly to raise revenues for the king, gave way to mercantilist policy, which tried to use them to improve the balance of trade.

From their view on the balance of trade mercantilists derived their attitude and formed their policy with respect to both goods and labor. Mercantilists like Frederick the Great of Prussia, Colbert, the great finance minister of Louis XIV of France, and the English Parliament, when it won control of economic policy after the Puritan Revolution, all were dominated by what has been called "the fear of goods." They aimed, as Adam Smith said, to create a "constant dearth in the home market" because domestic consumption decreased the stock

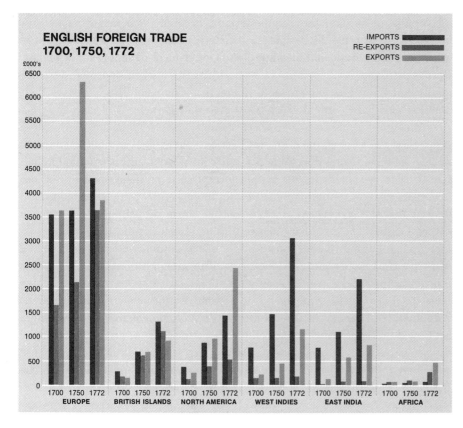

ENGLISH FOREIGN TRADE
1700, 1750, 1772

IMPORTS
RE-EXPORTS
EXPORTS

£000's
6500
6000
5500
5000
4500
4000
3500
3000
2500
2000
1500
1000
500
0

1700 1750 1772   1700 1750 1772   1700 1750 1772   1700 1750 1772   1700 1750 1772   1700 1750 1772
   EUROPE   BRITISH ISLANDS   NORTH AMERICA   WEST INDIES   EAST INDIA   AFRICA

The value and geographical distribution of England's foreign trade is depicted here at three stages in the eighteenth century. The British Islands included Ireland, the Isle of Man, and the Channel Islands. The growth of the colonial market reached the point, by the end of the century, where it absorbed 80 percent of the exports as against 20 percent in 1700.

of goods available for export, and therefore diminished the means for acquiring precious metals. To "unburden the country of its goods" by selling those goods abroad became a prime object of every country's statesmen. The general aim of discouraging consumption applied with double force to imported luxury goods. Such goods were complete; they could not therefore be worked on and sold abroad at a higher price. They were luxuries not necessities; they required the export of precious metals, yet contributed nothing to the strength of the country.

A crude set of deductions from the balance-of-trade idea resulted in a number of widespread notions on the proper policy with respect to the work force, notions which gradually emerged during the seventeenth and eighteenth centuries. Men observed, for example, that a pair of fine gloves brought a far better price in the market than did the skins of which they were made. What increased the price was quite clearly the labor applied in transforming the skins into gloves. This suggested that, since work added value to goods, the longer and harder men worked, the greater would be the value of the goods they produced. And the more valuable the goods a country produced, the more it would have for trading and the more favorable its balance of trade would be. So hours of labor should be long.

Wages on the other hand should be low. High wages were dangerous in two ways. With a high wage, the worker would either spend more or work less. But spending more would often take the form of a demand for foreign goods or for domestic products that could otherwise be exported. It would, therefore, create unfavorable pressures on the balance of trade. Secondly, if by five days of labor the worker could satisfy his wants for ten days, it was suspected that he would loaf the other five days, and thus five days of value-creating labor would be lost. Clearly, then, the way to prevent idleness among the workers and their overconsumption of goods was to peg wages so low that men would have to work their utmost all the time in order to keep body and soul together.

Mercantilism as a Policy of Power Although at the level of practical state action mercantilist statesmen tended to concentrate on measures directly or indirectly intended to ensure a favorable balance of trade, we shall miss the significance of their economic policy and lose sight of its relation to international politics in general if we do not understand the function of the balance of trade in the larger designs of the European powers. Colbert, the exemplary mercantilist statesman, stated the relation succinctly when he said that all the authority of the despotic monarchy should be used "to attract money into the kingdom and to spread it out into all provinces so as to pay their taxes," for "it is only the abundance of money in a state which makes the difference in its greatness and power." Businessmen may have wanted an abundance of money in the country purely for the commercial advantages that they believed accrued to them therefrom; statesmen were more moved by the ancient maxim, "Money is the sinews of war," revised in a mercantilist sense by Colbert to, "Trade is the source of public finance, and public finance is the vital nerve of war." Statesmen tended to regard the whole process of international exchange as a struggle, a kind of war for the lion's share of a constant quantity of riches.

Changes in the art of making war reinforced the statesmen in their view that money and consequently a favorable balance of trade were the indispensable means of power. The instrument with which the European princes met external pressure and exerted their own power was the professional standing army, a permanent force constantly at their disposal. The core of the army was the infantry, carefully trained in the use of its weapons (especially firearms) and extensively drilled to perform intricate maneuvers. Artillery prepared the way for and protected the infantry. The cannon, originally used to beleaguer heavy fortifications, was in the course of two centuries adapted and transformed into a fieldpiece, and the infantry-artillery team of modern ground warfare came into being. It was an expensive birth. It was hard enough to find means to pay troops for fighting in wartime, but it was even more painful to have to find the wherewithal to pay and train them in peacetime. Moreover, the weapons of the new warfare—firearms, cannon, shot, gunpowder—were costly to make and costly to use. Yet every major European ruler knew that his survival as a sovereign depended on finding a way to meet that cost, for the state had to provide its standing force with the new instruments of warfare. The broad designs and the penny-pinching schemes of the mercantilist statesmen both had as their basis the rising cost of war. They assumed that the ruler would spend the money that mercantilist policies brought into the country in wars to defend the state, extend its power, and win glory for himself. As Colbert put it to Louis XIV, "it is a beautiful maxim that it is necessary to save pennies on unessential things and to pour out millions when it is a question of your glory."

FIGVRAQVEMVESTRACOMO SEATALAIVNCE
QVAL QIERA PIECA DEARTILLERIA

A Spanish treatise on artillery dating from 1613 included this illustration demonstrating the proper way to yoke a team to move heavy guns.

When we recognize that the power of the state, not as a means to some other end but as an end in itself, became more and more the goal of European statesmen between the fifteenth and the eighteenth centuries, we can understand certain of these statesmen's economic policies that had no immediate connection with the balance-of-trade theory. In the arsenal of trade-war there were many weapons, and since the object of the statesman's policy was the power of his state relative to the power of other states, he gained a victory in that war if he improved the trading position of his own land, or if he ruined the trading position of a rival power. Colbert again put succinctly what many statesmen of his day were saying when he observed that a state flourishes not only in itself but in the want it inflicts upon all neighboring states.

5

The Rise of Modern Science

Today we live in a scientific age. Society possesses an extensive and coherent body of generalizations, sometimes called scientific laws, by means of which men can in considerable measure understand and in some measure control the physical world. Moreover, by the so-called scientific method, they can elicit from the physical world further generalizations and laws about their environment. Society depends on such generalizations in a very direct material way: as at no previous time in history, technology today is rooted in scientific knowledge.

Beyond these simple basic facts lie notions and ideas that powerfully influence our general habits of thought. These notions are vague and not easy to formulate, but, generally speaking, twentieth-century men believe that anything that can be positively known about nature can be known only through the methods of the sciences. In other words, the only real knowledge of nature is scientific knowledge. Further, they believe that everything, or almost everything, that ever has happened or ever will happen happens naturally and therefore can be explained or understood scientifically. Finally, most people today are imbued with scientific faith. If they believe scientists agree that a certain thing is true, they tend to believe that thing on their authority. In the face of this authority, most people in most matters are willing to reject the contrary evidence of their senses or their contrary previous beliefs and the contrary assertions of anyone who claims to have access to more authoritative information from other than scientific sources. To a great many people the mere statement "It has been scientifically proved" is enough to settle a point, even though they do not know what the scientific proof is and would not understand it if they saw it.

Western society entered the scientific age only three centuries ago, yet so important is science now that a non-scientific world has become almost unimaginable. Up to the seventeenth century, however, the findings of scientists were not generally accepted as authoritative, simply because the body of information about nature and about the scientific laws upon which the world is built did not exist. It could not exist because with respect to one subject, motion, investigators of nature had for centuries been spending their energies in a blind alley, pressing against a stone wall. A radically new way of approaching motion—especially the motion of bodies not physically attached to other bodies—had to be found before science could emerge from the doldrums.

With the naked eye men can perceive two kinds of motion: the motion of heavenly bodies, and the motion of things on the face of the earth or, when they are dropped, down to the face of the earth. The former is called celestial motion, the latter terrestrial motion. The science of astronomy depends on an understanding of the motion of heavenly bodies, that of mechanics on an understanding of the movement of earthly bodies. The two kinds of knowledge together once provided the foundation for physics.

The Traditional Theory of Motion

The finest observatory of the sixteenth century was that of the Dane Tycho Brahe. At right is a sextant; other instruments are under the protective domes. At left is the entrance to an underground chamber containing the more delicate instruments.

From classical antiquity until the seventeenth century, men working out their ideas about celestial and terrestrial motion operated under certain false assumptions. The trouble lay with these assumptions, not with any indifference or opposition to theorizing about motion. It was once believed that modern science was prevented from coming into being before the seventeenth century because in the Middle Ages men did not care how the world worked and were superstitiously opposed to the study of nature. This was not so.

Medieval intellectuals were interested in nature because they believed that the world was the handiwork of a Perfect Creator and must therefore be worthy of His design and purpose. This great design might be accepted on faith, but it could never be fully understood by faith. A great deal of it, however, could be understood by reason. In the world God made, things moved, therefore any rational understanding of God's creation called for an understanding of motion. The rediscovery of Aristotle's writings stirred Western intellectuals to a vigorous effort to grasp the teachings of the Greek master. Among his treatises were those dealing with moving bodies. If medieval intellectuals had not been very much interested in the world, and how and why things moved in it, modern science would not have been born in the seventeenth century.

Although philosophers of the Middle Ages and the Renaissance asked questions about all kinds of movement and thought hard about those questions, they came up with answers that the founders of modern science had to demolish bit by bit until finally the whole edifice of the older theory of motion came tumbling down. Yet their answers were anything but stupid and childish. On the contrary, they were highly sophisticated: they explained in a fairly sensible and convincing way many of the things that people noticed in the world about them, and they hung together in a rather orderly fashion. Some of them, in fact, especially those in astronomy, provided fair predictions. In other words, these earlier explanations of motion, although inadequate and unnecessarily complex, were themselves scientific explanations.

The explanation of motion generally accepted a little before the rise of modern science sharply divided the universe into two parts: the celestial, or heavenly, part, and the terrestrial, or earthly, part. Although the nature of motion was different in the two parts, all motion had one common trait: continuous motion was not wholly natural to any body at all. The natural state of all bodies was rest, and they would not move unless they were impelled by some outside force or unless they had somehow got out of their natural resting place and were headed back to it. The heavenly bodies appeared to move because they were imbedded in invisible rotating spheres. The characteristic motion of the spheres was circular, because circular motion was the most perfect motion and therefore suitable to the nobility of the heavens.

The free movement of terrestrial things was, depending on their constitution, upward from the earth or downward toward it. All terrestrial things were composed of mixtures of four elements, fire, air, water, and earth, and the terrestrial world comprised four concentric spheres, fire on the outside, next air, then water, then earth in the center. Each element sought its natural sphere in which it would be at rest—fire the fire sphere, air the air sphere, and so on—so that all natural terrestrial motion was directed, as it were, toward rest. The

A 1660 engraving pictures an earth-centered universe. Seven rotating spheres carry the moon, the sun, and the known planets; the outer sphere is the preserve of the stars. Water, air, and fire encircle the earth.

lighter elements, fire and air, tended upward and were said to have levity. Water and earth, on the other hand, tended downward and had gravity (weight). The heavier a body was, the faster it would tend downward, or fall to earth. With respect to all directions of movement other than up and down, terrestrial bodies had no natural motion: either they were at rest, or they would come to rest as soon as some external body ceased to impel them. The earth itself was, of course, at rest, since it was obviously the heaviest of all things and, therefore, the least likely to move.

Outside the sphere of fire, and invisible according to the classical theory, were the celestial spheres composed of a perfect and incorruptible fifth element—quintessence. Since in the heavens everything was where it ought to be, there was no up-and-down, or linear, movement in the celestial spheres, but only circular motion. The heavenly bodies were embedded in the celestial spheres. In the first sphere was the moon, and that sphere carried the moon around the earth every twenty-eight days. The rest of the known planets and the sun were carried in the next six spheres and the fixed stars in the eighth. Finally came the last sphere—the *primum mobile*. This had no specific heavenly bodies to carry about, but it had to be there to wheel the entire celestial system around the earth from east to west once every twenty-four hours.

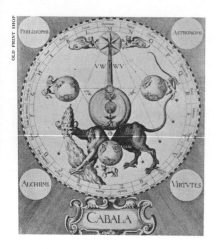

This seventeenth-century Christian cabala, an esoteric system of religious belief, unified the occult sciences to explain the world's mysteries. At center is a beastly Satan.

The system just described, part pre-Socratic cosmic speculation and part Aristotelian physics, had been elaborated by the ancient Greeks. The philosophers of the medieval schools took it over, harmonized it with Christian doctrine, and made it part of the medieval synthesis. On the whole they found it good, but they were amateurs. For the professionals, particularly for the professional stargazers from the fifteenth century on, it required a few modifications and raised a few difficult problems which it did not solve. The modification was demanded by observed peculiarities in the motion of the planets. For one thing, the motion was not regular as it should have been if the planets were firmly embedded in spheres rotating about the earth as their center. To account for this irregularity, men in the Middle Ages and up to the time of the Scientific Revolution accepted the explanation developed by the Greek astronomer Hipparchus in the third century B.C. and further elaborated by the astronomer Ptolemy in the second century of the Christian era. The Hipparchian-Ptolemaic theory became known to Western man when the *Almagest*, the Arabic collection of Ptolemy's main work, was translated into Latin in the twelfth century. It was this theory, under the name of the Ptolemaic system, that became the target of attack of the new astronomy during the Scientific Revolution.

Ptolemaic astronomy was a celestial geometry that sought to fulfill the following difficult conditions it inherited from classical physics: all movements ascribed to any part of the system must be perfectly circular, and the movement of each part of the system must be at uniform speed throughout its course; the system has to be constructed of spheres, each sphere completely contained within the next larger sphere; the earth, unmoving, must be the innermost sphere; and the calculated position of each heavenly body in this geometrical system of rotating spheres must coincide with the observed position of that body in the skies at a given time.

Almost all the heavenly bodies were easily placed in one sphere, that of the fixed stars. There were only seven heavenly bodies that gave real trouble—the sun, the moon, Mercury, Venus, Mars, Jupiter, and Saturn. The last five were especially irksome, for their orbits did not appear to be at all circular, and their movements appeared anything but uniform. In fact, they sometimes seemed to come to a dead stop in the skies and then disconcertingly to move backward for a while. Because of their peculiarly errant way of moving, these bodies were called planets, which means "wandering ones" in Greek. From the time of Hipparchus on, the task of astronomers was to work out a geometrical system that would account for the observed movements of the heavenly bodies, particularly of the erratic planets, without breaking any of the classical ground rules. It was a very complicated puzzle, and in trying to solve it astronomers had to employ such devices as the excentric, a circle rotating about a point that is not its center, the epicycle, the path of a point on the circumference of a rotating circle, the center of which is a point on the circumference of another rotating circle, and the equant, an imagined circle which reconciled the movements of the planets with the hypothesis of the uniform velocity of celestial motion.

For more than a millennium, the Ptolemaic system provided men with the most satisfactory available means of knowing approximately where in the sky at certain times they would find the sun, the moon, and the planets. This was a matter of serious "practical" importance, since many people in antiquity and the Middle Ages believed that their individual destinies were influenced by the position of the planets. If the planets were in a certain place on the day of one's birth, that would determine whether one was capable of certain undertakings; the position of the planets also determined when the time was ripe for such undertakings. The men who dealt in the "science" of discovering the proper adjustment of men's earthly affairs to the position of the heavenly bodies were called astrologers, and it was of the utmost importance to them to be able to predict the juxtaposition of those planets—what heavenly bodies they would be near at a given time—that were supposed to have a decisive effect on human destiny.

Although the Ptolemaic system allowed astrologers to predict with approximate accuracy the location of the planets on any given day, it failed to answer the question of whether the mathematical description that predicted their location actually described their physical motion as well. For the description to do that it had to be consistent with all observations of the heavenly bodies, not only with observations of their positions. For example, other things being equal, the apparent size of a source of light should diminish as its distance from the observer increased. But the Ptolemaic system failed to explain why changes in the magnitude of a planet or of the moon did not always correlate with the changes in its distance from the earth, which had to be assumed if the Ptolemaic system was correct. The more erudite medieval stargazers were aware of such anomalies, but until someone could contrive a mathematics for accurately predicting planetary position that also made sense of magnitudes, they had to be content with the Ptolemaic system. The irrelevance of the mathematical system of determining the place of the planets to the current physical explanation of the structure of the world was a quiet scientific scandal, a sort of skeleton in the intellectual closet of the Middle Ages.

Alongside the unresolved contradiction between Ptolemaic astronomy and medieval cosmology, there was a contradiction within medieval terrestrial physics. It resulted from the problem presented by the movement of projectiles on earth. According to medieval physics, things in the terrestrial sphere "naturally" moved only up or down toward their proper sphere. Terrestrial motion in any other direction was impelled and continued only as long as the impulse was present. Therefore anything that moved laterally was continuously pushed or pulled by some external agent, and it stopped moving as soon as the agent stopped. This notion seems very plausible if one is looking at a horse pulling a cart, but it is hardly plausible if one is looking at an arrow or any other projectile in flight. On the theory of motion just described, an arrow shot into the air should drop directly from the bow. The reason an arrow sailed on, one theory explained, was because when pushed from the bow it simultaneously packed the air in front of itself and made a vacuum—a hole in the air, as it were—behind itself. Then the packed air in front rushed to fill the vacuum behind and pushed the arrow through the air.

This explanation, imputing two mutually incompatible functions to the air, was hardly a satisfactory escape from the problem of projectile motion, and in the fourteenth century a few speculative physicists rejected it. They claimed that if linear motion could not be explained by some outside force pushing the projec-

A woodcut on ballistics demonstrates the theories of impetus and gravity held by medieval terrestrial physics.

tile, such motion must be due to something within the projectile itself. They suggested that this something was the impetus imparted to it by the projector—by the bow to the arrow, for example. The projectile dropped only when it had used up all its impetus. This explanation was not wholly satisfactory either. If it were correct, a projectile shot upward at an angle should go straight until it ran out of impetus and then fall straight down, but instead it could be seen to curve in an arc both up and down. Terrestrial mechanics, however, advanced no further than the theory of impetus until the seventeenth century.

The Impact of the Old on the New

Several traits of the classical way of thinking about motion were to affect the development of the new theory of motion that underlay the Scientific Revolution in the seventeenth century.

In the first place, though the old view was in part mechanistic—that is, it tended to conceive of natural motion as having the regularity of action of machinery—it was not altogether so. Although it is hard to imagine today, the idea of motion in nature before the Scientific Revolution involved spiritual, aesthetic, and even ethical elements. For example, since rest was deemed the natural condition of all things, the rotation of the spheres was taken by some thinkers to imply the presence of some force or spirit to keep them moving. Moreover, men thought of matter itself as having different degrees of excellence, ranging from the base element earth to the ultra-fine quintessence, the fifth element of the heavens. The ideas of baseness and fineness implied more than quantitative difference. The finer the element, the better, or more noble, it was. Quintessence was superior to earth in somewhat the same way that the princely office was superior to the function of the peasant. In the same way, since circular motion was "better" than linear motion, the heavenly bodies that moved in circles must participate in the special nobility of their superior kind of motion; they must be made of especially fine stuff. This kind of thinking was a serious obstacle to conceiving motion and the physical world in completely mechanistic terms. During the Scientific Revolution this obstacle was cleared away only with great difficulty.

Second, the accepted explanations of movement on earth and in the sky were good explanations in the sense that, despite a few skeletons in the closet, they provided a fairly intelligible and coherent account of almost all the kinds of physical movement that men had observed. They presented a true intellectual challenge to those who found that, in order to get rid of some of the skeletons, they would have to offer explanations of motion based on radically new assumptions.

Third, the traditional views of motion consistently failed to provide acceptable explanations for a number of observed facts. Their deficiencies lay not in the refinements of the theory, but in the axioms or postulates upon which the theory was founded—that the movement of all heavenly bodies is circular, that the natural state of bodies is rest, that celestial motion is governed by rules different from those governing movement in the terrestrial sphere, that the earth is at rest at the center of the universe, that the rate of fall of bodies is proportional to their weight, and that fire, air, earth, and water are real elements from which all terrestrial things are made. Consequently, a theory that aimed at solving the problems classical theory failed to solve could not achieve its goal merely by correcting the traditional views but only by flatly rejecting them. It was not easy to reject such plausible views, especially since the new assumptions did not at first provide answers to a number of problems for which traditional theory offered solutions. But, however slowly and hesitantly, the scientists of the new era did radically subvert the principal assumptions of their medieval and Greek predecessors, and it is quite appropriate to speak of the change these scientists wrought not as a reform but as a true revolution—the Scientific Revolution.

Fourth, the traditional views were orthodox in the sense that they were believed and taught by the professors in the universities. Like all orthodoxies they represented a vested interest to men who had spent much time in learning their content and who made a living out of teaching them. They were also orthodox in that they were accepted by the Church and incorporated into the way of looking at the world that the Church offered all Christians. In fact, the philosophers of the thirteenth century had done such a complete job of blending Greek physics, astronomy, and cosmic speculation with Christian revelation that to many the two seemed to form an inviolable whole, as likely to be endangered by an attack on the physics of Aristotle or the astronomy of Ptolemy as by an attack on the Epistles of St. Paul. Thus the pioneers of the Scientific Revolution, who had to start by rejecting first the astronomy of Ptolemy and then Aristotle's physics, were sure to run into trouble sooner or later with both the schools and the Church. On the other hand, if the pioneers were to make their case good, both the universities and the Church would suffer from the loss of esteem that the world tends to visit on those who publicly and vigorously back the losing horse.

Better than most historical developments, the formulation of the new laws of motion can be associated with particular men and circumscribed by exact dates. The men are Nicolaus Copernicus (1473–1543), Johannes Kepler (1571–1630), Galileo Galilei (1564–1642), and Isaac Newton (1642–1727). The dates are 1543 and 1687, which mark respectively the publication of Copernicus's *On the Revolutions of the Heavenly Bodies* and Newton's *Principia Mathematica*. Other lesser men, however, made important contributions to the work. Kepler, for instance, might have wasted his mathematical wizardry in a sterile number magic had he not had the painstaking and precise observations of the Danish astronomer Tycho Brahe to work with. And, especially after Galileo, scores of scientists all over Europe investigated, theorized, and suggested new insights into the as yet inadequately resolved problems of motion. The greatest scientific intelligence of them all, Isaac Newton, could rightly say that if perhaps he had seen a little farther than others, it was because he had stood on the shoulders of giants.

Early in the sixteenth century, Nicolaus Copernicus, a Polish scholar, had studied the Ptolemaic system at Padua, and did not like it, for motives that to-day would be called aesthetic, religious, and scientific. In the sixteenth century such motives were so entangled as to be well-nigh inseparable. Copernicus found revolting the Ptolemaic procedure of starting with a uniform circular movement around the earth for each planet separately and then hooking on to each circle as much gadgetry in the way of excentrics, epicycles, and equants as was needed to

The New Astronomy

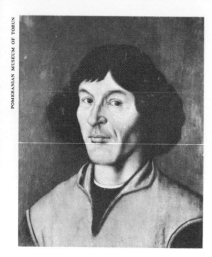

This portrait of Nicolaus Copernicus is by an unknown contemporary artist.

reconcile the observed positions of the planet to its presumed movement. In the Ptolemaic geocentric system such maneuvers were necessary to account even for the gross qualitative traits of observed planetary movements—for example, their regressions. Copernicus felt that to ascribe so many intricate dodges to the Creator impugned His skill and good sense. To move a few planets about He surely must have been able to devise a method more in accord with His mechanical gifts and (here Copernicus reflects the influences of anti-Aristotelian Neoplatonists of the Renaissance) His mathematical nature. Yet as long as the earth was immovable a very elaborate machinery of celestial geometry was indispensable to account for the character of planetary motion, no matter how much it ran counter to Copernicus's perfectionist sense of the mechanical skill that a Perfect Creator ought to display.

To vindicate his belief in the perfection of God, Copernicus propounded a theory that set the earth spinning on its own axis once a day, removed it from the center of the universe, and set it whirling, as he believed all the planets whirled, around the sun. In other words, he replaced a geocentric and geostatic (earth-centered and earth-stationary) theory with a heliocentric and heliostatic (sun-centered and sun-stationary) theory. Neither theory, of course, placed the earth or sun at the precise geometrical center of simple circular orbits of the planets, for neither view could have been reconciled with the observed positions of the planets. "Centricity" simply meant that the planets moved in successive orbits about the earth (Ptolemy) or sun (Copernicus), and that the earth or sun lay within the smallest of these orbits.

Scientifically Copernicus was one of the most conservative of radicals, or the most radical of conservatives. Because part of his radicalism had a great future and his conservatism had no future, we tend to emphasize the former and forget the latter. Yet for Copernicus they were inextricably intermeshed. The crucial principle of astronomy for Copernicus—as for his predecessors—was the excellence of simple circular motion. And he produced a celestial geometry qualitatively better with respect to this principle than any that had preceded it. Quantitatively it was not much if any better than the Ptolemaic system. To account for all the "observed" positions of the planets (some of the observations were quite inaccurate), Copernicus had to restore the epicycles and excentrics. On the qualitative side the heliocentric theory of Copernicus got rid of the inordinate complexity of the Ptolemaic system. Thus it was because of his position on a rotating planet that the earthly observer saw the sun rise and set. Heliocentricism dispensed with the entire paraphernalia of epicycles in explaining planetary regression. That wholly illusory regressing was simply due to the position of the observer on a planet, the earth, that was moving in the opposite direction from the observed planet at some particular period during their respective orbitings around the sun.

For its author, however, the "Copernican system" was not merely a method by which an observer on earth could calculate the place of the various heavenly bodies for the benefit of astrologers. It was a "system of the world." It purported to describe the physical movements of the planets and the moon. But at this point Copernicus crashed head on not only into Ptolemy's astronomy but into Aristotle's physics. As long as the planets were thought of as mere points (celestial geometry) or as weightless substances (Greek "Aristotelian physics"), their motion made sense in the context of current physical theory. To purify celestial geometry, however, Copernicus had set a very heavy weight, the earth, into a double and extremely rapid motion—around its own axis every 24 hours (a daily spin of about 25,000 miles at the equator) and around the sun once a year (a journey of millions of miles, even allowing for sixteenth-century underestimates of the distance of the earth from the sun). But it was the very essence of the physical theory of Copernicus's age that the earth was at the center of the universe because it was the heaviest of things, and the heavier a thing, the stronger its propensity to rest. How then could it be moving at the incredible rate that Copernicus ascribed to it? The answer is that within the bounds of Aristotelian physics it could not be moving at that or any other rate.

At this point, where he had to choose between his own system of the world and the orthodox physics, Copernicus became radical indeed. He chose his system. Thus he was forced to assert the "natural" mobility of heavy bodies (the earth first of all), and having done so there was no reason to deny gravity or weight to any of the planets or the stars. The division of the world into a celestial and terrestrial region was thus thrown in doubt. The heliocentric-heliostatic theory of Copernicus demanded the support of a new physics. And there was no new physics available to support it.

Copernicus's theory of movement of the heavenly bodies by no means won quick acceptance. This was due in part to the manner in which it was published: a disciple who saw the *De Revolutionibus* through its printing in 1543 sought

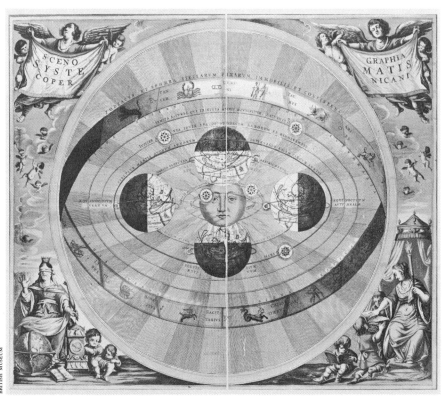

The universe according to Copernicus, with the earth and the five known planets orbiting the sun, was portrayed by Andreas Cellarius, who also did the Ptolemaic universe on page 123.

to avoid the objections of the orthodox by presenting it merely as a speculative essay—celestial geometry rather than astrophysics—and not as the great new truth about the universe that Copernicus thought it to be. In addition to this, the theory was coldly received because the Copernican astronomy made it no easier to compute planetary place than did the Ptolemaic system. But scientists who rejected his system did so primarily because it implied a radically new physics, and all that Copernicus provided along this line was speculation about the "naturalness" of spherical motion. The sole merit of these speculations was that they fitted Copernicus's theory, but they were wholly unverified and far out of line with subsequent scientific development. It is scarcely to be wondered, then, that the ablest observer and one of the best scientific minds of the generation after Copernicus devoted himself not to improving the Copernican system but to elaborating a system of his own that would account for the most meticulous observations of planetary position and at the same time preserve classical Aristotelian physics.

This observer was Tycho Brahe (1541–1601), who, as Astronomer Royal to the king of Denmark, brought descriptive astronomy—the part that deals with the observed location of heavenly bodies—to a new level of perfection. According to Tycho, all the planets circled the sun, while the sun itself circled the earth. Mathematically, the systems of Copernicus and Tycho are identical, except that Copernicus's system applies to an observer on the sun, Tycho's to an observer on earth. But in their impact on the traditional physics the systems were literally worlds apart. By keeping the earth immobile at (or near) the center of the universe, Tycho was preserving the traditional physics; by transforming the earth itself into one planet among others moving in its annual round about the sun, Copernicus undermined that physics.

It is for that daring act that Copernicus, despite his conservatism, may still be regarded as the chief precursor, if not the progenitor, of the Scientific Revolution. In effect, he made it possible for the first time since Aristarchus—perhaps for the first time since Aristotle—for men seriously to consider taking a radically new view of the order of nature. If the earth might be in motion, then a great many other things in nature might be happening in ways that according to accepted tradition were just as impossible as the movement of the earth. The importance of Copernicus's system cannot, therefore, be measured by the degree of its theoretical perfection. It must be measured by its impact on the scientists who came after him and whose work advanced the study of nature along the path that science was to follow for centuries. It is not wholly an accident that the next two great leaders of the Scientific Revolution, Kepler and Galileo, were "Copernicans" in the sense that they both believed that the earth moved in a curved orbit and that the sun stood at or near the center of movement of the planets, including the earth.

When Tycho Brahe left the service of the Danish king, he entered that of Rudolf of Hapsburg, the Holy Roman Emperor, who was deeply interested in the occult sciences, including astrology. Tycho brought with him to Prague the vast masses of new and improved data on the positions of the heavenly bodies that he had collected in Denmark, and his new tables were the indispensable instruments for the life work of Johannes Kepler, who became his assistant in 1600. Armed

Tycho Brahe collected his wealth of astronomical data without benefit of the telescope, which only came into use about a decade after his death.

with Tycho's observations on planetary positions, which for the first time in history made it possible to plot the apparent movements and times of the planets throughout their orbits, Kepler set out to discover regular numerical or geometrical relations in planetary movement. The fruitful consequences of years of pouring over Tycho's tables and of applying to them the most refined mathematical skills the age afforded are now known as Kepler's three laws of planetary motion:

1) The orbits of all the planets including the earth are elliptical (not circular), and the sun is one of the focuses of each of these elliptical orbits.

2) The planets do not move in their orbits with uniform velocity, but in equal times every planet "sweeps out" equal areas between itself and the sun. (This law is demonstrated in the diagram at right.)

3) The squares of the periodic times of the planets (i.e., the times they require to traverse their orbits) are in the same ratio as the cubes of their respective mean distances from the sun. Thus:

$$\frac{T^2}{T'^2} = \frac{D^3}{D'^3}$$

with T the time it takes one planet to complete its orbit around the sun, T' the orbit time of another planet, and D and D' the mean distances from the sun of the two planets, respectively.

Kepler's work was amazingly sound. His laws of planetary motion stand firm three and a half centuries after he announced them. But the scope of his work takes on added grandeur when it is seen in relation to the work that had gone before. For centuries, in order to account for the observed movements of the planets, astronomers had been piling one geometrical construction upon another—epicycles on equants on excentrics—and still falling short of accurate prediction as to where a planet would be at a given time. Each planet was treated as a separate case, its unique and intricate mathematical gyrations wholly unrelated to those simultaneously being performed by other planets. Kepler jettisoned all this and at the same time vindicated the mathematical uniformity of the heavens. His first two laws held for all planets. His third law tied all the planets together in a unified mathematical relationship based on their distance from the sun, thus regarding with fulfillment his long quest for the divine canon, or rule, of celestial architecture.

The magnificent mathematical simplicity of Kepler's laws all assumed a heliocentric system. All the planets, the earth included, were related in all three laws to the sun. All, including the earth, were conceived to be moving about the sun in elliptical orbits at velocities whose regularity was related to their position with respect to the sun and in periods of time whose relations were connected with their respective distances from the sun. Copernicus had set out to show that the Creator was a far more skillful artificer than Ptolemaic astronomy allowed. In the process he had subverted the physical universe as seen by contemporary natural philosophy, removing the earth from the center and setting it in motion. But in his system with its thirty-four epicycles and arbitrary excentrics the Creator still looked like something of a bungler. Kepler had achieved what Copernicus sought—a description of the planetary system that displayed it as regulated by simple mathematical relationships worthy of the Heavenly Mathematician.

Kepler's discoveries ought to have settled the issue. They did not. The neglect

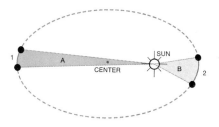

Kepler's second law of planetary motion: although a planet's orbital velocity is not uniform, if orbit times 1 and 2 are equal, areas A and B between planet and sun will be equal.

The elaborate title page of one of Kepler's works pictures (from left) Hipparchus, Copernicus, Brahe, and Ptolemy by pillars supporting astronomy. Kepler is in the panel at left center; in the map (center) is Brahe's observatory on the island of Hven.

his work suffered for a time was in part the result of the abstruse mathematical knowledge necessary in order to grasp his demonstrations and proofs. Few men of his day could follow the mathematical reasoning on which Kepler based his laws, and the few that could were probably thrown off by the peculiar substance in which these laws were embedded—the substance of Kepler's thought. That thought was Pythagorean. It not only sought numerical relationships in the physical world; it assumed that all the important numbers must have some deep inner meaning or reason. If there were five planets this could be no accident; there must be some special reason why there should be five, not four or six. Kepler found analogies between the triad of sun, fixed stars, and planets and the triad of Father, Son, and Holy Ghost. And those who opened his treatises looking for geometrical figures were likely to be confronted instead with pages of musical notes drawn to show that his discoveries demonstrated the harmony of the heavenly spheres. Small wonder that such works were closed quickly even by men who, had they had the pertinacity to go on, would have found, and might even have recognized as such, the most remarkable individual achievement in astronomy up to that time.

While Kepler—mystical, isolated, ill-understood—was providing the bases for modern celestial mechanics, a brash and brilliant Italian was laying the axe to the older physics. His name was Galileo Galilei, a Florentine by birth, a college professor by calling, a witty, ebullient genius by nature. He studied at Pisa, taught at Padua, and then returned to Florence in 1610 under the patronage of the Medici Grand Duke.

The New Dynamics

The quarrel of Copernicus and of Kepler had been with Ptolemy; they were primarily astronomers. Their conceptions had implications for natural philosophy and for the general theory of motion that was a central theme of natural philosophy; but they had avoided rather than systematically faced those implications. The quarrel of Galileo was with Aristotle; he was primarily a natural philosopher, or what we would call a physicist. As he saw the matter, the main obstacle to the acceptance of Copernicus's view was not offered by the astronomers but by the professors of natural philosophy, who for the most part bound themselves to an Aristotelian orthodoxy. In this diagnosis Galileo was correct. It was the inferences that might be drawn about the order of nature from the Copernican view of the movements of the earth that led men to reject or disregard those views.

Galileo's strategy in support of the new astronomy and against the Aristotelians of the university faculties had three aspects. First, he brought qualitative observations to bear on the old teaching so as to display its inadequacy. Second, he sought to ease the concern of those in whom the very idea of a moving earth stirred deep religious misgivings. Finally, he tried to show that Copernicus's theory seen as a statement about the physical order of nature conflicted with the Aristotelian account of terrestrial motion and with Aristotelian physics in general, and that the error, both in method and result, lay not with the new astronomy but with the traditional physics.

The principal qualitative observations that Galileo turned into weapons to attack traditional views about the heavens were secured through the use of the telescope. He learned that the Dutch had developed a device for making distant objects seem near, and working on very limited hints in a very short time he devised a telescope of his own. In 1609 he turned it toward the heavens, and within a few years he had discovered the moons of Jupiter, the mountains of the earth's moon, and the spots on the sun.

Every one of these manifestations was a sort of celestial mockery of the traditional cosmology. The "spheres" of the heavens were supposed to be composed of impenetrable stuff, and all the heavenly bodies were supposed to rotate about the earth. Yet here were moons sailing unconcernedly around Jupiter right through its "impenetrable sphere" as if that sphere were not there at all, as if they cared nothing for the rule that all heavenly bodies must circle the earth. If the moons of Jupiter did not act the way heavenly bodies should, neither did the moon and the sun. According to the Aristotelian tradition, heavenly bodies should be perfect simply because they were heavenly. The perfect form, of course, was the perfect unblemished sphere. But seen through the telescope the moon looked anything but unblemished. Its surface appeared to be miserably corroded, wrinkled, and pitted. It looked indeed like our most imperfect earth might look if one turned a telescope on it from the moon. And the heavenly bodies were supposed to be changeless, too, yet if one looked through Galileo's telescope at sun spots one could see that something was changing on the very face of the sun itself.

Galileo's observations shed little light on the scientific merits of the new astronomical theories. But they did cast the gravest doubts on the older theories of the heavens, for those theories were shaped to support a conception of the universe that graded its elements toward perfection in proportion to their distance from its imperfect earthly center. Yet if the perfection ascribed to the celestial bodies was visibly lacking, then the conception itself was faulty, and spinning out elaborate theories to support it was a wasted effort.

The partisans of the old tradition, however, found support not only in Aristotle but in the Bible, which seemed to assert the immobility of the earth. It spoke of the stars' movements through the firmament, whereas according to Galileo the stars were fixed; elsewhere it implied the movement of the sun and the moon, and in one passage in Joshua it specifically told of God making the sun stand in place, which surely seemed to suggest that the sun, not the earth, was moving. In the age of the Counter Reformation no Western man, and especially no Italian, could with impunity deny the divine inspiration of every verse of Scripture, and Galileo certainly did not want to make any such denial. He simply argued that the key texts did not mean what most interpreters had long taken them to mean, and that with a little verbal maneuvering they could be interpreted to mean what Galileo preferred to believe they meant and thus be reconciled with an immobile central sun and a moving planetary earth.

Galileo's not wholly persuasive venture into scriptural interpretation might soothe those already convinced of the validity of the Copernican system, and his explorations with the telescope might expose the naïve supporters of the traditional views to ridicule, but the solid foundation of those views did not crumble so easily. They offered, as we have seen, a full explanation of physical motion from that of the heavens to that of a snowfall. The new astronomy required the support of a radically new conception of motion because otherwise it would remain just another skeleton in the already fairly crowded closet of Hellenic-medieval natural philosophy; it would not be an integrated element of a new world system. Galileo boldly set out to develop the new science of motion that was needed. Near the end of his life, at the age of seventy-four, he proclaimed the fulfillment of his aim—a science of motion quite different from the one set forth in Aristotle's *Physics*.

LOUVRE

290

This crayon sketch of Galileo, by Ottavio Leoni, was made in 1624 when the astronomer met Pope Urban VIII to discuss the Copernican "heresy."

Two circumstances favored Galileo's quest. First, he seems to have been the first serious thinker in centuries who felt no impulse whatever to divide the universe between a superior celestial region and an inferior terrestrial one. He was not inclined, therefore, to exalt the heavens by seeking one set of rules for the movements of heavenly bodies or to debase the earth by seeking another and somehow inferior set for the movement of earthly bodies. To Galileo, a ball moving through space was just a ball moving through space, whether the particular ball was the planet Jupiter or a shot fired out of a cannon in Florence. If their trajectories were different, it was not because of the peculiar celestiality of the one and the peculiar terrestriality of the other.

Second, Galileo discerned the weakest point in the older theories of motion and

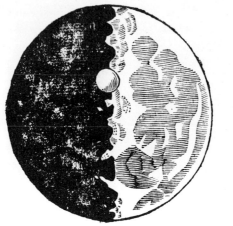
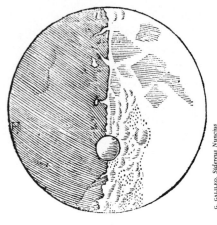

In 1610 Galileo published the first pictures of the moon as seen through a telescope, revealing its irregular surface and crater-like depressions.

concentrated his attack on it. That point, as we have seen, was projectile motion, and here Galileo set the traditional line of inquiry into reverse. The old question was, Why does a projectile keep moving? Galileo's question was, Why does a projectile stop when it stops? He found the answer in the law of falling bodies—his great discovery in the field of physics. He demonstrated that the rate of fall of a body to the earth is proportional to the square of the time of the fall. Therefore, a body dropped from a given height and a body fired horizontally from the same height will stop—that is, hit the earth—at the same time. A projectile fired horizontally, then, does not stop when it does because it is a projectile; it stops because it is a body, and all bodies near the earth's surface, projectiles or not, take the same time to reach the earth from a given height. But since it is the fall of a projectile that stops its movement, when would the forward motion of a projectile stop if it had no place to fall to? Galileo's answer was that it would not stop; it would go on forever at the same rate of speed. That, according to Galileo, was precisely what the earth and the planets—bodies made of the same stuff as the earth—were doing. They were circling through space forever, as any other projectile would if it had no place to fall to. The "natural" tendency of bodies was not to rest but to inertia, to doing what they had been doing before, whether it was resting or moving.

In his theory of the movement of projectiles, set forth in *Dialogues Concerning the Two New Sciences*, Galileo killed the traditional classical-medieval physics. The traditional physics had identified change with motion and therefore tried to explain motion. Galileo separated the two. To a body at rest motion was change, but to a body in motion rest was change. Physics had to explain change in motion; it did not have to explain motion as such. Moreover, the traditional physics had operated on the principle of rational fitness. For example, since circular motion was the most perfect motion and since the heavenly bodies moved circularly, it was fitting and therefore necessary that they be made of some perfect stuff. Galileo's physics, on the other hand, was a physics of brute fact and mathematical relation. There was no reason why the rate of fall of a body should be proportional to the square of the time it had been falling. It might just as well have been directly proportional to the time it had been falling, or to the cube of the time it had been falling, or not proportional to the time at all. What verified the law of falling bodies was not reason or rational fitness but controlled observation, experiment. Galileo's law of falling bodies is not the cause of fall; it is the mathematical expression of acceleration, of the changes in the rate of fall. The characteristics of motion are what they are as a matter of fact, but the fact is that those characteristics are related in a constant mathematical way.

Finally, the world is not divided into qualitatively different regions—a celestial superior region and a terrestrial inferior region—ordered by different rules because of their different qualities. Therefore, the effort to explain away evident similarities in the two regions is a waste of time, and it is particularly a waste when it involves suppositions for which there is no evidence at all. When Galileo showed the mountains on the moon, visible through his telescope, to an adherent of the traditional physics, the latter, seeking to defend the perfection of that heavenly body, said he supposed that the mountains were covered with a sheet of water, thus leaving the moon's surface perfect after all. Galileo agreed, but added that he supposed that out of the invisible lunar ocean rose invisible mountains of glass that roughed up the moon again. Thus he reduced to absurdity the practice of imagining phenomena for whose actuality there was no evidence whatever solely to buttress the belief in a qualitatively differentiated order of nature.

Even Galileo's mistakes are consistent with his bias against Aristotle's qualitative physics. His principle of inertia, for example, supposed inertial motion to be circular rather than in a straight line. This was not because he thought circles something particularly excellent. He thought, erroneously, that the orbits of the planets were circular and that the only force determining their orbits was inertia, so inevitably he arrived at the conclusion that the inertial force was circular. His mistake was the result of compounding physical errors of observation and investigation, not the result of any speculative bias on his part in favor of celestial circularity.

Up to Galileo's time Aristotle's thought had dominated the science of motion. Even when men deviated from Aristotle—as the medieval impetus theorists had —it was by way of exception. The substance, the ultimate assumptions of Aristotelian physics, remained unchallenged. The science of motion was a commentary on Aristotle, as the science of medicine was a commentary on the Greek physician Galen. Galileo put an end to this.

After Galileo it was no longer possible to take Aristotle for a starting point in physics, just as after Kepler it was no longer possible to take Ptolemy for a starting point in positional astronomy. Beginning with assumptions different from, sometimes opposite to, those of Aristotle, Galileo had constructed an account of motion as coherent as Aristotle's and more consistent with the known facts about the phenomenon it was supposed to account for. Galileo replaced "the commentary upon Aristotle's physics [with] the mathematical scaffolding of a new branch of science," writes A. R. Hall in *The Scientific Revolution* (1956).

The New Theory of Motion

We must emphasize the last eight words in Hall's statement. The difference between Galileo's theorems and the science of dynamics as it developed during the next century and a half was the difference between a scaffolding and a finished building. There was an enormous amount of work left to do, work that engaged the effort of dozens of keen intellects. But the work of those intellects was fruitful

"To myself, I seem to have been only like a boy playing on the seashore, and diverting myself in now and then finding a smoother pebble or a prettier shell than ordinary, while the great ocean of truth lay all undiscovered before me," Newton wrote.

instead of sterile because their framework was Galilean not Aristotelian, mathematical not qualitative.

In addition, it was the framework of a new science, not the framework of a viable "new system of the world." Galileo had sought to provide such a system, but since he took no account of Kepler's discoveries about planetary motion he was doomed to failure from the start. So, partly for the same reason, were others who tried their hand at the same task. The work of synthesis required a genius who could bring together the quantitative physics that found expression in Galileo's law of falling bodies and the mathematical astronomy in Kepler's laws of planetary motion. That genius was the Englishman Isaac Newton, who was born in 1642, the year that Galileo died.

In his youth at Cambridge University Newton read the writings of the leaders of scientific thought of his day. With his astonishingly quick mind and precise mathematical and physical insight he perceived the nature of the critical scientific problem raised by the new astronomy and the new physics; and at the age of twenty-four he arrived intuitively at a hypothesis to solve that problem: how to provide a physical explanation of planetary motion. Since he was at the time unable to verify his hypothesis, he simply set it aside for two decades. In the meantime another English scientist, Robert Hooke, had hit on the same hypothesis. In the interval Newton had turned to other investigations in optics and even in alchemy. Hooke's independent repetition of Newton's insight turned the latter back to his old interest. Under this impulsion he developed the mathematical procedures necessary to transform a mere hypothesis into a demonstrated theory of the kind that is called scientific law; and he also placed his explanation of planetary motion in the framework of a general theory of motion.

The first element in the Newtonian solution was inertia. Galileo's initial conception of inertia as circular motion had been corrected by Newton's day. "Every body perseveres in its state of rest or uniform motion in a straight line," Newton observed, "except insofar as it is compelled to change that state by impressed force." The second element in the Newtonian explanation was Kepler's three laws of planetary motion. The problem was to make the principle of inertia, applied to the planets, square with the laws that Kepler had discovered, that is, to identify the "impressed force" or forces that checked the inertial tendency of the planets and their satellites to fly off at a tangent to their actual orbits.

It was Newton's great achievement to demonstrate that a single force maintained the planets in their courses; that this same force determined the rate at which terrestrial bodies fell toward the earth; that this force operated between every particle of matter in the universe and every other particle; and finally, that this force could be precisely defined in a simple mathematical formula. All bodies tend to move toward each other. The force of this tendency Newton called gravity. The formula for the force of gravity between any two material bodies was that it varied directly as the product of their masses (or the quantity of matter in them) and inversely as the square of the distance between them. In abbreviated form:

$$gravity = \frac{mass \times mass'}{distance^2}$$

Thus, at last, the movement of the planets in their courses, the movement of fruit dropping to the ground in an orchard, the trajectory of a projectile fired from a gun were all brought within the scope of two great and universal principles of motion—inertia and gravity. Not only was the old Aristotelian view of the world of matter destroyed, but an altogether different view had been produced that gave an infinitely more adequate and more comprehensive solution to the problems that were their common subject. With the publication of Newton's *Principia Mathematica* in 1687 the amazing development of modern science was just beginning, but the Scientific Revolution, the overturning of the time-hallowed ways of thinking about and dealing with nature, was practically complete.

6

The World of the
New Sciences

The progress of the new sciences was by no means exhausted by the train of development that led to Newton's crowning achievement. On the contrary, throughout the later sixteenth and seventeenth centuries basic discoveries were made in almost all the areas that interested physicists up to about sixty years ago. Not merely motion but heat, pressure, light, and sound were investigated with great success.

Nor was it only with respect to the physical sciences that men made new advances. In the life sciences, too, they gained new insights and gathered new data that provided the starting place for a new forward movement in knowledge. The studies of Andreas Vesalius (1515–1564) opened new vistas in the investigation of human anatomy. In 1628 William Harvey's demonstration that in an hour the human heart pumped more blood than the full weight of a man established the fact and explanation of the circulation of the blood and raised new and basic questions in physiology that were to project that science far beyond the confines of older physiological theory and unsystematic medieval observation. Thus Vesalius and Harvey were undermining traditional authority in medicine, an authority mainly imbedded in the writings of the Greek physician Galen (A.D. *c.* 130–200), just as Kepler and Galileo were bringing down the traditional authority of Ptolemy and Aristotle. And while Galileo with his telescope was bringing into the range of vision phenomena too far away to be observed by the naked eye, a number of microscopists were bringing into the range of vision phenomena too small to be observed by the naked eye.

The flood of new knowledge generated during the Scientific Revolution appeared to be related to, and in some measure to depend upon, a new way of going about the study of nature. The natural philosophers—scientists—of the seventeenth century recognized the importance of these new ways of investigation and valued them highly. Among those who tried to generalize about them the French philosopher René Descartes considered his method of systematic rational inquiry the soundest way to elicit "scientific" knowledge of the physical world; according to him his method was "a more powerful instrument of knowledge than any other that has been bequeathed to us by human agency, as being the source of all others." The ways of investigating nature that elicit scientific answers are what we call today "the scientific method." It has been by the application of this method that our knowledge of the physical world and our ability to control and channel the operation of natural forces have reached their present-day level. How did this new method work?

From the time of Descartes and Francis Bacon in the seventeenth century down to the present there has been considerable disagreement on the subject of the scientific method. From the controversies two facts seem to emerge. First, in one sense every natural science has its own method of eliciting information from, and verifying its generalizations about, that aspect of nature which is its partic-

Sébastien LeClerc's view of the French Académie des Sciences was made about 1700. Among the welter of scientific equipment are musical instruments (far left) for harmonic studies and cannon models (lower shelf, rear) for experiments in ballistics.

ular concern. This is why the practice of every science demands special training in its own particular techniques, and why training in one science, say biology, does not provide the necessary means to conduct investigations in another science, say physical chemistry. Second, despite major and significant differences, the sciences share a common set of ground rules. These rules do not comprise the method of any particular science, but they do prescribe certain general conditions that must be fulfilled before any assertion will be accepted as scientifically verified. The ground rules thus constitute an element common to the methods of all sciences.

A plate from Rosa Ursina *(1630) by Christoph Scheiner, a German priest-astronomer, depicts a variety of telescopes trained on the heavens. In the bottom panel Scheiner's assistant adjusts a screen upon which sunspots appear. Unable to believe the sun was "imperfect," Scheiner thought the spots were small planets.*

During the Scientific Revolution the sciences with strategies for advancing the understanding of natural processes that won the highest prestige were physics and astronomy. By the second half of the seventeenth century those sciences had achieved such startling successes that their methods, in the minds of many, became synonymous with scientific method.° What was the method of seventeenth-century physics and astronomy?

The remarkable advances in physics and astronomy during the Scientific Revolution were achieved by linking two very different types of intellectual activity—mathematical reasoning by abstraction from actual experience, and concrete observation. From the time that Copernicus announced that no one without a knowledge of mathematics should seek to read his work, scientists have made the mathematical formulation of their results an ultimate goal. A crucial step in the new science involved "thinking away" all the incidental peculiarities that affect an event, that is, thinking what would take place if those peculiarities were not present. The law of inertia, for example, can never be seen in perfect operation because perfect conditions do not exist. The thrown ball does not keep going forever in a straight line because this could happen only in space totally empty of all other matter. Like the law of inertia, all the laws of the new science, therefore, supposed a set of physical conditions which exists nowhere in the universe. The prime function of the carefully controlled form of observation called experiment was to show that as actual conditions approached the limit of assumed conditions, the actual result came closer and closer to the result predicted by scientific law. Thus objects dropped through successively less resistant media—say water, air at the earth's surface, and a tube from which as much air as possible had been evacuated—came closer and closer to the limit set down in Galileo's law of falling bodies: all bodies, regardless of weight or shape, will fall equal distances in equal times.

To learn whether the actual was indeed approaching the ideal it was necessary to do three things: to see things as well as possible, to measure them as well as possible, and to find ways of bringing actual conditions closer to ideal conditions. In all three areas seventeenth-century scientists invented important devices or improved on devices earlier used for other purposes. So essential have such devices proved for the advancement of science that it is somewhat artificial to abstract the method of a particular science from the instruments indispensable to its investigations.

In the Middle Ages people had already learned how to use the magnifying properties that glass possesses when it is given a certain curvature in relation to its thickness. But at first this knowledge was only used to make spectacles. The greatest makers of optical glass in Europe were the Dutch lens grinders, and it was mainly in Holland early in the seventeenth century that devices were produced to enable men to see smaller and more distant things than they had ever seen before. Both devices worked by placing curved lenses a determined distance apart inside a cylinder. The microscope became an indispensable key to the biological sciences, but even more important during the Scientific Revolution was the telescope. At first used merely as a spyglass for amusement or for military

Human musculature as illustrated in Andreas Vesalius' Fabrica (1543). Vesalius was the personal physician to Holy Roman Emperor Charles V.

°Even today some scientists believe that a body of knowledge is truly scientific to the extent that it adopts methods and achieves results similar to those of physics.

purposes, in the hands of Galileo it became, as we have seen, a terrible weapon against intellectual orthodoxy and the medieval world view.

By thinking qualitatively about nature, the old physics had obscured the need for measuring. Heat and cold, heaviness and lightness, were conceived as basic attributes of things. But the new science with its emphasis on mathematics could not get along on such a descriptive procedure; it had always to ask, "How much heavier? How much hotter?" and it had to devise machines and instruments that would answer such questions accurately. At the very heart of the Scientific Revolution was the simple continuous scale of equal intervals on which quantities of weight, heat, distance, pressure, or time could be accurately measured. Given such a scale, measurable increments became primary, while qualities such as heaviness and lightness, heat and cold, were consigned to scientific irrelevance.

There was not much improvement to make in the measuring of terrestrial distances and angles, since men had done that rather well before the Scientific Revolution; but for measuring celestial angles and microscopic sizes a micrometer was invented. In the matter of weighing, the founders of modern science were especially fortunate, since the basic method of comparing masses of matter one with another dates back thousands of years. The balance—the "teeter-totter" beam in equipoise on top of a thin edge—provided the scientists, as it had long provided the money-changers, with a sound instrument for weighing.

It was otherwise with the instruments for measuring air pressure, temperature, and time. Short intervals of time had never been measured accurately before, and temperature and air pressure had never been measured at all. Besides all the other work he did, Galileo had the scientific insights that led to the invention of new instruments of measurement in all three areas. He observed, for example, that an increase of heat would cause the fluid in a bulb to expand into a thin closed tube. On the basis of this observation, scientists were soon making thermometers by putting water, alcohol, or mercury into bulbs that opened into glass tubes and marking off scales on the tubes.

Evangelista Torricelli, one of Galileo's students, following up and correcting the work of his master, explained a fact that men who were engaged in deep mining had known to their sorrow for a long time—that a pump would carry water up so far and no farther. What a pump did was to take the downward pressure of air inside a pipe off the water. Then the weight of the air outside would push the water up the pipe against the diminished resistance. The water would rise no more, said Torricelli, when the water per unit of surface inside the pipe weighed just as much as the air outside. What one had was a very special kind of balance with the water in the pipe counterpoising a column of air extending from the top of the atmosphere to the bottom of the mine. The column of water thus measured the weight of the air above the earth, that is, the atmospheric pressure. A gauge which stood thirty-odd feet high at sea level was a bit cumbersome as a measuring device, however, and Torricelli substituted for water a far denser liquid, mercury. Thus he reduced the column to thirty-odd inches and produced a workable barometer. The implication of the barometer was that air, to which the Aristotelian-medieval physics ascribed negative weight or levity, actually pressed down, that is, had positive weight or gravity. Experimental confirmation of this view was provided by the barometer itself. Two

R. BOYLE, Works, 1744

Englishman Robert Boyle confirmed Torricelli's air pressure findings with this experiment. An air pump atop a London building raised a column of water some 33 feet, and Boyle then compared the pressure reading with Torricelli's mercury barometer.

French scientists carried a barometer up a high peak. The fall of the mercury column indicated that the shorter column of air on the mountain top weighed less than the longer column in the valley.

Perhaps the most crucial problem for the new scientists was to find an accurate way to measure short intervals of time. Many of the things that interested them—projectiles and sound for example—moved very fast indeed, and a device that would catch time on the wing, as it were, was essential. Here again Galileo's insight was crucial. It is said that as a youth he had observed a lamp swinging back and forth in church, and noted, checking on his pulse, that the time of the swing remained constant even when the arc of the swing diminished. He later demonstrated that every swing of the pendulum, no matter how big or small its arc, took just as much time as every other, and that the duration of the interval depended on the length of the pendulum. A device that would accurately register the number of swings a pendulum made would therefore count equal intervals of time. Developed by the great Dutch scientist Christian Huygens, the observation of Galileo became the pendulum clock.

The very measuring devices that the scientists contrived ultimately created whole new areas of investigation. The barometer and its cousin, the pressure gauge, opened up the study of the behavior of matter in the gaseous state. While, via the pendulum, one door from Galileo's study of periodic vibrations led to the accurate measurement of physical time, another door led to the accurate study of musical notes (another kind of periodic vibration), and thence to the whole science of acoustics. The image of rooms with many doors is apt. It was as if the early scientists had entered the hall of a great palace, full of remarkable treasures and containing many doors. Each of these doors led to other rooms filled with more treasures and with many doors leading off to yet other rooms. . . . Scientists were torn between the desire to examine one room in detail and the urge to see what was on the other side of the many doors. One can get a vivid sense of the excitement of science in its youth from the First Day in Galileo's *Discourses on Two New Sciences* (1638). The day's talk, he tells us, will have to do with stresses and strains. But the dialogue soon gets away from stresses and strains and on to the problem of the nature of infinity, thence to falling bodies, thence to pendulums, to vibration, to the nature of musical harmonies, sound, and hearing. Each subject is connected with the one that precedes it, and about each one Galileo has something new and exciting to say; but with each step he digresses from stresses and strains, to which indeed he does not return at all in the First Day.

As essential as was the physical apparatus of the Scientific Revolution, its most important instrument was number. The physical apparatus of the new sciences—telescope, thermometer, clock, barometer—was all geared to provide the quantitative data with which scientists could either construct hypotheses or verify hypotheses based on numerical relationships. Number was the instrument of two operations indispensable for the development of the Scientific Revolution—computation and mathematical analysis.

The Roman number system was hopeless for purposes of computation. As long as the men of the Middle Ages retained it, they could not perform the ordinary

Galileo's plan for a pendulum clock, as sketched by his son in 1641. By means of the finger-like arms on the pendulum's pivot the pin wheel (at top) was turned, driving the clock.

The Role of Number

operations of addition, subtraction, multiplication, and division of whole numbers directly but instead had to use the abacus or counting board. Fortunately the Arabs had taken over from the Hindus of India a system of numerical notation based on the number 10, in which position played a consistent part in the determination of value, as it did not in the Roman system. In the later Middle Ages the Western world borrowed the system from the Islamic world; and we still acknowledge our debt by calling our numbers Arabic numerals.

The Arabic system greatly eased the difficulties of whole-number computation, but the mathematics of the Scientific Revolution increasingly had to deal with fractions. In the 1590s the Dutch scientist Simon Stevin helped to overcome the cumbersome procedures of fractional computation by inventing the system of decimal fractions. This was a great help, but it was not enough, for at the very time that Stevin's invention became available, the magnitudes of the quantities with which science had to deal underwent an enormous expansion. Since Ptolemaic astronomy had not concerned itself with actual physical distances, it did not have to cope with an arithmetic whose smallest significant quantity—the distance between the earth and the moon—was over 300,000 miles. But Kepler and subsequent investigators of the heavens had not only to deal with such figures but with their powers and roots. Not for the last time, Western man's curiosity about nature put him in a position where his methods of computation were inadequate to deal with the questions he wanted to answer. The difficulties of the twentieth-century physicist in this area were surmounted by the development of the electronic computer. The difficulties of the astronomers and physicists of the seventeenth century were conquered by the invention of logarithms. The first logarithmic system was developed by John Napier and published in 1614. The "common logarithms" with a base of 10 became available in 1624, thus more than halving the time required for multiplication, division, raising to powers, and taking roots of numbers, thus greatly increasing the store of intellectual energy available for the further explorations of nature.

The problems of the new sciences of motion, however, demanded more than improved methods of computation. They required wholly new developments in mathematics in order to deal with the problems raised by the study of motion. New discoveries were made in several old fields of mathematical study, but most important, two whole new mathematical disciplines were invented—the analytical geometry of the French philosopher René Descartes, and the calculus, independently worked out by Isaac Newton and the German philosopher Gottfried von Leibniz. Descartes' great feat was to find a common ground for the numerical analysis of algebra and the spatial analysis of geometry; it thereby became possible to give spatial representation to algebraic equations or to describe in algebraic equations the forms of curves. Thus the methods of both algebra and Euclidian geometry reinforced one another in this new field of mathematics. The calculus provides a method of determining the slope of a curve—its rate of deviation from a line tangent to it—at any point on that curve. A man who knew Descartes' analytical geometry could plot almost any measurable continuous process as a curve. By employing the calculus he could then determine the rate of continuous process at any given moment of that process. The relevance of the new mathematics to the new sciences of motion is evident if one considers the

CULVER

Gottfried von Leibniz was active in such varied fields as mathematics, philosophy, law, and diplomacy. The calculus he devised was published in 1684, nine years before Newton's.

mathematical implications of the transformation in astronomy. In Ptolemaic and even in Copernican astronomy men were still on the safe ground of Euclid's geometry. All movement was circular, and the rate of movement of each part of the system was assumed to be at uniform speed. In the astronomy of Kepler neither of these conditions held any longer. The orbits of the planets continuously deviated from circularity, and the time they took to traverse a given distance continuously varied throughout their orbits. Such phenomena called for a mathematics that could take into account both kinds of continuous variation—spatial and temporal—and it was precisely this kind of mathematics that analytic geometry and the calculus supplied. The new mathematics also had its applications to more earthly matters. The action of a spring under continuously increasing tension, the acceleration of a falling body, the behavior of fluids under varying conditions of pressure, the wave characteristics of sound—all these physical phenomena and many more were amenable to the kind of analysis that the new mathematics provided.

The methods of science are perhaps most fully revealed in the instruments it employs and the operations it undertakes. Most of the important instruments of the Scientific Revolution, as we have seen, were devices which made possible the exact measurement of increments of pressure, temperature, weight, time, and distance. The most important operations of the new mechanical sciences were mathematical. So both in its instruments and in its operations the Scientific Revolution was oriented toward number. The central role of number on both the experimental (instruments) side and on the theoretical (mathematics) side points to the underlying creed of seventeenth-century science. For the new scientists it was important to measure accurately because they were profoundly convinced that the relations among the phenomena they measured—pressure, temperature, time, weight, distance—were mathematical relations, and that these relations were constant because nature itself was constant. The universe of Aristotle had been an orderly pyramid of entities from the simplest material stuff at the bottom to God at the top; its symbol was a sort of pyramid of Being, qualitatively differentiated, from mere matter to pure spirit. The universe of the Scientific Revolution was masses of matter moving through space and time, their motions rendered orderly by constant quantitative relations among their weights, distances, temperatures, and pressures. The symbol of the order of nature to the men of the Scientific Revolution was the mathematical equation which balanced the force of the causes on one side with the force of the effects on the other. As Galileo expressed it, "The book of nature is written in mathematical language . . . the letters being triangles, circles, and other geometrical figures, without the grasp of which it is impossible to comprehend a single word."

It has been said that since they looked only for quantitative relations in nature, it is hardly to be wondered that the men who created a new system of the universe in the seventeenth century found nothing but quantitative relations. This is indeed true. On the other hand, in common sense it is hard to see how these men and the hosts of scientists who have followed in their footsteps could have experimentally verified their hypotheses about the quantitative relations among natural phenomena unless those relations existed in nature, that is, unless nature, whatever its other aspects, has one aspect that is quantitative in character.

So far we have looked at those traits of the methods of the men of the Scientific Revolution that seem to have made the deepest impression on their immediate successors. Those traits all emphasized quantity and number. There were then, however, important areas of scientific investigation where quantitative methods were premature or irrelevant or impossible, and there still are such areas today. Besides the quantitative approach, the early modern scientists developed other habits of thought, patterns of procedure, and standards of proof that since their time have gradually but methodically been applied to almost every field in which men have systematically attempted to advance the frontiers of knowledge. These came to constitute what may be called the ground rules of scientific investigation. Although there might be truths and ways of getting at truth that avoided the ground rules or even broke them, they were not scientific truths, and they could not be admitted to be so until they were verified according to the procedures laid down in the rules of scientific investigation. What were these ground rules?

1) Gradually the explorers of natural phenomena learned to draw sharp distinctions between speculation and hypothesis, between hypothesis and confirmed theory. In this respect, the difference between science before 1500 and science after 1700 is enormous, and the transformation is visible within the Scientific Revolution itself in the difference between free-wheeling speculators like Kepler and Descartes and hard-headed testers like Galileo and Huygens. In general, the rule was that to have scientific status any statement must be testable by experiment or observation. A statement for which no test could be devised was simply speculation; it had no place in the body of scientific knowledge at all. A hypothesis was a statement for which it was possible to devise a test, and a theory or scientific law was a general statement that had held up under every test of observation and experiment devised to try it.

2) Scientific knowledge and scientific testing had to be public. No one's assertion about his own private experiences had any standing unless others could repeat those experiences with similar results and thus check on them.

3) Since there was no way of experimentally verifying God's intention, to refer an event or a natural phenomenon to Divine Providence or Divine Purpose did not constitute a scientific explanation of that event or phenomenon, and assertions

The German Otto von Guericke, a contemporary of Torricelli, sought by experiment to disprove the old belief that a vacuum could not exist in nature, but initially his equipment was unequal to the task. The barrel (left) could not be made airtight, but he did achieve a partial vacuum in a metal sphere (right) before it crumpled under atmospheric pressure.

O. VON GUERICKE, *Experimenta Nova*, 1672

concerning God's intention were no part of the business of the scientist as such.

4) An adequate scientific explanation was one that most simply accounted for all the verified facts without conflicting with other adequate explanations for other sets of facts. To insist on a more complicated explanation when a simpler one would adequately deal with all the known facts was a waste of time, since in the equations that constituted the scientific description or explanation of any phenomenon observed, a complication on one side of the equation would cancel out a complication on the other, leaving the simplest equation fully adequate.

Such were some of the ground rules of scientific investigation that gradually developed to guide standard scientific practice in the seventeenth century and after. Today they may seem mere common sense, but that is because we are all grandchildren of the Scientific Revolution and have acquired our notion of what is common sense from our scientific grandfathers.

The methods of investigation developed during the Scientific Revolution were quickly adopted and extended by men concerned to increase natural knowledge. The kinds of argument about the nature of the physical world that had been customary among the learned since classical antiquity—arguments about qualities and purposes—diminished. By the time Newton died, the new sciences of motion had triumphed among men capable of understanding them. They had even begun to triumph among those incapable of understanding them. Such men began to have "faith" in the results the scientists achieved. This faith in science that conquered Western civilization within two centuries preached only a little, persecuted not at all, and employed neither force nor threats to make its way.

The Spread of the Scientific Revolution

The remarkable spread of science resulted in part from the fact that it could now furnish answers to a great many practical problems. Sailors wanted to know their longitude, mine operators wanted to work out efficient and economical pumping systems, builders, especially shipbuilders, wanted to know what size beam they needed to carry a particular stress and at what point on the beam the stress would be minimized. To all these questions and more, scientists supplied answers that experience sustained.

Science spread also because it offered what looked like a new kind of certainty about the world, a certainty that men could test for themselves. A hundred-odd years of theological bickering and religious war had shaken men's sense of the certainty of religious faith. The Protestant Revolution had cast doubt on the capacity of both human tradition and human authority to justify the confidence that men had long put in them. In place of this authority the Protestants offered the authority of Scripture as understood with the eyes of faith, yet the faithful turned out to be singularly lacking in unanimity about what their eyes saw in the Bible and extremely vocal about their differences of opinion. With many people finding it difficult to choose the "right" opinion from among all of the religious opinions rampant, the idea grew that perhaps in such matters as religion there was no way of telling who was right. But there did seem to be a way of telling whether the scientists were right. Where the practical man saw that science "worked" practically, the man in quest of certainty found that it "worked" intellectually as well. With his own hands and eyes such a man could prove that nature did act in the way that the general laws of the scientists suggested it *must*

The founding of the French Académie des Sciences in 1666 is commemorated in Charles Lebrun's painting. The central figure is Louis XIV; at his right is his finance minister, Colbert, a strong backer of the Académie.

act. Moreover, if anyone could show that in a particular case a scientific conclusion or law did not prove out, scientists were ordinarily (although sometimes not cheerfully) ready to go back over the ground to find out what was wrong. The discovery of errors, even trifling ones, in the teachings of churches and religious sects tended to shake faith in religious creeds. This happened because churches and sects were inclined to overcommit themselves to the details of their own doctrine, ascribing many such details to divine revelation. Paradoxically, when—as was frequently the case—scientists of the new kind fell into error, the discovery of the error confirmed faith in the new sciences. By re-examining in the light of criticism the whole process in which his error was imbedded a scientist often came up with a new answer that improved on the previous one, so that through the discovery and correction of error science became more accurate and precise and increased the sense of certainty of those who believed in it. For no matter how eminent or how conservative a scientist was, he could not permanently commit any science to his particular notions. He had no authority beyond that which he could achieve by demonstrating the soundness of his views according to the methods deemed valid in his field of investigation.

The scientists themselves did much to spread scientific knowledge and with it scientific faith. With men all over Europe turning their attention to the same

150   THE WORLD OF THE NEW SCIENCES

kinds of scientific problems, there was an increasing danger that a man in one place might waste a lifetime studying questions that, unknown to him, someone elsewhere had already answered. Moreover, as the investigations of nature advanced, its interconnectedness became increasingly apparent. A small discovery in one field might turn out to hold the key to a problem that had stumped the experts in another field. For these reasons and others, scientists came to feel a pressing need for ways of rapidly communicating their results to one another.

The first international communication was achieved by correspondence. This was especially effective if the recipient of the letter was the local focus of scientific activity. Letters sent to Galileo in Italy, Mersenne in France, Kepler in Germany, Huygens in the Netherlands, or Boyle in England were likely to be read by most of the important scientists in their respective countries. This tendency of scientists to cluster in one place or about one man was soon institutionalized. Scientists who had informally gathered to talk shop organized their meetings on a formal basis, often with governmental encouragement, and became scientific societies: the Accademia dei Lincei (or lynx-eyed) in Rome (1603), the Royal Society in London (1662), the Académie des Sciences in Paris (1666). Such societies took part in a steady flow of correspondence with individual scientists and societies in other lands. In their *Proceedings* and *Transactions* they published papers their members had written, exchanging these publications with foreign scientific societies. The use of Latin in many scientific communications facilitated the flow of knowledge, since Latin remained the common second language of all men of learning. Thus, in the era of the Scientific Revolution, the scientific faith spread along with scientific knowledge to every corner of the Western world, and it reached some men in every social stratum in which there were people literate enough to have any idea of what was going on.

That it is possible to be both a practicing scientist and a believing member of almost any Christian church is proved by the fact that many men have indeed been both. Yet, beginning with the publication of Copernicus's *On the Revolutions of the Heavenly Bodies*, many theologians developed a hostility to science and scientists. Later there emerged a reciprocal contempt on the part of many scientists for theologians and orthodox religion. To some extent the conflict still goes on today.

Science and Theology

Although the conflict between church and science has flared up again and again, the best known and perhaps the most dramatic episode in its history—the struggle over the new astronomy—took place during the Scientific Revolution. In the seventeenth century only one Christian church, the Catholic Church, had the means, will, and power to impose drastic penalties on a person for maintaining a scientific hypothesis or a cosmic speculation that the Church had declared to be erroneous or heretical. In 1632 the Pope used the Inquisition, the instrument the Church had devised to safeguard orthodoxy, to make an example of the most eminent advocate of the Copernican view, Galileo Galilei. In 1616 Galileo had been summoned before the Inquisition after he had made clear his fundamental disagreement with both the astronomy of Ptolemy and the physics of Aristotle. The Inquisition declared erroneous the Copernican view that the earth has a daily rotation and an annual circuit. Galileo submitted to the decree that he

The title page of Galileo's Dialogue *has Aristotle (left) exchanging views with Copernicus (right) and Ptolemy.*

should not "hold or defend" the condemned position as physical truth, but in his *Dialogue on Two Systems of the World* (1632), under a transparent veil of impartiality, he made clear his conviction that the Copernican view was correct. The Inquisition then forced him, through threat of torture and the infliction of extreme penalties, to again recant the doctrine that it believed to be "contrary to sacred and divine Scripture." For his conduct in evading the promise he previously had made, Galileo was confined to his home for the rest of his days.

Next to the trial and execution of Socrates, the trial and punishment of Galileo is the most celebrated episode in the recurrent conflict between the power of vested authority and the drive of men to teach what they believe they know. People have been arguing the rights and wrongs of the Galileo case for over three hundred years. Dubious motives have been ascribed to the group in the Church interested in suppressing Galileo's opinions; crookedness has been imputed to the course Galileo followed. Instead of attempting to judge and condemn, however, let us try to discern what drove both sides to act as they did. In seeking to vindicate himself Galileo attempted to prove that, contrary to the generally accepted interpretation, the Bible supported the Copernican view. What Galileo really believed was that if an interpretation of God's written Word conflicted with the conclusion of science, arrived at by mathematical demonstration and verified by experiment, then that interpretation was erroneous no matter what authority maintained it, and it had better be changed. But this meant that for Galileo, within the area of its competence, science was the final authority. And yet this final authority was not a permanently fixed authority. On the contrary, it was constantly changing. A hypothesis dogmatically but tentatively held to be authoritative for years had to give way to a different hypothesis arrived at by the same method but offering a better explanation of the matter in question. But although the doctrine of science might at any time be modified by further scientific discovery, that was the only thing scientific doctrine could be modified by. Thus from any teaching of science there did lie an appeal; but it was not to the past, to time-honored doctrines, whether those doctrines rested on the authority of Aristotle, on the accepted interpretation of Scripture, or on the decree of the authorized agent of ecclesiastical power. The appeal was to the future and a possible new scientific truth, a truth not yet discovered.

Here was the root of Galileo's trouble. He felt very differently than did the Inquisition about the very nature of truth. For the Inquisition the main truth was not something to be newly found or discovered; it had been set forth with finality centuries ago, and the primary function of thinking was correctly to interpret a truth long since revealed. And the Inquisition's own function was to protect the authority of the Church into whose custody God had given His precious revelation against just such careless and intellectually prideful men as Galileo. If such men, in pursuing their lesser and partial inquiries into the truth, arrived at conclusions at variance with the truth of Scripture, authoritatively interpreted, then such conclusions might rightly be condemned and the men who held them subjected to penal discipline. At the beginning of Galileo's great chapter on dynamics he sets forth his very different attitude toward the kind of truth he is concerned with. He has, he says, discovered many facts worth knowing, but "what I consider more important, there have been opened up two excellent sciences, of which my work is merely the beginning, ways and means by which other minds more acute than mine will explore their remote corners." Thus Galileo's intellectual pride in the face of all claimants to authority of an extra-scientific sort became humility in the face of the possibilities for discovering truth in the area of science by means of scientific inquiry—and the pride and the humility were inseparable, heads and tails of the same coin.

One of the most famous legends in the history of science tells how, after he had humiliated himself before the power of the Inquisition and recanted his error in espousing the Copernican theory of the double movement of the earth, Galileo muttered under his breath, "*E pur se muove*" ("Yet it does move"). Galileo almost certainly said no such thing. Nevertheless, the remark well represents his position and that of other scientists with respect to the standing of any alternative authorities in the face of scientific demonstration. In fact, they had no standing.

Galileo was the last eminent scientist put on trial by the Church for his scientific opinions. Within fifty years of his death his point of view had triumphed among the intellectual leaders of Western society and enfeebled all effective opposition. It was not merely that after Newton no one of any consequence seriously denied the movement of the earth. Although that was the case, it was merely an important symptom of a broader change. What had happened was that Galileo's views on the nature and the authority of scientific truth had won wide acceptance over all conflicting ideas about truth. In Galileo's time scientists had felt obliged to show that the Copernican view did not clash with the scriptural story about the sun and moon stopping in their courses at the command of Joshua; by 1700 men who upheld the authority of Scripture felt bound to show that the Joshua story might square with the scientifically demonstrated movements of the solar system. The position on the new astronomy that the Catholic Church took in 1633—a position it no longer upholds, but one that it long shared with the clergy of many other Christian groups—was thus badly undermined and crumbling within a century of its enunciation.

As the scientist's view of the relation between his discoveries and matters held true on non-scientific grounds gradually won acceptance, so too did certain working corollaries of that view. These corollaries helped for a long while to fix the posture that the Western world took toward scientific investigation. In the first place, in the realm of science the danger of error came to be held far less important than the freedom of the scientist to follow his search wherever it led him and to state his conclusions as he saw them. Religious error from the point of view of the Christian churches might destroy a man's soul; scientific error, from the scientists' point of view, was likely only to destroy a man's professional reputation. Even if error won temporary assent, its ascendancy would be short-lived, since by its very method of repeated verification science was self-correcting. But unless scientists could freely communicate their conclusions to one another, verification became impossible, thereby destroying or hopelessly impeding the progress of science itself. Freedom of inquiry was recognized as the necessary condition of scientific work.

The second corollary was that a scientist had no responsibility for the social or cultural consequences of his discoveries. His job was to investigate the operations of nature. He was bound to measure accurately, to think carefully, to report exactly, and not to "cook" his data. His work aimed solely at the improvement of the knowledge of nature. It was to be judged solely by its success in increasing natural knowledge. What use men made of the knowledge was neither the scientist's responsibility nor his concern. Galileo successfully analyzed the characteristics of the trajectory of a projectile, founding the science of ballistics. He was deservedly praised for the scientific advance that his analysis achieved. If at some later time it should turn out that, applying ballistics to cannon fire, artillerymen were able to mangle a great many more human bodies, open a great many more towns to pillage, rape, and murder by the infantry than they had been able to do heretofore, that was not Galileo's affair. No one suggested that he was in any sense responsible for the social results that followed from his discoveries, much less that he should have suppressed what he had learned, although, men being what they are, the social result—the increase in pillage, rape, and murder—was in the cards. Only within the last quarter century has the exploration of a possible alternative position begun.

The New Look of the World and Man

By 1700 the social and economic effects of scientific discovery could be seen in the way some men went about their daily work. By 1700, too, practically all the verified scientific theories resulting from more than a century of investigation could have been set down in a dozen or so pages of mathematical formulas. But very early the suspicion took hold that there was more to the Scientific Revolution than its immediate technical effects, and that it had something to say that was not and could not be included in a series of formulas. Men began to think that science revealed or hinted at some very important secrets about the nature of the universe and the nature of God and man.

One of the secrets that science seemed to reveal about the universe was its pervasive regularity—its operation according to rule (Latin, *regula*) or law. The idea that there is an element of regularity in nature must have been grasped by men almost as soon as they began to think about anything at all. Pre-literate man recognized that night and day, the cycle of the seasons, the waxing and waning of the moon not only recurred but recurred in a constant order and at regular intervals of time. This sense of the orderliness of nature increased through the centuries, although not without regressions, and was an integral part of the medieval synthesis. But to think of nature as orderly is one thing and to think that it is totally orderly and that its order may be totally intelligible to human reason is quite another. At no time up to the seventeenth century did the dominant intellectuals of any society conceive of the physical world as both totally orderly and totally intelligible. The few isolated thinkers who did so believe were handicapped by their inability to propose a set of plausible rules describing the order of nature or to prove the rules that they did propose.

Lacking a firm scientific base and a scientific method of demonstration, the so-called naturalistic systems of nature before the seventeenth century did not take a strong hold on men's minds. The more prevalent ways of thinking about nature, while recognizing certain elements of regularity in the world, left large and apparently irregular areas unexplored. This was so in the Middle Ages, even in the very orderly view of the world that one finds in St. Thomas Aquinas and Dante. Moreover the inexplicable—divine intervention, miracles, demoniac action—was not always separate from the explicable. There was a sphere of nature uniformly subject to known rules and laws and a sphere of super-nature where no rules (or at least a very different set of rules) held good. But super-nature always could and often did act on nature, penetrating it and, as it were, suspending the ordinary rules. So, although by and large natural law prevailed and the regular thing did happen in the universe as medieval men viewed it, still anywhere, anytime, through the intervention of supernatural forces the regular might not happen and the apparently irregular might happen. Consequently medieval science had two focuses—the regular and the irregular—with the latter deemed quite as worthy of attention as the former. Sound observation was mixed up with an indiscriminate interest in such "freaks of nature" as talking pigs, two-headed calves, and hailstorms of solid stone.

In general, in explaining why things are the way they are, one may say either that they were pushed from behind to their present state or that they were drawn from in front to their present state. The Aristotelian view, and therefore the late medieval view, was that ultimately things were drawn from in front. All things had a natural end or completion or perfection to which they at once struggled and were drawn. The acorn both sought to become an oak and was in a sense attracted toward becoming an oak, the proper end and goal of all acorns. All things were ultimately determined by their purposes. The here and now and everything in it was, therefore, to be understood in terms of purpose, of the end for which it was made and toward which it was developing. In the Middle Ages the ultimate purpose of all things was God's purpose. In part His purpose was revealed in Scripture; in part it disclosed itself to human reason; and in part it remained mysterious to man in this life. Even the inability to find any purpose for some natural events did not, therefore, prove that no purpose was there; it simply demonstrated the incapacity of mere man to understand the whole divine plan. The explanation of the human eye was easy enough to discern—it existed so that man might see. But the explanation of the human vermiform appendix in the divine scheme of things might be a sacred secret beyond the reach of human thought. Divine Providence thus became a convenient place of deposit for whatever was unintelligible. This view of nature is called teleological; it holds that nature is to be understood in terms of its purposes, or that the "final causes" of things, which draw them on, explain what those things really are and what they do.

It would be wrong to say that the scientists of the Scientific Revolution "proved" that there was no supernatural, no contact between the supernatural and the natural, no purpose behind natural events. What they did was actually far more devastating to the older view. They simply thought about nature in a way that did not involve either the supernatural or final causes, and in so doing they kept coming up with explanations which men found satisfying for events

The Romantic poet and artist William Blake portrayed Newton as an unfeeling, somewhat satanic draftsman of a universal order that, said Blake, made a "mathematical diagram" of God.

TATE GALLERY

that in former times had been explained by divine intervention or purpose. The more events the scientists were able to explain without reference to supernatural intervention or purpose, the more men were inclined to look only for the scientific explanation and to believe that the universe was a place where everything that happened could be explained by increasing the number of tested formulas that the scientists were producing.

Eminent philosophers of the seventeenth century—men like Descartes, John Locke, and Thomas Hobbes—tried to state precisely what, in their opinion, such a world would be like. They did not come up with identical answers, but certain elements in their various explanations blended into a common outlook, one that was shared by many of the more intelligent men of the following age and became a habit of thought in Western civilization, a pattern of its culture, a part of its climate of opinion. Roughly, what the philosophic ferment of the era of the Scientific Revolution left for subsequent generations was the theory that the only stuff in the physical universe is matter. Matter is something that takes up space and moves about in it. There is more of it in some places than in others, more in the same place at one time than at another time. But the whole physical universe is nothing but matter in various quantities or masses moving about in space and in time. Color, taste, sound—most of what makes up man's experience of the physical world—are not in the physical world at all. Rather, they are just the way that the colorless, tasteless, silent reality—matter in motion—is perceived by man's senses and received by his mind. Moreover, nothing in this world is what it is or where it is because it wants to be that or to be there, nor does it move because it wants to go somewhere else. Matter is not infused with spirit, and it has neither a purpose of its own nor any purpose imposed on it. Far different from the picture of the world of the medieval synthesis, the matter that comprises the physical universe is not pulled from in front by a purpose, as was previously thought, but pushed from behind by the impact or force of other matter.

Yet this wholly material and incredibly vast universe was not disorderly. On the contrary, it was orderly with a simplicity and intelligibility beyond anything man had dreamed of before the seventeenth century. All one had to know about matter was how much of it was in particular places, how far those places were from each other, and how fast the various masses of matter were moving, and one would be able to know where the matter was going and how long it would take to get there. This was because the laws of change in the shape and position of matter were sets of simple numerical relations among distance, time, and mass. Far from being chaotic, the universe was ruled by intelligible, universal law. It was like a splendid piece of self-regulating, self-winding clockwork, a perfect material mechanism, what has since been called the Newtonian "world machine."

The impulse the Scientific Revolution gave to seeing the physical universe as a machine was so strong that the philosophers beat the physicists and astronomers to it. Before Newton had discovered how the world clock was put together, some of the philosophers had simply assumed that it was a clock and that the laws of its operation would soon be discovered. But having made the physical universe a machine, the philosophers of the Scientific Revolution had on their hands, undisposed of, two major parts of that medieval world view which science had destroyed—God and man. In the medieval synthesis, God, man, and nature had

René Descartes, painted by Frans Hals. Descartes spent most of his adult life in Holland, a country more tolerant than his native France.

all been bound together in a great comprehensive vision that included all things, all feelings, all thoughts, all hopes.

Among those who tried to deal with the meaning of the new science there was less agreement about the nature of man than about the nature of nature, and less agreement about the nature of God than about the nature of man. Thomas Hobbes (1588–1679) propounded a philosophy that attempted to explain both physical and mental events on mechanical principles. In his system, God, although formally present, was at once so incomprehensible and so inactive as to be practically unnecessary. René Descartes (1596–1650) needed God to bridge the gap between the physical universe and the realm of thought inhabited by man's mind. The Dutch philosopher Baruch Spinoza (1632–1677) identified God with the whole system of laws that governs reality and makes science possible.

Despite differences among the leading philosophers of the age, their attempts to describe God's place in relation to a system of nature in which purpose played so small a part tended to depersonalize God, to make Him remote and abstract, in contrast with the concrete personal God of the Middle Ages and the Reformation. In fact, none of the efforts of the philosophers to find a place for God in the new view of nature proved wholly acceptable to the first generations of Western men raised in the intellectual climate created by the Scientific Revolution. Robert Boyle (1627–1691), one of those wide-ranging intellects who thrived in the invigorating atmosphere of the Scientific Revolution, a man who made fruitful investigations into many unexplored corners of nature, perhaps came closest to expressing what was to become the consensus in the matter. The universe, Boyle said, was governed by the rules of motion and the laws of nature. The universe being once framed, and the laws of motion settled, "the mechanical philosophy teaches that the phenomena of the world are physically produced by the mechanical properties of the parts of matter." But it was God who had established the rules of motion and the laws of nature. Whether Boyle's way of reconciling the activity and the creativity of God with a self-regulating universe can in the long run satisfy men with deep religious yearnings is doubtful. Nevertheless, it gained considerable currency in the eighteenth century.

Historians used to say that the triumph of the view of the universe set forth during the Scientific Revolution caused those who witnessed and understood that revolution to devaluate sharply man and his place in nature. It is true that the discovery of the immensity of the universe set some men to thinking in terms of an infinity of worlds, many of which might be inhabited by rational beings. Besides making the earth seem but an insignificant speck of dust in the cosmos and man's habit of thinking of the earth as created for his particular benefit peculiarly vainglorious, such speculation raised awkward theological questions about the role of the Incarnation and Crucifixion of Christ in a universe of infinite worlds. For overbold speculation on an infinity of worlds, the renegade monk Giordano Bruno was condemned by the Inquisition to a heretic's death at the stake in 1600. The great French mathematician Blaise Pascal was filled with a sense of anxiety and terror by the contemplation of the aloneness of man in boundless space. But Bruno and Pascal were somewhat unusual in thinking that the new astronomy had diminished man's importance. Far from resulting in a devaluation of man, the Scientific Revolution provided the basis for perhaps the highest valuation that man had ever put on himself. Instead of suggesting a despairing pessimism about the nature and destiny of man, the new science was soon used to justify an almost incredible optimism. The full bloom of this optimism did not come until later, after Newton and John Locke between them had fitted the chief ideas of the new science into a coherent picture gradually accepted by thoughtful men of the age. Its seed time, however, occurred during the Scientific Revolution itself, and it was Gottfried von Leibniz (1646–1716), one of the most powerful minds of the seventeenth century, who professed to have demonstrated that we are living in the best of all possible worlds.

The thinkers trying to discern man's place in a mechanical universe had to do without one of the more convenient features of the medieval synthesis. In the medieval world view the physical axis of the cosmos and its spiritual axis coincided exactly; they both ran through the earth. The earth, the physical center around which the whole universe turned, was also the place where the Christian drama—the great struggle between God and Satan for men's souls—was enacted. The new astronomy destroyed this nice balance. The physical axis of the universe moved off to some indeterminate point in space, and the earth was left as one planet among others whirling around a not especially major star, the sun. Yet this shift did not destroy man's sense of his own ultimate importance. Although the once geocentric physical system became heliocentric, the spiritual world remained essentially anthropocentric (man-centered).

The new philosophy found in the new science itself the ground on which to re-establish man's faith in his own importance. One thing was quite clear about the Scientific Revolution: it was men who made it. All its wonderful new insights into the nature of things, all its splendid discoveries were themselves the creation of men. But how had men done this wondrous work? They had done it against tradition, against authority, and without the help of any special revelation. The instrument of this magnificent achievement was the human intellect, aided only by the human senses. And if men's intellect could achieve so much, what else might it not achieve? Supported by the new method, the new mathematics, the new instruments of measurement, all of them of the intellect's creation, was there any limit to what that intellect could do?

Because their line of work requires fine distinctions, the historians of philosophy *Bacon and Descartes* have tended to obscure the fundamental elements of unity in the ideas of the early interpreters of the Scientific Revolution. Francis Bacon (1561–1626) is said to exemplify empiricism, a philosophy that emphasizes experience and observation; René Descartes is identified with rationalism, the philosophy based on reasoning from clear and distinct ideas. This distinction is helpful, however, only if it is understood that, between extreme empiricists like Bacon and extreme rationalists like Descartes, there are important similarities as well as distinct divergences, and that the vaguely defined common ground they share represents the common faith of the propagators of the Scientific Revolution. Both men, for example, agreed on the need for the drastic changes in traditional scientific thinking. Both found in scientific thinking the justification of their faith in man's high destiny. Both believed that it was in the exercise of his faculty for discovery through thinking that man reached the highest excellence. Both re-

The frontispiece of a history of the Royal Society of London depicts Francis Bacon (at right) as the Society's spiritual founder. The bust is of Charles II; on the left is the first president of the Society.

jected final causes or purposes as a means of explaining the physical world, and therefore rejected the major elements of the Aristotelian-medieval system that were built on that conception.

There were, however, two differences between Bacon and Descartes with respect to the proper way to go about attaining natural knowledge and, once attained, with respect to the use of it. Both differences pointed toward important future developments in Western civilization. Descartes believed that reason or the intellect advanced understanding by operating mathematically on certain ideas so clear and distinct that the mind could not reject them. This way of thinking is popularly called *deduction*. Bacon believed that the reason or the intellect advanced understanding by operating on the visible world, accumulating carefully verified information from which general inferences could be made. This way of thinking is popularly called *induction*. Both methods are based on confidence in the human intellect, and both ultimately seek to produce results that will stand up under experimental testing, but they start out from opposite points. In the history of science since the seventeenth century, the methods of the various sciences have tended to fluctuate between the extreme positions of Bacon and Descartes without ever completely conforming to either extreme. The strong impulse to seek the key to nature in mathematics, the most deductive of sciences, led most of the early leaders of the Scientific Revolution toward the Cartesian extreme, even when—as in the case of Newton—they rejected its principal dogma. But the quantitative deductive method was for a long time to prove a dead end in the life or biological sciences. Here the method advocated by Bacon and, long before him, by Aristotle, turned out to be the royal road to discovery. For a long while, the patient and systematic accumulation and classification of data were indispensable to progress in the life sciences. Indeed, the next great revolution in man's way of thinking about himself and his world was set off by a work that exemplified the Baconian approach at its best—Charles Darwin's *Origin of Species* (Chapter 16).

Descartes and Bacon disagreed not only on the best way for the intellect to learn about nature, but also on the best use of the new knowledge. In some measure both acknowledged the improvement of understanding and the amelioration of living conditions as proper ends of the new investigations into nature. But Bacon emphasized the importance of scientific discovery as a means of control or power over nature. In one sense he is the heir to the medieval alchemists and magicians, men who sought to wrest nature's secrets from her in order to gain control of her forces. In science Bacon saw a way more powerful than any the magicians had ever dreamed of for attaining this end. He foresaw a world in which the application of scientific knowledge would make man's life and work easier and more agreeable by improving productive processes. A nature controlled by science could, he believed, be made to provide men with riches and an easing of the material conditions of human existence such as had scarcely been imaginable in an earlier day. While he, too, expected material advantages to accrue to man from the investigation of nature, for Descartes the Scientific Revolution meant primarily the emancipation and expansion of the human intellect itself. By means of the new method, all bars to the full development of man's mind were destroyed. The human mind could penetrate to the outmost bounds of the universe, could enter into the operation of the tiniest particle of matter, certain at last that it could understand any occurrence in the world of nature that it undertook to investigate. In this Descartes is the heir of the medieval Scholastic philosophers, who found men's supreme fulfillment in the contemplation of being, of what is. Facing the future, Descartes is the precursor of those who believed that the mind of man could be emancipated from error and superstition only through the possession of scientific truth.

Together, Bacon and Descartes foreshadowed the era in the history of Western culture that followed the publication of Newton's work on natural philosophy and John Locke's philosophical writing and political theory. Both Bacon and Descartes believed that human reason was the principal agent for bringing about the ends they had in view—the amelioration of man's lot and the emancipation of his mind. That is to say, they believed that man, by using his reason, can progress toward a happier, more convenient life and toward the steady improvement of his understanding. In their emphasis on the sovereign power of human reason, on the rational intelligibility of nature, on the evils of relying on tradition and authority, and on the possibilities of human progress, Bacon and Descartes presaged the faith of the succeeding era. In the midst of the Scientific Revolution, the seeds of the Englightenment are sown and begin to grow.

7

The Enlightenment

By the twelfth century certain fundamental patterns had become firmly established in the civilization of the West. Those patterns survived for more than six hundred years until the eighteenth century, when they were vigorously attacked and ultimately destroyed during the revolutionary era after 1750. The patterns in question were six in number: a divinely sanctioned monarchy; a privileged, state-supported church; a privileged hereditary aristocracy; a stratified social hierarchy maintained by formal laws; a legal system that favored the collectivity—family, village, town, or guild—rather than the individual; and, finally, a decentralized state administration preserving a considerable measure of local variety and regional autonomy. In the Western world today most or all of these traditions have been obliterated. Those that survive do so feebly in subordination to other and opposite patterns—the republican state form, freedom of conscience, democracy, social equality, centralized administration, and the autonomy of the individual.

The great changes that occurred after 1750 involved more than institutions. The transformation of institutions was preceded and accompanied by an equally radical transformation in patterns of thought. Among the old ways of thinking were the convictions that stability—maintaining things as they are—is good and change usually bad; that the final meaning of life lies beyond life and outside history in the hands of God; that those things that are most important for men to know are already known; that the main path to truth lies through understanding the teachings of men who already possess the truth; and that therefore diversity of opinion and belief is bad. Today, men tend to identify change with progress and to regard it as good, while they identify stability with stagnation and look upon it, for the most part, as bad. Despite religious professions to the contrary, most men today are unabashedly this-worldly—for them the goal of the individual is self-fulfillment on earth, that of mankind progress toward some splendid future on earth. Moreover, since men progress in knowledge, nothing that was held true in the past can be taken as certain: certainty is ultimately beyond the reach of man. The way to the improvement of understanding lies through active doubt about things currently believed, which leads to inquiry and investigation. Unity of opinion is therefore a sign of cultural stagnation and diversity of opinion a sign of cultural life and growth.

The shift in the pattern of thinking that we have just described did not take place all at once, is not complete today, and may never be complete; but it was nevertheless drastic. The shift began as a change in the habits of thought of those engaged in working out the new science of motion and of those engaged in assessing the significance of that new science. It was not until the eighteenth century, during the so-called Enlightenment, that the new pattern of thinking was clearly and concisely defined and was placed before the literate public of the West in open and intentional opposition to older views.

Jean Huber's engraving, The Philosophes at Dinner, *pictures leading figures of the Enlightenment in France, among them Voltaire (center, with hand raised), the encyclopedist Diderot at his left, and the mathematician d'Alembert (left foreground).*

The eighteenth-century's fascination with the noble savage is reflected in Tiepolo's fresco America *(1752) that adorns the ceiling of a German palace. America is symbolized by a buxom Indian maiden astride an immense Mississippi alligator and surrounded by a melting pot of peoples.*

Most of the circumstances that concurred to create a situation favorable for the development of the Enlightenment were negative in the sense that they created or extended skepticism about what for centuries had been orthodox and rarely challenged matters of faith with respect to both religion and the social order. One of the most corrosive sources of this skepticism was the long agony of religious conflict. Since the first half of the sixteenth century, rivers of human blood had been spilled to secure unity of faith. The massive blood-letting slowly abated, but the harassment of heretics and the war of words did not. Persecution that Catholic and Protestant alike in the sixteenth century regarded as a necessary consequence of man's duty to God's will, by the beginning of the eighteenth century seemed to many men of both persuasions mere acts of futile and destructive fanaticism. And the seemingly endless din of controversy that accompanied the religious conflict led some thinking men to doubt that the will and word of God were quite as clear and accessible to men as the contestants insisted they were.

Such doubt was re-enforced when two countries, the Dutch Republic and England, denied to the clergy and to the civil magistrates effective powers of persecution and, instead of declining, became the two most prosperous states in Europe. In the sixteenth century even men with only limited religious zeal believed that religious uniformity was indispensable to civil order. Although both the Dutch Republic and England maintained established churches, neither countenanced severe penalties for religious dissent, and both thrived mightily. If God was very much set on being worshiped in one way only, He seemed rather remiss about punishing the two states that paid least heed to His wishes in so important a matter. England was a special scandal or temptation to skepticism, since its concurrent prosperity and toleration coincided with dramatic exactness with the descent of France into religious persecution and economic and military disaster in the 1680s.

If the Dutch and the English were a challenge and a scandal within the European community to all kinds of Christian orthodoxy, those who looked beyond Europe found even more to shake the old simplicities of their faith. They saw countless millions who went about the business of living without even having heard of Christianity and caring little about it when they did hear. Men disaffected by the futilities of religious strife in Europe saw in this outside world two stock types (partly the creation of their own imaginations, no doubt): the noble savage and the Oriental sage. The former, an innocent child of nature, lived more virtuously without the churches and their priests and parsons than the Europeans did with them; the latter, a product of a civilization more ancient and as refined as that of Europe, seemed to enjoy a good and decent life without benefit of Christianity. As knowledge about non-Europeans increased, a kind of cultural relativism began to spread among educated Europeans, a relativism re-enforced by their standard education in the literature of classical (and pagan) antiquity. Moreover, a sense of the sheer number of non-Christians in the world and of the number of generations that had preceded them was disturbing, for none of these millions had heard the Gospel or been baptized or taken communion, and so all, according to the orthodox view, were eternally damned. But if this were so, it suited ill with the Christian view that God had sent His son to die for the salvation of all men who believed in Him. How could those millions believe in Him that had never even heard of Him?

By the early decades of the eighteenth century, much had happened to attenuate the religious orthodoxy of Europeans. Since the Christian outlook and the Christian Church were deeply enmeshed in the whole intellectual and institutional structure of Europe, the growth of doubt threatened more than theological dogma. The Enlightenment, however, was not merely the gradual decay of Christian orthodoxy. The men who propagated it were not mere skeptics. They were simply skeptical about religious orthodoxy; they had a faith of their own. For that faith they drew sustenance from the Scientific Revolution. What gave the Enlightenment its power to capture the mind of the educated classes was the vitality of its commitment to the belief that the new science held the key to truth, and that the truth would make men free.

The era after the publication of Newton's *Principia* in 1687 was marked by the continued though irregular progress of the natural sciences. No discoveries comparable to Newton's law of gravitation were made, and the scope and precision of his generalizations discouraged men from attempting to construct new systems of the world. One of his successors observed ruefully that there was but one universe, so the laws of its operation could be discovered only once.

Scientific Progress and Scientific Faith

Nevertheless, certain fundamental principles of physics, such as the law of least action and the law of conservation of mass, were elaborated in the eighteenth century. In chemistry progress was for a century less rapid. Robert Boyle, Newton's contemporary, had cleared away much of the rubbish of alchemy that stifled the growth of chemistry, but it was not until the work of Joseph Priestley (1733–1804) and Antoine Lavoisier (1743–1794), culminating in the discovery that burning (combustion) did not subtract something from the thing burned but added something (oxygen) to it, that chemistry received a new impetus. Nor did medicine advance at the rate that it had in the days of the great anatomist Vesalius or of William Harvey, who discovered the true relation between the movement of the heart and the circulation of the blood, and the early microscopists.

Patient students of nature, however, began to accumulate that enormous store of accurate factual observations of living creatures and their habitats that was indispensable to the development of the biological sciences. The greatest of the collectors was the Frenchman Georges de Buffon (1707–1788), whose wide-ranging study of the earth and the various forms of life were published in his *Histoire Naturelle*, which appeared between 1749 and 1804 (posthumously). In his first volumes Buffon did not challenge the orthodox view of Creation based on Genesis; he simply disregarded it. Taken to task by the guardian of orthodoxy, the theological faculty of the University of Paris, Buffon agreed to abandon "whatever might be contrary to the narration of Moses." Then he went on publishing the facts about nature as he found them. Carolus Linnaeus (1707–1778), the Swedish botanist, worked out a system for the classification of living creatures into genera and species. But progress in this area—the development of an improved natural history—was gradual rather than sensational. It was not until the mid-nineteenth century that, in the hands of Charles Darwin, the accumulation of knowledge about living things received a simple unifying and satisfying interpretation, comparable in scope to Newton's generalization of the phenomena of motion in the physical world.

In the century following its publication, the Newtonian system captured the imagination of thinking men more completely than any scientific discovery before or since has ever done. There ceased to be any insight into the nature of things, scientific or otherwise, to challenge its ascendancy. We have already seen that by Newton's day the problem that brought Galileo into conflict with the Church had been resolved in favor of Galileo's fundamental position, even though some churchmen failed to acknowledge defeat. On those matters within its competence, the findings of science were accepted as the final authority by the recognized leaders of Western thought. Revelation, intuition, mystical experience, philosophy, and theology were not competent witnesses to the truth in matters to which scientific method was applicable. Two essential questions remained: What were the limitations of science? To what did it apply? If we are to understand the development of Western thought in the eighteenth century, we must realize that it followed two lines in answering these questions.

Along one line philosophers investigated the operations of what they called the mind, which was the apparent generator of scientific knowledge. They asked what the mind could know, and how it could know it. Some were driven toward the conclusion that the mind could know nothing outside itself, and that, therefore, while scientific knowledge and all other knowledge might be an adequate description of what went on in the mind, it gave no reliable clues to the nature of any reality outside the mind. Since Descartes' time, most men who gave thought to such matters had made an assumption that led into this trap. They assumed that mind and matter were absolutely different, separate and distinct from one another. But since mind could hardly be expected to know anything about matter, with which by definition it had no contact whatever, it followed that so-called scientific laws—products of the mind—were only a reflection of the mind and incapable of proof. They could not with certainty be held to be a description of physical nature or of any reality outside the mind. Before the eighteenth century was half over, the Scottish philosopher David Hume (1711–1776) had arrived at this zero point in analyzing what science proved about external reality. The significant fact is that for years no one took Hume's brilliant argument seriously, least of all Hume himself. In fact, he spent the rest of his life investigating such diverse matters as miracles and the balance of trade without any noticeable doubt about the soundness of his results.

The second line of thought pursued by eighteenth-century thinkers was the opposite of the first. It assumed that science—that is, the mind reasoning scientifically—provided answers to all the questions worth asking about God, man,

The celebrated Jardin des Plantes *in Paris, shown here in 1794, contained thousands of exotic botanical specimens. Georges de Buffon was its director for almost half a century.*

The title page from Hobbes'
Leviathan *(1651), dealing
with "A Commonwealth
Ecclesiasticall and Civil,"
matches the symbols of the
secular world (left) with
those of religion (right).*

and nature. In view of the soundness of Hume's argument from premises that almost everyone accepted, this reasoning was regarded simply as an act of faith. And, indeed, the epoch in Western thought that followed Newton's great discoveries in the late seventeenth century might well be described as the age of faith—in science. The French called the apostles of this new faith *philosophes.*

The *philosophes* were men of a different sort from those we ordinarily think of as philosophers today, especially in the English-speaking world. Few of the most eminent *philosophes* were academics associated with the universities. None consistently pursued lines of inquiry primarily of a technical character or primarily of interest to other philosophers. Habitually, they all addressed themselves to the wider public of intelligent and intellectually active laymen, and most of them cultivated a literary style aimed to appeal to such laymen. It was only late in the Enlightenment that philosophy went back to the universities, and even then this took place in Germany rather than in France. The French *philosophes*, the pacesetters of the Enlightenment, were highly cultured men of letters with wide-ranging interests. Intellectuals rather than scholars, they lacked the restraint and discipline a strong academic tradition imposes, but they also enjoyed freedom from the intellectual inhibitions of such a tradition.

In the area of intellectual enterprise, as in commercial enterprise, nothing succeeds like success. Over and over again in the history of Western civilization, an outstanding success in one sphere of intellectual effort has led to attempts to apply this success to other areas of human knowledge and concern. So it was, as we have seen, in the thirteenth century with the work of Aristotle; so it was in the nineteenth century with Darwin's theory of evolution, and in the twentieth with Freud's theory of neurosis. And so it was, of course, in the Enlightenment with the new—the Newtonian—science of that age. The remarkable success of that science in coping with the problem of motion in the physical world inevitably led to an attempt to extend the scope of its inquiries. As early as the seventeenth century, before Newton's day, the English philosopher Thomas Hobbes had already made a bold attempt to apply what he took to be the findings of the new science to human thought, human conduct, and the problems of politics. In the *Leviathan* he offered a purely materialist conception of man and his conduct, reducing the mind to a sort of photographic plate that mechanically recorded (and jumbled) the impressions made by the physical world on the senses.

Attempts to achieve unity of knowledge by binding all other areas of thought to the new physics during the Enlightenment received a powerful impetus from the way men previously had thought about the relation of science to those areas and of all branches of knowledge to each other. The contrast between that time and our own can best be grasped if we put two sets of words opposite each other.

Natural Science	Natural Philosophy
Theology	Theology or Divine Philosophy
Metaphysics	First Philosophy
Ethics	Moral Philosophy
Politics	Political Philosophy

The words in the left column are our words, the words of our contemporary civilization; the words in the other column are their equivalents, terms that were current during and for several hundred years before the eighteenth century. The fact that there is no visible and verbal link among the terms we use indicates a peculiarity of our present-day way of thinking. We may feel that what we think on all these matters *ought* to stick together more or less; but we are glad to leave the problem of sticking the matters together to professors who are supposed to think about such problems for a living. On the whole, in the Western world today intelligent men tend to accept a measure of chaos in their own thinking and to be a little doubtful about systems that try to tie everything into a neat bundle.

It was quite otherwise in the Age of the Enlightenment. The medieval faith in the unity and relatedness of all truth was handed on unalloyed to the eighteenth century. The terms the *philosophes* used to describe what we today call Natural Science, Theology, Metaphysics, Ethics, and Politics express this sense of interconnectedness; they were all parts of one great whole—Philosophy. Far from being separate and independent, the nature of each depended on the nature of all the others; and a vast change in one could not conceivably take place without demanding equivalent adjustments in the others.

A tremendous change—the Scientific Revolution—did take place in Natural Philosophy between 1550 and 1700. The men who came under the spell of the new science believed that this change was from Ignorance and Error to

Knowledge and Truth. They were quite sure, therefore, that an equivalent transformation must take place in the other branches of knowledge through the application of the methods of Natural Philosophy. "Natural Science," said one of Newton's disciples, ". . . is chiefly to be valued as it lays a sure foundation for Natural Religion and Moral Philosophy." With this conviction the *philosophes* set out to make the transformation themselves. When they had finished their work, they had presented Western civilization with a new outlook on the world—an outlook very different from the one which prevailed up to the seventeenth century, and vigorously in competition with it. Parts of the world view of the eighteenth century survive to this day and are incorporated in our habits of thought. Others have broken down and lie at rest in the vast rubbish heap of things men no longer believe. But the survivals and the discards together once formed a coherent pattern of thought. Different from our own day and from the Renaissance, but like the thirteenth century, the Enlightenment had a way of looking at all things that held together, that was pretty much of one piece intellectually. This is true despite a number of divergent opinions and unresolved problems that were ultimately to undermine the Enlightenment synthesis, as they have undermined attempts at comprehensive synthesis before and since.

The two essential elements in the Enlightenment's view of the world were Nature and Reason. To the *philosophes* Nature was not the mere hurly-burly that we see when we naïvely look about us. Nor was it the medieval Scholastics' hierarchy ascending an Aristotelian ladder from almost pure chaotic matter to the absolutely pure and perfect form of God. The Nature of the Enlightenment was the Nature that the scientists, especially Newton, had discovered. As the poet Alexander Pope wrote,

> Nature and Nature's Laws lay hid in night,
> God said, Let Newton be! and all was light.

Nature, the *philosophes* believed, was mechanical, rational, uniform, simple, and subject to unvarying mathematical laws. It was a manifestation of Reason, and because man had Reason, he could understand "Nature and Nature's Laws." Man's Reason was not an abstract unintelligible thing; it was simply good, common sense disciplined by mathematical analysis that had achieved such startling results when the scientists turned it to studying Nature. And as Reason provided the key to Nature and was part of Nature, it also was a part of man, who was himself a product, a child, of Nature. Reason was a natural faculty of natural man. Indeed, the conception of Nature was so intermingled with that of Reason that it might be better to think of them as one. In the eyes of the *philosophes*, Reason and Nature were neither evil nor neutral. They had moral meaning. Whatever was natural and rational was good, and what was good was always natural and rational.

Natural Religion   The Reason and Nature of the *philosophes* strangely altered that theology which for centuries had been both the beginning and the end of philosophy. Nature required, most *philosophes* thought, a Creator appropriate to the Creation. Such a Creator would have made the universe, established the laws by which it always and invariably worked, set it whirling, and then retired from it. Indeed, the very perfection of God's work made His retirement inevitable, for it seemed absurd to imagine that He ever interfered with the laws He had laid down from the very beginning. Some believed that the existence of such a God could be proved by the existence of Nature and its perfection. Only by accepting God as the "First Cause" could one account for the fact that Nature existed, and that all of its parts, from the planets to the human eye, were perfectly designed for their function. The men who rejected revelation, but retained belief in a personal God on what they considered rational grounds, were called deists.

Even in the Middle Ages men had sought to prove the existence of God by much the same arguments used by some of the *philosophes*. To the philosophers of the medieval Church such proofs were essentially a vindication of human reason. That reason could reach to such heights demonstrated its dignity and value, but faith in God preceded and was altogether independent of any proofs reason could offer. The *philosophes* felt no need to vindicate reason; they believed in it with unlimited faith. It was God who gave them trouble. They had to *prove* God's existence to convince themselves that He really did exist. Since they no longer believed His existence could be taken on faith, only reason alone could satisfactorily certify God. From the religious point of view, perceptive men saw the weakness in this approach. It was not merely that the particular proofs stood up poorly under careful analysis. It was rather—as the French mathematician and philosopher Pascal had already pointed out in the seventeenth century—that rational proof of God's existence never led anyone who denied or seriously doubted His existence to believe in Him. To make rational conviction the first condition for religious belief was to put faith on a foundation of sand. That this was the case was soon demonstrated in the Enlightenment. By the middle of the eighteenth century certain *philosophes* maintained, on what they alleged to be rational grounds, that the God of their fellow *philosophes* was incredible, expendable, or downright obnoxious. Thus the Enlightenment contributed to that increase in skepticism, indifference, and atheism which earlier had been stimulated by the unresolved differences within the Christian churches and by men's growing preoccupation with secular matters.

For the *philosophes* who continued to believe in God and even in Christianity, a peculiar change took place in the form of their religious ideas. Natural theology did not originate in the eighteenth century. St. Thomas Aquinas in the thirteenth century had sought to establish that reason alone without revelation could know many things about God and His relations to man. But up to the time of the Enlightenment, natural religion was held to be inferior and inadequate to save men from Hell. The religion of reason was the stage before the highest stage, which was the religion of faith, and its insufficiency was shown by the fact that many had passed beyond it not to Christian truth but to heresy or to pagan error and idolatry. The *philosophes* reversed the order of excellence. For most of them, the best and highest religion was natural religion, the religion men could arrive at by use of their natural reason. Other religions were good to the extent that they approached this standard. Many *philosophes* suggested that, by that standard, Christianity was inferior to a number of other contemporary religions. Even *philosophes* who defended Christianity accepted these grounds of debate of the exponents of natural religion. They argued that Christianity was the best because of all religions it was the most rational and natural, the least superstitious and miraculous. To prove their point, they often stripped away the miracles and always depreciated their importance for what was essential (that is, rational) in Christianity. But such a course was disastrous to the Christian faith, since in the end it must seek to minimize the greatest miracle of all—that God so loved the world that He gave His beloved son as a sacrifice to atone for and redeem the terrible sins of man. Most religious Christians cared nothing at all for the kind of Christianity that dispensed with a Redeemer, an Incarnation, and an Atonement. Where Christianity enjoyed a revival in the eighteenth century it was through fervent anti-rational Christian enthusiasts like John Wesley (1703–1791), the founder of Methodism, who utterly rejected the watered-down philosophical Christianity of the intellectuals.

Men who felt their minds enlightened by the new science found religious enthusiasm unreasonable and revolting. Whether they themselves concluded that rational Christianity, deism, or atheism represented the most natural attitude toward religion, they felt that to wage wars and kill men over differences in theology was a species of madness. Theological preferences were matters for a man to decide by his own choice, according to his own lights. In England Newton's contemporary, John Locke, had argued that if a man remained a good and virtuous citizen, the state ought not to interfere with his religious preferences. The *philosophes* agreed with this argument and spread it throughout the Western world. They sought to transform religion, in previous centuries the most public of all matters, into one of the most private. Instead of making uniformity of religion their first concern, rulers should make it no concern at all, granting toleration to all creeds, since all were local variations of one natural religion. Despite serious differences among the men whose religious views reflected their enthusiasm for the new sciences, such men were united in their hostility to all Christian orthodoxies, because such orthodoxies remained exclusive in their claims to truth and impenitent in their assertion of the supernatural character of Christianity.

The Science of Man

In attempting to develop a science of man to correspond to the new natural sciences, the men of the Enlightenment were drawn in divergent directions by conflicting impulses—the impulse to disinterested investigation and the impulse to reform. They sought to attain the simplicity and exactness that they discerned in the natural sciences. Those sciences, however, owed much of their achievement to their avoidance of moral valuation: gravitation was not good or bad; it simply *was*. The *philosophes*, on the other hand, were very much concerned with what *ought* to be, and they hoped that the science of man would provide them with as complete assurance about what ought to be as the natural sciences provided about what is. The *philosophes* seem to have confused the law of nature, the standard of right conduct for rational men, with scientific natural law, the uniformities actually observed in the behavior of things.

As a matter of habit the *philosophes* did not distinguish sharply between "ought" and "is," between value and fact, because they did not see nature as merely what happens to be or what happens to happen. They regarded it rather as the ground and source of all demonstrable truth, the truth about man and his moral and intellectual world as well as about the physical world. For them the underlying laws of human conduct guiding men in the way they should go were as natural, as rooted in nature, as the laws that governed the movement of the planets. The laws of nature were all of one piece, descriptive as well as prescriptive. By the same token, human regulations were mere conventions and had no standing except insofar as they conformed to the laws of nature.

The working out of the laws of motion during the Scientific Revolution had depended on the discovery of uniform and universal traits common to every particle of matter. Only on the basis of such common traits could general laws applicable to all matter be discovered. The Newtonian traits of matter were density and extension—that is, occupation of space. To deal with man scientifically as Newton had dealt with matter, the *philosophes* had to find a similar set of common traits in humanity. They believed that these common traits were the capacity to receive sense impressions from the external world, reason, and self-interest (or self-love or the desire for self-preservation). Since all men possessed these three basic natural traits, men were by nature equal. Moreover, these equal men, in order to preserve themselves, to follow their own interests according to the laws of their nature, had to be free to do what their reason told them was necessary. To deprive men of their liberty or of their property, like depriving them of their lives, was to take from them the means of self-preservation that naturally belonged to them and that were essential to their happiness. Liberty and property were therefore natural rights, and constraint was unnatural. Men were not only by nature equal; they were also, as Thomas Jefferson put it, "endowed by their Creator with certain unalienable [that is, natural] Rights, that among these are Life, Liberty, and the pursuit of Happiness." Those French disciples of the *philosophes* who made the French Revolution said, in the Declaration of the Rights of Man, "The end of all political associations is the preservation of the natural and imprescriptible rights of man; and these rights are Liberty, Property, Security, and Resistance of Oppression." On the basis of such fundamental ideas, the *philosophes* set out to construct a science of man modeled on Newton's mechanics.

John Locke strongly influenced American political theory as expressed in the Declaration of Independence and the Constitution. He also drafted a scheme of government (unused) for the Carolina Colony's proprietors.

The political science of the Enlightenment began with a conception of man endowed by nature with reason and self-interest (or desire for happiness) and with the natural rights of liberty and property. These rights being his by the law of nature, which was above the law of the state, no political authority could rightfully deprive him of them. Government was simply a mechanism to which men submitted because it protected their natural rights better than they, acting individually, could protect them. "To secure these rights, Governments are instituted among Men, deriving their just powers from the consent of the governed," Jefferson wrote. Government existed to protect natural rights and for no other end. At the basis of all government lay the contract in which the governors guaranteed the governed to safeguard those rights. A government that aimed to do more than preserve individual liberties exceeded its rightful authority. Such a government, moreover, was dangerous, since it acted as if it knew better than the individual himself what would make him happy.

The *philosophes* rejected the notion that the state could do better for the individual than the enlightened individual, rationally pursuing his own interests,

William Hogarth's Election Entertainment *(1754) is a savage indictment of the notoriously corrupt English electoral system of the period.*

could do for himself. For them, "that government is best which governs least," in Locke's words. Of course, actual governments might in fact exercise powers not derived from the consent of the governed and might use those powers to deprive men of their natural rights, but no such exercise of power could ever be right. It constituted a breach of the contract that was the very foundation of government and transformed the ruler into a tyrant. In such a case, the citizens were no longer bound to the agreement by which they subjected themselves to political command. They had a right to rebel against the government and to establish another more regardful of its function of protecting the natural rights of the individual. "Whenever any Form of Government becomes destructive of these ends," Jefferson wrote, "it is the Right of the People to alter or to abolish it, and to institute new Government. . . ."

These notions about politics received their earliest systematic exposition from the English philosopher John Locke (1632–1704) in his *Second Treatise on Civil Government*. Locke was an admirer of Newton and the new science. He was also a Whig and an opponent of the theory of divine right despotism of which the Stuart kings were feeble proponents. The *Second Treatise*, his major effort in political speculation, most of it written about 1680, served to justify the English Revolution of 1688. The political arrangements of the Revolution Settlement— religious toleration, civil liberty, minimum government—received in advance a reasoned foundation from Locke, and in the century that followed they enjoyed among enlightened men the popularity that came of being desired along with the prestige that came from being deemed scientific. In the generalized form that Locke gave them, they became the underlying political principles of the *philosophes* for several generations.

What specific machinery of government could best secure for men the individual liberty, toleration, and security of person and property that were their natural rights? For the English the problem seemed to be solved after the Revolution of 1688. The government that secured men's natural rights was the government they happened to have. The Revolution Settlement was a great deal more libertarian than the legislation connected with it would indicate. No law proclaimed the freedom to publish books without censorship, but the government ceased to require a license for printing, and freedom to publish followed. A similar course of events later made available to the public the hitherto secret deliberations of Parliament. An act of Parliament guaranteed religious toleration to Protestant dissenters from the established church and, although a fairly fierce set of laws against Roman Catholics remained on the statute books, Catholics were not seriously harassed for attending mass. Active persecution of deviation from religious orthodoxy practically came to an end.

The peculiar institutions of the English, however, did not easily lend themselves to imitation. In the first place, they were in a considerable state of flux throughout the eighteenth century. In the second place, up to nearly the end of that century the English ruling classes themselves do not appear to have figured out how the institutions they controlled managed to function. And, finally, it is doubtful whether the queer English political apparatus—made up of rotten boroughs,° large-scale political corruption, and the complicated maneuvers of greedy parliamentary factions for a place at the public trough—would have commended itself to zealous Continental reformers, even if they had understood how it worked. They wanted liberty English style, without the encumbrances which accompanied that liberty.

The earliest French *philosophes* had spread the good word about English liberty in their own land where liberty tended to be repressed by both church and state. In 1733, in his *Philosophical Letters on the English*, France's leading playwright, François Voltaire (1694–1778), celebrated Newton's science of nature, Locke's science of man, and the liberty, toleration, and dedication to business of Englishmen. His contemporary, the French lawyer and political philosopher Baron de Montesquieu (1689–1755), author of a large and thoughtful study of politics called *The Spirit of the Laws* (1748), also admired the results the English achieved, although he did not have entirely accurate notions about the institutions that brought them about. Voltaire's admiration for England did not prevent him, however, from accommodating himself for a while to the foggy and erratic absolutism of Louis XV and, later, to the quite clear-cut despotism of Frederick the Great of Prussia, who for several years kept him at his court. And Montesquieu was too cautious and too deeply impressed by the diversity in human arrangements that geography and time produced to take much stock in the bodily transplantation of institutions from one land to another. When, in *The Spirit of the Laws*, he tried to discover the best course for the French, he did not propose that they imitate the English. As befitted a former distinguished judge in the *parlement* of Bordeaux, he put his faith in the ancient institutions of the French monarchy and intimated that the best hope for liberty

° Boroughs with miniscule populations that by tradition enjoyed parliamentary representation at the expense of newer, more heavily populated districts.

in France lay in a revival and strengthening of the nobility, the clergy, and the great courts.

To most of the French *philosophes*, Montesquieu's solution was quite unacceptable. They were convinced of the natural equality of man, and they did not believe that true liberty stood to gain much from the special privileges of an anti-rationalist church, an incompetent aristocracy, and an entrenched judicial caste that occasionally consigned the free-thinking works of enlightened men to the fire. In fact, despite their splendid confidence in the possibility of discovering a science of man, the French *philosophes*, from whom all enlightened leaders of Continental thought took their cue, proposed few practical measures to acquire or guarantee that freedom for which their thought was supposed to be a scientific foundation. Most of the leaders of the Enlightenment on the European mainland put their hope in good government and good laws and their faith in their ability to convert monarchs into legislative liberators of their own subjects. They were inclined to assent to Alexander Pope's doctrine:

> For Forms of Government let fools contest;
> Whate'er is best administer'd is best.

Robert Turgot, sculpted by Houdon.

One element of Locke's theory vanished almost completely from the political thinking of his French disciples, at least up to the time of the American War of Independence. Consistent with his contract theory of the basis of political authority, Locke recognized in the people a right to resist a ruler who broke the contract—in effect, a right of rebellion. The Continental *philosophes*, however, shied away from a theory that would alienate the very rulers through whose power they hoped to achieve an orderly and rational reform of state and society. Moreover, in a state ruled by an absolute monarch, it was not safe to defend the right of revolution, whatever one's sentiments might be. But the *philosophes* had more than mere prudential motives for being averse to rebellion: they distrusted the people, the masses. The masses were, no doubt, potentially good because they were men, and men were naturally good. Actually, however, they were ignorant, superstitious, brutal, and stupid. Only the enlightened few could lead the many out of the darkness in which they had dwelt for centuries.

A group of French writers who put their faith in the possibility of harmonizing despotism and liberty pioneered the establishment of the one science of man to which the Enlightenment made a decisive and permanent contribution. The science was economics, the science of wealth. The pioneers were called physiocrats, that is, believers in the rule of nature. Of all the writers of the age of reason they were the most dogmatic. True law for them was natural law "instituted by the Supreme Being, immutable and unbreakable. All these laws exist eternally and implicitly in the Code of Nature. They are general and absolute, never allowing exception or change." The duty of the ruler is to make the eternal natural law the actual law of his land.

The fundamental principle of the physiocrats was that land and land alone was the source of riches and agriculture the only productive activity. From this assumption they drew the inference that, since other activities produced no net gain, such activities should not be regulated or taxed. The major achievement of the physiocrats was to give primary emphasis to production. They moved away from the mercantilist point of view with its heavy emphasis on foreign commerce and the balance of trade as the gauge of national wealth and put foreign trade in its proper perspective in relation to domestic trade. The physiocrats François Quesnay (1694–1774), Robert Turgot (1727–1781), and Pierre Samuel du Pont de Nemours (1739–1817), convinced that government intervention along mercantilist lines impeded healthy economic growth, coined the phrase that was shortly to become the all but universal watchword and war cry of economic individualism: *Laissez faire, laissez passer"* ("Let men act freely, let goods move freely").

A man of far more penetrating economic insight than the physiocrats was the Scottish moral philosopher Adam Smith (1723–1790), whose systematic investigation of the problem of riches, incorporated into his great treatise *The Wealth of Nations* (1776), laid the foundations of modern economic thought. Smith came nearer than any writer of the age of reason to achieving a Newtonian science in the realm of human affairs. One of the traits that distinguishes men from other creatures, Smith pointed out, is their "propensity to truck, barter and exchange." Alone among animals and on the basis of rational calculation, men will trade what they have and do not want for what they want and do not have. Allow each individual to dispose of his resources as he wills, said Smith, and following the course of rational self-interest he will seek the best deal he can get for them, the best price they will yield him. He will find that best price where the supply of the resources he has to sell is shortest, and he will find that the supply is shortest where demand is greatest. If people do not have enough of what they want, they suffer privation; that is, they are unhappy. If there is no interference with the market, however, the demand created by their wants will soon diminish their unhappiness: attracted by the high price created by this demand, men will offer more and more resources—capital, labor, land—to satisfy these wants. Then, as their needs become increasingly satisfied through increased production, people come to want less of that article and more of something else. As the demand for the first article drops, the price men will pay for resources to make it will also drop. The price for resources to make things people now want correspondingly rises and, always guided by their natural propensity to trade and by rational self-interest, those with resources will turn them to making what now brings the best price.

Smith had worked out something like a Newtonian science of man. Through its effect on prices, he said, the single law of supply and demand automatically tends *at every moment* to direct all resources precisely to the uses in which they will most contribute to human happiness—or, as economists say nowadays, in which they will "maximize utilities." Newton said that density and extension, operated on by the law of gravitation, produces a self-regulating cosmic system. Smith said that the propensity to trade and self-interest, operated on by the law of supply and demand, produces a self-regulating economic system. The new economic science had built into it that ability to quantify, to use number in its generalizations, that is characteristic of modern physical science. It could quantify market value just as physics could quantify distance or mass. Its instrument of measurement was price in dollars or pounds or rubles. To the extent that material goods make for happiness, the free, "natural," self-regulating economic system described by Adam Smith was the best system according to the *philosophes'*

BULLOZ

Baron de Montesquieu, by Lemoyne.

science of man, since it best provides man with what he wants when he wants it. According to Smith, the whole vast daily range of human activity devoted to the production of goods, their transportation, and their marketing proceeds without human interference or regulation as if guided by an invisible hand to the goal that is best for all. Any interference with it by anyone at all can diminish, but cannot increase, its capacity to contribute to human happiness. The new science of economics thus stood opposed to the older economic conceptions of mercantilism, and Adam Smith devoted a long section of *The Wealth of Nations* to a sharp criticism of the mercantile system.

Progress and Perfectibility   As the men of the Enlightenment took a fresh look at man's nature and found it good, so they also took a new look at man's destiny on earth and found it most hopeful. They believed that the circumstances of man's life had continuously been getting better, and that mankind could and would go on improving it without limit. Here again they found support in John Locke. He had held that there are no ideas that are not derived from experience, that the mind at birth is a blank sheet of paper that gradually acquires its content from the impressions that the outside world stamps on it by way of the senses. But if this is the case, the mind is malleable. See to it that men receive the right impressions from the world, enlighten their minds with the correct experiences, and there need be no limit to the improvement of humankind. Let man's mind be instructed in the ways of rational self-interest, and gradually all the bad irrationalities of his present way of life will be shorn off, and he will steadily climb toward perfection.

At the same time that Locke was saying that humanity could be indefinitely improved, other writers were working out a new theory of history that provided support for Locke's optimism. This theory, which emerged from the sixteenth to the eighteenth centuries, completely revised Western man's view of the human past. It was the theory of progress.

The Christian view of history, generally accepted in the Western world for more than a thousand years before the sixteenth century, took a rather uncheerful view of man's past on earth. According to that view, man started at the very height of bliss in the earthly paradise—Eden. Thence he had plummeted down through sin to live in pain and suffer death. During his alienation from God he had built up four empires—the Babylonian, the Assyrian, the Persian, and the Roman. By Divine Providence these empires had been permitted to attain great power on earth, but because they were rooted in sin they were doomed ultimately to destruction. Three of these monarchies had already vanished. When the last vestige of the fourth—the Roman—was destroyed, the reign of the Antichrist would come. After the rule of Antichrist, the Messiah would return, and the fifth monarchy, the reign of Christ on earth, would begin. Although many men had come to doubt and even reject this view of history, especially since the Renaissance, no general scheme or philosophy of history had been proposed to take its place, or at least none that captured the imagination of Western man.

The new view of history stood in marked contrast to the Christian theory. It was most optimistic about the potentialities of man for future improvement. Its proponents created a foundation for their optimism by developing the idea that the whole past of mankind was marked by an ascent, by a movement upward, by progress. To work out the underlying scheme of the new history, the *philosophes* drew on many sources and pulled together ideas that lay scattered through the work of many sixteenth- and seventeenth-century writers. The key ideas of the intellectual leaders of the Enlightenment as to the nature and the course of history are as follows:

First, the history of man is natural. Its transformations and changes are therefore to be explained through the operation of natural forces. It is not necessary to resort to Divine Providence to explain the course of events or any single event, as the Christian view of history frequently did. (The concept of the naturalness of history is, of course, compatible with any belief concerning the direction of historical change. The pattern, if any, that natural forces impose on history may be upward, or downward, or irregular, or even cyclical.) This purely natural view of history cannot be squared with the Christian view that in miraculous acts Divine Providence has broken into and altered the natural course of human events.

Second, there are natural laws of history which can be discovered by examining history itself. Since history is part of nature, and since the rule of law in nature has been revealed to the scientists who studied nature, it is to be supposed that the study of history must also reveal the laws of its development.

Third, man's lot on earth can be improved and his happiness increased by the advance of knowledge. Already new knowledge enabled him to control nature in some measure and to turn it to his uses. The mariner's compass extended man's power over the seas and allowed him to engage in trade and move goods to distant markets with increased security. The invention of printing brought to millions an opportunity to escape from the terrible unhappiness that goes with ignorance, superstition, and error. What had already been achieved held forth the promise of yet greater achievement in the future.

Fourth, history provides positive concrete evidence of advances in the things men know. The development of the natural sciences from the sixteenth to the eighteenth centuries offered sure proof of this. Here the superiority of the Enlightenment to all earlier times was beyond doubt, the *philosophes* maintained. Thousands of quite ordinary eighteenth-century men had a clearer notion of the actual operations of nature and of the laws of the universe than the great sages of antiquity had had. And future generations would know yet more, since the methods of the scientists opened an endless prospect for the advancement of learning.

Fifth, history also provides evidence of improvement in the things men do and the way they do them. The mechanical arts of eighteenth-century Europe were manifestly superior to what they were in any previous era of human history, and were still advancing. The textile industry and agriculture had improved their methods and increased their output. Productive processes of all kinds were simplified and accelerated by new tools and new methods. The proliferation of books made possible by the printing press in effect ruled out the chance that advances in science and technology might be lost. The improvement in technology, moreover, had been in process long before the Scientific Revolution. Thus, in this sphere at least, the whole of human history was marked by progress.

Sixth, men's natural abilities are not declining. They are always and everywhere the same. And, since science and technology are cumulative, the constant application of these natural abilities must necessarily result in a continuous advance in mankind's knowledge and the constant improvement of man's condition.

Seventh, in this latest and most glorious age of man, two new aspects of progress had been ensured. With the discovery of the new sciences of man—the true moral sciences—man's progress in virtue, wisdom, and enlightenment was made certain. This was most important, for in earlier times it had not been so. Periods of virtue and reason, such as classical antiquity, had been followed by long ages of ignorance, superstition, and darkness. Such was "the Gothic Age," what we call the Middle Ages, dominated by priests and nobles, which men of the Enlightenment viewed with detestation. Now men might look forward with confidence to a continual accretion and extension of man's moral growth. New heights would be reached with new discoveries in the moral sciences, and these discoveries would become accessible to more men through the spread of education and through geographical discoveries that guaranteed that men everywhere would eventually be bathed in the new moral illumination emanating from Paris, the City of Light.

Such were the ideas about the course of history that came to be held generally by the leaders of the Enlightenment. Turgot first gave them effective formulation in 1750 in a discourse delivered in—of all places—the University of Paris, the heart of darkness and Catholic orthodoxy, whose faculty was much given to burning the books of *philosophes* less temperate than he in their modes of expression. The acceptance of the idea of progress received a sort of symbolic stamp in 1778 when the old high priest of the Enlightenment, Voltaire, returning to Paris for the first time in years from self-imposed exile, kissed and wept over the hands of Turgot, whose recent attempts to bring the light of reason to the service of the French monarchy had resulted only in his prompt dismissal from office. The enormous force of the new idea of progress received its most dramatic exemplifications, however, from the man who most systematically formulated it, and in the very act of formulating it. The Marquis of Condorcet, Turgot's disciple, had always believed in progress, but he did not get around to a full exposition of his belief until 1793. Then the member of a revolutionary faction dislodged from power in France, under threat of death and in hiding from the revolutionary faction that had seized power, with a faith that nevertheless did not falter, he wrote the classical statement of the new confidence in humanity's capacity for the unlimited improvement of its own condition, the *Sketch of a Historical Tableau of the Progress of the Human Spirit*.

Of the conceptions that the Enlightenment engendered, that of progress was perhaps the most subversive in that it was radically incompatible with the framework within which Western men had hitherto ordered their views of man and his relation to society and the cosmos. In effect it replaced the great Chain of Created Being with the great Chain of Creative Becoming. We have already seen how the former conception built a bias against change into the habits of thought of the West. This of course did not prevent change from taking place; it did prevent men from planning and undertaking change with a view to the continuous improvement of the human condition. Change itself had been seen not in terms of improvement but as the restoration of divinely instituted order, which was always in danger and frequently in disrepair as a result of human wickedness. For this bias against change the idea of progress substituted a powerful incentive in favor of change. It urged men to action rather than to patience, to the assumption of control over their own destinies instead of the acceptance of things as they were, and it transformed discontent with things as they were from a vice to a virtue. It thus introduced a revolutionary leaven into the life of the Western world which from that day to this has never ceased to work, which spread with Western civilization until now, one way or another, it produces its ferment in all the corners of the earth.

When all the ideas and theories of the Enlightenment were put together, they led the *philosophes* to the following conclusions: (1) That the human past was characterized by an upward movement, by progress; (2) that this progress was not casual or accidental but embedded in the very nature of things, a law of history; (3) that, therefore, progress would continue indefinitely into the future; and (4) that progress was in the direction of a constant growth in human happiness and well-being, achieved through the enlightenment of men's minds and the improvement of the material conditions of life. By combining Locke's conception of the malleability of man's mind with the conception of the natural upward development of man in history, the *philosophes* completed their theory of the nature of man with a glowing vision of his high destiny. This vision, despite frightful setbacks and many transformations, still powerfully affects human thought and human action.

Enlightenment, Evil, and Convention

As we have seen, writers imbued with the spirit of the Enlightenment propounded doctrines about the nature of man and of the good society that were supposed to be in harmony with the teachings of the new physical sciences. These doctrines were themselves supposed to be sciences of man and of society. There was, however, a very significant difference between the natural laws of Newtonian physical science and the natural laws of the human sciences of the *philosophes*. Every individual bit of matter did in fact conform in its behavior to Newton's laws, and this could be verified by observation, but not every individual bit of humanity conformed to the natural laws of the *philosophes*, and this could also be verified by observation. In the whole universe, it appeared, only man, endowed with reason, did not uniformly follow the rational laws that a beneficent nature laid down for his welfare. Thus, in a new setting, the *philosophes* had to face an old, old problem—the problem of evil. And they had to face it with one hand tied, as it were, for in throwing orthodox Christianity overboard the *philosophes* also had disposed of the devil and the sinfulness of man. They no longer believed that a force for evil, personified in Christian tradition as Satan, operated powerfully among created things and on man. Nor did they believe that man was possessed by an inclination toward evil, called sin, that might be set right by God's grace but never by man's unaided nature. As we have seen, most *philosophes* were sure that by nature men were rational and good.

Then why were men, born with a capacity for reason, everywhere enmeshed in ignorance and superstition? Why were men, born free, everywhere in chains? Why were men, naturally good, everywhere so busy cutting one another's

The French court often exhibited the artifice condemned by the philosophes. *This grandiose barque, for example, was built especially for an entertainment staged for Louis XV.*

throats? Why were men, born for happiness, everywhere so miserable? Having rejected sin and Satan as possible explanations for brutality and meanness, the *philosophes* had to find some alternative explanation for the perennial evil doings of mankind, recorded in history and enacted before their own eyes. They found it in artifice, convention, and custom. The artificial and the conventional were the opposite of the natural; they were against nature. The customary was the opposite of the rational; it was against reason. The whole fabric of eighteenth-century society, as the *philosophes* viewed it, was one rotting mass of artifice, convention, and custom. This endless affront to nature and reason endured, however, because some men—and those the most powerful—benefited from its perpetuation.

Most men are ignorant, enslaved, and wretched, the *philosophes* said, because it is in the interests of a few men to keep them in this deplorable condition, to withhold from them the freedom, happiness, and enlightenment that is their natural and lawful birthright. To discover the villains of the piece it was necessary only to seek for those who gained by convention and exploitation, those whose power and riches would be imperiled by the progress of mankind toward perfection and who therefore sought to block that progress by every means at their disposal. The Continental *philosophes* had no difficulty in discovering the villains they sought. Very few of them had completely escaped from the unfavorable attentions of the established religious and civil powers. Their works were denounced from the pulpit, put on the Index by the Church, and burned by the common hangman at the behest of the law courts. The *philosophes* lived in fear of arrest, and some of them actually suffered exile or imprisonment because of what they had written. The villains, then, were the powers that be, the sinister interests that fed and fattened on the ignorance and servitude of humanity.

All churches were sinister interests, and, because it was the most powerful, the Roman Catholic Church was the most sinister. To many of the *philosophes*, the Church was the very symbol of opposition to progress. They regarded it as a consciously fraudulent corporation using craft—priestcraft—to impose on men's gullibility and suppressing by force anyone who refused to be gulled. In the "new history" of the Enlightenment, the Middle Ages become the Dark Ages, when the black pall of priestcraft stifled the light of reason. And although the *philosophes* believed that the power of the Church had been crumbling ever since the Renaissance, it was still rich and still established by law. It still claimed sole possession of the Final Truth, a truth antagonistic to the one the *philosophes* thought they had discovered. Worst of all, it still controlled two great channels of communication, the schools and the pulpits. Into these channels it poured, according to the enlightened, the falsehood and mumbo jumbo that kept mankind ignorant and insensible.

The second root of evil, an inveterate impediment to the course of nature, progress, reason, and reform, was the entire corporate order of society, rooted as it was in ancient and wholly irrational law and custom. To such questions as "Why should some men enjoy exemptions from taxes that others have to pay?" or "Why should guild members be allowed to practice a trade from which non-members are excluded?" or "Why should one social class have access to positions and privileges from which another social class in barred?" the answers seemed to be that such arrangements were sanctioned by immemorial custom, and that people allotted privileges by custom and the chances of birth were determined to hang on to their unnatural advantages. From the dreary and expensive frivolities of the court aristocracy, through the unmerited tax exemptions of certain provinces, to the unwarranted monopolies of local guilds, the French *philosophes* saw the social system of the society they lived in as an irrational mess.

The third powerful sinister interest was the state, which in most Continental countries was a bureaucratic monarchical absolutism overlaying the political wreckage of the institutions of the Middle Ages and the new monarchy. Concerning the state, the *philosophes* were not so single-minded as they were concerning the Church. Many of them favored the utter destruction of the Church, which in their eyes had no reasonable right to exist at all, but few favored the destruction of the state—a necessary evil perhaps, but necessary still in a world not yet perfect. Moreover, the *philosophes* knew that to win the Church to their side was manifestly impossible, because the Church was founded on truth, just as the Enlightenment was founded on truth, and between a truth in the saddle and a quite different truth trying to get into the saddle there could be no compromise. But they believed that it might be possible to win over the state in the person of the king, because the state was founded on power and was therefore likely to support the truth that happened to be most favorable to its own interests. Besides, the interests of the king were by no means so clearly opposed to the Enlightenment as were the interests of the Church. The *philosophes* were convinced that only good laws were required to make good and happy men, and absolute sovereigns had the power to make good laws. During most of the eighteenth century, the *philosophes* put their faith in winning monarchs to their way of thinking.

8

⸺⊷◉⊶⸺

The Enlightenment
in Practice

Although the Enlightenment took its main inspiration from the new science, and although the *philosophes* thought of their work as scientifically sound, in fact their actual procedures and conclusions did not follow the pattern of the new science at all. As we noted in Chapter 7, scientists deal with things as they are but the *philosophes* were primarily concerned with things as they ought to be. It is possible to investigate convention and rationality as the physicist investigates gravitation—in a completely disengaged way, without making moral judgments—but the *philosophes* chose not to be disengaged. They were interested only incidentally in how men act and why they act that way. Primarily, they wanted to teach and persuade men to act in a fashion as orderly and rational as the Newtonian world machine acts and to think as freely, boldly, and clearly about all things as Newton had thought about motion. They were less concerned to understand men than to emancipate mankind. For them, science was no mere technique for knowing, but an ideal for living, a guide to lead men out of ignorance and bondage. Where the seventeenth-century scientists sought to communicate with and persuade each other by private correspondence and learned treatises, the *philosophes* wanted to tell and teach the world. Above all, they were propagandists, perhaps the most effective band of propagandists the world has ever known.

The force of the propaganda of the Enlightenment was the more remarkable because, as we have seen, the two traditional instruments for disseminating ideas —the pulpit and the school—were in the hands of its most unrelenting enemy, the Church. As a means for spreading their ideas, the *philosophes* were practically confined to private conversation and the printed word. Moreover, in most of Europe their publications encountered a persistent though inefficient censorship, and they themselves faced the threat, rather capriciously enforced, of imprisonment.

By word of mouth they were able to advance their views among the great and important of Europe. In the eighteenth century the center of intellectual fashion shifted from Versailles back to Paris. The court of Louis XV was simultaneously dull and depraved, but the salons—the drawing rooms—of a dozen Parisian hostesses were centers of a lively and sophisticated society. There the most intelligent and eminent Frenchmen from the law courts, the world of finance, the royal administration, even some from the army and the Church, gathered to chat informally for hours on end. Eminent foreigners from every part of Europe imbibed the heady talk of the new age at its very source and carried it back to their homelands. The intellectual tone of the most important and influential salons was set by the literary lions of the Enlightenment. In one salon Louis's chief minister and several of his secretaries of state might rub shoulders with the erudite Baron de Montesquieu, whose *Lettres Persanes*, satirizing European society, had referred to the Pope as "that old idol to whom we offer incense out

The prototype of the so-called enlightened despot was Frederick the Great of Prussia. Frederick refused to sit for artists after he ascended the throne; Antoine Pesne painted him when he was crown prince in 1739, one of Frederick's rare portraits from life.

of habit." In another, one might see Bernard de Fontenelle, the secretary of the Academy of Sciences and a great popularizer of the dazzling achievements of the new natural philosophy, or Viscount Bolingbroke, the English politician and man of letters, a fluent if shallow discourser on the uses of history and the duties of a patriot king. Elsewhere, two eminent mathematicians might be holding forth in the same house—Pierre de Maupertuis and Jean d'Alembert, who wrote one of the most clear-cut and complete expositions of the claims, concepts, and hopes of the age of reason. And sooner or later one would be sure to run into Baron Melchior von Grimm, the slightly doubting apostle of the Enlightenment to Eastern Europe, whose correspondence kept numerous intellectually curious monarchs east of the Rhine and as far off as Russia abreast of the latest developments of thought in the City of Light.

Word of mouth, however, was perishable. The printed word endured longer, spread farther, and made a deeper impression. Of words the *philosophes* were supreme masters. Most of them were prolific writers, and the best of them produced literary masterpieces. Believing the truth was simple, they expressed it simply in words that transmitted and did not veil their thoughts. Thus Fontenelle (1657–1757), whose long activity spanned the whole period from the publication of Newton's *Principia* and Locke's *Civil Government* to the triumph of the Enlightenment in intellectual circles, by his skill at popularization brought the new sciences within reach of all literate Frenchmen and the many literate Europeans who knew French. Edward Gibbon (1737–1794), author of *The History of the Decline and Fall of the Roman Empire*, delighted lovers of history, wit, and fine prose by tracing the collapse of Roman dominion to the ravages of Christian superstition in sentences majestic but never difficult. In *The Wealth of Nations* Adam Smith laid the foundations of economic science with a felicity of expression and a wry humor that few economists since have displayed. And in philosophical treatises, dialogues, and essays, David Hume quietly cut away at all the most cherished assumptions of the *philosophes* themselves in language so exactly like theirs that for a long while no one except a Prussian professor, Immanuel Kant, fully grasped what he was up to. But of all the penmen of the Enlightenment, the most persistent and effective in their propaganda were two Frenchmen, Voltaire and Diderot.

Voltaire, born François Marie Arouet in 1694, was the son of a notary. Educated in a Jesuit college, he had already made himself a great name as a dramatist when an indiscretion, followed by an altercation with a nobleman, brought him imprisonment in the Bastille. After his release he went to England, where Bolingbroke, the leader of the Tory party, opened the English world of letters to him. On his return to France his *Philosophical Letters on the English* launched him on his career as an intellectual Jack-of-all-trades. Within the next three decades he became *the* literary figure of his age, holding a position in the world of letters such as no man had enjoyed since the sixteenth-century humanist Desiderius Erasmus.

Voltaire shared most of the common beliefs and enthusiasms of the age of reason, and he directed his attack on the old order at its most vulnerable point: the repressive power of the Church in an era increasingly attached to the principle of free inquiry and free discussion. Despite the growth of sentiment against persecution, the Church did not openly withdraw from its position that forceful repression was a proper way to deal with heresy. As late as 1767, the Catholic theological faculty of Paris proclaimed it to be the duty of the state to lend its sword to the repression of dissent, and, although the defense of orthodoxy had grown haphazard and disorganized, in the 1760s French Protestant ministers were still being executed for serving their faithful congregations. Voltaire waged a relentless war of satire, ridicule, and invective against the Church, the last refuge of religious intolerance. He took up the defense of men whose chances for a fair trial were endangered by their heretical views. A tireless worker who often put in a twenty-hour day in study and writing, he turned out an endless flow of poems, satirical tales, plays, essays, diatribes, histories, critical works, and popularizations of science. In 1778 his bust was crowned at the Comédie Française, the principal theater of France, while from a loge seat he observed his own transfiguration from a human being into an institution. For fifty years, over and over again in a thousand ways, he recited the same message: "*Écrasez l'infâme*" ("Crush the infamous thing"). The "infamous thing" was the Church. All France, all Europe heard the message.

As indefatigable as Voltaire was Denis Diderot (1713–1784). The well-educated son of a rich cutler, Diderot was a man of insatiable curiosity who wrote on dozens of subjects with an intellect less facile but more penetrating than Vol-

The Frenchman J. B. de Troy portrayed the enlightened eighteenth-century family, gathered in their drawing room to hear Molière read aloud.

taire's; he possessed at once greater range and deeper insight. His most brilliant achievement was the task to which he gave over twenty-five years of his life—the editing of the famous *Encyclopédie*. Struggling on the one hand with censorship and on the other with as truculent a group of contributors as an editor ever had to cope with, Diderot finally won through. The first volume appeared in 1751 and the last in 1772. In seventeen volumes of text and eleven of illustrations, Diderot assembled the efforts of the ablest minds of his day and made available to the Western world the full panorama of the intellectual achievement of modern science, the material advance of industrial technology, and the reorientation of thought that was eroding the foundations of the old order in the West.

The Enlightenment's Spread and Impact

The Enlightenment was a cosmopolitan movement, contemptuous of national boundaries. Writers—"citizens of the Republic of Letters"—are frequently cosmopolitan in outlook, and the *philosophes* were especially so because of their views on the essential unity and equality of mankind. But despite the aspirations of the Enlightenment to universality, much of its initial inspiration came from England, its language and spirit were predominantly French, and in the eighteenth century its impact was felt only among those who belonged to the Western tradition. By the 1770s to be "enlightened" was to be in the intellectual swim throughout the Western world. The *philosophes* were held in an esteem such as no group of literary figures had enjoyed since the days of the humanists, and it was a backward princeling indeed who did not provide one or two of them bed, board, and pension to tutor his children and to foster in him the illusion that he, too, was enlightened.

The intensity of the Enlightenment's impact, however, varied with geographical or cultural proximity to the Anglo-French center, being greater in northern Italy and in the American colonies of England, for example, than in Poland. In the morass of illiteracy and ignorance that was Russia and in the poor, polyglot sprawl of the Hapsburg holdings in Central Europe, the Enlightenment could not strike deep roots. In such lands it stirred a few of the intellectual élite and promoted the conviction, already well established, that modern science was a good thing or, at least, a sound small-scale investment.

The lands of its greatest triumph remained the lands of its birth—England and France. Yet even here there was a big difference—the difference between the smug satisfaction derived from having a treasure that others want and the longing for that treasure when it is just out of reach. England had much of what the *philosophes* wanted for mankind at large. The "natural rights" to life, liberty, and property had been built into the Revolution Settlement or were allowed to become standard practice through default of government action. Persecution for religious opinion had practically ceased, and government regulation of either opinion or economic activity was out of the question in a land where the police operated sluggishly through a decentralized amateur administration that had undergone no radical alteration in four hundred years.

It was France, therefore, that felt the full force of the current of new ideas. There, an increasingly prosperous middle class of lawyers, merchants, and industrialists combined with an increasingly skeptical and free-thinking aristocracy and clergy to provide the *philosophes* with a literate audience that shared their

An engraving dating from about 1745 shows an oath taken at swordpoint in a Freemason lodge. Other shrouded candidates await the oath at left.

discontent with things as they were. The light from the capital shone on the provincial towns. The larger ones had their *académies*, which offered prizes and published proceedings like the great *académies* in Paris. They also had their libraries, which subscribed to the better literary journals, purchased the newest books, and usually had a set of that enormous bible of the Enlightenment, the *Encyclopédie*. The town libraries also became centers of local literary societies, where provincials with a taste for letters or for talking discussed the pressing problems of the day. The narrow horizons and limited local interests that had hitherto enfeebled the political and social potency of the French middle class began to dissolve as, under the influence of their new intellectual culture, their minds came to encompass an interest in the welfare of mankind in general and of France in particular.

The same men who joined the literary clubs were also likely to join the Freemason movement. Secret Freemason lodges spread in an elaborate network over France. French Freemasonry was deist in outlook, and it provided men touched by the new thought an occasion for gathering together and reveling in their emancipation from what they regarded as outworn superstition. Many clergymen were infected by the new ideas of the Enlightenment too; and when between 1761 and 1764 Louis XV suppressed and expelled the Jesuits, a good deal of the pedagogy in France fell into the hands of churchmen half-*philosophes* at heart. Even in villages and manor houses far off the beaten track, the works of Voltaire and d'Alembert and Montesquieu found purchasers. In so unlikely a place as the small town of Périgord in southwestern France there were no less than forty subscribers to the *Encyclopédie*. Twenty-four of the subscribers were priests. Well might Voltaire exclaim, "The trade in thought has become prodigious." Western men, and especially Frenchmen, were ready to take a new look at themselves and the world they lived in, and Voltaire was among those who were providing the spectacles.

The Problem of Reform

The *philosophes* of the eighteenth century were convinced that a new social order, far better than the one in which they lived, was possible. They were sure, too, that they knew the fundamental rules for establishing such an order. Their mission was so boldly conceived that no one before in history had dared cherish so extravagant an aspiration. It was not merely to imagine a rational social and political order, not merely to persuade others of the excellence of that order, but to promote and achieve its actual realization. Never before had the intellectual leaders of a whole civilization seriously believed that by reason alone men could bring into being a good society. Only because the *philosophes* firmly believed in progress as the law of history and in the natural goodness of man could they dare to hope to create a wholly new society by an effort of the human mind.

The acute problem of the *philosophes* was to negotiate the abyss between thought and action, to translate what they believed should be into real changes in the real world. With an astounding confidence some of them produced works laying down the uniform doctrines of universal social betterment under such titles as *Leading Principles of a Constitutional Code for Any State*, convinced their teachings could be applied "to man in all climates and all lands."

One course was to win as many men as possible to their way of thinking, to flood with light a humanity whose mind was darkened by centuries of ignorance and superstition. Given the atomistic individualism of many of the *philosophes*, this was a sound way to proceed. To them the social whole was no more than the sum of the human particles comprising it, and if each of those particles moved in the course determined by enlightened self-interest, the whole society would necessarily mirror the perfection of its individual components. A second course was to enlist for the work of reform the men who had power in eighteenth-century Europe. To do so might immensely speed the job. The powers-that-be could both repress existing sinister interests (especially the Church) and provide through wise legislation the conditions under which enlightened self-interest would have free play. "If laws are simple and clear," said one *philosophe*, "there is no need for much study to make good men." In most of Europe the princes alone had the authority to make the laws that could cure the ills of society.

The leaders of the Enlightenment set out on both courses simultaneously. They conducted an elaborate propaganda campaign to convert anyone who would listen to them, but they directed a special campaign at Europe's secular princes in inverse proportion to the level of literacy and culture of their realms. In geographical terms, they relied on popular enlightenment less and less as the distance from England and France increased, trusting to it scarcely at all in Prussia, Russia, and the lands of the Hapsburgs. If the work was to be done at all in these lands, the ruler must do it.

Enlightened Despotism

To a surprising extent the *philosophes* did convert the European princes to their way of thinking. Enlightened despotism flourished not merely as a dream of social theorists but as an actual ideal of autocratic rulers, and many lands enjoyed the ministrations of would-be philosopher-kings. The high tide of the movement was in the 1770s when these new-style kings ruled in the great Eastern European monarchies of Russia, Austria, and Prussia as well as in Spain, Portugal, Piedmont, Tuscany, and a number of the principalities of western Germany.

In its power to propagate itself and to win the ostensible favor of the great, the Enlightenment was even more successful than the humanist movement of the Renaissance. The attraction the movement had for rulers is the more remarkable because the *philosophes* held in open contempt the established order of which the power of the princes was a part. They showed no great enthusiasm for monarchical institutions as such, and their essentially rational temper did not foster deep reverence for the "divinity [which] doth hedge a king." As time was to show, the Enlightenment fostered a spirit dangerous and hostile to monarchical authority. This spirit displayed itself in the French Revolution. Only the unfolding of events, however, made clear the peril, and until it did, the princes clearly found something congenial in the gospel of the *philosophes*.

Some part of the Enlightenment's attraction for European rulers lay in the fact that it was the fashion in France. It was the French *philosophes* who regained for their country that intellectual and cultural leadership that for a few decades at the turn of the seventeenth century had passed to England. The French tutors to whom many a European ruler entrusted the rearing of his offspring transmitted to their pupils the new spirit stirring in Paris. The sons and grandsons of kings who had imitated Louis XIV and savored the notion of divine right were thus systematically exposed to doctrines that held that kings justified their existence only if they ruled their subjects according to the precepts of nature as discovered by reason.

If the enlightened despots found the new rules of their craft in the writings of French theorists, they found the exemplar of enlightened despotism in Frederick the Great of Prussia, the first protégé of the *philosophes*. Frederick did quite well for himself in the arena of European politics. And he did it with no nonsense about divine right, practiced a religious toleration that only faintly masked his belief that all orthodoxies were stupid or fraudulent, and ruled without artificial pomp and ceremony and with a "natural" and simple industry that endeared him to the enlightened.

It was no accident that enlightened despotism got under way in Europe in the wake of Frederick's victories in the War of the Austrian Succession and reached full flood in the decade following the Seven Years' War. Frederick's military successes gave the new way in statecraft an impetus that no amount of philosophic argument could provide. They seemed to prove that enlightenment might increase the ability of a state to come up on the winning side in the European power game. Moreover, this documentation took place just at the time when the struggle for power in Europe was rising in intensity, when the decline of Poland and the Ottoman Empire was exciting the cupidity of Eastern European princes, and when Britain's maritime ascendancy was threatening all states that had overseas or Mediterranean interests. A philosophy carrying an increment of power in its baggage was thus doubly attractive to the Continental despots.

Enlightened despotism was in some respects more favorable than the concept of divine right to the current needs of European rulers. In the sixteenth century the theory of sovereignty had established the authority of kings to make law, and the theory of divine right had made them answerable only to God for their actions. While it had made the will of the rulers the source of law, the older theory strongly suggested that the ruler ought to will the preservation of things as they were and ought not to will their change. Custom, the way things had long been done, seemed natural—the local embodiment of that respect for natural law that the princes owed God. But behind custom were entrenched all those special privileges and vested interests that stood in the way of orderly administration, uniform laws, sound finance, and rational taxation and hampered the free action of the state by means of an incredibly tangled network of prescriptive rights, complicated rules, and archaic procedures. What the *philosophes* proposed was precisely the opposite of what the older concept of natural law implied. It was the rational, not the traditional, that was natural and right, they said, and there was nothing more rational than the subjection of all citizens to uniform laws, a uniform administration, a uniform and orderly fiscal system.

Thus the Enlightenment gave the rulers a line of radical action to follow that was far more favorable to the effective mobilization of political power and far more subversive of the existing order than the conservative course suggested by the older theory. Almost any vested interest, almost any institution held up to the pure light of reason was sure to appear full of flaws and unworthy to be maintained. Of course, absolute monarchy itself examined in that same merciless light appears just as unnatural and irrational as the rest, so that in the last analysis the Enlightenment was dangerous to the very kings who welcomed it. It took the French Revolution, however, to send the monarchs of Europe scurrying back to the safe snug harbor of legitimacy and divine right. Some, of course, did not have to scurry back because they had never ventured out. Neither Louis XV nor Louis XVI of France, at the very center of the Enlightenment, ever took a very firm stand either with respect to the Enlightenment or to despotism, and the kings of England could not have been enlightened despots because their subjects would not have allowed them to become despots at all.

Still, between the 1750s and the 1780s, the high noon of the Enlightenment, monarchs who more or less conformed to the pattern of the philosopher-king, or wanted to conform if it could conveniently be done, reigned over more than a dozen European states. They assumed the postures and adopted in varying measure policies dear to the hearts of the *philosophes*, and they hoped thereby to gain praise from posterity in the future and an accretion of power in the present. The most important lands whose rulers took on the trappings of enlightened despotism were Prussia under Frederick II (1740–1786), Russia under Catherine II (1762–1796), and Austria under Joseph II (1780–1790). These rulers, all extraordinary persons, played the game in very different ways with markedly divergent results.

Frederick the Great and Prussia   Frederick II of Prussia, successor to his drillmaster father Frederick William I, replaced the barracks-room spirit of the Prussian court with the intellectual atmosphere of a French salon. His tastes in literature and thought were those of the *philosophes*. A third-rate poet with a first-rate wit, he despised the boorishness of his backward kingdom. In the early part of his reign, Frederick was too hard pressed by the wars he fought to hold Silesia against a coalition that for a time included the three greatest Continental powers—Austria, France, and Russia—to apply the philosophy of the Enlightenment. Only when he had secured that rich territory could he turn his full attention to reforming his dominions. The remaining peaceful years of his reign provided him the time to vindicate by deeds the reputation for advanced ideas that he had achieved principally by words.

Frederick seems to have wished to live up to the role in which the *philosophes* had cast him. He considered himself not a monarch by divine right but merely the first servant of his country, and few lands have ever had such an assiduous and relentless first servant. He drove all Prussian officials hard but none so hard as himself. He delighted the intellectuals by his utter indifference to pomp and the Spartan simplicity of his life. In their eyes, his "natural," easy way contrasted favorably with the stiff formality of the monarchical style of Louis XIV.

One of Frederick's first concerns was the law and the judicial system. The codifications he fostered were not completed until after his death, but the courts that were to administer them were thoroughly reformed in his lifetime. Judges formerly paid by fees were put on adequate salaries, venality and corruption were reduced to a minimum, and Prussian justice became the most prompt and efficient in Europe. The law the courts applied also became increasingly enlightened. It showed a considerable respect for the "inalienable rights" of man—private property, liberty of conscience, and the civil rights of individuals.

In the field of economics, too, Frederick was a reformer of sorts. He was the greatest landlord in Prussia, and he used his position to modernize farming techniques and to improve stock breeds. As an enlightened despot Frederick was also interested in education. He improved the secondary-school system and tried to provide basic training in the primary schools. The intellectual pretensions of the new Prussia were crowned by Frederick's revival of the Berlin Academy, an institution for the advancement of knowledge that Frederick William I had found too elevated for his tastes. In his later years Frederick II diverted almost a quarter of the state budget into projects of social and economic amelioration and improvement.

And yet much that Frederick did and much that he did not do seems curiously at variance with the ideals of the Enlightenment. His commercial and industrial policy, for instance, was based on mercantilist principles rather than the principles of laissez faire. His tariff system tended to strangle foreign trade. Both mercantilism and the tariff were aimed at making Prussia self-sufficient, the latter by seeking to establish in Prussia industries that would reduce its need for imports. But Frederick did not allow the elements of production—capital, labor, and land—to allocate themselves freely according to their own best interests, as Adam Smith had proposed; rather, he drove the elements of production where he wanted them, using the tax system to supply him with the means of subsidizing and even of creating industries. Merchant and industrialist alike had to submit to the guidance of the bureaucracy. In short, the prototype of the enlightened despot, instead of conferring economic freedom on his subjects, guided and directed their economic activity with a firm, hard hand.

Even more significant, Frederick completely accepted the social order of his realm as he found it. If anything, he accentuated its peculiarities. The Prussian

Junkers were more firmly entrenched in their monopoly of military office at the end than at the beginning of his reign, not by accident but because he had willed it so. They continued to enjoy, in varying measure, tax privileges or outright tax exemption. The social system with its sharp class lines was made even more rigorous by precise legal definitions of status. Frederick's most conspicuous shortcoming as an enlightened ruler was in the matter of serfdom. As a good *philosophe*, he knew and said that serfdom was an abomination, but he did almost nothing about it. He did not even emancipate the serfs on his own estates, although he did give them some security of tenure. To the serfs of the *Junkers* he gave nothing at all, and on their backs fell the crushing burden of Prussian taxation. Frederick's program of primary education for the peasantry was designed mainly "to teach the youngsters religion and morals" in order to "keep them in the villages."

Finally, during Frederick's reign, his army and the taxes he exacted for its support nearly trebled, although Prussia's population only doubled. In fact, the more closely one examines Frederick's rule, the less he conforms to the *philosophe's* idea of an enlightened monarch and the more he looks like the true son of his father. The elaborate mercantilist policy, the grinding taxes, the tight bureaucratic controls on private activities, the complete deference to the interests of the *Junkers* had also been characteristic of the reign of Frederick William I. They were the consequences of the situation of Prussia in Europe. No land so small and poor could maintain its position as an independent great power in the eighteenth century except by straining all its resources to the utmost. The basis of Prussia's position as a great power was its army; the lifeblood of the army, Frederick thought, was a loyal and obedient officer corps that could only be recruited among the *Junkers*. The rigid bureaucracy, the taxes, the inflexible social system, the king towering over the whole watching every move and every penny—these were the stern necessities of a military state with no margin for waste. Having gambled on becoming a great power, Prussia could not relax at any point without risking degradation or even annihilation. In the last analysis, Frederick's pretensions to enlightenment could be effective only in the small interstices of the very tightly knit Prussian system he dared not change. To critics who felt that he fell short of their hopes, Frederick replied, in a way scarcely flattering to his countrymen, that after all he ruled over Prussians not Englishmen. When he died, his regimented and docile subjects had acquired no more "English" political and civic courage than they had possessed when he came to the throne.

Catherine the Great and Russia
In 1762 the daughter of a petty German prince arranged for one of her lovers to seize and murder her husband, Tsar Peter III. Thus Catherine of Anhalt-Zerbst, who had no hereditary claim to the throne whatever, became the Empress of Russia. Catherine's mode of succession, which in the West would have seemed somewhat crude, hardly raised an eyebrow in Moscow or St. Petersburg, for the Russian people had grown quite used to sudden displacements of the supreme ruler. Only a handful of them even remembered that Ivan VI, who had reigned briefly twenty years before, was still alive, a prisoner somewhere in Russia. But Catherine remembered, and not long after her accession had him murdered too.

A magnificently plumed and armored Catherine adorns a gold medal struck to celebrate her accession as Empress of Russia.

Much was unsettled in semi-Oriental Russia, but the most unsettled thing of all was the rule of succession to the tsardom. This uncertainty had gone on for nearly two hundred years, since the extinction of the old ruling house after the death of Ivan the Terrible. The accession of the Romanov dynasty only slightly stabilized matters, since in that numerous family the claim of any one Romanov, male or female, was treated as if it were as good as that of any other. After the death of Peter the Great in 1725, things went from bad to worse because Peter, who had been on bad terms with his only son, had done away with the law of succession. From then until 1762 the throne passed neither by election nor by inheritance but by palace revolution. The revolutions were conducted by the guard regiments that Peter had organized as an élite corps of this new Europeanized army. These tsar-makers were members of the *dvoriane* class (the service nobility), who used their power over the succession to promote their own interests. So effectively did this class bring pressure on the Russian tsars between Peter and Catherine that they succeeded in turning into slaves the peasants whose labor Peter had granted them in return for their military and administrative services. At the same time, they secured release from those very obligations to serve the state. A give-and-take arrangement was thus speedily transformed into one in which the new aristocracy took all and gave very little.

Catherine, soon to be called the Great, was the darling of the *philosophes*. She corresponded with many of the most eminent of the French leaders of the Enlightenment, including d'Alembert, Voltaire, and Diderot; she read with keen understanding the writings of Montesquieu on government and of the Italian *philosophe* Cesare Beccarria on prison reform; and she exchanged witty letters with that prototype of enlightened despotism, Frederick the Great. That such a ruler, raised in the West and acquainted with all the fashionable ideas of her time, should carry forward the process of Westernization that Peter had ardently begun, was to be expected. To Peter, Westernizing had meant importing the solid structures of Western technology, military methods, and bureaucracy, but to Catherine it meant introducing into Russia the whole complex of reforming rationalism associated with the Enlightenment.

Catherine seemed undaunted by the enormous obstacles raised against basic reform by the very nature and history of the lands she ruled. Soon after her accession she issued a broadly conceived manifesto looking to codification of Russian law. This manifesto drew heavily on Montesquieu's *Spirit of the Laws*. It proclaimed the principle of equality before the law, stated that rulers exist to serve the people, defined the nature of freedom, announced that serfdom should be rare, and urged the abolition of torture and the limitation of capital punishment to truly heinous crimes. Catherine summoned an assembly of nobles, townsmen, and free peasants to work on a recodification and reform of the law. She also summoned two Frenchmen to advise her on reform. One was Mercier de la Rivière, a laissez-faire economist, and the other was that eminent *philosophe* Denis Diderot, the editor of the *Encyclopédie*. To assist her in developing a general system of education in Russia, she brought into her service the man who had just provided Austria with perhaps the finest school organization in Europe. Anticlericalism and hostility to the established church were, of course, earmarks of the enlightened, and Catherine did her bit in this area by confiscating the property of the Russian Orthodox Church. Not satisfied with discussing reform in private or even with her own concrete achievements, Catherine turned to writing to prod the sluggish intellects about her into activity. She wrote ironical comedies of manners and took part in the direction of Russia's first satirical journal.

Catherine's sprawling empire had no effective system of local government. Inspired by the description of local self-government in Blackstone's *Commentaries on the Laws of England* and frightened by the lack of authority in the provinces revealed by the Pugachev peasant uprising (see below), she decided to give Russia local government on the English model. She broke down the enormous provinces into territorial units of manageable size and turned over local administrative duties to elected representatives of the landed aristocracy. She also vested in the towns certain rights of self-government, and granted charters to the merchants and the aristocracy that clearly defined their legal status and rights.

It seems surprising that a backward society that had reacted so violently to the reforms of Peter the Great should accept so calmly the activities of Catherine. This tolerance of the Russians becomes more intelligible once we examine Catherine's deeds instead of her winged words. The commission for law reform, for example, never developed into a regular legislative body. It did not even reform the law. It accomplished nothing, and Catherine finally dissolved it. The reform of municipal government proved equally futile. The town inhabitants stayed away in droves from elections, which in any case could only return figureheads, since effective police and regulatory power remained with the state bureaucracy. The scheme for public education remained largely a paper project. At the end of Catherine's reign there were only about three hundred public schools and six hundred teachers in all of Russia, and her plan to have all classes attend them came to nothing in the face of the refusal of the nobility to have their children educated with the common people. The other Western instrument of the Enlightenment that Catherine sponsored, the periodical press, fared even worse. Magazine editors who took too seriously their function of social criticism were simply put out of business by the executive order of Catherine herself.

The limits of Catherine's reforming ardor revealed themselves when the concerns and welfare of the nobility and peasantry, together comprising about nine-tenths of Russia's population, were at issue. She did not even try to reverse the aristocratic trend which reached a new high point just before her accession. In 1762 Peter III removed the state-service obligation from the nobility. Under Catherine the strangle-hold of the nobility on the peasantry became both stronger and more inclusive. A few bold spirits might speak of the need of giving the serfs at least security of tenure, but it all ended in talk. The serf gained no such security. His master could sell him separately from his family. He could punish him with the knout or condemn him to forced labor in Siberia without accounting to anyone. The boundary that separated serfdom from chattel slavery became almost imperceptible. Even as the masters were strengthening their grip on the peasantry, Catherine was extending the scope of serfdom. Her vast grants of crown estates to her officials and lovers clamped the fetters of bondage on a multitude of hitherto relatively free crown peasants. Without opposition from Catherine, the nobility began to impose serfdom in newly annexed lands such as the Ukraine. Her confiscation of Church lands worked further to enrich and aggrandize the nobles. Finally, the reform of local government on the English model proceeded on the frequent Enlightenment assumption that an institution

The palace at Tsarkoe Selo near St. Petersburg, exemplifying Russian imperial splendor, was rebuilt by Catherine in a distinctly Western style.

A Cossack named Emelyan Pugachev, who promised to free the serfs, led a violent revolt against Catherine in 1773. Pugachev was finally hunted down, caged (above), and executed.

found good in one place could simply be transplanted to any other place. But Catherine could not transplant the English gentry's sense of responsibility born of five hundred years of experience in local government, and she did not even attempt to transplant the foundations of that institution—equality before the law, the legal liberty of all subjects, and a flexible social system.

The reign of the philosophical Catherine marked the high tide of the ascendancy of the Russian nobility and the low tide of the peasants' condition. The situation was appropriately accented by the most violent of all of Russia's many peasant revolts before 1905, the Pugachev rebellion, which at one time threatened Moscow and which was put down in the customary welter of blood. The harsh realities of Catherine's position simply did not permit her to deal boldly with the disorders of Russia's social structure. Without the shadow of a legitimate claim to the throne, she had to appease the nobility, who would have gotten rid of her in a moment if they thought she was a serious threat to their position. She managed to subject the nobles somewhat to the bureaucratic control of the central government, but as the price for their acquiescence they demanded and got the final enslavement of the peasantry.

Yet Catherine accelerated the Europeanization of Russia in a way that was strangely to mark the subsequent course of Russian history. Where Peter the Great had highhandedly imposed the power techniques of the West on his native land, Catherine wooed and won Russia—at least the literate sector of the Russian nobility—for European culture. This group came to pride itself on its Western manners and elegant French. But to read French in Catherine's day was to learn that freedom was the birthright of all men, that the arbitrary exercise of power was tyranny, that of all things odious the enslavement of man by man was the worst. Only the most obtuse could miss the point. The leaders of the culture the Russian nobility came to revere condemned totally the Russian social order. At the very moment when the exploitation of the serf reached its height, the exploiters were infected with ideas that made them doubt the legitimacy of their position as a ruling class. Peter had instilled in the Russians an ambiguous fear and respect for Western power. Under Catherine the Russian aristocracy acquired an equivalent fear and admiration for Western thought and culture. This strange but natural attitude, a mixture of intense attraction and intense revulsion, became a permanent and dominant characteristic of the Russian ruling class. Their means of livelihood, the subjection and exploitation of the peasantry, could not be reconciled with the ideas of liberty and equality they had received from the West, and from the late eighteenth century on, this combination of peasant exploitation and Western ideas gradually rotted Russian society. Thus one source of the cataclysmic Bolshevik Revolution of 1917 can be traced to the reign of Catherine the Great.

Joseph II and the Hapsburg Empire

In the seventeenth century, while their Bourbon rivals in France were busy imposing a centralized bureaucratic administration on their realm, the Austrian Hapsburgs had remained merely the heads of a conglomeration of territories, a state surviving into the eighteenth century with central institutions little more sophisticated than those of England in the thirteenth century. The reorganization of the sprawling heritage of the Austrian Hapsburgs began in 1740. In the wars that Austria waged to regain the lost province of Silesia, upstart Prussia inflicted defeat after defeat on a fumbling Austrian army supported (or, more often, not supported) by the various other Hapsburg lands and hampered rather than helped by an officialdom given over completely to the promotion of provincial interests. Maria Theresa of Austria and her advisers reformed and remodeled in the hope that a strengthened state might recapture the rich province that Frederick the Great had boldly stolen. Although the hope was frustrated, the reform left Austria the most fully bureaucratic state in Europe. Indeed, this bureaucracy was the sole cement of the state. It alone bound together the Germans, Magyars, Czechs, Slovaks, Slovenes, and Croats who populated the Hapsburg realm; it alone infused into the heterogeneous multilingual mass a semblance of unity. But although Maria Theresa partly transformed her patrimony from a loose dynastic confederation into a bureaucratic despotism, she was no enlightened despot. Her models were Louis XIV and Frederick William I, not her hated enemy Frederick the Great. Conservative and pious, she was shocked at the irreverent mockery of the old sanctities that was the hallmark of the Enlightenment. She made changes because the self-preservation of her heritage demanded it, but her changes were aimed at preserving the established order, not overthrowing it.

Maria Theresa was a flexible conservative. Emperor Joseph II—her son and co-ruler from 1765 to 1780 and her successor (1780–1790)—was an inflexible radical. Of all the enlightened despots, he alone was a true doctrinaire, a literal-minded disciple of the *philosophes*. Where Catherine of Russia talked and Frederick of Prussia temporized, Joseph of Austria acted. The enemies he attacked were ignorance, intolerance, exploitation, misery, superstition, tradition,

A contemporary engraving shows Emperor Joseph II of Austria, on a tour of his realm, giving instruction in plowing.

and vested interest. His weapons were the social ideals of the *philosophes* and the power of the remodeled Hapsburg monarchy.

Joseph fought ignorance by giving Austria the finest school system in Europe. Normal schools were created to train teachers for the great network of primary schools. It was the duty of the teachers to make learning a pleasure rather than a torture for their charges. Secondary education was divided between technical schools and Latin schools, and the system was crowned by the University of Vienna. There the law faculty was charged with training bureaucrats to serve the monarchy. Joseph made the schools serve the cause of tolerance, too, by admitting Jews and Protestants on equal footing with Catholics. In a revolutionary decree he established complete religious freedom for all his subjects, except deists and atheists. He went further—to a point that even England did not attain until well into the nineteenth century—for he added civil equality: equality before the law and equal rights to military and political office. Thus in one sweeping act of his despotic will he sought to obliterate the edifice of the Catholic restoration that his ancestors had struggled for generations to achieve.

Though Joseph was a wholly devout Catholic in matters of dogma, his policies ran counter to those of the Catholic Church. He broke the Catholic monopoly of public office, and he secularized the educational system, removing it from the control of the religious orders. His aim was to establish a Hapsburg Catholic Church, which would be orthodox in doctrine but in all other matters subject not to the Pope but to the head of the Hapsburg dynasty. He limited the right of appeal to the Roman Curia, the Catholic court of last resort. He reorganized the administration of the Church, naming the bishops from among his own followers. He expelled the Jesuits, the shock troops of the Pope, and subjected the other religious orders to rigid state supervision. He closed down a third of their houses and used the huge endowment of the closed houses to subsidize education, poor relief, and the parish priests, and he decreed that priests were to be trained in state-founded seminaries under state supervision. The Pope's protests were of no avail; as far as he could, Joseph made the Catholic Church the ecclesiastical branch of the Hapsburg state.

The enlightened emperor also waged bitter war on all the remnants of the corporative society in his domains—the provincial autonomy of Hungary, Lombardy, and the Austrian Netherlands, the privileges of the Magyar aristocracy, the liberties of the towns, the monopolies of the guilds. Laissez faire and the ideal of economic freedom decided the fate of the guilds, and the rest of the corporate structure went down as a sacrifice on the altar of rational order and efficient administration—the enlightened police state.

There remained the toughest problem of all—serfdom. Bound to the soil, owing a heavy labor service to his lord, subjected to that lord's court in both criminal and civil cases, bound to pay as much as 70 percent of his income in Church tithes, state taxes, and manorial dues, the serf in Austria, Hungary, and Bohemia was a pitiable being. Joseph attempted a complete and radical solution of the peasant problem. He withdrew the peasants from their lord's control by giving them the right of appeal to the state courts. He removed from them the two harshest marks of subjection, their attachment to the soil and the lord's control over their freedom to choose a mate, giving them freedom of movement and free choice in marriage and earning a livelihood. Finally, he issued a decree that commuted their labor services into a fixed payment, transforming them, in effect, from serfs holding their land at the lord's pleasure into peasant proprietors. He abolished outright their obligation to pay Church tithes. For many peasants, these reforms would have reversed the proportion of payment: instead of owing almost three-quarters of their income for various payments, they were to retain three-quarters of it for themselves. The state's loss in peasant taxation was to be made up by an equitable single tax on all land, sweeping away the much-cherished tax exemptions of the privileged aristocracy and clergy.

Joseph was perhaps the only legitimate monarch in history who tried to bring off what he knew to be a social revolution by simple edict. His radical program evoked a violent reaction, the first of its kind in Europe and a foreshadowing of the organized reaction that the radicalism of the French Revolution would soon spawn. In attacking every vested interest in his empire, he left himself without effective support among his own people. "I have weakened deep-rooted traditions by the introduction of enlightened principles," he wrote proudly, but in seeking to weaken all deep-rooted traditions and to introduce all enlightened principles at once, he only succeeded in weakening the one tradition that he firmly believed in—the obligation of the subjects to render unquestioning obedience to the ruler. At the end of his reign he found himself isolated amid class wars and revolts against his reforms. Unable to resist the pressures, he delayed the application of his most significant reform—the emancipation of the serfs and their transformation into free peasant proprietors. The day of emancipation for the Hapsburg peasantry was thus put off for more than half a century.

Some recent historians have had doubts about the accuracy or usefulness of the conceptions "enlightened despots" and "enlightened despotism" on the grounds that as applied to the theory and practice of politics in the age of the Enlightenment they are misleading. They have proposed alternative labels such as "enlightened monarchy" or "enlightened absolutism," and have pointed out that the only ruler of a great power who came close to consistently making "enlightenment" the basis of his policy was a magnificent failure, Joseph II. As to the label, changing it does not change the fact that many of the *philosophes* believed that to realize their political goals the most effective instrument would be a resolute ruler who would use his authority to make and abrogate law for the public ends they supported—the subjection of the Church, the rationalization of law, the diminution or destruction of group privilege, the secularization of education, the establishment of religious freedom, the abolition of censorship. Whether one calls this despotism or absolutism or just monarchy, for almost half a century it was the standard set for the rulers of states by the leaders of intellectual fashion. It was the model of politics just as the rule of Louis XIV had been the model of politics in the late seventeenth century. But enlightened despotism was a transitory political ideal. Even before the death of Joseph II in 1790, it had begun to lose favor in Spain, Portugal, Prussia, and Russia. By 1815 there was scarcely a ruler in Europe who made the slightest pretension to enlightenment. Yet in its relatively short career, remarkable things had been done and even more remarkable things said by some of the rulers of Europe.

Enlightened Despotism in Ideal and Actuality

With Papal control of the Catholic Church in Austria threatened by the policies of Joseph II, Pope Pius VI journeyed to Vienna in 1782 (he is shown here on his arrival) but failed to budge the emperor's position.

The enlightened despots universally rendered lip service and occasionally real service to the idea that they were the servants rather than the masters of the state, that they existed for the welfare of the people. This was not a new idea in Europe; medieval and much early modern political theory had frequently made the same point. But the enlightened despots gave a specific and new content to the idea of the people's welfare, a blend of physiocracy, natural-rights philosophy, rationalism, and philanthropy. They believed that the welfare of the people lay not in religious uniformity and hierarchical order but in economic freedom and civil rights and prosperity, in orderly, rational, and uniform laws and administration, and in enlightenment. They also believed that the state (that is, themselves) had the duty and the authority to confer these blessings on the people. The extent to which the despots actually attempted to attain these ends differed, as we have seen, from country to country. Yet everywhere the tendency and the purposes of the enlightened despots were the same, and there is a strong resemblance among the measures they actually took.

They all to some extent improved the efficiency of state administration, making it more uniform and rational and hacking down some of the lush growth of special political privilege, sinecurism, waste, and financial chaos that characterized the governments that most of them inherited. They also tried to reduce the confused wilderness of custom, edict, and precedents that passed for law to some rational and coherent order. Believing that good laws would make good men, they aimed to produce codes so reasonable that men would want to obey them. In this area, they eliminated a good deal of the barbarity that characterized the old order. Torture, a standard practice in criminal proceedings in most of Europe, was abolished, and the outrageous penalties meted out for petty crimes were reduced. Prosperity and economic freedom were linked together in the minds of the enlightened despots; the former was the end, the latter the means. The way to economic freedom, they thought, lay through the destruction of those traditional "liberties" and franchises that impeded economic freedom: guild monopolies, toll rights, and barriers to a free market in goods, labor, and land within the state. At this point the influence of the physiocrats on the enlightened despots made a junction with that of the natural rights philosophers. Clearly serfdom—the binding of great numbers of workers to particular patches of land—hopelessly impeded a free labor market. It also clashed with the fundamental conception of the *philosophes*—the basis of all their political ideas—that all men have a natural right to freedom. Some enlightened despots inveighed against serfdom; others at least tried to ameliorate the serfs' condition and one, Joseph II, actually decreed their emancipation.

To enlighten their people and free them from superstition, the despots followed two different but related courses: they attacked what they saw as the chief enemy of light—the Church, and especially the Jesuit order—and they promoted secular education. This involved removing the young from the tutelage of the Church schools, which for centuries had done most of the primary educating and practically all of the secondary and higher educating in Europe, and taking money and land from the Church to help support the new schools. In a number of other ways the enlightened Catholic rulers diminished the wealth, curtailed the power, and curbed the influence of the Church. They limited appeals to the Papal Curia, withdrew cases from the ecclesiastical courts, eliminated Church censorship of the press, confiscated the lands of religious orders, and curtailed the freedom of the clergy to select their own bishops. It was a happy concomitant of this whole attack on superstition that the power and wealth taken from the Church fell into the hands of the despots themselves.

What we have just described, to repeat, is what the enlightened despots wanted to do, and what some of them tried to do. One need only turn back to the description of the actual achievements of Frederick in Prussia and Catherine in Russia to recognize the enormous gap between words and deeds. Catherine, who talked the best and played the worst game of any of the late eighteenth-century rulers, tried to account for this discrepancy by pointing out to Diderot that he put his reforms down on paper, whereas she had to impress hers on the hides of men.

Catherine put her finger on another aspect of the problem when she told her lover and foreign-policy adviser, Grigori Potëmkin, that if her subjects were well educated neither she nor Potëmkin could keep them in their places. An educated people would want to do things for itself, but the very essence of enlightened despotism was that it was government *for* the people, not *by* the people. It was not democracy; it was not even oligarchy; it was administrative government by a bureaucracy wielding the unlimited authority of the monarch. For all the despots' talk about natural rights and liberty, they did not surrender one iota of the absolute sovereignty they had inherited, and they even expanded the area of that sovereignty at the expense of local and ecclesiastical authorities. Censorship and inquisition into private affairs did not cease when the rulers curbed the Church; the ruler himself gathered up the powers he had forced the Church to forego. The king penalized different kinds of insubordination and suppressed different kinds of "dangerous" opinions than the Church did, but the power was no less arbitrary and unlimited for all that, and liberties held only by the sufferance of the king were, if anything, more precarious than liberties limited by the Church.

There was a marked contrast between the way the enlightened despots handled the privileges of the Church and the middle class and the way they approached the privileges of the nobility. By the standards the enlightened despots professed, all privilege was irrational, and most irrational of all was privilege for the few that involved actual servitude or serfdom for the many. Yet only one enlightened despot, Joseph II, dared lay hands on this sacred preserve of aristocratic power, and Joseph learned that the resistance of the aristocrats to an attack on serfdom recognized no bounds, certainly not the bounds of loyalty. And the loyalty of the aristocracy was indispensable to the eighteenth-century ruler because at a certain point, both by inclination and by necessity, the enlightened despots completely parted company with the theorists and philosophers from whom they drew their ideas. The physiocrats envisaged a world of universal brotherhood. The real world, however, was a world of contending great and small powers each ready to pounce at the first sign of weakness. The enlightened Frederick, Joseph, and Catherine, without blinking an eye, negotiated among themselves the carving up of Poland and Turkey. What a prince gained depended on his capacity to back his claims with regiments, and in Russia, Prussia, and Hungary those regiments were still led by the aristocrats. Only an improvident despot would bet his military strength on social reform, as did Joseph II, and he paid dearly for his quixotic act. The Magyars revolted, paralyzing his army in the midst of a campaign against Turkey. Catherine and Frederick never suffered such embarrassment, but neither did they seriously attack unenlightened serfdom.

Despite the discrepancy between their words and their deeds, the enlightened despots all put into their law books decrees entitling them to the claim of enlightenment. They complied with the pattern prescribed by the *philosophes* by enforcing regulations intended to bring about human progress and betterment by reasonable legislation. In addition to the immediate practical results they achieved or failed to achieve, the despots had a real impact on the minds of some of their subjects. They were, in fact, the most effective propagandists of the enlightenment in their own lands.

The Ambiguities of the Enlightenment

The limitations of enlightened despotism revealed a structural weakness in the common political concepts of the propagandists of enlightenment and in the very foundations of their philosophy of man. In setting forth the reforms that enlightened governments ought to adopt, the *philosophes* had given too little attention to the structure of government, to the source of authority, to the bases of political obligation, to questions of what gave rulers the right to rule and imposed on the ruled the duty to obey. The *philosophes* were so alienated by the abuses of the society in which they lived that they almost ceased to inquire into what social requirements men were bound to submit themselves to if there was to be a society at all, if men were not to stumble into a condition in which power was wielded simply for the gratification of its possessors. One of the premises held by most of the *philosophes* could indeed be considered to lead to just that conclusion: if it was natural to man that self-interest was the sole guide of conduct, if happiness was man's ultimate goal, if happiness was reduced to the accumulation of pleasure, and if pleasure was reduced to the satisfaction of whatever desire possessed one, then would not the freeing of man from the false and artificial restraints of society result in the strong satisfying themselves at the expense of the weak? After all, this was the way it was in nature; nature itself was red in tooth and claw. The strong animal, too, finds its most intense pleasure in the sex act and sometimes in cruelty and murder, the ultimate act of power. The premises of the *philosophes* not only could be forced to yield such conclusions; they were ultimately forced to yield them by a strange, partly mad child of the Enlightenment, the Marquis de Sade (1740–1814), from whom sadism received its name. Sade's work and his life constituted a dark, demonic underside of the Enlightenment. Even before his day, some of the *philosophes*—especially Diderot, in writings that were not published in his lifetime—occasionally showed an uneasy awareness that some of the most cherished concepts of the *philosophes* could be perverted to yield consequences that they rejected with horror.

None was more aware of this than Jean Jacques Rousseau (1712–1778), perhaps because he felt the danger in his own breast, because by his own nature he himself was driven to afflict both other human creatures and his own tormented spirit. Of all those who led the assault on the opponents of the Enlightenment, Rousseau was the most effective, more effective even than Voltaire. Born in Geneva, the ancient capital of Calvinism, he became a convert to Roman Catholicism in his youth, but the conversion did not last. In 1740 he went to Paris to try his fortune as a man of letters. Despite a remarkably disorderly and vagrant

In a French comment on the partitioning of Poland, the monarchs of Central and Eastern Europe (from left, Catherine the Great, Frederick the Great, Joseph II of Austria, and the puppet Polish king) gather about a map of Poland to divide the spoils.

Jean Jacques Rousseau sat for the English artist Allan Ramsay in 1766; this engraving is after the portrait.

way of life, he won friends among the *philosophes*, including Diderot and Fontenelle, but he gained little fame. Then, in 1750, he won a literary prize with an essay in which he argued that the advance of the arts and sciences had not contributed to the purification of morals. This essay established his position in the literary world, but he owed the adoration that he ultimately received to *La Nouvelle Héloïse* (1761), a romance of the conflict between carnal love and virtue, and to *Émile* (1762), a rambling, unorthodox disquisition on education.

In his writings, Rousseau turned his eloquent scorn against all the principal targets of the Enlightenment: the artificiality of contemporary manners, the absurdities of aristocratic pretensions, the love of luxury, the wickedness of despotic rule, the tyranny of the rich, the exploitation of the powerless by the powerful. He attacked what he regarded as the superstitions of Catholic orthodoxy and expressed his disbelief in the miraculous. He was an advocate of almost everything the *philosophes* held dear: natural religion, the dignity of man, the superiority of nature to convention, the sanctity of liberty and property. By reaching men through their feelings, Rousseau won enthusiastic converts among those scarcely touched by the writings of most of the *philosophes*. Where the *philosophes* spoke mainly of reason and enlightened individual self-interest, he spoke of "glowing and sublime ardor" and of the "transports of susceptible hearts." His large and enthusiastic following poured forth buckets of sympathetic tears at both the joys and sorrows of the enlightened characters portrayed by Rousseau as trapped in a corrupt and artificial world. Voltaire, Montesquieu, Diderot, and the Encyclopedists won much of the mind of the Western world for the Enlightenment, but Rousseau won its heart.

Rousseau had in him a strong streak of the prophetic. As with most prophets, a good deal of what he had to say was murky and ambiguous at the time he said it, perhaps even murky and ambiguous to him when he said it. Its import became clear only with the unpredictable and unpredicted unfolding of events which retrospectively conferred meaning and clarity of what in origin were gropings in the dark. This is especially so with respect to his greatest work, *The Social Contract*. Its meaning is difficult to grasp because it uses the vocabulary of its time, the language of the *philosophes,* to project views which lay beyond the limits of their vision. Rousseau was convinced that all the institutions of the world, all the institutions of culture and society and government, were corrupt and contrary to nature, and that they debased human potentiality instead of raising it. Though he did not suggest that men should or could forsake culture, society, and government, he urged them to find a new foundation for their common life grounded not in force, fraud, superstition, and legal and spiritual enslavement, but in freedom. The source of that freedom was not human reason, which the *philosophes* had shown to be self-regarding and calculating, but the human will, which created communities among men based on fellow-feelings that transcended the isolation of selfish reason. The concrete expression of these shared feelings created the most valuable relations of man: friendship, love, the relation between husband and wife, parents and children, teacher and pupil. It was only such a will that could make any form of subjection or subordination right and legitimate, since then subordination became the expression not of coercion but of freedom, the result not of force but of consent.

What was true of smaller associations was also true of larger ones, especially of the largest of all, the state. The state must be based not on calculations of the individual interest of its members, for such interests were diverse, fragmenting men rather than giving them solidarity. What Rousseau called the general will was the free will of men to participate in the laws that a community made through its designated magistrates. Such a will either transcended the individual wills of the members of the group, in which case a viable political community existed; or it did not transcend the individual wills or the wills of subgroups (like the clergy and the nobility which refused to subject themselves to common obligations), in which case there was no such community, no legitimate authority at all, merely the rule of force. By Rousseau's standards, few governments in Europe had even a vestige of a claim to rightful authority. And, indeed, if love of country, which was the natural external manifestation of the general will, was the basis of rightful authority, Rousseau was right. In a sense, events proved him right not merely in theory but in practice. The tepid efforts of most of the enlightened despots to reform their realms demonstrated that the old basis of government was no longer adequate to the demands of a new era. And in the New World the thirteen colonies of Britain showed a startled world what the new-born patriotism of a free people could do to create a general will and to build on it a viable structure of political authority based on consent.

In the meantime, no love was lost between Rousseau and the *philosophes*. The latter sensed something more than personal animosity in Rousseau's jibes at them. Although his professed goals were very similar to theirs, he had arrived at them by a very different route and, from the point of view of the *philosophes*, a most dangerous route. Appealing to the emotions of his following, urging men to act on the convictions of their hearts, was, according to the *philosophes*, to encourage them to follow a most erratic guide. From their point of view, the *philosophes* were quite right in dreading the consequences of making emotion the foundation of judgment and decision, and events were to justify their distrust. The anti-rationalism that Rousseau encouraged certainly provided much of the emotional drive behind the social and political transformations of the revolutionary age in Europe that opened in 1789, transformations that put into effect many of the principles of the *philosophes*, but also afforded a base of action both to those who hated the transformations and to those who felt that the transformations did not go far enough. Reactionaries and revolutionaries as well as reformers have hearts, and slogans such as "the faith of our fathers" and "our country, right or wrong" can capture the heart just as readily as love of liberty or reverence for reason. In fact both did so. In the Western world, during the age of revolution and after, the enlightenment of the mind was extinguished in many men by an enlightenment of the heart, and in the nineteenth century the liberal reforms that stemmed from the Enlightenment were to find as many enemies as friends among the Romantics—revolutionary or nationalistic or mystical —whose spiritual father was Rousseau.

Émile, which expressed Rousseau's views on education, was the inspiration for this monument erected in Geneva in 1779. In contrast to the former harsh regimen portrayed on a cracked medallion, a Rousseau-like teacher gently guides the child by means of a symbolic garland of roses.

The Enlightened Spirit

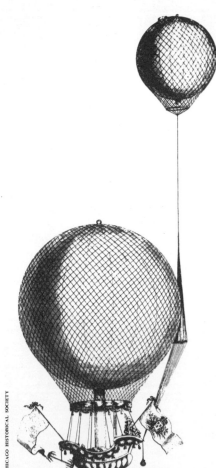

"If someone asks are we living in an enlightened age today," wrote the German philosopher Immanuel Kant, "the answer would be, No." But, he added, "we are living in an Age of Enlightenment." The year was 1784 and Kant was looking back over a century studded with men and women whose art and thought were as charming, as brilliant, and sometimes as explosive, as the new aerial balloons (left) that filled eighteenth-century skies.

Although the Enlightenment was cosmopolitan in its outlook, France —where refinement, taste, and learning flourished alongside tryanny, superstition, and poverty—was its center; "What the Greeks were to the Romans, the French are to us," wrote the German critic Johann Christoph Gottsched. The *philosophes*' natural habitat was the city, particularly Paris, and in the city it was the salon. There, said Lord Shaftsbury, "We polish one another, and rub off our corners and rough sides by a sort of amicable collision." On the opposite page is a detail from a painting done in 1814 by the Frenchman Anacète Lemonnier showing the *philosophes*, appropriately upstaged by Houdon's bust of Voltaire, as they might have been seen at Madame Geoffrin's Paris salon in the previous century.

Conversations sharpened the *philosophes*' wit, but the printing press was their artillery against what they believed to be the tyranny and ignorance of the *ancien régime*. Chrétien Malesherbes, a lawyer and a *philosophe* who was also France's official censor from 1750 to 1764, wrote: "In a century in which every citizen can speak to the entire nation by means of print, those who have the talent for instructing men or the gift of moving them—in a word, men of letters—are, amid a dispersed people, what the orators of Rome and Athens were in the midst of a people assembled."

The *philosophes* agreed with the ancient philosophers that the man who is "afraid of the gods is afraid of everything." Believing that they had only to unmask error to establish truth, their tactics were uncompromising. "We must cut off by the roots a tree that has always borne poisons," wrote Voltaire. Although secularly inclined, the *philosophes* approached their task with a sense of divine purpose. "Since, once and for all, we have seats in God's House of Commons," wrote the physicist Lichtenberg, "shall we not express our opinions?" The *philosophes* expressed themselves so freely and fervently that the English writer Horace Walpole complained: "The *philosophes* are insupportable, superficial, overbearing, and fanatic; they preach incessantly." Preach they did, yet in the hands of master satirists their sermons managed "to enliven morality with wit, and to temper wit with morality" with devastating effect.

Prince of Letters

W
hen Monsieur Arouet asked his seventeen-year-old son what career he wished to pursue, François Marie replied, "I want none but that of a man of letters." Angered, his father retorted, "That's the position of a man who wishes to be useless to society, a burden to his parents, and to die of hunger." In fact, of course, François Marie Arouet became world famous as Voltaire, made a fortune, helped to transform European society, and died not of hunger but to acclamation.

From 1718, when his first successful play, *Oedipe*, was produced, to his "crowning" (opposite) just before his death in 1778, Voltaire amused all Europe while he waged unremitting war against the authorities and the authoritarian spirit of the *ancien régime*. Having twice experienced the dreaded *lettre de cachet* and the "cool apartments" of the Bastille by the time he was twenty-five, Voltaire became a master of his own maxim on literary guerrilla warfare: "Strike and conceal your hand."

How to ridicule Paris? Write about the mythical city of Persepolis. How to attack Christian dogma? Conduct imaginary interviews with Christ. How to attack faith and advocate skepticism? Write a philosophical dictionary and define "faith" as consisting "in believing not what seems true, but what seems false." How to express hatred of cruelty committed in the name of religion? Have the innocent hero Candide flogged "in cadence to the accompaniment of hymns." How to attack the hypocritical religiosity of the aristocracy? Have an honest man hanged, although this was not "the custom" at an auto-da-fé at which "refreshments were served to the ladies between the mass and the execution." And how to remind men of their arrogance and greed? Have the hero become enlightened by discovering "men as in fact they are, insects devouring each other on a tiny atom of mud."

Voltaire's wit was destructive precisely because he felt the *ancien régime* must fall before a new order could be built. "If you are desirous of having good laws," he wrote, "burn those you have at present and make fresh ones."

At the left is Gabriel Saint-Aubin's pen-and-ink drawing of the crowning of Voltaire as he attended a performance of his play Irène *at the Comédie Française on his triumphal return to Paris from exile in 1778. At the right is Jean Antoine Houdon's marble bust of Voltaire, done in 1782. "It is impossible to describe the light in his eyes or the charm of his face. What an enchanting smile!" wrote an admirer.*

VERSAILLES; GIRAUDON

At the left is Quentin de [la]
Tour's 1755 painting of L[ouis]
XV's long-time favorite, [Ma-]
dame de Pompadour, a wo[man]
of beauty, charm, and learn[ing.]
At the right is Jean Honoré [Fra-]
gonard's frivolous but charm[ing]
canvas, The Happy Accid[ents]
of the Swing. The painti[ng's]
carefully mannered techn[ique]
and its unaffected licenti[ous-]
ness is a perfect reflection [of]
the Enlightenment's taste in

Elegance Enthroned

I n 1756 Elector Palatine Karl Theodore wrote to Voltaire, "It seems to me that this polished century, which may well have been called the golden age, bears some likeness to a mermaid, the upper part of whose body is that of a bewitching nymph, while the lower part ends in a loathsome fish-tail." The Enlightenment was indeed Janus-like and had two faces, but in general the face it chose to show was polished, urbane, and deliciously sensual, with a refined yet easy elegance unique in the history of the West. A French aristocrat, the Signeur de Saint-Évremond, expressed the period's carefully cultivated hedonism when he wrote, "An imperfect enjoyment is attended with Regret; a surfeit of Pleasure with Disgust; there's a certain nick of time, a certain medium to be observed with which few people are acquainted. We must enjoy the present Pleasures, without impairing the future."

This delicate balancing of sensibilities was largely the creation of women such as Louis XV's mistress, Madame de Pompadour (above), Voltaire's Madame du Châtelet, or Rousseau's Madame de Warens, who, whether at court or in their salons, created the Enlightenment's patina of exquisite sensibility and good taste. Although men of letters dominated the age, the influence of such elegant and witty women was pervasive. Warmly appreciative of this fact, Jean Jacques Rousseau wrote of the enlightened lady: "Everything depends on her; nothing is done except by her or for her."

The most poetic idealization of courtly love was the work of an extremely shy, tubercular artist named Jean Antoine Watteau, who painted his triumphal masterpiece, A Pilgrimage to Cythera, *in 1717 at the age of thirty-three, only four years before his death. Redolent with fantasy and sensuality, Watteau's canvas depicts the moment when a lady (in brown taffeta)*

whose scruples have been overcome by her gallant (in red satin) turns to take a last look at Cythera, the mythical island of love symbolized by the statue of Venus garlanded with roses at right, before joining other amorous couples as they saunter arm in arm toward their gilt-encrusted gondola where lusty Pans and innocent Cupids wait to speed them on their homeward way.

Rakewell's road to ruin begins at ar left with young Tom, who has inherited the fortune of his de-ed father, paying off the mother of h Young, whom Tom had gotten nant while at Oxford. The next aving (immediate left) shows , now a fashionable gentleman spending his fortune recklessly, at morning levee with his harpsi-dist, fencing master, dancing her, and shady jockey (kneeling).

next sequence begins (far left) in ndon tavern where Tom's light-ered companions of the night's ls relieve him of his gold watch. d from debtor's prison by the ful Sarah, Tom seeks to recoup fortune by marrying a wealthy, sy-eyed crone. At the ceremony ncorrigible Tom ogles the brides-l while Sarah and her mother kground) try to force their way the church to forbid the wedding.

he final sequence the old crone's ne has served only to plunge the e deeper into debt and degrada-Having gambled and lost, Tom, wigless and frantic, shakes his fist te while a dog barks in his face. e final scene Tom has been com-ed to Bedlam where, after a sei-, the still loyal Sarah tends him as dants clamp manacles to his legs wo slumming society ladies take in nad show with undisguised relish.

The Satirist's Eye

The elegant portraits of Boucher, Fragonard, La Tour, and Watteau pictured their patrons as they wished to be seen: aristocratic, refined, carefree. But in England a stubby and pugnacious bulldog of an artist tired of his highly successful career as a "phiz-monger" (as he called society painters) and rebelled against portraying patrons as "divinities." Believing that humanity was "placed between the sublime and the grotesque," William Hogarth set about depicting the human comedy. "I wished to compose pictures on canvas similar to representations on the stage," he once wrote, "and further hope that they will be tried by the same test, and criticized by the same criterion. . . . My picture is my stage, and men and women my players. . . ."

In 1732 Hogarth published his first cycle of satirical engravings, entitled *A Harlot's Progress*. Three years later he added *The Rake's Progress* (six of the eight *Rake* engravings are reproduced on the opposite page). Other cycles on marriage, industry and idleness, and sobriety followed. The novelist Henry Fielding, a friend and fellow satirist, explained Englishmen's relish for Hogarth's moral tales. "In his excellent work," Fielding wrote, "you see the delusive scene exposed with all the force of humor, and casting your eyes on another picture, you behold the dreadful and fatal consequences."

A no-nonsense member of the middle class, Hogarth risked a pot-shot at England's Establishment in his 1725 engraving above. On a platform, supported only by clouds of illusion, sit King, Bishop, and Judge surrounded by foppish courtiers and ministers. The King has a coin for a head and a scepter topped with a crescent symbolizing the weak and vacillating George I. The Bishop's head (center) is a jew's-harp which is attached by a rope, binding a Bible, to the church coffer: put a coin in the plate and the Bishop will mouth pious platitudes. Hogarth rounds out his unholy triumvirate with the be-wigged, block-headed Judge at right.

The Light of Science

The joy with which the *philosophes* abandoned the universe as explained by Scripture was only matched by the rapture with which they embraced the heavens as revealed by science. Even the miracle-deriding Voltaire could not contain his enthusiasm. "The marvelous order of nature, the rotation of a hundred million globes around a million suns, the activity of light, the life of animals—these," he said, "are perpetual miracles."

As the craze for science swept across Europe, hundreds of learned and not-quite-so-learned societies sprang into being. Ladies and gentlemen who really preferred horses or cards pored over Newton's *Principia Mathematica* or bravely tackled Georges Buffon's 44-volume *Histoire Naturelle*. They gathered together and peered earnestly into telescopes—sometimes, as in the engraving at the right (*c.* 1750), through the wrong end. They sat around tables and with cloth rubbed iron rods and then thrilled each other with electrostatic charges. Science became so fashionable that on visiting France the English poet Oliver Goldsmith wrote: "I have seen as bright a circle of beauties at the chemical lectures of Rouelle as gracing the court of Versailles."

Behind, or perhaps despite, all the fanfare, science was taking giant strides. The English astronomer William Herschel discovered Uranus, catalogued 2,500 nebulae and star clusters, and informed the world that some stars were more than 11,750,000,000,000,000,000,000 miles from the earth. The Swedish physician Carolus Linnaeus painstakingly identified more than 12,000 living things. And Erasmus Darwin anticipated his grandson's theory of evolution with a poem celebrating abiogenesis: "Hence without parents, by spontaneous birth,/ Rise the first specks of animated earth/. . . . Organic life beneath the shoreless waves/ Was born and nursed in ocean's pearly waves." Small wonder that enlightened men and women felt, as Alfred North Whitehead has written, "as though the very heavens were being opened."

The magnificent microscope at the left was made about the middle of the eighteenth century by Alexis Magny, a Paris engineer and maker of clocks and watches as well as of mathematical and physical instruments. In keeping with rococo elegance, the microscope's base was made of gilt bronze with curlicued supports; its case was fine leather. Magny's microscope had compound lenses and was quite advanced for its time. Advances in glassmaking and lens grinding were to make the compound microscope considerably more powerful by the nineteenth century, yet these early examples made possible Linnaeus' classification of plants (including their sex) and in medicine opened the way to microbiology and to the subsequent understanding of such dreaded diseases as cholera and smallpox.

KUNSTHISTORISCHES MUSEUM, VIENNA

At the left is an elegant brass declination sundial dating from 1764. Despite a rather complicated procedure, this kind of sundial measured time quite accurately. First, the four knobs supporting the base were to be adjusted until the plumb line at the left indicated that the sundial was level. Next, the face of the sundial was raised to correspond to the angle of declination. Finally, the pointer on the dial's face was moved so that it was parallel to the sun's rays. The result was the correct hour, indicated by the arrow at the pointer's tip, and, by means of the cogs on the sundial's circumference, the exact minute registered on the small numbered disk at the side of the dial.

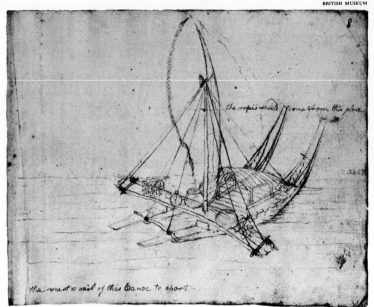

The wonders of the Pacific were variously interpreted by the artists who went with Cook on his three epochal voyages. The careful drawings of a kangaroo and of a Polynesian sailing canoe are the work of the natural history draftsman Sidney Parkinson, whose representations of hundreds of then unknown species of tropical birds, fish, and plants, done during Cook's initial voyage in 1773, were a significant addition to zoological knowledge. But it was the more theatrical renderings of the "noble savage" by William Hodges, who accompanied Cook on his second voyage to Tahiti, that captured the public's imagination. Below is one of his vivid works, showing part of a fleet of 330 Tahitian war canoes, manned by some 8,000 warriors and their gorgeously plumed chieftains, as they set out to do battle with the people of another island.

Venus Observed

O n April 13, 1769, Lieutenant James Cook, commander of H.M.S. *Endeavour*, dropped anchor in the crystal blue waters of Matavi Bay. Tahiti had been discovered only two years before, yet reports of the island had so impressed the scientists of Britain's Royal Society that they had chosen it as one of three sites from which to observe Venus as the planet made its approximately centennial pass between the earth and the sun.

Within three months Cook was at sea again, Venus had been observed, and a legend that was to profoundly influence the Enlightenment was in the making. When the *Endeavour* returned to England two years later, Tahiti, with its warm, sensual climate and its happy, love-adoring people, was presented and eagerly accepted as living proof that the "noble savage" not only existed but thrived. Cook's private views were more balanced, and he was well aware of some of the Tahitians' less felicitous customs ("They are thieves to a man . . . with such dexterity as would shame the most noted pickpockets in Europe"). On his return, however, his journal was reworked into a romantic tale; in any case, the enlightened welcomed the more exuberant views of Joseph Banks, an amateur scientist who had accompanied Cook. "On the Island of Tahiti where love is the chief occupation," Banks wrote, "both the bodies and the souls of the women are moulded into the utmost perfection."

BRITISH MUSEUM OF NATURAL HISTORY

MUSÉE D'ART ET D'HISTOIRE, GENEVA

Enlightenment for All

Denis Diderot, the man responsible for the Enlightenment's greatest collective achievement, described himself as "calm, reflective, tender, violent, passionate, enthusiastic." The Russian artist Dmitri Levitski attempted to capture this elusive mixture in his portrait above, painted in 1773 when Diderot was the reigning intellectual at the court of Catherine the Great. But in 1747, when the thirty-three-year-old bohemian became editor-in-chief of an encyclopedia which was to "assemble the knowledge scattered over the face of the earth," Diderot was a man of high hopes but few accomplishments. For the next twenty-five years, despite imprisonment, attacks by the clergy, censorship by the state, and quarrels and defections among his contributors and editors, Diderot, often alone, plugged on. By 1772 the twenty-eight volumes were done, and the world had its first encyclopedia worthy of the name.

It was, to be sure, an encyclopedia with a point of view—that of the most enlightened in an age of enlightenment. There were attacks against superstition: "Nothing is so firmly believed as the things one knows least about." There were savage, if veiled, attacks on the French monarchy: "A sovereign, absolute though he may be, has no right to touch the established law of a state, no more than its religion. . . . He is, besides, always obliged to follow the laws of justice and reason." But above all there was Diderot's determination to make knowledge serve mankind. To explain manufacturing processes, for example, Diderot went to great lengths: "We had to procure machines," he wrote, "set them up, learn to work them, become apprentices . . . and fabricate bad products ourselves in order to show others how to make good ones."

At left is the Encyclopédie's view of the composing room of an eighteenth-century French print shop. At the far left a typesetter picks out letters from pigeonholed cases of type, while the man in the center puts the lines in a galley. At the right, the locked-in galleys of type are tapped down to make them even and secure, ready for the press.

ALL: *Encyclopedie, 1751–1772*

Diderot was determined that the Encyclopédie would "at last give the artisans their due." When finished, the eleven volumes of engravings included elegant, accurate celebrations of craftmanship. The ornate silver candelabra above is an example of the lavishness of rococo furnishings. In the engraving reproduced at right, horses provide the only mechanical power for a typical eighteenth-century mine, where the lighting was poor, safety measures primitive, and accidents common.

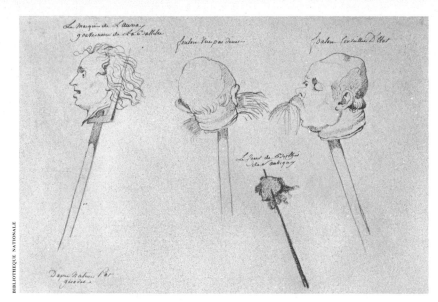

Rousseau and Rebellion

Jean Jacques Rousseau died in 1778, eleven years before the Revolution began, yet his radical, emotional writings caused Frenchmen to consider him the Revolution's spiritual father. He is pictured as such at left in Jeaurat de Bertray's *Allegory of the Revolution*. Rousseau presides over a jumble of symbols that include a monument to Equality (at left), two maidens representing Goodness and Good Faith, a bundle of rods and war axes symbolizing fair but forceful government, a Liberty Tree, unfinished pillars for regeneration and revolution, and, in the distance, a guillotine.

Rousseau's fame began in 1750 with his *Discourse on the Sciences and the Arts*, which won first prize from the Dijon Academy. "Why has man himself, while increasing his material knowledge, not grown happier and better?" asked Rousseau. His answer was that civilization's knack for artifice had taught men the worthless art of "how to speak well" and thereby corrupted the all-important ability "to do well." Two years later Rousseau followed his first triumph with a still more radical essay on inequality in which he blamed private property for the "crimes, wars, murders, miseries, and horrors of the human race." The wealthy Voltaire found Rousseau's advocacy of communism far from amusing and wrote him, "I have received, Sir, your new book against the human race." But Rousseau was not about to return to the Enlightenment's balanced rationalism. "I hate books," he wrote in *Émile*; "they only teach people to talk about what they don't know." In the *Social Contract* Rousseau went still further and wrote that all men were born free but were everywhere enslaved; while in the same work he advocated banishment by the state for those who did not accept its dogmas.

Doubtless Rousseau would have been horrified by the excesses of the French Revolution, such as the parading (above) of severed heads. Yet his emotional radicalism, which justified both complete freedom and absolute power, was an essential ingredient of the revolutionary cataclysms that gripped Europe in 1789 and after.

9

—◈—

Prologue to
the Era of Revolution

In 1775 a revolt or rebellion broke out in the continental American colonies of England. It was symptomatic of what was to come that soon after its outbreak the revolt was described by some as the American *Revolution*. It was in fact to be the prologue to a long period of revolutionary upheaval in politics and society that in one way or another involved the whole European world. This upheaval was of unprecedented dimensions, and it followed a period of remarkable tranquillity. Since the middle of the seventeenth century revolt and rebellion in the European world had been rare, sporadic, and, except in England in 1688, ineffectual. Moreover, the interconnection between the risings of the mid-seventeenth century had been obscure and was perhaps slight; the interrelation of revolutions from the late eighteenth century on was as evident to contemporaries as it is today. Everywhere it shook—and in many lands it temporarily or permanently shattered—the frame of government and society.

Because the systematic professional study of history began in the nineteenth century when national consciousness was heightened by frustrated national aspirations, historians for a long time tended to emphasize national differences among peoples of the European world and to pay slight attention to similarities. There were differences of course; but in the eighteenth century there were also notable similarities almost universal in that world, especially in the related spheres of government and society, and it is only by taking those similarities into account that similarities in response to the revolutionary surge in the last quarter of the century become in some measure intelligible.

In the eighteenth century Venice and Genoa were republics, the Swiss Confederation was a confederation of republics, and in the United Provinces the old conflict between republicans and the House of Orange continued. With these four exceptions, three unimportant and one equivocal, from the two continents of America eastward through Europe, every state was nominally or effectively a monarchy, and almost all the monarchies were effectively hereditary in the currently ruling dynasty. Government was in the name and under the authority of the king, the emperor, the tsar, the sultan, or, in Germany, of assorted dukes, margraves, and counts. Religion—one form of Christianity or another—was everywhere established by law, and the established church enjoyed legal privileges denied to other creeds. In some lands, England for example, the disabilities imposed on dissenters were light; in others they were ferocious, extending from banishment for dissentient forms of Christianity to death for atheists.

Again, in almost every European land, but not everywhere in the colonial world, immediately under the monarch in the hierarchy of secular honor there stood a class of hereditary nobles who enjoyed special privileges—political, social, economic, and ceremonial—attached to their status by law, although the range, variety, and economic value of privilege as between the nobilities of different lands diverged very considerably. Members of these hereditary nobilities

A major cause of the disintegration of the Polish state was the nobility's hold on the monarchy through its right to elect the king. This panoramic scene shows the election of Stanislas Poniatowski in 1764, held with great ceremony outside Warsaw.

almost everywhere held the places of highest honor in the courts of the monarchs. Although the law with respect to such places of honor did not usually grant much direct political power to those who held them, their ceremonial character often gave access to the ruler, and thus opened avenues of backstairs intrigue and opportunities for factional maneuvers to their possessors. Since the indirect power of the titled nobility, or part of it, depended on the malleability of the monarch and especially on the weakness of holders of important positions with direct governing authority, it was usually to the interest of the "court nobility" to keep strong men out of such positions.

A fourth common feature of most of the governments and societies of the European world was that "office," that is authority, theoretically originating and emanating from the monarch, was in a greater or less degree actually vested in men who claimed it as a matter of hereditary right, transmittable from father to son, from the possessor to his heir, and from owner to purchaser. In such situations many offices of state, both civil and military, had become the property right of their possessors. They were a source of both income and status which, with the perquisites, fees, and opportunities for corrupt dealing attached to them, were, like land, part of the family fortune. The right enjoyed by English peers of the realm to a place in the House of Lords in Parliament, the sovereign legislature, is an outstanding example of office that was hereditary but not venal, since a peer usually inherited his right to his seat in the Lords, but could not sell it. A place in one of the *parlements*, sovereign courts of France from whose judgment there was no appeal, was both hereditary and venal.

Besides families enjoying rights to a specific office, there were families from among the members of which offices, less specifically pre-empted, had to be chosen. This requirement might be a matter of law that rulers treated as binding or a matter of custom that they accepted. The effect was to limit much political and military power in Europe to a very small part of the population who held it by hereditary right. Nor was this true merely of power at the center, in the administrative capitals, or solely of temporal power. High ecclesiastical office, especially bishoprics, were in many lands held almost exclusively by the same families that enjoyed access to offices of state or the honor of nobility. Almost everywhere in Europe municipal authority was tightly vested in a few families, nowhere more so than in the ancient republican trading centers of Venice, Genoa, Geneva, and the towns of the United Provinces. Although local and regional variation was ubiquitous, the effect everywhere was similar: by law and custom to vest access to local authority and power as well as to central authority in a very small minority of the population.

Consequently, the overwhelming majority of the population of Europe had no say at all in the choice of the men who ruled them; but then they never had had much to say in the matter. Moreover, with respect to some offices the monarchs themselves lost all freedom to choose whom they would to exercise the authority that theoretically emanated from them; in respect to others they found their range of choice severely limited by law or custom. To rule as well as merely reign they had to rule through these irremovable vested authorities, or find means and men to circumvent them. Seen from another angle, men of ambition, talent, and considerable wealth found many principal avenues to power and authority altogether blocked. They either had to satisfy their ambitions in activities that gave them no direct political power and none of the prestige that attached to such power, or they had to chafe in discontent to see men of less ability inherit the authority they so vehemently desired. Far from loosening its hold or easing access to the inner oligarchic circle, it seems that during the first three-quarters of the eighteenth century all across Europe, the "Establishment," or "power élite," was maintaining its grip on the levers of power, both religious and secular, both civil and military. At some points—such as the officer corps of the French army, and local authority over the peasantry in Hungary, Russia, and elsewhere in Central and Eastern Europe—it appears to have strengthened its grip.

Still, up to the last quarter of the century it is easy to exaggerate the contemporary importance of the social group alienated by being blocked from attaining the inner circle. The number of men with enough ability, education, and wealth to suffer such frustration was not very large anywhere. Moreover, even very tight-meshed institutional fences surrounding the socially and politically privileged usually had a few small gaps through which the ablest, most ambitious, and most ruthless could push their way. Thus the danger of discontent was reduced by skimming off a few of the potential leaders of the discontented. Nor is it to be supposed that the situation evoked in the masses of the poor destined to be ruled by the privileged any revolutionary ideas or aspirations. No doubt these masses hated and cursed the worst of their local oppressors and exploiters. Their hatred occasionally broke out into mob violence, particularly when food was short, as it always was in bad years for the crops, and as it came to be more consistently short in areas like France, where the rise in population was not compensated by a rise in agricultural productivity or by uncleared land to absorb the overflow. Nevertheless, from 1700 on, the only major peasant revolts were in Eastern Europe, the greatest led by the Cossack Pugachev in the depths of Russia in 1773. Up to 1775 in Europe the *ancien régime*, the old order of monarchy, titled nobility, and ruling hereditary or quasi-hereditary oligarchy in established church and state, appeared not to be visibly threatened or challenged. What went on along the North American seaboard had not been highly visible in Europe up to that time, although it was about to become so.

Although there were similarities of the utmost importance in the governments and societies of the European world, there were also diversities that proved to be of decisive consequence when the revolutionary wave of the last quarter of the eighteenth century crashed against the power structures of the *ancien régime*. In the leading states of Central and Eastern Europe—Prussia, the Hapsburg lands, and Russia—there were obstacles to effective and cohesive political rule: scanty human and natural resources, indefinable frontiers, and lack of territorial continuity in Prussia; diversity of ethnic and linguistic grouping and of political and social structure, and, again, territorial discontinuity, in the Hapsburg Empire; enormous geographical distances, rickety institutional structures, and profound economic, technological, and educational backwardness in Russia. Under the façade of claims to absolute power the rulers of these heterogeneous states managed to weld their territories into sufficient unity to provide for their defense and even to engage in expansion at the expense of the soft and decaying states

Diversities in Government and Society

nearby that fell into their spheres of influence. We noted in the last chapter how Frederick the Great, Catherine the Great, and Joseph II added to the façade of absolutism the decorative motif of philosophical enlightenment. We also observed that Frederick and Catherine did not let philosophical enlightenment or anything else blind them to the harsh actualities of their position and of their need to work with rather than against the vested-power interests in their respective lands, and that Joseph II, who took his commitment to enlightenment more seriously, failed disastrously in his efforts at reform because he did not accurately measure the strength of those interests or come to terms with them.

In what follows therefore we shall give most of our attention to Britain and France. These two powers were the richest and, not only in the eyes of their own people but in those of the rest of the world, the most advanced in Europe in the first three-quarters of the eighteenth century. We begin, however, with Poland, the extreme case, a state toppling toward disaster during the *ancien régime*, unable to muster enough internal cohesion and force and external support to be saved from complete dismemberment by its neighbors in the years when the revolution struck in Europe.

The Collapse of Poland   In the first half of the eighteenth century Poland was in area the third largest state in Europe, with the fourth largest population. Before the end of the century Poland as a state had ceased to be. In three operations between 1772 and 1795 it had been partitioned among its neighbors, Austria, Prussia, and Russia. Two decades before the first partition it had been evident that Poland was no longer a viable political body, and its parlous condition had been deemed evidence that bigness in area and republican government were incompatible.

Two hundred years earlier, in the mid-sixteenth century, Poland was the farthest eastern outpost of the Western world, in touch spiritually and intellectually with the Renaissance and the Reformation, politically, socially, and economically no less viable than its neighboring states. It had the characteristic institutions of a state of the old regime—a monarch, an established church, a hereditary nobility, and privileged bodies. As in most medieval states, the orders of society—clerics, townsmen, nobles, free peasants—possessed "liberties," rights held by local custom or by charter, which protected their most vital interests from outrageous encroachments by other social groups. The disaster of Poland between 1550 and 1750 was the consequence of the catastrophic weakening of the major props of the old order and the destruction of the medieval liberties of all other orders of society by a hereditary nobility, the *slachta*, which comprised about one-tenth of the population.

The *slachta* controlled the ecclesiastical structure, as did the hereditary nobles in several other Roman Catholic states, by securing for themselves a monopoly of high church offices. By the eighteenth century the Roman Catholic Church in Poland reflected the intellectual decline of the *slachta* by its rigid persecuting intolerance, especially dangerous in a land with a large Greek Orthodox population in its eastern provinces.

The *slachta* destroyed the monarchy in all but name. This was made possible by the failure of the dynastic principle to establish itself in Poland. The *slachta* instead established the principle that monarchy was elective for life only, that they were the sole electors, and that before coronation every elected ruler had to come to terms with the electors in a pact that defined and limited the authority he could exercise. The effect was that the first qualification demanded of anyone who would be king of Poland was a willingness to dismantle the powers of the monarchy either by letting them fall into abeyance or by handing them over to the nobles, whether as individuals or collectively in the Diet, the national assembly, or in the local assemblies, the dietines.

The monarchy thus became too weak itself to safeguard the liberties of the lesser social orders, the towns and the free peasantry. Urban life, which had been reasonably vigorous and healthy at the beginning of the sixteenth century, had almost ceased by the eighteenth. The nobles destroyed town liberties, the rights to a measure of self-government that in medieval Poland as elsewhere in Europe were the foundation of urban life. They not only rescinded whatever protective legislation merchants of the Polish town had once enjoyed; they even conferred positive advantages on foreign traders, on one occasion barring native merchants from foreign trade altogether. They also barred the towns from the Diet, thus depriving them of all means for voicing or redressing their grievances.

The Polish peasantry suffered the fate common to the tillers of the soil in the other lands of Europe east of the Elbe in the early modern age: they were transformed into bondsmen. They lost all freedom of movement; they lost most of the land they had once tilled, and held what they held at the will of their lords, who were all nobles; they had to render heavy labor services on the lord's land; they had no appeal from the court of their lord to the king's courts or to any higher court; their lord could inflict corporal punishment on them at will; and they were bought and sold. Such being their condition, it makes little difference whether one describes the process as reduction to slavery or reduction to serfdom.

The cancerous growth of the power of the *slachta* did not engender in them any sense of corporate responsibility for the welfare of society or any capacity or will to rule effectively the society of which they had made themselves sole masters. So insistent were they on their own inflated "liberties," so suspicious of possible encroachment on them by members of their own order, that having made it impossible for the government to do anything effective about governing without the consent of the Diet they made it equally impossible for the Diet to do anything effective. The capstone of their creation of a power vacuum in Poland was the notorious *liberum veto*. This veto could be imposed by any member of the Diet, and its first effect was to block passage of any piece of legislation that any single member opposed. During the seventeenth century the effects of the veto were extended. Its imposition no longer merely reached the proposal against which it was directed; it also rendered null measures the Diet had consented to before the veto. And finally it dissolved or, as the Poles said, exploded the Diet itself. In an age of jostling for political power, when Frederick William I and Frederick the Great in Prussia, Peter and Catherine in Russia, Maria Theresa and Joseph II in Austria were achieving the power to grab anything in their neighborhoods not vigorously defended, the Polish *slachta* were dismantling the moderately viable political order they had inherited and rendering it and themselves impotent in its defense. The partitions of Poland were foreordained by the feebleness imposed on their native land by its own ruling class.

Karol Radziwill of the Polish hereditary nobility (the slachta) *was painted in 1785 as his country was crumbling under foreign pressures.*

The Ancien Régime in France

Historians for a long while construed the era of Louis XIV as the time when "absolutism" was fully achieved and firmly established in France, that thenceforth it remained the pattern of rule until it was shattered by revolution in 1789. This account of the matter, however, raises problems. First, the theory of royal absolutism in France was already rather fully worked out by the end of the sixteenth century. Moreover, even at the height of his power there were some policies of his government which Louis XIV and his officials were quite unable to carry through; for example, the transformation of France into an area of free trade by the abolition of internal trade barriers. Finally, after his death, despite their "absolute" power, his successors were unable sufficiently to restrain either the nobility or the vested privileged bodies through which the monarch ruled to secure the reforms necessary for the effective governing of the kingdom. Under the circumstances, instead of viewing Louis XIV as the political model of French monarchy, the object not only of cultural but political imitation by his successors and all European kings, it may be more enlightening to regard him as an exception—what biologists call a "sport." During the first half of his personal reign (1661–1688), as a result of fortune, his own energy and assiduity, and the ability of his advisers, he was able to bring his exercise of actual power into close conformity to the theoretical authority of the monarch stated in general terms in the theory of absolutism. His appetite for glory, fed by his very success, however, launched him on a pursuit of Continental conquest and domination. The disastrous consequences of this pursuit forced on him a series of policies and actions in order to raise money. These already foreshadowed and in part necessitated limitations on the effective power of his successors, which they either tacitly accepted or struggled against in vain. So viewed, France is reintegrated into the almost universal pattern of European politics and society whose four major constituents are the monarch, the established church, the hereditary nobility constituting a pyramid of honors, and the privileged bodies controlling political office. The French kingdom—in fact the greatest and richest, in appearance the most stable in Europe—was nevertheless in a peculiar position. The relations among monarch, nobility, and privileged bodies (including the Catholic Church) were such as to make France particularly vulnerable in the wave of revolution, and it was France that that wave struck in 1789 with cataclysmic force and an impact that in the following years was felt throughout the European world. One of the conditions, therefore, for understanding the onset of the era of revolution in Europe is to understand the relations among monarch, nobility, and privileged bodies in France from the death of Louis XIV on.

By 1715 Louis XIV outlived his eldest son and that son's son, so by the law of succession the heir to the throne was his great-grandson, Louis XV, a child of five. Absolute monarchies are especially handicapped when the king is a child, and France was no exception. Nobles and privileged bodies alike had long waited the death of the old king to reclaim the power and place he had denied them. The regent, Philippe of Orléans, gave the old nobility the chance it sought. Part of Louis XIV's legacy were the agents through whom he had tried to set the impress of his will on the government of France: in the provinces they were the *intendants*; at the center the Secretaries of State and the Controller

Hyacinthe Rigaud painted King Louis XV in 1715, upon his accession to the French throne at the age of five.

General of Finance. Neither Secretaries nor Controller held their positions by purchase; their tenure depended entirely on the royal will. Alongside them the regent established administrative councils with whom they were to work, and members of the old nobility of the sword received appointments to these councils. The experiment of making use of the old nobility failed. The noble appointees proved incapable of learning the first lesson about the effective exercise of governing power: that it falls to those who take the pains to get it and exercise it, that one has to work at it. The Secretaries worked; the nobles on the councils did not. Since the councils were evidently useless, the regent abolished them. The *parlements*, the most important of the privileged bodies, fared better. Louis XIV had straitly limited the right they claimed to remonstrate against royal edicts and to withhold registration, forcing the king formally to exercise his personal authority to register them in a *lit de justice* in order to give them the force of law. Because the regent needed to have the consent of the *parlements* to rescind Louis XIV's provisions for governing France after his death, and perhaps out of conviction, he restored to the *parlements* their right of remonstrance.

Despite some difficulties due to the dilapidated state of royal finances at Louis XV's accession (reigned 1715–1774), France emerged from his minority and the regency without disaster (itself a considerable achievement) and continued to enjoy unusual peace, prosperity, and tranquillity in the early years of the new king's "personal" reign. This happy situation resulted from the fact that Louis did not even try to reign but left virtually all authority in the hands of his old tutor, Fleury, bishop of Fréjus. The cardinal-bishop insisted on maintaining amicable relations with the old enemy, England, and allowed France to become involved in only one brief limited war until two years before his death at the age of ninety, when the reins of power began to slip from his aged hands. About the administrative shambles that Louis XIV had left at the end of his reign and about the shaky fiscal structure Fleury did almost nothing. As long as France remained at peace he did not need to, and before the bills for the cost of France's first large war (the War of the Austrian Succession, 1740–1748) fell due, he was dead.

The job of finding money was then handed to a dour, honest *intendant*, Machault d'Arnouville. In 1749, as Controller of Finance, he decreed the imposition of a flat 5 percent tax on all income without exception—the *vingtième*. The result was an explosion of rage and indignation on the part of the clergy. In an assembly of its own the clergy had traditionally bought their way out of direct taxes by a "free gift," which came to about one-sixtieth rather than one-twentieth of normal income, one-third of what the *vingtième* would have cost them. The clergy were not alone touched by the change in tax structure; a whole cluster of privileged bodies was also affected.° Among these were all who enjoyed immunities or advantages within the current structure, or rather chaos, of taxation. This included almost the entire nobility, both the old hereditary nobility and the relatively new hereditary nobility of office that manned the great courts. It also included provinces where local assemblies of estates sur-

Bishop Fleury (also painted by Rigaud) was Louis' tutor and then his chief minister for seventeen years.

° Note that in the United States, religious and private, nonprofit, educational, and charitable institutions receive exemptions from direct taxation today.

vived, since these assemblies had been able to strike favorable tax bargains with the monarch, and the provinces most recently annexed to the crown, whose ancient customs the monarchy had respected. Finally, it included most of the great towns, which also had come to favorable agreements with the crown. All these preferred the existing direct tax—the *taille*—from which they were exempt, and which consequently fell regressively upon the peasantry. The same cluster of interests had effectively frustrated the attempts amid the disasters of Louis XIV's last wars to draw them into the direct tax structure. While they passively resisted the *vingtième*, the clergy mounted active resistance to it in a campaign of prayer and by the threat of a sort of episcopal strike. When Louis XV withdrew his support from Machault, the first effort to meet the financial needs of the state by tax reform collapsed in the face of the clerical opposition.

The first serious crisis of the French monarchy of the *ancien régime* since the death of Louis XIV had openly set the royal governing bureaucracy against one of the privileged bodies, the clergy, and that body alone had been able to bring off a victory when the king failed to support his own servants. The next crisis followed hard on the next war, the Seven Years' War (1756–1763). This conflict, at once more disastrous for France and more costly than the War of the Austrian Succession, precipitated a far more severe upheaval and brought out into the open deeper cleavages in the old order. To meet what was clearly going to be a long-term financial crisis, the government issued several tax decrees. One indefinitely extended the *vingtième*, temporarily instituted during the war to meet immediate military costs. The second called for a reassessment of the land values on which direct taxes were based. A third levied a 1 percent tax on property in office. The clergy, the "old" aristocracy, the nobility of office, and the privileged towns and provinces were all hit by the new reforms. This time, however, the campaign against the bureaucrats supporting and exercising the king's authority was waged backstairs by factions of the old aristocracy with access to the king and publicly by the hereditary magistrates in the *parlements*, and by the surviving provincial estates. Two of the characteristic institutions of the old order, the hierarchy of honor and the privileged governing bodies, were drawn into a direct assault on the claim of authority of another of those institutions, the monarchy.

The *parlements* refused to register the tax edicts, published elaborate remonstrances against them, and harassed and even arrested royal officials charged with their enforcement. In pursuit of their opposition to the monarch's measures they engaged in correspondence with one another to concert measures of resistance and provide a common front of theory to justify their common action. Stirred out of his ordinary apathy by this statement of their right by the *parlements*, Louis XV confronted the *Parlement* of Paris with a statement of his absolute authority. On the *parlements* themselves, and on the course of obstruction to which they had committed themselves, the statement had no effect at all. At last, in 1768, Louis took the only step left for him short of capitulation. He put in office a new administration, headed by Maupeou as Chancellor, which simply abolished the *parlements* and sent their members into exile, the more cantankerous ones into parts of France with extremely disagreeable winter climates. Without offer of reimbursement to the hereditary members of the old

courts, Maupeou abolished property in judicial office and established new supreme courts paid by salary rather than fee and given assurance of fixed tenure. Controller General of Finance Terray carried through the financial reforms attempted seven years earlier, enforcing the edicts despite furious opposition.

For four years the new administration ruthlessly pursued its aim of indispensable fiscal reform, regardless of claims of privilege. Then Louis XV died. His successor, Louis XVI, immediately dismissed Maupeou and Terray, dissolved the new courts, and recalled the *parlements*. The monarchy thus surrendered its last chance of achieving solvency in the only way it could have been achieved: by the abolition of the exemption of the privileged bodies. It thus also surrendered to those bodies ultimate power and control over its destinies.

Louis XVI may not have known that that was what he was doing. If he did not, he soon received instruction. Having given up on achieving fiscal order directly by edict and in defiance of the privileged bodies, he tried to gain the same end by appointing as Controller General an experienced administrator, the *intendant* of the Limousin, Turgot, who was also a reformer in close touch with the advanced thought of his day in both political and economic matters. Turgot proceeded cautiously to seek a loosening of restrictions on the French economy, which might then yield enough taxes to meet government needs, a policy, familiar today in many countries, of aiming to increase the taxable gross national product by benign government action. Two actions Turgot deemed benign were (1) the abolition of guild monopolies in industry, and (2) the conversion of the obligation of peasants to do a few days' work a year to maintain royal roads (the *corvée*) into a very small tax on all landowners to provide wage-labor for road maintenance. The *parlements* struck out against the edicts. Very soon after, court intrigue struck down Turgot. It struck down with him the last serious

A contemporary engraving captures the pomp and circumstance attendant on Louis XVI's coronation at Reims Cathedral.

effort of the monarchy to achieve orderly and comprehensive reform in the face of a financial crisis and a rising crisis of confidence.

For the former crisis, the *parlements*, assuming leadership of the hereditary aristocracy and of all privileged bodies in the realm, were heavily responsible; they had succeeded in preventing a reform in the tax structure which alone would have resolved the government's fiscal problems. For the latter crisis, taking the same position of leadership, the *parlements* were also heavily responsible. They provided the rationale and the example for resistance to and defiance of the edicts of the king and for denials of his rightful authority. In so doing they had forced from Louis XV counterclaims of unlimited and despotic power. Only such a counterclaim sufficed to override the veto of *parlement* on necessary tax reforms. But in the second half of the eighteenth century in France in the midst of the Enlightenment, among the most enlightened people in Europe, the claim to unlimited and despotic power by any authority was not likely to be gratefully welcomed. Coming from the slothful and inept Louis XV out of the muddle of intrigue at a suspect court in the wake of national military disaster, it was not even credible. Public opinion, insofar as it was evident or articulate, supported the *parlements*, not the monarch. The *parlements* indeed incited public resistance to royal authority. In justifying their position they invoked the law, the motherland, the rights of the nation and of the citizen; and they claimed to speak as representatives of the people and to speak for liberty. It was a dangerous game, for concretely the only liberties they stanchly and ever more intransigently maintained were their own—the liberties of a narrow corps of entrenched hereditary judicial and administrative officers, the liberties of the titled nobility, the clergy, the officeholders, and certain favored towns and provinces to escape certain taxes, and in general the liberty of all legally privileged groups to cling to their privileges regardless of the common welfare. The privileged bodies were showing unprivileged Frenchmen the road to revolution, instructing them in revolutionary tactics and providing them with a revolutionary rhetoric. That their privileges were among the earliest items to go up in flames when the fires they set broke out among the unprivileged is not in retrospect surprising.

The Inimitable English   The rising against James II in 1688 is usually called the Glorious Revolution, and the arrangement and limitations of political authority in England after his flight to France and the assumption of the throne by his daughter Mary and her husband, William III of Orange, Stadholder of the Netherlands, is often called the Revolution Settlement. On the face of it, it was not much of a revolution; and it did not settle very much. The only legislative enactment that emerged directly from the Glorious Revolution was the Bill of Rights, the legal enactment of the Declaration of Rights adopted by the Convention Parliament, which conferred the crown on William and Mary. The Declaration had done little more than assert that most of the royal actions which most of the ruling class or the political nation called illegal for between sixty and a hundred years were indeed illegal, such as the power to suspend laws or to dispense men from their penalties, to erect commissions with judicial authority, to levy money without parliamentary grant, to raise a standing army in peacetime without consent of Parliament. That they were reaffirmations and precise definitions of what many Englishmen had long claimed to be law do not make the Declaration and Bill of Rights trivial. When William and Mary accepted the embodiment of the Declaration of Rights in the Bill of Rights, they accepted clear limitations on their personal powers and in effect on those of their successors. To abridge any of the rights declared in 1688 would henceforth and unmistakably require not merely the will of the king but an act of Parliament. Since the clauses of the Declaration made careful provision for the security of life, person, and property, which men in those days and subsequently deemed the primary safeguard of liberty, their effect was to put the liberty of the subject permanently beyond the grasp of the individual monarch.

Actually the Revolution Settlement settled a good deal more than was evident on the face of its immediate legislative work; it marked out with more or less clarity the bounds within which any subsequent government would have to work unless it was prepared to risk civil war. Because one governing group or another unceasingly pressed against some of these bounds or threatened to, it became necessary later to enact further restraining legislation. Thus to protect from the zeal of the supporters of the Church of England the minority that could not in conscience join that church, Parliament had to pass an Act of Indulgence (1689), subsequently called the Toleration Act, which legalized Dissenters' meetinghouses, exempted from the penal laws laymen who would take an oath of loyalty to the reigning monarchs and against the Popish doctrine of transubstantiation, and required of ministers an oath that only Catholic priests, Unitarians, and atheists could not take. Again, it was not until 1701, when some Englishmen threatened civil peace by taking seriously the claims of James II's Catholic son to inherit the throne, that Parliament passed an Act of Settlement denying the succession to any Roman Catholic or any ruler who married a Roman Catholic.

Beyond matters tacitly but not explicitly agreed on at the time of the Revolution of 1688 that required legislation later were a number of very important matters that did not require legislation at all. The English did not pass any laws positively defining or establishing "free speech" or a "free press," and before the Revolution these freedoms had only rarely evoked systematic defense. The licensing of the press, however, had in practice fallen to the crown and its agents. By 1688 very few politicians were ready to trust the power of licensing to the crown or to other politicians, so the Licensing Act was simply permitted to lapse. Utterance in print remained subject to prosecution under the laws of libel, sedition, and treason, and by word of mouth under the law of slander. There were further small restrictions under other existing laws. But since no one was ready to trust anyone else with the power required for stringent regulation, speech and the press became "free" in England, freer perhaps than anywhere in Europe at the time, simply by default.

The boundaries within which political matters had to be managed had also received considerable clarification as a result of the Revolution. In the crises of the reign of Charles II and especially in those which were provoked by the prospect of the succession of his Catholic brother James, considerable groups of English politicians took extreme positions on the extent and limits of royal

The English Parliament, from a 1742 view on the occasion of a speech by Walpole, standing at left center.

WILLIAM L. CLEMENTS LIBRARY

Fleury's contemporary, Sir Robert Walpole, dominated the British government from 1721 until 1742. John Wooton portrayed him in his role as the Master of Staghounds.

power. While many politicians preferred fudging, or "trimming," as it was then called, some argued that under no circumstances whatever were subjects justified in resisting the commands of the king, regardless of what he commanded. At the other extreme were men, republicans in all but name, who by one device or another would have so restricted royal authority as to subordinate it to the Houses of Parliament, especially to the lower House, the Commons. They wanted to make the king, as people then often said, into "a mere Doge of Venice," an executive errand boy for an all-powerful legislative body. These were the extreme "Tory" and "Whig" positions. From the succession of James II to his overthrow, English politicians learned that most of them did not seriously accept either of these extremes, and that even among those who did, very few were ready to fight for the sake of them. Tories were not ready passively to obey a Catholic king bent on destroying the established church and restoring Popery; Whigs were not ready actively to resist a Protestant ruler unwilling to leave the formation of policy or the choice of his ministers to Parliament, as long as he did not encroach on the liberties of the subject.

Such were the main boundary rules of the game of politics as it was played in the century between 1688 and about 1780. There was no lack of willingness on the part of politicians to try to change lesser rules—those applying to the duration of Parliaments, to the qualifications for membership in one House or the other, to the limits of religious toleration—for their own advantage. Nevertheless, politicians who pressed changes in the rules to the point where groups opposed to them would rather fight than suffer the change always got dropped from power. Consequently, there were no successful and few ardent attempts to change the rules, and none at all after about 1720. Compared with the tumultuous corresponding span in the seventeenth century, the years between 1720 and 1780 in Great Britain were of an internal tranquillity verging on stagnation.

The central problem for politicians after the Revolution of 1688 was posed by the very boundary terms of the Revolution Settlement. These implied that the king was to rule with the advice of ministers of his own choosing, but also with the consent of the two Houses of Parliament, most of the members of which were not of his choosing. The problem was to see to it that the king did not seek what neither a present nor a newly elected Parliament was likely to grant him and that the Parliament did not flatly refuse the king the means to do what on advice of his ministers he judged best. On the way in which to bring about this happy harmony between theoretically independent branches of government, the Revolution Settlement had nothing to suggest, no viable principle to propose.

This perhaps was just as well, since after 1688 English politicians were not much addicted to principle, and, in fact, the solution was found not in the statement of principle but in manipulation, maneuver, and adjustment of interests. The eighteenth century was, above any other, the century of interests in Britain. An interest was almost anything lawful° to which a sufficiently large, powerful, articulate, and organized group of men attached itself by the outlay of time, effort, money, or even mere loyalty. Among the great interests were the landed interest and the trading interest, the Church of England interest and the Dissenting interest. There were family interests and company interests, woolen and slaving interests. Further down there were the interests of men in their jobs, the "electoral" interest of peers and politicians in the parliamentary electorates they controlled by inheritance, purchase, or bribery, and the interests of considerable swarms of small and larger fry in places in government which they held or wanted, which they paid for and in return expected a payoff. Most of these interests had spokesmen in Parliament. Those charged with seeing to it that the king's government was carried on had the task of mobilizing enough of the parliamentary supporters of various interests, along with the considerable number of floaters who with, or more rarely without, reward were attached to the king's interest, to secure a majority in the two Houses of Parliament for what the king wanted or at least found acceptable. This required finding government jobs or positions and titles of honor for recognized spokesmen of various interests in Parliament, and jobs enough for their followers to keep them satisfied. If jobbery was not quite all there was to eighteenth-century English politics, it was an indispensable part of it. Another part of it was keeping the king's confidence, since the last word on who got government jobs was his. During the reign of the masterful William III, who knew quite exactly what he wanted, no problems rose. He wanted, above all, support for his Continental policy and managed matters to see that he got it. After a somewhat shaky two decades things settled down rather comfortably for almost four decades, from 1720 to 1760. First in Sir Robert Walpole and then in the Pelhams, George I and George II found men who, with aid of crown patronage, were able to patch together coalitions of interest in Parliament able to get for the kings most of what they wanted, or to persuade the kings not to want what it would be too difficult to get.

During the eighteenth century this odd political apparatus won wide admiration in Europe, often among intellectuals and reformers who did not actually

°Sometimes not so lawful either, as in the case of the Jacobite interest—the interest of those seeking the restoration to the throne of James II's male descendants—after the passing of the Act of Succession. The existence of a quiet smuggling interest including many members of Parliament may account for the complacency with which that body overlooked effective nullification of the Molasses Act of 1733 by smuggling American colonists.

Under Walpole's administration the English cabinet, shown here in session, evolved toward its modern form.

understand how it worked and were not aware of the tacit understanding and quiet deals that made it work.

Yet of certain highly visible achievements of the English these admirers were aware. England was more prosperous than any great Continental country, and Englishmen were freer—freer from arbitrary acts of the king's officers or of the church, freer to speak their minds, write what they thought, and worship as they chose or not worship at all if they chose not to—than any other people in Europe. Although there were privileged bodies in England and a hereditary nobility, membership in neither exempted men from taxation, and thus the most obnoxious and least defensible feature of the structure of privilege of the *ancien régime* did not exist. It was hard to believe that all these good things had nothing to do with the way Britain was ruled; they almost certainly had something to do with it. The richest men in Britain were either in Parliament or had their concerns represented by spokesmen for their "interest" there. Therefore they were more ready to grant taxes of which they had to pay a share to support the policies of government which gave them satisfaction or at least a hearing. Moreover, as much as to anything else the English owed their liberties to the strong sense of the governors that one of the prime conditions of governing at all was that they not govern very much. This was not the result of principle— laissez faire, or the general maxim that "that government governs best which governs least." It was the result of the discredit and distrust that the first four Stuarts had built up against the purposes for which strong goverment was likely to be used. This sense of things was reinforced by the evident incapacity of a minimal political apparatus, constructed on and by jobbing and for the management of interests in and out of Parliament, to undertake the complex administrative work that active government demands. Consequently, most governing was simply left to ancient and traditional local bodies—justices of the peace in the country and self-perpetuating oligarchies in the towns. The disposition, if any, of such bodies to hyperactive government was kept in check by lack of an effective local force to carry out their orders or even to repress riots. Thus the resources of the English state were not squandered on an effort, for better or for worse, to rule Englishmen. They went to buying allies and armies on the Continent and to maintaining the English navy, with a view to winning as much as possible in the game of European and colonial power politics.

About 1780 Britain's peculiar institutions, its way of adjusting the foundation elements of the old order—monarchy, established church, hereditary nobility, and privileged governing bodies—to one another showed signs of incipient disarray. In the first place, a number of important interests outside Parliament began to suspect that their wants were being poorly cared for in the House of Commons and by the king's ministers. They further suspected that, given the existing constitution of the House, this situation would continue. In large part the House was made up of the relatives, clients, and hirelings of great peers who controlled elections in boroughs where often there were few or, at worst, no electors,° of men who treated their ownership of a borough as a form of mercantile investment for sale to the highest bidder, of men who owed their

°Old Sarum, the property of the Pitt family, which returned to Parliament the great English minister of the Seven Years' War, William Pitt, was a borough without any inhabitants at all.

seats to boroughs controlled by royal patronage, of representatives of old entrenched and shrinking interests rather than new and expanding ones, and of a number of public-spirited but rather old-fashioned men whose good intentions marched far ahead of their abilities, their information, and their understanding. In the second place, major changes were taking place in the economy and society of England that were beginning to call for attention and action beyond the capacities and scope of the county magistracies, the justices, into whose hands internal government had fallen by default. The hitherto unstated but active principle of politics had been that the king and his ministers were to pay little direct attention to the condition of Britain and its governing. This principle was becoming outmoded, but how to adjust the necessary increase in concern and activity to a central apparatus of administration constructed almost entirely on the basis of patronage and jobbery was not in the least clear. Finally, the faith, so generally shared by all who enjoyed power and place in the old order in England, that that order was somehow the ultimate good attainable by human wisdom and contrivance, began to crumble. That faith had been reinforced for decades by the praise lavished on the order of things in England by the most enlightened foreign observers—men like Voltaire and Montesquieu. The praise of foreign observers, however, declined after the debacle of the American Revolution, and the United States, representing a new order of things, began to attract an enthusiasm that the English had once enjoyed. The question was whether the English way was in every respect the best possible, and that very question invited a much closer inspection of the way things actually worked and were working in English politics and society. It took a mind at once very subtle and very peculiar, like that of Edmund Burke, the Whig theorist, to argue that every major element in the going structure of power and politics was excellent beyond the possibility of serious improvement. Men of less subtle ingenuity, like Jeremy Bentham, the Utilitarian, concluded that from a rational point of view the structure could scarcely have been worse. Such men became reformers. More important, they arrived at something new, a consensus that the institution that before all others had to be reformed was the House of Commons, which was the center of power from which all further reform would have to flow and yet itself embodied all that was wrong with the old order, all that required reforming.

The aspiration to reform the old order in England did not result in disaster and destruction from without, as in Poland, or in revolution, as in France. Instead, that aspiration was frustrated for almost a half century by events. The main events were the outbreak of revolution in France and the conversion of France's internal revolution into an ideological war on the old order and all its institutions throughout the European world. These events ill served the cause of reform in England, the traditional enemy of French power. In the early 1790s the energies of England were diverted to resisting French expansion on the Continent, and the English movement for reform was compromised and discredited by its association in men's minds with the violent doings of the French revolutionaries. It was 1832 before the movement gained power and the Age of Reform in England began. Then it vindicated the leaders of the aborted reform movement of the 1780s: the initial reform of that day, the precondition of subsequent reform, was the reform of the House of Commons (Chapter 12).

A British officer who fought in the French and Indian War made this caricature of King George II about 1760.

The long and bitter struggle against the threat of French hegemony that ended
with the Treaty of Utrecht (1713) and the winding down of the Northern War
after Peter the Great's decisive defeat of the Swedes at Poltava (1709) introduced a period of relative tranquillity, partly induced by exhaustion, into the
power politics of the European states. With only minor interruptions, peace
prevailed until 1740. Then a major war erupted in Germany over Frederick the
Great's seizure of Silesia from Austria. Interspersed by truces and one formal
peace treaty (Aix-la-Chapelle, 1748), which was itself scarcely more than a long
truce, hostilities lasted from 1740 to 1763. The first phase of the struggle is
called the War of the Austrian Succession (1740–1748), the second the Seven
Years' War (1756–1763). Once Frederick had grabbed Silesia, the issue in Germany was defined: Would he be able to keep it? If he did, there would be for
the first time a German rival, the House of Hohenzollern, to the House of
Hapsburg in Austria for the dominant place in German affairs. If he did not,
Prussia would probably crumble to a third-rate power in the wake of his defeat.
In the end, and at terrible cost, Frederick managed to hold Silesia. He thus established the situation of rivalry and hostility between Hohenzollern and Hapsburg that was to characterize German history for a hundred years.

All the other great powers were eventually drawn into this struggle. The
British got involved partly because their king was also ruler of Prussia's neighbor, Hanover, and partly to prevent France from making the war the occasion
for another bid for European hegemony. France got involved first as Frederick's
ally and then as his enemy in a halfhearted attempt by frivolous statesmen to
revive the glory of the days of Louis XIV, an attempt that they had neither the
will nor the ability nor the resources to sustain. And finally Russia joined the
fray, because it now felt strong enough to play the old game of intervention in
German affairs that other powers had heavily indulged in since the beginning of
the Thirty Years' War.

The war in Germany more or less concurred with and overlapped with a world
struggle for empire between Britain and France, the only states with naval
strength and other resources sufficient for that costly form of enterprise. Britain's engagement in war for stakes overseas actually began in 1739 against
Spain, and after the peace of 1748 the colonial clash between France and Britain resumed in 1754, two years before either was embroiled in Germany.
Foolishly the French got much more deeply immersed in the German war than
the British did, and in consequence weakened their efforts in the New World
and India, the two principal theaters of imperial war. Britain had been trading
with India since early in the seventeenth century, France since the days of Colbert. Neither had sought to extend its political power there either directly or
through the chartered East India Companies that monopolized the trade. Nor
had there been any serious conflict between the two companies. The midcentury wars changed all that. Central power over India, held by the Mogul
emperors, had been disintegrating since early in the century, and princelings
now struggled for local power in the crumbling empire. When general war between France and Britain extended to India, sooner or later one commander in
the field or another was bound to try to weaken his opponents by alliance with a
native prince. In the event the French, the weaker power in the area, moved

*A well-adapted colonizer of the Brit-
ish East India Company is the subject
of a Bengal miniature of about 1760.*

VICTORIA AND ALBERT MUSEUM

first; the British perforce followed with profound consequences. First, both Western powers, or rather the trading companies they had chartered, found themselves inextricably embroiled in native power politics. Second, the embroilment revealed what previous commercial relations had concealed, that European troops were to an incredible degree superior to the Indians in the art of war, so that small numbers could defeat great hordes. Finally, it became clear that the exploitation of political power could with a little ruthlessness—no more perhaps than the native rulers deployed—be made to yield rewards far more substantial than mere trade afforded. It was the last two discoveries that gradually transformed the British, the victors in a trade war between two commercial companies, into the political masters of a vast subcontinent.

The superiority at sea, which was ultimately decisive in Britain's Indian victory, also defeated the French in the New World. There, with some support from the continental colonies, Britain destroyed French rule in Canada. The French were also ousted by the British from the great wedge of territory extending from the Appalachians to the Mississippi, which had been the initial object of violent contention between the two realms. Finally, France ceded to Spain its claims to land stetching west from the Mississippi. Thus by the Treaty of Paris (1763) France's first empire fell almost completely into other hands.

The great wars of the midcentury were followed by another era of relative tranquillity that lasted almost thirty years, to 1792. The removal of the center of major conflict from Germany had the effect of disengaging the groupings of European powers, one to find its main area of action in Eastern Europe, the other overseas. Prussia, Russia, and Austria concentrated on the complex maneuvers required for the partition of Poland among them, a process accomplished in three stages (1772, 1793, 1795), at which point the Polish state as an independent power (but not as a "problem") vanished from Europe. Further preoccupation with adjustment of claims and effective influence on the fringes of the European world was provided for Russia and Austria by the decay of the Ottoman Empire. Wary dealings prevented each power from taking so much so fast from the debilitated Turks as to provoke the other to war.

While the great states of Central and Eastern Europe were keeping out of major mutual conflict by negotiating the downfall of Poland and of Ottoman power in Europe, the Western maritime states with surviving overseas possessions were looking for ways to get back at Britain, whose naval victories in the Seven Years' War threatened these possessions. The opportunity came when in 1776 the thirteen continental colonies of Great Britain declared their independence of the mother country.

Revolution in North America, 1763–1788

The wars of European states that came to a short halt with the peace treaties of 1763 had major repercussions. None of these was in the long run more important than a crisis in the relations between Great Britain and its colonies on the North American continent which those wars generated. That crisis culminated in a struggle for independence in which, with the aid of France and the more than benevolent neutrality of the rest of Europe, the colonists were victorious. Having freed themselves of British rule, the people of the thirteen separate colonies bound themselves together under a common written law, a constitu-

A sharp opposition attack on the government's colonial policy, showing North America in flames, appeared in the Westminster Magazine *in 1774.*

tion, into a federal republic, the United States of America. These events and the construction that some people in Europe put on them created a situation favorable to revolution in Europe and helped to give form and concreteness to some of the aspirations of the revolutionaries. In particular, the cost to the French government of its aid to the colonists plunged it into a fiscal crisis; its failure to resolve this crisis was to render all too conspicuous the weaknesses of the *ancien régime*. At the same time, the achievement of the North Americans, as construed by French observers at a distance of 3,000 miles, provided some Frenchmen with new perspectives on the possibility of change in France and gave a new concreteness and definition to vague, ambiguous, and sometimes contradictory aspirations for change and reform expressed and publicized by the *philosophes* of the Enlightenment and also, ironically, by the principal victims of revolution in Europe, the privileged bodies such as the French *parlements*.

The process that began in America in 1764 can be regarded as an education of the colonists in what they thought about a number of matters that hitherto they had not given or needed to give much thought to at all. Their active though inadvertent teacher was the British government. Between 1688 and 1764 British governments had provided no instruction in such matters because within the widest limits they had let the colonies go their own way. The limits were those set by the Navigation Acts, which regulated trade within the empire. Those acts in fact required the colonists to do very little that they would not have wanted to do anyhow. The sole apparent exception to the rule was the Molasses Act of 1733 imposing a heavy duty on molasses brought into the colony from the French West Indies. The unfortunate effect that this would have had on the major American industry of rum-making was avoided because the act was not enforced. The importers got their French molasses by paying a very small traditional bribe to customs officials, an arrangement with which everyone was reasonably happy except perhaps the British West Indian sugar planters in whose behalf Parliament had originally passed the act. For the rest the governors appointed by the crown for each colony obeyed instructions from home, which did not amount to very much, as far as they could, which meant as far as the colonists would let them. Any excess of gubernatorial zeal was easy for the colonists to cool, since each governor relied for his pay on appropriations by the assembly of his colony, and delaying salary was a very effective persuader.

These arrangements, so generally attractive since they maximized profits and minimized effort for almost all the interested parties, were disrupted after the Seven Years' War. That conflict, including its American phase, the French and Indian War, had cost England heavily in outlays to defend and extend its empire. The very large extension in America—Canada and the land from the east bank of the Mississippi to the Appalachians—would clearly require continuing defense. To His Majesty's government in England, sensitive to the preferences of English taxpayers, the idea occurred that it would be gratifying to those taxpayers, convenient, and appropriate if the American colonists bore the charge of what after all was their own defense. Without more ado, and without expecting repercussions in the colonies, in 1764–1765 the government put through Parliament two acts: one tightening the colonial customs system so that it would not merely channel trade but yield revenue, and the other requiring colonials to affix stamps, purchased from the government, to legal instruments and other sorts of documents in common use, as the British at home had to do.

The colonists decided that both acts were tax measures aimed at producing revenue, which indeed they were. The colonists easily made up their minds that they did not want to pay these taxes, less easily that they ought not pay them because Parliament had no right to levy them. They refused to pay the taxes while they sought their repeal. They boycotted British imports and they mobbed a few of the unfortunate colonials whom the British government had appointed as stamp distributors. This so discouraged the other appointed distributors that no money came in; and besides doing nothing for the Treasury, the boycott hurt many English merchants. In less than a year the government had taught the colonists that on a theoretical level they did not believe the British Parliament had the right to tax the colonies, and on a practical level that a dozen separate colonies, which had been quite incapable of acting together in any matter before, could act together to resist what colonials sensed was a common danger and a common wrong.

Because the uproar in the colonies subsided quickly with the withdrawal of the stamp tax, the leaders in Parliament erred in gauging the nature of the crisis and a few years later again tried to solve British fiscal problems by taxing the colonials, this time indirectly. The new taxes all took the form of import duties collectable at colonial ports rather than a direct tax like the Stamp Act. By boycotts and pamphlets the colonists reasserted their refusal to pay any tax, direct or indirect, to which they had not consented through their colonial assemblies. Again Parliament pulled back, but this time not fast enough or far enough. It continued the import duty on tea, and then, to help bail out the East India Company, improved it in a way that gave the company a monopoly, cut the American merchant middlemen out of the trade, and maintained the principle of parliamentary supremacy over the colonies. With a fine mixture of zeal for freedom, profit, and counter-principle, some Bostonians unloaded into the harbor the first shipment of tea to arrive under the new law. This action of seditious violence and resistance—or nascent patriotism, depending on one's point of view—persuaded Parliament and the king alike that they could rule the Bostonians only by force. This was almost certainly true. Unfortunately, the measures adopted by Parliament to rule Boston, the so-called Coercive Acts, were such as to persuade not only the Bostonians, who needed little persuading, but all the colonies that they would just as soon not be ruled by Parliament at all. The only way for the colonies to stop being ruled was to resist and to organize for resistance. The only way the colonies could justify resistance was to allege that no power in England, king or Parliament, any longer had the right to govern them; but since they had to be governed, this meant that they had to assert the right to govern themselves, which they thereupon proceeded to do. By July 4, 1776, the British government had educated the American colonists into believing in their own independence, a notion they could have scarcely defined, much less entertained, twelve years earlier, but which they declared with great confidence, or at least a show of it, on that day. The war between the colonies and the mother country which had started a little earlier continued.

British will to coerce the colonists collapsed in 1781. Fighting considerable

Another Whig cartoon, this one done early in 1776, has the government's ministers slaying the American goose that lays the empire's golden eggs.

Drawings by a German, Johann Ramberg, portray two of the highlights of the American Revolution: above, the signing the the Declaration of Independence, and below, the surrender of Lord Cornwallis' army at Yorktown.

forces at a distance of 3,000 miles or more across water was not impossible (the British had done it before), but it was difficult, and doubly so without full command of the sea. The French joined the American colonists in the war against Britain, and the rest of the European powers adopted a policy of excessively amiable neutrality toward the rebels. When local British supremacy at sea failed at Yorktown and Lord Cornwallis surrendered his army there, the thirteen colonies had to face up to the cold fact that they were indeed independent. They were not, however, and did not intend to be wholly independent of each other. When the Declaration of Independence spoke of "The *United States*," it paid the ultimate tribute to the instruction that Britain had given the colonists. Men who twelve years earlier had never thought of the colonies as anything but separate entities, each going its own way, as a consequence of common experience began to think, and now perforce for the common defense had to think, of thirteen states acting in concert. The British had produced a new nation—the United States.

They had not produced a new government for the new nation nor indeed for each of its constituent states. Producing the latter was not very difficult. By and large the Americans were satisfied with such government as they had had before 1765. Experience with written colonial charters suggested to them the expediency of getting the rules of government down on paper, especially rules to prevent any governing body whatever from exercising the unlimited power that Parliament claimed to have before the War of Independence. The consequence was a rash of written constitutions with bills of rights attached, the bills securing from invasion by the governments established by the constitutions the liberties for which the Americans decided they had fought.

While adequately providing for the governance of the several new states, the Americans provided less than adequately for the custody of their common affairs. The Articles of Confederation of 1777 under which the United States was governed during its first decade did not provide the central government with enough of the cement of power to hold together the states with their divergent concerns and conflicting interests. Within a few years it appeared to many thoughtful Americans that unless a government more effectively constituted to care for the common interests of all the citizens of the United States was created to replace the weak Congress of the Articles, centrifugal forces would break up the union of states and leave the new nation prey to external enemies, to internecine war, or to both. Given both the mutual jealousies of the states and the inevitable objections of local politicians to surrendering power that they had in hand, it was fortunate that those who were convinced of the need to reconstruct and strengthen the fabric of the central government included in their number most of the major political leaders of the new nation.

Debate ordinarily takes place over points of doubt and disagreement, and it is likely to obscure wide areas of agreement. Such was the case with the deliberation of the Constitutional Convention that gathered in 1787. Disagreement over details concerning the mode and allotment of representation obscures the fundamental agreement of the delegates that the federal union had to be strengthened, that this required a more powerful executive, that the chief executive and the legislature should hold office in consequence, direct or indirect, of elections, and that the lower house of the legislature should be chosen by direct election from districts of equal population. That executive, legislative, and judicial authority should be seated in separate branches of the government, that the new federal government should have adequate taxing power, and that the new Constitution itself should go into effect as a consequence of ratification by conventions elected by the voters of each of the several states—these things, too, caused little difficulty. The failure to include in the federal Constitution a bill of rights modeled on those in the state constitutions making explicit the limits of the authority of the federal government did make difficulty; but this was an unfortunate oversight rather than a point of disagreement. It was quickly rectified by the amending process for which the Constitution did provide. The failure to deal forthrightly with the problem of Negro slavery was not an oversight. The issue was kicked under the rug, as it had to be if the new Constitution was to be adopted in the southern states. Ultimately, in 1861, that issue was to bring about the only major breakdown of constitutional process in the history of the United States up to the present.

The neatly dressed bewigged gentlemen-farmers, merchants, and lawyers responsible for the transformation of the thirteen continental colonies into the United States of America do not exactly conform to our present notion of revolutionaries; but they had made a revolution. Even they knew it, and they imprinted their knowledge on the Great Seal of the United States, "*Novus Ordo Seclorum*," a new order of things. Perhaps, however, they were not fully aware how revolutionary they were, since much about the new nation that struck the Old World as very revolutionary was indeed only a codification and a firm establishment of what had been prevailing practices in most of the colonies. As long as the Americans remained colonials, these practices were not highly visible from Europe. When the new nation established itself in an eye-catching way by successful disobedience to England in the midst of an eye-catching war, its features both old and new attained high visibility in Europe. Alongside something of a new discovery of America by Americans there took place a new discovery of America by Europeans. Although there were several ways of construing them, government and society in the United States could not be construed to fit well any of the prevailing patterns of ordering government and society in contemporary Europe. They could, however, be construed as embodying in concrete organization and effective action much that the *philosophes* of the Enlightenment had put into words about the need of a new order.

Just by being there, just by surviving without disaster, the new United States stood as a challenge and a threat to the *ancien régime*. The United States dispensed successfully with the most universal institutions of Europe—a single established and privileged church, membership in which was a condition of full civil rights; a hereditary nobility; ruling legislative, administrative, and military bodies, admission to the upper echelons of which was based on birthright and ownership or sharply restricted by law to a tiny fraction of the population; and, finally, monarchy itself. Of course, as colonials, the Americans had already been getting along without or with a scarcely visible minimum of all these things. Several colonies had got along from the start without any religious establishment and by the time of the Revolution all practiced toleration. Thereafter, any question of a national established church and of religious qualifications for the enjoyment of civil liberties as American citizens would have disrupted the union, and to forestall this the very first clause of the Bill of Rights was enacted: "Congress shall make no laws respecting an establishment of religion or prohibiting the free exercise thereof." In the United States the radical principle of religious freedom replaced the Old World principle of religious establishment with or without toleration for dissent, and a clerical order with heavily vested interests in a society rooted in privilege gave place to free churches.

Differences in informal social status based on the differential values of the community existed in the colonies as they do in all complex societies; in each colony there had emerged a "natural aristocracy." The kings of England had not chosen, however, to transform this aristocracy into a hereditary order endowed with legal privileges in virtue· of the possession of titles of honor. During the rebellion, moreover, the Americans most attached to England and English ways, the group most likely to lend any support to the notion of a hereditary nobility, were skimmed off. As loyalists the most vigorous and involved among them had to flee as the British lost control of the colonies. Thus one of the most characteristic institutions of Europe, a hereditary nobility with claims, not only moral and social but legal, to both privilege and deference never had existed in colonial America, and any likelihood of the emergence of the institution was stifled by a specific prohibition in the Constitution itself.

The removal and proscription of loyalists also helped to nip in the bud the flowering of those privileged bodies exercising governmental authority in which membership was achieved by purchase or co-optation or passed as heritable property from father to son. The small and not very promising beginning of a faintly similar institution had made its appearance in the form of the native-born councils of the colonial governors. The governors had tended to select these councils from a rather small inner circle of eminent families. Whatever the future might have held for them under more favorable circumstances, they were hopelessly compromised by the excessive number of loyalists who served on them. Unlike the monarchies of Europe, unlike its republics—Venice, Genoa, Geneva, and the Dutch Republic—the new republic in America was to have no small group of men possessed of any special vested right to hold office and to enjoy its privileges, powers, and emoluments, much less to pass them on to their heirs. The issue of republicanism against monarchy had scarcely risen in the colonies in the half century before the Stamp Act of 1765, nor did it rise seriously after 1776. It did not rise earlier because no one of much consequence in the colonies had ever imagined being under anything but monarchical govern-. ment; it did not rise after 1776 because no considerable group in the new nation conceived monarchy as even barely tolerable for free Americans.° The establishment of a republican polity was the most novel and radical act of the Revolution, but it led to no domestic trouble at all.

That the new nation in America had made a clean sweep of several of the most common institutions of Europe—institutions long held to be indispensable to the orderly conduct of any considerable community—was evident to any

---

°A few, like Alexander Hamilton, who did so conceive it, realized that opinion was overwhelmingly adverse and did not press the point.

European who had the curiosity to inform himself. What the salient traits of the new order were and what they implied were more difficult questions that different observers might answer in different ways. Still, there were some traits hard to overlook. In the first place, except (always) for the black slave, in senses in which almost any European would have understood the terms "liberty" and "freedom" every American enjoyed a wider liberty and a more general freedom than did almost any European—freedom of religion, of assembly, of the press, of speech, and from arbitrary acts of government, along with other liberties written into the bills of rights of both state and federal constitutions. Second, Americans were subject to a system of taxation that required the consent of assemblies of the representatives of those to be taxed. The representatives to the assemblies were elected on the basis of franchises far broader than those for selecting members of such bodies in Europe, in some states coming close to adult male suffrage. And since the same bodies that taxed also legislated, the "consent of the governed" to the laws that governed them was not just an elegant fiction, as it was in England, for example. Third, in the absence of any legal claim to prescriptive rights to any office, all offices were open to talent, at the very least to the talent for job-getting or for winning popular elections. Fourth, the notion of equality had a richer content and a more general acceptance as a political and social ideal in the United States than anywhere else in the world. Even economically, although there were some very rich men and some very poor ones, the gap between rich and poor was less conspicuous and probably narrower, excepting always the slaves. The presumption was in favor of equality; inequality was not to be assumed; it needed to be justified as a special case, an exception to the rule. Fifth, the constitutions of the states and of the federal union established protections for what their constitutions guaranteed to their citizens by establishing courts which assumed the power to declare unconstitutional any acts of the executive or legislature which in their view exceeded the authority vested in the three branches of government by the fundamental law. Finally, the very source of that law, what it derived its authority from, was "the people," not in the abstract way that the Roman jurists said law derived from the people, but by very concrete acts. The Constitution proclaimed the basis of its own authority: "We the people of the United States . . .," and in fact it was ratified by "conventions," by assemblies elected by "the people" in each state for that particular purpose.

Whatever judgment Europeans might make of what happened in America, in these respects it was quite evidently radically different, different to the very roots from anything they had known. And Europeans did make judgments about America, favorable and unfavorable, ignorant and informed. Books, the periodical press, American ambassadors, and Frenchmen and Poles who served in the American armies informed Europeans about the new order of things. The information, however, spread very unevenly: thinly indeed in Eastern and Central Europe, more thickly in Western Europe, and thickest of all in France. France was America's ally in the War of Independence. It was also the land of the Enlightenment and the *philosophes*. And it was a land headed for a political crisis which in 1789 precipitated a revolution in the affairs of Europe that overshadowed what had happened in America.

The Marquis de Lafayette, shown here directing a battle in Virginia, was one of those who helped import American revolutionary ideas into France.

10

The French Revolution

From 1789 to 1815 the Western world was convulsed by a revolution briefer but greater in geographical extent and more intense than the religious revolution of the sixteenth century. Before the conflict subsided, its repercussions were felt in places as far from the center of Western civilization as Brazil, Argentina, and Peru. The struggle even influenced politics in the newborn United States.

The tempo of events was such that at its center the revolution brought about in a few months changes in society that men in some of the remoter parts of the Western world are still struggling to achieve today, a century and a half later. Liberalism, democracy, socialism, nationalism, and dictatorship were all launched on their modern careers between 1789 and 1800, and the world that emerged in 1815 was vastly different from the world of 1789. Some new values developed in the course of the revolution, and a few old values were practically destroyed. Those older elements of Western civilization that survived emerged greatly changed. States, social classes, economic relations, habits of thought, political beliefs and alignments, religious institutions—the great revolutionary explosion touched them all, reshaping them, transmuting them, altering their value. After 1815, for example, there were still nobles in most of the Western world and clergy in all of it, but nearly everywhere their social position, their relations to other social groups and to the state, and their own outlook on society had undergone extensive alterations. The revolution that brought about this transformation of Western institutions and values and ideas began in France in 1789 and is known to history as the French Revolution.

The events that precipitated both the overthrow of the French monarchy and the revolutionary outburst that coincided with it were a response to a crisis in French institutions. As it spilled across the borders of France into lands with different histories and institutions, the Revolution was itself altered in character by the alteration in its setting and circumstances. Much that was typically French in it, being irrelevant in the new setting, was abandoned. The northern Germans, for example, displayed little of the violent anticlericalism so characteristic of many French revolutionaries. Much that originated in France was also transformed in passage to other lands. The nationalist upsurge, for instance, received an aristocratic development in England and a romantic monarchical development in Germany that almost concealed its republican and equalitarian French origin.

In 1789, despite its vast authority, the French monarchy was verging on bankruptcy: the government was unable to pay its debts and unwilling or unable to repudiate them, or to wipe them out by inflation, or to impose taxes heavy and broad enough to pay them. The financial crisis stemmed from the debt incurred in supporting the revolt in America. It is one of the ironies of history that, in insuring the triumph of the American patriots, the French monarchy precipitated

August 10, 1792: as drawn by François Gérard, Louis XVI (behind the barred window at right) takes refuge in the hall of the Legislative Assembly to the jeers of the Paris mob fresh from the sacking of the Tuileries; later that day he was deposed.

The orders of the Estates General, in typical garb: from top, a noble of the First Estate, a priest of the Second, and a commoner of the Third.

an act of unintentional suicide. By supporting the American Revolution, it popularized ideas entirely antipathetic to the French social order. Thus, the same action that impaired irretrievably its financial position also corroded the traditional moral foundations of the monarchy.

In proportion to France's resources and income, the government debt was not a really serious matter; with smaller national resources the English government managed a much larger debt. The French revenue system, however, blocked the monarchy from access to the country's wealth. The monarchy financed itself through a hodgepodge of irrational devices—a salt tax that fell upon different areas with differing severity; a customs system that did not treat the country as a unit but broke it up into three zones, each with a different tariff relation to the others and to foreign powers; and the *taille*, or land tax, which fell unequally on different regions and different social groups. As we have seen, this chaotic tax structure, the result of measures of expediency adopted in the near or distant past, was firmly established in custom by the 1780s.

Those subjects who could least afford to pay taxes were the ones most heavily burdened with fiscal exactions. Several of the principal indirect taxes were excises levied on the necessities of life, such as salt, and these lay much heavier on the poor than on the rich. The personal *taille*,° which provided the greatest part of the royal revenue, did not fall upon the privileged orders at all but fell with full force on the peasantry. By the 1780s it was clear that no adequate increase in the royal revenue was attainable within the framework of the existing tax structure. Further, the tax structure reflected the social constitutional structure of France and could not be remodeled except by reducing or abolishing the most cherished privileges of certain provinces and classes.

Throughout the eighteenth century the nobility had been strengthening its political position. In the previous century there had arisen alongside the military nobility a *noblesse de robe*—a "nobility of office." The mere possession of certain offices conferred on their holder and his heirs all the legal privileges of the older nobility. The most important offices of this kind were the judicial positions in the high courts—the *parlements* especially. In the seventeenth century the military nobility and the *noblesse de robe*, mutually distrustful, counterpoised each other. After Louis XIV's death, however, the two nobilities united socially and politically to protect and advance their common interest. That interest, as they saw it, was to gain a monopoly of power in the state by controlling all the high places in the armed forces, the judiciary, the central administration, and the local administration, and by closing the paths of entry into the nobility and thus preventing newcomers from diluting their power. The spearhead of their drive was the judiciary. As we saw in the last chapter, the judges of the *parlements* claimed the authority, denied them by Louis XIV, to veto royal edicts by not entering them in the court registers and refusing to enforce as law an unregistered edict. On presentation of an edict, the judges could remonstrate against it. Even if the king himself came in person to command registration (the *lit de justice*), the judges sometimes went on strike, refusing to enforce the law and suspending the work of the courts. The maximum punishment that the king could impose on the

°The personal *taille* was a land tax levied on the underprivileged landholder for whatever land he held. The real *taille* was levied on unprivileged land, whatever the status of the landholder.

judges for this final act of resistance was exile. Both remonstrance and judicial strike were, in a sense, appeals to public opinion, and the strike had about it a revolutionary tinge, since it invited Frenchmen to ignore the expressed will of their monarch. A king uncertain of his prestige would hesitate long before driving the courts to take extreme measures, and Louis XV and Louis XVI were quite rightly uncertain of their prestige. In 1776 the *Parlement* of Paris blocked the reforms proposed by the economist Turgot and brought about his resignation as finance minister. Thus, led by the *parlements*, the privileged orders brought to nothing Louis XVI's halfhearted attempts to save his finances from chaos.

The inability of the government to meet its financial obligations in the 1780s gave the nobles an opportunity to assert their power. When Louis called their leaders to an Assembly of Notables in 1787 to ask them to surrender some of their tax privileges, they demanded in return the privilege of supervising the royal revenue, and they demanded that local administration be transferred to local assemblies under their control. Thus they sought to change their role: instead of being the instruments of the king, they would be his master.

Louis could not accede to this attempt to transform France from an absolute monarchy to a government by and for the nobility. When his ministers attempted by edict to gain the taxing authority that the nobles refused to concede, however, they ran head on into a revolt of the aristocracy. The *parlements* would not register the edict, and the government's attempt to coerce the judges resulted only in popular demonstrations and mob violence. The courts were popular not because of the political views of the judges, but because they alone could discuss and criticize the action contemplated by the government in advance. The nobility encouraged the outbreaks of mass support in their favor and put themselves forward as champions of freedom against royal tyranny. They thus uncorked the bottle and released the genie that was to crush them. In but a few years men far more skillful at inflaming a mob organized the masses and destroyed the king, the church, and the nobility.

The revolt of the nobility was a success. The king revoked his tax edict, recalled the *Parlement* of Paris, and turned for help where the nobles had directed him to turn—to the Estates General of the realm, which had not met since 1614. At that gathering clergy, nobility, and Third Estate had assembled, debated, and voted by class order. According to custom, consent of all three orders was necessary to bind the whole body, just as the consent of both Senate and House is necessary to bind the American Congress. The nobles, who believed this custom would apply to the Estates General of 1789, thus believed they held a veto power over the king and the Third Estate and that any reform would have to be tailored to their specifications. As soon as the Estates General met in May, 1789, however, the middle-class, or bourgeoisie, part of the Third Estate moved to take over the revolution that the aristocrats had instigated.

The bourgeoisie was in law and in fact part of the Third Estate, which included about 98 percent of the population of France. The clergy were separated from the mass of Frenchmen by their way of life and by their privileges; they were internally divided into an upper clergy—bishops, abbots, and other prelates, practically all of noble birth—and a lower clergy drawn from the unprivileged

The Estates General and the Bourgeois Revolt

Balancing on a plank over the Bastille's moat, a revolutionary leader takes the surrender of the garrison.

mass of the people. The nobility was an almost closed caste. On the other hand, although there was a great social distance between the upper-middle class and the laboring poor, the two were not separated by any insurmountable legal barrier, and there were always men making their own way up—and down—the ladder between them. Moreover, a change in social geography had broken down an ancient barrier between the bourgeoisie and the rest of the common people. Until the late fifteenth century the bourgeoisie, as their name indicates, were almost exclusively townsmen—burghers. By 1789 this was no longer true. As minor officials, lawyers, wholesale dealers in wine, grain, and wool, entrepreneurs in the cloth industry, estate managers, and landowners in their own right, the French bourgeoisie had been pushing roots into the countryside. While the English peasantry, for example, could look only to the gentry-aristocracy for leadership, the French peasant looked to the bourgeoisie.

The bourgeoisie of France, although it may not have known it, was ripe for revolution. Its leaders were rich and well-educated. In their hearts they had rejected the social order in which they lived—a society that allotted political power and social prestige not in proportion to wealth, education, or ability, which many of the bourgeoisie had, but on the basis of birth and legal status, which the bourgeoisie did not have and could not acquire. The *philosophes* had taught the best intellects of the middle class to regard this situation as an outrage against nature. The snubs that they suffered and the obstacles that they met when they pressed against the barriers of privilege stamped into their hearts the beliefs that the *philosophes* had impressed on their minds. The bourgeoisie did not intend to allow the assembly that was to provide France with a new constitution to become a mouthpiece for their class enemy, the nobility. Moreover, the entire legal, judicial, and administrative structure with its multiplicity of customary laws, its complex and costly system of class justice, its chaos of trade barriers and trade restrictions, its confusion of locally varying weights and measures, and its mass of obsolete offices inhibited that pursuit of profit which the *philosophes* deemed natural and the bourgeoisie desirable.

That basic constitutional reform was to be the business of the Estates General became apparent as the local electoral bodies that chose the delegates formulated instructions and grievance lists (*cahiers de doléances*). All three orders in almost every district demanded a limitation on the king's despotic authority, participation by a representative body in lawmaking and taxation, and freedom of the individual and of the press.

Everything else that might go into reconstituting the French monarchy was undecided and in dispute. The decisions would hinge on how the Estates General was organized for business. To appease the Third Estate it had been allotted a membership equal to that of clergy and nobility combined; but the effect of the concession was nullified by the Paris *Parlement*'s ruling that voting was to be by order rather than by head. In such a case *either* privileged order—nobles or clergy—could veto any measure it disliked. When the Estates met at Versailles, the Third Estate, chosen by 98 percent of the people, refused to accept an arrangement that would make its vote of no greater force than that of those elected by 400,000 nobles or of those who spoke for 100,000 priests. Pursuing the tactics that the *noblesse de robe* had used against the king in 1787–1788, the deputies of the Third Estate struck by refusing to organize for business in the Estates General. At the same time they set afoot a popular agitation—establishing clubs, writing pamphlets, and declaiming in public places, especially in Paris—against the organization of the assembly by separate orders.

The role of the king in the crisis over the organization of the Estates was ultimately decisive for the destiny of the Revolution. A chubby, stupid person with a kind heart and a flaccid will, Louis XVI was not the man to master a crisis that would have taxed the firmness of Louis XIV or the resourcefulness of Henry IV. He always yielded to the more vigorous (or violent) force, but only after clearly betraying the fact that his sympathy was with the vanquished. And thus gradually and reluctantly, without ever gaining the credit that a show of good will might have won for him, he stumbled from one concession to the next, until he had finally divested himself of all effective power to influence the course of events. In the crisis over the method of voting in the Estates General he clearly aligned himself with the privileged orders. The deputies of the Third Estate refused to budge, declared themselves a National Assembly, and vowed not to separate until they had given France a constitution. Gathered to hear the king's proposals for reform—the first positive program Louis had set forth during two years of crisis—these deputies refused to disband when told to adjourn. At first, orders were given to remove them by force. Then Louis capitulated with an "Oh, well, the devil with it, let them stay," and ordered the nobles to join with the deputies of the Third Estate.

Representatives of the Third Estate had won. The working out of the constitution would be in their hands; the three orders united and, voting by head, became the Constituent (i.e., Constitutional) Assembly. Moreover, the pattern of the Revolution had been set both by the king and the Third Estate. Louis had committed himself to the aristocrats and henceforth was to be weighted down by their unpopularity. The members of the Third Estate, bourgeois in origin, had countered the dangers of force in the king's hands by drawing support from the masses, especially from the working-class quarters of Paris. This alignment of forces—the king, leading or driven by the privileged orders; the bourgeois deputies, leading or driven by the Paris mob—endured as long as the monarchy survived. In order to put pressure on the Constituent Assembly, to restore obedience in the capital, or to protect himself, the king summoned several regiments of his army to the region of Paris. The leaders of the Assembly suspected a design to defeat and destroy them by overawing their supporters. The Parisian mob reacted on July 14, 1789, by destroying the Bastille, a royal fortress in the heart of the working-class quarter. Although not an event of vast consequence, in men's minds the fall of the Bastille became a symbol of the collapse of the old order, and Bastille Day is now a national holiday.

A few months after the attack on the Bastille, revolutionary groups replaced the old government of the city of Paris; and in October a crowd of Parisians marched to Versailles and forced the king, followed by the Constituent Assembly, to return with them to the capital. Henceforth Louis and the Assembly alike acted in the presence of the threat of violence if they dared to oppose what the leaders of the mob strongly desired. The course of events had destroyed the basis

Revolution by Consent of the Bourgeoisie

of trust on which a peaceful settlement would have had to rest. Moderate men found their support slipping out from under them. Slowly but surely the extremists gained the upper hand. The conflict ultimately resolved into a struggle between the demagogues who controlled the Paris masses and the reactionaries who gained the support of disgruntled elements in France and abroad.

In the meantime, however, the Constituent Assembly had seriously set about the work of providing France with a constitution. Its foundations were laid in August, 1789, between the time of the storming of the Bastille and the march on Versailles. Despite haste, fear, and violence, the work was well done. The abolition of feudal and manorial dues achieved and the human rights proclaimed in this short span of time provided the aim and the guiding principles for reformers and revolutionaries in Europe for generations to come.

On August 4, in the face of agrarian risings in the provinces and bread riots in the towns, the Constituent Assembly voted the destruction of the legal and economic remnants of the corporative order of the Middle Ages. Liberal nobles, some of them great landowners, took the lead. Personal serfdom and labor services without compensation were abolished, while certain other peasant obligations were made redeemable by money payment. Other measures abolished the manorial courts and ended the proprietary right of the judicial nobility to their offices. Towns and provinces followed the nobles in renouncing their privileges. Finally, the Assembly decreed equality of legal punishment and the equal eligibility of all citizens for all public offices. Despite some small qualifications as to the degree that selflessness moved the Assembly of August 4, the measures taken were in fact a social revolution. The regime that based right on special group privilege, that measured status by birth, that regarded society as a graded hierarchy of unequal members—the *ancien régime*—was destroyed in France to the extent that legislation could destroy it.

In the Declaration of the Rights of Man and the Citizen, intended as a preface to the constitution that was the goal of its labor, the Constituent Assembly offered a preview of what it intended to put in the *ancien régime*'s place. The heart of the famous document is its first two articles: "Men are born and remain free and equal in rights. . . . The natural imprescriptible rights of man . . . are liberty, property, security, and resistance to oppression." The *ancien régime* was to be replaced not by some other status-based regime, but by a political and social order founded on the equality of free men. But freedom and equality are words of variable meaning. The Assembly used the remainder of the document to spell out what it had in mind. The relation of freedom and equality to security and resistance to oppression were not defined, nor was there any explanation of the last two terms. Liberty was well taken care of in provisions much like those that appeared in the bills of rights of the several American state constitutions after the break with England. Freedom of speech, freedom of the press, freedom of worship, and guarantees of civil rights against the arbitrary acts of the government belonged to all citizens. So presumably did the right to choose their own representatives to the sovereign lawmaking and taxing body. With respect to these liberties, at least, all men were born and remained equal. They were also equal before the law. No longer would there be one law for Normans, another for Bretons, one for nobles, another for commoners. As to property, the Declaration

A medal struck to celebrate the opening of the Estates General depicts the three estates cooperatively pulling Louis to the Temple of Happiness.

says little; it only prohibits its confiscation without compensation and due process of law.

In this and other matters the Declaration omits to say some things its promulgators meant, and says a few things they did not mean. The lawyers who framed it did not really mean that all men should actually have an equal vote in the choice of the legislature. These same men, when they came to write the constitution of 1791, imposed a property qualification limiting the right to vote. They did mean that the *right* to hold property should belong equally to all, but not, of course, that all men should hold property in equal amounts. They were bourgeoisie, not communists or socialists. The equalities that concerned them most were legal equality—one law for all citizens—and equal right of holding office for men of equal abilities.

Yet the very inadequacies of the Declaration of the Rights of Man as a definition of the aims and convictions of the bourgeois leaders of 1789 made it a great rallying point for future reformers and revolutionaries of all shades. Through it, all the aspirations of the great men of the Enlightenment were transmitted to the nineteenth century. Not only the reformist doctrines of Locke and Montesquieu, but also the radical democracy of Rousseau were embodied in the Declaration. At the time of its adoption it made explicit what the decrees of August 4 had already implied. Taken alone, those decrees might seem merely adjustments of the old order to a change in circumstances. Taken with the Declaration, they were intended as the first and necessary move toward establishing the new society that the men of the Enlightenment had dreamed of—more rational, more natural, more humane, freer than what had gone before.

Struck four months later, a second medal commemorates the destruction of the ancien régime's feudal privileges by the Constituent Assembly.

Until 1791 the Assembly pressed on with the work of reconstituting France in the midst of deepening crises. It had to establish new instruments of local government to replace the old which had disintegrated. It had to do something about finances. It had to decide what to do about the Church. To meet these problems it broke with the old administrative divisions of France into provinces, the ancient units from which the French state had been pieced together, and established the smaller, more regular units with no tradition roots, the *departments* of today. It confiscated Church lands and used them to back a new issue of paper currency. It made the priests into public officials elected by the people and paid by the state; it excluded Papal jurisdiction from France. This clerical legislation was called the Civil Constitution of the Clergy.

The effects of the legislation of the Constituent Assembly were not always exactly what the deputies intended. The intent of the law on local government was to bring about a devolution of authority. But in practice the local government law put effective power in the hands of the best organized political groups in each locality. In most places the best organized group was the Jacobin Club, an institution born of the Revolution itself. The Jacobin headquarters in Paris, led by some of the most important members of the Assembly, informed and directed the local clubs, which became the effective governing bodies of their localities. The new currency, called assignats, secured on confiscated lands, by no means solved the money troubles of the state; indeed, in the midst of revolution these problems were not soluble in any ordinary sense of the word. Those who redeemed their assignats for confiscated Church land, however, acquired a permanent financial stake in the Revolution and defended it in a most vulnerable sector—its relations with the Roman Church. Those relations, uneasy from the outset, came to a complete break when the Assembly voted to require the clergy, as public servants, to take an oath of fidelity to the constitution. Thus the revolutionaries achieved what the enlightened despots had aimed at—complete control of the national church by the state. Their success, however, not only cost them a break with the Papacy but also won them the bitter enmity of the most deeply religious segment of both the Catholic clergy and the laity of France.

The Organization of Villainy

For Louis XVI, the Civil Constitution of the Clergy was the last straw. He had seen his nebulous good intentions misconstrued; he had suffered indignities and threats from the Paris mob; he had had to stand by while his wife, Marie Antoinette, was menaced by ruffians; he had watched the Constituent Assembly work out a constitution that gave him only a suspensive veto over legislation and thus reduced his power to less than that of the President of the American republic. As a pious Roman Catholic, faithful to the Papacy, he was now called on to assent to the destruction of Papal authority over the Church in France. In June, 1791, after much secret preparation, he fled eastward toward the Rhine, where embittered French aristocrats had taken refuge and were seeking to build up a coalition against the revolutionaries. At Varennes, close to the border and safety, he was captured and forced to return to Paris. His flight and its failure destroyed whatever small credit and power he still possessed. A year later law caught up with fact; the powerless king was deposed. France, now a republic, was a land without a basic law, since the constitution of 1791 was at least formally monarchical.

That a foreign coalition should sooner or later be formed against revolutionary France was almost inevitable. The country was prey to serious internal disorders, and it was the good old custom of European powers to seize on the weakness of a neighboring state in order to annex part of it. By 1790 the three Eastern powers —Prussia, Russia, and Austria—were preparing to divide what was left of Poland. Wracked by revolution, France now seemed to offer another attractive field of activity. In 1792 the French Legislative Assembly (chosen in October, 1791, to succeed the Constituent Assembly) beat Prussia and Austria to the draw by declaring war on them.

The so-called War of the First Coalition precipitated a crisis in the Revolution. In its last months the Legislative Assembly proved hopelessly weak; in its first months its successor, the National Convention, which assembled in September, 1792, was paralyzed by an internal factional fight. As Prussian columns marched into France in June, 1792, the ill-led, demoralized troops of the new republic had fled in disorder, slaughtering their own officers, and opened the way of the enemy to Paris. Generals, holdovers from the days of the monarchy, directed their forces halfheartedly, and some deserted to the anti-French alliance. A brief rallying enabled a French army to invade the Netherlands, but it was quickly routed. In the west of France a devout Catholic peasantry was in revolt against the Revolution.

As the foreign enemy threatened France, the internal enemy prepared to welcome him. The latter was everywhere: priests who had rejected the Civil

Sketched by an eyewitness, the royal family takes its exercise outside the prison tower in which it was held.

Constitution of the Clergy and priests who had accepted it and then regretted their acceptance; aristocrats and the servants of the aristocrats; profiteering grain merchants who turned the emergency to their own gain while republicans starved; men who would sell themselves to the foreigners at a price; moderates— some of them still members of the Assembly and the Convention—who failed to understand that there was no longer any middle ground to stand on, that if they refused to go forward with the republic they were inviting a violent monarchical reaction. From the imminent dangers without and within, the people of Paris saved the Revolution late in 1792. To save it they intimidated the enemies of the Revolution by violence or fear of violence.

By 1792 intimidation was not a novel instrument of revolutionary politics. In the crises of 1789 radicals and reactionaries alike had sought to intimidate their opponents, the latter pinning their hopes on the royal army, the former on the city mob. Even before his troops set foot in France, the Prussian commander, the Duke of Brunswick, had tried intimidation from afar by threatening to subject Paris to "military execution and total annihilation" if any harm came to the royal family. Paris had answered the threat with far more efficient measures of counter-intimidation. In a municipal *coup d'état* the political leaders of the industrial sections of the city overthrew the government of Paris and replaced it with an insurrectionary Commune.

The inevitable though passive center of all counterrevolutionary plots was Louis XVI himself. The men who controlled the Parisian masses led an attack on the royal palace and forced the Legislative Assembly to imprison and depose the king, and a few months later, in January, 1793, forced the Assembly's successor, the National Convention, to decapitate him.° The rulers of the Commune had all suspected counterrevolutionaries in Paris seized and imprisoned, and they established a Revolutionary Tribunal to administer summary justice. In September, 1792, they connived at the massacre of all the inhabitants of the over-flowing Paris jails, both the counterrevolutionaries and the common criminals. They encouraged the people of the provinces to proceed in a like manner against all who were suspected of treason. Finally, pressure from the Parisians resolved by a blood bath a struggle of factions that, in the midst of the war crisis, had paralyzed the Legislative Assembly and threatened to do the same to the Convention. The rulers of Paris demanded from the Convention death for the members of that body, the Girondist party, who had led France into war and proved so incompetent to direct the struggle; and they got what they demanded.

This final act of victory ended the brief and bloody period of power of the insurrectionary Paris Commune. The proscription of one organized party—the Girondists—left the only other organized party, the Jacobins, in full control of the Convention. The Jacobins in the Convention were both a political faction and leaders of the directing unit—the Paris Jacobin Club—of a network of organizations widely spread through France. Because of the dissolution of the old local authorities and the insufficiency of the new ones, as we have seen, the Jacobin Clubs had become the effective governing bodies in the provinces. Their following in Paris and out, and after the purge of the Girondists in 1793 their control of the Convention, enabled them to take over the leadership of the Revolution

Louis XVI is shown in June, 1792, being forced to don a liberty cap and drink a toast to the Revolution.

°The following October Louis's wife, Marie Antoinette, met the same fate.

David's celebrated painting, Death of Marat *(1793), shows the Jacobin leader slumped in his bath, assassinated by a patriotic peasant girl.*

which for a year had gone by default to the radical politicians of the city. The Jacobins also took over the methods of the Commune. Intimidation of enemies of the Revolution became the order of the day. The so-called Reign of Terror became the official policy of the rulers of the young republic.

When the Jacobins attained power, victory or disaster still hung in the balance. France faced a coalition of foreign enemies that included every other great power in Europe except Russia. The peasants of the Vendée in the west of France were still in arms against the Revolution, waging a deadly guerrilla war on the forces sent to destroy them. The great provincial towns, egged on by those Girondists who had escaped the guillotine, rose against the dominance of Paris.

To meet the threat of catastrophe the Jacobins created a new Revolutionary Tribunal in Paris that knew only one sentence—death—and rarely gave any verdict but guilty. The Jacobin Terror extended to every corner of the land. In about a year it claimed 20,000 victims, most of whom were doubtless guilty of what was charged against them—that is, opposition to the rule and the rulers of the Convention. At the height of the danger from the foreign enemy the internal enemies of the Revolution who were not actually destroyed were undoubtedly held in check by the Terror.

The executive committee of the Convention—the Committee of Public Safety—learned more than intimidation from the insurrectionary Commune. They applied to the nation a system of war emergency measures that the Commune had already tried on the Parisians. They mobilized the abundant manpower of France for national defense. "All Frenchmen whatever their age and sex," ran the decree, "are called by their country to defend liberty." Enforced throughout the land, the decree provided the army with a mass of youth in their physical prime such as Europe had never before seen under arms. Nor had any Western state ever before been called upon to maintain an army so enormous. The Committee organized the supply of food, clothing, and munitions to the troops with the same indifference to individual private rights that they displayed in recruiting its manpower. The farmer's crops, the manufacturer's wares, and in many emergencies the very shoes of the citizens were commandeered. The scientific brains of the country were also requisitioned: metallurgists, chemists, and mathematicians devoted themselves to finding new sources of supplies and ammunition, speeding up production, and improving communication.

War and mass conscription added to the economic disruption brought on by the Revolution itself. The Jacobins had to find means of subsistence for the home-front force as well as for the army. To this end the dictatorial Committee seized grain supplies, not for the army only but for grain-deficit areas and especially for Paris. To secure a fair share of the basic necessities for the poor in Paris, to halt the decline in value of the assignats, to check the inflation of prices, and to stabilize the market the Committee instituted rationing of bread and grain, and established price and wage controls. The Convention abolished the redemption payments that the Constituent Assembly had required the peasantry to pay the lords for the commutation of manorial dues. It also for the first time made confiscated land available in lots small enough and on terms of payment liberal enough to permit poor peasants to acquire land directly. The aim of the policy of the Convention was something new in the history of the Western world. The most that governments in the days before the Revolution had done was to form policy in such a way as not to arouse the discontent of the masses, to seek to keep them passive. During the Terror the government by positive measures sought to elicit the active and enthusiastic support of the masses. In so doing it revealed what enormous power fell to rulers who succeeded in gaining that support.

The intensification of national effort brought with it a surge of patriotic fervor, which the revolutionary government vigorously fostered. Education, revolutionary festivals, songs, even the calendar, were given a patriotic twist. As passion against the enemy rose, the category of patriot narrowed and that of enemy expanded. All who deviated to the left or the right of the line laid down by Maximilien Robespierre, the most powerful man on the Committee of Public Safety, were treated as enemies of the people. The Committee put the press, so free in 1789, in a tighter strait jacket than Louis XVI had ever attempted. The stage also underwent a stringent censorship. Government spies lurked wherever men were likely to be plotting, or even saying, things adverse to the Committee's dictatorship. The tension and hostility that the fierce regime of the Committee evoked in the Convention and in the country soon entered the Committee itself. Those who felt that the mission of the Committee was to organize victory over the enemies of the Revolution ran head on against Robespierre and his followers. The latter conceived their mission to be the establishment of democracy based economically on small peasants and artisans and spiritually on a fanatical patriotism—a "republic of virtue." As a result of a sudden stroke—the *coup d'état* of 9 Thermidor (July 27, 1794)—men who regarded the dictatorship of the Committee primarily as a military measure won control of the Convention. Their victory resulted in the destruction first of Robespierre and his group, then of the dictatorship of the Committee and the Terror, and finally of the ascendancy of that radical, leveling, democratic republicanism ever since known as Jacobinism.

Before the Jacobin regime bled itself to death, it saved the Revolution from destruction at the hands of the First Coalition. The most amazing achievement of the dictatorship was the creation of the revolutionary army. It took the demoralized remains of the old army and amalgamated it with the mass of enthusiastic recruits raised by universal conscription. It provided the new military force with a brilliant set of young generals, drawn from among the lesser officers of the pre-revolutionary army. Having escaped by grace of the Revolution from ancient curbs on the military advancement of commoners, these men became dedicated and efficient servants of the new order that had opened the way for their talents. The Jacobins also gave the army an effective tactic. It had been worked out twenty-five years before during the *ancien régime*, but it was peculiarly suited to the new army, since it did not depend on the intricate defensive movements of close-packed human robots but on the shock-power of men high in morale, heavily supported by artillery, attacking en masse and using the bayonet.

Before this new and terrible weapon, forged in the fierce heat of the Terror, the old-style armies of the coalition melted away. In the fall of 1793 the invaders, pushing into France from Spain on the southwest, Piedmont on the southeast, and from the Austrian Netherlands and the Rhineland, were stopped cold. In 1794 the armies of the Revolution turned the British and the Dutch from the Austrian Netherlands, attacked Holland, occupied parts of the Rhineland, and invaded Spain and Piedmont. The collapse of Jacobinism did not impair in the least the deadly effectiveness of the army it had created. In the next three years that army dismantled the European coalition piece by piece. Spain dropped out; Holland was overrun; and Prussia signed a peace that put the whole left bank of the Rhine in French hands. In these three years the republic achieved what Louis XIV had utterly failed to accomplish in almost fifty—control of the middle and lower Rhine and of the Channel coast. Badly defeated in Italy by the brilliant generalship of a rising young commander of French forces, Napoleon Bonaparte, Austria finally made peace by 1797. French arms reached deep into Italy and organized much of it into satellite states wholly subjected to the power of France.

The Thermidorean Reaction

In France itself, however, the Revolution had lost its impetus. In their frantic organization of the national power, the Jacobins infringed upon personal liberty and rights of property. In so doing, they had gone far beyond the point that most Frenchmen found acceptable in the way of reform. The fall of Robespierre was the signal for a reaction. It is called the Thermidorean reaction from the month of the revolutionary calendar in which Robespierre was executed.

Men in the National Convention who had gone along with radicalism and with the Terror as an emergency measure were unwilling to continue it now that the victories of the army had ended the emergency. They abolished the Committee of Public Safety and destroyed the machinery of intimidation, including the Revolutionary Tribunal. But these men of Thermidor had steeped their hands in royal blood, and, as ordinary, mediocre men, they liked political power and the financial advantages that went with it. For five years, from 1794 to 1799, by various means, legal and illegal, peaceful and violent, those deeply implicated in the Revolution before Thermidor clung to control of the state. They thus succeeded in preventing a Bourbon restoration. But they also thoroughly discredited themselves with the French people. The new constitution of 1795 (the third since 1789) and the new government, called the Directory, got off to a bad start when the outgoing Convention packed two-thirds of the incoming legislative body with its own members. The old rulers under a new name failed to cope with the runaway inflation that had plagued France since 1793. They could not even make the final peace that most Frenchmen wanted, because the revenues that kept their regime afloat came from tribute money exacted in lands that the army had conquered. When in 1799 a new alliance, comprised of England, Austria and Russia—the Second Coalition—inflicted on the French armies a few serious though temporary reverses, the popularity of the Directory, never considerable, hit bottom. A faint flurry of Jacobin revival sent the ruling clique scurrying to the military to prevent a new surge of violence and to protect their jobs. The soldier they turned to was the most brilliant and most popular of the new generals, Napoleon Bonaparte. It was, as we shall see in the next chapter, like a flock of black sheep turning to the tiger to protect them from the wolves.

The Fruit of the Revolution

The era of the Revolution left behind it a heritage not only to France but to the whole Western world, and to people of the non-Western world who were not to hear of the French Revolution until it was only a memory.

Robespierre climbs the steps to the guillotine as the executioner exhibits the head of one of his followers and others of his party in the tumbrels at left await their turn.

The dream of a truly just and righteous social order is older than Western civilization itself. In the eighth century B.C. the Prophet Isaiah had foretold a time when

> They shall beat their swords into plowshares, and their spears into pruninghooks: nation shall not lift up sword against nation, neither shall they learn war any more.

This vision never wholly vanished. But for almost 2,500 years the belief in an age of righteousness to come was linked to the belief that that age would be the result of the direct action of God or of one especially sent by God to turn the course of history from the path of iniquity. Only in the eighteenth century did a new generation of prophets—the *philosophes*—foretell a time when justice would reign on earth, not by the grace of God, but by the effort of human thought and human action. In the French Revolution the vision of the *philosophes* was put to the test of practice. The leaders of the Revolution made a serious effort to root out iniquity, oppression, and ignorance and to establish the foundations of a free and just society. For the last century and a half the demand that rulers remold society in order to attain a reasonable and equitable social order has never ceased. The failures that have dogged every effort to attain such a goal, and the disillusion that has followed each successive experiment, have not extinguished hope. They have only convinced the hopeful that the particular *means* so far employed have been wrong; but the faith persists that some new way of remolding political or economic or social institutions will bring a decent and just organization of human affairs within the reach of human effort. The faith generated by the Revolution that men can achieve the good society, first by taking thought and then by taking action, has stunted the growth of conservatism in the Western world. The conservative position, that things are not as bad as they might be, and that changes are likely to be for the worse, survives with difficulty in a moral atmosphere suffused with the belief that men—so miserable at every present moment—can be made both happy and virtuous in the future by a properly constructed set of social institutions.

Although the Enlightenment and the French Revolution posed to the Western world the problem of achieving a just and reasonable social order by remodeling the machinery of society, the solutions that the Revolution itself came up with were various and conflicting. At the very end it turned about on itself and went back to its beginning when Napoleon, returning from Elba, offered to incorporate into his imperial constitution, from which he had hitherto excluded them, the personal liberties that the legislators of 1789 had written into the Declaration of the Rights of Man. In some ways the Declaration, made a dead letter by events soon after its adoption, was the greatest and most enduring monument of the Revolution. It embodied the aspirations of enlightened men of the eighteenth century. Personal liberty, civil equality, religious freedom, security of property, representative government under law, these principles became the goal of merchants, manufacturers, lawyers, doctors, and intellectuals—the middle class— all over Europe during much of the nineteenth century. To regain the ground won—and lost again so quickly—in the early days of the French Revolution became the political objective of that class which was to be the chief beneficiary of the vast economic changes called the Industrial Revolution. Thus the August days of 1789 provided a ground plan for a brave new world to the leaders of nineteenth-century liberalism.

The days of the Terror too put their mark on the new century. They taught whoever was willing to learn that an overwhelming force slumbered in the hitherto non-political masses of the peasantry and the urban poor. Whatever party could capture those masses and win their active support could crush to powder any interests less broadly based. The Terror pointed not only to the extent of the power of the people but also to one means of harnessing that power. The Committee of Public Safety had tried to provide the populace of the countryside with land and the masses of the town with bread; it had aligned itself with the masses against the classes, with the poor against the rich. In the nineteenth century the Terror provided a model, a tradition, and a method for radical democracy.

The Committee owed a large part of its success to its identification of patriotism and the cause of the French nation with the people's cause. The hopes and fortunes of the French masses were bound up with the victories of the armies of France. A fervor and a fanatic love, which only occasionally had appeared among the masses before, and then in a religious guise, were focused on the nation. *La patrie* became the object of a blind and unreasoning devotion. The force that gave momentum to France during the age of the Revolution, nationalism, has generated one drastic rearrangement after another in the political map of the world during the past century and a half.

On the extreme fringes of revolutionary radicalism in the early 1790s there had appeared a group, insignificant at the time, which rejected political means of building the perfect state on the grounds that such a state needs most of all to have sound economic roots from which a good social and political order would naturally grow. The perfect state must be based not merely on equality of rights but on equality of things. The radical sponsors of these notions got involved in a conspiracy against the Directory. Its members were arrested and its leader, Gracchus Babeuf, was executed in 1797. He thereby became the first martyr of the vast movement, generally called socialism, which since his time has seen hope for man in the radical reconstruction and equalization of the economic order and the property system.

In addition to giving birth to the four great movements—liberal, democratic, nationalist, socialist—whose interplay would provide the pattern of politics in the Western world to the end of World War I, the French Revolution firmly established three institutions that were to provide a common framework for the shifting political trends of the nineteenth and twentieth centuries: the national mass army based on universal obligation to military service; the centralized professional bureaucracy, open to talent and prepared by training to assume the increasingly complex administrative burdens of modern government; and the secular state, finally and fully emancipated from subjection or limitation by an established church and conducting its affairs solely with a view to its own interests.

The Revolution also gave France a new ruling class, the bourgeoisie, and elsewhere stirred in the hearts of the middle classes a desire to attain the position and achieve the gains of their French counterparts. Legal privilege and the corporative order had been destroyed or undermined not only in France but wherever the armies of the Revolution or the empire established French hegemony. Nowhere were they completely restored after 1815. The efficiency and rationality of the administrative and legal arrangements of the new order were obviously better adapted than the overgrown clutter of custom, tradition, and group privileges of the *ancien régime* to the changing economic pattern of the coming age. As the proponents and beneficiaries of the new sort of rational, efficient institutions in both the economic and the political spheres, the middle class dominated the nineteenth century.

Their dominance, as we shall see, was never comfortable, easy, or very stable. The world they made and ruled never came up to the optimistic expectations of those men whom the Enlightenment and the Revolution had taught to look forward to the early establishment of a truly righteous and just social order. And here the Revolution played a historic trick on the middle class which most substantially and immediately benefited from it. For the French Revolution was the first European revolution openly to justify itself *as a revolution*, not as a restoration. Whereas the religious revolutionaries of the sixteenth century and the English revolutionaries of the seventeenth had claimed to restore an old order maliciously destroyed or to maintain the existing order against attack, the French revolutionaries set up the bold claim of a right to subvert violently the legitimate institution blocking the realization of their ideal purposes. In the nineteenth century men ill-satisfied with the world this middle class made were well-satisfied to take up the weapon of revolution that that class had forged on the eve of its struggle for supremacy in France, a weapon it would willingly have destroyed on the day its victory was won. The bourgeoisie, however, had made revolution part of the pattern of Western politics, usable against any established order including a middle-class order. One of the richest and most troublesome legacies of the French Revolution to coming generations was the idea of revolution itself.

An allegory of the French Revolution is crowded with symbols of mob violence and wholesale slaughter.

11

The Napoleonic Era

The French Revolution wrought with remarkable speed and finality a number of fundamental changes in French life, but it failed to provide the country with political stability, the kind of stability that countries which have undergone a radical dissolution of traditional social bonds particularly require. In France, during the decade that followed the storming of the Bastille in 1789, several groups greatly enhanced their status and wealth: the peasants who had been freed from feudal obligations and acquired land of their own, the artisans who took advantage of the abolition of guilds to go into independent business, professional people for whom the Revolution opened many avenues of advancement, and investors and speculators of all kinds, especially those dealing in real estate. By the mid-1790s these groups, having gained all there was to gain from the revolutionary upheaval, were desperately anxious for a resumption of political stability. What they wanted was the restoration of a monarchy capable of legitimizing and safeguarding their gains. They could not accept, however, a restoration of the Bourbon dynasty, for along with the Bourbons would come the very administrators, nobles, and clergymen at whose expense they had enriched themselves. "Bonapartism," a system based on the personal dictatorship of Napoleon Bonaparte, provided an excellent way out of this dilemma. It legitimized the social achievements of the Revolution while restoring the political absolutism of the *ancien régime*.

Bonapartism did not remain confined to France, for under Napoleon's leadership the ideas and institutions of the French Revolution were carried by French armies to many remote corners of Europe. This fact lends special historic significance to the Napoleonic era: within France Napoleon solidified a social revolution, but abroad he initiated one. Wherever he was in control he transplanted French revolutionary achievements, abolishing feudal traditions and sharply curtailing the power of the aristocracy and clergy. Thus Bonapartism may be said to have been conservative in France and revolutionary elsewhere, the difference being that Napoleon came to power in France after the Revolution had done its work, while in other parts of Europe he took power away from traditional rulers and had to accomplish the revolution himself.

Nevertheless, both in and out of France the long-term effect of Napoleonic rule was the same. It promoted everywhere the urban and rural middle class—the manufacturer, the lawyer, the shopkeeper, the artisan, the peasant proprietor—at the expense of the old privileged estates. Behind the imperial façade and the military glory, the middle class moved inexorably to a dominant position in European society, which it was to hold throughout the nineteenth century.

Napoleon's paternal and maternal ancestors were of Italian origin. The Buonapartes had left Florence early in the sixteenth century to settle in Corsica, then the possession of the Italian republic of Genoa. In Corsica they continued to

Napoleon's Rise to Power

Jacques Louis David, the more or less official artist of France's Revolutionary era, painted this unfinished portrait of Napoleon in 1798, when the young general was the talk of Paris after his victories over the Austrians in his first Italian campaign.

speak Italian and to marry Italians and retained the sense of family cohesion typical of their people. Napoleon's father, Carlo, a lawyer, married Letizia Ramolino. Their fourth child, born in 1769, was registered as "Nabulione." The boy learned French in school and in time acquired excellent command of the language, but even as emperor he occasionally reverted to his native Italian in moments of stress.

In 1768, the year before Napoleon's birth, Genoa sold Corsica to France. The displeased islanders revolted. Napoleon's father at first sided with the rebels, but then switched his allegiance, for which he was rewarded with the privilege of having a son educated in France at royal expense. Upon reaching the age of ten, Napoleon was sent to a military school in Burgundy to prepare for a career in the French army. The five years he spent there were not happy ones, for being both foreign and poor he was treated contemptuously by his aristocratic schoolmates. He reacted by becoming an ardent Corsican patriot.

In 1784 Napoleon went to Paris to attend officer school. Although not an outstanding student, he showed great aptitude for mathematics, geography, and history. As his military specialty he chose the artillery, in part because it suited his mathematical skills, in part because it was a less aristocratic service than either the infantry or the cavalry. In 1785 he received a commission as sublieutenant. During the next eight years he drifted, spending much time on leave of absence, some of it unauthorized. He took an active part in Corsican politics, settled the financial affairs of the family (his father had in the meantime died), and read voraciously on many subjects. It was during these years that he laid the foundations of that extensive knowledge of politics, history, and law that was to be of invaluable service to him as sovereign of France.

Shortly after the Revolution erupted, Napoleon placed himself at the disposal of the new regime, and he established close relations with the Jacobins. Yet despite the opportunities open to young officers in the revolutionary army, he was

The Louvre, founded in 1793, was at first heavily stocked with art treasures systematically plundered by Napoleon's armies. This proposed design for a Sèvres vase shows a procession of loot from Italy entering the Louvre, including the Vatican Museum's Apollo Belvedere (far left).

slow to advance. His career finally began to flourish in the summer of 1793, when he distinguished himself as a junior artillery officer in the siege of Toulon against a counterrevolutionary force supported by British and Spanish troops. As a reward for this service, the Jacobin government promoted him to general. In 1794 he was placed in command of artillery units engaged in operations against the Austrians in Italy. The fall of Robespierre (July, 1794) and the collapse of Jacobinism threatened to put an end to Napoleon's ambitions. He was arrested and faced execution, but he soon regained his freedom and even won the confidence of the new government, the Directory. In October, 1795, he attracted attention by dispersing on behalf of the Convention a counterrevolutionary officer movement that had broken out in Paris (the so-called insurrection of 13 Vendémiaire).° A prominent Director, Paul Barras, took the handsome and brilliant young general under his wing and secured for him command of the Army of Italy. It is at this point that Napoleon's spectacular rise to power got under way.

The Italian campaign of 1796–1797 was the first of Napoleon's great military triumphs. Advancing with speed, he ejected the Austrians from Lombardy and secured a position from which, had he so desired, he could have marched to the gates of Vienna. Napoleon immediately demonstrated that he possessed not only military but also political and administrative abilities by consolidating the territories taken from the Austrians into a new, independent Cisalpine Republic, centered on Milan, and introducing a modern administration modeled on that established in France. In the occupied territories he was at first enthusiastically welcomed as a liberator, but his fiscal exactions and ruthless looting of art soon dampened Italian enthusiasm. Napoleon paid no more heed to popular protests than he did to instructions sent him from Paris. He behaved as if he were an

° Some scholars question Napoleon's participation in these events and suspect that the story was concocted later as part of the Napoleonic legend.

independent sovereign, even establishing in Milan a formal court revolving around himself and his large family. His behavior, however, was excused in Paris, for his victories had brought about a dramatic reversal in France's international position. In October, 1797, the Austrians had to sign the Treaty of Campo Formio conceding to France Belgium, most of the region of Venice, and the territories on the left bank of the Rhine.

The Italian victories, accomplished with an army that had been utterly demoralized when he took command, won for the young general great acclaim in France. At this time the Directory was in the throes of another of those internal crises that periodically afflicted the post-1789 French governments. Lack of firm leadership and uncertainty over the future awakened in the country a growing desire for traditional centralized, authoritarian government. When Napoleon returned to Paris from his Italian triumphs, he was openly mentioned as the man best able to restore political stability to France.

The Directory felt a natural apprehension over Napoleon's popularity, though it was not averse to exploiting it to bolster its own waning prestige. It eagerly welcomed, therefore, a bold strategic scheme he proposed early in 1798, a scheme that promised significant military and diplomatic advantages and at the same time removed him from the Paris scene. France at this juncture was at war with Britain and contemplating an invasion across the Channel. Napoleon persuaded the Directory to give up the invasion plan and instead strike at Britain in the Middle East. The Directory approved his proposal, and in May, 1798, Napoleon sailed at the head of 35,000 men for Egypt, from where he intended to undertake an invasion of India. Here disappointments awaited him. Despite a number of military victories, the expedition foundered and failed in its objective. To make matters worse, the British, under Admiral Nelson's command, destroyed or captured virtually the entire French fleet participating in the action (Battle of Abukir, August, 1798), thus isolating the French expeditionary corps. The fiasco of the Egyptian campaign did not, however, tarnish Napoleon's reputation in France. The glamor of the battles waged in the shadow of ancient pyramids and in the Holy Land captured the public imagination, and legend began to grow around his name.

While Napoleon fought in Egypt, a group of influential public figures in Paris conspired to overthrow the Directory. The leading figure among the conspirators was Emmanuel Sieyès, a one-time priest and a member of the Directory, a man of great political ambitions. Associated with Sieyès were the diplomat Talleyrand, the police chief Fouché, the writer Madame de Staël, Napoleon's brother Lucien, and several bankers who provided financial backing. The aim of the group, whose program may be summed up in Sieyès' formula, "Confidence from below, authority from above," was to put an end to anarchy by entrusting leadership to the moneyed and social élite. Its leaders wanted Napoleon's support because of his popularity with the army, whose assistance was essential to the success of the plot, but they intended that he should be no more than a figurehead.

Napoleon kept in close touch with Paris. When the political crisis seemed near resolution, he transferred command over the decimated Egyptian army to a fellow general and hurried home. On October 9, 1799, he landed at Fréjus in

Description de l'Égypte, 1809–1826

During his Egyptian campaign, Napoleon put an "intellectual task force" to canvassing the monuments of antiquity. Here it explores a pyramid passageway.

southern France. A week later he was in Paris. His ties with Corsica were by now entirely severed, and as Napoleon Bonaparte (his family name having been discreetly Gallicized some time earlier) he was ready to enter national politics.

The young general and his fellow conspirators spent several weeks following his return to Paris on careful preparations for a seizure of power. The manner in which the plot was carried out is of great interest not only because of its consequences for the history of nineteenth-century Europe, but also because it provides a classic example of the modern *coup d'état*. Different as may have been the circumstances under which such twentieth-century dictators as Lenin and Hitler came to power, the essential features of their ascent were remarkably similar to Napoleon's. The modern dictator emerges against a background of intense social unrest. He identifies himself with the fears and aspirations of insecure social groups, posing as the champion of liberty or peace or property, as the case may be, against fictitious challengers: "Jacobins" in the case of Napoleon, "imperialists" and "counterrevolutionaries" in the case of Lenin, "Jews" and "Communists" in the case of Hitler. Under the pretext of fighting these enemies, he secures a measure of mass support. To defend society, he demands and receives extensive authority, and before the country realizes what has happened, it finds itself subjected to a dictator who cannot be removed and who may soon adopt the very policies he had once pledged to fight.

Claiming that the Jacobins were plotting a counterrevolution, Sieyès and his associates persuaded both legislative chambers of the Directory—the Council of Elders and the Council of Five Hundred—to move away from Paris to the safety of suburban St. Cloud and to entrust the military garrison of Paris to Napoleon and his generals. This decision, made on the night of 17–18 Brumaire (November 8–9), 1799, placed Paris in the hands of the conspirators. On 18 Brumaire the five-man Directory dissolved. The next day Napoleon made his appearance at St. Cloud to obtain from the legislative chambers authority to crush the alleged Jacobin rebellion. But the deputies of the Council of Five Hundred now realized that they had been duped, and that the troops surrounding their temporary quarters were there not to protect them from the Jacobins but to force their acquiescence to a *coup d'état*. When Napoleon appeared before the Five Hundred, he was booed and almost lynched. Hysterical and near fainting, he was dragged outside. The plot seemed to have miscarried.

At this point Napoleon's brother Lucien came to the rescue. He told the soldiers that a minority of the legislators, bribed by the British, had threatened to overrule the majority and had tried to kill the general. He urged them to march in and disperse the Council. The soldiers hesitated, whereupon Lucien seized a sword and, placing it against Napoleon's breast, vowed that he would kill his brother if he ever plotted against French liberties. Inspired by this theatrical gesture, the troops charged into the building and did their work. Lucien next appeared before the Council of Elders and explained that force had to be used to save Napoleon from a violent death by enemies of the state. That evening rump sessions of the two chambers appointed a provisional government of three consuls, headed by Napoleon as First Consul, and adjourned.

Theoretically, the new government, known as the Consulate, constituted a collective in which Sieyès expected to play the leading role. But within a few days it became clear that Napoleon had no intention of serving as Sieyès's puppet. Taking advantage of his title as First Consul, he moved into the old royal residence at the Luxembourg Palace and at once assumed masterly command over the entire country.

A committee headed by Sieyès but supervised by Napoleon quickly drafted a new constitution. "Short and confused," as Napoleon said a good constitution ought to be, it re-established behind a republican façade all the essentials of royal absolutism. As First Consul, Napoleon was authorized to promulgate laws, appoint and dismiss state officials, initiate legislation, dispose of state revenues, command the armed forces, conduct foreign policy, declare war, and make peace. The representative assemblies—the Conservative Senate, the Legislative Body, and the Tribunate—received purely formal functions. The constitution made one ominous omission: it failed to refer to the rights of citizens, a custom in France since 1789. How great was the nation's yearning for stability and order may be gathered from the fact that a national referendum held in December approved the new constitution, known as the Constitution of the Year VIII, with a majority of 99.9 percent.

In 1800 a series of supplementary laws reorganized the administrative structure of the state. The effect of these laws was to further strengthen the authority of the First Consul. He was empowered to appoint all the principal agents of local administration: the prefects, subprefects, mayors, and police officials, as well as the majority of judges. The power of local elective councils created during the Revolution was correspondingly reduced. The system of administration established in 1800, vesting power in a centrally appointed bureaucracy, survived all the subsequent vicissitudes of the French state and remains to this day the basis of French local government.

Having secured a formal base of power, Napoleon departed hastily for Italy to deal with the Austrians, who had recently resumed hostilities. In a bold flanking movement, he marched 40,000 men with full equipment across snowbound St. Bernard Pass and appeared once more on the Italian plains. Despite the surprise gained by his thrust across the Alps, his second Italian campaign almost ended in disaster. In the Battle of Marengo (June, 1800) Napoleon was on the verge of defeat and was saved only by the unexpected arrival of a relief force under General Desaix. Since Desaix himself fell in the fighting, Napoleon in his dispatches home could claim full credit for the victory. In February, 1801, he signed at Lunéville a second treaty with Austria, confirming the provisions of Campo Formio and terminating the Italian wars. A year later (March, 1802) at Amiens he negotiated a peace treaty with England, gaining excellent terms because of England's eagerness to resume normal trade relations with France. Europe was now pacified, and Napoleon stood at the pinnacle of his popularity.

While engaged in vigorous military and diplomatic activity, Napoleon did not neglect domestic affairs. In his internal policy he concentrated on two related tasks: further enhancing his personal authority and restoring public order. In his mind these two tasks were intimately linked.

The quality that makes Napoleon's domestic politics so modern derived from his instinctive sociological grasp of the country's wants and needs. The wants, as he correctly surmised, were all reducible to one: an end to innovation and anarchy. This he promised the nation in a statement attached to the Constitution of the Year VIII: "Citizens, the Revolution is anchored to the principles which have given rise to it; it is terminated." There was thus to be neither backsliding into the old regime nor further upheaval. The country's needs could likewise be reduced to one: social order. The Revolution, in Napoleon's opinion, had atomized French society into an agglomeration of isolated individuals, into aimlessly shifting "grains of sand." It was necessary to fix this fluctuating mass by throwing on French soil some "boulders of granite." These boulders took the form of five institutions: private property, family, church, nobility, and monarchy.

The legislation bearing on property and family was incorporated into the Civil Code, work on which got under way shortly after 18 Brumaire. It was drafted by a committee of experienced jurists, to whom Napoleon gave frequent advice. On its publication in 1804, it became the first national code that France ever possessed; it also became one of the most enduring of Napoleon's achievements. It was so widely accepted both in France and abroad that Napoleon later decided to take personal credit for it and in 1807 had it renamed *Code Napoléon*.

The Code concerned itself mainly with questions of property. This concern is not surprising if one keeps in mind the large number of proprietors who had come into being since the Revolution and who were most anxious to have their acquisitions legally recognized. The Code upheld the Roman concept of property; that is, it gave the owner an absolute right to do with his belongings as he pleased, subject only to the most general public limitations. The Code also confirmed the right of citizens to pursue freely any branch of trade and manufacture.

In matters of family law, to which it also devoted much attention, the Code tended to strengthen family ties by vesting much authority in the father. Napoleon viewed the head of the household as a counterpart of the head of state: as the First Consul ruled the nation, so the father ruled his wife and children. The husband of an adulterous woman, for example, was given the right to send her to jail without a trial. In the Code women received rights inferior to men, both in legal and financial matters. In only one respect did the Code violate the principle of family cohesion, and that was by facilitating divorce. The reason for this exception is not hard to find. In 1802, when the Code was being drafted, Napoleon was contemplating divorce proceedings against his wife, Josephine, a Parisian courtesan whom he had married in 1796 and had good reason to suspect of infidelity.

The Civil Code became an essential instrument in rooting the post-feudal order in France and in abolishing feudal institutions abroad. It made a permanent imprint on French life and has directly influenced the legal systems of several Western European countries.

Napoleon had concluded early in his political career that, insofar as the Catholic Church enjoyed the support of the great majority of Frenchmen, the pacification of the country required that it be accommodated. In 1800 he ini-

Among David's sketches for his painting of the coronation was one of Josephine, kneeling to be crowned empress by Napoleon.

tiated negotiations with the Vatican that in the following year produced a treaty known as the Concordat. The Concordat made some concessions to the Church as a price for its reconciliation with the revolutionary order, but none of these concessions weakened the principle of state supremacy. The clergy was placed on a state salary, appointments of Church dignitaries were subject to Papal confirmation, and permission was granted to reopen religious seminaries. To some extent these measures represented steps leading to a re-establishment of the Church, but in all matters of importance Napoleon made certain that power rested in his hands. All high Church officials were to be appointed by the government, and existing archbishops and bishops, most of them uncompromisingly hostile to the regime, were retired and replaced by a new hierarchy drawn from government slates. The Vatican recognized the seizure of Church and monastic properties and the abolition of clerical privileges. It also accepted the Church's demotion from the status of France's official church: the Concordat defined Catholicism merely as the religion of "the majority of Frenchmen." By this treaty, Napoleon, at relatively small cost, won the sympathy or at least the neutrality of the Catholic establishment and laity.

European political theorists had accepted the necessity of a hereditary nobility for the maintenance of social and political stability at least since the days of Montesquieu. Lacking a nobility of birth, Napoleon created a nobility of

Although his finished painting was more discreet, David's initial sketch of the coronation reflects the stage management of the entire affair. Napoleon crowns himself with his sword very much in evidence and with his back turned rudely on Pope Pius VII.

merit. In 1802 he established the Legion of Honor, a corporate body of civilian and military Frenchmen who had performed significant services for the country. Its members, headed by Napoleon himself, were divided into fifteen "cohorts," each consisting of officers and 350 "legionnaires," all on a generous, lifelong government pension. This patronage scheme proved cumbersome and ineffective, and in 1808 Napoleon created a new hereditary nobility, undoing thereby an essential feature of revolutionary legislation. The medal of the Legion of Honor is given today to those who have distinguished themselves in the service of France.

Temperament and political instinct alike impelled Napoleon to reinstitute the monarchy. He wanted to perpetuate his absolute authority by making it hereditary in his family, a goal that required first of all the elimination of internal opposition. In 1800, taking advantage of several attempts on his life, he destroyed both the left (Jacobin) and right (royalist) opposition. Having rounded up leaders of these two groups, he had them either summarily executed or exiled to overseas possessions from which few ever returned. Simultaneously, he purged the army of officers suspected of harboring political ambitions. By the end of 1802 Napoleon felt strong enough to request and receive from the powerless legislative chambers the title "First Consul for life," a change approved in a national referendum. A new constitution (of the Year X) further increased his authority, empowering him to nominate his own successor. Two years later, in 1804, he realized his ultimate ambition by having himself proclaimed hereditary emperor. A plebiscite overwhelmingly approved this act as well, 3,400,000 to 2,569.° A splendid coronation followed, in the course of which Napoleon, by prearrangement with the Pope, took the crown from the Pope's hands and placed it on his own head. The appeal to imperial tradition, with its deliberate Roman and Carolingian associations, was a clear portent that Napoleon had ambitions beyond France—that he was, in fact, beginning to think in all-European terms.

The restoration of the monarchy led to a revival of court life with all its luxury and oppressive formality. At the imperial residences in the Tuileries, St. Cloud, and at Fontainbleau, strict etiquette was enforced as severely as it had been under Louis XIV. Napoleon attached great importance to pomp and ritual. When criticized (in connection with the institution of the Legion of Honor) for having brought back the "baubles of monarchy," he replied, with characteristic cynicism, "Men are ruled with baubles." Courtiers and sycophants reappeared at the seat of power, and several of Napoleon's closest relatives became corrupted by the wealth that surrounded them. Only Letizia, his mother, kept her head in the midst of the imperial splendor and continued to put aside money for a rainy day. Asked her opinion of his incredible career, she curtly replied: "Let us hope it lasts."

By 1805 the internal stabilization of France was accomplished, and Napoleon launched the first of a series of wars that were to continue almost without interruption until his final deposition ten years later. Whether the expansion of France under Napoleon was due to an over-all design for the unification of

MUSÉE CARNAVALET

J. B. Isabey satirized a fashionable Parisian couple in bizarre garb, he affecting a look of dandified old age, she aping the styles of classical Greece.

Mastery of Europe

° Actually, the affirmative vote was only 3,100,000, but later Napoleon arbitrarily increased the official figure.

Europe (an interpretation Napoleon himself liked to advance in retrospect, when in exile on St. Helena) or to a demonic, insatiable ambition is a matter of dispute. There can be no question, however, that it evoked enormous enthusiasm among the French. The Napoleonic campaigns won for France in a few years what the Bourbons had vainly endeavored to attain for two centuries, namely, hegemony over the European Continent. But the triumph was brief and the price terrible. Napoleon's wars cost Europe an estimated 3 million lives. They siphoned France's human and material resources from industrial to military pursuits, thereby seriously delaying the modernization of the French economy and severely handicapping it in future contests among the great powers.

Although several of his engagements ended in a draw, until Leipzig (October, 1813) Napoleon never lost a battle—a record that has deservedly earned him the reputation of the greatest military commander in European history. His successes were due partly to the social changes accomplished by the Revolution and partly to his skillful exploitation of the advantages that these changes had made possible.

The traditional eighteenth-century army, for example that of Frederick the Great, consisted of a relatively small body of highly trained and disciplined professionals. Its operations were slow and deliberate, for it marched with cumbersome supply trains, and its objectives were limited, often simply a fortress or some other strategic point. Composed of soldiers who made a living from war, such an army tended to avoid direct confrontation on the battlefield, preferring to outmaneuver rather than to outshoot the enemy so as to keep down casualties. When forced to give battle, it fought with clocklike precision instilled by endless drills. The generals who commanded were considered scientists.

The revolutionary army could not fight in this manner even if its leaders had wanted it to. The introduction in France of general conscription (1793) filled the ranks with recruits who lacked the training of the professionals and consequently could not be maneuvered on the battlefield with the precision demanded by eighteenth-century tactics. But what these recruits lacked in skill, they more than compensated for in other ways. The revolutionary and Napoleonic armies were mass armies and as such could be thrown into battle with a recklessness unthinkable to generals of the old school. Prepared to live off the countryside and to sleep under the open sky, they also depended less on supply trains and enjoyed greater mobility. Their morale too was superior. Fired with nationalism, they made sacrifices and bore hardships that would have been intolerable to professional soldiers.

The citizen armies of post-revolutionary France could be used most effectively in short campaigns aimed at annihilating the opposing force, and this is precisely how Napoleon employed them. He had no interest in seizing strategic points or in occupying territory, nor did he engage in protracted wars of movement. Instead, he strove to reach as quickly as possible the principal enemy force for the purpose of giving it battle and destroying it. Such a strategy precluded elaborate planning and depended on quick decisions on the battlefield. Napoleon, in any event, disliked scientific warfare by temperament; planning, he confessed, filled him with apprehensions that disappeared once the engagement got under way.

A contemporary engraving of a sharpshooter of the élite Imperial Guard, wearing a uniform that was less than practical during arduous campaigning.

Upon reaching the prospective battlefield, he usually divided his army into two parts, one composed largely of draftees, the other of veterans and élite guard units. When the battle began, Napoleon engaged his conscripts along the entire line in order to draw the opponent's fire and so learn his dispositions and intentions. Standing with aides and couriers on a commanding height, he would observe how the opponent behaved in the opening skirmishes. As soon as he decided where the enemy was most vulnerable, he would order the artillery to pound that position and then send the reserve units into action for the purpose of achieving a break-through. This delayed blow usually led to the collapse of the enemy, whose forces were, in the traditional eighteenth-century manner, fully extended and committed. Napoleon's methods were most devastating against concentrated, professional regiments led by traditionally trained generals. Against irregulars and guerrillas or in wide-open spaces against an enemy who refused to give battle, he was much less effective. The consistency with which Napoleon defeated the best armies surrounded him with an aura of invincibility that in no small measure contributed to further victories. His soldiers began to consider him indestructible, immune to bullets, even immortal. They went into battle with a confidence that turned doubtful engagements into triumphs.

Napoleon received an opportunity to display in full his military genius in 1805, when England, Russia, Austria, and Sweden combined in the Third Coalition against France and Spain. Behind the new international conflict lay the ancient rivalry between France and England, which had not only survived the Revolution, but had reached new heights of intensity. For Britain, commerce with the Continent was an absolute necessity. It could not permit the Continent to fall under the dominion of any one power, because such hegemony could be used to keep out its goods and thus reduce its influence and wealth. France, however, had striven since the seventeenth century to obtain this kind of hegemony. The peculiarity of the conflict between the two countries lay in their inability to get at each other directly. Britain had no large standing army and therefore could not challenge Napoleon on land, while Napoleon lacked a navy powerful enough to secure control of the Channel, which he had to dominate if he was to subdue the British Isles. As a result, the Anglo-French conflict tended to assume indirect forms. Britain used its financial resources to subsidize the armies of anti-Napoleonic coalitions, while Napoleon sought to isolate Britain from its European markets. In the Wars of the Third Coalition, these economic weapons were used to good effect by both sides.

Hostilities between England and France broke out even before the Third Coalition had been formally constituted. The British, taking advantage of their naval superiority, seized with impunity the remnants of the French colonial empire in the Caribbean and India. In 1802 a revolt of Negro slaves in Santo Domingo (Haiti) led to the separation of this island from France. Napoleon dispatched an expedition that succeeded in reintroducing slavery but at the cost of 40,000 men, who perished from yellow fever. In an effort to intimidate Britain, Napoleon undertook earnest preparations for a cross-Channel invasion. He stationed a large expeditionary force at Boulogne and simultaneously launched an ambitious program of naval construction. The British watched these prepa-

"It is with artillery that war is made," Napoleon insisted, and his mobile artillery and expert gunners became decisive factors on the battlefield.

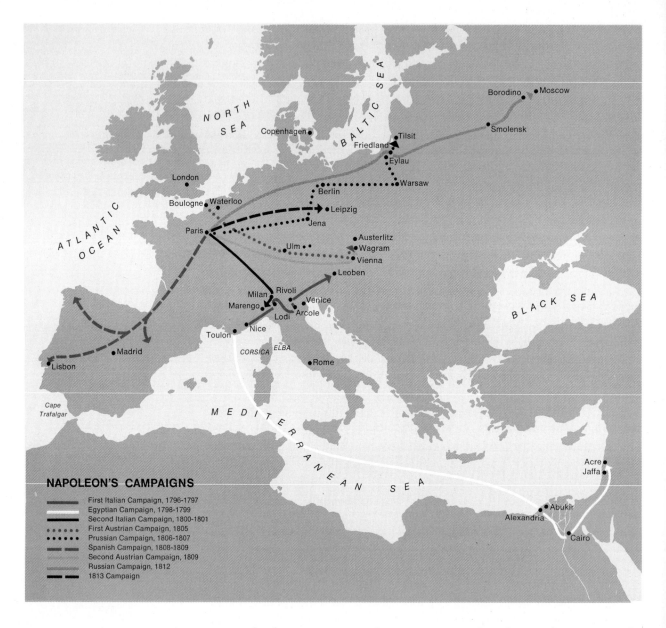

NAPOLEON'S CAMPAIGNS

———	First Italian Campaign, 1796-1797
———	Egyptian Campaign, 1798-1799
———	Second Italian Campaign, 1800-1801
··········	First Austrian Campaign, 1805
••••••••	Prussian Campaign, 1806-1807
– – –	Spanish Campaign, 1808-1809
———	Second Austrian Campaign, 1809
———	Russian Campaign, 1812
– – –	1813 Campaign

rations closely, stationing naval units near French and Spanish ports to make certain that the enemy fleet did not slip out and join the invasion force. In the fall of 1805 the main Franco-Spanish fleet made an attempt to elude British vigilance, but Nelson caught it at Trafalgar, near the Strait of Gibraltar, and dealt it a crushing defeat. The Battle of Trafalgar not only ended forever Napoleon's hopes of invading Britain, but established British supremacy on the high seas for the remainder of the nineteenth century.

On the European Continent, however, Napoleon had his own way. He reacted to the formation of the Third Coalition with his customary decisiveness and speed. While the allies were assembling their forces, he broke camp at Boulogne and by forced marches rushed his troops toward Austria. At Ulm he trapped the Austrian general Mack and compelled him to surrender with nearly

50,000 men (October, 1805). He then headed for Vienna, which he captured almost without a shot. At this juncture Napoleon faced a choice—either to withdraw to southern Germany or France, or to advance against the superior, fresh Russo-Austrian armies assembling in Moravia. Though prudence dictated withdrawal, Napoleon decided to attack, counting on the inexperience and impetuosity of the Russian tsar, Alexander I, the dominant figure in the enemy headquarters, to bring him victory. Advancing north, he stopped at the village of Austerlitz (near Brno in present-day Czechoslovakia), where he intended to intercept the allies advancing toward Vienna.

AUSTERLITZ
2 December 1805

— French Attack
— Allied Attack
---- Allied Retreat

After surveying the topography of the area, Napoleon concluded that the enemy generals would attempt to turn his right (southern) wing so as to make it impossible for him to regain Vienna. He decided to play along with this strategy by simulating a withdrawal toward Vienna and allowing the allies to push back his right wing until their forces became so extended that a strong thrust in the center could separate and annihilate their left. So confident was he of his plan that on the eve of the battle he revealed it to his troops. The battle was fought on December 2, 1805, the first anniversary of Napoleon's coronation. The French had 73,000 men, the allies 86,000. The engagement unfolded exactly as Napoleon had anticipated. The allies concentrated two-fifths of their troops on their left wing (Napoleon's right), while Napoleon placed his main force at the center. His wings took a terrible pounding from the superior enemy forces, but he kept the center inactive until the enemy left became sufficiently exposed. He then ordered the reserve to charge and cut the allied force in two. His victory was complete. The allies lost 26,000 in dead and wounded and nearly the same number in prisoners, compared to a total French loss of about 9,000. Austerlitz is generally regarded as Napoleon's greatest battle. It marked a decisive shift in the European balance of power.

Other victories followed. The Prussians, who had remained neutral while Napoleon was beating the Russians and Austrians, now entered the fray, provoked by Napoleon's highhanded methods in other parts of Germany. On October 14, 1806, Napoleon defeated them decisively at Jena. He then occupied Berlin and pushed into eastern Prussia in pursuit of the Russians. Two more victories over the latter—at Eylau (February, 1807) and at Friedland (June, 1807)—forced Alexander to seek peace. In the Treaty of Tilsit (July, 1807) he virtually capitulated to Napoleon, agreeing to join France in an alliance against Britain and recognizing the Napoleonic order in Europe. Prussia, in a separate treaty, had to cede its Polish regions to Napoleon, who formed of them the duchy of Warsaw, and agreed to limit its army to 42,000 men.

The campaigns of 1805–1807 in which the three great Continental powers—Russia, Prussia, and Austria—suffered humiliating defeats gave Napoleon mastery over Europe and enabled him to become emperor in fact as well as in name. They laid the foundations of the "Grand Empire."

The core of the Napoleonic empire lay in France, which was enlarged by the incorporation of Belgium, Holland, the German lands adjoining the North Sea and the left bank of the Rhine, and parts of Italy, including Rome. This core was surrounded by dependencies that, although nominally sovereign, stood at Napoleon's disposal. The oldest of them was the kingdom of Italy, which had been pieced together of areas won from the Austrians. The kingdom of Naples became another satellite when Napoleon expelled the Bourbon dynasty and placed his brother Joseph on the throne. Spain originally had been an ally of France, but in 1808 it was occupied by Napoleon's troops. At that time Joseph was transferred to Spain, and the Neapolitan crown was given to Marshal Murat, Napoleon's brother-in-law.° The most important of Napoleon's satellites was western Germany. In July, 1806, under French pressure, fifteen German principalities (among them Bavaria, Württemberg, Westphalia, and Saxony) formed the Confederation of the Rhine. Subsequently, other principalities joined the Confederation, either voluntarily or under duress, so that by 1812 it embraced all the German territories except Austria and Prussia. The Holy Roman Empire was dissolved. Farther to the east, Napoleon had at his disposal the duchy of Warsaw.

For all his boldness in organizing the internal affairs of France, Napoleon failed to evolve an effective constitution for the empire. His imperial government was an unimaginative and anachronistic combination of clannish and feudal institutions. He ran the empire along family lines, distributing kingdoms to his relatives as if they were parcels of real estate. He completely disregarded the fact that such a manner of governing was incompatible with the nationalistic and democratic spirit that the French Revolution had unleashed and his armies had spread across Europe. Most of his relatives showed no talent for government, quickly succumbing to the lure of pleasures and luxury. In the end, he had little success in achieving what was perhaps his life's ambition, the transformation of Europe into a hereditary domain of the Bonapartes.

Still, the long-term effects of Napoleonic rule on Europe were not inconsiderable and were in many respects beneficial. In areas under their control, the French greatly improved the administrative machinery by entrusting it to capable officials. They also helped establish law and order, introducing French legal codes and suppressing banditry, equalizing tax burdens and standardizing methods of raising revenues. Even more important from a historical perspective was the transplantation of French social laws in the imperial dependencies. In these areas Napoleon abolished serfdom and feudal dues, dissolved guilds, and did away with disabilities imposed on minorities. In all, he initiated that process of political and social modernization which was to occupy Europe for the remainder of the nineteenth century.

Although this was not his intention, Napoleon fostered the national unification of Italy and Germany. The creation of large satellite states in these two regions led to the destruction of many small principalities and city-states and thus initiated the formation of national states, a process that was completed half a century later.

On the debit side of Napoleon's imperial rule are political repression and fiscal exploitation. To maintain control over his satellites, he persecuted with utter ruthlessness all expressions of political independence and introduced an odious

---

°The rulers of the member states of the empire were personal vassals of Napoleon. He invested them in office and transferred or dismissed them at will. Those who by birth or marriage belonged to the imperial family were subjected, in addition, to special laws that gave Napoleon complete paternal authority over his relatives, including the right to dictate whom they could or could not marry.

PROMPTE ARRIVÉE DES DENRÉES COLONIALES.

A French comment on the Continental System anticipated that England, cut off from the Continent, would receive goods from its colonies at the same pace achieved by this cart and its lethargic team.

regime of spying and censorship. He also compelled satellites to make heavy contributions in taxes and in recruits for his army. Altogether, Napoleon exploited his imperial possessions in a most unscrupulous manner. Even his beneficent policies—administrative reform, legality, and social equalization—were designed in the ultimate analysis to enable him to squeeze from the conquered lands the maximum in men and money.

After the Wars of the Third Coalition, Napoleon dominated Europe, but Britain still eluded his grasp. To reduce its power and at the same time to solidify the empire, he had recourse to economic warfare. In November, 1806, Napoleon issued the Berlin Decrees, which, supplemented by later laws, introduced the Continental System. This was essentially a self-blockade of the European Continent. It forbade France and countries under French control to carry on any business with Great Britain. No ship, even a neutral one, could put in at a French-controlled port if it had previously touched English territory. Intercepted English goods were subject to confiscation and destruction. By this means Napoleon hoped both to ruin England and to promote the development of French industry.

Napoleon did not achieve the first of these aims because Europe had become too dependent on British goods and shipments, especially from overseas colonies, to observe his regulations. Furthermore, the British responded to the Continental System with countermeasures, blockading French-held ports and requiring ships heading for them to put in at a British port and pay customs. In the words of the president of the English Board of Trade: "France by her decrees has resolved to abolish all trade with England; England said, in return, that France should then have no trade but with England."

The Continental System produced a gigantic contraband operation, sponsored by Britain, in which British-supplied goods were first shipped to neutral countries and then re-exported with false certificates of origin to territories under French control. Napoleon exerted great efforts to stop this illicit trade. To replace colonial products he encouraged the development of indigenous substitutes (e.g., the sugar beet for cane sugar, and chicory root for coffee), but he never succeeded in eliminating contraband. Even the adherence of Russia to the Continental System after the Treaty of Tilsit did not help matters, for the Russians were lax in enforcing its provisions. At times, Napoleon himself had no choice but to violate the system and to sell French merchants "licenses" to import British goods. In this manner he secured much of the clothing and footwear for the army with which he invaded Russia in 1812. The second aim of the Continental System—that of stimulating French industry—was better realized. The system provided protective walls around Europe and enabled French textiles, iron products, machines, and other manufactured goods to sell in countries where previously they had had to compete with cheaper British merchandise. In some French-held territories, such as Belgium, the Continental System made possible the emergence of incipient industrial economies.

The conquest of the Continent and its subjugation to French rule before long caused a reaction that was French in inspiration but anti-French in intent.

The Rise of Modern Nationalism   The Napoleonic empire rested on a contradiction. On the one hand, it assisted the destruction of feudalism and the spread of democratic ideas; on the other, it subjected much of Europe to French domination. In other words, Napoleon at one and the same time promoted and violated the principle of national sovereignty. It is not surprising, therefore, that as soon as Europe experienced the full brunt of French imperialism, it turned violently against it.

The sentiments of national allegiance, whether in its positive, patriotic, or its negative, xenophobic, form, were of course not new. What was new about modern, or post-1789, nationalism was its claim to cultural and political primacy. Until modern times most men felt a primary allegiance to their religion or their territory or their class, but not to their linguistic group. Nor was the idea accepted that the boundaries of a state ought to coincide with the boundaries of a given national culture. These concepts are new, having spread in Europe only during the nineteenth century, and in the non-Western world during the twentieth.

At the time of its emergence—roughly from the outbreak of the French Revolution until the revolutions of 1848—political nationalism was democratic in its spirit and developed in intimate association with democratic movements. The democratic idea, the idea that sovereignty resides in the will of the people, inevitably raises the question, Who are the people? The most obvious answer is that the "people" are the "nation," that is, all those who share a common historic past and speak a common language. In practice, therefore, the "sovereignty of the people" comes to mean the "sovereignty of the nation." For this reason, the terms "people" and "nation" are used interchangeably in the Continental constitutions of the late eighteenth and early nineteenth centuries, beginning with the Declaration of the Rights of Man.

The center of the nationalist opposition to Napoleon lay in Germany, a land that more than any other suffered from the heavy hand of French domination. In 1807, after the humiliating defeat suffered by Prussia in the Battle of Jena, a wave of patriotic fervor swept Germany. It derived from the sudden discovery by intellectuals and statesmen of the German people.

The most influential manifestoes of German nationalism were the *Addresses to the German Nation* delivered in Berlin in 1807–1808 by the philosopher J. G.

Fichte. Fichte advanced the proposition that the Germanic race was unique because it possessed a true "primeval culture," uncontaminated by other influences. For this reason, it was called upon, he said, to fulfill a unique historical mission of creating a world-wide empire. Fichte's heady words were well received. The nationalist spirit that seized Germany in the first decade of the century exceeded in intensity any movement that that country had experienced since the Reformation. Secret societies were formed to promote national regeneration, and German literary, scholarly, and even athletic associations turned from their traditional cosmopolitanism to dedicate themselves to nationalist tasks. The leading German philosophers began to depict the state as the highest achievement of the human spirit.

German nationalism found its most constructive expression in Prussia, where it produced a comprehensive movement of internal reform. Prussia's defeat at Jena had demonstrated the impotence of the older system of civil and military organization based on the principles of paternalism and of bureaucracy. To fight Napoleon, it was necessary to adopt some features of the French post-revolutionary political system and above all to draw the educated and moneyed élite into active participation in the life of the state.

The main inspiration of the Prussian reform movement came from Karl vom

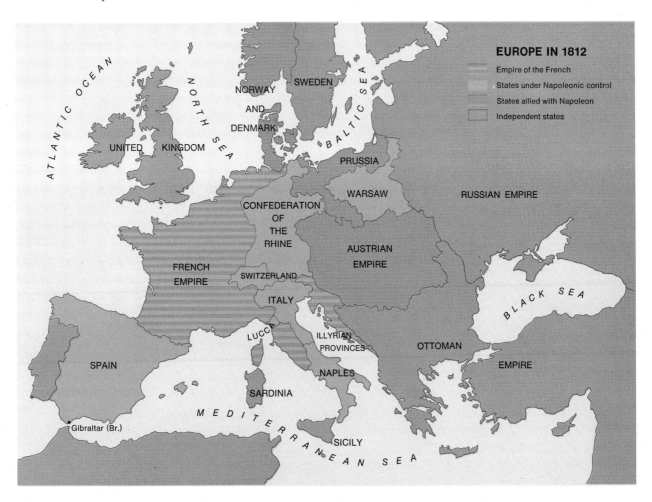

Stein, an enlightened and energetic high civil servant who in October, 1807, became chief government minister. Stein concluded that the Jena debacle was due to the failure of the Prussian monarchy to avail itself of the support of its citizenry. Instead of treating the population as a partner, the monarchy had treated it as an amorphous body of passive subjects. "The king has lost a battle; calm is the foremost duty of every citizen," was how the results of Jena were announced to the population of Berlin. Stein wanted to create conditions in which every Prussian would feel that the king's loss was also his loss. To achieve this aim, it was necessary to depart from the traditional stress on bureaucracy and to give the population the maximum of opportunity in both the civil and military establishment.

During his fourteen-month tenure in office, Stein acted with admirable energy. He abolished serfdom and many feudal laws (though retaining manorial jurisdiction and some peasant feudal obligations), established the civil equality of all citizens, and reformed local government to permit ordinary citizens to participate in it. At the same time two of his fellow reformers, Generals Scharnhorst and Gneisenau, carried out reforms in the Prussian army. To circumvent the provisions of the Treaty of Tilsit, limiting the standing Prussian army to 42,000 men, they introduced an ingenious reserve system. Under this system, citizens served in the army only long enough to undergo their basic training, on the completion of which they were retired into the reserve and their places taken by new recruits. By this device, Prussia kept within the treaty limits and yet developed an armed force which in wartime could swell to nearly 200,000 men. The military reforms also made it possible for commoners to obtain army commissions. This system was later copied by most European powers. It revolutionized warfare by permitting the maintenance in peacetime of enormous reserve armies.

Napoleon watched the activities of the Prussian reformers with growing apprehension, for he favored social reforms only when they strengthened his own power. In 1808 he forced the Prussian king to dismiss Stein and two years later to fire Scharnhorst. But the reform movement was not suppressed. Between 1810 and 1817, Prussian Chancellor Hardenberg streamlined the civil service, centralizing it on the French model. He also passed a law (1812) extending civil equality to Jews.

Stein and his colleagues revitalized the Prussian monarchy. Prussia, which in 1807 had seemed near disintegration, emerged in time as the most dynamic and best administered state in Central Europe. Its internal reforms enabled it later in the century to take away from Austria the leadership of Germany.

A reform movement of similar nature but much less successful in execution was initiated in Russia. After Tilsit, the volatile Alexander I decided to model his country's political and social institutions on their French and Prussian counterparts. He entrusted the task to his new adviser, Michael Speransky. With Alexander's backing, Speransky prepared a secret constitutional project that provided civil rights for all Russians and political rights for the upper class. Speransky also drafted a law code plagiarized from the *Code Napoléon*, revamped the central administration, and modernized the bureaucracy. But the gentry and civil service, feeling their privileges threatened, rose in arms against

Goya's series of etchings, titled The Disasters of War, *depict the horrors of guerrilla warfare in Spain in particular and the horrors of all war in general. This scene, of Spanish peasant women fighting against French soldiers, he labeled, "And they are like wild beasts."*

these reforms, and in 1812 Alexander had to dismiss Speransky. Only the bureaucratic provisions of Speransky's reform projects were actually carried out, and in the end the Russian bureaucracy proved to be the greatest beneficiary.

Anti-French nationalism, which emerged in Europe after the Wars of the Third Coalition, was bolstered by the Spanish revolt of 1808. The rebellion was ignited by Napoleon's decision to cross Spain on his way to conquer Portugal, one of the principal loopholes in the Continental System. The French armies were attacked by partisan detachments led by nobles and clergymen who regarded Napoleon as a Jacobin and the French as a nation of atheists. Napoleon transferred his Grand Army to Spain, but it proved unable to cope with the Spanish guerrillas, especially after the British had come to their assistance. He eventually withdrew the Grand Army, replacing it with an occupation force consisting mostly of recruits drafted in Germany, who for years waged a campaign of terror against the partisans and their sympathizers. The difficulties that Napoleon experienced in Spain when confronted with a united national-religious resistance were a foretaste of those he was to encounter with more disastrous consequences in Russia.

The resistance of the Spaniards emboldened Austria to take up arms. Napoleon quickly assembled his forces and marched into Austria. But even though he won again (Wagram, July, 1809), his victory was not decisive. He failed to destroy the enemy army, which withdrew in good order, having exacted from the French 34,000 casualties against 50,000 of its own.

Buffeted by nationalism, the empire was proving to be less solid than its imposing façade suggested. To deal with growing opposition at home and abroad, Napoleon had to resort to terror. In France, where the mood of self-confidence of the early years of his rule gave way to uncertainty and apprehension, he relied increasingly on the police. His minister of police, Fouché, created a network of informers who penetrated every stratum of French society and furnished the government with a steady flow of information. An excellent source of knowledge were the janitors (concierges) whom Fouché assigned to residential buildings in the dual capacity of caretakers and police agents. The information thus secured was digested for the emperor in a daily bulletin forwarded to him even when he was on distant campaigns. In 1810 the *lettre de cachet*, which could commit a citizen to imprisonment without trial, was revived. The Napoleonic police system was admired by the more reactionary statesmen in Europe, including Metternich and Tsar Nicholas I, who introduced it in their own countries after Napoleon's fall.

The police regime maintained by Napoleon was not conducive to cultural activity. Napoleon made great efforts to promote the arts and literature by means of state subsidies and rewards, but he had little success. The First Empire marks a low point in the history of French culture. Most creative talent either migrated from France or fell silent. Nor were the results of Napoleonic rule spectacular in education. The educational establishment was centralized, and the curriculum was subjected to strict controls intended to prevent schools from turning into centers of sedition. Napoleon favored the transformation of secondary and higher schools into training grounds for future state officials. He had no interest in learning as such; in fact, he rather feared it. He also saw no utility in primary education, which made no progress during his reign.

Outside France, Napoleonic terror took especially brutal forms. A good notion of Napoleon's political views can be seen in the candid advice he gave his brother Joseph, king of Naples:

> It is only by a salutary terror that you will keep in awe an Italian populace. . . . It is not by being civil to people that you obtain a hold on them. . . . The people of Italy, and in fact of every other country, if they do not feel that they are mastered, are disposed to rebel and to murmur. . . . You should order two or three of the large villages that have behaved the worst to be pillaged; it will be an example, and will restore the gaiety and desire for action of your soldiers.

During the latter years of the empire, Napoleon changed much in appearance and behavior. He grew fat, and became moody and irritable, ready to insult friend or foe at the slightest provocation. Bored by the slavish adulation that he had exacted and which now surrounded him, he spoke of plans to conquer Asia and the rest of the world. In this mood he undertook the campaign against Russia.

Disaster in Russia   Napoleon's quarrel with Russia had no single specific cause. To be sure, there were frictions and incidents of all kinds between the two powers, and the Tilsit peace gradually eroded. Napoleon was annoyed by Russia's failure to observe the Continental System, and Alexander on his part resented Napoleon's support of Polish nationalists and his threats to re-establish the Polish commonwealth. But such disagreements could have been peacefully resolved, had there been the will to do so. They were not, simply because Napoleon was constitutionally incapable of remaining still. "A government like ours," he once remarked, "to strengthen itself, must dazzle and astonish. . . . It must be the first, or collapse."

Napoleon as he looked in 1812, before his invasion of Russia.

At the beginning of 1811 Napoleon made the decision to attack Russia. All that year he directed his inexhaustible energies to the necessary diplomatic and military preparations: raising money, pressing recruits and supplies from his satellites, and diplomatically isolating Russia and its British ally. He banked on the hope that discord between England and the United States would divert Britain's resources from Europe and did everything possible to turn the two countries against each other. His efforts were crowned with success in June, 1812, when the United States and England went to war.

Napoleon meanwhile was assembling an army of nearly 600,000, the largest force under single command seen in Europe until that time. A third of these troops were recruited from the satellites. Alexander's army initially consisted of only 118,000 soldiers. Napoleon did not intend to penetrate deeply into Russia, let alone march on Moscow. Counting on Alexander to display the same impetuosity that had brought him disaster at Austerlitz, he expected to engage and defeat the main Russian army near the frontier. But the Russians were so frightened by the numerical superiority of the French that they resolved to avoid battle and retreat. By this strategy they compelled Napoleon to pursue them deep inside the country. It has been said with some justice that Napoleon lost in Russia because he was too strong.

Napoleon crossed the frontier on June 23, 1812, at the head of 420,000 men (the remainder of his army had been left behind to garrison Germany and Poland). Long columns of infantry, cavalry, and artillery poured into Russia for days on end. The commander of the main Russian army, Barclay de Tolly, a Livonian of Scottish ancestry, skillfully eluded French attempts to encircle him and retreated eastward. In the middle of August the French reached Smolensk, where they met for the first time with a stout defense. Though Napoleon hoped the Smolensk battle would be decisive, he soon realized that he was fighting the rear guard and that the main Russian force had eluded him once more. He now decided to march on Moscow, acting on the assumption that the Russians would not give up their ancient capital without putting up a determined fight. His calculation proved in part correct. The Russian army was growing impatient with Barclay de Tolly's evasive strategy, clamoring for battle and accusing Barclay of treachery. Alexander replaced him with General Kutuzov. The latter, against his better judgment, gave in to the pressures and ordered the army to make a stand at Borodino, west of Moscow. The engagement, fought on September 7, 1812, was the bloodiest military engagement of the entire nineteenth century. It cost 75,000 casualties, among them 10,000 French and 15,000 Russian dead. Despite these losses, the battle did not achieve for Napoleon the desired result, for the main body of the Russian army again retreated.

By the time Napoleon entered Moscow on September 14, his army was reduced by illness, casualties, and desertions to 115,000 men. He still did not

A Russian artist sketched the tsar's cavalry harrying the French out of the Kremlin during the first stage of Napoleon's withdrawal from Moscow.

worry, for he felt certain that Alexander would have to sue for peace. The fire that broke out a few hours after the French entered Moscow soon destroyed three-fourths of the city and placed the French in a precarious position. Though Napoleon waited day after day for Alexander to initiate negotiations, he waited in vain. Finally, in mid-October, he ordered a retreat, hoping to reach Poland before the onset of winter.

The road back led over 500 miles of territory that had been thoroughly ravaged during the advance and now offered neither food nor shelter. To make matters worse, the winter that year was early and unusually severe. At the beginning of November, when the French and their allies had regained Smolensk, Napoleon's troops were beginning to suffer from the cold. The army of 420,000 with which Napoleon had invaded Russia five months earlier had now dwindled to 70,000. During the difficult retreat Napoleon shared the discomforts of his troops and often dismounted to walk with them. The march from Smolensk to the frontier turned into a nightmare. Cossacks and peasants who trailed the army picked up stragglers and wounded and tortured them to death. The most disastrous incident occurred during the crossing of the Berezina River. The Russians attacked the pontoons that the French had constructed across the frozen stream, causing panic in which at least 12,000 men were drowned or trampled to death. Had Kutuzov at this point shown more initiative, Napoleon and the remainder of his army might well have been captured, sparing Europe the terrible campaigns of 1813–1814.

Worried about a coup in France, Napoleon abandoned his troops after the Berezina crossing and hurried to Paris. In the weeks that followed, between 50,000 and 100,000 men straggled back from the campaign. The invasion had cost the empire over 300,000 casualties, and, although Napoleon was as yet unwilling to acknowledge the fact, it marked the beginning of his end.

The whole empire now crumbled. Prussia, which had been forced to help Napoleon against the Russians, was the first to desert him. An appeal from the Prussian king to the people to form a volunteer army met with an enthusiastic response from the nationalistic youth. In August, 1813, Austria joined Russia and Prussia and declared war on France. With British subsidies, another anti-French coalition came into being.

Napoleon, who still had every intention of reasserting his authority over Europe and even of subjugating Russia, set about raising an army to replace the one he had lost. By the spring of 1813 he had assembled 180,000 men and with this force went to engage the allies in Germany. But the spirit of the opposing forces was very different from what it had been in previous campaigns. The allied troops were now confident and skilled, while his own proved to be demoralized and inexperienced. On October 16–19, 1813, a great battle—the so-called Battle of Nations—took place at Leipzig. Napoleon was decisively defeated by a superior Russo-Prussian army and lost his German dependencies. An offensive launched by Spanish and British forces in the Iberian peninsula drove across the Pyrenees into France in November, 1813.

The war went on for another six months, but the issue could no longer remain in doubt. On March 31, 1814, the allied armies took Paris. Napoleon now offered to retire in favor of his three-year-old son, but the offer was rejected, and on April 11, abandoned and betrayed by many of his associates, he abdicated. He was permitted to retain his imperial title and to retire on a generous French pension to the island of Elba, off the Italian coast.

The famous "Hundred Days" constitute an anticlimax to the Napoleonic story. Napoleon spent only a few months in his miniscule domain before he embarked on a desperate attempt to regain the French throne. Encouraged by the quarrels that broke out among the allies after his exile and by favorable reports from friends, he made a secret escape from Elba, landing on March 1, 1815, at Cannes, a few miles from Fréjus, where sixteen years earlier he had begun his rise to power. From Cannes, he marched at the head of a small force to Paris. Having quickly assembled a fresh army, he moved northward, toward Belgium, with the intention of engaging the English and Prussian forces assembled there. He hoped that a spectacular military victory would secure his return to the French throne.

The retreat from Moscow: a page from a soldier's 1812 sketchbook.

Jean Auguste Ingres' Apotheosis of Napoleon, *in which the emperor ascends to heaven, typifies many turgid renderings of the Napoleonic legend.*

The allied force in Belgium consisted of two armies: one under Wellington, centered on Brussels, with 93,000 men (half of them English, half of them German); and the other farther east, under Blücher, composed of 113,000 Germans. Napoleon wedged himself between these two armies, each numerically superior to his own, intending to destroy first Blücher and then Wellington. The opening engagements went well for him. He defeated the Prussians and compelled them to retreat. But Blücher was less hurt than Napoleon believed and, instead of fleeing east as Napoleon had expected him to do, he managed to regroup his forces nearby. Napoleon next attacked Wellington's army in defensive positions on the approaches to Brussels, near the village of Waterloo. Here, on June 18, 1815, Napoleon's last battle took place. Though he sent wave after wave in frontal attacks against the Anglo-German force, he failed to achieve a breakthrough. At one point, he might have carried the day had he been willing to throw his élite Imperial Guard into battle. But this he did not do, either from a loss of nerve or from a desire to retain this reserve for future use. When, later in the afternoon, Blücher suddenly appeared to help Wellington, the battle was over. The French fled in panic, and Napoleon himself barely escaped capture.

Napoleon once again had to abdicate. He was now sent to the island of St. Helena in the south Atlantic from where he had no opportunity to repeat his Elba escape. There he spent the remainder of his days, dictating his memoirs, quarreling with the British governor, and hoping his day would dawn once more. He died in 1821 of intestinal cancer.

In appraising Napoleon, it is necessary to distinguish the man from the myth and both from Bonapartism, the historical phenomenon. Judged by his actions and pronouncements, Napoleon was an utter cynic and misanthrope, with nothing but contempt for mankind. Neither in his private nor in his public life can one detect the slightest sympathy for other human beings. He manipulated religion, law, democratic institutions, and learning purely to promote his own ends. What these ends were, it is difficult to say. Originally, in his youth, he wanted power and glory. But having attained both quickly, he grew bored and desperately sought adventure. People were for him no longer instruments to help secure authority and wealth, of which he had a surfeit, but expendable items to serve his restless imagination. Neither in his youth nor in his middle age, however, had he viewed human beings as anything but tokens in his gambles against history.

The Achievement and Reputation of Napoleon

The legend of Napoleon—the myth of the superhuman liberator—has long overshadowed the reality. Napoleon himself was the original source of the legend. While in exile on St. Helena, he reinterpreted his record to make it appear more consistent and more liberal than it in fact was. He intended this revision to appeal to European liberals chafing under the conservative regimes of the restoration era (discussed in the next chapter) in the hope of stimulating a movement to bring him back to power. Although this hope was disappointed, the myth survived because of its powerful appeal to the Romantic imagination. Romantic writers and artists viewed Napoleon as the incarnation of an absolutely free individual, a man who emerged from nowhere to triumph over convention and humdrum reality. He has represented such a figure for those who hate their environment and want to rise above it. He was and remains the archetypical hero of the modern world who, lacking the advantages of birth and money, became a man who could do anything he wished.

Bonapartism is that legacy which remained an intrinsic part of Western history after the fall of Napoleon. Broadly speaking, Napoleon prevented a reestablishment in France and the rest of Europe of the pre-1789 order. Until he had come to power it was still possible for a restoration to undo the achievements of the French Revolution; after he had fallen from power, this was no longer the case. His triumphs and conquests, employing revolutionary institutions, exposed the weakness of old regimes everywhere and provided a lasting inspiration to liberal and national forces in their struggle with conservatism. To this struggle we will now turn our attention.

12

Liberalism and Conservatism: 1815-1848

Alasting consequence of the French Revolution and the Napoleonic era was the internationalization of European politics. The ideas formulated and put into practice in France between 1789 and 1814 were not regional but international in scope—a fact recognized by the monarchs of Europe, who time and again formed coalitions to restore the *ancien régime*. When Napoleon finally fell from power, and these same monarchs assembled at Vienna to reconstruct the Continent, they continued to think in all-European terms. Indeed, all the issues agitating Western opinion between 1815 and 1848—liberalism, conservatism, socialism, nationalism—had repercussions affecting every country. A rebellion of liberal officers in Spain immediately provoked a similar revolt of Portuguese and Neapolitan officers and frightened the Russian tsar into offering troops to help suppress these seditious movements. The overthrow of the Bourbons in France in July, 1830, prompted the House of Commons in England to pass a long overdue parliamentary reform bill. An uprising of Greek patriots against the Turks brought to their aid volunteers from all over Europe. The growing internationalization of politics culminated in the spring of 1848 in an all-European revolution, the first and only one of its kind.

The central issue of European politics, the controversy that between 1815 and 1848 polarized opinion in all countries into two hostile camps, was the conflict between the ideologies of liberalism and conservatism.° The conflict revolved, on its most fundamental, philosophical level, around the question of man's capacity to control his destiny and environment.

The roots of the liberal outlook lie in the awareness of the human self, in that individuation which constitutes perhaps the outstanding trait of Western culture. No other civilization has produced an equivalent to the autonomous Western individual: the man who thinks of himself standing face to face with God and nature, possessing the power of independent judgment, and answering ultimately only to his own conscience. Liberal ideology takes this individual as its basic fact. It believes that man has an unlimited capacity for self-development and self-improvement, provided he is free. Personal freedom is a precondition of all progress: with it, man can create on this earth near-perfect conditions. The purpose of liberalism is to remove all the shackles—political, legal, social, economic, even aesthetic—that constrain man and prevent him from giving full play to his personality. At the same time, however, liberalism is not anarchistic. It recognizes that man is a social being and that his search for freedom, unless somewhat restrained, would impinge on the freedom of others. It devotes its main attention, therefore, to securing for the individual the maximum of liberty that is compatible with the liberty of his fellow men. In politics, it seeks to attain this aim by

Ideological Controversies

°The word *liberal* as a political designation originated in 1812 in Spain and from there spread in the 1820s to the other parts of the Continent. *Conservatism* gained currency from the journal *Conservateur*, founded in 1818 by the French Catholic writer René de Chateaubriand.

Metternich's overriding concern was preserving intact and unchanged the Austro-Hungarian Empire, which he served as chief minister. "Pull one stone out of the structure and the whole will crash," he said. His portrait is by Sir Thomas Lawrence.

subjecting the state to the rule of law and the control of representative institutions and by granting the citizen civil liberties. In economics (discussed in the next chapter), it advocates free trade and manufacture (laissez faire). In art and literature (discussed in Chapter 14), it asserts the right to creativity untrammeled by classical or other norms.

The liberal faith in the individual derives from several distinct sources, including classical and religious humanism. But its principal source is science. Modern scientific endeavor, by penetrating some of the deepest mysteries of nature, accomplished two things. First, it demonstrated the astounding power of human reason, inspiring in Western man great self-confidence. Second, it revealed the existence of a natural order, rationally ordained and therefore capable of being grasped by reason. The discovery of this order also suggested that the operations of society are not arbitrary, but rest on rules and laws that can be discovered and applied to eliminate social friction. It would not be far-fetched to define liberalism as a by-product of the mechanistic concept of nature that dominated Western thought from the seventeenth to the end of the nineteenth centuries.

The link between liberalism and the mechanistic outlook is especially evident in the notion of "natural harmony." Common to liberal ideologies is the belief that the interests of men coincide and that if men are given the freedom to act on their own behalf, they will contribute, whether they intend to or not, to the general welfare. The liberal economist Adam Smith went so far as to assert that men are more likely to benefit society when they act from selfish motives than when they pursue what they believe to be the common good. Behind this view lay the assumption of a natural order that was prevented from making itself felt by artificial restraints of all kinds, such as antiquated laws or institutions.

In its practical program, liberalism concentrated on protecting the individual from arbitrary authority, whether of the absolute king or of the unruly mob. Liberal thinkers exalted the law. Their ideal was to transform men from passive subjects into active citizens, protected in their dealings with state and society by legal procedures. They saw the progress of mankind, in the formula of the English jurist Henry Maine, as a development from status to contract. The liberal model everywhere was the English constitution—not as it really was, inconsistent and vague, but as it had been systematized by eighteenth-century thinkers such as Montesquieu and Blackstone. The fact that Britain had withstood the Napoleonic challenge without sacrificing its liberties greatly enhanced the popularity of its system and of liberal causes in general.

The leading theorists of liberalism in its prime were the Germans Immanuel Kant and Wilhelm von Humboldt, the Frenchmen Benjamin Constant and Alexis de Tocqueville, and the Englishman John Stuart Mill. Their writings, translated into the principal European languages, exerted an enormous influence on both political thought and political practice. To such liberals, the state was a necessary evil whose effect was to prevent the natural harmony of interests from making itself felt. To safeguard the individual from the state, they sought, first, to reduce to a minimum the scope of state authority, and second, to subject the authority left the state to a variety of controls.

Liberalism advocated civil liberties—freedom of speech, press, and religion, for example. First formulated in the American Bill of Rights, these liberties were subsequently incorporated in all liberal constitutions. The most fundamental right was that of property, in which liberal theorists saw the surest means of protecting the individual citizen from the encroachments of the state. All these rights were considered inalienable in the sense that no citizen could be deprived of them, except in a national emergency and then only for its duration. They sharply delimited the scope of the state's authority by establishing side by side with the traditional public realm an inviolate private one on which political authority could not trespass. One of the most outspoken defenses of such a separation of the public from the private was made in 1792 by the German scholar and statesman Wilhelm von Humboldt in his essay on *The Limits of the Competence of the State*. The philosopher Kant also repeatedly and persuasively wrote on this subject.

The controls devised by liberal theorists to keep the government within the realm of its legitimate authority may be reduced to three: a written constitution, separation of powers, and legislatures elected by popular vote. A written constitution, one of the hallmarks of nineteenth-century liberalism, was intended to ensure that the political authority functioned not capriciously but in accord with legal norms. The separation of powers—the legislative from the executive and both from the judiciary—was believed to ensure that the government, through a system of "checks and balances," did not grow despotic. (The belief rested on a misunderstanding of the English constitution popularized by Montesquieu in his *The Spirit of Laws* in 1748.) Elected representative bodies were an institutional expression of popular sovereignty—that is, the notion that political authority derives from the people.

Early nineteenth-century liberals must not be confused with democrats. After the Napoleonic experience, which had shown that the masses could be manipulated for despotic purposes, liberals came to distrust the common people. Benjamin Constant repeatedly warned that democracy could degenerate into despotism, as did also Alexis de Tocqueville in his great book, *Democracy in America* (1835, 1840). For these reasons, liberals opposed the universal vote, preferring to limit the franchise to the propertied classes.

Like other modern ideologies, liberalism was created by intellectuals, but it triumphed because it won the support of the bourgeoisie, the class of property and education. The manufacturer, merchant, or lawyer instinctively sympathized with pleas for individual freedom and understood its advantages. Liberal arguments suited the individualistic entrepreneur, for it promised him a voice in the government—from which he had been excluded alike by the absolutist and aristocratic systems—as well as free scope for his business activities. The European bourgeoisie backed liberal causes, and liberalism achieved its most lasting successes in countries where the middle class was strong—that is, where trade and industry were well developed.

The premises of liberalism seem so reasonable that it is difficult to understand how anyone would oppose them except from the basest self-interest or obtuseness. Yet this was not the case. The conservatives had in their ranks thinkers of great insight and integrity, whose critique of liberal premises merits serious

The French liberal spokesman Alexis de Tocqueville, shown in 1844 after the publication of his prescient study of American democratic institutions.

consideration. Many of their arguments have stood well the test of time.

The conservatives took a pessimistic view of man. To them he was not the "measure of all things," but, in the words of the Latin poet Horace, "dust and shadow." A fallible, mortal creature, he could neither alter his destiny nor master nature. His efforts to do so were doomed. They were symptoms of his "presumptuousness" (a favorite word of conservative publicists), of that self-destructive pride the Greeks called *hubris*. The conservatives saw great danger in man's claim to question everything in the name of reason. In this as in their other views, they were profoundly influenced by the experience of the French Revolution, which began by asserting reason and freedom and ended in bloodshed and despotism.

The conservatives also rejected the liberal view of man as an isolated individual endowed with "natural" rights. For them, man existed only in society; he was born into it and functioned in it. The emphasis on the relevance of the social to the individual was characteristic of all conservatism of the late eighteenth and early nineteenth centuries and represented its lasting contribution to political theory. It called attention to the fact, often forgotten by liberals, that man is not an abstraction but a product of specific historic circumstances. The view was eloquently expressed in the 1790s by Edmund Burke in his *Reflections on the Revolution in France:*

> I cannot stand forward, and give praise or blame to anything which relates to human actions and human concerns on a simple view of the object, as it stands stripped of every relation, in all the nakedness and solitude of metaphysical abstraction. Circumstances (which with some gentlemen pass for nothing) give in reality to every political principle its distinguishing color and discriminating effect. The circumstances are what render every civil and political scheme beneficial or noxious to mankind. . . . As the liberties and the restrictions [on men] vary with times and circumstances, and admit of infinite modifications, they cannot be settled upon any abstract rule; and nothing is so foolish as to discuss them upon that principle.

According to Burke, man, whether he wants to or not, undertakes obligations of all kinds and submits to laws and rules in the making of which he had no part. Concrete duties, not abstract rights, are and must be the political reality; on them rests social life without which man cannot survive. The same views were advanced by such conservatives as the Frenchmen Joseph de Maistre and Louis de Bonald, the Austro-Germans Friedrich von Gentz and Metternich, and the Russian Nicholas Karamzin.

The conservatives regarded the state not as a mechanism but as an organism. To them it was not something constructed but something that grew. Constitutions were a product of historic developments, and it was absurd to propound universal canons of good government. Each society has its own peculiar, time-hallowed constitution, which must not be tampered with. The so-called inalienable rights are a fiction. Liberty, according to Burke, is not a right of nature, but an "entailed inheritance" passed on from generation to generation, exactly as is property or the peerage. In fact there is no one Liberty, there are only discrete liberties. Their preservation depends on the preservation of the inheritance, that is, of the political and social body that binds the living of a nation to the dead in an indissoluble bond, in what Burke called a "kind of mortmain forever." By breaking this bond in the vain pursuit of absolute individual freedom, man falls into the clutches of despotism. To the Continental conservatives, liberty was altogether a chimera. As Maistre once put it, all efforts to gain liberty ended in enslavement.

Conservatives also regarded the state as a great creative force. They did not share the liberal view that it was an evil and that the less of it, the better. The state preserved the social order and thereby assured conditions in which man could live well. To be effective, it had to enjoy strong power. Otherwise, the various classes and religions or ethnic groups would tear at each other and create anarchy. The conservatives preferred the monarchic system as best calculated to ensure authority. Catholic conservatives also stressed the need for a strong universal Church. To Maistre and Bonald, the Papacy was the supreme terrestrial authority.

If liberalism received its principal support from the bourgeoisie, the conservative movement was backed by the nobility, the bureaucracy, and the clergy. They feared that the pressures of the middle class for a greater share of political power would encourage the masses to do likewise and eventually cause a complete breakdown of European civilization.

In central, eastern, and southern Europe liberalism in the first half of the nineteenth century usually developed in close association with nationalism. In these areas many people lived under governments that were not only arbitrary (that is, subject to no legal restraints) but also foreign. For the Poles, Hungarians, Italians, or Czechs, liberty was, as it were, twice removed: before authority could be subjected to constitutional and other controls, foreign domination had to be thrown off. This was not quite the case in Germany, which, strictly speaking, was self-governing after 1815. But insofar as a large part of the German nation desired a united Germany, the division of the country into numerous principalities was widely considered a violation of national rights; so here, too, nationalism accompanied liberalism.

The conservatives, on the other hand, rejected national self-determination as a fatally divisive principle that would splinter the Western world and destroy its common culture. Metternich, as head of the multinational Austrian Empire, fought it as zealously as he fought liberalism and democracy, for he perceived a close connection among the three movements. The conservatives tended to think in supranational, all-European terms. Metternich often referred to Europe as his "fatherland," and Maistre's last words were "I die with Europe."

The argument between liberals and conservatives acquired great relevance after the defeat of Napoleon, when the victors had to decide on a new order for liberated Europe. Not surprisingly, the conservative position was at first dominant, for it had been in great measure the philosophy of the victorious coalitions. But the forces of liberalism were strong and offered constant challenges, especially in countries with a vigorous middle class conscious of its strength and impatient with the bonds of tradition. In England, France, Belgium, and later Piedmont, this middle class supported intellectuals agitating for reforms or constitutions and by midcentury succeeded in gaining access to the sources of po-

BIBLIOTHEQUE NATIONALE; BULLOZ

At right is J. B. Isabey's preliminary sketch for a painting of Europe's diplomats convened at the Congress of Vienna. Metternich is seated at the right, with his arm on the table; France's Talleyrand stands at the left, in front of the empty chair. At left, a French cartoon attacks the Machiavellian twists and turns of the diplomacy practiced by Talleyrand. He holds a crosier in one hand (he was once a bishop) and a child's toy in the other.

litical power. In countries where the middle class was undeveloped, (e.g., Spain, the Balkans, Russia), the liberal intellectuals either succumbed to the combined weight of bureaucracy, landed aristocracy, and clergy, or adopted more radical socialist and communist ideologies that aspired to a total transformation of the human condition.

The Peace Settlement The principal task of the statesmen who assembled in Vienna in September, 1814, to draft peace treaties was to prevent France from ever again breaking out of its frontiers and subjugating the Continent. The danger of renewed French aggression was considered very real. France had a record of expansion dating back to the seventeenth century and as a rich and populous state was thought likely to test its strength again. The attempt to contain France took the form of a variety of diplomatic measures: the re-establishment of a balance of power, that is, the distribution of wealth, population, and territory among the states in such a proportion that none would be powerful enough to menace the others; the formation of buffer states—kingdoms and principalities located next to the French frontier and intended to pen France in; and the creation of international institutions perpetuating the practice, introduced during the anti-Napoleonic coalitions, of consultation among the crowned heads.

Containment of France was an aim shared by all the great powers. In addition, each had its own national interests to uphold. England was anxious to keep the Continent open to its trade in order to avert a recurrence of the Continental

System. It had no territorial ambitions in Europe, but its interests required that no one power (especially Russia, whose very size was worrisome) acquire so much land as to endanger the equilibrium. Prussia and Russia had claims to land. Austria, for reasons which will be spelled out below, required the general acceptance in Europe of conservative principles. France wanted as quickly as possible to change its status from that of a defeated, inferior power to that of a full-fledged partner of the great powers.

The peace settlements arrived at by the Congress of Vienna between September, 1814, and June, 1815, represented a skillful compromise of these general and specific needs. They are more admired by historians and diplomats today than they had been in their time, if only because they proved more durable than the supposedly superior peace treaties drafted after World War I.

The first and most immediate task confronting the diplomats was to set terms for France. In dealing with this issue they showed great restraint, refusing to yield to pressures for revenge that twenty-five years of French conquest and oppression had engendered. The Second Treaty of Paris, signed in November, 1815 (the first, concluded in May, 1814, had been abrogated by Napoleon's *coup d'état* after his escape from Elba), pushed back France to the frontiers of 1790. It also imposed an indemnity and forced France to maintain an allied army of occupation on its soil until the sum was paid. In all, the terms of the treaty were quite reasonable. Talleyrand, the French Minister of Foreign Affairs, had good reason to declare that if France had ceased to be colossal, it was still great. The allies restored the Bourbon dynasty in France and required the king to issue a constitutional charter.

Much time at Vienna was devoted to the fate of the duchy of Warsaw, which Napoleon had created. The Russians were very eager to obtain the duchy as well as other Polish territories, claiming them as reward for their critical contribution to Napoleon's defeat. In this they were backed by Prussia. Both England and Austria opposed this demand, however, for it threatened to bring Russian power dangerously near the center of the Continent. Talleyrand, perceiving in this dispute a chance to improve his diplomatic status, persuaded England and Austria to join France in a secret military convention directed against Russia and Prussia (January, 1815). In the end, the Russians and Prussians had to yield to pressure and be satisfied with smaller acquisitions. The Russian tsar received the duchy on the promise to grant internal autonomy to its inhabitants. However, he had to give up his claim to other Polish lands. Prussia received territories in other parts of Germany, most importantly the rich commercial and manufacturing lands lying on the right bank of the Rhine. These acquisitions greatly enhanced Prussian power and made it a major Western European state. It was now ruler of nearly one-half of all the Germans living outside the Austrian Empire.

The frontiers of Austria also changed. Austria gave up its hereditary possessions in the Low Countries, which were formed into the kingdom of the Nether-

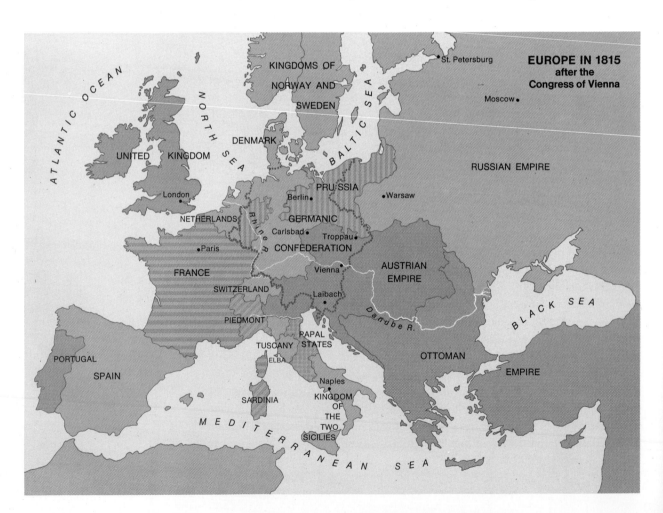

lands. The new state, embracing Dutch and Belgian provinces, was designed as a buffer against France. As compensation, Austria received holdings in the Italian peninsula: Tyrol and several provinces on the northern shore of the Adriatic (Venice, Lombardy, Illyria). In addition, several Italian principalities were placed in the hands of members of the Hapsburg house, while others were entrusted to monarchs with close personal ties to Vienna. As a result of these arrangements, Austria became the dominant power on the Italian peninsula. Only Piedmont-Sardinia escaped Austrian domination, partly because the great powers wanted yet another independent buffer against France, and partly because they did not wish Austria to enjoy a monopoly in Italy. In time, Piedmont-Sardinia became the center of opposition to Austria, and its rulers led the struggle for Italian independence.

Austrian and Prussian gains at Vienna were in large measure due to Britain's desire to develop them into effective counterweights to France and Russia. Yet the broader "German problem"—the desire of many Germans for unification and national statehood—remained unsatisfied despite these gains. The Congress of Vienna created a Germanic Confederation (*Deutscher Bund*) that embraced all the German-speaking territories, including Prussia and parts of Austria. This Confederation, however, was a paper state. Its unifying organ, a Diet that sat in Frankfort under Austrian chairmanship, had no authority. It was merely an assembly of representatives of the thirty-nine constituent kingdoms and principalities, whose rulers retained full sovereignty over their lands. The only importance of the Confederation was psychological, for by its very existence it kept alive the ideal of a united Germany.

The Congress of Vienna fixed the general outlines of the map of Europe for the next ninety-nine years. The durability of its provisions alone suggests that they were not wholly unsound. Their most glaring weakness was the failure to take into account the democratic and nationalist sentiments that had emerged with such vigor in the preceding quarter-century. The time was past when people and lands could be traded off among major powers like so much real estate, and the Vienna treaties would have had wider acceptance had they taken this fact into account.

The so-called Act of Vienna and the Second Treaty of Paris settled the immediate political problems arising from the defeat of Napoleon and the collapse of his empire. But after twenty-five years of war, there was a widespread feeling that a mere redrawing of the map of Europe was not enough. To keep peace and order, the Vienna settlement required a more permanent basis—nothing less than a regular supervision of the Continent by the great powers, a "Concert of Europe." This conviction resulted in the formulation of important new principles regulating international relations. These principles were embodied in the Quadruple and Holy alliances.

The initiative for both these alliances came from Tsar Alexander, who as early as 1804 had urged the heads of states to subscribe to a code of international morality. In January, 1814, as Russian troops entered France, he renewed his proposal, calling for a "general alliance to guarantee ourselves and save [ourselves] from the ambition of a conqueror." It so happened that British Foreign Secretary Viscount Castlereagh was thinking along similar lines, although for more pragmatic reasons. Whereas Alexander envisaged a permanent code of international ethics and an alliance to guarantee the *status quo*, Castlereagh thought of keeping alive the coalition that had defeated Napoleon as another safeguard against the renewal of French aggression. At the urging of Alexander and Castlereagh, the four allies signed in Vienna the Quadruple Alliance, which committed them to enforce the Second Treaty of Paris. The Alliance was a diplomatic innovation in that it represented a standing commitment of the great powers to cooperate in time of peace. One of its provisions introduced the novel principle of regular peace-time conferences. Drafted by Alexander ·and revised by Castlereagh, it read:

> To facilitate and secure the execution of the present Treaty [i.e., the Second Treaty of Paris], and to consolidate the connections which at the present so closely unite the Four Sovereigns for the happiness of the world, the High Contracting Parties have agreed to renew their meetings at fixed periods, either under the immediate auspices of the Sovereigns themselves, or by their respective Ministers, for the purpose of consulting upon their common interests, and for the consideration of the measures which at each of these periods shall be considered the most salutary for the repose and prosperity of Nations, and for the maintenance of the Peace of Europe.

This clause was responsible for several international congresses or conferences held between 1818 and 1822, but it also had long-range implications. It foreshadowed the institutions fully developed in the twentieth century to maintain general peace, not just on an emergency basis, but as a day-by-day concern of the great powers.

Alexander proposed to go even beyond the Quadruple Alliance and to obtain from the heads of state a commitment to abide by Christian principles in domestic as well as international dealings. This wish found expression in the declaration of the Holy Alliance, initially signed by Russia, Prussia, and Austria (September, 1815) and then by all the European powers save Britain, which pleaded constitutional obstacles; the Papacy, for whom it was deemed redundant; and the sultan, who, being a Muslim, was not invited. The Holy Alliance, which Metternich, even though he signed it, dismissed as "loud-sounding nothing," and which the annoyed Castlereagh called "a piece of sublime mysticism and nonsense," pledged the signatories

> both in the administration of their respective States, and in their political relations with every other Government, to take for their sole guide the precepts of [the] Holy Religion, namely the precepts of Justice, Christian Charity and Peace, which, far from being applicable only to private concerns, must have an immediate influence on the council of princes.

This declaration spelled out, in the language of the time, principles of international behavior that in our century found expression in the Atlantic Charter (1941) and the Charter of the United Nations (1945).

Alexander also took the initiative in proposing international disarmament. Although without practical consequences, the suggestion merits attention as the first of its kind to come from a sovereign ruler.

The arrangements made at the Congress of Vienna were conservative but not reactionary in spirit. They were intended to restore peace and order, and so required at least some concessions to the liberal forces released by the French Revolution. As evidence of this, we can point to the fact that in a number of states—e.g., with regard to the duchy of Warsaw, some German principalities, and, above all, France—the peace settlement required the sovereigns to grant their subjects constitutional charters. Nevertheless, within a few years after the peace treaties had been concluded the sentiment of its framers swung violently to the right. The liberal concessions were emasculated, and repression carried the day.

This transformation was largely the personal achievement of Prince Metternich. As Austrian Minister of Foreign Affairs without interruption for almost forty years (1809–1848), Metternich so thoroughly dominated the Continent, especially Central Europe, that the entire post-Napoleonic period has sometimes been called Metternichian. A native of the Rhineland, Metternich rose rapidly in the Austrian service thanks to his diplomatic skills, loyalty to the Hapsburgs, and personal charm. Metternich fully subscribed to ideas identified as conservative, including the primacy of society over the individual, the necessity of firm political authority and rigid social distinctions, and cooperation between the crowned heads of Europe. As Austrian ambassador to Paris under Napoleon, he had come to admire the repressive side of Napoleon's politics, such as police and censorship, which he emulated in Austria and other areas under his influence.

Metternich's success lay in his ability to convince many of the European sovereigns that what benefited Austria also benefited them and Europe as a whole. The Austrian Empire was virtually the only country in Europe that had emerged from the Napoleonic wars almost untouched by revolution or reform. Its government was a classical eighteenth-century absolutist monarchy, only less enlightened. Authority rested with the German-speaking nobility, from which the monarchy drew its high officials of the administration and church and its army officers. This nobility, in turn, depended on the personal labor or rents of the peasants working their estates. No effort was made to modernize the administration or to allow the citizenry to participate in some kind of partnership with the crown, as had been done in Prussia and in some other European countries. Liberalization spelled loss of privilege to the all-powerful bureaucracy, nobility, and clergy, and for that reason they strenuously resisted it. Furthermore, Austria was a multinational empire in which the dominant ethnic group, the Germans, constituted a minority. Concessions to nationalism within the empire would seriously have weakened the authority of these Germans. Outside it—in Italy and Germany—nationalist principles implied unification and thus the weakening of Austria's influence. The interests of Austria required the triumph of conservative principles. On them depended its survival as a great power.

But all around Austria and even in Austria itself blew the winds of change. To stifle them, Metternich conjured up the spectacle of a vast international conspiracy aimed at overthrowing the existing social and political order. Every unmasked plot, every assassination, every rebellion in Europe drove frightened kings and princes into his arms. Part of his political technique was to deny any difference between moderate liberalism, aiming at constitutional reform, and

A contemporary engraving depicts the assassination of the German poet August von Kotzebue in 1819. Kotzebue was serving as an agent for Russia.

radicalism, whose goal was political and social democracy. "The husk of liberalism is appearance," he once wrote, "the truth is radicalism; inside the husk lies the reality." The effect of this attitude was on the one hand to magnify the extent of sedition, and on the other, by forcing moderates into more radical positions, to encourage it.

The liberal movement of the restoration era had two principal centers, the army and the universities. In the latter stages of the war against Napoleon, the allies had greatly increased their armed forces. The young officers in Germany, Russia, Spain, and Italy, who had enlisted in 1813–1815 to fight for freedom and national ideals, loathed the conservative system. The universities were even more important as centers of liberal resistance. The beginning of the nineteenth century witnessed a great expansion of institutions of higher learning, especially in Germany. The University of Berlin, founded in 1809 under Alexander von Humboldt (the scientist brother of the liberal theorist Wilhelm), provided a model for modern universities. Open to all comers, it assured to professors and students alike complete freedom of inquiry. Around Berlin and other universities of the new type gathered thousands of young men from various walks of life, their heads filled with political ideas and their hearts eager for action. Some liberal-minded officers and students formed associations to fight the old order. Among the best known of these were the *carbonari*, secret organizations operating in southern Italy against the Austrians. The German student fraternities, known as *Burschenschaften*, although in theory neither secret nor political, in practice often became centers of resistance.

The years 1819–1820 witnessed throughout Europe and in some of the overseas possessions an outburst of liberal and nationalist violence. In 1819 a German student belonging to an extremist republican organization assassinated the reactionary poet August von Kotzebue. The next year another assassin killed the Duc de Berry, the son of the heir to the French throne, the future Charles X. That same year a rebellion of officers broke out in Spain, the rebels forcing King Ferdinand VII to swear allegiance to a new liberal constitution. The

Spanish revolt had immediate repercussions in Portugal and Naples, where liberal-minded officers also overthrew absolutist monarchies and replaced them with constitutional regimes patterned on the Spanish. In response to the Iberian uprisings, several Latin American colonies of Spain and Portugal rose in arms and proclaimed their independence (Mexico, Colombia, Peru, and Brazil, 1821–1822). Finally, in 1822, the Greeks took up arms against the Ottoman Empire.

The closeness with which these liberal and nationalistic rebellions followed one another convinced many conservatives that Europe stood on the verge of another major revolution. Metternich reacted quickly and decisively. After the murder of Kotzebue, he persuaded several German princes, among them King Frederick William III of Prussia, to endorse the so-called Carlsbad Decrees (September, 1819). These ordinances placed German and Austrian universities under the tutelage of curators, dissolved the *Burschenschaften*, severely limited the freedom of the press, and established a commission to look into treasonable activities in the Germanic Confederation. The decrees caused deep dissatisfaction among liberals, but at the same time greatly enhanced Metternich's personal hold on the German governments.

Simón Bolívar, known as the Liberator of South America, was painted in 1823 by Peruvian artist José Gil de Castro.

Metternich at first hesitated to intervene similarly elsewhere, for he was afraid of initiating action that could bring Russian troops into Western Europe. For this reason, he rejected Alexander's offer of armies to help suppress the Spanish rebellion. But when the Spanish rebellion spread to Naples and so threatened Austria's hold on Italy, he had to act. Metternich had the brilliant idea of using the system of regular allied conferences, provided for in the Quadruple Alliance, to obtain international sanction for his intervention in Italy. At his urging, the congress of the Alliance, which convened at Troppau and then transferred to Laibach (1820–1821), approved the novel principle of intervention to suppress subversive movements throughout Europe. The key phrases of the Troppau Protocol read:

> States which have undergone a change of Government due to revolution, the results of which threaten other states, *ipso facto* cease to be members of the European Alliance, and remain excluded from it until their situation gives guarantees for legal order and stability. If, owing to such alteration, immediate danger threatens other states, the Powers bind themselves, by peaceful means, or if need be by arms, to bring back the guilty state into the bosom of the Great Alliance.

Castlereagh, who shared Metternich's loathing of revolutions, was taken aback by this interpretation of the congress system of which he had been a principal architect. He had intended the system simply to assure the Continental balance of power. Castlereagh refused to sign the Troppau Protocol on the grounds that it arrogated on behalf of the diplomatic congresses the sovereignty of independent states—a step which he considered both impractical and dangerous. Behind Castlereagh's argument lay some very pragmatic considerations. Britain at this time was in the midst of its great economic expansion, the so-called Industrial Revolution. The products of this expanding industrial economy required markets, and these were easier to obtain when England dealt with independent states and their businessmen rather than with the bureaucracy or nobility of large and self-sufficient empires. The national interest of Great Britain thus impelled it to support liberal and nationalist causes much as the national interest of Austria induced that government to fight them.

Britain's refusal to endorse the Troppau Protocol marked the first fissure in the Concert of Europe created at Vienna. The gulf deepened in 1822 when George Canning succeeded Castlereagh as Foreign Secretary. Canning came out openly in favor of national self-determination and promised Britain's help to nations struggling against oppression. He not only refused to join in deliberations, initiated by Metternich, to restore Spanish and Portuguese authority in South America, but proposed to the United States a joint declaration pledging the two countries to keep European powers out of that continent. At Canning's suggestion, President James Monroe formulated his celebrated doctrine in 1823.

In the meantime, Metternich, undeterred by Britain's refusal, initiated with Russian and Prussian support armed intervention in Italy. In March of 1821 Austrian troops crossed the Po River and marched south. They easily dispersed the military forces that the rebel Neapolitan government had sent against them, occupied Naples, and restored the local Bourbon dynasty. The restoration was followed by a massacre in which several thousand persons lost their lives. The Austrians also helped suppress a liberal rebellion in Piedmont. Spain's turn came next. At the Congress of Verona (1822), the allies agreed to intervene in Spain on behalf of absolutism. With their authorization, French armies invaded Spain in the spring of 1823 and once more restored to the throne the ferocious Ferdinand VII. Here too the liberals were slaughtered en masse by the infuriated royalists. Faithful to its principle of suppressing revolutionary movements, the Alliance stood by while the Turks massacred the Greek rebels.

The congresses of Troppau, Laibach, and Verona marked the apogee of Metternich's influence. Having at his disposal, through the machinery of the Alliance, the combined power of Austria, Prussia, France, and Russia, he was in a position to dominate the politics of the Continent. To deal with sedition, real and imaginary, Metternich developed an efficient system of police espionage and censorship that many other rulers copied. A deep gloom descended on Europe.

Metternich was undisturbed by his reputation among liberals, being supremely confident of his rectitude. "I cannot help telling myself twenty times a day," he wrote in 1819, "dear Lord, how very right am I and how very wrong are the others." On another occasion he remarked: "For some years now I have made the singular observation. It is that men who are diametrically opposed to me die. The explanation is quite simple: these men are mad, and the mad die."

The Metternichian system found its purest fulfillment in Russia. Alexander I was too deeply imbued with the ideals of the Enlightenment to embrace Metternich's politics wholeheartedly, but this was not the case with his brother, Nicholas I, who succeeded him in 1825. During the brief interregnum that followed Alexander's death in December of that year, a group of Russian officers staged a mutiny in St. Petersburg and the Ukraine. The uprising had been in preparation for several years. Its leaders were mostly army officers of aristocratic background, some favoring constitutional monarchy, some of republican orientation. In all its principal features, this so-called Decembrist uprising was modeled on similar rebellions in Spain, Italy, and other parts of Europe. But its failure was even more dismal. Energetic military countermeasures by Nicholas squashed the rebellion on the day of its outbreak. This event had a lasting effect in that it strengthened Nicholas' inborn authoritarianism. From the moment of his accession he devoted himself with a single-minded dedication to the cause of absolutism both at home and abroad. Like Western conservatives, he believed that the salvation of mankind rested on the maintenance of order, authority, and a sense of duty. He established in Russia a police state even more repressive than Metternich's, on which it was modeled. It drove into desperation educated society, especially student youth, among whom Nicholas persecuted relentlessly any sign of independence.

In the third decade of the nineteenth century the cause of liberalism on the Continent seemed destined to frustration and failure. But this was only an appearance. The power of the conservative cause rested with the rulers of the three great agrarian monarchies of Eastern Europe, Austria, Russia, and Prussia. With the spread of industry and trade, however, wealth and power passed inexorably to the industrial and commercial nations led by England. And these nations moved toward liberalism.

Reaction and Reform in Britain

During the years 1815–1820, the rulers of Great Britain shared the conservative outlook of contemporary Continental statesmen and participated in the Concert of Europe. For them the threat came not from liberalism, since Britain had long realized the basic aims of the liberal movement, but from social unrest. At the end of the eighteenth century, Britain had entered the first phases of its intense industrialization, a process that had created large masses of workers whose livelihood depended on the vagaries of the national and international economy. The Napoleonic wars had stimulated its productivity, but this stimulus ended abruptly with the restoration of peace. The cancelation of defense orders and the simultaneous flooding of the labor market by some 400,000 discharged soldiers and sailors caused considerable unemployment. The industrial crisis was aggravated by an agrarian one. Wheat prices, which had risen steeply during the war, now fell, forcing landlords to abandon much arable land that was no longer profitable to cultivate. These factors caused social unrest in the towns and countryside that at times threatened to explode into revolution.

The British government reacted to this threat with repressive measures. In 1817 it suspended—for the first time in British history—the Habeas Corpus Act, and in 1819 it enacted a series of repressive measures known as the Six Acts which curtailed public assemblies and gave crown officials extraordinary authority to deal with sedition. Sometimes the repression of dissent took violent forms. In August, 1891, a large crowd, gathered at St. Peter's Fields in Manchester to hear speeches in favor of reform, was charged by soldiers. Several participants were killed and hundreds of others injured. This incident was popularly dubbed the "Peterloo Massacre."

In the 1820s, however, the atmosphere in England underwent marked change. For one thing, the economic situation improved, at least in industry. The spread of technical innovations (e.g., steam power and textile machinery) lowered drastically the price of British manufactured goods and permitted them to penetrate Continental and overseas markets. Secondly, the leadership of the dominant

MANSELL COLLECTION

British troops charge a gathering of reform-minded workers in the so-called Peterloo Massacre. The banners call for universal suffrage and for civil and religious liberty.

Tory party passed in 1822 to a new breed of men, some of them of middle-class background, more pragmatic in their outlook and more conciliatory in their spirit than their predecessors. Among them may be singled out George Canning, first Foreign Secretary and then Prime Minister (1827), raised in a banking family; Robert Peel, the Tory leader in 1835–1846, the son of a self-made man; and William Huskisson, president of the Board of Trade (1823–1827). These statesmen were in varying degrees influenced by the ideology of English radicalism, whose leading spirit was Jeremy Bentham.

The term *radicalism* as used in England in the early nineteenth century had little in common with Continental radicalism. On the Continent this word implied political democracy and social equality. English radicalism, on the other hand, was a kind of liberalism, suited to English conditions and temperament. As a young law student in the 1770s, Bentham concluded that the political and legal institutions of his country were a hopeless muddle, bearing little if any relationship to the actual needs of its inhabitants. He had for the English constitution none of the admiration of Blackstone or Burke. Tradition in itself meant nothing to him, but—and in this respect he differed from Continental liberals—neither did abstract rights or liberties. To him, the basic fact was the concrete individual, that is, the individual constantly engaged in pursuit of personal self-interest. Man seeks the greatest amount of pleasure and the least amount of pain, and everything apart from the pain-pleasure calculation—traditions, rights, liberties, and so forth—is meaningless. Those laws and institutions are best that secure the greatest amount of pleasure or happiness to the greatest number of living people. This is the test of "utility." Laws and institutions are justified only insofar as they can meet this test. If they fail to meet it, they must be changed or abandoned. In his numerous writings, Bentham subjected British political and legal institutions to a critique from the "utilitarian" point of view, showing that, whatever might have been their original justification, they no longer satisfied the needs of the majority of contemporary Britons.

Bentham's ideas had little influence on British public opinion during the French Revolution and the era of Napoleon when few were willing to tamper with a system that had proved itself so resilient. But gradually a small band of Benthamites or Utilitarians gathered around the lonely thinker. In 1824 this group put out the *Westminster Review*, in the pages of which they subjected the British constitution and judiciary system to a relentless critique. It was in no small measure due to their efforts that Britain in the 1820s began cautiously to reform its laws. In 1824–1825 the House of Commons repealed the so-called Combination Acts, which had outlawed the formation of labor associations for collective bargaining. In 1828–1829 it also repealed the Test and Corporation Acts and by so doing opened public offices to dissenters and Catholics. All through the decade, the penal system was humanized and the number of crimes carrying capital punishment reduced.

These reforms paved the way for the most important English legislative act of the first half of the century, the Reform Bill of 1832. The electoral system in force in Britain in 1830 was for all practical purposes the same as it had been in the seventeenth century. In other words, it did not make any allowance for the great shifts of population—from the southeast to the northwest and from the villages to the cities—that had occurred along with the industrialization of the country. In many instances, towns that had had large populations in the seventeenth century but had since become mere villages retained the right to send representatives to the House of Commons, whereas cities like Manchester or Birmingham with more than 100,000 inhabitants were unrepresented. This electoral system enabled wealthy politicians to purchase a following in the House of Commons by buying up so-called pocket or rotten boroughs which enjoyed a traditional right to parliamentary representation. Like any system from which men derive advantages, this inequitable arrangement had its defenders. They argued that it had stood the test of time, that it gave a chance to impoverished candidates, through patronage, to gain access to the House of Commons, and that it assured a fair representation to the many distinct groups of the population. Any more rational system of franchise, they claimed, would divide the nation along property lines into two distinct classes, those who had the vote, and those who did not. But the Utilitarians attacked this arrangement as absurd and in time secured the backing of the manufacturing interests, eager to have a voice in the making of laws.

The need for parliamentary reform became urgent in 1830, following the outbreak of the July Revolution in Paris. The Whigs, who at this time formed the cabinet, decided to press for such reform partly to forestall a revolution in England, partly to gain the votes of the newly enfranchised middle-class voters. After long wrangling, Parliament finally passed a comprehensive measure. The Reform Bill of 1832 achieved both a redistribution and an equalization of the franchise. First, it eliminated boroughs with less than 2,000 inhabitants and halved the representation of boroughs with a population between 2,000 and

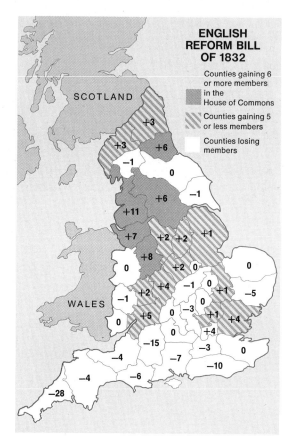

ENGLISH REFORM BILL OF 1832

■ Counties gaining 6 or more members in the House of Commons

▨ Counties gaining 5 or less members

☐ Counties losing members

The most obvious beneficiaries of parliamentary reform were the urban, industrialized Midlands and the north; the chief losers were southern counties.

4,000. The 168 seats thus gained were assigned to heavily populated areas, particularly the industrial cities. Second, it established uniform franchise in the boroughs and counties, giving the vote to all men who owned or leased a house with an annual rental value of at least £10 and setting precise voting qualifications for rural inhabitants.

The first and most obvious consequence of the act was to enlarge the electorate from 500,000 to 700,000—a figure that by 1866 increased to 1,100,000, thanks to the growth of the population. The increase in the number of voters, however, does not tell the whole story. The elimination of rotten and pocket boroughs and the election of representatives from the new urban centers began the transformation of the Commons from a private club into the national forum it became in the second half of the century. Landed gentry continued as before to dominate it, and rich peers still could manipulate votes, but the reformed House of Commons was broader in its composition and therefore in closer touch with the life of the country.

This triumph of the middle class had its effect on the working population of England, which was to a surprising degree inculcated with the liberal spirit and with liberal ideas. It too wanted a voice in the making of laws and in the 1830s pressed for them with great vigor. The movement for the universal vote, known as "Chartism," was the first significant political effort on the part of the industrial working class anywhere.

The Chartist movement derives its name from the six-point Charter drawn up in 1836 by the London cabinetmaker William Lovett. It called for universal male suffrage, the establishment of equal electoral districts (that is, districts with the same number of inhabitants), abolition of property qualifications for parliamentary candidates, annual Parliaments, the payment of members of Parliament, and the secret ballot. The Charter was widely disseminated, especially among workers and miners in the north. The Chartists held mass rallies, occasionally after dark when they appeared carrying torches and even weapons. The movement was from its beginning torn by quarrels between proponents of peaceful means and proponents of militant means, or, as it was then called, "moral force" and "physical force." The former were led by Lovett, the latter by a demagogic Irish landlord named Feargus O'Connor.

Chartism was formally launched in Birmingham in August, 1838. The following February its adherents held a convention in London, at which they drafted a petition embodying the Charter's six points. This petition, bearing 1,300,000 signatures, they presented to Parliament. In the event Parliament rejected it, the Chartists threatened to call a nationwide general strike.

The government watched these proceedings anxiously and mustered a large force to deal with anticipated violence. But none occurred. The vast majority of the Chartists followed Lovett, and when Parliament in fact did reject their petition (July, 1839), they did nothing whatever. A small local rebellion by a few of O'Connor's followers ended in a fiasco. In the 1840s Chartism, though still alive and menacing, lost some of its impetus, no doubt because the immense prosperity that England now enjoyed temporarily diverted the attention of the workers from parliamentary reform to trade unionism.

Britain's shift toward a more liberal position in the 1820s and early 1830s was accompanied by a similar movement in some parts of Continental Europe, most notably France.

The Decline of the French Monarchy

The Bourbons, whom the allies restored to authority in the person of Louis XVIII, did not intend to undo the achievements of the Revolution. The new king, a younger brother of the executed Louis XVI, had concluded in the course of his prolonged wanderings in Europe that monarchical absolutism was a thing of the past. After his return to France, he made a sincere effort to adjust to constitutionalism.

Louis XVIII ruled by virtue of a constitutional charter hastily drawn up in 1814. The framers of the constitution assumed that sovereignty came from God and rested in the king, who "granted" the charter to the nation. The king, vested with extensive powers, ruled with the assistance of a House of Peers, which he appointed, and a Chamber of Deputies, which was elected by approximately 100,000 voters out of a total population of 29 million. The administration created by Napoleon in 1800 was left intact.

The most important characteristic of the restoration monarchy was the fact that it made no attempt to undo the social achievements of the Revolution. The land taken away from the nobles and clergy remained in the hands of its new proprietors. No citizen could be punished for participating in the revolutionary or Napoleonic governments. The equality of Frenchmen was guaranteed, as

The July Revolution of 1830, as seen by an unknown Parisian artist. The locale is the Pont-Neuf (foreground). At the center a revolutionary scales the statue of Henry IV. In the right background is the Louvre.

were their basic liberties. In short, the middle class and the peasantry retained both the properties and the rights they had acquired after the overthrow of the *ancien régime.*

The political system established in 1814 ran into immediate difficulties, mainly because a large body of French opinion refused to accept its basic premises. The liberals wished to widen the competence of the Chamber of Deputies to the point where, like the British House of Commons, it became the focus of legislative and executive power. The extreme conservatives, on the other hand, wanted to do away with the charter and the parliamentary institutions and re-establish the absolute monarchy. They also desired the restoration to their original owners of the lands that had been confiscated during the Revolution. These conservative elements were dubbed Royalists, Ultraroyalists, or simply Ultras.

The Ultras began to gain ascendancy over Louis XVIII in about 1820. The king, discouraged by the conflicts of political groupings, gradually ceded much authority to the Comte d'Artois, the leader of the Ultras and heir to the throne. It was the Ultras who persuaded Louis to send troops to crush the Spanish revolution in 1823.

The chance of the Ultras came in 1824 with the death of Louis and the accession of the Comte d'Artois as Charles X. From the beginning of his reign, Charles made no secret of his intention to re-establish royal absolutism and the authority of the Church. Even his coronation at the cathedral of Reims was carried out with pomp intended to recall the *ancien régime.* Such acts produced dissatisfaction, especially in Paris. Discontent reached its peak in the summer of 1830 when Charles entrusted the government to Prince de Polignac, the most "ultra" of the Ultras. Polignac, in the so-called Ordinances of July 25, suspended the freedom of the press, appointed several prominent Ultras to high office, and reduced the number of Frenchmen eligible to vote from 100,000 to 25,000.

Two days after these ordinances had been issued, Paris was in rebellion.

Common laborers joined with artisans, students, journalists, artists, shopkeepers, and Napoleonic veterans to fight the detested regime. The royal troops proved unable to suppress the rebels in street fighting in the old quarters of Paris, and Charles abdicated. The republican wing of the rebel forces now wished to abolish the monarchy, but the moderates prevailed, and the crown was entrusted to Louis Philippe, the Duke of Orleans.

Louis Philippe was a very different man from either of his predecessors, both of whom had been products of the *ancien régime*. He had sided with the Revolution and fought in its ranks at Valmy. Afterwards, he had spent several years in the United States, where he had come to know and admire its constitutional system.

The July Revolution led to significant changes in the charter. Louis Philippe became the "King of the French by the Grace of God and the Will of the People," not merely "by the Grace of God," as his two predecessors had been. The constitution, therefore, was no longer a "granted" one. The king lost the monopoly on legislative initiative and the right to nominate and retain ministers; henceforth, a ministry that did not enjoy confidence of the Chamber of Deputies had to resign. Censorship was abolished, and France acquired the freest press in Europe.

The monarchy of Louis Philippe made a conscious effort to rest its power on the upper-middle class. François Guizot, a historian who formulated its political philosophy and served it for many years as a leader, believed the bourgeoisie to be singularly well suited to bear the responsibilities of governing. He defined it as a class combining the leisure of the aristocracy with the industriousness of the common people. The monarchy did all it could to promote the interest of the bourgeoisie and to win its sympathy. The electoral law, though broadened over what it had been, was still narrowly construed, and only 240,000 Frenchmen had the right to vote. The government also established a National Guard, membership in which was restricted to citizens who paid direct taxes and purchased their own uniforms. Both these stipulations limited the Guardsmen ("grocer

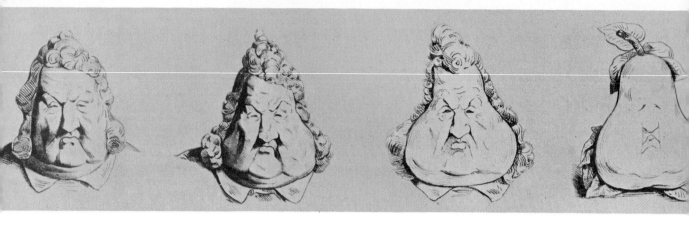

An anonymous artist took deadly aim at the jowly Louis Philippe in one of Paris' satirical journals in 1832.

janissaries," as their opponents called them) to the middle class. With characteristic venom but with some justice, Marx defined the regime of Louis Philippe as a "company for the exploitation of French national wealth," of which the king was director and whose dividends were distributed among the ministers, deputies, and 240,000 voters.

Neither his good will and respect for the constitution, nor the freedom which he granted the subjects, nor the great prosperity that France enjoyed under his rule made Louis Philippe popular. France was (and still is) a country of small owners, of several million *propriétaires* of land, workshops (*ateliers*), and stores. These petty bourgeois did not like to be lorded over by the big bourgeoisie and demanded equal rights. Furthermore, the nation as a whole disliked Louis Philippe's efforts to ingratiate himself with the moneyed class by assuming the stance of a "citizen king," mixing with the crowds and displaying good fellowship on all occasions. Nor did it approve of his pacifist foreign policy, which reduced France's influence in the world. Repeated efforts were made to assassinate him, causing the unfortunate man once to remark that on him alone there was no closed hunting season.

By skillful maneuvering, Louis Philippe and his ministers usually managed to secure a working majority in the Chamber of Deputies, but they remained oblivious that a parliament elected by so small a porportion of the country did not reflect public opinion. They made a fatal mistake in not availing themselves of the support of the conservative peasant-proprietors, so effectively exploited by Napoleon I and by Louis Philippe's successor, Napoleon III. French liberalism had so deep a fear of the masses that it forfeited national leadership to become a narrow class ideology.

This miscalculation provided a fertile soil for various radical movements, which, after July, 1830, made their international headquarters in Paris. Here gathered from all over Europe intellectuals disenchanted with liberalism and the whole social order and aspiring to a fundamental transformation of mankind—patriotic mystics from Poland, German idealists, Italian nationalists, Russian anarchists. The 1830s and 1840s saw the emergence in Paris of modern socialist theory and the development of a break between liberalism on the one hand and democracy and socialism on the other. The ideology of socialism is discussed in Chapter 19; suffice here to call attention to the fact that the modern radical movement emerged at a time and in a place where the bourgeoisie was more firmly in control than it had ever been, before or since.

The triumph of liberalism in Britain and France in the early 1830s destroyed the Concert of Europe. Unity gave way to duality. There were now two contending blocs: a liberal one, led by Britain and France, and a conservative one, consisting of Austria, Russia, and Prussia. The liberal bloc by no means assumed a passive role. It borrowed from its rival the technique of international intervention. As early as 1827 Canning dispatched a British expeditionary force to Portugal to help local liberals in their conflict with the king. After 1830 the British, acting either alone or with the French, intervened repeatedly in various areas on behalf of constitutional causes.

The West Against the East

The July Revolution produced immediate repercussions throughout Europe, encouraging liberals to fight for constitutions and, in areas under foreign domination, for national self-determination. Their success depended partly on the ability of Britain and France to extend them help and partly on the skill with which absolute monarchs defended their absolutist prerogatives. In August of 1830 a revolt broke out within the southern provinces of the Netherlands. The rebels ejected Dutch forces and proclaimed the independence of Belgium. The Belgian state received the most liberal constitution in Europe, providing for the popular election of both the lower and upper houses of parliament and a king required to act entirely through ministers responsible to the legislature. This constitution, together with that of the United States, served as a model for liberals everywhere during the subsequent revolutionary upheavals of 1848. Liberals also achieved partial successes in the Iberian peninsula. With the help of British and French armies, they overcame absolutist opposition and introduced a semi-constitutional system of government. Denmark and some Swiss cantons also granted constitutions to their citizens at this time.

Elsewhere, the prevailing type of government until 1848 remained that favored by Metternich: absolute monarchy, usually operating through a bureaucracy and police and in partnership with the landed nobility and the clergy. A Polish revolt against Russia in November, 1830, was militarily suppressed with the aid of the Prussian and Austrian troops. The conservative eastern powers stamped out revolts that broke out in the early 1830s in a number of German and Italian principalities. In Sweden and the Netherlands, absolutist rulers, for the time being, also managed to neutralize constitutionalist opposition.

13

❖

The Beginnings of Industrialization

While the French Revolution was shaking the political and social foundations of Europe, a development of equal and perhaps even greater long-term significance for humanity was occurring in Britain. Its consequences were so startling that as early as the 1820s some French publicists were calling it the "Industrial Revolution." The term caught on and entered the general vocabulary after the appearance in 1884 of a book by that title. Although the term is useful in conveying the dramatic effects of industrialization, it is also misleading; from the perspective of our time, the advent of industrialism resembles less a single revolutionary event than a continuous process.

As long as intense industrialization was largely confined to Great Britain—that is, until approximately the middle of the nineteenth century—it was reasonable to treat it as an event localized in time and space. But industrial methods soon began to spread to other countries. Unlike revolutions in the proper sense of the word, the so-called Industrial Revolution had neither a beginning nor a conclusion. On the contrary, industrial methods of production have been gathering momentum since they were first developed. Rather than speak of a "First," "Second," and "Third" Industrial Revolution, some historians in recent times have preferred to use more general terms such as "industrialism," "economic development," or "economic modernization."

The transition from an agricultural to an industrial economy that began in England in the eighteenth century represents one of the most fateful steps in the entire evolution of human society. Obviously, a brief analysis can do no more than call attention to some of its salient features. The adjective *industrial* evokes first and foremost a picture of machines and factories. In one sense, this picture is justifiable, because machines and factories are indeed prominent features of an industrial economy. But they do not constitute its essence. Machinery, including some contraptions that we like to think of as modern, has been known for many centuries. In the late seventeenth century, for example, steam power was experimented with to pump water, propel ships, and even to pressure-cook. Factories, too, are old. Textile and tapestry factories employing hundreds and even thousands of workers were in operation in seventeenth-century France and probably elsewhere in Europe as well. Yet neither early mechanical inventions nor early factories altered in any significant manner the quality of economic life. They were extensions of the human arm, not substitutes for it.

Machines and factories moved from the fringe to the center of economic life only when the pace of economic life quickened to the point where the traditional methods of production no longer satisfied the demand—in other words, when the market for goods outgrew the existing productive capacity. The most fundamental feature of industrialism is the replacement of an economy producing either for immediate consumption or for a local market by an economy producing for a national or world-wide market. This immense broadening of outlets

Steam power's first triumph was in the coal industry. This view of a British mine, by an unknown artist, dates from the 1790s. The Newcomen engine at center hoisted coal from the shafts at far left and right. A cartload of coal is weighed at the right.

for goods that characterizes modern economic life encourages the organization of productivity on an efficient basis and brings about the introduction of machines, new sources of motive power, improved means of transportation, and all the other features of the industrial system as we know it. In short, it is not machines that cause industrial productivity, but the need for intensified productivity that causes the employment of machinery.

The first important reason for the extension of markets was trade. The great maritime discoveries of the fifteenth and sixteenth centuries created unprecedented commercial opportunities for the European states bordering on the Atlantic. The early trade with the West Indies, North America, Southeast Asia, and India enabled Western Europe to accumulate much wealth and at the same time stimulated productivity. Much the same was the effect of the emergence of the national state. The abolition of such restraints on internal trade as tariffs and tolls, accomplished first in England, then in France, and finally in the remainder of Europe, created large national markets and also led to improvements in the methods of producing goods. There are at least two other factors responsible for the widening of the market: the increase of population, and defense orders. But these became decisive only later. Early industrialization (from about 1750 to about 1850) occurred against the background of intense national and international trade developed in the preceding three centuries.

The trading opportunities presented by the new markets also raised the problem of costs; the expanded markets were open to many producers, and, all other things being equal, those who could supply the goods at the lowest price won the business. At bottom, the whole gigantic transformation of human life brought about by industrialism derived and continues to derive from the need to reduce the price of goods and services to make them competitive in the largest possible market. Such was the immediate purpose of all the great inventions: the harnessing of steam and electric power, the construction of machines capable of performing quickly and accurately the most complicated operations, the development of efficient means of transport, the rational utilization of labor. Even in countries where protective tariffs shield native industry from foreign competition, cost is a factor of great importance, because inefficient methods of production drain capital and manpower that could be used to good advantage in some other way.

The overriding concern with costs involves an industrial economy in the life of the country to a degree previously unknown. A truly industrial country is one that not merely imports industrial techniques, but one that gears the entire life of its society to the requirements of more efficient—that is, less costly—productivity.

Industrial progress has not proceeded everywhere at an equal pace, some countries undergoing this process earlier and more intensely. Great Britain was the pioneer, the first country in the world in which the industrial sector of the economy came to outweigh the agricultural one in terms of manpower employed and value of goods produced. It attained this stage by the middle of the nineteenth century. Belgium followed close behind, becoming highly industrialized in the second quarter of the century. Next, industrialism spread westward to the United States and eastward to France and Germany in Western Europe, which

underwent intense industrialization after 1850. There remained large parts of Europe that began to industrialize in earnest either at the turn of the century (e.g., Italy, Russia) or only after World War II (the states of the Balkans). Countries that industrialized late served as suppliers of manpower, raw materials, and food to their more industrialized neighbors. The United States, which industrialized and at the same time produced a surplus of food to export to other industrial countries, was an exception.

Considering the economic prerequisites of industrialization, it is clear why Great Britain should have been the first country to industrialize. To begin with, after the union of England and Scotland in 1707, Britain boasted the largest internal market in Europe. Although inferior in terms of territory, population, and wealth to France, Britain, by uniting with Scotland, had eliminated those internal restraints on the free flow of goods that continued to obstruct the domestic commerce of France and such other countries of Western Europe as Germany and Italy. Within its insular boundaries, Britain was a free-trade area. This area was further expanded in the seventeenth and eighteenth centuries by virtue of colonial conquests, the territories that Britain acquired overseas providing both a source of raw materials and an outlet for manufactured goods. Lord Chatham, one of the builders of the British Empire, was well aware of the commercial importance of the colonies: "I state to you the importance of America," he once declared; "it is a double market: a market of consumption and a market of supply."

In the second place, Britain enjoyed a rapid growth of population. The population of England and Wales doubled between 1750 and 1832, and this growth, in effect, also doubled the domestic market for consumer goods available to English industry.

In the third place, Britain had the capital to finance the expansion of its productive capacity. This money came largely from overseas ventures, much of it from the slave trade in which Britain played a leading role. In the last two decades of the seventeenth century, British vessels transported 300,000 slaves from

This 1776 engraving shows the Severn River terminus of the Staffordshire & Worcestershire Canal, built by England's canal pioneer, James Brindley. Another of Brindley's canals had no less than 75 locks, 5 tunnels, and 275 bridges and aqueducts.

Africa to the colonies, and after the Asiento Treaty (1713) had opened up South America, traffic in human beings became a virtual British monopoly. The wealth of Liverpool, the main port of Lancashire and the birthplace of the modern factory system, derived largely from its proceeds. England also profited from business in colonial wares, of which it became the chief supplier to the Continent. Many individual fortunes that later helped finance British industry were made in India. Unlike the French, who dissipated much of their wealth on wars or on luxuries, the British invested theirs in trade and manufacture.

Technological Progress As has been pointed out, technical innovations occurred in close connection with the expansion of the market. Just as the existence of outlets for goods encouraged technical improvements capable of yielding better and cheaper commodities, so in turn the production of better and cheaper commodities made available additional markets. As industrialism developed, the relationship of technology to the market turned out to be not one of simple cause and effect but of constant mutual stimulation.

The classic industry of the early phases of the industrial era was cotton spinning and weaving. Compared to wool, cotton was a relative newcomer to England. Originally, cotton textiles had been shipped from India, but their popularity threatened the woolen interests, which in 1700 pressured Parliament into passing a law prohibiting the importation of printed cotton fabrics. This measure, however, instead of destroying the competition of cotton, encouraged the growth of a native cotton industry in Lancashire, a region that enjoyed both the proper climate for cotton spinning and access to good ports. From the beginning the cotton manufacturers had to struggle against the ancient and heavily protected woolen industry, and to survive they had to run their enterprises in a highly efficient manner. For this reason they proved receptive to all kinds of innovations.

The technical inventions that in the course of the eighteenth century revolutionized textile manufacture are difficult to explain because they require acquaintance with the many steps involved in the production of cloth. Basically, these inventions were intended to remedy a chronic imbalance between the two principal phases of this process: the spinning of yarn from fibers and the weaving of this yarn into fabric. In the early days of the Lancashire cotton industry, spinning could not keep up with weaving, and it took at least five spinners to keep one weaver supplied with yarn. This disparity was further increased with the invention in 1733 of John Kay's "flying shuttle," a device that enabled the weaver to increase his output substantially. The spinners now had even greater difficulty keeping up with the demand.

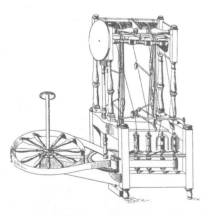

Arkwright's water-frame spinning machine (this is his 1769 patent drawing) was so named because it ran by water power.

To redress this imbalance, James Hargreaves constructed in 1764–1765 a mechanical spinner named "Jenny" in honor of his daughter. An even more advanced spinning device was produced by Richard Arkwright, the inventor of the so-called water-frame. Combining the Jenny and the water-frame, Samuel Crompton designed the "mule," a spinner that in time acquired great popularity. With mechanization, spinning more than met the needs of the weavers. In fact, the balance was now upset in favor of spinning, and efforts were exerted to mechanize weaving so that it could keep up with the flow of yarn. The greatest

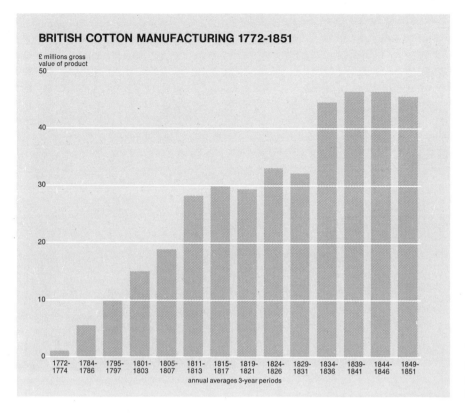

BRITISH COTTON MANUFACTURING 1772-1851

£ millions gross
value of product

annual averages 3-year periods

The transformation of Great Britain's cotton industry is charted here for selected periods. By 1820 cottons had taken the textile lead from woolens.

advance in this direction was made in 1785, when Edmund Cartwright succeeded in building the first practical mechanical loom. But Cartwright's invention gained slow acceptance, partly because of its engineering defects and partly because it required more power than was readily available at the time. The mechanical loom became perfected and began to outnumber the hand loom only in the 1820s.

The ramifications of the major inventions of the industrial age may be illustrated by the effects mechanization of English cotton manufacture had on the United States. The introduction of machinery increased the capacity of the Lancashire mills to the point where the existing supplies of cotton staple from India no longer met their needs. The most obvious alternate source was the United States, but American cotton was uneconomical to process because it was of the so-called short-stapled variety, the seeds of which were difficult to remove. Its commercial value was so low that in the eighteenth century the United States barely grew enough of it to meet its own needs. The situation changed drastically in 1793 when Eli Whitney invented the cotton gin, a machine capable of efficiently removing the seeds. This invention at once made it profitable to use short-staple cotton and led to a startling increase in American cotton cultivation. Two decades after the introduction of the cotton gin, the annual production of cotton in the United States rose from 1.5 million to 85 million pounds. The vast southern plantations on which this cotton grew required masses of cheap labor, bringing about a great increase in the importation of slaves. Thus, technical advances in Lancashire led to an intensification of slavery in faraway America.

SCIENCE MUSEUM, LONDON

The earliest view of the workings of the Newcomen engine was published in 1717 by the English scientist Henry Beighton. Above the brick furnace is the cylinder, with its piston connected to the heavy pumping beam.

The improvements in textile manufacture would not have been so effective were it not that they coincided with revolutionary changes in the methods of supplying motive power. Although not their originator, the textile industry derived from these changes the greatest immediate benefit. Mechanical devices, especially the new looms, required greater power to operate than could be provided by the traditional sources, such as water. The solution was found in steam, the harnessing of which is generally recognized as the single most important invention of the early industrial age.

It had been realized long before 1769, when James Watt constructed the first economical steam engine, that the principles of atmospheric pressure and heat expansion could serve as sources of energy. Engines built on these principles were in operation in about 1700, especially in coal mines, where they were used to cope with the problem of flooding. One such engine, the Newcomen pump (1712), was the direct precursor of Watt's great invention. This pump consisted of a boiler connected to a cylinder containing a piston. Steam was first injected under the piston and then condensed by a jet of cold water to create a vacuum, whereupon the piston descended. A rod connected to the piston operated the pump. The Newcomen engine made twelve strokes a minute, each capable of lifting ten gallons of water. It was an instantaneous success. By 1765 it was in operation in many British collieries and some potteries and had even found its way abroad.

The Newcomen pump had one obvious drawback—it required constant reheating of the cylinder, a procedure that consumed a great amount of fuel. James Watt, a maker of precision instruments and a man of wide learning, set himself to rectify this shortcoming. After much reflection and experimentation, he arrived at a solution that was remarkably simple in its conception and was destined to have incalculable consequences. Instead of cooling the steam within the cylinder, Watt provided for it a separate chamber, or condenser. During this cooling-off period, the cylinder itself remained warm, thus greatly diminishing the amount of fuel needed for the operation. That Watt fully realized this advantage may be gathered from the fact that, in applying for a patent in 1769, he described it as a device "to lessen the consumption of steam, and consequently fuel, in fire engines."

Watt's engine might well have had no immediate economic repercussions had it not attracted the attention of two prominent businessmen. One of them was John Roebuck, a wealthy iron manufacturer and owner of a coal mine. Roebuck's colliery experienced serious flooding that the slow-acting Newcomen pump could not cope with. Impressed by Watt's idea, he entered into partnership with him, undertaking to finance further experiments to improve the steam engine. But Roebuck soon ran into financial difficulties and was on the verge of pulling out of the enterprise when Matthew Boulton appeared on the scene. Boulton, who had made his fortune in hardware, offered to purchase Roebuck's share of the partnership. He saw an immediate use for Watt's "fire engine" in his Soho hardware shop, but he also realized the long-term commercial possibilities in the construction of such engines for sale. In 1768 he and Watt formed their celebrated partnership, Watt providing the technical genius and Boulton the money and business experience. Many difficulties had to be overcome before the steam engine based on Watt's principle of the separate condenser finally became a commercial reality (1776). Boulton invested in it the equivalent of several hundred thousand of today's dollars and probably never realized any profit. But he was a man of great vision, who understood the implications of Watt's invention. When James Boswell, Samuel Johnson's biographer, visited Boulton's Soho foundry in 1776, Boulton proudly declared: "I sell here, Sir, what all the world desires to have—POWER."

Watt's original engine was essentially a pump and as such of limited applicability. But in 1781–1784 Watt patented further improvements that greatly increased the usefulness of his invention. One of these was the so-called double-acting engine, which injected steam on both sides of the piston; another was a device to transform the simple up-and-down movement of the piston into a rotary motion. These improvements made the steam engine more versatile and led to its widespread acceptance. The first to employ it was the iron manufacturer John Wilkinson, who, in return for furnishing Boulton & Watt with cylinders, acquired a steam engine to blow his furnaces. In 1782 Josiah Wedgwood ordered one of Watt's engines to grind pigments and mix clay in his pottery establishment. But the greatest applicability of steam was in the cotton industry. The coupling of Boulton & Watt steam engines to spinning and weaving machines had a startling effect on the price of cotton goods. Between 1780 and 1812 the price of cotton yarn fell by 90 percent. It was such reduction of prices that permitted British cotton goods to flood international markets. Machine-produced cotton textiles were the first clothing material in history available cheaply and in quantities to the mass of the population.

The great advantages of steam over water, above all its economy and independence of geography, soon led to its employment in other industries, where it invariably increased productivity and lowered costs. In 1814 it was installed at the printing shop of the London *Times*, permitting press runs of a thousand copies an hour. Flour mills, breweries, coin mints, and other industries hastened to convert to steam.

One of the most important applications of steam took place in transportation, for the development of railroads and steamships contributed more to the opening of new markets than any other invention of the age. In the early part of the eighteenth century, it took a stagecoach leaving London three days to reach Dover (75 miles) and two weeks to reach Edinburgh (450 miles). Under these circumstances, merchandise could scarcely move from one part of the country to another on land. England, like every other country, consisted of a multitude of small, self-contained economies, each of which satisfied its own needs. In the second half of the eighteenth century, this situation was somewhat improved in England and in some Continental countries by the construction of canals. The pottery manufacturer Wedgwood estimated that one tow horse could pull as much merchandise on a canal barge as could forty horses on land—and with less breakage. But canals had obvious limitations: they were slow, expensive to build, and limited by topography to certain areas, which was not necessarily where they were the most needed.

The first important British rail line linked Manchester and Liverpool in 1830. This is the Mount Olive "cutting" the next year, still being laboriously dug by hand.

Coloured Views on the Liverpool and Manchester Railway, 1833

The railroad was free of these limitations and for this reason it soon dominated land transport. Although English collieries used small steam locomotives in the eighteenth century, the first practical railway engine, George Stephenson's *Rocket*, was not constructed until 1829. Stephenson's achievement lay in applying the motion of the piston directly to the wheels without recourse to the usual rod and crank mechanisms—a procedure that increased the power of the engine and at the same time reduced its fuel consumption. The *Rocket* proved its worth by pulling a thirteen-ton load at a speed of twenty-nine miles an hour. First used to transport coal, railroads soon pulled other loads as well, including passengers. In 1849, only twenty years after the debut of the *Rocket*, locomotives operating between London and Bristol attained average speeds of fifty miles an hour. At this rate, they covered as much distance in half an hour as a typical coach of the 1820s had covered in a day. Naturally, costs of transport dropped, as did prices of the shipped commodities. Wherever it penetrated, the railroad resembled a battering ram that broke down the invisible walls protecting local markets from outside competition. In many instances it became cheaper to buy products manufactured hundreds of miles away than those produced locally, for transport costs were negligible. One of the consequences of this development was regional specialization, each area tending to concentrate on those goods that it could produce most cheaply.

Although it antedated the railroad, the steamship was slow in exerting an impact on the economy. Robert Fulton, an American engineer, ran his paddle-wheel steamer between New York and Albany as early as 1807, but the first ocean-going steamships consumed so much coal that they could not compete with the new and improved sailing ships known as clippers, and they only gained acceptance in the 1870s. In the first half of the nineteenth century, they were used largely on inland waterways and other short routes (e.g., coastal waters), where they could stay close to fueling stations.

Most of the technological innovations, particularly the railroads, required large quantities of coal and iron, thus stimulating the search for improved methods of extracting these two basic commodities of the industrial era. The British iron industry was stagnating in the first half of the eighteenth century, for England had depleted its forests and lacked the timber needed for smelting. Early attempts at smelting iron with coal proved unsuccessful, because no way was known of removing the impurities present in coal. Britain, therefore, had no choice but to import iron from such timber-rich countries as Sweden and Russia, though attempts to devise means of employing coal for iron smelting never ceased. In 1781 an important advance was made by Henry Cort, who used coke, a by-product of coal distillation, to smelt iron. Cort's method, called the puddling process, gained wide acceptance, and within twenty-five years British iron production more than trebled. The Russian iron industry, on the other hand, suffered a corresponding decline. A further improvement was the invention in 1829 of a process that enabled coal to be used successfully to smelt iron. These innovations made Britain the world leader in the production and exportation of coal and iron. How great its lead was may be gathered from the fact that in 1840 it produced ten times as much coal as any of its closest competitors (Belgium, France, and Prussia). By that date, it was clear that a country short of coal

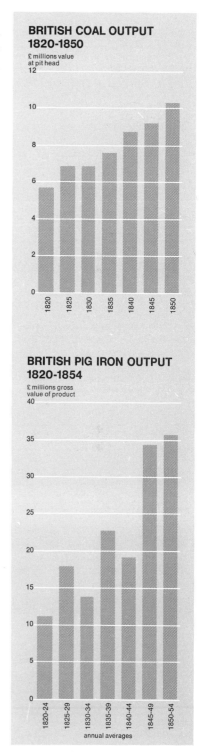

BRITISH COAL OUTPUT 1820-1850

£ millions value at pit head

BRITISH PIG IRON OUTPUT 1820-1854

£ millions gross value of product

annual averages

Whereas British coal output in the second quarter of the eighteenth century (above) showed steady growth, pig iron production (below) rose erratically due to technological problems.

and iron, the two basic materials of industrialism, could aspire neither to economic nor political might.

Britain, the pioneer in industrial development, was not allowed to enjoy its monopoly for long. Other Western countries, aware of how greatly industrialism had increased British wealth and power, soon emulated its example. At first, Britain tried to thwart competition by passing laws forbidding the emigration of skilled laborers and the export of new machines. But these measures proved unenforceable. Industrial espionage and financial inducements eventually secured for rival powers the designs of the machines and lured to the Continent managers and skilled workers who were instrumental in setting up mechanized textile mills, foundries, and factories of all kinds. The British eventually had to acknowledge their inability to maintain a monopoly on industrial processes and in 1842 repealed the last of the restrictive measures.

In the first half of the nineteenth century, the rest of the Western world profited greatly from British experience, willingly as well as unwillingly offered. During this time, the United States and several Western European countries laid the foundations of an industrial economy. None, however, became industrialized in the sense that Britain had, for each seemed to lack one or more of the vital ingredients, the fortuitous possession of which had accounted for Britain's early successes. Some lacked the necessary raw materials; others lacked a national government capable of destroying feudal institutions and assuring a large internal market; still others were short of capital. In addition, certain cultural factors inhibited industrial development on the Continent: the attachment to the land here was stronger than in England, as was the viability of old social organizations like the guilds. In most of Europe, it took half a century or more to break down these obstacles to industrialization.

The only Continental country to industrialize in earnest in the first half of the nineteenth century was Belgium, which benefited from a number of unique advantages. First, it possessed large markets by virtue of the fact that from 1793 to 1815 it had formed part of France and from 1815 to 1830 part of the Netherlands and its overseas empire. Access to these markets permitted Belgium to lay the foundations of a sizable industrial complex, which managed to keep going even after it had severed its ties to the Netherlands and gained independence, because an exceptionally high concentration of population provided a satisfactory domestic market. Second, Belgium had a progressive government eager to promote industry. The liberal monarchy generously invested its own capital and encouraged the influx of capital from abroad. It also assisted in the construction of transport. In 1835 Belgium inaugurated the first complete trunk railroad network on the Continent, and soon the length of its railways, hard-surfaced roads, and navigable waterways exceeded (in proportion to its total area) those of England. Belgium was also fortunate in having good iron and coal deposits, which, until their exhaustion later in the century, enabled it to develop heavy industry.

Until the middle of the eighteenth century, France probably had produced more industrial goods than Britain, but from then on it fell behind. The causes of this lag were partly economic and partly cultural. The soil of France has always been so fruitful that Frenchmen found little inducement to leave it for the

cities. The majority of Frenchmen wanted to be and in fact did become owners of agricultural land. Even that part of the population that went to work for industry retained its rural ties and returned to the land when given the opportunity to buy into it. Second, France had poor coal and iron deposits. Third, the French possess a highly individualistic temperament that rejects industrial discipline and dissolution in a faceless crowd. They have traditionally preferred small family-owned and -operated shops to gigantic factories. In the middle of the nineteenth century, three-quarters of all Frenchmen still lived on the soil, and as late as 1870 the value of France's agricultural product exceeded that of its industry. The aversion of Frenchmen to large industrial enterprises may be illustrated by the fact that, in the middle of the nineteenth century, 3 million Frenchmen classified as workers were employed by nearly 1.5 million establishments— a ratio of two workers to each business. Although it developed a number of efficient industries (textile, chemical, railroad construction) and acquired an excellent transport network, France remained for a long time a country with a mixed economy.

The countries of the Germanic Confederation possessed all the elements necessary for industrial growth but one: political unity. What became in 1871 the German Empire comprised at the beginning of the century no fewer than 300 sovereign principalities, each with its tariffs and tolls barring the way to the free flow of goods. Farsighted individuals, realizing that these conditions hindered economic development, concentrated on the creation of a free-trade zone embracing all the German territories, regardless of political divisions. This effort

The completion of Italy's first railroad in 1830, connecting Naples and Portici, was commemorated in a painting by Salvatore Fergola, the official painter to the Italian royal court.

THE ZOLLVEREIN

The Zollverein *customs union at its founding in 1834; it later was expanded to take in the northern German states, Baden, and Alsace-Lorraine.*

culminated in 1834 in the establishment of a customs union known as the *Zollverein*. This important institution developed gradually from tariff agreements that Prussia entered into with neighboring lands. In 1818, when Prussia liberalized its own customs system, a number of principalities that were fully enclosed by Prussian territory lost their customary commercial outlets. At Prussia's suggestion, these states now entered with it into reciprocal tariff agreements, the first of which was signed in 1819. Similar agreements were signed with other principalities that found it expedient to associate with the large Prussian-dominated market. Each of the states entering into such commercial agreements abolished tariffs against the others, but, of course, retained its political sovereignty. In the 1820s several principalities hostile to Prussia established their own customs union, and for a while it looked as if the German lands would be divided into two large commercial blocks, but in the end this group too joined Prussia and its associates. Thus, step by step, the common German market expanded until it embraced all the lands of the Confederation except Austria, which Prussia deliberately kept out as a political rival. The *Zollverein* went into effect on the morning of January 1, 1834, when, all over Germany, carts and barges loaded with goods assembled for the occasion were given the signal to proceed and swept joyfully past the old customs and toll barriers.

The *Zollverein* represents a unique instance of a single national market anticipating the national state. The *Zollverein*, however, only created a market framework; it did not create an industrial economy. This came into existence only after 1850. Despite its internal market, rich mineral deposits, and cadres of excellent scientists and artisans, in the first half of the century Germany remained overwhelmingly agricultural. In the 1840s Belgium produced more iron than the entire *Zollverein*, and coal consumption in the city of London alone exceeded the total coal output of Prussia, Germany's most industrialized state.

The other areas of Europe had only industrial pockets surrounded by traditional agrarian economies. Italy, like Germany, suffered from national disunity but, unlike Germany, created no customs union to remedy it. It has been calculated that merchandise transported from Mantua to Parma, a distance of thirty-seven miles, was subject to no less than six separate custom duties. Italy further suffered from a lack of coal and iron deposits. Its only serious industry was textile manufacture, which was concentrated in the northern regions of the peninsula. The Hapsburg Empire had the rudiments of an industrial center in Bohemia. Russia, although richly endowed with natural resources, a vast market, and an inexhaustible supply of cheap labor, suffered from a shortage of capital and the attitude of its government, which opposed industrialization as a cause of social unrest. At midcentury Russia had half a million industrial workers, the majority in the textile industry, the capital and management of which was supplied mainly from abroad. Elsewhere in Europe, mechanized textile manufacture established a foothold here and there, serving as a wedge of industrial culture without significantly altering the quality of life. The varying pace of economic development created a disparity between the predominantly industrial and the predominantly agrarian countries which, in the second half of the nineteenth century, divided Europe into two fairly distinct zones.

In Britain the advance of industry, which had transformed a small and relatively poor island into the leading manufacturing and trading power in the world, was attended by a re-examination of the principles on which the nation's economic life had hitherto rested. The result of this re-examination was the triumph of economic liberalism over mercantilism. So strong was the influence of Britain at that time that many other countries imitated its liberal economic policy, even though their situation was different from Britain's and demanded different measures.

Economic Liberalism

The fundamental principles of economic liberalism had been worked out in the second half of the eighteenth century by the French Physiocrats and by the Scotsman Adam Smith. They rested on the same assumptions of individualism and the natural "harmony of interests" that underlay the philosophy of political liberalism. Their practical recommendations were simple: to reduce to a minimum all interference of state, society, or any other external factor in the free operations of the economy. Tariffs, monopolies, fiscal controls, and guilds all had to go, because they prevented the "natural" order from asserting itself.

The principles of economic liberalism had wide ramifications. Although most directly pertinent to tariff policy, they challenged in one way or another all the basic principles that had guided Western economic life for centuries. In 1787, in his *Defence of Usury*, Jeremy Bentham, who in many matters followed Smith, argued that "no man of ripe years and sound mind, acting freely, and with his eyes open, ought to be hindered, with a view to his advantage, from making such a bargain, in the way of obtaining money, as he sees fit." By proposing free competition for money, Bentham rejected the traditional Christian view that lending money at interest was unethical. Bentham and such French popularizers of economic liberalism as J. B. Say and C. F. Bastiat eventually condemned all restraints on the free economic activity of individuals. "In political economy,"

Adam Smith's portrait medal of 1797 has on its reverse side (opposite) symbols representing Smith's Wealth of Nations.

Bentham wrote, "there is much to learn and little to do." The ultimate triumph of economic liberalism was not due, of course, to the mere force of its arguments. Economic liberalism won in England because it suited the most dynamic and productive class, that of traders and manufacturers.

As we have seen, British industrialists had tried to prevent foreign competition by prohibiting the export of men and machines. But these measures failed, and in any event the more farsighted industrialists preferred to capitalize on the head start that Britain had gained over potential rivals. As early as the 1770s, British manufacturers pressured Parliament to ease tariffs and the Navigation Laws. Their argument was that "from their present ascendancy of skill [they] have nothing immediate to fear from competition, and everything to hope from the speculation of an increased demand." These groups won the ear of Prime Minister William Pitt, who in 1786 signed a treaty with France reducing tariffs between the two countries. But in the protracted conflict between Britain and France that followed the French Revolution, economic warfare provided an important weapon, and economic liberalization had to be postponed.

The agitation for greater freedom of manufacture and trade revived after 1815. Britain's lead was by now so great that British industrialists clamored for the abolishment of the restrictions imposed when British industry had been weak and in need of protection. The manufacturers wanted repeal of the Navigation Laws, which required them to use British ships in trade with British colonies. They objected to duties on the importation of raw materials, especially on wheat, where the duty artificially kept up the cost of bread and forced them to pay workers higher wages. In general, the manufacturers could demonstrate that, with an increasing number of Englishmen gaining a livelihood from industry, the well-being of industry was of vital concern for England as a whole. If their argument did not immediately carry the day, it was because it challenged the interests of the landed aristocracy, which benefited from protection, and the state, which depended on custom receipts for much of its revenue.

The cause of economic liberalism began to make headway with the appointment of William Huskisson to the chairmanship of the Board of Trade. During his tenure of office (1823–1827), Huskisson reduced trade restrictions, proceeding so cautiously that he did not antagonize those whose interests they protected. He based his actions not on general, theoretical arguments, but on concrete evidence. For instance, when reducing tariffs on raw silk, wool, and several additional items, he demonstrated that this action would kill a vast contraband trade in these items. This kind of fiscal pragmatism typified the whole British movement toward free trade. Huskisson also eased the Navigation Laws, enabling the British colonies to engage in direct trade relations with the United States and European countries.

The crucial test in the mounting conflict between economic liberals and protectionists came over grain (or corn, as it is called in England). The early proponents of free trade, the Physiocrats and Adam Smith, had never anticipated such an occurrence; both had regarded the agrarian interests as more open to arguments in favor of free trade than the manufacturers, whom they believed firmly committed to monopolistic practices. As it turned out, however, liberal ideas won increased acceptance among the industrialists, whereas the landlords turned into last-ditch defenders of protectionism. The specific issue over which the decisive battle was fought was the Corn Law.

The Corn Law in force in the 1820s had been passed in 1815 to alleviate the agrarian depression that followed the conclusion of the Napoleonic wars. As long as the wars had been in progress and wheat prices rose, British landlords expanded arable land, even into areas of low productivity where farming would not have been profitable in normal times. This had been one of the main reasons for the increase in enclosure acts. The process of enclosures had reached its peak between 1802 and 1815, when acts of Parliament authorized the enclosure of some 50,000 acres annually, most of it for the purpose of transforming pasture land into arable land. With the return of peace, food prices dropped sharply. Wheat, which had sold during wartime for as much as 130 shillings a quarter (a fourth of a ton), fell in May, 1814, one month after Napoleon's abdication, to 73 shillings. To prevent a further decline in prices, the government in 1815 passed the Corn Law, which decreed that if the price of domestic wheat fell below 80 shillings a quarter, no wheat was to be imported; if it rose above that figure, foreign wheat could be admitted free of duty. The intent of the law was to assure the landlords of high prices, but it failed to fulfill this expectation, for domestic wheat prices continued to fall even without foreign competition. The Corn Law was very unpopular among both manufacturers and workers. In the early nineteenth century wheat was still the staple food of the common man. The artificial maintenance of higher wheat prices forced the manufacturer to pay bigger wages and the worker to spend a greater part of his income on food than would have been the case if English wheat had to compete freely with imported wheat.

Huskisson modified the Corn Law by abandoning the absolute 80-shilling figure in favor of a sliding-scale tariff, the amount of the duty charged being proportional to the price of domestic wheat. But this measure did not greatly improve matters from the manufacturer's point of view. During the decade that followed Huskisson's death in 1830 (he was killed in a railroad accident, perhaps the iron horse's very first victim), nothing significant was done to change further the Corn Law or any other tariff. The issue was reopened only in 1838 with the founding in Manchester of the Anti-Corn Law Association. For the next eight years, the conflict over wheat tariffs fairly dominated English public life.

The Anti-Corn Law Association (or League, as it was later called) was the child of Richard Cobden, a gifted agitator and organizer, who brought to the cause of free trade an almost religious fervor. Cobden felt convinced that freedom of trade would inaugurate an era of unprecedented prosperity for all mankind. At his side stood John Bright, one of the great orators of the time. Cobden, a successful industrialist, devoted his own fortune to the cause of free trade and persuaded Manchester businessmen to make large donations to the league. With Bright's assistance, he poured out a steady stream of pamphlets and books, organized mass rallies, and sent agitators to towns, factories, and even the hostile rural districts to plead for the abolition of duties on wheat. He had an uncanny sense of class interests and appealed to each social group in a manner calculated to win it over. His main argument was of a persuasive simplicity: If England, by abolishing the Corn Law, were to purchase more food abroad, foreigners would use the money thus obtained to buy more English manufactured goods. In this

manner, everyone would benefit, except for a small group of selfish landlords.

The campaign—a pioneering effort at modern propaganda—won much popular support, but it owed its ultimate success to the growing awareness of government authorities that tariff reduction would not cut into its revenues. A parliamentary committee appointed in 1840 found that 90 percent of the country's total customs income derived from a mere 19 of the 862 articles subject to duties. These findings caused Tory Prime Minister Robert Peel to lower tariffs on many raw materials and manufactured goods in 1842 and again in 1845. The reductions did not adversely affect customs receipts, because they led to an increase in imports; the revenue lost on individual items was more than compensated for by the larger quantity of imported goods. Evidence of this kind strengthened the hand of the free traders. For the time being, however, the Corn Law remained intact, for it protected the well-being of the landed aristocracy that dominated English social and political life.

The event that gave the final stimulus to the abolition of the Corn Law was the Irish famine. In 1845 the so-called black rot ruined the potato crop of Ireland. England had traditionally bought much foodstuff in Ireland and had no choice but to lower tariffs on food imports to make up for the loss of the Irish produce. Peel now became convinced that the repeal of the Corn Law was inevitable. Despite the fact that his party, the Tories, had been put into office on a platform pledging retention of the Corn Law, he introduced in 1846 a bill calling for the immediate reduction of wheat duties and their abolition three years later. Backed by the Whigs and liberal Tories, the bill passed the Commons.

The repeal of the Corn Law reduced the principal stronghold of the protectionists. The remaining tariffs and other restraints on trade now fell in quick succession. By 1852 Great Britain was for all practical purposes a free-trade country, admitting foreign goods without restrictions of any kind. A series of reciprocal commercial treaties with other countries, notably France (1860), facilitated also the entry of British goods into foreign markets. But although only a handful of countries followed Britain's lead in instituting full freedom of trade

The installation of increasingly complex machinery raised the issue of the safety of working conditions. These calico printing machines, depicted in 1836, have their driving gears and belt systems completely exposed.

E. BAINES, *History of the County Palatine*, 1836

(Holland, Belgium, Switzerland, and Sweden), Britain was not seriously hurt. At midcentury it enjoyed so great an industrial lead that it could compete with protected economies on their home grounds, despite the handicap of tariffs.

As the liberals had anticipated, the establishment of free trade brought immediate benefits to Britain's foreign commerce. The total value of its imports and exports, which before 1846 had fluctuated between £50 million and £120 million a year, rose in 1860 to £370 million and in 1873 to £620 million. But the import-export figures do not reveal the full extent of Britain's commercial relations with foreign countries. Britain derived additional income from two major sources: shipping and investments. British commercial shipping outclassed all competitors and dominated maritime trade, gaining for the country much money. Britain's foreign investments (in government bonds, railroad construction, mines, and other enterprises) also brought large returns. These foreign investments increased from £300 million in the early 1850s to £1,300 million in 1875. Shipping and other forms of "invisible exports" such as insurance, together with income derived from foreign investments, more than compensated for Britain's negative trade balance (i.e., the practice of buying abroad more than one sold there). For example, in 1860, when the value of imported goods exceeded the value of exported goods by £122 million, Britain earned £77 million from international shipping and £75 million from foreign investments. Its net gain was thus £30 million. Britain's principal exports were textiles and products of the metallurgical and mining industries (iron, coal, machines, hardware), and its principal imports were raw materials, chiefly food and cotton.

It should be noted that events refuted the protectionists who had claimed that the abolition of the Corn Law would ruin British agriculture. The landlords and farmers of Britain continued to benefit from the country's general prosperity until the early 1870s.

The Social Consequences of Early Industrialization

The emergence of industrial economies has everywhere altered the life of societies in a great variety of ways. The most apparent and incontrovertible change involved the growth and distribution of population. The advent of industrialism coincided with an unprecedented growth of the European population. In the middle of the eighteenth century, when rapid industrialization first began, the population of Europe (exclusive of Russia) was estimated to have been only slightly larger than that of Africa. A hundred years later it was twice as large. Roughly speaking (and one has to speak roughly in these matters, for early demographic statistics are notoriously unreliable), from 1750 onward the inhabitants of Europe doubled each century. Human history has never known an increase of similar proportions. We shall discuss the probable reasons and consequences of this phenomenon in a later chapter.

The second important change occurred in the distribution of the population: the shift of inhabitants from the countryside to the city. Urbanization, as this process is called, did not assume dramatic proportions until the second half of the nineteenth century, and for this reason we shall deal with it, too, later. Since the social history of the first half of the nineteenth century cannot be understood without taking urbanization into account, however, some observations about it are in order here.

The reasons for large-scale urban growth were primarily economic. In preindustrial conditions, with low labor productivity, it was more efficient to locate manufactures near the sources of food, that is, in the countryside, because the worker consumed more food (in terms of bulk and weight) than raw materials. This explains why, between 1500 and 1800, manufactures dispersed and the city population of Europe remained static and in some places even declined. The introduction of mechanization and steam power altered this situation. The productivity of labor now increased to the point where the worker required far more raw materials, such as cotton and coal, than food. It became, therefore, more expedient to locate him as close as possible to the sources of raw materials and to bring the food to him. The size and cost of machines, the construction of canals and railroads, and the desirability of concentrating in one place technical, administrative and financial operations contributed further to urban growth—as did the lure of wealth, amusement, and an opportunity for self-improvement.

Britain, the first country to industrialize, was also the first to urbanize. By 1851 its city population outnumbered the rural population, and from then on the urban-rural gap steadily widened. At the same time, the center of the British population shifted from the agrarian regions in the southeast to the industrial centers in the northwest. In Germany and France the growth of cities occurred more slowly, and intense urbanization got under way only in the second half of the century. In Prussia, whose territories included the manufacturing centers and mines of Silesia and the Rhineland, the percentage of urban inhabitants increased between 1815 and 1851 by only 2 percent (from 26.5 percent to 28.5 percent). In France, despite the dramatic growth of Paris, the urban element in the middle of the century accounted only for a fourth of the population. Here and there, however, individual cities expanded at a rapid rate, even in countries with thoroughly agrarian economies.

A far more difficult subject to discuss with any degree of assurance is the effect of early industrialization on the life of the masses of population. To arrive at any convincing conclusions, we would have to examine full statistical data on living standards. Such statistics are scarce and inadequate, even for a country with excellent records such as England. But even if we had complete data on standards of living, the criteria used to evaluate them would be subjective. How can we judge human well-being in statistical terms? How can we compare, for example, the loss of fresh air and a familiar environment with the acquisition of better clothing or more food, or the decline of security with the gain of material goods?

The term *Industrial Revolution* evokes for many people a picture of utter human degradation. It brings to mind children working fifteen hours a day in textile mills; young girls chained to coal wagons in deep underground tunnels and women carrying baskets filled with coal from pits a hundred or more feet deep; families expelled from villages into vermin-infested slums. The picture gains in intensity from the skill with which it was depicted in the popular social novels of the time, such as Charles Kingsley's *Alton Locke* (1850), Elizabeth Cleghorn Gaskell's *Mary Barton* (1848), and Emile Zola's realistic cycle of novels, *Les Rougon-Macquart* (e.g., *The Dram-Shop* [1877] and *Germinal* [1885]). This popular image is not without its elements of truth. The working conditions in early industrial establishments were indeed often appalling and arouse in

the modern observer a sense of outrage, as does the indifference of many of the propertied to the suffering of the poor, a subject documented exhaustively by social historians.

In rendering industrial subjects, Romantic artists tended to give them a nightmarish, satanic interpretation. This is a British ironworks in 1833.

Yet degradation and suffering are only a part of the story, and probably not the essential one. In dealing with any social phenomenon, it must be borne in mind that what attracts the attention of contemporaries and historians alike is not the typical, but the new and unusual. An early nineteenth-century observer, who may have passed unconcerned a village hovel, was startled by a city slum. Untroubled (if, indeed, not charmed) by the sight of women and children working from dawn to dusk in the fields or cottage industries, he was shocked when he saw the same women or children tending machines or carrying coal. It is these novel features of industrialization that tend both to dominate and to distort our view of what really happened. But the economic historian must acquire, as Sir John Clapham, a great practitioner of the discipline, once observed, "what might be called the statistical sense, the habit of asking in relation to any institution, policy, group, or movement the questions: How large? How long? How often? How representative?" Applied to social conditions of early industrialism, particularly to England, for which the available evidence is most abundant, these questions provide an important corrective to the traditional view.

Researches undertaken by modern economic historians have convincingly disproved the contention that early industrialism caused a general lowering of living standards among the working population. Employing statistical data rather than the case histories favored by social historians, they have discovered that living standards in Britain, the key country in the debate, improved in the first half of the nineteenth century. (There is no serious question of their improvement in the second half of the century.) The conclusion is based mainly on the fact that, apart from minor fluctuations, real wages (that is, wages adjusted to the cost of living) moved steadily upward. This phenomenon resulted from modern methods of manufacture and transport, which drove down the price of commodities. Thus, even with stable wages, the worker could buy more goods. The authors of a recent study conclude that real wages in Britain rose by some 25 percent in the first quarter of the nineteenth century, and by 40 percent in the second.° Students of French and German working conditions arrived independently at similar conclusions regarding their countries. In addition to a rise in real wages, workers in industrial nations improved their situation by virtue of the fact that modern manufacturing methods required an increasing number of high skills. As more and more workers moved from the unskilled to the skilled category, the median income of the working class went up.

Nevertheless, while the conditions of the working class *as a whole* improved, the conditions of certain of its segments undoubtedly deteriorated. The existence of dire poverty in the midst of general prosperity is a familiar phenomenon. It explains why many contemporaries felt convinced that industrialization had brought impoverishment to the masses. The rise in real wages and wage scales was slow and unspectacular in the nineteenth century, but the misery of certain groups of the population was a shocking reality, visible to all.

The group that suffered most was the unemployed. The introduction of machinery in manufactures that had previously relied on manual labor created havoc in certain trades. Most affected were the hand-loom weavers, who were made obsolete and destitute by the spread of the power looms after 1820. Another cause of unemployment was periodic recession. The industrial economy, producing not for a local and relatively predictable market but for an uncertain national or international market, was subject to wild fluctuations. Each such fluctuation caused layoffs and threw thousands of laborers out of work. The existence of large numbers of jobless, victims of vocational or cyclical unemployment, induces some modern historians to deny that a general improvement in living standards had taken place.†

Statesmen did little to help the unemployed, partly because they did not believe that social ills could be cured by government action, and partly because they considered social welfare measures incompatible with economic progress, Indeed, in 1834 Britain may be said to have taken a step backward in this respect. To curb abuses in the dispensation of public relief to the destitute and unemployed, the House of Commons that year passed a Poor Law that ended

---

°Phyllis Deane and W. A. Cole, *British Economic Growth, 1688–1959: Trends and Structure* (1962). See also T. S. Ashton, "The Standard of Life of Workers in England, 1790–1830," *The Journal of Economic History,* Supplement IX, 1949.

†See, for example, E. J. Hobsbawm, *The Age of Revolution, 1789–1848* (1962), and E. P. Thompson, *The Making of the English Working Class* (1965).

the traditional "outdoor relief" given by the parishes. Relief was henceforth to be earned in public workhouses. The proponents of this bill argued that there was no real unemployment in the country and that those seeking relief merely wanted to avoid work. In fact, the majority of paupers refused to go into the "bastilles," as they called the workhouses, and found jobs. But in times of severe economic depression (e.g., 1836–1837), the new Poor Law caused great distress in areas where previously parishes had been relied upon to provide relief.

Legislation to protect labor came slowly. It took a long time to realize that industrial workers constituted a distinct social group with specific needs. Nor did the manufacturers favor such protection, on the grounds that it would interfere with the "natural" operations of the economy. Nevertheless, some laws were introduced to curb female and child labor (e.g., the Factory Act of 1833). An important step was the Ten Hours Act, passed in 1847 under the pressure of the agrarian interests, who were eager to revenge themselves on the manufacturers for the repeal the previous year of the Corn Law. This act, applicable to women and children but in practice also extended to men, limited the working day to ten hours. On the Continent the worker remained for the time being entirely unprotected, except in countries like Germany, where the old guild legislation still remained in force.

The initial reaction of workers to the insecurity created by industrialism and economic liberalism was to attack its most visible cause: the machine. In the first quarter of the century Britain was plagued by industrial saboteurs, popularly known as Luddites, who destroyed machinery with a savagery that frightened Parliament into passing a law (1812) making the willful destruction of certain machines a capital offense. In 1831 French workers in Lyons smashed machines used in the manufacture of silk. Violence directed against machinery and factories was a common occurrence in all revolutionary disturbances in the first half of the nineteenth century.

Anti-machine feeling rarely survived the initial impact of industrialism. In time, workers everywhere recognized that the machine had come to stay, and they abandoned industrial sabotage to struggle for economic improvement and sometimes political democracy.

14

Romanticism

Historical movements are sometimes easier to identify in terms of what they oppose than what they espouse. The term *Romanticism* has been used to describe so great a variety of attitudes and styles that no single positive definition can give a precise idea of its meaning; indeed, some historians despair whether it has any meaning at all. Yet the Romantic movement certainly existed. Its adherents, whatever their internal differences, were bound by opposition to a common enemy, classicism, the aesthetic doctrine that had dominated Western culture in the seventeenth and eighteenth centuries.

Classicism was a formalized expression of that admiration for the achievement of the ancient Greeks and Romans which had characterized the art and thought of Europe since the Renaissance. But ancient culture, which in the fifteenth and sixteenth centuries had provided a fruitful stimulus, had become by the end of the seventeenth century a rigid doctrine inhibiting free creativity. Underlying the classical doctrine was the belief that there exist absolute, eternal standards of beauty, that these standards had been most closely realized by the ancients, and that, therefore, classical culture provided permanent models for all creative achievement. The aesthetic rules of classicism were formulated in France between 1660 and 1690, most authoritatively by Nicolas Boileau in his *L'Art Poétique* (1674). They embraced, in addition to poetry, other forms of literature, the visual arts, architecture, and music.

The aim of classicism was not so much to please as to instruct; it concerned itself not with the individual and the fleeting, but with the general and the unchanging. Because it assumed that aesthetic rules were absolute and eternal, it imposed on the writer and artist strict limitations. The classical dramatist, for example, was to adhere to the Aristotelian unities of time, place, and action. The poet had to occupy himself with "poetic," that is lofty, subjects and employ an appropriately lofty vocabulary and meter. The painter had to conform to certain rules of composition. One such rule forbade him to depict two figures in a group facing the same direction. That such regulation inhibited creative freedom did not escape the attention of the exponents of classicism, but they saw no harm in it, for they believed that mastery was attained precisely by conformity to prescribed rules. "No one unable to limit himself has ever been able to write," Boileau asserted, and Goethe stated the same principle when he said: "It is limitations that prove the master." Assuming that nothing really new could be said, classicism concerned itself more with form than with content, more with the manner in which an idea or emotion was expressed than with the idea or emotion itself.

Classicism owed its influence in no small measure to the control that its adherents exercised over patronage. Writers and artists require money to support themselves and to display their work to the public. For this reason, unless they have private means, all creative talents depend on a ready market for their prod-

The Englishman J. M. W. Turner was one of the founders of the Romantic school. The Shipwreck (c. 1805), one of his early canvases, is a highly imaginative version of an event he had witnessed. Later Turner's work became more abstract and impressionistic.

Jacques Louis David's Death of Socrates *(1787) is the archetype of classicist painting. The Christ-like philosopher has a final word for his twelve mourning disciples as he reaches for the cup of hemlock.*

uct. In our times, the spread of education and wealth have created outlets for artistic and literary works unknown before the nineteenth century, when talent relied for support on individual patrons: the royal court, the landed gentry, the church, merchants. Much of this patronage was dispensed not directly, through commissions, but through the agency of academies. The model was the French Académie des Beaux Arts, founded in 1648, which secured the remunerative privilege of nominating artists for royal commissions. Similar academies were founded in other countries: the Academia de Nobles Artes de San Fernando in Madrid (1752), the Imperial Academy of Arts in St. Petersburg (1757), the Royal Academy of Arts in London (1768), and so on. These academies, as a rule, maintained schools that trained their students according to classical precepts and held exhibitions to which they admitted only works conforming to these precepts. Drama was similarly kept within classical bounds by subsidized theaters. Printed literature—poetry and the novel—could always appeal over the heads of official establishments directly to the reader and for that reason never succumbed fully to the classical domination.

Conceived in the very broadest terms, Romanticism represented a cultural revolution against the whole classical model on behalf of modern, that is, post-classical, Western culture. Without disparaging the achievement of the ancients, the Romantics claimed equal distinction for the culture created by Christian Europe. This self-awareness of the Romantics as modern Europeans constituted a very important factor in the emergence of the Romantic movement. It lay at the heart of the discussions of a brilliant circle of German writers and critics who in the 1790s formulated the theoretical principles of Romanticism and gave the movement its name. These men constantly discussed the contrast between the "natural" and the "civilized," between feeling and thought, between spontaneity and consciousness. They believed that European classicism had upset this balance by overemphasizing the civilized, intellectual elements at the expense of the natural and emotional ones. From this awareness stemmed their distinction between the "classical" and the modern or, as Frederick Schlegel called it, the "Romantic." The classics, they argued, were rooted in a common mythology and tended to generalize about man and life; they were concerned with the typical. The moderns (by which they meant artists and writers of the whole Christian era), by contrast, were inclined to be subjective, to stress the individual, the unique, the original.

Like all great cultural movements, Romanticism rested on a specific concept of man. Classicism regarded man as a finite, static being, whereas Romanticism viewed him as a being endowed with endless potential. The realization of this potential was, according to the Romantics, the highest purpose in life. Johann Fichte, the German whose writings are among the philosophical foundations of Romanticism, stated that man's supreme virtue was to become himself, and the Englishman Samuel Taylor Coleridge spoke of man as in part "his own creator." This process of self-realization, of the unfolding of one's potential, the Germans called *Bildung*—a term that embraced not only formal education but also the development of one's character, will, aesthetic sensibility, capacity for true friendship, and so on. Frederick Schlegel, one of the founders of Romanticism, put the matter as follows:

> I believe that I live not to obey or to dissipate myself, but to be and to become; and I believe in the ability of the will and of education [*Bildung*] to bring me once more close to the eternal, to free me from the fetters of miseducation, and to make me independent of the limitations of the human kind.

The highest means of self-realization was artistic creativity. To the Romantics, art was not merely an act of craftsmanship, measurable in terms of its ability to cope with well-defined rules; it was an act of reaching beyond "the limitations of the human kind." "The poet is the only true *man*," the German dramatist Johann von Schiller wrote in a letter to Goethe. "Compared with him, the best philosopher is a mere caricature."

Obviously, such a concept of art precluded restrictions on the artist. It demanded that he be free to find the means best suited to his purpose, whether or not they enjoyed the approval of an Aristotle or a Boileau. What mattered was not form but content. The Romantics had nothing but scorn for those who hoped to achieve greatness by adhering to formal rules. "They swayed upon a rocking horse, and thought it Pegasus," Keats wrote of the classicists in his poem "Sleep and Poetry."

For the Romantics, pleasure was the only criterion of art; a work of art must please, not instruct, as the classicists maintained. The French novelist Stendhal defined this principle facetiously:

> *Romanticism* is the art of presenting to different peoples those literary works which, in the existing state of their habits and beliefs, are capable of giving them the greatest possible pleasure. *Classicism*, on the contrary, presents to them that literature which gave the greatest possible pleasure to their great-grandfathers.

An anonymous French spoof at classicism has an actor teaching Napoleon the proper pose for an emperor: the stance of classic Greek statuary.

Also fundamental to Romantic aesthetic theory was the denial of any absolute and immutable standards of beauty; it held that each work is an end in itself and must be judged on its own terms.

Although the flowering of Romanticism occurred at the very time when industrialism was beginning to transform Europe, Romantic writers and artists took little cognizance of it. Indeed, if one were to reconstruct the appearance of England solely from Romantic art and literature, one would imagine it to have been an age of bucolic serenity. The vast majority of Romantic novelists and painters simply ignored the factory or the coal pit, as well as the men working in them. This discrepancy between art and reality suggests how dangerous it is to judge the life of a period from its art.

The Romantics rejected the whole industrial order with its discipline, ugliness, and money-grubbing. They sought escape from it in distant times and distant places that they suitably "romanticized," that is, cleansed of sordid elements. Their favorites were the Middle Ages, the Orient, the Polar regions. They loved the world of children with its spontaneity and sense of wonder. Most of all, they liked to retreat from the city to the countryside, to "nature," as did Childe Harold, the hero of Byron's poem of the same name:

> Where rose the mountains, there to him were friends;
> Where rolled the Ocean, thereon was his home;
> Where a blue sky, and glowing clime, extends,
> He had the passion and power to roam;
> The desert, forest, cavern, breaker's foam,
> Were unto him companionship; they spake
> A mutual language, clearer than the tome
> Of his land's tongue, which he would oft forsake
> For Nature's pages glassed by sunbeams on the lake. . . .
> But in Man's dwellings he became a thing
> Restless and worn, stern and wearisome,
> Drooped as a wild-born falcon with clipt wing,
> To whom the boundless air alone were home.

In general, it may be said that the Romantics avoided the moderation and sensibility that had been the ideal of the classicists and inclined toward extremes of all kinds: experimental literary forms, musical sounds, visual images; extremes of the primitive, grotesque, abnormal. In an effort to transport themselves into the realm of extremes, some Romantic writers (e.g., the German E. T. A. Hoffmann and the Englishman Thomas De Quincey) deliberately induced hallucinations by means of opium and other narcotics.

Romanticism produced its own hero, writes the critic Paul van Tieghem, with principal characteristics common in all countries:

> The Romantic hero is sometimes a great lord, but more often he is of low or unknown origin. A foundling, an illegitimate child, a plebeian, a valet, clown, or brigand, he feels bitterly the contrast between his social position and his true worth. Everyone owes him something—he owes no one anything. He is full of pride, bitterness, and anger. Isolated in society, he often loathes it. Surrounded by mystery, he is a pawn of an irresistible fatality

The Swiss John Henry Fuseli combined a passion for Shakespeare with a taste for the erotic and grotesque in his Midsummer's Night Dream. *In a trance inflicted by her husband Oberon, the fairy queen Titania embraces a humble weaver masked in the head of an ass.*

which has preordained him for blind passion, for a destiny of adventure and danger, for unavoidable crimes; and yet he is often, at bottom, sensitive and tender. Despite the intensity of his life and the external activism which he unfolds, he remains more passive than truly active; often, like Hamlet, with whom perhaps he has something in common, the Romantic hero hesitates and trembles when confronted with the need for action. In general, he is a frenetic lover, and his love is fatal for its object. He embodies the rights of love against the prejudices of society. Often ironic and haughty, he defies morals and laws.

The Romantic hero was a person estranged from the society in which he was compelled to live and from which he was forever trying to escape. He was the antithesis of the down-to-earth, prosaic, sensible, ordinary man, or "Philistine," as he came to be known later in the century.

The Romantic hero found his incarnation in George Gordon, Lord Byron. Byron not only helped to create the image of his hero in his writings (*Childe Harold, Don Juan*), but he shaped his own life in accord with it. For this reason, he was the most widely emulated person of the whole Romantic era. Between 1815 and 1830, youths all over Europe took to wearing open or "Byronic" col-

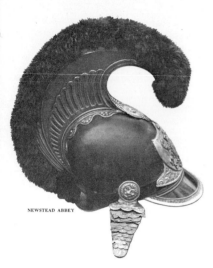

NEWSTEAD ABBEY

Byron designed a helmet appropriate to his role as a champion of Greek independence.

lars, affected "Byronic" haughtiness and spleen, and sought (fortunately, more often in words than in deeds) an early "Byronic" death.° Byron had all the qualifications necessary for his role: he was an aristocrat, a man of great gifts, a victim of social prejudice, and a champion of liberty. Until 1816 he had been very much a member of the English Establishment. He wrote successful verse, had access to the highest social circles, served in the House of Lords, and married an heiress. All was well, but had all remained well Byron would hardly have exerted much influence on Romantic youth. In 1816, just a year after they had been married, his wife sued for divorce. Although her reasons were not and are not to this day precisely known, London society turned against Byron. Deeply hurt, he left England in 1816, never to return. From then on until his death eight years later, he wandered over Europe, deliberately flaunting convention, attacking hypocrisy, and ridiculing the forces of reaction at a time when they were most potent. In his writings he could, when he wished, create lyric verse of the highest order, but much of the time he preferred to assume an air of cynical detachment toward his hero and himself—an attitude that contrasted with the usual solemnities of poetry and won him a great following among the reading public. He died of fever in 1824, fighting in the ranks of the Greek insurgents against the Turks.

The general principles of Romanticism—the assertion of the autonomy of European culture, the stress on individual self-fulfillment and complete creative freedom, the escapism from the industrial and urban toward the exotic and rural—had implications beyond literature and art. The Romantics, in the early phases of their movement, supported liberal causes all over Europe and were in the forefront of revolutionary upheavals directed against the conservative establishment. Romanticism had profound repercussions in philosophy and historical writing, in religious thought, in social theory, and even in science.

Romanticisim at its height influenced all the countries within the orbit of Western civilization, from Russia in the East to Latin America in the West. But it was peculiarly a movement of northern Europe. Its home was Germany and England, and its impact was most felt in Teutonic countries. This is not surprising, in view of the fact that classicism, against which the Romantics rebelled, had its roots in Latin culture. Romanticism had difficulty penetrating France, Italy, or Spain; it did so belatedly, and never with the same force as in the north.

Chronologically, the Romantic movement may be divided into three periods: proto-Romanticism of the eighteenth century; Romanticism proper (approximately 1790–1830), with a high point in the 1820s; and decline, which set in during the 1830s, when it weakened and began to lose ground to realism and materialism.

Literature and the Theater

The first flowering of Romantic literature occurred in the late 1790s. To contemporaries, it seemed a strange and sudden phenomenon, but it came not with-

---

° It must be noted, however, that a remarkably large proportion of Romantic writers died young, sometimes of natural causes, sometimes as a result of self-destruction. John Keats and the Hungarian poet Sándor Petöfi died at twenty-six, the Russian poet Mikhail Lermontov at twenty-seven, Novalis at twenty-nine, and Percy Bysshe Shelley at thirty. Among those who died in the fourth decade of their lives are the German poet Heinrich von Kleist (thirty-four), Byron (thirty-six), Alexander Pushkin (thirty-eight), the Italian poet Giacomo Leopardi (thirty-nine), and Edgar Allan Poe and the Polish poet Julius Slowacki (both at forty).

out warning. European literature of the eighteenth century had running through it a persistent strain of anticlassicism. England produced in the second third of the century an influential Sentimentalist school distinguished by love of nature and the Middle Ages as well as a stress on emotions. Among its best-known works are Edward Young's long poem *Night Thoughts on Life, Death, and Immortality* (1742–1745), Thomas Gray's "Elegy Written in a Country Churchyard" (1751), and the epics of the legendary Irish bard, Ossian, written (or rather, forged) by James Macpherson in the 1760s. Even more directly related to Romanticism were the writings of Jean Jacques Rousseau with their rejection of civilized life. This proto-Romantic tendency culminated in the 1770s and 1780s in the German "Sturm und Drang" ("Storm and Stress") movement, whose leaders were Johann von Goethe and Schiller and whose most influential work was Goethe's *The Sorrows of Young Werther* (1774).

Until the 1790s this current was decidedly subordinated to classicism. The fact that it gained ascendancy in the 1790s was not entirely fortuitous. Classicism had been identified with the absolute monarchy, and especially with the Bourbon monarchy, its principal patron. To many young Europeans, the fall of the Bourbons represented a signal to raise the banner of rebellion against classical authority in the arts. The struggle for the artist's right to create in complete freedom was, psychologically viewed, a counterpart of the civic and political liberties proclaimed by the French Revolution.

The Romantic movement, as we have seen, had its origin in Germany, but its leaders, the most notable being the brothers Frederick and August William Schlegel and the contributors to their journal, *Athenaeum* (1798–1800), distinguished themselves more as critics and theorists than as creative talents. The first significant and truly Romantic literary work appeared not in Germany but in England. It was *Lyrical Ballads*, a small volume of poems published anonymously in 1798. The product of a collaboration between two young poets, William Wordsworth and Samuel Taylor Coleridge, it achieved its effect of novelty by a deliberate violation of one of the cardinal rules of classicism: that under no condition must language appropriate for lofty subjects be used for subjects regarded as common, nor, conversely, must simple, everyday speech be employed for those subjects considered "sublime." Wordsworth and Coleridge had undertaken deliberately to challenge this rule by dealing with everyday matters in sublime language and with fantastic matters in ordinary language. The effect proved too startling for the tastes of the time, and the initial public reaction was unfavorable. Wordsworth's "Idiot Boy," Coleridge's "Rime of the Ancient Mariner," and other poems in the collection were criticized both for their choice of subject and their unsuitability of expression. Nevertheless, the breach in the classical fortress was made. With poets like Wordsworth, Coleridge, John Keats, Percy Bysshe Shelley, and Byron, English poetry, freed from its confines, achieved in the following three decades a level of distinction second only to that of the Elizabethan age.

Poetry was the first of the arts to abandon classicism in favor of Romanticism. After 1800 there emerged in various parts of Europe a new generation of writers who united in opposition to the old literary establishment. Romanticism, by rejecting classical models, stimulated the emergence of national literatures in coun-

A medallion portrait of Goethe done at Weimar in 1829, three years before the poet's death.

The historical novelist Sir Walter Scott is depicted as a Scottish country squire, the role he most enjoyed playing.

tries with weak or nonexistent classical traditions. Russian poets of the eighteenth century, for example, had to follow a classical model that had no roots in their own culture. Adherence to Romantic tenets permitted them to abandon this pretense and to write in a national idiom. Alexander Pushkin, who bridged the classical and Romantic ages of Russian literature, was not only Russia's greatest poet, but also the founder of its modern literary language. Romanticism had a similar effect on other cultures in eastern, southeastern, and central Europe.

While poetry was the principal medium of Romantic literature, prose also was affected by it. Here, the most important innovations were the historic novel and the fantastic tale. The creator of the historic novel was Sir Walter Scott, in his day widely regarded as Europe's leading prose writer. A native of Scotland, he avidly studied his country's past and collected its ballads. Scott's novels combined several elements dear to the Romantic taste: chivalry, the Middle Ages, and a northern setting. Its heroes were vastly different from early nineteenth-century Britons of nearby industrial Manchester. Scott found many emulators, among them the leader of the French Romantics, Victor Hugo, the author of *The Hunchback of Notre Dame* (1831).

The Romantic love for the unusual, especially the fantastic and grotesque, was connected with the belief that life was not what it seemed to mere reason, but instead contained mysteries revealed only to the imagination. This belief found literary expression in fantastic tales. The rage for this genre began in the 1790s with the novels of Ann Radcliffe, which were filled with supernatural incidents against a background of ruined medieval castles and abbeys. The genre was subsequently adopted by writers of major stature, who often heightened the horror by placing supernatural incidents in a realistic environment. Thus, the hero of Adelbert von Chamisso's *Peter Schlemihl* (1814) disposes of his shadow in a commercial transaction with the devil, while the subject of a short story by the Russian writer Nicolas Gogol wakes up one morning to find his nose gone

("The Nose," 1836). *Frankenstein* (1818) by Mary Shelley, the wife of the poet, which deals with a man-made monster, also belongs to this category. Perhaps the outstanding practitioners of fantastic tales were the German E. T. A. Hoffmann and the American Edgar Allan Poe.

The Romantics were much interested in folk literature, which they regarded as a repository of the primitive, "natural" spirit of Christian or "Romantic" culture lost by civilized man. They transcribed the poems, songs, and tales passed by the common people from generation to generation and reconstructed from such oral traditions and literary fragments their national epics. We owe to these efforts the preservation of a great literary heritage, much of which might otherwise have been lost. In Germany the brothers Jacob and Wilhelm Grimm, both professional philologists, collected folk stories, which in 1812–1815 they published in a celebrated book of fairy tales. Finnish folklorists reconstructed the text of their national epic, *Kalevala*, and the Russians transcribed the *byliny*, early heroic poems narrated by village bards. The predilection for the local and native also produced a body of regional literature written in dialects previously regarded as unsuitable for serious literary expression. Poems and stories appeared written in Provençal, Ukrainian, Alamannic, and various other peasant dialects.

Of all the literary genres, the drama succumbed last to the onslaughts of Romanticism. The stage had always been peculiarly in the domain of classicism. The aesthetic doctrines of Boileau found their purest realization in the plays of Jean Baptiste Racine. Altogether, in the theater the connection between classicism and the whole courtly and aristocratic establishment was firmly fixed. It was natural, therefore, that one of the most bitter contests between the old and new literary movements should have occurred in the theater and in France. The contest was climaxed by the so-called Battle of *Hernani*, which took place in Paris in February, 1830.

At issue was Shakespeare, whom the classicists regarded as an uncouth and inferior writer because he had consistently violated the Aristotelian unities, mixed the sublime with the ridiculous, and allowed emotion altogether too much scope. The anti-Shakespearean sentiment reached its greatest intensity in the 1760s and 1770s, when Voltaire attacked the English poet with all his wit and venom. He called Shakespeare a "barbarous charlatan" and described his dramas as a "dunghill containing a few pearls."

All the qualities of Shakespeare that had repelled the classicists endeared him to the Romantics. Indeed, in the early part of the nineteenth century, one's attitude toward Shakespeare became a touchstone of one's position in the whole classical-Romantic dispute. August von Schlegel, who translated Shakespeare's plays into German, regarded the English dramatist as the greatest representative of modern or Romantic genius. Coleridge, in a series of magnificent lectures in which he laid the foundations of modern Shakespearean criticism, extolled him as a peer of the greatest writers of antiquity, and in his book *Racine and Shakespeare* (1823), Stendhal depicted contemporary literary conflicts as a confrontation of the two styles represented by these writers.

The Romantic cause in France received a boost in 1827 when a visiting English theatrical group staged several of Shakespeare's plays. That same year,

Mary Godwin Shelley's Frankenstein *bested the efforts of both her husband and Byron in an informal horror-story contest. She wrote fiction and edited Shelley's works after his death.*

Victor Hugo, the leader of the literary rebels, wrote a play in the Romantic manner called *Cromwell*. He failed to have it staged, but his introduction to it created much stir and became the manifesto of the French Romanticists. Hugo rejected all classical rules, glorified Shakespeare, and called for a theater combining the "grotesque and the sublime, the awe-inspiring and the clownish, the tragic and the comical." "There exists today," he asserted, "a literary old regime, as there once existed a political old regime."

Hugo's opportunity to topple the "literary old regime" came three years later, in 1830, when the state-subsidized Théâtre-Français agreed to stage *Hernani*, his play written in the Shakespearean manner. For the Romantics, the first performance of *Hernani* was the literary equivalent of the storming of the Bastille. The novelist Théophile Gautier, a nineteen-year-old admirer of Hugo, assembled a band of writers, artists, bohemians, and ordinary hobos, for whom he purchased large blocks of seats to the opening night. Several hours before curtain time, Gautier, affecting a scarlet satin vest and green silk trousers, marched his band to the theater, where they amused themselves eating, drinking, and singing. By the time the well-to-do patrons began to arrive for the performance, the interior reeked of garlic and wine, as well as urine, for the Romantics thought nothing of relieving themselves against the walls of the auditorium. Gautier described the scene:

> In spite of the terror inspired by Hugo's partisans, who were scattered about in small parties and who were easily recognized by their peculiar costumes and their fierce looks, there sounded in the theater the low roar of the excited crowd, which is no more to be stilled than the roar of the sea. . . . It needed only to cast a glance at the public to learn that this was no ordinary performance; that two systems, two parties, two armies, two civilizations—it is no exaggeration to put it so—were facing each other, filled with cordial reciprocal hatred of the intense literary kind, ready to come to blows and longing for a fight. The general attitude was one of hostility; elbows were stuck out, the least friction would have sufficed to cause an outbreak, and it was easy to see that the long-haired youth considered the clean-shaven gentleman an atrocious idiot, and would not long refrain from giving expression to his private opinions.

Hugo's partisans had been cued beforehand which passages in *Hernani* had programmatic significance; whenever the actors pronounced these lines, they clapped, shouted, and made such a din that the classicists, if not persuaded, were at least silenced. Five months later came the July Revolution and the final extinction of Bourbon rule, and classicism in its traditional form suffered a defeat from which it has never recovered.

Music, Painting, and Architecture Romanticism found its most characteristic expression and reached its greatest creative heights in poetry and music, because these arts offered the artist the fullest freedom. In this respect, music was a vehicle superior even to poetry, for the musical language is infinite in its variety and utterly personal. In none of the other arts was the conquest of Romanticism so rapid and enduring.

Until Romanticism, music had performed essentially an auxiliary function, serving as an accompaniment or background to religious or social occasions. This functional role limited the freedom of the musician. Romanticism made music an end in itself and thereby emancipated him from such limitations. Musical performance now shifted from the church and salon to the concert hall, and the performer emerged from the obscurity of the organ loft or the orchestra pit into the limelight of the concert stage. Romanticism inaugurated the era of the musical genius, the virtuoso, and the great conductor. From one of the more marginal of the arts, music became, while Romanticism was at its height, the quintessence of art.

The Romantic composer took advantage of his freedom in several ways. For one, he experimented with new musical forms. In addition to sonatas, concertos, symphonies, or quartets, he composed songs, tone poems, incidental pieces, and vast secular works employing choruses and symphony orchestras. To list the names of the works of Frederick Chopin, the greatest Romantic composer for the piano, is to give an idea of the variety of musical forms used by the new school: they include ballades, nocturnes, preludes, scherzos, waltzes, and études. Romantics also took liberties with traditional forms. Beethoven, the greatest of all the Romantic composers, broke precedent by introducing in the second movement of his *Eroica Symphony* a funeral dirge and closing his *Ninth Symphony*

BIBLIOTHEQUE NATIONALE; GIRAUDON

A contemporary engraving gives the flavor of the riotous first-night performance of Hugo's "Shakespearian" play Hernani *in Paris in 1830.*

MUSIC, PAINTING, AND ARCHITECTURE   349

A highly Romantic subject, the virtuoso violinist Nicolò Paganini, was sketched with a cool insight by Jean Auguste Dominique Ingres, a student of David's and the last great neoclassicist.

with a chorus singing Schiller's "Ode to Joy." In addition to experimenting with forms, Romantics also occasionally violated accepted practices in matters of melody and harmony, introducing combinations of sounds that the classical ear found dissonant and jarring.

Romantic composers favored the piano as an instrument that offered intimacy combined with great tonal range. Beethoven wrote thirty-two piano sonatas, some of which he or his audiences gave such descriptive titles as "Pathétique," "Pastoral," "Moonlight," and "Appassionata." The piano compositions of Robert Schumann also tended to convey emotion and imagery. Chopin composed almost exclusively for the piano, which he endowed with extraordinary intimacy.

Other popular Romantic genres were chamber music and serious songs, the latter often based on contemporary poems. The quartets of Beethoven are generally considered the finest of their kind, and some critics regard the last in the series (Nos. 12–16) as Beethoven's supreme achievement. The leading composers of songs were Franz Schubert and Robert Schumann.

Though they preferred intimate instruments and forms, the Romantic composers, given their penchant for extremes, also wrote for large orchestras. The symphony orchestra as we know it today is in large measure the creation of the Romantic age. It was then that the classical string ensemble of some thirty performers expanded, through the enlargement of the string section and the addition of winds and percussion instruments, to become the modern orchestra of a hundred or more players. The orchestra thus enlarged could no longer perform on its own and required a full-time director to give it cohesion. This was the task of the conductor, who first appeared in the 1820s to coordinate the large body of singers and musicians employed in Karl Maria von Weber's Romantic operas (*Der Freischütz*, 1821, and *Oberon*, 1826). From then on the conductor became an indispensable feature of orchestral performance and a virtuoso in his own right. Romantic composers sometimes went to wild extremes in orchestration. Louis Hector Berlioz was a great innovator in this respect. His *Symphonie Fantastique* (1830), which sought to convey musically the visions of an opium-eater, achieved unusual orchestral brilliance and paved the way for the later innovations of Richard Wagner. In search for even richer effects, Berlioz employed in his *Hymn to France* (1844) no fewer than 1,200 performers. He was also one of the inventors of so-called programmatic music, that is, music intended to narrate a story. Another outstanding Romantic composer for the orchestra was Felix Mendelssohn-Bartholdy. His *Incidental Music to Midsummer Night's Dream* (1826, 1842) and his overture to the *Hebrides* (1830) (also known as *Fingal's Cave*) are superb examples of Romantic music and convey most faithfully the whole spirit of Romanticism with its Shakespearean elves, Ossianic heroes, misty northern islands, and so much else that stirred the imagination of the time.

Of course, one of the basic forms remained the classical symphony, which the Romantics expanded in length and orchestral scope. The nine symphonies of Beethoven, the four of Schumann, the eight principal ones of Schubert, and the last three of Mendelssohn are among the most majestic achievements of Romanticism. They constitute a staple of the modern orchestral repertoire.

Romanticism dominated music throughout the nineteenth century. The great composers of the second half of the century—Richard Wagner, Johannes Brahms, Giuseppe Verdi, Peter Ilyich Tchaikovsky—were Romantics, despite the fact that they lived in an environment that had become hostile to Romanticism.

In the visual arts Romanticism had a less pronounced impact than in either literature or music, for the academies managed to retain their influence over painters by continuing to control art schools, exhibition halls, and commissions. The Romantic school of painting concerned itself most characteristically with nature. The landscape, which in the classical era had served mainly as a backdrop for figures, now became an independent and favorite subject matter. The Romantics neither idealized nature nor reproduced it with realistic accuracy, but sought to penetrate its spirit and to convey its infinite variety of moods. They placed less emphasis on design and more on color, and in this respect they clearly anticipated the Impressionists. The French Romantic painter Ferdinand Delacroix expressed the Romantic attitude accurately when he said a painting should be a "feast to the eye." The pioneers of the Romantic school were two Englishmen, J. M. W. Turner and John Constable. Turner was obsessed with color and went to great lengths to capture it on canvas. It is said that to paint his *Steamer in a Snowstorm* (1842), a work of almost abstract quality, he had himself tied to the mast of a storm-tossed ship. Unfortunately, the colors have deteriorated on many of his paintings and do not render justice to his original visions. Constable's landscapes shimmer and pulsate as few landscapes had ever done before. Both Turner and Constable made sketches in the open, but they painted indoors, because the paints available in their time had to be ground and resolved in oil immediately before use, a task that could be performed only in the studio. Water colors, however, were not subject to this limitation and could be finished on the spot, like a pencil sketch. Early nineteenth-century English water colors convey a freshness and immediacy equal to the best Impressionist works.

In 1828 Paris held an exhibit of English landscape painting that, like the performances by the visiting Shakespeare players the previous year, exerted much influence on French tastes. Constable became the rage. In 1836 Theodore Rousseau launched a native school of Romantic landscape painters when he left Paris for the village of Barbizon in the nearby Fontainbleau Forest to paint in the open. He and his followers founded the Barbizon school, whose greatest representative was Camille Corot, a master of landscapes in delicate silvery gray and pale green hues. Similar Romantic landscape schools arose in other countries, including the United States, where its adherents formed the so-called Hudson River school.

Romantic painters also liked Oriental and Mediterranean themes and painted Arabs, Spaniards, and Greeks, often in settings of violent action. The leading exponent of this genre was Delacroix, who did many colorful canvases depicting scenes from North Africa and episodes from the Greek war for independence (see Portfolio Three). A minor school concentrated on grotesque and spooky themes, its adherents painting moonlit nights and ruins, ghosts, and mysterious shapes of various kinds, all calculated to frighten the onlooker. The most popular artist in this genre was the German Caspar David Friedrich (pages 370–371).

The perfection in 1819 of lithography—the art of striking prints from draw-

J. RUTTER, *The Delineations of Fonthill*, 1823

The English architect James Wyatt designed the emphatically Gothic Fonthill Abbey for an eccentric squire. Completed in 1807, the octagonal tower collapsed in 1825; the whole immense structure was later demolished.

ings done with a fatty substance on stone—offered a medium for quick and cheap reproduction. It became one of the favorite media, particularly useful for caricature. Its leading practitioner was Honoré Daumier, whose savage satires of the bourgeoisie under Louis Philippe initiated modern propaganda art.

Concurrently with Romantic painting there developed a movement that is difficult to classify. It was characterized by a desire to return to the simplicity and naïveté of early Italian painting. Its founders, a group of German artists known as Nazarenes, settled in Rome in 1810 and emulated the style of the artists of the fourteenth and fifteenth centuries. A related school, the Pre-Raphaelite Brotherhood, was established later (1848) by Dante Gabriel Rossetti in England. Both these circles were in some respects quite academic in their tastes, but in their admiration for the Middle Ages they resembled the Romantics.

In architecture Romanticism found its main expression in the Gothic Revival, which imitated medieval designs (or what its exponents regarded as medieval designs) and décor. The taste for Gothic building developed slowly, having to contend with a virile classical tradition in architecture, which achieved some of its greatest triumphs in the early nineteenth century. The first significant success of the new style occurred when its exponents won the commission to design a House of Parliament to replace the one that had burned in 1834. The result was exceptionally happy and was widely emulated in other parts of Europe. The Hungarian parliament building, the Vienna city hall, Memorial Hall at Harvard University, and many churches were built in the Gothic style. In Russia, which had no Gothic tradition, this movement yielded a parallel Byzantine Revival. Devotees of these various revivals stopped at nothing. They produced neo-Gothic interiors true to the smallest detail, including "Gothic" kitchens and bathrooms. Ludwig II, the king of Bavaria, constructed between 1869 and 1886 at Neuschwanstein a huge Alpine castle, with innumerable towers, turrets, spires, and all the other trappings of Gothic architecture. Many tourists regard Neuschwanstein Castle as an impressive example of medieval art, but it is actually only the last gasp of Gothic revivalism.

Romanticism was primarily an aesthetic movement: it concerned itself with art as the highest expression of the human spirit. The Romantics looked down on philosophers, partly because they had been the leaders of the Enlightenment, and partly because they lacked "creative genius." Nevertheless, Romanticism itself rested on very definite philosophical foundations, and it cannot be understood unless one obtains at least a general notion what these were.

Philosophic Idealism

The philosophical current associated with Romanticism is known as idealism. It came into existence in Germany between approximately 1780 and 1820 and dominated European thought throughout the Romantic era. It counted among its adherents all Romantics, even those who had never read a philosophical book.

Idealism emerged from a critique of the theories of empiricism, the dominant philosophical school of the eighteenth century. Empiricists such as Locke and Hume maintained that all knowledge derives from experience, that the mind has no "innate ideas." Until experience writes on it, the human mind resembles a clean slate. The most extreme empiricists went so far as to deny the existence of anything not capable of being perceived by the senses. Empiricism broadly

The philosopher Immanuel Kant led a life of almost perfect punctuality, his daily routine so unvarying that his friends set their watches by him.

defined may be said to have been the underlying philosophy of early modern science and owed much of its acceptance to scientific progress.

The most important critic of the empirical school, and the forefather of idealism, was the German philosopher Immanuel Kant. Kant conceded that knowledge derives from experience but argued that this proposition required qualification. He could point, for example, to an important realm of knowledge, mathematics, that has no basis in experience: nothing in our experience teaches us that the corners of a triangle add up to 180 degrees, or that any of the other axioms of algebra and geometry are correct. Mathematical truths obviously belong to a different order of knowledge. Awareness of this distinction induced Kant to analyze in detail the means by which we learn, the principal conclusions of which he presented in the *Critique of Pure Reason* (1781), one of the most seminal books in the entire history of thought.

Kant analyzed the cognitive apparatus and stated that the mind has built into it categories through which and through which alone it apprehends the data that the senses feed into it. The most obvious among these categories are the notions of space and time: we conceive everything by mentally locating it either in space, or in time, or in both. Space and time are, therefore, not qualities of reality itself, but of our mind. The external world as we know it is not the world as it actually is. Its real identity is beyond our grasp; it is the world as it appears after having been processed or filtered through the built-in apparatus of the human intellect. The mind, seen in this light, is not merely a passive recipient of information supplied by the senses. It is a very active organ, filled with understanding that precedes and is independent of experience. Mathematics is an aspect of this non-experimental knowledge.

From the point of view of cultural history, the most important consequence of Kant's theory lay in the shift that it accomplished in the role of the intellect. It was viewed no longer as the clean slate of the empiricists, but as a wonderfully complex apparatus with much understanding—a peer, as it were, of nature itself. This elevated notion of the mind suited the Romantic mood, and the Romantics turned into enthusiastic adherents of Kantian philosophy.

A succession of German philosophers, departing from Kantian principles, constructed individual systems of idealistic philosophy that were exceedingly abstruse and complicated. The most influential of such systems was that of G. W. F. Hegel, formulated in the first and second decades of the nineteenth century. Hegelianism was an ambitious attempt to reconcile "ideas" and "reality" within a single all-embracing scheme. The Hegelian philosophy was dynamic, in the sense that it conceived reality as moving in time and acting through history. Other important idealist philosophers were J. G. Fichte and F. W. J. von Schelling. The various idealist systems had one quality in common, and that was the stress on the creativity of the mind (or "Self" or "Absolute," as it was sometimes called). In this respect they went far beyond Kant. In its extreme form, idealism denied the existence of objective reality altogether and claimed that thought alone had true existence.

Historicism

Until the late eighteenth century history was a branch of philosophy; that is to say, it was regarded as a kind of gloss or illustration of abstract truths. The old saying "History is philosophy taught by examples" perfectly reflects this attitude. A seventeenth- or eighteenth-century reader opened Plutarch less to learn about antiquity than to obtain time-hallowed guidance in the art of statesmanship. In so doing, he denied (whether or not he was aware of it) any qualitative difference between the ancient and the contemporary worlds. Such an attitude conformed, of course, to the whole classicist spirit.

The Romantics, more than anyone else, discredited this view. The modern attitude toward the past, which has come to be called "historicism," is not only one of the most important legacies of Romanticism, but a landmark in the evolution of human thought.

The creator of historicism was Johann Gottfried von Herder, a German philosopher active in the last three decades of the eighteenth century. Herder developed his concept of history in the "Storm and Stress" period, that is, before Romanticism proper got under way. In several works, the most important of which is *Ideas Toward a Philosophy of the History of Mankind* (1784–1791), he spoke of the unique contribution that each culture made to human history. Every nation and every age has its own merit; each is equally near God. "No object in the whole divine order is a means only—everything is both means and goal." Thus there are no "superior" and "inferior" histories. Man should not aspire to some fixed model, but develop the qualities inherent in the spirit of his own culture or its "ethos." "Every nation has within itself the center of happiness, just as every sphere has its center of gravity." For Herder, the history of humanity was an endlessly varied mosaic, to which each nation makes its own contribution. Although he was not without forerunners, Herder must be given main credit for the concept of world history as a dynamic process involving all mankind.

This concept was further developed by Schelling and particularly by Hegel, who regarded history as a purposeful process whose main phases were marked by the great civilizations. The progress of history represents an irresistible movement toward freedom: in the ancient Oriental states one man only was free; in classical Greece and Rome some were free; in the "Germanic" world all were free. The modern Prussian state represented the culmination of the historic process. This historical philosophical approach, although originally devised for Germany for the purpose of extolling its contribution to world civilization, lent itself perfectly for export and was adopted for their own purposes by nationalists all over Europe.

The basis of historicism is the assumption that every historical phenomenon is unique and self-contained. What the ancient Greeks did helps us understand the Greeks; it tells us nothing about medieval Frenchmen or modern Germans. Historicism denies abstract "man" and eternal truths, much as did Edmund Burke, the British statesman who was one of its progenitors. Its essential quality is relativism, and in this respect it accords with the whole Romantic penchant for the unique and its hostility toward absolute standards.

The historicist outlook exerted its most immediate effect on the writing of history. The school of historians that arose in Germany in the early years of the nineteenth century made a deliberate effort to understand past eras as they actually had been, that is, on their own terms, and not as they appeared from the vantage point of either classical or modern cultures. Barthold Niebuhr's *History of Rome* (1811–1812) is generally recognized as the first work of modern historical scholarship. It owes this reputation to the author's endeavor, by a critical use of sources, to reconstruct Roman events cleansed of the patina put on them by modernizing classicists. The greatest exponent of the new tendency was Leopold von Ranke, who, in a lifetime extending over ninety-one years (1795–1886), produced a vast quantity of works on all epochs, including a monumental *History of the Popes* (1834–1836) and *German History in the Time of the Reformation* (1839–1847). For Ranke, the aim of the historian was to penetrate and to convey the uniqueness, the specific quality of the subject, to seize that essence which differentiates it from all others. Modern historical scholarship rests on the foundations laid by the great German scholars of the early part of the nineteenth century, for what distinguishes modern history writing from pre-Romantic history writing is precisely the belief in the uniqueness of phenomena.

The principle of historicism did not remain confined to professional historiography. In some ways it affected all branches of learning. Let us take law, for example. The concept of "natural law," on which had rested much French revolutionary legislation and the basic liberal doctrine, implied eternal, absolute, immutable standards of good and right. The statement "all men are born free," self-evident as it may seem, in fact silently assumes an abstract "man" whom it contrasts with actual (i.e., non-free) man. The Romantic historicists (as Burke before them) questioned whether this abstract man existed. The founder of the his-

The Englishman William Blake—artist, poet, mystic—portrayed the drama of Genesis; here, a winged, patriarchal God shapes Adam from primordial dust and, literally, the coil of mortality.

torical school of law, Frederick Savigny, maintained that all law was the product of a specific environment and that its roots had to be sought not in abstract rights, but in the "spirit" from which it had emerged. From this point of view, customary (that is, unwritten) law is superior to Roman law, because it derives from and presumably corresponds to the "spirit" of the people who had given rise to it. Similarly striking conclusions were obtained from the application of historicism to other areas of knowledge, such as economics and philology.

Nationalism drew considerable encouragement from historicism. The notion of cultural uniqueness—all nations, as all eras, being equally near God—encouraged intellectuals of small or backward countries to advance bold claims. It is on such grounds that Fichte, in his *Addresses to the German People* (1807–1808), could preach the world supremacy of Germans. Slavic intellectuals, under similar influences, predicted the coming superiority of their race. In Italy Vincenzo Gioberti's book *On the Civil and Moral Primacy of the Italians* (1843) made even more extravagant claims, asserting that Italians had led Europe in all the arts and skills, including warfare. Each such claim rested on different criteria of national greatness, but no one seemed troubled by their mutual incompatibility.

It would be difficult to exaggerate the importance of historicism. It is so much a part of our whole way of looking at things that we may have difficulty realizing how novel the theory was in its day. Some of the most influential ideas of the nineteenth century, including Darwin's theory of evolution and Marxism, derive from it, in the sense that they view reality not as fixed but as dynamic and meaningfully evolving.

One of the characteristic qualities of the Romantics was religiousness. For some of them, Christianity was the essence of all modern or Romantic civilization, the Western counterpart of classical mythology. For others, it was the supreme expression of all the mysterious and beautiful in life. They favored Roman Catholicism, both because it was the religion of the Middle Ages, which they admired, and because it had such splendid ritual. *Religion*

Signs of a religious revival became apparent almost immediately after the outbreak of the French Revolution. In the early 1790s Joseph de Maistre and Louis de Bonald, leading conservative theorists, independently and concurrently developed a theory that explained the Revolution as the will of Divine Providence. In 1799 the German Romantic Novalis (Baron von Hardenberg), in an essay called *Christianity or Europe*, extolled the Middle Ages as a period of spiritual unity, when a single Christian faith united all Europe. But the most influential work of the religious revival was René de Chateaubriand's *The Genius of Christianity* (1802), a paean in praise of Christianity as more profound and more beautiful and in every other way superior to classicism:

> Of all the religions which have ever existed, Christianity is the most poetic, most human, the most conducive to freedom, to the arts and literature. . . . The modern world owes it all, from agriculture to the abstract sciences, from hospices for the unfortunate to the temples built by Michelangelo and decorated by Raphael. . . . There is nothing more divine than its morality, nothing more lovely, more grand than its dogmas, its doctrine, its ritual. . . . It encourages genius, purifies taste, develops virtuous emo-

tions, infuses thought with vigor, furnishes the writer with noble forms and the sculptor with perfect shapes.

Chateaubriand's book, promoted by Napoleon to justify his Concordat with the Vatican, had a wide audience throughout Europe. It was followed by other works extolling Christianity, usually in its Catholic form, at the expense of antiquity. In its extreme form, the Catholic revival became known as ultramontanism, a movement inspired by Joseph de Maistre that preached the supremacy of the Pope over secular rulers. Many Romantics converted to Catholicism. The early nineteenth century witnessed the re-establishment of the Jesuit order (1814) and the founding of numerous societies for the propagation of the faith. In 1826 King Ludwig I of Bavaria founded the University of Munich to serve as a center of Catholic learning and a counterpart to the Protestant University of Berlin. The Catholic revival even reached Orthodox Russia. There, between 1829 and 1831, Peter Chaadaev wrote a series of *Philosophical Letters* in which he predicted the continued stagnation and backwardness of Russia because it had taken Christianity not from Rome but from corrupt Byzantium. In Poland the cause of national liberation fused with that of Catholicism. The leading Polish Romantic poet, Adam Mickiewicz, extolled his country as the "Christ of nations" whose suffering would redeem the world, as Christ's had redeemed mankind.

In England the religious revival found expression in the Oxford Movement, whose adherents protested against the worldliness and rationalism of the Anglican Church and wished to reinfuse the church with a sense of mystery and beauty, to free it from its dependence on the state, and altogether to give it greater importance in the life of the individual and the nation. The movement was launched in 1833 at Oriel College, Oxford, when John Keble, a newly appointed professor of poetry, delivered a celebrated sermon on "National Apostasy." In it, he protested against the recent emancipation of the Catholics and the subservience of the Anglican Church to the state. Keble was joined by John Henry Newman, with whom he published a series of widely read *Tracts for the Times* (from 1833 on). Newman was not satisfied even with a revitalized Anglicanism, and in 1845 converted to Catholicism. The Oxford (or, as it is sometimes called, the Tractarian) Movement brought ritual back into the Anglican Church and in general stimulated religious sentiment.

In Russia the challenge of Catholicism engendered an important lay religious movement known as "Slavophilism." Slavophilism was more than a religious phenomenon: its doctrines embraced philosophy of history, politics, and social matters. Though it was in effect a theory of Russian national identity, at its base lay a religious doctrine formulated in the 1840s by Alexis Khomiakov. Khomiakov asserted (in answer to Chaadaev) the superiority of the Orthodox faith to both Catholicism and Protestantism, by virtue of its being uncorrupted by worldly concerns and classical philosophy and thereby adhering more faithfully to the spirit of original Christianity. Khomiakov and his circle formulated the first Orthodox philosophy attractive to intellectuals. It became the source of all modern Russian religious thought.

Romanticism also gave rise to mystic movements, most of them variants of neo-Platonism. The discoveries of science, such as magnetism and electricity,

VERSAILLES

"I was in love with fame as with a woman," wrote Chateaubriand. This 1807 portrait is by Anne Louis Girodet.

also received pseudo-religious connotations and provided the basis of a "Romantic science," some of it silly, some of it plainly dishonest.

The religious revival essentially affected the upper class and the educated. Among the lower classes, the early nineteenth century witnessed rather a loosening of religious ties and a weakening of religious sentiments, especially in countries that underwent significant industrialization. The shift from the village into the city tended to break the bonds linking working families with the church and to encourage a mood of indifference toward religion and its institutions. The English census taken in 1851 found that more than 5 million persons, representing a third of the population of England and Wales, did not attend any church and that half of those who did were dissenters or Catholics. Much the same probably held true of other industrialized and urbanized countries.

Romanticism in the narrow sense of the word was a new literary and artistic style that rejected formalized classicism in favor of spontaneous forms and themes. But in a broader sense it was the beginning of a cultural revolution, the first assertion of an autonomous Western civilization. As the Renaissance had freed Western culture from its subservience to religion and facilitated the emergence of secularism, so Romanticism reduced the authority of classicism and inaugurated an era of artistic and literary freedom, which is the essence of modernity.

The Historic Significance of Romanticism

The full implications of this revolution were not then seen, because the Romantics still adhered to many classical values—more so than they realized, or than one could infer from their anticlassical zeal. But the principle of creativeness as an end in itself and subject only to its own criteria, once launched, has been subsequently pushed to ever greater extremes. Our own culture is a linear descendant of Romantic culture in the sense that it is uncompromisingly individualistic and rejects all restraints on creative freedom.

Romanticism enormously enriched Western art and thought, if only because it enlarged the variety of means available to creative talent. It permitted the use of a vocabulary and a meter, of color combinations, and of harmonies that the preceding age rejected as barbarous. It also opened up to serious inquiry subjects (e.g., folklore or the history of smaller nations) that had previously been deemed unworthy of attention.

But everything has its price. Until the advent of Romanticism, Western culture had rested on a consensus of values and tastes, whether Christian or classical. Romanticism began to destroy that consensus. By rejecting absolute criteria and making self-realization the aim as well as the standard of all creativity, it not only undermined the cultural unity of Western civilization, but contributed heavily to the eventual breakdown of understanding between the creator and his audience. The aesthetic theories of Romanticism, when revived on the eve of the twentieth century, caused a growing estrangement between art and literature on the one hand and the public on the other. For better or worse, twentieth-century modernism derives from the aesthetic of Romanticism pushed to its logical conclusion.

The Romantic Impulse

"I will not Reason and Compare: my Business is to Create," wrote the English poet William Blake. On the other side of Europe in Vienna, Ludwig van Beethoven proclaimed, "In a man, music should strike fire from his spirit." In France the painter Eugene Delacroix noted in his diary, "In some people the inner spark scarcely exists. I find it dominant in me. Without it, I should die, but it will consume me (doubtless I speak of the imagination, which masters and leads me)." Though Blake, Beethoven, and Delacroix shared neither a common country nor a common medium of expression, as Romantics they were united in their rejection of the rigid rules of classicism and in their espousal of the unrestricted imagination.

The Romantics viewed imagination both as a purely individual quality and as a "Divine Vision." Blake expressed this double quality poetically: "The Sun's light when he unfolds it/ Depends upon the Organ that beholds it." The German critic Frederick Schlegel made the same claim in prose: "It is precisely individuality that is the original and eternal thing in men. . . . The cultivation and development of this individuality, as one's highest vocation, would be a divine egoism."

The Romantics considered the French Revolution and the meteoric rise of Napoleon the signal for a new era ruled by divine egoism, or genius, as it came to be called. In his poem *The French Revolution*, written in 1804, Wordsworth expressed the elation with which Romantics greeted the opportunities created by the fall of the *ancien régime:* "Bliss was it in that dawn to be alive, but to be young was very heaven!" Joyfully he contemplated the debacle of the old order's "meagre, stale, forbidding ways of custom, law, and statute" and called upon those "who had fed their childhood upon dreams . . . who had made all powers of swiftness, subtilty, and strength their ministers" to create a new order. "Poets," wrote Shelley in full agreement a decade later, "are the unacknowledged legislators of the world."

With the accent on individual vision, the impulses of the Romantics proved highly varied, yet certain themes have come to express the quintessence of Romanticism. In *Mephistopheles Flying Over the City* (left) Eugene Delacroix engraved not just an illustration for Goethe's *Faust*, a favorite Romantic subject itself, he also portrayed the Romantics' relish in the demoniac pursuit of supernatural power. In a like manner, Delacroix's 1827 canvas at right, *Greece Expiring on the Ruins of Missolonghi*, records not just the successful Turkish siege of the insurgent Greeks at Missolonghi in 1826 and the earlier death there of Lord Byron (the poet's still bleeding hand protrudes from beneath the ruins), but the Romantics' highly theatrical devotion to national liberation as well.

Byron the Hero

"Whilome in Albion's isle there dwelt a youth,/ Who ne in virtue's ways did take delight;/ But spent his days in riot most uncouth,/ And vex'd with mirth the drowsy ear of Night." Thus in March of 1812, at the age of twenty-four, George Gordon, Lord Byron, introduced himself as the wicked hero of his epic poem, *Childe Harold's Pilgrimage.* By April London society had a new hero. "The subject of conversation, of curiosity, of enthusiasm," wrote the Duchess of Devonshire, "is not Spain or Portugal, warriors, or patriots, but Lord Byron."

The fascination had cause. Born with a deformed foot, fatherless at three, heir to a barony and a Gothic abbey at six, tortured by a sadistic quack, seduced by his nurse, subjected to the violent outbursts of his dour Scots mother, and possessed by a tempestuous mind, young Byron considered himself a fallen angel, a miscreant Mephistopheles. At the age of twenty-one he had left England for the Mediterranean where he swam the Hellespont, chatted with the sultan in Constantinople, and crossed Albania with an outlaw chieftan. Byron refurbished these wanderings of the child and the man as the pilgrimage of Childe Harold.

London's ladies found Byron "mad, bad, and dangerous," but swore in the next breath, "That beautiful pale face is my fate." One scandal followed another, including probable incest and a disastrous marriage. Gossip turned to outrage. In 1816 Byron left England never to return. Abroad, the fallen angel wrote and lived as extravagantly and brilliantly as ever, laying bare "the pageant of his bleeding heart" and rebelling against hypocrisy and tyranny wherever he found them. At the age of thirty-six, "a young, old man," as he put it, Byron sought and found a hero's death aiding the rebellious Greeks against their Turkish masters.

Romantic painters found Byron and his poetry irresistible subject matter. John Martin's 1837 water color above, Manfred on the Jungfrau, depicts the guilt-ridden, oblivion-seeking Manfred (Byron's 1817 literary version of his tormented self) being restrained from suicide by a kindly chamois hunter. At the left is Thomas Phillips' portrait of Byron in Albanian dress, done in England after Byron's return from the Mediterranean. At the right is an illustration from an early edition of Byron's epic poem Don Juan, that shows the hero wooing—and undoing—the Greek maid Haydai.

In 1845, twenty-three years after Shelley drowned, his friend and admirer Joseph Severn painted this memorial canvas, Shelley Composing 'Prometheus Unbound' in the Baths of Caracalla. The Romantic critic William Hazlitt had less love for the expatriate Shelley. "The author of Prometheus Unbound," wrote Hazlitt, "has a fire in his eye, a fever in his blood, a maggot in his brain, a hectic flutter in his speech. . . . His bending, flexible form appears to take no strong hold of things, does not grapple with the world about him, but slides from it like a river."

Sweet Exile

Byron was not alone in swearing "I will not descend to a world I despise" and then thumbing his nose at his native land, its politics, and its customs. Despite the jocular vein of George Cruikshank's 1816 cartoon (below) lampooning Byron's departure from England, or the lush sentimentality of Joseph Severn's painting of Shelley composing verse amidst Roman ruins, exile was serious Romantic business. Almost entirely self-imposed, exile was both a way out of ordinary life—"this cold common hell" Shelley called it—and a way into the incandescent realm of the Romantic imagination. In *Alastor*, writing of his poet hero, Shelley described both the pattern and the reason for exile: ". . . When early youth had passed, he left/ His cold fireside and alienated home/ To seek strange truths in undiscovered lands."

Among the delights of exile was consorting with other exiles. On the shore of Switzerland's Lake Geneva Madame de Staël received a steady stream of precocious and disgruntled fellow Romantics. From Germany came the Schlegel brothers spouting Romantic ideals, from France came Chateaubriand oozing sentimentality, from England came Lord Byron licking his wounds, and the young lovers, Percy Bysshe Shelley and his talented consort and wife-to-be, Mary Godwin. A few years later Shelley set up his own refugee camp for Romantics in Italy, and found it so delightful that he wrote, "Thou Paradise of exiles, Italy!"

But the true bonanza of Romantic exile was the finding of Shelley's "strange truths in undiscovered lands," which foreign soil yielded in profusion. Byron's wanderings, for example, inspired not only *Childe Harold's Pilgrimage*, but also *Manfred, The Prisoner of Chillon,* and *Don Juan*. It was in Italy that Shelley wrote *Adonais, Ode to the West Wind,* and *Prometheus Unbound,* and a soiree of exiles at Lake Geneva prompted one of the stranger "truths," Mary Shelley's *Frankenstein*.

KEATS-SHELLEY MEMORIAL HOUSE, ROME

BRITISH MUSEUM

Morocco so delighted Delacroix that he spoke of it as "my Morocco" and filled seven sketch books there. According to the French ambassador, Delacroix made his sketches during the day and then "At night, in the silence of his tent, when everyone was asleep, he would touch them up with water colors." On his return Delacroix painted more finished versions, such as Horsemen Resting Near Tangiers (above). At the right is an 1832 water color, Arab at Prayer. Another 1832 water color, Fantasia (below), records the arrival of his party at Meknes in the desert. "Our entry was a lovely sight." Delacroix noted, "At every turn we encountered groups of armed tribesmen who squandered incredible quantities of gunpowder to celebrate our coming. Sometimes we even heard bullets overhead; they'd forgotten to use blanks!"

The Lure of the Exotic

Like Lord Byron, whom he greatly admired, Eugene Delacroix was fascinated by the Muslim world. For years, in vast canvases filled with color, violence, and sensuality, such as *The Death of Sardanapulus* (overleaf), Delacroix had painted the exotic even though his inspiration came only from Romantic literature and paintings. But in 1832 he made a fateful six-month journey to Morocco. On his arrival in Tangiers he wrote, "I am like a man dreaming, who sees things he is afraid to see escape him."

In fact, Delacroix let little escape. Day and night he prowled the bazaars, slums, and seraglios of Algeciras. Even when he rode 200 miles inland to the desert fortress of Meknes, he continued to sketch, resting his notebook on the pommel of his saddle. The immediate results were the deft water colors on the opposite page, but for Delacroix, as for all Romantic artists, observation was the springboard for imagination. Back in Paris he fused notes, sketches, and memories into hundreds of canvases such as *The Lion Devouring a Horse* (below), painted about 1850, that blended, as Baudelaire pointed out, "dreams and drama in a mysterious reality."

OVERLEAF: *In 1826, inspired by Byron's tragic play, Delacroix painted his own spectacular version of* The Death of Sardanapulus. *On his divan the world-weary and defeated Assyrian king impassively watches the slaughter of his harem and his charger before setting fire to his palace, his treasures, and himself.*

The Inward Vision

At the heart of the Romantic impulse lay a profound desire to commune with God or what the Romantics felt to be *the* reality that lay behind reality as observed by the senses. German Romantics had their own version of this theme, the cult of *Sehnsucht*—a dreamlike longing for the ineffable and unattainable. Probably no painter expressed this mood or tasted more fully of the despair it brought than Caspar David Friedrich. With Romantic fervor he cried out against optimistic rationalists: "O, you good-natured people, who do not recognize the inner drive and tension of the soul, and want Man not as the loving God has created, coined, and stamped him, but as time and fashion will have him." To portray the tension-ridden landscape of the soul Friedrich advised artists to "shut your physical eye and look first at your picture with your spiritual eye, then bring to the light of day what you have seen in the darkness." Like many soul-searching Romantics, Friedrich found God "everywhere, even in a grain of sand." But his profound melancholy, which eventually became insanity, turned what might have been joyful pantheistic visions into moody, almost sinister landscapes that fused the natural with the supernatural and beauty with despair.

370

Deepening melancholy marks Friedrich's artistic development. About 1811 he finished The Cross and the Cathedral in the Mountains *(right) using the church as a symbol of redemption from the oppressive forest of life.* Man and Woman Gazing at the Moon *(below, painted in 1819) shows his growing obsession with the nocturnal aspect of natural phenomenon. In 1821 Friedrich painted* The Wreck of the 'Hope' *(left), which recorded not only the news of the foundering of a ship and the memory of his brother crushed by ice-floes on the Elbe, but also his own engulfing despair.*

Nature Discovered

Dr. Johnson neatly summed up the Enlightenment's attitude toward nature when he said, "A blade of grass is always a blade of grass; men and women are *my* subjects of enquiry." Then came Rousseau, and the race for wood, field, and stream was on. By 1798 William Wordsworth was extolling a new mistress of the mind in a poem entitled, significantly, *The Tables Turned.* "One impulse from a vernal wood," he wrote, "May teach you more of man,/Of moral evil and of good,/ Than all the sages can."

The Romantics considered nature an "active principle" and they felt that she must be perceived by "a heart that watches and receives." Nature not only yielded a profusion of sensations and "thoughts that do often lie too deep for tears," but, in keeping with the active principle idea, she was also seen as a friend and consoler in times of misery. In his poem *Adonais,* commemorating the death of Keats, Shelley gave a vivid example of the Romantic belief in the mystic bond between man and nature when he described how, in a fit of grief, "Morning . . . dimmed the aëreal eyes that kindle day," while the "Pale Ocean in unquiet slumber lay,/ And the wild Winds flew round, sobbing in their dismay."

Believing that "Nature is Spirit visible," the Romantic English landscape painters pursued their subject with unusual devotion. John Constable, whose 1826 painting The Cornfield *is shown at left, believed that "The landscape painter must walk in the fields with a humble mind. No arrogant man was ever permitted to see nature in all her beauty." Constable considered the more impressionistic landscapes of J.M.W. Turner, such as* The Lake of Zug *(above), painted in 1843, "golden visions" which, said Constable humbly, "one would like to live and die with."*

The painting above, done by Joseph Danhauser in 1840, is an example not only of the fusion of the arts, but also of sentimental Romanticism. At the piano is Franz Liszt, staring dreamily at a bust of Beethoven. At his right is one of his great loves, the Comtesse Marie d'Agoult. Seated behind Liszt are the novelists George Sand (in man's clothing) and Alexandre Dumas. Behind them Paganini stands between Victor Hugo and the rotund Rossini, the evening's host. Liszt may well have been playing Chopin, whose music he described in true Romantic vernacular: "A bitter and irreparable regret seizes the wildly-throbbing human heart, even in the midst of the incomparable splendour of external nature."

New Forms in Music

"From the heart, may it go to the heart," Beethoven wrote as the inscription to his monumental mass *Missa Solemnis.* In those few words he summed up the credo of Romantic music. When the great composer conducted his *Battle Symphony* following Wellington's victory at Vittoria, "the applause rose to the point of ecstasy"; when Paganini, the Italian violin virtuoso, performed, "screams of delight and astonishment burst from the audience"; when the German writer E.T.A. Hoffmann listened to Chopin, he found himself embraced by "a confusion of colors, sounds, and perfumes . . . as though they all sprang up mysteriously from some ray of light and then united to form a marvelous concert."

The success of Romantic music lay in the wide range of innovations in musical forms developed by the composers. In turn, these changes were facilitated by technical innovations. New fingering mechanisms greatly improved the flute, oboe, and clarinet; valves provided the horn and trumpet with a complete chromatic scale; the iron frame, steel strings, and an improved sounding board turned the piano into a one-man-orchestra; and improved metals added tone and power to the tympanny, kettle drums, and cymbals. The range of orchestral possibilities was so great that in his opera *La Muette de Portici* the French composer Daniel Auber did not hesitate to throw in an eruption of Vesuvius.

Romantic composers made use of the almost infinite variety of orchestral possibilities to invent new musical forms that could express the whole gamut of Romantic moods and fantasies. In the course of writing some 700 piano compositions, Chopin expressed every kind of feeling: melancholy, rebellion, exaltation. In his *Symphonie Fantastique* Berlioz blithely combined a delirious waltz, a pastoral fantasy, and a chilling dream of a witches' sabbath. And in opera Wagner fused the whole panoply of orchestral effects with spectacular dramatic action to create grand opera on, quite literally, an earthshaking scale.

An unknown contemporary did the sketches at the right of Franz Liszt conducting. Liszt employed dramatic facial expressions and explosive gestures to lead the orchestra, and the audience, to dizzying heights of musical excitement.

The Legacy of Romanticism

I n 1846 the French critic Charles Baudelaire wrote, "To say the word Romanticism is to say modern art—that is intimacy, spirituality, color, aspiration towards the infinite, expressed by every means available to the arts." Intimacy, color, and complete artistic freedom have indeed been parts of Romanticism's legacy to modern culture. But Romantic idealism has fared less well. In the words of one modern critic, the Romantics who followed Wordsworth's generation "turned from vast mysteries and intoxicating ideas to delicate sentiments and careful description."

If Romanticism proper became overly sentimental and lost its earlier vigor, a new vision was in the making which owed much of its vitality, if little of its intent, to Romanticism. No artist better exemplifies this shift toward Realism than the Frenchman Honoré Daumier. In his *Don Quixote and Sancho Panza* (left), finished about 1860, Daumier painted a Romantic subject with Romantic freedom and expressiveness, yet the painting is realistic in that it portrays rather than praises the combination of the sublime and the ridiculous that is Cervantes' windmill-tilting knight.

By 1860 Europe was in the middle of a revolution as profound as the French Revolution that had fired the imagination of the Romantics sixty years before. Inevitably Romantic idealism proved no match for the Industrial Revolution, yet there remained Romantic masterpieces that even a materialistic age would treasure. In 1819 John Keats (depicted on his death bed in Joseph Severn's drawing above) created such a work in his *Ode to a Grecian Urn*. Describing a love-scene pictured on an ancient Greek vase, Keats wrote,

> What leaf-fring'd legend haunts about thy shape
> > Of deities or mortals, or of both,
> > > In Tempe or the dales of Arcady?
> > What men or gods are these? What maidens loth?
> What mad pursuit? What struggle to escape?
> > What pipes and timbrels? What wild ecstasy?
> Heard melodies are sweet, but those unheard
> > Are sweeter; therefore, ye soft pipes, play on. . . .

15

The High Tide of Liberalism:
1848-1870

The political system prevailing in most of Europe in the 1830s and 1840s was too rigid to respond to the changes that were occurring in European life and thought. It allowed neither for the social shifts brought about by industrialization (the population movement to the cities, the growing power of the capitalist, the increase in the number of wage earners) nor for the emergence of a vocal intelligentsia imbued with new ideas (romanticism, liberalism, nationalism, socialism). The revolutionary disturbances that periodically shook the peace should have served to warn the remaining conservative regimes that they were out of tune with the times. But by and large these signals went unheeded. Aside from a few countries in Western Europe—notably England and Belgium—symptoms of unrest merely hardened the resolve of the conservatives to oppose reforms. Even in France, a country that after 1830 had a moderate government and belonged to the liberal bloc, the clamor for the extension of the franchise was ignored. As a result, beneath the imposing surface of European life there gathered powerful forces ready to erupt and to destroy those political systems that continued to base their authority on a coalition of monarchy, bureaucracy, landed gentry, church, and the uppermost layer of the bourgeoisie, and to install in their places regimes dominated by the whole middle class and the intellectuals.

This eruption occurred in 1848. In the spring of that year the Continent was the scene of a series of related revolutions that were especially violent in those parts (the Austrian Empire, Germany, and Italy), where the conservative system was most firmly entrenched.° These revolutions ushered in a new era in the political life of the West.

The historian Lewis Namier subtitled his book *1848* "The Revolution of the Intellectuals," and, indeed, intellectuals played in it an extraordinarily prominent role. They formulated the revolutionary theories and slogans, led the mobs, and took charge of the national assemblies and provisional governments that came into power once legitimate authority collapsed. These intellectuals came mostly from the universities, the professions (especially law), and journalism—that is, from those institutions and occupations that had experienced unusual expansion in the first half of the nineteenth century.

Intellectuals generally were addicted to what Napoleon I had scornfully labeled "ideology"—all-embracing systems concerned with the betterment of the human race. They not only disapproved of things as they were but believed that genuine improvement had to be total and instantaneous; piecemeal reform or trial-and-error methods were not for them. Ideologies can be defined as secular religions—movements that retain the zeal and chiliasm of true religions but, rejecting God and life after death, direct their energies toward establishing the

The Revolutions of 1848

°Russia, which in the 1840s was the most conservative country in Europe, escaped revolution because opposition was as yet scattered and weak, while the repressive apparatus of the state enjoyed exceptional strength.

The street barricade became the hallmark of the revolutionary outbreaks that convulsed Europe in 1848. As shown in a contemporary lithograph of the Vienna uprising, they were thrown up of whatever was handy—paving stones, timbers, even carriages.

millennium on earth. They flourished greatly in the 1830s and 1840s. François Guizot, Louis Philippe's Prime Minister, watched with bewilderment the scheming of the international intelligentsia headquartered in Paris. "They yearn for events, immense, sudden and strange," he wrote; "they busy themselves with making and unmaking governments, nations, religions, society, Europe, the world." Such ideas intensified the feeling of uncertainty produced by economic and social changes and created an atmosphere propitious for revolutionary upheavals.

The dissident intellectuals, united as they were in opposition to the monarchic-feudal system, differed in their positive programs. Their aspirations had three principal tendencies. One was liberal. A large body of opinion wanted the abolition of all remaining restraints on individual liberties and the introduction of constitutional government with representative assemblies. University professors and members of the professions were especially active on behalf of these goals, from the achievement of which they expected a profound transformation of the human condition.

The second tendency of the intellectuals was democratic. Its adherents fought for the realization of the ideals of the French Revolution. They wanted a republic and the universal vote. A radical wing of the democratic group wanted to go further, toward socialism (the abolition of private property), or anarchism (the abolition of private property and of the state as well), but they were a minority. Many students and journalists adopted the democratic ideology.

The third tendency was nationalistic. Among ethnic groups that either suffered foreign domination (the minorities in the Hapsburg, Russian, and Ottoman empires) or that felt frustrated in their aspirations toward statehood (the Italians and Germans), intellectuals assumed leadership of the cause of national liberation and unification. Their nationalism combined either with liberal or democratic ideologies.

The intellectuals owed their strength in the late 1840s to the fact that their own essentially moral discontent happened to coincide with unrest among the urban lower classes. It would be tempting to ascribe this social unrest to conditions created by industrialization. But if industrialization had indeed been its decisive cause, then England and Belgium, as the industrially most developed countries of the period, should have experienced the greatest violence. In fact, neither experienced a revolution. On the other hand, some of the bloodiest upheavals occurred in countries hardly touched by industrialization, such as Italy and Hungary. Clearly, industrial conditions as such were not the cause of the revolutions of 1848.

A more likely cause was the mass uprooting of populations that accompanied intense urbanization. As we have noted, the first half of the nineteenth century was throughout Europe a period of rapid urban growth. The rural population streamed into the cities partly in search of better-paying jobs, partly in the hope of self-improvement. So great was the influx that between 1800 and 1848 Paris and Berlin more than doubled their populations. One-third of the inhabitants of London in 1851 were not native born. Striking growth occurred also in Vienna, Milan, Budapest, and other metropolitan centers.

Urbanization at this pace and rate inevitably created a variety of problems with which governments of the time were not prepared to cope. Among these, housing was especially acute. Most Continental cities at the time were still confined to a compact area enclosed by the defensive walls of the Middle Ages. The incoming population had to be squeezed into this limited space, into basements or garrets, cheap tenements constructed for quick profit by speculators, or makeshift hovels. The result was enormous congestion. The effects of excessive crowding on human beings are even today poorly understood, but there can be little doubt that they awaken deep-seated anxieties and aggressive instincts. Close contact with wealth in its moneyed, ostentatious form, much in evidence in the cities, aggravated the distress of the new urban population. Little wonder then that it formed a volatile element, receptive to ideological incitement by the intellectuals. In *Vanished Supremacies* Lewis Namier wrote:

> For men rooted in the soil, there is, as a rule, a hierarchy of allegiances: to their village community or estate, to their district, to their "country." . . . Traditional beliefs and hereditary ties persist; class and the way of living determine alignments; things are individual and concrete in the village or the small, old-fashioned town. But in the great modern cities men grow anonymous, become ciphers, and are regimented; thinking becomes more abstract and is forced into generalizations; inherited beliefs are shaken and old ties are broken; there is a void, uncertainty, and hidden fear which man tries to master by rational thought. He starts by proudly asserting the rights of the abstract, average individual freed from the bondage of tradition, and then integrates him into the crowd, a collective personality, which unloads itself into mass movements. The mass is the refuge of the uprooted individual; and the disintegration of spiritual values is as potent a process as the splitting of the atom; it releases demonic forces which burst all dams. The program may be social revolution, or national revolution, or both.

These psychological tensions were exacerbated by economic crises of the kind that recurred periodically in the nineteenth century. The years 1846 and 1847 saw crop failures and industrial layoffs. Many among those hurt by the crises headed for the cities either to seek help or to vent their wrath on the whole urban-capitalist-industrial complex.

The intellectuals and the workers constituted the two main forces of the 1848 revolutions—their brains and muscles, as it were. A force apart were the propertied classes: those industrialists, merchants, professionals, and well-to-do peasants who were committed to no specific ideology, but who nevertheless disliked the *status quo* and supported the revolution so long as it was directed against the absolutist bureaucracy and the feudal nobility. The moment the revolution took a more radical, democratic turn, however, these groups withdrew from it. For this reason, the revolutions of 1848 in every country went through two distinct, consecutive phases: a liberal (or liberal-national) phase, in which intellectuals, workers, and the propertied groups combined to overthrow the existing conservative or conservative-liberal regimes and replace them with typical liberal governments; and a democratic phase, in which the radical and democratic intelligentsia, backed by more desperate working-class elements, pressed on with the

François Guizot, the dominant figure in French politics during the 1840s, was also a historian of great repute.

This daguerreotype of Louis Kossuth, leader of the 1848 revolution in Hungary, was made about 1851 during the exile's tour through the United States.

revolutionary struggle for the purpose of winning full political and social democracy. Once the revolution entered this second phase, the propertied groups invariably threw their support behind the forces of order, usually the army, and helped to suppress the insurrectionary elements. This explains why to many radicals the upheavals of 1848 seemed an unfinished business, and why they so confidently, and vainly, awaited the outbreak of another European revolution.

The first rumblings of revolt sounded in Italy in January, 1848, but the revolutions really began the following month in Paris. In the summer of 1847 French opposition circles, determined to force a broadening of the franchise, launched a campaign of "banquets"—large public dinners at which speakers toasted liberty and criticized Louis Philippe and his Prime Minister, Guizot. The authorities grew annoyed by these doings and outlawed a banquet scheduled for February 22. On that day large crowds took to the streets to demand Guizot's dismissal. Louis Philippe, surprised by the ugly mood of the crowds, yielded and discharged his Prime Minister, but this act failed to placate the populace. The next day the streets filled with an even angrier mob. That evening a procession of students and workers ran into a body of soldiers guarding the Ministry of Foreign Affairs. When one of the demonstrators fired a shot, the troops volleyed and killed fifty persons. During the night the infuriated crowds built barricades all over the city. On February 24 the seventy-year-old king, facing a mutinous capital and no longer confident of his troops, abdicated and sailed for England.

After the king had departed, power passed to a provisional government composed of liberals, democrats, and socialists, who immediately proclaimed the abolition of the monarchy and the establishment of the Second Republic. This done, however, they began to quarrel. The socialists, inspired by the ideas of Louis Blanc (Chapter 19), demanded that the Republic assure jobs to all and found "national workshops" to provide work for the unemployed. The liberals intensely disliked the national workshop project, but for the time being went along with it for fear of the mob. The workshops attracted additional unemployed to Paris and at one time provided relief for a hundred thousand persons. The cost, nearly a million francs a day, was borne by the bourgeoisie and the peasantry, neither of which felt fonder of the Second Republic for making them support what they regarded as an indolent Parisian mob.

Friction between liberal and radical elements came to a head in June, 1848. In the spring of that year the country had voted for a National Assembly. The elections, based on universal suffrage, gave the liberals 500 seats, the royalists 300, and the socialists fewer than 100. The Assembly appointed an executive committee containing no socialists and on June 21 ordered the closing of the national workshops. In reaction to this order, the Parisian workers and unemployed rebelled and seized the eastern half of the city. The uprising threatened to topple the provisional government, but it was suppressed by troops under General Cavaignac, the Minister of War. Except for Marseilles, the rest of France failed to respond to the June revolt.

In Austria the revolution began under nationalistic slogans. It started on March 3 in Budapest, when the popular leader Louis Kossuth demanded a liberal constitution and full autonomy for Hungary. The emperor at first refused to make such concessions, but after rioting had spread to Vienna he had to yield.

On April 11 Vienna granted Hungary a constitution. Kossuth now pressed for independence, and at the end of July the Hungarians broke relations with Austria. Similar nationalist demands were voiced in Bohemia, where the Czechs founded their own national committee. Italy seethed with rebellion, as did other regions of the Austrian Empire.

The uprisings in Paris and the unrest in the Austrian borderlands emboldened Viennese intellectuals to challenge the detested regime of Metternich. In mid-March mobs led by students caused such a riot that Emperor Ferdinand had to dismiss Metternich and grant Austria a constitution. But the revolution did not stop there. In June it took a radical turn, as artisans and craftsmen set fire to industrial establishments and with their violence helped intellectuals gain control of the city. Ferdinand fled to the safety of Innsbruck. In July a constituent assembly met in Vienna. The deputies, most of them sent from the Slavic areas, passed laws abolishing many feudal rights and granting peasants civil equality.

Having reached its height in the summer of 1848, the tide of Austrian revolution began to recede. The army, which had never wavered in its loyalty to absolutism, now led a counteroffensive. Behind it stood the urban middle class, frightened by radicalism, and the mass of the peasantry, who had gained what they wanted and desired a restoration of order. In June, 1848, the army dispersed the Czech national committee in Prague. In October it captured Vienna and from there proceeded against Hungary, which it cleared of rebels with the assistance of Russian troops. By the spring of 1849 the monarchy had regained control of the empire.

In Germany the years 1848 and 1849 passed under the spell of nationalism. Here the goal of revolutionaries was political liberty and national unification.

The short and unhappy life of a typical 1848 revolutionary: orator and fighter for freedom in March and May, followed by capture (center), summary trial, and the firing squad in autumn.

The revolution broke out in Berlin in mid-March. Events followed a pattern familiar in other countries: mass meetings and processions; public clamor for freedom of the press, trial by jury, and other planks of the liberal platform; efforts at suppression; the breakdown of administration. Frederick William IV, impressed by the strength of the opposition, had to agree to the convocation of a constituent assembly, which, like its counterparts in Budapest and Vienna, turned out to have a fairly radical complexion. But by the end of the year, emboldened by the Austrian example, Frederick William used troops to reassert his authority, and the assembly was dissolved. Elsewhere in Germany, local rulers invited liberal statesmen to form governments and granted constitutional charters. The notable exception was Bavaria's King Ludwig I, who preferred to abdicate.

The most dramatic event in Germany was the convocation in Frankfurt am Main of the first all-German parliament. Called the National Assembly, it was organized on the initiative of liberal intellectuals. Elections for it were held in the territories of the Germanic Confederation in the spring of 1848 on a broad, nearly universal suffrage. The voters returned a majority of liberals and nationalists. Since Germany had no regular parties, they cast their ballots for well-known individuals, usually men who had distinguished themselves as champions of freedom. Most of these were academics and members of the professions, and therefore 550 out of 830 deputies turned out to belong to these two categories. The task of the Assembly was to transform the impotent Confederation into an effective all-German government. But the deputies sorely lacked parliamentary experience. Each deputy spoke in his own name rather than for a party, and precious months were spent on rhetoric. The question of admitting Austria into the new state was decided negatively. Much time was spent drafting constitutional projects until an acceptable one was produced in the spring of 1849. At that time the Assembly voted to offer the Prussian king the title "Emperor of the Germans." When Frederick William refused to accept the crown from an illegitimate, revolutionary body, the National Assembly dissolved.

In Italy the revolutionary forces were encouraged by Charles Albert, the king of Piedmont. At heart a dyed-in-the-wool conservative, Charles Albert had personal reasons to dislike the Hapsburgs. Furthermore, he hoped to benefit from the anti-Austrian revolution to augment his territory. Intending to annex Venetia and Lombardy, he declared war on Austria and proclaimed himself leader of an Italian liberation movement. But the Austrians reacted in Italy with more efficiency than had been anticipated in view of their performance elsewhere, and by the summer of 1848 they had brought the Piedmontese offensive to a halt. Frightened by the emergence in several Italian principalities (Venice, Rome, and Tuscany) of radical republics, Charles Albert made peace with Austria. He stood by while the republics were liquidated with the help of Austrian and French troops and reactionary regimes restored throughout the peninsula.

The immediate consequence of the 1848 revolutions everywhere was a conservative restoration. In this sense, the revolutions brought cruel disappointment to many of their participants. The Russian radical Alexander Herzen, who in 1847 had gone to the West expecting to witness the dawn of a new era, was so disillusioned that, in a book published in 1850 (*From the Other Shore*), he

A remarkably candid self-caricature, by Frederick William IV of Germany.

denied human history any meaning. In fact, however, the revolutions of 1848 inaugurated an era of liberal hegemony and of modern mass politics.

The year 1848 marked the end of conservatism in its classical, Metternichian guise as a factor in European politics. After a brief initial reaction, the decades that followed witnessed the triumphant spread of liberal principles and practices. From Western Europe they penetrated to Eastern Europe and eventually to distant, non-European countries such as Persia and Japan. Liberalism, both political and economic, came into high fashion. It was an up-to-date, operative theory adopted by statesmen of the new generation. In the air were legal reform, civil equality, constitutionalism and parliamentarism, democratic franchise, and national self-determination.

Why did this occur? Probably the most likely explanation is that rulers and professional politicians alike came to realize that liberal institutions and procedures would strengthen their authority. The examples of the United States (especially after the victory of the North in the Civil War) and Great Britain held much attraction. The wealth and the international prestige of the two liberal powers demonstrated better than could any theories the political benefits that accrued to the state from involving the citizenry in politics. And if those examples were not enough, the revolutions of 1848 served as a reminder that in any event one could not forever freeze the political and social systems nor hope to rule through a bureaucratic-police apparatus. If the art of politics is the art of winning support, then modern life, which in all realms increased the importance of the common man, required that the state gain his support as well.

Another factor in favor of liberalism was its natural affinity with business. Merchants, manufacturers, and investors greatly preferred liberal regimes because they provided a variety of guarantees absent in traditional conservative regimes—notably, safeguards against arbitrary seizure and taxation, and the general protection of law. Governments that wished to increase their wealth and power had, therefore, strong inducements to make liberal concessions as a means of promoting business activity and attracting capital.

The liberalization of European politics in the third quarter of the nineteenth century may be described as an adjustment of the state to conditions created by the spread of industry and the growing self-awareness of all groups of the population. The state became liberalized in order to gain new strength and to acquire allies against the radical minorities that in 1848–1849 had shown such destructive capacity. This adjustment did not occur everywhere at the same pace or with the same thoroughness, for conditions varied from country to country, as did the political skill of the rulers. In some countries it hardly touched the surface. But it may be stated as a general principle that only countries that liberalized in earnest subsequently escaped political and social revolutions. Those that did not—among them the Austrian, Russian, and Ottoman empires—went from crisis to crisis until they eventually disintegrated.

We shall now trace the progress of liberalism in the principal countries of midcentury Europe, stressing three issues: the struggle of nationalities for self-determination and unity, the democratization of the suffrage, and the evolution of parliamentary institutions and parties.

Mid-Victorian England   In the middle of the nineteenth century England came closer than any other European country to the fulfillment of liberal ideals: a society that offered the citizen the safe enjoyment of life, liberty, and property. Rich and peaceful, England developed a system of government that most of the world envied. In 1848 the only sedition it experienced occurred in Ireland, where a minor local insurrection was speedily and bloodlessly suppressed.

In England the problems that agitated Continental politics were largely solved. Legislative authority resided firmly in the two Houses of Parliament and executive authority in a cabinet formed by members of the House of Commons. The overwhelming majority of the members of Parliament shared a common political philosophy. Conflicts between them involved not matters of ideology but of practical policy. The two parties remained non-ideological, that is, they had no commitment to a systematic program. The party that happened to be in power at any given time pursued a broad, national line of policy, while that out of power criticized its real or alleged failures. The broad consensus of opinion contributed more than any other factor to the efficient functioning of the British government.

In the late 1840s the political parties underwent realignment. Peel's "great betrayal"—his support of the Corn Law repeal in 1846—broke up the old Tory party that had dominated English politics in the first half of the century. One faction containing Peel's supporters went over to the Whigs. The fusion that resulted was called the Liberal party. The anti-Peel Tories constituted the Conservative party.

The Liberal party consisted of a coalition of two main groups: a smaller contingent of Whig landlords, very close in their outlook and way of life to their Tory rivals, and a larger contingent made up of traders and manufacturers. The latter set the tone. They were the liberals par excellence: they supported full economic liberty, a broad franchise, and the interests of the urban, industrial population. The Conservative party was composed almost entirely of landed gentry, with some backing of shopkeepers and other lower-middle-class elements. It was socially more prominent, and some businessmen, once they had made enough money and could afford a landed estate, switched their allegiance to it. The Liberals completely dominated English politics from the repeal of the Corn Law in 1846 to 1874. During this twenty-eight-year period the Conservatives formed only four short-lived ministries serving a total of fifty-six months. The rest of the time they were in opposition.

The organization of English political parties at this time underwent little change. In the 1830s, in response to the First Reform Act, the two major parties founded their national headquarters—the Tories the Carlton Club, and the Whigs the Reform Club. But since until the mid-1880s most candidates for Parliament ran unopposed and since contests for constituencies were an exception, these headquarters had little to do and functioned as ordinary social clubs.

The English parliamentary system owed much of its excellence to Queen Victoria, who ruled for sixty-four years (1837–1901). She ascended the throne at a time when the popularity of the monarchy was at its lowest, following the mad years of George III and the profligate ones of George IV and William IV. But Victoria quickly won the sympathies of the population by her modesty and by her respect for the constitution. Uninterested in the details of politics, and indeed unable to comprehend them, she left the actual conduct of the government to others. She acknowledged the supremacy of Parliament and adjusted herself as no English monarch had done before to playing a secondary role in the country's political life. Yet at the same time she had no intention of giving up her residual rights. When Lord Palmerston, the powerful Prime Minister, once took the initiative in a foreign-policy matter without bothering to inform her, she reprimanded him; when he repeated the offense, she had him dismissed. Victoria provided just enough leadership to keep the parliamentary system functioning smoothly without ever seeming to threaten the jealously guarded prerogatives of Parliament itself. The result was a balance of power between court, cabinet, and the two legislative houses—that balance which Walter Bagehot in his influential *English Constitution* (1867) described as the secret of the British system of government.

The most important legislative act of the midcentury was the extension of the suffrage, enacted in 1867. The manner in which this bill secured passage is very characteristic of the non-ideological quality of English party politics of the time. The proposal to widen the suffrage was made in 1865–1866 by the Liberals under the leadership of Lord John Russell. It immediately caught the imagination of the working class, especially the trade unions, which took up the old Chartist clamor for the franchise and threatened violence if their demand was not met. The Reform Bill submitted by Lord Russell, however, failed in the Commons, being defeated by an alliance of Conservatives and landed Whig elements among the Liberals. The leading Conservative figure, Benjamin Disraeli, saw in the Liberal defeat an excellent opportunity to restore the fortunes of his power-hungry party. He proposed to the Conservatives that they take the cause of suffrage reform away from the Liberals and submit an even more radical bill in their own

A biting French satire on England's Irish problem shows Queen Victoria, carefully shielded from unpleasant sights, touring the troubled island.

name. In this manner, Disraeli hoped, the Conservatives would win the loyalty of the newly enfranchised voter. Backed by the Conservatives as well as the pro-reform elements within the Liberal party, the Second Reform Bill was passed in August, 1867. It doubled the electorate by enfranchising in effect all house-hold owners and tenants paying taxes above a certain minimum sum. The bill gave England a very broad male suffrage and introduced an era of political democracy.

The Second Empire in France

In France the midcentury witnessed a reversion to authoritarian government in the personal rule of Napoleon III. In this respect, France was an exception to the general tendency of the period toward liberalization. But authoritarian regime in its pure form lasted only nine years (1851–1860). By 1860 it became apparent that purely bureaucratic methods could no longer effectively administer France. From 1860 until his deposition in 1870, Napoleon III continuously surrendered power. The whole second half of his reign represented an irresistible sliding toward constitutionalism and parliamentarism, an eloquent proof of the all-pervasive liberal tendency of the age.

The specific political development of France was mainly due to the peculiarities of its social structure. As we have noted, France was a country of small proprietors, extremely sensitive to any threat to their holdings. Whenever they felt such a threat to exist, the French sought protection in authoritarian government. This happened in 1799, again in 1850–1851, and again in 1958. The challenge to property came invariably from the same source, namely the socialist and anarchist elements concentrated in Paris. As soon as these elements seemed to get the upper hand, the majority of the country (that is, the provinces) veered sharply to the right.

The Paris uprising of June, 1848, frightened the countryside in precisely this way. Confronted with a choice between dictatorship and anarchy, it opted for dictatorship and once more entrusted its destiny to a man bearing the name of Napoleon. Louis Napoleon was the son of Louis Bonaparte, Napoleon I's younger brother and king of Holland in the days of the First Empire. In his youth he joined radical causes and imbibed the whole spirit of socialism and nationalism of the Romantic era. During the reign of Louise Philippe he was the principal Bonapartist claimant to the French throne. He twice tried unsuccessfully to overthrow the July monarchy. The second attempt (1840) led to his imprisonment, his eventual escape, and his flight to England.

Louis Napoleon developed an interesting political philosophy, which he outlined in two books, *Napoleonic Ideas* (1839) and *The Extinction of Pauperism* (1844). Underlying his theory were two fundamental thoughts: that modern politics must rest on the masses (rather than on the landed nobility or the moneyed élite), and that the masses must be led by the state. "Today the reign of castes is finished," he wrote; "one cannot govern except by means of the masses. . . . [The masses] must be organized so that they can formulate their will, and disciplined so they can be directed and enlightened about their true interests." In these statements one can detect anticipations of modern totalitarianism, and indeed Louis Napoleon may be regarded as one of its forerunners.

Louis Napoleon was much influenced by the French social thinker Claude

Henri de Saint-Simon. Saint-Simon, whose main activity occurred during the restoration period, maintained that the French Revolution had opened a new age in the history of mankind, what he called the "age of industrialism." By industrialism he meant not so much a specific mode of production, but everything antithetical to the feudal, aristocratic, and parasitic. His industrial class included all who were "productive" or "creative"—bankers, businessmen, engineers, scientists, scholars—as contrasted to the "idlers" (*oisifs*) and "militants," who either lived off the work of others or destroyed that work by war. The new world would be an alliance of industry and science, and all authority would be vested in experts or, as they are known today, technocrats. Inheritance would be abolished, but private property and inequalities in wealth would remain—a provision that disqualifies Saint-Simon from being included among the socialists, with whom his name is customarily linked. He was really an apostle of technological and scientific modernism. His views won him a following among French engineers and bankers, but they were much distorted and subsequently discredited by a group of close disciples who after his death set up a "Saint-Simonian" religious cult.

Louis Napoleon's opportunity to put his own and Saint-Simon's ideas into practice came in 1848. As soon as he learned of Louis Philippe's abdication, he headed for Paris, where the immense popularity of the Napoleonic name helped him gain election to the Chamber of Deputies. In November, 1848, he was nominated to run for the presidency of the Second Republic against General Cavaignac, the suppressor of the June revolt. He won handily.

Under the constitution adopted in 1848, the President's authority was severely curtailed by a single-chamber Legislative Assembly. He could hold office only for a single four-year term. Such restrictions did not suit Louis Napoleon's authoritarian temper, and he awaited an opportunity to be rid of them. In the meantime, he solidified his internal position by skillfully appealing to various social groups. He gained the support of the Catholic hierarchy by backing the Pope in his conflict with the Italian nationalists and by conceding the clergy

"The name Napoleon," said Napoleon III, "is a program in itself: it stands for order, authority, religion, the welfare of the people. . . ." In Constantin Guys' eyewitness sketch, he takes the oath as President of the Second Republic on December 20, 1848.

Baron Haussmann's so-called modernization of Paris inspired these comments by Honoré Daumier. Above, dispossessed tenants; below, hazards of a stroll on the Champs Élysées.

greater influence over the schools. He also won the favor of the royalists by appointing their adherents to high office and of the military by enlarging the army.

The chance for a power seizure presented itself in the summer of 1851 during a prolonged parliamentary crisis caused by an attempt of the Legislative Assembly to do away with universal suffrage. Louis Napoleon now was able to conceal his bid for absolute power behind the mask of a champion of popular freedoms. When the Assembly refused to change the constitution in order to enable him to run once more for the presidency, he illegally dissolved it and ordered a popular plebiscite on the revision of the constitution, coupling it with a proclamation restoring universal suffrage. This *coup d'état* occurred on December 2, 1851, the anniversary of Napoleon I's coronation. There was some scattered resistance, but it was quickly overcome. In the plebiscite that followed, 7,500,000 ballots (against 650,000) approved the President's request to revise—that is, subvert—the constitution.

The new constitution, drafted under Louis Napoleon's instructions, resembled closely the Napoleonic constitution of the Year VIII (1799). It vested in the President, as previously in the First Consul, the essentials of political power. The two legislative chambers had little authority and no control over the ministers. In 1852, once again emulating his uncle, he asked the nation to make him hereditary emperor. Again the country complied, giving him 7,800,000 Ayes against 253,000 Nays, with 2 million voters abstaining. He chose the name Napoleon III.

The new emperor—"Napoleon the Small," as Victor Hugo called him—had nothing but contempt for party politics, considering them a squandering of national energies. Politics were to be authoritarian, legitimized by a broad mandate of national referenda. The center of political authority shifted to the imperial court and to the immense civil service dependent on it. The government of the Second Empire was a government by bureaucracy to an extent unknown in Europe until that time. The bureaucracy controlled local government through departmental prefects who selected reliable pro-government candidates to run for the Assembly and marshaled the vote for them. It could squash any opposition by exercising its right to arrest, detain, and deport political opponents, and to suspend publications. Information gathered by a network of police officials and agents permitted the Minister of the Interior to forestall potential sedition. Under such conditions political opposition did not and could not exist. There is no evidence that the country at large missed political liberties, for the 1850s was a period of great prosperity and a splendid social life. In elections government candidates generally received majorities, and some of the emperor's most solid electoral support came from the working population in the industrial centers.

If Napoleon III had contempt for politics, he was very serious about what we would call today economic development. He surrounded himself with Saint-Simonian technocrats with whose aid he undertook to stimulate economic activity. He founded several large national investment banks, notably the Crédit Foncier to provide mortgages for real estate, and the Crédit Mobilier to finance industrial undertakings. As a result of these and other measures, the value of France's industrial production doubled in the first two decades of the Second Empire. From the socialists Napoleon III borrowed the idea of public works as a remedy for unemployment. The most spectacular public works project of his reign was the modernization of Paris carried out under the direction of Baron Haussmann, in the course of which many medieval sections were razed and replaced with broad boulevards. Despite his early interest in the working class, Napoleon III did little to improve France's social legislation. The French working class remained dangerously isolated from the rest of society, bourgeois as well as peasant.

So far, France's course was running against the general liberal trend of the times, but in the 1860s this situation changed as Napoleon's prestige and power, unassailable in the 1850s, began visibly to erode. The main reason for this decline lay in foreign failures. Napoleon III was at heart a pacifist, but this did not prevent him from engaging in an ambitious foreign policy that at times required recourse to arms, for which he had neither heart nor skill. His intervention on behalf of Italy against Austria in 1859 (see below) aroused protests from politicians who preferred a dismembered to a united Italy as a neighbor. Napoleon's commercial treaty with Britain, signed in 1860, alienated many French businessmen who were not prepared to compete with the world's leading industrial power without the protection of high tariffs. In 1861 Napoleon intervened disastrously in Mexico, hoping to found there a Catholic empire. The French candidate, Maximilian, was put on the throne with the help of French troops, but when these withdrew under United States pressure, the Mexicans seized and shot him.

The unpopularity of his foreign policy made it imperative to relax the reins of authority at home, where a liberal opposition was becoming more audible and the bureaucracy less able to guarantee the election of loyal Assembly candidates. As a result, an anti-government bloc took shape. To govern the country as well as to maintain confidence in its finances, Napoleon had to secure the support of the opposition, and to this end he now began to make concessions. In 1860–1861 he increased the financial competence of the legislatures and allowed their debates to be published. In 1867 he granted the Assembly the right of "interpellation," that is, of questioning government ministers. The following year he lifted the most onerous restrictions on the freedom of speech and assembly.

These liberalizing measures, instead of placating the opposition, emboldened it. In the elections of 1869 government candidates received only 4.4 million votes compared to 3.3 million cast for opposition candidates. A majority of deputies now pressed for the creation of a responsible ministry. Napoleon was not prepared to go that far, but in 1869–1870 he further enlarged the authority of the legislatures, granting the Assembly the right to initiate legislation, to vote on the budget, and to demand from ministers a certain amount of accounting. These measures moved France toward an equilibrium between the executive and the legislative, a development that met with the approbation of the majority of the population. In a national plebiscite held in the spring of 1870 the country gave its assent to the new political system with 7.3 million voting for and 1.5 million against.

Despite this impressive triumph, the days of the Second Empire were numbered. A few months later it was shattered by a blow delivered by Prussia, a country that had been quietly gathering strength and now emerged as the first power on the Continent. But before we turn to the story of Prussia's rise, we must deal with chronologically antecedent events on the Italian peninsula.

The Risorgimento   The suppression by the Austrians of the revolutionary governments that had sprung up in northern and central Italy in 1848–1849 left on the peninsula only one liberal state, Piedmont. Unlike the other rulers who quickly retracted the constitutions that had been foisted upon them by the revolutionary mobs, Victor Emmanuel II, the king of Piedmont since 1849, honored the pledges of his predecessor, Charles Albert. The Piedmontese constitution, promulgated in March, 1848, was based on the French charter of 1830. It provided for a bicameral legislature, one appointed, the other elected on a restricted franchise. The ministers were responsible to parliament. Elsewhere in Italy—the Papal domain, the Kingdom of the Two Sicilies, and the principalities of Parma, Modena, Lucca, and Tuscany—the forces of reaction had the upper hand.

Italian nationalism matured slowly. In the 1820s the Italians still lacked any real sense of national identity, and Metternich justly referred to Italy as a "geographic expression." This national sense developed only in the 1830s and 1840s, largely under the influence of Romantic intellectuals and publicists, of whom the most important was Giuseppe Mazzini. A republican and a democrat, Mazzini believed that the unification of Italy would come about through a mass movement of all regions and all classes. To promote such a movement, he founded in 1832 a society called "Young Italy." The goal of this organization, whose membership was limited to patriots less than forty years old, was to stimulate anti-Austrian and anti-absolutist uprisings and help create a united Italian republic. It was linked with a broader international society, "Young Europe," which Mazzini founded two years later with branches among the Swiss, Germans, Poles, and other nationalities to promote democratic, republican, and national goals in the rest of Europe.

Mazzini did much to spread the ideal of Italian unity, but, despite his personal magnetism and courage, his insurrectionary strategy had no success. The Austrians brutally stamped out every uprising organized by Young Italy. The response among Italians, too, was discouraging. Few educated Italians felt as yet sufficient affinity with artisans, shopkeepers, and peasants to join with them in a common struggle for statehood. Young Italy suffered its decisive fiascoes in 1848–1849, when the republics that it had helped to establish were swept away in the subsequent reaction. After that, leadership of the Italian national movement passed to men of a new breed, with another temperament and program.

The greatest figure of Italian politics in the 1850s, and the creator of Italian unity, was Count Camillo Cavour. In contrast to the fiery Romantic intellectual who dashed from insurrection to insurrection, Cavour resembled a typical middle-class English liberal. He admired the constitutional monarchy, believed in industrialism and free trade, and carefully calculated his chances before undertaking any action. Prior to entering politics, he had spent seventeen years running his father's estate, acquiring in this manner a good understanding of management and practical economics.

Cavour entertained no illusions that Italy could win national unity and independence by means of a popular uprising. These aims required a power base at home and abroad. He decided that Piedmont offered the best chance of serving as the national base from which to launch the movement for unification. It was liberal and progressive, fairly prosperous, and enjoyed a strategically advanta-

geous position in regard to Austria. In 1847 Cavour founded a newspaper, *Il Risorgimento (Renascence)*, whose name was later applied to the whole Italian unification movement. In it he propagated the idea that Piedmont lead the work of unification. In 1850 he entered the Piedmontese cabinet and two years later took over as Prime Minister, a post he held, with one brief interruption, until his death in 1861. During these years he laid the foundations of Italian statehood. He tackled with great energy the task of economic development in Piedmont, reorganizing finances, lowering tariffs, and promoting the construction of railroads. In a short time his efforts gave Piedmont the most lively economy in Italy. These policies won him much sympathy in England and France. Cavour also firmly reduced the power of the Catholic clergy.

At the end of the 1850s, feeling his home base secure, Cavour undertook negotiations to obtain a foreign ally against Austria. This he found in the Second Empire. At a secret meeting with Napoleon III held in July, 1858, at Plombières, he received the promise of French military assistance against Austria in return for the cession of Nice and Savoy. With this guarantee, Cavour provoked Austria into war by fomenting disorders in its Italian provinces (April, 1859). As soon as Austrian troops crossed the Piedmontese frontier, the French intervened, and in two major battles fought at Magenta and Solferino in June, 1859, defeated them. In the peace treaty that followed (Treaty of Zurich, November, 1859), Aus-

Giuseppe Garibaldi began his career as a military adventurer in South America. After conquering Sicily he was briefly dictator of the island.

tria ceded the rich commercial regions of Lombardy, including Milan, to Piedmont.

Cavour took advantage of the Austrian defeat to organize insurrections throughout Italy. For this purpose he employed the National Society, founded in 1857, which had branches all over the peninsula. In the fall of 1859 uprisings broke out in Parma, Modena, Tuscany, and the northern regions of the Papal domain. Each uprising was followed by a plebiscite in which the population approved a merger with Piedmont. When in the spring of 1860 a rebellion broke out against the Bourbon dynasty in the Kingdom of the Two Sicilies, Cavour encouraged Giuseppe Garibaldi to go to its aid as the head of an expedition of 1,000 "Red Shirts." Garibaldi quickly seized Sicily and from there proceeded to Naples. He intended also to march on Rome, but the French, who had stationed a contingent of troops in Rome since 1849, thwarted this plan. Naples and Sicily, however, were secure and in October, 1860, voted to amalgamate with Piedmont.

In February, 1861, the process of unification, so skillfully directed by Cavour, culminated in the convocation in Turin of the first all-Italian parliament. The assembly proclaimed an Italian kingdom with Victor Emmanuel at its head. The constitution of the new state rested on that adopted by Piedmont in 1848 and retained the principle of ministerial responsibility.

At the time of Italy's founding, two regions still remained outside its borders: Venetia and the Papal domain, with its center at Rome. Venetia was acquired in 1866 after a brief war with Austria. The acquisition of Rome took longer, for the situation was greatly complicated by the French presence. Finally, the French withdrew, and Rome fell under Italian rule and became the capital (1871).

The Papacy The Papacy was the only power in Europe to resist the midcentury trend toward liberalization. Indeed, it tended to grow increasingly conservative and in the 1860s became the most uncompromising representative of anti-liberal forces.

The Papacy emerged after the defeat of Napoleon Bonaparte stronger than it had been for two hundred years. It profited greatly from the religious revival that had begun during the French Revolution and continued during the Romantic era. In Catholic countries conservative rulers of the restoration era returned to the Church its properties and privileges in recognition of the role that it had performed in resisting the forces of revolution. In addition, at the Congress of Vienna the Popes were awarded the lands that had been taken from them by the French. The Papal States after 1815 embraced much of central Italy, including Rome. In these territories the Popes established an administration, thoroughly clerical and conservative, that collaborated with the Austrian and pro-Austrian princes in stamping out any signs of liberalism and radicalism.

The commitment of the Catholic Church to temporal affairs and its alliance with the conservative states was by no means universally approved by the Catholic community. Some outstanding Catholic writers, such as Félicité Robert de Lamennais, urged the Church to assume leadership of the liberal and democratic movements and to become spokesman of the masses (*The Words of a Believer*, 1834). Others wanted the Church to abandon politics altogether and transform itself into a purely spiritual power.

The liberal tendency in Catholicism seemed to gain the upper hand in 1846 with the election to the Papacy of Pius IX. The new Pontiff had a reputation of being a moderate, liberal man, and he at first justified this opinion by relaxing censorship and granting amnesty to political offenders. But his failure to support the anti-Austrian rebels in Italy in 1848 so enraged the nationalists that they forced him to flee from Rome. Upon his return in 1850 he revealed himself as a stanch conservative, determined to oppose at every point the dominant trends of his age. In 1864 he issued two celebrated encyclicals, *Quanta cura* and *Syllabus errorum*, in which he condemned rationalism, liberal economics, socialism, liberty of conscience, popular sovereignty, and secularism. In 1869–1870 he went further and convoked the Vatican Council (the first since the Council of Trent in the sixteenth century) which, at his urging, proclaimed the doctrine of Papal Infallibility—i.e., the doctrine that the Pope could not err when pronouncing on matters of faith or morals in the performance of his duties.

These developments brought the Catholic Church into direct collision with the secular authorities. The Church resisted the *risorgimento* and rejected the offers of compromise made by Cavour and his successors. As a result, in 1870 it lost its last territorial possession, and Pius IX became a virtual prisoner in the Vatican. He subsequently forbade Italian Catholics to participate in national elections. His reactionary measures evoked protests in Austria and Germany and gave Bismarck a pretext for engaging the Catholic Church in a long-drawn-out political conflict (the *Kulturkampf*, Chapter 20). The relations between the Papacy and secular authorities began to improve only in 1878 with the accession of Leo XIII, who adopted some policies advocated by liberal Catholics.

The Unification of Germany

The difficulty in achieving a unification of Germany lay not so much in an inadequate sense of national identity or in foreign interference, both of which had delayed Italian statehood, but rather in the necessity of reconciling the interests of many sovereign principalities, several of them large and with old traditions. Some of the thirty-nine states of the Germanic Confederation were Protestant, others Catholic; some were industrial and commercial and oriented westward, others predominantly rural and oriented eastward; in some, liberal ideas prevailed, whereas others were thoroughly conservative. To fuse such diverse entities in a single national state required patience and skill. The difficulties were compounded by the rivalry between the two most powerful states of the Confederation, Protestant Prussia and Catholic Austria, either of which had the capacity to perform the function that Piedmont had performed in Italy. One group of German nationalists wanted to unite all the lands with a German-speaking population, including the Austrian, under Hapsburg leadership. This was the so-called "Great German" (*Grossdeutsch*) solution. Another group, proponents of the "Little German" (*Kleindeutsch*) solution, wanted Prussia to lead and Austria to be excluded from the unified German state. The Austrians championed the "Great German" program, of course, but they lacked the power to carry it out. The Prussians therefore triumphed, but the victory of their cause was by no means inevitable.

Prussian political life was characterized by the preponderance of the military. The independent officer corps, which was drawn from the *Junkers*, the landowning class, formed a tightly knit group with a great deal of *esprit de corps* and

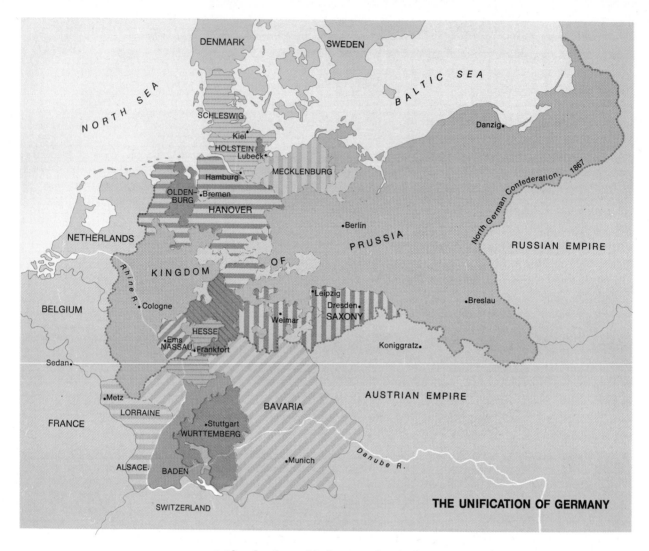

THE UNIFICATION OF GERMANY

a rigid code of social behavior. They had enjoyed great influence in the Prussian state since the eighteenth century and retained it even after Prussia had begun to industrialize, in part because they married into commercial and manufacturing wealth. Prussia was the first country in the world to put modern technology to work for the military. The Prussian General Staff, a highly professional body virtually free of control by the civilian authorities, exploited fully the latest technical innovations, such as railroads, steel armaments, and the telegraph. Helmuth von Moltke, the Chief of the General Staff from 1858 to 1888, was a characteristic specimen of the modern Prussian officer—a romantic visionary for whom war was the noblest expression of the human spirit, and at the same time a pragmatic technician. It was this combination of the feudal and industrial mentalities that made the Prussian and subsequently the German army such a terrible instrument of destruction.

William I, who ascended the throne in 1861, shared the traditional Prussian love of the military. In an attempt to strengthen his armed forces, he approved a series of military reforms, among them measures prolonging the duration of army service and dissolving the popular militia, which was officered by nonprofessionals. These proposals, upon being submitted to the Landtag, the lower house of the Prussian parliament, caused a prolonged parliamentary crisis. (The Landtag had been created in March, 1848, at the height of the revolutionary disturbances in Berlin.) The majority of the deputies at this time were liberals and belonged to the Progressive party. As nationalists, they welcomed measures designed to strengthen Prussia and increase its weight in the Germanic Confederation. But as liberals, they objected to the influence wielded by the military. Interpreting the proposed reform as an attempt by the *Junkers* to gain more power, the Progressives rejected the bill and, to give force to their action, vetoed the budget. The king, hoping for popular support, dissolved the Landtag and ordered new elections. But the voters backed the Progressives, giving them two-thirds of the seats in the new house. William was so dispirited by this turn of events that he was on the point of abdicating, when his military friends persuaded him to seek the help of Bismarck.

Otto von Bismarck came from an old if undistinguished family of Pomeranian *Junkers* and displayed all the virtues and vices of that class. His loyalty to the Prussian monarchy was complete and unflinching, superseding even his loyalty to Germany as a whole. His outlook was fundamentally feudal and rural. He had an instinctive mistrust of people living in the cities, of intellectuals, and of parliamentary institutions. At the same time, however, he understood well how to manipulate for conservative ends liberal institutions and ideas, such as representative assemblies, the universal vote, and nationalism, and even radical ones such as social welfare. He was an outstanding example of the new breed of conservative statesman: a statesman who knew how to exploit liberalism and socialism to strengthen the authority of the state.

When William ran into trouble with the Landtag, Bismarck was serving as Prussian ambassador to Napoleon III. He eagerly accepted William's invitation to take charge of the government and saw as his immediate and principal task to undermine the popularity of the liberals, whom he considered the main threat to royal authority. This aim he achieved by depriving them of their most powerful weapon, namely nationalism. Under Bismarck's leadership Prussia carried out a series of quick and victorious but limited wars, the result of which was to engender enormous patriotic enthusiasm throughout Germany and to give Prussia's claim to hegemony an irresistible impetus. The wars also placed the liberals in a position where to oppose Bismarck was equivalent to opposing the cause of national unification. When Bismarck retired in 1890, German liberalism was demoralized and no longer an effective counterforce to the monarchy.

As soon as he had taken over the Prussian government, Bismarck dissolved the Landtag and imposed a severe press censorship that made it difficult for the Progressives to campaign in the new election. In 1862, between sessions of the house, he introduced new taxes in order to free himself from dependence on the regular budget, which was subject to the Landtag's veto. This unconstitutional procedure was for all practical purposes a *coup d'état*, and for a while there was a danger of a nationwide revolt. But the Berliners were not Parisians, and the expected uprising never came. By his successful defiance of the Landtag, Bismarck dealt a devastating blow to the cause of constitutionalism and liberalism and assured the monarchy of a decisive voice in the country's political life. It was

An attack on Bismarck has the Chancellor carefully making his way toward military dictatorship and war.

at this time that he made his oft-quoted remark: "The great issues of the day will be decided not by speeches and votes of the majority—that was the great mistake of 1848 and 1849—but by iron and blood."

Next, in 1864, Bismarck involved Prussia and Austria in a brief war against Denmark over the disputed territories of Schleswig-Holstein. The victory of the Prussian-Austrian forces greatly raised the prestige of Prussia, which had engineered and directed the engagement.

The crucial conflict—the one that assured Prussia of the lead in the task of unification and guaranteed that Austria would be barred from the united German state—was the Austro-Prussian War of 1866. The pretext was an argument over the administration of Schleswig-Holstein, which the two powers had exercised jointly. But in reality the Prussians wanted war. Moltke later admitted that the conflict had been coldly worked out in the Prussian cabinet. Prussia had to humiliate Austria in order to discredit once and for all the "Great German" solution. In the Battle of Königgrätz (Sadowa), fought in July, 1866, the modernized Prussian army, equipped with the latest breech-loading guns, decisively defeated the Austrian troops, whose guns were of the old muzzle-loading type.

The victory of 1866 unleashed an explosion of nationalistic frenzy in Prussia and many other German regions. To the liberals it presented a dilemma: either to support Bismarck to the hilt and give up hope of establishing a true parliamentary government, or to oppose him and lose influence over the electorate. This dilemma led to a split in liberal ranks. One group formed a National Liberal party, which allied itself with Bismarck and supported his internal policies, even when they violated cardinal principles of liberalism; the other remained in the old Progressive party. The latter gradually lost ground, being squeezed between a right composed of monarchists and National Liberals and a left dominated by the emergent Social Democratic party.

Bismarck promptly capitalized on the pro-Prussian sentiment engendered by victory over Austria. He annexed to Prussia several principalities, connecting in this manner Prussia's eastern and western portions. In 1867 he replaced the Germanic Confederation, which had dissolved as a result of the Austro-Prussian War, with a new political union called the North German Confederation. This association included all of northern Germany, that is, Prussia and most of the Protestant principalities. The constitution of the new Confederation was designed to assure the preponderance of both the Prussian king and the Prussian state. William I became the President of the North German Confederation and the commander of its armed forces. The parliament consisted of two chambers: an upper one (Bundesrat, or Federal Council), representing the principalities, and a lower one (Reichstag), representing the population. Prussia assured itself of sufficient votes in the upper house to exercise an effective veto. The lower house was elected on the basis of universal democratic male suffrage. Bismarck granted this suffrage in the hope of obtaining broad public support against the liberals. (Later on he admitted that this miscalculation had been the worst error of his life.) As Chancellor, Bismarck was accountable only to his king; in other words, there was no ministerial responsibility and therefore no parliamentary system of government. The constitution of the North German Confederation became in 1871 the basis of the constitution of the German Empire.

Under Bismarck the Prussian soldier —well trained and equipped, rigidly obedient—became Europe's best.

To complete the unification of Germany, Bismarck needed one more great victory—over France. Such a victory would assure that the Catholic states of southern Germany would have no choice but to associate themselves with the North German Confederation. Napoleon III himself was not averse to war, partly because he had grown increasingly alarmed over the rise of Prussia and wanted to reduce its power, and partly because a victorious war would bolster his waning prestige at home.

The diplomatic incident that caused the outbreak of the Franco-Prussian War of 1870 was Prussia's promotion of a Hohenzollern candidate to the vacant throne of Spain. The French objected and applied pressure on King William to withdraw it. William agreed to do so. The dispute would have ended amicably, were it not that militant groups on both sides were eager to find a pretext for war. The pretext was provided by the famous "Ems telegram." In the course of private talks with King William at the resort town of Ems, the French ambassador demanded that Prussia not only withdraw its candidate for the Spanish throne but pledge never again to propose a Hohenzollern as ruler of Spain. William refused to give such a pledge. An account of these talks was wired to Bismarck, who released it to the press, but only after having doctored it to make the French demand appear as an insolent ultimatum and the German response as an equally insolent reply. The French, outraged by this action, declared war on Prussia (July, 1870).

The Prussians moved with greater speed and in August thrust through Alsace and Lorraine into France. The French resisted, but a large part of their army found itself encircled and trapped in the Metz-Sedan area. Among the prisoners taken at the beginning of September was Napoleon III himself. Bismarck, who waged war for limited political objectives, had now achieved his aim and wanted to suspend operations. But Moltke and the other military would not agree. They wanted to annihilate the enemy and pursued him deep into French territory, beyond the Loire River. In mid-September the Prussian forces laid siege to Paris, which they had surrounded. Four months later the starving city capitulated.

In January, 1871, while the siege of Paris was still in progress, the Prussian king was proclaimed German emperor.° The new empire, the fulfillment of the dream of German nationalists since the beginning of the century, expanded the North German Confederation to include the kingdoms and principalities of southern Germany, such as Bavaria, Württemberg, and Baden. The empire's constitution derived from that of the Confederation. It gave a preponderant position to Prussia and established the responsibility of the Chancellor (Bismarck) and the other ministers to the emperor. Universal suffrage was retained for the lower house. The constitution made no mention, however, of the "rights of the citizen"—an omission unique in the constitutional charters of the great European states of that time and an evil omen for the political future of Germany. The extent to which the unification of Germany had been the work of the military may be gathered from the fact that among the participants of the ceremonies attending the proclamation of the empire in the Hall of Mirrors at Versailles there

°The proclamation specified that he was "German Emperor" not "Emperor of Germany" in order not to offend the monarchs of the constituent states, who continued to regard themselves as sovereigns of their own territories.

were only two or three civilians. All others, including Emperor William I and Bismarck, wore uniforms.

The events of the 1860s, culminating in the formation of the empire, mark a watershed in the history of the German spirit. Until then the Germans had been universally regarded as a nation of sentimental dreamers: musicians, poets, scholars, craftsmen, and they so regarded themselves. Voltaire expressed the prevailing eighteenth-century view when he said that God, in creating the world, had entrusted to the French the kingdom of the land, to the English the kingdom of the seas, and to the Germans the kingdom of the clouds. This had now changed. Even during the anti-Napoleonic Wars of Liberation (1813–1815), ugly strains of chauvinism had been heard among German intellectuals; they resounded again at the sessions of the Frankfurt parliament in 1848–1849. In the 1860s, and especially in the 1870s, following an uninterrupted succession of military victories, nationalism in Germany disassociated itself from liberalism and became arrogant and aggressive. The new nationalism found expression in an exaggerated notion of Germany's past, contempt for the "lesser breeds" (such as the Slavs), and growing reliance on "iron and blood." The theories of Charles Darwin (discussed in the next chapter) with their notions of "struggle for existence" and "survival of the fittest" were readily assimilated by a nation that felt it had finally arrived. As the new mood gained ground, the older idealistic tradition receded into the background. Kant, Goethe, Schiller, and the Humboldts were still greatly admired, but not so much for what they had said as for having said it in German.

The Austro-Hungarian Empire   The Hapsburgs, as we have seen, succeeded in preserving their empire during the revolutions of 1848–1849, despite the severe shocks it had received from nationalists in the borderlands and from radicals in the capital. The Austrian state at midcentury was still a giant, the second power in Europe in terms of territory and the third in terms of population. Its national economy, while not of the first rank, was considerable. Nevertheless, the revolutions of 1848–1849 marked the beginning of Austria's decline. It never regained the exalted international position that it had enjoyed thanks to the diplomatic skill of Metternich and the disunity of Italy and Germany. The unification of these two neighboring countries significantly reduced Austria's influence in Central Europe. Even deprived of such influence, however, the Austrian Empire would have remained a major power had it not been for conflicts among its own ethnic groups that steadily sapped its strength and eventually (1918) assured its dissolution.

The German-speaking population that ruled the Hapsburg domain was numerically a minority group. The non-German nationalities—the Magyars (Hungarians), Slavs (Poles, Czechs, Slovaks, Serbians, Croatians, Slovenes, Ukrainians), Latins (Italians, Romanians), and other ethnic groups (Jews)—outnumbered the Germans approximately three to one, and the proportion tended to increase further to the detriment of the Germans because they had fewer children. During the time when authority was firmly in the hands of the nobility and the autocracy, such ethnic disparity did not much matter. But with liberalization and democratization it threatened the very survival of the state, because, as more citizens received the vote, national interests and antagonisms came to the fore.

The bond that more than any other united this diversified population was religion: three-fourths of the emperor's subjects were Catholics. It was for this reason that Metternich had so closely connected Austria's politics with Catholicism. But in a secular age such a policy had little prospect of success. With each passing decade an increasing number of Austrian subjects thought of themselves not so much as Catholics but as Poles or Czechs or Croatians.

Probably the best solution for Austria's nationality problem would have been federation, a system that would have granted the principal ethnic groups territorial autonomy. But for several reasons this solution was not accepted, despite the strong support it received from some circles. For one, it would have reduced

THE PEOPLES
OF AUSTRIA-HUNGARY

Germans
Magyars
Romanians
Italians

SLAVS

Croatians
and Serbians
Czechs
Slovaks
Poles
Slovenes
Ukrainians

Dual Monarchy, 1867

the influence of the German element. For another, it would not have satisfied the most radical nationalists among the non-German groups, who refused to settle for anything short of full political independence. Furthermore, with industrialization and urbanization, the various ethnic groups were increasingly intermingled, so that equitable territorial divisions became less and less feasible.

After suppressing the revolutionary movement of 1848–1849, the Hapsburg government veered sharply to the right. The 1850s were a period of black reaction, with authority placed in the hands of the bureaucracy. The Minister of the Interior, Alexander Bach, who exceeded even Metternich in his loathing of liberalism, pursued a policy of Germanization and relied heavily on his officialdom, popularly known as "Bach's Hussars." The new ruler, Franz Josef, was a stanch autocrat, ready to concede political rights to his subjects only when he had no other choice. He ruled even longer than Queen Victoria (sixty-eight years as against her sixty-four).

The first serious breach in the autocratic system occurred as a result of Austrian defeats in the war with Piedmont in 1859. To gain popular support, Franz Josef consented in 1861 to the establishment of an imperial House of Deputies, or Reichsrat. This assembly was elected not directly by voters, but indirectly by regional Diets, each of which had allotted to it a certain number of seats in the Reichsrat. These Diets, in turn, were elected by a quota system or "colleges." The whole electoral system was designed to give preponderance to propertied groups and to German nationals. The franchise was very limited. The Reichsrat initiated and voted on laws (subject to imperial approval), but it did not direct the executive branch: Austrian ministers were and remained responsible solely to the monarch until the collapse of the empire in 1918.

The Hungarians, whose nationalism was highly developed, refused from the beginning to participate in the Reichsrat and demanded full internal autonomy. Their leading statesman, Count Gyula Andrássy, proposed to Franz Josef that he reject the federal schemes pressed on him by other national groups in favor of a "dual solution" that would make Austrian Germans and Hungarian Magyars equal partners in ruling the empire. The emperor consented to this proposal, partly in order to strengthen his internal position after another military defeat, this time at the hands of the Prussians (1866), and partly to please his pro-Hungarian wife, Elizabeth. In 1867 he approved the *Ausgleich*—the "leveling" or "evening out" of the Austrian and Hungarian portions of the empire. The empire now became a "Dual Monarchy" consisting of an Austrian (or Cisleithanian) part and a Hungarian (or Trans-leithanian) part. The two were linked by the person of the monarch, who was emperor in Austria and king in Hungary, as well as by three joint ministries (foreign affairs, armed forces, and common treasury). In internal matters the Hungarians received full autonomy. In 1867 the government also issued a decree guaranteeing full civil rights to all subjects, regardless of nationality or religion.

Admirably as the *Ausgleich* may have met the wishes of the Magyar nationalists, in the long run it precluded a satisfactory solution of the national problem for the empire as a whole, for, unless all the ethnic groups received rights similar to those given the Magyars, they were reduced to political subservience to an Austro-Hungarian partnership. For a while, the government seemed ready to

A French traveler sketched the inside of a Russian peasant hut, home to both the family and its livestock.

grant a Hungarian-type arrangement to the Czechs, but in 1871 this proposal was dropped, whereupon the Czechs began to boycott the Reichsrat. From then on, national conflicts in and out of parliament became the principal issue of internal politics in Austria-Hungary.

The Great Reforms in Russia

Of all the countries in nineteenth-century Europe, Russia alone failed to make the transition to constitutional and parliamentary government. It remained an absolutist monarchy until October, 1905, long after even less advanced countries, like the Ottoman Empire and Japan, had experimented with liberal institutions.

Russia's failure to follow the prevalent pattern was due less to the weakness of liberal forces than to the strength of conservative ones. The government and a large part of the educated public had a deep-seated dread of mass anarchy. It feared that the uncouth and unpredictable Russian peasant, who constituted nine-tenths of the country's population, would go on an uncontrollable rampage of murder and arson the instant he sensed a weakening of authority over him. Liberalism seemed to involve precisely such a weakening of authority. The spectacle of dissident political parties, social unrest, and periodic revolutions in the countries of Western Europe indicated to many Russians the necessity of retaining in their own country firm, centralized government. The absolutist state alone could accomplish the enormous task of educational reform and economic development required for Russia's internal stability and external power.

Russian liberalism gained its main support among the Westernized landed gentry. This class, however, was on the decline. In its struggle against the bureaucratic-police regime, it received next to no support from the other groups of the population. To the peasants, the liberals appeared as selfish lords who wanted to limit the power of the tsar in order the better to exploit them. To the young intellectuals, heavily imbued with anarchist ideas, the liberals were anathema because their program—constitutionalism and parliamentarism—would enhance the power of the state that they wished to destroy. As for the bourgeoisie, it was not strong to begin with and in any event tended toward conservatism in gratitude for the protection that the imperial government extended it against foreign competition as well as against the demands of the Russian working class.

Russia's failure to undergo genuine liberalization does not mean, however, that the country did not liberalize at all. The 1860s in Russia was a decade of liberal reform that profoundly altered the face of the country. These reforms were carried out on the initiative of Alexander II (1855–1881), a ruler of essentially conservative views who came to the realization that it was no longer possible to govern a country of Russia's size and international position along purely bureaucratic lines. He introduced a series of reforms intended to increase the participation of society in the country's public life. These "Great Reforms" resembled in their essential features those that Stein and his colleagues had carried out in Prussia half a century earlier.

The stimulus to reform, as in the case of post-1806 Prussia and post-1866 Austria, was military defeat. The active policy that Nicholas I had pursued in the Near East from the moment of his accession finally involved Russia in war with the Western powers. Britain, whose commercial interests in that area made it sensitive to Russian encroachments, repeatedly clashed with Russia on behalf of

In an 1853 Punch *cartoon, Britain and France try to diagnose the ills of their patient, the Ottoman Empire, menaced by the Russian scourge.*

the Ottoman Empire. Gradually France too became involved. In March, 1854, Russia found itself at war with a coalition consisting of Britain, France, and Turkey, which was later joined by Piedmont. The allies dispatched an expeditionary force that landed on the Crimean peninsula and after prolonged fighting seized the chief Russian port of Sebastopol (September, 1855). Completely isolated, Russia had to agree to peace terms (Treaty of Paris, 1856) that greatly reduced its influence in the Near East.

Although the Crimean War was in no sense a military disaster for Russia, it discredited the autocratic system enforced by Nicholas I, a stanch supporter of the Metternichian system. It showed that Russia had to modernize or cease to be a great power in any meaningful sense. This realization penetrated even high bureaucratic circles in St. Petersburg and made possible the Great Reforms that got under way with the death of Nicholas I in 1855 and the accession of his son, Alexander II.

Of all the questions confronting the country, the foremost was serfdom. Serfdom had come to Russia, as to most of Eastern Europe, late, having been legalized only in the seventeenth century. In the middle of the nineteenth century, slightly over one-third of the peasant population consisted of private (proprietary) serfs, who had no civil rights and could not legally acquire property. The worst feature of serfdom was not economic—the peasants, by Western standards, had more than enough land to till—but civil and moral: deprived of rights, serfs lacked incentives to improve their lot and felt isolated from society at large. Accustomed since the Middle Ages to treat all authority as hostile, the Russian peasant, for all his devotion to the Church and tsar, indeed harbored powerful destructive instincts.

There was talk of emancipating the serfs as early as the eighteenth century, and it is known that both Alexander I and Nicholas I in principle favored such action, though they did not have the courage to act. After the Crimean War the measure could no longer be delayed. The Emancipation Edict, issued on February 19, 1861, freed the serfs and gave all peasants basic civil rights. It also gave them land. The government reimbursed the landlords for that portion of the land they had lost to their one-time serfs by means of state bonds, which the peasants in turn were required to repay to the government over forty-nine years in the form of annual "redemption payments." For administrative and fiscal reasons, the land was not given directly to the peasants themselves but to village communes. To make certain that he met all his tax obligations and redemption payments, the peasant was forbidden to leave the commune without its permission. Thus, although he was freed from the landlord's authority, the peasant remained tied to the soil and to the commune. Despite these conservative features, the Emancipation Edict was a very bold measure that, without bloodshed, transformed millions of Russians from passive subjects into citizens.

By destroying the legal authority that the landlord had traditionally exercised over the peasantry, the edict necessitated a number of related reforms. In 1864 Alexander introduced into cities and provinces organs of local self-rule (municipal councils and *zemstva*). These institutions were elected by all the groups of the population. They were not meant to compete with the imperial bureaucracy, but to assist it by assuming a variety of responsibilities previously left unattended:

primary education, public health, the maintenance of roads and bridges, and so forth. To fulfill these obligations, the municipal councils and *zemstva* were empowered to collect taxes. Until abolished by the Communists, these organs helped significantly to raise the material and cultural level of the country. They also provided an excellent school of political training for public-minded citizens. Court reform (1864) introduced such advanced Western practices as irremovable judges and trial by jury. The army recruitment procedure was also reformed (1874), the system of draft quotas previously imposed on the serfs being replaced by compulsory military service for all citizens. Censorship was considerably eased. The Great Reforms helped the monarchy obtain a measure of public support in the difficult task of administering so vast a realm and yet did not deprive it of its monopoly of political power. They liberalized the administration without making it liberal.

Even the Turkish government—proverbially the most corrupt and backward in Europe—could not escape the general tendency of the time. In the first half of the nineteenth century, the government of the Ottoman Empire proved itself increasingly unable to cope with the internal and external challenges to its authority. The Greek rebellion of 1821 lasted for a decade and ended with the Turks conceding independence to Greece. In the 1830s Constantinople lost effective control over Egypt. Especially great was the threat of Russia, which in the 1830s established a virtual protectorate over the empire. Had it not been for repeated intervention by Western powers, notably Great Britain, there is little doubt that the Ottoman Empire would have fallen apart, the bulk of its territory being seized by Russia.

The Ottoman Empire

In Turkey, as elsewhere, military defeats provided the most persuasive argument in favor of internal reform. At first, the sultans were content to transplant Western culture, hoping that the adoption of Western manners and techniques would of itself infuse the state with the necessary vigor. Mahmud II (1808–1839), who is sometimes called the Turkish Peter the Great, introduced Western military practices, Western schools, and Western dress for state officials.

The reform movement proper, known as *Tanzimat*, got under way after Mahmud's death. In 1839 the Ottoman government proclaimed the equality of its subjects. The intention of this measure was to create, by decree as it were, a common Ottoman nationality, and in this manner to neutralize national sentiment among the non-Turkish citizens. Its effects, however, were nil, for the overwhelming majority of citizens continued to owe allegiance to their respective religious communities. It aroused much opposition among the Muslims, who could not admit that the Christians, or "Franks" as they called them, were superior to those who followed Islam (literally, "submission to God's will").

Under Western pressure, the Ottoman government carried out further reforms after the Crimean War, the hope being that these reforms would strengthen the empire and make it more resistant to Russian encroachments. In 1856 it issued a far-reaching general reform edict that assured Christian subjects of their civil rights and gave them access to positions in the army and civil service. These measures seemed to point to a steady development toward liberal forms, but, as we shall see, these expectations were not fulfilled.

16

Science and the
Scientific Outlook

At the time of its emergence, Romanticism was a great liberalizing force. It helped to emancipate Western culture from the restraints of classicism and restored to the writer and the artist the right to creative self-expression. Politically, it had close affinities to liberalism and nationalism, both of which strove to free man from subjection to arbitrary authority. Early Romanticism was an ally of those who fought tyranny in all its forms.

But time and success killed the generous impulses of the Romantics. As soon as it had dislodged classicism, Romanticism became part of the established order and acquired the status of a new kind of orthodoxy. The poetry of Coleridge and Wordsworth, the novels of Scott and Hugo, and the stories of Hoffmann and Poe became, by the middle of the century, part of a cultivated European's cultural background. Before the century was over, they were included in the secondary-school curriculum—a certain sign of public acceptance. As they grew older, Romantic writers often turned conservative. Coleridge, who in 1789 had celebrated the fall of the Bastille, opposed Catholic emancipation and parliamentary reform in the 1820s. Pushkin, the singer of gypsies and the free Caucasian mountaineers, exhorted Nicholas I in 1830 to suppress the Polish uprising. The late German Romantics grew particularly reactionary.

European youth of the 1830s and 1840s, who found little to admire in the old Romantic idols, sought new heroes and new ideals in the world of science. The first half of the nineteenth century was a period of spectacular discoveries in chemistry, biology, and physics—discoveries that had particular bearing on such traditional philosophic questions as the nature of life and the physical universe. Science had a daring, a freshness, an authority that Romanticism had lost, and gradually talented youth abandoned Romanticism in favor of science and of philosophies based on scientific premises.

The device of the Royal Society of London, the world's oldest scientific institution, bears the words *Simplex sigillum veri* (simplicity is the seal of truth). And, indeed, the quest for the simplest, most economical explanations of the largest number of phenomena is the goal of scientific endeavor. Science seeks to penetrate the screen of appearance which confronts man with a seemingly inexhaustible variety of unrelated objects and processes, to reach the underlying unities. Its progress is marked by ever higher levels of abstraction. To the prescientific or non-scientific mind, for example, breathing, burning, and rusting are unrelated phenomena, each requiring a unique explanation. To the scientist they are merely different manifestations of an identical process, namely combustion. The term combustion permits an abstract (non-sensory) correlation of these three apparently different occurrences.

If abstract principles with the widest applicability are the goal of science, measurement is its means. The scientist learns with the help of quantities. A law

George Richmond's portrait shows Charles Darwin at the age of thirty, at the time the naturalist first formulated his theory of "natural selection." Darwin, wrote the biologist Julian Huxley, shook the world with the "magic force of a single idea."

In his notebook John Dalton sketched representations of two adjacent atoms (top) and below them a molecule, or, as he called it, a "compound atom."

is of little use to him unless it can be expressed in terms of mass, velocity, or some other quantitative unit.

The importance of the scientific discoveries made in the first half of the nineteenth century derives from the fact that they yielded a few fundamental laws capable of embracing an enormous variety of natural phenomena. These laws revealed for the first time the basic structural element of all organic substances and living organisms (atoms, molecules, and cells) and formulated general principles regulating the relations of chemical and physical matter (the laws of the conservation of matter and energy). They also revealed a far greater degree of unity in nature than had been suspected and encouraged philosophers to devise a philosophic system capable of providing a scientific explanation of all phenomena, including the actions of man.

THE STRUCTURE OF PHYSICAL MATTER

The problem of the ultimate structure of matter had troubled thinkers since antiquity. Are there substances in nature, men wondered, which are final and incapable of being reduced to different substances? Among the thinkers who dealt with this question was Aristotle, who postulated that four "elements"—water, air, earth, and fire—were the basic ingredients of all material objects. This fourfold classification or one of its numerous variants survived well into the modern period and was finally abandoned only on the eve of the French Revolution, when Antoine Laurent Lavoisier, the father of modern chemistry, began to investigate the nature of fire. Like Aristotle, eighteenth-century scientists believed that fire was an element, involving the release of a substance called "phlogiston." They expended rivers of ink trying to define phlogiston and to explain why it was so elusive. Experimenting with oxygen, which had been recently isolated, Lavoisier showed that there was no such thing as phlogiston. From his researches he drew two conclusions: that in nature no matter is lost (the law of the indestructibility or conservation of matter), and that Aristotle's elements are not final entities at all but compounds of more basic chemical elements. Lavoisier drew up a table of thirty-two such elements (oxygen, nitrogen, hydrogen, etc.), most of which he identified correctly.

It had long been suspected that elements—that is, substances that cannot be changed into different substances—are made up of identical, minute entities. In the seventeenth and eighteenth centuries, scientists discussed such entities at great length, using the old Greek term "atoms." But the concept had no practical value for want of a method of identifying and measuring its units.

Atoms became an operative concept early in the nineteenth century, thanks to the researches of John Dalton, an English schoolmaster. Pondering the results obtained in experiments on gases, Dalton concluded in 1803 that they could be explained only by assuming that each element was in fact composed of identical atoms. He devised means of estimating the relative weights of the atoms of a number of elements and formulated a theory about the manner in which they combined to form chemical compounds. What distinguished one element from another, according to Dalton, was the weight of their respective atoms.

In the decades that followed Dalton's discoveries, chemists made great progress in ascertaining the precise atomic weight of the elements. This work culminated in the brilliant hypothesis of the Russian chemist Dmitri Mendeleev, who discovered that, if one listed all the then known elements in order of their atomic weight, they seemed to group themselves into several categories, each endowed with common properties. Mendeleev published in 1869 a list of the elements grouped in the form of a "Periodic Table." Some of the categories did not have their full complement of elements—a fact that suggested (for science assumed a symmetry in nature) that other, as yet unknown, elements existed. The Periodic Table in effect predicted the atomic weight of elements not yet discovered. Subsequent researches confirmed Mendeleev's intuition, and in time the empty spaces of the Periodic Table were filled in with elements newly found or artificially produced.

BIOLOGICAL DISCOVERIES

The identification of the atom as the ultimate entity of inorganic matter encouraged a search for a similar entity in living tissue. It had been known since the early seventeenth century, when the microscope first allowed men to take a closer look at tissues, that certain plants consisted of identical cell-like structures. But the "cellular theory" gained general acceptance only as a result of the researches of two German scientists, the botanist Matthias Schleiden and the biologist Theodor Schwann. Schleiden published a paper in 1838 showing the ubiquity of the cell nucleus and suggesting its relationship to the formation of cells. The following year, Schwann demonstrated the cellular nature of animal tissue. It now became evident that plants and animals, from the simplest to the most complex, are constructed of the same elementary "building blocks." Shortly afterward it was shown that all cells consist of protoplasm, a complex of chemical substances that was recognized as the basis of life.

Investigations along these lines yielded important insights into the nature of disease. In the third quarter of the nineteenth century, the German botanist Ferdinand J. Cohn isolated minute plants known as "bacteria," showed that they are responsible for many diseases, and indicated ways of neutralizing them by means of antibodies. On the basis of his findings, Louis Pasteur and Robert Koch developed the science of immunology which succeeded in greatly reducing deaths from communicable diseases.

ENERGY

One of the greatest mysteries confronting physical science in the eighteenth and early nineteenth centuries was the nature of light and heat. Early science had regarded them as material objects, and even Lavoisier listed them in his table as regular elements. This view, however, had one obvious flaw: unlike all other known material substances, light and heat seemed to have no measurable weight. To reconcile this contradiction, some scientists had recourse to the concept of "imponderability." By "imponderables" they meant material objects that were by definition incapable of being weighed. Heat was regarded as an "imponderable" fluid that passed from object to object as if it were some kind of juice. But not everyone was satisfied with this explanation, and experiments continued in the hope of isolating the material substance of heat.

A significant advance in solving this problem was made by Benjamin Thompson, Count Rumford. A native of Massachusetts, Thompson left the United States during the Revolution because of his loyalist sympathies and spent the remainder of his life in the service of various European monarchs. In 1798–1799 he carried out experiments that cast serious doubt on the materiality of heat. In one of these experiments, he placed the tip of a metal borer and the mouth of a cannon in a box filled with water and then proceeded to bore the cannon, at the same time measuring the resultant changes in the temperature of the water. He found that there was no limit to the amount of heat that the action of boring could generate. From this evidence, Thompson concluded that heat was not a material body, for no material body could be produced in unlimited quantities. He suggested instead that it was a "kind of motion."

To James Joule, an English physicist active in the 1840s, belongs the main credit for demonstrating the correctness of Thompson's hypothesis. Joule dissolved a piece of zinc in acid and measured the amount of heat produced by this dissolution. Next, he measured the heat produced by the dissolution of an identical piece of zinc in a battery wired to an electric generator. The second measurement turned out to be smaller. What happened to the missing heat? Joule showed that its exact equivalent could be recovered either in the heat which the passage of the electric current produced in the wire, or in the work performed by the generator which the current had activated. In other words, no heat disappeared, and some heat changed into mechanical motion. These findings led the German Hermann von Helmholtz in 1847 to formulate the law of the conservation of energy. The term *energy* was applied to a variety of phenomena previously regarded as unrelated: first heat, electricity, and magnetism, and subsequently light. These forms of energy were discovered to be interchangeable and capable of being transformed into mechanical work. The law of the conservation of energy (a counterpart of Lavoisier's law of the conservation of matter) held that one form of physical activity can be converted into another, the total amount of such activity in the world remaining unchanged. It is widely regarded as the single most important scientific generalization of the nineteenth century. If conservation of matter gave birth to the science of chemistry, conservation of energy produced the science of physics.

At midcentury there existed in the West a fairly consistent scientific outlook. Its method was defined as inductive and empirical: the careful accumulation of carefully gathered data, and the rejection of anything that could not be verified by the senses or scientific apparatus. Nature, which was regarded as having an objective reality, was seen as operating according to firm, undeviating laws, the most fundamental of which were the conservation of energy and of matter.

The Theory of "Natural Selection"

The theory of evolution, especially in its Darwinian form, exerted the same impact on the biological sciences that the conservation theories had exerted on the investigation of chemical and physical processes. It too linked phenomena previously not considered significantly related to each other, namely the structure and organs of animals and their natural environment.

Until the early nineteenth century, theologians, philosophers, and scientists alike accepted the biblical account that the universe had come into being in the single act of Creation. Every kind of animal and plant, every river and mountain, was believed to have been created in its finished form, exactly as it appeared. This view implied the permanence of animal and plant species. Insofar as everything was eternally fixed, the main function of the naturalist was to classify. The great eighteenth-century Swedish botanist Carolus Linnaeus, true to this concept, devoted his life to the task of classifying and naming the known plants.

However, in biology, as in chemistry and physics, evidence continued to accumulate that could not be reconciled with the traditional view. Toward the end of the eighteenth century, Chevalier de Lamarck, a professor at the Parisian Botanical Gardens, found it impossible to fit some of the plants placed in his care into the accepted classification system. In search of explanations, he concluded that the separation between the species was less clear than the science of the time believed. Gradually, he developed a theory of evolution that he published in 1809 in a book titled *Philosophie Zoologique*. Plants and animals, he argued, were different not so much because God had made them differently, but because in an effort to adjust to their environment they had to assume different shapes and develop different organs. Thus, for example, a whale whose diet consisted of soft plankton shed its teeth, while a giraffe, to reach leaves high up on trees, kept on stretching its neck until it acquired its present monstrous proportions. Lamarck assumed that the characteristics that an animal acquired during its lifetime were passed on to its progeny.

Additional evolutionary evidence accumulated from geology. The existence of layers apparently from differing epochs suggested that the earth also was not created at once in its present form, but underwent constant change. Sir Charles Lyell's *Principles of Geology* (1830–1833) helped to disseminate the view that the earth was not the result of a single act of Creation, but had evolved slowly over a long period of time.

The growing evidence did not for a long time overthrow the static outlook in biology, because no one could satisfactorily explain how the variations of animal species had come about. (Lamarck's theory was regarded as a joke.) The appearance in 1859 of Charles Darwin's *Origin of Species*, which contained a massive body of evidence in support of evolution and a persuasive theory to explain its workings, made, therefore, a tremendous impression.

Darwin's grandfather, Erasmus, had been one of the leading exponents of the theory of evolution, and he himself became well acquainted with it at an early age. Intrigued, as were many of his contemporaries, by its mysterious operations, he accepted in 1831 (at the age of twenty-two) the post of chief naturalist on a scientific expedition exploring the South Pacific and the coast of Latin America in the ship *Beagle*. The *Beagle* cruised leisurely for five years in the southern waters, affording Darwin an excellent opportunity to study closely a number of animal species. On the Galápagos Islands, off Ecuador, he discovered a perfect biological laboratory, for here animals had been able to develop on different islands for millions of years with a minimum of external interference. A comparison of the Galápagos animals with related animals from the mainland of South America or with fossils permitted Darwin to discard the notion of a special Creation. He concluded that animals do indeed evolve with time, and that they do so in response to their environment.

In analyzing the processes of evolution, Darwin found it useful to employ a concept first formulated by Thomas Malthus in his *Essay on the Principle of Population*, published in 1798 (see Chapter 17). Malthus had used this concept

Early in his career the botanist Carolus Linnaeus explored Lapland collecting specimens. He is decked out in his Lapp costume in this portrait.

Ranked as the leading comparative anatomist of his time, Thomas Huxley also made major contributions to physiology, physiography, geology, and cellular study.

—"the struggle for existence"—to explain how the rate of population growth was related to the availability of food supplies. This notion suggested to Darwin the principle of "natural selection," which he formulated (but did not announce) in 1837–1838. Aware that evolution could not gain acceptance unless it was shown precisely *how* animals changed in response to the environment, he spent twenty years after the return of the *Beagle* patiently sifting his data.

In June, 1858, Darwin received a letter and an unpublished scientific paper from Alfred R. Wallace, a young naturalist residing in Malaya, which indicated that Wallace was on the same track. Darwin therefore decided to make his theory public, and the following year brought out *On the Origin of Species by Means of Natural Selection.*

The fundamental assumption of Darwin's theory is that since all organisms live in intimate dependence on their natural environment, to survive and propagate they must engage in a "struggle for existence." Plants fight for light and water, while animals seek to escape their predators and compete for food. To succeed in this endless struggle, organisms must adapt. Adaptation is made possible by the appearance of "variants," that is, some organs or qualities that are particularly suitable to given conditions. As to precisely how these "variants" first occur in organisms, Darwin was not clear. But this was not a fatal flaw in his doctrine, because he was not so much concerned with the problem of why animals happen to be different as with why some differences help them survive and flourish while others cause them to disappear. In other words, he was concerned not with how the fittest "arrive," but with how they "survive."

Given the fact that variants do occur, some are obviously better suited to assist the organism in coping with its particular environment than others. If certain insects, for example, happen to develop coloring that blends with their environment, they can better elude the birds that prey on them and are likely to produce more progeny with similar characteristics. On the other hand, insects whose coloring stands out perish and with time become extinct. In this manner, nature may be said to engage in a constant process of "selecting" those organisms that are most suitable for the particular conditions it creates. This process of natural selection constitutes the heart of Darwin's theory of evolution. He summarizes it in *Origin of Species* as follows:

> If under changing conditions of life organic beings present individual differences in almost every part of their structure . . . if there be, owing to their geometrical rate of increase, a severe struggle for life at some age, season, or year . . . then, considering the infinite complexity of the relations of all organic beings to each other and to their conditions of life, causing an infinite diversity in structure, constitution, and habits, to be advantageous to them, it would be a most extraordinary fact if no variations had ever occurred useful to each being's own welfare, in the same manner as so many variations have occurred useful to man. But if variations useful to any organic being ever do occur, assuredly individuals thus characterized will have the best chance of being preserved in the struggle for life; and from the strong principle of inheritance, these will tend to produce offspring similarly characterized. This principle of preservation, or the survival of the fittest, I have called Natural Selection. It leads to the improvement of each creature in relation to its organic and inorganic conditions of life.

Natural selection explains why we encounter such immense variety of biological forms: variety of forms results from the adjustment of living organisms to that variety of conditions created by nature.

Darwin, of course, did not "discover" evolution. But by the weight of carefully observed evidence, he made what had been a dubious hypothesis a widely accepted scientific theory. The immediate reaction to *Origin of Species* was mixed. A number of scientists found it convincing and accepted it without reservations. Among them was Thomas Huxley, who called himself "Darwin's bulldog" because he championed Darwin's theories wherever they were assailed. (Darwin himself disliked controversy, preferring a sheltered life.) And the opposition was stanch. Evolution challenged the biblical account of Creation and placed man on a par with the other primates such as apes and monkeys. Religious authorities on the whole rejected the theory of natural selection at first, especially in Protestant countries, where the Bible was widely read and often literally interpreted.

A famous early encounter between the Darwinists and their opponents, indicative of the passions that Darwin's theory had aroused, took place in 1860 at Oxford. The leading figure among the opponents was Samuel Wilberforce, bishop of Oxford, popularly known as "Soapy Sam." He had not read Darwin's book, but expected to have an easy time demolishing it by ridicule. In the course of his speech, which the elegant audience received warmly, he turned to Huxley and asked him whether he traced his descent from the apes on his grandfather's or his grandmother's side.

Huxley held his fire until the audience clamored for a reply, then rose to say:

I asserted—and I repeat— that a man has no reason to be ashamed of having an ape for his grandfather. If there were an ancestor whom I should feel ashamed in recalling, it would rather be a *man*—a man of restless and versatile intellect—who, not content with success in his own sphere of activity, plunges into scientific questions with which he has no real acquaintance, only to obscure them by an aimless rhetoric, and distract the attention of his hearers from the real point at issue by eloquent digressions and skilled appeals to religious prejudice.°

In the ensuing pandemonium one lady fainted, another jumped on her chair, and the bishop for once was left speechless.

It would be wrong to regard all opposition to Darwinism as due either to ignorance or prejudice. Darwin himself was well aware that his theory failed to answer many questions. How did variations occur in the first place? How did animals *gradually* develop adaptive organs or features (e.g., the shock-giving organ of the electric eel) that were of no use until *fully* developed and therefore could have no effect on natural selection until then? And why could man produce no new species by selective breeding? Darwin grappled with such problems to the end of his life. Some remain unsolved to this day.

The problem of the emergence of variations, or the "arrival" of the fittest, was in large measure solved around the turn of the century by so-called neo-Darwinian biologists. In the 1890s German biologist August Weismann proved that characteristics acquired by organisms during their lifetime could not be passed on to their progeny. Body cells and germ cells were distinct entities, without influence on one another. These findings fairly finished the old Lamarckian hypothesis that even Darwin had at times found attractive. (Lamarckian theories were revived in Stalinist Russia.) In the early 1900s a Dutch botanist, Hugo de Vries, showed that variants are caused by sudden changes or "mutations" in the germ cells. A mutation produces offspring with some distinct quality that its parents lack. Natural selection then determines whether the variant is useful and worthy of preservation or a freak and doomed to disappear.

Science and Philosophy

The great discoveries in the fields of chemistry, physics, and biology produced a veritable cult of science and engendered something that had no precedent in human history: a scientific culture—that is, a comprehensive interpretation of life parallel to a religious or philosophical outlook. This culture dominated Western thought between approximately 1840 and 1880. It demanded that all opinions accord with the method and the findings of natural science. To gain acceptance, philosophical, religious, political, economic, and aesthetic views had to be "scientific."

The new intellectual current is known by a variety of names, of which "positivism," coined by the French philosopher Auguste Comte (see below), is probably the most widely accepted. Positivism holds that man is not a unique being but an ordinary product of nature. His life, both as an individual and as a member of society, is subject to laws as consistent as those of the inorganic world. He

---

°Leonard Huxley, *Life and Letters of T. H. Huxley,* (1908). Of course, the Darwinists did not claim man's descent from apes, but the descent of both man and ape from a common primate ancestor.

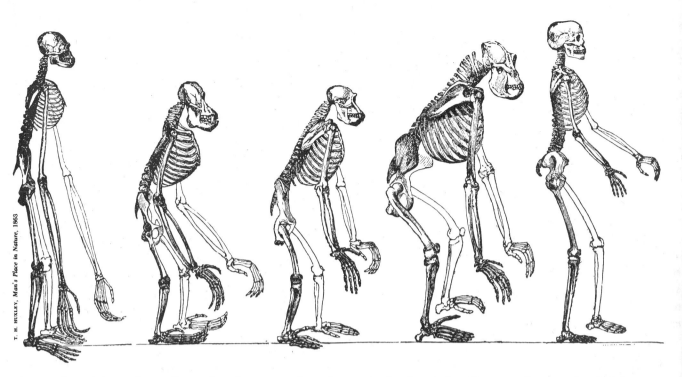

has neither soul nor free will. In the ultimate analysis, he is merely chemical compound. Such a view was diametrically opposed to the Romantic concept of man as his self-creator.

Interestingly, practicing scientists were much more cautious in drawing inferences from their researches than were scientific amateurs and popularizers. Scientists had an instinctive dread of going beyond the evidence at hand. Observation told them nothing about God or life after death or freedom of the will, and therefore they preferred to leave such subjects alone. Darwin himself professed to be an agnostic—one who holds God to be unknowable. Some scientists remained religious. Scientific discovery, instead of destroying their faith, merely intensified it, for it revealed the universe as even more complicated and mysterious than had been suspected. In 1872 the German physiologist Emil Du Bois-Reymond delivered a famous address called "On the Limits of Natural Science" in which he denied that thinking could be explained in chemical terms and asserted that man could never penetrate the ultimate mysteries of nature because he himself was a part of that nature which he was investigating.

The most extreme claims on behalf of science were advanced by the so-called materialists, philosophers who argued that all phenomena without exception are ultimately reducible either to matter or to energy. The idea that man was a mechanism composed entirely of material substances had occurred to philosophers even before the discoveries of modern chemistry and biology. In the eighteenth century there appeared in France "materialists" who denied the existence of the soul. Julien de La Mettrie, the author of *L'Homme-machine (Man a Machine*, 1748), pioneered the movement; Baron Paul Holbach's *Système de la Nature (System of Nature*, 1770) made it notorious. Both La Mettrie and Holbach defined consciousness and thought as physical phenomena. The influence of these two philosophers, due to persecution by church and state and to the primitive

Thomas Huxley reproduced skeletons of (from left) a gibbon, an orangutan, a chimpanzee, a gorilla, and a man in an 1863 work on man's place in nature, pointing out the similarities and differences in body structures.

condition of eighteenth-century science, was limited, and the triumph of Romanticism put their works into temporary oblivion.

Materialism revived around 1840. Its main propagators were a group of young German philosophers called "Left Hegelians," whose leading spirit was Ludwig Feuerbach. Though Feuerbach himself was not a materialist in the strict sense of the word, he gave the principal stimulus to the emergence of modern materialism. Feuerbach addressed himself to the question: What is the origin of the idea of God, and, by extension, of many other ideas which the senses are unable to perceive? He was not content to dismiss religion as prejudice, ignorance, or mythmaking, as were some of his contemporaries, but investigated the psychological roots of religious sentiment. He was struck that man ascribed to divinity the very qualities that he himself most sorely lacked, for example, omniscience, omnipotence, generosity, beauty, and so on. From this observation he concluded that religion represented what today would be called a "wish fantasy." Man "projected" his own aspirations onto an imaginary being. "Religion," he wrote in *The Essence of Christianity*, "is the relation of man to his own nature . . . but to his nature not recognized as his own, but regarded as another nature, separate, nay, contradistinguished from his own. . . ." By creating this fantasy-wish "other" nature, according to Feuerbach, man estranged or "alienated" himself. The task of modern thought was to return to man all those qualities of which he had divested himself—to recreate "true man." Feuerbach called his system "anthropological" because it freed man from the tyranny of religious and philosophical abstraction with which he had surrounded himself, placed him at the center of the universe, and literally made him his own god.

The Feuerbachian notion of man had great appeal to radical intellectuals and provided the philosophical foundation of both anarchism and Marxism. (See Chapter 19). The vision of a "true man," unencumbered by illusion of any kind, free in the fullest sense of the word, is common to all modern radical movements. In the twentieth century it re-emerged most explicitly in existentialism.

Materialism reached its apogee in the 1850s. Bookstalls were flooded with works condemning idealism and religion and reducing life to chemical processes. The materialists delighted in shocking the public with statements like: "Thought bears the same relation to the brain that bile bears to the liver or urine to the kidneys," and "Man is what he eats." "Is life worth living?," asked one popular pun, whose answer was, "It depends on the liver."

Public opinion was shocked and disturbed by materialism, but not persuaded. Even the educated public of the time found it difficult to accept that man could be scientifically studied at all, let alone that he could only be so approached. Faith in the uniqueness of life processes was deeply ingrained. It was generally believed that living organisms possessed a "vital force," a life-giving substance (not unlike phlogiston) that fundamentally differentiated them from inorganic objects. This belief made people skeptical about the possibility of medicine becoming a "science." The most influential attack on this attitude was Claude Bernard's *Introduction to Experimental Medicine*, published in Paris in 1865. Bernard, a celebrated physiologist, denied the existence of any "vital force" and asserted that living organisms could and should be studied experimentally.

The new concept of man led to the emergence of experimental psychology. In

Leipzig in 1879, Wilhelm Wundt opened the first "psychological laboratory" and proceeded to measure and classify various manifestations of human consciousness.

Once man had been deprived of his unique status and reduced to a mechanism, it was inevitable that the society made up of such mechanisms would also be subjected to scientific interpretation. The study of society became a science, sociology. Its task was to apply to society empirical methods of investigation, to discover its operating principles, and thus to predict its future behavior.

Sociology originated in the second quarter of the century. Its founder, Auguste Comte, decided that the progress of man from the beginnings of recorded history was essentially a progress of enlightenment involving a gradual transition from lower to higher stages of understanding. All knowledge goes through three phases: theological, metaphysical, and "positive" or scientific. In the earliest phase, man attributes happenings to the will of God or gods. In astronomy, to take one example, he interprets the motions of the planets as responses to divine directives. In the metaphysical phase of knowledge, he discovers that nature obeys firm rules. He still believes that behind these rules lies a will, but he now sees this will as rational and predictable. Astronomy reached the metaphysical stage in the seventeenth century with the help of Kepler and Galileo. Knowledge enters its final, positive stage when it is realized that nature obeys no superior will, irrational or rational, but its own immutable laws. This happened in astronomy with the discoveries of Newton. The more complex a branch of knowledge, the slower it is to attain this positive stage. Mathematics, being the simplest (in the sense that it depends on no previous body of knowledge), became positive earliest, for no one had ever attributed algebraic or geometric laws to divine volition. The study of society, being the most complex, remained longest in the throes of theological or metaphysical explanations.

Comte felt that the time had come to develop a positive science of society that would reveal the immutable laws governing human relations. In his principal work, *Treatise on Positive Philosophy* (1830–1842), he outlined a grand scheme for the development of knowledge, culminating in the development of sociology. In a society of the future, he believed, human actions will rest on positive or scientific knowledge, and differences of opinion will disappear. Men will no more quarrel over what was right or wrong than they quarrel over the properties of chemical elements. Any disputes that may arise will be settled by experts.

Comte led a sheltered life, refusing even to read newspapers, so as not to be distracted from his supreme task of creating a sociology. But life had its revenge. Three years after he had brought out the final installment of the *Treatise*, he fell in love with a much younger woman, who did not reciprocate his feelings and who soon passed away. Comte was so shaken by this experience that he began to tamper with his admirably lucid system, introducing into it mystical elements that took it right back from the "positive" to the "theological" phase. With some of his followers he created a new "positivist religion" which replaced the worship of God with that of humanity. This religion had its churches, priests, and ritual; Comte's deceased love became humanity's "patron saint." Another group of followers, led by the lexicographer Maximilian Littré, broke away from

Comte, declaring him insane, and remained faithful to pure "positivism." Under Littré's guidance the movement flourished, spreading far beyond France. Because of the importance it attached to knowledge as a factor of progress, positivism had much appeal to intellectuals in non-industrial countries, where indeed knowledge was all that lent itself to development. Positivism boosted the intellectual's sense of self-importance. In Russia, Poland, and Brazil, to mention only three examples, it fairly dominated opinion in the second half of the nineteenth century.

The most promising tool for predicting human behavior seemed the newly developed discipline of social statistics. Henry Thomas Buckle, in his influential *History of Civilization in England* (1857–1861), argued that statistics "reveal the great social law that the moral actions of men are the product not of their volition, but of their antecedents." As an example of the predictable recurrence of human actions, Buckle pointed to the fact that London and Paris post offices received year after year the same proportion of letters bearing neither the name nor the address of the intended recipient. Similar patterns could be found in statistics of marriages, murders, and suicides. Indeed, a French mathematician of the time showed that an occurrence seemingly as haphazard as the proportion of soldiers in the Prussian army who died every year from the kick of a mule remained constant. Statistics and sociology developed from the first in intimate association.

Biological evolution also received social application. This task was attempted by Herbert Spencer and Thomas Huxley. Even before the appearance of *Origin of Species*, Spencer had speculated about the resemblance of society to a biological organism and the possibility of studying history in evolutionary terms. Darwin's book provided him with the necessary theoretical framework to formulate a theory known as Social Darwinism. To Spencer, the "struggle for existence" that Darwin had found in nature was a natural concomitant of social life as well: man, too, was engaged in a constant struggle against his fellows, from which only the fittest emerged victorious. Free economic competition performed the same function in society as natural selection performed in nature. From this analogy, Spencer and Huxley concluded that the less one interfered with the operations of society, the greater the assurance that the fittest, i.e., the best, would come out on top. This was laissez faire at its most extreme, far beyond what Adam Smith and his immediate followers had envisioned. Social Darwinism had great appeal to a part of the business community, for by equating wealth and power with "fitness" and both with "goodness" it provided a pseudo-scientific excuse for disclaiming responsibility for one's less fortunate fellow men. It was rejected by socialists and anarchists, who considered social conflict artificial and transitory and social harmony the natural condition of man. A most persuasive argument against Social Darwinism was made by the Russian anarchist Peter Kropotkin in his study *Mutual Aid as a Factor in Evolution* (1890–1902). Basing his argument on evidence from nature and history, Kropotkin maintained that cooperation was an even more powerful factor in life than struggle, and that it best assured the survival of species.

Darwinism, both in its original and in its Spencerian-Huxleian forms, gave rise to a great variety of pseudo-scientific theories. It lent itself admirably to the justi-

The French philosopher Auguste Comte not only originated sociology as a science but coined the term as well.

fication of oppression or brutality by enabling those on top to claim that the mere fact of being in power proved their greater right to existence. It thus encouraged the mood of violence that became very pronounced after 1870. According to Jacques Barzun,

> No one who has not waded through some sizeable part of the literature of the period 1870–1914 has any conception of the extent to which it is one long call for blood, nor of the variety of parties, classes, nations, and races whose blood was separately and contradictorily clamored for by the enlightened citizens of the ancient civilization of Europe.°

The most pernicious of the hate theories that developed at this time was racialism. Its beginnings antedate Darwin's book, but it flourished best in the atmosphere produced by such concepts as "struggle for existence" and "survival of the fittest" (the latter phrase coined by Huxley). Its founder, the French writer Count Joseph de Gobineau, argued in *The Inequality of Human Races* (1853–1855) that there is a hierarchy of "races." The highest race consists of the Germans (by which term he meant not the population of modern Germany, but the blonde, blue-eyed inhabitants of northern France, Belgium, and England). Because these "Germans" had avoided mixing with "inferior" Semitic and Negroid races, they were destined to rule the world. This theory was later developed by a Germanized Englishman, Houston Stewart Chamberlain, in his *Foundations of the Nineteenth Century* (1899). Chamberlain held that modern-day Germans were the only pure Aryans, and that they alone could save Europe and European civilization from the destructive assaults of such lower races as the Jews, Negroes, and Orientals.

In the long run, the so-called science of society failed to produce anything resembling scientific laws of human behavior, but often buttressed vested interests, social as well as ethnic, and prepared the ground for theories of extermination.

One of the by-products of the scientific spirit, especially in its Left Hegelian form, was a new interpretation of biblical history.

Science and Religion

Textual criticism carried out in the 1830s and 1840s, mostly at German universities, revealed the Bible to be a compilation written at different historic periods. Like the earth and its inhabitants, it now appeared as not having been created at once, but having grown. Readers of the Pentateuch (the first five books of the Bible) had long noted, of course, that it gives alternate and differing versions of a number of events, such as the Creation of man or the Flood. Theologians had exerted a great deal of ingenuity in trying to reconcile these discrepancies. The new, critical school of biblical scholarship, by contrast, sought to peel away the ambiguities and to disassemble the Pentateuch into its component parts. It demonstrated that the Pentateuch consisted of several distinct texts that had been woven together by an unknown editor or editors. Textual analysis of the Gospels raised the possibility that they were not accounts of four separate eyewitnesses. The Left Hegelian Bruno Bauer, in two books written in the 1840s, advanced the proposition that the Gospels according to John,

---

°Jacques Barzun, *Darwin, Marx, Wagner: Critique of a Heritage* (1941).

Luke, and Matthew derived from one common source, namely Mark.

These findings coincided with a new interpretation of the origins of Judaism and Christianity. The new philosophers and historians denied that they were divinely inspired creeds and treated them instead as ordinary legends. In his *Life of Jesus* (1835), David Strauss, another Left Hegelian, presented Christianity as a "myth" unconsciously created by a community raised on Jewish expectations of a Messiah. Others tried to cut through this "myth" to the authentic historical kernel in biblical history. Miracles were rejected in favor of scientific explanations. The most famous attempt to rationalize and humanize Christianity was made by the French positivist Ernest Renan in his *Life of Jesus* (1863). Renan, who had visited Palestine, sought to depict the story of Jesus against a genuine historical and geographic background. He also tried to provide scientifically plausible explanations of supernatural incidents in Christ's story. His account of Christ's death, for example, rested on medical evidence, providing a clinical account of the hemorrhage that crucifixion would cause in the human body. Although he was a deeply religious person who thought to enhance man's admiration for Christ by his realistic portrayal, Renan shocked his contemporaries and lost his university post.

Realism in Literature   The aesthetic counterpart of the scientific spirit was known as Realism. A movement based on Realist principles emerged in the 1830s, matured in the 1850s, and dominated Western literature and art from then until the late 1880s.

Realism rested on the premise that man was an intrinsic part of the natural order and a product of his environment. It rejected the Romantic idealization of man as a being endowed with limitless potential. Hippolyte Taine, the founder of positivist literary criticism, assumed that writers—like mankind in general—were molded by three forces: heredity, milieu, and the spirit of their times. Human values, ideals, behavior, and even manner of thinking could always be traced to these three factors. "Vice and virtue," he wrote, "are products like vitriol and sugar." The task of the Realist writer was to penetrate and depict truthfully the human environment in all its complexity. The writer's attention was to shift from the individual and his inner life to the web of circumstance in which this individual found himself and which made him what he was—that is, in effect, to the society within which he lived and worked.

The Realist school demanded from the writer first and foremost a portrayal of the "real" world. By this it emphatically did not mean a world populated by demons, by men who lost their noses or sold their shadows, or by solitary heroes who roamed Alpine peaks or carried a curse for having killed an albatross over the South Pole. It meant essentially a depiction of nineteenth-century working Europe. Its dramas were small: the cumulative effect of daily misunderstandings, petty squabbles, little injustices committed and suffered without awareness of their ultimate implications. Proceeding from this view, the Realists concentrated on ordinary people, usually from the working class or the petty bourgeoisie, in their ordinary surroundings.

In a world in which little of a dramatic nature happened, action became of secondary importance, and the writer's attention shifted to detail, to things which—insignificant in themselves—in their totality give life its specific quality.

With furious energy Balzac worked as much as 18 hours a day for months on end on his Comédie Humaine. ***This study is by Louis Boulanger.***

This detail had to be rendered accurately and objectively. The writer was expected to stay out of the picture and to function as a dispassionate recorder; under no circumstances was he to moralize. Since everything that happens is "natural," in the sense that it has definite causes, everything must be recorded, including the ugly and the repulsive. The novel proved to be the medium best suited to depict the environment in all its realistic detail. In the second third of the century, it was by far the most popular literary form.

Realism originated in France, which had never fully surrendered to Romanticism and now once more assumed its traditional role as the aesthetic leader of Europe. From there it quickly spread to other countries. The founder of Realism was the Frenchman Honoré de Balzac, whose social novels began to appear in the 1830s. Balzac depicted the times so accurately and in such detail that his novels constitute an excellent source of information on social conditions in France under Louis Philippe. In 1842 Balzac brought out the first volume of his monumental *Comédie Humaine* (intended as a modern counterpart of Dante's *Divine Comedy*), which at the time of his death (1850) comprised 47 volumes. One can obtain some notion of the complexity of this narrative from the fact that it has a cast of more than 2,000 characters.

Realism acquired an articulate program in the early 1850s. It was first formulated by the painter Gustave Courbet, who publicly announced that he had his fill of saints and angels and intended henceforth to paint only "the modern and the common." His canvases, including the well-known *Stone Breakers* (page 422), were barred from the official Salon, but he won a circle of supporters, including some writers who translated his sentiments into theoretical manifestoes, and launched literary Realism on its way.

GEMALDEGALERIE, DRESDEN; DEUTSCHE FOTOTHEK (DESTROYED, WWII)

The Stone Breakers *(1849) by Courbet. When the International Exhibition of 1855 barred his pictures, Courbet held a one-man show by the gates under the sign, "Realism—G. Courbet."*

The new movement had its first great success with the appearance in 1857 of Gustave Flaubert's *Madame Bovary*, the story of a lonely provincial woman who betrays her husband and is herself in turn betrayed by her lover. The incident was commonplace (in fact, it was based on an authentic case) and the characters most ordinary, yet the whole had a profoundly moving effect. Flaubert showed that the lives of small people could furnish material for an intensely dramatic narrative. The shock that *Madame Bovary* produced and that caused the book to be impounded by the authorities derived not so much from its description of adultery, a topic frequent enough in literature, but from Flaubert's deliberate refusal to pass moral judgment on it.

From the 1860s onward, the European literary market was flooded with realistic novels depicting an immense variety of human situations previously considered unworthy of serious literature. Readers could learn from them how Swiss shopkeepers, Russian foresters, Polish peasants, Jewish traveling salesmen, Italian fishermen, and Prussian merchants lived. The stress was on the seamy side of life: poverty and drabness when dealing with the poor, immorality and corruption when dealing with the rich.

In England Realism found its main expression in the social novel. Less "objective" than the French Realist novel, it was written with the intention of awakening public conscience and spurring social reform. Some of the novels of Charles Dickens belong to this category, at least in part (for example, the prison scenes in his *Pickwick Papers* (1836–1837) and the description of the workhouse in *Oliver Twist* (1837–1838), as do the novels of Charles Kingsley and Mrs. Gaskell. William Thackeray's and Anthony Trollope's canvases of British life are more typically Realist in the French sense, tending to emphasize description and atmosphere.

Realism reached its greatest creative heights in Russia, a country that had few outlets for its thoughts and feelings besides literature. In fiction it was possible to communicate ideas that censorship would have forbidden in any other guise. Belles-lettres, and in particular the novel, performed in Russia the combined functions of the political pamphlet, the religious tract, and the uncensored newspaper.

Russian literature boasts several novels that qualify as Realist in the best sense of the word, among them Sergei Aksakov's *Family Chronicle* (1856), a description of the life of the author's ancestors on the Eastern frontier, and I. A. Goncharov's *Oblomov* (1859), the story of a slothful landlord. But the greatest Russian novelists were adherents of Realism only in a limited sense. While they set their stories in the contemporary world and placed their heroes in a specific social environment, they did not, as a rule, obey the injunction to refrain from moralizing. Count Leo Tolstoy's novels are full of preaching. *Anna Karenina* (1875–1877), like *Madame Bovary*, deals with the theme of adultery, but, unlike Flaubert, Tolstoy does not hesitate to condemn his heroine. Fëdor Dostoevsky's early novels (e.g., *Poor Folk*, 1846) were written in a Realist manner. In his later work, that is, in all his great novels, he turned political pamphleteer. In Ivan Turgenev the moralistic element is least noticeable. *Fathers and Sons* (1862) is a remarkably accurate portrayal of the conflict between generations—the old Romantic-liberal one and the new positivist-socialist one. The author's attitude is so detached that one cannot decide on the basis of the novel where his sympathies lie.

Toward the end of the century, writers in pursuit of extreme realism produced works that were virtually static. In *A Lovely Day* (1881), Henri Céard recounts an abortive affair between a middle-aged, married housewife and her neighbor. The two plan an outing, the woman expecting to be seduced, the man expecting to seduce her. As the day progesses she grows bored with him and he with her. In the evening they return home, separately. The description of that uneventful episode in the life of two completely uninteresting people occupies 200 pages. Realism pushed to such lengths departed from its original intent and imperceptibly shaded into new forms of literary expression that we shall discuss under the heading of Modernism (Chapter 25).

Nineteenth-century Western culture was too rich and too diversified for any single movement to obtain a monopoly on it. If we divide the century into Romantic and Realist periods, it is only to isolate its dominant trends. Just as, at the height of idealism, scientists were quietly pursuing their laboratory experiments, so in the age of scientific hegemony voices of protest were heard inveighing against science and all it stood for. These voices came from thinkers who did not believe that science had all the answers or that man was a mere plaything of circumstances.

The anti-positivist protest movement in the second half of the nineteenth century lacked unity or a formal program. What it had in common were certain general attitudes. It stressed deep-seated, non-rational drives: man's instinct for violence, longing for power, craving for beauty. It glorified those periods in history when these drives seemed to have been best satisfied (such as pre-Socratic

In his diary Leo Tolstoy urged himself to "leave a piece of flesh in the inkwell every time you dip your pen."

Greece and the Renaissance) and looked pessimistically at a future dominated by liberal-socialist egalitarianism.

A leading thinker in this category was Friedrich Nietzsche, an expatriate German philologist and philosopher residing in Switzerland. In the 1870s and 1880s Nietzsche wrote a number of works in which he savagely criticized the moral codes of Christian civilization as stifling natural instincts and leading to spiritual degeneration. He looked back to antiquity and to the Renaissance as great eras of "free spirits." So did his friend and teacher, the Swiss historian Jacob Burckhardt. Burckhardt's *The Civilization of the Renaissance in Italy* (1860) is not only a classic of historical writing and a pioneering attempt at cultural history; it is also a nostalgic evocation of a time when man was an unfettered individual, when people "knew little of false modesty or of hypocrisy in any shape, [when] not one of them was afraid of singularity, of being and seeming unlike his neighbors."

The anti-positivist reaction took many forms, including a cult of the beautiful, an aesthetic revolt whose adherents admired early Christian and Japanese art, neo-paganism, and everything primitive. There was also a current of pessimism, most notably seen in the writings of the German philosopher Arthur Schopenhauer and the Danish philosopher Søren Kierkegaard.

Some of the bitterest criticism of the scientific culture came from Russia, a country exposed to all the intellectual currents emanating from the West, yet sufficiently distinct to entertain the possibility of choosing a different road. Konstantin Leontiev, an original thinker active between 1850 and 1870, felt revolted by the spectacle of contemporary bourgeois Europe. An aesthete, he believed that there could be no morality without beauty. He considered it unthinkable that bourgeois civilization represented the ultimate achievement of history:

> Would it not be dreadful and offensive to think that Moses climbed Mount Sinai, that the Hellenes built their graceful Acropolis, that the Romans waged the Punic Wars, that the handsome genius, Alexander, in some plumed helmet crossed the Granicus and fought at Arbela, that the apostles preached, the martyrs suffered, the poets sang, the artists painted, and the knights dazzled at tournaments, only in order that a French or German or Russian bourgeois, "individually" or "collectively", garbed in his hideous, comical suit should wallow placidly on the ruins of all this past greatness? . . . One would burn with shame for mankind if this base ideal of general utility, trivial labor, and ignominious commonplace were to triumph forever.

Leontiev's ideal was the Ottoman Empire, whose despotic regime prevented the spread of egalitarianism and thus preserved a marvelous variety of life. He advised Russia to "freeze itself" so as to protect its own diversity from the Western solvent.

All of Dostoevsky's mature works are devoted to attacks on the scientific culture of his time. Dostoevsky detested Buckle and Claude Bernard, ridiculed the positivist prediction of a problemless world, and painted a horrifying picture of the moral consequences of atheism and rationalism. Man was not the reasonable creature of the positivists. He was thoroughly evil; only Christianity with its

Dostoevsky's view of the human condition was influenced by his personal experiences with revolutionaries and a sentence to hard labor in Siberia.

gospel of love and promise of afterlife restrained him. Once man begins to question Christian morality and substitutes for it his own reason, he turns into a killer. Such is the message of Dostoevsky's greatest novels, *Crime and Punishment* (1866), *The Possessed* (1871), and *The Brothers Karamazov* (1880). Dostoevsky rejected as preposterous the vision of a world in which men would live in utter harmony according to reason and their own best interests, for he knew within himself powerful irrational and self-destructive drives. In his *Notes from the Underground* (1864), he carried on a fictional dialogue with a positivist in which he made the following point:

> You are firmly convinced that man will accustom himself [to act as reason and science tell him] once the old, stupid habits are shed, and common-sense and science completely re-educate and direct human nature along its normal paths. You are confident that man will at that time *voluntarily* cease to err, and, so to say, be compelled to desire no conflict between his will and his interests. More than that: at that time, you say, science itself will teach man . . . that he has neither will nor caprice of his own and never had any, and that he is nothing more than a kind of piano key or the stop of an organ; and that besides the world has only laws of nature, so that all he does happens not at all because he wants it, but of itself, by virtue of the laws of nature. In consequence, one only has to discover these laws of nature, and man will no longer bear responsibility for his acts and enjoy a very easy life. All human actions, of themselves, will then be reckoned according to these laws, mathematically, like tables of logarithms, up to 108,000, and entered into an index.
>
> As for me, I will not be surprised in the least if suddenly, for no reason, in the midst of all this general future reasonableness, there should appear a gentleman with an ignoble, or better yet, a reactionary and mocking face, plant his arms at his sides, and tell of all you: "What about it, fellows— let's get rid of all this reasonableness, let's kick it to bits, just so that all these logarithms go to the devil and we can again live as we damn please!" That would be nothing yet, but what hurts is that such a man would be certain to find followers: that is how man is made. And all this for the most insignificant reason, the kind one should think unnecessary even to mention: that is, that man, always and everywhere, no matter who he was, liked to do what he pleased, and not at all what reason and interest told him. . . . Man needs only his *free* will, no matter what it costs and where it leads.

In the nineteenth century such warnings received little attention. When Nietzsche lost his mind in 1889, prevailing opinion saw his insanity as the natural consequence of his ideas. Kierkegaard and Leontiev remained unknown outside of a small circle of friends, while Dostoevsky earned himself the reputation of a novelist addicted to the morbid and abnormal. The overwhelming majority of Westerners, optimistic and confident, believed in progress and science.

MUSEE D'ART ET D'INDUSTRIE, SAINT-ETIENNE

17

The Industrialization of
the Continent

Until the middle of the nineteenth century Great Britain and Belgium were the only countries in the world possessing sizable industries. As we have noted, the introduction of industrial processes into France, Germany, and some other Continental nations did not at first alter significantly either their social structures or the tenor of their everyday life. This occurred only in the second half of the century, with the intense industrialization of Western Europe and the United States. On the European Continent there now emerged an industrial heartland (northern France, the Low Countries, and western Germany) that closely resembled the older area of heavy industrial concentration in the English Midlands and around London. It had the same density of population and concentration of transport and faced many of the same social problems. Together with England, it constituted something like an industrial core, surrounded by a belt of economically peripheral countries where, apart from isolated industrial pockets, the economies remained rural.

For all the resemblances, however, the industrial development of the Continent showed some important deviations from the pattern originally set by England. To begin with, countries that industrialized after England profited from the English experience. What Britain had acquired by trial and error, others could obtain in finished form. No one, for example, had to retrace the steps involved in the construction of the first steam engine—it could be bought ready-made from Boulton & Watt. The result was a telescoping of technological and economic development: processes developed in England in a certain logical order became fused and accelerated.

On the other hand, however, Continental industries experienced a problem that had not confronted Britain until much later: a shortage of markets. Britain enjoyed so great a head start that it had little to fear from competition; it had only to produce to sell. But the spread of industrial methods caused a struggle for outlets. Left to their own devices, few fledgling industries could have survived English competition, and for this reason they relied increasingly on state protection. After 1879 free trade everywhere went on the defensive, giving way to a policy sometimes called neo-Mercantilism. To the modern state, the possession of an industrial economy became a matter of national prestige and even necessity, for on it depended modern military technology. The state could assist the development of native industry in a variety of ways, the most obvious being protective tariffs, military procurements, and colonial conquests. Every country that industrialized after Great Britain did so with active government support, the extent of this support being directly proportionate to the scantiness of the country's resources and the lateness with which it started along the road to industrialization. State intervention reached its culmination in the twentieth century when Communist governments took over direction of the entire process of industrial development.

Constantin Meunier titled his late-nineteenth-century painting of an industrialized landscape in Belgium The Black Country. *At midcentury, heavily exploiting its natural resources, Belgium outpaced all the Continental powers in industrial growth.*

The second half of the nineteenth century was a period of technological progress of a scope unprecedented in the history of mankind. Inventors and industrialists, exploiting the scientific discoveries made in the preceding century and a half, constructed the foundations for the technical civilization of our own time.

The achievement was international, for all the major inventions resulted from contributions of nationals of many countries. For example, electrical energy, one of the seminal discoveries of the age, was first tapped by Italians, related to magnets by a Dane and a Frenchman, made inductive by an Englishman, turned into an economic source of power supply by Germans, and applied to everyday consumer needs by Americans.

The landmarks in industrial history were the discoveries of new sources of motive power. The first of these was steam, which provided the energy that built the industrial might of Britain. In the second half of the century steam was supplemented by electricity and liquid fuels, both of which became economically exploitable between 1870 and 1890.

The harnessing of electrical power had its origins in scientific experiments carried out in the eighteenth century. It had been known since antiquity that a piece of amber that had been vigorously rubbed attracted other bodies. An English physician in the reign of Queen Elizabeth called this mysterious force "electric" (from the Greek word *elektron*, meaning "amber"). In 1745 two scientists devised a method of collecting "electrical" charges in so-called Leyden Jars, but the energy thus stored was static and of little use. In 1780 the Italian Luigi Galvani accidentally discovered that if he touched a frog with wires connected to a Leyden Jar, the frog twitched. He ascribed this reaction to "animal electricity." Another Italian, Alessandro Volta, showed that the frog's reaction was due not to the electricity allegedly stored in its body, but to the contact of the wires. Utilizing this knowledge, Volta constructed in 1800 a simple primary battery known as the Voltaic Pile. For the next two decades, electricity provided a great deal of amusement at parties and gave rise to a Romantic pseudo-science. The Romantics were attracted to these discoveries because they confirmed their belief in the existence of mysterious forces supposedly beyond the grasp of reason.

The next phase in the growth of knowledge about electricity was the discovery of electromagnetism. In 1820 Christian Oersted of Denmark showed that an electric current from a battery transmitted through a wire placed above a magnetized needle had the effect of deflecting the needle. A few years later the French scientist André Ampère devised a method of measuring the relationship between electricity and magnetism. Finally, in 1831, the Englishman Michael Faraday demonstrated that the movement of a coil of wire through a magnetic field produced in the wire a flow of electric current (electromagnetic induction).

Although fully appreciated at the time, these discoveries had no immediate effect on the power supply, because early electromagnetic generators were too cumbersome and expensive to operate. This difficulty was removed only in the 1870s, when a German engineer, Werner von Siemens, produced an efficient generator. In the 1890s the first large high-voltage power stations capable of distributing electricity over large areas made their appearance. From then on electricity became an intrinsic part of modern life.

The discovery of electromagnetism was first utilized in communications. By sending electric impulses over wires it became possible to produce a controlled reaction a great distance away. This was the basis of the telegraph that the American inventor Samuel F. B. Morse constructed in the mid-1840s and for which he devised a special alphabet in a code consisting of dots and dashes. The railroads were the first to employ the telegraph, which found an unforeseen use in 1845 when a murder suspect was reported by railway telegraph to have been seen on a London-bound train. The London police arrested him on arrival, and he was subsequently tried and sentenced to death, the first victim of scientific detection. In 1851 an underwater telegraph cable was laid between France and England, and fifteen years later England and the United States were similarly linked by means of a transatlantic cable. In 1862, 150,000 miles of telegraphic cable were in use throughout the world. The rapidity of communications that resulted from the spread of the telegraph revolutionized warfare, diplomacy, and journalism.

A similar principle to convey voice by electric impulses was utilized in the telephone, patented in 1876 by a Scottish-born professor at Boston University, Alexander Graham Bell.

Electricity found another important use in illumination. Here again, engineers from many countries made essential contributions, the basic ones being those of the Englishman Joseph Swan and the American Thomas Alva Edison. Working independently, Swan and Edison devised the carbon-filament lamp (1878–1881), which eventually replaced other means of providing artificial light, including natural gas and kerosene. Toward the end of the century, most of the big and many of the small cities of Europe converted to electrical illumination. For the first time streets and public buildings were brightly lit at night. Electric lighting provided additional hours of "daytime" and made possible the bustling night life of the late nineteenth-century metropolis. It had particular significance for the working population of the big cities whose hours of leisure previously had coincided with the hours of darkness.

The world had hardly become familiar with electricity when a new source of power made its appearance—gasoline, a product of petroleum that was first used in the 1880s in the internal-combustion engine. Internal combustion, which operates the automobile and many other motors, takes advantage of the pressure produced in the cylinder by an explosion. The principle of internal combustion had been known for some time, but it could not be exploited for lack of a suitable fuel. In 1876–1877 the German engineer Nicholas Otto developed, on lines first indicated by French scientists, the basic four-stroke engine, employing coal gas as a fuel. The internal-combustion engine, however, gained widespread acceptance only after experiments that another German engineer, Gottlieb Daimler, conducted in 1883–1885 with gasoline. The use of gasoline permitted Daimler to design an engine using considerably less fuel than Otto's and thus to construct economical automobiles. In 1894, in a race between Paris and Rouen, gasoline-driven cars defeated all competitors, covering on the average thirty miles per gallon of fuel. Until the outbreak of World War I, driving remained a fashionable sport of the wealthy. Adventurous automobilists organized expeditions across continents: one team of German cars traversed Africa (1907–1909) and another the United States (1908). A further development was an engine

In a daguerreotype of about 1860, the Englishman Michael Faraday holds a bar used in his magnetism research.

The German Justus von Liebig established a celebrated organic chemistry laboratory, shown here in 1842, at Giessen. At the extreme right, in the top hat, is A. W. von Hofmann, Liebig's assistant, later famous as the founder of industrial chemistry.

fueled by heavy oil, which did not explode but burned gradually. Called the Diesel engine after its German inventor Rudolf Diesel (1892), it found extensive application in industry, railroads, and ocean shipping.

Next to the new sources of power, the most important inventions of the second half of the century resulted from the application to industry of organic chemistry. If the generator and the internal-combustion engine eased the problem of power supply, industrial chemistry provided an entirely new source of raw materials. Like electricity, it had the effect of making man less dependent on nature.

Industrial chemistry originated in the dye industry. Its founder was A. W. von Hofmann, a German scientist living in London. Von Hofmann discovered that coal tar, obtained cheaply by distilling the bituminous coal used in illuminating gas, yielded many new compounds. While experimenting with one such compound, aniline, in 1856, an eighteen-year-old student of von Hofmann's named William Perkin accidentally produced an excellent purple dye. Von Hofmann himself attached no significance to this discovery, but Perkin patented it, built a factory to manufacture the dye, and became a wealthy man. The new synthetic dye found quick acceptance among textile manufacturers. It was also used for a variety of other purposes, including early British postage stamps. Soon, other synthetic colors were produced. Being cheaper as well as more dependable than vegetable and animal dyes, they pushed the latter out of the market. Germany became the world leader in the development and production of industrial chemicals.

Synthetic dyes were only the first of many products subsequently created by industrial chemistry. In the 1860s, for example, the Swedish chemist Alfred Nobel discovered that the addition of kieselguhr, a porous kind of earth, to nitroglycerin made it possible to control that unpredictable and dangerous explosive. The new substance, called dynamite, had an immediate effect upon the design of weapons and greatly influenced military tactics as well as civil engineering. In the 1880s chemists developed artificial drugs (quinine), and in the 1890s synthetic textiles (artificial silk, also known as rayon).

Chemistry also found important uses in agriculture. Justus von Liebig, a German chemist and the author of *Organic Chemistry and Its Relation to Agriculture and Plant Physiology* (1840), analyzed the process by which plants obtain food from the air and the soil and thereby made possible the production of artificial fertilizers. His discoveries freed agriculture from total dependence on the manure of domestic animals, which had never been available in sufficient quantities and diminished further in the nineteenth century as a consequence of the shrinking of pasture land. Countries with a progressive rural economy could now double and triple the yield per acre.

Important technical innovations revolutionized the steel industry. Steel is iron with a carbon content of between 0.1 and 2 percent. It is more malleable than pig iron, which has a higher carbon content (2.5–4 percent), and harder than wrought iron, whose carbon content is lower (less than 0.1 percent). The virtues of steel have been known for centuries as have the technologies of its manufacture, but production costs were always so high that steel had to be confined to expensive items, such as weapons and cutlery. The early railroads used iron exclusively. So did Gustave Eiffel as late as 1889 in constructing his famous tower for the Paris Exhibition.

The main difficulty in the manufacture of steel lies in the removal of the precise amount of carbon from the pig iron. This problem was first solved by the English engineer Sir Henry Bessemer in his well-known ''converter,'' a device that transformed or ''converted'' pig iron into steel by injecting a jet of compressed air into the molten iron mass. The air blast oxidized the correct amount of carbon in a matter of minutes, yielding high-grade steel quickly and cheaply. He patented his process in 1855–1859. It had a striking effect on steel prices, because Bessemer could manufacture steel costing £5 or £6 a ton, compared to the prevailing rate of £50 to £60. Toward the end of the century, the Bessemer process yielded in popularity to the ''Siemens-Martin,'' or ''open-hearth,'' method, invented between 1864 and 1868.

The Bessemer converter as well as the Siemens-Martin hearth could be used only with a superior nonphosphorus iron ore, because high phosphorus ore, found in abundance on the Continent, resulted in a product too brittle for commercial purposes. In 1876 this problem was solved by two Englishmen (one of them a police-court clerk with an amateur interest in chemistry) who invented a way of removing phosphorus from iron by adding substances to the ore and lining the converter with manganese. This discovery permitted the exploitation of iron deposits with a high phosphorus content—including those in Lorraine, which had been ceded to Germany in 1871. It helped build the great industrial power of modern Germany.

The decline in steel prices led to a sharp increase in demand for steel, which gained acceptance in a variety of industries, such as construction and transport. World production rose from 0.5 million tons in 1870 to 28 million in 1900 and 58 million in 1912.

Innovations in the electrical, chemical, and steel industries by no means cover the range of technical advances made in the second half of the nineteenth century. Photography, sewing machines, refrigeration, canning—all invented in the nineteenth century—caused a great change in human life when they became generally available in the twentieth century.

Mention must also be made of the development of techniques of scientific management and mass production. These techniques, though not strictly technological, had intimate links with technology and influenced productivity and prices as much as did any mechanical device. They were developed in the United States, a country whose perennial shortage of labor induced it to experiment ceaselessly with labor-saving procedures. Scientific management was formulated by the American engineer Frederick W. Taylor and is known abroad as "Taylorism." In two influential books, *Shop Management* (1903) and *Principles of Scientific Management* (1911), Taylor indicated how manufacturing costs could be reduced by putting labor to its most efficient use. The so-called time-and-motion studies that he had conducted in the 1880s for the Midvale Steel Company in Philadelphia pioneered various labor-saving procedures. An important American innovation of this kind was the moving assembly line, designed to reduce to a minimum the movement of the workers by bringing the product to them and limiting their task to a simple repetitive operation. The conveyor belt was inaugurated in the Chicago meat-packing industry, but it found its first important industrial application in the automobile plant that Henry Ford built at Highland Park, Michigan, on the eve of World War I. There in 1913 Ford produced the world's first cheap car, the famous Model T (it sold at $500). The methods of scientific management and standardized production penetrated other industries after World War I and became an intrinsic feature of modern industrial culture.

Emergence of the World Market   In the latter part of the nineteenth century the destruction of the barriers that had obstructed the flow of goods proceeded so relentlessly that for the first time in human history there came into existence a single world-wide market. The expansion of cheap land and sea transport, the search for diverse raw materials, the quest for profitable investments, the growing dependence of the industrial countries on supplies of labor and food from agricultural areas, the demand for ever-new outlets for the goods turned out by industrial economies—all these factors tended to draw countries and continents into an economic unit. The result was an unprecedented degree of international interdependence. The collapse of several banks in Vienna in the spring of 1873 caused a financial panic in Germany, which in turn brought down scores of small railroad companies in the United States, and in New York City led to the dismissal of 200,000 employees. When German agrarian interests persuaded Bismarck to impose a tariff on Russian grain, landlords and peasants on the Volga and Don rivers felt the effects at once. The use of manganese in hardening steel and the discovery by Liebig of the role of nitrates in fertilization led to the development of manganese mining in the Congo and nitrate mining in Chile, bringing industry to areas that in other respects were wholly in a pre-industrial era. Such examples could be multiplied many times.

The factor that contributed most to the economic unification of the world was the spread of railway and steamship lines. Intensive railroad construction began in the 1840s, but the real boom came only after midcentury. (See the chart at right.) Between 1860 and 1878 alone, the railway network in Europe tripled in length. Vast trunk lines were built to connect the great industrial centers with each other and with sea ports. The production of cheap steel made possible by the Bessemer process gave a great boost to this development, because rails made of steel proved many times more durable than those of iron and, by reducing maintenance costs, increased profits.

In Britain railroad construction was left entirely to private initiative; the government not only did not encourage it, but for a long time saw no need to regulate it. One consequence of this attitude was that Britain ended up with two different gauge systems. On the Continent, by contrast, the state took an active part in the process, helping railroads and at the same time imposing on them a degree of control. In Belgium the government initiated the construction of trunk lines and left it to private interests to provide the feeder lines; in the 1870s it reversed its policy, purchased the feeder lines from private owners, and placed the entire Belgian railroad network under state authority. In France public and private interests cooperated, but the government never ceased to exert close supervision. A law passed in 1842 provided that the government would supply the land and the road bed, and private concessionaires would provide the rolling stock, the government reserving for itself extensive authority over the tariffs and the geographic distribution of lines. When the concessions expired, the railroads were to become national property. In 1883 the French government transferred to private interests the lines under its control and guaranteed minimum profits to the companies that assumed responsibility. This arrangement lasted until the eve of World War II, when all French railroads were nationalized. In most of Germany the state built and owned the lines; Prussia, where until 1879 private interests predominated, was a surprising exception. Until 1920 Germany had no formally unified railway system, and the operations of the various systems were regulated by the powerful Imperial Railway Office. In Russia, too, state and private capital cooperated, the imperial government tending in time to gain the upper hand.

If the railway broke down commercial barriers inside continents, the steamship broke them down between continents. The first steamship crossed the Atlantic in the 1820s, but it took time for this mode of transport to become economical because its fuel consumption was so high. The sea-going steamship gained acceptance only in the 1870s when improved engines and the construction of coaling stations along maritime routes permitted its fuel load to be significantly reduced, releasing corresponding space for cargo. Once accepted, steamship transport had an immediate effect on the movement of foodstuffs and mineral raw materials, that is, on bulky and heavy items whose transportation costs had been prohibitive in the days of the sailing ship. It reduced the price of a bushel of American wheat in Western Europe by three-quarters. This price

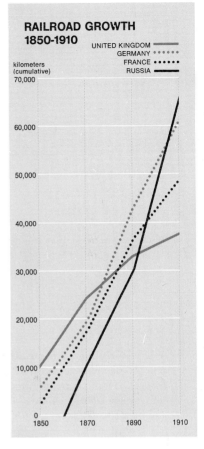

RAILROAD GROWTH
1850-1910

UNITED KINGDOM
GERMANY
FRANCE
RUSSIA

kilometers
(cumulative)

70,000

60,000

50,000

40,000

30,000

20,000

10,000

0
1850   1870   1890   1910

reduction made possible large-scale grain exports from the Americas to Europe in the 1870s. The simultaneous development of refrigerated trains and ships also permitted transoceanic shipment of meat. Argentinian beef and Australian mutton, which until then had practically no commercial worth for lack of markets, suddenly acquired great value and became the main source of the wealth of these countries. The steamship exerted great influence on the whole economy of the Western Hemisphere, encouraging the development of intense cereal and meat production for export. Conversely, it had a deleterious effect on the agriculture of many European countries, where growing food ceased to be profitable.

The drastic reduction in shipping rates brought about by the steamship led to the development of regional specialization among suppliers of raw materials to the industrial countries. Egypt came to depend on its cotton, Cuba on its sugar cane, Bolivia on its tin, Chile on its nitrates. Such specialization brought sudden prosperity to areas that until then had remained outside the routes of international trade, but it also made them vulnerable to technical innovations and to the slightest fluctuations in the world economy.

During the half century preceding the outbreak of World War I, international trade experienced enormous expansion. Its total volume increased from an estimated $1.5 billion in 1830 to $4 billion in 1850, $14 billion in 1880, and $40 bil-

Stock speculation on the Paris bourse was viewed unsympathetically by the noted illustrator Gustave Doré, who drew it as a frantic scramble for wealth.

lion in 1913. The bulk of the trade occurred between the great industrial powers. The complicated financial operations that such a volume of international business required were facilitated by the general adoption of gold as the standard of exchange. The discovery of large gold deposits in California (1848–1849) and South Africa (1886) injected into the international money market vast quantities of bullion. At the beginning of the twentieth century the currencies of most great powers were convertible to gold, a fact that both facilitated and encouraged investments and trade.

Economic activity received another stimulus from two important innovations: the investment bank and the joint-stock company with limited liability. The great expansion of business accompanying industrialization demanded a constant flow of capital for which the traditional sources—private and family fortunes or simple partnerships—no longer sufficed. One device developed to overcome the shortage of capital was the joint-stock or investment bank. Such banks raised the funds for long-term investments in business enterprises either by selling stocks and bonds to the public or by setting aside for this purpose a part of their savings deposits. The model new bank was the French Crédit Mobilier, founded in 1852. It was widely emulated elsewhere, especially in Germany.

In addition to drawing on banks, mid-nineteenth century businesses began to seek capital directly from individual investors by means of stocks or shares, the purchase of which gave the holder a right to share the company's profits. This method of raising funds, simple and advantageous to all concerned, had been known for some time, but it did not gain popularity because partners of companies had been deemed legally responsible for the firm's debts to the full extent of their personal fortunes, no matter how much or little of the stock they owned. Various attempts had been made (e.g., in France under Napoleon I and later in Belgium) to reduce this liability, but the legislation was hedged with so many formalities that it gained little acceptance. The first effective law of this kind was passed in 1855 in England. The law established the principle of limited liability: purchasers of shares in a limited-liability company bore responsibility for the company's debt only in proportion to the amount of their holdings. This law greatly enhanced the popularity of joint-stock companies in England and attracted into industry and trade much new capital. Corresponding laws were adopted in France in 1867, in Germany and Italy in the 1870s, and subsequently in other European countries. The modern stock exchange and its by-product, stock speculation, was one of the results of this legislation.

As the main beneficiary of the expansion of world trade, Europe became the world's supplier of capital. The leader in foreign investments was Britain. By 1914 it had placed abroad the equivalent of $20 billion, a quarter of its estimated national wealth. The bulk of British investments went to self-governing dominions and to the countries of the Western Hemisphere, where they financed a great variety of economic activities. The French preferred to invest in bonds of foreign governments. In 1914 $9 billion, an estimated one-sixth of the French national wealth, was placed abroad, a quarter of it in Russia. Germany had in 1914 investments totaling $6 billion and the United States $2.6 billion. Britain, whose foreign investments exceeded those of all the other countries combined, led in trade, shipping, and insurance and came to perform the function of an

A piece of anti-Semitic propaganda, dating from 1898 and of French origin, caricatures the Rothschild banking house as seeking world dominance.

international clearinghouse. London acquired the status of the world's central money market. Capital, flowing where it was in greatest demand, became something of a commodity. It was bought, borrowed, sold, imported, and exported like any other commercial product.

But the sky was not entirely cloudless. In the overwhelming progress attending the advances of technology, the expansion of markets, and the accumulation of wealth, there were two phenomena that gave cause for anxiety. One was overproduction. As more and more industries developed, it became apparent that sooner or later the markets for their products would become saturated. This fear was a very genuine factor in European economic and diplomatic activities after 1870 and perhaps the single most important motive behind the intense drive for colonial conquests in the last quarter of the nineteenth century (see Chapter 21).

The other was recurrent economic crises. These were not new but never before had they been so frequent, so shattering, and so global in scope. In 1857 the world experienced a distressing international depression; from then on they occurred every decade or less. On May 11, 1866 ("Black Friday"), a London banking house suspended payments, producing widespread financial panic that brought down the Crédit Mobilier in Paris. The worst crisis, which occurred in 1873, caused a temporary halt in the expansion of trade and took many years to overcome. The world was shaken by further depressions in the mid-1880s and mid-1890s. These crises were caused by temporary maladjustments between the productive, commercial, and financial elements of the economy. Businessmen, having had little experience with the workings of the international market and spurred by prospects of immense profit to operate to the limit of their financial resources, easily miscalculated. There was as yet no system of international monetary cooperation, state regulation of banks and of stock exchanges, or market research. Much economic activity was inherently speculative and unstable. At the time, however, these causes were not readily apparent. The socialists won many adherents by their claim that crises were an inevitable concomitant of the capitalist economy and would grow in severity until the whole capitalist system collapsed. Anti-Semitic movements also profited by persuading the gullible that recessions were due to an international Jewish conspiracy.

Industrialism and the National State

The emergence of a world-wide market coincided with the consolidation of national states. The two processes—the internationalization of economics and the nationalization of politics—stood in stark contradiction. As a rule, the conflict resolved in favor of nationalism; that is to say, most states, when confronted with the choice of achieving the maximum of self-sufficiency or raising living standards, chose self-sufficiency. The requirements of national interest caused barriers to be put up against the free flow of goods and men, restricting the world market.

The economic historian W. W. Rostow, after comparing the experience of a number of Western and non-Western countries, discerned three basic common phases in the process of industrialization (chart opposite): "take-off," "maturity," and "high mass-consumption." In England the "take-off" stage occurred between 1785 and 1800, "maturity" was attained around 1850, and "high mass-consumption" after 1930. Using these convenient terms, we may say that the take-off stage—the critical transition from an agrarian to an industrial economy,

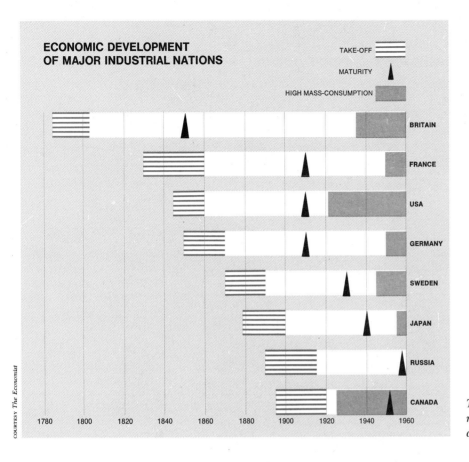

ECONOMIC DEVELOPMENT
OF MAJOR INDUSTRIAL NATIONS

TAKE-OFF

MATURITY

HIGH MASS-CONSUMPTION

BRITAIN

FRANCE

USA

GERMANY

SWEDEN

JAPAN

RUSSIA

CANADA

1780 1800 1820 1840 1860 1880 1900 1920 1940 1960

The patterns of industrial development of leading Western nations, as defined by economist W. W. Rostow.

the Industrial Revolution proper—took place in France and Germany between 1850 and 1870 and in Russia in the 1890s. Yet, in using such general concepts, we must not forget that the experience of each country was unique.

Imperial Germany was the only country on the Continent that fully satisfied the requirements for full-scale industrialization. With these advantages, Germany outpaced its rivals, and on the eve of World War I had surpassed Great Britain in most fields of industrial productivity. The German Empire possessed in the Ruhr, Lorraine, Saxony, and Silesia the richest iron and coal deposits on the Continent. It also had a large and rapidly growing population. At midcentury the Germans outnumbered the French, traditionally the most populous nation in Western Europe. In 1890 Germany had nearly 50 million inhabitants compared to 37 million each in France and in the United Kingdom. Thanks to its tradition of craftsmanship, Germany had numerous skilled artisans who could be shifted from small shops into large industrial establishments. Finally, the state took an active interest in economic development. The government of Prussia had much experience in this matter, for it owned large properties; it was, for example, the leading producer of coal in pre-1870 Germany. The imperial government engaged in many kinds of economic activities, setting an early example of that marriage between industry and politics that later provided the model for totalitarian states. Its agencies operated railways and telephone and telegraph lines and exploited forests and mines. In 1913 more than one-half of Germany's

INDUSTRIALISM AND THE NATIONAL STATE 437

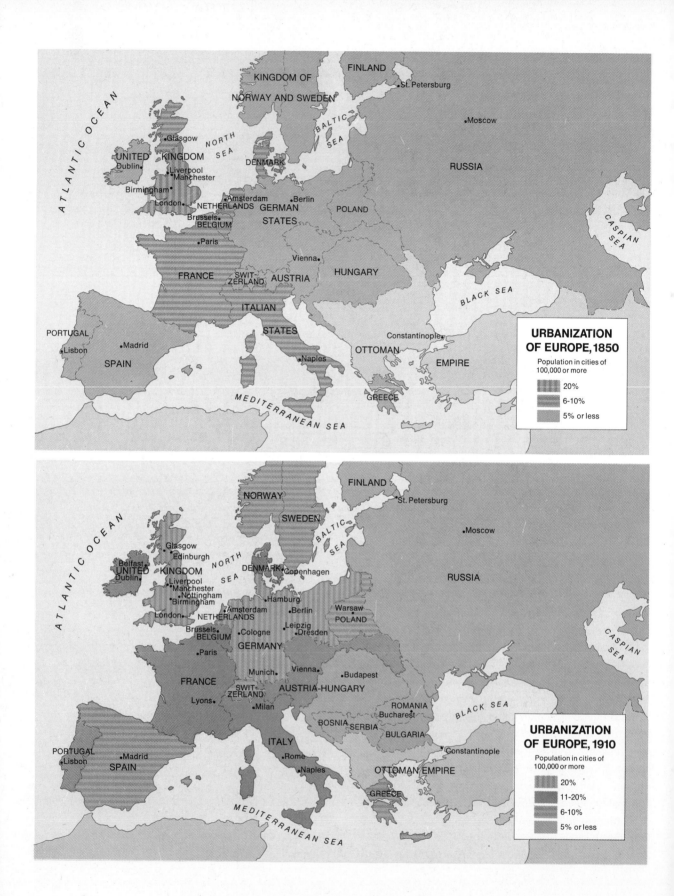

URBANIZATION OF EUROPE, 1850

Population in cities of 100,000 or more

20%

6-10%

5% or less

URBANIZATION OF EUROPE, 1910

Population in cities of 100,000 or more

20%

11-20%

6-10%

5% or less

state revenue derived from its own properties—an income that enabled the monarchy to escape excessive dependence on parliament. The government assisted industry by establishing a network of technical schools that furnished Germany with the largest body of engineers and technical specialists in the world.

The rapidity with which German industrialization progressed once it got under way was indeed staggering, the only parallel being the United States. The charts on page 441 illustrate this growth and require no elaboration. What does call for explanation, however, are two techniques on which the Germans relied to promote their industry: protective tariffs and economic "rationalization."

Until the late 1870s Germany followed the prevalent trend toward free trade. The *Zollverein* was designed less to create protective walls on the outside than to remove them from inside German territory. With a few exceptions, the *Zollverein* imposed moderate tariffs on foreign goods. When the *Zollverein* was still in its infancy, however, voices began to be heard advocating a radical departure from free trade. The most telling argument for such a change was made by the German economist Friedrich List, whose *National System of Political Economy* (1841) deserves to be ranked, in terms of historic importance, alongside Smith's *Wealth of Nations*. If Smith had formulated most succinctly the theory of economic liberalism dominant until the 1870s, List formulated the principles of economic nationalism dominant since.

List began to champion protective tariffs in the early 1820s, but he developed his economic theory only after he had emigrated to the United States in 1825. He arrived in America at a time when that country was experiencing a powerful movement toward protectionism that culminated in the Tariff Act of 1828 (the "Tariff of Abominations"). He read a great deal of the American literature favoring and opposing protective tariffs and was particularly impressed by the writings of Alexander Hamilton, an ardent advocate of tariff protection. On his return to Germany in 1831 (he received an appointment as United States consul to Leipzig), List began to propagate similar ideas, giving them a theoretical exposition in his *National System*.

The premise of List's doctrine is that the economy must concentrate not merely or even primarily on the production of goods, but on the development of "productive forces": "The power of producing wealth is infinitely more important than wealth itself." By "productive forces" List meant all the human and material resources involved in economic activity, including knowledge and education, which he regarded as the "mental capital of a nation." On this premise, List proceeded to build a powerful argument in favor of protectionism. Though he agreed with Adam Smith that tariffs prevent a country from obtaining at the most advantageous price industrial goods on the world market and thus indirectly lower living standards, in the long run, he maintained, the sacrifice is worthwhile; protected by tariffs, native industry will mature and acquire the capacity to produce goods at prices below those goods purchased abroad. In effect, List advocated a temporary reduction in living standards in favor of longterm economic growth—an argument that re-emerged in the twentieth century as a central proposition of so-called development economics. As for the contention that Britain had become a great industrial power by pursuing a contrary course, List had no difficulty showing that Britain had laid its economic foundations under stringent protectionism and ventured into free trade only when it no longer feared competitors.

List was an "historicist," that is, he viewed phenomena from a dynamic, relativist point of view. He did not regard protective tariffs as an end in themselves, but rather as measures required at a transitional phase. He approved of free trade for backward countries like Spain, to help raise them from a condition of "barbarism," as well as for countries like Britain, which had already attained a high level of productivity. He advocated protectionism, however, for countries in the early phase of industrial development.

List had little influence in his own time and, distraught and disappointed, committed suicide in 1846. But his views gradually won a following among academic economists and those business groups (e.g., iron manufacturers and cotton spinners) that had been hurt by competition, especially during and after the depression of 1873.

In 1879 Germany formally went over to protectionism. The decisive factor was fiscal: Bismarck saw in customs a good source of revenue (the imperial constitution had made no provisions for levying taxes on the empire as a whole) and yielded to German businessmen who had been long clamoring for higher tariffs. Although in itself quite moderate (it taxed mainly iron, textiles, and foodstuffs), the tariff of 1879 produced a chain reaction. France responded in 1881 with a more severe tariff act, and a few years later Italy, Sweden, and Russia followed suit. The reversion of the great powers to protectionism culminated in the most stringent tariff act of all, the American Dingley Act of 1897.

Although in many cases the motives inspiring protection were narrowly fiscal rather than broadly economic (in List's sense), they everywhere had the effect of promoting national economic development. Of the great powers England alone resisted the new fashion, but even there it had its proponents, especially Joseph Chamberlain, the founder in 1903 of the Tariff Reform League. It is testimony to the dynamism of the European economy at the time that, notwithstanding the emergence of tariff barriers, international trade continued to expand at an intense rate.

Equally important as tariffs for the world economy were the pioneering attempts of the Germans to subject production and distribution to planning or "rationalization." This end was furthered by forming organizations designed either to secure control over the manufacture of a given product (monopolies) or else to diminish or eliminate competition among independent producers (trusts or cartels). Such practices were common in all countries, but nowhere were they

An engraving after a sketch by German economist Friedrich List shows what appears to be an excursion on the Leipzig-Dresden-Berlin line in 1833.

as prevalent as in Germany. In Great Britain, for example, agreements for the restraint of productivity or trade, while not illegal, were not legally binding. The United States outlawed them in 1890 by the Sherman Anti-Trust Act. The Germans not only allowed them and enforced them in courts, but regarded monopolies and cartels as superior forms of economic organization. The participation of German banks in much economic development encouraged the formation of cartels, for the banks were interested in reducing as much as possible competition likely to pit one of their clients against another.

German cartels grew rapidly after the passage of the tariff of 1879. In 1905 there were in Germany 385 cartels embracing every major branch of the economy. The larger ones, such as the Rhine-Westphalian Coal Syndicate, were by then organized on a joint-stock basis, with a formal board of directors and regular meetings of members. For a while the Prussian government itself, as owner of collieries, sat on the board of the syndicate. The key unit of most cartels was the Sales Bureau, appointed jointly by the participating firms, which fixed production quotas, prices, or both. Some cartels expanded vertically, that is, they acquired control over the raw materials and means of transport used in their particular field of production. Originally devised as a means of regulating the market, cartels furnished models afterward used by countries adopting planned socialist economies.

By virtue of its industrial expansion, Germany began toward the end of the century to offer Britain serious competition in markets that until then had been Britain's preserve (Latin America, the Middle East). It also gained a firm foothold in eastern and southeastern Europe. German merchandise, well made and reasonably priced, often suited local needs better than the conservatively designed, high-quality British goods. In 1900 Germany gained second place in world trade, the volume of German business being far ahead of the next two competitors, the United States and France. On the European Continent Germany forged ahead of Britain and stood in first place.

Although a great power, France never industrialized in the full sense of the word. In France industrial processes, instead of replacing the agrarian order, accommodated themselves to it, resulting in a mixed rural-urban economy. The attachment of Frenchmen to the land and their individualism, mentioned previously, persisted. As late as 1911, when France was fully in the "mature" stage of economic development, the majority (56 percent) of its population continued to live in the countryside, and most industrial establishments employed four workers or less. The shortage of coal and iron hindered the growth of heavy industry, while capital tended to flow into luxury goods that did not lend themselves to methods of mass production.

The industrialization of Russia began around 1890, when indexes of economic activity showed a sudden spurt characteristic of the take-off phase of development. Much of the capital, management, and skilled labor came from abroad (France, Germany, Belgium, England). The importance of foreign investments in Russia's economy may be gauged from the fact that when the Revolution of 1917 broke out, foreigners directly controlled nearly half of the capital held by Russian banks. The imperial government on the whole did not favor industrialization, fearing that it would denude the countryside of peasant recruits and

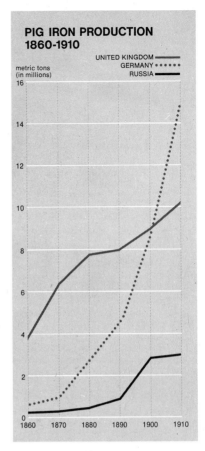

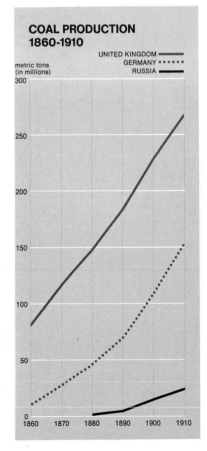

cause unrest in the cities. The main promoter of industry was the Ministry of Finance, headed by Sergei Witte, which had to fight constant battles with the agrarian interests defended by the Ministry of the Interior. The latter opposed industrialization on the theory that, if Russia produced enough manufactured goods of its own to cease buying them in Germany, the Germans would be likely to stop purchasing wheat in Russia. Despite these difficulties, imperial Russia managed in the last quarter of its existence to acquire the foundations of a respectable industrial economy.

In most of the countries outside the industrial heartland (Russia included), industry tended to be consumer-oriented until the outbreak of World War I. It concentrated on the manufacture of textiles and household articles, and on food-processing. Here and there, the presence of rich mineral deposits led to the emergence of industrial nuclei in the midst of agrarian economies (e.g., iron ore in Sweden, copper and coal in Spain, petroleum in Romania, etc.).

Agriculture and Land Ownership European agriculture was less affected by scientific and technical innovations than was manufacturing. Indeed, in much of Europe farming in the nineteenth century continued to be carried on exactly as it had been since the Middle Ages. The resistance of agriculture to change stemmed partly from the innate traditionalism of the peasantry and partly from the unsuitability of most mechanical, technical, and organizational innovations to rural conditions.

The great shock to European agriculture was the influx in the 1870s of American grain, which was so low in price that, in areas where land was scarce and therefore expensive, growing grain ceased to be profitable. This was the case in England, where agriculture, notwithstanding the abolition of the Corn Law, had continued to enjoy great prosperity until then. The 1870s marked a collapse of English agriculture; with the curtailment of arable acreage, England became now more than ever dependent for its foodstuffs on imports. Denmark experienced a similar crisis but overcame it by switching to dairy farming and exporting to England and other industrial countries milk, eggs, butter, and similar items that could not then be shipped across the Atlantic. Other countries met the overseas threat to their agriculture by resorting to protective tariffs on foodstuffs. The Germans led the way, and before the end of the century most Continental countries had followed suit. Such tariffs hurt countries dependent on agrarian exports and forced them to impose tariffs on foreign manufactured goods. The result was a succession of "tariff wars" in the 1880s, the ones between Russia and Germany and between Italy and France being the most spectacular.

Economic developments in the nineteenth century produced different results on the distribution of ownership in industry and in agriculture. In industry the tendency everywhere was to wipe out small, independent producers and to concentrate ownership in large enterprises. In agriculture—with the notable exception of England—the general tendency was the opposite: large estates were broken up into small or medium-sized holdings. This held especially true of the industrial countries on the Continent, where the one-time serf and tenant farmer gradually turned into an independent proprietor. The transformation was striking in France, the traditional home of the small landowner. Even before 1789 some 40 percent of the arable soil in France had been in the actual (if not legal) possession of the peasantry. The Revolution legalized this ownership and increased further the holdings of the peasants by enabling them to purchase land confiscated from the Church and the *émigrés*. In 1892 France's nearly 5 million individual landholdings measuring 25 acres or less accounted for 90 percent of the farms in the country. Fewer than a thousand properties exceeded 1,000 acres. To what extent the French farmer was also a proprietor may be gathered from the fact that at the end of the century, with a total of 5.5 million holdings, France had only 3.5 million agricultural laborers, that is, peasants working on land not their own. A similar situation prevailed in Germany by 1895, when 94 percent of all the farms were of less than 50 acres and where nearly all of them belonged to their cultivators. Both countries, of course, also had giant holdings; these, in the case of Germany, were concentrated in the east and northeast. In Belgium the parceling of agricultural land reached its extreme. Of a total of 830,000 holdings, 500,000 measured less than 2.5 acres, and only 3,500 exceeded 125 acres. The small farms could survive owing to constant improvement in techniques that increased yields beyond anything known previously. Germany, the pioneer in scientific farming, extracted three times as much wheat from an acre as Russia and twice as much as the United States (1912).

England had a rather special situation. The enclosure acts and early urbanization had decreased the number of small farmers and tenants, giving England the highest concentration of land ownership among the industrial countries. In 1871 approximately one-half the land in Great Britain belonged to 7,400 persons. In 1895, of a total British agricultural area of 32.6 million acres (exclusive of Ireland), 28 million were rented and only 4.6 million were occupied by the owners. The land rent enabled the British aristocracy to maintain a high style of life in the midst of industrial expansion.

In the non-industrialized, rural countries of Europe the bulk of the land re-

French artist Jean-François Millet, himself of peasant background, made the peasantry a frequent theme of his work. This is an 1855 etching.

mained concentrated in the hands of state, church, and large landowners. The peasants in these areas—Ireland, Portugal, Spain, Italy, Austria, Hungary, eastern Germany, and Russia—were predominantly full- or part-time tenants or laborers or partial owners. It has been estimated, for example, that in the central provinces of Spain two-thirds or more of the land was contained in holdings of more than 25,000 acres. In Italy some 10 million men and women worked on land owned by 400,000 proprietors. In Ireland less than 10 percent of the land was tilled by owners; the remaining 90 percent was leased (1904). Such examples illustrate the reason for the acute land hunger that developed in the peripheral countries of Europe toward the end of the nineteenth century. It was a prime cause of the great migratory wave that began to build after 1850.

Population Growth and Migration   From the late eighteenth century onward, the world experienced an unprecedented growth of population. The original cause of this phenomenon is not clear; some scholars ascribe it primarily to a decline in mortality, others to an increase in births. Proponents of the former view maintain that the establishment of firm political order, the introduction of sanitary measures, and improvements in the quantity of food and quality of clothing produced a demonstrable decline in deaths. A. M. Carr-Saunders, an English statistician, has estimated that the death rate (the number of deaths occurring annually for every 1,000 persons) declined in Europe from 32 in 1820 to 20 in 1900. Other authorities, without denying the decline in deaths, ascribe the growth of population primarily to an increase in birth rates. This they account for partly by earlier marriages, made possible by economic prosperity, and partly by a reduction in infanticide and abortions caused by more enlightened legislation pertaining to illegitimacy. They also point out that there were few medical advances in the eighteenth century, when the population growth first got under way.

Whatever the cause, there is general agreement that in modern times the traditional balance between birth rates and death rates has been upset. Before 1800 the birth rate averaged in most countries between 35 and 50 per 1,000 (that is, for each 1,000 inhabitants there were 35 to 50 live births) and the death rate between 30 and 40. The slight surplus of births over deaths was periodically wiped out by one of the traditional enemies of man: war, disease, or famine. This ceased to hold true in the nineteenth century. Mortality rates dropped (in England to as low as 18 per 1,000), while birth rates either remained constant or rose, so that the gap between births and deaths kept growing wider. At the end of the century Italy had an annual surplus of births over deaths of 300,000, Hungary of 230,000, and Russia of more than 2,000,000. As a result, the nineteenth-century population of Europe more than doubled, growing from an estimated 193 million in 1800 to 423 million in 1900. In other words, Europe accumulated more inhabitants in the course of a single century than in all the centuries of its previous existence.

This increase created fears that the day would come when the earth no longer could house or feed its inhabitants. The most striking argument of this nature was made in 1798 by Thomas Malthus in his *Essay on the Principle of Population*. Malthus argued that the population grew at a considerably more rapid rate than the food supply, with the inevitable consequence that mankind continually faced mass starvation. No real improvement in the condition of the working class was possible. Malthus urged that society abstain from social welfare because it encouraged population growth among the poor, who were the most fertile group, and concentrate instead on reducing the marriage rate. Misery and vice (to which he later added "moral restraint") were in his opinion the only efficacious means of preventing an exhaustion of resources and ultimate catastrophe. These ideas influenced early liberal thought against social reform and played a part in the passage of the Poor Law of 1834. Though much criticized for their inhumane implications and doubtful scientific premises, the theories of Malthus came back into vogue later in the century in the form of "neo-Malthusianism." The Malthusian League, founded in London in 1877, initiated the modern birth-control movement.

A painting by a Russian artist (1889), reminiscent of American Western art of the same era, depicts a stranded and starving Russian peasant family.

The dire predictions of Malthus have not been borne out (at least so far), because they made no allowance for the ability of an industrial economy to absorb more people in a given area than an agricultural one. There were several reasons for this phenomenon. First, the introduction of the railroad and steamship facilitated the importation of food from distant areas. Cheap transport, in effect, annexed to Europe the prairies of the American Midwest, Argentina, and southern Russia. Second, the increase in agricultural yields brought about by scientific farming disproved Malthus' fears of an insufficient progression in food production. Third, the harnessing of the energy latent in steam, electricity, and mineral fuels allowed a reduction in the number of horses and freed much pasture land for other purposes. It has been estimated that the steam engines operating in England in 1870 produced the equivalent power of 6 million horses. Thus millions of acres that would have been required to provide fodder for these horses became available for other uses.

These factors enabled countries with advanced industrial economies to maintain population densities that would have proved fatal to purely agrarian ones. Belgium attained in 1900 an over-all density of 589 inhabitants a square mile, and in some provinces of nearly 1,000. By contrast, Spain could barely support 97 and Russia 55 inhabitants a square mile. The growing population provided industrial countries with both a labor force and an expanding market.

But in countries with poorly developed industries, the new population had nowhere to go. The land, heavily concentrated, was out of reach; the cities had few jobs to offer. In such areas in the second half of the nineteenth century, a huge landless proletariat began to emerge. This group might well have caused violent social revolutions had it not been for the safety valve provided by emigration. The excess rural population could migrate to three principal places: to the cities, to other European countries, and overseas. The movement to the cities is an aspect of urbanization that we shall discuss in the next chapter. Within the European Continent, there was a sizable migratory movement of rural inhabitants—some temporary (seasonal), others permanent—to the industrial countries. France was particularly receptive to immigrants, for its own population grew so slowly that there were well-founded fears that France some day would no longer be able to defend itself. To provide labor for its industries and mines, France imported workers from Italy and Poland. Germany also drew on Poland for additional agricultural and industrial labor. But the principal

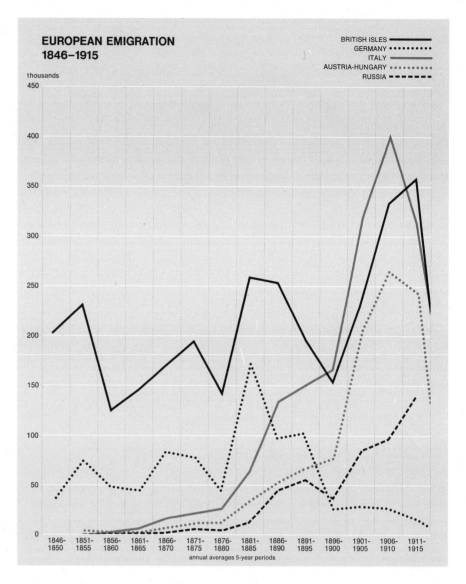

**EUROPEAN EMIGRATION
1846–1915**

BRITISH ISLES
GERMANY
ITALY
AUSTRIA-HUNGARY
RUSSIA

thousands

450

400

350

300

250

200

150

100

50

0

1846-
1850
1851-
1855
1856-
1860
1861-
1865
1866-
1870
1871-
1875
1876-
1880
1881-
1885
1886-
1890
1891-
1895
1896-
1900
1901-
1905
1906-
1910
1911-
1915

annual averages 5-year periods

form of migration was overseas, especially across the Atlantic. This migratory wave constituted the largest population movement in recorded history.

In the first half of the nineteenth century overseas migration was not yet a significant factor in European life. It tended to be sporadic and selective, the majority of the migrants leaving Europe less for economic than for political or religious reasons. The mass exodus began in 1846–1847 with the Irish migration caused by the potato blight. From then on every economic and political crisis sent from Europe fresh waves of overseas migrants. The development of cheap steamship transport contributed to this movement, for ships bringing wheat to Europe, rather than return empty, took on migrants at low fares. In the second half of the century an average of 400,000 persons departed annually from European ports to settle overseas. At the height of emigration (1900–1914), this figure exceeded 1 million. It has been estimated that between 1870 and 1914, 34 million Europeans left for overseas, 27 million of them for the United

States. In this manner Europe lost two-fifths of the additional population that it had acquired during that period.°

Great Britain was the first to experience significant migration overseas. By midcentury it had become customary in England for each economic crisis to be followed by a mass exodus. The Irish famine induced a fifth of that island's population to migrate. Between 1846 and 1860, 3.5 million persons left the United Kingdom (including Ireland). This outflow was undoubtedly responsible for the peaceful solution of social conflicts in Great Britain. After the middle of the century the number of migrants from England declined steadily, though it remained large in Ireland.

German migratory statistics show clearly how much industrialization increased a country's capacity to absorb people. Until Germany had industrialized, its citizens migrated overseas in such large numbers that certain provinces showed an actual decrease in population. By the mid-1890s, when German industry reached maturity, this migratory movement died down, and Germany not only ceased to let out excess labor but began itself to import workers from neighboring countries.

After 1880 few emigrants left industrial Europe: Englishmen and Germans found work at home, while Frenchmen were never inclined to migrate anyway. From then on the bulk of the migrants came from the peripheral countries, especially from Italy and the Slavic regions. The Italian migrants originated mostly in the southern provinces and Sicily, where the rural overpopulation was particularly acute. Nearly half the Italian migrants found work in Europe; the others settled mostly in the United States and Argentina. Between 1880 and 1914 Italy furnished the largest number of overseas immigrants: in 1913 alone 873,000 Italians left home.

Among Russians, despite rural overpopulation, migration overseas was less significant. The overseas migrants consisted largely of Jewish artisans and unskilled workers, inhabitants of the small towns of western Russia who were legally prohibited from either owning land or moving away to other parts of the country. At the turn of the century 15 out of every 1,000 Russian Jews left each year for overseas destinations—one of the highest migratory rates on record.

Migration had a twofold effect. First and foremost, it relieved population pressure and reduced the risk of social upheavals in Europe. Second, it increased Europe's hold on the rest of the globe. Thanks to migration, three continents—North America, South America, and Australia—became Europeanized; a fourth, Africa, acquired compact colonies of European settlers. The problem of "decolonialization" and much of the racial friction afflicting the twentieth century are among the legacies of the great migrations of the nineteenth century.

° It must be noted, however, that an estimated 9 million of the 34 million migrants eventually returned to Europe. The long-term net emigration, therefore, totaled 25 million persons.

The Fruits of Industrialism

U. OF NEWCASTLE UPON TYNE

In common with any great revolutionary movement, the industrialization of the Western world penetrated areas and produced affects quite beyond what anyone could have expected or predicted. To the poet Wordsworth

> An inventive Age
> Has wrought, if not with speed of magic, yet
> To most strange issues. . . .

As these "strange issues" became more familiar and their potential more widely understood during the second half of the nineteenth century, they inspired hope and fear and every emotion in between. To the Italian Futurist Antonio Sant'Elia the new age promised a dynamic New City; to the German artist Kaethe Kollwitz it meant the ugly exploitation of the mass of mankind; to the Frenchman Ferdinand de Lesseps it brought reality to a dream as old as the pharaohs of antiquity, a canal at Suez. A sampling of the fruits of industrialization, both the sweet and the bitter, appears on the following pages.

Great Britain, as the first nation to industrialize, was first to reap the fruits of the new age. Its landscape was changed (at left, a steampowered colliery in Northumberland, 1839), its economy revolutionized, its cultural and social patterns altered. It is not surprising, therefore, that Britain made the first effort to assemble in one place—the Great Exhibition of 1851—the most celebrated products of the Industrial Revolution. Prince Albert, Queen Victoria's consort, conceived the Exhibition "to give us a true test and a living picture of the point of development at which the whole of mankind has arrived . . . and a new starting point from which all nations will be able to direct their future exertions." The immense building erected in London to house the exhibits, with its 300,000 panes of glass and its 5,000 iron columns and girders (designed by a greenhouse builder, it was dubbed the "Crystal Palace" by *Punch*), was itself a monument to the new technology. The Crystal Palace was such an attraction that it was disassembled and rebuilt at Sydenham (right) where, embellished with coy neoclassic statuary, it was a popular resort until 1936, when it burned to a heap of molten glass and iron.

The Great Exhibition had its detractors, who followed up their visits with predictions of a dim future for Western civilization. According to the Swiss writer Henri Amiel, "The useful will take the place of the beautiful, industry of art, political economy of religion, and arithmetic of poetry." Amiel, however, was in the minority. For most observers at midcentury, the potential promise of the new age greatly outweighed the potential menace. Here, it seemed, was further evidence of the Enlightenment's theory of man's inevitable progress toward perfectability.

Marvels of the Machine Age

In the six months of 1851 that the Crystal Palace remained open in London's Hyde Park, 6 million people flocked through it to see the marvels of the Great Exhibition. The displays by nearly 14,000 exhibitors ranged from the American sculptor Hiram Powers' life-size Greek slave girl, who was not only nude but revolved as well, to the celebrated Koh-i-noor diamond from India, reputedly worth more than all the other exhibits put together, to cuffs "knitted from the wool of French poodle dogs." "I came back quite dead beat," wrote Queen Victoria in her journal, "my head really bewildered by the myriads of beautiful and wonderful things. . . ."

In the machinery sections were great marine engines and printing presses and locomotives and one of Cyrus McCormick's reapers from America, all of them in the process of revolutionizing the way people traveled, what they read, and what they ate. For the most part, the machinery was crisply and simply designed for maximum economy and efficiency; the same could not be said of the machine-made products for the consumer. A contemporary remarked that the "savage population" of Canada showed "more attention to the useful than to the ornamental," but if the Canadians resisted ornamentation, hardly anyone else did. Furnishings swarmed with machine-turned bric-a-brac of every description. There was an iron stove disguised as a medieval castle and a metal bedstead with head and footboards of cast scrollwork in which "the little cupids are prettily introduced. . . ." The Great Exhibition was more than the "authentic voice of British capitalism in the hour of its greatest triumph," as one observer has described it; it was as well the authentic voice of Victorian taste in the machine age.

The articles in the Hardware Section (left) of the Great Exhibition, whether they were "absolute requirements of large industrial populations" or for the "convenience of society," were pleated, plated, tasseled, fringed, and fluted to the maximum. By contrast, Moving Machinery (above), run by steam power from a boilerhouse outside the Crystal Palace, displayed a minimum of frills. In the right foreground is a large British lathe for turning railroad wheels. Below is a portion of the French exhibit, much admired and second in size only to the British. The display of Sèvres vases and porcelain visible at the far left in the print was a particular favorite of Queen Victoria, who placed a large order.

At right is Brunel's Great Eastern ready for launch late in 1857. The huge ship had paddlewheels as well as a single propeller. The launch was broadside and took two lives and four months to complete; great hydraulic rams, chains, and winches "were all broken in regular succession," reported the Times of London. A vessel of greater displacement was not built until 1907. Below is Rain, Steam, and Speed (1844) by the Romantic artist J.M.W. Turner, depicting a train on Brunel's Great Western Railway. On the opposite page, in an 1849 view, a span of a so-called tubular style railroad bridge in Wales is floated into position for lifting by hydraulic jacks.

The Transportation Revolution

Isambard Kingdom Brunel (1806–1859) has been called the Great Engineer, the spiritual father of modern mechanical engineering. An Englishman whose energy was exceeded only by his imagination, Brunel broke new ground in every field he put his hand to; his bridges were the longest, his trains the fastest, his steamships the largest. Among the 2,000 miles of track laid under his direction was the Great Western Railway, running from London into the west of England and carrying in the midcentury period the first great crack trains—*The Flying Dutchman, The Cornishman, The Zulu.* His *Great Britain*, launched in 1843, was the first iron-hulled and screw-driven ocean steamship. Fifteen years later came the *Great Eastern*, accommodating 4,000 passengers and five times the size of any ship afloat, exceeding even the bulk of Noah's Ark as calculated by Sir Isaac Newton. Designed for the long run around Africa to Australia, the "Wonder of the Seas" was made obsolete for that trade by the completion of the Suez Canal, through which she was too big to pass. In the case of the *Great Eastern*, Brunel's vision was too far ahead of his time for commercial success, but the huge vessel proved ideal for the task of laying transoceanic cables, including the Atlantic Cable (1866).

Brunel's engineering accomplishments presaged a growing flood of technological advances in the fifty years after his death that stimulated, and were stimulated by, the spread of industrialization. The year 1869, for example, saw the completion of two remarkable engineering feats in totally different climes, a canal at Suez and a transcontinental railroad across the United States. Railroad mileage doubled and doubled again, until by 1900 it exceeded 170,000 miles in Europe and 600,000 miles in the world. Steel rails, more powerful locomotives, air brakes, refrigerator cars—all in their turn improved service and lowered costs to shippers. In hardly more than half a century similar radical changes took place in ocean-going vessels, changes from sail to steam to steam turbines and Diesel engines, and from wood to iron to steel hulls. Cheaper and stronger steel revolutionized bridge building; new machinery revolutionized road and tunnel construction. Urban transport was altered dramatically by electric streetcars, elevated railroads, the first subways, and the internal combustion engine. Each new development spawned a dozen more until the process had induced a Transportation Revolution.

Canal at Suez

Many of the major elements comprising industrialism were focused on the problems of building the Suez Canal, so that in time it became a virtual microcosm of the industrial age. It involved the highest engineering skills, steam-powered heavy machinery, the resources of finance capitalism, policy decisions by national governments, the demands of the world market and of imperialism, and, as important as anything else, the single-minded dedication of a promoter-builder. For a decade the Frenchman Ferdinand de Lesseps drew his plans and wheedled support for his dream—a canal through the 100 miles of desert between the Mediterranean and the Red Sea, which, by more than halving the sea journey between Europe and the Far East (cutting, for example, the Marseilles-Bombay route from 10,400 miles to 4,600), would bring nation and nation, mother country and colony, into far closer communication. "It will open the world to all people," de Lesseps promised.

Somewhat more than half the shares in the Suez Canal Company were bought by the French public, the average holding being nine shares. The rest of the money was put up by the Egyptian government. The British, fearing an attempt at French hegemony in the Middle and Far East, opposed de Lesseps every step of the way. "It is the greatest bubble [swindle] which was ever imposed upon the credulity and simplicity of the people of this country," Prime Minister Palmerston told the Commons. (Thirty years later, through a blend of fiscal opportunism and imperial highhandedness, Britain seized control of the bubble.) De Lesseps was backed by Napoleon III instead.

In April, 1859, construction began. The canal itself involved moving some 100 million cubic feet of sand and blasting through three rock ridges. A small canal had to be dug to bring fresh water to the site from the Nile, and a harbor and dock facilities created at Port Said, the Mediterranean terminus. Egyptian laborers with shovels and baskets worked alongside 10,000-horsepower steam dredges The job took ten years of prodigious effort and weathered repeated financial storms. The total cost came to $100 million.

The print at left offers an aerial perspective. Suez, the southern terminus, is at lower left, Port Said at upper right. At upper left is the Nile Delta. On November 17, 1869, to enormous fanfare, the job was finished and the canal opened to the traffic of the world.

Claude Monet, one of the masters of French Impressionism, painted Gare Saint-Lazare *(above) in 1877. The station, with its vaulted iron and glass roof, was one of seven terminals in Paris. Such was the status of the railroad in its youth that great stations were built in the heart of most cities—along with their sprawling marshaling yards. The vista at right was part of the working quarter of Newcastle upon Tyne. Slum houses and tenements were built "of the commonest materials," complained a British Royal Commission, "with the worst workmanship . . . altogether unfit for people to live in." The progressive piling up of housing units in such factory towns as Newcastle reached incredible proportions in the cities. "I have seen the lowest quarters of Marseilles, Antwerp and Paris," wrote the French philosopher Hippolyte Taine after a visit to London. "They come nowhere near this. Squat houses, wretched streets, stifling alleys, troops of pale children crouching on filthy staircases. . . ."*

The Birth of Coketown

One of the bitter fruits of industrialism was its physical impact on the urban centers of the world. The centralization so necessary to efficient and profitable manufacture spawned what the urban critic Lewis Mumford has christened Coketown. At night, Mumford writes, "its prevailing color was black. Black clouds of smoke rolled out of the factory chimneys, and the railroad yards, which often cut clean into the town, mangling the very organism, spread soot and cinders everywhere. . . . The manufacture of illuminating gas within the confines of the towns became a characteristic new feature: the huge gas tanks reared their bulk over the urban landscape, great structures, on the scale of a cathedral: their tracery of iron, against an occasional clear lemon-green sky at sunrise, was one of the most pleasant aesthetic elements in the new order."

Of themselves, Mumford notes, the elements of the industrial age "were not necessarily evil; . . . in their segregation they might have been comely." Brunel's viaducts were graceful in their proportions and his tunnel entrances bore pleasing Romanesque designs. In skilled hands the new materials—iron, steel, sheet glass—became original and eloquent structures. But these were the exceptions. In Manchester and Lille and Essen and Pittsburgh and a hundred other cities the slums and factories and railroads spread cancerously, uncontrolled and uncontrollable. In the rush toward profit and in the name of progress the city planner was ignored and aesthetic considerations forgotten. The architect, writes a critic, "suddenly becomes a dim figure . . . retreating into his ivory tower." "Never before in recorded history," concludes Mumford, "had such vast masses of people lived in such a savagely deteriorated environment. . . ."

Captains of Industry

One of the gold medal winners at the Great Exhibition of 1851 in the Crystal Palace was Alfred Krupp of Essen, honored for his design of a 6-pounder steel cannon. At the time Krupp found no interested buyers, but it was not long before the world heard more from the "Cannon King." In the long Krupp dynasty he was known as Alfred the Great. His policy was to sell arms to anyone who would pay for them; "he would not stretch his patriotism at the cost of potential Krupp profit," said a biographer. After the Battle of König-grätz in 1866 a Prussian general wrote Alfred the Great: "Those children of yours conversed for long hot hours with their Austrian cousins. . . ." An arms race was music to Krupp ears.

In the course of the second half of the nineteenth century, Krupp and a few score other titans came to wield enormous power. Supported by the popular theories of Social Darwinism ("the survival of the fittest"), blessed with government support or at least non-interference, they manipulated the levers of industrial capitalism to gain power, fame, and fortune. Their favorite lever was the one controlling competition. Through such devices as the joint-stock merger (Britain), trusts and holding companies (United States), and cartels (Germany), they divided the market and eliminated competition. These devices soon became international in scope; Alfred Nobel, for example, the Swedish inventor of dynamite, set up the Dynamite Trust, Ltd. in 1886 to control the explosives markets of five nations.

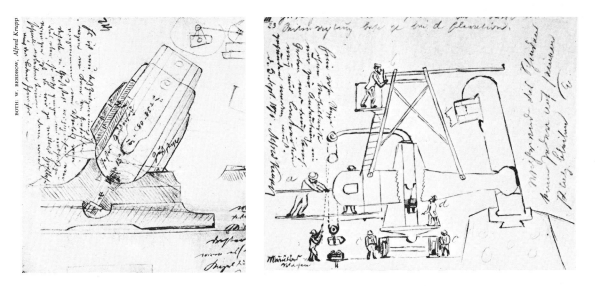

The two sketches above are from the notebook of Alfred Krupp. On the left is his design for a huge 550-millimeter mortar that was used in the siege of Paris in 1870, one of dozens of heavy guns that hurled an average of 300 shells nightly into the French capital during the four-month siege. Above right is Krupp's drawing of an advanced "panzerkanone," dated 1875. The scene below, painted by Otto Bollhagen, is the Krupp foundry in Essen in 1873.

These French advertising posters all date from about 1900. The poster for home furnishings on the opposite page reflects strong Art Nouveau influences, while the one at the right, for bathroom appointments, is strong on snob appeal. Many artists of the day, since famous, tried their hand at posters— for example, Toulouse-Lautrec (pages 578–579) and two represented in color on this page, Albert Guillaume, promoting Nil cigarettes, and Theophile Steinlen, appealing to lady cyclists.

For Public Consumption

From midcentury on, the benefits of industrialization affected most strongly and most immediately the urban middle class. Possessing the creature comforts before industry began mass-producing them, the aristocracy and the upper classes realized no radical change in their living standards. The lower classes, the masses, were the last to reap benefits, and these were at first in areas that the other classes took for granted: sewer systems, water lines, the rudiments of sanitary plumbing, heating units, gas and then electric illumination. In any case, daily life and (except for the upper classes) standards of living were radically altered by the mass and variety of consumer goods that the new technology was inventing, the new factories producing, and the new transportation delivering.

Refrigeration, the ubiquitous "tin" can, pasteurization, and packaging innovations changed eating habits. The sewing machine, the vacuum cleaner, and the washing machine gave housewives a new outlook. Ready-made clothing and machine-made shoes wrought a sartorial revolution. Advances in printing technology brought mass-circulation newspapers and magazines and inexpensive books into the bourgeois parlor and "fine art" prints to its walls. Carpeting, wallpaper, and furnishings became available in good quantity if not in good taste. The pleasures of the cities came within reach, thanks to street lighting and public transportation. The bicycle, railroad, and steamboat encouraged excursions into the countryside and more elaborate vacations. And simply to reach all these customers required new techniques of marketing and more sophisticated advertising—witness the examples reproduced here.

MR. AND MRS. WILLIAM LINCER COLLECTION, NEW YORK

Pictures of Misery

Europe, remarked the Conservative party's Benjamin Disraeli, was fast splitting into "two nations—the Rich and the Poor. . . . The claims of the future are represented by suffering millions." Commenting on the same phenomenon, Karl Marx observed: "everything seems pregnant with its contrary; machinery gifted with the wonderful power of shortening and fructifying human labour, we behold starving and overworking it." The facts of urban poverty, of a large mass of workers stripped of economic security and defenseless against economic fluctuations, had become a part of the new age.

Disraeli and Marx saw the problem in its broad dimensions; the artist Kaethe Kollwitz, the wife of a Berlin doctor, saw it on an individual, personal level. With much of her husband's practice devoted to social work and a primitive form of socialized medical care for the poor, she witnessed the dreary cycle of illness, unemployment, alcoholism, and desertion, and confided in her diary, "The more I see of it, the more I realize that this is the *typical* misfortune of the workers' families. As soon as the man drinks or is sick and unemployed it is always the same story. . . . For the woman the misery is always the same." Working in charcoal or crayon, limiting herself to browns, blacks, and greys, she strove to capture the blunt images of poverty and exploitation. "I must try to keep everything to a more and more abbreviated form," she wrote, "so that all the essentials are strongly stressed and the inessentials almost omitted."

In the manner of many socially conscious artists (Hogarth, for example), her major work was in series form. Her first series, "The Weavers" (1898), took its inspiration from an abortive revolt by Silesian weavers in 1842, but its individual plates—*Poverty, The Conspiracy, Riot*—had universal, contemporary implications. The series won a gold medal at an exhibition in Berlin, but Kaiser William II squelched the presentation, noting his distaste for "gutter art." (This was not Kaethe Kollwitz' last experience with censorship; after 1933, under Nazi edict, her art was removed from German museums.)

The three examples of her work shown here all date from about 1909. *Lunch Hour* (opposite) is a study of factory workers. The common practice of wives of the poor doing piece work, such as sewing on lace, is the subject of the drawing above right, *The Home Worker.* Below right is *The Homeless*, published in a German magazine in 1909 as one of a series she titled "Pictures of Misery."

A New Dynamism

Historians examining the latter half of the nineteenth century have
given the period a variety of labels: the Age of Exploitation, the
Age of Progress, the Age of Materialism, the Age of Optimism.
Contemporaries were of several minds as well; to the optimists industrialization promised progress, growth, dynamism. "Machinery was indeed
dynamic, not static," writes the historian C. J. H. Hayes. "By a kind of
parthenogenesis, it multiplied itself; so that everybody was now minded to
talk, in the manner of the enlightened Englishman described by Chester-
ton, 'as if clocks produced clocks, or guns had families of little pistols, or a
penknife littered like a pig.'" It was widely believed that in time the
material benefits of industrialization would produce an earthly order not
unlike the precisely ordered universe Newton had promulgated in the sixteenth century. If the industrial machine still misfired and ran raggedly—
and the periodic economic depressions testified that it did—all that was
needed was a few adjustments; the machine itself appeared sound.

Dynamism was the credo of a group of Italian artists and writers who
founded about 1909 a movement termed Futurism (Chapter 28). Futurists
exalted science, technology, and mechanics; the painter Giacomo Balla, for
example, sought the speed and movement of the city in his abstract canvases (above). The young architect Antonio Sant'Elia saw the marriage
between industrialism and urbanization producing *The New City* (left;
1914). "We must invent and remake the Futurist city to be like a huge
tumultuous shipyard, agile, mobile, dynamic in all its parts," he wrote.
"Every generation should build its own city."

One of the less felicitous tenets of the Futurists was their glorification
of war as "the only health giver of the world"—a belief that was to cost
Sant'Elia his life at the front in 1916. Yet without doubt industrialization
brought with it a many-fold increase in military power. It was this fact and
its implications that has been termed "the lurking nemesis" facing the
Western world as it turned into the twentieth century.

18

Urban Culture
and the Middle Class

Some of the most significant changes in the quality of Western life in the nineteenth century resulted from the process of urbanization, that is, the shift of the population from the countryside to the city. As a consequence of this shift, the city—traditionally an enclave in a rural sea—became for many Western countries the normal place of habitation and for the whole modern world the main source of cultural values. The distinction that we draw between the term *urbane* and the term *provincial* reflects the predominantly urban character of modern civilization, much as the contrast between *noble* and *menial* or *villainous* reflected the rural character of medieval life The term *urbane* in modern usage is synonymous with *polite, courteous, civil, mannerly,* while *provincial* means *intolerant, illiberal, narrow-minded, insular.* It is not difficult to determine whose values this terminology reflects.

Though the city had grown in importance with the rise of industrialization and the revolutions of 1848, until the middle of the century the urban population was everywhere in a minority. From 1851, when Britain first registered more urban than rural inhabitants, urbanization proceeded everywhere at a rapid pace, especially in countries with developed industrial economies. In 1914 the urban element accounted for 80 percent of the population in Britain, more than 60 percent in Germany, more than 45 percent in France. By that time even countries with relatively weak industries, like Russia, Poland, and Denmark, had one out of three citizens residing in cities. The increase was particularly striking in large towns. Budapest and Berlin, for example, increased their population tenfold in the course of the nineteenth century. Prior to 1800 not a single European city had a million inhabitants; since then, more than 50 have exceeded that number. The multimillion-person metropolis has determined the course of Western history during the past century.

The typical old European town had been confined to a compact area enclosed by one or more rings of defensive walls. These walls, which remained in place long after they had lost their military significance, artificially constrained urban growth. In the second half of the nineteenth century they were generally pulled down and turned into parks and boulevards. Freed from their confinement, European cities spilled into the adjacent countryside, engulfing villages, farmlands, orchards, pastures, and forests. The outward movement became especially pronounced toward the end of the century, when the construction of streetcar lines and commuter trains made it possible to house the working population far away from its place of employment.

The map of Cologne (following page) will illustrate this development. The area marked with the numerals I through III represents the whole city area as of 1800; it hardly differs from that of the ancient Roman town of Colonia Agrippina that had occupied the same location. The population that gravitated toward this important commercial center in the course of the nineteenth century

W. H. Egley's In the Omnibus, *painted in 1859, manages to capture—in its costumes, its expressions, even in its composition—the very essence of the urban middle class that dominated English social and cultural life during the reign of Queen Victoria.*

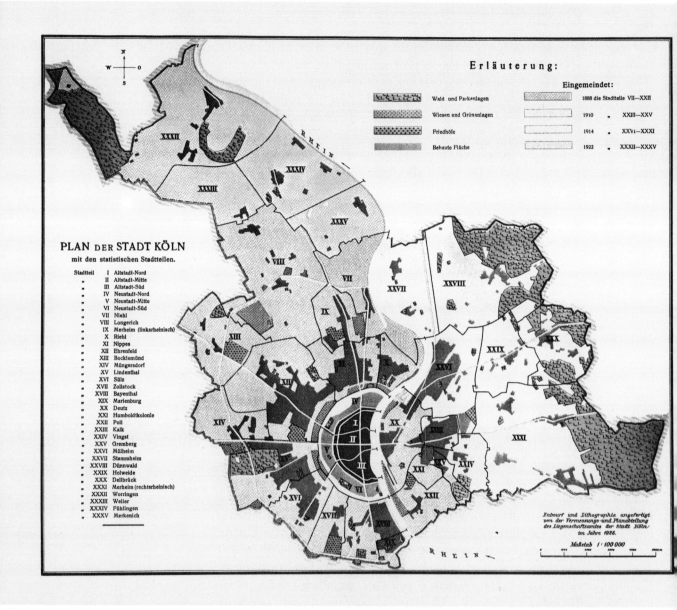

PLAN DER STADT KÖLN
mit den statistischen Stadtteilen.

Stadtteil
	I	Altstadt-Nord
	II	Altstadt-Mitte
	III	Altstadt-Süd
	IV	Neustadt-Nord
	V	Neustadt-Mitte
	VI	Neustadt-Süd
	VII	Niehl
	VIII	Longerich
	IX	Merheim (linksrheinisch)
	X	Riehl
	XI	Nippes
	XII	Ehrenfeld
	XIII	Bocklemünd
	XIV	Müngersdorf
	XV	Lindenthal
	XVI	Sülz
	XVII	Zollstock
	XVIII	Bayenthal
	XIX	Marienburg
	XX	Deutz
	XXI	Humboldtkolonie
	XXII	Poll
	XXIII	Kalk
	XXIV	Vingst
	XXV	Gremberg
	XXVI	Mülheim
	XXVII	Stammheim
	XXVIII	Dünnwald
	XXIX	Holweide
	XXX	Dellbrück
	XXXI	Merheim (rechtsrheinisch)
	XXXII	Worringen
	XXXIII	Weiler
	XXXIV	Fühlingen
	XXXV	Merkenich

Erläuterung:

Eingemeindet:

Wald und Parkanlagen   1888 die Stadtteile VII—XXII
Wiesen und Grünanlagen   1910   „   XXIII—XXV
Friedhöfe   1914   „   XXVI—XXXI
Bebaute Fläche   1922   „   XXXII—XXXV

Entwurf und Lithographie angefertigt
von der Vermessungs-und Planabteilung
des Liegenschaftsamtes der Stadt Köln
im Jahre 1926.

Maßstab 1 : 100 000

A plan of Cologne shows the city's growth in stages from 1888 to 1922. I-IV designates the pre-1888 city. The key at upper center delineates (reading down) forest and parks, meadowland, cemeteries, and arable land.

could not be accommodated within these narrow limits and settled in adjacent villages. In the early 1880s Cologne constructed new walls, gaining a bit of additional space (IV–VI), but this space was so quickly filled up that the authorities had to give up the effort to contain the city within definite, neatly drawn boundaries. In the 1890s Cologne burst from its confines, losing the appearance of an enclosed area and acquiring the sprawling, amorphous shape of the typical modern city. Quarters designated VII–XXII were incorporated in 1888, XXIII–XXV in 1910, and XXVI–XXXI in 1914. A similar pattern of growth took place in other European towns. The outline maps of the expansion of London (opposite) resemble ink spots spreading on a sheet of blotting paper.

In the regions of intense industrialization, for example, the western Midlands of England or the Ruhr in Germany, the towns grew so large that they soon absorbed the entire countryside separating them from each other. The result were urban clusters—"conurbia," or "megalopolises" as they are called today. Where this occurred, the usual distinction between town and country lost meaning.

The social group identified with urban life is known as the middle class (in French, *bourgeoisie*). This term is not easy to define, because it is so often loosely used. For our purpose we shall define the middle class as consisting of those who derived their income from non-agrarian property, or professional skills and services and distinguish it from the landed aristocracy and the peasantry on the one hand and from manual labor on the other.

The middle class can be subdivided further into an upper and a lower part. The upper bourgeoisie consisted of industrial entrepreneurs, bankers and wealthy investors, big merchants, and representatives of the free professions. Although it lacked formal criteria of exclusiveness comparable to those the aristocracy had in family ancestry, the upper-middle class did maintain its identity and cohesion by a variety of devices. Until approximately 1870, for instance, it shared with the nobility a virtual monopoly on political representation. It also controlled access to the secondary schools, attendance at which in turn assured entrance to institutions of higher learning and, beyond them, to the professions. And, of course, it controlled capital and credit, the sinews of modern economic life.

The lower-middle class or petty bourgeoisie embraced a large and amorphous body of persons who furnished the aristocracy and upper-middle class with goods and services. It included shopkeepers, artisans, and domestic servants. Wedged between the prestigious upper-middle class and the mass of manual laborers, the petty bourgeoisie was habitually insecure: eager to climb up the social ladder, dreading proletarianization, it was despised alike by the bourgeoisie proper, whom it wished to emulate, and by the manual workers, from whom it wished to separate itself.

Many large cities had, in addition to the upper- and lower-middle class and the manual laborers, a fourth social group consisting of intellectuals, students, artists, and others, who were usually of middle-class background but detached from it. This "bohemian" element sometimes settled in separate districts, usually on the edge of a slum (e.g., Montparnasse and Montmartre in Paris), and in periods of acute social unrest often allied itself with the working classes against the bourgeoisie.

The rapid growth of cities in the nineteenth century destroyed the cultural homogeneity that had previously characterized urban life. The modern metropolis performs a great variety of economic, administrative, and cultural functions and attracts a corresponding variety of cultural groups, each with its own values and codes of behavior. It is really many towns in one. In dealing with it, therefore, one must distinguish the component groups that, although equally "urban," have differing and often incompatible aspirations. We shall discuss the working class and its supporters among the intelligentsia in the next chapter. Here we shall concentrate on the upper-middle class, the social group that more than any other set its stamp on the nineteenth century.

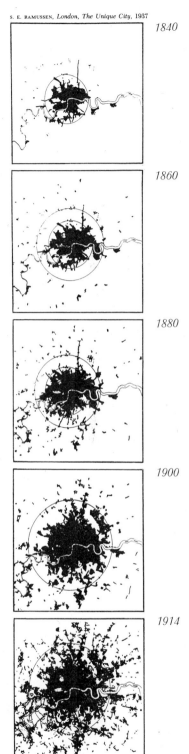

S. E. RAMUSSEN, *London, The Unique City*, 1937

1840

1860

1880

1900

1914

The built-up area of London, traced over three quarters of a century. In 1840 the circled zone was four miles in diameter, in 1914, nine and a half.

The Upper-Middle Class: Morals and Manners

The model for the upper-middle class was primarily English, but it was international in scope. The ethics, manners, and tastes of the nineteenth-century bourgeoisie were remarkably uniform. The English Victorian businessman exerted a powerful influence even in countries where life remained largely rural and agrarian, for it was easier to transplant values and modes of behavior than economic or social institutions. The same held true, although to a lesser degree, of the lower-middle class, which also displayed throughout the Western world many common cultural characteristics.

Although the bourgeoisie achieved a dominant position only in the nineteenth century, it is a class with a venerable past. According to the historian Werner Sombart, it originated in Italy in the fourteenth century. It was then that literary works appeared espousing virtues that ever since have been regarded as typically middle class: orderliness, industry, thrift, and the avoidance of sensual temptations and "bad company." Similar ideals were popularized in the so-called merchants' manuals that proliferated between the sixteenth and eighteenth centuries. Among literary works in this tradition are Daniel Defoe's *Robinson Crusoe* and Benjamin Franklin's *Poor Richard's Almanack*. These writings laid stress on the inner purity of the "good man": the "good man" thought cleanly and acted fairly, and by so doing also served best his own interests. In Protestant countries the ideal bourgeois was often depicted as endowed with divine blessing, his wealth being heaven's reward for virtue. His antitheses were the irresponsible, dissipated aristocrat and the slothful, depraved pauper.

Perhaps the most prominent feature of bourgeois culture, in the period of its gestation as well as its maturity, was its inclination to view everything in moral terms. How one disposed of money or brought up children, what relations one established with persons of the opposite sex, and what one did with leisure time testified not only to one's judgment but also and above all to one's virtue. This obsession with morality was a source of both strength and weakness in bourgeois culture.

Thanks to its moral sensitivity, the middle class never remained content simply to bask in its privileges and wealth. It is true that much of the bourgeoisie proved smug and callous and refused to accept responsibility for those less fortunate, treating poverty as punishment for laziness or depravity. But it is equally incontrovertible that the bourgeoisie produced in generation after generation a body of reformers who, by touching its conscience, were able to persuade it to share its advantages. It would be difficult to find in history another social group as firmly entrenched in power as the European bourgeoisie in the first half of the nineteenth century that did not use its power merely to entrench itself further. But the European bourgeoisie abolished serfdom at home and slavery abroad, did away with discriminatory laws against religious and national minorities, extended public education to the masses, and permitted labor to organize and everyone to vote. By these and other similar measures it forfeited both its economic and political monopoly. In a sense, the bourgeoisie undermined its hegemony, but by so doing, it spared most of Europe a revolution.

But there is also another aspect to this moral sensibility. The pre-industrial businessman had lived and worked in a world of relative equals: whether negotiating with another merchant, directing a small body of apprentices, or farming out tasks to domestic craftsmen, he could act in accord with the precepts of justice and charity. This became difficult and sometimes impossible under conditions of industrialism. Industrialization, with its open-market economy, encouraged and indeed forced businessmen to compete, and competition was difficult to contain within ethical bounds, especially if defeat spelled ruin. Free trade brought the abolition of elaborate schemes of price and labor regulations by which early business had enforced fair dealing. Furthermore, industrialization separated the entrepreneur from the mass of wage earners and increasingly left the direction of business to salaried managers who executed but did not initiate policy. All these developments tended to deprive economic activity of moral connotations. The businessman of the industrial era had to be aggressive and in his everyday dealings act on principles very different from those that his religious conscience dictated. William Thackeray in his novel *The Newcomes* (1853–1855) offers the following bit of worldly advice, which, even if given tongue in cheek, gives a fair idea of the practical Victorian's outlook:

> To push on in the crowd, every male or female struggler must use his or her shoulders. If a better place than yours presents itself just beyond your neighbor, elbow him and take it. Look how a steadily-purposed man or woman at court, at a ball, or exhibition, wherever there is a competition and a squeeze, gets the best place; the nearest the sovereign, if bent on kissing the royal hand; the closest to the grand stand, if minded to go to Ascot; the best view and hearing of the Rev. Mr. Thumpington, when all the town is rushing to hear that exciting divine; the largest quantity of ice, champagne and seltzer, cold pâté, or other his or her favorite flesh-pot, if gluttonously minded, at a supper whence hundreds of people come empty away. . . . Is there a good place at table? Take it. At the Treasury or the Home Office? Ask for it. Do you want to go to a party to which you are not invited? Ask to be asked. Ask A., ask B., ask Mrs. C., ask everybody you know: you will be thought a bore; but you will have your way. What matters if you are considered obtrusive, provided that you obtrude? By pushing steadily, nine hundred ninety-nine people in a thousand will yield to you. . . . If your neighbor's foot obstructs you, stamp on it; and do you suppose he won't take it away?

The code of behavior described by Thackeray contradicted the assimilated canons of religious ethics, and the conflict between "Sunday and Monday," between ethics and reality, ran like a thread through nineteenth-century middle-class life. The conflict was aggravated by the spread of science with its challenge to religious beliefs. In some these conflicts led to a psychological crisis from which they sought escape in religion, aestheticism, or socialism. But most members of the middle class resolved the dilemmas by ignoring their existence, that is, acting as though there were no contradictions. Such was the source of hypocrisy, the most outstanding Victorian vice, the natural safety valve of a society whose "practical ideals were at odds with its religious professions, and [whose] religious belief was at issue with its intelligence."°

°G. M. Young, *Early Victorian England, 1830–1865* (1934).

The central upper-middle class institution was the family. This had been the case even in the Middle Ages, as testified by the prevalence of representations of the Holy Family in religious paintings commissioned by medieval bourgeois patrons. One of the earliest middle-class manuals, written by Leon Battista Alberti, a fifteenth-century Florentine humanist, was called *Della Famiglia (On the Family)*; it depicted family cohesion as indispensable to a virtuous life. Alberti called for the submissiveness of wife to husband and children to father, good domestic management, proper education and manners, and sexual purity.

In the nineteenth century economic changes modified the function of the family without depriving it of its traditional importance in middle-class life. When the ideal of the middle-class family first emerged, the family had been an effective economic unit in the sense that its members could and often did engage in joint business activities such as banking, trading, or handicrafts. The modern division of labor and separation of ownership, management, and manual work loosened the economic ties binding the family and transformed it into a primarily cultural unit. It performed this function by a variety of religious, artistic, and literary activities.

Christmas had been originally a purely religious holiday, and had been celebrated in church. During the Reformation in Germany, it first became common

A water color by an unknown artist, dating from about 1865, shows the living room of a well-to-do Lombard family. An engaged couple sits in perfect propriety amidst the ornate furnishings and décor, chaperoned by the girl's mother busy at embroidery.

practice to celebrate Christmas at home. From Germany the custom of domestic Christmas celebrations was transplanted to England by Queen Victoria's German husband, Prince Albert, and from England it spread to the United States. Charles Dickens' *A Christmas Carol* (1843) did much to popularize the custom among English-speaking peoples. It subsequently became in Protestant countries and some Catholic ones an important formal manifestation of family loyalty.

A good middle-class family engaged in cultural activities every day of the year, as well as on weekends and holidays. Very common, especially in England, was the custom of reading aloud. It was both a form of entertainment at a time when there was little of it, and an assertion of domestic cohesiveness. Musical activities were also much in vogue. Middle-class women were expected either to play an instrument or to sing, and in Germany families sometimes formed complete musical ensembles. Culture so relentlessly pursued within the walls of the household inevitably influenced the content and form of literature and art. Books and journals read to the whole family had to avoid subjects unsuited for the ears of children. This consideration accounts in large measure for the well-known prudery of nineteenth-century literature. Older works that did not meet these standards were sometimes expurgated or "bowdlerized," as the procedure came to be known when Thomas Bowdler in 1818 brought out a *Family Shakespeare*.

The genteel life of the middle-class family would not have been possible were it not for the availability of cheap domestic help. The supply came from the overpopulated rural areas. Wages were low and working conditions bad. A full-time chambermaid in mid-Victorian England, in addition to room and board, received a wage of 30 shillings a month—the price at the time of a standard "triple-decker" (three-volume) novel. Domestics were housed in cramped quarters in attics or basements, or even in the kitchen, so as to be available whenever needed. Nevertheless, there was never any shortage of help, because rural girls were lured to the city by its excitements, the hope of marriage, and the opportunity of acquiring a city appearance and manner and thereby improving their social status. The richer middle-class neighborhoods had hordes of domestics. In 1861 England had more persons employed in domestic service than in the textile industry. At the end of the century a seventh of the entire British labor force was engaged in paid domestic work—2,600,000 persons, compared to 1,600,000 engaged in agriculture and fishing.

An important feature of middle-class culture was its attitude toward sex. Here, too, family considerations were decisive. The middle-class household could not tolerate sexual laxity because it threatened its cohesion and even survival: scandal, divorce, an illegitimate child were tragedies afflicting not only persons directly involved, but the entire family. The reaction to the threat was ruthless, both on the part of relatives and society at large; it involved expulsion from the home, disinheritance, and social ostracism. In France the law went so far as to virtually absolve a husband for the murder of an adulterous wife. The bourgeoisie prided itself on its sexual chastity, seeing in it yet another proof of its superiority to the aristocracy and to the lower class. It viewed sex as an unavoidable but regrettable means of procreation and tolerated it only for this purpose.

This attitude had various effects, not all salutary. The sexual life of human

William Holman Hunt painted The Awakening Conscience *in 1853. It depicts the moment when a slightly soiled dove sees her error and leaps in horror from her paramour's lap. The purchaser, however, had Hunt repaint her expression; she now appears to be reconsidering her decision.*

beings is more complicated than nineteenth-century middle-class morals allowed, and it would not stay confined within such narrow bounds. Nowhere was hypocrisy carried farther than in this respect. Middle-class men found it easy to satisfy their appetites with women of the lower classes, and society tolerated such escapades as preferable to family breakup. Prostitution increased enormously in the big cities at the very time when sexual standards were ostensibly at their strictest. The rate of illegitimate births was also high. Records show that in 1851, 42,000 illegitimate children were born in England—a figure interpreted by a contemporary to mean that "one in twelve of the unmarried females in the country above the age of puberty strayed from the path of virtue." In Austria at the end of the century one out of every eight children was born out of wedlock and in France one out of four. How many such children were not recorded and how many were aborted or killed we shall never know.

Sexual escapades were available in the upper-middle class only to men. Women were expected to adhere to prevailing standards and indeed did so to a remarkable degree. They had to be chaste not only in their behavior, but also in their thoughts. If not always as saintly as middle-class imagination depicted them, they were at any rate expected to repress their feelings and conform. This double standard placed a great burden on middle-class women. Only in the 1880s did psychiatry begin to discover the repressive causes of many inexplicable ailments, such as hysteria, and help gain acceptance for a more tolerant attitude toward sex.

In theory, middle-class society was open to anyone with the requisite personal qualities and accomplishments. The criteria were not external (such as ancestry) but internal. It is for this reason that so much importance was attached to good manners, which served as an outward manifestation of inner purity. Etiquette manuals, which proliferated in this era, often identified good manners with religious virtues. One of the most popular manuals, Mrs. H. O. Ward's *Sensible Etiquette of the Best Society*, includes this passage:

> If we examine the laws which good society lays down for our guidance and governance, we shall find without doubt, that they are those which a simple Christian, desiring to regulate the meetings of a number of people who lacked the Christian feeling would dictate. . . . The considerations which dictate [the laws of society] are reducible to the same law, and this law proves to be the fundamental one of the Christian doctrine. . . . The great law of Christianity which inculcates brotherly love and self-denial, finds its counterpart in the first law of politeness—to be agreeable to everybody, even at the expense of one's comfort. Peace is the object of Christian laws; harmony that of social observances. . . . Pride, selfishness, ill-temper are alike opposed to Christianity and good breeding.

Such manuals laid particular stress on the necessity of treating all people as equals and savagely condemned "snubbing," "sniffing," or "cutting." It is easy to understand why a class composed of so many self-made persons, forever dreading the aristocratic sneer, should have attached so much importance to this matter.

Those who did not conform to the accepted norms of behavior were regarded as "bad company," distinguished by such traits as vulgarity, arrogance, and disrespect for public opinion. The "fast woman"—a species of "bad company"—was depicted as a person who flirted, sought out male friends, engaged furiously in sports, and used cosmetics.

Although in theory a "company of equals" and open to all who met its standards of morality and breeding, middle-class society placed many obstacles in the path of those who aspired to rise to it from the lower ranks. Its standards could be attained only by those persons who were successful in the struggle for survival. Money was an unspoken assumption of middle-class morals and manners: money to buy a good education, to secure independence, and to pay for a staff of domestics.

Although such matters are admittedly subjective, there is general agreement that the high tide of middle-class influence (between approximately 1830 and 1890) marked a nadir in taste. The age seems quite to have exhausted its inventiveness in science and technology and to have remained content with borrowing aesthetic guidance from the past. It created no style of its own, preferring to adapt or "revive."

The tastes of the middle class were influenced by three criteria: realism, moral significance, and ostentatiousness. A pragmatic being, the bourgeois wanted his art to represent life as it was, that is, as perceived by the eye and by common sense. He had little use for allegory, mythology, or the frank sensualism of aristocratic art. Middle-class art was realistic in the sense that it strove at verisimilitude. Yet its realism was diluted by a penchant for moralizing. It was not art for art's sake but art that carried a message. John Ruskin, the most in-

The Upper-Middle Class: Tastes

fluential art critic of the century, never tired of stressing the moral element in aesthetic experience: The more a work of art elevated the spirit, the greater, according to his *Modern Painters*, was its artistic merit:

> The difference between great and mean art lies, not in definable methods of handling, or styles or representation, or choices of subjects, but wholly in the nobleness of the end to which the effort of the painter is addressed. We cannot say that a painter is great because he paints boldly, or paints delicately; because he generalizes or particularizes; because he loves detail, or because he disdains it. He is great if, by any of these means, he has laid open noble truths, and aroused noble emotions.

Although Ruskin had subtler criteria in mind, most of his contemporaries interpreted his rule to mean that art must convey a moral lesson. This view reached its extremes in Russia, where the radical publicist Nicholas Chernyshevskii had much success in the 1850s with an aesthetic doctrine that judged art solely by its ability to awaken public conscience against social injustice. Leo Tolstoy in *What Is Art?* (1898) rejected all creative efforts that did not make men better Christians. Among the authors he dismissed on these grounds was Shakespeare.

The desire to reconcile realism and morality resulted in a sentimentalized, pseudo-realistic art. Content once more took the upper hand over form and color. In its choice of themes, bourgeois art showed a preference for historic subjects, domestic scenes, and episodes from the life of the peasantry. Because of their

METROPOLITAN MUSEUM OF ART

Two examples of popular bourgeois art are offered here. At left is Pierre Auguste Cot's The Storm *(1880), respectable but titillating. On the opposite page is Sir Edwin Landseer's* The Old Shepherd's Chief Mourner. *Such scenes of bathos won Landseer a wide following.*

didactic value, contrasts were in vogue: age and youth, life and death, wealth and poverty, virtue and sin were all depicted in a manner calculated to induce moral reflections. Landscapes and religious subjects declined in popularity, the former because they could not be moralized, the latter because they were difficult to present realistically. Great attention was paid to a smooth finish and faithful rendition of detail.

The names of the nineteenth-century painters whose canvases brought the highest prices are hardly remembered today. Manuals of art history pass them by, and museums store their works out of sight. Yet for the historian they are of the greatest importance as indicators of prevailing taste. The painters most in demand were not the Impressionists, who did not come into their own until the turn of the century, and then only among advanced connoisseurs, but such artists as Sir Edwin Landseer, Sir John Millais, Sir Edward Burne-Jones, Constant Troyon, Rosa Bonheur, and J. L. E. Meissonier. Their works fetched in the latter part of the century today's equivalent of $50,000–$100,000 and more. The buyers who paid these sums were levelheaded businessmen who thought they were making a wise investment. They could hardly have been more wrong. When tastes changed early in the twentieth century, their paintings lost nearly all value. Burne-Jones' *Love and Pilgrim*, bought in 1898 for £5,775 (in purchasing power, the equivalent today of some $120,000), sold in 1941 for £21 (less than $100). Troyon's masterpiece, *Les Hauteurs de Suresnes*, bought in 1889 for £3,045 ($50,000), was disposed of in 1944 for the equivalent of two cases of black-market whiskey. These examples are by no means exceptional, but typical.

The taste of the middle class was most evident in the architecture and home furnishings of the time. The guiding principle was ostentation, for, although in theory money was frowned upon, in reality those who had it liked to display it, especially if they had made it themselves. They strove for heaviness and elaborateness, an effect they achieved with the aid of machines. Until the nineteenth century, an elaborate object was expensive because it required more labor than a plain object. Ornament, therefore, symbolized wealth. The invention of machines able to produce cheaply various kinds of ornament altered this situation, but the basic attitude remained. The bourgeoisie seized on the opportunities that technology offered to surround itself with visible tokens of affluence by decorating everything, including objects of the simplest utility. The result was a veritable orgy of ornamentation. The decorations of this period strike the modern eye as particularly disagreeable because they bear no relation either to function or basic design. The low point was reached at the Great (Crystal Palace) Exhibition of 1851, which demonstrated the possibilities of over-ornamenting every imaginable object from railroad locomotives to bathroom fixtures.

The cluttered appearance of bourgeois interiors was heightened by a predilection for bric-a-brac. Every open space and surface had to be filled. Walls that were not completely covered with paintings encased in rich gilded frames were hung with Oriental swords and shields, carved mirrors, tapestries, and stag heads. Floor space was crowded with cupboards containing china and glass, with potted tropical plants, and endless *objets d'art*. Draperies made of heavy, opaque

Upon careful inspection it is possible to pick out from among the ferns and fretwork and animal skins decorating her Paris studio the celebrated Victorian actress Sarah Bernhardt.

materials increased the impression of richness and solidity. Windows were seldom opened.

The greatest achievement of middle-class culture was the novel. Although not a new literary genre, it came into its own in the nineteenth century. The novel— especially that which we have described as Realistic—concerned itself with the relationship of individuals to each other and to society at large, and as such admirably suited an age of great social transformations and preoccupations with moral problems. By virtue of its length, the nineteenth-century novel required an audience of leisured readers, which it found largely among middle-class women. It broadened intellectual horizons by exposing the middle class to the life of the lower orders with whom it had little personal contact, and in this manner stimulated social reform movements.

> Man for the field, and woman for the hearth;
> Man for the sword, and for the needle she;
> Man with the head, and woman with the heart;
> Man to command, and woman to obey;
> All else confusion.

The Emancipation of Women

Thus, in "The Princess," Alfred, Lord Tennyson, the poet laureate of mid-Victorian England, defined the relationship of the sexes. The vision was a man's vision, and one may doubt whether the majority of women willingly subscribed to it. Nevertheless, it is true that in the first half of Queen Victoria's reign the Western middle-class woman was more confined to the household than either her immediate predecessor or successor.

As with so much of middle-class culture, the search for a cause leads back to the family. Woman was the pivot around which this whole institution revolved: it was her task to offer the breadwinner a refuge from the rough competitive world of business, to make sure that the children received a good education and acquired the proper manners, and to supervise the domestics. Ultimately, she guaranteed family cohesion. It was sincerely feared that if women engaged actively in public affairs they would neglect the household, and the home would collapse. The domestication of women stemmed not only from a low regard for their intelligence (which was a factor) but also from a high regard for the home as the basis of civilized life.

Women were expected to be submissive, and this demand was enforced by a variety of discriminatory laws. British and French laws in force in the first half of the century prohibited married women from owning property, even that which they had earned with their own labor. (France, however, did make an exception for real estate.) Upon marriage, a woman's property passed at once to the control of her husband. (According to the English historian G. M. Trevelyan, "The law was in curious contrast to the words of the marriage service, when the man was made to say 'with all my worldly goods I thee endow'; it was really the other way around.") Women were also discriminated against in laws pertaining to the family that virtually barred them from initiating divorce proceedings or claiming legal authority over their children. And, of course, they could not vote.

The discrimination enforced against women violated the tenets of liberalism,

A heavily tasseled, decidedly over-stuffed French rocker, evidence that Victorian taste crossed the Channel.

Perfect decorum in beachwear was one of the last bastions of the old social order to fall. This is a beach at Villerville in 1908, photographed by a precocious French youth named Jacques Henri Lartigue, age eleven.

and in a liberal age it was bound sooner or later to be challenged. The challenge, in the form of the feminist movement, emerged in the first half of the nineteenth century, acquired momentum in the second, and gained most of its objectives in the twentieth. Like other movements of the time, it was international in scope.

The first outspoken feminists were the Romantics. As proponents of feeling over convention, they disparaged marriage and extolled free love. Frederick Schlegel did so in his novel *Lucinde* (1799), and virtually every Romantic felt bound to speak up for the rights of love over authority, including that of parents and husbands. Many of the Romantics practiced what they preached, with the result that wife-stealing became among them a common occurrence. Schlegel, for example, stole the wife of a German banker, and Victor Hugo that of his friend, the critic Sainte-Beuve. The Romantic era also produced a number of prominent "emancipated women," including some outstanding novelists. The most celebrated among these were Frederick Chopin's mistress, George Sand, a French novelist who dressed in trousers and smoked cigars, and George Eliot, the author of, among other works, *Silas Marner* and *Middlemarch.*

Isolated feminist symptoms began to coalesce into a movement at the time of Louis Philippe. The Saint-Simonians were particularly active on behalf of female equality, although it is significant that they allowed women no positions of responsibility in their own organizations. Under their inspiration, Parisian women organized feminist clubs and petitioned Louis Philippe to add to his title "King of Frenchmen" that of "King of Frenchwomen."

Feminism got under way in earnest in 1848, when suddenly in Europe as well as in the United States voices were raised demanding equal political and legal rights for women. The leaders of the movement were mainly resourceful and intelligent ladies of middle-class origin. Some joined because they had become aware, through literature or philanthropic work, of the wretched condition of working-class wives; others because they hoped to exert influence on legislatures to curb drinking and gambling; still others because they sought an outlet for their idle energies.

The movement received a great boost in 1869 with the publication of John Stuart Mill's *The Subjection of Women.* With his customary incisiveness, Mill demonstrated the inconsistency of discriminatory legislation. He argued that the subservient position of woman in modern society was a relic of ancient slavery, from which men alone had succeeded in emancipating themselves; that this position was convenient to men, and they therefore brought up women believing that they were by nature submissive the better to dominate them; and that as long as woman remained in an inferior situation her true nature and capacity would remain unknown. "What we now call the nature of women," Mill wrote, "is an eminently artificial thing—the result of forced repression in some directions, and unnatural stimulation in others. It may be asserted without scruple, that no other class of dependents have had their character so entirely distorted from its natural proportions by their relation with their masters."

These arguments, reinforced by current sentiments against Negro slavery, won feminism a fanatical following among a small body of women, but they hardly persuaded public opinion. The humorous English journal *Punch* had a field day ridiculing the new generation of women; if one is to believe its cartoons, by 1870 most of them had turned into Amazons, hardly distinguishable from men. Manuals of etiquette, those reliable guides to current social ideals, rejected woman's claim to political rights. *The Habits of Good Society; A Handbook for Ladies and Gentlemen* (1869) intoned:

> What do women want with votes, when they hold the sceptre of influence with which they can control even votes, if they wield it aright? It is by women that nature writes indelible lessons in the hearts of men. Not only when she fills the sphere of a wife, a mother, a teacher, but in every state of life it is woman who has it in her power to influence for good or evil the men with whom she is thrown.

The anti-feminists replied to Mill's question, "Why can a woman rule over England, but not sit in Parliament?," by forming the Man's League for Opposing Woman's Suffrage.

But even without the vote, the position of women gradually began to improve. One of the best ways for a woman to break out of her domestic confinement was to get a job, and this became easier as the job market expanded. Nursing, which Florence Nightingale had made respectable, was one of the first professions open to women. Later some universities opened their gates to them (those of Italy and Switzerland were among the pioneers). Great gains were made in the United States, a country so short of labor that it had no choice but to allow women into occupations previously monopolized by men, including a large proportion of teaching and secretarial jobs. By gaining financial independence women strengthened their social position, and by the end of the century won in most Western countries the right to own and freely to dispose of property.

After 1870 social attitudes also underwent change. Sports came into fashion, bringing middle-class men and women into freer, more casual contact. In the 1860s a lady's physical exertions had been confined to croquet and archery. In the 1870s women adopted two new sports, lawn tennis and roller skating; in the next decade gymnastic exercises were added to the list. In the 1890s came the bicycle rage. A chaperon could hardly keep up with such strenuous activities and by the 1900s had disappeared, at any rate in England. Ladies were now permitted to travel and to attend theaters and restaurants unaccompanied. Indeed, in high English society it became fashionable to be seen in public without one's husband. Elegant hotels and restaurants came into existence to cater to the socially emancipated woman. It was in one of them, the Savoy of London, that in 1896 the Duchesse de Clermont-Tonnerre made history by becoming the first society lady to light a cigarette in public. Ladies now began to use cosmetics, which in the middle of the century had been restricted to "fast women" and prostitutes.

The change that occurred in the position of women in the closing three decades of the century was reflected in fashions. At midcentury the bourgeois woman had

An 1856 comment by Punch on the rage for crinolines in feminine fashion bore the caption, "Fragment of an unpublished novel of fashionable life."

Punch, nov. 22, 1856

deliberately dressed in a manner that precluded any useful work. When the burden of superfluous frills, laces, ruffles, and petticoats had become so great that she was unable to work or even to move, Parisian couturiers invented the "crinoline." This was a bell-shaped frame of metal or whalebone intended to support the overelaborate skirt. Crinolines came into fashion during the Second Empire, providing wits with an inexhaustible subject. A Parisian dramatist even wrote a play called *A Journey Around My Wife*. The crinoline disappeared suddenly about 1870, and from then on female attire became simpler and better suited to an active life. In the 1890s women adopted a skirt-and-blouse costume complete with collar and tie.

Despite these gains in social status and freedom, the right to vote came slowly. The first to grant equal suffrage were frontier areas where women were more active and therefore enjoyed greater freedom. New South Wales in Australia pioneered (1867), followed by Wyoming in the United States (1869) and New Zealand (1886). The first country in Europe to give women the vote was Norway (1907). In the heartland of Western Europe, however, men stanchly held on to their political power. In France women had been promised the vote by the republican government of 1848, but when time for elections came, the idea was quietly dropped. The English Reform Bill of 1832 actually disenfranchised some women who had had the vote under the old system. In 1869 propertied English ladies received the right to participate in municipal elections, but not in parliamentary ones.

To win the vote, the feminists organized toward the end of the century pressure groups modeled on the Anti-Corn Law League. These were the "suffragettes," as they were at first contemptuously called and then proudly called themselves. They agitated and demonstrated, and when these methods failed to bring the desired result, they had recourse to civil disobedience. They accosted public figures, tied themselves to lampposts, and altogether made nuisances of themselves. Some even refused to pay taxes on the grounds that they were taxed without representation. In 1904 the suffragettes formed an International Association for Woman's Suffrage and held regular congresses. But these determined efforts notwithstanding, women did not gain the vote in most countries until after World War I.

Until the 1860s the ability to read and write had been confined in most of Europe to an élite; the majority of the people could do neither. In England at the time of Victoria's accession (1837) a third of the men and half of the women were unable to sign their marriage registers. A similar proportion held in France. In less advanced countries the number of illiterates was much larger: in Italy 61.9 percent for men, 75.7 percent for women (1871); in Romania 78 percent for both sexes (1899); in Serbia 88.7 percent for men and 98.1 percent for women (1874). In effect, the majority of Europeans—from 50 percent in the most industrialized countries to more than 90 percent in the least—were excluded from participation in cultural life. The written word, the chief medium of cultural communication, remained for practical purposes the monopoly of the propertied.

The notion that education is a public responsibility has a surprisingly recent origin. Until the middle of the nineteenth century it was generally assumed that

Education and Literacy

responsibility for education rested on the family or the church. Until 1870 a country so advanced in all respects as Great Britain had virtually no provisions for public education, entrusting the matter to the initiative of private bodies.

Apart from the Jews, who always had taken special care to instruct the young, the first to concern themselves with public education were Protestant nations. In both cases, the ability to read the Holy Scriptures was considered indispensable, and learning to read constituted an essential aspect of a person's religious upbringing. Luther urged compulsory schooling, and a number of Protestant states introduced it. Scotland passed laws requiring every parish to provide a primary school as early as the sixteenth century; Sweden issued corresponding ordinances in the seventeenth century and Denmark and Prussia in the eighteenth. Although not always fully realized, these provisions gave Protestant countries an educational foundation superior to Catholic and Orthodox ones. In states with a religiously mixed population, for example, Switzerland, Protestants as a rule sent a higher proportion of their children to school than did the Catholics.

In the course of the nineteenth century it became apparent that a basic education was indispensable: it simply was not possible to develop the skills necessary for modern technology, military as well as civil, nor to operate democratic institutions with an illiterate population. Since private bodies could not support the burden of educating a population growing as rapidly as that of Europe in the nineteenth century, the state had no choice but to take over.

The first country to assume public responsibility for the education of its citizenry was France. The French had made much progress in this direction during the Revolution and the First Empire, but the most important measure was enacted in the reign of Louis Philippe. This was the Primary School Law of 1833, initiated by François Guizot (who, incidentally, was himself a Protestant), which required every commune to provide at least one primary school for its inhabitants. In the 1870s most European countries followed the example set by France. The result was a network of primary schools, financed partly by the state and partly by the communities, providing compulsory education for children between the ages of approximately six and fourteen. In a number of countries, however, public education remained a dead letter for lack of money and teachers. This was the case, for example, in Spain and Portugal, which had been among the first countries in Europe to pass laws requiring primary schooling.

The progress of education was often slowed by conflicts between proponents of clerical and lay control. The clergy, having enjoyed for many centuries the right of educating children, was loath to surrender this right to the state and insisted on playing a dominant role in public schools as well. The conflict became especially savage in France, where it provided an outlet for the basic hostility between the Republican and Conservative political blocs.

The European educational system tended to separate primary and secondary schooling into two watertight compartments. Even after about 1870, when it had become generally accepted that society owed its children a primary education, it was nowhere acknowledged that society also should assure graduates of primary schools an opportunity to continue their schooling. Secondary schools and the universities remained in effect reserved for the aristocracy and upper-middle

In the view of the French satirist Honoré Daumier, the wide dissemination of popular literature had a negative effect on the social graces.

class. Ordinary citizens were barred from secondary schools by a variety of devices, including tuition fees and language requirements (Latin and Greek). The vast majority of children, therefore, dropped out of school after completing six or eight grades and went to work. Around 1900 the proportion of primary-school pupils who proceeded to secondary schools in most of Europe varied between 2 and 5 percent. The remaining 95–98 percent, if they were persistent, had some avenues open for continuing their studies (e.g., evening schools or the so-called Mechanics Institutes), but such institutions could accommodate only a small minority. The ladder to a higher education, and through it, to professional careers, was only available to those fortunate two to five out of a hundred able to obtain a secondary-school diploma.

Primary education for the masses influenced culture long before it influenced the social structure. In the more advanced countries it virtually wiped out illiteracy. By 1901 the percentage of illiterates in England and France had declined below 6 percent. The decline was even more striking among the young; the proportion of illiterates among army recruits dropped in England and France to around 1–2 percent, and in Germany it was so insignificant that the armed forces ceased to keep illiteracy statistics. In the predominantly rural states the proportion of illiterates at the end of the century remained high: 79 percent in Russia, 68 percent in Spain, 50 percent in Italy and Hungary, 30 percent in Austria. But even here there was evident improvement among the younger generation. The proportion of recruits unable to read and write declined to 27 percent in Russia by 1913 and to 30 percent in Italy and Greece.

We know less about the culture of the lower-middle class than of the upper, because the upper-middle class controlled the institutions of opinion and taste: the influential journals and newspapers, the theater, the art salons, the universities. This fact tends to distort our view of the nineteenth century. We think of it as an age of earnestness, refinement, and gentility, because such were the qualities characterizing the élite. They by no means held true of the age as a whole if we take as our criterion the outlook of the majority. Underneath the surface of what passes for nineteenth-century culture one can clearly discern the seeds of the mass culture of our own time.

Compulsory primary schooling gave Europe a large body of citizens who were literate without being educated. They could read and write, but they had not been exposed to the humanizing influence of the liberal arts and had no taste for serious novels or informative newspapers and reviews. They preferred a simple and exciting literature that would enable them to escape their humdrum existence. This demand was met by a new literary industry designed specifically to cater to the large, semi-educated petty-bourgeois public of skilled workers, shopkeepers, clerks, and domestic servants.

In the first third of the century the mass reading public, at least in the Protestant countries, still consumed largely religious literature. A religious tract in fictional form, the Reverend Leigh Richmond's *Dairyman's Daughter*, sold 2 million copies within 18 years of its appearance in 1809. The popularity of the propaganda literature spread by the Chartists and the Anti-Corn Law League attests also to a widespread interest in politics. But even then the mass reader

The Culture of the Lower-Middle Class

The French popular press capitalized on the notorious affairs of Napoleon III. This is a title page of 1900.

hungered for sensationalism. In 1828 an enterprising English publisher sold over a million copies of a murderer's *Last Dying Speech and Confession* and in 1837 even more copies of an illustrated account of the purported thoughts of another criminal before his execution.

The 1850s mark in England a watershed in the history of mass culture. The increase of prosperity, as well as the spread of scientific views, reduced the interest in political and religious literature and created an insatiable demand for cheap escapist works. Among the principal suppliers of such works was the writer and publisher G. W. M. Reynolds, who regularly outsold Charles Dickens, the most popular author of the Victorian upper-middle class. Reynolds introduced the so-called penny dreadful, a closely printed and garishly illustrated weekly of sensational adventures. These publications provided for the first time exciting literature at a price everyone could afford. Whereas Dickens' family review *Household Words* attained in its best year a circulation of 40,000, Reynolds' penny dreadful *The London Journal* sold in the 1850s around 500,000 copies a week. Reynolds also outsold Dickens with his books. On the day of issue, his *Soldier's Wife* sold 60,000 copies, compared to 35,000 copies sold of Dickens' *Bleak House*. Among Reynolds' books were *The Mysteries of London, The Necromancer, Pope Joan, The Loves of the Harem, Omar, Leila,* and *Agnes, or Beauty and Pleasure.* Had Victorian England kept lists of its "best sellers," our notion of its literary tastes would have to be substantially revised. It seems fairly certain, however, even without such lists, that for every reader of *Vanity Fair* there were ten who read *Wagner, the Wehrwolf* or the *Empress Eugénie's Boudoir.* In France a similar taste was satisfied by the superior novels of Eugène Sue, whose most popular work was *The Mysteries of Paris* (1842–1843).

The literature devoured by the mass reader avoided the moral and social issues preoccupying the middle class. Being frankly escapist, it either skirted real human problems or settled them by means of facile solutions. In the end, love and decency conquered all. The heroes and heroines were generally of humble origin, so that the reader could identify with them. Their personalities were simple and two-dimensional: the heroines pale, weak, and chaste, the heroes virile and courageous. The narrative often introduced characters from the upper classes, but generally class lines were observed. The style inclined toward the turgid and rhetorical, the characters speaking in theatrical sentences that unconsciously parodied the language of the educated.

The success of this cheap, sensational literature did not escape the attention of the guardians of public morality either in England, where it originated, or on the Continent, to which it spread. The upper-middle class in Germany condemned it as "backstairs novels," and the Poles called it "sidewalk literature." Efforts were made to elevate public taste by promoting religious tracts, manuals of self-improvement, and popular "home magazines." Some of these publications gained success, among them the *Family Herald,* known also as "sunshine in the kitchen," a wholesome, low-priced journal that attained a circulation of 125,000. Immensely popular among the lower-middle class, especially skilled workers, was Samuel Smiles' *Self-Help* (1859), a book that advocated perseverance, diligence, thrift, and other traditional middle-class virtues as a road to fame and wealth. *Self-Help* was translated into the major European languages, its popularity attesting to the prevalence of middle-class values among a sizable segment of the working population.

The newspaper was another factor in the molding of mass culture. Until the 1880s its purpose was to serve primarily as a source of information. It was expensive (fourpence was the standard price of a London daily) and hard to read. The *Times*, the leading English paper, achieved in the middle of the century a circulation of 50,000; most of its competitors sold around 5,000 copies.

The emergence of a mass reading public made possible an entirely new kind of news writing that was designed not so much to inform as to distract. Known as "yellow journalism," it stressed subjects that for some reason have come to be known as "human interest": murder, theft, divorce, and scandal, particularly when they involved the rich. Accuracy and truthfulness were sacrificed to headlines and "scoops." The style was brief, simple, and colorful. Originated in the United States in the 1880s and 1890s by Joseph Pulitzer and William Randolph Hearst, it was introduced to Europe by Alfred Harmsworth (later Lord Northcliffe). Harmsworth founded in 1896 the *Daily Mail*, a racy paper selling at a halfpenny that quickly won an immense following among people who previously had not read newspapers. While the *Times* by then had reached a circulation of 70,000, the *Daily Mail* three years after its founding exceeded 500,000 and soon climbed well above 1 million. Harmsworth owed his success to unabashed sensationalism, keeping his readers excited by clever appeals to curiosity and national pride. With the fortune that the *Daily Mail* had brought him, Harmsworth launched other papers and in 1908 bought the *Times*. His success encouraged imitators on the Continent: France produced its *Petit Journal* and *Petit Parisien* and Germany its *Lokal-Anzeiger*, all of which sold over a million copies daily.

Among the diversions available to the masses, mention must be made of competitive sports. Traditionally an amusement of the rich, "games" became "sport" with the introduction of paid public contests. Soccer became a spectator sport in the 1870s; boxing, baseball, and tennis followed suit, and soon virtually all physical contests were commercialized.

Mass culture was not regarded in the nineteenth century as worthy of much attention, let alone respect. But with the steady improvement of the living standards of the Western population, the influence of this culture grew. In the twentieth century the lower-middle class became the most dynamic element in Western society, and its culture gradually superseded that of the bourgeoisie proper.

19

Labor and Socialism

Three distinct groups are involved in modern movements of social protest: the total body of wage earners and self-employed, the minority among them who belong to trade unions, and another minority consisting of socialist intellectuals and politicians. This fundamental distinction is often obscured by a tendency, especially prevalent among socialists, to consider modern history in terms of a dichotomy between the "bourgeoisie" and the "working class" or "proletariat." There is, of course, no homogeneous body of "proletarians." The working class is and always has been a stratified body whose upper ranks mesh imperceptibly with the lower-middle class. There are substantial differences between urban and rural workers, salaried and self-employed workers, skilled and unskilled workers, and between workers in large industrial establishments and those in small artisan shops. Furthermore, there is a basic difference in the condition and outlook of workers in countries with advanced social legislation and those in countries where such legislation is rudimentary or absent. The constant growth of the category of wage earners who provide services instead of producing goods and of the white-collar class—salaried but hardly proletarian—further complicates the picture.

A part, but only a part, of the total working population ever joined trade unions and/or became socialist. Germany, the country with the most developed socialist movement in Europe, had in 1895 an estimated working population of 35 million. Of this number, 850,000 were unionized (1900), and at most 2 million cast their votes for the socialist party. Analysis of German election returns at a time when the Social Democrats were making their biggest advances shows that, even in the most industrialized regions of the country (Silesia, Westphalia, and the Rhineland), no more than a third of the workers voted for the socialist ticket. In Britain before World War I the Labour party never won more than half a million votes, or one vote in fourteen (1910). In France in 1914 the Party of Socialist Unity, which represented most socialist groupings, gathered 1,250,000 votes from an electorate of 7 million laborers; its active membership was 69,000. In the predominantly agrarian countries of Europe the relationship between labor, trade unions, and socialist parties was even more tenuous. In Italy, out of a wage-earning population of 7,700,000, 546,000 belonged to unions (1909), and approximately 1 million voted for the socialists and anarchists (1913). In Russia the Union of Struggle for the Liberation of the Working Class—formed in 1895 —did not include among its members a single worker. In view of these facts, both trade unionism and socialism must be regarded as organizations or movements representing only a small, albeit a dynamic and articulate, element of the total working population and intelligentsia.

In the nineteenth century there emerged for the first time a self-conscious labor movement that was determined to advance the interests of the working class. Its leaders were usually skilled, well-paid workers, a kind of labor élite

Jean Jaurès, the leading figure in the French socialist movement, was photographed as he spoke to a party rally in 1913. On the very eve of World War I, as he tried to stem the drift toward war, Jaurès was assassinated by a demented super-patriot.

A membership certificate of the Amalgamated Society of Engineers, Great Britain's first modern trade union.

imbued with liberal values and ideals. Having observed the bourgeoisie wage a struggle against aristocratic privilege and win, these labor leaders insisted on acquiring similar rights for themselves—especially the right to vote and to engage in collective bargaining. The anti-bourgeois spirit among the workers, insofar as it existed, was inspired not so much by animosity toward the middle class and its culture as by resentment against the bourgeoisie for not extending to the rest of the population the rights it had gained. The innate liberalism of the small, self-conscious labor élite presented the main obstacle to the penetration of socialist ideas into labor ranks.

The labor movement usually passed through three phases: mutual-aid associations, trade unions, and political action. The earliest associations of workers were formed by journeymen, that is, members of guilds who had lost the chance of becoming masters and had to resign themselves to the status of lifelong hired hands. These associations were a by-product of the dissolution of the guilds; in countries where the guild system remained strong (e.g., Germany), labor organizations had a slow start. The purpose of the mutual-aid associations was to furnish financial assistance to members in case of illness, accident, or any other emergency. In England in the eighteenth and early nineteenth centuries they were known as "friendly societies," in Italy as "società di mutuo soccorso," and elsewhere under similar names. Most governments tolerated such associations, but through "anti-combination laws" forbade them to engage in concerted action against employers for economic benefits.

Trade unionism in the proper sense of the word became possible only when workers received the right to engage in collective bargaining. This right they won first in England. In 1824–1825 the House of Commons repealed the stringent anti-combination laws of 1799–1800. While still forbidding "conspiracy," Parliament now allowed worker associations to organize openly and to engage in peaceful negotiations with employers. In the 1830s British trade unions experienced rapid growth. On the Continent union activity remained illegal for a long time. Piedmont authorized unions in 1848, but most countries did so only after 1860 (France partly in 1864–1868 and fully in 1884, Belgium in 1866, Austria in 1870, Germany fully in 1890, Russia in 1906).

The trade union in its mature form was a counterpart of the capitalist enterprise. It was an organization established for the express purpose of negotiating collectively on behalf of its members with industrial establishments or with a branch of industry. Its aim was not to undermine the industrial or "capitalist" order but to secure within it the greatest share of economic benefits for the workers. In that sense, the trade union was inherently economically oriented and reformist rather than politically oriented and revolutionary. Trade unionism was a by-product of the prosperity created by the industrial and capitalist system; it flourished under conditions of affluence and languished under those of recession or underdevelopment.

The first modern trade union was the Amalgamated Society of Engineers, founded in England in 1850–1851. A wealthy organization with a membership of skilled and well-paid workers, the Society in 1852 demanded an industry-wide abolition of regular overtime and piecework. The employers, interpreting this demand as an infraction of their right to run their businesses as they saw fit, refused, whereupon the Society ordered a strike. For three months the Society supported its striking members. In the end, the employers broke the strike, but the Society had won the admiration of the other trades, and national "amalgamated" societies soon mushroomed throughout Great Britain. Unions of the new type were run by professional labor organizers who had sizable funds at their disposal and directed a staff of full-time lawyers, accountants, field representatives, and clerks. In 1874 British trade unions had nearly 1 million members.

Until the 1890s Britain alone had a significant trade-union movement. On the Continent its development was inhibited by various factors such as government repression, a low degree of urbanization, or by the prevalence of small productive units that were unsuitable for amalgamation on a wide scale. In 1879 when German industry was in full swing, German trade unions had only 50,000 members. (On the eve of World War I, however, they had 4 million members.) The proportion of non-agrarian wage earners belonging to unions averaged 4 percent in France (1906) and 7 percent in Italy (1909).

Trade unions were primarily concerned with securing economic advantages; on the whole, they shied away from politics. In England they hesitated to support the Chartists. After the Second Reform Act (1867), which granted the suffrage to many workers, trade unions preferred to back the Liberals rather than enter parliamentary contests. On the Continent, with some exceptions (the most notable being Germany), trade unions professed either political neutrality (the policy adopted in 1906 by the French and Italian trade-union congresses), or else, as in Spain and Russia, committed themselves to syndicalism, which sought to transfer political authority from the state to associations of producers. The notion that the interests of labor were political and national—let alone international—in scope was as a rule brought to labor from the outside, by intellectuals. It never penetrated very deeply, and for that reason socialist intellectuals mistrusted trade unions, preferring to appeal directly to the "laboring masses." The social history of the last hundred years is marked by constant tension between the economic preoccupations of organized labor and the political preoccupations of the socialists. V. I. Lenin, the most successful revolutionary of modern times, realized this conflict early in his career and built a whole strategy on the assumption that socialism could not be entrusted to workers because, left to their own devices, they would never outgrow the trade-union mentality. Socialism, Lenin held, required a tightly organized body of full-time professional revolutionaries.

Socialism may be described as an ideology whose goal is to change the existing capitalist order, either peacefully and gradually or violently and suddenly, and to create conditions under which labor appropriates all the wealth that it produces. For all their doctrinal differences, socialist theorists of different schools agree that private property should disappear. (By "private property" they usually mean the means of production—that is, natural resources, including land, and the instruments of labor, but not unproductive wealth such as private quarters or personal clothing.) Anarchists and Romantic socialists wish to do away with the state altogether and transfer authority to associations of producers; Marxist socialists wish to have the state expropriate private property and assume control of the means of production.

From its inception socialism has been a doctrine of middle-class intellectuals in rebellion against the middle class. To be sure, among the leaders of the socialist movement one may find a few aristocrats and a few workers, but its most prominent spokesmen have descended from and belonged to the bourgeoisie. They were people raised on liberal values who, unlike the majority of their kind, found themselves unable to accept the disparity between ideals and reality inherent in nineteenth-century middle-class life. Like many conservative critics of liberalism, they rejected the hypocrisy, smugness, ugliness, and dullness of industrialism and looked for a return to a fuller, simpler, more beautiful and satisfying way of life, which they imagined had once existed. Socialism was and remains a normative doctrine: socialist doctrines, including the ostensibly scientific one of Marx, contain strong moralistic elements. They are concerned not so much with life as it is, but as it ought to be.

There is a voluminous and interesting literature that probes into the psychological relationship between intellectuals and socialism. Many middle-class intellectuals converted to socialism because they wanted to serve a cause and could no longer find one in religion. Memoirs abound of youths brought up in conventional bourgeois homes who found in socialism an identification with the masses and a deep moral release. In Russia in the 1870s this phenomenon reached epidemic proportions, with thousands of youths leaving school to seek expiation among ordinary peasants. Contemporary Russian accounts even refer to this "going-to-the-people" movement as a "religious crusade." Other intellectuals turned to socialism because they disliked the disorder of the competitive system and sought a more rational and equitable system of managing the economy. The Belgian sociologist Hendrik de Man argues in *The Psychology of Socialism* (1926) that in a capitalist society, in which everyone is motivated by gain, the intellectuals alone retain the sense of over-all community interest. Socialism attracts them because it banishes the profit motive and replaces it with their own spirit of public service. Finally, for some, especially for ambitious workers eager to exchange the factory bench for an office job, the socialist movement was a means of upward mobility, leading from the proletariat into the ranks of the lower-middle class. In 1915 another sociologist, Robert Michels, observed that "That which the Church offers to the peasant and petty bourgeois, namely, a facility for ascent in the social scale, is offered to intelligent manual workers by the socialist party."

Despite points of contact, the pragmatism of labor and the idealism of the socialist intelligentsia led the two movements toward different goals. The socialists wanted to do away with the bourgeoisie, the workers wanted to become bourgeois. In the end, revolutionary socialism obtained a hold only on the agrarian periphery of Europe where, because of the slow development of industry and democracy, the working class had little hope of raising itself to a higher social status without recourse to violence. In the industrial countries, socialism fused with liberalism and turned reformist.

The theories of the pioneers of socialism are not easy to define. In the first half of the nineteenth century the movement lacked organized parties and formal programs and was composed of an eccentric breed of individuals who gathered around themselves ephemeral bands of equally eccentric disciples. What unites the diverse schools of early socialist thought is their Romantic outlook. They believed in the self-realization of the individual and the brotherhood of mankind (often conceived in terms of a religious renaissance or a "new Christianity"). To the writers and artists of the Romantic movement, the enemy was classicism; to its politicians, the enemy was the *ancien régime*; to Romantic socialists, the enemy was economic competition. They were appalled by the debilitating effect of competitiveness on human character and human relations and felt that, as long as man was compelled by the economic system to fight his fellow man, he was bound to fall far short of his full potential. *Romantic Socialism*

The principal purpose of the schemes that the Romantic socialists tirelessly devised was to replace "wasteful" competition with cooperation. They paid surprisingly little attention to that conflict between labor and capital which became the hallmark of the later socialists. What troubled them were not so much the inequalities of wealth as the existing system's failure to make intelligent use of the means of production—not so much the injustice of capitalism as its irrationality. Most of the early socialists opposed revolution, because they felt that the change they desired could not be accomplished by replacing one type of government with another, but only by a slow transformation of the human mind and heart.

There is some question whether Claude de Saint-Simon was or was not a socialist, but because his influence was greatest among bankers and engineers of the Second Empire who were anything but socialists, we discussed him earlier (in Chapter 15). Saint-Simon left behind a large and active body of followers who moved definitely in the direction of socialism but whose influence was dissipated by their erratic behavior.

In the 1830s one of the most influential socialist theorists was Charles Fourier. The son of a merchant, Fourier had been troubled since childhood by the wastefulness of capitalist competition, examples of which he had occasion to observe in his father's business, and by the disharmonies in human relations. In his writings, Fourier concerned himself primarily with finding means to assure for all men work fitted to their individual talents and preferences. To this end, he proposed the creation of special communities or *phalansteries*. Each *phalanstery*, consisting ideally of 1,600 members, would form working teams to take care of the various needs of communal life. Under this arrangement, members could join the teams that best suited them, achieving the maximum of self-fulfillment in work. The *phalansteries* were to have communal kitchens and nurseries, but families would be allowed to reside together in private apartments. The role of the central government would be reduced to a minimum. Fourier's vision anticipated in some respects the *kibbutzim* established in Israel a century later.

The desire to harmonize social relations was also uppermost in the mind of Robert Owen, the leading socialist in Britain. Owen saw in economic competition the main cause of social conflicts and of the deterioration of human character. Born into an artisan family, he rose rapidly in the world of business and before he was thirty became one of the main manufacturers of cotton yarn in Great Britain. At New Lanark, Scotland, the site of his plant, Owen established a model community that attracted much attention. Later on, he threw himself with great zeal into the task of forming cooperative associations, trade unions, and "labor exchanges" designed to make workers independent of the state and the capitalists. He stood at the height of his influence in the early 1830s, when a vast labor movement arose in Britain, animated by his ideas. Though Owen's schemes (including a socialist community at New Harmony, Indiana) failed, they were not without issue. To Owen belongs much of the credit for having launched in England both the trade-union and the cooperative movements.

Etienne Cabet, a lawyer who once had held the position of attorney general of Corsica, spent many years in England, where he became acquainted with Owen's theories. In his *Voyage to Icaria* (1840) he outlined in minute detail his plan for a totally regulated community. Such imaginary communities had been popular in the eighteenth century, the best known, as well as the most terrifying, having been described in Abbé Morelly's book, *Code de la nature* (1755). In Cabet's vision, as in Morelly's, there was no room for private initiative of any kind, happiness being attained through the individual's complete integration into the community. Each citizen of Icaria was to be told when to rise in the morning, what to eat, how to dress, what to read, when to marry. It was regimentation carried to the point of madness. For the sake of minimizing social conflict and maximizing productivity, Cabet eliminated freedom. To distinguish it from the socialist and anarchist schemes of the time, Cabet's scheme was called "communist."

Another influential socialist thinker of the Romantic era was Louis Blanc. In his writings Blanc discussed the inability of the worker and artisan to gain economic independence under capitalism because the tools of production were in the hands of the rich. To overcome this handicap he wanted the state to establish "social workshops" that would furnish the workers with all that was required for industrial production. These workshops, operating under the direction of workers and serving their interests, would in time, Blanc believed, prove their superiority over capitalist-owned industries and create conditions of material abundance. Once this occurred society would ask every citizen to contribute according to his ability and reward him according to his needs. Blanc's workshops were instituted in a travestied form in 1848 as "national workshops," less from a desire to make workers self-sufficient than to keep the Parisian unemployed from rebelling. (See Chapter 15.)

Saint-Simon, Fourier, Owen, Cabet, and Blanc are often called "Utopian Socialists." This pejorative term, coined by Marx to discredit his rivals, has no place in a scholarly vocabulary. The early socialists were often eccentric, and their schemes were often fantastic and chimerical. But underneath their wild Romantic visions one can discern a view of the future in many respects less "utopian" than Marx's. They were the first thinkers to realize the social and economic implications of industrialism and the necessity of devising new institutions to cope with them. The disciples of Saint-Simon created sociology, the scientific study of society, and pointed the way to state management of economic development, a concept realized in the twentieth century. Fourier pioneered labor psychology, Owen the cooperative movement, Blanc unemployment relief. As far as the Western world is concerned, their view of the future as a gradual accommodation of society to industrialism proved more realistic than did Marx's prediction of class warfare and revolution.

Robert Owen had an architect friend portray what New Harmony, his model socialist community in the Indiana wilderness, would look like. Public buildings and botanical gardens are enclosed by a rectangle of members' dwellings. Owen's dream never progressed beyond the log cabin stage.

Marxism   Until the middle of the nineteenth century socialist thinkers sought to reduce social antagonisms and to create a world of cooperation. With Karl Marx and his associate, Friedrich Engels, this no longer held true. The ideals of harmony, persuasion, and peaceful evolution yield to programs involving deliberate violence. Marxism is the first modern ideology to advocate conflict as both legitimate and progressive.

Karl Marx was born in 1818 in Trier, a Prussian town near the French frontier, the son of a Jewish lawyer. When he was six years old his family converted to Christianity. Marx began to study law at the University of Bonn, but soon transferred to the University of Berlin, where he engaged in a broad program of study centered on philosophy. In Berlin he drew close to the Left Hegelians and was much influenced by their ideas, especially those of "alienation" and anthropocentrism. Marx had hoped for an academic appointment, but, failing to receive it, he turned to journalism. While reporting for a liberal Rhineland paper he became interested in politics and economics and the relationship between the two. Concern with these matters led him to current French socialist literature, then virtually unknown in Germany. Under its influence he became by 1843 a socialist. Later that year he moved to Paris and from there to Brussels, where he developed in the mid-1840s his own anti-Romantic, "scientific" socialist theory.

Marx detested the bourgeoisie—the "eminent spinners, extensive sausage makers, and influential shoe-black dealers," as he once called them. In Paris he published an essay called "On the Jewish Question" in which he identified the Jewish spirit with that of the bourgeoisie and called on Europeans to overcome both. Marx learned much about class conflict from Friedrich Engels and Lorenz von Stein. Engels, who became his devoted friend, was the son of a wealthy German textile manufacturer. He had spent several years in Manchester and Liverpool as his firm's agent, where he became acquainted with Owenism, Chartism, the Anti-Corn Law League, and the British labor movement. He summarized his impressions in a book called *The Condition of the Working Classes in England* (1845). Stein, a conservative Prussian jurist, brought out in 1842 an important study called *Socialism and Communism in Contemporary France* in which he summarized the teachings of French radicals and argued that the principal issue of the future would be class conflict between the proletariat and the bourgeoisie. Although Stein hoped that by an active social policy the monarchy could prevent class conflict in Prussia, his general historic conception could be used (and was used by Marx) to develop a positive theory of social revolution. Utilizing the knowledge obtained from Engels, Stein, and other sources, Marx developed an original theory based on the notion of class war as a constant and fundamental feature of history. In so doing he had recourse to economic analysis, and was the first socialist to fuse sociology with economics. This specific amalgam constitutes the essence of Marxism and the source of its great appeal.

The fundamental premise of Marxism holds that the relationship of men to the basic means of production determines human actions and institutions. This relationship is for Marx a dynamic, historic one—that is, one constantly in the process of development. Originally, in prehistoric society, goods belonged to all; no one owned anything, and men were equal. Gradually, however, certain people

Karl Marx and his wife, photographed about 1860. Marx fled the Continent after the revolutions of 1848, living the rest of his life in London in modest circumstances and working on Das Kapital *in the British Museum.*

succeeded in seizing control of the land, the basic source of wealth in an agricultural economy. By controlling land, they were able to enslave or otherwise subordinate the majority of the population and force it to work for them. In this manner early communism disappeared, being replaced by the division of society into classes and the exploitation of man by man. Henceforth, all societies have been based on class distinctions. Such societies surround exploitation with an elaborate structure of institutions and ideas designed to justify and perpetuate it. Among them are the state, law, religion, and the church, all of them, according to Marx, serving the interests of the class that at a given time happens to control the means of production.

Although it may appear that the landed aristocracy, having seized control of the basic means of production, could retain its privileged position forever, this did not in fact happen. Every economic system based on a division of classes and exploitation bears within itself the seeds of its own destruction. This is because the means of producing wealth constantly improve, technologically and otherwise, and at a certain stage outgrow the social system constructed on it. Thus, within the feudal system—a term Marx applied to agricultural economies employing unfree labor—there emerged an urban commercial and manufacturing class, the class of capitalists, whose power rested not on land but on money. The capitalist methods of production proved superior and eventually brought down the feudal system.

The triumph of capitalism over feudalism, assured by the French Revolution, did not abolish exploitation; it merely changed its character. The capitalists abolished serfdom and slavery because they found it more profitable to use hired labor, but in his own way the capitalist exploited the hired worker, just as the feudal lord had exploited his serf. To prove this contention, Marx had recourse to the so-called labor theory of value. The notion that value derived from human work was not new (John Locke was among its early exponents). Marx adopted it from the writings of the early nineteenth-century English economist David Ricardo. The theory held that physical labor is the source of all value: the commercial price of a product is directly related to the amount of physical labor that was expended on it. According to Marx, capitalist exploitation operates by appropriating a certain portion of the value that labor creates. The capitalist employer buys labor as he would any other commodity, that is, at the lowest available price, which in the case of labor happens to be the minimum wage necessary to keep the worker alive. This price—or wage—represents only a fraction of the value that the worker actually creates. If, for example, it takes wages of $1 a day to furnish a worker with a subsistence living, but the worker produces in a day goods that can be sold on the market for $5, the difference of $4 represents "surplus value." The capitalist, by appropriating it, commits in effect an act of theft. "Surplus value," which may be defined broadly as the difference between wages paid to the workers and the market price of the goods produced by them, is the basis of the capitalist system and the specific form of capitalist exploitation.

Marx devoted a great deal of attention to demonstrating the inevitable internal disintegration of capitalism. As the feudal system of exploitation had collapsed, so, he said, would the capitalist system. His principal work, the economic treatise called *Das Kapital*, the first volume of which (the only one to appear in Marx's lifetime) came out in 1867, predicted the inevitable collapse of capitalism. Marx's

Among the leading lights of the socialist movement gathered in Zurich in the 1890s are Friedrich Engels (fourth from left) and his friend Eduard Bernstein (far right), theorist of the German Social Democrats.

prediction rested on two related principles, "concentration" and "pauperization," both of which he adopted from the writings of the Franco-Swiss critic of capitalism Jean Sismondi (*New Principles of Political Economy*, 1819).

When it first emerged, according to Marx, capitalism had been a progressive force because it opened new markets and brought to the fore the most dynamic economic elements. Marx greatly admired the achievement of capitalism in its prime in developing an international economy and culture. In contrast to many early socialists, he also welcomed urbanization, having little sympathy for what he called the "idiocy of rural life." But he also maintained that at a certain stage of its history, capitalism became regressive. Under a system of unrestricted competition, the stronger and more efficient producers win out, and the means of production concentrate in fewer and fewer hands. Eventually, effective competition is eliminated. In this manner a fatal conflict arises between the methods of production and the social system resting on it: the method of production, highly concentrated, outgrows the capitalist system that presupposes competition and the diversification of ownership.

In the meantime the laboring force is steadily "pauperized," that is, impoverished. The labor supply increases with the constant accretion of small producers and traders who are ruined by big business. The more workers that are available, the more cheaply can they be purchased and the more ruthlessly can they be exploited. The rich grow richer while the poor grow poorer, a development that compounds the inner contradictions of the capitalist system. The larger the proletariat, the less money needs to be spent on wages; the less money is spent on wages, the more "surplus value" can be reinvested to produce more and more goods for which there are fewer and fewer consumers (insofar as the majority of the wage earners are growing poorer). The result is overproduction and economic depression that grow in intensity and frequency until capitalism crashes.

By the time capitalism is ready to disintegrate the means of production are already so concentrated that nothing is simpler than to nationalize them for the benefit of society as a whole. This event follows a revolution in which the proletariat seizes power and establishes the "dictatorship of the proletariat" of undefined duration. The new government destroys the bourgeoisie, appropriates its ill-gotten wealth, and introduces public control over the means of production. These measures lay the foundations of a new classless society. They open a new era for mankind, an era of return to the freedom and equality of original communism. When that age arrives the state dissolves or "withers away."

Such, in briefest outline, is the theory that Marx and Engels first announced in the *Communist Manifesto* of 1848 and subsequently developed more fully. Engels, in an introduction to a new edition of the *Communist Manifesto* published in 1883, defined Marxism as resting on the following propositions:

> That in every historical epoch the prevailing mode of economic production and exchange, and the social organizations necessarily following from it, form the basis upon which is built up, and from which alone can be explained the political and intellectual history of that epoch; that consequently the whole history of mankind (since the dissolution of primitive tribal society, holding land in common ownership) had been a history of

"Priests, monarchs, statesmen, soldiers, officials, financiers, capitalists, moneylenders, lawyers"—all of them, according to the anarchist Mikhail Bakunin, were "mankind's tormentors."

class struggles, contests between exploiting and exploited, ruling and oppressed classes; that the history of these class struggles forms the series of evolution in which, nowadays, a stage has been reached where the exploited and oppressed classes (the proletariat) cannot attain its emancipation from the sway of the exploiting and ruling class (the bourgeoisie) without, at the same time, and once and for all, emancipating society at large from all exploitation, oppression, class distinction and class struggles.

Critics in Marx's lifetime and since have pointed out numerous flaws in the doctrine: the unfounded historical assumption of an original propertyless and classless society, the inconsistency of certain economic propositions, and the improbability that the proletariat, at the depth of its supposed degradation, would have the capacity to assume power and establish a social order calling for exceptional moral and intellectual maturity. In particular, professional economists have rejected the labor theory of value on which the Marxist theory rests; outside Marxist circles it has become a historical curiosity. John Maynard Keynes, who of all economists has had the greatest influence on twentieth-century economic policy, dismissed Marx and Engels' writings as "out-of-date controversializing." But criticism notwithstanding, Marxism has exercised an extraordinary influence on socialist intellectuals and on much of modern thought in general. In an age dominated by the scientific outlook, it has provided a theory that, even if not considered scientific by professional economists, did use scientific evidence and methods of analysis. Engels, on Marx's death, compared his achievement to that of Darwin, meaning that Marx had provided a key to the process of social evolution as Darwin had done for biological evolution.

In London in 1864 Marx helped organize and acquired control of the International Working Man's Association (popularly known as the First International). Its purpose was to bring together representatives of the world proletariat to prepare for the collapse of capitalism that Marx and Engels believed to be imminent, but from the beginning it suffered from the controversy that developed between the Marxists and their anarchist opponents.

Anarchism   Marx predicted that socialism would inevitably replace highly developed industrial and commerical capitalism; thus his ideology had its greatest relevance to countries with advanced economies, such as England and Germany. Anarchism, by contrast, appealed most to the economically underdeveloped countries.

Marxism and anarchism had much in common. Both advocated violence and class war and the replacement of one social order with another. Both desired the abolition of private property. Where they differed fundamentally was in their attitudes to the state and to intellectuals. Like the anarchists, Marx considered the state an instrument of exploitation and oppression and predicted its eventual disappearance. But between capitalism and triumphant socialism, he posited the transitional state called the "dictatorship of the proletariat," during which the new ruling class would use the whole might of the state to destroy forever the apparatus of human exploitation. The anarchists rejected this prospect. They repudiated political authority in all its forms, socialist no less than capitalist. The so-called dictatorship of the proletariat seemed to them certain to degenerate into a new instrument of oppression, a tyranny of intellectuals, the "most aristocratic, most despotic, most arrogant, and most evil of all" as Mikhail Bakunin, their main theorist, once put it. Instead, they advocated the immediate destruction of central government and the transfer of political authority to small communities or associations of producers.

Elements of anarchism can be discerned in the theories of Fourier, Owen, and Blanc, but the most important early anarchist thinker was Pierre Joseph Proudhon. Proudhon was an exception among socialist theorists in that he came from a humble family (his father was a tavern-keeper) and made his living from manual labor (he served as a printer). In 1840 he published *What Is Property?*, a frontal attack on the whole institution of ownership as the basis of man's tyranny over man. In this work and in his subsequent writings Proudhon predicted that property would disappear and give way to a system in which possession of land and productive tools would be vested in the producers, that is, those who actually did the work. (Possession is not a legal right, as is property; it means the right to use but not to sell or bequeath.) These producers would form voluntary associations that would enter into voluntary unions with other associations, until all mankind was linked in a single vast federation. "The twentieth century will begin the era of federations," Proudhon once prophesied, "or it will mark the beginning of a thousand-year purgatory." He opposed the nationalization of private property on the grounds that once the state appropriated wealth, its tyranny would increase: if it owned everything, everybody would depend on it.

Proudhon still envisaged anarchism as emerging gradually and peacefully from within capitalism. But after his death in 1865, leadership of the movement passed to Bakunin, who to an even greater degree than Marx espoused violence. The son of a well-to-do Russian landowner, Bakunin began his career as an officer in the army, but he resigned early and spent the rest of his life (when not in jail or in exile) traveling from country to country in search of revolution. He was an international figure, as well known in Spain as in Russia, in Lyons as in Naples. A huge, burly man with a wild beard and flashing eyes, he personified the archetypical revolutionary. His life was as spontaneous as the one he preached. He never had money of his own, preferring to live on loans that he immediately spent and rarely repaid. "Liberty he always proclaimed the great principle of living," writes a historian of socialism, "and assuredly no one ever lived with more liberty on so little money that was his own."[°]

Bakunin lacked the systematic habits of Marx and left behind no consistent body of doctrine. He believed in the absolute value of freedom, in releasing spontaneous forces held down by the weight of laws, customs, and institutions, above all, the institutions of church and state. He was a determined atheist, believing (as did the Left Hegelians, with whom he was associated in his youth) that religion was the worst instrument of oppression. Bakunin preached destruction, giving little thought to the order that would follow, because he considered destructiveness to be a great creative force in itself.

Although in his revolutionary strategy Bakunin relied on the industrial proletariat, he paid particular attention to the landless peasantry, the unemployed, and other *déclassé* elements. He felt certain that in the masses of the population

[°]G. D. H. Cole, *Socialist Thought: Marxism and Anarchism, 1850–1890* (1954).

This print was inspired by the suppression in 1843 of a Rhineland newspaper edited by Marx. Portrayed as Prometheus, Marx is bound to his press as the Prussian eagle gnaws at his vitals. The maidens despairing at his feet represent the various Rhineland towns served by the paper.

lurked instinctive social hatreds; it was only necessary to unleash the "evil passions" for the whole world to be engulfed in the flames of class war. He was much encouraged by the prevalence of banditry in the regions he knew best (Russia, Spain, and southern Italy), interpreting it as symptomatic of latent destructive mass instincts. Bakunin was the first radical to have realized the revolutionary potential of the landless peasant. By so doing, he made a unique contribution to socialist strategy, from which the Marxists, despite their rejection of Bakuninism, greatly profited later on. He mistrusted socialist intellectuals, accusing them of a desire to use the revolution as a means of seizing power and replacing the bourgeoisie as the principal exploiting class.

This emphasis on spontaneity was the crux of his quarrel with Marx. To Marx, Bakunin's program was utopian, for it failed to take into account the relentless spread of capitalism and the realities of modern class structure. He considered the anarchists exponents of the interests of the petty bourgeoisie: the small producer, the artisan, the peasant. But for Bakunin, Marx and his followers were laying the groundwork for a "knuto-Germanic empire":

> [The rulers of the socialist state], the Marxists say, will consist of workers. Yes, perhaps of *former* workers. And these, as soon as they become the rulers or representatives of the people, will cease to be workers, and will begin to look down upon the entire world of manual labor from the heights of the state. They will no longer represent the people, but themselves and their own pretensions to rule the people. . . . They [the Marxists] will concentrate the reins of government in a strong hand, because the ignorant people are in need of quite a firm guardianship. They will establish a single State Bank that will concentrate in its hands all commercial, industrial, agricultural, and even scientific productivity: and the mass of the people will be divided into two armies, the industrial and the agricultural, which will be under the direct command of government engineers who will constitute a new privileged class.

The quarrel between the two leaders of socialism often assumed ugly personal overtones. Marx accused Bakunin of serving as an agent of the tsarist police, sent to wreck the International. Bakunin reciprocated by calling Marx a greedy, scheming Jew. Their dispute led in 1876 to the dissolution of the First International.

Labor and Politics   Socialism as an ideology came into being in the middle third of the nineteenth century at a time when the future of the working class was uncertain and the violence of some working-class activities, especially in 1848, suggested the imminence of social revolution. It became an influential movement in the closing third of the century at a time when the laboring class was making unprecedented progress in terms of living standards, education, and political rights. Contrary to the expectation of Marxists and some other socialists, the proletariat (i.e., the impoverished working element), instead of growing in numbers, decreased. In England—the country for which Marx had predicted inevitable pauperization—real wages between 1850 and 1900 increased by an estimated 84 percent. In fact, the period 1850–1875—the very time when Marx was working out his theory

of pauperization—witnessed the most rapid rise in real wages. A British parliamentary commission appointed in 1894 concluded after an exhaustive study that the proportion of persons receiving very low wages in England (that is, Marx's pauperized proletariat) had been "very much larger" fifty years earlier; their number had declined partly from general improvements in pay and partly from the tendency of higher skills to replace lower ones. The same held true of the second most industrialized power in Europe, Germany.

These developments confronted European socialists with a dilemma. Insofar as they had the interests of the working class at heart, they had to welcome improvements in its condition, and insofar as they hoped to gain the worker's vote, they had to press for more such improvements. But as they increasingly identified themselves with the cause of social reform, they became tied to the existing social system, and their clamor for revolution turned hollow. If they rejected reforms, they lost labor support; if they advocated them, they integrated themselves into the whole capitalist order and could hardly be taken seriously when they preached its overthrow.

The anarchists were less troubled by this dilemma than the Marxists, for having repudiated parliamentary action in principle, they had no need to adjust their program to please the electorate. Adopting a policy known as "direct action," the anarchists declared war on the existing political order. They boy-

Anarchists twice tried to kill King Alfonso XIII of Spain. This is the second attempt, in Madrid in 1906; a bomb thrown at the royal carriage killed twenty bystanders but did not harm the king or his bride (it was their wedding day). The bomb-thrower shot himself.

Carrying banners and a portrait of Tsar Nicholas II, Russian workers stage a triumphant march through the streets of Odessa after wresting a constitution from Nicholas in 1905.

cotted parliamentary elections and sabotaged parliamentary assemblies. They also carried on a relentless campaign of terrorism against heads of state. Anarchist assassins murdered Tsar Alexander II of Russia (1881), President Marie Carnot of France (1894), Empress Elizabeth of Austria (1898), King Humbert of Italy (1900), and President William McKinley of the United States (1901). In addition, they slew scores of high government officials, including Prime Ministers Cánovas of Spain (1897) and Stolypin of Russia (1911).

Alongside sabotage and terror, late nineteenth-century anarchists had recourse to industrial unrest, aiming at the "general strike." The general strike was first conceived in England in the 1820s but was fully formulated toward the end of the century in France. Its goal was a simultaneous and universal work stoppage by all the trades. The "anarcho-syndicalists" expected the general strike to bring the economy to a standstill, cause a collapse of capitalism, and replace the state with a republic based on trade unions. In 1892 the French Congress of the National Federation of Trade Unions formally adopted the general strike as its goal; three years later the first French national trade-union organization, the General Confederation of Labor (CGT), pledged itself to abstain from participation in the country's political life. The French socialist Georges Sorel evolved a theory based on the general strike as a great social "myth" capable of uniting the working class and educating it for the class struggle (*Reflections on Violence*, 1896–1906).

In several European countries it was more than a myth. In 1893 the proclamation of a general strike by left-wing groups in Belgium forced the government to concede universal suffrage. In 1905 in Russia, similar tactics finally persuaded Nicholas II to grant the country a constitution. In 1909 in Spain, the syndicalists seized the city of Barcelona and held it for a week before they were dislodged by government troops. Echoes of the general strike were still heard after World War I in the great English strike of 1926 and in France in 1938.

Anarchism, both in its Bakuninist and syndicalist forms, acquired its greatest following in the non-industrial countries. It enjoyed particular success where democratic traditions were weak and where the population regarded the state as an alien, hostile force (Spain, Italy, Russia). It also won followings in countries such as France that had a large class of artisans and small producers opposed to big industry. These are the same areas that after the Russian Revolution of 1917 developed the most powerful Communist movements.

In the industrially developed countries the influence of anarchism, never great to begin with, waned, while that of Marxism increased. Marxism gained the upper hand over anarchism precisely because it was a more moderate and pacifistic and, one may almost say, a more respectable theory. Instead of throwing bombs, Marxists participated in parliamentary elections. Their leaders were undistinguishable from those of the "bourgeois" parties: neatly dressed, academic-looking gentlemen, in contrast to the disheveled anarchists. Whenever organized labor chose to collaborate with the socialists, it preferred to do so with the Marxists, finding them more stable and politically more adept.

In theory, Marxism should have rejected reformism, insofar as it postponed "pauperization" and, with it, the socialist revolution. But in fact, from the beginning Marxism contained two disparate elements: an uncompromising theoretical one, and a compromising practical one. Marx himself had welcomed the English Factory Laws designed to improve the condition of the workers, although it is difficult to see how he reconciled this approval with the belief that a deterioration of the working class was a necessary precondition of the destruction of capitalism. Be that as it may, his followers also tended to back social reform. By so doing they gained a foothold among the workers.

Germany was the first country in which socialists succeeded in overcoming labor's traditional antipathy to involvement in party politics. This was largely the achievement of Ferdinand Lassalle. Lassalle was less of a theorist than Marx and more of a practicing politician. He became convinced that labor could radically change its condition only by acquiring the vote and forming its own political party. He was instrumental in persuading Bismarck to grant universal male suffrage to Germans by arguing that the enfranchised labor would vote against the Liberals. In 1863 he founded the General German Labor Association, designed to unite all workers in a political party to represent them in elections to the parliament. Lassalle's eloquence and dedication, however, failed at first to break the apathy of German labor to politics, and at the time of his death in 1864 the association had only 4,500 members.

But the seeds were sown. In 1875, at the so-called Gotha Congress, Lassalle's

Proclaiming "The World Is Ours!" a German Social Democratic paper records the unofficial returns in the party's electoral triumph of 1890.

Labor Association merged with the German Social Democratic Labor party founded by several of Marx's followers. This merger laid the foundations of close cooperation between socialism and labor in Germany. The program adopted at Gotha did not entirely please Marx (who also had envied Lassalle's influence over German workers), but insofar as it committed organized German socialism and labor to political action it represented a victory over both anarchism and apolitical trade unionism.

Despite harassment by the government, German Social Democracy gained successes at the polls. It became the first socialist party in the world to carry weight in parliamentary politics. In 1877 it won nearly 500,000 votes and 12 seats in the Reichstag in its first national election. This unexpected strength induced Bismarck to pass an Anti-Socialist Law (see Chapter 20). In 1890, when the Reichstag allowed the Anti-Socialist Law to lapse, German Social Democracy began its triumphant advance. In 1890 it gained 1.4 million votes and 35 seats in the Reichstag, in 1893 1.8 million votes and 44 seats, in 1898 2.1 million votes and 60 seats. Neither various obstacles placed in its path by the government nor attempts to block its progress by National Liberals and Conservatives succeeded in stopping the relentless advance of the socialist movement. In 1903 the Social Democratic party polled 3 million votes and gained 81 seats—nearly a third of the votes cast and as much as the next two parties combined. These electoral triumphs stimulated the emergence all over Europe of Social Democratic parties patterned on the German model.

German Social Democracy owed much success to superb organization. It offered its adherents not only an election ticket and program but a whole way of life. It ran a gigantic publishing enterprise, welfare and insurance agencies, clubs and associations, and even its own taverns. This comprehensive program of activity helped the party gain the loyalty of half the trade-union membership—a figure not duplicated in any other country—and induced it in 1906 to acknowledge trade unions as a progressive force. From its rich treasury the party also subsidized several poorer foreign Social Democratic organizations.

A party of such scope and resources, capable of spending millions of marks on a single national election, required a large professional staff. The more successful its candidates proved at the polls, the fatter its treasury, the longer its membership rolls, the more the party needed a regular bureaucratic apparatus. Robert Michels, in his study *Political Parties* (1915), concluded that Social Democracy did not escape the fate of its conservative and liberal counterparts: like them, it gave rise to a professional élite of organizers and politicians who lost contact with the electorate. He was especially struck by the speed with which socialist politicians of worker background acquired "bourgeois" characteristics.

English labor turned to politics from disappointment with the Liberal party. The first labor candidates made their appearance in the 1870s to protest the passage of the so-called Criminal Law Amendment Act (1871), which gave judges the right to decide when a strike or picketing constituted "intimidation" and was subject to criminal prosecution. To punish the Liberals for sponsoring this law, the trade unions put up candidates for the election of 1874 and gave much support to the Conservatives. The defection of labor voters cost the Liberals this election, and the next year the Criminal Law Amendment Act was repealed.

The trade unions gradually concluded that their interests required political action. In 1899 they decided to participate in elections, though they had as yet no clear idea how to go about it. Labor's resolute entry into British politics is generally attributed to another legal landmark, the Taff Vale judgment rendered by Parliament in 1902. This decision made a union financially liable for the acts of its members, even when they acted without its authorization. Angered by this blow at the essence of trade unionism, the leaders of the unions decided to enter Parliament in sufficient numbers to be able to exert pressure on labor's behalf. The "Labour party" participated in elections for the first time in 1905. It won 29 seats. This election marked the beginning of a fundamental transformation in the structure of British party politics: eighteen years later Labour was to secure a parliamentary majority, form a cabinet, and replace the Liberal party as the main opponent of the Conservatives.

Neither German nor British parliamentary labor deputies worked for the socialist goals of the abolition of private property and the transfer of the means of production to the state. Rather, they fought conventionally for social reforms. The greater were their successes at the polls, the more moderate became their demands, for to win votes they had to appeal to the largest electorate, and this meant toning down radicalism in favor of liberal and democratic slogans. Successful socialist parties tended to liberalize, and in some countries (e.g., Germany and Belgium) they assumed the role traditionally performed by liberal parties.

In the 1880s and 1890s most European countries had their own socialist parties. The majority of these were linked by means of the Second International, formed in Paris in 1889. (Anarchists, however, were excluded.) The Second International advocated active participation of socialists in parliamentary elections where the workers possessed the suffrage and a struggle for universal suffrage where they did not. The Second International dominated the socialist movement during the quarter of a century from its formation to the outbreak of the war. It held regular congresses at which socialists of various nations gathered to discuss common problems and to plan common strategy.

Socialist Revisionism

As the century drew to a close it was becoming apparent that the theory underlying the socialist movement bore little relation to its practices. In theory revolutionary, the movement was in practice reformist. It remained doctrinally committed to the concept of "pauperization," although in reality the gap between the employer and the worker was steadily narrowing. Many socialists realized this discrepancy but hesitated to do anything about it, partly from inertia bred by success, partly from fear of tampering with a doctrine believed scientifically validated for all time.

The first to take cognizance of the changes in social conditions brought about by advanced industrialism was a group of English intellectuals gathered in the "Fabian Society." Composed of outstanding intellectuals led by Sidney Webb and including George Bernard Shaw, the Fabians revived English socialism, dormant since the days of Robert Owen. Constituted into an organization in 1883–1884 for the purpose of propagating socialist ideas, they brought out in 1889 a volume of *Fabian Essays*, the first manifesto of "revisionism" in the socialist movement. (Their name derived from Fabius Cunctator, the Roman general known for his delaying tactics against Hannibal.) The principal essay in the collection, written by Sidney Webb, represented a reversion to the central idea of the Romantics: socialism would emerge from an evolution of the existing economy, not from its destruction. Webb maintained that the whole development of modern life—the extension of the franchise, the growth of joint-stock companies, the state's assumption of responsibility for social welfare, etc.—steadily broadened the scope of public authority at the expense of private. Society was gradually, inexorably, almost unwittingly taking over tasks once entrusted to individuals. In this manner, and in this manner only, could socialism triumph; it had to grow, it could not be engineered. Since time was working for socialism, they urged slow, dilatory, "Fabian" tactics.

The Fabians were not Marxists, and for this reason their *Essays* did not cause much stir among Continental Social Democrats. But they impressed Eduard Bernstein, a German socialist then residing in England, a friend of Engels, and a leading theorist of German Social Democracy. In 1896 Bernstein stunned his German colleagues by proposing that the party formally disassociate itself from the "disaster theory," that is, from the view that capitalism would collapse violently from the force of its internal contradictions. In his chief work, *The Premises of Socialism and the Tasks of Social Democracy* (1899; published in England as *Evolutionary Socialism*), Bernstein denied that capitalism continuously disintegrated from economic depressions, that big business was taking over,

Beatrice and Sidney Webb were major figures in the Fabian socialist movement in Britain. The Fabian method —"gradually permeating cultivated people with our own aspirations"— was more intellectual than activist.

and that the proletariat was becoming pauperized. Capitalist society was fundamentally healthy, he asserted. Drawing on Fabian arguments, Bernstein charged his colleagues with utopianism for adhering to the vision of a sudden leap from capitalism to socialism. Bernstein professed to remain a Marxist but insisted that, like any other scientific theory, Marxism had to be verified by empirical evidence or degenerate into sterile dogma.

A few years earlier the German Social Democrats had adopted a new party program (Bernstein had participated in its drafting) committing them to the "disaster theory." With it they had won several electoral triumphs. Not surprisingly, therefore, they rejected Bernstein's proposal. So did the Amsterdam Congress of the Second International (1904). Nonetheless, Social Democrats everywhere increasingly acted in accord with the principles laid down by the Fabians and the Bernsteinian revisionists. In the happy formula of Karl Kautsky, the leading theorist of German Marxism, Social Democracy was a "revolutionary party, but not a party that made revolutions." Whenever it was expedient, socialists collaborated with "bourgeois" parties; in Belgium (1911–1912) they formed joint electoral blocs. With the growing number of socialist deputies sitting in European parliaments, it was inevitable that sooner or later they would enter cabinets and perhaps even form ministries. The first contingency was in fact realized in France in 1899, when the socialist Alexandre Millerand, to the dismay of many of his colleagues, accepted a post as Minister of Commerce in an ordinary "bourgeois" cabinet.

The myth of proletarian or socialist internationalism was as unrealistic as the myths of "pauperization" and "capitalist collapse." According to Marx, the interests of the working class, and of the socialists as its vanguard, cut across national lines. This belief lay behind the founding of the Socialist International, whose leaders time and again proclaimed their opposition to the diplomatic and military intrigues of their national governments and pledged themselves to resist war. At the height of the Russo-Japanese conflict of 1904, the Russian and Japanese delegates at the Amsterdam Congress of the Second International demonstratively shook hands in front of the assembled audience. The gesture brought a storm of applause, but it merely underscored the unreality of the whole proceeding. The International was a loose association of socialist intellectuals, whose decisions were not binding on their respective socialist parties, let alone on labor as a whole. Its leaders were in their majority sincere internationalists; but the electorate to whom they had to cater was not. The German Social Democrats learned this lesson in the elections of 1907: having condemned the government's brutal suppression of a Negro revolt in an African colony, they lost 28 seats. Industrialism created great differences in living standards, and the working class of the more advanced countries felt less and less affinity with those of the less advanced ones (if indeed it had ever felt such affinity at all). In 1914, with a handful of exceptions, socialist leaders everywhere would vote for war measures they had pledged to oppose, and the workers would proceed obediently to slaughter their proletarian brethren.

20

—◦◦◦—

The Crisis of Liberalism:
1870-1914

Liberal ideas and institutions reached the height of popularity in the 1860s. Although they continued to make gains, after 1870 their conquests became increasingly hollow. Long before the outbreak of World War I liberalism entered a phase of crisis.

The basic cause of liberal decline was the steady extension of political democracy. As we have noted in Chapter 12, the early liberals were anti-democratic. They mistrusted the masses, whom they considered ripe for exploitation by despots like Bonaparte, and preferred to keep the franchise restricted to the propertied and educated classes. Nevertheless, the pressures for political democracy proved irresistible, and the liberals had to yield to them. France introduced the universal vote in 1848, the North German Confederation in 1867 and the German Empire in 1871, Great Britain in 1884, Spain in 1890, Belgium in 1893, Norway in 1898, Russia in 1905, Austria and Sweden in 1907, Italy in 1912, Denmark in 1914. The democratization of the franchise altered the whole quality of European political life. Politics became mass oriented. To gain votes, parties had to appeal to the wage earners, who lacked the confidence and the security of the middle classes. These appeals were most successful when based not on individualistic, self-reliant premises of classical liberalism, but on collectivist ideas, whether socialist or nationalist or both in combination.

The extension of the franchise was accompanied by a widening of the scope of state authority. This phenomenon was caused partly by technological and partly by social factors. The railways, telegraph lines, telephone networks, and other utilities introduced in the second half of the nineteenth century required some degree of central control. The state either took over the management of these new services, or assumed responsibility for their regulation. The introduction of compulsory primary education also called for state intervention. So did the adoption of social welfare schemes, pioneered by Germany in the 1880s and emulated in most European countries. Only the central government could initiate, finance, and supervise programs of old age pensions, insurance against sickness and accidents, sanitary regulations, or factory inspection. The whole drift of modern life pointed toward centralization, and away from private initiative, voluntary associations, and local self-rule. It thus ran counter to the liberal contention that the less government the better.

The liberals were not well suited either temperamentally or ideologically to engage in competition for the newly enfranchised mass voter, and kept on losing ground to the collectivist parties of the left and the right.

The socialists have been discussed at length in the preceding chapter. Here suffice it to say that in the latter part of the nineteenth century they succeeded, in large measure, in appropriating the ideas of civil liberty and equality of opportunity which previously had served the liberals so well. In some countries (for example, Germany and Belgium) the Liberal parties virtually disintegrated, their

Édouard Vuillard's sketch, almost poster-like in execution, depicts a riot in Paris' Place de la Concorde in the 1890s. It may relate to the notorious Dreyfus Affair, or it may simply symbolize the frequent disorders in the Third Republic at the time.

place being taken by the Social Democrats. Elsewhere (for example, Great Britain and Scandinavia) liberalism absorbed so much of socialism that it lost its identity.

To the right, liberalism now faced the challenge of a reinvigorated conservative movement. The conservative doctrines, which we examined in connection with the restoration era (Chapter 12), had been static and backward looking. They had rejected the industrial and urban culture, and the forces associated with it. This no longer held true of post-1870 conservatism. Like its predecessor, the new conservatism gave priority to state and society over the individual and exalted duty and order above rights and freedom. But it proposed to realize its principal aim—a strong state—by different methods.

First, the new conservatives were nationalistic, often virulently so. In the latter part of the nineteenth century nationalism broke its traditional association with liberalism and fused with conservative doctrines: it became a leading weapon in the right-wing arsenal. Modern nationalism no longer aspired to the Mazzinian ideal of an all-European brotherhood of free and equal nations. Rather, it asserted the right of stronger nations or races to dominate the weaker. It was xenophobic. It was usually also anti-Semitic, for the new conservatives saw in the Jew the embodiment of liberalism, capitalism, individualism, cosmopolitanism, radicalism, and many other things they feared and hated.

Second, the new conservatives acknowledged the industrial, urban order and wished to harness its forces in the service of nation and state. In particular, they used social reform as a means of gaining the support of the lower classes against the liberals. They often made common cause with the Church, especially over the issue of secularization of schools advocated by the liberals, but they were not pro-clerical as the old conservatives had been. On the other hand, they maintained close relations with the military establishment.

The post-1870 conservative movement spanned a wide ideological spectrum. In its moderate wing were statesmen like Disraeli—an imperialist and believer in alliance between aristocracy and the working class, but essentially a man with a liberal temperament. Farther to the right stood Bismarck, a typical "strong man" of the time, who defended monarchical absolutism by exploiting parliamentarism, nationalism, and even socialism—yet, for all his ruthlessness in fighting the liberals, a compromiser. On the extreme right were nihilistic nationalists, exemplified by the French publicist Charles Maurras, whose theories anticipated national socialism and fascism.

Socialism on the one hand and neo-conservatism on the other stripped liberalism of its broad ideological appeal. Toward the end of the century liberalism increasingly turned into a movement representing special interests: of the middle class in England, of the free professions in Germany, or of the affluent landed aristocracy in Russia.

An important reason for the general discrediting of liberalism was disappointment with parliamentary institutions. The parliament is the central organ of the liberal state, embodying popular sovereignty, and at the same time ensuring that the executive stays within its constitutional limits. Impressed by the achievements of the parliamentary system in Great Britain and in the United States, all European countries had by 1906 introduced parliamentary institutions. Their achievements fell far short of expectations. Except in a few small and rich states, parliaments on the European Continent neither won the prestige nor attained the effectiveness of parliaments in Anglo-Saxon countries.

We can isolate four distinct causes of this failure:

1) *The absence of ministerial responsibility.* The proper functioning of parliamentary institutions requires that those ministers who were charged with administration enjoy the confidence of the deputies, and resign when they lose it.° This principle of ministerial responsibility was not universally adopted. By 1914 it existed in Great Britain (where it had originated), in Belgium, the Netherlands, France, Italy, Switzerland, and the Scandinavian countries. It was absent in Germany, Austria, and Russia, the three conservative monarchies whose rulers refused to concede to representative bodies the crucial right of appointing ministers. Here the cabinet was named by the emperor and held office at his pleasure. This arrangement, under the best conditions, gave the parliament no more than a power of supervision over the executive; under the worst conditions, it produced constant strain between the legislative and executive, which sometimes brought government to a standstill.

2) *The absence of strong and well-organized political parties.* The parliamentary system presupposes the existence of an effective opposition, a kind of shadow government able to assume responsibility the instant the party in power is voted out. This requirement can be met only where there are effective party organizations, able to command parliamentary majorities and to enforce discipline among their members. In most Continental countries such parties did not exist. Instead, there were numerous groupings and cliques representing either specific ideologies, personal followings, or narrow social interests; they were usually small and loosely organized and rarely had the power to assume responsibility for the administration. In such countries the retirement of one cabinet was not followed automatically by another stepping in. Rather, it led to protracted negotiations between statesmen charged with the task of forming a new cabinet, between parliamentary factions, and even between individual deputies for the purpose of securing a workable majority. This procedure vitiated in large measure the parliamentary arrangement in the constitutions of France and Italy, the two major parliamentary states on the Continent. Cabinets composed in such a manner were artificial coalitions and as such inherently unstable. The resignation of a single minister was sometimes sufficient for the whole laboriously constructed cabinet to fall apart. The system also encouraged private deals and corruption among deputies.

3) *The absence of agreement on political principles.* The function of parliamentary bodies is not the resolution of questions of political philosophy; their function is to pass laws. This they can do only if there is broad agreement among political parties on constitutional principles. On the Continent powerful groupings, especially the anarchists and the extreme conservatives, rejected the entire parliamentary system and worked for its overthrow. Furthermore, in countries with minority problems, nationalists sabotaged parliamentary assemblies to gain independence. This was the case with the Irish in the British House of Commons, with the Norwegians in their Storting, and at one time or another with most of the national minorities in the Austrian Reichsrat. The clerical groups

°The American system, whereby the Chief Executive is elected directly by the voters, is rather exceptional.

also sometimes blocked orderly parliamentary procedure out of resentment over the secularization of schools. In France, Belgium, and the Netherlands this issue dominated domestic politics in the latter part of the nineteenth century.

4) *The inability of parliaments to cope with the increased responsibilities assumed by the state.* The extension of the scope of state authority, mentioned previously, required a staff of professional civil servants: parliaments were too unwieldy to deal with the day-to-day exigencies of running social welfare schemes or regulating the economy. As a result, the bureaucracy everywhere made spectacular progress. The German sociologist Max Weber was so impressed by its growth that he foresaw parliaments turning into mere adjuncts of an omnipotent civil service.

For all these reasons, at the turn of the century there was widespread skepticism about the future of representative government. For many Europeans parliaments meant petty squabbles, empty rhetoric, legislative impotence, and graft. Few, even among the conservatives, advocated that they be done away with, but there was a noticeable tendency to treat them as auxiliary institutions, as buttresses of authority rather than its foundation. Some thinkers now argued that the citizenry had neither the knowledge nor the interest to participate actively in political decisions, and that consequently power should be vested in an élite or "ruling class." This idea, later appropriated by twentieth-century dictators, was advanced by the Italian political scientist Gaetano Mosca as early as 1884.

In only one respect did liberalism continue to make significant gains, and that was in winning increasing acceptance for the idea of civil liberty. In country after country restrictions on freedoms were lifted and the citizenry accorded equal rights. The European of the early twentieth century was freer than he had ever been before. The precariousness of his freedom in view of the steadily growing power of the state was not apparent at the time.

We shall now turn to the political history of Europe from 1870 to 1914, proceeding from countries that established the most successful liberal governments to those in which liberalism fared worst.

Great Britain   The outstanding feature of post-1870 British politics was the steady shift of the political spectrum to the left, toward democracy and socialism. The spread of the franchise accomplished by the Second and Third Reform Bills (1867 and 1884) forced the two major parties to abandon their predominantly aristocratic and middle-class orientations and to court the working-class voter.

As we have noted (Chapter 15), the Conservative party was virtually out of power between 1846 and 1874. After 1874 its fortunes improved considerably, and during the period 1874–1905 it held power for twenty-four out of the thirty-one years.

The driving intellect behind the initial Conservative successes was Benjamin Disraeli. An imaginative statesman, Disraeli offered the Conservatives a program and a sense of direction which they had lacked since the days of Peel. Disraeli's goal was "Tory Democracy," a formula denoting an alliance of the landed aristocracy with the urban proletariat against the moneyed middle class. It was with this alliance in mind that he persuaded his colleagues in 1867 to snatch from the Liberals the sponsorship of the Second Reform Bill enfranchising much of the working population. Despite his intellectual domination of the party, Disraeli had to wait a long time before he was allowed to form a ministry, for, being a converted Jew, a novelist, and something of a dandy, he inspired little confidence in the rank and file of Conservative politicians.

Disraeli headed one short-lived government in 1868, but his great achievements came during his second (and last) ministry. He was nearly seventy when called upon in 1874 to form another cabinet. In the following six years he introduced a series of legislative acts which, moderate as they appear in retrospect, marked a break with the tradition of laissez faire. Among these were laws authorizing municipalities to clear slum areas and construct adequate housing for workers, establishing elementary sanitation procedures, and increasing the power of trade unions. Disraeli also sought mass support by reviving the idea of imperialism, which had fallen into disfavor during the era of Liberal hegemony.

Disraeli's main rival was William Ewart Gladstone, the leader of the Liberal party and the personification of British nineteenth-century liberalism. The son of a wealthy Liverpool merchant, Gladstone had pursued the classical political career, moving from Eton through Oxford to the House of Commons. He hated injustice and oppression, whether at home or abroad, and fought them with a passion rooted in deep moral conviction. At the same time he was a pragmatic politician, skilled at parliamentary tactics and highly efficient in budgetary matters. A combination of preacher and banker, he had great appeal for the Victorian middle class and much of the working population. He failed, however, to win over the queen. Victoria despised him for his self-righteousness and constant moralizing, for addressing her as if she were a "public meeting." She much preferred the companionable Disraeli, who prepared for her political reports that read like novels.

Gladstone headed four ministries (1868–1874, 1880–1885, 1886, 1892–1894). Under his leadership the Commons passed measures extending public assistance to schools, abolishing the purchase of army commissions, introducing examinations for candidates to the Civil Service, and establishing the secret vote. These laws had the common purpose of doing away with privilege and creating equal opportunity. Gladstone also led the fight against the remaining religious restrictions on membership in Parliament. In 1884 he introduced the Third Reform Bill, which gave the vote to four out of five male adults.

Gladstone's favorite cause, the one that offered the greatest outlets for his passion for justice, was Ireland. He did more than any other statesman to curb abuses in Ireland and to pave the road for its eventual independence.

The Irish nationalist movement, which got under way in the 1850s, was heavily supported with men and money by Irish immigrants in the United States. In 1858 they formed in New York the Fenian Brotherhood, the first major organization dedicated to the task of fighting for Irish independence. The nationalists in Ireland gained a strong following in the countryside after the passage of the Ballot Act in 1872 which, by making voting secret, prevented English and pro-English landlords from intimidating the voters. Shortly afterward there emerged in the House of Commons an Irish Home Rule party, which carried out obstructionist tactics designed to force Britain to grant Ireland independence or face a breakdown of parliamentary government.

Benjamin Disraeli, spokesman for the British Conservative party, shown in the 1860s, before his first ministry.

Gladstone set his heart on solving the Irish question. After various palliative measures failed to satisfy the Irish nationalists or to quell disorders, he concluded that nothing short of self-rule would set the matter at rest. He threw his whole prestige behind two Home Rule bills (1886 and 1893), the second of which would have made Ireland virtually sovereign. Both failed to secure a majority in the Commons. Irish politics continued to trouble Great Britain until after much violence it conceded Ireland independence (1921–1922).

The Disraeli-Gladstone rivalry led to an important innovation in British party politics. Until then it had been the practice for British politicians to confine campaigning to their particular constituencies. But in 1879 Gladstone, outraged by Disraeli's support of the Turks, who were then massacring Bulgarians, and by his entire aggressive imperialist policy, decided to storm the country in a railway coach to attack the Conservatives and solicit votes for the Liberal party. This was the so-called Midlothian campaign (named after Gladstone's constituency), a landmark in the evolution of British politics. The Liberals won the election, and from then on both parties regularly conducted national campaigns and put up candidates in as many constituencies as possible, forming regular party organizations. Politics ceased to be an avocation and became a profession.

The Conservatives never had much success with "Tory Democracy," for the working population supported first the Liberals, and then the Labourites. They were more successful with imperialism, the second component of Disraeli's policy. The voters responded favorably to the party's appeal to their pride in Britain's colonial accomplishment. The leading proponent of imperialism after Disraeli's death (1881) was Joseph Chamberlain, a Birmingham manufacturer who had broken with the Liberals over their pro-Irish policy and joined the so-called Liberal Unionist party, which he helped form in 1886. He cooperated with the Conservatives and served in their cabinets. Chamberlain urged closer ties with the overseas possessions, including tariff preferences for colonies. He also urged vigorous expansion in Africa.

The cause of social reform, which the Conservatives had abandoned after Disraeli, was taken up by the Liberals. In identifying themselves with this policy, the Liberals were in some measure motivated by a desire to neutralize the threat of the Labour party, which had emerged at the turn of the century and immediately cut into the workingman's vote. But beyond this pragmatic factor lay deeper reasons. In the second half of the nineteenth century a large part of liberal opinion had become persuaded that one could not depend on diligence, sobriety, thrift, and other middle-class virtues in themselves to solve social problems. The initial handicaps of poverty and ignorance were so great that for a large part of the population the noble ideals of liberalism had no meaning. Genuine freedom presupposed security, and general security could be achieved only if society came to the aid of the less fortunate. The evolution in liberal thought from stress on freedom to stress on equality and social justice can be traced in the writings of the leading English liberal theorist, John Stuart Mill. Beginning as a classic liberal, Mill in his later writings (he died in 1873) urged the state to equalize the distribution of wealth by means of taxation on inherited property and by social laws. The task indeed was great: a contemporary writer estimated that almost one-half of the income of the United Kingdom went to one-ninth of the population, and over half of Britain's capital belonged to one-seventeenth.

The development of the Liberal party occurred along the lines charted in the later writings of Mill and the contemporary German "state socialists" (see below). In the elections of 1906 the Liberals went to the voters with a program that included a bold scheme of social reform, diametrically opposed to laissez faire. They won a sweeping victory and immediately introduced a series of bills that marked the inauguration of welfare measures in Great Britain. The purpose of these measures was frankly declared by a Liberal spokesman to be a "greater equalization of wealth." These laws gave the worker protection against injury suffered during work, allowed him to engage in peaceful picketing, and gave him an old age pension upon reaching the age of seventy. They also fixed procedures for enforcing minimum wages.

This legislation ran into a great deal of opposition, because it violated some fundamental principles of liberal ideology dominating British life and thought for nearly a century. The controversy seethed during the first three years of the new administration and exploded in 1909. In preparing the budget for that year, David Lloyd George, the Chancellor of the Exchequer, found that he lacked money to pay for two extraordinary expenditures: naval construction necessitated by competition with Germany (Chapter 21), and old age pensions. To raise additional revenue, he drafted a "People's Budget," a revolutionary measure designed both to raise revenue and to achieve a certain degree of social leveling. Its most controversial provision called for heavy taxation of so-called unearned income, such as inherited wealth and profits accruing from the rise in the value of real estate. This proposal aroused vehement protests, especially in the House of Lords, which rejected the budget. A constitutional crisis ensued, which

GERNSHEIM COLLECTION, UNIVERSITY OF TEXAS

Gladstone disconcerted his opponents and shocked Queen Victoria by conducting a whistle-stop campaign in 1879. He continued to follow the practice; he is shown here in 1885.

only ended two years later with the passage of the Parliament Act (1911) that reduced permanently the power of the House of Lords so that it could thenceforth delay but not veto laws passed by the Commons.

The remarkable pliancy of British parties and institutions gave the country a stability and cohesion that few others possessed. There were strains—the Irish question, industrial unrest (especially acute in 1911–1912), and great disparities in wealth—but all in all the system functioned remarkably well.

The Smaller Democracies   Next to Britain liberalism established itself best in the small states of western and northern Europe: Switzerland, Belgium, Holland, and the Scandinavian kingdoms. Being compact and relatively unpopulous—the number of their inhabitants in 1910 ranged from 2.5 to 7.5 million—these countries were able to preserve the close relationship between voters and government that was no longer possible in the more populated countries. Indeed, in some Swiss cantons government continued to be based on "direct democracy," that is, on the personal participation of the entire citizenry in legislative processes. Prosperity and a high level of literacy also played their part; so did that imponderable, the liberal "spirit"—the attitude of tolerance for dissenting opinion and respect for law without which, in the ultimate analysis, self-government is not possible.

The tendency in these six countries was for liberal forces to move toward political and social democracy, and for the state to gain power.

Switzerland was particularly successful in working out its political problems. In the first half of the nineteenth century it had been organized as a loose confederation of twenty-two cantons, some liberal, others conservative, subject to a bare minimum of central control. By midcentury such decentralization was no longer satisfactory. The country had to construct an exceptionally complex and expensive system of railways and hydroelectric stations, and to organize a national army able to resist the forces of the neighboring great powers—tasks beyond the capacity of the self-governing cantons. Accordingly, in 1874 Switzerland revamped its constitution, adopting a federal system like that of the United States, with a strong central executive. Peculiar to it was the use of national referenda as a means of assuring popular participation in important legislative acts. At the end of the century Switzerland introduced a number of social welfare measures.

In the Low Countries in the latter part of the nineteenth century political conflicts revolved around the issue of school secularization. In the Netherlands the Catholics allied themselves with their arch-enemies, the conservative Calvinists, to prevent the separation of church and state and the assertion of public control over schools pressed by the Liberals. In Belgium the school controversy was long and bitter, and ultimately led to the crushing of the Liberal party. In 1879 the Belgian Liberals passed an education act disqualifying church schools from receiving public funds. This move caused the Clerical party to defect from the Liberals, with whom they had hitherto jointly dominated Belgian politics. In the election of 1880 the Clericals won a majority. They then passed a new education act, extending state support to church schools in predominantly Catholic districts. In 1895 religious instruction in schools was made compulsory. The Liberals rapidly lost strength and virtually disappeared from the political scene, while the traditional anticlerical forces gathered around the Labor party.

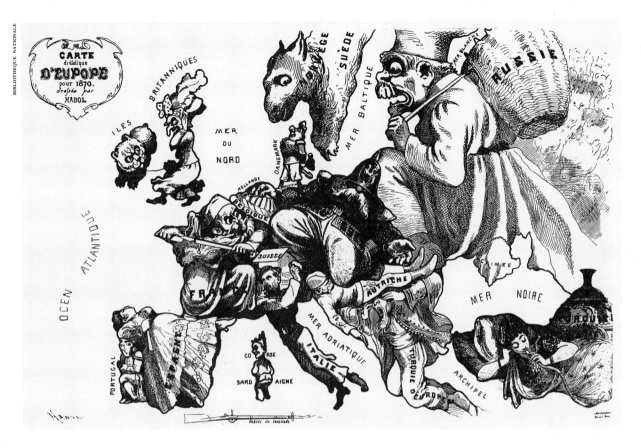

A French view of the European scene in 1870. Militant Prussia dominates the Continent, crushing Austria and threatening France, who draws his sword in defense. To the east lurks the Russian giant; to the west the Irish problem worries Britain.

In Scandinavia one of the principal political controversies centered around the desire of Norway to separate from Sweden, to which it had been subjected since 1815. Although enjoying virtually complete autonomy, including a separate parliament and ministry, the Norwegians no longer wanted to be subject to the authority of the Swedish king. For several decades this controversy caused great tension between Oslo and Stockholm. In 1905 the Norwegians unilaterally proclaimed their independence, whereupon the Swedes gave their assent—a unique instance of peaceful separation of one nationality from another.

The Scandinavian countries became converted to liberal and democratic institutions slowly, but at least without the backsliding characteristic of states in which the transition occurred suddenly. In the first half of the nineteenth century Sweden was one of the more conservative countries in Europe. Its liberalization began in 1864 with the promulgation of a constitution and the establishment of a two-chamber parliament. The franchise was restricted. The three Scandinavian monarchies adopted parliamentary government and universal suffrage only in the twentieth century (Norway 1898, 1905; Sweden, 1907; Denmark, 1914–1915).

The Scandinavians were among the first to introduce schemes of social reform modeled on those of Germany. Between 1886 and 1892 the Danes enacted national programs of unemployment and health insurance and pensions for the aged. The Swedes took some steps in this direction in the 1880s, but they did so in earnest only in the decade preceding World War I. At this time they passed laws providing for the protection of workers, for the settlement of labor disputes, for assistance in home construction, and for old age pensions.

The Third Republic   Superficially, France, with its parliament elected by universal suffrage and a responsible ministry, had a liberal, democratic government, not unlike that existing in Great Britain. No one questions that France was democratic in practice as well as in theory, but there is considerable doubt whether the system prevailing under the Third Republic can be described as a genuinely parliamentary one. For reasons that we shall indicate, the Chamber of Deputies could not exercise the extensive powers vested in it by the constitution, with the result that a great deal of authority devolved on the bureaucracy. The French historian Daniel Halévy goes so far as to state that the Third Republic operated on two distinct constitutional systems:

> Republican France has in reality two constitutions: one, that of 1875, is official, visible, and fills the press—it is parliamentary; the other is secret, silent, that of the Year VIII—the Napoleonic constitution which hands over the direction of the country to the administrative corps.

The fundamental flaws of the French political system—the factors that largely vitiated the parliamentary provisions of the constitution—were the polarization of forces between an intransigent left and right, and the absence of effective political parties.

The Third Republic, born of one German invasion (1870) and killed by another (1940), had two basic political blocs, the Conservative and the Republican. The two differed over basic constitutional principles. Broadly speaking, the Conservatives wanted firm authority, preferably monarchical, allied with the Catholic Church, whereas the Republicans wanted a republic and the separation of state and church. These blocs were not parties, properly speaking, for they had neither structure nor discipline; rather, they were agglomerations of parties, factions, and cliques held together mainly by agreement on the question of church-state relationship. The Conservatives drew their support from the upper-middle class, peasant proprietors, and practicing Catholics. The Republicans had the backing of the lower-middle class, minor civil servants, urban and rural workers, and the intellectuals. The enmity between the blocs was sealed in blood spilled in 1848 in the course of the June uprising and again in 1871 in the suppression of the so-called Paris Commune.

The Commune came into existence as the aftermath of the Franco-Prussian War. Two days after Napoleon III had capitulated at Sedan (September 2, 1870) a group of Parisian politicians proclaimed the establishment of the Third Republic and appealed to France to defend itself against the advancing Germans. But the country at large had no more heart for war. Nearly two-thirds of the deputies sent to the National Assembly elected in February, 1871, favored immediate peace. On the basis of these returns Adolphe Thiers, the leader of the Liberal opposition under the Second Empire, initiated peace negotiations. In the Treaty of Frankfurt, concluded in May, 1871, France ceded to Germany the provinces of Alsace and Lorraine and undertook to pay an indemnity of 5 billion francs (approximately 1 billion dollars).

Among the varied works of the French artist Édouard Manet are portrayals of civil disorders. This is his lithograph of the summary execution of Communards in Paris by loyalists in 1871.

To much of the populace of Paris, worn out by months of siege, the results of the vote for the Assembly and the signing of the peace treaty were acts of national apostasy. Early in March Paris rebelled against France. The uprising was dominated by anarchists who desired the abolition of the centralized state and the transfer of authority to the communes, the smallest unit of French administration. They now proclaimed the overthrow of the Third Republic and the establishment of the Paris Commune. Allied with the anarchists were Jacobin elements. The latter reintroduced the revolutionary calendar of 1793, shut down churches and monasteries, and arrested prominent citizens as hostages.

The legitimate government drawn from the National Assembly and headed by Thiers was at this time sitting at Versailles. Its first reaction to the Commune was to sit back and wait. But when the Communards began to lynch pro-government prisoners, Thiers decided to send troops to quell the rebellion. As soon as the collapse of the Commune seemed certain, the Communards went on an orgy of slaughter and destruction. They set fire to numerous public buildings, and were barely dissuaded from gutting Notre Dame and the Louvre. They executed many hostages, including prominent clergymen. The spectacle that greeted the loyalist troops upon their entry into the city so infuriated them that they launched a massacre of their own. During the so-called Bloody Week (May 21–28, 1871), an estimated 15,000 Communards and sympathizers were killed. Subsequently several thousand more were exiled to a penal colony in the South Pacific. The events of March-May, 1871, left a legacy of hatred between the right and left that has poisoned French politics ever since.

A Conservative paper's comment on the Dreyfus case shows a Prussian officer manipulating a mask of author Émile Zola, a stanch Dreyfus defender, over the face of a Jewish conspirator bent upon the destruction of France.

After the suppression of the Commune France seemed certain to adopt the monarchical form of government, for royalists enjoyed an absolute majority in the National Assembly (400 out of 650 seats). But, unfortunately for them, the leading pretender to the throne was an "ultra," a man of such conservative views that he would not even consent to the retention of the tricolor as the national flag, insisting on the Bourbon white. In the stalemate that ensued, the royalists had to agree to the appointment of a President. In 1875, in view of the continued stalemate, the Assembly passed legislative acts that gave France a new republican constitution. The Third Republic established itself thus almost as if by default. The republican government consisted of a bicameral parliament, whose lower house (Chamber of Deputies) was elected by universal male suffrage. Executive power was entrusted to a ministry formed by a majority in the Chamber. The two houses, sitting jointly, elected a President. His powers were so limited as to make him into a virtual figurehead.

Throughout its existence the Third Republic suffered from the absence of political parties strong enough or organized enough to assume the responsibility of forming a ministry. The formation of a new cabinet each time involved negotiations of the kind described earlier in this chapter, and yielded highly precarious coalitions. The average life of a French cabinet before 1914 was one year; in Great Britain it was five.

The failure of the monarchists gradually sapped their strength and increased that of the Republicans, who for the next forty years dominated French politics. The Republicans put their main effort into reducing the power of the Catholic Church. In the 1880s they issued a number of decrees separating the state from the church, including laws secularizing public schools and requiring their teachers to be laymen. The clergy resisted vigorously, supported by the monarchists and other conservative groupings. Throughout France pro-clerical and anti-clerical elements entered into conflict. This antagonism found expression in the classic French confrontation between village teacher and priest. The Republican drive culminated in 1905 in the repudiation of the Concordat, signed by Napoleon in 1801, and the disestablishment of the Catholic Church. The Republicans also took overdue steps to protect the French working class. In the 1890s they passed laws fully sanctioning trade unions and giving the worker basic security. In 1911 they enacted old age pensions.

The Conservatives, who had once been so near victory, grew embittered by the steady advance of their opponents. They loathed the Third Republic, sought to discredit it, and plotted its overthrow. In the late 1880s the Republic faced great danger from a conspiracy formed around a nationalist general, Georges Boulanger, who prepared to seize the government and assume dictatorial powers. Though everything seemed ready, Boulanger at the last moment lost his nerve, and the plot collapsed. In 1892–1893 the Conservatives exploited the "Panama Scandal" against the government. The scandal resulted from the bankruptcy of a company chartered to dig the Panama Canal, in which a number of high Republican politicians were implicated. But the greatest anti-Republican issue was the celebrated "Dreyfus Affair," around which the whole political life of France revolved for over a decade.

Alfred Dreyfus, a Jew and a captain attached to the General Staff, was arrested in 1894 on the charge of treason. The evidence against him consisted of a document, allegedly in his handwriting and containing military secrets, that was said to have been retrieved from the German embassy by a French agent. Although there was no conclusive proof that the document in question had been written by Dreyfus, he was convicted, dishonorably discharged, and exiled to a penal colony. The fate of an unknown captain would hardly have aroused the whole country had it not become evident from the start that the Conservatives meant to exploit him to convict the Republican government of treasonable activities and to give vent to anti-Semitic feelings. The controversy divided France into two camps, the Dreyfusards and the anti-Dreyfusards, roughly corresponding to the Republican and Conservative blocs. Dreyfus' relatives and friends gathered sufficient evidence to prove that the accused was an innocent victim of a conspiracy to protect another member of the General Staff who had, in fact, committed espionage. Yet Dreyfus was not fully exonerated until 1906, because the Conservative forces had staked so much on his guilt. No other issue in modern French politics aroused so much antagonism.

The collapse of the case against Dreyfus did not destroy the Conservative cause, but led to the emergence of a neo-Conservative movement, whose leading theorist was Charles Maurras. Organized as *L'Action Française* (1899), the new conservatives propagated what they called "integral nationalism," extolling France above other nations. Maurras detested parliaments and democracy, which he considered incapable of providing firm authority. He adopted from the socialists and anarchists the techniques of propaganda and mass politics, and advocated a *coup d'état* leading to the establishment of absolute authority. In the writings of Maurras and his associates one can perceive clearly the roots of modern right-wing totalitarian ideology.

While being challenged by an exasperated conservative right, the Third Republic also confronted a constant threat from the left. The growth of a syndicalist movement dedicated to anarchist ideals and methods severely tested its ability for survival, especially in the early years of the new century.

An Anglo-Saxon observer, accustomed to judging the health of a country by the soundness of its legislature, is likely to underrate the basic solidity of the pre-1914 Third Republic. Owing to its wide distribution of property and an efficient administrative corps, France enjoyed greater political continuity and stability than the yearly shifts of ministries or the irreconcilable hostility between the right and left may indicate. The political system was not satisfactory, but fortunately for France its life depended less on the legislative branch of government than did that of many other countries.

Italy

The constitution of the Italian kingdom resembled that prevailing in republican France. The king, like the French President, was a figurehead, and power rested in a ministry formed by the lower house. The franchise was gradually extended until in 1912 it became universal. The Italian bureaucracy, however, was far less efficient than the French.

Political parties in Italy were casual and formless. The would-be Prime Minister could secure the required majority only by making "deals" with individual deputies, promising them patronage or other rewards in their districts in return for their support in parliament. Known as *trasformismo*, this system of "transforming" the opposition into a malleable body of adherents became in the 1890s the normal method of conducting government. The Italian parliamentary regime, writes H. Stuart Hughes in *The United States and Italy* (1965),

> developed in conformity with neither of the more usual European models. It did not take form as the alternation of two large parties on the English model. Nor did it evolve into a game of constructing coalitions among a number of parties basically ideological in nature, as in France. . . . The Italian Parliament degenerated into an amorphous mass of deputies, dependent on the skillful orchestration of an official majority-monger.

Needless to emphasize, such tactics had little in common with genuine parliamentary procedures. They served to bring discredit to parliament, and it is not surprising that Italian theorists were among the earliest and most outspoken critics of the whole representative system of government.

A bitter issue in Italian politics was the relationship between church and state. As we have seen (Chapter 15), Pius IX had opposed the unification of Italy, and after the Italian kingdom had annexed Rome in 1870, he shut himself up in the Vatican and forbade Italian Catholics to participate in national elections. Leo XIII, who succeeded him in 1878, was a man of somewhat more moderate views. In 1891 he issued the encyclical *Rerum novarum*, which affirmed the concern of the Church for the working class. Nevertheless, on political questions Leo XIII remained fairly intransigent as did his successor, Pius X. The relations between the Italian government and the Vatican remained tense until the Lateran Treaties signed in 1929.

Imperial Germany The decline of liberalism occurred nowhere as swiftly and with such disastrous consequences as in Germany. In 1848–1849 the future of that country seemed to rest in the hands of the high-minded intellectuals gathered in the National Assembly at Frankfurt. Fifty years later their heirs, divided, demoralized, and uncertain of their course, formed a minor party, squeezed between a powerful conservative right and an inexorably expanding socialist left. The collapse of German liberalism was a disaster not only for Germany, but for the world at large. In the second half of the nineteenth century Germany set the pace in industry, trade, technology, and science. It seemed to many a model state of the future. The withering of liberalism there contributed heavily to discredit the liberal movement everywhere.

A major responsibility for the destruction of German liberalism rests on Bismarck. Bismarck desired at all costs to preserve the unity of the empire. Afraid of the pull of diverse ideological, social, religious, and regional partisanship, he saw in strong, centralized monarchical authority the best guarantee of national cohesion. He was not against political parties and parliament as such, for he understood that under modern conditions effective government could not be conducted without them. But he envisaged them principally as sources of support. In his mind, the function of political parties was to speak on behalf of specific social groups, and that of the Reichstag to serve as a channel of loyal opinion and social interest. "I consider parliamentary *cooperation*—if properly

Bismarck, looking no less uncompromising in his retirement, was painted in 1895 by Franz von Lenbach.

practiced—necessary and useful," he wrote, "as much as I consider parliamentary *rule* harmful and impossible." Bismarck viewed resistance to the will of the monarch as an act of disloyalty and crushed it without hesitation. The result of this attitude was to create in Germany a widespread impression that opposition to the central government was morally wrong and unpatriotic. Such an attitude, of course, had fatal consequences for the cause of liberalism in Germany. A great German historian, Friedrich Meinecke, surveying the wreckage of his country after World War II, concluded that Bismarck, by destroying in Germans the capacity for responsible government, bore much of the blame for Hitler's rise to power.

Bismarck was able to pursue his illiberal policies by virtue of the German constitution, much of which he himself had designed. In theory the German Empire was a federation of twenty-five states, but in practice it was a unitary state dominated by Prussia. Prussia had five-eighths of the population of the empire and two-thirds of the seats in the Reichstag; it commanded the armed forces, and controlled much of the agricultural and industrial wealth. The king of Prussia was German emperor, and his chief minister was Germany's Chancellor. The Chancellor owed no responsibility to the national Reichstag. He was appointed by the emperor, and as long as he enjoyed his confidence he could rule the country with near-dictatorial authority. The power of the Prussian king within his own kingdom was unassailable. Whereas the elections to the imperial Reichstag were based on universal vote, the Prussian Diet was elected by a complicated indirect suffrage, which heavily favored the propertied groups and the landed aristocracy. Given the power that he enjoyed in Prussia, and that Prussia in turn enjoyed in Germany, the emperor or a man whom he chose to be his Chancellor could govern the empire with less interference than any head of state of a major European country except the tsar of Russia.

As we noted in Chapter 15, the Progressive party, the principal liberal organization at midcentury, disintegrated in the 1860s. The majority of its members formed the National Liberal party, which stressed the nationalism in its name rather than the liberalism, and supported Bismarck most of the time. It usually spoke for big business interests. The residue, consisting of genuine liberals, formed the Radical party, which enjoyed little influence outside the free professions. The Conservatives represented agrarian interests, mainly the land-owners from the east. The Center party was an organization of Catholics, generally conservative in its orientation, but opposed to excessive centralization and rather progressive on labor questions. Social Democracy formed the most powerful group on the left. Founded as a revolutionary organization, it gradually evolved, as we have seen (Chapter 19), into a party espousing liberal and democratic aims.

Bismarck usually got along with the Conservatives and the National Liberals and had no reason to worry about the weak Progressives. It was the Catholics and the socialists whom he feared. He saw them as foes of the unified and authoritarian German state and fought them ruthlessly, although with little success.

The conflict with the Catholic Church—the so-called *Kulturkampf* ("struggle for culture")—began in Prussia in the early 1870s and in time engulfed most of Germany. The pretext for Bismarck's assault on the Church was the promulgation in 1870 of the dogma of Papal Infallibility (Chapter 15), which he interpreted as a challenge, by the Church, to state authority. Behind his action, however, lay some pragmatic considerations. The German Catholics opposed excessive Prussian power and wished to strengthen the constituent states of the empire. They also maintained close relations with the Austrians and the Polish minorities in Prussia. On Bismarck's initiative the Prussian government expelled the Jesuits, dissolved other Catholic orders and associations, and placed the education of the clergy under state supervision. Recalcitrant priests were forcefully removed from their parishes. By 1876 all the Catholic bishops in Prussia were either in jail or in self-imposed exile. Bismarck also prevailed on the imperial Reichstag to pass a number of laws directed against the Catholics, including a decree requiring civil marriages. The Center party came into existence to resist these measures. Continued persecution of Catholics increased its following, and Bismarck finally had to recognize the folly of an attack on a church claiming the allegiance of more than one-third of the empire's population. In the 1880s he called a halt in his unsuccessful struggle.

While the struggle with the Catholics was at its height, Bismarck launched another political offensive, this time against the socialists. This action was inspired by the success of the newly formed Social Democratic party, which in 1877 had polled half a million votes. He responded to this threat with a double policy: a negative one, designed to repress the Social Democrats, and a positive one, designed to win over their actual and potential supporters.

In 1878, using as a pretext two attempts on the life of the emperor (neither, in fact, involving Social Democrats), Bismarck pressured the Reichstag into passing an Anti-Socialist Law. This act prohibited Social Democrats from holding public meetings, raising funds, or sponsoring publications. It did not, however, prevent them from running for the Reichstag. In response to the law the Social Democratic leaders moved abroad, from where they directed political activities in Germany and put up candidates for elections. It is a telling commentary on the difference between nineteenth-century authoritarianism and twentieth-century totalitarianism that while the Anti-Socialist Law was in effect, German Social Democrats continued to win seats in parliament and from its rostrum publicly to criticize the government.

In his positive program against the Social Democrats, Bismarck availed himself of the ideas of the so-called state socialists. These were mostly academic thinkers—their opponents sometimes called them "socialists of the [professorial] chair"—who accepted the premises of radical socialism but drew from them different conclusions. They agreed that capitalism deprived the worker of a fair share of the wealth he produced. But whereas the radical socialists wanted to right this injustice by nationalizing the means of production, the state socialists advocated social reform carried out under state auspices. They urged the government to achieve a better distribution of wealth by taxing the rich and legislating measures of social security. Their goal was a peaceful achievement of many socialist measures within the framework of the capitalist order. Their program provided the theoretical basis of the modern welfare state.

For Bismarck state socialism offered as effective a weapon against the Social Democrats as nationalism had once been against the liberals. To win the mass voters' sympathies for the monarchy, he initiated measures of social legislation. Most important of these were laws establishing compulsory insurance against sickness and accidents (1883–1884) and unemployment caused by disability or old age (1889). The money for these schemes came from contributions of employers, workers, and the state. These laws gave Germany the most advanced system of social security in existence, and were subsequently copied throughout Europe.

The political results of these policies, however, proved disappointing to Bismarck. Whereas the four other principal parties remained static, the Social Democrats consistently attracted the new voters, especially country people who, upon moving to the cities, first availed themselves of the suffrage. In 1890 the Reichstag let the Anti-Socialist Law lapse. The Social Democrats surfaced and in their first open campaign in twelve years showed that they had not been harmed, for they gained one-fifth of the ballots. In nearly every subsequent election they continued to improve their standing, and in 1912 they won almost as many votes as the other parties combined. Bismarck grew so alarmed by the socialist advances that in his last years in office he considered depriving the socialists of the suffrage, and even abolishing the Reichstag.

Bismarck's career came to an abrupt end in 1890. In that year he was dismissed by the new emperor, William II, who wished to take over the reins of government himself.

In view of the extraordinary power vested in the German emperor, the personality of the new Kaiser was a matter of some consequence. William was twenty-nine when he came to the throne. Raised in the Potsdam Guards Regi-

Britain's Punch, *equating socialism with anarchy, looked with favor upon Bismarck's Anti-Socialist Law of 1878.*

ment, he absorbed the values of the Prussian officer class. He believed in force, and the "survival of the fittest" in domestic as well as foreign politics. For party politics or parliament he had little use. "My *Reichstag* behaves as badly as it can," he wrote on one occasion (in his rough-hewn English) to Tsar Nicholas II, "swinging backwards and forwards between the socialists egged on by the Jews, and the ultramontane Catholiks; both parties being soon fit to be hung all of them as far as I can see." William was not lacking in intelligence, but he did lack stability, disguising his deep insecurities by swagger and tough talk. He frequently fell into depressions and hysterics, and on one occasion, after a humiliating defeat at the hands of the Reichstag, suffered a nervous breakdown. He was also incurably vulgar. An idea of his taste may be gathered from his fondness for practical jokes. The spectacle of his Chief of Staff, dressed in tulle, giving imitations of a ballerina never failed to double him up with laughter.

William's personal instability was reflected in vacillations of policy. His actions, at home as well as abroad, lacked guidelines, and therefore often bewildered or infuriated public opinion. He was not so much concerned with gaining specific objectives, as had been the case with Bismarck, as with asserting his will. This trait in the ruler of the leading Continental power was one of the main causes of the uneasiness prevailing in Europe at the turn of the century.

William did not help matters by his irresponsible public pronouncements. In 1891 he created a sensation with an address to army recruits:

> You have sworn to me loyalty. This means, children of my guard, that you are now my soldiers, that you have dedicated yourself to me body and soul.

Bismarck (center) playing host to the new emperor, William II, at his country estate in 1888. Two years later William dismissed him as Chancellor.

You have now only one enemy, and he is my enemy. Under conditions of present-day socialist disturbances, it may happen—which God forbid— that I shall order you to shoot down your relatives, your brothers, yes, even your parents. Even then you must obey my orders without murmur.

In 1900, when the Chinese Boxers murdered the German minister in Peking, William urged the following advice on an expeditionary corps dispatched to China:

When you encounter the enemy, he shall be beaten! Give no quarter! Take no prisoners! He who falls into your hands is yours! As the Huns under Attila had made themselves a thousand years ago a name that even today covers them with glory in legends and fairy tales, so may you estab- lish in China for a thousand years to come the name of the German, that a Chinese never again as much as give a German a queer look!°

William unfortunately lacked a steadying influence at the court. His Chancellors were, on the whole, weak and ineffective, and the courtiers and military friends mostly yes men. The atmosphere surrounding the Kaiser was a compound of superciliousness and uncertainty in which voices urging moderation tended to be drowned out. A similar mood prevailed among the German middle class; it was elated by the incredible advances of the country in all fields of endeavor, and yet afraid that Germany might not win for itself in the world a place commensurate with its position and needs. The Social Democrats, who stood for democracy and parliamentary rule, were widely regarded as internal enemies; so was much of the working class.

In the Dual Monarchy, created by the *Ausgleich* of 1867, the basic factor of political life was national antagonisms. In the Austrian part the Germans clashed with Slavs and other ethnic groups, which outnumbered them two to one; in the Hungarian part the Magyars fought with the non-Magyar half of the popula- tion. The democratization of the franchise in Austria only made matters worse because the electorate among the ethnic minorities, responding to nationalist appeal, sent to the Reichsrat deputies pledged to uphold the national cause. The Magyars noted this fact and refused to widen the suffrage in their part of the state. In Austria real political authority concentrated in the hands of the bureaucracy, and in Hungary in those of the nobility. In neither half of the Dual Monarchy was the parliament an effective instrument.

The issue that aroused especial passion in both Austria and Hungary was elementary education. The introduction of compulsory primary schooling re- quired agreement on the language to be used in the classroom. Minority intellectuals insisted on the use of native languages, sometimes coupling this demand with one for cultural autonomy. There were also disagreements over languages to be used in government offices located in areas inhabited by minority populations.

The imperial government made valiant efforts to satisfy the wishes of the non-German groups in Austria. It conceded them full civil equality, opened up to

Austria-Hungary

°These remarks were the origin of the appellation "Huns" used by the Allies in referring to the Germans in World War I.

them the civil service, and made considerable linguistic concessions in schools and administrative offices. In 1907 the Austrians introduced universal franchise. This was a courageous move, because it gave the non-Germans a majority in the Reichsrat. But nothing really succeeded, and at the beginning of the century there was a widespread feeling that the days of the empire were numbered.

As the century drew toward a close the Austrian Liberals, after taking the lead in enacting anti-clerical measures and legislation favoring the minorities, passed from the scene. The majority of German Austrians now turned toward conservative solutions; a significant minority shifted to the socialists.

The Germans in Austria felt themselves to be a group in danger of being outnumbered, outvoted, and inundated by the Slavs, Jews, and other minorities. They resented both the *Ausgleich*, which had detached Hungary and left them to confront a Slavic majority, and the introduction of universal suffrage, which had reduced their political influence. Some of them looked to the north for help, longing for a "Greater Germany" in which German Austria would be included. But Bismarck gave them no encouragement, for his foreign policy required a strong and integral Austrian Empire. National anxiety, therefore, found its main outlet in a powerful conservative movement dedicated to the assertion of Germanic supremacy.

A distinguishing characteristic of this movement was its anti-Semitism. Behind it lay the fear that the Jews were seizing control over the country's economic and cultural life. After 1867, when they received full civil equality, Jews had moved from all directions into Vienna and the provincial capitals of the empire, many of them fleeing anti-Semitic excesses in Russia. In the following thirty years in Vienna alone, the Jewish population grew from virtually nothing to 150,000 inhabitants, or 10 percent of the population. The importance of the Jews exceeded mere numbers. They controlled much of the banking that financed Austrian economic expansion. They also took over a good part of the urban retail trade. They rarely received gratitude for the economic benefits they brought Austria, but invariably had to bear the blame for economic dislocations and disasters, such as the panic of 1873 (Chapter 17). Much of the resentment of the Austrian middle class and the peasantry against the capitalist-industrial order that penetrated the country at the end of the century focused on the Jew as its symbol. Furthermore, Jews dominated Vienna's culture: they owned most of its daily press, and played a prominent role in literary, musical, and scientific life. Indeed, they were largely responsible for transforming Vienna from a charming provincial town into one of the cultural centers of *fin de siècle* Europe. Although anti-Semitism was on the rise everywhere in the late nineteenth century, it was nowhere as virulent as in Austria. In 1900 a bill was introduced in the Reichsrat making marriage between Gentile and Jew a crime under laws prohibiting relations between man and beast. At the time such a bill had no chance of passage; but it became reality thirty-five years later in the form of the Nürnberg Laws.

In the 1890s the German conservative nationalists founded the Christian Socialist party dedicated to fighting the Slavic and Jewish "danger." Its most popular leader was Dr. Karl Lueger, an anti-Semitic politician whom the Viennese repeatedly elected mayor, despite Franz Josef's refusal to install him in office. When the emperor finally yielded, Lueger launched a vigorous policy of municipalization of public utilities to remove them from the control of Jews and foreigners. The Christian Socialists and their conservative allies held great attraction for the upper and lower German middle classes in Austria. After the introduction of universal suffrage in 1907, the right-wing parties formed the most powerful voting bloc in the Reichsrat. Lueger's political tactics—a combination of nationalism, anti-Semitism, and socialism—greatly impressed a young drifter from Upper Austria named Adolf Hitler, who at the time was unsuccessfully trying to make an artistic career in Vienna. Later he declared Lueger to have been the greatest "statesman" of his time.

To escape the pressures of anti-Semitism many Austrian Jews converted to Catholicism. But a small minority, headed by Theodor Herzl, a Viennese doctor, proposed to solve what had become known as the "Jewish problem" by founding in Palestine a Jewish national home. Herzl's book, *The Jewish State* (1896), although not the first to make this proposal (it had forerunners in Russia and Germany), marked the beginning of Zionism as an organized movement. Thus the ideas that were to lead alike to the destruction of most of European Jewry and to the salvation of its remnant came into being at the same time and at the same place.

After the decline of the Liberals, the main proponents of political and social democracy in Austria were the Social Democrats. Theirs was the single largest party in the post-1907 Reichsrat, but they too were torn by national dissensions, a repetition on a smaller scale of what went on in the empire as a whole.

The Great Reforms of the 1860s marked a break with the thoroughly autocratic-bureaucratic government in Russia, but they brought no political liberalization. Russians enjoyed basic civil liberties but still lacked political rights. They remained the only citizens in Europe without a constitution or parliament—a situation the educated classes in Russia found intolerable. *Russia*

In the 1870s the protest against the autocratic system took the form of an anarchist movement. Its leaders, mostly students, were inspired by the belief that the peasantry was ready to rise in rebellion and overthrow the existing political and social order. They were, like anarchists elsewhere, anti-liberal, in the sense that they regarded constitutions, parliaments, and even civil liberties as instruments used by the ruling class to solidify its dominant position. They desired the immediate abolition of state and private property, the transfer of land and tools to peasants and workers, and the shift of authority to associations of producers, as exemplified by the Russian peasant commune.° In their contacts with the peasants, the anarchists quickly discovered that the working people had a deep respect for tsar, state, and church. To undermine it, they launched a campaign of terror against government officials, culminating in the assassination of Alexander II in 1881.

As was often the case, radical excesses strengthened the hand of the reactionaries, who could now claim they had been correct in opposing the liberalization of the 1860s, since liberalism bred anarchy. In the 1880s the government

°These radicals are often referred to as "Populists," although they did not so call themselves, preferring the name "Socialist Revolutionaries."

veered sharply to the right. Alexander III, the son of the murdered tsar, was a firm believer in autocratic rule. He revoked many of the powers granted previously to organs of local self-rule, tightened censorship, and repressed any signs of political independence. The same held true of his son and successor, Nicholas II, who came to the throne in 1894. In an effort to win popular support the government condoned and sometimes encouraged anti-Semitism. From the 1880s onward, Jews were occasionally subjected to violent pogroms, which the police made no effort to prevent.

Notwithstanding strict ordinances outlawing them, political parties began to take shape around the turn of the century. The most influential was the party of Constitutional Democrats, formally organized in 1905, but in operation since 1902. It combined demands for parliamentary government and universal suffrage with a rather radical social program, especially on land distribution. To the left stood two socialist parties. The Socialist Revolutionaries continued the older anarchistic tradition: they wanted decentralization of government and the socialization of land, and resorted to terror against government officials. They enjoyed a considerable following among the peasantry. On the other hand, the Russian Social Democratic party was built on the model of its German counterpart. It demanded political democracy as its immediate aim and a socialist order as its long-term objective. Its principal adherents were among intellectuals and skilled urban workers. Russia had no single conservative party, but instead various reactionary, nationalistic groupings whose adherents treated all demands for change, whether moderate and liberal or extreme and radical, as conspiracies of Jewish, Polish, or "Masonic" origin. Although even smaller in the number of active members than parties of the left, right-wing groups enjoyed considerable influence on policy by virtue of their connections at the court.

Like Austria-Hungary and Turkey, Russia was a multi-national empire with numerous minority groups, some of which began to evidence stirrings of nationalist sentiment.

The most troublesome of these minorities were the Poles. Descendants of a nation that in the seventeenth century had dominated Eastern Europe, the Poles would not reconcile themselves to the loss of independence. The Russians had made several efforts to arrive at an accommodation with their Polish subjects, most notably in 1815 when they granted the duchy of Warsaw a constitution with broad internal autonomy. But these efforts failed, because the Polish leaders refused to accept any status within the Russian Empire. They not only insisted on independence, but on independence within the frontiers of 1772, before the First Partition, when Poland had extended "from sea to sea"—from the Black Sea to the Baltic. The Russians on their part could not acquiesce in a demand that would cut off their western provinces, with the result that through the century relations between the two nations remained extremely strained. A Polish rebellion in 1830–1831 caused the Russians to suspend the 1815 constitution; another in 1863 moved them to abolish Poland as an administrative entity and to incorporate it into Russia. At that time tens of thousands of Poles were expelled from the western provinces of Russia and sent into penal servitude in Siberia. The defeat of the 1863 uprising temporarily cooled nationalist passions in Poland. Many Poles felt that instead of fighting for ephemeral independence, they should concentrate on raising the economic and cultural level of the nation. The 1870s and 1880s were an era of such practical concerns. But in the 1890s nationalism in its political form re-emerged, this time in close association with socialism. And as the century drew to a close Poles and Russians once more began to clash.

In addition to the Poles, Russia had many other minority groups: Ukrainians and Belorussians, both of them Slavic and Orthodox, culturally close to the Russians but by no means identical; and numerous Finnic, Jewish, Turkic, Iranian, and Caucasian groups. At the end of the century, Russians proper (without Ukrainians and Belorussians) constituted somewhat less than 45 percent of the population of the empire. Although many of the minorities were not yet sufficiently self-conscious to advance national demands, most of them produced, early in the twentieth century, a thin layer of nationalistic intelligentsia. Influenced by the example of the nationalists in Austria-Hungary, these intellectuals began to think in terms of cultural or territorial autonomy for their ethnic groups. To these claims the imperial government usually reacted with repression and Russification.

Until 1904–1905 the imperial government managed to beat off challenges to its authority. But the failure in the war against Japan (Chapter 21) so weakened it that it was no longer able to do so. The military debacle encouraged urban unrest, which the government could not suppress because its armed forces were many thousands of miles away. By the autumn of 1905 the autocracy lost control of the country. Political parties, though still technically outlawed, began to meet in the open; censorship broke down; workers formed strike committees; the countryside blazed in revolt as peasants burned estates and seized private land. In October, 1905, the tsar, faced with the threat of a general strike, capitulated. He now issued an "October Manifesto" granting Russian subjects full civil liberties and promising the establishment of a representative legislative body. Having by this measure won the support of moderate groups, the government used the returned troops to stamp out disorder.

The October Manifesto marked the second phase in the liberalization of Russia, the era of constitutional rule. The constitution ("Fundamental Laws") of 1906 provided for a parliament—the first in the country's history—consisting of an upper and lower chamber. The latter, called the Duma, was elected by universal and secret male ballot. The Duma had the right to debate and vote on legislation. No law could become effective without its approval. It also voted on the budget. But it lacked the power of appointing and dismissing ministers, who remained responsible to the tsar. The tsar retained other prerogatives, including the right to declare war and to direct the armed forces. In its principal provisions, the Russian constitution resembled those in force in contemporary Germany and Austria, on which it was modeled.

Although a phenomenon without precedent in Russian experience, the constitutional regime engendered great enthusiasm in the country. In the elections to the first Duma, held in April, 1906, the liberals (Constitutional Democrats) won a stunning victory, capturing more than one-third of the seats. The constitutional experiment thus seemed off to a good start, for, unlike the parties of the extreme left and right, the leaders of this party accepted the new order. But the imperial government, having regained its footing, had second thoughts about the con-

Conservative politician Peter Stolypin headed Russia's government from 1906 until his assassination in 1911.

cessions it had made when under duress. The tsar and his closest advisers never reconciled themselves to sharing authority with the Duma, and indeed tended to treat its very existence as something of an affront. The first Duma was dissolved after a session of ten weeks; the second, meeting early in 1907, after one of fifteen weeks. Furthermore, various devices were invented to bypass its authority.

Finally, in June, 1907, the government ventured on a virtual *coup d'état*, reminiscent of Bismarck's action in 1862. While the country was preparing for its third election in fourteen months, the government promulgated a new electoral law. Its purpose was to reduce the representation of the peasants, workers, and minorities and to increase that of the Russian propertied classes. The measure was incontrovertibly illegal because, according to the constitution, changes in the electoral system required the approval of the Duma.

Management of policy in the new government was entrusted to an able conservative politician, Peter Stolypin. Stolypin, who in many ways emulated Bismarck, believed that the function of parliament was to assist the monarchy. The new electoral law gave him what he wanted, a docile majority, and the next two Dumas lasted out their normal terms of five years each. With Duma support Stolypin took energetic steps to solve the persistent agrarian crisis. He abolished the laws requiring the peasant to belong to the commune, enabling him to consolidate his land holdings, and made various provisions to promote the emergence of a vigorous rural middle class, which he hoped would stabilize the countryside. But he had many enemies, and in 1911 he fell victim of a bullet fired by a terrorist on the police payroll.

On the eve of World War I Russia was a vigorous and dynamic country saddled with a backward-looking monarchy and an anarchistic peasantry. The economy had expanded greatly since the 1890s, the currency was stable, and the education of the citizenry was making rapid progress. But the political situation seemed insoluble, despite the great hopes awakened in 1905-1906. The failure of the imperial government to treat the popularly elected Duma as a genuine partner created constant tension, which benefited the revolutionaries. The hostility between the leaders of public opinion and the bureaucracy created for the revolutionaries a propitious atmosphere for agitation among the politically inexperienced peasants and workers.

Spain It is an exasperating task to seek any meaningful trend in the political life of nineteenth-century Spain. Revolutions, restorations, followed by more revolutions and restorations, succeeded with monotonous regularity and without any discernible sense of progression. These events never failed to produce a great deal of excitement for those engaged in them, but they had little effect on the life of the population at large. In the second half of the century, while Spain ostensibly enjoyed parliamentary government and even intermittent universal suffrage, a traveler venturing into Andalusia was still well advised to engage a retinue of bodyguards.

Early in the century Spain had had a vigorous constitutional movement; the constitution drafted in Cádiz in 1812 by the anti-Napoleonic rebels had provided a model and an inspiration for a whole generation of European liberals. But the country, strongly influenced by one of the most conservative church establishments in Europe, repudiated liberalism and time and again helped reactionary elements to suppress attempts at genuine representative government. The army, which earlier in the century had been a liberal force, also gradually evolved toward the right.

Under such conditions the constitutional system established in 1876 after the accession of Alfonso XII turned out to be a farce. The guiding spirit behind it was Antonio Cánovas, a cultivated man with genuine liberal sympathies. Cánovas admired Disraeli and Gladstone but felt that his own country was not yet ready for a true parliamentary system. Until the population was sufficiently educated and prosperous, it had to be ruled by the rich. And since the rich themselves were divided into two camps, Liberals and Conservatives, Cánovas devised an ingenious plan. Under his prodding, the two parties decided which at a given time would govern and which would provide the opposition—an arrangement that saved them the trouble and expense of campaigning. Elections were mere formalities, which gave returns in accord with instructions sent from Madrid. On one occasion (1886), the government newspaper even carried the election results before the election itself had taken place. This elegant system of conducting government survived until 1931.

A complicating factor in Spanish politics was the tenacity of regional sentiments. Although Spain had no minority problem in the strict sense of the word, in some provinces, such as Catalonia, there existed a great deal of hostility to Madrid. These regions were also centers of Spain's incipient industry, where the anarchists obtained a powerful hold on the urban and rural proletariat and caused the government a great deal of trouble by organizing strikes and carrying out acts of terrorism. The country tended thus to split in two: a conservative and Madrid-oriented center and north, and a more radical, federalist east and south. In the Spanish Civil War in the 1930s the battle lines between the Nationalists and Loyalists would run approximately along the divide between these two zones.

The pseudo-parliamentary government, instead of reflecting the realities of the situation, papered them over. Power actually rested in the landed aristocracy, clergy, and army, which showed little interest in the common citizenry and lived as if Spain were still the proud possessor of the Netherlands and Latin America. Only a handful of intellectuals concerned themselves with public matters.

The Balkans and Turkey

The history of the Balkan peninsula was that of the disintegration of the Ottoman Empire. To stem this disintegration Turkish reformers tried to liberalize and modernize their government. They failed, and from the possessions of Turkey emerged several new national states. By 1914 Turkish holdings in the Balkans were reduced to the area immediately surrounding Constantinople.

At the beginning of our period, that is, around 1870, the Ottoman Empire still controlled most of the Balkan peninsula, except for Greece, independent since 1829. But its control over this domain was weak, for the Christian nationalities, incited by Russia, were growing increasingly restless. The attempt to establish a common "Ottoman" nationality embracing both Muslims and Christians (Chapter 15) bore no results whatever.

In 1876 the Turkish reform movement, or *Tanzimat*, reached its apogee. The

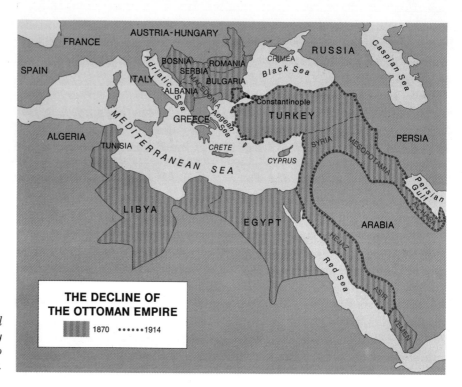

THE DECLINE OF
THE OTTOMAN EMPIRE
■■■ 1870 ●●●●●● 1914

The Ottoman hold on Egypt, nominal at most by the 1830s, was broken by Britain in 1882. Tunisia went to France (1881), Libya to Italy (1912).

Balkans were then in the midst of a rebellion, and to quell the disorders an attempt was made to transform the empire into a constitutional monarchy. This measure was the work of Midhat Pasha, an experienced civil servant, who saw in liberalization a means of consolidating the empire. The Ottoman constitution promulgated in 1876 on his advice was patterned on the constitutions of Germany and Austria. It reserved considerable authority for the sultan, but it also created a parliament with a voice in passing of laws and budgets. The constitution aroused general dissatisfaction. The new sultan, Abdul-Hamid II, a ruthless man and an authoritarian ruler, resented the loss of absolute power. The clergy, Muslim and Christian alike, were displeased by the new arrangement because it deprived them of their authority over their respective religious communities. The bulk of the peasantry, of course, cared little about the whole matter. The main support of the constitutional regime came from the Westernized officials, burghers, and intellectuals—elements which the rest of the population called by the pejorative term *effendis*. The new parliament barely assembled when it was permanently adjourned by Abdul-Hamid. Midhat, who had been dismissed, was presently murdered, and the absolutist regime came back.

A critical event in the history of the area was the Russo-Turkish War of 1877–1878 (Chapter 21). Turkey lost the war, and at the ensuing Congress of Berlin had to agree to painful territorial losses. Romania and Serbia, previously semiautonomous principalities carved out of Ottoman lands, were given recognition as independent states. An autonomous Bulgarian state was created, and Bosnia and Herzegovina were occupied by Austria. After 1878 Turkey's holdings in the Balkans consisted of little more than Albania and Macedonia.

The new Balkan states were in theory constitutional monarchies, but any resemblance to constitutional states as known from Western experience was coincidental. The usual method of settling political disputes was by recourse to arms. Dissatisfied groups frequently resorted to assassination and abduction. On one occasion the Bulgarian king himself was kidnapped. National and territorial disputes provided a constant source of friction.

The deterioration of the Ottoman Empire caused a succession of constitutional crises, none of which, however, resulted in stable and effective government. In 1908 Abdul-Hamid was forced by an army rebellion to restore the constitution of 1876 and to convene a parliament. For a while Turkey seemed at long last to be on its way toward a truly liberal regime. But the hope proved deceptive. In 1909 Abdul-Hamid encouraged a Muslim conservative rebellion against parliamentary institutions. The uprising was suppressed by the army, which deposed and exiled him. During the next four years, power was exercised by a weak sultan, Mohammed V, assisted by a cabinet and an assembly. The new government also failed to stop the disintegration of the empire. In 1912–1913, in the course of two successive Balkan wars, Albania became independent and Macedonia joined with Greece. In 1913 a group of politically-minded officers known as "Young Turks" seized power, and by ruthless means sought to suppress opposition in the center and borderlands. The intervention of the army in political life as a result of ineffective parliamentary institutions, first observed in Turkey, was to become a common phenomenon in Europe after World War I, and in Africa and Asia after World War II.

The instability of the Balkans was a source of great international concern, because it stimulated Russia and Austria to seek influence there. As we shall see, the conflict between these two powers over Serbia provided in 1914 the immediate cause for the outbreak of World War I.

History has a built-in bias in favor of "crises." The historian cannot help but select incidents and trends indicative of conflict or disorder because they make for change, and change causes the flow of events, which is his concern. A narrative of political history between 1870 and 1914 may suggest a more desperate state of affairs than in fact was the case. To correct any such false impression, we must keep in mind developments other than political: the unprecedented progress in industry and trade, the constant rise in living standards, the spread of civil liberties, the remarkable achievements in thought and art. We shall then understand why, notwithstanding serious doubts about basic issues of domestic politics, the majority of Europeans looked confidently to the future; and why, in all, it was a good time to be alive.

The Ottoman ruler Abdul-Hamid was known as the Red Sultan for his ruthless methods and bloody repressions, a view reflected in a French print.

PRESS ASSOCIATION LTD.

21

<figure>—◆◇◆—</figure>

Diplomacy and Imperialism:
1870-1914

The period of fifty-five years separating the Congress of Vienna from the Franco-Prussian War (1815–1870) was one of relative international stability. During this time the great powers devoted their principal attention to domestic problems resulting from industrialization and the introduction of political democracy. Expansion was not fashionable. There was a widespread belief that mankind stood at the threshold of a new era in its history. As Herbert Spencer put it, the age of "industry" was replacing that of "militarism." International conflicts of that period—as, for example, over the legacy of the Ottoman Empire, or the unification of Italy and Germany—involved objectives of a specific and limited nature, usually territorial, and as such were negotiable. They caused shifts in frontiers without upsetting the European state system as a whole.

This no longer held true of international relations in the years 1870–1914. Issues dividing the great powers now became both more basic and ill defined, involving vague aims such as "spheres of influence" or "a place in the sun." The extraordinary growth of population and of industrial productivity gave rise to fears that outlets capable of absorbing the excess people and goods would soon become saturated. These fears pushed statesmen to the conquests of new land and markets. The spread of racial and Social Darwinist ideologies encouraged such tendencies by providing them with a seemingly scientific justification. Expansionism revived in a more ambitious and brutal form than ever, and the world entered a period of disequilibrium from which it has yet to emerge.

Great Power Rivalry in the Balkans and Middle East

The most persistent cause of diplomatic tension throughout the nineteenth century was Russia's pressure southward, toward the Mediterranean, the Persian Gulf, and the Indian Ocean. This pressure encroached on British commercial interests and on Austria's territorial ambitions, and transformed the whole long southern frontier of the Russian Empire into a focus of keen international rivalry.

Russia's primary interest centered on the eastern Mediterranean, or, to be more precise, on Constantinople and the Straits. This concern is often explained in terms of a search for warm-water ports, but this reasoning is questionable, for Russia had neither a fleet nor a foreign trade of such dimensions as to require vigorous expansion. The matter may be better explained in terms of cultural factors. To Russia Constantinople was the source of its Christian faith and the fountainhead of its monarchy. Furthermore, Russians felt close kinship to the Balkan Christians, most of them Orthodox and Slavic. The European holdings of the Ottoman Empire were thus a natural object of aggrandizement, especially to the Russian Pan-Slavists who advocated a supra-national state embracing all Slavs under the scepter of their tsar.

The British reacted to Russian exertions in this area with an alarm that today seems quite out of proportion to the danger it posed and that can be explained only by the exaggerated notion they held of Russian military might. They tried a

Germany's Kaiser William II (left) and Britain's King George V, in full panoply, leave the royal palace at Potsdam to review the garrison. The occasion was the wedding of William's daughter in 1913; it was the last meeting of the two cousins.

variety of methods to stop the Russians from taking over European Turkey. On some occasions they cooperated with them against the Turks (e.g., in 1827–1829, during joint action on behalf of the Greek rebels). At other times they rallied diplomatic support behind the sultans to forestall Russian designs (as was done in the 1830s and 1840s). When neither method succeeded, Britain had recourse to arms (the Crimean War, 1854–1856). All along, the British applied pressure on the sultans to carry out internal reforms as a means of solidifying their empire and making it more resistant to Russian pressures.

Farther east, the British and the Russians competed over the approaches to India. The border separating that area from Russia was not well known at the time, and there was genuine fear in London that Russian expansion into central Asia could endanger Britain's hold on the Indian subcontinent. The swift conquest of Turkistan by Russian armies in the 1860s caused consternation in England, which deepened in the early 1880s when the Russians began from there to press on Afghanistan.

The constant need to resist these advances created an unfavorable view of Russia in England and other parts of the English-speaking world. Indeed, most of the preconceptions held about Russians today in England and the United States were formed in the Victorian era, in the heat of competition over the Middle East.

Notwithstanding their defeat in the Crimean War, the Russians soon renewed their pressures on Turkey. The event that gave them an opportunity to do so was

the outbreak in 1875 of an anti-Turkish uprising among the Balkan Christians. The Turks reacted to the revolt with brutal massacres, which outraged people throughout Europe. There were great pressures on the tsar to come to the aid of the persecuted Balkan Christians, and in April, 1877, he declared war on Turkey.

The war at first went badly for the Russians, but eventually they broke Turkish resistance, and in January, 1878, approached Constantinople. The sultan, in the Treaty of San Stefano (March, 1878), had to accept humiliating terms. Among them was the creation of a "Greater Bulgaria," a Russian vassal state carved out of Turkish territory. The treaty virtually eliminated the Ottoman Empire from the Continent and assured Russia of undisputed influence in the Balkans.

The Russian victories and especially the peace terms caused consternation among the great powers. As the Russian troops approached Constantinople, Disraeli ordered British naval units to the Bosporus as a warning that he would not tolerate seizure of that city. The Austrians, too, showed annoyance, and threatened mobilization, although they had originally consented to the Russian attack in return for the Turkish provinces of Bosnia and Herzegovina. The Russians had no choice but to yield to British and Austrian pressure. In secret talks with London and Vienna, carried out in the spring of 1878, they consented to reduce substantially the proposed Bulgarian state and to give up some other claims to the Balkans. An international congress convened by Bismarck shortly afterward (Congress of Berlin, June, 1878), ratified these earlier accords.

Until the war of 1877 Russian expansion into the Balkans had run mainly into British opposition. From then on it met increasingly with the resistance of Austria.

Austria's interest in the Balkans was an unexpected result of the unification of Italy and Germany. The emergence of strong national states south and north had deprived Vienna of its traditional spheres of influence and forced it to seek outlets for its ambitions elsewhere. Such an outlet it found along its southeastern frontier, in the unstable regions adjoining the Ottoman Empire. From 1877 onward Austria pursued its claims in the Balkans with increased vigor, sometimes with active British and German encouragement. In 1881 Austria, by means of a secret accord, established a virtual protectorate over Serbia, and two years later it signed a military alliance with Romania. These diplomatic moves greatly perturbed the Russians. They were even more angered by Austria's interference in 1885 in the internal affairs of Bulgaria, a state the Russians regarded as their dependency. The rivalry over the Balkans in the 1870s and 1880s led to a deterioration in relations between Russia and Austria, and ultimately had profound consequences for the whole diplomatic alignment of Europe.

The Alliance Systems

The tension in the Balkans, for all its implicit dangers, presented less of a threat to the general peace than did the post-1870 antagonism between France and Germany. The latter involved two leading powers with great military establishments. The quarrel between them, moreover, concerned not territories belonging to third parties, as was the case in the Balkans, but general issues that could hardly be settled except by a clear-cut victory of one over the other.

At stake, fundamentally, was hegemony over Europe. France had aspired to this hegemony since the seventeenth century and on one occasion, under

Russia's royal family poses for an official portrait in the early 1890s. At center is Tsar Alexander III; behind him is future Tsar Nicholas II.

Napoleon I, had actually attained it. Except for distant Russia it had been traditionally the largest, the most populous, the richest, and therefore the mightiest state on the Continent. In the second half of the nineteenth century it had ceased to be all these things. The German Empire equaled its territory, vastly surpassed its population (64 million to France's 39 million in 1911) and industrial productivity, and, as 1870 had demonstrated, excelled it in military power. The two rivals for European supremacy eyed each other with suspicion, and their leaders grew convinced that the final settlement of their disagreements required another war.

In France this *revanchist* sentiment was especially widespread within the Conservative bloc, which favored action against Germany to revenge the defeat at Sedan and to recover Alsace and Lorraine. In the 1880s the anti-German movement gained great momentum; it played a prominent part in both the Boulanger and Dreyfus episodes (Chapter 20). Nor were the Republicans immune to these sentiments.

The German attitude toward the Third Republic was at first essentially defensive. Bismarck considered his country to have attained its natural limits: it was "satiated," as he put it. The principal task of his foreign policy was to safeguard what had been won, that is, to protect the unity and the integrity of the empire. The greatest threat to this aim was France. France endangered the empire both because of its inherent hostility toward Germany, and because of its capacity, by means of alliances with Germany's neighbors, to force it into a two-front war. Bismarck, therefore, concentrated on diplomatically isolating France: "We require that France leave us alone," he wrote in 1872, "and we must prevent it from securing allies should it fail to remain still; as long as it is without allies, France poses to us no danger."

The most effective way of depriving the French of allies was to bind any potential friend of France to Germany. These were, first and foremost, Russia, Austria, and Italy. (England, a naval power without a significant army, was not a serious factor in these calculations.) Proceeding on this premise, Bismarck engineered two major alliance systems—the League of the Three Emperors (1873: Germany, Austria-Hungary, Russia; after 1881 known as the Alliance of the Three Emperors), and the Triple Alliance (1882: Germany, Austria-Hungary, Italy).

The League of the Three Emperors, the basic instrument of Bismarck's diplomacy, committed the signatories to come to each other's aid in the event one of them was attacked by a fourth power. It was valid for three years and could be renewed. The League served German interests superbly well, isolating both Austria and Russia from France and assuring Germany of their help should Bismarck's nightmare—a French attack—materialize. Russia gained least, since neither of its allies could offer it effective assistance against its main rival, Great Britain, in the Middle East. The Triple Alliance came about as a result of Italy's rivalry with France over North Africa. Piqued by French seizure of Tunisia in 1882, the Italians cast their lot with the Germans and Austrians. The Alliance also bound the three powers to help each other against external attack.

The two alliances constituted the foundation of the Bismarckian diplomatic system, which dominated international diplomacy during the years of his chancellorship. France was in fact isolated: it could initiate no action against Germany without rousing against itself virtually the entire Continent.

For all its seeming solidity, Bismarck's system had one fatal flaw: the incipient hostility between Austria and Russia, Germany's principal allies. Bismarck exerted great efforts to keep this antagonism from breaking into the open, for he was aware that should such a breach occur he would be forced to make a formal choice between them and thereby automatically drive the spurned ally into French arms. The task proved to exceed even his exceptional diplomatic skills.

The fissures in the League of the Three Emperors began to appear in the wake of the Russo-Turkish War of 1877. The unfriendliness that Austria had demonstrated during and after the conflict, and the neutrality displayed by Germany, produced in Russia strong dissatisfaction with the League. Political writers of a conservative and Pan-Slavic orientation began now openly to question the value to Russia of an alliance with the two empires, and to call for a general reorientation of Russia's foreign policy. Indeed, a good case could be made that the League brought Russia no returns for its very real services rendered Germany and hence should have been abandoned in favor of an alliance with France. But neither Alexander II nor his son and successor, Alexander III, were as yet prepared to alter radically Russia's diplomacy. Personal friendship with Kaiser William I and admiration for Bismarck and things German, combined with a loathing for the republican form of government, inhibited a *rapprochement* with France. In 1881, and again in 1884, Russia renewed the alliance to Bismarck's great relief, although in a watered-down version that permitted it greater freedom of action in regard to Germany.

Bismarck always attached great (perhaps excessive) importance to public opinion in the formulation of foreign policy. The outburst of anti-German feeling in Russia after the Russo-Turkish War of 1877, coupled with the helplessness of the tsarist government in dealing with its revolutionary movement, persuaded him that the League did not furnish a sufficiently stable basis for Germany's foreign policy. He now decided to negotiate, behind Russia's back, an additional treaty with Austria. In 1879, on his initiative, the two countries signed an accord committing them to help each other if attacked by Russia or a power supported by Russia and to preserve neutrality if attacked by any other country. The alliance in effect committed Austria to help Germany against a potential Russo-French alliance in return for a freer hand in the Balkans. Because the treaty was concluded in utmost secrecy, both countries could continue to adhere to the League of the Three Emperors.

Despite the secrecy of the Austro-German alliance of 1879, the growing affinity between the two countries did not escape Russian diplomats. When in 1887 the Alliance of the Three Emperors came up for its periodic renewal, the Russians made difficulties. To keep the tenuous link with St. Petersburg from snapping, Bismarck resorted now to a desperate move. He proposed to the Russians a secret "Reinsurance Treaty," committing Germany to maintain neutrality in the event of an Austrian attack on Russia in return for Russian neutrality in the event of a French attack on Germany. This treaty, which was signed in June, 1887, was clearly incompatible with the spirit of the Austro-German alliance of 1879. Bismarck's single-minded obsession with isolating France led him into a system of such complexity and inner contradiction that its collapse became inevitable.

The Reinsurance Treaty notwithstanding, Russo-German relations deteriorated steadily, causing a simultaneous improvement in Russo-French relations. In 1888 Bismarck issued a directive to the German Imperial Bank to refuse Russian state bonds as collateral for loans. This measure made it difficult for the Russian government to obtain funds on the German money market and compelled it to turn instead to France. The same year the French government authorized the floating of the first Russian state loan, and thenceforth the imperial government secured in France the bulk of its foreign capital. This financial dependence inevitably made the Russians more responsive to French pressures for a political and military accord. The decisive event in the relations of the two countries was the refusal of William II in 1890 to renew the Reinsurance Treaty. Convinced that autocratic Russia and republican France would never get together, and offended by the anti-Austrian implications of this treaty, William allowed it to lapse. By this action he paved the way for a Russo-French *rapprochement*. In 1894 the two countries concluded a military convention calling for the immediate mobilization of French and Russian armies in response to a mobilization order by any member of the Triple Alliance and for mutual military help against Germany if either country were attacked by Germany or one of its allies.

From 1894 onward, Europe stood divided into two hostile blocs. One, dominated by Germany, embraced Austria and Italy; the other joined France and Russia. The agreements binding the two blocs assured that if one of the signatories became involved in a war with another, the other signatories would become involved as well; in other words, that any clash between two major powers would inevitably turn into a general war. England, for the time being, stayed outside these pacts.

The Revival of Imperialist Sentiment

The dangers implicit in the rivalry over the Balkans and the antagonism between the Franco-Russian and Austro-German blocs were aggravated by conflicts over colonies. These became intense in the last quarter of the nineteenth century. The great powers, having attained their national borders in Europe, carried their struggle for territory and influence overseas to areas in which statehood either was unknown or in a condition of decay.

Great power competition for overseas possessions is defined by the term *imperialism*. This term has today a pejorative meaning, but this was not the case before the twentieth century. In the ancient Middle East, where they originated, "empires" had been superior forms of political organization, permitting the coexistence within one state of diverse races, nations, and religions. The Persian Empire represented a great advance over earlier states that had annihilated or enslaved conquered nations; so did the Hellenistic and Roman empires, the latter of which had survived as an ideal in Western tradition until the Napoleonic era. Imperialism acquired its bad name only around 1900, following a sudden outburst of Western expansionism. At that time it came to mean ruthless aggrandizement and the exploitation by whites of the colored races.

From the late eighteenth to the late nineteenth century, European opinion had been opposed on purely pragmatic grounds to colonial expansion. Along with other mercantilist notions the liberals rejected the view that a state gained power and wealth from the acquisition of overseas possessions. Their attitude rested partly on political and partly on economic arguments. The physiocrat Turgot stated the political case against the colonies even before the outbreak of the American Revolution when he compared them to fruits that "clung to the tree only until they ripened." The subsequent separation of the North American colonies from England and of the Latin American ones from Spain and Portugal having confirmed this expectation, liberals concluded that sooner or later all colonies would demand and obtain independence. The economic argument against imperialism held that the costs of administering and defending overseas possessions exceeded the profit they brought. Adam Smith, Bentham, Cobden, and other liberal theorists maintained—and had evidence to prove it—that a country gained more from trading with other sovereign states than from exploiting its own colonies. Since colonies brought no economic advantages and were certain to separate, there seemed little point in keeping those one had and none in acquiring others.

Such considerations were responsible for the loosening of bonds between the European states and their colonies in the course of the nineteenth century.

Although English Liberals were not prepared to quit the overseas possessions, they were willing to go quite far in conceding them self-rule. The process of emancipation, of transforming dependent colonies into virtually independent states, began in the 1830s. In 1837 a rebellion broke out in the Canadian provinces as a result of a prolonged conflict between crown-appointed officials and representative assemblies. Rather than suppress the rebellion by force, as it would have done in the past, the British government dispatched to Canada a new governor, Lord Durham, a man of moderate views prepared to conciliate Canadian opinion. Durham submitted to London in 1839 a *Report on the Affairs of British North America*, a document that provided the basis for a new kind of relationship between Britain and its possessions. It proposed to grant the Canadian legislatures nearly complete authority in domestic matters, and to confine that of the crown and its officials to Canada's foreign policy and foreign trade. On the basis of Durham's report, the House of Commons passed in 1840 a Union Act with Canada. Before long, similar arrangements were made with other overseas territories inhabited by European populations (Australia, 1850; New Zealand and Cape Colony in South Africa, 1852). In this manner a new type of self-governing colony came into existence. Later known as "dominions," they represented a transitional stage between colonial status and full independence.

In 1834 Britain abolished slavery in its possessions. Although enacted largely under pressure of philanthropic and religious groups, this measure owed its passage to the relative indifference of statesmen and businessmen of that time to colonial affairs.

The anti-imperial sentiment prevailing in liberal England was echoed on the Continent. Bismarck, although not unappreciative of the value of the colonies, showed little enthusiasm for overseas ventures. He preferred to encourage other powers to seize colonies so as to divert their attention from Germany. The French Empire also remained stationary after 1830, the year France had seized Algeria.

Evidence of a shift in sentiment made itself felt first in Russia in the 1860s. Partly from economic considerations (the desire for potentially rich cotton-

"Radical Jack" Lambton, Lord Durham, by Sir Thomas Lawrence. Durham called for Parliament to establish "responsible government" in Canada.

PUBLIC ARCHIVES OF CANADA

growing areas), and partly under pressure from the military, the imperial government authorized in 1865 an invasion of Turkistan. In a few years three Muslim central Asian principalities were conquered, and Russia established itself firmly in the heart of Asia. From there it carried out expeditions south and west, toward the Persian and Afghan borders, until it was finally stopped by British intercession.

In England in the late 1860s several writers began to speak up on behalf of the imperial cause, and to exhort Britons to greater appreciation of the achievements of its explorers, conquerors, and settlers. The movement gained impetus with the conversion of Disraeli to its tenets. In 1872, in his Crystal Palace speech, Disraeli accused the Liberals of a deliberate effort to dissolve the empire, and urged Britain to reforge its links with the colonies:

> The issue is not a mean one. It is whether you will be content to be a comfortable England, modeled and moulded upon Continental principles and meeting in due course an inevitable fate, or whether you will be a great country, an Imperial country, a country where your sons, when they rise, rise to paramount positions and obtain not merely the esteem of their countrymen, but command the respect of the world.

In an 1876 Punch *cartoon, Prime Minister Disraeli offers Victoria the crown of India. The next year the queen took the title Empress of India.*

Disraeli conducted a vigorous imperial policy, being especially concerned with checking Russian threats to the "imperial lifeline" extending from London to India. It is with this in mind that he acquired for Britain a dominating voice in the control of the Suez Canal (see below). At the end of the century imperialist sentiment was widespread in Great Britain. Joseph Chamberlain built his political career on it, and Rudyard Kipling owed to it the immense popularity of his stories and poems glorifying the colorful colonial life. Nevertheless, British enthusiasm was always somewhat checked by deeply rooted liberal convictions about national self-determination and free trade.

On the Continent the imperialist movement got under way somewhat later, but once started it was not greatly inhibited by liberal traditions. In the 1880s publicists and politicians throughout Europe began to extol the need for colonies and to call for colonial conquests. Very active on behalf of the imperialist causes were lobbies in the form of colonial societies, the first of which had been founded in Britain (Royal Colonial Institute, 1868). Imperialist enthusiasm even spread to the United States, a country born in rebellion against colonial rule, where President Theodore Roosevelt propagated it with all the vigor of his ebullient personality. Nor was the movement confined to Western countries. The Japanese became converted to it as well, and at the turn of the century participated alongside European powers in acquiring territory and spheres of influence on the Asiatic mainland. As a rule, the socialist parties furnished the most consistent opposition to imperialist ventures.

The Causes of Modern Imperialism

Before proceeding to trace the history of late nineteenth-century imperial expansion, we must ask what caused the shift in opinion and induced the great powers to put so much effort in establishing themselves in the poor, backward areas of Africa and Asia.

There is a widespread belief that the reasons for modern imperialism are economic: the search for outlets capable of absorbing excess goods, capital, and population. This view owes its prevalence to the fact that it was shared by both the advocates of imperialist expansion and its opponents. The former, in an effort to persuade a reluctant public to back overseas ventures, promised the acquisition of colonies would solve all economic and social problems. They claimed that "trade follows the flag" and that enterprising men would find overseas unlimited opportunities to better themselves. Such an appeal was explicit in Disraeli's speech cited above. The critics of imperialism, mostly socialists, accepted the premise but turned the argument around. They charged that imperial conquests were carried out solely for the private advantage of the bourgeoisie while at the same time diverting public opinion from pressing domestic problems. Pro-imperialists and anti-imperialists agreed that imperialism was economically profitable. They only differed in their judgment as to whom it benefited: the country as a whole or special interest groups. In view of this basic agreement, it is not surprising that the public at large accepted the general economic interpretation of imperialism.

Dispassionate analysis of the data, however, reveals that the economic benefits of colonialism were insignificant and that the liberals were more correct in their estimate of the matter. Colonies were significant neither as outlets for goods and capital, nor as centers of emigration.

As concerns trade, the available figures indicate that business with the colonies, especially those acquired in the late nineteenth century, represented a small part of the total trade of the imperial powers. This held true even of Great Britain, which of all the imperial powers did the most business with its possessions. Trade within the empire accounted for one-quarter of Britain's external commerce. Half of that trade, however, was with the self-governing dominions, such as Canada and Australia, which had been acquired long before 1870. Only one-eighth of the imperial trade was with the colonies proper, and the bulk of that was with India, a British possession since the eighteenth century. In the case of the other powers, the share of the colonial market in their total foreign trade was smaller yet: it was 11 percent for France, 4 percent for Japan, 0.4 percent for Germany, and 0.3 percent for Italy.° The colonies were simply too poor to absorb a significant quantity of industrial goods. The industrial powers did the greatest volume of business with one another, not with the underdeveloped colonies. Great Britain sold in the United States goods twice the value of those disposed of in India, its richest colony; and Germany, in turn, found Britain its best customer. From the strictly commercial point of view, the interests of the great powers required them to cooperate, not to engage in rivalry over colonies.

As concerns capital investments, the argument that colonial expansion was undertaken in an effort to find outlets for excess capital was popularized by the English economist John A. Hobson in his study *Imperialism* (1902). In a statement of breathtaking sweep, Hobson asserted: "It is not too much to say that the modern foreign policy of Great Britain has been primarily a struggle for profitable markets of investment." This theory was afterwards accepted by many socialists, including Lenin, and explains why the Communists attach so much importance to expelling Western powers from the colonies: to them, colonies are the last bastion of the whole capitalist order.

° Figures from Grover Clark, *The Balance Sheet of Imperialism* (1936).

The wickedly ironical Max Beerbohm portrayed the arch-imperialist Rudyard Kipling enjoying an outing "along with Britannia, 'is gurl."

Statistical evidence, however, indicates no meaningful relationship between capital investments and colonialism. The great years of overseas expansion (1875–1895) were, in the case of Britain, a low point in the rate of foreign investment. Britain exported more capital in the era of anti-imperial sentiment than in the heyday of imperialism. Nor is there any indication that British investors were guided by imperial preferences. Only 13 percent of all British foreign investments on record in 1914 were placed in the colonies proper (as distinct from the five older, self-governing dominions), compared to 20 percent placed in the United States and Latin America. France invested less than 10 percent of its foreign capital in its colonies; 90 percent went to sovereign states. France's investments in Russia exceeded two and a half times those placed in its own possessions. Germany's investments in its African colonies represented about 4 percent of its foreign capital commitments. Clearly, as in the case of trade, capital followed not the flag but economic opportunity: it went where the returns were best, regardless of who was in political control. In an age when currencies were readily convertible to gold, it made no difference to an investor in what currency he drew his profit. It may also be noted that two among the most aggressive imperialist powers, Russia and Japan, not only had no excess capital looking for investment opportunities, but borrowed heavily from their imperialist competitors.

In drawing up the economic balance sheet of imperialism, it is necessary also to take into account the cost of administering and defending the colonies. These charges cannot be exactly computed, but they were high. In the case of Germany, Italy, and Japan they must have considerably exceeded the negligible returns from trade and investments.

The expectation that colonies would absorb migrants was not borne out either. The territories suitable for settlement had been seized before 1800. Those taken between 1870 and 1914 did not lend themselves to this purpose. The total net migration of Europeans to all their overseas colonies between 1885 and 1935 was 500,000 persons—less than the United States sometimes received in a single year. European migrants settled on the American continents, not in Africa and Asia where the scramble for colonies took place.

To deny that economic necessity required colonial expansion, however, is not to deny the existence of economic factors behind it. It can be shown that *objectively*, imperialism did not significantly solve any of the problems confronting advanced economies. At the same time, *subjectively*, economic considerations played a very important role in the revival of imperialism. It was widely believed that imperial expansion could permit the absorption of excess goods, capital, and population, and this belief—even if now proven to have been unfounded—stimulated imperialism. One must keep in mind the deep anxiety felt by many Europeans as they observed the incredible outpouring of goods made possible by modern technology. Their worry over markets was genuine and understandable, the more so as with each decade new countries industrialized and thereby entered the list of potential competitors. The economic crises of 1873 and 1885, each severe and prolonged, gave substance to these fears. It was no coincidence that imperialist sentiment emerged in England around 1870, for that happened to be the very time when Britain, hitherto the unchallenged leader in world trade, for the first time confronted serious competition from Germany and the United States. To farsighted statesmen it seemed imperative that Britain expand: "Little England" had to become "Greater Britain" or the country would decline and perish. The fear was particularly acute in Germany, whose production rose at a staggering rate, much beyond the needs of the domestic market. The hunt for colonies began as a kind of preventive action or insurance against future crises from overproduction and overpopulation. Once it got under way every country that aspired to great power status had to join in, if only because the other great powers did so. Russia and Japan, countries with rudimentary industries, engaged in imperialist rivalry not because their economies required it, but because it was thought that unless they did so, their future generations would experience insurmountable economic and social difficulties. Not the needs of the existing economy but faulty economic calculation concerning the future constituted the economic factor in imperialism.

Modern historians tend also to stress heavily the political side of imperialism. They see it as expansion for the sake of power, strategic advantage, national glory, and many of the very same goals that had inspired national conflicts in Europe itself. Some among them also ascribe the outburst of late nineteenth-century expansionism to irrational drives in man, such as aggressive tendencies inherited from primitive ancestors.

Colonial competition in the late nineteenth century was global in scope. Every region not claimed by a power able to assert its sovereignty was open to seizure. But the two areas that attracted the most attention from the great powers were Africa and China. They were at the center of the imperial rivalries. *Overseas Expansion*

THE STRUGGLE FOR AFRICA

The rush for Africa began with the completion in 1869 of the Suez Canal. The new waterway cut the route from Europe to the Indian Ocean in half and immediately acquired great commercial and military value, especially for Britain. Britain had failed to participate in the construction of the canal because its experts doubted its feasibility. The undertaking had been launched by the French, who thereby strengthened their already solid position in the eastern Mediterranean. Britain could not tolerate this situation, for control over the Suez gave France mastery over the route connecting Britain with some of its most important overseas possessions. An opportunity to redeem the mistake presented itself in 1875 when the khedive (viceroy) of Egypt, faced with bankruptcy, offered for sale his shares in the Suez Canal Company. On learning the news, Disraeli immediately borrowed 4 million pounds from the Rothschild bank (he was afraid to miss the chance by waiting for a regular parliamentary appropriation) and with it purchased the khedive's shares.

Disraeli's move not only gave Britain 44 percent of the stock in the Suez Canal Company, and thereby the strongest voice on its board, but also a base from which to establish hegemony over northeast Africa. After the khedive had suffered further financial reverses, England and France compelled him to abdicate and placed Egypt under joint rule. In 1882 the British took advantage of a nationalist uprising to occupy Egypt and establish a protectorate over it. From there they extended their authority southward, into the Sudan. By 1900 northeast

Africa was British, except for two Italian enclaves (Somaliland and Eritrea), French Somaliland, and independent Ethopia.

The French, ousted from the northeast, realized their imperial ambitions in the northwest. In 1881 they seized Tunisia, and then expanded into Morocco and the Sahara. Despite strong native resistance, by 1914 France had established its authority over this territory.

The most intense imperialist competition occurred in the central regions of Africa. This area, believed to harbor great mineral wealth, became the object of keen rivalry involving colorful explorers, chartered companies, and, behind both, the foreign ministries of the great powers.

In the 1860s central Africa was still an unknown territory, penetrated only by a few intrepid missionaries and explorers. Its opening to Western influence was due to the enterprise of an Anglo-American journalist, Henry M. Stanley. Stanley first went to Africa in 1871 as a correspondent for the New York *Herald* to locate David Livingstone, a British missionary lost in cannibal country. Having completed this celebrated mission, he became fascinated with the economic potentialities of the vast and unchartered Congo River basin. He returned there on several exploratory expeditions, first on his own, then on behalf of the Belgian king, Leopold II, whose interest he had aroused. In 1878–1882 Leopold founded the International Association of the Congo—ostensibly a private company, but in fact an instrument by means of which he established control over the area. In time Leopold secured international recognition of the Association as the sovereign authority in the Congo under his personal rule. This arrangement benefited most the businessmen interested in the economic exploitation of the region, for it exempted them from Belgian parliamentary control. It led to such abuses and protests, however, that in 1908 the king felt compelled to transfer sovereignty over the Congo to the government of Belgium.

Belgian advances in central Africa aroused German interest. The first German explorations there were carried out by individuals acting without Bismarck's encouragement or authorization. In 1884–1885 they claimed on behalf of their country extensive territories in eastern and southwestern Africa. At first reluctantly, and then with increasing enthusiasm, the German government assumed responsibility over these colonies.

A German satirical magazine included these drawings in a "special issue" in 1904 devoted to colonialism in Africa. At the right, the German propensity for regimentation is applied to the local fauna. Opposite, the British utilize whisky and religion to gain a favorable balance of trade.

BOTH: *Simplicissimus*, 1904

France, Portugal, and Britain were also active in central Africa, exploring and setting forth claims. The absence of fixed frontiers of any kind made friction unavoidable. The most serious incident occurred in 1898 when British and French expeditions, racing from different directions to secure control of the upper Nile, ran into each other at Fashoda in the Sudan. After a tense period of diplomatic maneuvering, which for a time threatened war, France yielded and ordered withdrawal of its forces. Britain's triumph in the "Fashoda Crisis" assured its hegemony in that part of Africa, but the bad blood it created delayed for several years a Franco-British diplomatic understanding in Europe.

In South Africa the colonial problem was complicated by the presence of white settlers, descendants of seventeenth-century Dutch and Huguenot colonists, known as "Boers" (a Dutch word meaning "farmers"). The Boers engaged in agriculture and cattle breeding, employing Negro slave labor. Imperialism here, therefore, involved not the conquest of a native colored people, for these had already been subjugated by an earlier colonial wave, but the establishment of one white authority over another.

The British had seized South Africa from the Dutch in 1806, at which time they renamed it Cape Colony. From the beginning of their rule they clashed with the Boers over slavery, which the British first limited and then (in 1834) abolished. Once slavery was outlawed, 10,000 Boers left Cape Colony to migrate to the north and northeast (the "Great Trek," 1835–1837). Here they founded two independent republics, Transvaal and the Orange Free State, in which they built plantations worked by slaves.

The Boers were not permitted to enjoy their way of life in the new land for long. The discovery of the world's richest diamond deposits in the Orange Free State (1867) and of gold in Transvaal (1886) attracted to the two republics hordes of European fortune seekers. By the end of the century these outsiders, or *uitlanders*, most of whom settled in boom towns of which Johannesburg was the largest, outnumbered the Boers in both republics. The Boers refused to grant the newcomers political suffrage and discriminated against them in other ways as well.

Rivalry between the British and the Boers reached a high level of intensity in the 1890s. At that time, the Prime Minister of Cape Colony was Cecil Rhodes, an

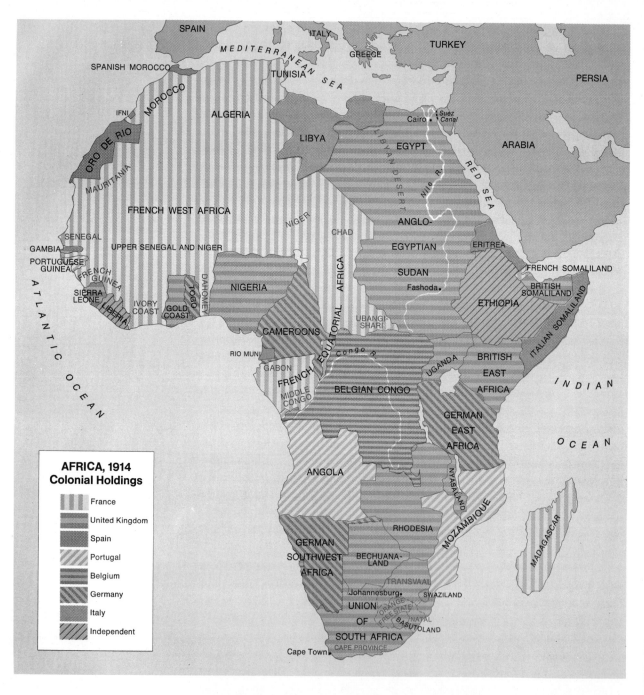

AFRICA, 1914
Colonial Holdings

France
United Kingdom
Spain
Portugal
Belgium
Germany
Italy
Independent

immensely wealthy entrepreneur with a directing voice in the South African diamond and gold syndicates. Rhodes was an ardent empire builder. His great dream was a solid British domain extending from Cape Town to Cairo. In 1889 he obtained a royal charter to form the British South Africa Company, through the agency of which he obtained control of Bechuanaland. This region he later renamed Rhodesia and attached to Cape Colony. After being appointed Prime Minister in 1890, he exerted constant pressure on the Boer republics hoping to bring about their collapse. With the aid of a few friends, among them a certain

Dr. Jameson, he formed a plan calling for a coordinated internal and external attack on the Transvaal. It involved an uprising of *uitlanders* in Johannesburg, to be followed by the dispatch of an armed expedition under Jameson to its aid. Unfortunately for Rhodes, Jameson bungled his assignment by penetrating the Transvaal before the *uitlanders* had revolted. He suffered defeat and capture (January, 1896), and Rhodes had to resign as Prime Minister. Despite its failure, the strategy that Rhodes devised for the subversion of the Boer republic is of historic interest, for it anticipates the methods used later on, with more success, by totalitarian rulers in Europe.

In 1899 Britain and the Boer republics went to war. The British quickly disposed of the regular enemy armies, but they required over two years to suppress the guerrillas who continued the struggle. In 1902 the Boers finally capitulated and acknowledged British sovereignty.

The African continent was so thoroughly carved up by the great powers that in 1914 only two countries, Ethiopia and Liberia, retained their independence.

The Partition of China

In the Far East the situation differed from that in Africa in that imperial competition was not over territories unclaimed by internationally recognized powers, but over the legacy of one of the most ancient of states. In the end, however, the results of imperialist rivalry were analogous to those observed in Africa. The great powers established definite claims to specific regions of China, and were it not for the outbreak of World War I, which diverted their attention, China's collapse and partition could hardly have been averted.

Until the nineteenth century China and Japan alike had isolated themselves from Western influences. But Japan's resistance to the West collapsed much sooner. After 1868 the Japanese rejected traditionalism and turned toward Europe. They modernized their political system, introduced compulsory military service, adopted European educational methods, and launched the beginnings of an industrial economy. The speed and thoroughness with which the Japanese Westernized has no historic parallel. Because of this they were not only able to resist encroachment by European states, but before the end of the century to join the ranks of the great powers and to become involved in imperialist ventures themselves.

The Chinese did not follow this road. Why Japan Westernized and China did not is a question beyond the scope of this survey. It may be mentioned, however, that one of the reasons for China's refusal to do so was the antiquity and accomplishment of its native culture. Japan's culture had been borrowed from China; its Westernization involved the substitution of one alien cultural influence for another. China's culture was indigenous, and Westernization implied a renunciation of the country's national identity and heritage. For a long time the Chinese refused to acknowledge the superiority of Western techniques, even when militarily defeated. They responded to humiliation not by acquiring these techniques and turning them against external powers, as the Japanese had done, but by indulging in fanatical xenophobia. The Chinese government proved less and less capable of exercising effective authority over its vast domain, which included several large dependencies (Sinkiang, Manchuria, Mongolia, and Tibet) and tributary states (Korea, Indochina, and Burma).

The French cemented their grip on Indochina in 1884 with a victory, painted here by a Chinese artist, over the Chinese near Hanoi, capital of present-day North Vietnam. The French troops holding the two forts at top, supported by warships, repelled the Chinese advancing from the right along the river.

Western penetration of China, spearheaded by Britain, initially took commercial and military forms. In 1842, following a brief war, Britain compelled the Chinese authorities to open several ports to trade, and to cede Hong Kong to them. The British soon strengthened their position and in the middle of the century gained additional privileges for their merchants and missionaries after the suppression of the so-called Taiping Rebellion, a violent anti-imperial and anti-foreign uprising.

After this rebellion the Chinese government began to lose control over its territories. The uprising had revealed the weakness of the regime and encouraged foreign claims to territories traditionally regarded by the Chinese as under their sovereignty. The territorial encroachments were inaugurated by the Russians, who appropriated the Maritime Province. There, in 1860, they constructed a port they named Vladivostok—literally, "Master of the East." The French began exploration in Indochina, which in the 1880s they appropriated as a colony. In 1886 Britain took over Burma. The greatest threat to China, however, came from Japan, which in the 1870s established a foothold on the Asiatic mainland. Japanese intrusions into Korea led in 1894 to the Sino-Japanese War. The modernized Japanese forces won without much difficulty. In the Treaty of Shimonoseki (1895) China had to cede Formosa to Japan and grant independence to Korea. The latter became a Japanese protectorate.

So far, encroachments on the Chinese domain had involved China proper less than its tributary states. The Sino-Japanese War of 1894 initiated a veritable scramble for native Chinese territories. The competition at first took the form of economic concessions. Through financial inducements and military blackmail, the great powers forced the Chinese government to lease them port cities and grant licenses to construct railroads and engage in mining. By means of such concessions, the holder assured himself of a "sphere of influence" over a region. In time, it was expected, such "influence" would lead to outright ownership. The Russians obtained the first important concession in 1896 in the form of a privilege to extend the Trans-Siberian Railway across northern Manchuria to Vladivostok. This arrangement gave them a claim to the entire Manchurian province, an important and rich dependency of China. Other powers won from the Chinese government similar economic concessions. The United States did not seek such concessions but instead exerted pressure on the other powers to accept the so-called Open Door policy guaranteeing all countries free access to Chinese markets (1899).

In 1897–1898 the Germans and Russians undertook joint action for the purpose of occupying the Chinese port cities of Kiaochao and Port Arthur, respectively. These seizures marked the beginning of the territorial partition of China proper. Their example was soon emulated by France, Britain, and Japan.

These constant encroachments by foreign powers stimulated in 1900 the outbreak of a second, even more violent anti-foreign uprising, the so-called Boxer Rebellion.° The movement was fundamentally religious, being directed against Christians, especially Chinese converts. The Boxers were so much imbued with fanaticism that they regarded themselves as immune to foreign bullets. They were crushed largely by intervention of foreign armies, including a detachment from the United States. As compensation, the Chinese government had to make further concessions as well as pay an exorbitant indemnity.

°The name derives from "Righteous and Harmonious Fists," a patriotic organization dedicated to exercises as a means of steeling the mind and body for combat.

This photograph was carefully posed to emphasize the international nature of the foreign armies that intervened in the Boxer Rebellion in China in 1900. The troops are, from left, British, American, Russian, Indian, German, French, Austrian, Italian, and Japanese.

Rivalry in the Far East led in 1904 to the outbreak of a war between Russia and Japan. At the turn of the century a group of unscrupulous adventurers, interested in exploiting the lumber resources along the Yalu River in northern Korea, persuaded Nicholas II to back their claims. These activities encroached on the Japanese sphere of influence. Japan proposed negotiations, but the tsar, egged on by militant circles at the court, refused, whereupon the Japanese in February, 1904, attacked Port Arthur. Subsequently, they inflicted a series of humiliating defeats on Russia's army and, in the Battle of Tsushima, sank a good part of its navy.

In 1911 a group of Westernized reformers in China overthrew the imperial government and proclaimed the establishment of the Chinese Republic. The leader of the group, Sun Yat-sen, had been educated in an English school in Hong Kong and had spent many years in Europe and the United States. The republican regime which he headed did not possess adequate resources for effective administration or for the implementation of its program of Westernization. There seemed little chance that it would be able to check the ambitions of Japan which, after its victory over Russia, appeared destined to dominate the Far East.

Anglo-German Rivalry   At the beginning of the twentieth century the international situation presented the following picture: in Europe two major blocs confronted each other, one linking Germany with Austria and Italy, the other linking France with Russia. The main rivalries pitted Russia against Austria over territory and influence in the Balkans, and Germany against France over general primacy on the Continent. The powers also engaged in competition over African and Asian possessions.

Britain so far had stayed out of alliances, preferring "splendid isolation" to military commitments. A pre-eminently commercial country, it needed peace; and as an insular state without a standing army it could neither benefit from the armed forces of potential allies, nor contribute much to them. Its foreign policy was flexible, sometimes backing the Austro-German bloc, sometimes the Franco-Russian.

The factor which finally caused England to abandon its isolation was the same that had moved it a century earlier to form anti-Napoleonic alliances: the fear of a single power becoming so overwhelmingly powerful as to be in a position to dominate the Continent. This danger now came from Germany.

Bismarckian diplomacy, as we have noted, had been defensive. In the 1890s this conservative foreign policy no longer suited the mood of Germany, which observed with frustration the overseas conquests of rival powers. Kaiser William II formally abandoned Bismarck's defensive Continental diplomacy in 1896 when he committed Germany to what became known as *Weltpolitik* or "world politics." The term had no precise meaning, but as used, it implied that Germany would no longer concentrate exclusively on self-defense. Instead it would engage actively in international competition for colonies, markets, and influence.

The trouble with *Weltpolitik* was not its general aim, which was pursued by all the great powers, but the absence of specific objectives. The theorists and executors of *Weltpolitik* had no clear notion of what they wanted, except to make Germany's weight felt. As a result they seemed to want everything and to threaten everybody at once. This applied especially to Britain. The Kaiser's irresponsible sallies into international affairs challenged Britain's position in a number of widely separated areas of the world without any hint of the conditions on which it would be possible to come to terms. In 1896 the Kaiser surprised and outraged Britain by sending the President of Transvaal a telegram congratulating him on his victory over the Jameson raiders. The move seemed to indicate an intention to enter South African politics, but this goal was not pursued. Instead, two years later William challenged Britain's whole Middle Eastern position by declaring himself, in a public address, ready to act as "protector" of the world's Muslims, the majority of whom lived under British rule. This threat of subversion was not carried out either, because the Kaiser's attention was soon diverted to the Far East, where his seizure in 1897 of Kiaochao had initiated the scramble for Chinese territory.

Such actions, coming in rapid succession and lacking a definable end, caused consternation in England. Yet the breach between England and Germany was not inevitable. Britain had greater disagreements with Russia, and even with France, than with Germany, and some British statesmen advocated an alliance with Germany. In 1898, at the height of the Fashoda Crisis in the Sudan, Joseph Chamberlain opened exploratory talks with Berlin to this end. The Germans, however, cold-shouldered British advances, and the negotiations collapsed. The Germans saw themselves as holding the balance of power between Britain and the Franco-Russian bloc and believed that by procrastinating they could exact from Britain greater concessions in their bid for a greater role in "world politics."

The critical event in the rupture between England and Germany was the naval race that broke out in 1900.

Under the influence of the books of the American historian Alfred T. Mahan, who depicted naval supremacy as the decisive factor in modern warfare, and of the German Minister of the Navy, Alfred von Tirpitz, William II undertook to construct a large battle fleet. The intention was to create an offensive navy of sufficient strength to menace the British Isles, in the expectation that such a threat would force Britain either to withdraw a good part of its navy to home waters and thereby endanger its empire, or yield to German demands for territory and commercial advantages. The navy, in other words, was to serve as an instrument of diplomatic blackmail. With this goal in mind, Germany enacted in 1898 and 1900 naval laws authorizing the construction of a high-seas fleet.

The British were highly perturbed by these measures, especially the Second Naval Law (1900), which provided for the construction, over a period of twenty years, of 38 battleships. For Britain, naval superiority was not a matter of mere ambition or prestige, but of survival. Since the early nineteenth century the British Isles had come to depend for their basic necessities on imports. Fourfifths of the wheat consumed in Great Britain, for example, came from abroad by ship. By obtaining control of the high seas, a hostile power could force Britain into submission without setting foot on its soil. It was to prevent this from happening that Britain in 1889 proclaimed the so-called "two-power standard," a formula committing it to maintain a naval force superior to that of the two next most powerful navies combined. Any country that challenged this rule invited the enmity of Britain.

Kaiser William II (at center, mounted on the white horse) initiated the First Moroccan Crisis in 1905 with a visit to Tangier, hoping to split the Anglo-French Entente Cordiale.

To meet the German threat Britain took diplomatic and military counter-measures. In 1902, abandoning its traditional policy of nonalignment, it signed a defensive alliance with Japan. Two years later it entered into an Entente Cordiale with France—a loose act of friendship without specific military commitments. At the same time the British government authorized the construction of a new class of battleships, the so-called dreadnaughts, superior to any warship then in existence. The first of these vessels was launched in February, 1906.

The Germans, viewing these moves as portents of a hostile alliance directed against them, sought to break the tightening noose by detaching from the anti-German bloc first England, then Russia, but their efforts backfired. An attempt to test and loosen the Entente Cordiale by intervening against France in Morocco (the so-called First Moroccan Crisis, 1905) yielded the contrary result: it so appalled the French and British that they initiated secret military talks.

When in May, 1906, the German government passed the Third Naval Law providing for battleships capable of matching the dreadnaughts in displacement and firepower, a breach with England became inevitable. British statesmen now became convinced that nothing short of acknowledging German superiority on the Continent and on the high seas would satisfy the Germans, and that it was essential for Britain to safeguard its vital interests by extending full support to the Franco-Russian bloc. In 1907 Britain settled its outstanding differences with Russia over the Middle East and signed with it a treaty similar to the Entente Cordiale. The agreement did not call for automatic military assistance, but it left no doubt with whom Britain would side in the event that the Austro-German and Franco-Russian blocs went to war.

After 1907 relations between the great powers underwent a succession of dangerous crises in scattered parts of the world, each capable of causing a major war. Of these the gravest occurred in 1908 in consequence of the Austrian annexation of Bosnia and Herzegovina, and in 1911 in the course of a Franco-German confrontation in Morocco.

Austria originally occupied Bosnia and Herzegovina in 1878 as a result of a deal with Russia (see above), later confirmed by the Congress of Berlin. Such *de facto* possession, quite satisfactory to Vienna, seemed threatened in 1908 by the deposition of Sultan Abdul-Hamid and the assumption of power in Turkey by nationalistic officers (Chapter 20). The Austrians now feared that the Young Turks would demand a return of the occupied territory. A group of aggressive Austrian statesmen, headed by Aehrenthal, the Minister of Foreign Affairs, therefore urged the annexation of Bosnia and Herzegovina to forestall such an eventuality. In secret negotiations with the Russians the Austrians secured their agreement to the annexation in return for a pledge to support the right of Russian warships to pass through the Straits. While the Russians made vain efforts to obtain British and French agreement to a revision of the Straits convention, Austria announced its annexation of Bosnia and Herzegovina (October, 1908). The Turks, who considered these regions their property, as well as the Serbs, who coveted them, were outraged; the Russians, having received nothing from their secret accords with the Austrians, now publicly ranged themselves against Vienna. For several months there was danger of war between a Russo-Serbian bloc and Austria, the latter backed to the hilt by Germany. But although for the time being war was averted, the Bosnia and Herzegovina incident left a lasting legacy of hostility in Eastern Europe, aggravating in particular the relations between Russia and Austria.

The Second Moroccan Crisis flared up in July, 1911, when William II ordered a German gunboat to Morocco. The ostensible purpose of his move was to protect German business interests during civil disturbances in this area, generally recognized as a French sphere of influence. The true reason was to force France to concede the French Congo to Germany. Britain strongly backed France. Germany ultimately obtained a part of the French Congo in return for a recognition of French rights to Morocco, but at the price of driving England and France closer together.

Incidents of this kind tended to solidify each of the two great alliance systems and to widen the gulf between them.

La Belle Epoque

ROGER VIOLLET

The Franco-Prussian War officially ended on June 28, 1871. Bismarck's Prussian legions had captured Napoleon III; Paris was shell-torn and occupied, Alsace-Lorraine lost, and the new government of the Third Republic found itself saddled with a massive indemnity. From March until the end of May the convulsions of the Paris Commune had revived all the horrors of civil war. The French capital presented a desolate landscape of "gaping roofs, battered walls, and charred frontages. . . . The theaters were closed and the shops were shuttered; no one even cried newspapers."

Paris was battered, but her spirit was unbroken. When the government floated a loan for Bismarck's 5 billion franc indemnity, Paris alone subscribed 12 billion of the astonishing total of 42 billion francs raised. More important, a new spirit was in the air. "War, revolutions, military intrigues, strategy, tactics, artillery, shells, petrol, we've had enough of them," wrote the popular journalist Philibert Audebrand. "The theaters are open again, ladies and gentlemen, the Parisiennes are more seductive than ever, visitors are arriving in crowds, and *gaiety is in the air.*" Rapidly the indoor world of the genteel salon gave way to the varied pleasures of the outdoor cafés, the café concerts, the parks, the circuses, the racecourses, the banks and islands of the Seine, the streets, the Opéra, the ballet, the theaters. *La belle époque,* the beautiful years, had begun. All Paris was to be a stage.

History's image of *la belle époque* is largely the work of a succession of bold artists who dared, as one contemporary critic wrote, "To compose the picture not in the studio but on the spot, in front of the subject; to shake off all conventions; . . . to give a meticulous interpretation of the impression, of the raw sensation, however strange it may seem; to present the living being, in gesture and attitude, moving in the fugitive, ever-changing atmosphere and light; . . . to make the figures inseparable from their background, as though they were the product of it. . . ."

La belle époque had many aspects, but at stage center of this theatrical age were the café concerts, a unique blend of music hall and night club featuring entertainers who aroused, shocked, and delighted all Paris. At the right is Edgar Degas' delicate yet lusty pastel, *Le Café-Concert aux "Ambassadeurs"* (1876), and at the left, Toulouse-Lautrec's 1894 lithograph of Montmartre's most famous dance team, La Goulue and her partner Valentin le Désossé, performing at the celebrated Moulin Rouge.

It was there that La Goulue made a gesture that in its own way epitomized the age. Executing a high kick, she knocked off the top hat of the visiting Prince of Wales, and said archly, "Hullo, Wales, are you paying for the champagne?"

Believing that "the motif should be observed more for shape and color than for drawing," Pissarro portrayed Paris with the bright palette and "comma" brush strokes of the Impressionists. Below is one of the many views Pissarro did of the Avenue de l'Opéra. At right is his rendition of the Pont-Neuf, looking across the Seine from the Île de la Cité.

The City of Light

The Paris that served as a stage for the festivities of *la belle époque* was the favored creation of nature, history, and the determined efforts of a slightly spurious baron. Nature provided Paris with a gentle climate, rolling wooded hills, and the broad reaches of the Seine. History left the city a rich legacy of buildings, monuments, and bridges such as the Pont-Neuf (above), built in 1607 by Henry IV. But it was reserved for Napoleon III's Préfet de la Seine, Baron Georges Eugène Haussmann, to turn Paris from an impenetrable labyrinth of sewerless alleyways and decayed tenements into a modern metropolis of broad, tree-lined boulevards, with spacious plazas setting off such elegant landmarks as the Opéra (left).

Between 1853 and 1870 Haussmann ruthlessly revamped Paris. By tearing down slums and ramming new boulevards through the medieval fortifications that girdled and cramped the city, Haussmann not only opened Paris to itself, but to the country and the suburbs as well; by making two huge parks, the Bois de Boulogne and the Bois de Vincennes, just outside the old walls, he gave the city racetracks, riding trails, and ice skating rinks. An 81-mile aqueduct brought fresh spring water and 300 miles of tiled sewers made perfume a luxury rather than a necessity. Mindful of beauty and a varied social life, Haussmann flanked his boulevards (which were wide enough for a troop of cavalry) with trees, spacious sidewalks, and buildings featuring multi-class residency and a consistent architectural style. No more than six stories high, each building had shops and offices on the ground floor, apartments for the wealthy on the floors above, and, following a pattern of gentle decline in social status with each ascending story, garrets under the eaves for artists and the poor. When the Second Empire fell Haussmann lost his job, but once the Franco-Prussian War was over Paris hurried to complete his grand scheme. By 1880 the result was a city that was at once spacious and intimate, efficient and beautiful.

The man who best caught the changing aspects of this new light-filled Paris was Camille Pissarro who, when conjunctivitis threatened his sight in the 1890s, turned to painting dozens of views of the city he loved from behind his closed windows.

563

Above: In the Conservatory (1879) was one of Manet's few paintings to win official acclaim. "This is a most attractive modern work," wrote one art critic. "The air moves, the figures are marvelously projected."

In 1876 Manet made the informal portrait at the left of his friend, the Symbolist poet Stéphane Mallarmé. Mallarmé was one of the few art critics to proclaim the virtue of Manet's abandonment of academic finish. "What is unfinished about a work," wrote Mallarmé, "if all its elements are in accord, and if it possesses a charm which could easily be broken by an additional touch?" This charm is evident in the scene on the Rue Blanche (right), where Manet skated.

La Haute Bourgeoisie

At the center of Parisian society were the wealthy, well-educated, and fashionable citizens of the upper-middle class, or *haute bourgeoisie*. Thoroughly respectable, moderately republican, and mildly progressive, they were the natural center of the Third Republic as it steered a precarious course between the radical left and the Bonapartist and monarchist right.

From the self-satisfied midst of the *haute bourgeoisie* there appeared a painter who dressed like a dandy, detested bohemianism, and sought official recognition, but who, nevertheless, dealt conventional art a blow from which it never recovered. A revolutionary in spite of himself, Édouard Manet thought it only natural that a painter "must be of one's own time and paint what one sees." His attitude toward the neo-classical convention of copying Renaissance models was equally straightforward: "We are not in Rome and don't want to go there. We are in Paris; let us stay there."

Manet painted many aspects of Paris, but none with surer knowledge than his own world of the *haute bourgeoisie*. In works such as *In the Conservatory* (left) he caught the essence of middle-class well-being by picturing a fashionable young couple as they posed calm and self-assured in their winter garden. In *Skating* (below) and *Bar at the Folies-Bergère* (overleaf) Manet skillfully mirrored the pleasures of the fortunate as well as the less amusing lot of those who served their "betters."

Suffering from an advanced case of locomotor ataxia, Manet began his last great canvas, *Bar at the Folies-Bergère*, in 1881, only two years before his death. A fancy music hall featuring elaborate revues, the Folies was one of Paris' more egalitarian institutions, catering not only to the wealthy bourgeois with "overworked digestions and underworked intelligences," but also to "foreigners, shop assistants on a spree, and little ladies on the make." Shown in the Salon of 1882, the picture was dubbed dull and in bad taste, but one critic realized what Manet had accomplished and prophetically wrote, "He does not immobilize forms . . ., he surprises them in their effective mobility. It is a very new formula of art, very personal, very piquant, a direct conquest of the artist which will not be lost on the future."

Degas believed "A picture is a thing that demands as much cunning, astuteness, and vice as the perpetration of a crime." He practiced this credo using candid-camera-like poses and techniques such as blowing steam over pastel, to catch, as on the facing page, the ephemeral vision of a ballet skirt in motion. At the right is an 1873 painting of Vicomte Lépic and his two daughters strolling along the Place de la Concorde. Below is a pastel study of a gentleman on his way to the hunt.

The Rich at Play

With the opening of the Paris Exposition of 1878 *la belle époque* moved into high gear. "The prosperity of the city is staggering," exclaimed the journal *Siècle*. "The hotels are full, the restaurants are turning people away, and the boulevards are crowded with visitors leisurely examining the beauties of the capital." From a city of charred ruins, in seven years Paris had become the playground of the world, especially of the rich—American millionaires, European nobility, the new industrial aristocracy. Their pleasures were numerous, sociable, and always fashionable: strolling along the boulevards, riding in the Bois de Boulogne, consuming quantities of truffled game and poultry along with vintage wines at an endless round of dinner parties, going to the races at Longchamp and Auteuil, attending the Opéra, reveling in the night life of the *demi-monde*.

In keeping with the Victorian double standard, "ladies" were expected to find music halls "mostly unsuitable," and the cafés of Montmartre were "to be avoided." The gentlemen were freer even if their freedom was lightly disguised. "Men, of course, went to the Opéra for the ballet, or rather to talk to the *danseuses*," wrote one aristocratic Englishman. Indeed the gentlemen so much enjoyed the ballet at the Opéra that its director was unofficially known as "Procurer to the Republic."

The almost gluttonous delight which the rich took in the best things in life was easily matched by the open-armed yet extraordinarily sensitive and rigidly disciplined passion of Edgar Degas for capturing the beauty of this society. "To produce good fruit," wrote Degas, "one should be like a tree trained on an espalier; your arms stretched out, you stay put all your life, your mouth open to gobble up whatever comes your way." A master at portraying an exact impression of movement and light, as in *Ballet Seen from a Loge* (right), or *At the Races* (overleaf), Degas sought to go beyond "instantaneous impressions" in order to "get hold of the customs of a race, that is to say, its charms."

Degas finished *At the Races* around 1880 when horse racing was at its most fashionable. The painting is probably of Longchamp in the Bois de Boulogne; the mustachioed jockeys are gentlemen riders, and the race may well be the *Prix de Drags*, a very smart occasion which the *beau-monde* viewed from a variety of elegant and stylish carriages. At the center of this enthusiasm for horse racing were the Prince of Wales, who sparked a craze for things English, and Paris' ultra-fashionable Jockey Club, which by 1905 included the reigning monarchs of England, Holland, Belgium, Denmark, and Serbia among its members. Keeping up with royalty was an expensive pastime and soon American millionaires—the Goulds, the Vanderbilts, the Biddles—became familiar figures on the turf and throughout the chic world of the very rich.

Joie de Vivre

aris was of course more than a playground for the rich; it was also a spirit of *joie de vivre* —an optimistic, almost childlike love of life which the English language has never been able to precisely or adequately translate. *Joie de vivre* expressed itself in the optimism with which Parisians rebuilt their devastated city, in their love of fun and pleasure, even in their response to the influenza epidemic that followed the World's Fair of 1889. Parisians laughed off the deadly disease with a cheerful cabaret song that ended in the chorus "Everybody's got the influe-en-za-ah!"

Joie de vivre was a common quality, but it took an uncommon artist to catch its full-bodied character. In the 1860s, when Pierre Auguste Renoir began to study painting, his teacher, on seeing one of his lighthearted efforts, caustically asked, "No doubt it's to amuse yourself that you dabble in paint?" Unabashed, Renoir answered, "Why, of course, if it didn't amuse me, I wouldn't do it." Not only the dreary poses but also the dark pasty colors of the neoclassical masters seemed to him a betrayal of life. "No shadow is black," he wrote. "It always has a color. Nature knows only colors." For years a struggling but happy artist, Renoir, in vivid, lively paintings such as the two reproduced here, and in sketches such as *Anglers Along the Seine* above, created scenes of Parisian gaiety that have given *joie de vivre* a visual if not a verbal translation.

In 1908 at the age of sixty-seven, when rheumatism had forced him to paint with his brush strapped to his wrist, Renoir summed up his technique by saying, "I arrange my subject as I want it, then I go ahead and paint it, like a child." For instance, in Bal à Bougival *(left; 1883) he posed his brother and the Impressionists' favorite model, Suzanne Valadon, as typical summertime Parisians enjoying outdoor dancing. In* Luncheon of the Boating Party *(right; 1881), he again posed friends (including Alice Chirigot, his wife-to-be, playing with a puppy) in order to mirror the festive joy which Renoir knew both as a child and as an exponent of his era.*

The year 1885 marked a turning point in the history of *la belle époque*. It was a moment of equipoise before Paris plunged into the frantic excitement of the *fin de siècle* and before France was rocked by the string of political crises that began with General Boulanger and ended with the First World War. No painting expresses this moment of balance more convincingly than Georges Seurat's monumental, frieze-like masterpiece, *A Sunday Afternoon on the Island of La Grande Jatte*, painted in 1885 when Seurat was only twenty-five. Artistically Seurat's work broke new ground. His pointillist technique of spreading tiny dots of pure color that combined not on the canvas but in the eye according to optical laws led to the search for new visual perspectives and uses of color that were to so fascinate the *avant-garde* after the turn of the century.

Toulouse-Lautrec finished his "autobiographical" painting, Au Moulin Rouge
*(above), in 1892, three years after the cabaret had opened its doors to the
demi-monde. Seated at the table are some of his closest friends. Behind them
are the dwarf-like Lautrec, his towering cousin-companion Tapié, and, re-knot-
ing her famous orange bun, Lautrec's favorite subject, the dancer La Goulue.*

Demi-Monde

In the 1860s Montmartre was a rural wooded hillside dotted with windmills on the outskirts of Paris. A generation later it was the center of the city's thriving night life, of the *demi-monde*, where nothing was illegal and everything available. As the nineteenth century drew to a close, a frenzy for fast living and good times gripped the City of Light. The triumph of realism in literature had encouraged a flood of lurid novels, scandalous journals, and a taste for forbidden fruits. In Montmartre dandies such as the *boulevardier* at right consorted with cabaret singers, comics, and chic and not so chic prostitutes to create the hybrid society of the *demi-monde*.

One of the fixtures of this society was a stubby, bearded, well-dressed gentleman, his figure cruelly deformed by stunted legs, who almost nightly clambered down from his horse-drawn cab, sniffed the air, and then, propped up by his cane, advanced unsteadily up one of Montmartre's narrow streets in search of a café and a drink. Born the son of the hard-riding, hard-drinking Count of Toulouse and prevented by his deformity from living a sportsman's life, Henri de Toulouse-Lautrec felt that "nature" had betrayed him. Montmartre, whose singular people were full of gaiety and eccentricity that bordered on monstrosity, made Toulouse-Lautrec feel at home and provided an unexplored terrain for his genius. A prominent figure of the world he pictured, he painted the *demi-monde*, himself included, with a relish that inevitably had little to do with idealized beauty. "I have tried to draw realistically and not ideally," he said. "It may be a defect, for I have no mercy on warts, and I like to adorn them with wanton hairs, rounding them off, and giving them a bright surface."

Working in gouache on cardboard, Lautrec painted Monsieur Boileau *in 1893. The artist's absinthe-drinking friend was one of Paris' better-known gossip columnists.*

Unlike the Impressionists who preceded him, Toulouse-Lautrec believed that "the figure alone exists." In his prints and posters he concentrated on strong, rhythmic lines enclosing areas of bold, contrasting colors. Some critics were dismayed and wrote of his "curious and evil talent" which "dissects his models in a sort of moral and psychological nakedness," but the artist was unmoved. When an actress asked, "Lautrec, why do you always make women so ugly," he replied, "Because they are." His caustic style was, however, in part a reflection of the rough-and-tumble nature of fin de siècle entertainment. Among Lautrec's closest friends was Aristide Bruant, proprietor of the cabaret Le Mirliton, where Bruant specialized in insulting the demi-monde. "Here's something fancy coming," Bruant would bellow as customers arrived. "No dregs this time. Something choice, three star tarts. And the gentlemen behind are undoubtedly pimps or ambassadors." Society loved it. In 1895 Lautrec did the lithograph at right of his colorful, haughty friend. The sketch below right, Yvette Guilbert en diseuse, is one of a series Lautrec did of the queen of the café concerts. She accepted the unflattering likeness philosophically, but added, "For the love of God, don't make me so appallingly ugly! God knows, everyone cannot see its value as a work of art!" Below is an 1896 sketch in which Lautrec featured his friends Chocolat the dancing clown and Achille the bartender.

The Entertainers

Occasionally Toulouse-Lautrec ventured into the dignified society of his class, but only long enough to call it "a crush of gloved hands manipulating tortoise-shell or gold lorgnettes." Soon his familiar figure would again be seen waddling exuberantly and with seemingly inexhaustible vitality through an endless round of Parisian pleasures. No amusement, from the ballet to the brothel, was too refined or too crude for his taste. Armed with a sketchbook and a hollow cane filled with "refreshments," he made a second home of theaters, circuses, cabarets, and brothels, becoming friends of the dancers, singers, bareback riders, actors, and prostitutes who entertained a generation bent on having its fling.

Fascinated by the artificiality of Paris' show business élite, Toulouse-Lautrec made thousands of drawings, many of which he later turned into lithographs, posters, and paintings of such famous show people as the singers Yvette Guilbert and Aristide Bruant (left) and the circus clown Chocolat (far left). His posters, such as *Troupe de Mlle. Églantine* (above), became the rage and revived the art of print making. In turn the entertainers paid homage to his genius. "The more one sees of him," wrote one friend, "the taller he grows. In the end he assumes a stature above the average."

579

The Charm of Everyday

While Toulouse-Lautrec was recording the gay, often bizarre, and sometimes lurid night life of *fin de siècle* Paris, another artist, who was just three years Lautrec's junior but who was to outlive his fast-living friend by nearly half a century, was quietly painting a wholly different facet of *la belle époque*. In his canvases Pierre Bonnard celebrated the thousand and one scenes of daily life that made Paris a synonym for charm. Unlike Lautrec, who feasted on the exotic and the forbidden, Bonnard cultivated the familiar and the natural. As one of his friends wrote, "He understands, loves, and expresses everything he sees, the pie for dessert, the eye of his dog, a ray of sunlight coming through a window blind, the sponge in his bathtub."

Although Bonnard showed a marked preference for familiar subject matter, stylistically he was an important innovator. As a member of a small group of artists who called themselves the Nabis ("Prophets" in Hebrew), Bonnard championed freedom from rational restraints so that painting might partake of the freshness of childlike perceptions. His work effectively communicated his intent. As early as 1893 one critic observed, "M. Bonnard catches the most fleeting expressions; . . . and in support of this gift he is able to draw upon a delicate sense of humor, sometimes ironic, always very French."

Bonnard had a fondness for maxims: "True importance is an unexpected impression"; "Its faults are sometimes what gives life to a picture"; "The unlikely is often the real truth." The Cab Horse, Boulevard des Batignolles (below), painted in 1895 while Bonnard was living in the Batignolles district, and Movement in the Street (left), finished in 1900, are examples of his maxims as well as delightful expressions of his private yet common vision.

581

The Avant-Garde

Paris celebrated the beginning of the twentieth century with yet another World's Fair. The year 1900 was, as one artist later wrote, "a time of great tranquility, employment, and money." However, a new world was being born. Electricity was making Paris literally as well as figuratively the City of Light. The Métro (subway), the telephone, and the automobile signaled an era of rapid transportation and communication, and Alexandre Gustave Eiffel's great iron tower proclaimed the arrival of the industrial age. The twentieth century was on its way, but few realized that the new century would be more of a departure from than an extension of the nineteenth. Among those few was a loose-knit international coterie of artists, writers, musicians, and thinkers who, attracted by the Paris of *la belle époque*, began to experiment with radically new artistic ideas.

Avant-garde painters owed much to the individualistic tradition that had begun with Manet forty years before, yet their bent was fundamentally different. Willing to believe that "Nature is only a hypothesis," they created new visual experiences where color no longer necessarily represented color as seen by nature, or shapes natural shapes, or experiences happenings as perceived by the rational, conscious mind. Using brilliant, broad strokes of color, as in André Derain's portrait of Henri Matisse (below), or the difficult visual perspectives of Cubism, as in Pablo Picasso's portrait of the art dealer Kahnweiler (lower right), or the dream-like vision of Henri Rousseau (far right), they abandoned the logical clarity of a century gone by for the revolutionary dimensions of a new age.

In his 1905 portrait of Matisse, André Derain made the same free use of explosive colors as Matisse himself. The Salon was scandalized; a critic labeled them "Fauves," wild savages.

*1906 Picasso painted his patron, the American writer
nd grande dame of the avant-garde, Gertrude Stein.*

*ater, in 1910, Picasso portrayed his dealer and friend,
ne German Henry Kahnweiler, in his new Cubist style.*

Henri Rousseau's Poet and His Muse *is an allegorical
portrait of the poet and critic Guillaume Apollinaire.*

End of an Era

When the *avant-garde* painter Maurice Vlaminck wrote his memoirs, he pictured Paris at the beginning of the new century as a place where "life was more engrossing than one's career or one's prospects." Though it was the center of the West, Paris still retained a "happy provincial routine." Times were good, people were friendly, and "half of Paris seemed to be perpetually strolling around with a little cash in its pockets."

It was this intimate, charming, unruffled world of little pleasures which Edouard Vuillard pictured in canvases such as *The Park* (left). Like his fellow Nabi, Pierre Bonnard, Vuillard painted only those scenes which familiarity had made a part of himself. Shy and retiring, he would say, "I prefer to be humble rather than to pretend to understanding." His subtle, intricately colored paintings prompted the novelist André Gide to write in his review of the 1905 Salon, "I do not know what I like most here. Perhaps, Monsieur Vuillard himself. I know few works where one is brought more directly in communion with the painter." Vuillard's success, wrote Gide, "is due to his emotion never losing its hold on the brush . . ., to his speaking in a low tone, suitable to confidences, and to one's leaning over to listen to him."

By 1905, however, events already threatened Vuillard's world. In that year the First Moroccan Crisis led to a rising flood of *revanchist* sentiment against Germany. By 1912, after the Second Moroccan Crisis, French nationalists could hardly wait for hostilities to begin. "The man of arms has taken revenge upon narrow ideologues and windy pacifists," wrote Etienne Rey in his popular book, *The Renaissance of French Pride.* "Once again men have come to realize the essential virtue of war, the exaltation which it induces in the spirit of mankind." When war did come in August of 1914 the French jubilantly greeted the news. As troops marched past Versailles, bedecked with flowers as in the photograph above, women shouted gaily, "Don't forget to send me the Kaiser's moustache!"

22

—◦◦◦—

World War I

Napoleon III once observed that one can do anything with bayonets but sit on them. Weapons, both military and diplomatic, invite use. In August, 1914, the tensions generated by international rivalries exploded into general war.

The immediate cause of World War I, the spark that led to the explosion, was the conflict between Austria and Serbia. Serbia, small but vigorous and highly nationalistic, stood in the path of Austrian expansion into the Balkans, competing with it for the legacy of the disintegrating Ottoman Empire. On occasions when the Serbians had gained territory from the Turks, the Austrians applied pressure and forced them to renounce it. Gradually, influential circles in Vienna concluded that Austrian interests required Serbia to be crushed and looked for an opportunity to open hostilities.

The occasion presented itself in June, 1914, when a Serbian terrorist assassinated Austrian Crown Prince Francis Ferdinand during the latter's visit to Sarajevo. Although the assassin was an Austrian subject, and Sarajevo, located in Bosnia, was Austrian territory, Vienna charged Serbia with responsibility for the crime. The dispute initially appeared to be leading to yet another Balkan crisis of the kind the world had learned to take in stride. But this time the outcome was different because the intricate chain of alliances forged in the preceding thirty-five years was brought into play.

Before attacking Serbia, Austria requested German assurances of support against Russia should Russia come to Serbia's aid. The request placed the Germans in a quandary. On the one hand, they were not eager to place themselves at the mercy of Austrian diplomacy, which could involve them in war with Russia and therefore with France. On the other hand, the trend of international relations since 1890 had made them increasingly dependent on Austria. Austria, in fact, was the only ally on whom they could count, for Italy, the other member of the Triple Alliance, seemed to waver in its loyalties. The Germans thus could not let Austria down without risking complete diplomatic isolation—a fact the Austrian diplomats exploited to the utmost. On July 5 William II yielded to their pressures and gave the Austrians the desired assurance—the so-called "blank check"—of unconditional support against Serbia. The Germans counted on this assurance to intimidate Russia and forestall its intervention. But if this device did not work, they were prepared to fight. Many German generals believed that time was working against Germany because the Russians were making great strides in modernizing their armed forces, and that the sooner war came, the better.

With the German guarantee in its pocket, Austria issued an ultimatum to Serbia on July 23. The Austrians made their terms intentionally unacceptable, for they were seeking not a peaceful solution to the quarrel but a pretext for an invasion. The next day Germany came out in Austria's support, making public a note in which it warned the other powers to keep out of the Austro-Serbian dispute or face "incalculable consequences."

Beginning with the Crimean War and the American Civil War and reaching new peaks of skill in World War 1, documentary photography revealed to the world the true face of war. These are German troops breaking the Allied line along the Somme in 1918.

The Russians could not acquiesce in the destruction of Serbia, for to have done so would have meant forfeiting all influence in the Balkans. But they too did not want to act without consulting their ally. The French, like the Germans, felt that they risked isolation if they failed to honor their treaty obligations, and on July 25 pledged to the Russians support against Austria.

On July 28, encouraged by the Germans, the Austrians declared war on Serbia, despite Serbian willingness to accept all but two of the most insolent demands of their ultimatum. The very next day Austrian artillery bombarded Belgrade. Austria's haste was due to its desire to destroy Serbia before the other powers had a chance to arbitrate and settle the dispute.

In response to the Austrian attack, Russia ordered a general mobilization (July 29). At that period a mobilization order was tantamount to a declaration of war. The call to the colors of reserves and the activation of reserve units required several weeks. The country that completed the process first enjoyed a decided advantage over its adversary because it could commence hostilities whenever and wherever it wanted. No country, therefore, could allow a potential enemy to mobilize without immediately following suit. Once mobilization was under way, military operations ensued almost automatically, since each power sought the benefit of strategic initiative.

At this juncture several last-minute attempts were made to stop the drift to

war. The Russians proposed submitting the dispute over Serbia to an international court, but the Austrians would not hear of it. Next, the British tried to mediate. Their proposal, containing a thinly veiled threat to support Russia and France in the event of war, had an effect opposite to the one intended. William II, his head filled with racial doctrines, interpreted the British move as evidence that the "Anglo-Saxons" had decided to join the "Slavs" and "Gauls" in encircling and destroying the "Teutons." He became nearly hysterical and made up his mind to fight. In both Berlin and Vienna war parties silenced the more conciliatory groups.

At this point events got out of control. On July 31 Austria ordered a general mobilization, followed the next day by France and Germany. At 7 P.M. on August 1, Germany declared war on Russia, and that very night, without a formal declaration of war against France, sent its troops into Belgium and Luxemburg on their way to Paris.

Europe, in the midst of the summer holidays, was not aware of what these events portended. Contemporary sources agree that the outbreak of the war caught the Continent by surprise.

Ever since 1894, when France and Russia concluded their treaty of alliance, Germany had had to prepare for the contingency of a two-front war. To meet this

On the opposite page are Austrian Crown Prince Francis Ferdinand and his wife (rear seat) minutes before their assassination in Sarajevo. The picture above was made in Berlin as war was announced; the news was greeted with similar enthusiasm by all the belligerents.

Military Preparations and Plans

Alfred von Schlieffen, Chief of the German General Staff from 1891 to 1905, author of the celebrated strategic plan to defeat France.

situation, the German General Staff formulated a strategic plan involving two rapid, closely coordinated thrusts—first against France, then against Russia. The success of this plan depended on speed. France had to be crushed in less than six weeks, the time it was estimated the Russians would require to complete their mobilization. This consideration explains why the Germans so seriously viewed the Russian mobilization order of July 29 that they declared war on Russia three days later. Any delay in reacting to it spelled ruin to their entire strategic plan.

A fundamental difficulty with this concept was the fact that France could not be knocked out in six weeks by an attack across the Franco-German frontier, for this frontier was short (150 miles) and heavily fortified. The French could be struck decisively only by outflanking their fortifications, that is, by crossing the Low Countries. It was with these thoughts in mind that Count Alfred von Schlieffen, the Chief of Staff, had formulated his famous strategic plan in the early 1900s. The "Schlieffen Plan" called for a wheeling movement by an overwhelming right wing across Belgium, coupled with a holding operation by the center and left disposed along the Franco-German frontier. The operation that Schlieffen envisaged has been likened to a swinging door, the right wing serving as the door, the center and left as its hinge.

The French had a general notion of what the Germans intended. To meet their anticipated thrust through Belgium, they devised "Plan XVII." Rather than collide head-on with the swinging door, they decided to concentrate forces in the center; as soon as the Germans launched their wheeling movement, they intended to strike at the German positions in Lorraine at the pivot of the swinging door, so as to separate it from the hinge. Thus one offensive was to be met with another offensive.

The German strategy had an obvious flaw in that the violation of Belgian territory was certain to bring Britain into the war on the Franco-Russian side. But the Germans were not much perturbed at this prospect. As the only major European power without conscription, Britain had only 160,000 men under arms—a miniscule force compared to Germany's 5 million or France's 4 million. Bismarck once expressed German contempt for Britain's military might when he threatened to order his police to arrest any expeditionary force the British might land on the Continent. The British navy was another matter. But the navy could make its weight felt only in a protracted war, and the Germans felt certain that by crossing Belgium they could finish the war in two or three months.

The Germans and the French alike believed that the decision would be reached on the Western front. Until then, Russia and Austria were expected to keep each other balanced in the East. The French rather overestimated the effectiveness of the Russian army because of its modernization, for which they had advanced much money. The Russian command was generally of low quality, and transport and communications were of a most primitive kind. Much the same may be said of the Austro-Hungarian army, which, in addition, suffered from the disloyalty of the Slavs who formed the majority of its conscripts.

Although it was not immediately apparent, the war that broke out in 1914 differed fundamentally from all other wars that had preceded it. The best way to define the difference is to say that World War I was the first industrial war—the first in which the manpower and technology of the industrial era were applied to the slaughter of human beings. In the second half of the nineteenth century the major European powers (Britain excepted), emulating the example set by Prussia in the Napoleonic era, had introduced universal military service coupled with reserve systems. This practice virtually transformed the entire male population into a potential fighting force. Within a few weeks after the outbreak of war in 1914, 6 million men stood poised to fight. Behind them were many more millions who could be drawn upon as the need arose. Such masses of soldiers could not be equipped and armed by conventional arsenals; they required the services of the country's entire industrial plant. Countries like Russia, Italy, and Austria-Hungary, which had the manpower but lacked the industrial backing, found themselves now at a great disadvantage. By contrast, Great Britain and the United States, even though they had no peacetime conscription and therefore lacked a ready pool of reservists, managed quickly to mount efficient armed forces thanks to their superior industrial capacity and the industry-bred discipline of their citizenry.

The application of industrial methods to warfare accounted for the unprecedented destructiveness of World War I. Battle experience gained in the wars of the nineteenth and early twentieth centuries (the American Civil War, the wars waged by Prussia against Austria and France, and the Russo-Japanese War) yielded a variety of new weapons of great destructive power, such as the breech-loading rifle and the machine gun. These instruments of death could now be put into mass production. So could the automobile and airplane, which with a few changes became suitable for military purposes. Warfare acquired a new dimension: it became total, calling for the full commitment of human and economic resources.

The Germans had little trouble overcoming Belgian resistance, stanch though it was, and pushing on toward Paris in accord with their timetable. Shortly after Germany had sent troops across the Belgian frontier, Britain declared war.

The Major Campaigns, 1914–1916

In response to the German offensive, the French put into execution their Plan XVII, launching an attack against Lorraine. But German resistance there proved stronger than had been expected, and the drive soon faltered. The failure of this offensive placed the whole French army in grave peril. The Germans carried out their drive through Belgium on a broader front and with more numerous forces than the French had anticipated. The French had disposed only 31 divisions on their Belgian flank against the 52 which the Germans employed in the wheeling movement, and these they grouped along the eastern half of the Franco-Belgian border, leaving the western portion virtually undefended. The German right wing moved forward with astounding speed. On August 27 advance units crossed into France, on September 3 they captured Reims, and two days later they were 15 miles from Paris. The bulk of the French army, vainly battering against German positions in Lorraine, now faced the danger of being trapped in a gigantic nutcracker formed by the enemy's steadfast center and irresistibly advancing right. How near collapse France was at the beginning of September may be gathered from the fact that the government at this time evacuated to Bordeaux.

To relieve the pressure on the French, the Russians hastily mounted an offensive against Germany in East Prussia. But the attack was badly executed and ended in disaster. The German forces, led by their two ablest generals, Paul von Hindenburg and Erich Ludendorff, met the Russians in early September in the Battle of Tannenberg, and inflicted on them a crushing defeat.

At this point, when the war seemed over, there occurred what became known as the "Miracle on the Marne." The Allies expected the Germans to keep their extreme right wing moving forward, first to the west and then to the south of Paris, so as to isolate the capital from the rest of the country and outflank the French armies of the center. But the Germans shifted the direction of the extreme right, sending it instead north and east of Paris. Their intention was to close the gap that developed between their extreme right and the other armies taking part in the offensive. The astonished French saw the Germans, instead of executing the dreaded flanking movement, exposing their own flank. With superb confidence, General Joseph Joffre launched on September 6 a general counteroffensive along the Marne River. The Germans, exhausted and confused, stopped their advance and then withdrew. Both Paris and the French army were thus saved from a disastrous encirclement.

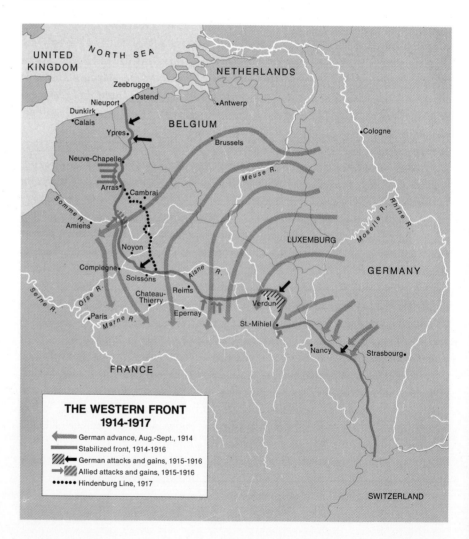

**THE WESTERN FRONT
1914-1917**

German advance, Aug.-Sept., 1914
Stabilized front, 1914-1916
German attacks and gains, 1915-1916
Allied attacks and gains, 1915-1916
Hindenburg Line, 1917

This turn of events ended Germany's hopes of crushing France in six weeks and forced it into a protracted two-front war, which it had sought so desperately to avoid. The failure of the Schlieffen Plan has been subsequently blamed on the German command's unwillingness to adhere strictly to its creator's recommendations. It has been said that Schlieffen's successors lost courage at the last moment and weakened the right wing to reinforce the left, and then deflected the right from its appointed course around Paris. Recent researches, however, have shown such criticism to be unfounded. They reveal that Schlieffen himself had considered a variety of alternatives in troop dispositions, and that he had actually intended to route the extreme right north of Paris. Furthermore, it appears today that his famous plan was not realizable under the best of circumstances. It ignored modern railroad transport and the advantages that it gave the retreating side, with shrinking and therefore faster lines of communications, over the advancing side whose lines became increasingly extended and slower. The plan was simply a desperate gamble. One can only marvel at the recklessness of a government willing to risk the fate of 68 million people on a strategy so rigid in its timing that a delay of a week or two spelled the difference between victory and defeat.

Walking wounded of the British Expeditionary Force, photographed in the retreat from Antwerp in 1914.

The following two months (October and November, 1914) of military operations on the Western front are known as the "Race to the Sea." The two opponents were not so much trying to reach the coast as to outflank each other. As each effort failed, they moved farther north and west, until the Channel put an end to their maneuvers. In Flanders the Germans had the disagreeable experience of running into the small but superbly trained British Expeditionary Force (BEF) consisting of regulars. At Ypres the BEF lost 50,000 men, the bulk of its contingent.

By Christmas, 1914, the Western front was stabilized, and a solid line stretched from the English Channel to Switzerland. This line was to remain virtually unchanged for the next two and a half years. Despite offensive operations that cost millions of casualties, neither side succeeded until March, 1917, in denting the front by more than ten miles either way. Flanking movements in the West were no longer possible. The enemy had to be assaulted frontally, that is, in the most difficult and costly manner. This fact helps explain the enormous casualty lists of World War I.

Although their great offensive had failed, as 1914 drew to a close the Germans were in a better position than their rivals. In the opening stage of the war they had augmented their economic capacity considerably by securing control of industrialized Belgium and the northern regions of France, the latter containing over half of France's coal and nine-tenths of its iron. No enemy soldiers stood on German soil. Under these circumstances, the Germans could adopt a defensive strategy on the Western front.

In the course of 1915 the battle lines in the West remained relatively static as both sides turned their attention to the East. On the French front troops installed themselves in trench complexes. Attempts at a break-through produced no significant results. In April, 1915, the Germans succeeded in opening a gap in the Allied lines by the use of a new weapon, poison gas, but the breach was soon sealed and the front re-established.

The Central Powers achieved their gains in Russia in 1915 against the forces of six-foot six-inch Grand Duke Nicholas. He was relieved by the tsar, who took command himself.

In drawing plans for 1915, the German General Staff decided to make a major effort on the Eastern front to help their hard-pressed Austro-Hungarian ally. Although the Russians had suffered a severe defeat at Tannenberg, their simultaneous offensive launched against Austria-Hungary had gone well. In the fall of 1914 Russian armies had conquered Galicia and threatened to break across the Carpathian Mountains into the Hungarian plain. Czechs and other Slavic conscripts were deserting the Austro-Hungarian armies in droves. The position of the Dual Monarchy was further aggravated by Italy's defection from the Triple Alliance. After a period of wavering, the Italians in May of 1915 declared war on Austria-Hungary and launched an offensive along the Isonzo River near Trieste. Pressed along its extended frontier and shaken by the disloyalty of its minorities, Austria, which had irresponsibly begun the war, stood on the verge of collapse. To forestall this disaster, the Germans withdrew eight divisions from France, and in May, 1915, launched an attack against the Russians. Confronted with superior firepower and better command, the Russians had to withdraw, evacuating both Galicia and central Poland.

Among the Allies, the stalemate obtained on the Western front in the winter of 1914–1915 caused deep differences of opinion. One group, including the majority of the generals, continued to believe that the war would be decided in France and favored building up forces there until they were strong enough to launch an overwhelming offensive. Another, led by David Lloyd George and Winston Churchill (then First Lord of the Admiralty), felt that it was useless to throw men and matériel against the well-entrenched Germans. Instead, they wanted a diversion against Germany's weak allies, especially the Ottoman Empire, which had joined the Central Powers in December, 1914. The Churchill-Lloyd George plan was to seize the Dardanelles and Constantinople by means of a sea-borne invasion force in order to open up a convenient sea route to Russia and wreak havoc in Germany's and Austria's backyards. But the military was not prepared to gamble precious divisions on such a risky venture. The Australian and New Zealand troops landed in February, 1915, at Gallipoli, near the entrance to the Dardanelles, proved insufficient for their task. The whole operation was badly bungled, and in December of 1915, after suffering heavy casualties, the Allied troops withdrew. Churchill had to resign from the cabinet.

The entrance of Italy and Turkey into the war greatly extended the scope of military operations in 1915. There was fighting in the provinces of the Ottoman Empire, especially in Transcaucasia and Mesopotamia, where the Russians and the British respectively made good progress. The British also ejected the Germans from most of their colonial possessions. The Bulgarians sided with the Central Powers, and the Romanians went over to the Allies (1916). In this manner a secondary front came into existence in the Balkans, pitting the Italians, Romanians, and Serbs against the Austro-Hungarians, Turks, and Bulgarians.

In the course of 1915, while engaging in relatively minor skirmishes elsewhere, the Germans, French, and British were marshaling their resources for a supreme effort on the Western front in 1916. With great energy, Britain made up for its peacetime lack of military preparations. A call for volunteers brought to arms over a million enthusiastic men, who were speedily trained and dispatched across the Channel. In January, 1916, when the flow of volunteers seemed to dry up,

Britain took a step without precedent in its history by introducing compulsory military service. Lloyd George, appointed Minister of Munitions, overcame the shortages that had developed early in 1915 and placed the entire munitions production on an efficient basis. France and Germany also recruited masses of men and geared their industrial production to military uses.

In 1916 both sides expected to achieve a break-through by concentrating an enormous superiority of men and artillery on a short sector of the Western front. These expectations, however, were cruelly disappointed. Under technical conditions prevailing at the time, the defender had a decided advantage over the attacker. The critical factor was the machine gun. Placed behind lines of barbed wire, it exposed the attacking forces to a deadly barrage that mowed them down and sooner or later forced them to stop. Gradually the trenches on both sides developed into elaborate subterranean fortifications: on the surface, barbed wire, mines, and a maze of trenches; underground, command posts, living quarters, and supplies. An attack against such a line was not so much a charge as a siege, but it took the generals a long time to realize this fact.

The first great battle of 1916 was inaugurated by the Germans early in the year in the area of Verdun. They struck at this relatively unimportant fortress with the deliberate intention of "bleeding white" the French army. For reasons best known to themselves, they counted on inflicting five French casualties for every two of their own. They intended to force France to keep pouring men into combat

Several of the reasons why the carnage of World War I exceeded that of all previous conflicts are shown in this German photograph: entrenchments, poison gas, the machine gun.

Farthest Russian advance, 1914-1915
The front, 1915
Brusilov offensive, 1916
Armistice line, 1917
Area occupied by Central Powers
under Brest Litovsk Treaty, 1918

by the hundreds of thousands until it could do so no longer and collapsed from sheer exhaustion. The Battle of Verdun in fact exceeded in ferocity and casualty rates any previously fought. Much of it was waged by pockets of isolated units that held on to the last and exacted a frightful toll from the opponent. As the French solidified their positions, German losses increased. Of the 500,000 men who lost their lives at Verdun by July, 1916, when the forces finally disengaged, nearly one-half were Germans.

The Battle of Verdun sapped the strength of the Allies while they were preparing for a great summer three-front offensive to end the war. The French, exhausted by Verdun, had to yield the initiative to the British, whose large and fresh forces concentrated in the area of the Somme River. The Italians were to launch an attack on the Austrians, while in the East the Russians undertook to mount a powerful offensive in Poland.

The first to strike were the Russians. They moved early in June, in time to relieve the hard-pressed defenders of Verdun. Commanded by Aleksei Brusilov, the ablest Russian general of the war, they advanced with great vigor, especially against the Austrians. Their victories in the summer of 1916 were the most brilliant won by the Allied armies in the entire course of the war. Had the drive not been allowed to bog down from lack of decision and political bickering, it might well have caused the collapse of the Central Powers. In the Brusilov offensive the Russians lost an estimated 1 million men.

While the Russians were rolling forward in the East, the British were preparing a major offensive on the Somme in northwestern France. They had assembled not only an eager army of volunteers but a quantity of weapons and supplies of all kinds exceeding anything previously seen on a battlefield. Among them were airplanes and new armored vehicles known as tanks. This superb fighting force, buttressed by French divisions, stood concentrated along a 23-mile front. The Allied intention was to pulverize the German lines by an artillery bombardment, and then send in the infantry simply to "mop up" what had survived the shelling. In other words, the artillery was to conquer, and the infantry to occupy ground.

On June 25, 1916, Allied artillery—one gun for each 20 yards of front in the British sector—opened fire. The bombardment went on without interruption for seven days and seven nights. Then it suddenly stopped, and the Allied troops went over the top. What was intended as a mopping-up operation soon turned out to be a "race with death." The Germans, concealed inside their excellent fortifications, had survived in considerable numbers. As soon as the artillery barrage lifted, they emerged and manned their machine guns. The attackers, especially the British, were severely handicapped in their dash toward the German positions, for each of them had to carry 66 pounds of supplies and ammunition—they could barely walk let alone run across the cratered no man's land. Their chances of survival were further diminished by being required to advance in orderly waves with fixed bayonets. The German machine gunners cut them down as they approached, wave after wave. On the first day of the Somme offensive the BEF lost 60 percent of its officers and 40 percent of its rank and file—the highest casualty rate of any battle recorded in history. Despite these losses, the Allies pressed their advance into the murderous fire in the ensuing weeks, until the onset of winter put an end to the operation. The Somme offensive gained the Allies a maximum penetration of seven miles. The total cost to both sides was over a million killed and wounded, approximately one casualty for every four square yards of contested ground.

The results of the Italian offensive along the Isonzo River in 1916 were also disappointing to the Allies. Despite strenuous efforts, the Italians did not succeed in denting the Austrian line or significantly pushing it back.

The great battles of 1916, especially Verdun and the Somme, attained a level of horror and sheer destructiveness never before experienced. They were simply "battles of attrition," in which the aim was no longer to outmaneuver, outflank, or break through enemy lines, as had been the case in previous wars, but systematically to drain the opponent's human and material resources. In such combat, casualties were computed on the same basis as expenditures of matériel: no matter how high, they were considered justifiable as long as they inflicted greater losses on the enemy. Human lives became statistical quantities, accounted for like shells or fuel.

A German artist sketched dispirited Russian troops captured as the Brusilov offensive was blunted in 1916.

Morale The depersonalization of warfare, which began in 1916 and continued until the armistice, profoundly depressed the morale of the troops.

Difficult as it is to believe today, the outbreak of hostilities in 1914 occurred amid widespread enthusiasm. The vast majority of Europeans knew of war only from books, for the Continent had been spared prolonged warfare for nearly a century, and in consequence they tended to romanticize it wildly. For many it brought a welcome change from the routine of factory or office. War was seen as the adventure of a lifetime, an escape from a "world grown old and cold and weary," in the words of Rupert Brooke, the most popular of the early English war poets:

1914

Now, God be thanked Who has matched us with His hour,
And caught our youth, and wakened us from sleeping,
With hand made sure, clear eye, and sharpened power,
To turn, as swimmers into cleanness leaping,
Glad from a world grown old and cold and weary,
Leave the sick hearts that honour could not move,
And half-men, their dirty songs and dreary,
And all the little emptiness of love!

Oh! we, who have known shame, we have found release there,
Where there's no ill, no grief, but sleep has mending,
Naught broken save this body, lost but breath;
Nothing to shake the laughing heart's long peace there
But only agony, and that has ending;
And the worst friend and enemy is but Death.

In the first two years of war, the combatants on both sides, many of them volunteers, fought with incredible discipline, fervor, and bravery.

After Verdun and the Somme the situation changed. The discipline remained, at least on the Western front, but the fervor disappeared and for bravery there was less and less scope. Burrowing for months on end in damp, rat-infested trenches, exposed to constant danger from gas and artillery, surrounded by decaying corpses, the fighting man gradually lost his identity and turned into a dull cog in an impersonal war machine. His thoughts concentrated on survival. His best chance of survival was receiving a wound serious enough to send him to the rear for a long convalescence.

To obtain a flavor of the war of attrition we can do no better than turn to the later war poets who, unlike Brooke and his contemporaries, depicted warfare in its true horror. The first poem cited below, written by Siegfried Sassoon, conveys the sensations of the soldiers moments before going over the top; the second, also by Sassoon, depicts the appearance of a battlefield after an attack; and the third, by Wilfred Owen, relates an incident which occurred during a routine gas bombardment.

At dawn the ridge emerges massed and dun
In the wild purple of the glow'ring sun,
Smouldering through spouts of drifting smoke that shroud

The menacing scarred slope; and, one by one,
Tanks creep and topple forward to the wire.
The barrage roars and lifts. Then, clumsily bowed
With bombs and guns and shovels and battle-gear,
Men jostle and climb to meet the bristling fire.
Lines of grey, muttering faces, masked with fear,
They leave their trenches, going over the top,
While time ticks blank and busy on their wrists,
And hope, with furtive eyes and grappling fists,
Founders in mud. O Jesus, make it stop!

❉   ❉   ❉

The place was rotten with dead; green clumsy legs
High-booted, sprawled and grovelled along the saps

And trunks, face downward, in the sucking mud,
Wallowed like trodden sand-bags loosely filled;
And naked sodden buttocks, mats of hair,
Bulged, clotted heads slept in the plastering slime.

❉   ❉   ❉

Bent double, like old beggars under sacks,
Knock-kneed, coughing like hags, we cursed through sludge,

Part of the grisly harvest of the Somme offensive of 1916, a slaughter on a scale that moved English poet Siegfried Sassoon to write, "I am staring at a sunlit picture of Hell."

Till on the haunting flares we turned our backs,
And towards our distant rest began to trudge.
Men marched asleep. Many had lost their boots,
But limped on, blood-shod. All went lame, all blind;
Drunk with fatigue; deaf even to the hoots
Of gas-shells dropping softly behind.

GAS! GAS! Quick, boys!—An ecstasy of fumbling,
Fitting the clumsy helmets just in time,
But someone still was yelling out and stumbling
And floundering like a man in fire or lime.—
Dim through the misty panes and thick green light,
As under a green sea, I saw him drowning.

In all my dreams before my helpless sight
He plunges at me, guttering, choking, drowning.

If in some smothering dreams, you too could pace
Behind the wagon that we flung him in,
And watch the white eyes writhing in his face,
His hanging face, like a devil's sick of sin;
If you could hear, at every jolt, the blood
Come gargling from the froth-corrupted lungs,
Bitter as the cud
Of vile, incurable sores on innocent tongues,—
My friend, you would not tell with such high zest,
To children ardent for some desperate glory,
The old Lie: Dulce et decorum est
Pro patria mori.°

In the spring of 1917 many armies experienced mutinies. A serious revolt took place in April in the French army, when many regiments refused to go into battle. Disorders also occurred in Italian and Russian units. The forces of the most industrialized countries, England and Germany, succeeded in maintaining excellent discipline. But according to Ludendorff, the German army lost at the Somme its old fighting spirit, never to regain it.

Mobilization of the Home Front   When the war had broken out no one anticipated either its intensity or its duration. The issue was expected to be settled in a matter of weeks or, at most, months, and therefore no provisions had been made beyond the usual military kind.

This attitude underwent radical change as the war went on, seemingly without end, making increasing demands on manpower and resources. In static trench combat, ultimate victory came to depend less on the skill of the men under arms than on the ability of the nation to furnish them with an uninterrupted flow of weapons, ammunition, and replacements. Since the resources of every country had their limit, this task could not be entrusted to the normal operations of a

°"It is sweet and proper to die for one's country."

peacetime economy, the more so as the war had disrupted the intricate commercial links connecting all countries with the world market. The economy had to be centralized and managed so that all the resources—human and material alike—were employed in the most efficient manner. In response to this need, the belligerents devised a variety of institutions and procedures, which in the most extreme case, that of Germany, brought the country close to a kind of state socialism. This development is of utmost historical importance. The economic measures devised during World War I as temporary remedies outlived the war, providing a new model of economic and political organization. This model was utilized fully by subsequent totalitarian systems and to some extent also by the democratic countries.

Germany, a country especially short of resources, pioneered this process. Before the war a large proportion of its raw materials, food, and labor had been imported from abroad, from areas which after 1914 came under enemy control or were inaccessible because of Allied command of the high seas. Without putting its resources to the most rational use, Germany would have been unlikely to remain in the war for long. German industrialists realized this fact sooner than did German generals, who relied entirely on force of arms and showed little awareness of the economic aspects of modern warfare. Walther Rathenau, the director of electrical industries, was the first to grasp the need for organizing Germany's domestic resources for war. At his urging, the Prussian government established in August, 1914, a War Raw Materials Department to stock and allocate raw materials on a priority basis. In November staple foods were placed under controls, and in 1915 food rationing was instituted. The Germans also carried out intensive experiments with chemical substitutes for scarce raw materials, including food. A spectacular result of these efforts was the discovery of a method of "fixing" nitrogen present in the atmosphere—a discovery that freed Germany from dependence on nitrates, previously obtained from Chile, and provided its industries with an essential of both high explosives and chemical fertilizers.

Sound management and applied science permitted Germany to overcome to some extent the shortage of raw materials. But there remained an acute shortage of labor. The armed forces continued without interruption to siphon off white-collar and manual workers to the point of endangering both the economy and the administration. The losses suffered in 1916 at Verdun and the Somme necessitated especially severe encroachments on the labor force. The problem was solved by a drastic method. In the fall of 1916 the Kaiser placed Ludendorff in charge of the entire German war effort. Ludendorff grasped much better than most Prussian generals the necessity of harnessing the total national resources to the war effort. He requested and obtained from the Reichstag in December, 1916, the passage of the National Service Act that mobilized the entire male population of the country for war service. The law required every male between sixteen and sixty years of age and not on active military service to take a job in an occupation officially designated as critical, be it in a factory or office or on a farm. A special war office (*Kriegsamt*) was established to supervise the execution of this law. In time, the *Kriegsamt* became the central agency for the management of the war economy. To augment its manpower further, Germany began forcefully to deport workers from occupied territories in Belgium, France, and Poland. In Octo-

Posters and prints played an important role in mobilizing public opinion against the enemy. This 1915 print, captioned "A Fine Victory," was inspired by reports of German atrocities against Belgian civilians.

ber, 1916, on Ludendorff's recommendation and with the enthusiastic backing of the industrialists, the German government established special concentration camps to receive the deportees and distribute them to factories, farms, and military construction sites. In all, 60,000 foreign laborers were brought in by February, 1917, at which time protests in neutral countries forced the cancellation of the program. Both the National Service Act and the deportations represented a significant innovation in the relationship between the state and the individual. The introduction of forced labor brought Germany the closest of all the belligerents to total mobilization.

The Allies acted more slowly in mobilizing the home front, in part because they lacked Germany's tradition of economic centralization, and in part because they never experienced equally severe shortages. Unlike the Central Powers, they had at their disposal the inexhaustible resources of the United States and the British Empire. But they too in time found it necessary to organize. Having centralized the manufacture of munitions and introduced conscription, the British government in February, 1916, passed the Defence of the Realm Act, authorizing it to purchase raw materials at set prices. By the time the war ended, all the belligerents had put into effect some control measures, among which the following may be mentioned: fiscal operations freeing currency from its dependence on gold; centralization of foreign trade; priorities on raw materials; price and wage controls; rationing of all kinds; restrictions on agriculture; and labor conscription. Merely to list these measures is to indicate how much the economic policies of the war period departed from traditional liberal practices and foreshadowed the regulated economies of more recent times. It was during World War I that the productive resources of a country first began to be viewed as an economic whole, and statesmen began to think in terms of production "crash programs" and national economic development.

What did the belligerents expect to gain from all their efforts and sacrifices? On what conditions were they prepared to make peace? Until January, 1917, no one knew. Incredible as it may seem, two years after the outbreak of hostilities neither the Allies nor the Central Powers had formulated anything resembling their war aims, anything that could serve as a basis for peace negotiations.

This became apparent in December, 1916, when President Woodrow Wilson, believing the conflict deadlocked and hoping to bring the belligerents to the conference table, invited both sides to formulate their intentions. It was only in response to his request that the statesmen of the great powers diverted their attention from the pursuit of war long enough to define their goals—and even then they did so more from a desire to appease American opinion than from an earnest belief in the value of such an exercise.

The Allied terms included the following demands: the evacuation by the Central Powers of all the territories occupied by them since August, 1914; the surrender of Alsace and Lorraine; the expulsion from the Continent of the Ottoman Empire; and the reorganization of Europe in accord with the principle of national self-determination—in other words, the disintegration of Austria-Hungary. The Central Powers could have accepted these terms only if they were ready to capitulate—which in December, 1916, they definitely were not.

The German terms were even stiffer. In their formal reply to Wilson, the Germans asked only for a vague "zone" lying between Germany and Russia, colonies, and financial compensation. (They were silent on Belgium.) But their actual aims were much more ambitious. Recent studies based on documents captured in Germany after World War II reveal that nothing short of European domination and possibly even world hegemony would have satisfied William II and his associates. They expected from the war a considerable expansion of German territory, including full political control over Belgium and the industrial regions of France in the West, as well as over Poland, the Baltic region, and the Ukraine in the East. In addition, they envisaged the formation of a large Central European Customs Union embracing Germany, Austria, Holland, France, and the Scandinavian countries. These political and economic gains would have given Germany a solid base for the conduct of *Weltpolitik*, as well as assuring it of an enormous market for its industrial goods.

Clearly, with such unacceptable aims in mind, neither side thought seriously of peace. The war had become a sheer contest of wills—a primitive struggle for national survival.

> There was absolutely no definable area of disagreement and therefore no problems to be solved, the solution of which would mean peace. It was this that turned the First World War into an insane orgy of destruction. With the lack of any rational declaration of intentions, the formulation of the whole conflict was left to the apocalyptic imagination. Blind hatred reached the level of delirium, because there was nothing, no handhold, to which articulate thought might cling.°

The only serious peace move was initiated by the Austrian emperor, Charles I, who in 1916 succeeded Franz Josef. Determined to save the Austro-Hungarian

°Herbert Luethy, "The Folly and the Crime: Thoughts on 1914," *Encounter* (March, 1965).

The Failure of Peace Initiatives

General Erich Ludendorff became a virtual dictator in both the military and civilian spheres in Germany. Fiercely opposing any course short of total victory, he urged unlimited submarine warfare in 1917.

WELTKRIEGSBUCHEREI, STUTTGART

Empire even if it meant betraying Germany and signing a separate peace treaty, he opened secret negotiations with Allied representatives early in 1917. He even offered meaningful concessions; but the Italians considered them insufficient, and the negotiations collapsed.

The War at Sea
The operations of the fleets, especially Britain's Royal Navy, were less spectacular than the great offensives on land, but they had a critical influence on the outcome of the war. Command of the high seas assured the Allies of steady supplies of raw materials, industrial products, and men, and enabled them to deny these very things to the enemy. In short, it permitted the Allies to bring to bear the resources of five continents against that portion of the sixth which was controlled by the Central Powers.

Its role as the guardian of the Allied supply routes demanded of the Royal Navy a cautious, defensive stategy. It strove to keep the high seas free of German vessels and to enforce a blockade of the Central Powers, while avoiding major engagements with the German battle fleet stationed in its home ports. There was little to be gained from a victory over the German navy, and everything to be lost from defeat at its hands. As Churchill once put it, the commander of the Royal Navy was the only man on either side capable of losing the war in an afternoon. The one major naval engagement of the war—the Battle of Jutland, fought in May, 1916—resulted not from design but from the confusion of British and German admirals. It ended indecisively.

The only serious challenge to British naval supremacy was the submarine. Cruising undetected on the high seas, it proved deadly to the unescorted, unarmed merchant ships on whose cargoes Britain's war effort depended. In February, 1915, in retaliation for the British blockade, the Germans proclaimed

English artist Joseph Pennell made this sketch of submarines in port in 1917. So effective was the Allied convoy system that of every thirteen ships sunk by German submarines in the final year and a half of war, only one was under convoy.

a counterblockade, threatening to sink on sight all ships entering British waters, including those displaying a neutral flag. This policy, ruthlessly carried out, aroused much anti-German feeling in neutral countries. The sinking of the passenger ship *Lusitania* (May, 1915) off the coast of Ireland with a loss of 1,200 lives, many of them American, nearly brought the United States into war against Germany. To mollify foreign opinion, in September, 1915, the Germans temporarily suspended such attacks on neutral ships, though they continued to dispatch Allied vessels at a disturbingly high rate.

In February, 1917, the German government reversed itself once more and decided to resume unrestricted submarine warfare. At that time it announced its intention of sinking any ship, regardless of flag, that entered the waters designated as a "war zone" around Allied ports in the Atlantic and Mediterranean. This step was a desperate gamble, not unlike that taken with the Schlieffen Plan. Superficially, the situation of the Central Powers early in 1917 looked sound: the great Allied offensives of 1916 had been beaten back, Romania had been defeated and occupied, and Russia seemed on the verge of collapse. But the long-run prospects were dim, because the Central Powers had at their disposal fewer human and material resources than did the Allies. The Allied blockade was making itself increasingly felt, causing serious food shortages in Germany and Austria. The German high command realized this fact, and considered defeat inevitable if the war lasted much longer. The only chance of victory lay in a supreme effort to knock out Britain, thereby freeing Germany and Austria from the asphyxiating blockade. The German navy thought it possible, by means of the submarine, to sink 600,000 tons of shipping a month, at which rate Britain would run out of food by the autumn of 1917. Unrestricted submarine warfare, of course, virtually assured America's entry into the war, because the United States would not stand by and tolerate the wanton destruction of its merchant and passenger ships. This risk, however, was considered worth taking because the United States was so unprepared militarily that the war could end before its power had made itself felt. As it turned out, the German leaders once more underestimated political and psychological factors in international relations, and placed too much trust in sheer force and chancy timetables.

At first, unrestricted submarine warfare was successful beyond Germany's most sanguine expectations. In April of 1917 the U-boats sank 850,000 tons of Allied shipping. The figure declined somewhat during the summer but remained sufficiently high to cause deep anxiety among British statesmen. With food reserves sufficient only until October, the island faced the prospect of starvation. But as is always the case with new offensive weapons, countermeasures were soon devised. Depth charges and mines proved effective, and even more so were convoys in which British (and later, American) men-of-war escorted fleets of merchant vessels. These methods eventually brought the submarine under control. How thoroughly the Allies commanded the seas by late 1917 may be gathered from the fact that in the last year of the war, Allied navies transported across the Atlantic over two million American soldiers without a single casualty.

As generally anticipated, unrestricted submarine warfare caused the United States to declare war on Germany (April, 1917). America's entry at first had negligible effects on the military situation (except for naval operations), but it

THE WESTERN FRONT 1918

— The front, March, 1918
━━ German spring offensive
➤ Allied counteroffensive
•••••• Armistice line, Nov., 1918

exerted, from the beginning, an important psychological influence. In the long run, it assured the defeat of the Central Powers.

The Campaigns of 1917–1918　　Although the experience of the first two years of war had demonstrated the futility of frontal attacks against entrenched positions, such attacks were repeatedly resorted to in 1917 and 1918. The generals always hoped that surprise, new tactics, or more devastating weapons would smash the enemy lines; and, in any event, they could think of no alternative. French generals, true to the Napoleonic tradition, were particularly fond of head-on assaults.

In early 1917 the French prevailed on their allies to launch another coordinated offensive. This major effort, from which great things were expected, also failed. During the preceding winter the Germans had constructed a heavily fortified defense system in depth (the so-called Siegfried or Hindenburg Line), to which they withdrew on the eve of the Allied attack. The British and French troops sent against it suffered frightful losses—30,000 killed in the first 48 hours—without being able to break through. The Russian offensive, launched on Allied insistence despite the grave internal crisis in Russia (Chapter 23), was the last gasp of a dying army. In the fall it dissolved, and the new Bolshevik government, which seized power at the beginning of November, sued for peace. The Italian offensive also went badly. In the Battle of Caporetto the Austrians and Germans threw back the attackers, capturing 300,000 prisoners and nearly destroying the Italian army.

During the second half of the war, the Western front became increasingly mechanized. If the Germans proved masters in the art of fortification, the British showed the greatest ingenuity in applying to warfare advanced industrial technology. It is they who first developed the tank, which was destined to play so critical a role in World War II. Having tried it with some success in the Somme offensive, the BEF secretly gathered a large number of tanks near Cambrai, and in November, 1917, sent them against the unsuspecting German trenches. The attack—the first in which tanks were used in massed columns—succeeded in achieving a break-through; but since no preparations had been made to follow up the assault, the Germans rallied and closed the breach.

Marshal Foch (left), Allied supreme commander, with General John Pershing, head of the American forces.

The British also led in the production and use of the airplane. Originally employed mainly for reconnaissance, the plane came to fulfill a variety of functions in the latter stages of the war: for example, to bomb supply depots behind enemy lines, and to provide tactical support of troops. The Germans, for their part, initiated the practice of bombing the civilian population with the intention of disorganizing industrial productivity and lowering morale. From October, 1915, onward they subjected eastern England, especially London, to systematic bombing by Zeppelins (dirigibles) and airplanes. These air attacks strained the nerves of British civilians and brought about a certain decline in production. In retaliation, the Allies bombed German industrial sites. When the war ended, they were readying one-ton aerial bombs to drop on German cities. Such bombing further obliterated the distinction between the military and home fronts.

The last major offensive of the war was launched by the Germans in March, 1918. Russia's withdrawal from the war the preceding winter had enabled Germany to transfer forces from the East and to mount the final supreme effort aimed at capturing Paris. Timing was once more essential to the German plan: the offensive had to succeed before American troops could reach the Western front in sizable numbers. Ludendorff, who directed the operation, was prepared to lose a million men to achieve his objective. The main brunt of the offensive fell on the British sector, which nearly caved in. The situation seemed desperate, and the Allies finally agreed to establish a unified command under the leadership of Marshal Ferdinand Foch—a step they had not been able to decide upon previously. At its height, the German offensive came to within 40 miles of Paris. But the Allies, reinforced in May by several fresh American divisions, fought back furiously. In July, 1918, they counterattacked, breaking through the Siegfried Line and sweeping toward the pre-1914 frontiers.

In September, 1918, the Bulgarians sued for peace, followed in October by the Turks. One by one the ethnic minorities of Austria-Hungary proclaimed their independence, and on November 3 the Austrians capitulated. The next day violent revolts and mutinies engulfed Germany. The Kaiser abdicated and fled to Holland. Finally, on November 11, 1918, a German delegation appeared at Allied headquarters to request an armistice.

The Effects of the War In assessing the consequences of World War I, we must distinguish between short, medium, and long-term effects.

The most immediate and tragic consequence was the loss in lives. There were about 10 million dead and nearly twice that number wounded, many of them permanently mutilated.° A generation of European youth had been wiped out. The war also caused immense material losses, destroying much of the wealth accumulated during the preceding century. The financial losses alone were staggering. To pay for the cost of the war, the belligerents had to spend most of their capital reserves to liquidate a part of their foreign investments. Europe, before 1914 the world's banker, became by 1918 its debtor.

Among the middle-term effects, the most important was the change in the international position of Europe. The war deprived Europe of the world hegemony it had enjoyed throughout the nineteenth century. Gone were the days when a conference of half a dozen European ministers could decide the fate of distant continents. There emerged in the course of the war two vast powers with large populations that threatened to take over leadership in world affairs. The United States came out of the war as the strongest Western state, in no small measure because sales and loans made to the other belligerents had gained it a great deal of wealth. In Eastern Europe the Russian Revolution had brought to power a radical regime that immediately declared war on the entire Western political and economic system. The international position of Europe was further weakened by provisions of the peace treaty (Chapter 26) which, by penalizing the defeated powers, perpetuated the hatreds and suspicions awakened by the war.

In the long run perhaps the most profound consequence of the war was the demoralization of Western man. The senseless destruction of life and property carried on for four long years by nations regarded as the most advanced in the world destroyed confidence in rationalism and progress, two basic tenets of modern Western civilization. In the course of the war there emerged influential intellectual movements that openly preached the irrationality of life. It is symptomatic of the mood of postwar Europe that one of its best sellers was a turgid treatise by Oswald Spengler, a German school teacher, bearing the title *The Decline of the West*. The success of the Bolsheviks, who proclaimed the old order bankrupt and called for a revolution, also owed much to this widespread mood of despair and futility.

The postwar atmosphere was ripe for power-hungry demagogues to exploit the accumulated resentments, especially among the war veterans, by focusing them on concrete objects. Some of them blamed the carnage or defeat on the capitalists, others on the Jews, yet others on the Communists. And since life had become terribly cheap, it became possible to clamor for mass extermination of the classes, races, and political groups allegedly responsible for the war. For if a million men could have been sacrificed for a few square miles of no man's land, why could not a similar number be liquidated to assure a "constructive" aim such as the creation

---

°The known dead (in millions) were as follows: Germany, 1.8; Russia, 1.7; France, 1.4; Austria-Hungary, 1.2; the United Kingdom 1.0; Italy, 0.5. Serbia lost 360,000 men, the Ottoman Empire 325,000, Romania 250,000, and the United States 115,000. The actual fatalities were certainly much greater, and have been estimated as high as 13 million. There were also heavy civilian losses, the worst in Anatolia, where in 1915 the Turks massacred nearly 1 million Armenians as retribution for their alleged treachery.

of a classless or racially pure society? In other words, why not kill off all the bourgeois or all the Jews or all the Communists? Such solutions were not generally acceptable in the immediate postwar years, when people still adhered to the older, pre-1914 values, even if unsurely; but for the first time they were openly proclaimed by some public figures.

The world of 1919 stood stunned and uncertain. Wilfred Owen, the greatest of the English war poets (he was killed one week before the armistice), expressed thus the deep doubts of the generation that had lived through the war:

British soldiers blinded by poison gas during the German spring offensive of 1918 wait for medical aid.

THE END

> After the blast of lightning from the East,
> The flourish of loud clouds, the Chariot Throne;
> After the drums of Time have rolled and ceased,
> And by the bronze west long retreat is blown,
>
> Shall life renew these bodies? Of a truth
> All death will He annul, all tears assuage?—
> Fill the void veins of Life again with youth,
> And wash, with an immortal water, Age?
>
> When I do ask white Age he saith not so:
> "My head hangs weighed with snow."
> And when I hearken to the Earth, she saith:
> "My fiery heart shrinks, aching. It is death.
> My ancient scars shall not be glorified,
> Nor my titanic tears, the sea, be dried."

And French essayist Paul Valéry wrote in 1919: "We, modern civilization, know now that we are mortal. . . . We realize that a civilization is as fragile as a life."

23

❖

The Russian Revolution

H ad it not been for World War I, tsarism might well have muddled through and peacefully yielded to some kind of parliamentary regime. Despite the existence among Russian intellectuals of a strong radical wing, the mood of the country was not revolutionary, and the 1906 constitution, for all its shortcomings, did provide a basis for a genuinely representative system of government. But the war precluded such a peaceful evolution. It subjected Russia to enormous strains that aggravated inherent political weaknesses and social tensions. All the belligerent states of Europe experienced such strains, and by 1917 most of the countries on the periphery of the Continent were near collapse. Russia collapsed first because its government (for reasons discussed below) proved both unable and unwilling to obtain the cooperation of the country in the war effort. By 1916 it became evident even to extreme conservatives that Russia could not remain in the war without major political changes. The events that led to the abdication of Nicholas II and the revolution that followed were thus originally a by-product of World War I—an unexpected consequence of what had begun as efforts to invigorate the pursuit of the war.

The war at first engendered great patriotic fervor. Initially it proved popular with most political groupings: with those of the right because it seemed to promise Russian hegemony in the Balkans, and with those of the center and left because the alliance with the Western democracies seemed to assure the country of a liberal future. The industrial workers showed their dedication to the war effort by suspending strikes. A wave of patriotism sweeping Russia temporarily reconciled tsar and nation.

But the mood did not last. Economic difficulties and the incredible ineptitude of the monarchy in all matters of organization reopened old wounds, and within a year after the outbreak of hostilities, government and society confronted each other once again in a spirit of traditional hostility.

Russia's wartime problems were partly due to inherent economic causes, and partly to mismanagement.

Although an ally of Britain and therefore in theory able to gain access to resources throughout the world, Russia was during the war more effectively blockaded than Germany or Austria. The Central Powers had severed Russia's principal land routes to the West, and by naval control of the Baltic and the Straits had closed its maritime routes as well. The only links with the outside were through distant Vladivostok and the northern port of Archangel, the latter connected with the interior by means of a single railway which was completed only in 1917.

Russia's isolation was not necessarily fatal, for the country had immense internal resources. But poor organization, combined with inadequate transport facilities, prevented their exploitation. When in the autumn of 1914 the military requisitioned railroad cars, Russian cities at once experienced a food shortage,

The Petrograd garrison, a key factor in the Bolshevik seizure of power, is shown demonstrating by the light of bonfires. This water color is by an American-born artist, E. B. Lintott, who was a witness to the revolutionary events in the Russian capital.

notwithstanding abundant harvests in the agricultural provinces. Such shortages became chronic during the war years. The country's industrial plant also never fully geared for the war effort. Of all the belligerent countries, imperial Russia did least to mobilize its home front.

Such mobilization as did take place was carried out by the Duma and the organs of local self-rule. In 1914–1915 these bodies appointed committees that took the initiative in organizing the domestic side of the war effort. They established military hospitals, assisted refugees, and helped retool industry for military needs.

The failure of the imperial regime to cope with the domestic side of the war was only partly due to incompetence. It also had deeper causes of a political nature. Harnessing the nation for war involved a partnership between government and citizenry, and thereby inevitably increased the power of society. Both the court and its bureaucratic-police apparatus feared such a development almost as much as they feared an Austro-German victory. For if the Duma, municipal councils, and *zemstva* (Chapter 15) obtained an active voice in the war effort, they could not be put back in their place once peace had been restored. For this reason, the imperial government hesitated to request or to accept public assistance. It may be said that it waged a war on two fronts: externally against the Central Powers, and internally against contenders for a greater share of political influence.

Nicholas II himself had anything but an autocratic personality. Simple and modest, he was temperamentally better suited for the life of a country squire than for that of an absolute ruler. His real passions were his family and the outdoors. If Nicholas defended autocracy with such stubborness, it was not from an appetite for authority but from an almost mystic sense of duty: he believed himself to have a sacred obligation to maintain and pass on intact to his successor the autocratic system he had inherited from his father. He never really became reconciled to the constitution that had been wrung from him in the turmoil of 1905.

In this attitude he was strongly encouraged by his wife, Alexandra. Born in Germany but raised in England, the empress had a congenital loathing for parliamentary government. She regarded as a conspiracy all attempts by the Duma to assist in running the country and urged her weak husband to oppose them with all his might. Her letters to him were full of exhortations to be strong and masterful—to be another Peter the Great. Because of her superior strength of will and undeviating political outlook, Alexandra gained increasing ascendancy over Nicholas until in the end she took away from him the reins of government.

The imperial couple's political isolation was compounded by a domestic tragedy. After giving birth to four daughters, the empress finally produced an heir to the throne. The boy, however, turned out to be suffering from hemophilia: the slightest cut or bruise caused him painful hemorrhage and threatened death. The despair of the parents knew no bounds. They tried every possible remedy to no avail, and when medicine failed, sought help from quacks and charlatans.

The only person able to stop the tsarevitch's bleedings turned out to be one Grigori, an itinerant preacher and healer. He was by origin an uneducated Siberian peasant, whose dissoluteness had earned him the nickname Rasputin—

A German cartoon on the Duma's attempt to gain power in 1915: the tsar looks up from his grim playthings to exclaim, "How my dolly has changed!"

the "Depraved." How Rasputin succeeded where everyone else had failed is not known, though it has been suggested that he used hypnosis. Because of his healing powers he became a household fixture at the court. The empress, temperamentally inclined to mysticism, came to regard him as a messenger sent by God to save the dynasty from extinction; and Nicholas, who deeply loved his wife, acquiesced in the presence of a man whom he disliked and mistrusted. As his prestige at the court rose, Rasputin indulged in every conceivable vice with impunity. The police could take no measures against him, for the empress treated all reports of his misdeeds as slanders spread by unfriendly politicians.

The critical moment in the relationship between the monarchy and the nation occurred in the first half of September, 1915, when Nicholas made two decisions: to assume personal command over the army, and to prorogue the Duma.

By departing for the front, Nicholas intended to bolster the morale of the troops who that year had suffered great reverses at the hands of the Germans. But another, and perhaps more important reason for his action, was the wish of the empress to remove him from Petrograd in order the better to be able to handle the detested Duma.

The Duma, in fact, grew increasingly discontented with the conduct of the war. In August, 1915, a group of parliamentary leaders ranging from monarchists to moderate socialists formed a coalition known as the "Progressive Bloc." On September 7 this bloc published a program; its principal demand was the introduction of parliamentary government, that is, the appointment of a cabinet responsible not to the tsar but to the Duma. The bloc asserted that only such a government could enjoy the confidence of the country and carry the war to a successful conclusion. To the imperial couple this demand was intolerable. Their reply was to prorogue the Duma. By taking this step, Nicholas deprived himself of the one institution capable of organizing Russia under trying wartime conditions, and virtually assured his downfall.

After September, 1915, political authority devolved into the hands of Alexandra and her sinister companion. They made and unmade ministries, appointing to the highest positions men whose sole qualification for office was their unquestioned loyalty to the imperial couple. In a short time the two disorganized the whole higher civil service.

In 1916 Russia was in deep crisis. The cities, their population grown in two years from 22 to 28 million, suffered acute food shortages. The army still fought with magnificent courage, winning in 1916 its greatest victories. But its morale was being undermined by ugly rumors. It was openly said at the front that the empress and her Prime Minister, Stürmer, were German sympathizers, that Rasputin was the empress's lover, and that all three betrayed military secrets to the enemy. In the Duma, which was reconvened in November, 1916, the leader of the Constitutional Democrats made a speech in which he virtually accused the government of treason. Even the Grand Dukes pleaded with Alexandra to get rid of Rasputin. She, however, remained deaf to all such entreaties, urging Nicholas instead to exile meddling politicians to Siberia.

Finally, in December, 1916, a group of conspirators which included a close relative of the tsar, a member of an aristocratic family, and an ultra-conservative Duma deputy lured Rasputin to a private residence and there murdered

A Russian cartoon, titled "The Russian Ruling House," depicts Nicholas and Alexandra posed puppet-like on the knees of a dominating Rasputin.

A photograph made in March of 1917, when the tsarist government was toppled, shows soldiers of the Petrograd garrison patrolling the streets.

him. The empress never recovered from the shock. To her it meant the end of the dynasty and of Russia.

Neither Nicholas nor his wife reacted vigorously when on March 8, 1917, disturbances broke out in Petrograd. It was as if they had expected heaven's wrath to descend on the country to avenge the murder of Rasputin. The riots started in the breadlines and from there spread to factories and army barracks. The city had at the time a swollen garrison of 170,000 men, many of them raw recruits recently drafted in the villages. They did not want to go to the front and took advantage of the riots to mutiny. Such disturbances were common among belligerent countries in the second half of the war. Indeed, at this very time a large part of the French army also refused to go into battle (Chapter 22). But the difference was that Russia had an inept and discredited government, completely isolated from the nation. Government troops brought in to deal with the rioters at first fired on them but then refused to do so and fraternized instead. Chaos spread unchecked, and before anyone knew what had happened, the mobs were in control of the streets. On March 12 a group of Duma deputies constituting a Provisional Government assumed interim responsibility for public order. Three days later a delegation of deputies journeyed to the army headquarters to inform Nicholas that the well-being of the nation and the successful pursuit of war required his abdication. He complied readily, almost happy to be rid of the heavy burden, and abdicated in favor of his brother, Michael. The following day Michael decided against accepting the crown, abdicating in turn in favor of the Provisional Government. Thus, on March 16, 1917, the Romanov dynasty came to an end, and Russia lost the pivot around which its political life had revolved for centuries.

The March Revolution was received in the cities with unbounded enthusiasm. *The Provisional Government*
The streets filled with joyous crowds. They demonstrated, paraded, or simply
milled around, intoxicated with their new freedom. It was as if a great load
had been lifted, and everyone could at last breathe freely. All hopes seemed
near realization.

The first Provisional Government was a coalition of the same groups that in
1915 had formed the Progressive Bloc. It was committed to the pursuit of the war.
It also had a deep commitment to civil liberties, and immediately after assumption of authority abolished all limitations on individual freedom, including the
restrictions on ethnic or religious minorities. But beyond these measures the
Provisional Government did not feel itself empowered to go. As its name implies,
it regarded itself merely as a transitional authority, something like a trustee of
national sovereignty until the convocation of a Constituent Assembly. This
legalistic attitude determined its subsequent fate.

The Provisional Government faced formidable problems. The country was in
the throes of an acute economic crisis: the treasury stood empty, the ruble continued to fall, transport was disorganized, food deliveries lagged. The administration was also in disarray. Shortly after assuming power, the new government
abolished the detested police, replacing it with an ineffective "peoples' militia."
The imperial civil service dissolved. The result was an administrative vacuum,
which well-meaning but inexperienced intellectuals tried to fill by forming various councils and committees to assume responsibilities for local government.

But beyond economic and political problems lurked even graver ones—problems that may be described as those of excessive expectations. The country had
awaited "democracy" for so long and so fervently that it expected miracles: it was
to cure all ills, resolve all disputes, and make everyone happy. The peasantry
wanted "democracy" to confiscate at once the land belonging to non-peasant
proprietors and distribute it among them. The workers demanded better wages,
shorter hours, and a voice in the running of factories. The national minorities
insisted on immediate autonomy. The radical intellectuals called for far-reaching
reforms leading toward a new social order. The demands of one group instantly
provoked demands of other groups, each fearing to lose out in the great scramble
for goods and rights. What happened was that wants and aspirations repressed
for decades under imperial rule suddenly rose to the surface, and no appeal to
reason, patience, or patriotism could stifle them any longer.

The Provisional Government would have had a difficult task controlling these
pressures even under the best of circumstances. But if it had any chances of
success, it spoiled them by committing two serious mistakes.

The first was to forget that a government must rule. The legalistic argument
that it was only a "provisional" authority meant little to a nation desperate, after
years of imperial mismanagement, for firm authority, the more so because the
government kept on postponing the elections to the Constituent Assembly to
which it intended to transfer sovereign powers. This failure is not surprising. The
leaders of the Provisional Government had a background of parliamentary
opposition which had taught them how to criticize authority but not how to
exercise it. On some occasions, when provincial representatives came to Petrograd
for instructions, they were told by ministers that in a democracy policy decisions

should be made locally, and therefore no instructions from the center would be forthcoming. Such an attitude invited anarchy.

The Provisional Government's second mistake was to remain in the war. It was apparent even in March, 1917, that the country had no strength to carry on. Nevertheless, the government not only decided to continue fighting but undertook to launch a major offensive. In making this disastrous decision, it was motivated by two desires: to secure Constantinople and the Straits, promised Russia by the Allies in secret agreements of March, 1915, and to participate in the general peace settlement. But Allied pressure also played its part. Allied statesmen, their eyes riveted on the Western front, knew little and cared even less about the desperate internal problems confronting the new Russian government. All they wanted was another offensive on the Eastern front to divert German forces. The Provisional Government, dependent as it was on its allies for military and financial support, could not resist these pressures, and promised to throw its last available forces against the external enemy. When later the time came to defend its authority from an internal enemy, the government found it no longer had any forces at its disposal.

From the beginning of its existence, the Provisional Government had to cope with a dangerous rival on the left, the so-called soviets. The first soviets (the word means "council") emerged in the Revolution of 1905 as strike committees of industrial workers. In the course of that first revolution, they had expanded through the admission to their ranks of soldiers and sailors from nearby garrisons and thus became popular organs of political action. Their organization was informal, not unlike that of the American town hall meeting. Socialist intellectuals quickly realized the value of soviets as instruments of mass agitation and bases for revolutionary activity. They joined them, providing leadership and ideologi-

L'ILLUSTRATION

Alexander Kerensky was photographed examining a military map in the fall of 1917, shortly before the Bolsheviks overthrew his Provisional Government.

cal guidance. The Social Democrats in 1905 were especially active in the soviets. They saw them as a means of exerting "socialist" pressure on the "bourgeois" government if and when the middle class succeeded in overthrowing "feudal" tsarism.

The Petrograd Soviet, liquidated in December, 1905, re-emerged on March 12, 1917, the very day the Provisional Government came into being. In its early days it was a committee representing the mutineers of the Petrograd garrison. Its first act was to issue the celebrated "Army Order No. 1," which contributed much to the collapse of discipline in the Russian army. This self-styled decree deprived officers of nearly all their authority and created in every military unit soldier committees endowed, among other rights, with exclusive control over weapons. The order was jubilantly received by the soldiers, who in many regiments proceeded to arrest and even lynch officers accused of "undemocratic" behavior toward them. Like its 1905 predecessor, the new Petrograd Soviet soon broadened its composition and transformed itself into the Soviet of Soldiers' and Workers' Deputies. It claimed the right to issue decrees and to countermand ordinances of the Provisional Government. The Petrograd Soviet, and the soviets that sprang up in the other cities of the empire, enjoyed close links with the troops and industrial workers, and from the very beginning assumed the prerogatives of a shadow government.

Until the fall of 1917 leadership in the soviets was everywhere in the hands of moderate, democratic socialists belonging to the Socialist Revolutionary party or the Menshevik faction of the Social Democrats. Their policy was inconsistent in the extreme and contributed greatly to the breakdown of the Provisional Government. On the one hand, they favored continuation of the war; on the other, they insisted on social reform measures that made the pursuit of the war all but impossible. They could conduct such a contradictory policy because they had no political responsibility and sought none; they were content to use the soviets as organs of pressure on the "bourgeois liberal" government. But the passions they aroused among the masses with their calls for a social revolution soon got out of hand, and in the end the moderate socialists found themselves swept aside by the very forces they had helped to unleash.

The dyarchy between the Provisional Government and the Petrograd Soviet reflected the profound cleavage that had long existed between Russian liberals and radicals. It courted disaster, and responsible statesmen made great efforts to overcome it and to consolidate political authority. In May, 1917, the coalition cabinet resigned, yielding to a ministry of a more radical complexion. Its outstanding figure was a young lawyer, Alexander Kerensky, who assumed the post of Minister of War. As a prominent agrarian socialist, Kerensky enjoyed a following in the Petrograd Soviet. It was hoped that he could bridge the gulf between the two centers of power and rally the country for the forthcoming summer offensive.

However, instead of subsiding, the acute internal crisis that developed in the spring became further aggravated upon the arrival in Petrograd of Lenin, the most radical and most ambitious of the socialist intellectuals.

The Bolsheviks

The novelist Turgenev once divided mankind into two categories: the Hamlets and the Don Quixotes—those who think without acting, and those who act without thinking. Most Russian revolutionaries fell neatly into one of these two groups. There were those who theorized, engaged in hair-splitting arguments, and drafted endless programs, manifestoes, and protests, but in the end did nothing. They loathed bloodshed, and for all their talk about class war or terror always recoiled when it came to employing force. The others detested talk and extolled action. They believed in a direct assault against the existing order, even at the sacrifice of their lives. They carried out terrorist acts with incredible bravery, usually ending their days either on the gallows or in exile.

Lenin belonged to neither category. He esteemed theory but only a theory linked to action. He had no aversion to violence, considering it a natural concomitant of life. Among his intellectual heroes was the Prussian military theorist Clausewitz, the author of the theory of strategic annihilation. But at the same time Lenin rejected useless self-sacrifice. He believed that force should be used with circumspection so as to yield the best results. No politician of his time had a better appreciation of the nuances of power: how to obtain it when weak, and how to augment it when strong.

Lenin was born in 1870 under the name Vladimir Ilich Ulianov in a middle-class family. His father was a school inspector in Simbirsk, the same town where by a remarkable coincidence the father of Kerensky, his future adversary, served as school principal. When he was sixteen his older brother was executed for participation in a plot to assassinate the tsar. After completing school, Vladimir Ilich went on to study law at the University of Kazan. There, like many students of his time, he became involved in political activity, joining a terrorist organization and taking part in a mass student protest, for which he was expelled. But he managed later on to pass examinations at the University of St. Petersburg where in 1891 he received his law degree.

During Lenin's university days Marxism became a serious intellectual force in Russia. Lenin became passionately converted to it. He accepted the theories of Marx and Engels literally, without doubts or reservations, in a spirit nothing short of fanatical—with greater dedication than Marx himself, who frequently asserted his theories were a method, not a dogma. He had a religious, ascetic disposition, incapable of tolerating either dissent or weakness. A century or two earlier he might well have been the leader of some extreme fundamentalist sect. Once he had grasped the historic mission of the proletariat as seen by Marx, he fully identified himself with it, and came to believe with an utterly sincere conviction that he embodied its spirit. Anyone who opposed him was by definition an enemy of the working class, a scoundrel whose life had no value.

In St. Petersburg Lenin joined an illegal circle of Social Democratic propagandists, for which in 1895 he was arrested. The years 1897–1900 he spent in rather comfortable exile in Siberia, studying and writing for legal Marxist journals. When he regained his freedom, he found the Social Democratic movement in disarray. The revisionist theories of Eduard Bernstein (Chapter 19) had persuaded many socialists to reject social revolution in favor of peaceful evolution. Other socialists, impressed by the rise of trade-unionism, decided to confine themselves to helping workers improve their economic condition. Such views revolted Lenin. He saw in them a betrayal of Marxism, an opportunistic surrender to the bourgeoisie. In 1900–1901 he experienced a profound spiritual crisis.

When he emerged from it, his mind was made up: he decided that neither the peasantry, nor the working class, nor the intelligentsia could be depended on to carry on a revolution, and that it was necessary to found a small, tightly organized, fully independent party of professional revolutionaries.

In 1902 Lenin brought out in Germany, where he had temporarily settled, his most important theoretical work, *What Is to Be Done?*, outlining the tenets of what was to become Bolshevism. The working class of itself, Lenin maintained, was not capable of developing a proletarian class consciousness or of maintaining revolutionary zeal. Of itself, it could not progress beyond trade-unionism, that is, the striving for peaceful economic self-improvement. The ideal of the socialist revolution had to be carried to the workers from the outside, from a body of professional, full-time revolutionaries. Like priests of some religious order, the socialist intellectuals had to guard the true faith.

In 1903 the Russian Marxists assembled in London to launch a Russian Social Democratic Labor party. In the course of debating its statutes, Lenin insisted that the party was to be a highly centralized and disciplined body, open only to persons prepared to place themselves without reservation at the disposal of its Central Committee. Many of the other participants rejected this concept as élitist and undemocratic; they preferred a party organized on another model, with easy admission and autonomy of local cells. In the complicated struggle that ensued, Lenin carried the majority and formed a faction that called itself "Bolshevik" (from the word *bol'she* meaning "more"—hence the "Majority"). Its opponents became known as "Mensheviks" (from *men'she* or "less"—hence the "Minority"). Thus, from the moment of its foundation the Russian Social Democratic organization split into two hostile wings, one centralist and the other democratic. Lenin's majority did not long survive the London congress, but with characteristic political acumen he retained the name "Bolshevik" as psychologically more attractive. His following consisted mostly of middle-brows, who admired him and accepted his leadership without question. The Mensheviks, on the other hand, claimed the major theoretical lights of Russian Marxism, and enjoyed closer ties with the labor movement. Lenin ran his organization with a strong hand. He vehemently attacked his opponents, including one-time associates, accusing them of opportunism, treachery, corruption, and all other manner of sin.

When the war broke out, Lenin joined a small international band of socialists who opposed the fighting and urged the soldiers of all countries to transform the war between nations into a war between classes. He spent the war years in Switzerland, impoverished and isolated. Before 1914 his activities had been financed by a few eccentric millionaires and by bands of Bolshevik youths who carried out daring holdups of Russian banks. Now these sources were dried up, and Lenin had to search desperately for literary jobs to support himself and his wife. He cut a rather pathetic figure as he buttonholed Russian travelers passing through Zurich to fulminate against the bourgeoisie and the Second International (Chapter 19), for which he had developed a consuming hatred. He had little hope of seeing a socialist revolution in his lifetime.

The German authorities had their eye on émigrés like Lenin, considering them potentially useful in sowing defeatism among Russian troops. In 1915, on the initiative of one Parvus, a Russian renegade socialist in their service, they established contact with Lenin, though apparently without any concrete results. (It may be mentioned, in passing, that the Germans pioneered in the use of political propaganda and spent much money and energy in efforts to undermine the morale of their various enemies.)

When the March Revolution toppled the imperial regime, Lenin was impatient to return to Russia. At the urging of Parvus the German authorities gave permission for a special sealed train, carrying Lenin and a number of other Russian revolutionaries, to cross Germany on their way to neutral Sweden. Their intention was to let loose in Russia the most outspoken opponents of Russia's participation in the war, and thereby to accelerate the demoralization of the Russian armies.

Lenin reached Petrograd via Stockholm in mid-April, and at once attacked the Provisional Government. He demanded the transfer of all power to the soviets,

"There is no other man," an observer remarked of Lenin, "who is absorbed by the revolution for twenty-four hours a day, who has no thoughts but the thoughts of the revolution. . . ."

the nationalization of land, the abolition of the army and the civil service, and the cessation of hostilities. In effect, he wanted nothing less than an immediate socialist revolution. Other socialists, including most of his own Bolshevik followers, were aghast at the thought of cutting short the "bourgeois" stage of the revolution. But Lenin was not to be restrained by theory. He realized instinctively that the Provisional Government was foundering, that no one wanted political responsibility, and that the country would soon be ripe for a *coup d'état*. When pressed for a theoretical justification, he could fall back on the concept of "permanent revolution" formulated before the war by Parvus and Leon Trotsky, according to which the bourgeois revolution immediately, without a halt, would deepen into a socialist revolution. In any other country at war, Lenin's public pronouncements would have landed him in jail or before a firing squad. In France that same month the government executed 23 persons for propagating defeatism and inciting mutinies. But in Russia, in its noonday of democracy, any restraints on speech were regarded as an intolerable violation of human liberties, and Lenin was allowed to speak and publish freely.

Lenin's ultimate aims—the disorganization of the army, subversion of the Provisional Government, and seizure of power—required money. This he now obtained from the Germans. The German high command was so delighted with Lenin's relentless criticisms of Russia's war effort that it placed at Parvus's disposal considerable sums for transfer to him. In April Parvus turned over to Lenin's representative in Stockholm 5 million marks. With this and subsequent subsidies from the same source, Lenin financed the party newspaper *Pravda*, flooded the trenches with antiwar propaganda, and built up a Bolshevik paramilitary force in the form of Red Guard units composed of workers.°

In mid-July, after the failure of the great military offensive, rioting troops demonstrated in the streets of Petrograd, demanding the transfer of power to the soviets. Even though the Bolshevik party did not organize these disturbances (it judged its forces too weak as yet for a seizure of power), the Provisional Government accused it of complicity and proceeded to arrest those Bolshevik leaders it could lay its hands on. Lenin, however, escaped in disguise and concealed himself in Finland.

By July Russia for all practical purposes had ceased to have a government. The cabinet having resigned, it took most of the month to replace it. The new Prime Minister was Kerensky, a dedicated democrat and excellent orator, but a man short on political skill. Despite the fiasco of the July offensive, he kept on exhorting the troops to fight in the unrealistic hope that victories at the front would somehow reunite the nation and quell social conflicts. Rather than address himself to urgent domestic issues, he spent his time at army headquarters. Kerensky satisfied no one: conservative opinion condemned him for tolerating anarchism, while the left taunted him as a servant of the international bourgeoisie.

At this time (August, 1917) there began to take shape to the right of the government a loose coalition of liberal and conservative elements. It included army officers disgusted with the destruction of discipline among the troops, businessmen afraid of economic collapse, and various political figures. These elements had no formal program or organization. What bound them together was alarm over the rapid disintegration of political and social institutions and the conviction that unless this process was checked, Russia faced civil war. They accepted the March Revolution, in the making of which they had played a decisive role, but they felt that at this point the establishment of order was more important than further extensions of freedom or equality.

The Bolshevik Seizure of Power

°That Lenin received money from the Germans had been suspected as early as 1917, but proof of the fact became available only after World War II, with the capture by the Allies of the archives of the German Ministry of Foreign Affairs.

General Lavr Kornilov, appointed and then dismissed as head of the army by the Provisional Government.

In countries with unstable government it is common for the armed forces to assume political responsibility. Unlike political parties, armies by their very structure require an effective chain of command that enables them to carry out decisions. In late summer of 1917, therefore, those who sought a way out of the chaos instinctively turned to the generals, around whom there now emerged a movement of national restoration. Its great hope was the colorful Cossack General Lavr Kornilov, Kerensky's new Commander in Chief. Like some other professional generals of the Imperial Army, Kornilov came of peasant stock, and mistrusted monarchs and aristocrats. But he disliked the socialists even more. He expressed contempt for the Provisional Government, which he accused of yielding to anarchist pressures, and talked openly of leading troops on Petrograd to restore order.

The Russian left was much disturbed by this development. Well versed in the history of the French Revolution, it tended to interpret the events of 1917 in the light of those of the 1790s. Radical intellectuals knew that at a certain point a revolution faced the danger of a right-wing reaction. When Kornilov began to menace the Provisional Government, the leadership of the Petrograd Soviet decided to back Kerensky to resist the "danger from the right" and to prevent a Russian 18 Brumaire. The "danger from the left," that is, from Lenin and the Bolsheviks, was considered at this point to be the lesser of the two evils. With the concurrence of Menshevik and Socialist Revolutionary leaders, Bolsheviks were admitted to the military formations established by the Petrograd Soviet to defend the city against Kornilov. Thus unexpectedly Lenin's party, nearly shattered in July, re-emerged in the center of events.

Kerensky's difficulties with the army came to a head in the second week of September. Convinced that Kornilov was plotting a *coup d'état,* Kerensky dismissed him from the post of Commander in Chief and himself assumed supreme civil and military powers. Kornilov refused to obey the dismissal order. There ensued complicated political maneuvers, some of which remain obscure to this day. In any event, on September 9, Kerensky openly broke with Kornilov, and Kornilov issued an emotional appeal announcing his intention of saving Russia from the Germans and their agents among the radicals. Simultaneously he dispatched troops toward Petrograd. But the Petrograd Soviet saw to it that the transport and communications of the advancing rebels were disorganized. Kornilov's units simply melted away as they approached the capital.

After the Kornilov affair the position of the Provisional Government became hopeless. By allying himself with the Petrograd Soviet against Kornilov, Kerensky had alienated a large part of his officer corps, without thereby gaining authority in the Soviet. Quite the contrary. The Soviet, regarding itself as the savior of the country from a "counterrevolutionary" plot, was less than ever disposed to obey the government. From early September onward the cabinet did not even hold meetings, all power being vested in Kerensky. To make matters worse, a violent rebellion broke out in the countryside, where peasants, abetted by military deserters, began to burn estates and seize land.

At the height of the Kornilov crisis the Provisional Government had released from jail the Bolshevik leaders arrested after the July disturbances, in order to create a common "democratic front" against the "Bonapartist" threat. Among the Bolsheviks who profited from the amnesty was Leon Trotsky. (Lenin, charged by the Provisional Government with being a German agent, had to remain in hiding.) An outstanding orator and publicist, Trotsky had had an irregular political past, sometimes allying himself with the Mensheviks, sometimes with the Bolsheviks, but generally pursuing an independent policy. In 1905 he had been a leading figure in the first Petrograd Soviet. Afterward, while in exile, part of which he had spent in the United States, he published penetrating essays on such subjects as the nature of the future revolution and the role in it of the soviets. In July, 1917, Trotsky cast his lot with Lenin. The two men complemented each other admirably. Lenin had a narrow intelligence and an unprepossessing exterior but a tremendous will power and a genius for organization. Trotsky, by contrast, had a brilliant mind and a charismatic personality, but he sorely lacked perseverance and patience.

While Lenin remained in his Finnish hideout, Trotsky assumed leadership of the Bolshevik cause. In this he was greatly aided by winning the election to the chairmanship of the Petrograd Soviet on October 3. He at once employed his energies to push the Soviet toward a decisive conflict with the Provisional Government.

On October 23 the Central Committee of the Bolshevik faction held a clandestine conference in Petrograd, attended by Lenin, to discuss the feasibility of a power seizure. Several participants were opposed to this proposal. They pointed to reports from party cells indicating poor morale and organization and predicted that a coup would fail and destroy the party. They preferred to wait until the Bolsheviks had obtained a solid majority in most of the country's soviets. Lenin, on the other hand, insisted on immediate action. He felt that the government was at its lowest ebb and that the Bolsheviks, enjoying majorities in the Petrograd and Moscow soviets and having at their command a force of Red Guards, were strong enough to strike and succeed. After acrimonious discussions Lenin's view prevailed. The committee resolved to prepare for the coup, without fixing the strategy or setting the date. Since Lenin had to remain in concealment, Trotsky took charge of the preparations.

Trotsky was certain it would be disastrous to carry out a power seizure in the name of the Bolshevik party. The country simply would not have tolerated any one party assuming political power. Even the most pro-Bolshevik workers and soldiers felt loyalty not to the party as such, but to the soviets, which the Bolsheviks had proclaimed as the country's legitimate authority. For this reason, a *coup d'état* had to be disguised as an assumption of authority by the soviets, or, more specifically, by the Second All-Russian Congress of Soviets, scheduled to assemble in Petrograd at the beginning of November. Until then, Trotsky's strategy was to incite the Petrograd Soviet (many members of which belonged to other socialist parties) against the government and at the same time surreptitiously to create a suitable power apparatus.

Trotsky implemented his plan superbly well. From the rostrum of the Soviet he kept on taunting the government, accusing it, among other things, of conniving with Kornilov and the Germans. He claimed that Kerensky, in order to rid himself of revolutionary Petrograd, had secretly arranged its surrender to the German armies. This treacherous plot had to be thwarted. Trotsky persuaded the Soviet to veto a government order sending troops from Petrograd to the front, and to constitute, under his chairmanship, a Military-Revolutionary Committee. Ostensibly, the committee's task was to organize the defense of the capital against the alleged government-inspired German occupation. In fact, it was intended to serve as the instrument through which the Bolsheviks, acting in the name of the Soviet, were to secure control of the military garrison and arsenals of Petrograd. It mattered little that Trotsky's charges were sheer inventions. His rhetoric held crowds spellbound and enabled him to manipulate them at will. Here is Nikolai Sukhanov's eyewitness account of Trotsky's effect on the mob on the eve of the Bolshevik power seizure:

> The mood of the audience of over three thousand, filling the hall, was definitely one of excitement; their hush indicated expectation. The public, of course, consisted mainly of soldiers, though it had not a few typical petty bourgeois figures, male and female. The ovation given Trotsky seemed to have been cut short, from curiosity and impatience: what was he going to say? Trotsky at once began to heat up the atmosphere with his skill and brilliance. I recall that he depicted for a long time and with extraordinary force the difficult . . . picture of suffering in the trenches. Through my mind flashed thoughts about the unavoidable contradictions between the parts of this rhetorical whole. But Trotsky knew what he was doing. The essential thing was the *mood*. The political conclusions had been familiar for a long time. . . . Soviet power [Trotsky said] was destined not only to put an end to the suffering in the trenches. It would provide land and stop internal disorder. Once again resounded the old recipes against hunger: how the soldiers, sailors, and working girls would requisition the bread from the propertied, and send it free of charge to the front. . . . But on this decisive "Day of the Petrograd Soviet" Trotsky went further:
>
> "The Soviet government will give everything the country has to the poor and to the soldiers at the front. You, bourgeois, own two coats? give one to the soldier, freezing in the trenches. You have warm boots? stay at home. Your boots are needed by a worker. . . ."
>
> The mood around me verged on ecstasy. It seemed the mob would at any moment, spontaneously and unasked, burst into some kind of religious hymn. Trotsky formulated some short general resolution or proclaimed some general formula, on the order of: "We will defend the cause of the workers and peasants to the last drop of blood."
>
> Who is in favor? The crowd of thousands raised its hands like one man. I saw the uplifted hands and burning eyes of men, women, adolescents, workers, soldiers, peasants, and typical petty bourgeois figures. . . . [They] agreed. [They] vowed. . . . I watched this truly grandiose spectacle with an unusually heavy heart.

Lenin, cut off in his hideout from day-to-day developments, burned with impatience. He feared that unless the Bolsheviks acted quickly, the military would overthrow the Provincial Government, restore order, and forever cut the ground from under his party. He wanted the Central Committee to start an insurrection at once, without bothering to wait for the Congress of Soviets. "The

Leon Trotsky, architect of the Bolshevik coup d'état, was photographed at his Red Army headquarters in 1919.

people [i.e., the Bolsheviks] have a right and a duty to decide such questions not by voting but by force," he wrote to the Central Committee. But Trotsky procrastinated, keeping opponents in and out of the Soviet in a state of constant suspense: one day he would hint that insurrection was near at hand, the next he would deny that any insurrection was intended. The resultant confusion was so great that neither the Provisional Government nor the groups in the soviets opposed to a coup took preventive measures. Trotsky's handling of the situation provided a model subsequently imitated by many dictators, and especially by Hitler in his foreign policy dealings. The technique of charging the opponent with one's own intentions and alternating between threats and promises became a stock in trade of modern totalitarian leaders.

On November 6—one day before the opening of the Congress of Soviets—the Military-Revolutionary Committee issued an appeal to the population of Petrograd. It claimed that the followers of Kornilov were assembling forces with which to suppress the Congress and to prevent the convocation of the Constituent Assembly. In order to meet this alleged threat it took upon itself the responsibility of defending the "revolutionary order." This fabricated accusation provided the pretext for the Bolshevik insurrection. That night detachments of the Military-Revolutionary Committee and the Red Guard (both under Bolshevik control) took over key buildings in Petrograd and arrested the ministers of the Provisional Government (Kerensky, however, eluded them and escaped). In contrast to the days of March, 1917, there was virtually no bloodshed, except at the Winter

Lintott's water color shows the Red Guard storming loyalists in the Winter Palace in Petrograd, the only violence in the Bolshevik take-over.

Palace, where a small body of loyalist troops held out until the following day.

In the early hours of November 7 Lenin emerged from his hideout, and together with Trotsky made a triumphal appearance at the Congress of Soviets. The Congress, representing about half of the country's soviets, approved of a Bolshevik resolution proclaiming the passage of all power to the soviets. The resolution said nothing about the Bolshevik party or its role in the new system: what that was emerged only later. At the time, the vast majority of the delegates, including many leading Bolsheviks, had no idea that Lenin intended a one-party dictatorship and thought they were merely formalizing the dissolution of the Provisional Government.

The leaders of the Menshevik and Socialist Revolutionary parties, however, sensed what lay behind the passing of "all power" to the soviets. Denouncing the resolution as a fraud perpetrated by the Bolsheviks to subvert democracy, they walked out of the Congress, accompanied by catcalls, over which could be heard Trotsky's taunt, "Into the dustbin of history!"

Lenin took charge of the government in November of 1917 with the same assurance Napoleon had shown in November of 1799. His problem was similar: how to restore stability to a completely disorganized society. But the conditions were different, and so were the means. Where Napoleon achieved stability by sanctifying property and reviving old institutions, Lenin did so by destroying property and creating a completely new institutional framework.

Civil War

In the first months Lenin gained the appearance of being master of the situation by identifying himself with those processes over which he had no control: anarchy on the land and in the factories, and mass desertions in the army. Rather than try immediately to establish order, he legitimized, as it were, disorder. On November 8, 1917, he signed a decree requisitioning without compensation landed properties belonging to the crown, church, monasteries, and wealthy landlords, for immediate distribution to the peasants. This decree changed nothing: it merely sanctioned the existing situation, for peasants were seizing estates anyway. Later that month Lenin authorized another *fait accompli*, namely worker control over industries. Both these measures were taken bodily from the anarchist program, but this did not trouble Lenin, who viewed them merely as stop-gap remedies, to be undone once he was more firmly established in power.

Similar considerations induced Lenin to sign a humiliating peace treaty. The Germans posed stiff demands: they wanted, among other things, Finland, Poland, the Baltic Provinces, and the Ukraine—regions containing over one-quarter of Russia's population and much of its wealth. Lenin's colleagues objected to making such concessions, but Lenin saw no choice: Russia had no army left to continue the war, and any attempt to recruit a new one would topple his government. Peace at any cost was the price of political survival. After bitter debates that threatened to split the party, Lenin won, and in March, 1918, the Russians signed at Brest Litovsk a peace treaty conceding the Central Powers their demands.

Where Lenin was not willing to make any concessions whatever was on the monopoly of political power. Although all through 1917 he had clamored for a Constituent Assembly and had publicly stated his willingness to accept the voters' verdict, even if unfavorable to his party, when the occasion presented itself he did not keep his word. The elections to the Consituent Assembly held late in 1917 gave a majority to the Socialist Revolutionaries. The Bolshevik party obtained only one-quarter of the seats. Lenin allowed the Assembly to convene and sit for one day and then ordered units of soldiers and sailors to disperse it (January 18, 1918).

Having secured in early 1918 a modicum of internal authority, Lenin could now concentrate on the main external threat to his regime, the so-called White movement.

After the Bolsheviks had seized power, a number of generals made their way south, to the region inhabited by the well-to-do and conservative Don Cossacks. There in January, 1918, they formed a volunteer army to "oppose the impending anarchy and German-Bolshevik invasion." The initial force was small, around 3,500 men, mostly commissioned and noncommissioned officers. It had no money and found it difficult to recruit volunteers in a nation heartily sick of war. But gradually its numbers grew, and by the end of 1918 the Whites had at their command an effective fighting force. It consisted of three principal armies: one in the south, under General Denikin; another in the Urals, under Admiral Kolchak; and a third west of Petrograd, under General Iudenich.

The White movement is often described as "counterrevolutionary," but the label is inappropriate. Unlike France in the 1790s, Russia had no significant movement for the restoration of the monarchy. The White leaders in all theaters of war pledged themselves to reconvene the Constituent Assembly and to respect the government chosen by a popular vote. They entrusted the political management of their forces to Constitutional Democrats or Socialist Revolutionaries, members of parties wholly committed to the democratic achievements of the March Revolution. On the other hand, it is true that the actual temper of the Whites was more conservative than their official pronouncements indicated. The officers, shocked by the tragedy that had befallen their country, sought scapegoats, and often found them in liberals and socialists, whom they treated as identical and sometimes refused to distinguish from the Bolsheviks. Had they won the Civil War they almost certainly would have established, at least temporarily, a military dictatorship of some sort.

To meet the White danger, the Bolsheviks formed the Red Army in the summer of 1918. Its organization was Trotsky's second great contribution to the Bolshevik cause. The original military force at Bolshevik disposal was an undisciplined rabble, mainly occupied with looting and extortion. Such troops could not hope to defeat the professional soldiers of the Whites. In April, 1918, Trotsky therefore suggested founding a regular armed force, based on compulsory conscription and staffed by ex-tsarist officers. Lenin and the other Bolshevik leaders received this proposal skeptically, fearing that an army might turn around and overthrow their government; but in the end, Trotsky's view prevailed. In the summer of 1918 decrees were issued introducing compulsory military service for all members of the working class. At the same time former imperial officers were ordered to accept commissions in the Red Army or face confinement in a concentration camp and the detention of their families as hostages. By the end of the year the Red Army had 800,000 men under arms, including nearly 50,000 ex-imperial officers. Throughout the Civil War, the command of the Red Army was entrusted to these officers, but they were subjected to close supervision by "military commissars" drawn from the ranks of loyal Bolsheviks. The soldier committees introduced in 1917 by Army Order No. 1 were abolished, and strict discipline, with the death penalty, was restored. In November, 1918, the government formed a Council of Workers' and Peasants' Defense to direct the entire war effort. Trotsky, as Commissar of War, had the responsibility over military operations, but he did not interfere with strategy, preferring to leave this matter to specialists.

The war was fought with incredible savagery. There was no stable front, and some areas changed hands dozens of times, each change being followed by bloody repressions. Murder of prisoners and hostages, torture, and mutilation were daily occurrences. Particularly vicious were the so-called "Green" armies, composed of anarchistic peasants who rejected alike the Reds and Whites, and murdered with impunity anyone they disliked, especially urban inhabitants.

A controversial aspect of the Civil War was the so-called Allied intervention. In the summer of 1918 contingents of Allied troops, largely British and Japanese, landed respectively in Archangel and Vladivostok. Their primary purpose was to safeguard the enormous stores of war supplies—over 1 million tons—that had been dispatched by the Allies in 1916–1917 to the Russian armies but for lack of transport had remained stockpiled in the ports of entry. Their secondary purpose was to reactivate the Eastern front against the Central Powers. By the end of 1918 the total Allied contingent in Russia was about 10,000 to 15,000 strong. Since such a force could not seriously undertake military operations against the Central Powers, the Allies extended support to the Whites, who were committed to the pursuit of the war. This support at first took the form of financial assistance, resembling that extended by the Germans to the Bolsheviks.

After the signing of the armistice in November, 1918, there was no longer any military reason for keeping troops in Russia, but there was an economic one. In February, 1918, the Soviet government had declared that it would not honor debts incurred by preceding Russian governments. At the same time it had

An incident photographed during the Civil War: after lynching Bolshevik captives, White troops parade villagers past the corpses as a warning against aiding the Communists.

CHARLES PHELPS CUSHING, NEW YORK

An American soldier at a snowy outpost near Archangel in north Russia during the winter of 1918–1919. The United States contributed 5,000 men to the Allied intervention force, of which some 2,000 became casualties.

expropriated major industries and all banks, in which Western investors had a large interest. These measures represented a serious loss to Western countries, already impoverished by the war. Since the Whites promised both to respect Russia's foreign obligations and to compensate owners of confiscated properties, in 1919 the Allies offered them military assistance. It would be tempting to believe that in so doing they were motivated by a desire to suppress Bolshevism. But there is no evidence to show that they, in fact, thought of Bolshevism as a long-term danger. The Allied leaders, especially Lloyd George and President Wilson, were ill informed about events in Russia and tended not to take seriously the Bolshevik government with its amateurish leadership and unorthodox policies. Among influential Western statesmen, Churchill alone urged a vigorous military intervention to stamp out Bolshevism; but in this he had no more success than he was to have in the 1930s with his pleas for a firm stand against the Nazis. While helping the Whites, both France and England had their ears tuned to Moscow for any signs of willingness to make financial compensation for loans and investments. The help extended to the Whites was too small and too sporadic to assure a White victory, but just sufficient to enable the Bolsheviks to rally much Russian national sentiment behind their cause. With the exception of a few minor engagements, more accidental than intentional, the Allied troops did not fight the Red Army. The Civil War was throughout a fratricidal struggle between Russians.

The Whites came nearest to success in October, 1919, when they launched a four-pronged offensive against Moscow and Petrograd. Denikin's army approached to within 250 miles of Moscow, and Iudenich's troops penetrated the suburbs of Petrograd. But later that month, when the Red Army counterattacked, the overextended White forces simply disintegrated. In the spring of 1920 the Whites were left holding only the Crimea, from which they were expelled in November of that year. This action ended the Civil War.

In the course of the war the Bolsheviks reconquered some of the borderlands that had proclaimed their independence during the Revolution. They had no success along the Western frontier, where direct Allied support helped protect the political integrity of Finland, Poland, Lithuania, Latvia, and Estonia. But they overcame local resistance of the nationalists in Belorussia and the Ukraine, and in 1919 transformed them into Soviet republics. In 1920 the Red Army conquered Armenia and Azerbaijan and in 1921, after bitter fighting, Georgia. These three areas were forcefully fused into a Transcaucasian Soviet Republic.

The victory of the Reds over the Whites was not due to their superior social program or greater appeal to the masses. Programs counted for little in those years, nor did the masses show greater liking for the Bolsheviks than for their opponents. According to Soviet statistics, over 2.5 million desertions took place in the Red Army during the war. The Bolshevik victory can be better explained by their superior understanding of modern warfare. The White leaders were essentially old-fashioned staff officers who viewed combat in strictly operational terms and had little patience with politics. The Bolsheviks, on the contrary, waged "total war," one that fused military operations with economic and psychological (propagandistic) activities. They also enjoyed the advantage of a unified command and of a centralized transport system.

While the Civil War was in progress Lenin instituted in Russia a one-party dictatorship—an entirely new political system that subjected the whole citizenry to the authoritarianism previously established within the Bolshevik party and that provided a model for all subsequent totalitarian regimes.

Constitutionally, the new state was a republic of soviets. The structure and operating procedure of the soviets was normalized, and they received constitutional status as organs expressing the will of the working population. The people's will, theoretically, filtered upward: from the numerous local soviets of workers' and peasants' deputies, through provincial congresses of soviets, to the country's highest legislative organ, the All-Russian Congress of Soviets. The latter appointed a cabinet called the Council of Peoples' Commissars. This government structure existed in the Russian Soviet Republic, as well as in the three borderland republics of Belorussia, Ukraine, and Transcaucasia. In 1924 the four were fused in a single Union of Soviet Socialist Republics.

The idea of a state composed of soviets was anarchist in inspiration. The Bolsheviks adopted it partly because of the role that the Congress of Soviets had accidentally played in their power seizure, and partly because it provided a convenient democratic façade for their profoundly undemocratic manner of government.

From November 7, 1917, onward, the true source of sovereignty resided in the Bolshevik party, or, as it became known in 1918, the Communist party. The party was organized in an authoritarian fashion, from the top downward. At the top stood the self-appointed and self-perpetuating Central Committee. The Central Committee made decisions by majority vote, but Lenin always had his way because a mere threat of resignation brought his recalcitrant colleagues into line. The orders of the committee were binding on the lower organs of the party, including the Communist parties of Belorussia, the Ukraine, and Transcaucasia. In fact, they were also binding on all of the country's institutions without exception. The party viewed itself as the "vanguard of the proletariat," that is, the embodiment of the aspirations and interests of the most advanced social class, the class destined to abolish forever all classes. It was subject to no legal restraints. Any opposition to it, whether from within or without, even that coming from the working class itself, was by definition counterrevolutionary. In its capacity as the "vanguard of the proletariat," the party reserved for itself exclusive control over the organs of the state. The composition of the Central Committee and the Council of Peoples' Commissars was virtually identical, Lenin chairing both. Key positions in all soviets, from the lowest to the highest, had to be occupied by Communists. In other words, the whole *state* apparatus built around the soviets was merely a casing that concealed the operations of the true power mechanism vested in the *party* apparatus.

To assure its monopoly of political power, the party had to eliminate competitors. This process makes melancholy reading, less shocking to us than it was to contemporaries. One by one, political opposition was suppressed. As early as December, 1917, political parties were deprived of an opportunity to make themselves heard by a law that suspended (with two exceptions) all non-Bolshevik newspapers. Next, the rival parties were liquidated. The first to be outlawed was the liberal Constitutional Democratic party (December, 1917). The Socialist Revolutionaries and Mensheviks were harassed but tolerated for a while, because their following among peasants and workers made it dangerous to take open action against them. But with the end of the Civil War, they too were subjected to persecution. In 1922 prominent Mensheviks and Socialist Revolutionaries were arrested or expelled from the country. A sham trial of Socialist Revolutionaries held in the summer of 1922 condemned twelve of the party's leaders to death—a sentence without parallel in the entire history of imperial Russia. The liquidation of parties was accompanied by destruction of private and civic organizations. By the time the process was completed in the early 1930s, there was no organization of any kind left in Russia that was not either closely supervised or directly run by the Communist party. Society was atomized into its individual components, and unable to resist pressures from above.

The basis of the party's power was economic. Its decrees had force because the party acquired control over all the capital and all the productive resources of the country—a control that enabled the party to decide who should eat and how much, who should wear a warm coat, and who should have a roof over his head. This fusion of political monopoly with economic monopoly, inaugurated by the Bolsheviks, is a distinguishing feature of all modern totalitarianism.

The economic policy pursued between 1918 and 1920 is known as "War Communism." In some of its techniques it was influenced by the domestic policies of the Germans during World War I and represented a belated mobilization of the Russian home front. But it went much further. Its ultimate purpose was not so much economic as political: to undercut the economic basis for any resistance to the Communist party. Indeed, as we shall see (Chapter 27), War Communism proved to be an unmitigated economic disaster, lowering productivity below anything Russia had known before or since. Politically, however, it was eminently successful.

War Communism was an attempt to centralize in the hands of the party the country's entire productive and distributive processes. Its policies may be grouped under five headings:

1) *Land.* The peasants, having seized the available land, were loath to supply produce to the cities and army in exchange for worthless paper money. To extract the produce from them, the government in the summer of 1918 undertook forceful requisitions. The Commissariat of Food acquired the exclusive right to stock and distribute foodstuffs and to confiscate them wherever found. These confiscations were usually carried out by armed detachments, originating in the cities or the army, that in effect robbed the peasantry of produce. In November, 1918, all land was nationalized.

2) *Industry.* A decree of June, 1918, revoked the earlier anarchist law authorizing worker control, and nationalized, without compensation, a great part of the industrial and mining establishments. Nationalizations continued during the next two years, so that by 1920 nearly the entire industrial plant of the country was in the hands of the party. It was administered by a Supreme Council of National Economy.

3) *Banking and trade.* In December, 1917, private banks were closed and their resources taken over by the State Bank. In April and November, 1918, the right to private foreign and internal trade, respectively, was abolished; commerce became

a state monopoly. Attempts were also made to replace money by barter and wages in kind.

4) *Labor.* Emulating the wartime National Service Act of Germany, the Communists introduced compulsory labor: everyone was required to work. Strikes were outlawed. Workers and peasants were conscripted to perform service and in 1920 were occasionally organized into "labor armies." A decree of July, 1918, singled out members of the "bourgeoisie" for the obligation to perform hard and menial physical work.

5) *Expropriations.* Monastic and church properties, as well as properties of the crown, were confiscated. A law issued in May, 1918, abolished inheritance and appropriated for the state properties of deceased citizens. Individual decrees expropriated many private possessions, including those of a "nonproductive" kind, such as jewelry and art collections.

It would be a great mistake to think that Russians accepted these political and economic repressions with equanimity. They resisted, and did so more fiercely than any other people subsequently subjected to totalitarian controls. Terrorism revived: Socialist Revolutionary gunmen killed individual Communists and gravely wounded Lenin himself. The peasantry fought so energetically against food requisitions that in 1920 almost half the Red Army had to be assigned the task of suppressing agrarian rebellions. In 1920–1921 serious dissensions developed within the Communist party among members dissatisfied with the muzzling of freedom. The climax of the resistance came in March, 1921, when the garrison of the Kronstadt naval base near Petrograd—one of the citadels of Bolshevism in 1917—revolted against the Communist dictatorship and proclaimed a "Third Revolution" in the name of true soviet democracy.

Lenin responded to this resistance with pitiless terror. Neither he nor Trotsky delighted in blood; but their ideal was to remake man and society, and to achieve

The expropriation of church treasures at bayonet point by the Red Army in Petrograd in 1922, viewed unsympathetically by a Russian artist.

it they felt compelled to remove enemies as swiftly and coldly as a surgeon removes morbid tissue. To Lenin all politics was a battle in which one either destroyed one's opponent or perished at his hands.

In the first ten months of Bolshevik rule repression was sporadic. But in September, 1918, after an assassin had shot the chief of the Petrograd secret police, Lenin proclaimed the inauguration of a systematic "Red Terror." This meant in practice giving state security organs the unlimited right to search, arrest, imprison, torture, and execute without trial persons accused of a broad range of activities deemed "counterrevolutionary." The weapon of Red Terror was the Extraordinary Committee for the Suppression of the Counter-revolution, or Cheka, established in December, 1917. Its head was Felix Dzerzhinskii, the son of a Polish landlord, a revolutionary mystic who sent his victims to the firing squad with the joyless cruelty of a Grand Inquisitor. These victims included persons of all social groups, among them peasants who had concealed food and workers who had gone on strike. How many persons perished in the Cheka's compounds will never be ascertained, for Lenin apparently ordered its records destroyed. The number must have been enormous. For example, after an anti-Bolshevik uprising in Iaroslavl in 1918, the Cheka shot 350 prisoners. Several hundred of the survivors of the Kronstadt rebellion suffered a similar fate. Among the early victims of terror were Nicholas II, his wife, and their five children. In July, 1918, the Bolshevik guards holding them imprisoned in the Urals butchered them, burned the bodies, and dumped the remains in an abandoned mine shaft.

As the prisons overflowed, the police began to send convicts to forced labor camps, the first of which was established in April, 1919, in northern Russia. Here White prisoners of war, ex-tsarist officers, political dissenters, and economic "saboteurs" did hard labor side by side with common criminals. These early camps were the nucleus of a vast concentration camp system that was to develop later under Stalin.

A by-product of Bolshevik dictatorship and terror was mass migration from Russia. During the Civil War an estimated 2 million persons left the country to seek refuge abroad. Among them was a large proportion of Russian intellectuals, including some of its greatest writers and artists.

The Communist International   It was a fundamental tenet of Marxism that the socialist revolution had to begin in countries with the most highly developed capitalist economy. By Western standards, imperial Russia certainly did not qualify as an economic power of the very first rank. How then could one reconcile with Marxism the fact that the first socialist revolution had occurred in Russia? Lenin explained away the contradiction by treating the Russian Revolution as the act of "snapping the weakest link" in the capitalist chain. He assumed that before long the other links would break too. He asserted more than once that unless the Russian Revolution was followed shortly by revolutions in the great industrial countries, it would fail in its historic mission.

Immediately upon assuming power, the Bolsheviks launched an intensive program of international revolutionary propaganda and subversion. But the opportunity for large-scale activity of this kind came only with the November, 1918, armistice. The demoralization that spread in Europe after the war, es-

pecially among the defeated Central Powers, provided fertile ground for social upheavals. Many people who before 1914 had turned deaf ears to radical agitation were now prepared to believe that the "bourgeois" order was indeed rotten and that the time had come to do away with it. This mood permitted the Communists to achieve some striking, if transitory, successes.

In early November, 1918, even before Germany had formally capitulated, Communist groups composed of radical workers and intellectuals initiated mutinies and formed soviet-like councils of workers' and soldiers' deputies in several German cities. (This was to provide the Nazis later on with a pretext for the claim that Germany had lost the war from a "stab in the back.") In January, 1919, the Communists staged an uprising in Berlin, and in April they proclaimed a Soviet republic in Bavaria. Throughout 1919 Communist agents and sympathizers promoted violent disorders in Austria. In Hungary in March, 1919, Lenin's associate Béla Kun overthrew a progressive liberal government and founded a Hungarian Soviet Republic. These revolutionary attempts were promptly suppressed by conservative military or paramilitary self-defense units, with the exception of Béla Kun's republic, which managed to survive for half a year.

Lenin had decided as early as 1914 to break with the Second International (Chapter 19) and to found a new socialist body, genuinely dedicated to the cause of world revolution. In March, 1919, when Communist-sponsored revolts in Central Europe were at their height, Lenin realized this ambition by launching in Moscow the Third, or Communist, International (Comintern). The task of this organization was everywhere to stimulate and assist revolutionary movements. Its head was Grigori Zinoviev, Lenin's closest collaborator and in 1917 his companion on the trip from Switzerland. In deference to Lenin's belief that modern capitalism depended for survival on its colonies (see Chapter 21), the Comintern paid great attention to the so-called national liberation movements in colonial areas. In the first year of its existence, the membership of the Comintern was small and haphazard, consisting mostly of Spanish, Italian, and French anarchists. In 1920, when contacts with the rest of Europe were re-established, its composition broadened. On Lenin's instructions, in every country the Communists initiated a policy of splitting the existing socialist parties so as to detach from them their most radical elements and form them into national Communist parties. These, in turn, were linked with the Comintern. This method attained a certain measure of success, especially in Germany.

The optimism of the Communists at that time knew no bounds. Every minor crisis abroad, every strike, every manifestation of sympathy for Soviet Russia portended to them an imminent revolution. Zinoviev made the following prediction on May Day, 1919:

> The [international revolutionary] movement progresses with such dizzying speed that one may say with assurance: a year from now we shall begin to forget that Europe had undergone a struggle for Communism, because in a year all Europe will be Communist. And the struggle for Communism will move on to America, and perhaps also to Asia and the other parts of the world.

Shortly after its founding, the Comintern experienced an internal conflict over two issues: the relationship of foreign Communist parties to the Communist International and to their own "bourgeois" governments.

Lenin envisaged the Comintern as an international Communist party, endowed with the same unquestioned authority over its constituent parties as the Central Committee of the Russian Communist party enjoyed over its regional branches. But many foreign Communists would not acquiesce in such authoritarianism.

The Germans especially resented being compelled to submit to Russian rule. The anarchists quit in large numbers over this issue. Lenin, however, would not yield. In 1920 the Comintern formulated a twenty-one point program to which all foreign Communist parties and affiliated organizations had to subscribe. In this fashion began the domination of the international Communist movement by the leaders of Soviet Russia, which continued until the mid-1950s.

On the question of domestic politics, a vociferous section of the Comintern membership—its so-called left wing—desired an uncompromising conflict with the bourgeois order. They wanted neither cooperation with other parties nor participation in parliamentary elections. Lenin repudiated this strategy. In an important treatise, *Leftism, a Childhood Disease of Communism* (1920), he outlined the manner in which Communists were expected to exploit all conflicts within non-Communist societies, exactly as the Bolsheviks had done:

> The whole history of Bolshevism both before and since the Revolution is *full* of examples of zig-zagging, accommodations, compromises with other parties, including those of the bourgeoisie! To wage war for the overthrow of the international bourgeoisie . . . and in advance to reject zig-zagging, the exploitation of conflicts of interest (even of a temporary kind) among the enemy, accommodation and compromises with possible . . . allies—is this not an infinitely ridiculous thing? . . . After the first socialist revolution of the proletariat, after the bourgeoisie of one country had been overthrown, the proletariat of that country will remain for a *long time weaker* than the [international] bourgeoisie. . . . One can defeat a more powerful opponent only by the greatest concentration of forces and the *imperative*, most circumspect, careful, cautious, skilful exploitation of every, even the smallest "crack" among one's enemies, of every conflict of interest among the bourgeoisie of various countries, among the various groups or species of bourgeoisie within individual countries—as well as of every opportunity, even the smallest, to win a mass ally, even a temporary, wavering, unsteady, unreliable, conditional one. . . .

The concept of world-wide revolution introduced a new and explosive element into international relations. It implied the rejection of the existing state system and the deliberate refusal to recognize peace and stability as goals of foreign policy. Like the *Weltpolitik* of William II, it challenged everything and everybody, but in a manner infinitely more ambitious and even less capable of being satisfied by concessions. The aim of the "overthrow of the international bourgeoisie" meant that the Russian people, whom the new government had in 1917 promised peace and bread, found themselves harnessed in the service of a messianic cause that would deprive them, for a long time, of both.

24

Modern Thought

Tthe great political and military events that occurred at the beginning of the twentieth century must not be allowed to obscure for us a development of comparable if less visible importance. The years 1890–1910 (the dates, of course, are approximate) witnessed a veritable cultural revolution. This event is still too close to be grasped in full. Indeed, we do not even have a name for it, except the vague term *Modernism*, which, for lack of a better term, we shall have to use. But its reality is all around us. The twentieth century cannot be understood without taking into consideration this revolution.

Modernism represents a renewal of the Romantic impulse: it is, in Edmund Wilson's phrase, the "second flood of the same tide." Like Romanticism, it proclaims the right of every man to his own values and taste, unfettered by classical or other models. But in making this claim it goes much further than did Romanticism, whose spirit of revolt, retrospectively, appears timid. Modernism is anti-traditionalist without reservations. It sheds impatiently the burden of the past and draws its material directly from raw life. It frowns upon "civilization" with its rules and inhibitions, lavishing admiration instead on whatever is simple and spontaneous. Innovation is not only permitted, as it was under the Romantics, but encouraged, being regarded as the test of true creativity.

Allied to the modern admiration for the simple and spontaneous is the frank acceptance of uncertainty. In this respect, twentieth-century culture differs from all that has preceded it. It has no fixed image of human nature, it recognizes no universal standards of morality or beauty, it even rejects the notion of objective reality. It views everything as in flux and devoid of permanent qualities. These attitudes represent an extreme reaction against the entire positivistic outlook dominant in the mid-nineteenth century.

The collapse of positivism was due to a number of causes. One was the doubts that affected the West toward the end of the century as a result of political, social, and economic crises. The irrationality of World War I played a critical role in the breakdown of the complex of ideas based on the assumption that reason will inevitably rule mankind. Another factor was boredom. In the 1880s the European public, tired of earnestness and purposiveness, began once more to experience pleasure in "art for art's sake," in mysticism and idealism, and in everything else that midcentury opinion had frowned upon. But in the long run, perhaps, the decisive causes were developments that occurred within science. In the 1890s physicists discovered a vast realm of nature which they could not satisfactorily explain in terms of traditional science. Phenomena of this order called for explanations based on concepts and rules that differed from—and sometimes stood in stark contradiction to—those of traditional science, previously considered validated forever. Suddenly the notion of an all-embracing realm of "nature," obeying definable and unexceptional laws, began to dissolve. Positivism, pushed to its logical conclusion, turned against itself. Subjectivism, un-

Three leaders of the modern revolution in science, photographed in California in the 1920s. The experiments of A. A. Michelson (left) led Albert Einstein (center) toward his theory of relativity. Robert A. Millikan was an important contributor to subatomic theory.

certainty, chance, believed banished from Western thought, re-entered the scientific vocabulary. This development was fatal for the whole positivistic-materialistic point of view, which had rested on the belief in the existence of one nature and of one set of laws regulating it. It may be said, therefore, that scientists betrayed the positivistic-materialistic outlook on life and unexpectedly joined the ranks of its enemies.

Modernism was flourishing by the time World War I had broken out, though it did not penetrate popular culture until after World War II. Our contemporary thought and art are fundamentally a development of intellectual and aesthetic principles formulated in the period 1890–1910. This period is likely to be seen by future generations as one of the most creative ages in the history of man. (By so saying, we do not pass judgment on the quality of modern culture, but merely state its historic significance.)

We shall divide the discussions of this subject into two parts. In the present chapter we shall discuss the changes that physics and psychology brought about in man's view of nature and of himself. In Chapter 25 we shall deal with the effect these changes had on art and literature. It must be borne in mind, of course, that such a division is an artificial one, for the Modernist revolution took place concurrently in all realms of thought and taste.

The New Conception of Matter The contrast between the views of nature held by the scientist and the common man has never been as great as today. It is no exaggeration to say that in the twentieth century, a century in which science is dominated by concepts of relativity and quanta, even well-educated men profess a common-sense, mechanistic outlook that would have brought them no credit three hundred years ago.

The main cause of the discrepancy between science and general culture is the widening gap between scientific concepts and everyday experience; and this gap, in turn, derives from the growing preoccupation of scientists with objects and processes that are too big, too small, or too fast for unaided observation. The realm beyond man's sensory perception is enormous: it is enough to realize that the unaided human ear perceives sounds only within the frequency of 16 to 20,000 cycles, whereas scientific instruments can detect sound waves in a range of 100,000,000 cycles. Similarly, what the human eye perceives as light is but a narrow, intermediate band of a vast radiation spectrum that includes invisible radio, infrared, and X-ray waves. Common sense, based on sensory experience, is therefore merely a crude, rule-of-thumb set of guidelines for that particular and limited environment in which man happens to find himself. The instant we leave the realm of familiar dimensions and velocities, common sense loses relevance. It tells us no more about objects that are smaller than the atom or move at speeds near that of light than life in the water teaches the fish what it is like on land or in the air.

Early science did not encounter this conflict with experience with the same sharpness because it concerned itself mainly with man's immediate environment. Even seventeenth-century mechanistic science did not have to depart radically from common sense: its laws may have taxed the imagination, but by and large they did not contradict rules valid in everyday life. Galileo and Newton, for all their revolutionary influence, viewed objects in a framework of absolute time and space, exactly like that known to ordinary man. It was the investigation of optical and electrodynamic phenomena carried out in the last quarter of the nineteenth century that first uncovered an entirely different realm of nature, one to which human experience proved largely irrelevant. To explain phenomena of this kind it was necessary to have recourse to abstract mathematical formulas and to laws which often make mockery of daily experience. Indeed, what are we to make of such propositions as: matter is only another form of energy; an object increases its mass as it increases its velocity; and time runs faster or slower depending on the speed with which the clock travels?

The discrepancy between science and experience, although extreme in our time, is not peculiar to it; nor is there reason to fear that it will always remain so wide. Max Planck, the discoverer of quanta, once said that the world of science differs as much from that of the average adult as the world of the average adult differs from that of the child. All growing up, whether of individuals or of civilizations, involves the weaning away from a total commitment to immediate experience and common sense, and the acceptance of many rules and principles that contradict them. An infant, when it reaches for the sun, acts on the common-sense premise that it can touch whatever it sees. As it grows, it learns that this is not the case, that the circumference of the sun and the distance that separates it from the earth are so great that nothing in man's immediate environment can give any meaningful equivalent for purposes of comparison. In maturing, people come to accept such abstractions as infinity, eternity, the number zero, and the strangest fact of all, the inevitability of their own death. Many opinions that we consider based on plain common sense are actually articles of faith that we have assimilated to the point where they seem natural and self-evident. The same holds true of mankind at large. That the earth is flat and stands still is common sense—it is a concept that accords with experience; that the earth is round and revolves around the sun is a scientific proposition that contradicts experience. How many habits of thought had to be broken before man would admit the possibility of people walking feet up and heads down on the other side of the earth! There is good reason to believe that the basic discoveries of modern physics will in time enter the mainstream of general culture as firmly as has the heliocentric theory of Copernicus.

In the 1860s no one entertained the suspicion that the view of nature then accepted would ever be questioned. Physics and chemistry seemed to have arrived at a conclusive understanding of matter. There was general agreement that matter consisted of irreducible atoms, that there was a different kind of atom for each of the 92 chemical elements, and that one element could not be transformed into another. Furthermore, it was believed that matter and energy were qualitatively different, each subject to a different law of conservation. These explanations accorded perfectly with the prevalent mechanistic philosophy of the period and were regarded as eternally validated. Yet the twentieth century found reason to question every one of them. Mechanistic physics now appeared inadequate to explain a vast range of phenomena, for which it had to be replaced by the quantum theory of Planck (1900) and the relativity theories of Einstein (1905 and 1916). It was gradually realized that atoms were not in fact the smallest, irreducible components of matter, but agglomerates of yet smaller particles; that these particles were identical in the atoms of all the elements; and that the elements themselves were not immutable. Matter and energy were discovered to be different aspects of the same phenomenon and subject to a single law of conservation. The notion of absolute time and space also had to be abandoned.

At the beginning of the twentieth century it was thought that these discoveries had overthrown traditional physics. Today this is no longer the accepted view. Science in general progresses not by abandoning older theories but by showing the limits of their validity. "The new world picture does not wipe out the old one," Max Planck observed, "but permits it to stand in its entirety, and merely adds a special condition for it." The discovery that the earth was round did not affect medieval road maps or navigation charts, which had perfectly served the purposes for which they had been designed. By analogy, modern or mathematical physics has not invalidated older physics. For this reason a leading physicist even denies that one can speak of a "revolution" in modern physical knowledge. In *Philosophic Problems of Nuclear Science*, Werner Heisenberg writes:

> Columbus' discoveries were immaterial to the geography of the Mediterranean countries, and it would be quite wrong to claim that the voyages of discovery of the famous Genoese had made obsolete the positive geographical knowledge of the day. It is equally wrong to speak today of a revolution in physics. Modern physics has changed nothing in the great classical disciplines of, for instance, mechanics, optics, and heat. Only the conception of hitherto unexplored regions, formed prematurely from a knowledge of only certain parts of the world, has undergone a decisive transformation.

Twentieth-century physics has abandoned a unified view of nature: it accepts the existence of several distinct physical realms, each subject to different sets of explanations. As yet no formula has been found to bridge these sets and to re-establish that unity of nature which underlay mechanistic science. This is one of the reasons why it can be said that modern science has helped to destroy the notion of an objective reality.

The most important achievements of modern physics have been the discovery of the structure of the atom and the formulation of two theories: relativity and quantum.

The Discovery of Electrons and of Radiation

The subatomic structure of matter was first revealed in the course of experiments conducted with electricity. In 1876–1878 electrical current sent through low-pressure gas tubes was observed to generate curious rays from the negative, or cathode, pole. These "cathode rays," as they were named, illuminated the gas, heated objects standing in their way, and even caused these objects to throw shadows. They obviously consisted of some kind of matter, but what it was no one knew. Curiosity about the phenomenon increased with the discovery made by Wilhelm Roentgen in 1895 that cathode rays released penetrating rays. Because of their enigmatic nature, Roentgen called them "X rays."

In 1897 the Englishman Joseph John Thomson finally solved the mystery. He identified cathode rays as particles of negative electricity and showed that they had an extremely small mass, 1/2000th that of the hydrogen atom, the smallest

Marie and Pierre Curie in their Paris laboratory about the turn of the century. She was awarded Nobel Prizes in both physics and chemistry.

material object previously known. He called these particles "electrons." Thomson's analysis demonstrated not only that the negative electric current consists of corpuscles, but, more importantly, that there exist material bodies smaller than atoms. Further researches also revealed the existence of other particles, which were named "protons." Before long it was realized that electrons and protons were constituents of all atoms, although their relationship to each other remained obscure. In any event the atom lost its position as the irreducible, minimal "building block" of matter.

Shortly after Thomson had identified electrons, two French scientists, Pierre Curie and his Polish-born wife, Marie, made the discovery that elements such as uranium and radium had the property of "radioactivity"; that is, they spontaneously discharged electrons and other particles and rays. The radioactivity of radium was so great that the energy it released could, within an hour, raise the temperature of an equivalent quantity of water from freezing to boiling. The process of radiation upset some seemingly impregnable laws of physics. It violated the principle of the conservation of matter, since radioactive elements were shown to disintegrate spontaneously. It blurred the distinction between matter and energy. It also disproved the whole notion of the immutability of elements: for in the course of their disintegration radioactive elements changed their atomic weight and moved down the Periodic Table.

These findings threw physics into disarray. They confused the picture of physical matter and its relationship to energy, and challenged the universal validity of mechanistic science.

The Theory of Relativity

Albert Einstein, who with Max Planck made the greatest contribution to modern physics, was the son of a German-Jewish businessman. In the early 1900s he held a job as a clerk in the Swiss Patent Office. The position was undemanding and left him much free time for scientific studies and speculations. Like the other great physicists of modern times, Einstein was not a laboratory technician but a thinker, whose only equipment consisted of pen and paper. He was much interested in philosophy, especially the writings of the contemporary Viennese, Ernst Mach. Mach, an extreme positivist, criticized Newton's concepts of absolute space, time, and motion on the grounds that they could not be empirically verified and therefore represented unscientific, metaphysical assumptions.

Reflecting on the contradictions introduced into the picture of the physical world by recent discoveries, Einstein concluded that these contradictions were due to the application of mechanistic concepts to phenomena not subject to mechanistic laws. In particular, mechanistic physics was not applicable to light and objects traveling at a speed near that of light.

According to the mechanistic view, light consisted of waves (which James Maxwell in 1864–1865 proved to be electromagnetic in nature), transmitted through a material but weightless substance known as "ether." This ether was thought to fill empty space in the universe and to permeate matter. It was regarded as motionless, providing a stable point of reference against which all motion was measured.

The experiment that cast doubt on the whole notion of ether, and a good deal of traditional physics besides, was performed in the 1880s by A. A. Michelson and E. W. Morley. By means of an ingenious apparatus these American scientists determined that the speed of light, known to be in the neighborhood of 300,000 kilometers (or 186,000 miles) a second, did not change, regardless of the direction in which light traveled—whether with the motion of the earth or at an angle to it. For if the motion of the earth (30 kilometers a second) indeed occurred through static ether, a light beam sent along its course should have traveled correspondingly more slowly. At first the paradoxical results of the Michelson-Morley experiment were thought to be due to imprecise measurement, but every subsequent test yielded the same negative result. Light, it was found, has a constant speed.

In 1905 Einstein published in *Annalen der Physik* a 30-page paper under the unassuming title "On the Electrodynamics of Moving Bodies." It was an early fruit of his speculations, known as the "special theory of relativity." In this paper Einstein showed that such findings as obtained in the Michelson-Morley experiment necessitated the abandonment of the whole concept of ether. This conclusion had far-reaching implications. For if ether did not exist, it was no longer possible to find a stable frame of reference in the universe: there was no longer any fixed coordinate to provide a standard for measuring absolute space or time. Space and time turned out to be not absolute, but relative—different for each "system."

To illustrate what Einstein meant when he spoke of the relativity of time, we may ask (as he did): What do we mean when we say that two events occur at the same time? Let us suppose that a person traveling on a train sends, exactly midway between two stations, two beams of light, one forward, and one backward. Since the speed of light is constant (that is, it is not affected by the motion of the train), an observer *outside* the train will see the two beams strike the stations at precisely the same instant. For him, they will be simultaneous events. They will not be simultaneous, however, for the person *inside* the train. Since he is in motion toward the forward station, for him the beam sent ahead will strike the station sooner, because in the interval between his sending the beam and receiving its reflection, he will have traveled some distance forward. Here we have an example of two "systems," each with its own timing.° In daily life, of course, such problems do not arise, because we deal with slow-moving objects; but they become very real when we turn to objects moving at a velocity approaching that of light. The same holds true of space, which is also relative. Einstein demonstrated that the length of material bodies cannot be objectively measured, for it depends on the speed with which they move in relation to the observer.

The special theory of relativity had an unexpected bearing on the puzzling connection between matter and energy. In his paper Einstein showed that mass, like time and size, depends on the object's velocity: the greater the velocity, the greater the mass. Mass he defined as "latent energy," showing that all mass has energy and all energy contains mass. Both are controlled by the same law, the law of the conservation of energy. The relationship between mass and energy Einstein defined in his formula $E = mc^2$—that is, energy equals the product of the mass multiplied by the square of the speed of light.

The special theory of relativity applied to all physical phenomena except gravitation. For the latter, Einstein devised in 1916 his general theory of relativity. One of its predictions was that light waves (which Einstein had previously identified as corpuscular) were subject to gravitational attraction. In 1919, as soon as the termination of hostilities permitted it, the British sent scientific expeditions to South Africa and Latin America to test this hypothesis. The photographs taken by these expeditions during a solar eclipse confirmed Einstein's predictions by showing that light "bent" in the vicinity of the sun. These findings captured public imagination as did no other scientific discovery of modern times, and brought Einstein unrivaled international fame.

The Structure of the Atom

The discovery of electrons, protons, and radiation, and the formulation of the special theory of relativity helped physicists to construct the model of the atom. In 1910–1913 Ernest Rutherford and Niels Bohr formulated the so-called solar model of the atom, according to which atoms consist of a positively-charged nucleus (proton) surrounded by negative particles (electrons), orbiting around it much as the planets orbit around the sun. The chemical elements were distinguished from each other not, as had been thought earlier, by the properties of the atoms, for these were identical in all the elements, but by the quantity of electrons or protons. The more of them in a given atom, the greater its atomic weight. In 1932 physicists discovered a third subatomic particle, which, because it had neither the negative charge of the electron nor the positive charge of the proton, they called the "neutron."

In 1919 Rutherford took another important step toward the understanding of

° This example is drawn from Leopold Infeld, *Albert Einstein* (1950).

Albert Einstein was photographed (opposite) in Berlin in 1920, when he was director of theoretical physics at the Kaiser Wilhelm Institute. He worked in the modernistic tower shown above, designed by the German architect Eric Mendelsohn, who was much influenced by Expressionist painters.

Physicist Max Planck, photographed just before World War 1, developed his quantum theory during his long tenure at the University of Berlin, where he taught for thirty-nine years.

BOTH: BROWN BROTHERS

atoms. He bombarded nitrogen atoms with helium nuclei and found to his amazement that in this manner he could disintegrate the atom of nitrogen and transform it into an atom of oxygen. This experiment marked the birth of nuclear physics. Subsequently the nuclei of other atoms were split with apparatus of increasing complexity.

In the 1930s it was realized that the splitting of atoms could release enormous energy. In 1939 the German physicist Otto Hahn found that the bombardment of the nucleus of uranium, the heaviest natural element, with neutrons caused a chain reaction yielding millions of volts of energy. These experiments, announced immediately in the journal *Nature*, aroused great curiosity in the international scientific community. On their basis, three years later, the United States government authorized work leading to the manufacture of the first atomic bomb.

THE QUANTUM THEORY

There is general agreement today that Max Planck's discovery of quanta was the single most important event in the development of twentieth-century physics. No theory, not even that of relativity enunciated by Einstein, has exerted a comparable influence on the modern conception of nature and the scientific method.

In studying the light effects of radiation, Planck noticed the absence of high-frequency light waves. This observation led him to the hypothesis that the exchange of energy between mass and radiation occurred not in a continuous stream, but discontinuously, in packets or quanta of energy. He formulated the manner in which this exchange took place in a mathematical equation.

Science was slow in realizing the full implications of the quantum theory. At first it attracted attention because it challenged one of the most firmly established principles of science, namely that natural processes occur continuously, without gaps or jerks. As the Latin proverb has it, *natura non fecit saltum,* "nature does not leap." But in time the quantum theory completely changed scientific thinking. Analysis of quanta revealed that in dealing with extremely small and fast-moving particles it is in principle impossible simultaneously to locate them in time and space and to determine their speed. We can know at any one instant only half the qualities of such objects, and therefore we cannot with certainty predict their behavior. Determinism had to be abandoned. "Indeed, the present quantum theory furnishes us only with laws of probability, allowing us to say what, the result of the first observation being given, is the probability that a later observation will furnish us such and such result."[*]

Mechanistic science conceived nature as an objective reality outside man: it was monolithic and subject to ironclad and universal laws. Man was seen to confront this reality as he would an unknown continent. By using accurate instruments to carefully assemble and process data, he was believed capable of obtaining a complete understanding of all natural phenomena without exception. According to the mechanistic view, if one could ascertain the position and movement of every particle of matter in the universe, he would be able (theoretically) to predict all future events from the present into eternity. This view struck deep

The Implications of Modern Physics

[*] Louis de Broglie, *The Revolution in Physics* (1953).

The Dane Niels Bohr reconciled the quantum theory with the solar model of the atom that he developed with Ernest Rutherford.

roots in the Western consciousness, and contributed much to that sense of self-confidence that characterized Western culture in the nineteenth century.

Modern physics, while leaving intact mechanistic explanations of certain natural phenomena, shattered the overall mechanistic conception of nature. It destroyed the notion of an objective reality with all that it implied: the unity of nature, the universality of natural laws, the determinism of physical processes, and the ability of science to solve all problems of the natural world. Its impact on general culture was therefore bound to be great, even greater than that of biology in the mid-nineteenth century.

Einstein struck the first telling blow against the concept of an objective reality —a concept that assumes the existence of universal time and space into which nature fits, independently of the observer. Einstein showed that there is no single spatial and chronological frame of reference. Every observer is confined to a specific and relative time-space system. As Einstein once put it, before relativity it had been thought that if one removed from the universe all material objects, time and space would remain; according to relativity, however, time and space would disappear along with the objects. Relativity replaced one objective reality with many subjective realities.

The quantum theory and quantum mechanics which issued from it in the 1920s had an even more devastating effect on the traditional concept of reality. They demonstrate that we cannot know both the position and the motion of certain particles and therefore we are not able to predict their behavior. In such cases, statistical probability replaces determinism. This means that some physical phenomena are exempt from that absolute and unexceptional certainty that had been considered the hallmark of science.

The implications of these discoveries profoundly influenced the whole intellectual climate of the twentieth century.

Old-fashioned empiricism with its belief in "facts" and the power of induction—the ability to elicit general laws from a mass of evidence—is not generally shared by modern scientists. No one heaped more scorn on it than did Einstein. He thought that scientific understanding is achieved only through insight and deduction, and went so far as to agree with the ancient philosophers that "pure thought" could grasp reality.

Gone today too is the belief in the capacity of science to unravel all enigmas of nature. Modern physicists are cautious and even humble in their claims:

> The knowable realities of nature cannot be exhaustively discovered by any branch of science. This means that science is never in a position completely and exhaustively to explain the problems it has to face. We see in all modern scientific advances that the solution of one problem only unveils the mystery of another. Each hilltop that we reach discloses to us another hilltop beyond. . . . The aim of science . . . is an incessant struggle toward a goal which can never be reached. Because the goal is of its very nature unattainable. It is something that is essentially metaphysical and as such is always again and again beyond each achievement.°

With the disappearance of the concept of objective reality, there disappeared

°Max Planck, *Where is Science Going?* (1932).

also the old dichotomy: man-nature. In *The Physicist's Conception of Nature*, Werner Heisenberg has observed that the physicist of today does not view nature as something existing independently of him, and concerns himself, to an extent unthinkable among scientists a century ago, with philosophical questions, especially problems of knowledge:

> The common division of the world into subject and object, inner world and outer world, body and soul is no longer adequate and leads us into difficulties. Thus even in science *the object of research is no longer nature itself, but man's investigation of nature.* . . . Science no longer confronts nature as an objective observer, but sees itself as an actor in [the] interplay between man and nature.

The effect of these diverse implications of modern physics has been to render obsolete the whole positivistic outlook. Positivism had rested on the assumption that, unlike religious and philosophic "pseudo-knowledge," scientific knowledge was objective and certain. But as science itself abandoned objectivity and certainty in favor of relativity and probability, positivism in its classical meaning lost sense.

It would certainly be farfetched to assert that the twentieth century has consciously assimilated the findings of modern physics. For most people the discoveries of Planck and Einstein are a form of magic that they do not understand and therefore fear. But science plays too large a part in Western culture not to exert its influence, even when misunderstood and resented. Modern physics has radically altered the attitude of man to himself and to his environment, throwing him back on his own resources: by destroying the fixed conception of an objective reality it has also destroyed, especially for those who lack religious faith, external bearings, casting people adrift in a sea without charts or landmarks. Such is the main intellectual source of what is called the "alienation" of modern man. "For the first time in the course of history modern man on this earth now confronts himself alone . . . he no longer has any partners or opponents," writes Heisenberg. These words, uttered by a physicist, could as well have been spoken by an existential philosopher, a psychoanalyst, or an abstract painter. They touch on the most vital aspect of modern culture, that quality that lends it its sense of unity.

The New Conception of Man

As we have seen (Chapter 16), the mid-nineteenth century had produced a view of human nature that was in accord with the prevailing materialistic and mechanistic outlook. It treated man as a physiological entity pure and simple, and thinking as a by-product of chemical processes. In the second half of the century this view began to break down. The emergence of psychology as an independent discipline, freed from the tutelage of philosophy, led to intense investigations of human behavior which soon revealed the need for subtler methods of analysis than those provided by natural science. The growing dissatisfaction of natural science itself with mechanistic explanations and with materialism in its cruder forms further encouraged a revision of psychological assumptions. Gradually, a new conception of man emerged, as different from the traditional conception as new mathematical physics was different from its mechanistic predecessor.

American psychologist William James, brother of the novelist Henry, taught anatomy, physiology, and philosophy as well as psychology at Harvard.

The distinguishing feature of modern psychology is its abandonment of the notion of the "soul" as the central agency of mental and psychic processes. The traditional Western view held that man consisted of two separate entities, a body and a soul, the one responsible for physiological and the other for mental and spiritual functions. Nineteenth-century materialists, of course, denied the existence of an immaterial soul, but they in fact retained it in another guise. Academic psychology of the 1870s and 1880s assumed that mental processes originated in sensations, and that these sensations produced in organisms a sense of "consciousness," which was merely another term for "soul." The task of psychology was to localize in the body the organs of sensation and consciousness, to separate consciousness into its elementary components ("ideas," "concepts," "feelings," "emotions," and so forth), and to describe how these components interacted to produce higher states of mind. Much attention was also devoted to measuring psychological phenomena, such as the intensity of sensations. This view had a great deal in common with the whole mechanistic outlook, because it regarded higher psychological processes as resulting from the combination of lower ones. There was agreement that consciousness was an entity, that it had distinct properties, and that it could be analytically separated into its constituent elements.

The first forceful attack on this view of consciousness was launched around 1890 by the American psychologist William James and the French philosopher Henri Bergson. Both of these influential thinkers denied that consciousness could be broken down into its components, on the grounds that mental states constitute an indivisible totality. The mind is in constant flux—it is a living stream, not a building constructed of individual bricks.

In his *Principles of Psychology* (1890–1892), James included a chapter entitled "Stream of Consciousness" in which he eloquently described this psychological continuum. Bergson, in his popular books and lectures, laid stress on the inner logic of mental operations. He showed that these obey not formal categories but their own rules in which associations play an important part.

James and Bergson helped to emancipate psychology from its subservience to natural science by depicting the unique quality of mental processes and demonstrating their immunity to analytic methods. But although they criticized academic psychology for its treatment of consciousness, they did not deny that a single state of consciousness existed. This notion was rejected by their successors after the turn of the century.

The modern conception of man, as we have said, abandons altogether the view that man possesses a single "soul" or "consciousness," in favor of one of two alternatives. One school, originating in the United States and Russia and continuing the older positivist tradition, maintains that "consciousness" is a metaphysical abstraction that cannot be scientifically studied. It concentrates its attention instead on behavior. The other, born in Central Europe and more closely connected with the literary and philosophic tradition, maintains that the conscious is merely an outer shell for the real motor of the psyche, the unconscious.

The first of these two schools has its original source in American pragmatism, whose leading figure was William James. James developed a celebrated theory

The French philosopher Henri Bergson in 1905. "There are general problems which interest everybody and must be dealt with in language comprehensible to everybody," Bergson maintained, and this ability to popularize broadened his influence.

according to which our mental states are not causes of our actions but responses to them. In his view the physiological precedes and has priority over the psychological. An extreme formulation of this theory is James's aphorism: "We do not weep because we are sad, but we are sad because we weep." James laid great stress on the ability of the will, by guiding behavior, to influence the general condition of the mind. The so-called Behaviorist School of psychology, founded by the American John Watson, concentrated entirely on the study of human actions. An extreme development of this tendency occurred in Russia. The psychologist Ivan Pavlov demonstrated by experiments on animals the existence of what he called "conditioned reflexes," that is to say, responses to external stimuli independent of volition and any conscious process. These experiments caused fears, apparently unfounded, that by exploiting such conditioned reflexes it should be possible to transform human beings into soulless automata.

The second modern school of psychology, that which stresses the unconscious, has had a growing influence both on science and on public opinion in the twentieth century.

The idea that the psyche is divided into two separate compartments is by no

The Cry (1893), *by the Norwegian Expressionist painter* Edvard Munch, *is a visualization of subconscious fears like those in a nightmare.*

means new. It was a commonplace among Romantics, who habitually distinguished between what they called "imagination" and "understanding"—the former grasping reality instinctively and therefore deeply, the latter grasping it formally and superficially. It is quite incorrect to claim, therefore, that modern psychology "discovered" the unconscious. Even the most determined adherents of nineteenth-century academic psychology could not entirely dispense with it. What modern psychology has done, however, is to shift the unconscious from the periphery to the center of psychological explanation.

Much of the credit for popularizing the concept of the unconscious belongs to Henri Bergson. He drew a sharp distinction between "intelligence" (in which he included science) and "instinct." Man develops intelligence to cope with the problems of life. It is a practical instrument, concerned with reality only insofar as it can be used. It systematizes experience by means of formal logic and such categories as physical time and objective space. Instincts, by contrast, are free from such utilitarian influences. They are spontaneous drives, deeply buried in our subconscious. Bergson devoted much attention to memory, showing it to be a rich storehouse of knowledge which surfaces only when not restrained by intelligence, in dreams, hallucinations, or delusions.

The most influential modern theory of the unconscious is that associated with the psychoanalytic method of Freud, which, because of its present-day popularity, requires a more extended discussion.

Sigmund Freud was born in Vienna in 1856 in a middle-class, assimilated Jewish family—a biographical fact not without bearing on his intellectual development. The environment in which he grew up was exceptionally inhibiting. As a member of the bourgeoisie, he had to adhere to a demanding code of morals, especially strict in all that pertained to sex. As an assimilated Jew, he faced in addition the conflict between the inner awareness of being Jewish and the need outwardly to conform to a hostile, Catholic milieu. Such inhibitions also affected most of his friends and early patients, who came from a similar background and faced similar problems of adjustment. Undoubtedly this circumstance heightened Freud's sensitivity to tensions between inner drives and outward restraints. Like all theories claiming universal validity, Freudian psychology is the product of a specific place, time, and social environment, that is, of unique historic conditions, and remains most relevant to them.

In the 1880s Freud, then a medical student, participated in experiments carried out in Paris and Vienna to cure hysterical patients by means of hypnosis. It was discovered that in a hypnotic trance patients relived situations from their life, and that when being confronted with this information upon awakening they sometimes were cured of hysteria. For Freud this discovery had great significance, revealing the existence of an empirically verifiable subconscious level, a vast repository of hidden information that seemed to control the intelligence. It also suggested to him a central theory of psychotherapy: that the mere identification of the cause of a nervous sickness may result in its cure.

Freud's predecessors and contemporaries treated hypnotic experiments primarily as a method of healing nervous disorders. For Freud it served as an inspiration for a systematic study of the unconscious. The fact that hysterical patients concealed from themselves certain experiences, usually those that were in stark conflict with prevalent moral norms, suggested to him the existence of a "repressive mechanism." He was the first to study systematically, and in all its manifestations, the conflict between the conscious and unconscious and particularly to call attention to the ingenious methods by which the psyche resolves this conflict. This was the truly new contribution of his theory.

Freud began to investigate repression by analyzing dreams. Like Bergson, he believed that dreams convey messages from the unconscious; but unlike Bergson, for whom the unconscious was passive, he assumed it to be full of drives. Dreams embody wishes, but wishes disguised in a symbolic form, for the conscious "censors" the unconscious and forces it to express itself in an indirect, circuitous way. By relentlessly probing into his own dream recollections and those of his patients, and then connecting them with incidents from life, Freud concluded that dreams spoke in an elaborate code, which, if properly deciphered, permitted an insight into the deepest recesses of the mind. He found, in particular, that many seemingly innocent or nonsensical dream sequences disguise sexual fantasies. He published the results of these investigations in 1900 in his most famous book, *The Interpretation of Dreams.*

From dreams, Freud proceeded to analyze art and literature, religion, politics, and many other kinds of human activity, seeking in each case to identify the manifestations of the repressed unconscious. In this manner he gradually constructed a comprehensive theory of human behavior and culture centered on the concept of repression. Although he began his investigations with persons suffering from nervous disorders, in time he concluded that the distinction between the normal and abnormal is one of degree, and sometimes merely one of social convention.

Freud distinguished in the psyche three distinct components: the *id*, the center

"Insight such as this falls to one's lot but once in a lifetime," Sigmund Freud wrote in his celebrated study, The Interpretation of Dreams *(1900).*

of unconscious drives; the *ego,* the seat of reason—that which we call "I" in ordinary speech; and the *superego,* the locus of conscience. Both the ego and superego are molded by culture, and exert a restraining influence on the unconscious id. They have the ability to keep out of consciousness that which they dislike.

The most important repressions involve sexual drives, because these drives are both extraordinarily powerful and subject to strict cultural taboos. Freud believed that the repression of sexual instincts begins early in childhood. (His assertion that children experience strong sexual desires conflicted with the prevalent view of the time that preadolescents were asexual, pure creatures, and brought his theories into early disrepute.) According to Freud, all male children suffer from what he called the "Oedipus complex," that is, from a conflict brought about by their being in love with their mothers and desiring to kill their fathers. Girls, on the other hand, suffer from a sense of sexual inferiority. Childhood neuroses are unavoidable. They are the main cause of psychological troubles experienced in adulthood.

The task of psychoanalysis is to probe deeply into the memory in order to retrace all the way to childhood the chain of repressions, make the conscious aware of the unconscious, and thus resolve psychic conflicts. This task it accomplishes in a variety of ways, including the analysis of dreams and free-thought associations.

Freud believed that psychoanalysis provided the key to the understanding of all human phenomena, and would in time become the keystone of the humanities. It explained everything that man "makes or does." In view of this claim, it is not surprising that he likened himself to Copernicus and Darwin.

Freud's influence on Continental thought has never been very strong. On the other hand, it has been great in England and even more so in the United States, where a whole cult has arisen around his theory. Critics of Freud point out that his "topography of the mind," with its threefold division, is purely metaphysical, since the id, ego, and superego cannot be empirically verified; that his interpretations in psychoanalytic categories of phenomena such as religion and primitive society are speculative to the extreme; and that the usefulness of psychotherapy remains to be demonstrated. For all their novelty, Freudian theories can be shown to rest on old-fashioned, nineteenth-century premises. They assume the power of reason to control irrational drives, the unchangeability of human nature across the ages, and the acquisitiveness and individualism of man. A sympathetic student of Freud calls psychoanalysis

> the last great formulation of nineteenth-century secularism, complete with substitute doctrine and cult—capacious, all-embracing, similar in range to the social calculus of the utilitarians, the universal sociolatry of Comte, the dialectical historicism of Marx, the indefinitely expandable agnosticism of Spencer.[°]

Needless to say, Freud's adherents think otherwise. Although they have subjected the master's theory to many revisions, they regard it as the most profound insight ever gained into the human mind.

[°]Philip Rieff, *Freud: The Mind of the Moralist* (1961).

Carl Jung was a disciple and close collaborator of Freud's from their first meeting in 1907 to 1913, when the two strong-willed men parted bitterly to follow divergent paths.

Among Freud's students and associates, the most influential was Carl Jung, who broke with Freud and founded his own psychoanalytic school. Jung was nearly twenty years younger than Freud, a Swiss whose background was free of the inhibitory factors so significant in Freud's case. His psychology is more affirmative and optimistic, and in some respects more modern. In contrast to Freud's positivistic-mechanistic outlook, Jung adopted a conception of nature close to that of modern physics, complete with nuclear analogies. If to Freud man was fully conditioned by his past, to Jung he was constantly made and remade by the free exercise of his will. Jung's psychology was therefore less deterministic.

Jung divided the psyche into two categories, the conscious and unconscious, the ego sharing in both. The conscious and the unconscious are in constant conflict because their relationship is inherently antithetical. When the conscious is outgoing, interested in the external world—"extrovert"—then the unconscious is withdrawn, self-centered—"introvert"; on the other hand, when the conscious

The logical positivism of Bertrand Russell (left) and the existentialism formulated by Martin Heidegger (right) dominate twentieth-century philosophy.

is "introvert," the unconscious turns "extrovert." This disharmony causes psychological tension, especially acute in middle age; it can be a source of creativity, but it can also cause neuroses and nervous breakdowns. Jungian psychology strives to harmonize the conscious and unconscious parts of the psyche and to bring the two drives into some kind of equilibrium.

Jung's conception of the unconscious was broader than Freud's. To Jung it was not only the seat of appetites, but also of religious and other spiritual needs. He viewed it as twofold, consisting of the "personal unconscious" and the "collective unconscious." The latter—a central concept for Jung—is the repository of memories that all men share. It consists of "archetypes," images common to all humanity, that appear in dreams of individuals as well as in works of primitive art and in mythology. Examples of archetypes are the mother-goddess, paradise, the wandering hero, the number three. To Jung, symbols, whether personal or collective, were not substitutes for repressed drives, but primordial images that force their way to consciousness because we live not only as individuals but also as members of humanity, and as such share in mankind's unconscious.

If Freud's psychology dominates psychotherapy, Jung's has had fruitful application in the study of primitive and mass cultures.

Modern Philosophy　In the twentieth century physics and psychology have appropriated the two central concerns of traditional philosophy—the nature of matter and the nature of thought. Philosophy in Western culture has correspondingly lost status, and has become an academic discipline of limited influence.

The leading philosophical movement of modern times is logical positivism (or logical empiricism). This school originated in Vienna in the early 1920s under the influence of the writings of the British philosopher Bertrand Russell. Today it dominates professional philosophic thinking, especially in Great Britain and the United States. Like the older empirical tradition from which it descends, logical positivism rejects metaphysics, and acknowledges only propositions that can be either empirically verified (e.g., scientific facts) or shown to have logical validity (e.g., mathematical equations). The Viennese Ludwig Wittgenstein, who with Russell is the most influential philosopher of the century, argued in his *Tractatus Logico-Philosophicus* (1922) that the majority of philosophical propositions constitute verbal deceptions, which, when subjected to strict logical analysis, turn out to be devoid of meaning. The adherents of this school concentrate their attention on the use of language, seeing in it the key to the understanding and critique of philosophical concepts. Rudolf Carnap, a leading figure of this movement, sought to develop an artificial logical language that would avoid the pitfalls of everyday speech and achieve the precision of mathematics. The tendency of logical positivism, like that of modern philosophy in general, has been to shun humanistic preoccupations, especially moral concerns, on the grounds that they lead to conclusions that are either self-evident or unverifiable, or even absurd. Instead, it has turned its attention to logical and mathematical problems closely related to those confronting physical science, with which it maintains close contacts.

The only important modern philosophical movement to continue the traditional concern with moral questions is existentialism. This movement was founded by the German thinker Martin Heidegger, whose main work is *Being and Time* (1927). From Germany it penetrated into France, where, during and immediately following the German occupation (1940–1944), it acquired an influential following grouped around the writer Jean-Paul Sartre. (Heidegger, like Jung, compromised his reputation by collaborating with the Nazis; Sartre, on the other hand, always has been sympathetic to the left.) Existentialism is a philosophy born of the desperation caused by two world wars and the breakdown of traditional values. It provides guidance for the uprooted, "alienated" individual, cut off from religion and any other system of stable, absolute values, by showing him how to establish his identity through engagement in life.

Like modern physics and psychology, existential philosophy views the individual not as a finished product with set qualities, but as a creature in the process of becoming. Life is meaningless, absurd. Man finds himself in it utterly alone (existentialists profess atheism), without any stable frame of reference. The elemental facts of life are boredom and anxiety—a view that the existentialists have adopted from the nineteenth-century Danish philosopher Søren Kierkegaard. To overcome both, man must act, he must become "engaged"; in so doing he acquires an identity. "Man is potential" (Heidegger); he is "nothing else but that which he makes of himself" (Sartre). The intellectual heroes of the existentialists, in addition to Kierkegaard, are Nietzsche and Dostoevsky (Chapter 16), leading critics of mid-nineteenth century Western culture.

The analogy between the new view of matter and the new view of man must not be pressed too far, but it is apparent that the two have close affinities. Just as modern physics has abandoned the older view of matter as a final substance with fixed qualities, so has modern psychology abandoned the older view of the "soul." The study of nature and the study of man simultaneously lost sight of their respective objects.

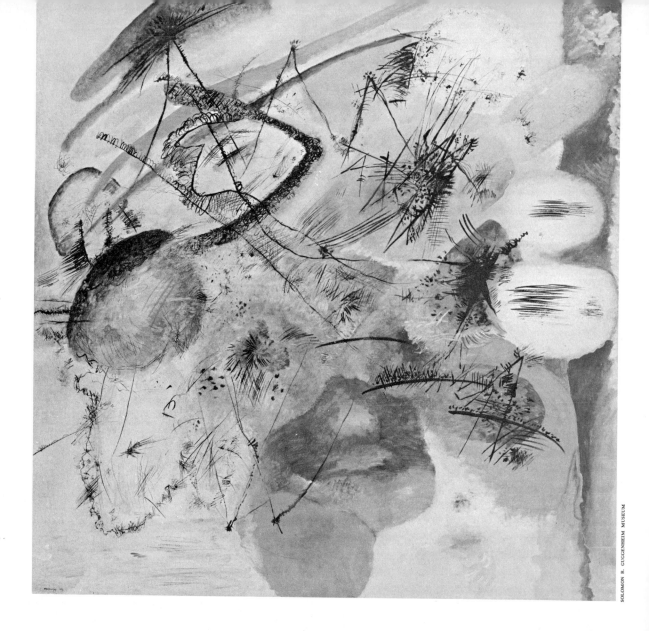

25

Modern Taste

The Modernist movement in art and literature began once artists and writers sought to push the positivistic view of reality to its logical extreme and to locate a "real" reality behind the veil of appearance. This quest led them to tamper with the conventions of space and time. But gradually they abandoned altogether the notion that their task was to render reality. Modern art and literature create their own reality—a fact which accounts both for their tremendous inventiveness and their estrangement from the public at large.

Impressionism

The history of modern painting divides itself into three successive periods, each characterized by increased dissociation from visual realism. The first period (approximately 1860–1886) was Impressionist; the second (1886–1910), Post-Impressionist; and the third (1910 to the present), Abstract. The innovations achieved between 1860 and 1910 had a decisive effect on all subsequent painting. The history of visual arts since the introduction of Abstraction represents little more than an elaboration of themes and techniques developed in the preceding half century. Once a revolutionary movement, the modern style has itself gradually become orthodox and conservative. Today it dominates artistic expression as thoroughly as classicism had done in its time.

As we mentioned before (Chapter 14), Romantic artists failed to reduce significantly the power of the academies for the reason that the purchase of a canvas or a statue, unlike the purchase of a book or a ticket to the theater or a concert, involves a considerable investment of money, and investors like to seek the advice of experts. This was especially true of the bourgeoisie, the main patron of the arts in the nineteenth century, whose keen appreciation of money was not matched by a corresponding aesthetic judgment. The Academy of Fine Arts met this need for expertise. By selecting a painting for exhibition at the Salon, it stamped on it, as it were, a seal of approval and thereby emboldened middle-class patrons to buy. In making its selections, the Academy tended to favor works that in terms of content met the middle-class preference for the narrative and the morally uplifting, and in terms of technique adhered to the classical criteria of draftsmanship and finish. The more money invested in paintings conforming to these standards, the greater grew the intolerance of patrons and dealers of any innovation, for the triumph of a different aesthetic spelled to them great financial loss.

The rebellion against the academic art establishment broke out in the 1860s in Paris. As we have seen, its slogan, "Realism," paved the road for an anti-Romantic rebellion in literature (Chapter 16). The leader of the rebels was Courbet, around whom had gathered an articulate body of admirers, ready to proclaim his principles of painting as universally valid aesthetic laws. Repeatedly rejected by the Salon, Courbet organized anti-Academy exhibits, and in 1862 opened a school where young artists, bored with copying antique models at the

The modern artist's quest for "true" reality took on new dimensions with the advent of Abstract Expressionism, which rejected the traditional canons of representational art. Its pioneer was Vasili Kandinsky, whose Black Lines, No. 189 *(1913) is reproduced here.*

The Impressionists were particularly intrigued by the effects of light on water. This is Alfred Sisley's Flood at Port-Marly *(1876), one of a series of paintings he did of the effects of spring floods on the Seine near Paris.*

Ecole des Beaux Arts, could paint from live models. The following year Napoleon III authorized a *Salon des Refusés* to exhibit works rejected for the official Salon. Clearly, the monopoly of the Academy was on the wane.

The founders of what later became known as Impressionism—Claude Monet, Alfred Sisley, and Camille Pissarro—spent their formative years in this atmosphere of rebellion and developed early a strong sense of artistic independence. At the beginning of the 1860s the future Impressionists turned their backs on studios and museums and took to the country. Scattering around Paris—Pontoise, Argenteuil, Barbizon—they painted nature directly, under the open sky. The recent invention of a method of storing ready-mixed paints in metal tubes enabled them to complete their canvases on location. The imagination of these painters was captivated by the role of light in determining the appearance of objects. They never tired of observing and reproducing light effects in their infinite variety. They concluded that in nature all was color—they saw neither white nor black, nor the halftones prized by academic painters, and therefore discarded them. They also paid little attention to the line, that is to drawing, because like Romantic painters they found that the eye did not distinguish sharp borders between objects. Their main effort was directed at capturing the living, fleeting instant in its totality as expressed in light effects. We can obtain an excellent notion of their aims and methods from the advice Pissarro gave a fellow artist:

> Look for the kind of nature that suits your temperament. The motif should be observed more for shape and color than for drawing. . . . Precise drawing is dry and hampers the impression of the whole, it destroys all sensations. Do not define too closely the outlines of things; it is the brush stroke of the right value and color which should produce the drawing. . . . Paint the essential character of things, try to convey it by any means whatsoever, without bothering about technique. When painting, make a choice of subject, see what is lying at the right and at the left, then work on everything simultaneously. Don't work bit by bit, but paint everything at once by placing tones everywhere, with brush strokes of the right color and value,

Claude Monet painted La Grenouillère *in 1869. It was a popular bathing spot on the Seine frequented by the Impressionists, who found its rippling waters an ideal subject to depict with unrefined strokes of color.*

while noticing what is alongside. . . . The eye should not be fixed on one point, but should take in everything, while observing the reflections which the colors produce on their surroundings. Work at the same time upon sky, water, branches, ground, keeping everything going on an equal basis and unceasingly rework until you have got it. Cover the canvas at the first go, then work at it until you can see nothing more to add. Observe the aerial perspective well, from the foreground to the horizon, the reflections of sky, of foliage. Don't be afraid of putting on color, refine the work little by little. Don't proceed according to rules and principles, but paint what you observe and feel. Paint generously and unhesitatingly, for it is best not to lose the first impression. Don't be timid in front of nature: one must be bold, at the risk of being deceived and making mistakes. One must have only one master—nature; she is the one always to be consulted.°

The painters of this group did not confine themselves to landscapes. They also depicted contemporary genre, especially everyday scenes in Paris and its environs. They loved big city life. They frequented cheap cafés and dance halls on the Montmartre, then still a village overlooking Paris, the parks, playgrounds, market places, and any other location where life could be caught in its uninhibited spontaneity. One of their favorite haunts was La Grenouillère on the Seine, where they swam and engaged in rowing, then a sport newly come into fashion. In general, their subject matter was popular rather than aristocratic: they preferred people at work and at play to the frozen attitudes of the well-to-do—a fact which did not endear them to the art patrons.

In the handling of genre subjects, the future Impressionists were strongly influenced by Japanese prints, knowledge of which had penetrated to the West in the 1860s. (The influence of Japan, paramount for all modern art, began with the so-called Meiji Restoration of 1868, when Japan abandoned its isolation and opened regular contact with the outside world.) The deliberate disregard of perspective by the Japanese in favor of a two-dimensional, flat effect, their

°Cited in John Rewald, *History of Impressionism* (1961).

unorthodox manner of placing figures off-center, their use of primary colors and avoidance of shadows—all fascinated the young painters and encouraged them to take similar liberties. Degas, perhaps the greatest of the group, was especially influenced by Japanese examples.

The Salon from time to time accepted works of the young rebels, but it did so capriciously. In 1874, tired of fighting the Salon, they organized their own exhibit. The event was what the French call a *succès de scandale*. The public, which came in droves, found the exhibition an outrage. What shocked it most was the lack of finish, the seeming "sloppiness" of the exhibited works. The Impressionists, in their effort to render the vibrations of light, deliberately avoided the satin-smooth gloss that convention demanded. As a rule they did

Edgar Degas' L'Absinthe (1876) is a striking study of withdrawal in a café on the Place Pigalle patronized by many of the Impressionists.

LOUVRE; GIRAUDON

not coat their canvases with the customary base and sometimes even squeezed the paint directly from the tube, spreading it with a spatula. To the visitors at the 1874 exhibit the canvases resembled rough sketches or essays for paintings rather than genuine works of art. In addition they complained that the subjects were trivial, the models ugly, the colors unrealistic, and the draftsmanship amateurish. One journalist, reporting on the exhibition for a satirical magazine, borrowed the title of a canvas by Monet, *Impression, Sunrise*, to label the whole school "Impressionist." The name stuck, although those to whom it applied disliked it, preferring to call themselves "Independents."

Impressionism reached its peak of development during the decade following the first exhibition. Its adherents formed a closely knit group. Confident of their method, they experimented ceaselessly, discovering ever new subjects and techniques, and creating in the process a new vision of man's environment. Even today, nearly a century later, one is amazed by the inventiveness of the Impressionists, for nearly all their paintings are in some measure original and contain surprises for the viewer. But this was not apparent at the time, and the public remained hostile. Dealers boycotted the Impressionists except for one in particular, Durand-Ruel, a loyal friend who bought their works when no one else wanted them and advanced them money for living expenses and art supplies.

In the mid-1880s the Impressionist group began to break up. Some of its members left Paris for the Côte d'Azur (Riviera) in search of more intense light contrasts; others quarreled on personal or doctrinal grounds. In 1886 they held their last joint exhibit. This date is generally taken to mark the end of Impressionism as an original, living force.

The year 1886 also marked Impressionism's first commercial successes. That year Durand-Ruel, exasperated by the hostility of the French public, organized an exhibit of his friends' works in New York. The show enjoyed an unexpected success. American patrons purchased a number of Impressionist paintings, and continued to do so in subsequent years—a farsighted attitude that permitted the United States to acquire in time the best collection of Impressionist paintings in the world. In 1891 Monet's nearly abstract *Haystacks*—fifteen successive images of the same subject under different light conditions—were purchased at high prices. From then on the Impressionists were "in" with discerning connoisseurs. The general public was not won over until after World War I.

At the very time of their first successes, the Impressionists found themselves under attack from a new generation of painters who accused them not of being too radical but of being not radical enough.

Post-Impressionism and Abstract Painting

Impressionism carried the seeds of its own destruction. In one respect it was "realistic," and belonged to the whole positivist trend that characterized science and the scientific outlook (Chapter 16). But in another and deeper sense, it denied realism. By rejecting the objectivity of nature and concentrating on optical effects, it cast doubt on the whole notion of visual reality. If the task of painting was not to reproduce things as they were "in themselves" but as they struck the viewer, why confine oneself to external, that is, sensory impressions? Why not look deeper, into the mind's eye, into reality as it appeared to the inner self? Or, for that matter, why bother with objective reality at all? Why not concen-

In an ironic self-portrayal as a saint, painted on a door in a favorite Brittany inn, Paul Gauguin jibed at symbolism in painting he had helped initiate.

trate entirely on the subjective world of the artist? By shifting from objective reality to subjective response, the Impressionists paved the way for a complete withdrawal of the artist from his traditional task of depicting the external world about him.

Impressionism was followed by a movement usually called Post-Impressionism, and sometimes Expressionism. This movement marked the shift from a purely sensory, visual perception to a psychological perception of reality. The Post-Impressionists were concerned not with the surface appearance of objects but with their reflections in the viewer's mind. They were especially influenced by the literary concept of "symbols," understood as words or images by means of which external reality is suggested to and assimilated by the mind.

Impressionism was a French movement; Post-Impressionism was international. Although originating in France, it spread rapidly to other countries, notably Germany and Russia. It had much less coherence than Impressionism. The Impressionists constituted a well-identified group which held together for nearly a quarter of a century, adhered to a fairly concrete aesthetic program, exhibited jointly, and sold through one dealer. The Post-Impressionists formed small, ephemeral bands, which rarely survived a couple of seasons. By the time Post-Impressionism yielded to Abstract art (around 1910), the whole notion of movements and schools disintegrated. Painting became thoroughly individualized, each artist developing his personal style or mannerism.

Post-Impressionism was launched by Paul Gauguin, Georges Seurat, and Paul Cézanne, and included among its adherents the Dutch painter Vincent van Gogh.° In contrast to the Impressionists, born mostly in the 1830s, the leading Post-Impressionists (with the exception of Cézanne) belonged to a younger generation, born around 1850.

Gauguin led the attack on the Impressionists, whom he dismissed as the "official painters of tomorrow." He rejected their illusionism as superficial and sought a deeper grasp of reality in the psychic unconscious and in the mysteries of primitive life. In revolt against modern rational civilization, he fled in 1887 to Central America and in 1891 to Tahiti, to paint unrealistic works, almost medieval in their mysticism. He pioneered in the discovery of primitive art, claiming that it expressed the sense of wonder that civilized man no longer possessed. The taste that the twentieth century has acquired for African and pre-classical Greek art owes a great deal to Gauguin. So does the whole current of "modern primitivism," contemporary painting in a deliberately childlike manner by amateurs, the most gifted of whom was Henri Rousseau.

Seurat's main contribution was the technique of "pointillism." Study of scientific light theories convinced him that the mixing of colors ought to occur not on the painter's palette but in the viewer's eye. He worked out an elaborate system of conveying both shape and hue by means of carefully juxtaposed dots of primary color. In a sense, Seurat was at one with the Impressionists in seeking to capture the effects of light. But his method was fundamentally incompatible with Impressionism, because it required the artist to compose slowly and methodically, and this could only be done in the studio. Seurat's works are

° These painters are often mistakenly called "Impressionists." The term, however, should not be applied indiscriminately to all modernistic painters of the second half of the nineteenth century.

classical in their static quality. They contradict every principle stated by Pissarro in the passage quoted above.

Cézanne is today generally recognized as having had the greatest influence on twentieth-century painting. He was older than Gauguin and Seurat, belonging to the generation of the Impressionists. But even while Impressionism was at its height, he stood to the side, pursuing his own individual path. Cézanne was fascinated not by light but by form. "Nature," he once asserted, "must be treated in terms of the cylinder, the sphere, the cone." This principle he applied to landscapes, figures, and especially to still life. His colors were deliberately dull, the emphasis being placed on the shape and spatial relationship of objects. He pioneered the transition from the visual to the intellectual grasp of reality, from appearance to underlying structure.

The Post-Impressionists, unlike the Impressionists proper, paid great attention to composition, which they worked out as carefully as the academic painters. This held less true of van Gogh, who adopted their emphasis on the "inner" reality of objects, but in matters of composition preferred to follow the Impressionists and the Japanese. Toulouse-Lautrec, another outstanding Post-Impressionist, also adopted Japanese models in his works, especially in his brilliant drawings, lithographs, and posters.

Gauguin's The Day of the God *is composed around the Maori god of creation. For Gauguin the South Seas idyll he painted was a mockery; he died there in 1903, nearly blind, a victim of syphilis and alcoholism.*

Julien Tanguy was one of the few dealers (Durand-Ruel was another) who saw the promise of modern painting. Vincent van Gogh painted Tanguy (left) against a backdrop of the Japanese prints much admired by the Post-Impressionists. Opposite is one of the carefully structured landscapes of Paul Cézanne, a view of Mont Sainte-Victoire in Provence.

In the early years of the twentieth century painting fell into as great confusion as physics. The notion that the artist's task was to represent "reality" became meaningless, for no one seemed certain any longer what reality was. The aversion of post-1900 painters to visual realism was heightened by the spread of photography. Although invented in the 1830s, photography did not become a popular pastime until half a century later, when George Eastman produced the first Kodak (1888), a cheap and simple amateur camera. Now that everyone could produce naturalistic portraits and landscapes with a snap of a shutter, it no longer made sense to do so laboriously by paint and brush. Painters increasingly began to think of a canvas not as a reproduction but as an end in itself:

> Beginning in 1905 the great goal was an art that would express human inwardness without recourse to metaphors drawn from the outside world. The essential was no longer to reproduce objects, *but to make the picture itself into an object* which, through the resonance inherent in its construction, would awaken a feeling similar to that aroused by the things and processes of visible nature.°

The picture thus tended toward an autonomous existence, its purpose being not to mirror reality but to create it.

The possibilities inherent in this aesthetic led to the emergence of a bewildering variety of pictorial schools. Each appeared on the scene with great fanfare, accompanied by a manifesto, worded in high-flown but imprecise terms, which

°Werner Haftmann, *Painting in the Twentieth Century* (1960). Italics added.

rejected the past and promised an entirely new art. It shocked the public for a season or two, until pushed into oblivion by another even more radical school equally intolerant of all that preceded it and equally short-lived.

In 1901 the great sensation were the painters of a group dubbed "Les Fauves" (the Savages), which included Henri Matisse. They announced that the purpose of painting was to depict not things but "emotions." They used color without reference to natural appearance, for the mere sake of effect—like "sticks of dynamite, exploding them to produce light," in the words of one of their adherents. The French Fauvists had their counterpart a decade later in the German "Expressionists."

Around 1907 the new sensation was Cubism, whose leading exponent was the Spaniard Pablo Picasso. Pushing Cézanne's geometric view of reality to its logical conclusion, the Cubists painted geometric designs with the intention of having them serve as visual "stimuli" to recreate reality in the viewer's mind. They liked to experiment with collages, that is, paste-ups of material objects like

Henri Matisse's Dance *(1909), a study for a mural, exhibits the "genius of omission" and rhythmic spontaneity of composition he strove to achieve.*

newspaper clippings, scraps of wood or metal, pieces of string, and anything else that was handy.

The flight from visual reality culminated in 1910–1911 with the introduction of "Abstraction." Cubism still paid some obeisance to reality by aspiring to stimulate the viewer into "imagining" physical objects not depicted on the canvas. Abstraction gave up reality altogether. It regarded a painting as a completely self-contained, self-justified object—an end in itself, like a tree or a house. The pioneer of Abstract painting was the Russian Vasili Kandinsky, who lived and worked in Germany. Under the impression of Monet's *Haystacks*, Kandinsky concluded that the subject matter of a painting was irrelevant—decisive was the arrangement of shapes and colors. The movement caught on, especially in Moscow, which, on the eve of World War I, became the international center of Abstraction. It achieved its ultimate fulfillment in the work of another Russian, Casimir Malevich, whose *White Square on a White Background* represents the ultimate fulfillment of the whole Abstract movement.

After 1910 it is no longer possible to generalize about the history of painting. Although Abstraction dominates, side by side there exist other schools. Some painters, notably Picasso, have traversed a great variety of styles in an unending search for the new. Others formulate their personal techniques and adhere to them. With the triumph of extreme subjectivism, aesthetic standards have disappeared: since every artist is acknowledged to have a right to his own "reality," there can be no generally acceptable criteria to help distinguish good art from bad. One of the by-products of this whole development has been a decline in professional skills, especially of draftsmanship. Nineteenth-century artists, even when they rebelled against the line (as did the Romantics and Impressionists), knew how to draw well. This no longer holds true of most contemporary painters, who do not undergo the long and exacting training necessary to achieve mastery of drawing.

Much of the misunderstanding of Abstract art derives from the desire to apply to it standards of traditional representational painting by inquiring about its meaning. Abstract art bears close kinship to Byzantine and Muslim art. It no more "means" anything than does a stylized icon, a Persian carpet, or a Turkish tile. It must be liked or disliked as an object in itself, not as a reproduction of something else. Fundamentally, visual art as it had been understood for hundreds of years in the West has disappeared in our time, giving way to a purely decorative style.

The evolution of the visual arts from conventional realism to abstraction has had a powerful influence on the applied arts, producing a veritable revolution in design. The essential feature of this revolution is a merger of art and engineering.

In the nineteenth century art and engineering were natural enemies, one belonging to the realm of beauty, the other to that of utility. The function of art

Modern Design

BOTH: MUSEUM OF MODERN ART

Les Demoiselles d'Avignon (1907) was *Pablo Picasso's first venture into Cubism. It has been called "a battlefield of trial and experiment" (the two faces at right, for example, are suggestive of African sculpture). The title is an ironic reference to a cabaret or brothel in Barcelona.*

was to conceal by all available means, mostly ornament, the true appearance of ordinary objects, especially those produced by industrial methods. John Ruskin, the high priest of Victorian taste, even declared ornament to be the essence of art. The majority of engineers probably shared this sentiment. But in the course of their work they sometimes had to employ expedients that violated it. When constructing a cheap bridge or factory building, they occasionally dispensed with ornament, leaving the stuctural elements exposed to the eye. These unpretentious, utilitarian buildings, some of which have survived, strike the viewer as remarkably modern. "Artlessness" of this kind, of course, was tolerated only in buildings of little importance. It was unthinkable in public buildings and private residences. These were the domain of "art," that is, of skills designed to disguise true structure and function.

The essential quality of modern design is rebellion against aesthetic camouflage. It marks the positive acceptance of industrialism and the reunification of art with engineering, identifying beauty with that design which best—that is, most economically—fulfills the function of a given object. It refuses to disguise a load-bearing pillar as a Greek column, to conceal an ordinary toilet inside a pseudo-Gothic chair, or to distort the shape of a sewing machine with wrought-iron tracery. It exiles ornament from objects of utility, leaving it to art. (This fact has further encouraged the visual arts to abandon the representational in favor of the ornamental.)

The pioneer of modern design was the English poet and artist William Morris. Morris married in 1859, and like a good middle-class citizen proceeded in an earnest manner to furnish his household. He found to his disgust, however, that the wares offered by commercial stores consisted entirely of ugly machine-made "antiques." He then founded, with a few associates, his own workshop to produce various household goods, such as furniture and wallpaper. By standards of the time his products were remarkably plain and functional. He grew so enthusiastic about the mission of improving public taste that he transformed the workshop into a commercial enterprise. Later on he designed his own house. He also founded the Kelmscott Press, which pioneered modern book design. Morris was inspired by an anti-industrial animus: like a typical Victorian, he idealized the Middle Ages and wanted a return to guild production. Nevertheless, his efforts anticipated Modernism in the sense that they posed, and in some measure solved, the question of preserving beauty under industrial, mass production, conditions.

A notable phase in the development of modern taste was a movement that originated in the 1890s in Germany and Belgium and today is generally known by its French name, "Art Nouveau." (In Germany it is called *Jugendstil*—"Youth style.") Like Morris, the artists of this movement were steeped in the mentality of their time, and yet departed from it, moving toward Modernism. Art Nouveau was essentially a decorative style, highly flamboyant, characterized by sinuous floral lines, asymmetry, and the use of unshaded colors. It involved the transfer of some of the visual effects of Post-Impressionism to the applied arts. Art Nouveau had its furniture, posters, jewelry, bookbindings, and many other objects of use, usually exquisite in workmanship and expensive. It also had an architectural style, whose greatest exponent was the Spaniard Antoni Gaudí,

An Art Nouveau chair, made c. 1900 by the Frenchman Hector Guimard.

the designer of fantastic churches and apartment houses in Barcelona. By its stress on ornamentation, Art Nouveau ran contrary to what we have defined as the essence of modern design, but it is regarded as pre-Modernist because of the boldness of its design and the use of ornament not to conceal but to accentuate structure.

The greatest innovations in architecture were made in the United States. Toward the end of the century the unprecedented expansion of industry and population in America necessitated the development of cheap and fast building methods. There was no place for the classical temple or the Gothic cathedral styles in the office buildings and residences designed for booming Chicago, where modern architecture was born in the 1890s. The so-called Chicago school, led by Louis H. Sullivan, made use of the latest technical innovations, such as steel frames and safety elevators, to construct office buildings, warehouses, and department stores of great height and almost free of ornament.° These buildings revealed honestly their structure as well as purpose. The Chicago style spread to England and to the Continent, where it found even more radical application. Here, as in the United States, business proved most receptive to innovation, being attracted to it by considerations of economy and efficiency.

Antoni Gaudí's Casa Milá apartment in Barcelona, with its avoidance of straight lines and its improbable shapes, looks like a pastry cook's masterpiece. It is built of cut stone.

°Chicago's great fire of 1871 necessitated rapid rebuilding and created an atmosphere conducive to architectural experiments.

Public institutions and private builders remained, on the whole, resistant until after World War II.

In the early 1900s the principles of Modernism were also extended to domestic appliances. The tendency here too was to discard superfluous ornament and to reveal function. The pioneering work in this field was done by Germans, especially by the gigantic electric cartels, which, even before World War I, streamlined such domestic objects as lamps, irons, and tea kettles. At the time the Germans excelled in industrial design, that is, the application of advanced aesthetic standards to mass-produced consumer goods.

The whole evolution of modern design from William Morris onward reached a

Walter Gropius wrote that buildings must be "receptacles for the flow of life which they have to serve." He practiced what he preached in his Bauhaus at Dessau, combining in one complex workshops, classrooms, offices, dormitories, and social areas.

synthesis in the "Bauhaus"—a collective of designers founded in Germany in 1919 by Walter Gropius. Its purpose was to bridge, institutionally, the distinction between art, craftsmanship, and industry by gathering under one roof in creative companionship craftsmen, artists, architects, and engineers. The Bauhaus produced buildings, furniture, and appliances, and sometimes even outfitted complete households. Its orientation was democratic in the sense that it aimed at providing well-designed industrial goods for the mass market. It dissolved in 1928, and shortly afterward, with the advent of Hitler, leadership in industrial design passed to the Scandinavian countries and the United States.

In music it is not possible, of course, to speak of "reality" quite in the same sense in which the word is used in the visual arts and literature, for music does not depict. And yet there is a musical equivalent of realism, and that is the rendering of emotions. Emotion may be described as the musical counterpart of visual and literary reproduction. Modern music, through a succession of technical innovations, has tended to move away from emotional expression and toward pure sound that pleases the ear and sometimes appeals only to the intellect.

The crisis of traditional music began in the mid-nineteenth century. Its immediate cause was the exhaustion of the possibilities inherent in the traditional idiom. By then, Romantic music had said everything it had to say, and composers found it increasingly difficult to create without repeating Beethoven, Schubert, or Chopin. A traditionalist of such genius as Brahms agonized for fourteen years over his *First Symphony* (1876) because he did not want to repeat his predecessors. The trouble with Romantic music was that it had not departed radically enough from the conventions of classicism. Although Romanticism had increased the independence of music, broadened the range of its forms, and permitted a certain degree of harmonic freedom, it never challenged the basic premises of classical music. Technically, Romantic composers continued to adhere to the canon of a Bach or a Mozart. Their harmony was "tonal," that is, based on a seven-note scale with major and minor keys. A trained listener can tell immediately from a few bars of classical or Romantic music the key in which it is written and the note on which it will end.

The first important departure from the classical-Romantic musical tradition is associated with the name of the German composer Richard Wagner. To begin with, Wagner had a novel conception of music, envisaging it as only one ingredient in a total artistic experience. In his "musical dramas" he fused music with poetry and visual effects to produce an experience of this kind. He dispensed with the customary recitative and arias, giving each character or event an identifying theme. Second, Wagner took great harmonic liberties, frequently departing from strict tonality. Though he had a great gift for melody, he did not indulge in it, preferring to concentrate on musical moods. Wagner's *Parsifal* and *Tristan and Isolde*, written in the late 1850s, were seminal works that even today seem remarkably *avant-garde*. His friends, headed by the king of Bavaria, established at Bayreuth a Wagnerian center, where his musical dramas were performed in a setting calculated to create an impression of utmost reality. Apart from a small coterie of fanatical devotees, however, the public was scandalized by his works, considering them jarring and formless.

Musical Impressionism originated in Russia, but reached its heights in France. Its founder was the Russian composer Modest Mussorgsky, whose *Pictures at an Exhibition* (1874) represents the first successful attempt at transposing pictorial images into sound. Claude Debussy, however, was the greatest composer of this school. Like the contemporary Impressionist painters, he sought to re-create in musical terms the fleeting impressions of nature. This he did not by means of such naïve sound-effects as imitating the chirping of birds or the clap of thunder but by establishing an overall sound-mood. He virtually abandoned melody and often ignored tonality. Among his outstanding works are *La Mer* (The Sea; 1905) and compositions for the piano with such typical im-

MARCEL BREUER

Tubular steel chair (1925) by Marcel Breuer, an alumnus of the Bauhaus.

Picasso sketched Igor Stravinsky in 1920 after the prèmiere of his ballet Pulcinella, *for which Picasso designed the costumes and settings.*

pressionistic titles as "Gardens in the Rain," "Reflections in the Water," "Bells Through the Leaves," and "The Sunken Cathedral."

Musical Impressionism faded out around 1910 and was replaced by a new fashion comparable to Fauvism. As Matisse and his friends delighted in color for its own sake, so the composers of this new trend found pleasure in sheer sound. Expressionism in music was also a Russian invention, the product of the musical genius of Igor Stravinsky and the organizational talent of the greatest of modern impressarios, Sergei Diaghilev. Diaghilev succeeded in assembling the best musical, choreographic, and decorative talent in Russia around the Ballet Russe, with which he revolutionized the art of the dance. This group turned its back on nineteenth-century choreographic conventions, with their predictably tulle-clad ballerinas performing predictable steps to predictable music, in favor of violent effects: fantastic costumes and unrealistic backdrops splashed with wild colors, dramatic leaps, and violent rhythms. The most sensational work in the repertoire of the Ballet Russe was Stravinsky's *Le Sacre du Printemps*, a work that made free use of primitive sounds and beats. Its first performance in Paris in 1913 created a theatrical scandal comparable to the Battle of *Hernani* of 1830 (Chapter 14). The public, outraged by the savagery of the music and dancing, booed so loudly that it nearly drowned out the sound of the orchestra. The assimilation of primitivism into serious music, however, proceeded apace, being accelerated during World War I when American troops imported Negro jazz to Europe. The total effect of these innovations was not only to broaden the range of musical expression but, more fundamentally, to free the composer from the obligation to convey emotions and impressions by allowing him to indulge in pure sound.

For all his innovation, Stravinsky still adhered to a harmonic reference system

—that is to say, he wrote in a definite key. The most radical of modern musical innovators, the Viennese Arnold Schönberg, went a step further and abandoned tonality altogether. Rather than treat all notes in a composition as tied to a common key, he decided to treat each as an independent entity. In his musical system the scale consists of twelve independent notes, unrelated to a tonal key. The purpose of such "atonal" music is simply to organize sounds. In this respect it is closely akin to Abstract painting, which took a similar attitude toward visual images. Schönberg composed the first "atonal" work in 1907–1908 (*The Second String Quartet*) and continued to experiment with this mode until his death in 1951.

After 1910 music, like painting, lost its unity and broke up into a bewildering variety of individual tendencies. Some composers, such as Richard Strauss and Jan Sibelius, continued to write Romantic music. Others, for example the Hungarian Béla Bartók, adopted no particular musical system, experimenting ceaselessly with techniques and forms. The same holds true of Stravinsky, who left Russia after the Bolshevik seizure of power and settled in the West. Yet others followed Schönberg and proceeded relentlessly toward extreme abstraction. Modern music has encountered even stronger resistance than painting, and hence contemporary concert managers usually schedule modern compositions in the middle of the program to prevent audiences from avoiding them by either arriving late or leaving early. The achievement of modern composers, however, has been considerable because they have greatly extended the range of their art. The time may well come when music will be regarded, along with design, as the most original aesthetic contribution of the twentieth century.

All that has been said above concerning modern thought and art applies, with minor modifications, to literature as well. We find here the same withdrawal from objectivity, the same uninhibited experimentation, and the same creative individualism. The attention of modern writers has shifted from the external to the internal: from society and man's place in it to the inner world of the individual. A characteristic feature of modern prose and poetry is the abandonment of the rigid chronological framework. It takes similar liberties with time that modern painting takes with space and modern music with tonality. Concentration on the inner states of the mind has encouraged the adoption of subjective, psychological time in place of objective, physical time.

The rebellion against literary realism began in poetry. In the heyday of positivism poetry had been out of favor with the public because it was less suitable to rendering the social environment than was prose. It regained favor in the 1880s, and before long poetry experienced a veritable renaissance. The revival began in France, but it quickly spread to the rest of the Continent, and from there, with some delay, to England and the United States.

The most influential poetic movement of the second half of the nineteenth century and the fountainhead of all literary Modernism was Symbolism, a movement that began in France. The Symbolists reacted against the so-called Parnassians, the poets of the positivist era, who stressed purity of form and precision of language as the highest aesthetic virtues. The founder of Symbolism, Stéphane Mallarmé, developed a poetic theory pithily summarized in the follow-

Modern Literature

ing sentence: "It is not *description* which can unveil the efficacy and beauty of monuments, seas, or the human face in all their maturity and native state, but rather *evocation, allusion, suggestion*." "Evocation," indeed, was the key concept of the entire Symbolist school. Symbolism strove to penetrate beyond the formal meaning of words to their evocative connotations. It also sought evocation by word combinations and rhythms that produced something akin to musical effects.

The contrast between the Parnassians and the Symbolists may be illustrated in their respective treatment of the same theme, the classical image of faun and nymphs. In his poem "Pan," the leader of the Parnassians, Leconte de Lisle, treats the subject as a tableau in two scenes: a faun is surrounded by dancing nymphs and falls in love with one of them; when darkness descends he carries the nymph away. This poem lends itself perfectly to pictorial treatment, for it concerns itself only with external appearance, telling us nothing about the subject's thoughts or feelings. By contrast, Mallarmé, in "The Afternoon of a Faun" (1876), his most celebrated work, deals with nothing but the confused flow of the faun's consciousness after the sudden and fleeting glimpse of two nymphs. Mallarmé's poem is not pictorial or descriptive but musical, evocative. Debussy, in setting "The Afternoon of a Faun" to music, is said to have followed the poem line by line.

Symbolism immensely enlarged the vocabulary of the writer by breaking with the tradition that held that each object or occurrence has one and only one word that most accurately renders it. It encouraged writers to invent allusions, word combinations, symbols, and other oblique devices that bore no definable relation to the object depicted, yet engendered in the reader's imagination and emotion the desired response. On this principle a great modern school of poetry came into existence. Among its leading practitioners may be mentioned Paul Verlaine and Arthur Rimbaud in France, W. B. Yeats and T. S. Eliot in England, R. M. Rilke in Austria, Alexander Blok, Boris Pasternak, and Anna Akhmatova in Russia.

The Englishman William Butler Yeats, photographed in 1908, was one of the modern poets influenced by Symbolism.

In extending the means of expression available to the poet, Symbolism caused poetry to become obscure and unapproachable. In pre-Symbolist days any literate person could approach a poem with the assurance that a modicum of concentration would be rewarded with a modicum of understanding. Symbolist and post-Symbolist poetry requires more than concentration. It calls for knowledge of the author and his personal language, for without such knowledge the allusions cannot be understood and the poem appears meaningless. As a result, poetry has ceased to play a part in popular culture; it has become instead a secret language understood only by initiates.

Although its greatest impact was on poetry, Symbolism also had a powerful effect on prose. This, together with the influence of modern psychology, did much to discredit realistic and naturalistic techniques in prose.

In the typical realistic novel of the nineteenth century, the characters were endowed with definable personalities and orderly minds. A representative realistic hero had a "character" with a fixed set of qualities, which permitted the reader to anticipate the hero's reaction to a given occurrence. His ideas, insofar as they were spelled out, formed themselves as a matter of course into grammati-

Marcel Proust, photographed in the 1890s at a picnic, was rather a dilettante before sequestering himself to write Remembrance of Things Past.

cally correct and logically consistent sentences. Such a conception of the literary personage accorded with the mid-nineteenth century view of the human psyche with its "states of consciousness." Toward the end of the century *avant-garde* writers found this whole conception unsatisfactory. Bergson and James had made them aware that the mind does not operate in a neat logical manner: consciousness is formless, hazy at the edges, flowing in a continuous stream. In real life thoughts jump from subject to subject in accord with an informal logic of psychological associations, the key to which lies buried in the individual's past experience. The notion of character as something static dissolved further under the influence of psychology. It now appeared not as a fixed condition but a process—a battlefield on which the conscious waged constant war on the unconscious. According to the English novelist Virginia Woolf, one of the leaders of the new school of novelists, "life is not a series of gig-lamps symmetrically arranged, but a luminous halo, a semi-transparent envelope surrounding us from the beginning of consciousness to the end." The task of the novelist therefore is to "convey this varying, this unknown and uncircumscribed spirit, whatever aberration or complexity it may display, with as little mixture of the alien and external as possible."° To achieve this aim he must have recourse to methods different from those employed by the realists.

One of these methods has been for the writer to isolate himself entirely from active life in order to delve undisturbed into the innermost recesses of his memory and to bring to the surface its unconscious recollections. Marcel Proust spent ten

°Virginia Woolf, *The Common Reader* (1948).

Above left, James Joyce with Sylvia Beach, whose Paris bookstore was a haven for expatriate writers and who published Joyce's Ulysses *in 1922. Above right, Anton Chekhov (in black hat) with Count Leo Tolstoy in 1900.*

years (1909–1919) in a cork-lined apartment in Paris in an effort to achieve this. The result is *Remembrance of Things Past*, an incredibly detailed evocation of past experiences.

Proust followed Bergsonian psychology, but the majority of innovators preferred the "stream-of-consciousness" technique derived from late nineteenth-century psychology. This technique seeks to render verbally the spontaneous flow of thought with all its capriciousness, fragmentariness, and imprecision. The most celebrated novel of this genre is James Joyce's *Ulysses*, published in 1922. Joyce tells in it the story of a single uneventful day—June 16, 1904, to be precise—in the life of ordinary citizens of Dublin by following the flow of their "internal dialogue." Memories, wishes, and impressions fuse in one inseparable whole. The narrative has that indeterminate quality that modern psychology finds in the operations of the mind. The method attracted many other practitioners, among them Virginia Woolf (*Mrs. Dalloway*, 1925) and the American novelist William Faulkner. It has the great virtue of permitting the writer to depict his characters not only as they presently are, but as they were in the past and as they are likely to be in the future. It thus accords with the modern view of the personality as something in the process of becoming.

The stress on inner psychological processes is responsible for the most radical innovations in the art of novel writing, but it has been by no means universally adopted. Side by side with the psychologically oriented school of writing there exist other tendencies, of which two are especially noteworthy.

One group of writers has pursued the older tradition of the social novel by using the device of grand family chronicles, which permits them to show the evolution of society as revealed in attitudes and actions of successive generations. Among the outstanding novels in this category are Thomas Mann's *The Buddenbrooks* (1901), John Galsworthy's *The Forsyte Saga* (1906–1921), and Roger Martin Du Gard's *Les Thibaults* (1922–1940). The Nobel Prize Committee has always shown partiality for authors of this genre, but their popularity has declined, and today they are more esteemed than read.

The other tendency may be described as visceral writing. Its exponents scorn as decadent the whole psychological orientation, preferring to write in a vigorous language taken from everyday life and stressing violent physical experience. The English novelist D. H. Lawrence, a leader of this school, considered "understanding" to be the greatest calamity to have befallen mankind and appealed for a revival of the dormant senses. "I stick to the solar plexus," he wrote. "Your solar plexus is where you are you." The Italian Gabriele D'Annunzio and the American Ernest Hemingway were leading representatives of this tendency.

The withdrawal of much of modern prose literature from contact with social reality has thus not gone unchallenged. Although Proust, Joyce, and the other writers of the psychological school dominate the current high-brow literary scene and academic criticism, strong voices nevertheless are heard condemning this trend. Some critics maintain that modern techniques like the "stream of consciousness" obscure instead of clarifying the processes of the mind and make much modern literature unintelligible. Others accuse modern writers of having forfeited the writer's traditional function as an intermediary between the reader and his fellow men. Some of the greatest prose writers of the post-Symbolist era —for example, Anton Chekhov and Thomas Mann—though not immune to modern trends, continued to write in a traditional manner.

In the theater the greatest innovations were introduced by Chekhov, who has had overwhelming impact on dramatic art in the twentieth century. Chekhov wrote what can best be described as "undramatic drama"—plays that have no plots and that derive dramatic tension from psychological conflicts within the characters themselves. Chekhov once said that life's real tragedies occur when one opens an egg at breakfast—that is, the tragic is the commonplace. His characters are frustrated people, constantly torn between their awareness of reality and their aspiration to some higher ideal that is unattainable, and that, even if it were attained, would not make them happy. In his *Seagull* (1896), *The Three Sisters* (1901), and *The Cherry Orchard* (1904) almost nothing happens, and yet there hovers over the proceedings a sense of deep disaster. The principles that Chekhov introduced were developed by successive dramatists and led to the emergence of the modern *avant-garde* theater. The plays of this genre take as great liberties with the formal dramatic unities as the modern psychological novel takes with the tradition of the narrative.

Interesting experiments along these lines have also been made in the cinema, which from a form of cheap amusement has developed into one of the liveliest arts. The technical flexibility of the moving picture permits great freedom in distorting formal time and space for narrative purposes. Efforts to utilize modern techniques in cinematography, initiated in Russia in the early 1920s by Sergei Eisenstein and revived in France after the Second World War, represent an attempt to transfer to the screen the methods of the psychological novel and drama.

verylowL'ILLUSTRATION

26

———◦◦◦———

The Twenties

The two decades separating the end of the First World War from the outbreak of the Second witnessed a disastrous decline of liberal attitudes and institutions. The liberal crisis, noticeable at the end of the nineteenth century, came to a head in the twentieth—what had been a sickness turned into an agony. By 1939 liberal regimes survived only in the few countries in which they had struck the deepest roots: Great Britain, the Low Countries, Switzerland, Scandinavia, and France (and in the latter, only until the summer of 1940). Elsewhere the rule of law, constitutional safeguards, and parliamentary bodies collapsed under internal or external pressure. Their place was taken by authoritarian regimes ranging from relatively innocuous, old-fashioned dictatorships to the most ruthless and destructive totalitarianisms.

The disaster that befell liberalism had several causes, all of which had made themselves felt before the Great War. Of these the most important were national and social antagonisms and the erosion of the middle class. The World War and the Russian Revolution gave added impetus to these processes. Disoriented and demoralized, liberal governments (including those composed of democratic socialists) proved unable to cope with their tasks and at the same time withstand a growing challenge from left and right extremists: Communists, Fascists, Nazis, and their many imitators. In country after country they fell under the onslaught of groups determined to seize power and exercise it without any constitutional or even moral restraints. The story of this dark episode in Western history is the subject of this and the following two chapters.

The principal peace terms concluding World War I were drawn up at a conference held at Paris in the first half of 1919. The Treaty of Versailles, signed in June, set the conditions for Germany and at the same time provided for the establishment of a League of Nations. Supplementary treaties with the other defeated countries were signed later: with Austria in September, 1919, at St. Germain; with Bulgaria in November, 1919, at Neuilly; with Hungary in June, 1920, at Trianon; and with Turkey in August, 1920, at Sèvres. (All these are localities in the vicinity of Paris.)

The Peace Settlement

Although the representatives of many countries participated in the deliberations and were consulted in cases directly involving their interests, the terms were in large measure set by the big powers, the so-called Council of Four, composed of President Woodrow Wilson and the Prime Ministers of Great Britain (David Lloyd George), France (Georges Clemenceau), and Italy (Vittorio Orlando). The defeated powers, Germany included, did not participate in the negotiations and had to sign conditions in the framing of which they had taken no part. Soviet Russia, which had dropped out of the war in March, 1918, by signing a separate peace treaty, was not represented either.

The Council of Four intended to lay the groundwork of a lasting peace, but

Woodrow Wilson acknowledges the cheers of Parisians as he arrives for the peace conference. With him is French President Raymond Poincaré. Wilson made brief tours of Britain, Italy, and France before the conference and was lionized everywhere.

its members differed greatly on how to go about it. Two general approaches were discernible: the "hard" line, espoused by the French, and the "soft" line, advanced by the United States. The Italians sided with France, while the British vacillated between the two positions.

Clemenceau, the head of the French delegation, saw the main cause of international instability in German aggressiveness, and considered it essential to weaken Germany to the point where it no longer would be able to wage effective war. Concretely, this meant creating a buffer state along the Rhine separating Germany from France, and breaking up Germany into a number of smaller states and demilitarizing it. It was on his insistence that the British maintained their blockade of Germany, preventing the flow of food into a country on the verge of starvation, so as to soften it and force it to accept onerous peace terms.

President Wilson, by contrast, did not regard Germany as the principal source of instability or as the country responsible for the outbreak of the Great War. To him the cause of the war lay in fundamental flaws of the system regulating relations between states: in secret diplomacy, thwarted aspirations to national statehood, and, above all, the absence of institutions capable of peacefully resolving international disputes. He was less concerned with punishing or disarming specific aggressors than with establishing a new order that would remove the causes and eliminate the means of aggression in general.

The peacemakers of 1919 lacked that freedom of action that their predecessors had enjoyed at Vienna in 1815. Each of the Four, in addition to serving as a diplomat, also headed a political party dependent on a democratic electorate. This electorate, by and large, had little understanding of the broader issues of international relations, and responded readily to the appeals of demagogic politicians and irresponsible journalists for vengeance (in the case of the European Allies) or withdrawal from foreign commitments (in the case of the United States). Public opinion thus exerted an invisible but ever-present influence on the negotiations. How disastrous this influence could be is evident in the example of Lloyd George. In December, 1918, in the course of a parliamentary election, the British Prime Minister found himself making extravagant promises to the discharged soldiers and recently enfranchised women voters. Before he knew what he was committing himself to, he had pledged to extract from the Germans all the money that Britain had spent on the war. "We will get out of her all you can squeeze out of a lemon and a bit more," a close associate of his promised the voters; "I will squeeze her until you can hear the pips squeak." Such incautious promises forced Lloyd George after his re-election to follow the "hard" line more than he really wished to do, especially on the issue of reparations. In the case of the United States, as we shall see, the failure of public opinion and congressional leaders to support Wilson had an even more disastrous effect on the fate of the peace treaty.

The Germans had originally agreed to an armistice on the basis of Wilson's "Fourteen Points," a general peace plan which he had made public in January, 1918. The French, British, and Italians did not much care for the proposal, but they went along for fear that unless they did, the United States would sign a separate peace treaty. The Fourteen Points called for national self-determination for all peoples and the redrawing of European frontiers to conform with it.

Lloyd George (right) and Clemenceau were photographed in June, 1919, at St. Germain after delivering their peace terms to the Austrian delegates.

They also urged freedom of trade and of navigation, open diplomacy, and the establishment of an international organization to guarantee the security of states. Wilson made no mention of any punitive measures against the Central Powers, and in his public speeches explicitly disavowed them.° The Fourteen Points constituted the legal basis of the peace negotiations, but they were promptly lost sight of. Later on, the Germans and Austrians could therefore claim with some justice that they had been tricked into signing an armistice.

The negotiations at Paris were conducted in an atmosphere of acrimony and tension. Clemenceau, pressed by the French generals, pursued relentlessly and with great cunning his main objective, the emasculation of Germany. Wilson tried to frustrate these designs, but he was not a skillful diplomat, lacked knowledge of foreign languages, and was handicapped by the absence of domestic sup-

---

°The European Allies, however, in accepting the Fourteen Points, did reserve for themselves the right to claim full compensation for damages to civilian property.

port. At one point he became so angry that he threatened to break off talks and sail for home. Orlando, peeved at the failure to win territory for Italy, actually did pack up and leave. Lloyd George, ignorant of European history and geography, shifted his position frequently. The spectacle was not a pretty one, and it contributed heavily to the general sense of postwar disenchantment.

Finally, in June, 1919, after much wrangling, the peace treaty was ready for submission to the Germans. Its provisions bearing on Germany may be grouped under three headings:

1) *Territorial.* In the west, Germany was to surrender Alsace and Lorraine and evacuate territories occupied during the war. American and British opposition forced Clemenceau to drop his plan for a buffer state in the Rhineland and the breakup of the rest of Germany. Instead, German territory west of the Rhine and within a belt thirty miles deep to the east of it was declared permanently demili-

The map of Europe as redrawn by the terms of the peace settlement; also shown are areas of subsequent dispute.

EUROPE AFTER WORLD WAR I

- German Empire, 1914
- Austro-Hungarian Empire, 1914
- Russian Empire, 1914
- Ottoman Empire, 1914
- Disputed areas after Treaty of Versailles

tarized. Here the Germans could neither station troops nor build military installations. The Saar region was placed for fifteen years under international administration, to be followed by a plebiscite. In the east, Germany was to cede to the new Polish state the area of Posen as well as a "corridor" to the Baltic. East Prussia and Upper Silesia were to be polled whether they wished to join with Germany or with Poland. German overseas colonies were taken away and placed under the League of Nations. These provisions deprived Germany of one-seventh of its territory in Europe and one-tenth of its population. The lost territories had considerable economic value, for they contained three-fourths of Germany's iron resources and one-fourth of its coal.

2) *Military.* Apart from an army of 100,000 men and a miniscule navy, Germany was to be disarmed. It was to have no heavy artillery, tanks, military aviation, or submarines. Military conscription was abolished.

3) *Reparations.* Originally it had been the intention of France, Britain, and Italy to recover from Germany in the form of an indemnity all the money they had spent in waging war. Unyielding American opposition forced the abandonment of the proposed indemnity. Instead, the European Allies contented themselves with reparations, that is, repayment of the losses that German military action had inflicted on civilian property. Germany's legal liability for these losses was fixed in a separate article.° A Reparations Commission was appointed to determine the extent of the civilian property losses. In 1921 it reported its findings, fixing the reparations at $33 billion; half of this sum was to go to France.

No peace treaty in modern times has evoked sharper criticism and produced more controversy. The German delegates confronted with these terms protested loudly but to no avail. They were told that if they refused to sign, Allied troops would occupy Germany and the British would maintain indefinitely their naval blockade. A scathing critique of the treaty, and especially of its reparations provisions, appeared in early 1920 from the pen of John Maynard Keynes under the title *The Economic Consequences of the Peace.* Keynes called Versailles the "Carthaginian Peace of M. Clemenceau." It was "neither right nor possible": in the first instance because it degraded the Germans to long-term economic servitude, in the second because its territorial and other punitive provisions prevented them from fulfilling the demands of that servitude. Keynes's acid sketches of the negotiators, his persuasive economic arguments (we shall encounter him later as the outstanding economist of modern times), and his moral indignation did much to discredit the Versailles settlement.

In recent years scholars have taken a more tolerant view of the matter. As for the moral issue, it has been pointed out that if Germany had won the war it would have almost certainly imposed harsher terms on the Allies. The extent of Germany's territorial ambitions was indicated by the Brest Litovsk Treaty (Chapter 23) by which Germany forced Russia to yield territories containing one-fourth of its population and much of its industrial and agrarian wealth. Financial exactions,

°The article (No. 231) reads: "The Allied and Associated Governments affirm and Germany accepts the responsibility of Germany and her allies for causing all the loss and damage to which the Allied and Associated Governments and their nationals have been subjected as a consequence of the war imposed upon them by the aggression of Germany and her allies." This controversial article does not, as has been often claimed, place on the Central Powers exclusive moral responsibility for the war. It was drafted by a young American lawyer, John Foster Dulles, to provide a legal basis for reparations.

Escorted by war veterans, Thomas Masaryk enters Prague in 1919 to take office as head of the Czechoslovakian republic.

too, were not immoral in themselves, since it had been a custom of long standing in Europe for the loser to pay: Napoleon imposed an indemnity on Prussia after Jena, and the Germans, in turn, collected from France after the war of 1870. As for the feasibility of the treaty, a French economist, Étienne Mantoux, demonstrated in a book called *The Carthaginian Peace, or the Economic Consequences of Mr. Keynes* (1946) that after Hitler had come to power Germany easily raised for rearmament the money and goods that it had been allegedly unable to provide for reparations.

Whatever the merits of the case, there can be no doubt that Versailles was widely regarded as a harsh and punitive peace. The bad conscience over Versailles weakened the will of Europeans later to resist Hitler, who rode to power on slogans pledging to rectify the treaty's real and alleged injustices.

The terms for the four other Central Powers involved essentially territorial changes. The application of the principle of national self-determination formalized the dissolution of the Hapsburg Empire and gave recognition to the emergence in Eastern Europe of a number of new states. Serbia, united with several Austrian provinces inhabited by Slavs, became Yugoslavia ("the country of southern Slavs"). The Czechs and Slovaks merged to form the Republic of Czechoslovakia. Farther north, Poland regained its independence lost in the eighteenth century. Its territory consisted of lands partly ceded by Germany and Austria in the provisions of the peace treaty, and partly won from Soviet Russia in a war waged in 1920. Romania enlarged at the expense of Hungary, acquiring the province of Transylvania. Hungary separated from Austria and became fully independent. The Italians gained several Austrian regions, including southern Tyrol and the port city of Trieste. As a result of these losses Austria, which in 1914 had been the second largest state in Europe, was reduced to the status of an insignificant power, smaller in size than Bulgaria. All that remained of its former glory was Vienna, once the capital of a vast empire, now a head without a body. The Treaty of St. Germain explicitly forbade Austria to unite with Germany.

One of the main criticisms leveled at the post-World War I settlements is that by destroying the Austro-Hungarian Empire they created in the East unviable and unstable states that endangered the peace of Europe. It is true that the Allies encouraged independence movements in this area, but the process unrolled on its own anyway. By the time the peace negotiations opened, the Austro-Hungarian Empire had already fallen apart and its constituent nationalities had proclaimed their independence. Nothing short of armed intervention by the Allies could have re-established the Hapsburg Empire, and such intervention was, of course, inconceivable.

The Russian Empire escaped wholesale disintegration because the Communists reconquered most of the separated borderlands by force of arms (Chapter 23). In addition to Poland, only Finland and the three Baltic states—Estonia, Latvia, and Lithuania—succeeded for the time being in asserting their independence. The Ottoman Empire, on the other hand, lost its remaining possessions, including Palestine, Syria, and Iraq, which came under British or French control. All that was left to Turkey was Anatolia and Constantinople with its environs.

Woodrow Wilson made many concessions to his colleagues on questions of territory and reparations in order to secure what mattered to him most: the League of Nations, on which he pinned his hopes for a lasting peace. Clemenceau realized this fact and exploited it to wring concessions from the President. Wilson, in turn, succeeded in making the League an integral part of the peace treaty with Germany.

The League of Nations

The idea of a permanent supra-national body to settle disputes between countries before they erupted into war was not new. As we have seen (Chapter 12), the Congresses of the Quadruple Alliance, convened after the defeat of Napoleon, were originally designed to meet this need. Throughout the nineteenth century an increasing proportion of activities involving many states—communications and treatment of prisoners of war, for example—were entrusted to international regulatory organizations such as the International Postal Union and the Red Cross. In 1914 over thirty such international bodies were in operation. In 1899, on the initiative of Tsar Nicholas II of Russia, a conference was convened in The Hague to discuss disarmament. Although no agreement was reached on arms limitations, measures were adopted limiting the use of certain weapons and assuring protection of civilians in wartime. The conference also established a permanent court of international arbitration to sit in The Hague and to pass on disputes submitted to it by the concerned parties. Neither the regulatory international organizations nor the Hague Court—a body of legal experts rather than judges—infringed on the sovereignty of independent states; but they were indicative of the growing need in the modern world for institutions whose authority cut across national boundaries.

Wilson received valuable support in his efforts from Jan Christian Smuts, a member of the South African delegation to the peace conference. In his booklet

The League of Nations (1919), Smuts outlined clearly the scope and functions of the proposed body. The League, he maintained, should be viewed not only

> as a possible means for preventing future wars, but much more as a great organ of the ordinary peaceful life of civilization, as the foundation of the new international system which will be erected on the ruins of this war. . . . It is not sufficient for the league merely to be a sort of *deus ex machina*, called in in very grave emergencies when the spectre of war appears; if it is to last, it must be much more. It must become part and parcel of the common international life of states, it must be an ever visible, living, working organ of the polity of civilization. It must function so strongly in the ordinary peaceful intercourse of states that it becomes irresistible in their disputes; its peace activity must be the foundation and guarantee of its war power.

The League, as created by the peace treaty, was conceived not as a super-government but as an association of free sovereign states—a fact not always understood by its friends or opponents. Its members merely undertook to help each other to repel aggression and pledged to submit to arbitration their own disputes. The League was intended to act as an organ of collective security, obviating the need for military alliances, considered one of the main causes of the war.

The widespread revulsion against war is expressed in Théophile Steinlen's 1922 poster calling for a "War on War" on behalf of an international labor syndicate.

The League of Nations consisted of two chambers: a General Assembly, composed of representatives of member states and convened annually; and a Council with executive functions made up of representatives of the five great powers (the United States, Great Britain, France, Italy, and Japan), as well as those of four additional states, elected by the Assembly. The headquarters of the League was to be located in Geneva. Operating under the League's auspices were numerous international offices (labor bureau, economic bureau, and so on). Its day-to-day business was carried out by a Secretariat. Among the important responsibilities imposed on the League were trusteeship of the colonies taken away from the Central Powers, and the supervision of plebiscites in disputed areas.

The success of the whole peace settlement of 1919–1920 depended in large measure on the willingness of the United States to help with its execution. The French had consented to moderate their claims on Germany only because the United States and Great Britain assured them of joint protection against German attack. A defensive treaty to this effect was signed by the three powers on the same day the Germans affixed their signatures to the Treaty of Versailles. Furthermore, the League of Nations had been from the beginning an American idea. Indeed, many European statesmen viewed it skeptically, and agreed to the League only as a means of ensuring the permanent involvement of the United States in European affairs.

Unfortunately, the American public was not yet ready to assume that world leadership which the self-destruction of the great European powers had thrust upon it. From the beginning of its history the United States has viewed itself as an antithesis of the Old World. Its reluctant entry into the war had been predicated on the assumption that the intervention would be short and decisive. In the words of a popular American war song, the boys would be back "when it's over over there." But, of course, nothing was or could be over. The bickering at Paris and the subsequent conflicts among big and small powers reinforced the deep-seated aversion that the majority of Americans had toward lasting involvement abroad.

Wilson did not help his cause by his unskillful handling of the opposition. He failed to secure cooperation of congressional leaders before making his commitments, and rejected their suggestions for emendations afterward. Such a policy was imprudent, for he had to contend in both houses with a Republican majority whose leaders were isolationist. When the Versailles Treaty came up for ratification, considerable opposition developed. Exasperated, Wilson took his case for the treaty and the League of Nations to the country. In September, 1919, in the midst of a speaking tour, he suffered a paralytic stroke that removed him from active politics.

Two months later the Senate refused to ratify either the Treaty of Versailles or the mutual-assistance pact with France. The most essential element of the entire peace settlement was thus knocked out: the League lost its main champion, and France lost the principal guarantor of its security.

Boundary Disputes

The difficulties in enforcing the peace settlements began almost immediately. National self-determination, accepted as one of the bases of the peace treaties, proved exceedingly difficult to carry out in practice. In many areas, after centuries of coexistence within larger multi-national empires, the various ethnic groups had become so thoroughly intermingled that even the best of will (often absent) could not produce a formula able neatly to separate one from the other. The usual solution was for the stronger nation—as a rule, the one on the winning side in the World War—to decide the issue in its own favor.

The new Polish Republic was particularly troublesome in this respect. Having lost its independence in 1795, Poland lacked frontiers on which to fall back and had to carve its territory out of what had been German, Austrian, and Russian possessions. With French encouragement (the reasons for which are stated below) it expanded in all directions, seizing in the process regions to which its ethnic claims were highly doubtful. The Poles ignored the results of the plebiscite in Upper Silesia, which had rendered a majority in favor of union with Germany, and sent troops to occupy this territory. Later on, Upper Silesia was divided between the two countries, Poland retaining the most valuable industrial and mining districts. The Poles also seized the region of Vilno, claimed by Lithuania. In the summer of 1920 Polish forces invaded Soviet Russia. Their aim was to detach from Russia the Ukrainian and Belorussian territories and to create out of them a buffer region against the Soviet Republic. However, the Russians threw the offensive back. They now swept forward into Poland, reaching the gates of Warsaw, to be stopped and thrown back in turn. By the Treaty of Riga (1921) Poland secured lands containing large Ukrainian and Belorussian minorities. As a result of all these acquisitions, one-third of Poland's population consisted of minorities.

Another area of keen boundary dispute was Transylvania, a district with a mixed Romanian and Magyar population. The Allies had promised Transylvania —a part of the Hungarian monarchy—to the Romanians as a reward for their entry into the war against the Central Powers. In January, 1919, the Romanians proclaimed the annexation of this territory, an action subsequently confirmed by the Treaty of Trianon. But the Hungarians would not reconcile themselves to the loss of a region inhabited by 2 million Magyars and continued to hope for its reacquisition. The Transylvanian question poisoned relations between the two countries throughout the interwar period.

Farther to the south the Italians engaged in a protracted feud with the Yugoslavs over the Trieste-Fiume region, another legacy of the defunct Austrian Empire. The Italians occupied this region on the evacuation of Austrian troops in November, 1918. President Wilson, however, refused to acknowledge Italy's claim to Fiume, a predominantly Slavic area, and it was this issue that caused Orlando to withdraw from the peace conference. Fiume kept on changing hands until the Yugoslavs in 1924 finally conceded it to Italy.

A particularly savage conflict broke out in 1919 between the Greeks and the Turks. The Allies had assigned to the Greeks numerous islands in the Aegean as well as the Smyrna region on the Ionian coast, territories with a predominantly Greek population. The Turks, who had reconciled themselves to the loss of their empire, refused to give up territories that were geographically a part of the Turkish homeland. A nationalist army formed in Anatolia by a one-time Ottoman officer, Kemal Atatürk, began to resist Greek encroachments. For over two years Greeks and Turks engaged in full-scale war, in the course of which the Greek population of Anatolia was partly massacred and partly expelled. Peace was restored only in 1922.

The League of Nations made valiant efforts to settle peacefully these and similar disputes, but it had neither the authority nor the machinery to enforce its decisions. Its judgments were effective only when both parties in a boundary dispute found it expedient to accept the League's verdict. The border disputes left a legacy of resentment which persistently troubled international relations, especially in Eastern Europe, and undermined respect for the peace settlements. The losers tended to view the principle of national self-determination as a fraudulent formula devised by the strong to rob the weak.

Heavy as had been its losses in the war, Britain emerged from it sufficiently intact to nourish the illusion that nothing had changed and that it could revert to its old routines. The desire to return to "normalcy," that is, to pre-1914 life, was the dominant trait of British public opinion in the interwar period, to be finally shattered only by the Second World War. It was a self-deception that served to conceal the gravity of the problems confronting Britain and to delay the application of drastic remedies. *Great Britain*

The crisis was fundamentally economic in nature. British prosperity, and the social stability resting on it, were uniquely dependent on foreign trade. Before the war one-third of Britain's entire national product had been sold abroad. After the war Britain found it increasingly difficult to recapture its old markets. Some countries, notably Germany, once Britain's leading customer, were too impoverished to make significant purchases. Others, such as the United States, had developed during the war great industrial resources of their own, and imported proportionately less. The decreasing foreign demand affected precisely those industries that had traditionally provided the bulk of British exports: coal, iron and steel, textiles, and ships. Britain's ability to sell abroad was further diminished by high prices, caused partly by antiquated methods of production and partly by the decision in 1925 of the Exchequer, headed by Winston Churchill, to restore the gold standard. In some areas overpriced British goods were pushed out of the market by Japanese merchandise manufactured at substantially lower costs. The net effect was a steady decline in British sales abroad: in 1924 the share of the national product sold through exports fell to one-fourth. The gap between exports and imports became wider than it had been before the war, although for the time being the unfavorable balance of trade was righted by shipping income, returns on foreign investments, and other "invisible exports."

The decline of foreign sales in the staple industries, employing the bulk of labor—mining, metals, shipbuilding, and textiles—caused chronic unemployment. Throughout the 1920s a tenth or more of the British labor force was regularly out of work. There were never fewer than 1 million unemployed, and sometimes their number exceeded 2 million.

Persistent unemployment caused social unrest of an intensity and on a scale not experienced in Britain since the early decades of the nineteenth century. There were frequent strikes and demonstrations, sometimes violent. The coal miners were especially disaffected. The example of the Russian Revolution encouraged the emergence in the British labor movement of a radical wing hostile

Workers parade by the Marble Arch in Hyde Park during the British general strike of 1926. Visible second from left is the banner of the Amalgamated Society of Engineers (page 490).

to the whole social and economic system. Social unrest culminated in May, 1926, in a general strike. The strike, which began with a work stoppage by the miners, expanded as several sympathetic trade unions joined in. It collapsed after nine days, but not without leaving a legacy of mutual mistrust between the upper and lower classes.

The social unrest of the postwar era provided the background to a major realignment in British politics. Until 1922 Great Britain was ruled by a coalition government formed in the midst of the war. Although Prime Minister Lloyd George was himself a Liberal, the coalition rested on Conservative support because much of the Liberal party had refused to follow Lloyd George's leadership. In 1922 the Conservatives decided to withdraw from the coalition. Three major parties participated in the elections that followed: Conservative, Labour, and Liberal, the latter split into pro- and anti-Lloyd George factions. The Conservatives won, polling 5.5 million votes and gaining 347 seats in the Commons. The Liberals suffered a crushing defeat. While they polled a respectable 4.1 million votes, in the individual constituencies they won more second and third places than first and ended up with only 117 seats. Labour, on the other hand, which polled only slightly more votes (4.2 million), captured 142 seats, and became, for the first time in history, His Majesty's Opposition party. The Liberals were never to recapture their old position, and have remained to this day a minor third party.

British politics in the interwar period was dominated by the Conservatives. The tone in the party was set by wealthy, rather unimaginative and tradition-bound businessmen. They believed in deflation, that is, dear money, strict economy in government spending, and the minimum of activism in foreign affairs. They refused to recognize the fact that Britain no longer was the leading industrial power in the world. They rejected bold fiscal measures advocated by farsighted Britons as a means of radically improving the country's economic position and blamed social unrest on Bolshevik agitation. The leaders of the

Conservative party believed all problems facing Britain to be problems of post-war readjustment. This attitude conformed to the mood of the majority of British voters, who longed for the pre-1914 world, and who liked being reassured that it would soon return.

The Labour party consisted of several disparate elements. The bulk of its support came from conservative trade unionists, from whose minds nothing was farther than class warfare or revolution. It was they who repeatedly rejected offers of affiliation with the British Communist party, founded in 1920. But the Labour party also had a radical wing, mostly from the depressed areas with high unemployment, whose representatives sympathized with Soviet Russia and had no aversion to class conflict. Finally, there was a small but influential intellectual faction of socialist professors and writers who, like their Fabian forerunners, injected an ideological element into the party. Although British Labour was more radical now than it had been in the late nineteenth century, its leadership, on the whole, was just as responsible and willing to operate within the British political tradition as it had been then. The two Labour cabinets—one in 1924 and another between 1929 and 1931—produced no revolutionary legislation. Indeed, they proved rather timid. This caution frustrated the more radical elements in the party, but it gained Labour the reputation of respectability that it had previously lacked among middle-class voters, and established it as the normal alternative to the Conservatives.

The 1920s marked the climax of the movement for Irish independence. During the war the Irish nationalists, who openly sympathized with the Germans, staged a rebellion against British rule. Violence erupted again in 1919, and for the next two years Ireland was in the grip of a savage civil war between the followers of the Sinn Fein and regular British forces. Finally, in 1921–1922, Britain agreed to a compromise. Ireland was divided, the northern part (Ulster) remaining British and the remainder receiving dominion status. In the next few years southern Ireland severed all political ties with Britain and became an independent republic.

France and French Diplomacy

The main concern of French statesmen in the 1920s was containment of Germany. Victory had given France for the first time since the middle of the nineteenth century an upper hand over its rival, and it worked feverishly to take advantage of its temporary superiority. France's long-term prospects were not favorable: its population was smaller and declining; its industrial capacity inferior, despite its acquisition of Lorraine; its political life unstable. The refusal of the American Senate to ratify the defense pact against German aggression had released Britain from a similar commitment and left France to fend for itself. All these factors encouraged French statesmen to adopt an intransigent attitude. They aimed at nothing less than to emasculate Germany internally and to isolate it externally, and they pursued both ends without much regard for their impact on the world at large.

The French government more than any other insisted that Germany fulfill punctiliously its reparations commitments. It had borrowed heavily to reconstruct the areas devastated by war on the assumption that it would recover the equivalent from reparations, and was unwilling to acquiesce in any German requests for the easing of terms or delays in deliveries. Early in 1921, even before the Reparations Commission had made its report, French troops occupied three German cities on the Rhine to ensure prompt payments. In January, 1923, on the excuse that the Germans had defaulted on coal deliveries, a Franco-Belgian force occupied the Ruhr, Germany's most productive industrial area. By then the French exercised direct or indirect control over most of the lands lying along the Rhine.

French diplomacy simultaneously pursued a policy of alliances designed to block Germany in the East. Before 1914 France had relied on Russia to provide the threat of a two-front war. Now, however, Russia was no longer its ally. Indeed, France was the most anti-Soviet country in Europe, for it had suffered the greatest losses from Communist expropriations and defaults on foreign debts. To replace Russia it now sought friends in Central Europe and in the Balkans, among the states that had profited at the expense of Germany and the Austro-Hungarian and Russian empires. These states welcomed French financial assistance and guarantees against potential future German, Austrian, or Russian claims, offering in return dubious promises of support in the event of German aggression. The anchor of France's alliance system was the "Little Entente," a coalition formed in 1920–1921 between Czechoslovakia, Romania, and Yugoslavia. France also cultivated Poland, whose territorial claims against Russia and Germany it supported militarily and diplomatically. The alliances with the smaller states of Eastern and Central Europe had for the French also a secondary function of a *cordon sanitaire* against Soviet expansion.

France's strong-handed methods on the Continent could succeed only as long as both Germany and Russia lay prostrate. This was certain not to be forever, and in retrospect French foreign policy of the early 1920s appears to have been exceedingly shortsighted. It played right into the hands of German militarists and nationalists bent on revenge, and undermined the democratic government then in power in Germany. Furthermore, it encouraged an alliance between Germany and Russia, the two outcast nations of Europe. In 1922 these countries surprised the world by signing at Rapallo a treaty pledging them to remain neutral should one of them be attacked by a third power. Rapallo marked the beginning of economic and military cooperation between Soviet Russia and Germany. Russia obtained from Germany credits and technical advice and in return provided facilities on Soviet territory for the *Wehrmacht* to carry out secret tank and aviation exercises which had been forbidden by the Versailles Treaty.

In 1925 France at last obtained international guarantees of its security. At a conference held in Locarno, Great Britain and Italy committed themselves to protect the existing frontier between France, Belgium, and Germany. In separate mutual defense treaties with Poland and Czechoslovakia, France obtained and gave the promise of help in the event of German attack. Locarno created the illusion of ushering in a new era of international good will and collective security. But that the French did not place excessive trust in it may be gathered from the fact that in 1929 they began construction of a massive chain of fortifications along the German frontier, the so-called Maginot Line. It was intended as an impregnable wall to stop the invader should all the guarantees fail and France find itself alone face to face with German might.

The government that succeeded the Hohenzollerns was appointed by a National Assembly popularly elected in January, 1919, and convened in the town of Weimar. In the Assembly, the Social Democrats had the largest bloc of seats (38.5 percent) and, together with the associated Catholic Center party, held a comfortable majority. The German Republic was therefore in large measure their creation. The constitution adopted by the Assembly in 1919 gave Germany a parliamentary democracy, with a strong executive. The President and the Chancellor received wide emergency powers to use against subversion, including the right temporarily to suspend civil liberties. The authority of the central government was increased, that of federal governments diminished. It was the most liberal and democratic constitution Germany had ever had, and an excellent one by any standards.

The Weimar Republic had from its inception to contend with the opposition of rabid anti-democratic elements on both the left and the right.

On the left, the most dangerous enemy was the Communist party, whose aim was to replace the republic by a Soviet-type government in which it would exercise dictatorial powers. In January, 1919, a proto-Communist group of "Spartacists" staged an uprising in Berlin, and before long Communist groups raised the banner of rebellion in other German cities. In Munich in April the Communists proclaimed a Soviet Republic of Bavaria.

The Weimar government reacted to radical subversion with great vigor and succeeded in suppressing it. Defeat, however, did not discourage the Communists from keeping up a steady offensive against the republic so as to undermine its popularity among the masses of workers.

Spearheaded by a tank obtained from the British, German troops advance into Berlin to quell the Spartacist revolt in 1919.

In coping with the Communists the government had to rely on the help of right-wing elements, especially of paramilitary formations composed of discharged soldiers and civilian volunteers. The leaders as well as the rank and file of these groups had no love for the republic. They detested the Social Democrats, the leading party in the government, whom they accused of having "stabbed in the back" the German army in the last months of the war by fomenting strikes and mutinies. They also refused to recognize the action of the National Assembly in ratifying the Versailles Treaty and scorned the government for complying with the Allied demands for reparations. The right-wing opposition consisted of two disparate elements: traditional monarchists and nationalistic radicals, who temporarily cooperated with each other out of hatred of the Weimar Republic. The two groups murdered political opponents and staged repeated uprisings. On one occasion they even succeeded in seizing temporary control of Berlin and forcing the government to flee (Kapp *Putsch*, March, 1920). The Weimar authorities tended to treat right-wing subversives with greater indulgence than the Communists, probably because they regarded the latter as more dangerous.

The socialist-liberal consensus that had prevailed in Germany at the end of the war evaporated remarkably fast, and soon political life began to polarize. Extremist parties did surprisingly well in the first postwar elections to the Reichstag (June, 1920), the Communists gaining one-fifth of the seats and the most militant nationalist party one-sixth (see chart, page 717). This election marked the beginning of the steady disintegration of the liberal-democratic center.

Weakened by a narrowing domestic mandate, the Weimar Republic had also to contend with steady pressure from its neighbors, especially France. Immediately after the cessation of hostilities Germany was required to surrender to the Allies the bulk of its merchant navy, as well as considerable quantities of gold and raw materials. Then came regular reparations payments. The occupation of the Ruhr by French and Belgian troops in 1923 caused an outburst of national resentment that carried with it even the working class: in the occupied areas workers refused to work and carried out acts of sabotage. Throughout Germany there was dissatisfaction with the inability of the Weimar Republic to stand up to what were widely considered unreasonable and degrading foreign demands.

In 1923, on top of all its other troubles, the republic experienced an inflation the likes of which had never been seen. The steady outflow of gold in the form of reparations payments or transfers of private capital, as well as the adverse balance of trade resulting from the need to import industrial raw materials and food, caused a steady depreciation of German currency. In the spring of 1921 one United States dollar equaled 65 marks; in September, 1923, it was worth 9 million marks, and in November, 1923, 4.2 trillion! By then, several hundred paper mills and printing establishments worked around the clock to supply the treasury with banknotes. The mark became worthless—and so did bank savings, investments, securities, and loans. The German middle class, whose livelihood had depended on such values, grew to detest the republic which had in effect expropriated it, and swung to the right, toward monarchistic and nationalistic movements.

A German magazine's bitter comment on American loans going directly to the French for reparations payments.

Simplicissimus, JUNE 28, 1922

In the fall of 1923 the Weimar Republic seemed on the verge of collapse. In October the Communists staged an uprising in Hamburg, and the following month right-wing extremists, led by General Ludendorff and Adolf Hitler, attempted a coup in Munich. Both revolts were contained, but the danger of sedition remained.

In 1924, however, the situation unexpectedly improved. A clever monetary reform introduced a new and stable mark to replace the worthless old currency. The Allies realized at last that it was not possible to keep on squeezing Germany without regard to its ability to pay. In 1924 they appointed a commission headed by the American financier Charles G. Dawes to draw up a plan for the economic reconstruction of Germany. Dawes's report established a schedule for reparations payments and recommended that Germany receive sizable international loans. Earlier in 1924 the French had pulled out of the Ruhr. Soon private and public funds from abroad began to flow into the country. The Germans used a part of these to meet their reparations obligations, thus easing the strains on their economy.° The treaties of Locarno further eased Franco-German relations. One of its consequences was Germany's admission into the League of Nations.

The stability and prosperity that began in 1924 re-established for the time being the prestige of the moderate parties and restored a certain degree of confidence in the republic. Nevertheless, the position of the Weimar government remained precarious because the majority of Germans in principle opposed the republican-democratic form of government. This became apparent in the presidential elections held in 1925. At this time 48.1 percent of the voters cast their ballots for the monarchist General von Hindenburg and 6.2 percent for the Communist candidate. A minority—45.2 percent—of the voters backed the candidate of the Social Democratic, the Catholic Center, and other parties supporting the regime. Hindenburg's election, made possible by the Communist refusal to join forces with the republican parties, had tragic consequences for the republic, for Germany, and for the world. As we shall see, it was Hindenburg's political naïveté that enabled Hitler in 1933 to become Chancellor and to acquire dictatorial powers.

The 1924 poster of a Nazi coalition makes an anti-Semitic appeal to the "exploited" German working classes.

The Drift Toward Dictatorships

The instability of postwar conditions placed stresses on parliamentary institutions which the weaker among them could not withstand. Ethnic, social, and political strife, either separately or in combination, created a demand for firmer authority than that provided by the liberal system with its multiplicity of rival parties and cumbersome parliamentary procedures. An increasing proportion of the citizenry of postwar Europe came to question the efficacy of liberalism and to seek salvation in dictatorships. This held especially true of countries where the parliamentary system either had failed to sink deep roots before World War I, or where it had had only come into being since the war.

Among the first countries to shift toward authoritarian forms was Hungary. Its first postwar administration, formed in January, 1919, was liberal and progressive, but two months after its formation it was overthrown by a Communist

---

°"The U.S.A. lent money to Germany which enabled her to pay reparations to the European ex-allies, which enabled them to make war-debt payments to the U.S.A.—and so the circle continued." William Ashworth, *A Short History of the International Economy Since 1850* (1962).

Marshal Josef Pilsudski, who assumed dictatorial power in Poland in 1926.

regime sponsored by Soviet Russia (Chapter 23). The Communist leader, Béla Kun, antagonized a large part of the population by his anti-religious policy and a program of land nationalization. In the summer of 1919 the Communists were ejected, in turn, by invading Romanian troops, who freely plundered the country. At the same time right-wing terrorists exacted revenge on the Communists and their suspected sympathizers, and carried out anti-Jewish pogroms. Finally a semblance of order was re-established in 1920. A nationally elected parliament nominated Admiral Nicholas Horthy as regent, to exercise supreme executive powers until the restoration of the monarchy. Since the Allies, however, prevented such a restoration, Horthy remained permanent regent with all the usual royal prerogatives.

In the next few years several other countries took the road to authoritarianism. In 1923 Kemal Atatürk, the commander of the Turkish national army, became dictator of the Turkish republic. The Republican People's party, which he headed, was declared the only legitimate political organization. The same year a military coup in Spain brought to power Miguel Primo de Rivera, who dissolved the parliament, suspended the constitution, and proceeded to rule the country by decree. In 1926 neighboring Portugal came under a dictatorship in which authority eventually fell into the hands of Antonio Salazar. In Poland Marshal Josef Pilsudski, commander of the armed forces which had fought for independence during the war, carried out a coup against the parliament in which the Peasant party had obtained a majority (May, 1926). Pilsudski left parliamentary institutions intact, but by assuming the combined functions of Prime Minister, Minister of War, and Chief of Staff, he enjoyed virtually dictatorial powers. Opposition parties were tolerated but harassed. In 1929 King Alexander of Yugoslavia, exasperated by endless friction among Serbs, Croats, Slovenes, and other minorities, suspended parliamentary government temporarily.

The only one among the successor states to resist the general trend toward authoritarianism was the Republic of Czechoslovakia. A country with a high level of culture and a relatively well-developed industrial economy, it created a democracy in no way inferior to the most advanced Western models.

Italian Fascism   In turning to the Fascist government established in Italy by Mussolini, we are moving into a gray zone separating ordinary dictatorship from totalitarianism. The differences between the two systems will be discussed in the next chapter. Here suffice it to note that totalitarian regimes are not content to deprive the citizen of his political rights, but also rob him of his civil liberties. Mussolini claimed to be a totalitarian ruler and tried to be one, but he never really carried out a totalitarian revolution of the kind accomplished by Lenin and Hitler, and for this reason his place is not among them.

Fascism arose against a background of violent social unrest that broke out in the industrial centers of northern Italy at the end of the war. This area had old traditions of syndicalism and anarchism, which the news of the Russian Revolution intensified. Beginning in 1919 Italy experienced a wave of massive strikes, culminating in September, 1920, in seizures of whole factories by syndicalist workers in Milan and Turin. From the cities the unrest spilled into the countryside, where tenants seized estates and refused payment of rents. In 1919–1920

Italy tottered on the brink of social revolution, which the frequently changing socialist and liberal governments seemed unable to do anything about. It was this situation that gave Mussolini his chance.

Benito Mussolini was born in 1883. His father, a poor village blacksmith, was a professed anarchist, and Mussolini spent his childhood in an atmosphere of rebellion against government, church, private property, and the whole culture of the middle class. As a youth he tried his hand at teaching and other occupations, including bricklaying, but his real passion was politics. He read avidly, showing a predilection for such modern prophets of violence and élitism as Nietzsche, Sorel, and Pareto.

He gained his initial political experience in the Italian Socialist party, where his literary and speaking ability helped him make a rapid career. In 1912 he was elected member of the party's Executive Committee and editor of its official newspaper, *Avanti*. Two years later, however, he was expelled from the Socialist party because as an ardent patriot and militarist he had objected to the party's pacifist policy and agitated for Italy's entrance into the war. In 1915 he went to the front, from where he returned in 1917 with grave wounds. He still remained a socialist, but of a militant kind, who, like Lenin, despised the liberal, reformist tendencies prevalent among European socialist parties. Unlike Lenin, however, he also rejected their cosmopolitanism.

Mussolini (center, wearing the national colors across his chest) and his Blackshirts parade in Rome after their takeover.

Mussolini at first admired the Bolshevik Revolution, but he quickly became disillusioned with it, and after the Communists became involved in fomenting industrial strikes and violence, turned against them. He gathered around himself students and ex-soldiers whom he organized into combat units, called *fasci di combattimento.*° Beginning with April, 1919, these black-shirted squads engaged in street brawls and attacked the offices of radical organizations and newspapers. Claiming that he was saving the country from communism and anarchism, Mussolini persuaded frightened industrialists and landlords to give him financial support. His movement gained momentum, especially after the factory seizures of 1920. It attracted nationalists embittered by the failure of Italy's allies to accede to all its territorial demands, unadjusted war veterans, poets and artists won over by Mussolini's romantic activism, and ordinary people who simply wanted an end to the anarchy. The situation was not unlike that prevailing in Germany at the same time, except that the Italian socialists, who dominated the government, were much less energetic in dealing with extremists.

Until the end of 1921 Mussolini lacked a party organization, and indeed denied any need for it. Fascism was a "doctrine of action" not to be confined by organizational fetters. But in November, 1921, he decided, against the advice of his more radical followers, to found a regular party organization, the *Partito Nazionale Fascista.* Its membership was then around 300,000.

His ambition was to acquire dictatorial powers. The Fascist following in parliament was small: with their allies, they controlled less than one-tenth of the seats. But the Italian parliamentary system being what it was, lack of a majority was not an insurmountable obstacle to a prime-ministership. It had been traditionally the task of the Italian Prime Minister to constitute a majority only after assuming office by making deals with individual deputies. In 1922 Mussolini demanded that the king appoint him to form a cabinet. The king, a weak and confused man, hesitated, and so did the leaders of the moderate parties. The trouble was that no one, Mussolini included, really knew what he stood for and what he would do once in office. To force the issue, in October, 1922, Mussolini organized a "March on Rome," a coordinated advance on the capital by thousands of Fascist Blackshirts. (Mussolini himself stayed behind in Milan.) Nothing was done to stop them. Once the Fascists were in control of Rome, the king agreed to Mussolini's request.

Mussolini, like Hitler after him, subverted democratic institutions only after he had succeeded in legally becoming head of government. Although he had risen on an anti-Communist, anti-anarchist platform, his real enemy was the liberal state. He skillfully exploited its weaknesses to destroy it from within.

In December, 1922, Mussolini obtained from parliament dictatorial powers for the period of one year to restore order in the country. Almost immediately turbulence subsided: strikes were either broken up or called off, factories were restored to their owners, street fighting and brigandage were suppressed, the civil service was infused with new life. The pacification was remarkably successful, and in the elections of 1924 the "National List" presented by the Fascists received an absolute majority (63 percent) of the popular vote. Although here

---

°The term *fasci,* from which derives the word *fascism,* refers to *fasces,* a bundle of rods containing an axe, which in ancient Rome symbolized authority. It was widely used in Italy by both radical and nationalist movements.

and there the Fascist militia used strong-arm methods, there is general agreement that the elections were honest, and represented a genuine vote of confidence in the new regime. With a parliamentary majority Mussolini could proceed to acquire permanent dictatorial powers. In 1925–1926 he issued a series of decrees that transferred to him, as Leader, *Duce*, all the essentials of legislative authority. In 1928 a new electoral law was introduced which abolished universal suffrage and limited eligibility for parliamentary elections to candidates officially approved by the Fascist Grand Council.

Like Soviet Russia, Fascist Italy was ruled by a single party that controlled the legislature and the administration. The party, in turn, was under the personal authority of the *Duce*. Mussolini, emulating Lenin, combined the functions of head of party and chief of state. He also closely followed Lenin's system of meshing the party and state apparatus. After 1926 other political parties were outlawed. The Fascist party also controlled numerous ancillary organizations, including youth organizations (*Ballila* and *Avanguardisti*) and trade unions. But the Fascists never attempted to establish control over the entire organized life of the country. The Catholic Church, relations with which were regularized by the Lateran Treaties of 1929, was left its autonomy and allowed to carry on many activities. The monarchy, too, was left intact. Nor did the Fascists tamper with the judiciary: they respected the independence and irremovability of judges, and made no attempt to interfere with court procedures. It is for this reason that Mussolini's power was never "total."

In their social and economic policy the Fascists displayed little initiative. Private property, including ownership of industry, was retained. Mussolini made an effort to tamper with the economy only in 1934, in the wake of the great depression which threw 1 million Italians out of work. At that time he introduced the system of "corporatism." The country's entire economy was divided into twenty-two branches, in each of which the employers and employees formed a "corporation," regulated by a National Council of Corporations. The ostensible task of this arrangement, which aroused much attention at the time, was to correct the faults of the free economy and to eliminate class conflict. Although clearly modeled on the Soviet Five-Year Plan (see Chapter 27), the corporations did not signify the introduction of economic planning. Insofar as the "Corporate State" had any reality, it meant a greater role of the state in the running of the economy —an anticipation of that mixed system of state direction and free enterprise which became common in the world after World War II.

It would be vain to seek in fascism any fixed ideology. Mussolini himself repeatedly insisted that the essential quality of fascism was dynamism—a sense of constant movement, daring, excitement. A popular Fascist motto, *Me ne frego* ("I don't give a damn"), typified the attitude that Mussolini desired of his followers. There was much stress on youth, and *Giovinezza* was made the anthem of the Fascist party. Mussolini made a great deal out of the imperial tradition, exhorting the Italians to re-establish in the Mediterranean a modern Roman Empire, but it is doubtful that he took this aim seriously. He was too intelligent to believe the slogans with which he confused the Italian public. At bottom he was a great cynic—a modern *condottiere* for whom life was a game. He thought to get the most out of it by living recklessly.

Striking a typically bombastic pose, Mussolini was photographed at a ceremony in the Italian colony of Libya.

27

<hr>

Totalitarianism

The term *totalitarianism* was coined by Mussolini to describe the kind of regime he sought to establish in Italy: a regime in which one party monopolizes all power, dissolves or subordinates all independent institutions, and asserts complete, direct authority over all its subjects and all their activities. Although totalitarian governments may differ from one another in some particulars, they represent a distinct political type, as consistent in their essential features as were the diverse enlightened despotisms of the eighteenth century or the parliamentary democracies of the nineteenth.

The Elements of Totalitarianism

Totalitarianism is the antithesis of liberalism, and its most implacable enemy. It rejects the philosophical principles on which the liberal order rests (as defined in Chapter 12). It denies the ultimate worth of the individual, valuing him only insofar as he is useful to the state or national community. Consequently it has no use for freedom or for law, whose purpose it is to protect the individual. It also denies the fundamental harmony of human interests, stressing instead the universality of conflict, whether social, national, or racial. From the point of view of these assumptions, totalitarianism is a conservative creed. At the same time, however, it borrows from socialism its techniques of mass appeal. It is a mass-oriented movement, harnessing the emotions and aspirations of the multitude not to satisfy them but, with their help, to destroy resistance to total power whether at home or abroad. It is conservative in its aims and radical in its means.

Totalitarianism is not only a political system but a whole set of values, a way of life. In economics it rejects laissez faire in favor of state controls. In culture it is anti-modernist.

To understand totalitarian regimes and to distinguish them from ordinary dictatorships, we must keep in mind the dual nature of the liberal state. The classical liberal state rested on twin foundations, political and civil. Liberalism in politics subjected the government to legal restraints (constitutions) and the authority of elected, representative institutions (parliaments). Liberalism in civil matters ensured the individual citizen the protection of the law and a great variety of personal freedoms. While ideally political rights and civil liberties went together, it was possible to have one without the other. As a matter of fact, most Europeans enjoyed civil liberties long before they had constitutions and the right to vote.

The dictatorships that spread in Europe in the wake of World War I, as described in the preceding chapter, cut down only the political pillar of the liberal state. They resulted from disenchantment with party politics and parliamentary procedures which seemed unable to provide the firm national leadership required under conditions of postwar instability. The purpose of these dictatorships was merely to remedy what was seen as a fatal flaw in the traditional liberal system, not to uproot liberalism as such. A Pilsudski in Poland, a Salazar

At a Nazi party rally at Nürnberg in 1934, American correspondent William L. Shirer described an audience listening to Hitler. "They looked up at him as if he were a Messiah," he wrote, "their faces transformed into something positively inhuman."

in Portugal, or a Horthy in Hungary were "strong men": they abrogated constitutions, reduced parliaments to virtual impotence, and appropriated executive and legislative powers. But they did not—and this distinguishes them from a Stalin or a Hitler—strive for total power. The political authority they exercised stayed within traditional limits. They left their citizens recourse to law; nor did they challenge on the whole their right to form independent associations, to criticize the government, or to travel abroad. Even in Mussolini's Italy the independence of judges and courts was never challenged.

In totalitarian states such lines are no longer observed. The barriers separating the individual from society, and both from the state, fall down. Civil liberties are dispensed with. In a mature totalitarian regime, such as Soviet Russia was under Stalin after 1933, or Germany during the last three years of Hitler's rule, the citizen turns into an object devoid of any rights whatever.

Totalitarianism emerged at a time when the ideas and social classes on which liberalism had traditionally relied were in a state of collapse. The pessimism and the mood of violence that had appeared before World War I, and which the war had intensified, undermined the faith in reason and progress and the respect for human life which constitute the essence of the liberal outlook. The simultaneous decline of the middle class (discussed in the next chapter) deprived liberalism of that social group which had traditionally served as its main support. The worldwide economic depression that began in 1929 further weakened the liberal cause by souring a large part of the working class on democracy and democratic socialism. By the early 1930s liberalism seemed spent, a thing of the past, and totalitarianism the wave of the future.

The first totalitarian state, and the universal model, was Soviet Russia during the period of War Communism, 1918–1920 (Chapter 23). It is not that Lenin assumed dictatorial powers, dissolved the duly elected Constituent Assembly, and transformed the Congresses of Soviets (proletarian parliaments) into a mere rubber stamp. It is not even that he suppressed rival parties. Had he done this and nothing more he would have been merely another garden variety postwar dictator. But Lenin went much farther in that he refused to be bound either by law or by inalienable rights of the individual. Following Marx he regarded law and human freedoms as frauds by means of which the class in power suppresses those it exploits, and he declared at once his intention of denying them to his opponents in the name of the proletarian dictatorship. The will of the party—that is, in effect, his will—was to Lenin superior to rights and freedoms and to law. The Communist party was not bound by any objective norms, not even those of its own making. All that remained, therefore, was the sheer will of the leader, unlimited in scope and unrestrained in application.

Although, as we had occasion to point out, the power of the liberal state after 1870 had increased steadily, nothing had prepared the world for such a startling development. The Bolshevik Revolution shattered the traditional conception of what was properly within the limits of state authority. Everything came within the purview of the state, and therefore everything acquired political significance. The many barriers which, since the American Revolution, had been carefully constructed to prevent this from happening, crumbled in Russia. The politicization of life characterizing totalitarianism finds succinct expression in the

The Nazis early attempted to capture the loyalty of German youth. This photograph was taken at a youth rally held by the party in Munich in 1925.

paraphrase of Christ's words that the ruler of the African state of Ghana, Kwame Nkruma, had engraved on his monument: "Seek ye first the political kingdom and all other things shall be added unto you." Or, in the words of Mussolini, "Everything within the state, nothing outside the state, nothing against the state."

Lenin's successes in establishing his power and especially his use of the Bolshevik party to obtain control over the government and the citizenry impressed ambitious politicians in other parts of Europe. Here the teachings of neoconservatism (Chapter 20) had created in certain groups an intense anti-liberal sentiment. First Mussolini, then Hitler, and finally some dictators of smaller countries learned to combine neo-conservative ideas—nationalism, anti-Semitism, and mass action—with the Leninist technique of one-party politics to create a Western version of totalitarianism or semi-totalitarianism.

The central institution of the totalitarian state is the party. The word "party" applied to the Communist or National Socialist organizations is a misnomer, for they have next to nothing in common with what is ordinarily meant by that term: a voluntary association of persons with similar opinions or interests formed to exercise pressure on the government or to assume temporarily political responsibility. The totalitarian party forms the very essence of the state, penetrating everywhere and controlling everything. In Mussolini's words, it is "the capillary organization of the regime," invading the tissues of the body politic as the blood vessels spread through a living organism. The party not only assumes responsibility for government; it becomes the government. If in the liberal state the party in power is a temporary lessee of sovereignty, in a totalitarian state it is its permanent owner. Membership in such a party is not open to everyone: it is bestowed on the select in conformity with strict standards, being regarded a privilege.

The totalitarian party owes responsibility only to its leader—*vozhd, duce, führer*—who may or may not also serve as the formal head of state, but who invariably directs affairs of government. His powers are unlimited, though they are rarely legally defined. This following description of Hitler's powers, voted by the Reichstag in 1942, gives a good idea of what they in fact are:

> The Führer must . . . at all times be in a position—without being tied to existing legal restrictions—in his position as Führer of the nation, supreme commander of the armed forces, head of the Government and supreme possessor of executive power, senior judiciary and Führer of the Party, to urge every German . . . to fulfill his duties by all means that he considers suitable, and, on violation of such duties, to inflict the punishment that he considers suitable.

What does the totalitarian state want? What does it offer the individual in return for his loss of rights and freedoms? The question is a difficult one to answer. While totalitarian regimes spend much effort on formulating and propagating their official ideologies, they rarely commit themselves to firm rules, for to do so would limit the leader's freedom. Even Lenin, who devoted a great deal of attention to theoretical writings, left no consistent body of doctrine, and his ideas can be cited to justify completely contradictory policies. Totalitarian movements prefer ideological flexibility, which allows constant shifts to meet changing conditions. They all, however, demand sacrifices: they invariably appeal to the present generation to give up whatever it cherishes for the sake of the generations to come. Despite their secular, anti-religious bent, they are therefore every bit as other-worldly as are traditional religions, for the blessings they promise are never to be enjoyed here and now, but only in some mythical future.

Instead of a fixed ideology totalitarian leaders prefer a sense of drive, of forward motion, of what Mussolini described as the "state of highest ideal tension" and called the most important ingredient of fascism. Liberalism tended toward a static situation in which state, society, and individual each would function within its proper sphere, and the whole body politic revolve like a well-oiled mechanism. Such an ideal is utterly alien to the totalitarian spirit. It seeks constant action. It thrives on enemies, and cannot do without them, whether they be designated as Jews, capitalists, Communists, or imperialists. When no enemies exist they are invented, for crises alone justify the power and obedience that leaders of such movements claim. In this sense totalitarian regimes are inherently dynamic, expansive, and unsettling.

To maintain itself in power a totalitarian regime needs a large police apparatus invested with broad powers. Its task is not only to ferret out actual opponents but to prevent sedition in advance. To this end it employs terror, striking alike at the guilty and the innocent, so as to create an atmosphere of pervading fear. (At the height of the Stalinist terror, Moscow furnished provincial police authorities with quotas indicating what percentage of the local population was to be arrested.) Naturally, a police enjoying such powers acquires control over the party that had created it, for to stand up to it is to invite the charge of disloyalty. In both Stalinist Russia and Nazi Germany the police in the end superseded the party and ran the state. The ultimate fulfillment of totalitarianism is the concentration camp, a self-contained, isolated realm where "enemies of the people" are incarcerated, to live, to suffer, and to die at the pleasure of their police masters.

A common feature of totalitarian regimes is their loathing of both the middle class and the intellectuals, two elements that resist dissolution in an amorphous mass. Representatives of these two groups often initiate anti-liberal revolutions, but they usually perish at the hands of those who succeed to power. The social group that profits most is the lower-middle class. In the Communist, Fascist, and Nazi parties the people who made the best careers and who set the tone were small businessmen and functionaries of all kinds. Their ambition was to displace the bourgeoisie, and it is they who lent totalitarian movements their hostility to the propertied, the titled, the well-educated. Yet at the same time they wished to separate themselves as sharply as possible from the working class, and as a result they ruthlessly destroyed democratic socialism within and without their parties.

Totalitarianism, insofar as the historical record is any indication, can be stopped only before its adherents seize the state apparatus. Once in power a totalitarian regime cannot be dislodged, except by defeat in war. Its control is so pervasive and its vigilance so keen that internal opposition against it has no chance of establishing a foothold.

After peace had been restored in 1919 the Western economy tended spontaneously to revert to the system that had prevailed before 1914, that is, to a free, self-regulating world market. For a while the effort succeeded, and by 1925 world productivity and world trade attained to their prewar levels. But the economic reconstruction rested on fragile foundations. In 1929 the collapse of values on the New York Stock Exchange caused a world-wide chain reaction leading to the most severe economic depression in history, and producing disastrous social and political consequences. No single factor contributed so heavily to the triumph of totalitarianism.

The World Economic Crisis

As we have pointed out previously (Chapter 17), international prosperity before World War I had derived from the existence of a world market in which goods, money, and labor moved virtually unobstructed to where they were in the highest demand, that is, where they were the most productive. This movement was not entirely free, for it had to contend with protective tariffs, especially toward the end of the nineteenth century. But prior to 1914 these tariff barriers were not high enough to impede significantly the natural flow of the international economy.

The disruption of this economy began in earnest during the war. The Central Powers were from the beginning cut off from their usual sources of supply and forced into self-sufficiency. In 1917 Russia, one of the leading commercial nations, withdrew from the world economy. All the belligerents had to channel their productive capacities to military purposes, overdeveloping industrial sectors which with the restoration of peace would be of little use. The neutrals, on the other hand, especially the United States, expanded their general production at a feverish pace to keep up with the demands of the belligerents, much beyond the needs of the normal world market. The war thus unbalanced the economic life of both belligerents and neutrals.

After the cessation of hostilities it proved difficult to reforge the disrupted trade links and to restore the economic balance. The immediate problem was the

The German artist Kaethe Kollwitz (pages 462–463) did this charcoal study, Unemployed, *in Berlin in 1925.*

uneven distribution of gold and "hard currencies," that is, currencies that were internationally accepted (e.g., the dollar, pound sterling, Swiss and French franc, etc.). Wartime purchases had siphoned off a great deal of the European gold to the neutrals: in the 1920s the United States alone owned 40 percent of the world's gold reserve. Furthermore, the newly independent countries of Eastern Europe began statehood with such small reserves that their currencies never gained international status. Germany, burdened with large reparations payments, had little gold to spare. As a result of these factors, convertible currency —the lifeblood of international trade—was in such short supply that many European countries were unable to engage in, significant foreign trade. Their currencies turned into tokens with a strictly internal circulation.

To remedy this situation and to stimulate trade on which the health of their own economies depended, the capital-rich countries—the United States, Great Britain, and France—poured in the 1920s a great deal of money in the form of loans and investments into the capital-poor countries, especially Germany. Another means of overcoming the shortage of capital was acceptance of the so-called Gold Exchange Standard, introduced in 1922. A country that adopted it backed its currency not with gold proper but with gold-backed currencies or securities of other countries. These measures succeeded in stimulating trade, but they also created an unhealthy dependence of much of Europe on the continuous flow of outside capital, especially from the United States, as well as on the economic stability of the gold-holding countries.

A second factor that inhibited postwar trade was the steady rise of tariff barriers. To protect its overexpanded industries from competition, the United States passed in 1922 a very stringent tariff act, thereby making it even more difficult for capital-poor countries to secure gold and dollars. Furthermore, the dissolution of the great empires in 1918 had produced numerous successor states, each of which immediately established its own tariff system. The total length of European frontiers in 1920 was exactly double that of 1914; each new mile of frontier represented another hurdle to the movement of goods. These successor states exacted higher duties than had the empires. It has been estimated, for example, that the Czech and Hungarian republics charged tariffs 50 percent in excess of those collected by the Austro-Hungarian Empire of which they had formed a part.

The shortage of gold and convertible currencies and the simultaneous increase of tariff barriers created a vicious circle: to raise gold or hard currency each country sought to obtain the most favorable balance of trade, that is, to sell abroad the most and to buy abroad the least. Obviously, the less it purchased from other countries, the less the latter could purchase from it in return. Gradually, the international economy began to move toward "autarchy," or self-sufficiency of individual states, which vitiated the whole idea of an open world market.

In the meantime productivity was rising everywhere. By 1925 world manufacture of goods, having surpassed that of 1913, continued to climb upward. It was only a question of time before productivity outpaced demand. For the time being (1925–1929), however, trade kept pace with output, thanks to constant injections of capital.

In October, 1929, the main source of this capital suddenly dried up. The collapse on the New York Stock Exchange of a stupendous speculative wave in common stocks caused a shortage of capital in the United States. Credit became difficult to obtain. United States imports and foreign investments shrank and by 1932 were only one-third of what they had been in 1929. Many European banks and enterprises whose credit had been overextended or that had relied on the currencies or securities of other countries now went bankrupt, pulling down other banking and commercial institutions. In May, 1931, when the Creditanstalt, the principal bank of Austria, declared its insolvency, Europe experienced a grave financial crisis. A few months later several German banks suspended payments. Soon gold disappeared: in September, 1931, Great Britain went off the gold standard, and two years later the United States followed suit.

Trade declined. Most countries carefully guarded their limited reserves of gold and hard currencies and confined their foreign dealings as much as possible to agreements with individual countries, that is, in effect, to barter agreements. Between 1929 and 1932 world trade declined in value from $68.6 billion to $26.6.

The reduction in trade necessitated a corresponding reduction in productivity, since there was no point in manufacturing goods that could not be sold. World productivity of raw materials and manufactured goods decreased by more than one-quarter; in the two leading countries (the United States and Germany), the output of industrial goods declined by nearly one-half. Workers had to be laid off or dismissed. The world had never experienced unemployment of such dimensions. In 1932, when the depression was at its worst, an estimated 22 percent of the world labor force, or 30 million people, were jobless. In the nineteenth century many of these unemployed could have migrated overseas, but this became much more difficult now because some of the leading recipients of immigrants in the past, notably the United States, severely restricted the inflow of foreigners.°

The depression occurred at a time when confidence in liberalism and all it stood for was already severely shaken. Liberalism had proved itself incompetent to cope with postwar political and social instability; now it also showed its economic impotence. In the early 1930s the only way out of chaos seemed to lie in strong, purposeful "total" authority. The depression completely discredited liberalism and gave the critical impetus to totalitarian regimes that were to dominate the next two decades.

Stalinist Russia

War Communism had secured Bolshevik power, but it left the country economically and spiritually shattered. Between 1918 and 1920 an estimated 7 million people died in Russia from sickness, hunger, and the cold. The peasantry, outraged by food expropriations, refused to produce beyond its own immediate needs, and in 1920–1921 a terrible famine afflicted the country. Only thanks to the American Relief Administration, organized by the future President Herbert Hoover, were hundreds of thousands of additional Russians saved from certain starvation. Compared to 1913 the productivity of heavy industry in 1920 declined four-fifths and real wages of workers two-thirds.

Lenin, confronted with this catastrophic situation, acted in a typically resolute manner. In March, 1921, he abandoned War Communism and adopted the New Economic Policy (NEP). The NEP was primarily designed to placate the peasantry and to restore agricultural productivity. Forced food requisitioning was replaced by a tax in kind. The peasants were allowed to lease land and hire labor, and to dispose of their produce on the free market. A good deal of private initiative was also permitted in trade and manufacture. The results of this policy were spectacular. By 1928 Russian agricultural and industrial productivity attained their pre-1914 levels. Never before or since was the Soviet government as popular, especially among the peasantry, which at long last realized the age-old dream of having at its disposal all the country's arable land.

The NEP awakened widespread expectations that the Communist experiment was over, and that Russia, like France after the fall of Robespierre, was entering its "bourgeois" stage of development. Such hopes proved deceptive. The Communist leaders never gave up their monopoly either of political power or of what

° In 1921 Congress passed an Immigration Act which established quotas by country of birth: the annual number of immigrants from any country was limited to 3 percent of the number of that nationality who were foreign-born United States residents in 1910. As a result of this and subsequent laws, the number of immigrants coming to the United States in the 1930's sank to one-tenth and less of what it had been before the war.

Russian peasants line up for bread during the 1920–1921 famine. The American Relief Administration distributed in Russia nearly half a million tons of food, clothing, and medicine.

they called the "commanding heights" of the national economy, that is, heavy industry, banking, and foreign trade. The NEP was merely a breathing spell, a period of national convalescence before the next phase of the revolution from above got under way.

In December, 1922, Lenin suffered a paralytic stroke that incapacitated him completely. He died in January, 1924. Even before his final illness the question of his successor arose in acute form. One of the weaknesses of a regime that comes to power by violence and maintains itself in power by violence is that it lacks a legitimate procedure of succession. Lenin's heir could be selected only by a process of ruthless in-fighting within the party hierarchy, with the victory going to him who gained the support of the party's functionaries.

On the face of it Trotsky had all the attributes of an heir-apparent. He had been the organizer of the October Revolution and the creator of the Red Army. He was the most intelligent of the Bolshevik leaders; he was also the best orator, and, next to Lenin, the most familiar figure in the country. He headed the armed forces. He had the assets, but he lacked the essential personal qualities: will to power and the ordinary talents of a politician. Trotsky had no patience for the details of administration, nor did he know how to pretend interest in the little bureaucrats who came to the center for guidance and leadership. He preferred to speak and write on behalf of world revolution, hoping to maintain his leadership by appealing to the emotion and imagination of the masses as he had done in 1917.

But times had changed. The masses no longer counted. What counted were the millions of functionaries of the party and government who carried responsibility for the day-to-day administration of what had become a large and relatively stable state. These "men of the apparatus," or *apparatchiki*, had had enough of turmoil. They craved normalcy, an opportunity to enjoy the fruits of the power they had won since 1917. They were now a ruling class. Why should they endanger their position on behalf of a world revolution to which Trotsky

Lenin (left) and Stalin were photographed together in Moscow in the summer of 1922. In December of that year Lenin suffered a paralytic stroke.

was exhorting them? An increasing proportion of these *apparatchiki* came to distrust the clever Jewish intellectual and turned instead to a stolid Georgian named Joseph Dzhugashvili, known in the party as Stalin.°

Stalin was born in 1879 in an artisan family. After receiving a sketchy education in a religious seminary, he associated himself with the Bolsheviks and became a full-time revolutionary. He had no literary or rhetorical gifts, but he was loyal, dependable, and ready to carry out Lenin's instructions without raising the kind of moral or theoretical questions that troubled most other Russian Social Democrats. In the Revolution he played a minor role. However, after the Soviet state had been established and administrative problems multiplied, Lenin came increasingly to rely on him. Stalin could always be counted upon to attend to details for which Lenin and Trotsky, preoccupied as they were with major political or military decisions, had no time. Gradually, he built up within the party a personal following consisting of non-ideological careerists. By the time the Civil War had come to an end, a great deal of the party apparatus had quietly slipped into Stalin's hands. Trotsky paid no attention to the inarticulate Georgian, whom he once characterized as a "grey blur." By 1922 Stalin grew so powerful that he had the temerity to ignore Lenin's instructions and even to

°The Georgians, who inhabit the Caucasus, have been under Russian rule since 1801. They are Orthodox Christians, but have nothing in common with the Russians either ethnically or linguistically.

insult Lenin's wife. One of Lenin's last acts was to break personal relations with Stalin.

By then it was too late. Skillfully exploiting personal rivalries among other Communist leaders, Stalin organized party coalitions against Trotsky, his main rival. He depicted Trotsky as an unprincipled opportunist who had repeatedly betrayed Lenin and who now wanted to lead the country into dangerous adventures. Rather than exert efforts to promote revolutions abroad, as Trotsky desired, Stalin counseled "socialism in one country"—the concentration of all efforts and resources on developing in Soviet Russia a huge industrial economy. Trotsky's arguments that "socialism in one country" was a contradiction in terms because socialism (in the Marxist sense) could triumph only as an international movement fell on deaf ears among the party rank and file. In 1927 Trotsky was expelled from the party and two years later exiled from the Soviet Union. After long wanderings he settled in Mexico, where in 1940 he was murdered by a Stalinist agent.

Stalin's victory over Trotsky marked the beginning in Russia of a new phase of totalitarian rule. Combining talents for incredible intrigue and sadistic destructiveness with outstanding administrative abilities, Stalin eliminated his rivals one by one and emerged in the late 1930s as the absolute master of 170 million people. No other man in history had ever held such power.

Stalin's rule may be divided into three phases: the basic economic transformation of Russia (1928–1932), political terror (1932–1938), and war and external expansion (1939–1953). We shall deal with the last of these phases in the chapters that follow and here concentrate on the first two.

The main aim of Stalin's economic measures was to provide Soviet Russia with an industrial base on which to erect a modern military machine, which World War I had revealed was alone capable of winning twentieth-century battles. To realize this aim it was necessary to centralize the productive resources of the country and to direct them in a rational manner toward specific economic goals. In other words, a wartime economy was to be introduced in peacetime.

In 1928 the NEP was abandoned and replaced by rigidly controlled economic planning. In that year Russia adopted the Five-Year Plan, a crash program concentrated on building up heavy industry. Emphasis was placed on coal and iron, electrification, and machine construction. Each branch of the national economy was assigned specific production targets, and detailed schemes were drawn up for the movement of capital and resources. The country, especially its youth, responded enthusiastically to this gigantic constructive undertaking whose ultimate purpose, as depicted in a massive propaganda campaign, was abundance of consumer goods and a socialist society.

The results of the first Five-Year Plan were indeed spectacular. Upon its completion a second Five-Year Plan with similar objectives was launched. In 1936 Russia produced three times as much iron and oil and four times as much coal and steel as in 1913. The electrical output was sixteen times that of 1913. Many new industries were established—for example, automobile and tractor plants and industrial chemicals—which had not previously existed in Russia.

The class that paid most dearly for the forced industrialization was the peasantry, which in 1926 constituted 78 percent of the population. Soviet Russia did not have enough resources to launch its industrial drive and at the same time to provide the consumer with anything beyond the barest necessities. The anticipated reduction in consumer goods, however, raised the danger that the peasant would once more refuse to sell his food to the cities and industrial centers because he could receive in return nothing but worthless paper money.

To prevent this from happening Stalin cajoled the party into launching simultaneously with the first Five-Year Plan a massive program of land "collectivization." The government now took over the peasant's land, that which he had acquired before and since the Revolution, as well as his livestock and agricultural implements. These were turned over to "collective farms" (*kolkhozy* and *sovkhozy*) supervised by party-appointed managers. The peasant became in effect a hired hand, tilling for the state what had been until then his own land. In return for his labor, he received that part of the produce that remained after the collective had met the quotas set by the government. If the village did not produce a surplus above the required state deliveries, it had to go hungry. The city's supply was assured in any event.

The peasants furiously resisted this expropriation which reverted them to the condition prevailing before the Emancipation Edict of 1861. Rather than surrender their cattle they slaughtered and ate them. In many villages armed resistance reminiscent of 1920 broke out. Army and police units had to surround such villages and shoot the peasants into submission. Rich peasants, the so-called kulaks, or "fists," who were also the most productive elements in the countryside, were forcefully removed from their properties and either killed or exiled to concentration camps. How many people perished in this action cannot at present be established. During the war Stalin, in an expansive moment, confided to Winston Churchill that collectivization affected 10 million peasants, "the great bulk [of whom] were very unpopular and were wiped out by their

The propaganda directed at the Russian peasant included such newspapers as The Collective Farmer, *shown being printed on the back of a truck in a Ukrainian wheat field at harvest time.*

laborers." We may therefore assume that close to 10 million peasants lost their lives. Peasant resistance lowered production of food to the point where in 1932–1933 Soviet Russia suffered its second major famine since the Revolution. The cities had their food quotas delivered, but many villages starved, especially in the Ukraine. Peasants quit their villages in droves and moved into the cities.

By 1932 virtually the entire industrial and agricultural resources of Russia were in the hands of the state—that is, of Stalin. The dictator's next task was to secure this personal power against any potential contenders. Beginning in 1932 Stalin launched a reign of terror, initially directed against the Communist party apparatus but later broadened to encompass the entire population. He had to rid himself of those who took their Marxism and Communism seriously, whose memories reached back to Lenin and Trotsky, who had links with foreign socialists, and to replace them with a new generation of functionaries—men from the lower strata who owed everything to him and who knew and believed only what he allowed them to know and believe.

This process was launched in 1932 with a mass purge of the party, in the course of which one-third of the party effectives were dropped from the rolls. The reign of terror proper began in the winter of 1934–1935. The pretext was the assassination of Sergei Kirov, the popular party chief in Leningrad. Stalin claimed that Kirov's murder was the work of a vast counterrevolutionary organization and that vigorous measures were required to root it out. (Today it is virtually certain that Kirov was assassinated in the best gangland fashion on the orders of Stalin himself.) In the years 1936–1938 the astonished world witnessed in Russia what looked like the enactment of some ghoulish scenario by Dostoevsky: a succession of show trials at which the men who had made the Revolution and helped found the Soviet state confessed to the basest crimes, including espionage on behalf of foreign powers. Each trial ended with mass executions. By 1938 not one of Lenin's close friends and associates was left alive. In the 1930s elaborate theories were advanced in the West to explain these proceedings, often with reference to alleged peculiarities of the Russian "soul." (Some Westerners, of course, accepted the trials at face value.) But in 1956 Nikita Khrushchev, Stalin's successor, explained the confessions in a very simple manner:

> How is it possible that a person confesses to crimes that he has not committed? Only in one way—as a result of methods of physical pressure, of tortures, which bring him to a state of unconsciousness, deprivation of judgment, which rob him of human dignity. [Stalin's] "confessions" were secured in this manner.

Before being brought to trial the victims were subjected to such inhuman beatings and tortures that they agreed to anything and looked forward to death as relief.

The show trials were only public spectacles behind the scenes of which unrolled a wholesale terror. Millions of party and state functionaries, army officers, trade unionists, intellectuals, simple peasants, and workers were arrested by the secret police, speedily "investigated," forced to sign fabricated "confessions," and either shot or sent to concentration camps. Both Bolsheviks and their one-time opponents now shared a similar fate. The Russian intelligentsia was virtually annihilated. The secret police, concentrated in the Ministry of the Interior (NKVD, later renamed MVD), replaced the party as the ruling organization. Even its chiefs, however, were not immune from persecution, each in turn being accused of treason and executed, until in 1938 Stalin settled on a fellow Georgian, Lavrenti Beria.

In 1938 the whole gruesome process finally ground to a halt. The old Communist apparatus lay in shambles, and a new generation had come into power: crude and ignorant, but totally dependent on Stalin and presumably loyal to him.

Neither the horrors of collectivization nor those of the terror discouraged Western pro-Communists. Indeed, in the 1930s the popularity of Stalin and Soviet Russia grew. Many foreign intellectuals, appalled by the economic depression and the rise of fascism and nazism, idealized the Soviet experiment, and saw in it a blueprint of the future. In the 1930s there was a widespread tendency in the West to dismiss any evidence unfavorable to Soviet Russia. "You cannot make an omelet without breaking eggs" was frequently heard in justification of Stalin's actions.

The more his power grew, the more Stalin withdrew from the public eye. Stalin was not a "charismatic" leader, that is, one able to command a fanatical following by the force of his personality. He had no rhetorical gifts whatever: he spoke with a monotonous voice and in a heavy Georgian accent, which to a Russian has a very comical sound. Instead of exposing himself personally he projected his identity through an enormous propaganda campaign that impressed on the public the image of an all-knowing, all-present, all-powerful, and, indeed, immortal being.

The Nazi Seizure of Power

The economic crisis of 1929–1932 undercut the last remaining props of the Weimar Republic. Exports declined by two-thirds, and by 1932 over 6 million Germans were unemployed. German workers were now in as desperate straits as the middle class had been during the inflation of the early twenties, and as discontented. Many defected from the Social Democrats and joined extremist parties.

One group that profited from this situation was the German Communist party. Well-organized, purposeful, aggressive, it continued to whittle away votes from the Social Democrats, the mainstay of the republic. Its share of the parliamentary seats grew steadily, especially during the depression (chart, opposite). The Communists were not concerned by a much more spectacular gain of the parties at the opposite end of the political spectrum, the traditional conservatives and the National Socialists. At the time they regarded the Social Democrats as their main enemy, the principal rival for the workingman's vote, and concentrated all efforts on their destruction. With Stalin's backing, German Communist leaders acted on the premise that Hitler was less dangerous, indeed preferable, to the liberal, reformist socialists.

The greatest benefit from the disintegration of the liberal center accrued to the Nazis, the German National Socialist Labor party (NSDAP). Between 1928 and 1932 they picked up 11 million votes and increased their share of parliamentary seats thirteenfold.

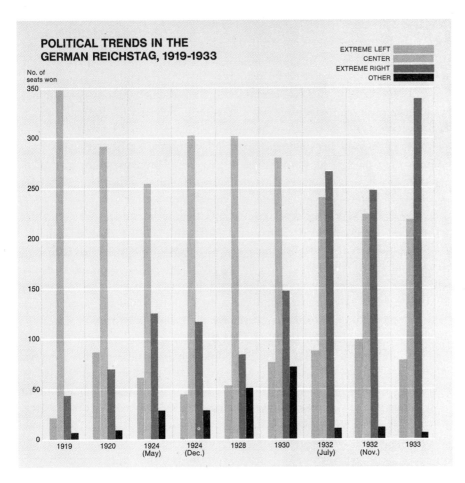

POLITICAL TRENDS IN THE GERMAN REICHSTAG, 1919-1933

EXTREME LEFT
CENTER
EXTREME RIGHT
OTHER

No. of seats won

The NSDAP came into existence as one of the numerous Austrian neo-conservative parties that would have vanished without a trace were it not that in the person of Adolf Hitler it acquired a leader of singular demagogic gifts and utter nihilistic unscrupulousness. Hitler was born in 1889 in the family of a petty Austrian customs official. As a youth he tried desperately to make an artistic career, but the Vienna Academy of Fine Arts rejected his application for admission on the grounds that he did not know how to draw. Temperamentally unable to hold a job, Hitler became a tramp. Living in Viennese flophouses, he earned just enough from casual manual work and peddling his landscapes to keep his head above water. During these years he developed a consuming hatred for the cultivated bourgeois society of Vienna that had rejected him and condemned him to the life of an anonymous cipher, and most of all for the Jews who were so prominent in Vienna's cultural life. He dreamed of gaining power and exacting revenge for his humiliations. Hitler had no political ideas either then or later, but he studied attentively the techniques of mob manipulation. He admired greatly the Christian Socialist mayor of Vienna, Karl Lueger (Chapter 20), for his ability to appeal simultaneously to German nationalism, anti-Semitism, and anti-capitalism to gain votes. He also observed closely the activities of the Austrian Social Democrats, especially the mass rallies at which orators whipped up their followers. Hitler knew that he could only realize his wild ambitions by mastering crowds. His intellectual baggage was common currency of right-wing

Austria in the turn-of-the-century period: Social Darwinism, racism, anti-parliamentarism.

From his youth onward Hitler evidenced a hysterical personality. He was subject to frequent, ungovernable outbursts of rage, which later astonished even his intimate associates. His utter confidence in himself and his cause, combined with overpowering emotionalism, made him into a spellbinding orator; and on his rhetoric he built his political career. Notwithstanding his extreme skill in utilizing political and military means to gain his objectives, there can be no doubt that he had a deranged mind: medicine is familiar with psychopaths who pursue totally irrational ends in a highly calculating manner.

During World War I Hitler served in the German army on the Western front. (He had earlier abandoned his Austrian citizenship out of disgust with the vacillating policies of the Hapsburgs, especially their leniency toward their non-German subjects.) After demobilization he joined the disaffected veterans who were plotting the overthrow of the Weimar Republic. His skill in rabble-rousing in Munich beer halls secured him contacts with nationalistic generals who needed popular support for their subversive plans but did not know how to go about obtaining it. In 1920 Hitler and his friends—a casual assortment of war veterans, journalists, ideologists, and plain thugs—formed squads of street fighters to assault Social Democrats and Communists. These units, modeled on Mussolini's *fasci di combattimento*, were organized in 1921 into regular Storm Troop detachments (*Sturmabteilungen,* or SA). In 1923, when the French occupation of the Ruhr seemed to have dealt the republic a fatal blow, Hitler joined Ludendorff in an abortive *coup d'état* in Munich. For this he was arrested and sentenced to five years in prison. There, comfortably installed, he began to write his main political work, *Mein Kampf* (*My Struggle*).

After the fiasco of 1923 the Nazis came to the conclusion that power had to be secured not by violence, that is, by a direct assault on the republic. Like Lenin and Mussolini, Hitler decided to make his "revolution" only after having come to power and now began to stress legality. The Weimar Republic played into his hands by dealing leniently with him and his followers, although the Nazis made no secret of their ultimate aims. Hitler himself was released from prison after serving only one year. Later, when the Nazis stood at the pinnacle of power, Hitler's Propaganda Minister, Joseph Goebbels, recalled the Weimar days:

> Until 1932 our political opponents did not realize where we were going, that our respect for legality was only a trick. We wanted to come to power legally, but we certainly did not intend to use power legally. We did not want to tolerate parties that in a year would deal with us as we intended to deal with them. They could have suppressed us. This would not have been so difficult. But this was not done. In 1925, a few of us could have been arrested, and everything would have been over. But we were allowed to cross the danger zone.

The Nazi program must be viewed on three distinct levels: the official party platform, most explicitly formulated in 1920; the concealed political aim—totalitarianism—which became apparent only in 1933, after Hitler had secured the chancellorship; and the ultimate racial goals, hinted at in the 1920s and

The biting Social Democratic poster below asks, "Do you want these to rule you?" The 1932 Nazi poster opposite equates a vote for Hitler with the fight against hunger and despair.

partly realized in the 1930s, but revealed in all their insanity only after the outbreak of World War II. The gradual, piecemeal manner in which the Nazis unraveled their program was one of the reasons for their success in deceiving the public at home and abroad.

The formal party platform of 1920 was designed to appeal to the broadest strata of opinion. It advocated nationalism based on race (rather than on culture) and called for the unification of all Germans in a single state, the renunciation of the humiliating treaties of Versailles and St. Germain, and the expulsion from Germany of residents with foreign citizenship. Its nationalism was fortified by unabashed anti-Semitism: German Jews were to be denied the status of Germans on the grounds that they did not and could not belong to the German "racial community." The platform also contained strong socialist elements. It favored state guarantees of employment, the confiscation of war profits and of income not earned by work, the nationalization of big business, and profit-sharing. To the peasants the Nazis promised land reform and to the lower-middle class (which they courted especially assiduously) the expropriation of department stores, the great competitor of the shopkeeper. The platform was emphatically anti-bourgeois and anti-liberal, making a strong appeal to the sentiments hostile to industrialization and capitalism among the lower-middle class and the working population.

The 1920 program also pledged to "abolish the corrupt parliamentary order," but it did not specify what would replace it. Nothing was said about the intended one-party dictatorship, the abolition of political rights and civil liberties, or the omnipotence of the police. Following the example of Lenin and Mussolini, Hitler was most reticent about the most essential.

He was more explicit about his ultimate, long-range racial aims, but these were so fantastic that hardly anyone, even among the Nazis, took them seriously. What he had in mind was no less than the physical destruction of a considerable part of the European population and its replacement by a new breed of human beings. These were to be sired by the purest representatives of the "Aryan" race and brought up in the spirit of National Socialist ideas: industry, thrift, and unquestioned loyalty to Hitler as the incarnation of the "Aryan" spirit. The "inferior" races and "defective" human specimens were to be enslaved or pitilessly destroyed.

Hitler succeeded in coming to power in a perfectly legal manner by taking advantage of the widening rift between right and left to present himself as the leader of a "revolution" leading to national unity and renascence.

In 1930 the government was assumed by the Catholic Center party, which at last took firm action against both the anti-republican parties, the Communists and Nazis, and outlawed their strong-arm squads. The extremists, however, continued to do well in elections: in July, 1932, the Nazis won the largest number of votes and became the strongest party in the Reichstag. They demanded that Hitler be named Chancellor, but President von Hindenburg refused on the basis that the Nazis were a divisive party, likely to exacerbate social conflicts. Soon new elections were held (November, 1932). This time the Nazis lost 2 million votes, while the Communists made another advance. The good showing of

The Establishment of Nazi Totalitarianism

the Communists frightened the traditional conservatives and induced them to seek an alliance with the Nazis. In January, 1933, Hitler was invited by the monarchists to head a coalition government. The men who engineered this deal had little sympathy for the Austrian upstart, but they believed that by bringing Hitler into the government they could thwart the Communist danger and at the same time exert a moderating influence on the Nazis. On January 30, 1933, Hindenburg appointed Hitler Chancellor of a cabinet in which the Nazis held only two additional posts.

Hitler at first kept up the pretense of being a good parliamentarian and insisted on holding new elections, the third in a year, to secure an absolute majority in the Reichstag. In the electoral campaign SA squads ruled the streets, intimidating opponents and fighting Communist gangs. The Nazis offered no specific program; they merely asked the country to give them four years to show what they could accomplish toward a national revival. Their brutal electoral techniques did not bring them the anticipated majority, but they secured a respectable following nonetheless: 17 million votes, or 43.7 percent of the ballots. With their allies, the Nationalists, they now controlled 51.9 percent of the Reichstag seats. This was a sufficient basis on which to make a bid for total power.

By 1933 the totalitarian model was well established. What Lenin, Mussolini, and Stalin had learned by trial and error, Hitler could put into practice in fin-

A picture made in 1933 shows the senile "Wooden Titan," German President von Hindenburg, taking the salute of SA troopers as his masters march behind him. Hitler is visible at center in mufti, next to the bemedaled Goering.

ished form. Within a few months after taking office as Chancellor, he gained enough authority to assert unlimited personal power over the German people.

The first step was to abolish civil rights protecting the opposition. This step was taken even before the Reichstag elections, in the guise of defending the country from an alleged Communist conspiracy. On February 27, 1933, unknown arsonists (most likely Nazis) set fire to the Reichstag building in Berlin. Hitler immediately blamed it on the Communists. He demanded that Hindenburg invoke constitutional emergency provisions and suspend civil liberties to safeguard the security of the country. On his Chancellor's advice, the President issued on February 28 an "Ordinance for the Protection of the People and the State" that indefinitely suspended civil liberties, authorizing

> restrictions on personal liberty, on the right of free expression of opinion, including freedom of the Press, on the rights of assembly and association; violations of the privacy of postal, telegraphic, and telephonic communications; warrants for house searches; orders for confiscations as well as restrictions on property.

Since the police, who were charged with carrying out these sweeping provisions, were by then largely in Nazi hands, the ordinance enabled Hitler legally to dispose of his opponents. The Communists now paid dearly for their shortsighted tactics: their party was the first to be outlawed and their leaders went to jail or to concentration camps, where most of them later perished; with them went many Social Democrats and other outspoken anti-Nazis. Regular courts were enjoined from interfering with the police and confined to civil suits. "Political" and "criminal" offenses (as defined by the Nazis) were handed over to the police and to "People's Courts," created in 1934. The Ordinance of 1933 remained in force until the collapse of the Nazi regime in 1945 and provided the legal basis for the repressions and executions of German citizens in the intervening period.

After the March, 1933, elections, Hitler turned his attention to the destruction of political rights. His aim was to be invested by the Reichstag with full legislative authority, that is, to usurp from the nation's elected representatives the right to issue laws. Such an amendment to the constitution required approval of two-thirds of the deputies. The Nazis persuaded the Catholic Center party to support their resolution, and by arresting Communist deputies they secured the necessary majority. On March 23–24 the Reichstag passed an "Enabling Act" divesting itself for a period of four years (but in fact permanently) of legislative authority. As Chancellor, Hitler could henceforth issue laws, even those violating the constitution, without consulting the Reichstag. The Social Democrats were the only major political party to vote against this self-imposed sentence of death that simultaneously destroyed German parliamentarism and German constitutionalism.

With the authority he now possessed Hitler could rapidly proceed to establish control over the whole of state and society. This process, euphemistically called *Gleichschaltung* (Coordination), involved the penetration by the NSDAP and its subsidiaries of all facets of German life, and the elimination of most foci of independent power. Among the first to go were the governments of the federal states. Their authority was severely abrogated, with the result that Germany be-

WIDE WORLD

Heinrich Himmler, one of Hitler's earliest adherents, headed the SS and the Gestapo, eventually directing the entire Nazi police apparatus.

came for the first time in its history a centralized, unitary state. In the spring of 1933 all political parties, including those that had invited the Nazis into the government a few months earlier, were disbanded, and the NSDAP was declared the only lawful political organization in the country. The once powerful trade-union organizations were abolished and dissolved as well. So were most other associations, including cultural and recreational ones. At the end of 1933 Goebbels could thus describe what the Nazis had achieved in the course of the year:

> The Revolution which we have accomplished is a total one. It has seized all the realms of public life and transformed them from the ground up. It has completely altered and reformed the relations of men toward each other, toward the state, and toward problems of existence. . . . The system which we have overthrown found in liberalism its most accurate representation. If liberalism took as its starting point the individual and placed the individual man in the center of all things, we have replaced the individual by the nation and the individual man by the community.

At the beginning of 1934 only three institutions were still outside Hitler's complete grasp: the SA, the church, and the army.

The Storm Trooper organizations, which had proved so useful in the Nazi march to power, at this time numbered over 2 million members. Among them were genuine radicals who had taken at face value the socialist slogans of the Nazis, as well as ambitious politicians who wanted a "second revolution" to bring to heel big business and the largely middle-class army. But for Hitler the concept of "revolution" had lost its usefulness, and in 1934 he publicly declared Germany would have no more revolutions for a thousand years. Furthermore, he needed the support of big business and the officer corps to launch the program of rearmament, now his immediate goal. After some hesitation he therefore decided to liquidate the SA. In June, 1934, on his orders, several hundred SA leaders were massacred. Henceforth this organization lost influence.

Like other totalitarian leaders, Hitler was anticlerical. He saw in Christianity a "Jewish swindle," and he privately expressed his ultimate intention of wiping out the church. But in the first years he was not yet strong enough to tackle the powerful Catholic and Protestant establishments, and contented himself with a demand for strict separation of church and state. In July, 1933, he signed a Concordat with the Vatican in which the Catholic hierarchy recognized the new regime and renounced all activity in Germany save that of a purely religious and philanthropic kind. The Protestant churches, however, from the beginning offered strong resistance to the Nazis on ideological and moral grounds. Later, as the Nazis began to interfere with Catholic organizations, they, too, resisted. In 1937 the Pope issued an encyclical in which he voiced his anxiety over Nazi policies. By then the Nazis and the two major churches were locked in a grim struggle that lasted until the collapse of the regime.

The army, or *Reichswehr*, remained autonomous for the time being, for Hitler and the generals happened to have had common interests: both wanted to rearm. It was only in 1938, when basic rearmament was completed, that Hitler took personal charge of the *Reichswehr*. (See Chapter 29.)

The Nazi party did not differ fundamentally either in its structure or in its functions from the Communist party of the Soviet Union, or the Italian Fascist party, and therefore need not be described. The NSDAP created a whole hierarchy of offices that duplicated and controlled the regular state apparatus. It was officially described as "the bearer of the idea of German statehood, indissolubly bound with the state." When Hindenburg died in 1934, Hitler assumed the title of President, thus uniting in his person, like Lenin and Mussolini (but unlike Stalin), the positions of party chief and head of state.

To assure his personal power Hitler established an élite corps, the *Schutzstaffel* (Guard Detachment), or SS, which was placed under Heinrich Himmler, a onetime chicken farmer and the most pathologically sadistic among the Nazi leaders. The SS began as a bodyguard whose members took the oath of personal loyalty to Hitler and swore to carry out without question any orders he issued. Into it were recruited the most vicious elements of the Nazi movement. They staffed police posts, both overt and secret, and gradually penetrated much of the party and state machinery. From their ranks were drawn the concentration camp guards and, during World War II, the mass murderers. The powers of the SS grew steadily and eventually came to approximate those that the NKVD enjoyed under Stalin in Russia.

Anti-Semitism occupied a very special place in Nazi doctrine and practice; indeed, it was the only constant element in National Socialism, the one policy that never changed. Hitler and his associates were rabid anti-Semites, to whom the Jew was a satanic figure, a bloodsucker and invidious despoiler of Aryan purity, the lowest of subhumans. Their attitude toward the Jew was of a most primitive kind, in which sexual anxieties and historic traditions, rooted in the darkest Middle Ages, played a significant part. But Hitler also exploited anti-Jewish feelings in a cold-blooded fashion, for he needed a racial foe, much as the Soviet Communists needed their "class enemy."

The advent of the Nazis to power led immediately to the issuance of anti-Jewish laws. These culminated in the infamous Nürnberg Laws of 1935, which in effect deprived Jews of German citizenship and forbade them to marry "Aryans." The law defined as Jewish anyone who professed the Jewish faith or who had at least one-fourth of Jewish blood in his veins. Subjected to constant indignities and gradually deprived of their livelihood, many Jews had to migrate, leaving their possessions behind. In November, 1938, the anti-Semitic policy entered a violent phase with an organized nation-wide pogrom and burning of synagogues. These anti-Semitic acts were merely a prelude to what was intended as an eventual annihilation of the Jews and other "lower races" in Europe.

Hitler's main objective, once he had secured dictatorial powers, was to give Germany a powerful armed force with which to conquer "living space" and subjugate the Continent. The rearmament program required the maximum concentration of the country's resources, not unlike that introduced by imperial Germany during World War I. Shortly after the Nazis came to power the German economy was put on a wartime footing. Private enterprise was left intact because it proved efficient and cooperated with the Nazis, but it found itself subjected to stringent controls. Production soared: between 1932 and 1935 alone German steel production trebled. In 1936, emulating Stalin, Hitler introduced a Four-Year Plan. Its purpose was to make the German economy self-sufficient in

Hitler at a carefully staged Nazi party rally at Nürnberg. "You have to go through one of these," correspondent Shirer wrote, "to understand Hitler's hold on the people, to feel the dynamic in the movement he's unleashed and the sheer, disciplined strength of the Germans."

strategic war materials, such as rubber and gasoline, by the development of substitutes. In 1940, when the plan was to be fulfilled, Hitler expected the armed forces and the economy to be fully geared for war.

In their social policy the Nazis spoke of creating a one-class society, but they did not pursue this aim with anything like the determination they displayed in their destructive policies. In 1934 they formed a "National Labor Front," uniting employees and employers in a single national organization. This institution, modeled on Mussolini's "corporations," did not greatly alter society, for the retention of private property kept intact the traditional social distinctions.

The Nazis owed much of their early popularity, especially among the workers, to the elimination of unemployment. The rearmament program absorbed many of the jobless; others found work with large public work projects, such as the construction of a network of superhighways (*Autobahnen*), ultimately also destined for military uses. Within a year of Hitler's coming to power the number of unemployed dropped by half; gradually unemployment disappeared. But pay was low, and the standard of living remained stationary, below that of 1929. The government made determined efforts to win labor support by means other than high wages. Especially popular with the working population was the "Strength through Joy" program, which combined vacations, education, and entertainment with Nazi indoctrination. A "People's Car" (*Volkswagen*) was designed to provide cheap transportation for the Nazi citizen. Of course, nothing came of the socialist promises, for the government could not afford to alienate the industrialists who furnished the military hardware.

Among the party's auxiliary organizations mention must be made of the Hitler Youth (*Hitlerjugend*). It was a copy of the Union of Communist Youth (*Komsomol*), founded by Lenin in 1918, and later emulated by Mussolini in his *Ballila* and *Avanguardisti*. Its purpose, too, was to indoctrinate the new generation with the party ideology and a sense of obedience, and to furnish cadres for the party and police.

No account of nazism can ignore its public spectacles. The party showed great skill in manipulating visual and auditory effects to hearten supporters, sway doubters, and overwhelm opponents. Parades, organized with a precision and on a scale never before seen, hypnotized participants and, through the radio and movies, audiences all over Germany. The greatest of those was the annual party rally at Nürnberg. There assembled tens of thousands of stalwart Nazis, lined up like so many identical automatons, with their insignia, banners, and battle gear, facing their leader, high up on a podium. Hitler's speeches to those and other gatherings, in which threats and promises always alternated, kept Europe in a state of constant tension. The synchronized roar of the crowds with their *Sieg-Heil!* (Victory-Hail!) and *Ein Volk, Ein Reich, Ein Führer!* (One People, One Country, One Leader!) created the impression of an elemental force that nothing could stop.

Repercussions

Stalin and Hitler were the only truly totalitarian leaders. But their seeming success in coping with domestic problems encouraged elsewhere a further move away from liberalism toward totalitarian forms. A number of dictatorships veered in the 1930s toward more restrictive policies, suspending or violating civil liberties and establishing governments of a semi-totalitarian kind. In Austria the threat of Nazi subversion induced the authorities in 1933 to suspend parliamentary government and many civil liberties. In the same year Portugal adopted a new constitution, based on the Fascist model. In Spain a civil war that broke out in 1936 (Chapter 29) brought to power a Fascist government with totalitarian aspirations. And in Poland, after the death of the dictator Pilsudski in 1935, authority passed into the hands of army officers who increasingly repressed political opposition and imprisoned people they disliked.

In other countries democratic institutions, hitherto intact, weakened appreciably and sometimes collapsed under the assault of conspirators. In 1934 democracies were done away with in Latvia and Bulgaria; in 1936 in Greece; and in 1938 in Romania.

In many instances this anti-liberal, anti-democratic subversion was financed by the Nazis, who exploited various sources of discontent and played on anti-Semitism abroad to undermine political stability and prepare the soil for eventual conquest.

In the 1930s traditional institutions and political morals were disappearing everywhere in Europe with dizzying speed. The world headed for a catastrophe that no one seemed able to prevent: another war, but one that would be also a revolution and possibly mark the end of civilization as it had been known in the West.

28

<hr>

The Dissolution
of the Middle Class

Behind the collapse of liberalism lay not only specific political and economic factors but also deeper social and cultural ones. Liberal institutions throughout the European Continent caved in with such speed and finality because of the coincident collapse of the middle class, that social group which traditionally had provided its backbone (Chapter 18). In the twentieth century the bourgeoisie suffered both impoverishment and demoralization. Its money went or lost value; the family, its fulcrum, fell apart as women asserted their independence and sought self-fulfillment outside the confines of the home; its moral scruples and its gentility appeared increasingly ridiculous in a world subjected to mass slaughter and the horrors of totalitarianism. Already in 1920 Keynes noted a drastic shift in the bearing of the once-proud middle class:

> [Twenty-five years ago] the capitalists believed in themselves, in their value to society, in the propriety of their continued existence, in the full enjoyment of their riches and the unlimited exercise of their power. Now they tremble before every insult; call them pro-Germans, international financiers, or profiteers, and they will give you any ransom you choose to ask not to speak of them so harshly. They allow themselves to be ruined and altogether undone by their own instruments, governments of their own making, and a press of which they are the proprietors.

This led Keynes to conclude that perhaps it was true "that no order of society ever perishes save by its own hand."

An essential aspect, perhaps the main cause of the decline of the European middle class, was its impoverishment. This was brought about in three ways: taxation, inflation, and expropriation.

Impoverishment

TAXATION

Until the end of the nineteenth century, income taxes were virtually unknown: whatever a man earned, he kept. Governments, national and local alike, derived their revenue from taxes on property, from customs duties, monopolies, state properties, or indirect taxes. The notion that the greater a man's earnings the more he should pay contradicted the whole liberal ethos, since it seemed to penalize industry and thrift. On occasion, during national crises (for example, in France and England during the French Revolution, and in the United States during the Civil War), income was taxed, but only for the duration of the emergency. The absence of an income tax made it possible to amass enormous fortunes in a short time; it was an essential in the ascendancy of the middle class.

Regular taxation of income was introduced only in the second half of the nineteenth century. It was necessitated by rapidly rising government expenditures on armaments and social welfare. Great Britain inaugurated a regular graduated

The disintegration of the European middle class was well under way in late 1921, when this drawing appeared in the German satirical journal Simplicissimus. *"We cannot socialize with these nouveau poor," the beggars complain. "They have nothing!"*

income tax in 1874, Prussia in 1891, France in 1909. At this time the treasuries of the great powers came increasingly to depend on this source for their operating revenue. In 1909 Lloyd George stated that the income tax, previously an expedient, had become "the center and the sheet anchor" of the British fiscal system. Germany, which had introduced a particularly efficient scheme of taxing income, derived from it early in the twentieth century one-half of its revenue.

But important as the income tax may have been for the budgets of some states, until 1914 it bore rather lightly on the individual citizen. In the 1890s an Englishman paid the equivalent of 3 cents on each earned dollar; in Prussia the wealthiest contributed 4 percent of their earnings. Elsewhere in Europe the income tax was usually lower, and in any event, it was rarely collected.° It has been estimated that prior to 1914 the total tax burden (income, local, and property taxes) even of the most affluent European did not exceed 8 percent.

Taxation became burdensome only after the outbreak of World War I. It was especially heavy in Great Britain, which had made an early decision to pay for military expenditures not from loans (as was done in France and Germany) but from taxing income. In the middle of World War I an Englishman contributed to the government 15 percent of his income, and at its conclusion an unheard-of 30 percent. With the restoration of peace the rate was somewhat reduced, but it never again reverted to its pre-1914 level. During the Second World War the British tax climbed once more, to claim one-half of earnings. Englishmen were, in addition, liable to a heavy inheritance tax (death duty), which on wealthy estates amounted to 50 percent. Understandably, it became increasingly difficult for an Englishman to make a fortune and virtually impossible to pass it on to his heirs. This fact greatly demoralized the middle class, removing an important traditional motive behind its economic drive: the prospect of accumulating capital for oneself and one's family.

The British income tax and death duties, exacting as they may have been, were at least legally enacted. On the Continent in most cases the middle class was shorn of its property by less legitimate and less predictable means.

INFLATION

A considerable part of the income of the nineteenth-century bourgeois derived from capital investments. The income which these investments brought was meaningful only as long as prices remained relatively constant; that is, as long as a given sum of money brought year after year a corresponding return in goods and services. It so happened that in the nineteenth century, especially in its second half, the Western world enjoyed exceptional monetary stability. Prices rose, but so slowly—on the average 1 to 1.5 percent a year—that the rise was not felt. A European living on capital had reasonable assurance that the income it yielded would enable him to live in the accustomed style for the remainder of his days.

World War I inaugurated the great modern inflation, which is still in progress. Its original causes were the classical ones of all inflations: too much money and too few goods. During the war governments everywhere to some extent helped cover their extraordinary military expenditures by printing paper money. Even Britain, which followed a conservative financial policy, between 1914 and 1918

°The United States introduced a modest income tax in 1894, but the Supreme Court voided it. It came back in 1913 with the ratification of the Sixteenth Amendment.

Worthless German marks are baled for scrap paper after the currency reform of 1924.

quadrupled the quantity of pounds in circulation. In Germany, in the same period, the amount of circulating banknotes increased five times, in Russia twelve times, in Austria-Hungary fifteen times. At the same time, with the economy working primarily for the military, consumer goods became scarce, and their prices steadily climbed upward. Between 1913 and 1920 wholesale prices more than doubled in the neutral European countries (e.g., Holland and Switzerland), tripled in Great Britain, quintupled in France, and sextupled in Italy. A person living on fixed income now found that he could buy less and less for his money; he was doubly hurt in countries with heavy income taxes, where he had less of the depreciated money to begin with.

Nowhere was the inflation more calamitous than in postwar Germany. The inflation of 1922–1923, which reduced the mark to the absurd level of 4.2 trillion to the United States dollar (Chapter 26), utterly ruined the German middle class. It now had to dispose of its treasured possessions—art works, libraries, musical instruments, furniture—merely to obtain money to buy food. In a few years the class of property and education which had been the supporting pillar of imperial Germany was reduced to a standard of living below that of the working class. The following random observations of a contemporary give some idea of the effects of the great postwar inflation on the lives of middle-class Germans: .

I know a former high government official. One day I noticed the leather covering on his big easy chair had been removed and cheap cloth substituted. I spoke about it. He smiled apologetically. "The children needed shoes." In October of 1922 the mark salaries of lower government officials were sixty-nine times as high as in 1914; of middle officials, sixty-two times

The sale of art treasures by the hard-pressed to gain stable dollars was of widespread concern in postwar Europe. The anguished figures represent Holbein, Dürer, and Cranach.

as high; and of higher officials, only fifty-seven times as high. Meanwhile, a bricklayer made one hundred and forty-seven times as many marks as in 1914. A skilled workman was paid more than three-quarters of the income of a principal of an elementary school or a medical officer. For a two-hour university extension lecture, the lecturer is paid the equivalent of ten cents, enough for a meal for himself and his family. One of the foremost economists in Germany writes newspaper editorials which bring in from a half-dollar to a dollar each. In November of 1922 the monthly stipend of a lower official would barely buy the coat and vest of a suit of clothes; trousers had to await the next pay check. A higher official was fortunate; *he* could buy the whole suit and a pair of paper shoes. . . . If the lower official's income all went for butter, he could buy two pounds every three days.

A middle-class widow in Berlin is writing of the hardships she had to undergo. In January of last year her monthly pension of 6,000 marks just sufficed to supply her with milk and two pounds of fat. Her other expenses for herself and her daughter, who is ailing from a disease caused by under-nourishment, amounted to 80,000 marks—obtained by letting rooms, sewing, and teaching. No meat was included in the diet. She says: "I am still forced to work hard from six o'clock in the morning until ten o'clock at night. . . . We live entirely upon potatoes, bread and margarine, and a little soup.°

Persons disposing of hard currencies could make fortunes in postwar Germany buying up belongings of the hard-pressed bourgeois. During this time, approximately one-quarter of the apartment houses in Berlin passed into the hands of foreigners. The resentment that this wholesale loss of its property caused among a people notable for their industry and thrift can be readily imagined. It played no small part in the subsequent swing of much of the middle class to the Nazis, who promised them retribution and recompense.

The effects of inflation were only slightly less devastating among the successor states of the dissolved East European empires. The Austrian crown, which in 1914 had been worth twenty U.S. cents, sunk in 1922 to 1/700th of one cent. In Poland it took 8 million Polish marks to buy one dollar. In those countries with runaway inflations, profiteers and speculators who possessed dollars had a field day.

The inflation in France and Italy was far less calamitous (here disaster was to come only during World War II), but it was serious enough to subvert the life of the middle classes. In both countries the currency (franc and lira, respectively) lost in the decade 1914–1924 between two-thirds and four-fifths of its purchasing capacity. What this meant concretely may be illustrated by the example of a hypothetical French family disposing of a capital of 500,000 francs. Before the war this capital yielded an annual income of 23,000 francs. Of this sum 14,000 went to meet living expenses, the surplus being available to be added to the capital. In 1924, partly due to the natural increase in the capital and partly to the rise in interest rates, the family's annual income rose to 30,000 francs. But because of the increase in living costs, it now required 40,000 francs to maintain

°F. A. Ross, "The Passing of the German Middle Class," *The American Journal of Sociology* (March, 1924).

its accustomed standard of living. The family had an option of either lowering its standards (for instance, by firing domestics) or eating into its capital.° Neither alternative permitted in the long run survival of middle-class life: either comfort or long-term financial security had to be sacrificed.

EXPROPRIATIONS

The middle class suffered the greatest economic disaster in Russia, where after the Bolshevik seizure of power nearly all private property was nationalized. Several million people, from wealthy industrialists, bankers, and landowners to shopkeepers and self-employed artisans, were made destitute overnight. The collectivization of agriculture carried out in 1928–1932 completed the proletarianization of this class by expropriating the land and livestock of the small rural proprietors.

The only other part of Europe where such drastic measures against property owners were instituted was Nazi Germany. During their twelve-year reign the Nazis expropriated the wealth of the Jewish population under their control.

Land reforms carried out in several East European countries after World War I often took the form of expropriations. The governments of Latvia, Romania, Yugoslavia, Czechoslovakia, and Poland established norms for maximum landholdings by one individual and declared properties exceeding them liable to confiscation. Where such land reform was actually carried out, the owners (especially if they were of a foreign nationality) usually received only a fraction of the true market value of their properties. The same held true of the proprietors of major industries, for example, the Romanian oil fields or the Czech Škoda works, which were nationalized in the 1920s.

Finally, rent controls often served as a concealed form of expropriation. During or immediately after war many governments passed strict regulations fixing the amount owed by tenants for their rooms or apartments. In countries subjected to extreme inflation, the real value of fixed rents sunk so low that they did not suffice to pay for basic house maintenance. Under these conditions real estate became a financial burden instead of a source of income, and many hard-pressed owners had to dispose of their property for much less than it had originally cost.

A price guide for the well-turned-out gentleman—admittedly temporary, as the dollar shines brightly and the mark sinks out of sight. Both cartoons are from Simplicissimus, 1922.

The Breakdown of the Middle-Class Family

On top of its financial disasters, the middle class suffered another misfortune: a loosening of the bonds that held the family together.

This process was in part brought about by economic developments. The family business, passed on from father to sons, and providing employment for needy relatives, could not withstand the competition of large, publicly financed corporations. It either collapsed or went public, entrusting its management to salaried executives brought in from the outside. The basic entity of modern enterprise is not the family, but rather on the one hand the impersonal corporation and on the other the salaried individual. The family as such has ceased to perform any meaningful economic function.

At the same time, the family has also gradually been deprived of its cultural and social functions. Public schooling has everywhere taken over the education of youth. Gone are the tutors and governesses who in the heyday of the bourgeoisie had filled middle-class households. Entertainment, too, has largely

°This example is drawn from Lucien de Chilly's *La classe moyenne en France après la guerre, 1918–1924* (1925).

ceased to be sought within the confines of the home. The middle class, which in the nineteenth century had spent its leisure hours at home in reading, conversation, music, or games, has acquired the habit of seeking amusement outside. Movies, sports, dances, night clubs, cocktail parties, and other modern forms of entertainment have in common that they all lure the individual out of his house and away from his family.

But perhaps the single most effective cause of the weakening of family bonds has been the progressive emancipation of women from their traditional confinement to the home. In the course of the present century, women have come to demand a full life of which the family forms only one aspect, and not necessarily the central one.

The older feminist movement attained most of its goals between the First and Second World Wars: the right to vote (apart from a few countries—Italy, France, Switzerland, and Yugoslavia), as well as legal equality. But the feminists did not stop there, content with their gains. Already in the 1870s there emerged among them a radical faction that wanted to move beyond political and legal parity with men to full social and sexual equality. This radical tendency originated and won its greatest following in northern Europe—Scandinavia and Germany—but in the course of the present century its influence spread throughout the Western and even the non-Western world.

To begin with, the radical feminists challenged the institution of marriage. They did so not merely on the grounds that in its actual workings it discriminated against women—grounds a John Stuart Mill might have chosen (Chapter 18)—but because they considered the whole institution inherently wrong. Marriage, they argued, created a false relationship between the sexes because it institutionalized love, a volatile and changing thing, and forced people to live

A women's suffrage demonstration in France during the 1920s. French women did not gain the vote until 1945.

together even after they had ceased to care for each other. Emotional honesty was more important than marriage vows and contracts.

Such sentiments were expressed in the influential plays of the Norwegian dramatist Henrik Ibsen. He penetrated behind the conventions and hypocrisy surrounding middle-class family life to reveal the dissembled frustrations, tensions, and suffering. Ibsen demanded for the wife the right to self-fulfillment, even at the risk of breaking up the family. Nora, the heroine of his *Doll's House* (1879), leads a seemingly content existence in a conventional middle-class household, until a crisis occurs which reveals the superficiality of her whole family relationship. She is wrongly accused of having forged a signature on a bond, whereupon her husband is ready to abandon her. After the mistake had been realized, he wants to forgive and forget, but Nora revolts. She now realizes how little she had known about herself, her husband, and her children. She tells him:

> Our home has been nothing but a playroom. I have been your doll-wife, just as at home I had been papa's doll-child, and here the children have been my dolls. . . . I am not fit for the task [of bringing up children]. There is another task I must undertake first. I must try and educate myself—you are not the man to help me in that. I must do that for myself. And that is why I am going to leave you now. . . . I must stand quite alone if I am to understand myself and everything about me.

To her husband's reproach that she cannot leave him because of her "sacred duties" to her family, Nora retorts that she has "other duties just as sacred . . . . duties to myself." In another Ibsen play, *Lady from the Sea* (1888), the heroine chooses in the end to remain with her husband but only after he consents to let her depart with her lover.

The quest for self-realization, of course, did not necessarily take the form of love affairs. It could involve the decision to pursue a higher education, to acquire a profession, or to take a paying job. What it meant in all cases, however, was a shift in prime responsibility from the family to oneself.

From criticism of marriage there was but one step to the advocacy of free love. One of the leading exponents of this theory was Ellen Key, a Swedish writer active at the turn of the century. She called loveless marriage a crime, and exhorted men and women alike to seek their happiness wherever they found it, in or out of wedlock.

The critique of marriage and the stress on woman's right to self-fulfillment was reinforced by revolutionary changes in the understanding of sexual life. As we have noted previously (Chapter 18), the nineteenth-century bourgeoisie held sex to be a necessary evil, which it tolerated only insofar as it was essential to procreation. Anything pertaining to sex beyond procreation (within marriage, of course) was thought debasing, repulsive, and physically harmful. Women, like children, were considered non-sexual beings. There was a widespread belief that women were organically incapable of experiencing sexual satisfaction. In general, all that pertained to sex was taboo and shunned.

The veil of mystery surrounding sex was lifted at the end of the century. Medical investigations revealed the enormous complexity of human sexual experience, the variety of its outlets, and the prevalence of drives and practices previously regarded as abnormal. A pioneering contribution was a work by the English physician Havelock Ellis, *Studies in the Psychology of Sex*, the first installment of which appeared in 1898. It described in a clinical manner all the known aspects of the sexual impulse, avoiding the customary moralizing: Ellis treated its varied manifestations as neither good nor bad, but simply as natural. Although the book scandalized the public and caused legal proceedings to be instituted against its author, it initiated a serious scientific investigation of sexual behavior.

An important by-product of Ellis' and related studies was the discovery that woman possessed as strong sexual instincts as did man. The view of woman as a pure, ideal creature who suffered with resignation man's advances was completely shattered by medical evidence. Indeed, as the researches of Freud showed, female sexual drives were so powerful that their repression could bring about nervous and physical disorders. As a result of these findings, advanced scientific and intellectual circles in early twentieth-century Europe began to acknowledge that woman, no less than man, had a right to seek sexual gratification.

In the course of World War I the social and sexual emancipation of Western woman made dramatic strides. Many women, including those from middle-class homes who had previously disdained gainful employment, took jobs to replace the men who had gone to the front. In Britain nearly 1 million found work in industry, and in Germany the National Service Act enrolled 6 million. These women earned their own pay, acquired an independent social life, and found themselves less tied to the household and the family. The war enhanced their sense of independence and self-reliance.

After the armistice the majority of women had to give up their jobs to the returning veterans, but the attitude of employers toward them underwent a lasting change. An increasing number of positions in business and industry became regularly available to women, and some—e.g., secretarial and sales positions—have turned into their preserve. The modern middle-class woman regards it as perfectly natural to take work outside her household even if she has no financial need to do so.

The First World War also affected sexual morals. The relations between men and women, whether those working side by side in industry or those meeting casually in places of entertainment, became freer, more spontaneous, less inhibited. Fighting men on furlough from the trenches were in no mood to respect the old codes of behavior. Sexual relations became very casual. An important contributing factor was the spread by the armed forces of contraceptive devices. Their main purpose was to safeguard the health of the troops, but their main effect was to remove the fear of pregnancy, a factor which more than any other had inhibited extramarital relations in the past. In the 1920s contraceptives became for the first time widely available in Europe.

During the war the loosening of moral codes was not assigned much importance because, like everything else that had happened then, it was considered a temporary deviation from the norm. But the revolution in morals only intensified with the restoration of peace. In the 1920s suddenly everything that had been regarded as right and proper in the nineteenth century was dismissed as hope-

The new French fashions for 1925, from Harper's Bazar *(as it was then spelled); the celebrated "flapper" of the 1920s was then evolving.*

lessly out of date. The older ideal of the self-effacing wife and mother yielded to a new ideal of an aggressive, self-seeking "bachelor girl" who lived fast and free without thought of the future, getting out of life all it had to offer. The term "sex appeal" was coined in the 1920s. The physical type of the ideal woman changed: she was rather boyish with her hipless and bosomless figure, her short hair, and her athletic carriage—the very antithesis of the young lady of the mid-nineteenth century. Smoking and drinking in public became fully accepted. There was little room for husbands and children in this ideal world of modern womanhood, which very few realized but to which many women aspired and took as their model.

The decline of the family after the war can be demonstrated statistically: it became smaller and less stable. Impoverishment forced many bourgeois to limit themselves to one or at most two children, because they could not afford properly to bring up and educate more. "Birth control," devised in the early twentieth century for the benefit of the poor, was in fact practiced largely by the middle classes. In Great Britain in 1927 the number of births per 1,000 inhabitants dropped to one-half of what it had been fifty years earlier. In France, the classical country of the propertied middle class, more people died each year than were born, so that the population actually declined. As the century progressed it became less common for relatives to live under the same roof, and the size of household units diminished.

Middle-class families became less stable due to the easing of divorce laws and procedures. These had once been both strict and costly. In most of Europe until the end of the nineteenth century adultery was the only legally recognized grounds for divorce. In Great Britain, prior to 1857, it required a private act of Parliament to terminate a marriage; this was so difficult to obtain that there were only fifty divorces granted in Britain in the whole first half of the nineteenth century. Toward the end of the century the variety of grounds on which a divorce could be obtained was much increased, and at the same time the legal procedures were simplified and made less costly. Divorce now came within the reach of a moderately well-to-do person. In France the new laws recognized, in addition to adultery, habitual drunkenness and violence as grounds for divorce. Sweden went further, authorizing divorce on grounds of "unconquerable aversion." Soviet Russia in its early years went furthest of all, requiring nothing more than mutual consent and official notification. (Later on, under Stalin, Soviet divorce laws were considerably tightened.)

As a result of these developments there has been a slow but steady rise in divorce rates. In France the number of divorces increased fivefold in thirty years (1874–1904). In the United States, which always had the highest divorce rates, it more than doubled over the same period. In Great Britain divorces were uncommon at first, but gained momentum later. Two out of every 1,000 British marriages ended in divorce in 1911; in 1921 the number rose to 8; in 1937 to 16; and in 1950 to 71. Among the affluent in urban, industrial, Protestant areas marriage has in fact become a conditional arrangement such as the radical feminists had preached.

A final factor requiring mention in connection with the weakening of family bonds is the shortage of domestic help. Young girls who would have previously served in private homes preferred after World War I to take employment in industry or trade, not so much because it paid better but because it gave them more independence and a higher social status. The industrial countries experienced, therefore, a severe shortage of domestics. The number of girls in domestic service in Great Britain declined from 1.4 million in 1911 to 352,000 in 1951; male servants all but disappeared. On the Continent the supply of servants remained adequate, but there inflation had so lowered incomes that many middle-class families could afford no more than one domestic, or none at all.

Neopaganism   Apart from economic and social blows, the middle class in the twentieth century suffered also a serious loss of self-confidence. The typical bourgeois had viewed everything in moral terms, and these morals in turn rested on religious foundations. The motive that inspired the nineteenth-century businessman was not only or even primarily greed, but the conviction that he was doing good: that he bettered the world by creating employment, producing wealth, raising living standards, and bringing nations into peaceful concourse. It was this assurance of the élite and the responsibility and discipline that it gave rise to that permitted the extraordinary economic achievement of the West in the nineteenth century.

The grandsons of the men who had built industrial empires and forged trading links between the most distant parts of the world, however, came to doubt the value of this activity. The socialists told them they not only did not produce wealth, but stole it from the working man, its true creator, and furthermore that they bore responsibility for wars which were simply struggles for resources and markets. Scientific discoveries upset their fathers' religious beliefs and commonsensical outlook. Taxes, inflation, and expropriations made it seem utterly pointless to accumulate capital that sooner or later was bound either to end up in the treasury or depreciate to nothing. Combined, these factors engendered in the middle class the mood of hedonism typical of periods of great uncertainty. A new morality emerged which preached the unrestrained enjoyment of the present, the surrender to everything that gratified the senses, that gave the sense of total fulfillment, of being fully alive.

The desire to live it up had made itself felt among the wealthy aristocracy and uppermost middle class already at the turn of the century. The "Edwardian Era"—the brief reign of Edward VII (1901–1910)—was a period of unprecedented elegance and luxury. The money then squandered belonged to a generation that thought of itself as the last one able to afford such a life. After the war this attitude spread to the broader layer of the bourgeoisie. The pursuit of pleasure took many forms, all strenuous and frenetic. In the 1920s a dancing mania swept the Western world, not unlike that which had followed the Napoleonic wars a century earlier. The tango and the fox trot, imported from the Americas, replaced the traditional waltz, and Dixieland acquired great popularity. Cocktail parties came into vogue; night clubs mushroomed. Outdoor sports like tennis, swimming, skiing, and mountain climbing were vigorously pursued. There was great interest in professional athletics, such as boxing. *Avant-garde* intellectual and artistic circles in Europe, in their search for new forms of excitement, took to using opium, morphine, and other drugs.

The postwar generation rediscovered the human body, which had been carefully concealed during the era of gentility. Sunbathing, previously considered unhealthy, became the rage in Europe after German physicians had discovered that it helped undernourished children overcome deficiencies in vitamin D. Swimming suits became skimpier, more revealing.

Max Beckmann's bitter comment on the social mores and nihilism prevalent in the between-wars period; the scene is a Baden-Baden bar, 1925.

Two examples of the developing anti-tradition in art: at the right, Unique Forms of Continuity in Space *(1913), by the Italian Futurist Umberto Boccioni; opposite is Meret Oppenheim's fur-covered teacup, hit of a 1936 Surrealist show in New York.*

The great depression of 1929–1932 brought this outburst of self-indulgence to a sudden halt. But the kind of life which the 1920s had created did not disappear without a trace. It was to revive on an even grander scale amid the affluence and uncertainty of the 1960s.

CULTURAL NIHILISM

From 1900 onward a great variety of ideologies spread in Europe which called for the destruction of the whole cultural heritage of the West in order to release man from the burden of the past and restore to him creative freedom. A kind of self-conscious barbarism took hold of the fringes of the Western intelligentsia, of which a typical expression was Futurism, a movement formed in Italy shortly before World War I. Its celebrated Manifesto of 1909 was not only a statement of literary principles, but an appeal for the annihilation of Western culture:

1. We shall sing the love of danger, the habit of energy and boldness.

2. The essential elements of our poetry shall be courage, daring and rebellion.

3. Literature has hitherto glorified thoughtful immobility, ecstasy and sleep; we shall extol aggressive movement, feverish insomnia, the double quick step, the somersault, the box on the ear, the fisticuff.

4. We declare that the world's splendour has been enriched by a new beauty; the beauty of speed. A racing motor-car, its frame adorned with great pipes, like snakes with explosive breath . . . a roaring motor-car, which looks as though running on shrapnel, is more beautiful than the *Victory of Samothrace.*

5. We shall sing of the man at the steering wheel, whose ideal stem transfixes the Earth, rushing over the circuit of her orbit.

6. The poet must give himself with frenzy, with splendour and with

lavishness, in order to increase the enthusiastic fervour of the primordial elements.

7. There is no more beauty except in strife. No masterpiece without aggressiveness. Poetry must be a violent onslaught upon the unknown forces, to command them to bow before man.

8. We stand upon the extreme promontory of the centuries! . . . Why should we look behind us, when we have to break in the mysterious portals of the Impossible? Time and Space died yesterday. Already we live in the absolute, since we have already created speed, eternal and ever-present.

9. We wish to glorify War—the only health giver of the world—militarism, patriotism, the destructive arm of the Anarchist, the beautiful Ideas that kill, the contempt for woman.

10. We wish to destroy the museums, the libraries, to fight against moralism, feminism and all opportunistic and utilitarian meannesses.

11. We shall sing of the great crowds in the excitement of labour, pleasure and rebellion; of the multi-coloured and polyphonic surf of revolutions in modern capital cities; of the nocturnal vibration of arsenals and workshops beneath their violent electric moons; of the greedy stations swallowing smoking snakes; of factories suspended from the clouds by their strings of smoke; of bridges leaping like gymnasts over the diabolical cutlery of sunbathed rivers; of adventurous liners scenting the horizon; of broad-chested locomotives prancing on the rails, like huge steel horses bridled with long tubes; and of the gliding flight of aeroplanes, the sound of whose propeller is like the flapping of flags and the applause of an enthusiastic crowd. . . .

Come, then, the good incendiaries, with their charred fingers! . . . Here they come! Here they come! . . . Set fire to the shelves of the libraries! Deviate the course of canals to flood the cellars of the museums! Oh! may the glorious canvases drift helplessly! Seize pickaxes and hammers! Sap the foundations of the venerable cities!°

The Futurists welcomed the Bolshevik Revolution in Russia and the Fascist one in Italy—not out of any sympathy for totalitarianism, but because these events portended the destruction of what they hated most: bourgeois values and the bourgeois way of life.

The Rise of the Salaried Estate

In the nineteenth century the Western class structure in its classical (and vastly oversimplified) form could be likened to a pyramid of three layers: on top, a small élite of wealthy landowners and capitalists, who worked little and earned much; below them, a thicker layer of the middle class, which both worked hard and earned well; and at the base, the most numerous element, the manual workers and peasants, who worked much but received little in return. In the twentieth century this pyramid has flattened at the top and narrowed at the bottom: the proportion of the idle rich and indigent poor has decreased, swelling correspondingly the interstitial middle layer.

But this middle layer is no longer the old bourgeoisie. It is a new estate whose

°Cited from Joshua C. Taylor, *Futurism* (1961).

distinguishing trait is that it derives its living from salary, the economic sinew of modern industrial society. Now whether one draws a six-figure salary, supplemented by a commensurate bonus, as company director, or a four-figure wage as factory foreman, makes, of course, a vast difference in the style of life. But the difference is less fundamental from that which had distinguished the old-style capitalist and the wage earner in the nineteenth century. The salaried estate is an open one, qualifications being the prime criterion for movement up the career ladder—for which reason some sociologists speak of the modern ruling class as a "meritocracy," an aristocracy of merit. Being open to talent, it does not provide the kind of security which the owner of capital had enjoyed. Even the highest-paid executives are dependent on the good will of the board of directors, and are liable to be fired at a moment's notice. They are constantly threatened from below by competitors for their positions; nor can they assure the future of their children. In this respect those at the top of the meritocracy are in no better position than those at its bottom. The reverse of social mobility is social insecurity.

The topmost layer of the modern business world consists of hired managers. As we have pointed out earlier, the tendency of modern business enterprise has been to become public. Family resources have seldom sufficed to finance the increasing costs of modern technology, with the result that major enterprises have found it necessary to issue stock. Once they do so, they place themselves under the scrutiny of shareholders and government bodies. They must assure the public that they are managed in the most efficient manner, and this they can do only by engaging the services of specialists, that is, salaried managers. The importance of managers in the modern world is so great that one American writer, James Burnham, even speaks of the occurrence of a "managerial revolution." The category of independent businessmen and self-employed has been steadily diminishing in the more advanced industrial countries. In Germany in 1870 they constituted 26 percent of the gainfully employed, and in 1939 only 14 percent. In Great Britain they decreased from 6.7 percent (1911) to 4.9 percent (1951); over the same period the percentage of managers and administrators has grown from 3.4 percent to 5.5 percent. The same tendency may be observed in other countries with developed industrial economies.

The descent of the capitalist proprietors into the ranks of the white-collar class was accompanied by a simultaneous rise in the social status of the higher echelons of the working class. The word "proletariat," frequently applied in the nineteenth century to manual workers, derives from the Latin *proles*, meaning "offspring"; it had been originally used for the lowest strata of the population of ancient Rome which had nothing to offer the state save their children. Already in the nineteenth century the situation of the manual worker in advanced industrial countries improved to the point where he ceased to be a proletarian in the original sense of the word. The rise in real wages brought about by a lowering of prices on basic commodities and the improvement in skills, as well as increased security due in part to unionization and in part to national welfare schemes, tended to transform the upper layers of the working class into a petty bourgeoisie. This fact was noted by the anarchists, and caused them to dismiss the European worker as a potential revolutionary.

In the twentieth century this tendency of labor *embourgeoisement* has been accelerated. Under modern industrial conditions machines are increasingly taking over functions previously performed by manual labor. Industry therefore needs proportionately fewer manual workers and more supervisory and administrative personnel. In countries with advanced economies the number of workers in the traditional sense of the word is therefore decreasing. German industry, for example, had in 1880 9.5 million workers and 0.5 million white-collar employees. In 1953 it employed 12 million workers and 4 million white-collar personnel. The ratio of manual workers to white-collar ones thus dropped from 19:1 to 3:1. A considerable part of those classified as white collar was drawn from the layer of skilled workers and craftsmen, or their children. In Great Britain between 1911 and 1951 the proportion of persons classified as manual workers decreased from 80 percent to 70 percent of all employed, while that of administrators, clerical workers, foremen, and inspectors doubled. The increase everywhere is greatest in the category of clerical help—testimony to the growing bureaucratization of modern life. Taking the advanced industrial economy as a whole, there is a visible shrinking in the number of persons engaged in production and a corresponding growth of those engaged in services of all kinds. In the contemporary United States the latter actually outnumber the former.

The group that shifts constantly from the productive to the service sector of the economy is no longer a "working class" in the traditional sense of the word; nor, for that matter, is the well-paid manual worker. Its manner of living is in no way distinguishable from that of the older petty bourgeoisie: its members own savings and property, usually a house and a car, enjoy regular vacations, and send their children to secondary schools and even to universities. With the rise in living standards and social status, the industrial worker rapidly sheds the proletarian mentality. Surveys conducted in Germany after World War II reveal that only a small minority of contemporary German workers think of themselves as workers: the vast majority, when asked what they were, identified themselves by their specific vocation; many did not even know what the word "proletarian" meant. If this holds true in a country which had the most highly developed socialist movement in the world, it is even more so in countries like the United States and Great Britain, where socialism had never struck deep roots. Today the self-awareness of the workers as a class apart still persists only in those countries (e.g., France and Italy) where social legislation had come relatively late and the worker had not yet become fully integrated into national life.

While, as we have noted, capital in the twentieth century witnessed a calamitous collapse, salaries and wages held their ground and made some gains. From 1914 onward they began to rise, keeping pace with prices even during the most extreme inflations. In the 1920s workers were relatively better off than professional people and self-employed; and apart from the disastrous period of unemployment in the early 1930s, the living standards of those depending on salaries and wages have everywhere in the Western world shown a steady improvement.

In this manner the decline of the middle class has been accompanied by the ascent of a new class, that of white-collar employees. The propertied have yielded to the salaried.

29

World War II

The origins of World War II are easier to ascertain than those of World War I: it was brought about by the man to whom the Germans had entrusted their destiny. "The Second World War was Hitler's personal war in many senses. He intended it, he prepared for it, he chose the moment for the launching of it; and for three years, in the main, he planned its course."[*]

During the first two years of his chancellorship, Hitler pursued a relatively cautious foreign policy so as not to alarm Britain and France until he had solidified his grip on Germany and made progress with the secret rearmament program. He withdrew from the League of Nations and on every possible occasion fulminated against the "Versailles *Diktat*," but he acted prudently. A nonaggression pact which he signed with Poland in 1934 was generally interpreted as a sign of peaceful intentions, although in fact it served as the first step in the isolation of France.

Hitler made his first overt aggressive moves in 1935. In March of that year he formally denounced the disarmament clauses of the Versailles Treaty and introduced compulsory military training. This measure did not produce abroad the expected violent reactions. Indeed that very year Britain signed with Germany a naval agreement which, by establishing ratios of naval power between the two countries, implicitly legitimized Hitler's breach of the Versailles Treaty. Emboldened, Hitler a year later sent German troops into the demilitarized zone of the Rhineland. Again nothing happened, although by so doing he had knocked out another prop of the French security system.

There is general agreement among historians that the years 1935–1936 offered the last chance to stop Nazi expansion short of general war. Had France displayed the same intransigence toward Nazi Germany that it had shown toward the Weimar Republic, Hitler would have had to retreat. We know now that German troops marching into the Rhineland had orders to pull back in the event of French countermeasures. The impunity with which Hitler violated the Versailles Treaty gained him immense prestige in Germany and vastly increased his self-confidence.

Behind Allied inaction lay the mood known as "appeasement." It was a crucial element in the chain of events leading to World War II, and played indirectly a major part in the conduct of international relations in the decade that followed the war. To "appease" meant yielding to the demands of the dictators in the belief that once these demands were satisfied the dictators would settle down and turn into good members of the international community. This belief rested on the assumption that the totalitarian dictators were at bottom motivated by a sense of self-interest and self-preservation. By their upbringing and experience the appeasers were unequipped to appreciate the self-destructive nihilism inherent in the totalitarian psyche.

[*]H. R. Trevor-Roper, *Hitler's War Directives, 1939–1945* (1964).

As the Nazi tide was rolled back across Europe in the last year of the war, the pattern of destruction by shellfire, bombing, and demolition mounted with grim regularity and precision. Here, American troops take what is left of a small German city in April, 1945.

The principal and universal element behind appeasement was pacifism. World War I had settled nothing, and had obliterated without trace that romantic militarism which had pervaded European youth in 1914. There was widespread expectation that another world war would be infinitely more destructive, particularly for the civilian population. Anything seemed preferable to fighting. The pacifistic mood of the time is well reflected in the amazing resolution adopted by the Oxford Union, the university's main political society, one month after Hitler's advent to power: "This House will under no circumstances fight for its King or country." Many of the appeasers wanted to meet hatred with love and rejected war even in self-defense. Antiwar sentiment also pervaded much of German public opinion. Hitler's early popularity at home derived in large part from the fact that he achieved his aims by diplomatic pressure and not by recourse to arms.

Pacifism was reinforced by additional factors, especially influential in Britain, where appeasement was most rampant. One was a feeling of guilt about Versailles. In the 1930s the passions of the immediate post-World War I years were spent, and the terms imposed on Germany appeared unduly harsh. Hitler took full advantage of these guilt feelings, and for some time disguised his aggressive moves as efforts merely to rectify the injustices of Versailles. By so doing he gained favor with many people of liberal and socialist convictions who had no sympathy whatever for nazism. Another factor was anti-communism. Hitler's successful pose as a crusader against the Communist threat neutralized the conservative, nationalistic circles in Britain and France who otherwise would have opposed German expansion. And, finally, a small but influential group wanted to appease Hitler because it admired nazism for the sense of purpose and the dynamism which it had seemingly given Germany, as well as for the effective manner in which it had dealt with unemployment.

In England the Conservative and Labour leaderships alike were addicted to appeasement. Both parties rejected a major rearmament effort long after it had become apparent that Germany was arming at full speed. The only prominent voice raised against the follies of appeasement and unilateral non-armament was that of Winston Churchill. He warned that unless Britain matched German military expenditures, it would lose air and naval superiority and become a helpless victim of Hitler's blackmail. He also courageously condemned diplomatic concessions to Hitler as whetting his appetite and encouraging him to further aggression. But Churchill had the reputation of a troublesome eccentric. He was remembered chiefly for the fiasco of the 1915 Gallipoli campaign and for his poor performance as Chancellor of the Exchequer. He was consistently kept out of office and ignored. As late as 1938 Britain's expenditures on armaments were only one-quarter those of Germany.

France had fewer illusions about the Nazis, but without British support it could not stand up to them. Hitler revealed how tenuous its international position was by his pact with Poland and remilitarization of the Rhineland. France was further weakened by internal dissent. In the 1930s the traditional rivalry between Republican and Conservative blocs was exacerbated by the emergence in each of extremist wings: a Communist bloc on the left, and a Fascist one on the right. Shortly after Hitler had marched into the Rhineland, France was paralyzed by the worst general strike in its history and seemed to teeter on the brink of civil war. This danger was averted by the formation in June, 1936, of a coalition government consisting of socialists and Communists, headed by Leon Blum. Blum's cabinet passed a number of long-overdue social reform measures, which alarmed the Conservatives. Under the slogan "Better Hitler than Blum" some right-wing circles in France began now openly to flirt with the Nazis. The Nazis fanned these sentiments by generously bribing susceptible politicians and journalists.

The fearful, accommodating foreign policy of the Western democracies had as one of its by-products the emergence of a coalition of authoritarian states led by Nazi Germany.

In October, 1935, Mussolini launched an unprovoked attack on Ethiopia, the last major independent state on the African continent. The League of Nations, in one of its more determined efforts, condemned Italy as the aggressor and voted to impose on it economic sanctions. Great Britain strongly denounced the Italian move, and even sent naval units to the Mediterranean. But Mussolini simply disregarded these threats and continued his campaign until all Ethiopia was in his hands. The attempted collective security measures proved too weak to halt Fascist aggression (the economic sanctions were never really enforced) but just irritating enough to push Italy into Germany's arms. Before long the two countries established close diplomatic links. Mussolini spoke of Rome and Berlin as forming a political "Axis." The term caught on and was subsequently applied to the whole anti-democratic, totalitarian bloc. The League of Nations suffered a grievous loss of prestige in the Ethiopian crisis and never recovered even that limited influence it had enjoyed until then.

The Ethiopian war was barely over when a civil war broke out in Spain. A group of conservative Nationalists, led by General Francisco Franco, invaded Spain from Morocco with the purpose of overthrowing a left-wing Popular Front

Picasso was moved to paint Guernica *(1937) by Nationalist terror bombing of civilians in the defenseless town during the Spanish Civil War.*

government, containing Communists, which had recently won the elections. The war was conducted with great savagery. Nazi Germany and Fascist Italy immediately aligned themselves with the Nationalists and sent them troops and equipment. The Soviet Union, on its part, came to the aid of the Republicans. The Western democracies sought to maintain and enforce neutrality. The war ended in March, 1939, when the Nationalists and their Nazi and Fascist allies captured Madrid.

Germany also managed to bring to its side Japan, which was increasingly moving in the direction of authoritarianism. In November, 1936, Germany and Japan signed the so-called Anti-Comintern Pact, ostensibly directed against the Communist International but actually designed as a vessel for a new coalition of powers in Europe and Asia. Italy signed a year later. (In 1941 the pact was renewed, and eleven other countries became signatories.)

Thus, while the democracies were ineffectually trying to preserve peace at any price, a group of expansionist countries formed a counter-alliance. Its leader, Hitler, played with consummate skill on foreign opinion, making demands that sounded limited and reasonable, but which were always coupled with threats of dire consequences if not met. The governments of England and France were confronted with a succession of artificial crises where the alternatives were either sacrificing a little (usually the property of third parties) or risking all-out war. The successes of Nazi diplomacy lay in its knowledge of precisely how far to push blackmail before its victims rebelled. Its crowning achievement was the Munich agreement of 1938.

Armored Japanese officers in Shanghai in 1932, during one of the "incidents" the Japanese used as pretexts to attack and carve up China during the 1930s.

On November 5, 1937, Hitler gathered around him the chiefs of the armed forces and outlined to them his long-range plans. One of those present, Colonel Friedrich Hossbach, took down the gist of Hitler's remarks. His record, the so-called "Hossbach Minutes," discovered after the war, represents a key document in the understanding of events leading to World War II. Hitler began by expounding his basic political ideas as he had formulated them in *Mein Kampf*: that the 85 million Germans had to acquire additional "living space" or face extinction. This space lay in Europe, not overseas: here alone were the raw materials and foodstuffs that Germany needed. Since history showed that space could be acquired only by violence, war was inevitable, the only question being when and under what conditions it should break out. Germany would attain the peak of military strength in 1943–1945, and this was the latest date for launching war, although it could begin earlier. In any event, the immediate task was to destroy Austria and Czechoslovakia so as to protect Germany's flank for the critical operations in the West.

These remarks are the earliest indication of Hitler's resolve to gamble for the control of Europe: in a sense they mark the beginning of World War II. But this significance was not apparent at the time, because Hitler cleverly camouflaged his assault on Austria and Czechoslovakia with slogans of national self-determination. All he wanted, he proclaimed, was to bring into the Reich the Germans who against their will had been separated from it: the Austrians and the German minority in the Sudeten region of Czechoslovakia. The deception worked. Two weeks after the talk recorded by Hossbach, Hitler invited to Germany British Foreign Secretary Lord Halifax, a leading appeaser. He warned Halifax that Germany had some outstanding issues to settle with its eastern and southern neighbors. Halifax let Hitler understand that Britain was not committed to the *status quo* in that part of the world, and would not object to a "peaceful" solution of the nationality problems there. Hitler correctly interpreted this statement to mean that Britain would not intervene.

In February, 1938, on the eve of the assault on Austria and Czechoslovakia, Hitler created a High Command of the Armed Forces to replace the Ministry of War, staffing it with loyal supporters. This measure severely limited the traditional autonomy of the German General Staff, and completed the *Gleichschaltung* of the country's institutions (Chapter 27). It assured Hitler of control of the army in the event of war.

The Austrian Republic was brought down in March, 1938, by the combined pressures of Germany from without and a Nazi "Fifth Column" from within. It was then fused with Germany into a Greater Reich. Hitler's claim that the political union (*Anschluss*) of Austria with Germany expressed the wishes of its population was given credibility by the hysterical welcome accorded Nazi troops, and by the zeal with which the populace of Vienna took to abusing its Jews.

Hitler was prepared to move immediately against Czechoslovakia, but here the difficulties were much more formidable. The Czechs, unlike the Austrians, wanted no dealings with the Germans and were prepared to resist them: their military equipment was first-rate, and they commanded excellent fortifications. Furthermore, Czechoslovakia had firm guarantees against external aggression from France, dating back to 1924–1925, so that an assault on it was likely to

Prime Minister Chamberlain on his return from Munich, waving the agreement that meant, he said, "peace with honour." Opposite, a Czech citizen reacts to Chamberlain's "peace" as Nazis subsequently occupy her country.

bring on a general war. Taking these factors into consideration, German generals opposed Hitler's designs: the *Wehrmacht*, in their opinion, was not yet ready to fight. But their advice was ignored, for Hitler felt confident he could have his way without recourse to arms.

In the spring of 1938 the Nazis began to stir up trouble among the 3 million Germans inhabiting the Sudeten region. Prague was prepared to go far in meeting the Sudeten Germans' demands for autonomy, but each time it made a concession the stakes were raised and more civil disturbances followed. Hitler, declaring "intolerable" alleged Czech persecution of the Sudeten Germans, threatened to intervene on their behalf. In September, 1938, war seemed imminent. The Germans carried out large-scale maneuvers along the French frontier, the French ordered a partial mobilization, and the Czechs made ready to fight.

How far Hitler was prepared to carry out his threats will never be known, because he was spared the necessity of a decision. At the critical juncture, as he was weighing the risks involved and contending with his own recalcitrant generals, Britain unexpectedly came to his aid. The Conservative Prime Minister Neville Chamberlain, although completely without experience in foreign affairs, believed himself destined to spare Europe another world war. He simply could not allow that the disagreements with Germany were insoluble. "How horrible, fantastic, incredible, it is that we should be digging trenches and trying on gasmasks here because of a quarrel in a faraway country between people of whom we know nothing," he exclaimed in a radio address at the height of the Czech crisis.

Encouraged by other appeasers, Chamberlain approached Hitler with a request for a meeting, hoping by a person-to-person discussion to solve once and for all the outstanding issues arising from Germany's claims. In negotiations held at Munich, later joined by Mussolini, he and the French Premier Edouard Daladier agreed to persuade Czechoslovakia to yield the Sudetenland to Germany. As Churchill protested in dismay, "the German dictator, instead of snatching the victuals from the table, has been content to have them served to him course by course." But Chamberlain thought otherwise, and so did the English public, which gave him an enthusiastic welcome when he returned home waving the Munich agreement and claiming that he had gained "peace in our time." For in return, Hitler had pledged not to make any further territorial claims in Europe.

Churchill was much closer to the mark when he described Munich as a "total and unmitigated defeat." Hitler was once more proved right in his tactics of blackmail and triumphed conclusively over his internal opponents. Henceforth his self-assurance knew no bounds, nor did his contempt for the democracies. French diplomatic guarantees became worthless, and the system of alliances which France had built up so assiduously in the 1920s in Eastern Europe crumbled: after Munich that area fell into the Nazi sphere of influence. Munich, as we shall see, also brought about a disastrous reorientation in Soviet foreign policy.

Barely one month after the signature of the Munich agreement, in total disregard of his pledges, Hitler ordered the German army to occupy the remainder of Czechoslovakia. The republic, shorn of its fortifications by the loss of the Sudetenland, could offer no resistance and capitulated (March, 1939).

As soon as he was installed in Prague, Hitler began to apply pressure on Poland, demanding Danzig and a corridor linking Germany with East Prussia. The Poles refused to bargain on these matters. This time the Western democracies came to the aid of Hitler's intended victim. Chamberlain, deeply offended by Hitler's breach of promise not to demand additional land in Europe, on March 30, 1939, wrote out with his own hand a guarantee to Poland, pledging Britain's entry into war in the event of a German attack on it. The French endorsed this pledge. But Hitler doubted that these pledges would be honored should he succeed in smashing Poland with one quick blow. On April 3, 1939, he issued secret orders to prepare the invasion of Poland.

Like almost everyone else, Stalin at first misunderstood Hitler and underestimated his aggressive intentions. In 1932 he had German Communists fighting the Social Democrats and thus indirectly helping the Nazis, and in 1933 he had declared publicly his intention of keeping out of European conflicts. But by 1934 he seems to have realized his mistake. Hitler's threats of an anti-Communist crusade, and later (1936) the conclusion of the Anti-Comintern Pact with Japan, posed a direct threat to the Soviet Union. Russia was diplomatically isolated, and in the event of a combined Nazi-Japanese attack could count on the support of no major power.

From 1934 on, Stalin took measures to overcome this isolation. In September of that year the Soviet Union joined the League of Nations, which it had previously denounced, and there became an ardent advocate of disarmament and collective security. In May, 1935, it signed mutual defense treaties with France and Czechoslovakia.° In the summer of 1935 the international Communist movement was instructed to enter into working alliances—Popular Fronts—with

The Nazi-Soviet Pact

°By terms of the treaty with Czechoslovakia, Russia was required to come to its aid only if France did likewise. The French betrayal of its ally at Munich thus absolved Russia, which in any event had no common frontier with Czechoslovakia.

socialist and liberal groups as a means of preventing Fascists and Nazis from coming to power. There is also reason to believe that the great Soviet purges of 1935–1938 were connected with the international situation, serving to eliminate rivals for power in the event of war and internal anarchy.

Western appeasement of Hitler aroused Stalin's suspicions. He began to think that it was part of a deliberate plot on the part of England and France to buy their own safety by deflecting Hitler's ambitions from the West to the East. The Munich agreement and the subsequent unopposed German occupation of Czechoslovakia seemed to confirm these suspicions. Stalin appears to have concluded that Eastern Europe had been conceded to Hitler as a springboard for an attack against Russia. If one keeps in mind that early in 1939 Soviet and Japanese troops were actually shooting at each other along the Mongolian border, Stalin's alarm becomes readily understandable. He now decided to extricate himself from his predicament by turning the tables on the Western democracies: instead of having them sit back and watch Russia being torn to pieces by Germany and Japan, he would make common cause with the Axis powers and enjoy the spectacle of a destructive war among the "capitalist" countries.

In March, 1939, a few days after Nazi troops had marched into Prague, Stalin made a speech in which he dropped hints that he was ready to come to an understanding with Germany. To Hitler, Stalin's overture presented another one of those unexpected gifts which he had come to view as signs of heaven's special favor. An agreement with Russia seemed to reduce even further any possibility of England and France risking a general war over Poland. The hint was therefore immediately taken up in Berlin, and soon Nazi and Soviet diplomats were engaged in secret negotiations. Overtly, Stalin made simultaneous approaches to the Western powers, but there can be little doubt that by this time he no longer had any intention of coming to terms with them and used these negotiations only as a means of exerting pressure on the Nazis.

As a price for his acquiescence in the Nazi destruction of Poland, Stalin demanded Poland's eastern regions as well as recognition of a Soviet "sphere of influence" over Finland, the Baltic states (Estonia, Latvia, and Lithuania), and Bessarabia. These were steep demands, but from Hitler's point of view there was no point in haggling over them, since ultimately he intended to conquer the Soviet Union anyway. The two powers signed a nonaggression pact, which on August 27 was announced to an unsuspecting world. The most important provisions, namely those calling for the partition of Poland and the division of Eastern Europe into spheres of influence, were not revealed, being incorporated in a secret part of the treaty.

Such was perhaps the most bitter fruit of appeasement. With the assurance of Soviet neutrality, Germany felt free to launch its projected attack on Poland, and thereby risk World War II.

Blitzkrieg The disarmament imposed on Germany by the Versailles Treaty had turned out to be a blessing in disguise for the Germany military, because once rearmament got under way they could immediately proceed to raise the most up-to-date armed force. In the 1920s, preparing for this eventuality, the German General Staff had studied carefully the lessons of World War I. Impressed by the possibilities inherent in mechanized warfare which the British had introduced but only partly exploited in the Somme offensive and at Cambrai, it decided that the future German army would be built around a nucleus of armored and motorized divisions operating with close tactical air support. The function of these mechanized units would be to break through enemy lines, spread out behind them, and form vast "pincers" isolating and trapping large enemy units. This strategy—blitzkrieg or "lightning war"—was ideally suited for a country with enormous technical resources and superb discipline but short of the raw materials essential for a protracted war of attrition.

If the Germans based their new strategy on that invented by the Allies, the Allies, in turn, adopted the defensive strategy that the Germans had put to good use during much of World War I. France, bled white and suffering a declining birth rate, could not afford another carnage. It decided therefore to post its forces behind the fortified Maginot Line, extending along the Franco-German frontier, and let the Germans do the attacking. Britain, once it began to rearm in late 1938, put its major effort into the air force. The military leadership of both countries was utterly second rate.

In the early hours of September 1, 1939, the Germans launched their attack on Poland. The first battle test of the new *Wehrmacht* exceeded all Nazi hopes. Slashing from the north, west, and south, the mechanized divisions cut through Polish defenses, and on the sixth day reached the suburbs of Warsaw. Those Polish units that had extricated themselves from German encirclements, as well as those that had not yet fully mobilized, retreated to the east, to make a stand in the wooded and marshy terrain there. But their hopes of resistance ended on September 17, when Russia sent troops into eastern Poland to claim territories accorded it by the secret agreement with Germany Polish units were disarmed,

The German conquest of Poland was followed by expropriations and deportations to labor and concentration camps. These families are driven from their Warsaw apartments at gunpoint.

and the officers sent to prisoner-of-war camps, where many were later massacred by Soviet police squads. Simultaneously, Soviet troops occupied strategic bases in the three Baltic republics.

Triumphant in the East, Hitler had an unpleasant surprise in the West. Two days after the invasion of Poland, Britain and its empire, followed by France, declared war. After the crushing defeat he had inflicted on Poland, Hitler hoped that France and Britain would change their minds and come to terms—a hope sustained by the fact that the Allies made no move to come to Poland's aid militarily, although the German frontier in the West had been only lightly defended. But the days of appeasement were over, and Hitler's peace offer made in early October was rejected.

Stalin too had a shock. The rapidity and finality with which the Germans had disposed of Poland had robbed him of a long period of grace on which he had counted and revived the possibility of collusion between Hitler and the Western democracies. To mollify Hitler he himself now began to pursue a policy of arrant appeasement. In October, 1939, Stalin informed the Nazis that in his view "a strong Germany was the absolute prerequisite of peace in Europe" and that "the Soviet Union could not give its approval to the Western powers creating conditions which would weaken Germany and place it in a difficult position." Communist parties abroad were accordingly instructed to defend the Axis cause. More concretely, Stalin signed with Germany a supplementary trade agreement, which had considerable influence on the subsequent course of the war. By its terms Soviet Russia undertook to supply Germany with scarce raw materials from its own territory and to facilitate for it the transit of strategic goods from the Middle East and East Asia. This accord enabled Nazi Germany to break the naval blockade that Britain had imposed on it in September, 1939. Henceforth, Soviet Russia regularly supplied Germany with grain, oil, phosphates, manganese, chrome, iron ore, and many other minerals, and arranged abroad for the purchase and shipment of natural rubber and materials used in the manufacture of synthetic rubber. In the first year of the treaty the Soviet Union shipped to Germany 1 million tons of cereals and sufficient quantities of oil and rubber to create there a large strategic stockpile, essential for the conduct of mechanized warfare. Soviet economic assistance to Germany in the first twenty months of World War II was of such dimensions that according to the historian who has investigated it, "it leaves open the question of whether without Soviet aid, particularly in the matter of oil supplies and rubber transit, the German attack in the West in 1940 could have been as successful as it was, and the attack on the Soviet Union [in 1941] would have been possible at all."[*]

In October, 1939, in accord with the secret clauses of the Nazi pact which had placed Finland within the Soviet sphere of influence, Stalin began to press the Finns for territorial concessions. When Finland resisted, the Russians attacked. The campaign went badly for the Russians, confirming European opinion in its low estimate of their fighting capacity. In the end, however, Soviet superiority in numbers (100 Red divisions against 3 Finnish ones) asserted itself, and the Finns had to capitulate (March, 1940).

In the West the winter and spring of the first year of war passed without

[*]Gerhard L. Weinberg, *Germany and the Soviet Union, 1939–1941* (1954).

action, in what came to be known as the "phony war" or "sitzkrieg"—"sitting war." The only important engagement occurred in Scandinavia. The British and the Germans simultaneously tried to seize Norway, but the Germans got there first with larger forces, occupying Denmark on the way (April, 1940).

Having eliminated all danger in Eastern Europe, Hitler was ready to tackle his original and principal objective, France. The strategic plan that the General Staff proposed and he accepted called for an ingenious reversal of the Schlieffen Plan (Chapter 22). This time the right wing, sent into the Low Countries, was to be a weaker, diversionary force. Once a major Allied force had rushed into Belgium to intercept it, the German left, containing the bulk of the armored and motorized divisions, was to strike westward and cut off the Allies.

The German offensive opened on May 10, 1940. Belgian fortresses were captured in a matter of hours by specially trained parachute units. The Dutch were given an ultimatum to surrender, and when they failed to capitulate in time, German bombers leveled Rotterdam, killing in the process 40,000 civilians. Refugees seeking to flee the zone of combat were deliberately machine-gunned from the air to create chaos, clog the roads, and hamper reinforcements.

As the Germans had anticipated, the Allies immediately dispatched strong infantry forces and much of their armor into Belgium. A week later Nazi mechanized armies concentrated in the west broke across the supposedly impassable Ardennes forest near Sedan and raced behind the Maginot Line for the Channel. The Allies had no reserve force to stop them. Five days later Nazi armored units reached the sea, cutting off the Allied army in Belgium. This done, the Germans wheeled south. Subsequently, the British managed to evacu-

As French resistance collapsed Paris was declared an open city to prevent its destruction. The occupying German forces emphasized the debacle by parading past the Arc de Triomphe.

Churchill inspecting the ruins of the House of Commons, wrecked by the Luftwaffe in 1940. "We shall not fail or falter," he promised; "we shall not weaken or tire. . . . Give us the tools, and we shall finish the job."

ate nearly their entire trapped Expeditionary Force, plus a considerable French contingent—338,000 men in all—through Dunkirk, but most of their equipment had to be left behind. The French army collapsed. On June 13–14 the Germans entered Paris, and shortly after France signed an armistice. The country was divided into two zones: the northern one was placed under German occupation, and the southern one was established as a satellite state ruled from Vichy by the senile Marshal Pétain. At this point (June 10) Mussolini, "rushing to the aid of the victors," declared war on France and Britain.

Britain was left alone to face the Axis powers. Had it made peace—as it could have—all of Europe would have been at Hitler's feet. But Britain, which had made concessions to Hitler when it had been in a position of strength, refused to do so when its prospects seemed hopeless—a reversal which Hitler could never quite comprehend.

In May, 1940, the prime-ministership in Britain had been entrusted to Churchill, the only man of sufficient stature to lead the country in the hour of its mortal peril. His youthful self-confidence and pugnacity, his honest warnings, his Gibbonian rhetoric, so dissonant during the years when Britain had sought "normalcy," were just what was needed by a nation left virtually unarmed to face the most powerful military force in the world. Churchill never wavered in his determination. Britain, he announced, would fight "if necessary for years, if necessary alone" until Germany gave up all its conquests. With the backing of his cabinet he rejected out of hand Hitler's second peace offer, made after the collapse of France.

Confronted with this intransigence, Hitler issued on July 16, 1940, orders for "Sea Lion," the invasion of the British Isles. The first phase of the operation was to secure mastery of the air, essential for the safe transport of the invasion force across the Channel. There could be little doubt that once the Germans secured a beachhead they would quickly conquer the British Isles, for Britain had no army left with which to oppose them.

Early in August the *Luftwaffe*, the German military air arm, launched its offensive against the Royal Air Force (RAF). For the next two months the air space over Britain was the scene of the greatest aerial battle in history. The RAF proved a tough nut to crack. Its main fighter plane, the Spitfire, had a slight edge over the German Messerschmitt, and so did the morale and training of its pilots. The RAF also had at its disposal a valuable defensive weapon: a chain of radar stations strung along the coast which, by giving timely warning of the approach of enemy squadrons, enabled it to make maximum use of its equipment. In the Battle of Britain the RAF managed to destroy on the average two German planes for each plane that it lost. At the beginning of September the *Luftwaffe*'s losses grew so high that it changed its tactics: instead of daytime attacks on air installations, it carried out nighttime attacks on cities. The intention was to break civilian morale and force Britain to make peace. For months London was subjected to nightly incendiary raids that destroyed large parts of the city. But British morale was not broken, and the RAF continued to exact a heavy toll of the raiders. In the end the bombing of cities proved a costly mistake, for it diverted the *Luftwaffe* from its primary task, that of gaining mastery of the air.

The crossing of the Channel could be effected, at the latest, in September, after which the weather became too unpredictable. Having failed to destroy the RAF by mid-September, Hitler ordered Operation Sea Lion indefinitely postponed. He had lost the Battle of Britain: Nazi Germany had suffered its first defeat.

The War Becomes Global

At the end of 1940, notwithstanding the failure of the aerial assault on Britain, Hitler was at the peak of his power. Yet he could not rest on his laurels. His power derived from a five-year priority in armament, but the gap between German and foreign military power was bound to narrow: everyone was arming now, including the United States, which in 1940 made large appropriations for defense and introduced America's first peacetime military conscription.

In other words, Hitler had to act while he still held his great advantage. He had a choice of options. His first instinct was to form a grand coalition to carve up the British Empire. In September, 1940, while the *Luftwaffe* was softening Great Britain for the kill, Germany concluded with Italy and Japan a Tripartite Pact dividing Asia and Africa into spheres of influence: Italy was to have the Mediterranean, Japan southeast Asia, while Germany reserved for itself central Africa. Hitler then turned to Soviet Russia, offering it as its share of the spoils territories in the Middle East, namely Iran, Afghanistan, and India.

By approaching Stalin only after the Tripartite Pact had been concluded, Hitler committed a major blunder. Stalin was offended at being treated like a second-class ally, and immediately became suspicious of Hitler's motives. Doubts seem to have arisen in his mind whether Hitler was not deceiving him as he, Stalin, had deceived England and France in 1939—that is, whether Hitler was pretending to seek an alliance with Russia while in reality forming behind its back an anti-Russian coalition. Stalin was particularly disturbed by aggressive

German and Italian moves in southeastern Europe, which he regarded as lying within his own sphere of influence. In October, 1940, the Italians launched an attack on Greece, and the following month the Germans pressured Hungary, Romania, and Slovakia into joining the Tripartite Pact. Thus the Axis partners obtained hegemony in the Balkans and established a potentially dangerous base on Russia's southwestern flank.

In secret negotiations conducted in October-November, 1940, the Russians expressed their willingness to join the Tripartite Pact, but insisted on the recognition of some of their rights in the Balkans. Hitler quickly lost patience with Stalin's reservations. He now began to contemplate the possibility of postponing the final assault on Britain and its empire, concentrating instead on the unavoidable destruction of the Soviet Union. When, at the end of November, Stalin formally demanded Bulgaria and the Turkish Straits as his price for joining the Tripartite Pact, Hitler did not trouble to reply. Instead, on December 18, 1940, he gave instructions to prepare for Operation Barbarossa, the invasion of Russia.

The strategy of the projected Russian campaign was to launch a lightning offensive that would bring German armies in eight to ten weeks to the banks of the Volga. German units were to conduct "daring operations led by deeply penetrating armored spearheads" that were to encircle and trap enemy forces, as they had done the preceding spring in France. The territories conquered west of the Volga were to provide Germany with abundant foodstuffs, raw materials, and slave labor, transforming German-dominated Europe into a self-sufficient, impregnable fortress. Areas east of the Volga were to be left to the Russians. Having destroyed the Red Army, Hitler intended to turn southward and take over the Middle East and North Africa.

The assault on Russia was conceived not merely as a war of conquest; it was to be a war of extermination, the first phase in clearing Eastern Europe of the "inferior races" for subsequent German settlement. The instructions given the *Wehrmacht* were unlike those ever given a European army. It was not only to destroy the enemy's armed forces but also to kill any and all "intellectuals" and "Communists" that fell into its hands. Two months before the invasion Hitler told his generals:

> We must abandon the point of view of soldierly comradeship. The Communist never was and never will be a comrade. This is a war of extermination. . . . We do not wage war to preserve the enemy. . . . Bolshevik Commissars and the Communist intelligentsia must be exterminated. The new states [of Eastern Europe] must be socialist but they must not have their own intelligentsia. A new intelligentsia must not be allowed to emerge. We must fight the poison of sedition. This is not a matter for war tribunals. The leaders of the troops must know what the issues are. They must lead the struggle. The troops must defend themselves with the same means with which they are attacked. . . . The fight will be very different from that waged in the West. In the East, toughness [now] means mildness in the future. The commanders must demand sacrifices of themselves to overcome their scruples.

The army issued appropriate directives to its forces, stating in addition that

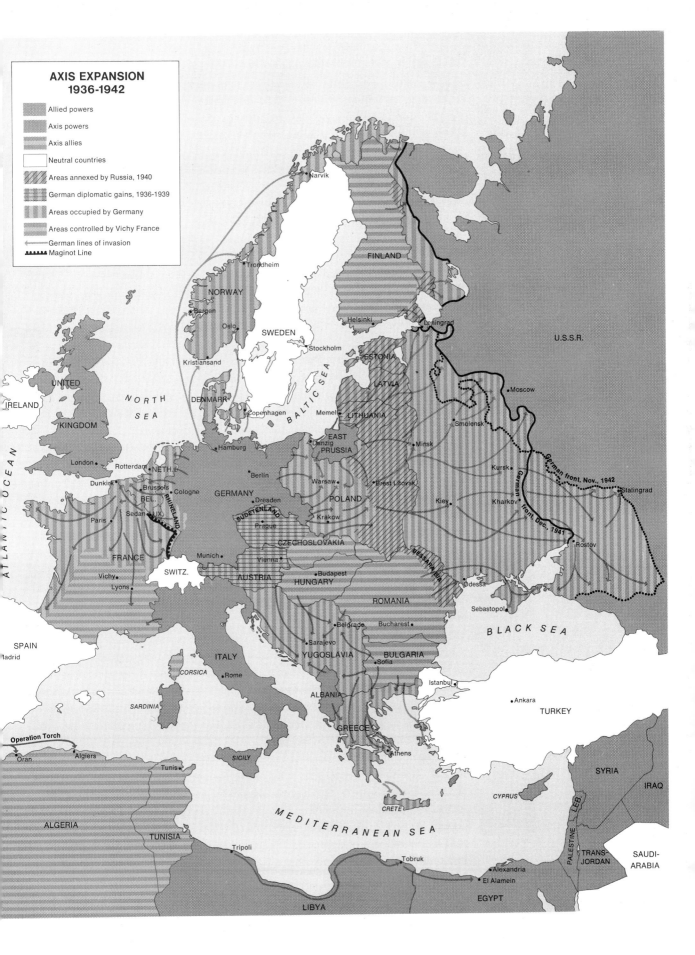

AXIS EXPANSION
1936-1942

- Allied powers
- Axis powers
- Axis allies
- Neutral countries
- Areas annexed by Russia, 1940
- German diplomatic gains, 1936-1939
- Areas occupied by Germany
- Areas controlled by Vichy France
- German lines of invasion
- Maginot Line

IRELAND

UNITED
KINGDOM

London

NORTH
SEA

ATLANTIC OCEAN

Narvik

NORWAY
Bergen
Oslo
Kristiansand

Trondheim

SWEDEN
Stockholm

FINLAND
Helsinki

Leningrad

U.S.S.R.

ESTONIA
LATVIA
Moscow

BALTIC SEA

DENMARK
Copenhagen

Hamburg

Memel
Danzig
LITHUANIA

EAST
PRUSSIA

Minsk

Smolensk

German front, Nov., 1942

Stalingrad

Rotterdam
NETH.
Dunkirk
Brussels
BEL.
Cologne
Berlin
Warsaw
Brest Litovsk

Kursk

German front Dec., 1941

Paris
Sedan
LUX.
RHINELAND
GERMANY
Dresden
POLAND
Krakow
Kiev
Kharkov

Rostov

FRANCE
Munich
SUDETENLAND
Prague
CZECHOSLOVAKIA
Vienna
AUSTRIA

Vichy
SWITZ.
Lyons

Budapest
HUNGARY

BESSARABIA

Odessa

ROMANIA
Bucharest

Sebastopol

BLACK SEA

SPAIN
Madrid

ITALY
CORSICA
Rome

SARDINIA

Belgrade
Sarajevo
YUGOSLAVIA

Sofia
BULGARIA

Istanbul

Ankara

TURKEY

ALBANIA

GREECE
Athens

SICILY

Operation Torch
Oran
Algiers
Tunis

TUNISIA

ALGERIA

Tripoli

CRETE

CYPRUS

SYRIA
LEB.
PALESTINE
IRAQ

TRANS-
JORDAN

SAUDI-
ARABIA

MEDITERRANEAN SEA

LIBYA

Tobruk

Alexandria
El Alamein

EGYPT

"as a rule, the use of arms against Soviet prisoners of war is legal." In other words, the Germans about to enter Russia were given the explicit authority—indeed, they were told that it was their patriotic duty—to kill anyone whom they considered to be or chose to define as being a "Communist" or an "intellectual," as well as all captured enemy soldiers.

Stalin had ample warning of German invasion plans from his own and British and American intelligence services, but he chose to ignore them, for he admired Hitler and thought he could trust him. Instead, he continued his policy of appeasement, delivering to Hitler strategic supplies and even turning over to him the German Communists who had sought refuge in the Soviet Union.

Hitler was so certain of his ability to quickly dispose of the Red Army that he discouraged the Japanese from joining him in the projected invasion, and egged them on instead to attack British possessions in southeast Asia. In April, 1941, the Japanese signed with the Soviet Union a neutrality pact that subsequently proved of utmost value to both parties.

The German offensive against Russia was originally scheduled for mid-May, 1941, but it had to be postponed by a month. The Italians bogged down in Greece, and in April Hitler sent troops to bail them out. In the process the Germans also invaded and occupied Yugoslavia.

On June 22, 1941, 145 Nazi divisions, 20 of them armored, plunged into Soviet territory. The Russians were not prepared for the attack, and had not even fully mobilized. Nazi armored divisions pushed forward according to plan, encircling large Soviet contingents and capturing prisoners by the hundreds of thousands. Within six weeks the road to Moscow lay open. But Hitler, intending to avoid Napoleon's mistake, decided to postpone capture of the capital in order first to destroy what was left of Soviet armies and industrial resources in the northern and southern parts of the country. Overruling the General Staff he ordered at the beginning of August a temporary halt in the advance on Moscow. One part of the center force was to turn northward, take Leningrad and link up with the Finns, and another to veer southward and join up with the armies operating in the Ukraine. The northern operation did not gain its objective, for Leningrad held out, and in the end was never captured. But in the south, near Kiev, the Germans trapped an enormous Soviet force. They also succeeded in capturing the great industrial area of the Donbas.

Hitler's decision to postpone the capture of Moscow gave the Russians two months in which to raise fresh troops in the east and organize their defenses. It also forced the Germans to open the drive on Moscow at the onset of the winter, for which they had made no provisions. The offensive resumed early in October. On December 2, in savage fighting, the Germans penetrated the suburbs of the city, but here they were stopped. By now winter had set in: German soldiers were exhausted from half a year of continuous combat and froze in their summer uniforms; their motorized equipment stalled for lack of antifreeze. On December 5–6 the Russians, who had secretly brought fresh troops from Siberia, unexpectedly counterattacked. Hitler gave strict orders not to yield any ground, but the order could not be obeyed, and in the middle of January, 1942, the *Wehrmacht* retreated, digging in a hundred miles west of Moscow. Hitler, infuriated by the reverse, sacked his top officers and assumed personal command.

On the Russian side, the Nazi invasion produced a tremendous surge of national sentiment. At first the population offered no resistance to the Germans, and in some areas even welcomed them. But as soon as the *Wehrmacht* and SS began to shoot civilians and prisoners, resistance stiffened. Russians who faced death at Nazi hands for their party or administrative connections fled to the forests and formed partisan detachments, joined by patriotic youths and soldiers who had escaped capture. Surrounded Soviet military units often refused to capitulate, fighting to the last man. Stalin, in his propaganda, abandoned all pretense of defending communism, and frankly exhorted the nation to fight for "Holy Russia." All these developments proved an unpleasant surprise to the Germans, for the miserable showing the Red Army had made in the war with Finland led them to expect a rapid collapse of Russian morale.

Immediately upon the German attack on Russia, Churchill offered the Soviets British friendship and help. The United States, too, though still neutral, made no secret of its sympathies. President Roosevelt realized the grave danger that the Axis powers presented to American security, and did all he could to assist those who resisted them. In the summer of 1941 Congress extended to the Soviet Union the benefits of the Lend-Lease program, enacted in March, by virtue of which American war supplies were sent to anti-Axis powers. In August, 1941, Roosevelt and Churchill issued the Atlantic Charter, which proclaimed the desire of their respective countries to assure all nations of self-determination. Communist parties the world over changed their propaganda and exhorted freedom-loving peoples to fight the Nazis. Thus, something like an anti-Axis alliance began to take shape.

This alliance became a reality on December 7, 1941, when the Japanese launched a surprise attack on Pearl Harbor, and thereby brought the United States into the war.

At a ceremony in Tokyo, the Japanese Foreign Minister offers a toast to the Axis Tripartite Pact, signed in September, 1940. At right are German and Italian ambassadors. The officer in uniform at center is General Hideki Tojo, the War Minister, who led Japan into the war in December, 1941.

"Battleship Row" at Pearl Harbor, as photographed from a Japanese plane during the surprise attack on December 7, 1941. Fuel oil gushes from the torpedoed ships; at lower left the stricken Oklahoma *is about to capsize.*

The Pearl Harbor attack culminated a decade of Japanese expansion. Suffering from overpopulation and a shortage of raw materials for its industries, Japan in 1931 had begun to penetrate China, placing under its control Manchuria and much of the Chinese coastline. This expansion met with opposition from liberal circles in Japan, but the voice of the liberals grew fainter as the country came under the domination of military and industrial groups sympathetic to European Fascists and Nazis.

The defeats which the Nazis had inflicted on the great imperial powers—Britain, the Netherlands, and France—opened for the Japanese expansionists unprecedented opportunities. Southeast Asia, with its rich natural resources of rubber, tin, oil, and so forth, on which they had long cast a hungry eye, suddenly was available for the taking. The Germans encouraged the Japanese to move into these regions, but the Japanese hesitated, afraid of the reaction of the Soviet Union and the United States.

Anxiety about Russia evaporated in 1941. At the end of that year Russia seemed to be breathing its last, and certainly was in no position to thwart Japanese expansion. But the United States was another matter. It had made it clear that it would not tolerate Japan's expansion indefinitely, and for some time fear of its great might paralyzed Japanese will. In the late summer of 1941, however, tentative offensive plans were drawn up. Not even the most sanguine Japanese militarists hoped to bring the United States to its knees, let alone occupy it. What was considered feasible, however, was a series of lightning strikes leading to the seizure of European and American colonial possessions in southeast Asia, and their integration into an impregnable realm modeled on

Hitler's "Fortress Europe." The plan had one hitch: it required the elimination of the United States Pacific Fleet. The more militant Japanese hoped to dispose of this difficulty by a surprise blow that would neutralize American naval forces in the Pacific. Having completed their conquests, they intended to open negotiations with the United States.

In November, 1941, under pressure from moderate elements (among them, the emperor), the Japanese opened final talks with Washington. It was agreed that if the United States gave indications that it was prepared to acknowledge Japan's hegemony in East Asia, the projected assault on the U.S. fleet would be called off. But Washington refused to make concessions and continued to insist on Japanese evacuation of China. On December 1, 1941—as German troops were penetrating the suburbs of Moscow—Tokyo decided to go to war.

The United States Navy, having broken the Japanese diplomatic code, was in a position to listen in on many of the discussions on the other side. Nevertheless, through negligence, it failed to take the necessary precautions. As Japanese bombers, brought to the proximity of Pearl Harbor by carriers, struck, no fighters rose to intercept them. (A message alerting Pearl Harbor had been sent to Honolulu by a commercial radio agency; the dispatcher carrying it to the base was caught by the air raid while pedaling there on his bicycle.) In the raid two battleships were sunk and five others damaged, but fortunately no carriers were in port. Shortly after Pearl Harbor, in a succession of superbly executed campaigns, the Japanese conquered the Philippines, Malaya, the Dutch East Indies, New Guinea, and a chain of strategic islands to the east. The democracies suffered now yet another defeat, as disastrous as that which the Nazis had inflicted on them in France.

The debacle notwithstanding, Churchill at once recognized Pearl Harbor as the death sentence of the Axis. A few days after the Japanese attack, Germany, with incredible recklessness, declared war on the United States. This meant that the Axis powers now confronted the combined forces of the United States, Great Britain, and the Soviet Union—a combination which nothing could vanquish.°

In the winter of 1941–1942 Hitler, considering the war as good as won, set into motion the first measures toward the "New Order"—a Europe refashioned according to the racial hallucinations which he had first experienced in his Vienna days.

The Nazi "New Order"

His authority in Germany was total. In 1942 the docile Reichstag voted him the right to deal with any German as he saw fit (see Chapter 27); and there certainly was no limit to his authority over the inhabitants of the conquered territories. Only in the statellite countries—Hungary, Romania, Bulgaria, southern France—were there still some centers of independent power, as there were in Italy and Spain, but they were generally friendly to the Nazis.

As the war progressed, power increasingly fell into the hands of the SS and the Gestapo, both headed by Himmler. Disgusted with the *Wehrmacht*, Hitler even built up during the war an independent SS armed force. The SS and the Gestapo initiated throughout Europe a rule of terror. Persons suspected of any political

°The Soviet Union, on its part, did not declare war on Japan; nor Japan on Russia. Russia entered the war in the Pacific only in August, 1945, when it was for all practical purposes finished (see below).

misdemeanor, actual or potential, were sent to concentration camps, where they were placed at the mercy of their guards. In the Eastern territories, notably Poland and Russia, the Gestapo arrested from previously prepared lists numerous intellectuals, such as professors and well-known writers, and had them shot. The SS was specifically assigned the task of massacring European Jewry. Its device—"Faith is our honor"—absolved it from all moral responsibility save obedience to the Führer.

To convey the mentality that lay behind the unspeakable atrocities committed by the SS, we can do no better than cite the words that Himmler addressed to a gathering of its officers in 1943:

An SS man must adhere absolutely to one principle: he must be honorable, decent, faithful, and comradely to members of his own race, and to no one else. What happens to the Russians, what happens to the Czechs is to me a matter of total indifference. . . . Whether other nations live well or die of starvation interests me only in so far as we need slaves for our culture—other than that, it holds for me no interest. Whether during the construction of a tank trap 10,000 Russian women die of exhaustion or not, interests me only in so far as the tank trap for Germany has been constructed. We shall never be tough and pitiless where it is not necessary, that is clear. We Germans are the only nation in the world with a decent attitude toward animals; we shall also be decent toward these human animals. But it is a crime against our own blood to worry about them or to bring ideals to them so that our sons or grandchildren have more trouble with them. When someone comes to me and says: "I cannot build tank traps with women and children, that is inhuman, they will die," I shall say to him: "You are the murderer of your own blood, because if the tank trap is not built, German soldiers shall die, and they are the sons of German mothers. That is our blood." That is what I would like to inculcate in the SS . . . our care, our duty, is our people and our blood. . . . Everything else is of no importance . . .

I turn now to the evacuation of Jews, to the extermination of the Jewish people. This is one of those things that are easily said: "The Jewish people will be exterminated," a party member says, "of course, it says so in our program, we shall eliminate, exterminate the Jews." And then they all come, the brave 80 million Germans, and each one of them has his decent Jew. Yes, of course, the other Jews are swine, but this one is a first rate Jew. Of all those who speak so, none has witnessed it, none has experienced it. Most of you know what it means when 100 corpses lie next to each other, or 500, or even 1000. To experience this, and—apart from human weaknesses—to remain decent, that has made us hard. This is a glorious page in our history. . . .

The "glorious page" in German history began in late 1941 when Jews in German-held territories were herded into walled ghettoes and required to wear the Star of David. After the attack on Russia the Nazi leaders decided to commence the physical annihilation of the 11 million European Jews. At a conference held in January, 1942, at Wannsee, a suburb of Berlin, it was resolved to begin the

Rentabilitätsberechnung der SS über Ausnützung der Häftlinge in den Konzentrationslagern	Table of profits (or yield) per prisoner in concentration camps (established by SS)
Rentabilitätsberechnung	**Rental accounting**
Täglicher Verleihlohn durchschnittlich RM 6,–	Average income from rental of prisoner, per day — RM [Reichsmark] 6.00
abzüglich Ernährung RM –,60	Deduction for nourishment, per day RM 0.60
durchschnittl. Lebensdauer 9 Mt. = 270 x RM 5,30 = RM 1431,–	**Average life expectancy:** 9 months: 270 [days] by RM 5.30 = RM 1431.00
abzüglich Bekl. Amort. RM –,10	Minus amortization on clothing RM 0.10
Erlös aus rationeller Verwertung der Leiche:	Profits from rational utilization of corpse:
1. Zahngold 3. Wertsachen	1. Gold teeth 3. Articles of value
2. Kleidung 4. Geld	2. Clothing 4. Money
abzüglich Verbrennungskosten RM 2,–	Minus costs of cremation RM 2.00
durchschnittlicher Nettogewinn RM 200,–	Average net profit RM 200.00
Gesamtgewinn nach 9 Monaten RM 1631,–	Total profit after 9 months RM 1631.00
zuzüglich Erlös aus Knochen und Aschenverwertung.	This estimate does not include profits from [sale of] bones and ashes.

deportation of Jews to special camps where they were to be most expeditiously and economically put to death.

The mass murder of Jewry was carried out with the precision which had always been the special pride of Germans. It was murder refined in an industrial, technological age, with bureaucratic procedures, careful accounting, a complex transport system, and maximum use of the human by-products. In 1940–1941 a number of new concentration camps were constructed, among them several designated as "extermination camps," which were in fact giant slaughterhouses. The largest of those was at Auschwitz, in the industrial region of Silesia; there were four others, all on the territory of what had been Poland.

Shortly after the Wannsee conference, special detachments of the SS began to round up Jews for what was euphemistically called "evacuation." The victims were merely told they were being shipped to points east, where they would be relocated and suitably employed. The shipment was done in cattle cars, into which the Jews were herded without food or water. Many died in transit. Upon reaching their destination the "transport" was at once divided in two parts. One group, consisting of able-bodied men and women, was sent to production centers to perform heavy labor on substandard food rations. The intention was literally to work them to death. When they collapsed from exhaustion, malnutrition, or disease, they were returned to the extermination camp for slaughter. The other group, that judged unsuited for work—it included all children and elderly—was sent directly to the gas chambers. To lull suspicion these chambers were disguised as shower rooms. The victims were told to undress and wash. As soon as they had filled the purported shower room and the guards had bolted the doors, poison gas was injected. For 15 or 20 minutes the condemned would choke amid inhuman struggles and shrieks. Once silence descended, the doors were unlocked and detachments of prisoners removed the corpses to search them for hidden valuables and to remove gold tooth fillings. Finally, the remains were cremated.

The operation was carried out with such efficiency that at Auschwitz alone 10,000 persons could be disposed of without trace each day. At this camp 2.5

The SS bureaucracy worked out this table (translated, right) as a model for profitable, organized murder of slave labor.

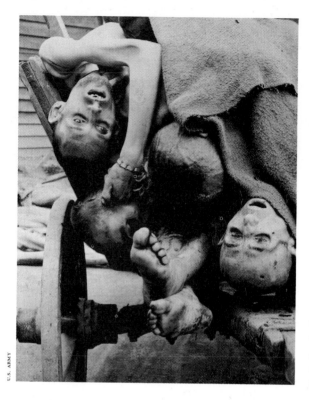

Victims of starvation at Gusen, a Nazi concentration camp in Austria, photographed after the camp was liberated by Allied troops in the last month of the war.

million persons, nearly all Jews, perished from gas poisoning, and an additional half million died from malnutrition and torture. To break the monotony of the daily slaughter, the Nazis invented ever-fresh methods of inflicting pain and humiliation. Only a diseased mind could even conceive of the variety of sufferings that the perverts of the SS devised for its innocent and helpless victims.

On Russian territory the Nazis did not bother to establish extermination camps. There, detachments of the SS, operating with the assistance of Ukrainian or other auxiliaries, rounded up the Jewish inhabitants in towns and villages, herded them into a nearby ravine or forest, and mowed them down with machine guns. Outside large cities giant pits were dug; the victims, lined up at the edge and shot, fell directly into their mass graves. In Kiev alone over 30,000 Jews were massacred in such a manner in a single day. The German army occasionally protested against these slaughters as dishonoring its name, but by and large it either turned its back on them, or, if required, lent a willing hand.

Between 1941 and 1945 the Germans killed an estimated 6 million Jews, a quarter of them children. This crime has no precedent in human history. Every period has had its massacres, and every nation has been guilty at some time of spilling innocent blood. But never before had a whole ethnic or racial group been condemned to die, for no reason and without possibility of reprieve, and the sentence carried out in so meticulous and cold-blooded a manner. Little was done to rescue those destined to die, and in the United States and Great Britain there was even a tendency to discount news of the massacres which was leaking out of occupied Europe. There were only a few honorable exceptions to the prevailing indifference. The Danes, having gotten wind of the deportation orders, ferried most Danish Jews to neutral Sweden. In Hungary, Horthy stanchly refused to condone deportation proceedings, and by his dilatory tactics saved the lives of some 200,000 Jews; another 200,000 perished in 1944, after the Germans had occupied Hungary. The Bulgarians resisted to the end German pressures to hand over their Jews to the SS, and so, in large measure, did the Italians.

It has been estimated that some 50,000 persons directly participated in the Jewish slaughters. After the war only a fraction of these was ever brought to trial, and only some 500 executed. Most of the remainder quietly slipped back into civilian life in Germany and Austria.

In addition to the Jews, other groups were subjected to mass murder. Three million Russian prisoners of war never returned home. A program of mercy-killing of demented and incurably sick persons, including Germans, claimed over 70,000 victims before it was restrained in 1941. Countless partisans were shot in Poland, Yugoslavia, and other parts of German-occupied Europe.

The Germans intended by this insane terror to assure their hold on the Continent and lay the foundations of a new Germanic civilization.

Upon its entry into the war the United States confronted two major decisions: whether to assign priority to the defeat of Japan or of Germany, and how to define its war aims.

The Grand Alliance

The first of these two issues was taken up during joint American and British staff talks held in early 1942. Here it was decided to recommend that priority be given to the European theater. Germany was by far the most powerful of the Axis partners, and if allowed to consolidate its hold on the Continent could transform it into a fortress that no subsequent effort would be able to reduce. Japan, on the other hand, was considered unable to withstand for long an Allied assault, once Germany was defeated. This decision was undoubtedly a correct one, as subsequent events demonstrated.

The second question was resolved in a manner that has since aroused much controversy. At a conference held in Casablanca in January, 1943, Roosevelt and Churchill agreed to pursue the war until the unconditional surrender of Germany and Japan. A few months later Stalin endorsed this declaration. The demand for unconditional surrender has been criticized on the grounds that it disheartened anti-Hitler opposition in Germany and needlessly prolonged the war. However, it is difficult to see how the Allies could have done otherwise. The alliance that the Western democracies had struck with the Soviet Union, Hitler's recent ally, was highly artificial, and there was a real danger that it would fall apart. Had the door been left open to a negotiated peace, Hitler would have gained the opportunity (on which he counted) of sowing suspicion among his enemies and dividing them. The unconditional surrender formula, which committed the three Axis powers to fight to the end, eliminated that opportunity and undoubtedly cemented the fragile anti-Axis partnership.

The immediate task of the Western powers was to bring relief to the hard-pressed Russians. Stalin wanted them to open at once a "second front" to divert German forces, but this was clearly impossible for some time to come. Britain and the United States were only beginning to build up their armies, and lacked the forces with which to assault the heavily fortified Atlantic shores of Nazi

IMPERIAL WAR MUSEUM

An Allied convoy on the "Murmansk Run," delivering arms to Russia, under attack by German bombers in September of 1942.

Europe. Stalin, who had little understanding of amphibious operations, found these explanations lame, and never ceased to suspect that his allies were deliberately delaying the second front to bleed Russia. It was only natural for him to think so, for this is very likely what he would have done—indeed, what he did do in 1939–1941—when in a similar position. His morbid distrust was merely a counterpart of his infinite duplicity.

For more than two years after the Nazi attack on the Soviet Union, the Western Allies could only help the Russians indirectly, by delivering war supplies and by attacking and destroying from the air the German war potential.

The greatest contribution the United States could make to the Allied cause was to put to military use its vast industrial plant. This was done immediately upon America's entry into the war. President Roosevelt pledged to make his country "the arsenal of democracy," and American production of armaments indeed grew at a staggering rate. One year after Pearl Harbor it equaled that of Germany, Italy, and Japan put together, and by 1944 it was double that. An important share of this output went to the Soviet Union in the form of Lend-Lease. During World War II Russia received from the United States over 400,000 trucks, 12,000 tanks, 14,000 planes, and an immense quantity of other goods, totaling 17.5 million tons. The motorized equipment was of particular value to the Red Army, putting it for the first time on wheels, and enabling it to mount large-scale offensive operations. In the later stages of the war, thanks in part to

Lend-Lease, the Russians enjoyed a pronounced superiority in matériel over the Germans.

While vastly increasing their own war productivity the Western Allies made a determined effort to reduce by means of aerial bombardment that of Germany. Strategic bombers carried out intensive raids on German industrial and urban centers, gutting large areas of the country. In May, 1942, the British carried out the first 1,000-bomber "saturation raid," against Cologne. In the spring of 1943 the Ruhr was heavily struck. In July, 1943, a series of incendiary raids leveled Hamburg. By and large the strategic bombing effort suffered from lack of consistent purpose, indiscriminate bombing of cities alternating with precision attacks on selected industries. By dispersing their plants the Germans managed to maintain high levels of productivity, at any rate until the summer of 1944.

Naval operations, carried out jointly by American and British forces, were a vital episode in the Second World War, as they had been in the First. Fortunately for the Allies, the Nazis began large-scale constructions of submarines late in the war (Hitler had little confidence in naval warfare) and they never had enough of them. Nazi submarines achieved their greatest successes in 1942, when they sank over 8 million tons of shipping. To fight them the Allies began to employ with excellent results small aircraft carriers and radar-equipped long-range bombers capable of spotting submarines at night and in cloudy weather. Early in 1943 Allied aircraft were destroying submarines at such a rate that in May the Germans had to withdraw them from the Atlantic. The "snorkel" device, which permitted the submarines to remain submerged for long periods and thus to escape detection from the air, came too late to affect the outcome. By the spring of 1943 the Allies had conclusively won the Battle of the Atlantic.

The second half of 1942 proved to be the decisive period of the war as far as land operations were concerned. Until then the initiative had lain in the hands of the Axis powers; now it passed into those of the Allies. Between June, 1942, and January, 1943, the United States, Great Britain, and Russia each in turn dealt the enemy a crushing defeat. The three decisive battles, in chronological order, were Midway, El Alamein, and Stalingrad.

The Axis Powers Rolled Back

In the spring of 1942 the Japanese controlled an enormous empire with a diameter of some 5,000 miles, a population of 450 million, and a self-supporting economy. Out of this territory they sought to create a community of interest, an empire to which they gave the catchy name of "Greater Asian Co-prosperity Sphere." Under the slogan "Asia for the Asians," they made a strong appeal to anti-European national and racial sentiments. They liquidated the old imperial administrations and replaced them with puppet governments staffed by native nationalists. The elements that collaborated with them provided the cadres from which, after the war, came the leadership of the anti-Western nationalist movements in this part of the world.

Having achieved their immediate objectives, the Japanese were anxious to assure the maximum security for their empire. Their predicament was not unlike that which had confronted Hitler after the fall of France: they too had to keep on moving and expanding while the odds were in their favor. They now decided to seize control of the eastern Pacific so as to deprive the United States of naval

Combat half a world apart: at right, British infantry seize a crewman of a disabled German tank at the Battle of El Alamein in North Africa. Opposite, a Japanese kamikaze (suicide) plane attempts to crash a U.S. carrier near the Philippines in January of 1945. It missed.

bases, and to sever its sea route to Australia. To this purpose they assembled in late May, 1942, a great fleet, including four of their six large, modern aircraft carriers. The mission of this task force was to lure what was left of the U.S. Pacific Fleet into combat, destroy it, and occupy the Aleutians and Midway.

The American commander, Admiral Chester Nimitz, had at his disposal a much smaller force, but he did have a unique weapon: knowledge of Japanese naval codes which enabled him to know enemy dispositions and intentions. In the first week of June the two fleets clashed in the vicinity of Midway in what turned out to be one of the decisive naval battles of history. It was a new kind of naval warfare, for the ships never fired at each other; fighting was done entirely by carrier-based bombers and torpedo planes. American pilots won a striking victory, sinking all four of the Japanese carriers. The United States lost one carrier, but it had four remaining and thirteen under construction, whereas Japan lagged hopelessly in the naval construction race. At Midway Japan lost air superiority over the Pacific, and in effect naval superiority as well. In August, 1942, an American force attacked and seized Guadalcanal. From there, under the brilliant leadership of General Douglas MacArthur and Admiral Nimitz, the Allies started the process of "island hopping" toward Japan. The Japanese henceforth went over to the defensive.

The British scored their victory in North Africa. Fighting in Africa had begun in the fall of 1940 with an Italian attempt to seize British possessions, Egypt,

and the Suez Canal. British imperial forces soon repelled it, and in turn invaded Italian colonies. The Germans once more had to come to the aid of their embattled allies, dispatching there an élite "Afrika Korps" under Erwin Rommel, one of their ablest generals. In the spring of 1942 Rommel launched an all-out offensive on Egypt. The Italo-German force reached El Alamein, within 60 miles of Alexandria, where it was thrown back (October, 1942) by a British army under General Bernard Montgomery. The invaders were driven headlong into Libya. At this point another Allied force, containing large American contingents, landed in their rear in Algeria and Morocco. After six months of fighting, the Axis North African army capitulated: the Allies took a quarter of a million German and Italian prisoners (May, 1943). The southern flank of Hitler's Europe now lay exposed.

The most portentous of the three battles waged in late 1942 took place at Stalingrad. The importance of Stalingrad was not so much strategic as psychological. As at Verdun in 1916, the two sides decided here to make their supreme contest of will. After they were beaten, many Germans for the first time realized that the war was lost.

In the spring of 1942, when operations on the Russian front resumed, the Germans were in a favorable position. They controlled the principal industrial and agrarian regions of the Soviet Union. They had suffered less than a million casualties, while inflicting 4.5 million casualties on the Red Army. They also were entrenched in the close proximity of Russia's two major cities, Moscow and Leningrad.

In making strategic plans for 1942 Hitler decided once more to postpone the capture of Moscow, and to concentrate instead on seizing the Caucasus, where lay Russia's richest oil deposits. The spring campaign began well, and advance German units planted the Nazi flag on the Elbrus, the highest mountain of the Caucasian range. But they failed to reach the oil-producing areas, and worst of all, they could not reduce Stalingrad, whose capture Hitler had demanded. The more troops they sent against it, the more troops the Russians committed to its defense.° The fighting grew steadily in intensity and in the fall developed into a major battle. In house-to-house fighting, troops of the German Sixth Army conquered nine-tenths of the gutted town, but the Russians held on to what was left. Both sides fought with incredible heroism.

Suddenly, on November 19–20, the Russians launched a powerful counterattack, breaking through the Hungarian, Romanian, and Italian units guarding the flanks of the Sixth Army. The German generals pleaded with Hitler for permission to stage a breakout from the trap while there was still time, but Hitler insisted that the troops hold on to every inch of gained ground. Outnumbered, freezing, so short of food that some of them resorted to cannibalism, the Germans held out for two months. Then, at the end of January, 1943, the Sixth Army surrendered. The Russians captured 91,000 prisoners, 1,500 tanks, and 60,000 vehicles. In Germany the news of the surrender was met with three days of national mourning. To straighten out the front after the loss of the Sixth Army, the *Wehrmacht* had to retreat, giving up most of the ground conquered the preceding spring.

Hitler's reaction to the Stalingrad disaster was to proclaim "total war." The German economy, until then relatively unregulated, was fully centralized under the Minister of Armaments and Munitions, Albert Speer. With his efficient and ruthless management, Speer increased armament productivity by one-half in five months. Forced labor was impressed from conquered territories, and concentration camp inmates were mobilized. At the height of the war Speer had at his disposal between 7 and 9 million slave laborers. "Defeatism," which spread in Germany, was pitilessly prosecuted. Germans accused of it were hauled before "People's Courts" and usually shot, following a perfunctory trial.

After Midway, El Alamein, and Stalingrad, the issue could no longer be in doubt. The days of blitzkrieg were over, and the Axis powers had to brace themselves for a war of attrition that they could not possibly win. As Churchill put it cautiously in a speech delivered in November, 1942, the world was witnessing "not the end, not even the beginning of the end, but possibly the end of the beginning."

Victory   Hitler, however, meant to hold out to the last. He counted partly on Allied disagreements and partly on a new secret weapon, a ballistic rocket known as the V-2, which his engineers were developing under highest priority; the first of these were sent against London in September, 1944, causing severe damage and

°For Stalin, Stalingrad had a personal significance. The city was named for him because in 1919 he had played an active part in directing its successful defense against the Whites.

greatly demoralizing the war-weary population. But if he had to lose, Hitler was determined all Europe would go down with him.

On the eastern front the Germans undertook in July, 1943, one more major offensive to boost their sagging spirits. They sent 17 armored divisions against the Russian defenses in the Kursk area, with the intention of executing a pincer movement. But by now the Russians were familiar with blitzkrieg tactics. In the greatest tank battle in history they repulsed the attack, after which they pushed the *Wehrmacht* back two hundred miles. The best the Germans could henceforth hope for was simply to hold in the East. The Russians had twice the manpower, and two to three times the weapons and equipment, including tanks and planes. Wherever the Germans were forced to retreat, they looted that which was movable and dynamited or set on fire what was left, including ancient churches and historic monuments.

The Western Allies in 1943 adhered to the strategy advocated by the British and concentrated on the Mediterranean, the "soft under belly" of Nazi Europe. In July they sent an invasion force from North Africa to Sicily. Italian armies offered only token resistance. A few days after the invasion a bloodless coup in Rome overthrew the Fascist regime, and the new government immediately opened negotiations with the Allies. The Germans reacted by sending troops into Italy to prevent it from falling into Allied hands. After the arrival of the Germans, the Allies had great difficulty making further progress, partly because the terrain favored the defenders, partly because their leadership was poor and indecisive. It took them a whole year to reach Rome.

The main preparations of the Western Allies in 1943–1944 went into "Over-

The Anglo-American invasion of Normandy in June, 1944: American troops wade ashore from a landing craft at Omaha Beach, the most heavily contested of the D-Day landing sites.

lord," the projected cross-Channel invasion of France. The difficulties and risks attendant on such an operation were enormous. In anticipation of the landings the Germans had withdrawn from Russia some of their best units, assembling along the Atlantic shores 60 divisions, 11 of them armored. The Allies could throw against them in the first critical day of the invasion only 7 divisions: to bring such an army across the Channel required no fewer than 5,000 ships and 12,000 planes. Unless a solid beachhead was secured in the first few hours to permit the landing of reinforcements, the Germans could concentrate an overwhelming force at the landing point and throw the invaders back into the sea. Everything therefore depended on the strength and speed of the initial blow.

The Allied strategic plan was worked out by General Montgomery, who had been placed in charge of the invasion forces under General Dwight D. Eisenhower, the Supreme Commander of the Allied forces. His proposal was for a British force to establish a beachhead near Caen in Normandy, with the purpose of attracting to itself the main German counterattack. While the British held the ground, the Americans, who were to land nearby, were to make an end run, swinging around the Germans and heading straight for Paris.

German preparations for the invasion were hampered by disagreements and miscalculations. Whereas the generals wanted to place the main defense forces in northern France, Hitler insisted on protecting the whole length of the Atlantic coast. As a result, German units were thinly dispersed. Furthermore, the *Wehrmacht* was so certain the Allies would land their main army at Calais that it concentrated there its own main force, leaving Normandy relatively unprotected.

"D-Day" came on June 6, 1944. Despite some errors in navigation, which placed American units off course, beachheads were established and held. In the course of the first day 156,000 men were landed, some from the sea, others from the air. With remarkable speed Allied engineers constructed off the beachhead two artificial ports, known by their code name "mulberries," through which poured an endless stream of men and supplies. One week after D-Day the Allies had more troops in France than did the Germans. They also enjoyed complete mastery of the air. In late July the American forces broke through German defenses and made a dash for Paris, which they took a month later.

At this point some generals wanted to make a direct drive on a narrow front for the heart of Germany, but General Eisenhower decided on a slower, more cautious strategy involving a steady sweep through France along a broad front. There is reason to believe that this strategy gave the Germans time to fortify their frontier and needlessly prolonged the war.

After D-Day the Allied air forces could concentrate all their resources on the destruction of Germany. In a few months the bombers reduced substantially the still formidable German industrial plant: from the summer of 1944 on, German industry could no longer meet the requirements of the military. Particularly damaging were the raids on oil installations: they reduced oil production to the point where many German planes, tanks, and trucks could not operate for lack of fuel. Saturation raids against cities also continued at full force. An incendiary attack on Dresden in February, 1945, killed an estimated 135,000 persons.

In July, 1944, a group of anti-Hitler conspirators attempted to assassinate the Führer and enter into negotiations with the Allies. Involved in the plot were

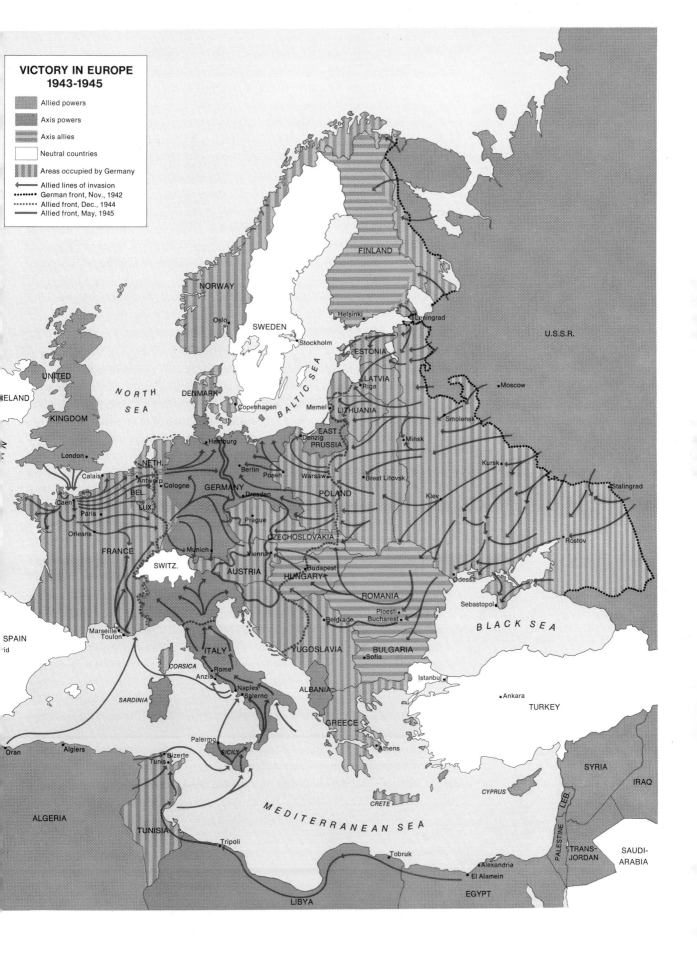

VICTORY IN EUROPE
1943-1945

Allied powers
Axis powers
Axis allies
Neutral countries
Areas occupied by Germany
← Allied lines of invasion
•••• German front, Nov., 1942
∙∙∙∙ Allied front, Dec., 1944
— Allied front, May, 1945

NORTH SEA

NORWAY
Oslo

SWEDEN
Stockholm

FINLAND
Helsinki
Leningrad

U.S.S.R.
Moscow

UNITED KINGDOM
London

ELAND

DENMARK
Copenhagen

BALTIC SEA

ESTONIA

LATVIA
Riga

Smolensk

LITHUANIA
Memel

EAST PRUSSIA
Danzig
Minsk

Kursk

Stalingrad

NETH.
Calais
Antwerp
Cologne
BEL.
LUX.
Caen
Paris
Orleans

Hamburg

GERMANY
Berlin
Dresden

Posen
Warsaw

POLAND

Brest Litovsk

Kiev

Rostov

FRANCE

Prague

CZECHOSLOVAKIA

SWITZ.

Munich

Vienna

AUSTRIA

Budapest

HUNGARY

Odessa

Sebastopol

BLACK SEA

SPAIN
rid

Marseille
Toulon

ITALY

CORSICA
Rome
Anzio

SARDINIA

Naples
Salerno

YUGOSLAVIA

Belgrade

ROMANIA
Ploesti
Bucharest

BULGARIA
Sofia

Istanbul

Ankara

TURKEY

ALBANIA

GREECE
Athens

SYRIA
IRAQ

Palermo

SICILY

CYPRUS
CRETE

LEB.

PALESTINE

Oran
Algiers
Bizerte
Tunis

MEDITERRANEAN SEA

TRANS-JORDAN

SAUDI-ARABIA

ALGERIA

TUNISIA
Tripoli

Tobruk

Alexandria
El Alamein

LIBYA

EGYPT

conservative statesmen and high army officers, who had become convinced Hitler would bring about the total destruction of Germany. A briefcase containing a powerful bomb was placed in Hitler's headquarters. It exploded, but failed to kill Hitler. The Gestapo quickly rounded up and executed the conspirators. For Hitler's private enjoyment, moving pictures of the ringleaders were taken while they were being strangled to death, suspended from meat hooks.

In April, 1945, with the Russians, Americans, and British converging on Berlin, Hitler decided to commit suicide. Germany, he declared, having lost a unique chance at world mastery under his leadership, did not deserve any better lot than that which it now had in store: enslavement by the subhuman Russians and decadent Anglo-Saxons. In the same month, Mussolini, seeking to escape to Switzerland, was caught by a band of Italian partisans and shot. On May 7 a delegation of German generals appeared at General Eisenhower's headquarters and signed a surrender act.

The war in Europe over, the United States and Britain could now turn their undivided attention to the Pacific front. At the time of Germany's capitulation, American troops, having seized Iwo Jima and Okinawa, were at Japan's doorstep. The Allied command wildly overestimated the Japanese willingness and capacity to fight. It was thought, on the basis of the experience gained in reducing Japanese-held island fortresses, that an invasion and occupation of Japan would cost a million casualties. In fact, however, the Japanese in the spring of 1945 were desperately seeking a way out of the war, and were putting out in vain a succession of peace feelers. One of these, sent through the Soviet Union (then still at peace with Japan), Stalin never saw fit to forward to Washington.

This gross miscalculation explains the Allied political and military strategy in defeating Japan. Great pressure was exerted on Stalin to secure Russia's entry into the Pacific war, although no pressure was necessary, Stalin being most eager

Dresden was crowded with refugees fleeing the advancing Russians when some 900 British and American planes fire-bombed it in February, 1945. The dead are shown being collected for cremation pyres in the streets.

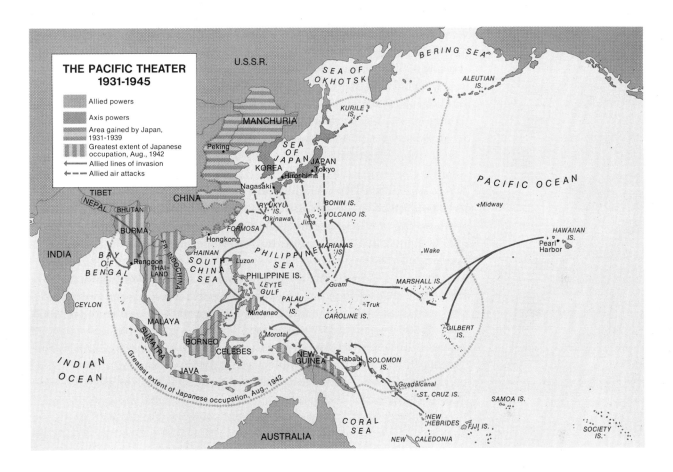

to do so anyway in order to profit from the collapse of the Japanese Empire. Furthermore, it was decided, after considerable deliberation, to subject Japan to bombardment by a new weapon, the atomic bomb. Work on this bomb had been carried out in utmost secrecy since 1942, when a group of physicists had set off in a laboratory a nuclear chain reaction. At first the possibility of dropping the bomb in an unpopulated place was considered, but uncertainty whether or not the bomb would go off induced President Truman to order its use against Japanese cities. In August, 1945, the two atomic bombs in the American arsenal were dropped, one on Hiroshima, the other on Nagasaki, causing 75,000 and 39,000 casualties respectively. Between these two atomic raids the Soviet Union declared war on Japan, occupying virtually without resistance Manchuria and Korea. Shortly afterward, Japan capitulated. A survey conducted after the war showed that Japan would have surrendered before the end of the year without an invasion, without the atomic bombs, and without Russia's entry.

The grim balance of World War II was 55 million dead, half of them civilians. Europe lay in rubble, many of its great cities leveled to the ground, its wealth and influence gone.

The War in Russia

It was autumn, 1941, and the German panzer columns (right) were sweeping eastward along a 1,500-mile front, unchecked even by the first snows. Russian author Boris Pasternak was moved to write:

> Do you remember that dryness in your throat
> When rattling their naked power of evil
> They were barging ahead and bellowing
> And autumn was advancing in steps of calamity?

The Soviet Union was reeling under the onslaught of blitzkrieg, and as far as Adolf Hitler or the Western allies were concerned, it seemed on the verge of total disintegration.

Yet this was to underestimate the historic capacity of the Russian people to endure. For four years, while the greatest land war in history raged about them, they suffered brutality, starvation, and devastation. They met repeated defeat, yet they were never beaten. In time the war in Russia became "the Great Patriotic War," nurtured on ideals supposedly done to death by the Revolution. Officers led their men into battle (left) invoking images of 1812, of the great heroes of the Romanov epoch, of "Mother Russia."

On July 3, 1941, almost a fortnight after the German assault began, Joseph Stalin delivered his first wartime broadcast to the Russian people. In this historic speech, un-Stalinlike in its warmth (never before had he addressed the people as his "friends," his "brothers and sisters"), the Premier laid down the rules for total war. Above all, Stalin said, this was a "life-and-death struggle" against an enemy who meant to "destroy the national culture of the peoples of the Soviet Union. . . . The Red Army and Navy must fight for every inch of Soviet soil, fight to the last drop of blood. . . . All enterprises must intensify their work and produce more and more. . . ." There would be partisan war in the occupied areas "where intolerable conditions must be created for the enemy and his accomplices." Finally, there would be a scorched-earth campaign. "The enemy must not be left a single engine . . . , not a pound of bread nor a pint of oil. . . . All valuable property . . . which cannot be evacuated, must be destroyed."

Only last-ditch resistance outside Moscow and Leningrad, where they willingly traded lives at the rate of four to one, saved the Russians in 1941. Disaster threatened once again the next summer when the Germans resumed their offensive, this time angling southward toward Stalingrad and the oil-rich Caucasus. Hitler had predicted that in six weeks "the whole rotten structure will come crashing down." Fourteen months later his *Wehrmacht* and the Red Army were locked together in a death struggle at Stalingrad.

Stalin's collaboration with Hitler provoked a flood of intensely critical comment from foreign political cartoonists. England's David Low was struck by the cynical, even ludicrous, aspects of a deal between arch ideological enemies (right). Suggesting, as did a number of others, that Stalin was the dominant figure in the pact, a French commentator (opposite) saw Goering and Hitler—"Now you will pay us, eh?"—as whores nuzzling the Premier.

Depicting Europe under the pall of the combined visage of Stalin and Hitler (right), an American newspaper correctly forecast the events of 1939 and 1940, beginning with the joint dismemberment of Poland. Above, a Dutch cartoonist has Hitler and his henchmen (from the left, Goebbels, Ribbentrop, and Goering) dancing to a Russian tune.

Yesterday's Enemies

The Soviet-German nonaggression pact, signed in Moscow on August 23, 1939—even as an Anglo-French military mission was feebly promoting its own defense treaty a few blocks away—left the Western powers shaken and dismayed over what seemed a strange and cynical partnership. Moscow entered a *rapprochement* with Berlin anticipating a protracted, crippling war between the Axis and the Allies. It provided welcome breathing space when both Germany and Japan stood poised at the Soviet borders. Moreover, a secret protocol in the pact gave the Russians an equal share in carving out certain "spheres of interest" in Eastern Europe. As Foreign Commissar V. M. Molotov smugly observed on August 31, the day before Germany invaded Poland, "The political art in foreign affairs . . . is to reduce the enemies of one's country, and to turn yesterday's enemies into good neighbors."

Sixteen months after the start of the Soviet-German honeymoon, Hitler put his General Staff to planning Operation Barbarossa, the invasion of Russia. Every sign indicated it was coming. Yet Stalin chose to ignore warnings from Churchill and his own highly detailed intelligence reports. Shortly after midnight on June 22, 1941, a trainload of Russian wheat crossed the border into Germany in accordance with trade agreements concluded shortly after the nonaggression pact. At 3:15 A.M. 3 million German troops started into Russia.

Blitzkrieg

Ill-equipped and ill-commanded, Russia's soldiers and airmen paid a ghastly price on June 22. Battalions, regiments, whole divisions simply melted away under the shock of the German assault. "We are being fired on. What shall we do?" a beleaguered unit radioed. From headquarters came the reply. "You must be insane. And why is your signal not in code?" In some of the defensive positions no one had bothered to issue ammunition. Air force losses ran to better than 130 planes an hour.

Day after day the rout continued, with three great German army groups bearing down on the Ukraine, Moscow, and Leningrad. By mid-July the lightning thrusts of the German armor had carried it across the Dnieper, a leap of some 400 miles. Fresh reserves from Siberia were rushed in to counterattack, only to be sucked into the cauldron. Two entire Russian armies were encircled and destroyed at Smolensk on the road to Moscow and at Kiev in the Ukraine, the Germans collecting over 600,000 prisoners in the latter engagement. The low ebb came in early October when the Germans launched their decisive attack on Moscow. Briefly there was panic and "unauthorized withdrawals" of the Red Army. Party cards were burned in preparation for the occupation. But the Russians hung on through November and December, until the panzers bogged down in the cold and snow.

Villages put to the torch, groups of dazed peasants fleeing eastward, prisoners carried hundreds of miles in open freight cars to slave labor camps—this was blitzkrieg as recorded by German photographers in the summer and autumn of 1941. Opposite, a German antitank gun crew whoops in triumph after knocking out a Red Army tank. By the end of September the Germans had taken a toll of 2.5 million men, 22,000 guns, 18,000 tanks, and 14,000 planes. Still, the Russians kept on fighting. "There was resistance, always resistance, however hopeless," a German commented at the time. "A single gun, a group of men with rifles, a chap by the roadside with a grenade. . . ."

The New Order

At first parts of the Ukraine and Russia's newly acquired Baltic states welcomed the Germans with open arms. Smiling Ukrainian girls presented their liberators with food (above) and politicians, temporarily relieved of the Stalinist yoke, began planning nationalist governments.

For the conquered East, however, the Nazis specified a so-called New Order, based on unremitting exploitation of human and natural resources and the extermination of "undesirables." Nowhere was that special instrument of the Nazi regime—organized terror—applied with greater intensity. Slavs and Jews were *untermensch*, subhuman. A Nazi bureaucrat pronounced the official line: "The Slavs are to work for us. In so far as we don't need them, they may die. . . ." The best policy for the Ukraine, Hermann Goering declared, was "to kill all the men . . . and then to send in the SS stallions."

The Nazis wasted no time putting the New Order into effect. On the last two days of September, 1941, tens of thousands of Jews were killed at Babi Yar near Kiev. The scene at the right was repeated time and again in the Ukraine and White Russia, where roving SS squads massacred whole villages. Ultimately 3 million persons, mostly youths, were shipped to Germany as slave labor. In doing so, however, the New Order succeeded in spawning a formidable resistance movement.

Reflecting and no doubt intensifying the national purpose, Soviet propaganda stressed the evil of the enemy and the need to destroy him rather than vague appeals to patriotism. An early example is the poster at right; the poster above, in which Hitler is greeted by the grim visage of defeat, appeared in 1943 as the tide was turning at Stalingrad. Below, models of the excellent T-34 medium tank take form on an assembly line east of the Urals. The Russian army and air force suffered terrible privations until the new factories and Lend-Lease shipments from Britain and America reached full stride in 1943. By the end of that year Soviet war plants were turning out tanks at the rate of over 2,000 a month.

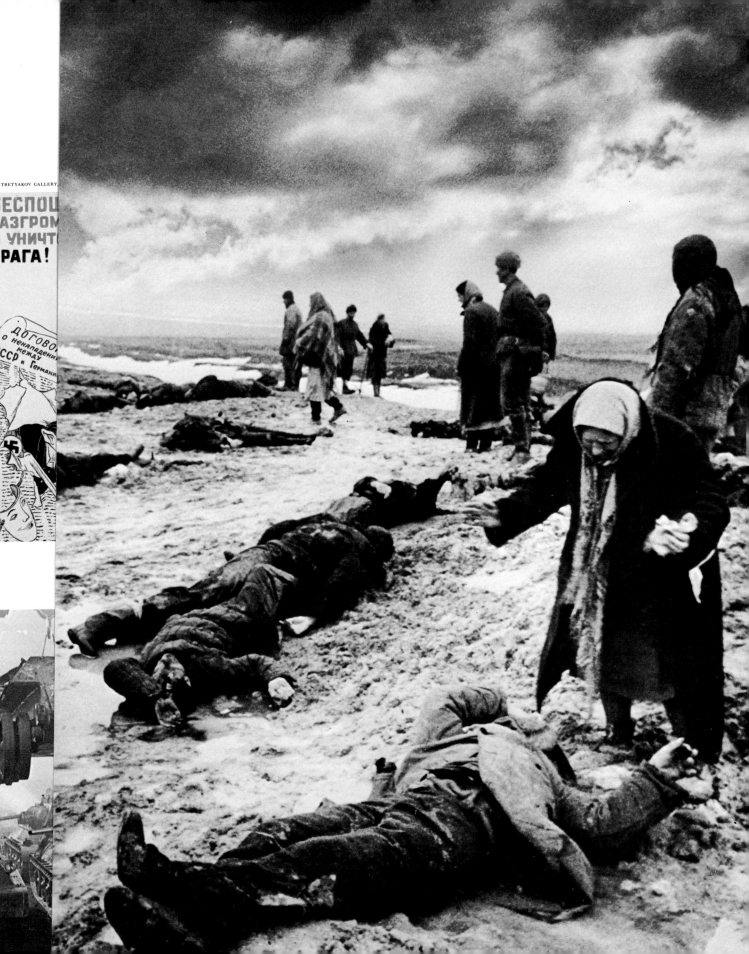

A horse-drawn column of partisans, equipped with captured German [rifles?] [in]
the Ukraine in 1941. In one four-month period the partizany wreck[ed . . .]

Mobilizing for [Survival]

Violence begat violence. Before long, propagandist Ilya [Ehrenburg exhorted the]
Russian people to a vengeful crusade: "Let us not speak. [Let]
us kill. . . . If you have killed one German, kill another. [There is nothing more amusing to us than a heap of]
German corpses." The mood reached even into the intellectua[l world, where the war inspired]
the brutal chords of Shostakovich's *Leningrad Symphony* and [the poet Konstantin Simonov's]
popular poems, "Kill Him!" and "I Hate."

Stalin rapidly overhauled the Soviet military machine. The [incompetent generals were re-]
lieved of their commands (or shot for "treasonable activities") a[nd replaced by such capable]
officers as Vasili Chuikov and Georgi Zhukov, and even with s[ome of those imprisoned]
since the army purges of the late thirties. Drawing on seemingl[y inexhaustible reserves, the Red]
Army mobilized a million men within a month of the invasion.

The evacuation of industry to the Urals and Siberia, one of the [great achievements of World]
War II, began at the same time. Steel mills, stamping plants, air[craft factories—all were]
dismantled en masse and later reassembled at remote spots far to [the east. The Zaporozhye works,]
for example, one of the Soviet Union's largest tube-rolling m[ills, was dismantled and]
shipped eastward in tens of thousands of boxcars. It was back ir [operation in a matter of]
four months.

No person, no institution escaped service. Stalin "revived" the [Orthodox Church]
as a spur to patriotism, creating a government post jocularly know[n as the Commissar]
for God. Women by the thousands dug new coal mines to repla[ce those lost to the Germans.]
Wives and daughters took over the nation's farms; lacking horses [they hitched]
cows as draft animals. Anticipating a long war, Stalin establishe[d a new medal, the Order]
of Motherly Glory, for those who bore more than seven children.

With the city's utilities smashed, women began drawing water from
broken mains in the streets. Despite the hopeless outlook, looting and
suicide—the symptoms of complete breakdown—never took hold.

Civilians dug hundreds of miles of trenches and tank
traps around Leningrad. The inner perimeter, defended
by troops under Marshal Zhukov, was never breached.

A dead child, a victim of the famine or the cold or the
bombs, is borne by its parents to one of the common
graves hastily prepared during the siege of Leningrad.

A People Besieged

Failing to take Leningrad by storm, the Germans determined to "hermetically seal" the city and starve it to death. When the noose tightened in September of 1941, three million people were trapped with about a month's supply of food. When the snows came people began consuming stray pets, hair oil, and homemade brews of furniture glue and wallpaper paste. At the height of the starving time deaths averaged between 3,500 and 4,000 a day. Men and women walking to makeshift factories collapsed and died in the streets, others went to sleep in the chill gloom of their homes and never awoke. Constant shelling and bombing (below) compounded the strain, but the city's nerve never broke. A factory official told British correspondent Alexander Werth of the will to resist: ". . . one day in December, in twenty degrees of frost, we had all our windows blown out by a bomb, and I thought to myself: 'No, we really can't go on. . . .' And yet, somehow—we didn't stop. A kind of instinct told us we mustn't—that it would be worse than suicide, and a little like treason." Finally, the Russians established a supply route across the ice of Lake Ladoga, the famous Ladoga Lifeline, but the siege was to last until January, 1944—over twenty-seven months in all—in which time an estimated one million Leningraders perished.

Soviet Life FROM SOVFOTO

DR. ALFRED OTT

War of Attrition

Stalingrad: the name, like Verdun, stands for all of the horrors of war, for the ghastly expenditure of men and equipment, for the grave of an army. Here, from the end of August, 1942, until the following February, the armies flailed at each other in sewers, cellars, and bombed-out houses and factories. And always, as the opposing generals sought the decisive blow, the soldiers responded to their call for "one last heave." For the Germans, who had already lost one and a half million men in Russia, defeat in this place was the beginning of the end. In his diary an officer of the doomed German Sixth Army described the nether world of Stalingrad:

"We have fought during fifteen days for a single house, with mortars, grenades, machine guns and bayonets. Already by the third day fifty-four German corpses are strewn in the cellars, on the landings, and the staircases. . . .From story to story, faces black with sweat, we bombard each other with grenades in the middle of explosions, clouds of dust and smoke, heaps of mortar, floods of blood, fragments of furniture and human beings. Ask any soldier what half an hour of hand-to-hand struggle means in such a fight. And imagine Stalingrad; eighty days and eighty nights of hand-to-hand struggles. . . .

"Stalingrad is no longer a town. By day it is an enormous cloud of burning, blinding smoke; it is a vast furnace lit by the reflection of the flames. And when night arrives. . .the dogs plunge into the Volga and swim desperately to gain the other bank. The nights of Stalingrad are a terror for them. Animals flee this hell; the hardest stones cannot bear it for long; only men endure."

Laid out on the frozen earth (above), German dead await spring for a proper burial. At left, one of Stalingrad's "scorching, howling, bleeding nights."

The Road Back

Stalingrad was the turning point. Thereafter, except for a few brief detours, the road led inexorably to Berlin. Braced by its monumental victory on the banks of the Volga, and now armed to the teeth with equipment from the Western allies and the factories beyond the Urals, the Red Army was rapidly becoming the most potent ground force in the world. Before long, the Russians could muster 12,000 trucks to supply a single assault and at one point boast a superiority over the Germans of 5.5 times more men, 7.8 times more guns, 5.7 times more tanks, and 17.6 times more planes. In July of 1943, at the Kursk salient southwest of Moscow, this awesome new strength was exhibited: with immense tank formations using adopted panzer tactics and massed artillery (the "queen of battle" in Stalin's view) the Russians utterly annihilated the last great German offensive in the East.

By December of 1943 the Russians had established bridgeheads over the Dnieper and liberated two-thirds of German-occupied territory. Six months later they were across the Dniester and into Poland. Alternating offensives north and south in the last half of 1944, they swept into Romania, Hungary, Latvia, and Lithuania. By February of 1945, two years after Stalingrad, Marshal Zhukov stood poised on the Oder for the final drive to Berlin.

"Avenging Russia is advancing. . ." the poet Alexei Surkov wrote in late 1943, and indeed the Red legions advanced into Germany exacting "bread for bread, blood for blood." Revenge for Kiev, for Leningrad, for the murder camps where uncounted Russian Jews perished drove some of the troops. Others indulged in an orgy of rape and pillage for its own sake. Already a drama of infinitely greater impact had been played out in the "liberated" countries of Eastern Europe, where NKVD squads and special political action groups labored with ruthless efficiency to establish Stalin's own New Order.

"German towns are burning, I am happy," Ilya Ehrenburg announced as Red tank columns (right) ground through the snowy streets of the Reich. Ahead of them a mass of human flotsam fled westward in carts, or clinging to the sides of overloaded trains (left), or simply walking. Benumbed survivors of the Wehrmacht, *represented above in a captured German painting, dug in for the final, overwhelming attack on the Eastern front.*

The Victors

In mid-afternoon of April 30, 1945, after dictating his political testament and having a dose of poison distributed to his new wife, Adolf Hitler sat down on a sofa in the Chancellery *Fuehrerbunker* and shot himself in the mouth. On the following day, after nearly a week of the bitterest street fighting, a Russian soldier clambered atop the Reichstag and waved the hammer and sickle in a victory salute over the desolation of the Third Reich's capital (opposite). "Today is the first of May, a great holiday for our two nations," a surrendering German officer informed General Chuikov, one of the heroes of Stalingrad and now the conquerer of Berlin. "*We* have a great holiday today," Chuikov replied dryly. "How things are with you over there is less easy to say."

Soon the victory celebrations got underway in Moscow, with thousand-gun salutes; with Stalin praising the "small people, the little screws and bolts" of the invincible Soviet machine; with hundreds of German banners piled on the steps of Lenin's tomb; and, more ominously, with an endless procession of huge Stalin tanks passing in review. Yet no amount of exultation could obscure the scars of this most brutal campaign in history. At least 20 million Russians had lost their lives. Millions more were maimed, countless millions left homeless. A charred wasteland stretched from the Dniester to the Volga, from the Baltic to the Black seas.

Yet Russia had absorbed this frightful toll and emerged from the Great Patriotic War as the strongest power in Europe. It was the Russians who, in Churchill's charitable phrase, "tore the guts out of the German army." This they made manifestly clear during the proceedings at Yalta (above) and Potsdam. Indeed, Stalin's truculent behavior at the war's end gave reason to believe that the Soviets saw themselves as worthy challengers for the position of leading power in the postwar world. Already in the summer of 1945 the first confrontations, the probing tests, were taking place in the rubble of Germany.

30

The Cold War

In dealing with international relations after World War II we run into a number of special difficulties. One is the scarcity of evidence. The great powers have so far made public only a fraction of the pertinent documents, so that our interpretation of post-1945 diplomacy must of necessity rest on much guesswork. In the second place, post-1945 events are part of our own time to such an extent that we are unable to view them as dispassionately as those of the more remote past. And, finally, there is a peculiar problem arising from the revolutionary changes that have occurred in the twentieth century in the nature of international relations. In modern times the customary distinction between diplomacy and warfare has become blurred. Since the *Weltpolitik* of Kaiser William II, but especially since the Bolshevik call for world revolution in 1917, international relations have increasingly tended to approximate the condition that Trotsky had defined as "neither war nor peace." The large powers, combined in vast blocs, contend against each other with as great determination as they would in war, using all available means short of direct military confrontation: hostile propaganda, sedition, economic warfare, rivalry over neutral states and outer space. This conflict, which has become a permanent feature of modern life, constitutes the Cold War. It reached the height of intensity during the first decade that followed World War II.

Signs of serious friction between the Soviet Union and the Western Allies manifested themselves while the war was still in progress. At first, during the early months of the Nazi invasion, Stalin showed every intention of accommodating his new allies. But once the Nazi drive on Moscow had been stopped and the United States had entered the war (these events occurred simultaneously, in the first week of December, 1941), his attitude visibly hardened. Unlike President Roosevelt, whose attention was concentrated on winning the war as quickly and expeditiously as possible, Stalin never ceased to think in long-range political terms. As early as January, 1942, he had warned Anthony Eden, the British Foreign Secretary, that after the victory he intended to press for major revisions of East European frontiers. The closer the moment of victory approached and the less Allied help he needed, the more uncooperative Stalin became. The evolution of his attitude can be traced in his wartime correspondence with Roosevelt and Churchill, whose tone, in the words of the historian Herbert Feis, gradually changed "from amiability—to reserve—to bluntness—to bold rudeness."

The Western Allies, and particularly President Roosevelt, were for a long time inclined to overlook Stalin's growing obduracy. They entertained considerable guilt feelings about the Soviet Union, not unlike those that Hitler's appeasers in the 1930s had experienced over Versailles. The record of Western hostility toward communism, and especially the Allied intervention in the Russian Civil War, troubled Roosevelt and some of his associates. They believed

Postwar Western Effort at Cooperation

The major upheaval of the Cold War in Soviet-dominated Eastern Europe took place in Hungary in 1956. Here, jubilant Hungarian "freedom fighters" pass a disabled Russian tank in Budapest; a few days later the reinforced Red Army crushed the revolt.

that by displaying patience and good will they could overcome what was regarded as Soviet Russia's understandable suspicion of the West and gradually draw it into responsible partnership with the United States and Great Britain in maintaining peace. Stalin, who had a totalitarian dictator's uncanny feel for the soft spots in the liberal conscience, fed these illusions. His quick mind and peasant gruffness as well as his democratic professions altogether charmed Roosevelt, who saw in the heroic Russian resistance to the Nazis ultimate proof of Stalin's right to speak for his people. In a radio address delivered on Christmas day, 1944, the President referred to Stalin as "a man who combines a tremendous relentless determination with a stalwart sense of humor." He added his belief that Stalin was "truly representative of the heart and soul of Russia" and that the United States would "get along very well with him and the Russian people—very well indeed."

Churchill had a more realistic estimate of Stalin and his government and no regrets about his role in urging Allied intervention in 1918–1920. But since he was certain that Russia would inevitably dominate postwar Europe, he was content with whatever concessions could be extracted from Stalin. After his plan for a major Allied invasion of the Balkans, intended to seize that area ahead of the Russians, had been vetoed by the United States, he made a secret agreement with Stalin dividing the Balkans into spheres of influence. But in general, his opinion carried less weight and did not vitally influence the major decisions.

Roosevelt, Churchill, and Stalin held during the war two major conferences, partly to coordinate military plans, partly to lay the groundwork for the postwar peace settlement. The first of these took place at Teheran (November, 1943). Here the basic positions were outlined and broad accord was reached on the principles on which peace was to be based. The second conference, held at the Russian resort of Yalta (February, 1945), produced detailed inter-Allied agreement on a number of outstanding issues. The three leaders decided at Yalta to divide Germany into occupation zones, and to take concerted measures against a revival of German militarism. In areas liberated from the enemy, it was agreed to apply the principles of the Atlantic Charter (Chapter 29), guaranteeing "the right of all peoples to choose the form of government under which they will live" by means of free democratic elections.

Stalin, however, was not content with such vague generalities. At Yalta he also demanded and received specific territorial and diplomatic concessions. Of these the most important concerned Poland. Stalin had no intention of giving up that part of Poland which he had secured in 1939 from Hitler. Under his pressure, Roosevelt and Churchill formally acquiesced to Russia incorporating this area, with the understanding that Poland would be compensated in the west at Germany's expense. Stalin, in return, promised "free and unfettered" elections in Poland, in which the leaders of the Polish government-in-exile, resident in London, would participate. In exchange for a promise to enter the war against Japan, Russia also secured territorial gains in East Asia, including a restitution of the "special rights" (i.e., a sphere of influence) that imperial Russia had enjoyed in Manchuria (Chapter 21). The Allies agreed on founding a United Nations Organization to take the place of the moribund League of Nations. In the United Nations Assembly the Soviet Union was promised three votes: one for itself, and one each for its constituent republics, Ukraine and Belorussia.°

Few international agreements have aroused such controversy as those reached at the Yalta Conference, once its secret clauses calling for territorial adjustments in Russia's favor had been revealed. Its critics charge that at Yalta the Western leaders made genuine concessions in return for worthless promises. In particular, they condemn the territorial awards that Roosevelt and Churchill made at Poland's and China's expense without the consent of the governments or peoples of these two Allied countries. Some critics attribute Western behavior to the physical debility of the President (he died three months after Yalta of a brain hemorrhage) and even to treason on the part of some high American officials (one of the members of the United States delegation, Alger Hiss, was indeed later convicted of perjury for denying connections with a Soviet espionage ring).

There is, however, no reason to suspect any foul play. The appeasement of Stalin was inspired by the same combination—an overwhelming desire for peace, an ignorance of history, and a constitutional inability to understand the totalitarian psyche—which a decade earlier had led to the appeasement of Hitler. Given the predisposition in his favor, it was a relatively easy matter for Stalin to extract concessions from the Allies. For, indeed, what was the concession of some Polish or Chinese territory, or a couple of extra seats in the United Nations Assembly, in return for the Soviet Union's promise of full cooperation in the maintenance of peace?

No wonder the Allied delegations returned from Yalta in a jubilant mood. Harry Hopkins, Roosevelt's closest adviser, described the feelings that he and his colleagues shared at the conclusion of the Yalta negotiations as follows:

> We really believed in our hearts that this was the dawn of a new day we had all been praying for and talking about for so many years. We were absolutely certain that we had won the first great victory of the peace— and by "we" I mean *all* of us, the whole civilized human race. The Russians had proved that they could be reasonable and farseeing and there wasn't any doubt in the minds of the President or of any of us that we could live with them peacefully as far into the future as any of us could imagine.

According to Hopkins, the Western Allies' only worry was whether Stalin's successor would prove to be as "reasonable and sensible and understanding" as he had been. That Stalin, with his record, should have been able to persuade the President of the United States and his staff that he had any of these qualities must surely rank him as one of the greatest diplomats of all time.

As anyone even superficially acquainted with the history of the Communist movement might have anticipated, Stalin had no intention of honoring his Yalta pledges of "free and unfettered elections" in areas conquered by his armies. From the time it had dissolved the Russian Constituent Assembly (Chapter 23), the Communist leadership had never allowed itself to be constrained by respect for democratic institutions which, in its eyes, were merely instruments

The Stalinization of Eastern Europe

° By this arrangement, the Ukraine and Belorussia were and still are in effect represented twice: once through the Soviet delegation, and then again through their own.

of bourgeois exploitation. Stalin had made it very clear in his dealings with Hitler that he regarded Eastern Europe as lying within his sphere of influence. He certainly had no reason to give up, after having won a great victory over the Nazis, that which he had demanded and partly obtained from them in 1939 without losing a man. Stalin was much too realistic not to see that democratic elections would not yield him the majorities that he needed to secure a solid grip over this area. It had to be taken by force. To prepare for this eventuality Stalin formed in Moscow several "Patriotic" or "National Liberation" fronts, staffed with dependable Communists and fellow travelers from Eastern European countries, to serve as instruments for the eventual power seizure. These organizations had been created some time before the Yalta Conference convened.

The methods that Stalin employed in subjugating Eastern Europe closely resembled those that he and Lenin had employed in the course of eliminating internal opposition in Russia. They were later defined by a Hungarian Communist official as "salami tactics." Beginning with the broadest alliance of anti-Fascist parties, Stalin and his subordinates gradually sliced away from governmental power one party after another, until all that remained was its Communist core. This accomplished, Stalin got rid of Communists who had strong local roots and replaced them with those who had made their careers in Moscow. By the early 1950s, when the process was completed, the countries of Eastern Europe had been transformed into miniature versions of the USSR, or, as they came to be known, its "satellites."

The Stalinization of Eastern Europe began while the war was still in progress.

Truman and Stalin and their unruly "children," seen by the cartoonist Walt Kelly in early 1949, a period of tense East-West relations.

As soon as each country had been liberated by the Soviet army, the Moscow-based Fronts were brought in and established as provisional governments. In Warsaw, where a tremendous anti-German uprising of the underground Home Army erupted in August, 1944, while Soviet forces were approaching, Stalin ordered his troops to halt their offensive. Only after the Germans had slaughtered 200,000 inhabitants of the city and obtained the surrender of what was left of the pro-London Home Army was the Soviet advance resumed. In this manner Stalin let the Nazis liquidate the most serious threat to his power in Poland. By the time the Moscow-appointed "Committee of National Liberation" had entered Warsaw, there was no force left able to challenge it; indeed, there was virtually no city, for in the course of suppressing the uprising the Germans had dynamited and burned it to the ground.°

Initially, the provisional governments established by the Communists in Eastern Europe were coalitions embracing a multitude of socialist and peasant parties, including those representing the exile governments based in London. But it is worth noting that in all these coalitions the two key ministries—defense and security (police)—were from the beginning staffed by Communists. Sooner or later elections were held, as provided for by the Yalta agreement. In one or two cases they were indeed "free and unfettered." In Hungary the voters had an opportunity of giving a majority to the Smallholders party, a peasant group sympathetic to the West. In Czechoslovakia, where the memories of the Western betrayal at Munich were still fresh, the Communist ticket actually won a majority. But in most Eastern European countries the elections proceeded in an atmosphere of police intimidation, reminiscent of what had occurred in Nazi Germany in 1933. Candidates likely to pursue an independent policy, especially those affiliated with the London governments, were struck off the voting lists and personally harassed. When the Western Allies learned of these irregularities they protested to Moscow, but to no avail.

In 1945–1946 Stalin still maintained a pretense of coalition governments in areas occupied by his armies because he did not want to jeopardize the chances of those Communist parties which after the war had been invited to participate in ministerial cabinets in the West. Of these the most important were the Communist parties of France and Italy. At that time it seemed quite likely that these two organizations, in alliance with other left-wing groups, would win a parliamentary majority and come legitimately to power. But in early 1947 two events occurred which dashed this hope. One was the inauguration by the United States of the Truman Doctrine and the Marshall Plan (see below); the other was the dismissal of Communist ministers from coalition governments in France and Italy (May, 1947). Stalin now no longer had any reason to engage in the complicated and potentially dangerous game of coalitions. Everything dictated that he quickly consolidate his hold on Eastern Europe, for here disenchantment with Soviet Russia had begun to set in, and the non-Communist left was displaying an unmistakable yearning for closer links with the West. In 1947 Stalin

---

° During their alliance with the Nazis, the Russians massacred over 10,000 Polish officers whom they had interned in September, 1939. The bodies of the victims were unearthed by the Germans in the Katyn forest, near Smolensk. The Polish government-in-exile in London demanded a Red Cross investigation, causing Stalin to break relations with it (1943). This slaughter was intended to eliminate potential leaders of national resistance in Poland.

ordered the dissolution of the influential peasant parties in all countries occupied by his armies. The peasant leaders either fled abroad or suffered imprisonment and in some instances execution. The following year came the turn of the socialist parties. These were not outlawed but forced to merge with the Communist parties to form a common labor front, known by a variety of names (United Workers' party in Poland, Socialist Unity party in East Germany, People's Front in Hungary, etc.), in which the Communists controlled the key positions. These mergers were everywhere completed by the end of 1948. By then the one-party system was in operation throughout Soviet-controlled Eastern Europe.

The transformation of independent states into satellites was not accomplished without resistance. In Czechoslovakia the Social Democrats refused to merge with the Communists. The non-Communists in the Prague government also showed an alarming proclivity to seek United States economic aid. To nip in the bud this tendency toward independence, Stalin had the Czech Communists stage a *coup d'état*. In February, 1948, the Communists arrested the leading figures of the independent parties and established a one-party government.

In one country—Yugoslavia—Stalin's technique did not work, and he suffered a humiliating defeat. Here the liberation from the Nazis had been accomplished not by the Soviet army but by a local Communist partisan movement, whose members subsequently occupied major military and police posts. The head of the partisan movement, Joseph Broz, known as Tito, had been trained in Moscow and showed every intention of collaborating closely with the Soviet Union. But he was not willing to become a docile vassal of Stalin. In 1947–1948 a variety of conflicts developed between the two Communist leaders. They came to a head over the issue of economic planning, when Tito refused to subordinate the needs of the Yugoslav economy to those of the economy of the Soviet Union. Lacking an internal lever in the form of an army and police apparatus, Stalin had no way of forcing Tito out. In 1948 the quarrel broke into the open. Stalin excommunicated Yugoslavia from the Communist bloc, while Tito asked and received economic aid from the West.

To guard against a repetition of "Titoism" in his domain, Stalin inaugurated in 1948 a series of purges of the Communist apparatus in Eastern Europe. Communists who had been active in the partisan movement, who enjoyed strong local following, or who had resisted in any manner Moscow's pressures, were now ruthlessly weeded out. Between 1949 and 1952 a succession of mock trials took place in the satellite countries, in the course of which leading party and government officials confessed to the most outrageous crimes. Some were sentenced to long prison terms, others executed. Several of these "trials," notably that of the Czech Communists, carried unmistakable anti-Semitic overtones, for in his diseased imagination Stalin believed himself menaced by a world-wide Jewish plot.

Next to Poland, no single issue caused such bad blood between the West and the Soviet Union as the fate of Germany. It had been agreed among the Allies that as soon as feasible elections would be held in that country, the occupation zones merged, and a peace treaty signed. But the negotiations for a German peace treaty, which got under way in November, 1946, at once ran into snags, and after a while it became apparent that Stalin had no desire to settle the Ger-

FENNO JACOBS—BLACK STAR

The Berlin Airlift (June, 1948–May, 1949) delivered more than a million and a half tons of supplies to the blockaded city in 196,000 flights.

man question. Nor did he give any evidence that he intended to hold elections in his zone. To the Western Allies it was an urgent matter to put Germany on its feet as soon as possible in order to reduce the high costs of occupation and economic aid and to stabilize the political situation in the heart of the Continent. When it became obvious that Russia would indefinitely procrastinate on this issue, the three Western Allies merged their zones into one (1947). At the same time steps were taken to restore the German economy. In 1948 a reformed currency was introduced into West Germany, leading promptly to a revival of industry and trade.

To these measures Stalin responded with a determined effort to eject the Western Allies from Berlin and to consolidate his hold on East Germany. In the spring of 1948, without warning, he closed to Allied vehicles all land access to Berlin across the Soviet zone. The Allies asserted their rights in Berlin by undertaking a massive airlift. For almost a year, every day, a steady stream of transport and cargo planes supplied the blockaded city with all its necessities. Finally, in May, 1949, Stalin capitulated and lifted the blockade.

By then not only Berlin but Germany as a whole was split down the middle into two separate states. In the Western zone elections gave a majority to the Christian Democratic party headed by Konrad Adenauer, which formed a government of the German Federal Republic with residence in Bonn. The constitution of the Republic was based on that of Weimar. In the Eastern zone the Communists persisted in their refusal to hold elections, installing there instead a puppet Communist regime, modeled on those in their other satellites. The popularity of the German Democratic Republic may be gauged by the fact that from the time of its establishment until 1961 (when the construction of the Berlin Wall put an end to the population movement) 2,700,000 persons, or an average of 700 a day, fled from East to West Germany.

Once the countries of Eastern Europe had become full-blown satellites, their entire internal life came to be subordinated to Soviet interests. The economic development plans of each satellite had to be fully coordinated with the Soviet Five-Year Plan. The military and police security apparatus of each was integrated

The Berlin Wall, erected in 1961, blocked the mass exodus from East Germany. These East German police of the large patrolling force were photographed through the barricade.

with corresponding Soviet institutions; in the case of Poland the armed forces came directly under the command of a Soviet marshal. To ensure that none of the satellites defected despite these precautions, Stalin left in each a large Soviet army contingent, a kind of friendly occupation force.

The subjugation of Eastern Europe threw the Western Allies, and especially the United States, into a state of bewilderment. Unlike Stalin's earlier acts, his flagrant breaches of the Yalta agreements could not be explained by suspicion or ill-feeling arising from Western transgressions, real or alleged, dating back to the early years of Soviet history. What aggravated matters was evidence of Soviet expansionism in other parts of the world. In the summer of 1945 the Soviet government applied strong pressure on Turkey, coupled with military threats, to surrender territories adjacent to the Caucasus and to agree to a revision of the treaties regulating passage through the Straits. In early 1946 the Soviet army refused to evacuate northern Iran, which it had occupied during the war and promised to leave six months after the end of hostilities. In May, 1946, Communist guerrillas in Greece initiated a civil war against the duly elected, pro-Western government. A steady stream of anti-American invective in the Soviet press and radio depicted the United States as the successor of Nazi Germany and the main enemy of peace and freedom in the world.

The initial tendency in Washington was to respond to these acts with a show of firmness. President Truman shared neither his predecessor's sense of guilt nor his hopes about Soviet Russia, and in his dealings with Stalin he immediately adopted a resolute tone. Its monopoly of the atomic bomb appeared to assure the United States of an ultimate weapon should Soviet expansion ever directly menace its security. The American armed forces, which on the day of Japan's surrender had numbered 12 million men, were demobilized subsequently at a rate of a million a month, until nothing more than a skeleton army remained. To strengthen its position the United States conducted a series of atomic bomb tests in 1946–1947 in the Pacific, whose purpose was at least as much political as military, namely to impress Russia with the awesome destructiveness of this new weapon.

But neither verbal toughness nor atomic bomb demonstrations had any noticeable effect on Stalin, who calmly went on absorbing areas under his control and menacing areas outside it. Some circles in Washington, especially among the military, began now to urge a more forceful response, but the President and his foreign policy advisers preferred not to break openly with the wartime policy of great power cooperation as long as on some issues the Soviet Union continued to be cooperative.

One of these issues was the prosecution of the Nazis. In 1945 the Allies opened in Nürnberg, the city that had been used by the Nazis for their party rallies, a trial of the major war criminals. The testimony produced at the trial for the first time revealed to the general public the full horror of Nazi rule. The court sentenced the surviving Nazi government and military leaders either to death or long prison terms.

An even more important subject of agreement between West and East was the United Nations. This organization had first met in San Francisco in April, 1945.

Its structure and functions closely resembled those of the League of Nations, but with some significant differences. One was the participation in it of both the United States and the Soviet Union. Another was that in the Security Council —the institution specifically charged with the responsibility for maintaining peace—the five great powers had the right of veto. Both of these features made the United Nations more of an instrument of big-power politics than the League of Nations had been. This was not necessarily a fault, because it may well be argued that the weakness of the League derived from its unrealistic attempt to create a parity between great and small states. The Soviet Union from the beginning frequently availed itself of the veto right to kill resolutions that it disapproved, but it did actively participate in all the activities of the United Nations, and there was the hope that through its agency outstanding great power conflicts could be peacefully resolved.

The wartime policy of collaboration with the Soviet Union was finally abandoned only in February-March, 1947, when it gave way to the policy of "containment."

The theory of containment was first suggested in an 8,000-word telegram dispatched to Washington from the United States Embassy in Moscow in February, 1946. Its author, George F. Kennan, was one of the State Department's leading Russian specialists. Kennan argued that the Soviet Union's foreign policy was not significantly affected by the realities of the international scene; in other words, its policy was not a response to Russia's treatment by the great powers. Rather, it derived from internal traditions, particularly from a deep-seated sense of insecurity whose roots reached back to the Middle Ages, when Russia had lain exposed to the ravages of its nomadic neighbors. The expansion in which Russia had engaged since the end of the war was a natural consequence of its historical heritage. Kennan warned that Russia would maintain a relentless pressure on its neighbors, exploiting their internal weaknesses and divisions in order to conquer them. Russia was fundamentally committed to the view that no lasting peace between it and the rest of the world was possible. Given such an attitude, compromises and concessions could not mollify it, nor *ad hoc* emergency measures blunt its drive. In his subsequent writings Kennan argued that what was needed was an equally relentless and sustained counter-effort to "contain" the Soviet Union within its existing realm.

The views which Kennan articulated found support among the leading diplomatic and military figures in Washington, including Dean Acheson, an influential Undersecretary of State. They caused in time a complete reversal of earlier assumptions about the sources of Soviet behavior. Previously, Russia's obduracy had been interpreted as a reaction to Western wrongs; now it was explained as inherent in Russia's traditions and outlook. In 1948, surveying Soviet postwar policies, Acheson argued: "the direction and goals of Soviet action . . . were chosen and desired and were not forced upon her rulers as defensive measures . . . the main thrust of Soviet policy was self-generated and not a reluctant response to the acts or omissions of others."°

The event that decided the shift in American foreign policy was the economic crisis confronting Western Europe at the beginning of 1947. The winter that

°John C. Campbell, ed., *The United States in World Affairs, 1947–1948* (1948).

year was more severe than it had been in several decades. It destroyed fall-seeded crops and made extraordinary demands on the limited coal supply; Europe's scanty fuel reserves had to be diverted from industrial to consumer needs. The remaining dollar reserves, instead of being used for economic reconstruction, had to be spent on purchases of food and coal. Great Britain was in such straits that it had to curtail industrial production, even at the risk of mass unemployment. To save its economy from collapse the British government resolved to reduce its foreign commitments, and in particular to suspend the aid which it had been giving to Turkey and Greece to resist Communist diplomatic pressures and guerrilla warfare. On February 2, 1947, the British Foreign Office communicated this decision to the United States Department of State.

Britain's withdrawal from the eastern Mediterranean confronted the United States government with an urgent choice: whether to abandon Turkey and Greece to their certain fate, or to take on the international responsibilities traditionally shouldered by Great Britain. On the answer to this question depended the fate not only of the two Balkan countries but of Western Europe as well. In French national elections held in late 1946 the Communists emerged as the single most powerful party, while in Italy they were within a hairbreadth of an actual parliamentary majority. If Western Europe were allowed to suffer a serious economic depression, it was more than likely that Italy and France would come under Communist or Communist-dominated governments.

Confronted with this situation, President Truman initiated intense discussions involving high officials of the Department of State and the armed forces, and congressional leaders of both parties. The overwhelming consensus was that the United States had no choice but to confront the Communist threat and to declare its readiness to come to the aid of any and all countries menaced by it. The decision was inspired by a firm resolve to avoid the mistakes committed by the appeasers of Hitler, whose concessions and compromises had proved to encourage aggression.

On March 12, 1947, President Truman made his appearance before a joint session of Congress. He asked for an immediate appropriation of several hundred million dollars to provide assistance to Turkey and Greece. But in the course of his address he went beyond this request, outlining the basic principles of the containment policy, or, as it became subsequently known, the Truman Doctrine. He wanted a firm commitment of the United States now and in the future

> to help free peoples to maintain their institutions and their national integrity against aggressive movements that seek to impose on them totalitarian regimes. This is no more than a frank recognition that totalitarian regimes imposed on free people, by direct or indirect aggression, undermine the foundation of international peace and hence the security of the United States.

With Republican backing Truman received the appropriation for Turkey and Greece, and by implication, approval of his policy directives. Henceforth, containment became the official policy of the United States in its dealings with the Soviet Union and its satellites. The policy, however, was not entirely negative. It was designed not only to stop further Soviet expansion but also to remove the economic and social causes that facilitated it. To this end, the United States government launched in June, 1947, a program of economic aid known as the European Recovery Program, or Marshall Plan (Chapter 31).

The importance of the decisions taken in Washington in February–March, 1947, for the United States and the world at large, can hardly be overrated. The United States decisively and probably permanently broke with its traditional refusal to enter into peacetime alliances, committing itself to defend from external aggression a large number of countries extending from the northern tip of Norway to the borders of the Caucasus. This commitment was formally made in the North Atlantic Treaty, ratified by the Senate in July, 1949. By virtue of Article 5 of this treaty the signatories recognized that an armed attack on any one of them was an attack on all of them, and pledged themselves to come to the aid of the victim. A North Atlantic Treaty Organization (NATO) army came into being simultaneously. The United States dispatched its own contingents to the Continent to help its allies match the multimillion Soviet force stationed in Eastern Europe. Thus in 1947 the United States assumed nothing less than the responsibility, partly formal, partly moral, for safeguarding the external integrity of the entire non-Communist world—a responsibility that was bound in a thousand different ways to affect the life of the American people.

For Europe, the Truman Doctrine with its economic and military complements—the Marshall Plan and NATO—provided a unique opportunity for economic reconstruction. Shielded by the military might of the United States and assisted by its loans and grants, Europe made a spectacular recovery. By 1950 its production exceeded prewar levels, and the threat of economic collapse vanished. Western Europe was spared the fate of its Eastern half.

The Cold War Shifts to East Asia

Thanks to its "Eurasian" location Russia has the unique ability to engage in direct diplomatic and military activity in three of the world's major geopolitical areas: Europe, the Middle East, and the Far East. Already in the nineteenth century, having suffered a setback in one of these regions, the imperial government was known to shift its attention to the others. Thus, the thwarting in the Crimean War of Russian ambitions in the Balkans was followed by an outburst of expansion in Central Asia; as soon as that had been checked by the British, Russia reverted to the Balkans and then to China and Korea.

This pattern recurred in 1948–1950. By then the Soviet drive in Europe, which at one time had threatened to bring the entire Continent under Russian domination, had been blunted all along the line. The Allied stand in Berlin and the emergence of a viable government in Bonn had stabilized the situation in Germany. Yugoslavia's defection from the Communist bloc had deprived the Greek guerrillas of their main base of operations and caused the civil war in Greece to collapse. Turkey, backed by the United States, refused to bow to Soviet demands. In France and Italy the Communists, having lost hope of coming legitimately to power, went over to sterile opposition. The good will that they had gained in Europe during the war, thanks to their partisan activities and the Russian stand against the Germans, eroded as it became obvious that the Communists had no real interest in economic and political reconstruction. In

1948, in a crucial Italian election on which the Communists counted to yield them a parliamentary majority, victory went to the liberal, pro-Western Christian Democrats; the Popular Democratic Front, sponsored by the Communists, won less than one-third of the vote.

In the Far East, by contrast, the situation looked promising. The defeats that the Japanese had inflicted on the Western imperial powers in 1941–1942 and those which the West in turn had inflicted on them in 1942–1945 had created in this area something approaching a political and military vacuum. Japan itself, ruled imperiously by General MacArthur, was closed to Soviet influence. But the whole eastern periphery of Asia, from Korea to Burma, was unsettled and vulnerable. Here a determined Communist drive seemed to offer excellent chances of success.

Although we have no documentary proof to this effect, it is fairly certain that sometime in the winter of 1947–1948 Stalin and the leaders of the local Communist parties decided to launch a coordinated offensive against Western and pro-Western governments in East Asia. The strategy adopted seems to have been fundamentally identical for all the countries concerned. Where the Communist movements were already well established and in control of some definite territory, they were to declare themselves the legitimate government and undertake a military campaign intended to conquer the rest of the country. Where this was not the case, they were first to form a National Liberation Committee, gain a foothold in some inaccessible area, and then go over to the offensive. The social base of these operations was to be the peasantry, but essential to their success was the sympathy of the urban intelligentsia and the neutrality of the middle class. For this reason the programs advanced by East Asian Communist movements at this stage were not Communist or even socialist, but rather broadly democratic and nationalistic.

Beginning with the spring of 1948 a succession of guerrilla movements erupted and spread in various regions of East Asia: in March in Burma, in June in Malaya, in September in Indonesia, in October in the Philippines. In China, where they had controlled since the 1930s territory in Yenan, near the Mongolian border, the local Communists in September, 1948, proclaimed the establishment of the North China People's Government. The same month, in North Korea, a Communist government installed by the Soviet army announced the creation of a People's Republic with authority over the entire peninsula.

Today, viewed from the perspective of decades, these events seem too closely timed to have been coincidental. But this was not seen then, the more so as East Asia, considered less important than Europe for Western security, was not so closely watched. It was only when all China came under Communist domination that the magnitude of the problem confronting the Western democracies in East Asia became apparent.

The Chinese Communist movement was, of course, pro-Soviet, but it was at no point a tool of Moscow. With its own army and administration it could maintain toward Russia an attitude of considerable independence. Its leader, Mao Tse-tung, enjoyed the same maneuverability toward Stalin as did Tito, something not true of Communist leaders who were placed in power by the Soviet army. Stalin must have sensed this fact and all along conducted in China a

An American soldier checks a rocket during NATO maneuvers in Germany.

U.S. infantrymen advance in Korea in 1951 as refugees flee the fighting zone—a scene as old as war itself.

double policy: he helped the Chinese Communists (for example, equipping them with captured Japanese weapons) but at the same time maintained friendly relations with the pro-American government of Chiang Kai-shek. Probably Stalin hoped that Mao and Chiang (himself a defected Communist) would eliminate each other and enable him to install in China a tractable Communist government of his own making.

The conflict between Chiang and Mao went back to the 1930s, and during World War II the two fought each other more doggedly than they fought their common enemy, the Japanese. After Japan's collapse the United States made several attempts to bring the two sides together into some kind of coalition government, but these efforts failed, and in the summer of 1947 full-blown civil war was in progress in China. The United States supported Chiang with money and weapons, while the Soviet Union increasingly and overtly backed Mao. After they had established the North China People's Government, the Communists made rapid progress in conquering the rest of the country. In October the Soviet Union let the Chinese Communists into Manchuria, which Russian forces had occupied by virtue of the Yalta agreement. The antiquated and corrupt government of Chiang collapsed under the combined onslaught of well-organized Communist armies in the countryside and pro-Communist intellectuals in the cities. In 1949 all China fell under Communist control and a Chinese People's Republic was instituted. Chiang, with the remainder of his troops, evacuated to the island of Formosa (Taiwan).

The Communist triumph in China was not only a major debacle for the United States, which had staked much on the Chiang regime; it was a portent of worse things to come. With a base in China the Communists could give direct support to the guerrilla movements in eastern and southeastern Asia and completely eject the Western powers from this area.

That the Communists meant to take advantage of this situation became apparent in June, 1950, when the North Koreans launched a surprise invasion of South Korea. Korea had been a Japanese dependency since early in the century. After the war it had been divided into two zones, separated by the 38th parallel: a northern zone, under Soviet control, and a southern zone, under that of the United States. As in the case of Germany, it had been agreed that as soon as conditions permitted, the Koreans would be given an opportunity to hold democratic elections and create a national government. But exactly as had occurred in Germany, the Soviet occupation forces refused to allow their occupation zone to vote, being well aware that victory would go to Syngman Rhee, the hero of anti-Japanese resistance and a stanch foe of the Communists. In September, 1948, the country split in two, each establishing its own government.

The establishment of the North Korean People's Republic, as in the case of the North China People's Government, was a prelude to a general offensive aimed at seizing the whole country. But in the case of Korea this offensive had to be somewhat postponed because South Korea still had a contingent of United States troops. At the suggestion of the Soviet Union, made in September, 1948, both occupying powers withdrew their armed forces. In June, 1950, the North Korean army, built up with Soviet help, struck. The Communists had good reason to expect that the United States neither would nor could defend Korea, for it had no forces able to come immediately to South Korea's aid. But, to their surprise, the invasion produced an instantaneous reaction in Washington. With the backing of the United Nations Security Council, which declared North Korea the aggressor, a token force was immediately dispatched to bolster the South Korean armies.[*]

By early September the small United Nations contingent in Korea was reduced to a beachhead in the southwestern corner of the peninsula. But just as victory seemed within sight, the North Korean drive ran out of steam. In mid-September General MacArthur launched a surprise landing operation in central Korea, compelling the Communist forces to withdraw or risk being cut in two. The United Nations army (consisting mostly of United States troops) now pursued the invaders northward, toward the Chinese frontier, MacArthur's intention being to reunite both parts of the divided country. As Allied troops approached the Yalu River, the Chinese armies intervened. In the ensuing seesaw battle the line was eventually stabilized along the 38th parallel. General MacArthur insisted on carrying the war into China by bombing Chinese air bases, but this permission was denied by President Truman, and MacArthur was eventually dismissed from his post.

The invasion of Korea was a major blunder on the part of the Communists. The United States and its Western allies might have tolerated guerrilla movements, especially those disguised as movements of national liberation, but they were not disposed to permit a brutal onslaught reminiscent of Hitler's blitzkrieg. In response to the Korean War, the United States undertook a major rearmament program. NATO forces in Europe were considerably bolstered, and it was decided to rearm Germany. In the Far East the United States signed in September, 1951, a separate peace treaty with Japan. The Asian guerrilla movements, which until then had been making good progress, were before long suppressed by the alerted national governments.

By the early 1950s the Cold War had reached a level of intensity at which the slightest provocation could have unleashed a thermonuclear conflict.[†]

Domestic Repercussions in the United States

The events that we have described produced in the United States a mood of confusion and frustration. As long as the country had been at war, the American public had been prepared to do whatever was needed to bring a military victory. It was not, however, prepared for the drawn-out contests of the Cold War in which the issues were vague and the methods of combat entirely unfamiliar. At first, Americans were told on highest authority that the United States and the Soviet Union would cooperate after the war as they had during the war. Then, scarcely two years after the Nazi capitulation, they were told on equally high

[*]The United Nations vote was made possible by a tactical mistake of the Soviet Union. In January, 1950, in protest against the presence of Chiang Kai-shek's representative, the Soviet delegation walked out of the Security Council. When, six months later, the Council voted on the resolution condemning North Korea as the aggressor, the Soviet representative was not on hand to veto it.

[†]It is now known that at the height of the Cold War the head of the British intelligence department charged with responsibility for neutralizing Soviet espionage activities, as well as a leading American specialist in the Foreign Office, were Soviet spies (both have since defected to Moscow). Through them Stalin must have been well informed of United States intentions—an invaluable asset in the Cold War competition.

authority that the Soviet Union represented a mortal danger to peace and freedom and had to be stopped from further expansion. The Communist subjugation of Eastern Europe and invasion of South Korea seemed to corroborate the new policy. Yet, when General MacArthur wanted to employ full force against China, which had intervened on behalf of the aggressors in Korea, he was unceremoniously fired. The confusion which these policy shifts in Washington engendered was compounded by two events that occurred almost simultaneously in 1949. One was the end of the American monopoly on atomic weapons. The explosion that year by the Russians of a thermonuclear device suddenly exposed the United States to a deadly danger from which it had considered itself immune. The other was the Communist victory in China, a country toward which the United States had a special sympathy, which it had aided in its struggle against the Japanese, and for the sake of which it had in 1941 refused to come to terms with Japan.

The anxiety that these rapidly succeeding developments produced enabled demagogic politicians to attract attention and improve their fortunes by blaming American reverses on treason. The most notorious of these was the Republican Senator from Wisconsin, Joseph McCarthy. In the summer of 1950 he publicly announced that he possessed a long list of Communists allegedly on the State Department payroll. He never produced this list, but went on to make wilder and wilder charges, claiming, among other things, that both the Communist victory in China and the Russian acquisition of atomic weapons were made possible by betrayal by United States officials. The image of a country infested with agents and spies seemed to many ill-informed people to provide an explanation for the puzzling events of the postwar era. McCarthy's demonstrated ability to cause the electoral defeat of candidates who had opposed him or his friends gave him immense power in Congress. This he used with utter recklessness to smear reputations and secure the dismissal from the government of persons he disliked. The Republican leadership did not much care for McCarthy's methods, but since they hurt the Democrats, it tended to look the other way.

In 1952 the country elected a Republican administration. The new President, Dwight D. Eisenhower, entrusted the conduct of foreign policy to John Foster Dulles, an experienced international lawyer. During the electoral campaign the Republicans had advocated a more dynamic policy abroad, urging that "containment" be replaced by "roll back." But, as we shall see, when subsequently the occasion to recapture territory from the Communists presented itself, it was not taken advantage of In effect, the Eisenhower administration continued to adhere to the containment policy introduced by Truman. A tacit assumption of this policy was mutual recognition of the *status quo* established by 1947 between the Western and Eastern blocs.

The New Course in Russia Stalin's postwar foreign policy, after its initial successes, had ultimately placed the Soviet Union in a position of isolation. His tendency to view the outside world in categories of white and black—those who obeyed Stalin and those who did not—forfeited to the United States leadership of the entire third, gray category, consisting of neutral countries uninvolved in the Cold War. Communist parties outside the Soviet bloc were reduced to the status of propaganda mouth-

"Over the East-West Wall": cartoonist David Low's 1954 comment on the Soviet "thaw" after Stalin's death. The gregarious housewife is Georgi Malenkov, briefly Stalin's successor.

pieces, as isolated from the societies in which they functioned as was the Soviet Union from the world at large.

Russia and its satellites lay supine at Stalin's feet. The police, to maintain its grip, carried out constant purges and arrests without rhyme or reason. Millions of people were confined in concentration camps, where they had to perform backbreaking labor and where many died from malnutrition or physical abuse. The old tyrant, completely out of touch with humanity, grew increasingly paranoid, sending to their death even his close relatives. Cut off externally from all contact with the rest of mankind, Russia, internally, hovered on the brink of physical and spiritual collapse.

In March, 1953, Stalin suffered a fatal stroke. Immediately, Lavrenti Beria, the head of the security police, made a bid for power, but he was thwarted by his colleagues in the Central Committee, arrested, and shot. The police, which in Stalin's last decade virtually administered the country, was subsequently reduced in power, and many of its camps were quietly shut down. The party now reasserted its authority. Between 1953 and 1955 a kind of "collective leadership" or leadership by committee emerged, in which two factions vied for control. One consisted of "conservatives," who wished to continue running the country much as it had been run under the late Stalin. The other, comprised of "liberals," pressed for a major reform of the existing system so as to return to that which had been in force in the early years of Stalin's dictatorship (1928–1933), before the senseless purges and indiscriminate terror.

Under conditions which remain obscure, but in which personal rivalries undoubtedly played as large a part as ideological considerations, the liberal wing triumphed. At the Twentieth Party Congress, held in 1956, the new leaders, at

In 1960 the peripatetic Khrushchev attended a United Nations session. Here he confers with Secretary General Dag Hammarskjöld (left center).

first cautiously and then with unexpected frankness, attacked Stalin and what they euphemistically called the Stalinist "cult of personality." The high point of the proceedings was a report delivered at a closed session by Nikita Khrushchev, the outstanding personality of the liberal faction. Khrushchev depicted Stalin as a demented despot who had killed thousands of good, loyal Communists, and would have killed many more if death had not intervened. Whether this information was indeed news to the Congress delegates, as their recorded expressions of indignation seem to indicate, may be doubted. But the shock of hearing these facts publicly conceded by the party leadership was indeed great. Khrushchev's report was subsequently read to party organizations throughout the country, producing general confusion.

The "de-Stalinization" launched at the Twentieth Party Congress was intended to clear the decks for a major reorientation of internal and external policy. The change was indeed bold, bolder than one might have expected from men who had spent their lives in the Communist apparatus. But it involved no basic change in the aims of either the Communist movement or of its institutions. The men who took over the reins of government had all been Stalin's men. Much as they may have resented Stalin's behavior toward them, they could not help but regard the world in his terms or they would not have survived as his close subordinates. Nothing comparable to even the moderate de-Nazification of post-Hitler Germany took place in post-Stalinist Russia. Except for Beria and a few of his closest henchmen, none of the persons involved in Stalin's acknowledged crimes was tried and punished. The apparatus of the party, police, and administration remained virtually intact; so did the constitution, which vested sovereignty in a self-perpetuating, oligarchical party organization; and so, finally, did the economic structure, by virtue of which that organization controlled the industrial, agricultural, and commercial wealth of the country.

Internally, the new course involved a certain measure of relaxation. To shake the population out of its lethargy, the Soviet government took steps to raise living standards above their bare subsistence level. It restored some intellectual freedom. It also made a rather ambitious attempt to assure the average citizen, previously left to the mercies of the secret police, legal protection in offenses of a nonpolitical nature. The cult of Lenin replaced the cult of Stalin, and a conscious effort was made to reinfuse the Communist movement with the enthusiasm of its early years.

The greatest change occurred in the realm of foreign policy. It was imperative for the sake of Soviet security to emerge from the self-imposed isolation in which Stalin had placed the country. The actual foreign policy directives that Stalin's heirs adopted between 1953 and 1956 are not known. But subsequent Soviet actions permit us to reconstruct in broad outlines their principal features.

There can be little doubt that the new Soviet rulers resolved to terminate the Cold War and thereby to break up the whole political and military establishment that the Western powers had formed while it was in progress. Relations with the West were to be normalized to the point where the latter would not feel threatened, and therefore would consent to dismantling its network of air bases and military outposts, dissolving NATO and other regional defense organizations, and slowing down the pace of armaments. To promote this end, Khrushchev advanced in 1956 a novel theory of "peaceful coexistence." According to this theory, the ultimate triumph of the Communist cause in the world does not require a general war. Instead, it can be brought about by a gradual shift of economic (and, implicitly, military) hegemony from the "capitalist" to the "socialist" bloc, and the disintegration of the former from the force of internal contradictions. Although the main purpose of the peaceful coexistence formula was and continues to be neutralization of the Western defense effort, behind it probably lay also a genuine realization that atomic warfare could destroy all life on this planet, and war therefore was no longer feasible.

The rejection of general war did not preclude the possibility, indeed the desirability, of local wars. The new Soviet regime, like its predecessor, declared itself ready to support "just wars," especially wars of national liberation. The stated intention of the Eisenhower administration not to participate in small "brush-fire" conflicts but to rely on what it called "massive retaliation" by atomic weapons encouraged Soviet leaders to believe that they could undertake and assist such actions with impunity.

Beginning in 1955 Khrushchev and his government carried out a series of measures designed to give credibility to the peaceful coexistence formula. They evacuated Soviet troops from Finland, signed a peace treaty with Austria, normalized relations with West Germany, and initiated a program of international economic and cultural cooperation. They also suspended the vituperative propaganda campaign against the United States and dissolved the Communist International (Cominform), which Stalin had revived in 1947.

An integral feature of the peaceful coexistence policy were personal encounters between Soviet leaders and their Western counterparts. In July, 1955, on Soviet initiative, the first "summit conference" took place in Geneva. In September, 1959, Khrushchev visited the United States and held a three-day private meeting with President Eisenhower at Camp David, in Maryland. The official communiqué issued on the completion of the Camp David talks affirmed the resolve of both parties to settle "all outstanding international questions . . . not by application of force but by peaceful means through negotiations."

While pursuing a *détente* with the West, the Soviet Union launched a vigorous diplomatic and economic drive to establish a foothold in the Middle East. This area had been neglected by Stalin, who preferred to expand in Europe and East Asia. But now there were excellent reasons for a resumption of an offensive in this region. During the postwar decade, Great Britain and the other colonial powers had withdrawn from most of their Middle Eastern possessions (Chapter 31), yielding to numerous young and unstable national governments. These were perenially short of money and arms, and liable to be won over by a power willing to supply both. Furthermore, the emergence of the state of Israel in 1948 had created in the eastern Mediterranean a permanent fulcrum of unrest. A determined drive in support of the Arab cause stood a good chance of winning the Soviet Union millions of friends in this important strategic region.

From 1955 on, Khrushchev, as head of the party, and Nikolai Bulganin, as head of state, undertook a series of visits to the Middle East, ranging from Burma to Egypt. "Bulgy and Khrushy," as they came to be known, behaved on these journeys like two experienced American campaigners, waving to the crowds, delivering flattering speeches, bowing to local divinities, and, above all, promising economic and other aid. That these promises were not empty became obvious in September, 1955, when Gamal Abdel Nasser, the dictator of Egypt, announced the conclusion of an agreement with Czechoslovakia providing for substantial military aid to his country. From then on, Soviet influence in the Middle East, especially in the Arab world, increased rapidly.

The new Soviet policy in the so-called "third world" called for cooperation with governments that in Communist parlance were clearly "bourgeois-nationalist." In a sense it involved a betrayal of the local Communist movements pledged to overthrow these regimes. This was a cruel decision to take, but it was worth the gamble because nowhere were the Communist movements strong enough to seize power on their own. On the other hand, they stood a good chance of success in a broad popular front involving socialists and nationalists and directed against the "imperialist" powers. Once the third world was won over, the United States would find itself as isolated as the Soviet Union had been under Stalin.

The third element in the new foreign policy was a massive modernization program of the Soviet armed forces. Although Stalin had authorized the manufacture of atomic weapons, he tended to think in nineteenth-century strategic terms of territory and manpower. His successors adopted a new strategy, consonant with the military technology of an age of atomic warheads and ballistic missiles. After Stalin's death the modernization of the Soviet army, navy, and air force along these lines proceeded at full speed. Its costs were so huge that the promise

A 1954 incident in the continuing war in Vietnam: prisoners repair road damage blocking a French column.

of a genuine improvement in the country's living standards could not be fulfilled.

The new foreign policy contained elements that were not fully compatible. The aggressive drive to penetrate the Middle East on the one hand, and the modernization of the Soviet military establishment on the other, were not likely to promote a *détente* with the Western powers. The arming of Egypt, and even more significant, the launching in 1957 of an artificial satellite (*sputnik*)—the by-product of an intense effort by the Soviet army to develop military missiles—alarmed the United States and induced it to launch a major missile program of its own. Nor did Khrushchev's frequent threats, sometimes ominously Stalinist in tone, help matters.

In a survey of this kind it is not possible to treat events of the most recent period. Suffice it to say that the policy of the United States toward the Soviet Union since 1956 has represented a continuation of "containment" as modified by "peaceful coexistence." The United States is still committed to thwart, by force of arms if necessary, any Communist expansion. But it accepts, even if only tacitly, the Soviet contention that an all-out war between Russia and America is unthinkable. Hence, confrontations between the two blocs are no longer direct, as they had been at the height of the Stalinist Cold War, but indirect, through the intermediacy of third parties. With the accession of President John F. Kennedy in 1961 the United States abandoned the strategy of "massive retaliation," developing instead a mobile armed force able to challenge Communist forces wherever they threaten legitimate governments. All East-West conflicts since

1956 have been of such an indirect character: the Vietnamese War, in progress uninterruptedly since 1946, the two wars between Israel and its Soviet-backed Arab neighbors (1956 and 1967), and the so-called Cuban missile crisis of 1962.°

Polycentrism   The liberal course adopted by the Soviet regime after 1953 had profound repercussions on the relations between Moscow, on the one hand, and the satellite countries and affiliated foreign Communist movements on the other. The monolith that Stalin had sought to fashion out of his domains, and to a large extent had succeeded in fashioning, revealed after his death serious internal fissures. De-Stalinization had the effect of widening them and causing a breakdown of the unity of the Communist bloc. The "socialist camp," once unanimous in thought and action, disintegrated into a loose alliance with several centers, several theories, and several strategies.

As soon as it had gained the upper hand in Moscow, the "liberal faction," headed by Khrushchev, began to introduce reforms in the satellites. As in the Soviet Union itself, the satellite governments reduced the power of the security police, released from jail and concentration camps many political prisoners, relaxed censorship, and permitted economic reforms. Among those freed from prison were Communist leaders who had been confined on Stalin's orders for nationalistic, "Titoist" tendencies.

In the Soviet Union the population appreciated such liberal measures. But in the satellites the relaxation of rule only released the pent-up hatred of the Communist regimes and of the Soviet army which stood behind them. Beginning with 1953 a series of uprisings, which startlingly recalled the revolutions of 1848, shook Eastern Europe: they involved the same social elements—intellectuals and workers—and the same ideologies—nationalism in combination with liberalism or socialism. Only this time the enemy was not the conservative monarchy with its church and nobility but the Communist dictatorship with its bureaucracy and police.

The first of these uprisings broke out in June, 1953, in East Berlin, where the construction workers engaged in building the monumental Stalin Boulevard rose up in arms. Before long the disturbance developed into a general anti-Communist revolt. Soviet armored units brought out to quell the melee were showered with pavement stones and rocks. It did not take them long, however, to restore order.

The resentment that smouldered throughout the satellite world erupted next in Poland. It began in Poznan, where in the summer of 1956 a large number of workers engaged in an illegal strike. As in East Berlin, what had begun as an industrial work stoppage quickly transformed itself into a broad protest movement against the Communist regime, with various disaffected elements gathering around the strikers. Fanned by intellectuals, the spirit of rebellion spread to other Polish cities and penetrated the party apparatus itself. In October, 1956, the Central Committee of the Polish Communist party fired from its membership the most notorious "conservatives" and elected as its First Chairman Wladyslaw Gomulka, a prominent Communist whom Stalin had jailed for his alleged nationalism.

° In Cuba, when a direct conflict between the United States and the Soviet Union seemed imminent, the Soviet Union quit the field.

The Soviet government did not quite know how to react to these developments. The liberal course taken by the Polish Communists was, of course, in line with the Soviet government's own desires. But in the satellites the conservatives were the very people who accepted subservience to Russia, whereas the liberals were nationalists and wanted genuine independence. Khrushchev and his colleagues procrastinated to see how things developed. When the appointment of Gomulka was imminent, the leaders of the Soviet government made a dramatic journey to Poland. To forestall a possible Polish break with the Communist bloc, they seem to have issued strong warnings, coupled with threats of military intervention. But Gomulka expressed his unflinching loyalty to the Communist bloc and readiness to accept Soviet guidance in foreign policy dealings. This prudence apparently saved the Polish Communist government from being overthrown by the Soviet army units stationed in Poland.

The greatest of the anti-Communist revolutions occurred in October, 1956, in Hungary. Here the party leadership was violently split between conservative and liberal factions, the latter demanding greater freedom and greater autonomy from Moscow. The quarrel among the leaders disorganized the party and state machinery and led to the collapse of authority. Soon throughout the country Communist offices were under attack. The population was particularly savage with the secret police, whose officials it sometimes literally tore to pieces. On a number of occasions Soviet army units came to the assistance of the Hungarian

Hungarians burn pictures of Stalin and other Communist memorabilia during their abortive revolt in 1956.

police, but as the Hungarian army swung to the support of the rebels it had to ask for reinforcements. At the end of October a new liberal-national government headed by the Communist Imre Nagy came into existence. Nagy announced the abolition of the one-party system and Hungary's withdrawal from the Warsaw Pact, the Communist counterpart of NATO. As soon as a sufficiently strong Soviet army contingent had been assembled, it swung into action. A savage war ensued between Soviet divisions and the Hungarian army, supported by worker and peasant detachments. After the rebels had been crushed, a new Communist regime was installed. Nagy and the generals who participated in the uprising were subsequently shot, and many other Hungarians suffered imprisonment. Nearly 200,000 Hungarians took advantage of the revolution to seek refuge abroad.

After the suppression of the Hungarian uprising the situation in Eastern Europe stabilized. The failure of the United States to come to the aid of the East German and Hungarian rebels, despite its commitment to "roll back" communism, discouraged any thought of further armed action. The nationalists in these areas now preferred to concentrate their attention on slow economic, cultural, and political gains within the Communist framework. The Soviet Union demanded and obtained from its satellites subservience in all matters affecting foreign policy and military strategy. But it was not averse to a certain amount of internal liberalization and even nationalism, and it no longer insisted on economic mastery.

The loosening of control over the satellites was accompanied by a similar process within the international Communist movement. Leaders of Communist parties outside the Soviet bloc, especially in countries where they had a wide following, began to demand equality of status. In 1956 the head of the Italian Communist party, Palmiro Togliatti, called for frank recognition of the fact that the Soviet Union had no right to dictate policies to Communist parties abroad. "The Soviet model should no longer be obligatory," he said; "the complex of the system is becoming polycentric, and in the communist movement itself one can no longer speak of a single guide." The notion of "polycentrism" gradually gained acceptance, largely because of the general recognition that only by adopting utmost flexibility in dealing with local situations could the local Communist movements restore their waning fortunes.

Notwithstanding the violence in East Berlin and Hungary, and the relative emancipation of Poland, the relaxation of control over the satellites and foreign Communist parties proved on the whole successful. The satellite governments broadened their base of support, while the international Communist movement rid itself of the heavy onus of being a Soviet tool.

The fatal flaw in the whole post-Stalinist foreign policy was that it led to a violent clash between Russia and China which split the Communist movement in two. It is certain that Russia's rulers not only did not desire such a clash but sought at all costs to avoid it. But once it got under way, they were unable to stop it from taking its natural course.

Sino-Soviet friction may have existed earlier, but it became overt only in 1960. The Chinese Communists were watching with profound suspicion the Soviet pursuit of "peaceful coexistence," in particular as it affected relations between the Soviet Union and the United States. Being versed in Communist theory, the Chinese must have known what the concept meant and why it was invoked. But they seem to have suspected all along that behind the high-flown language of the new diplomacy the Soviet Union was arranging with the United States to divide the world into spheres of influence. What particularly chagrined them was Soviet readiness to negotiate with the United States limitations on the spread of nuclear weapons. In their view the inevitable outcome of the American-Soviet *détente* was the reduction of China to the status of a second-rate power.

The first open Chinese criticism of Khrushchev and his foreign policy followed the Camp David meeting. In early 1960 official Chinese organs stated that China did not feel bound by international agreements concluded without its participation. Next, they questioned the whole Soviet theory of "peaceful coexistence," restating the Leninist theory that communism could not triumph in the world without an ultimate and conclusive military conflict. In one particularly virulent statement the Chinese Communists asserted that a Third World War, involving atomic weapons, was not to be feared because it would cause the ultimate collapse of capitalism.

Gradually other sources of friction developed between the two countries. The Chinese resented the economic aid that the Soviet Union extended to India, partly because they had aggressive designs on that country (which they attacked in a brief war in 1959) and partly because such aid diminished whatever assistance the Russians could furnish them. Soon recriminations over frontiers also made themselves heard, the Chinese laying claim to all of Mongolia and even Central Asia.

As the conflict deepened, the Chinese advanced their own theory of Communist action. Following Lenin's tactics in 1900–1903 within the Russian Social-Democratic movement, they deliberately broke with the moderate (Soviet) wing in the Communist movement, accusing the Russians of having turned into Social-Democratic opportunists. The world, as Stalin had said, was indeed divided into two camps: the progressive and the reactionary. Soviet Russia had joined the latter camp, and was as much an enemy of the working class as was the United States. There was to be no peaceful cooperation with bourgeois national governments in the underdeveloped countries but a direct onslaught on them. The method advocated was guerrilla wars, based largely on the peasantry, which would isolate and bring down city-based governments, exactly as they did in China in 1947–1949. To wean aggressive elements away from Soviet influence, the Chinese leaders have sought everywhere to split the Communist parties and form small but dynamic organizations dedicated to their ideas. They have also aided, to the limit of their modest resources, guerrilla movements in various areas of the world, including Central Africa, the Middle East, and Vietnam.

The Sino-Soviet split derives from differences not of aims but of means. Nevertheless, given communism's stress on monolithic organization and unity of theory, it marks a very deep crisis in the movement. What used to be a conflict between two blocs—a Western and an Eastern—has turned into a more complicated struggle. This struggle is bound to affect profoundly the character of communism and its relations with the rest of the world, and may therefore be regarded as one of the most significant events of the twentieth century.

31

Europe and the World

Viewed on the scale of global history, the predominance of Western peoples and Western culture is a relatively recent phenomenon. Its origins date back to the end of the fifteenth century, when a sudden outburst of maritime exploration carried Europeans to the remotest parts of the globe and enabled them to link to themselves and to each other hitherto isolated communities and continents. The hegemony of Western nations in the post-Renaissance era derives from the fact that it is they who first made real the potential unity of the world. Later, thanks to the development in Europe of science and technology, Europe's leadership became virtually unassailable.

Natural and permanent as the hegemony of the West may have appeared when at its height in the nineteenth century, it is obvious today that it was neither. The attitudes, ideas, and techniques that had originally assured the West its preponderance could be learned by others and turned against it. Indeed, since the beginning of the present century the global position of Europe has steadily eroded. Around 1900 Western nations were still scrambling for the last unclaimed portions of Africa and Asia; half a century later they were abandoning with alacrity everything their ancestors had conquered since the fifteenth century. Today their direct political control is with a few exceptions (notably in the Soviet Union and South Africa) limited to Europe and to areas in which Europeans constitute an overwhelming majority of the population.

In a sense, therefore, one may speak of the four-centuries-old domination of the world by the West as finished. But such a statement calls for considerable qualification. Politically, the world hegemony of the West has indeed come to an end, and it is difficult to conceive how it can ever be restored. But economically and culturally the primacy of the West, far from being done for, has not even been diminished. Quite the contrary: by surrendering its political powers the West has succeeded in permeating other civilizations with its way of life to a far greater extent than before. The real Westernization of the world has taken place only after the West has given up its political hegemony over it.

The relationship between the West and the world at large is a subject of great subtlety which must not be dismissed with simplistic generalizations about the "end of imperialism." For better or worse, all modern culture is Western culture, and the contemporary non-European world, even when rebelling against Europe, is assimilating its values and copying its ways.

In this chapter we shall discuss two related topics: the withdrawal of the imperial powers from their colonies, and the adjustment of Europe to its changed position in the world.

The Causes of De-colonization

Western authority in the colonies declined for two principal reasons: internecine conflicts among the imperial powers, and the emergence of a European-type nationalism among the native élites. The two factors reinforced each other, un-

One example of the West's cultural influence is the new Indian city of Chandigarh, the capital of Punjab, whose public buildings bear the distinctive stamp of the Swiss-French architect Le Corbusier. This is the entrance portico of the Assembly building.

Thinly disguised and chanting "Africa for the Africans!" in unison, China's Mao Tse-tung (left) and Russia's Khrushchev enter the African power vacuum; a 1964 Dutch cartoon.

dermining among the subject peoples that awe of the white man which had furnished the psychological foundation of colonial rule.

The relative ease with which Europeans had conquered and subjugated overseas peoples was due not only to their military superiority but also to the absence on the part of the native peoples of an inner resistance to foreign rule. In their world, in which past and present generations mingled imperceptibly and magic permeated all life, the natives of Africa and Asia often regarded white men as a reincarnation of dead ancestors, come to provide help and protection. A French sociologist, having analyzed closely the mind of the inhabitants of Madagascar, concluded that the net effect of colonial rule was to make them totally dependent on their rulers. The natives, regarding their white conquerors from the beginning as superior beings because they were immune to magic, developed toward them a profound sense of inferiority. In actual practice, the psychological relationship between the domineering master and the subservient native resembles that established between Prospero and Caliban in Shakespeare's *The Tempest.*°

As long as the Western nations acted in harmony and beat down all opposition to their overseas expansion, this sense of awe, dependence, and inferiority remained intact. But at the beginning of the twentieth century it began to break down. The victory the Japanese gained over the Russians in the war of 1904–1905 made a tremendous impression on the non-Western world because it showed

°O. Mannoni, *Prospero and Caliban: The Psychology of Colonization* (1956).

for the first time that an Oriental people, properly armed and led, could humiliate a great Western power. So, to a lesser extent, did the stubborn Turkish resistance against Italy in the Tripolitan War (1911–1912). World War I, in which the white powers fought and slaughtered each other, and even had to import black troops to help them out, did little to enhance their prestige overseas. But nothing lowered this prestige more than the Second World War. The speed and almost contemptuous ease with which the Japanese disposed of Western armies and navies and seized Western colonial possessions irreparably damaged the reputation of the West throughout Asia. Europeans were now seen as having lost the "mandate of heaven." After the war it became simply impossible to re-establish Western authority in colonies that had been under Japanese occupation and difficult in those that adjoined them.

As Western prestige in the colonies waned, the sentiment of nationalism gained ground. Its leading exponents were intellectuals trained in Western schools, who in the course of their education had absorbed the European ethos with its stress on historicism, national culture, social equality, statehood, and other typical nineteenth-century ideas. Such intellectuals found themselves in a highly ambivalent situation. By virtue of their Western upbringing and outlook, they no longer fitted into the traditional society in which they were born; and yet, because of their race, they could not fully integrate into the ruling white society. To overcome its estrangement the native intelligentsia turned nationalistic, seeking on the one hand to sever its country's dependence on the imperial metropolis and on the other to transform its own peoples in accord with a Western model.

The colonial powers, of course, were not unaware that the education they were providing to the native élite could have such unwelcome consequences. But most of them continued to furnish education nevertheless: the British because they considered it necessary to train cadres of civil servants for ultimate self-rule, the French and the Russians because they hoped by its means to assimilate culturally their colonial élites. The Belgians and Portuguese followed a different policy, seeking to prevent the emergence of a native intelligentsia by confining education in their possessions to the elementary and vocational levels.

A powerful factor in the breakdown of the Western position in the colonial areas was also the anti-imperialist propaganda waged by the totalitarian powers. Both the Communists and the Nazis (and to a considerable extent the Japanese as well) vigorously attacked Western imperialism in Asia and Africa, although they engaged in far more brutal forms of domination along their own borders. This propaganda tended to lessen respect for Europeans and to intensify local nationalism.

The Progress of De-colonization

Britain was the first imperial power to recognize the changes that had occurred in the spirit of its colonial peoples and to acknowledge the need for adjustments in its imperial constitution.

In the 1920s and 1930s the idea of the empire was very much alive in Britain. The shrinking of its export markets, especially during the international depression, forced it to think in terms of maximum self-sufficiency. Free trade was given up and some external tariffs imposed (1932). The empire now appeared to provide a potentially gigantic internal market. In 1932, at the Ottawa Conference, Britain accepted the principle of imperial preference advocated earlier in the century by Joseph Chamberlain. By virtue of the Ottawa agreements, the Dominions agreed to offer advantageous terms for entry of British manufactured goods in return for preferential access to Britain of their foodstuffs and other raw materials. Thus, for the first time since protectionism had been abandoned a century earlier, the British Empire became something of a formal economic entity.

Simultaneously, the British government recognized formally what it had acknowledged informally for some time, namely that the Dominions were not bound by laws enacted in the British Parliament. The Statute of Westminster, passed in 1931, affirmed that Dominion legislatures enjoyed complete sovereignty. In this statute Britain and its Dominions were defined as "autonomous communities" within the British Empire, equal in status and "united by a common allegiance to the Crown." During the 1930s the term "British Commonwealth of Nations," as more accurately describing the new imperial arrangement, gradually superseded "British Empire."

The framers of the Statute of Westminster and the Ottawa agreements believed that they were laying the groundwork for a new and lasting kind of imperial relationship. Their expectation was that as the colonies inhabited by non-white peoples became politically and economically mature, they too would rise to the status of Dominions, and in time the whole empire would become transformed into a world-wide association of free and equal partners.

Under conditions other than those prevailing in the twentieth century, this noble vision might well have been realized. But it needed time, and time is something history rarely grants. The outbreak of World War II, less than a decade after the imperial reforms of 1931–1932, cut the ground from under the long-term program. Britain emerged from the war so impoverished that it could no longer afford to carry the financial burden of administering and defending most of its colonial possessions and therefore had to cut down drastically its imperial commitments.° Between 1946 and 1948 Britain pulled out from most of its Far Eastern and Middle Eastern possessions, proclaiming its intention of ultimately withdrawing from those remaining in Africa as well. This withdrawal was, on the whole, accomplished voluntarily and under the pressure of domestic economic considerations. But the speed with which the nationalist movement developed in the colonial areas after the war left no doubt that unless the British departed willingly, they would eventually be ejected. This consideration played no small part in Britain's resolve.

The critical decision concerned India, the keystone of the British Empire. During the war Indian nationalists of the Congress party showed disquieting sympathies for the Japanese and even a willingness to collaborate with their armies which had invaded and occupied a part of India. To prevent its defection, Britain promised to grant India independence after the war. In August, 1947, the promise was made good with the proclamation of the Indian Independence Act. The subcontinent subsequently split in two halves: a Hindu-dominated India, and a predominantly Muslim Pakistan. The cleavage occurred

°There is no better argument against the economic interpretation of imperialism (Chapter 21) than the fact that Britain sought colonies when it was rich and abandoned them when it became poor.

amidst mutual carnage between the two religious groups. In 1948 Ceylon and Burma also received independence. India, Pakistan, and Ceylon became Dominions within the British Commonwealth—a status that imposed no restrictions on their sovereignty, but allowed them to gather handsome benefits from trading within the pound sterling area.

Robert Capa photographed Israeli militia marching toward the front during the Palestinian War of 1948.

While withdrawing from the Middle East, Britain also liquidated, though more gradually, its holdings in the eastern Mediterranean. The greatest trouble occurred over Palestine, which Britain administered under a League of Nations mandate (it had been taken from the Turks during the First World War). Since the early years of the century an increasing number of European Jewish Zionists had migrated to Palestine in the hope of establishing there a national home for themselves and their persecuted brethren. They purchased fallow lands from the Arabs and by dint of hard work and modern techniques transformed them into flourishing agricultural communities. In 1917, through the so-called Balfour Declaration, Britain pledged itself to assist the creation in Palestine of "a national home for the Jewish people." Later on, however, Britain found it difficult to honor this pledge because the Jewish influx inflamed Arab nationalists, who viewed the Jews not as refugees from Western persecution but as Western colonists come to push them out of their ancestral lands. In view of the importance of Arab good will, Britain tried to thwart Zionist designs and restrict the flow of Jewish immigrants. After World War II and the unprecedented losses that they had suffered in it, the Jews became desperate for a place of refuge. They applied pressure on the British and, when this did not work, resorted to terrorism. In 1948 Britain announced its intention of withdrawing from Palestine. The United Nations voted a partition plan creating two states, one Jewish, the other Arab. The Arab countries rejected this plan and formed a coalition which invaded Palestine, seeking to occupy it and prevent the formation of a Jewish state. They were soundly beaten by an amateur Jewish army. The state of Israel, which came into existence in the midst of this war, has since been recognized by the whole international community, with the exception of the Arab countries.

During the course of 1947–1948 Britain liquidated the "imperial lifeline" that it had acquired with such effort during the preceding two centuries. The transfer of power to the local population occurred earlier than British imperial planners had anticipated, and for this reason in a number of areas such as India and Palestine it caused a collapse of public order. But on the whole the transition from colonial status to independence in the British Empire proceeded smoothly. Having trained honest and responsible civil servants in territories under their control, the British had officials to whom to entrust authority when the time came to withdraw. This was least true of Africa, which the British evacuated rather hastily in the 1950s, before such local cadres could be trained.

In the 1960s all that remained of the British colonial empire were strategic naval and air bases, and even these are now in the process of liquidation. The British Commonwealth survives essentially as the world's second largest trading area, enjoying preferential tariffs and employing the pound sterling.

With the exception of the United States, which in 1946 promptly granted independence to the Philippines, its one major colony, the other imperial powers surrendered their possessions much more reluctantly than did Britain.

The French Empire rested on very different principles from those of the British. Britain thought in terms of ultimate self-rule, whereas France thought in terms of ultimate assimilation. The ideal of French imperialists was not a commonwealth of many free and equal states but a single community of white, black, and yellow Frenchmen. Unlike the British, the French practiced little or no racial discrimination, regarding as one of themselves any person who had acquired French culture. These considerations explain why, if for the British the postwar transfer of sovereignty to the colonies involved advancing their timetable, for the French it involved abandonment of their whole conception of themselves as a world-wide, multi-racial civilization.

In 1946 the French government proclaimed the establishment of the "French Union" (*L'Union française*), which it defined as a voluntary association of France and its overseas territories. The idea behind the Union resembled that underlying the British Commonwealth. But France was not prepared to recognize the right of its possessions to self-rule, insisting that they exercise their political rights within the institutions of metropolitan France. Rather than constitute their own legislatures, the colonial areas were to send representatives to the French parliament.

This arrangement did not suit the nationalists in the major French possessions. They demanded self-rule, and when this was refused they took up arms. In
1946 a savage colonial war broke out in Indo-China (Vietnam), where the nationalist forces were directed by a veteran of the Communist International, Ho
Chi Minh. In 1954 the French were defeated and forced to withdraw. Chastened
by this experience, France in 1956 conceded independence to two of its North
African colonies, Tunisia and Morocco. But in Algeria such a solution was
thwarted by the objections of the large resident European population. When
self-rule was refused to the Algerian Muslims, they launched a guerrilla campaign. An extremely brutal civil war ensued, whose repercussions even threatened
to cause a breakdown of order in metropolitan France. In 1958 the French army
in Algeria staged a coup which overthrew the Fourth Republic and brought to
power General de Gaulle. De Gaulle originally won the sympathies of the army
by intimating his support for a French Algeria, but as soon as he came to power
he reversed his stand and offered the Algerians independence (1959–1962).

After withdrawal from its other colonies in Africa the French Empire dissolved
into a trading community, loosely tied by allegiance to the franc.

The least enlightened colonial policy was conducted by the smaller European
powers, such as Holland, Belgium, and Portugal. The Dutch, upon their return
to the East Indies, encountered a powerful nationalist movement organized during the war by the Japanese occupants. In 1945 the local nationalists proclaimed
the independence of Indonesia and launched a guerrilla campaign against the

*Algerian nationalists, photo-
graphed in the capital city of
Algiers, celebrate their independence from France in 1962.*

MARC RIBOUD-MAGNUM

The anarchy in the Congo following the Belgian withdrawal was accompanied by a threat of famine. Here, a Swedish soldier attempts to maintain order at a UN food-distribution center in 1960.

Dutch. The latter at first tried to resist by force of arms, then sought a compromise by offering Indonesia something close to dominion status, but finally recognized their defeat and withdrew (1954).

The Belgians in the Congo conducted what is usually described as a paternalistic colonial policy. Their aim was to raise the material level of the native population but at the same time to prevent any political ambitions from striking root among them. In 1960, when the Congo appeared on the verge of a major revolt and the Belgians decided to evacuate it, there were in the entire area only a dozen or so natives with a college education. No wonder that the precipitous Belgian withdrawal was followed by anarchy. The Portuguese to this day pursue in their African colony of Angola a colonial policy generally similar to that of the Belgians.

The liquidation of the Italian and Japanese empires during the war, and of the British, French, Dutch, and Belgian empires after it, left only one major empire in the world, the Russian. In the Soviet Union the Russians constitute approximately one-half the population. They rule over 100 million non-Russians, originally conquered by the imperial government, including 45 million Ukrainians and 30 million Muslims. Soviet imperial policy, since the Revolution as before, follows the French model: it promotes the economic and educational progress of its subject peoples while depriving them of any meaningful self-rule. In the long run, the Soviet government expects its subject peoples to be assimilated and become Russified.

A Europe deprived of its colonies and wedged between the more powerful United States and Soviet Union no longer could afford the luxury of division into a multitude of sovereign, contending states. If Europe was to maintain its identity and avoid becoming a satellite of one or the other of its two giant neighbors, it had to unite.

The process of European integration, which began shortly after the end of World War II, was inspired by a political ideal—the United States of Europe—but it was launched on its way by economic exigencies. The post-World War II integration of Europe resembles closely the unification of Germany in the nineteenth century, where a customs union (*Zollverein*, Chapter 13) also preceded political union. In the catastrophic situation in which Europe found itself after the war, it became obvious even to the most unsentimental businessman that the retention of internal tariff barriers would fatally handicap European countries in any competition with the United States and the Soviet Union, each with the labor force, market, and capital of nearly 200 million people. As a result of this realization (and no little American prompting) the wheels of history, which for a century and a half had driven the countries of Europe further and further in the direction of political and economic self-sufficiency, unexpectedly reversed themselves. Europe today is more united than it has ever been since the emergence of the democratic national state at the end of the eighteenth century.

PHASE ONE: THE MARSHALL PLAN

The initial impetus toward economic integration came from the United States. It took the shape of a massive scheme of economic assistance, the European Recovery Program, popularly known as the Marshall Plan, which originated in the spring of 1947, a few weeks after the proclamation of the Truman Doctrine (Chapter 30). This was a time when the growing disenchantment with Soviet behavior had induced Washington to undertake a general reappraisal of its policy toward the Soviet Union and to assume world-wide responsibility for protecting the integrity and security of independent states from the Communist threat. General George C. Marshall, the Secretary of State, had returned in April from Moscow after another futile meeting of foreign ministers. He now became convinced that the Soviet Union not only had no desire to cooperate in promoting European economic recovery, but was interested in positively preventing such recovery in order to improve the chances of the Western European Communist parties. Marshall instructed the newly formed Policy Planning Council of the Department of State, headed by George F. Kennan, to formulate a broad proposal on how best to cope with the problems of the European economy and the attendant political dangers.

In their recommendations Kennan and his colleagues urged that the government be guided not by a desire to combat communism but by a desire to eliminate "the economic maladjustment which makes European society vulnerable to exploitation by any and all totalitarian governments." In other words, the need was not for stop-gap aid to neutralize momentary Communist influence, but for a long-range program designed to revive Europe economically. Essential to the success of such a program was active European participation and inter-European cooperation:

It would be neither fitting nor efficacious for this government to undertake to draw up unilaterally and to promulgate formally on its own initiative a program designed to place Western Europe on its feet economically. This is the business of the Europeans. The formal initiative must come from Europe; and Europeans must bear the basic responsibility for it. . . . The program which this country is asked to support must be a joint one, agreed to by several European nations. While it may be linked to individual national programs . . . it must, for psychological and political, as well as economic, reasons, be an internationally agreed program. The request for our support must come as a joint request from a group of friendly nations, not as a series of isolated and individual appeals.°

On the basis of these recommendations General Marshall, in an address at the Harvard commencement in June, 1947, issued an invitation to the European states to formulate a common recovery program to present to the United States government.

The offer was taken up promptly. The British, French, and Italian governments immediately instituted consultations, in which fourteen additional countries subsequently joined. (Poland and Czechoslovakia also expressed a desire to participate in these talks, but were prohibited from doing so by Stalin.) Before long the seventeen countries submitted a joint proposal scheduled for a four-year period and budgeted for $22 billion. President Truman requested this sum from Congress, which cut it down to $17 billion. During the four years that the European Recovery Program was in operation (1948–1952), the United States actually spent about $12 billion, half of which went to three countries (Great Britain, France, and Germany).

After the Marshall Plan had been authorized the participating countries founded an Organization of European Economic Cooperation (OEEC) to distribute Marshall Plan funds and to facilitate economic activity among member states. The OEEC became a rudimentary apparatus of economic coordination, an institution which, although not specifically designed for that end, taught the sovereign states to think and act in an all-European rather than a national fashion.

Aid under the Marshall Plan was extended in two forms, as outright grants or as loans. In general, funds for articles of immediate consumption, such as food or fuel, were given in the form of grants, while purchases of equipment were financed by loans. Private enterprise in both the United States and Europe was heavily involved. More than half the monies appropriated under the Marshall Plan were spent inside the United States, stimulating productivity and providing jobs during the period of postwar readjustment.

The results of the Marshall Plan were spectacular. Two years after its initiation the productivity of Western Europe exceeded its prewar average by 25 percent; at its termination, in 1952, productivity was twice that of 1938. The European dollar gap—the difference between dollars earned and dollars spent—was significantly reduced. In the remarkably short period of four years Europe, which had seemed on the verge of total economic collapse, had not only recovered but had launched what turned out to be the greatest boom in its history.

°Quoted in George F. Kennan, *Memoirs, 1925–1950* (1967).

Viewed from the perspective of its short-range interests, it was not to the advantage of the United States that Europe should recover its productive capacity or closely coordinate its economies. A vigorous, coordinated Europe was certain to become America's competitor in world markets. This was so obvious that a large part of the European public at first doubted the intentions of the United States, suspecting that its real purpose in launching the Marshall Plan was to seize control of the European economy. But in reality the thinking of American statesmen who had formulated and executed the plan was different. They acted on the sound commercial assumption that a prosperous neighbor was not only a competitor but also a customer; that is, that in the long run the United States stood more to gain from trading with a well-to-do Europe than from supporting a weak and dependent one. The fear of communism played its part, but it was not the main motive behind the European Recovery Program and does not vitiate the fact that the Marshall Plan was one of the most imaginative and constructive acts in human history, an instance of enlightened self-interest at its best.

PHASE TWO: THE COMMON MARKET

The Marshall Plan initiated Europe's economic *cooperation*; the next step was its economic *integration*. This was conceived in the shadow of the Marshall Plan, and saw the light of day in 1957 with the creation of the European Economic Community (EEC), better known as the Common Market.

The dream of a united Europe goes back to the medieval ideal of the restored Roman Empire; Napoleon played on it to justify his conquests, and so did Hitler. It was a genuine aspiration of those who loved Western civilization and feared its self-destruction from nationalistic conflicts. There had been a Pan-European movement during the interwar period, but the time then was not propitious, and its influence remained confined to a small body of visionaries. After World War II the movement revived. It now gained a number of proponents among eminent statesmen, including Winston Churchill, German Chancellor Konrad Adenauer, and several high French, Belgian, and Dutch officials. With this support a political movement aiming at a federation of European states actually got under way in 1948–1949. At this time, a Council of Europe was set up at Strasbourg to serve as the proto-parliament of a united Europe. But the movement for political consolidation never got far because of vehement British opposition. Britain still had a strong aversion to surrendering any part of its sovereignty and an equally deep fear of confronting a united Continent. Moreover, the Labour government, in power during the crucial years 1945–1951, had additional reasons for not wishing to become involved in a supra-national organization in which non-socialists would constitute a great majority.

Having failed in their political aspirations, the Pan-Europeans succeeded in their economic ones. The first genuine accomplishments achieved by the proponents of a united Europe came as an accidental by-product of Franco-German rivalry. The French viewed with mounting anxiety the rapid recovery of German industry after 1948. Initially, they proposed to control and limit the industrial productivity of Germany so as to prevent its eventual remilitarization, but this proposal was vetoed by the United States, which considered a strong German industry vital to the economic recovery of Europe. In 1950 the potential German military threat became acute, for in that year (the Korean War had just

A 1947 Russian cartoon, "The Modern Trojan Horse," sees American aid dollars threatening Europe's sovereignty.

broken out) the United States decided on rearming Germany. Although the new German divisions were to be integrated into NATO forces, from the French point of view the mere re-emergence of a German army was enough to raise frightening specters.

To deal with this problem French Foreign Minister Robert Schuman in 1950 formulated an interesting proposal. As a means of forestalling a future war between the two countries he proposed a merger of the French and German steel and coal industries, the two indispensable ingredients of modern military technology. His scheme called for the creation of a supra-national "High Authority," an administering body free from control or even influence by the governments of the two respective countries, which would direct the pricing, marketing, and distribution of their joint steel and coal output.

The Schuman Plan was ratified by the French and German parliaments. In 1951 Italy, Belgium, the Netherlands, and Luxemburg also subscribed to it. In this manner a six-nation European Coal and Steel Community came into existence, whose member countries agreed to transfer a small part of their sovereignty to the High Authority. Britain was invited to join the Community but declined.

The integration of the coal and steel industries worked so well for all concerned that in 1955 the six participating countries resumed negotiations to see whether they could not further expand their economic cooperation. These talks culminated in the signing of the Rome Treaty in March of 1957, establishing the European Economic Community. In the process of European integration the Rome Treaty represents the most important milestone. It made provision for

A series of talks between French President de Gaulle (at microphone) and West German Chancellor Adenauer (left) symbolized the postwar rapprochement between France and Germany.

ERICH LESSING-MAGNUM

the gradual elimination over a period of twelve to fifteen years of all tariffs among the six participating countries. When the process was completed, goods, capital, and labor were to move freely from one country to another, undeterred by frontiers. The Treaty of Rome laid the foundations of a free trade area inhabited by 170 million people—a market nearly equal to that of the United States. While doing away with tariffs among themselves, the signatories undertook to raise uniform tariffs for goods originating outside the EEC. In addition to a free trade area the six also agreed on several other joint ventures, including a common atomic energy effort (EURATOM).

Great Britain had a chance to become associated with the Common Market but once more decided against involvement in Continental Europe. The main reason for its decision was the obligation of states that joined the EEC to adopt common external tariffs. Acceptance of this obligation conflicted with Britain's commitment to extend preferential tariffs to its Dominions. It would have spelled the end of the whole idea of the British Commonwealth of Nations and transformed Britain into a purely European power. Britain was not as yet prepared to acquiesce to such a policy, so contrary to its entire historic tradition. Torn between its allegiance to the empire and its craving for access to the West European market, Britain opted for the empire (for the time being, at any rate).

Instead of joining the EEC, Britain hastily organized in 1959 a European Free Trade Association, consisting of, in addition to itself, Sweden, Norway, Denmark, Switzerland, Austria, and Portugal. The members of this association pledged themselves to abolish gradually all tariffs against each other, but they were not obligated to adopt common tariffs against non-members—a provision that left Britain free to retain its preferential tariffs for Commonwealth states.

The British decision not to join the Common Market was a major blunder that had dire consequences for Britain's economy. The Free Trade Association added only 38 million potential customers to Britain's market, whereas the EEC would have added 170 million. After ratification of the Rome Treaty, American capital shifted from the United Kingdom to Western Europe, where potential growth was much greater. The output of industrial goods and the exports of the Common Market countries indeed grew more rapidly than did those of the Free Trade Association. In the early 1960s, realizing its mistake, the British government applied for admission to the Common Market, but its application was vetoed by French President de Gaulle (in 1963 and again in 1967).

The success of the EEC inspired the establishment of two other free trade areas. The Communist countries had since 1949 a common economic organization (COMECON) originally created as a counterweight to the Marshall Plan. In 1960 the countries of South America formed the Latin American Free Trade Area. Neither of these blocs, however, has yet had much success, because the economies of their member states are neither as complementary nor as dynamic as are those of the West European economic community.

Neo-liberalism

In the 1950s liberal political and economic doctrines, seemingly dead and buried during the interwar period, underwent an unexpected resurrection. The experiences with authoritarian regimes had a sobering effect on Europeans and made them more tolerant than before of the shortcomings of the liberal system. The

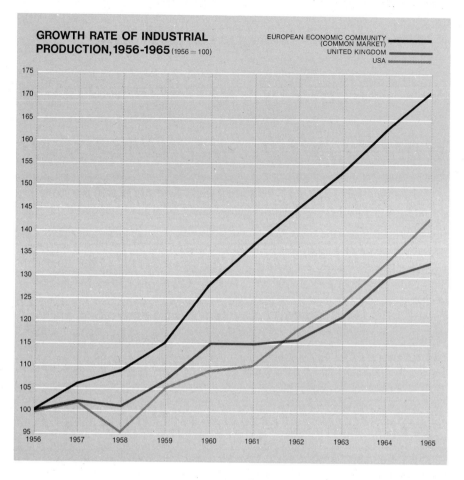

GROWTH RATE OF INDUSTRIAL PRODUCTION, 1956-1965 (1956 = 100)

EUROPEAN ECONOMIC COMMUNITY (COMMON MARKET)
UNITED KINGDOM
USA

United States, which in the immediate postwar years had had an overwhelming influence on Europe, encouraged and promoted this tendency. After the totalitarian "wave of the future" had receded, the older liberal values re-emerged surprisingly intact.

When we speak of a renascence of liberalism after World War II, we do not have in mind, of course, the classical, Manchester-type liberalism of the mid-nineteenth century (Chapter 13), but rather that liberalism modified by socialism which made its appearance later in the century (Chapter 20). This neo-liberalism adhered to the basic premises of the older doctrine—individualism, law, parliamentary institutions—but it no longer rejected state intervention. It regarded as essential government involvement in the life of society, especially in regulating its economic and social affairs.

After the immediate post-World War II anarchy had been overcome, the majority of voters in Western Europe expressed their preference for parties espousing such ideologies. In Germany and Italy—the two countries that had suffered most from the oppressive weight of regimentation—political power was entrusted to Christian Democratic parties. These were middle-of-the road groupings committed to a modernized version of traditional liberalism. The Social Democrats, the principal opposition party in Germany, became hardly distinguishable from their rivals after 1959, when they formally disassociated themselves from Marxism and disavowed social revolution. In France the Fourth Republic that emerged in 1944 continued to suffer from the same parliamentary instability that had plagued its predecessor. In 1958, however, the military *coup d'état* originating in Algeria brought to power General de Gaulle, the leader of the Free French movement during the war. On de Gaulle's initiative, a new constitution was formulated which greatly strengthened the executive and introduced the American principle of direct popular elections for the Presidency. In its domestic politics the government of the Fifth Republic has shown itself to be fundamentally liberal. Finally, in Great Britain the Labour government which came to power in 1945 carried out an ambitious program of nationalization of heavy industry and social welfare. But as Britain's international economic position deteriorated, experimentation was abandoned, and succeeding administrations conducted a more moderate policy. The 1950s and 1960s thus have witnessed throughout Western Europe a re-emergence of political tendencies which had dominated before World War I. The basis of the neo-liberal state is an alliance of government and big business for promoting productivity and trade.

The revival of liberalism occurred against a background of unprecedented prosperity. After 1950 the economy of the West underwent an expansion that exceeded considerably anything experienced during the great boom of the nineteenth century. The annual rate of growth in the output of goods produced in the West (including the United States) had been 2.7 percent between 1870 and 1913; between 1950 and 1960 it averaged 3.9 percent. The growth was especially rapid among countries of the Common Market, showing during this period a rate of 4.4 percent in France, 5.9 percent in Italy, and an incredible 7.6 percent in Germany.°

This "economic miracle" had several causes. Among them were generous United States help in the form of loans and outright grants, the great reservoir of skills and the discipline of Western workers, and the expansion of the market by the reduction of tariffs. No little credit is also due to the farsighted steps begun during World War II to prevent another drying up of the sources of liquid capital such as had occurred in the 1930s. In 1944, at a conference held at Bretton Woods in New Hampshire, the Western Allies had established an International Monetary Fund designed as a pool from which member countries could buy gold or dollars in local currencies to overcome temporary disequilibriums in their balance of payments. Agreements of a similar nature entered into after the war stimulated the free flow of money. Thanks to these measures, world trade developed vigorously, nearly doubling in volume between 1948 and 1958. Increased trade meant increased productivity and this, in turn, meant increased employment. Thus the contraction of the world economy, which had begun in 1929 (Chapter 27), was now dramatically reversed.

Two additional factors influenced the spurt of the Western economy after the war: new techniques of economic control, and the emergence in Western Europe of a new business mentality.

During the depression of the 1930s much ingenuity had been exerted on finding means of alleviating unemployment. The most influential theoretical contribu-

°Figures from Angus Maddison, *Economic Growth in the West* (1964). In the period 1913–1950—an era of wars and depression—the over-all Western rate of growth had sunk to 1.9 percent.

tion to this discussion was that made by the English economist John Maynard Keynes. Keynes, whom we have encountered as a critic of the Versailles Treaty (Chapter 26), urged the government to intervene to promote full employment as soon as the natural operations of the market failed to do so. Among the steps he proposed were controls on interest rates on money, public work projects, and heavy government spending. The advice Keynes offered contradicted the traditional method of combating recession: limit spending and practice thrift. His advice was not taken in Britain at the time, though it had much influence on Roosevelt's New Deal. After the war Keynesian doctrines gained wide acceptance in both Britain and the United States. The two countries created elaborate mechanisms to keep a permanent check on the pulse of the national economy: as soon as that pulse slows down, the government intervenes, revivifying it by easing interest rates, or expanding credit, or lowering taxes, or increasing its own expenditures. When there is a danger of excessive inflation, the government reverses its policies. These techniques have helped substantially to reduce the business cycle and to save the economy from costly fluctuations.

On the Continent Keynesian methods gained less acceptance. Continental states, true to their tradition of centralism, have tended to adopt regular, over-all economic planning instead of manipulating money. None of the Western European states imitated the Soviet system of planning, with its firm production schedules. This system was quite inappropriate for countries that retained private enterprise and where the government could not command the entire national economy. In addition, the rigidity of the Soviet system was considered counter-productive. The model most widely adopted was that evolved in France in the 1950s. Its intention is not to direct from above the country's productive resources, but to make private business aware of general economic trends and thereby to induce it to think and plan its investments in line with the needs and tendencies of the national economy as a whole. The central organ of French planning, the *Commissariat du Plan*, although a branch of the government, has no executive authority: it advises (and given the power and wealth of the French government, its advice carries no mean weight), but it cannot command. On the basis of the French experience the other members of the Common Market group, as well as Britain, Sweden, Norway, and Austria, have introduced planning agencies.

The system of fiscal and budgetary control adopted by the United States and the United Kingdom, and the system of economic planning prevailing among the West European countries, have greatly enhanced the role of the state in the economic life of the West. The change is so great that some economists question whether the old term *capitalism* can be appropriately used today. They maintain that the modern Western economy is no longer capitalist in any meaningful sense, because it does not work for the free, competitive market. Rather, it is a mixed economy, depending on cooperation of the private and public sectors, without a clear line of demarcation between the two. Indeed, it is doubtful whether big business in the West could survive for long without government subsidies and other forms of assistance; nor is it conceivable that the state could manage an economy of such magnitude and complexity as that of the modern West without the help of private initiative. The mixed economy presently operating in the West may well provide the model for the world as a whole, replacing both the free, unregulated market economy of ideal liberalism and the fully regimented economy of ideal communism.

The other factor behind the economic boom of the 1950s and 1960s was a fundamental reorientation in the mentality of European business. Traditionally, European business enterprise had been more concerned with securing a share of the existing market than in expanding that market. This conservative policy contrasted with that pursued in the United States. The aim of business in the United States has been to enhance by all available means both the capacity and the desire of the consumer to buy. Among these means are full employment, high wages, liberal credit, and advertising. The American technique has been to place the maximum money or credit in the hands of the consumer and then to entice him to spend it on goods and services. By this method the United States has created an enormously productive economy, relying mainly on the domestic market (exports have always been secondary in the United States economy).

In the 1950s a similar philosophy began to permeate European business. A conscious effort was then made to increase the purchasing capacity of the working population. By pumping money into society through social welfare schemes, higher wages, and easier credit terms, the purchasing capacity of the average European has been considerably enhanced. The European consumer is today

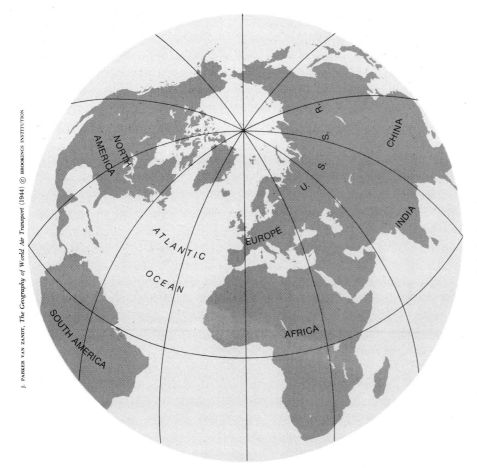

J. PARKER VAN ZANDT, *The Geography of World Air Transport* (1944) © BROOKINGS INSTITUTION

Europe's central position in what has been called the "principal hemisphere" is seen here. Within a hemisphere centered in northern France are 98 percent of the world's population, 94 percent of its industry, and the vast majority of its capital, natural resources, and management skills.

encouraged not to save but to spend. Much of the boom of the postwar Western European economy is due to the vast increase in the production of what is known as "durable consumer goods": automobiles, television sets, furniture, clothing, and so on. Many articles that had previously been confined to the middle class, notably the automobile, have now come within reach of the common man. This "Americanization" of the European economy has also had significant social consequences. With the spread of consumer goods an important distinction between classes—between those who have goods and those who do not—is disappearing. In its style of life postwar Western Europe is rapidly approaching the one-class pattern that has prevailed for some time in the United States.

The tempo at which its economy has developed after World War II has permitted the West to retain the international economic leadership that it had enjoyed at the height of the imperial era. The loss of colonies has had no appreciable effect on the position of the West in the world economy. With one-seventh of the world's population, Western Europe and North America produce 59 percent of the world's industrial goods, carry on two-thirds of the world's trade, and own three-quarters of the world's gold and foreign exchange. The rate of growth of the economies of the "underdeveloped countries" has been much slower, with the result that the distance between their standards of living and those of the West has tended to widen.

Concluding Remarks   We have brought our narrative to a close with a discussion not of politics or of ideas but of the changes in the Western economy. The justification for this procedure is the fact that under modern conditions the economy is the single most powerful lever of history. Technology, capital, productivity, and marketing, with all that they involve, determine to a large extent how we live. They also provide a clue to the direction in which civilizations are likely to move in the second half of the twentieth century.

We have seen the West lose its global pre-eminence and almost simultaneously coalesce into a rudimentary supra-national bloc. In the postwar era the tendency everywhere has been for such large blocs to take shape, each united by political and economic interests and, to a lesser degree, by a common ideology. There is the Western bloc, consisting of two overlapping parts: the Atlantic community and the Common Market. There is also the Communist bloc, with its antagonistic halves: one under Soviet, the other under Chinese leadership. Other such entities are in the process of formation in Latin America and the Middle East. These blocs are in some measure supplanting the national state just as the national state in its time replaced the city-state and the feudal principality.

It is too soon to tell whether such blocs will solidify and become prevailing forms of political and economic organization, or turn out to be merely a transitional phase leading toward a single, world-wide community. In the long run the creation of a united world, in which people and goods will move as freely as they now do within the confines of the national state and free trade areas, appears inevitable. The process of world integration has been initiated by imperialism, and although imperialism itself appears a phenomenon of the past, the forces it has launched are irreversible. "Imperialism's one great achievement was to open up all parts of the world," writes William L. Langer, "and to set all humanity on the high road to eventual association and collaboration." And another historian, Herbert Lüthy, speaks of Europe's colonization of the world as "the painful birth of the modern world itself . . . the tumultuous and frightening genesis of a world which knows for the first time that it is one world and that its compass no longer stops at the edge of the visible horizon."

Whatever the future brings—many sovereign nations, several large supranational blocs, or a United States of the World—it seems certain that the interdependence of the peoples of the world will continue to increase. Self-sufficiency can be purchased only at the cost of prosperity and in the long run is untenable. A division of labor has been taking place throughout the world since early modern times with a steady relentlessness that occasional reversals can delay but not prevent. Labor, goods, and capital are finding their way everywhere, seeking locations where they are most needed and most productive. The era of free trade inaugurated after World War II promises to cement the world market even more solidly than did the first great wave of free trade in the nineteenth century.

This means that human beings will be increasingly wrenched out of the security and isolation of their communities and thrown together—often in competition—with people whose cultures are altogether different from their own. We are already witnessing an expansion of the labor market that would have appeared fantastic fifty years ago, with Turkish workers operating machines in German factories, German stewardesses staffing domestic airlines in the United States, American workers drilling for oil in Arabian deserts, and Arab waiters serving tables in Swiss mountain resorts. The mobility of labor is bound to increase beyond anything known previously and to heighten the possibilities of conflict between nations and races.

In such a thoroughly intermingled world the need for liberal values will be greater than ever before. It will be imperative to learn respect for views and behavior other than one's own, to obey laws that make it possible for a variety of people to coexist in one community, to accept situations in which one does not have one's way in everything. Extreme authoritarian tendencies, such as National Socialism or communism, are not suited to the modern world. They are outdated survivals of an age when it still seemed possible for one person, or one nation, or one idea to transform life in its image. They are ideologies of people bewildered by modern life and anxious to do away with its inherent unpredictability. But life is too rich, too spontaneous to be held still. Nor is irresponsible anarchism the answer, for it undermines respect for law and institutions, without which coexistence of individuals and communities espousing differing interests and values is not possible. Only liberalism—with its tolerance and orderliness, with its mechanism for correcting outdated institutions and laws through democratic elections, with its ability to balance the wants of the individual against the needs of the whole society—is a suitable system for the contemporary world. Under modern conditions the liberal way is not only the best way—it is the only way—to regulate human affairs.

Maps and Charts

Bibliography

§ INDICATES PAPERBACK EDITION AVAILABLE

CHAPTER 1. THE STRUGGLE FOR EMPIRE

Bakeless, John, *The Eyes of Discovery: America as Seen by the First Explorers*§ (1961). In contrast with Brebner (see below), Bakeless concentrates on descriptions of various sections and inhabitants of North America as revealed to their first European beholders; noteworthy for its accounts of the incredible beauty and fecundity of the continent as it once was.

Brebner, John B., *The Explorers of North America, 1492–1806*§ (1955). An account of the voyages and treks of discovery in North America, through Lewis and Clark.

Gómara, Francisco López de, *Cortés*, trans. and ed. Lesley Byrd Simpson§ (1965). A contemporary journal portraying the personality of the conquistador, his achievements, and the society and peoples he encountered and subdued.

Latourette, Kenneth Scott, *A History of the Expansion of Christianity*, Vol. 3: *Three Centuries of Advance, A.D. 1500–1800* (1939). Describes in detail the missionary urge and activities of the Christian churches in newly discovered lands.

Morison, Samuel Eliot, *Admiral of the Ocean Sea* (1942). The best biography of Columbus and account of his voyages, written by a good naval historian and knowledgeable sailor.

Parry, J. H., *The Establishment of the European Hegemony, 1415–1715: Trade and Exploration in the Age of the Renaissance*§ (1961). A brief, solid account and analysis of European exploration and colonization.

Penrose, Boies, *Travel and Discovery in the Renaissance, 1420–1620*§ (1952; 1962). More detailed than Parry (see above), though also more limited in scope; little on colonization and settlement, but a good deal on geographical literature and the development of cartography.

Rowse, A. L., *The Expansion of Elizabethan England*§ (1955). Rowse's enthusiasm conveys the Elizabethan spirit of enterprise and courage, though his patriotism and admiration for Elizabethan sailors are irritatingly intrusive.

CHAPTER 2. THE IMPERIAL WEST

Elliott, John H., *Imperial Spain, 1469–1716*§ (1963; 1966). More up to date and sophisticated than Mariéjol (see below) and equally well written. Elliott challenges many interpretations in Mariéjol. Probably the best English work on Spain during the fifteenth to sixteenth centuries.

Haring, C. H., *The Spanish Empire in America*§ (1963). A solid account of Spanish government in the American colonies up to the nineteenth-century wars of independence.

Mariéjol, Jean H., ed. Benjamin Keen, *The Spain of Ferdinand and Isabella* (1961). Originally published in 1904. The Introduction notes changes in more recent interpretations, but Mariéjol is still valuable for readability and detail on Spanish government and society of the period.

New Cambridge Modern History, Vol 5: *The Ascendancy of France, 1648–1688* (1961), and Vol. 7: *The Old Regime, 1713–1763* (1959). Has various chapters on the colonial powers, their economic policies, and their government abroad.

Nussbaum, Frederick L., *The Triumph of Science and Reason, 1660–1685*§ (1953); John P. Wolf, *The Emergence of the Great Powers, 1685–1715*§ (1951); Penfield Roberts, *The Quest for Security, 1715–1740*§ (1947); and Walter L. Dorn, *Competition for Empire, 1740–1763*§ (1940). Four volumes in the Harper Rise of Modern Europe series, which contain material on various colonial empires and related European conflicts and policies.

Pares, Richard, *Yankees and Creoles* (1956). A brief and readable account of trade between North America and the West Indies before the American Revolution. Explains English mercantile decrees and the difficulties of enforcing them.

Rossiter, Clinton, *The First American Revolution*§ (1956). Rossiter is primarily concerned with the history of the English colonies in America and with the background of the Revolution of 1776, but his analysis gives considerable insight into English imperial policy and its effects.

CHAPTER 3. POPULATION, INDUSTRY, AND AGRICULTURE

Bruford, W. H., *Germany in the 18th Century*§ (1935; 1959). A good study of German social and economic structure and institutions.

Clough, S. B., and C. W. Cole, *An Economic History of Europe*, 3rd ed. (1952). Any general history of so broad a subject must oversimplify and distort, but of several such works, Clough and Cole do so the least.

Davies, R. Trevor, *The Golden Century of Spain, 1501–1621*§ (1965). A thoughtful revisionist description of Spanish policies and problems, especially under Philip II; its aim is to defend Philip against contemporary and present critics.

Gras, N. S. B., *A History of Agriculture in Europe and America*, 2nd ed. (1946). Quite technical and detailed, but more useful and reliable than most discussions of the subject for this very reason.

Notestein, Wallace, *The English People on the Eve of Colonization, 1603–1630*§ (1954). An excellent survey of the social fabric and political life of England during this period.

Taylor, Philip A. M., ed., *The Origins of the English Civil War: Conspiracy, Crusade, or Class Conflict?*§ (1960). Useful for English economic and social history during this time.

(*See also* bibliography for Chapter 2: Elliott, Nussbaum, Wolf, Roberts, Dorn; *New Cambridge Modern History*, Vols. 5 and 7.)

CHAPTER 4. THE AGE OF THE MERCHANTS

Barbour, Violet, *Capitalism in Amsterdam in the 17th Century*§ (1963). Gives concrete details, and solid analysis, of trade and merchants in the city that was briefly the economic center of Europe.

Cole, Charles W., *French Mercantilism, 1683–1700* (1965). As discussions of mercantilism go, this one is brief and free from detail that is of little use except for the specialist.

Ehrenberg, R., *Capital and Finance in the Age of the Renaissance* (n.d.). Primarily a study of the Fugger bank's organization and operations, but the book is of general interest not only because the Fuggers had such vast influence on their times, but also because Ehrenberg makes many observations on sixteenth- and seventeenth-century capitalism and its impact.

Nef, John U., *Industry and Government in France and England, 1540–1560*§ (1957). Nef argues for the existence of a real industrial revolution, starting in the sixteenth century. Whatever the merits of his case, the book is valuable for its relatively brief but solid descriptions of industrial organizations and governmental economic policies.

Tawney, R. H., *Religion and the Rise of Capitalism*§ (1955). Tawney summarizes Max Weber's theory of the "protestant ethic," and suggests a plausible modification of Weber. He also provides a good account of conscious and unconscious assumptions about business between the later Middle Ages and the seventeenth century.

CHAPTER 5. THE RISE OF MODERN SCIENCE

Andrade, E. N. da C., *Sir Isaac Newton*§ (1958). A short biography of Newton, which also places his major ideas and discoveries in perspective.

Boas, Marie, *The Scientific Renaissance, 1450–1630*§ (1966). Gives a more generalized account than Bronowski and Mazlish (see below). Especially good in its treatment of the relation of magic to science and in its discussion of Galileo's trial.

Bronowski, J., and Bruce Mazlish, *The Western Intellectual Tradition: From Leonardo to Hegel*§ (1960). Concentrates on main themes in European intellectual history from Leonardo da Vinci to the nineteenth century; its strength is that it is not a textbook in the usual sense, but a collection of chapters, or essays, on the thought and significance of individual thinkers. Stresses the Scientific Revolution. Includes a good critical bibliography for each chapter.

Burtt, E. A., *The Metaphysical Foundations of Modern Science*, rev. ed.§ (1954). Comparatively difficult and technical, but profound. Covers the ideas of major figures from Copernicus to Newton.

Butterfield, Herbert, *The Origins of Modern Science, 1300–1800*, rev. ed.§ (1966). Especially good in its stress on the role of original assumptions and questions, rather than new evidence, in the Scientific Revolution; also valuable for its general evaluation of the significance of the Scientific Revolution in European history.

Cohen, I. Bernard, *The Birth of a New Physics*§ (1960). A compact survey of astronomical studies from Copernicus to Newton. Especially appropriate for students who know some math and physics, for it contains a relatively large number of the crucial formulas and scientific diagrams.

Hall, A. R., *The Scientific Revolution, 1500–1800*, rev. ed.§ (1966). Somewhat broader and more massive than Boas (see above). Probes the ways in which scientific discoveries affected the philosophers and attitudes of various thinkers.

Kuhn, Thomas S., *The Copernican Revolution: Planetary Astronomy in the Development of Western Thought*§ (1957). The best and most recent account of Copernicus' thought, its background, and its impact.

Tillyard, E. M. W., *The Elizabethan World Picture*§ (1961). Tillyard's concern is to describe the assumptions of Shakespeare and other Elizabethan authors about what the universe was like; in doing so, he presents a brief and striking picture of how the universe was viewed prior to the dominance of the new sciences.

CHAPTER 6. THE WORLD OF THE NEW SCIENCES

Bacon, Francis, *Complete Essays, Including The New Atlantis, and Novum Organum*, ed. Henry L. Finch§ (n.d.) Bacon's own hopes for science are clear in his own writings; the scientific essays outline his ideas and capture his enthusiasm.

Drake, Stillman, ed. and trans., *Discoveries and Opinions of Galileo*§ (1957). Drake has edited some of the most significant papers of Galileo, particularly those relating to his mathematical concept of the universe and to his argument that scientific certainty does not conflict with properly defined and understood Christian beliefs.

Farrington, Benjamin, *Francis Bacon: Philosopher of Industrial Science*§ (1961). A good brief biography of Bacon which explains his key assumptions and theories.

Hazard, Paul, *The European Mind, 1680–1715*§ (1963). A lengthy and thorough survey of all the major areas of European culture in this period, which Hazard argues was a decisive one in the transition to a modern world-view. Hazard has a good deal on the effects of science on areas of thought such as philosophy, biblical study, and theories of society. Written in an impressionistic and dramatic style.

White, A. D., *A History of the Warfare of Science with Theology in Christendom*, 2 vols.§ (1965). This massive nineteenth-century work, although much out of date in many respects, particularly in its main thesis that Christianity consistently and inevitably struggled against scientific advance, is still worth dipping into if only to understand the fervor and assumptions of this largely discredited point of view.

CHAPTER 7. THE ENLIGHTENMENT

Becker, Carl, *The Heavenly City of the Eighteenth-Century Philosophers*§ (1932; 1959). Famous both for its literary style and for its provocative thesis that the Enlightenment transformed, rather than rejected, the world-view of medieval Christianity.

Frankel, Charles, *The Faith of Reason* (1948). An analysis of the origins of the eighteenth-century idea of progress, with stress on its dependence of scientific ideas.

Havens, G., *The Age of Ideas: From Reaction to Revolution in Eighteenth-Century France*§ (1955; 1965). Deals with many of the same issues that Martin (see below) does, but with a rather different method. Includes biographies, and considerable incidental detail about the major French figures of the Enlightenment.

Hazard, Paul, *European Thought in the Eighteenth Century: From Montesquieu to Lessing*§ (1954). A sequel to Hazard's book cited in the bibliography for Chapter 6 and much the same in style and approach to intellectual history.

Manuel, Frank, *The Prophets of Paris: Turgot, Condorcet, Saint-Simon, Fourier, Comte*§ (1965). A broader and more detailed study of the idea of progress, more balanced than Frankel (see above). Manuel analyzes the ideas of two eighteenth-century believers in progress and several early nineteenth-century socialists, including both wildly visionary schemes and the first systematic efforts to found a discipline of sociology.

Martin, Kingsley, *French Liberal Thought in the Eighteenth Century: A Study of Political Ideas from Boyle to Condorcet*, ed. J. P. Mayer§ (1963). A study of the origins of political liberalism, tracing political and social thought from the time of Boyle to the eve of the French Revolution.

Schapiro, J. S., *Condorcet and the Rise of Liberalism* (1963). Provides a more specific guide to early eighteenth-century liberal ideas than does Martin (see above). Condorcet's ideology of progress and hopes for social science is a classic distillation of this eighteenth-century school of thought.

CHAPTER 8. THE ENLIGHTENMENT IN PRACTICE

Cassirer, Ernst, *The Question of Jean-Jacques Rousseau*, ed. and trans., Peter Gay§ (1963). Cassirer is brief but brilliant in dealing with the main ideas of Rousseau and their various interpretations. Gay's Introduction provides a useful discussion of previous scholarship on Rousseau, especially concerning the problem of whether he was primarily democratic or totalitarian in his political thought.

Ford, Franklin L., *Robe and Sword: The Regrouping of the French Aristocracy After Louis XIV*§ (1953; 1965). A solid, scholarly study of the resurgence of aristocratic power in France after Louis XIV. Provides an understanding of the basis of the continuing power of aristocratic families and institutions and also of why the Revolution was eventually aimed at a monarchy that could not dislodge this aristocratic power.

Gagliardo, John C., *Enlightened Despotism*§ (1967). A brief account, and interpretation, of the enlightened despots and their policies.

Gershoy, Leo, *From Despotism to Revolution, 1763–1789*§ (1963). Another volume in the Harper Rise of Modern Europe series. Discusses the enlightened despots within the broad context of their society and times.

Gooch, G. P., *Frederick the Great* (1947). A biography of Frederick II which includes an analysis of various aspects of his rule; in particular, there is a good deal of material concerning the personal and philosophical relationship of this enlightened despot to his most famous mentor, Voltaire.

Grey, Ian, *Catherine the Great* (1962). A biography of Catherine II of Russia, dealing with the interaction between her personality and her policies.

Sorel, A., *Europe Under the Old Regime*, trans. Francis H. Herrick§ (1947). The first chapter, in condensed version, of an eight-volume classic work on European diplomatic history before and during the French Revolution. Sketches the nature of national interests and diplomatic practice before 1789.

See also bibliography for Chapter 7: Havens; Martin

CHAPTER 9. PROLOGUE TO THE ERA OF REVOLUTION

Bailyn, Bernard, *The Ideological Origins of the American Revolution* (1967). A sophisticated analysis of various ideas of liberty in America and Europe, and their implications; explains the climate of opinion which made revolutions like those of 1776 and 1789 possible.

Greenlaw, Ralph W., *The Economic Origins of the French Revolution: Poverty or Prosperity?*§ (1958). Presents extreme "left-wing" and "right-wing" views of the condition of Frenchmen prior to 1789, as well as much more moderate and accurate material. Like Tocqueville (see below), the book is also relevant to many contemporary issues in a direct way, such as the problem of how poverty ought to be gauged or defined.

Kronenberger, Louis, *Kings and Desperate Men: Life in Eighteenth-Century England*§ (1959). A description of the world of artists and aristocrats in eighteenth-century society.

Lefebvre, Georges, *The Coming of the French Revolution*§ (1957). Narrative history, in contrast with Tocqueville (see below), but also contains a great deal of analysis. Lefebvre studies the origins and momentum of the French Revolution through October of 1789.

New Cambridge Modern History, Vol. 8: *The American and French Revolutions, 1763–1793* (1965).

Plumb, J. H., *England in the Eighteenth Century*§ (1950). A solid survey of society, politics, and the Industrial Revolution and its first effects.

Tocqueville, Alexis de, *The Old Regime and the French Revolution*§ (1955). Now over a century old, Tocqueville's work remains a classic for its acute analysis of the weaknesses of the monarchy and the forces which fomented revolution. A great deal of Tocqueville's observations are equally pertinent today to what has been called the "revolution of rising expectations" in underdeveloped areas of the world, including the American ghettos.

(*See* Rossiter, in the bibliography for Chapter 2, for background of the American Revolution.)

CHAPTER 10. THE FRENCH REVOLUTION

Amann, Peter, *The Eighteenth-Century Revolution, French or Western?*§ (1963). Contains excerpts from scholars both criticizing and supporting Palmer's thesis (see Palmer, *Age of the Democratic Revolution*, below).

Brinton, Crane, *A Decade of Revolution, 1789–1799*§ (1935). One of the best, and certainly the best written, of the Harper Rise of Modern Europe series; few scholars can match Brinton's ironic wit. Brinton's work complements Becker's (see bibliography, Chapter 7) in that Brinton stresses the parallels between revolutionary and religious psychology.

Brinton, Crane, *The Jacobins: An Essay in the New History* (1962). A careful analysis of the social basis and political and social ideals of the Jacobins.

Goodwin, Albert, *The French Revolution*§ (1962). Rather cut-and-dried in its approach compared with Lefebvre (see bibliography, Chapter 9) but far from dull. Gives a good account of the Revolution through the fall of Robespierre.

Greer, Donald, *The Incidence of Terror During the French Revolution* (1935). A small but significant scholarly monograph which corrects many common misimpressions as to what kind of people were executed during the Terror, and why.

Palmer, R. R., *Age of the Democratic Revolution: A Political History of Europe and America, 1760–1800*, 2 vols. (1959). A massive work on Europe and America between 1760 and 1800, arguing that the French Revolution was but one aspect of a revolutionary wave that swept through Atlantic civilization.

Palmer, R. R., *Twelve Who Ruled*§ (1965). A history of the Terror during the French Revolution, keyed to the personalities and policies of the Committee of Public Safety under Jacobin rule.

EUROPE IN THE NINETEENTH AND TWENTIETH CENTURIES: GENERAL LITERATURE

COMPREHENSIVE SURVEYS

The New Cambridge Modern History, Vol. X: *The Zenith of European Power, 1830–1870* (1964); Vol. XI: *Material Progress and World-wide Problems, 1870–1898* (1962). The most recent attempt at a global history; Vol. X is better organized and altogether superior to Vol. XI.

POLITICS, DIPLOMACY, AND WARFARE

Clark, Grover, *A Place in the Sun* (1936). "This book is the result of an attempt to get, from the actual records, an answer to the question: Do colonies pay? Most emphatically, the answer is: No."

Craig, G. A., and Felix Gilbert, eds., *The Diplomats: 1919–1939*, 2 vols.§ (1953; 1965). A collection of sketches of leading diplomatic figures of the twentieth century by diverse authors.

Falls, Cyril, *A Hundred Years of War*§ (1953;

2nd ed. 1961). The development of military technology and strategy from the American Civil War through World War II.

Fieldhouse, D. K., *The Colonial Empires* (1966). A general survey of Western imperialism since the eighteenth century; post-World War II developments briefly treated.

Fuller, J. F. C., *Armament and History* (1945). "A study of the influence of armament on history from the dawn of classical warfare to the Second World War."

Hawgood, J. A., *Modern Constitutions Since 1787* (1939). A survey of constitutional development in the West, by types of constitutional systems.

Ruggiero, Guido de, *The History of European Liberalism*, trans. R. G. Collingwood§ (1927; 1959). Surveys European liberal ideas and attitudes.

Taylor, A. J. P., *The Struggle for Mastery in Europe, 1848–1918* (1954). A controversial study of diplomatic history by an English historian.

Winslow, E. M., *The Pattern of Imperialism* (1948). A study of the theories of imperialism—its causes and significance.

ECONOMIC AND SOCIAL

Armytage, W. H. G., *A Social History of Engineering*, 2nd ed. (1961). How technology and technical innovation originate and how they influence history; with emphasis on Britain.

Ashley, Percy, *Modern Tariff History* (1904). The emergence of protective tariffs in Germany, the United States, and France.

Ashworth, William, *A Short History of the International Economy, 1850–1950* (1952). A succinct account of all branches of economic activity.

Birnie, Arthur, *An Economic History of Europe, 1760–1939*§ (1930; 1957). Brief survey, topical rather than regional, which emphasizes industrialism and industrial growth and their social aspects.

Bowden, Witt, Michael Karpovich, and A. P. Usher, *An Economic History of Europe Since 1750* (1937). A comprehensive survey which pays much attention to frequently neglected subjects, such as agriculture and Eastern Europe.

The Cambridge Economic History of Europe, Vol. VI: *The Industrial Revolutions and After*, 2 Parts (1965). The most up-to-date, authoritative treatment of Western economy since the mid-eighteenth century; partly topical, partly regional.

Cipolla, C. M., *The Economic History of World Population*§ (1962). An introduction to historical demography.

Clapham, J. H., *The Economic Development of France and Germany, 1815–1914*§ (1921; 4th ed., 1935). Comparative study of the two economies.

Condliffe, J. B., *The Commerce of Nations* (1950). The impact of the international economy on national economies in the nineteenth and twentieth centuries.

Derry, T. K., and T. I. Williams, *A Short History of Technology* (1961). A general introduction "from the earliest times to A.D 1900."

Dickinson, R. E., *The West European City: A Geographical Interpretation* (1951; 2nd ed., 1961). A historical survey of the Western city and its various types.

Glass, D. V., and D. E. C. Eversley, eds., *Population in History* (1965). A collection of essays dealing with various historic aspects of population growth and movement.

Mumford, Lewis, *The City in History* (1961). The city from earliest times to the present, by a critic of modern industrial civilization and the sprawling megalopolis.

Palm, F. C., *The Middle Classes Then and Now* (1936). The bourgeoisie across the ages.

Rostow, W. W., *The Stages of Economic Growth*§ (1960; 1965). An attempt, by an economic historian, to provide a scheme of economic development valid for all countries.

Rudé, G. F. E., *The Crowd in History, 1730–1848*§ (1964). Analysis of crowd behavior on the basis of French and British experience.

Willcox, W. F., *International Migrations*, 2 vols. (1929–1931). Vol. I contains statistics, Vol. II, interpretation by country or ethnic group; the fullest account of modern population movements.

THOUGHT, SCIENCE, AND ART

Aron, Raymond, *The Opium of the Intellectuals*§ (1957; 1962). The myths of intellectuals: "revolution," "proletariat," "history," and so on.

Bowle, John, *Politics and Opinion in the Nineteenth Century*§ (1954; 1964). The ideological antecedents of twentieth-century politics: the Romantics, the Darwinists, the socialists, and extreme nationalists.

Caute, David, *The Left in Europe Since 1789*§ (1966). A sociological survey of radical movements and ideologies.

Cole, G. D. H., *A History of Socialist Thought*, 3 vols., (1953). A sweeping survey from the French Revolution to the outbreak of World War I.

Höffding, Harald, *A History of Modern Philosophy*, trans. E. B. Meyer, 2 vols.§ (1900;

1924). Vol. II deals with idealism and positivism in the nineteenth century; relatively non-technical.

McKenzie, A. E. E., *The Major Achievements of Science*, 2 vols. (1960). Stresses the nineteenth and twentieth centuries. Vol. I has a lucid historical exposition; Vol. II contains selections from original scientific writings.

Reichen, C. A., *A History of Physics* (1963); *A History of Chemistry*, (1963). Profusely illustrated brief introductions to the subjects.

Shryock, R. H., *The Development of Modern Medicine* (1936; 1947). Stresses social aspects of medicine.

Singer, C. J., *A Short History of Scientific Ideas to 1900*§ (1959; 1962). A comprehensive history of scientific thought, the latter part of which is devoted to the nineteenth century and the mechanistic outlook.

Singer, C. J., *A History of Biology to about the Year 1900* (1931; rev. ed. 1962). The evolution of knowledge about the nature of living things.

Whitehead, Alfred North, *Science and the Modern World*§ (1926; 1949). A popular exposition of the meaning of modern science by an eminent philosopher.

BRITAIN

Ashworth, William, *An Economic History of England, 1870–1939* (1960). A survey.

Briggs, Asa, *The Age of Improvement, 1783–1867* (1959). A topical description of England during its Industrial Revolution, stressing social and cultural subjects but also encompassing political history.

Carrington, C. E., *The British Overseas* (1950). Not so much a history of British empire-building as one of British colonization.

Checkland, S. G., *The Rise of Industrial Society in England, 1815–1885* (1964). The industrial sector of British society—the social history of all the elements involved in the industrial process, including inventors, businessmen, and workers.

Cole, G. D. H., and Raymond Postgate, *The British Common People, 1746–1946*§ (1947; 1961). The "people" here means the working class, whose social and political movements are traced.

Deane, Phyllis, and W. A. Cole, *British Economic Growth, 1688–1959* (1962). By economists employing modern methods of analysis.

Ensor, R. C. K., *England, 1870–1914* (1936). A survey.

Knaplund, Paul, *The British Empire, 1815–1939* (1941). A survey of imperial history.

Lewis, Roy, and Angus Maude, *The English*

Middle Classes (1949). A historical essay on the vaguely defined group.

Maccoby, Simon, ed., *The Radical Tradition, 1763–1914* (1952). Excerpts from English radical writings with brief commentaries.

Mowat, C. L., *Britain Between the Wars, 1918–1940* (1955). A comprehensive survey, with much attention to economics.

Schlote, Werner, *British Overseas Trade from 1700 to the 1930's* (1952). A statistical study.

Seton-Watson, R. W., *Britain in Europe, 1789–1914* (1937). British relations with the Continent, with emphasis on the "Eastern Question."

Taylor, A. J. P., *English History, 1914–1945* (1965). A survey.

Thompson, F. M. L., *English Landed Society in the Nineteenth Century* (1963). Deals with landed interests, often overlooked by historians emphasizing the moneyed middle class.

Thornton, A. P., *The Imperial Idea and its Enemies* (1959). Changing attitudes toward the empire in Britain, with emphasis on the past century.

Woodward, E. L., *The Age of Reform, 1815–1870* (1938; 2nd ed. 1962). A survey.

Young, G. M., *Victorian England*§ (1936; 2nd ed. 1953). An essay synthesizing the social and intellectual climate of England in the long reign of Queen Victoria.

FRANCE

Brogan, D. W., *France Under the Republic* (1940). A rambling, witty, idiosyncratic account of the Third Republic.

Cameron, R. E., *France and the Economic Development of Europe, 1800–1914*, 2nd ed., rev. and abr.§ (1961). Deals primarily with French banking and investments.

Cobban, Alfred, *A History of Modern France*, rev. ed., Vols. II and III§ (1957–1965). A survey from the rise of Napoleon I to 1962.

Plamenatz, J. P., *The Revolutionary Movement in France, 1815–1871* (1952). An essay on the republican, anti-monarchist ideologies and forces.

Priestley, H. I., *France Overseas* (1938). The growth of the French Empire in the nineteenth and early twentieth centuries.

Soltau, R. H., *French Parties and Politics, 1871–1921* (1930; 1965). The role of parties under the Third Republic.

Soltau, R. H., *French Political Thought in the Nineteenth Century* (1931).

Thomson, David, *Democracy in France Since 1870*§ (1946; 4th ed. 1964). Not a political history but an analysis of the interaction of conservative and revolutionary traditions in modern France, treated topically.

GERMANY

Craig, G. A., *The Politics of the Prussian Army, 1640–1945*§ (1956; 1964). The role of the military in German politics, and its disastrous consequences.

Hamerow, T. S., *Restoration, Revolution, Reaction*§ (1958). Argues that the triumph of anti-liberal forces in Germany between 1815 and 1871 was due primarily to the dissatisfaction of the lower classes with industrialism and the bourgeoisie.

Krieger, Leonard, *The German Idea of Freedom* (1957). Seeks to penetrate and explain the peculiarities of German political ideology.

Pinson, K. S., *Modern Germany, Its History and Civilization* (1954; 2nd ed. 1966). Concentrates on the post-1848 period.

Rosenberg, Arthur, *Imperial Germany: The Birth of the German Republic, 1871–1918*§ (1931; 1964). The internal history of Wilhelmian Germany and the reasons for its collapse. Should have been called: "The Death of the Imperial Regime."

LOW COUNTRIES AND SWITZERLAND

Bonjour, Edgar, H. S. Offler, and G. R. Potter, *A Short History of Switzerland* (1952).

Edmundson, George, History of Holland (1922).

ITALY

Chabod, Federico, *A History of Italian Fascism* (1963). The title misleads, for this is really a general history of Italy from the end of World War I until 1949.

Clough, S. B., *The Economic History of Modern Italy* (1963). From the Risorgimento to the present.

Hughes, H. S., *The United States and Italy* (1953; rev. ed. 1965). Contains a great deal on the internal life of Italy.

Jemolo, A. C., *Church and State in Italy, 1850–1950* (1960). The crises in church-state relations from Risorgimento through most recent times.

Seton-Watson, Christopher, *Italy from Liberalism to Fascism, 1870–1925* (1967). A survey.

Smith, Denis Mack, *Italy; A Modern History* (1959). Italian political history, mainly from 1861 to 1925.

THE IBERIAN PENINSULA

Atkinson, W. C., *A History of Spain and Portugal*§ (1960). A survey.

Brenan, Gerald, *The Spanish Labyrinth*§ (1943; 2nd ed. 1950, 1960). An essay on the forces of Spanish history which pays much attention to social and economic subjects.

Carr, Raymond, *Spain: 1808–1939* (1966). A survey.

AUSTRIA-HUNGARY

Jászi, Oszkár, *The Dissolution of the Habsburg Monarchy*§ (1929; 1961). Emphasizes the Hungarian half of the empire.

Kann, R. A., *The Habsburg Empire* (1957). An inquiry, from the point of view of political science, of integration and disintegration of a multinational state on the example of Austria-Hungary.

Kann, R. A., *The Multinational Empire*, 2 vols. (1950; 1964). Nationality problems in the Hapsburg monarchy and the efforts to solve them between 1848 and 1918.

Taylor, A. J. P., *The Habsburg Monarchy, 1809–1918*§ (1941; 1965). A short survey.

RUSSIA

Blum, Jerome, *Lord and Peasant in Russia*§ (1961; 1964). Agrarian conditions in Russia from earliest times to the emancipation of serfs (1861).

Florinsky, M. T., *Russia: A History and an Interpretation*, Vol. II: 1801–March, 1918 (1953). A detailed account by a historian critical of the imperial regime.

Kennan, G. F., *Russia and the West Under Lenin and Stalin*§ (1961; 1962). A history of Soviet Russia's relations with the Western powers, by a diplomat who at certain stages played a crucial role in shaping them.

Kornilov, A. A., *Modern Russian History from the Age of Catherine the Great to the End of the Nineteenth Century*, 2 vols. (1916–1917). An older account by a liberal Russian historian, almost exclusively devoted to internal policy.

Lederer, I. J., ed., *Russian Foreign Policy*§ (1962; 1964). A collection of papers dealing topically and regionally with Russian diplomacy.

Seton-Watson, Hugh, *From Lenin to Khrushchev*§ (1960; 1962). The history of Communism as an international movement, embracing the Soviet Union as well as Communist movements outside its borders.

Seton-Watson, Hugh, *The Russian Empire, 1801–1917* (1967). A general history which stresses successes and failures of "modernization."

Treadgold, D. W., *Twentieth Century Russia* (1959). The last decades of the imperial regime and the Soviet period, surveyed as an entity.

Wallace, D.K., *Russia*§ (1912). The *Times* correspondent describes turn-of-the-century Russia known to him from long residence. (The paperback version is abridged.)

SCANDINAVIA

Arneson, B.A., *The Democratic Monarchies of Scandinavia* (1939). Some historical background, but concentrates on the twentieth century.

Hovde, B. J., *The Scandinavian Countries, 1720–1865*, 2 vols. (1943; 1948). An introduction to the emergence of modern Scandinavia.

CENTRAL EUROPE AND THE BALKANS

The Cambridge History of Poland, Vol. II: *From Augustus II to Pilsudski (1697–1935)* (1941). A survey.

Davison, R. H., *Reform in the Ottoman Empire, 1856–1876* (1936). A history of the *Tanzimat* in the nineteenth century.

Halecki, Oscar, *A History of Poland*§ (1943; 1961; 1966). By a Catholic historian.

Lewis, Bernard, *The Emergence of Modern Turkey* (1961). The dissolution of the Ottoman Empire and the rise of the Turkish Republic.

Marriott, J. A. R., *The Eastern Question* (1917; 4th ed. 1940). The decay of the Ottoman Empire and international competition over its legacy.

Seton-Watson, R. W., *A History of the Czechs and Slovaks* (1943; 1965). A survey by a great sympathizer of the Czech Republic.

Seton-Watson, R. W., *A History of the Roumanians* (1934). A survey.

Stavrianos, L. S., *The Balkans Since 1453* (1958). A survey.

Wolff, R. E., *The Balkans in Our Time* (1956). Balkan history in the twentieth century.

CHAPTER 11. THE NAPOLEONIC ERA

Bruun, Geoffrey, *Europe and the French Imperium, 1799–1814*§ (1938; 1963). An account of Napoleon's domination of the Continent. (In the Harper Rise of Modern Europe series.)

Chandler, D. G., *The Campaigns of Napoleon* (1966). A study of Napoleon's military strategy and an account of his main battles.

Connelly, Owen, *Napoleon's Satellite Kingdoms* (1965). Analyzes Napoleon's rule over Italy, Holland, Westphalia, and Spain.

Deutsch, H. C., *The Genesis of Napoleonic Imperialism* (1938). The expansion of France from 1801 to 1805.

Ergang, R. R., *Herder and the Foundations of German Nationalism* (1931). The emergence of nationalism in late eighteenth-century Germany, centered on the creator of modern "historicism."

Gershoy, Leo, *The French Revolution and Napoleon* (1933). A general survey of French history from the fall of the Bastille to the fall of Napoleon.

Geyl, Pieter, *Napoleon: For and Against*§ (1949; 1964). The changing reputation of Napoleon among historians.

Hayes, Carlton, *The Historical Evolution of Modern Nationalism* (1931). A "typology" of national ideologies and movements.

Heckscher, Eli, *The Continental System* (1922; 1964). By a leading Swedish economist.

Herold, J. C., ed. and trans., *The Mind of Napoleon*§ (1955; 1961). "A selection from his written and spoken words."

Kohn, Hans, *The Idea of Nationalism*§ (1961). A history of the antecedents of the idea of nationalism from the earliest times to the French Revolution.

Ludwig, Emil, *Napoleon*§ (1915). A popular biography, based on good knowledge of the facts. (Available in several editions.)

Kircheisen, Friedrich, *Napoleon* (1932). A biography, translated from the German, written by a major Napoleonic scholar.

Simon, W. N., *The Failure of the Prussian Reform Movement, 1807–1819* (1955). Argues that the Prussian reformers fell "disastrously short" of their objectives.

Tarlé, Evgenii, *Napoleon's Invasion of Russia* (1942). From a Communist-nationalist point of view; stresses the role of peasants in the destruction of the Napoleonic armies.

Thompson, J. M., *Napoleon Bonaparte: His Rise and Fall* (1952). One of the recent general accounts, by an English historian.

CHAPTER 12. LIBERALISM AND CONSERVATISM: 1815–1848

Artz, F. B., *Reaction and Revolution, 1814–1832*§ (1934; 1957). A general survey, in the Harper Rise of Modern Europe series.

Bertier de Sauvigny, G. de, *The Bourbon Restoration* (1967). France from the fall of Napoleon to the July, 1830, Revolution, interpreted by a Catholic historian not unsympathetic to the Restoration government.

Bertier de Sauvigny, G. de, *Metternich and his Times* (1962). A sympathetic account.

Briggs, Asa, ed., *Chartist Studies*§ (1960). A collection of essays by different authors, mostly devoted to local activities of Chartist groups.

Burke, Edmund, *Burke's Politics,* ed., R. J. S. Hoffman and Paul Levack (1949). An anthology of his outstanding writings and speeches.

Butler, J. R. M., *The Passing of the Great Reform Bill* (1914). "More concerned with negotiations behind the scenes and effect of popular opinion, than with the course of events in Parliament."

Halévy, Elie, *The Growth of Philosophic Radicalism*§ (1928; 1955). Bentham and the Utilitarians.

Halévy, Elie, *History of the English People in the Nineteenth Century*§ Vol. II: *Liberal Awakening, 1815–1830*; Vol. III: *The Triumph of Reform, 1830–1841* (1926; 2nd ed. rev.). Britain between 1815 and 1841, by its outstanding French historian.

Hovell, Mark, *The Chartist Movement* (1918; 2nd ed., 1925). Despite its age, still not superseded.

Howarth, Thomas, *Citizen-King* (1961). The biography of the hapless Louis Philippe.

Hudson, Nora, *Ultra-royalism and the French Restoration* (1936). The rise and fall of the Right in Restoration France.

Johnson, D. W., *Guizot* (1963). An effort to redress the unfavorable prevailing view of the leading ideologist of the July monarchy.

Kissinger, H. A., *A World Restored*§ (1957; 1964). The efforts of Metternich, Castlereagh, and other participants of the anti-Napoleonic alliance to stabilize Europe, 1812–1822.

Magnus, Philip, *Edmund Burke, a Life* (1939). Biography of Europe's most seminal conservative thinker.

Mazour, Anatole, *The First Russian Revolution, 1825*§ (1937; 1961). An account of the liberal and republican officer uprising in Russia, the so-called Decembrists.

Nicolson, Harold, *The Congress of Vienna*§ (1946; 1961). By a participant in the Paris negotiations of 1919; hints at interesting parallels.

Packe, Michael St. John, *The Life of John Stuart Mill* (1954). The life and thought of the outstanding English nineteenth-century liberal thinker.

Phillips, W. A., *The Confederation of Europe* (1914). An account of the efforts made in 1815 and after to assure the "concert of Europe."

Pipes, Richard, ed. and trans., *Karamzin's Memoir on Ancient and Modern Russia*§ (1959; 1966). A translation and analysis of the most important Russian conservative document of the nineteenth century (1811).

Romani, G. T., *The Neapolitan Revolution of 1820–1821* (1950). Stresses the reasons for the failure of the Neapolitan rebels.

Webster, C. K., *The Congress of Vienna, 1814–1815*§ (1919; 1963). A diplomatic account.

White, R. J., *Waterloo to Peterloo* (1957). An essay in "suspended revolution"—social unrest in England after the Napoleonic wars.

Woodward, E. L., *Three Studies in European Conservatism* (1929). "Metternich, Guizot, [and] the Catholic Church in the nineteenth century."

See also bibliography, General Literature—Politics, Diplomacy, and Welfare: Ruggiero.

CHAPTER 13. THE BEGINNINGS OF INDUSTRIALIZATION

Ashton, T. S., *The Industrial Revolution, 1760–1830*§ (1937; 1964). A brief general survey.

Brady, Alexander, *William Huskisson and Liberal Reform* (1928). Not a biography but an analysis of the collapse of British mercantilism and triumph of liberalism, centered on the head of the Board of Trade.

Clapham, J. H., *Economic History of Modern Britain*, Vol. I: *The Early Railway Age, 1820–1850* (1926; 1939). A massive study of British industrialization at the time of its most dramatic progress.

Deane, Phyllis, *The First Industrial Revolution*§ (1966). The century 1750–1850 in the light of modern theories of economic growth.

Dunham, A. L., *The Industrial Revolution in France, 1815–1848* (1955). Stresses the causes behind the slow development of French industry.

Hammond, J. L., and Barbara Hammond, *The Town Labourer, 1760–1832* (1917; 1967). A devastating picture of living and working conditions of labor in England in the first phase of industrialization.

Henderson, W. O., *Britain and Industrial Europe, 1750–1870* (1954; 2nd ed., 1965). Deals with Britain's role in the development of the European economy.

Henderson, W. O., *The Zollverein* (1939). A history of the economic association which preceded and stimulated German political unification.

McCord, Norman, *The Anti-Corn Law League, 1838–1846* (1958). A fresh look at the League which endeavors, by pragmatic analysis of the evidence, to steer between liberal glorification and radical condemnation.

Mantoux, P. J., *The Industrial Revolution in the Eighteenth Century*§ (1927; 2nd rev. ed. 1961; 1962). The antecedents of nineteenth-century English industrialism.

Morley, John, *The Life of Richard Cobden* (1881). A detailed biography of the founder of the Anti-Corn Law League.

Singer, C. J., *et al.*, eds., *A History of Technology*, Vol. IV: *The Industrial Revolution, 1750–1850* (1958). A comprehensive survey of all branches of technological invention.

Thompson, E. P., *The Making of the English Working Class*§ (1963). The emergence of class consciousness among English labor in the first half of the nineteenth century.

(*See also The Cambridge Economic History of Europe*, Vol. VI, Pt. 1.)

CHAPTER 14. ROMANTICISM

Brinton, Crane, *The Political Ideals of the English Romanticists*§ (1926; 1966). The disillusionment of English Romantic poets with the French Revolution.

Brion, Marcell, *Romantic Art* (1960). A picture book with commentaries.

Chadwick, Owen, *The Victorian Church*, Pt. 1, 1829–1860 (1966). Religion and church in England and their problems.

Clark, Kenneth, *The Gothic Revival*§ (1928; 1964). An essay on early Victorian taste, with stress on architecture; confined to England.

Einstein, Alfred, *Music in the Romantic Era* (1947). By the son of Albert Einstein.

Gleckner, R. F., and G. E. Enscoe, eds., *Romanticism*§ (1962). The meaning of the term as interpreted by successive generations.

Halsted, J. B., ed., *Romanticism*§ (1965). A collection of excerpts by modern historians dealing with the meaning and significance of Romanticism.

Hugo, H. E., ed., *The Romantic Reader*§ (1957). Anthology containing excerpts on the idea of Romanticism, the Romantic hero, the artist, and other related subjects.

Royce, Josiah, *Lectures on Modern Idealism*§ (1919; 1964). A popular introduction to idealistic philosophy by a leading exponent of American pragmatism; originally delivered in 1906.

Stendhal, Henri, *Racine and Shakespeare* (1962). A contrast between the Classical and the Romantic, as seen by the French novelist.

CHAPTER 15. THE HIGH TIDE OF LIBERALISM: 1848–1870

Bagehot, Walter, *The English Constitution* (1867). The classic summation of the English political system in the mid-Victorian era. (Available in several editions.)

Benson, E. F., *Queen Victoria* (1935). A brief biography.

Binkley, R. C., *Realism and Nationalism: 1852–1871*§ (1935; 1963). A survey, in the Harper Rise of Modern Europe series.

Eyck, Erich, *Bismarck and the German Empire*§ (1950; 1964) An abbreviation of a 3-volume German work by a historian somewhat critical of the Chancellor.

Friedjung, Heinrich, trans. A. J. P. Taylor and W. L. McElwee, *The Struggle for Supremacy in Germany, 1859–1866* (1935). The conflict between Austria and Prussia, by an Austrian historian of German sympathies; originally published in 1897.

Griffith, G. O., *Mazzini: Prophet of Modern Europe* (1932). "What has been attempted in the main is the setting forth of the development of Mazzini's inner life."

Hales, E. E. Y., *Pio Nono*§ (1954; 1962). A sympathetic view of the Pope and of the position of the Church in its struggle with the liberal, national state, by a Catholic historian.

Halévy, Elie, *History of the English People in the Nineteenth Century*§ Vol. IV: *The Victorian Years, 1841–1895* (1926; 2nd ed. rev.)

Howard, M. E., *The Franco-Prussian War* (1961). An account of military operations.

King, Bolton, *A History of Italian Unity*, 2 vols. (1899; rev. ed. 1912). A sweeping panorama of Italian political life from the fall of Napoleon to 1871.

Kitson Clark, George, *The Making of Victorian England* (1962). An effort to reinterpret the Victorian period in depth by using a variety of new methods, including statistical.

Longford, Elizabeth, *Queen Victoria* (1965). A full-dress biography, based on the queen's personal archives.

Mackay, D. C., *The National Workshops* (1933). The abortive socialist institutions set up in Paris in 1848.

Manuel, F. E., *The New World of Henri Saint-Simon*§ (1956; 1963). An intellectual biography of the thinker who exerted an enormous influence on French thought and politics of the mid-nineteenth century.

Mosse, W. E., *Alexander II and the Modernization of Russia*§ (1958). A brief survey of the reign which saw the most important liberal reforms.

Mosse, W. E., *The European Powers and the German Question, 1848–1871* (1958). The attitude of the other great powers toward the unification of Germany.

Namier, Lewis, *1848: The Revolution of the Intellectuals*§ (1944; 1964). Concentrates on the revolutions in Germany; reveals reactionary nationalist elements present in the German liberal movement.

Pflanze, Otto, *Bismarck and the Development of Germany*, (1963). Deals with Bismarck and his role in the unification of Germany, stopping with 1871.

Rath, R. J., *The Viennese Revolution of 1848* (1957). Emphasizes opinion.

Robertson, Priscilla, *Revolutions of 1848*§ (1952; 1960). A survey of the revolutionary year throughout Europe.

Salvemini, Gaetano, *Mazzini*§ (1910; 1957). His political thought and political action.

Simpson, F. A., *Louis Napoleon and the Recovery of France* (1923). The career of Napoleon III until the end of the Crimean War.

Simpson, F. A., *The Rise of Louis Napoleon* (1909; 3rd ed. 1950). The youth of Napoleon III.

Smith, Denis Mack, *Cavour and Garibaldi, 1860* (1954). Conflict between two political ideologies and personalities against the background of revolution in Sicily and Naples.

Smith, Denis Mack, *Garibaldi* (1956). "A great life in brief."

Temperley, Harold, *England and the Near East: The Crimea* (1936). The "Eastern Question" from 1839 onward, culminating in the outbreak of the Crimean War.

Thayer, W. R., *The Life and Times of Cavour*, 2 vols. (1911). A full-bodied life-and-thought, old but still not superseded.

Thompson, J. M., *Louis Napoleon and the Second Empire* (1955). Concludes "he was a man too small for the great things he set out to do."

Valentin, Veit, *1848: Chapters of German History*, trans. E. J. Scheffauer (1940). An abbreviated version of the standard German account.

Zeldin, Theodore, *The Political System of Napoleon III* (1958). An attempt to analyze the political techniques employed by Napoleon III.

(*See also* bibliography, General Literature—Britain: Young; and Russia: Kornilov.)

CHAPTER 16. SCIENCE AND THE SCIENTIFIC OUTLOOK

Bagehot, Walter, *Physics and Politics* (1873). Politics seen from the point of view of Social Darwinism.

Becker, G. J., ed., *Documents of Modern Literary Realism* (1963). An anthology of writings by authors and critics of the nineteenth and twentieth centuries.

Berdiaev, Nikolai, *Leontiev* (1940). The life and thought of a Russian aesthete and enemy of industrial civilization.

Burrow, J. W., *Evolution and Society* (1966). The impact of Darwinian theories on social thought of the Victorian era.

Charlton, D. G., *Positivist Thought in France During the Second Empire, 1852–1870* (1959). Positivism and its influence on sociology, scientism, and literature.

Darwin, Charles, *On the Origin of Species by Means of Natural Selection*§ (1859). The classic statement of the theory of "natural selection." (Available in several editions.)

Darwin, Charles, *The Voyage of the Beagle*§ (1860). An account of the scientific journey which provided Darwin with evidence for the theory of "natural selection." (Available in several editions.)

Dostoevsky, Fedor, *The Diary of a Writer*, 2 vols. (1949; 1954). The political articles of the Russian novelist and conservative thinker.

Irvine, William, *Apes, Angels, and Victorians*§ (1957). Joint biography of Darwin and Huxley.

Kaufmann, W. A., *Nietzsche*§ (1950; 1964). A study of a leading critic of nineteenth-century civilization.

Marvin, F. S., *Comte* (1936; 1965). The philosophy of the founder of sociology.

Merz, J. T., *A History of European Thought in the Nineteenth Century*§ 4 vols. (1896–1914). A survey of scientific and philosophical thought in the age of positivism.

Sears, P. B., *Charles Darwin* (1950). An introduction to Darwin and Darwinism.

Woodcock, George, and Ivan Avakumovič, *The Anarchist Prince* (1950). The life of Peter Kropotkin, the Russian foe of Social Darwinism and the apostle of cooperation.

CHAPTER 17. THE INDUSTRIALIZATION OF THE CONTINENT

Buer, M. C., *Health, Wealth and Population* (1926). An explanation of the population growth 1760–1815 in England and Wales in terms of rising living standards during the Industrial Revolution.

Feis, Herbert, *Europe, the World's Banker, 1870–1914* (1930). Europe's investments in its colonies and other economically underdeveloped countries.

Carr-Saunders, A. M., *World Population* (1936). A standard analysis of the problems posed by population growth in the modern world.

Clapham, J. H., *Economic History of Modern Britain*, 2nd ed., Vols. II (1932) and III (1938). The zenith of British industrial and commercial might and the beginning of the decline.

Hirst, M. E., *Life of Friedrich List* (1909). Still the only biography in English; includes selections from his writings.

List, Friedrich, *The National System of Political Economy* (1841). The classical modern argument for economic protectionism and national economic development.

Singer, C. J., *et al.*, eds., *A History of Technology*, Vol. V: *Late Nineteenth Century, 1850–1900* (1958).

Stolper, Gustav, *The German Economy, 1870 to the Present* (1940). Stresses the role of the state in German economy.

(*See also* bibliography, General Literature—Economic and Social: Ashley; Ashworth; *Cambridge Economic History of Europe*, Vol. VI; Condliffe; and Glass and Eversley.)

CHAPTER 18. URBAN CULTURE AND THE MIDDLE CLASS

Banks, J. A., and Olive Banks, *Feminism and Family Planning in Victorian England* (1964). The domestic economics of the Victorian middle class.

Briggs, Asa, *Victorian Cities* (1965). An account of the life in several urban centers as an aspect of the total Victorian experience.

Briggs, Asa, *Victorian People*§ (1955; 1965). Biographical sketches of outstanding mid-Victorian figures intended to redress the prevailing unfavorable view.

Clephane, Irene, *Towards Sex Freedom* (1935). The social emancipation of European women, mostly before World War I.

Cruse, Amy, *The Victorians and Their Books* (1935). Literary history concentrated not on the writer but the reader; tells what was read in England in the first fifty years of Victoria's reign.

Dalziel, Margaret, *Popular Fiction 100 Years Ago* (1958). The literary tastes of the mass reading public in mid-Victorian England.

Dudek, Louis, *Literature and the Press* (1960). The effects of modern printing methods on culture in the English-speaking world.

Houghton, W. E., *The Victorian Frame of Mind, 1830–1870*§ (1957; 1963). The values and outlook on life of early Victorian England.

Lowndes, G. A. N., *The Silent Social Revolution* (1937). "An account of the expansion of public education in England and Wales, 1895–1935."

Morazé, Charles, *The Triumph of the Middle Classes* (1966). The European bourgeoisie during its zenith, 1780–1880.

Pevsner, Nikolaus, *High Victorian Design*

(1951). The nadir of nineteenth-century taste, the Crystal Palace Exhibition of 1851.

Reitlinger, Gerald, *The Economics of Taste*, 2 vols., (1961; 1964). "The rise and fall of the *objets d'art* market since 1750."

Smiles, Samuel, *Self-help* (1859; 1959). From rags to riches to fame by way of honesty, industry, and thrift, as shown through examples of self-made men.

Sombart, Werner, *The Quintessence of Capitalism* (1913). The cultural background and the ethos of the European bourgeois.

Stutterheim, Kurt von, *The Press in England* (1934). Mostly devoted to the nineteenth and twentieth centuries.

Weber, A. F., *The Growth of Cities in the Nineteenth Century* (1899; 1963). The sociology of the modern city.

Wingfield-Stratford, Esmé, *The Victorian Tragedy* (1930). Victorian social life and values at mid-nineteenth century.

(*See also* bibliography, General Literature—Economic and Social: Dickinson; Mumford; and Palm.)

CHAPTER 19. LABOR AND SOCIALISM

Berlin, Isaiah, *Karl Marx*§ (1939; 3rd ed. 1963; 1966). The man, his ideas, his achievements.

Bernstein, Eduard, *Evolutionary Socialism*§ (1909; 1963). The original statement of Marxist Revisionism.

Braunthal, Julius, *History of the International*, Vol. I (1967). Traces the history of the first two socialist internationals up to 1914; by a participant in the Second International.

Carr, E. H., *Michael Bakunin*§ (1937; 1961). A biography of the leading Russian anarchist.

Cole, G. D. H., *A History of Socialist Thought*, Vol. I: *The Forerunners, 1789–1850* (1953). A broad survey of modern socialist movements until the emergence of Marxism. Vol. II: *Marxism and Anarchism, 1850–1890* (1953). The conflict between Marx and Bakunin.

Cole, G. D. H., and A. W. Filson, *British Working Class Movements: Select Documents, 1789–1875*§ (1951). Excerpts from official reports, worker publications, and other sources bearing on the labor movement.

Gay, Peter, *The Dilemma of Democratic Socialism*§ (1952; 1962). Bernstein and Marxist Revisionism.

Hook, Sidney, *From Hegel to Marx*§ (1936; 1962). Philosophic and political radicalism as background to the emergence of Marxism.

Laidler, H. W., *Social-economic Movements* (1960). A general account of all the major and many minor socialist ideologies and movements.

Lichtheim, George, *Marxism*§ (1961; 1962). An introduction to Marxist theory.

McBriar, A. M., *Fabian Socialism and English Politics, 1884–1918*§ (1962; 1966). The role of Fabianism in the emergence of labor as a political movement.

Man, Henri de, *The Psychology of Socialism* (1927). By a disenchanted socialist.

Manuel, F. E., *The Prophets of Paris*§ (1962). Turgot, Condorcet, Saint-Simon with his disciples, Fourier, and Comte as social visionaries.

Marx, Karl, *Capital*§ (Vol. I, 1867, Vols. II–III, ed. by Engels, 1885–1894; Vol. IV, ed. by Karl Kautsky, 1905–1910). The main theoretical opus of Marx. (Available in several editions.)

Marx, Karl, and Friedrich Engels, *The Communist Manifesto*§ (1848). The prophesy of the imminence and inevitability of a Communist revolution. (Available in several editions.)

Maximoff, G. P., ed., *The Political Philosophy of Bakunin*§ (1953; 1964). An anthology of Bakunin's writings.

Mayer, Gustav, *Friedrich Engels* (1936). A biography of Marx's collaborator.

Mehring, Franz, *Karl Marx*§ (1935; 1962). An "official" biography, by the historian of the Second International.

Michels, Robert, *Political Parties*§ (1915). A study in political sociology revealing the bureaucratization of modern parties, including the Social Democratic.

Pelling, Henry, *The Origins of the Labour Party, 1880–1900* (1954; 2nd ed. 1965). Emphasis on political sociology: how the Labour party became a party.

Perlman, Selig, *A Theory of the Labor Movement* (1928). On the basis of historical evidence stresses the role of trade unionism and the gulf between laborers and socialist intellectuals.

Shaw, George Bernard, ed., *Fabian Essays in Socialism* (1889). The principal theoretical work of the Fabian socialists.

Sorel, Georges, *Reflections on Violence*§ (1908). A French syndicalist, who influenced Mussolini, stresses the need for the "myth" to keep the working class movement going. (Available in several editions.)

Webb, Sidney, and Beatrice Webb, *The History of Trade Unionism* (1894). The evolution of the trade-union movement in Britain by two leading Fabian socialists.

(*See also* bibliography, General Literature—Britain: Cole and Postgate; and Chapter 13: Thompson.)

Chapman, Guy, *The Dreyfus Case: A Reassessment* (1956). An attempt to provide a balanced view of the issues and personalities.

Croce, Benedetto, *A History of Italy, 1871–1915*, trans. C. M. Ady (1929). A broad political and cultural analysis of Italy by a liberal historian.

Cross, Colin, *The Liberals in Power, 1905–1914* (1963). Emphasis on social legislation which laid the foundations of the welfare state.

Curtis, Michael, *Three Against the Third Republic* (1959). Sorel, Barrès, and Maurras.

Dawson, W. H., *Bismarck and State Socialism* (1890). An old account, still valid, of the ideas behind Bismarckian social measures and the whole modern welfare state.

Ensor, R. C. K., *England 1870–1914* (1936). A general survey.

Eyck, Erich, *Bismarck and the German Empire*§ (1959; 1964). A political biography.

Fischer, George, *Russian Liberalism from Gentry to Intelligentsia* (1958). From the middle of the nineteenth century to the Revolution of 1905.

Halévy, Elie, *History of the English People in the Nineteenth Century*§ Vol. V: *Imperialism and the Rise of Labour, 1895–1905*; Vol. VI: *The Rule of Democracy, 1905–1914* (1926; 2nd ed. rev.).

Hanham, H. J., *Elections and Party Management* (1959). "Deals solely with problems of the ordinary party politician and the growth of party organisation" in the era of Disraeli and Gladstone.

Hayes, C. J. H., *A Generation of Materialism, 1871–1900*§ (1941; 1961). A survey, in the Harper Rise of Modern Europe series.

Jellinek, Frank, *The Paris Commune of 1871*§ (1937; 1965). The story of the uprising of anarchists and Jacobins in the French capital during its siege by German armies.

Jones, Thomas, *Lloyd George* (1951). A biography of the man who first led and then wrecked the Liberal party.

Magnus, Philip, *Gladstone*§ (1954; 1964). The standard biography.

May, A. J., *The Hapsburg Monarchy, 1867–1914* (1951). A comprehensive survey.

Miliukov, P. N., *Russia and Its Crisis*§ (1905; 1962). Russia at the turn of the century as seen, at the time, by the leader of the Constitutional-Democratic party and an outstanding historian.

Monypenny, W. F., and G. E. Buckle, *The Life of Benjamin Disraeli, Earl of Beaconsfield* (1910–1920; 1929). The standard older biography.

Nowell-Smith, S. H., ed., *Edwardian England, 1901–1914* (1964). A collective work depicting various aspects of British life on the eve of World War I.

Pobedonostsev, K. P., *Reflections of a Russian Statesman*§ (1898; 1965). The political ideas of the man who most influenced the policies of Alexander III.

Pulzer, P. G. J., *The Rise of Political Anti-Semitism in Germany and Austria*§ (1966). Traces the emergence between 1867 and 1914 of anti-Semitic politics in German-speaking Central Europe, casting light on neo-conservative movements in general.

Robinson, G. T., *Rural Russia Under the Old Regime* (1932). Agrarian conditions and problems after the emancipation of the serfs.

Rogger, Hans, and Eugen Weber, eds., *The European Right* (1965). A collection of essays by diverse authors on conservative movements throughout Europe.

Somervell, D. C., *Disraeli and Gladstone* (1925). A double biography.

Venturi, Franco, *Roots of Revolution*§ (1960). The Russian social-revolutionary movement in the age of Alexander II.

Walkin, Jacob, *The Rise of Democracy in Pre-Revolutionary Russia* (1962). Stresses the forces tending toward greater democratization after 1861.

Weber, E. J., *Action Française* (1962). The story of the most aggressive neo-conservative group in Europe.

CHAPTER 21. DIPLOMACY AND IMPERIALISM: 1870–1914

Albertini, Luigi, *The Origins of the War of 1914*, trans. ed., I. M. Massey, 3 vols. (1952–1957). Vol. I: *European Relations from the Congress of Berlin to the Eve of the Sarajevo Murder*. Deals with the diplomatic antecedents from the Congress of Berlin (1878) to 1914; rather severe on Germany.

Bodelsen, C. A. G., *Studies in Mid-Victorian Imperialism* (1924). An intellectual history of the movement from "Little England" to "Greater Britain."

Brandenburg, Erich, *From Bismarck to the World War* (1927). Diplomatic history (1870–1914) concerned with the question of responsibility for World War I.

Brunschwig, Henri, *French Colonialism, 1871–1914* (1966). Stresses nationalism as a factor in French expansion and contrasts with British imperialism.

Clark, Grover, *The Balance Sheets of Imperialism* (1936). Shows the unprofitability of colonialism by means of statistics.

Craig, G. A., *From Bismarck to Adenauer*§ (1958). A brief, critical survey of German foreign policy and its lack of realism.

Hobson, J. A., *Imperialism*§ (1902; 1965). The classic argument for the economic interpretation of imperialism.

Hoffmann, R. J. S., *Great Britain and the German Trade Rivalry, 1875–1914* (1933). Upholds the thesis that Britain did not go to war for commercial reasons, but shows influence of economic fears on British opinion.

Hudson, G. F., *The Far East in World Politics* (1937). Great power activities in East Asia in the nineteenth and twentieth centuries.

Kipling, Rudyard, *Barrack-room Ballads* (1892). Sadistic, brawling verse meant to exult virility; reflects the mood of Social Darwinism and imperialism of the late nineteenth century.

Langer, William L., *European Alliances and Alignments, 1871–1890*§ (1931) and *The Diplomacy of Imperialism, 1890–1902* (1935). These two volumes provide a comprehensive survey of conflicts of the great powers and the formation of the principal alliances.

Langer, William L., *The Franco-Russian Alliance, 1890–1894* (1929; 1966). Supplements Langer's general studies (above) of diplomatic history of late nineteenth-century Europe.

Lovell, R. I., *The Struggle for South Africa, 1875–1899* (1934). Centers on Cecil Rhodes and the antecedents of the Boer War.

Lucas, C. P., *The Partition and Colonization of Africa* (1922). Devotes main attention to the late nineteenth-century "scramble."

Moon, P. T., *Imperialism and World Politics in the Nineteenth and Twentieth Centuries* (1919). Western imperialism in its final burst of expansion.

Petrovich, M. B., *The Emergence of Russian Panslavism, 1856–1870* (1956). The ideology behind Russia's push into the Balkans and conflict with Austria.

Saul, S. B., *Studies in British Overseas Trade, 1870–1914* (1960). Commerce within and without the empire as aspects of the emergent world economy.

Schmitt, B. E., *Triple Alliance and Triple Entente, 1902–1914* (1924). A brief account of the formation of the diplomatic alliances before World War I.

Sumner, B. H., *Russia and the Balkans, 1870–1880* (1937). From the antecedents to the consequences of the Russo-Turkish War of 1877.

Sumner, B. H., *Tsardom and Imperialism in the Far East and the Middle East, 1880–*

1914 (1942). Russia's contribution to the imperialist competition over land and influence.

Townsend, M. E., *The Rise and Fall of Germany's Colonial Empire, 1884–1918* (1930). From imperial indifference to imperial ambition to imperial collapse.

Wertheimer, M. S., *The Pan-German League, 1890–1914* (1924). The story of the powerful nationalistic and imperialistic lobby in Wilhelmian Germany.

Williams, Basil, *Cecil Rhodes* (1921). A biography of one of the leading British imperialists, by an admirer.

Woodward, E. L., *Great Britain and the German Navy* (1935). The "naval race."

(*See also* histories in modern diplomacy and imperialism listed in bibliography, General Literature—Politics, Diplomacy, and Warfare.)

CHAPTER 22. WORLD WAR I

Albertini, Luigi, *The Origins of the War of 1914*, trans. and ed., J. M. Massey (1952–1957). Vols. II and III.

Armeson, R. B., *Total Warfare and Compulsory Labor* (1964). "A study of the military-industrial complex of Germany during World War I."

Chambers, F. P., *The War Behind the War, 1914–1918* (1939). An account of home mobilization among the belligerents during World War I.

Cruttwell, C. R. M. F., *A History of the Great War, 1914–1918* (1934; 2nd ed., 1936). A general survey of all the fronts.

Falls, Cyril, *The Great War: 1914–1918*§ (1959; 1961). A general survey.

Fay, S. B., *The Origins of the World War*, 2 vols.§ (1928; 2nd rev. ed., 1938). Tends to be somewhat more generous to the German and Austrian side than most foreign historians.

Feldman, G. D., *Army, Industry, and Labor in Germany, 1914–1918* (1966). Social aspects of the German military effort.

Fischer, Fritz, *Germany's Aims in the First World War* (1967). On the basis of archival documents shows how broad and uncompromising were German ambitions.

Forster, Kent, *The Failures of Peace* (1942). "The search for a negotiated peace during the First World War."

Golovin, N. N., *The Russian Army in the World War* (1931). Not a military narrative but an analysis of the condition of the Russian armed forces.

Hašek, Jaroslav, *The Good Soldier: Schweik*§ (1930; 1962). The archetypal bewildered little man in World War I: a Czech recruit in the Austrian army.

Hemingway, Ernest, *A Farewell to Arms*§ (1929; 1967). World War I on the Italian front.

Kedourie, Elie, *England and the Middle East* (1956). "The destruction of the Ottoman Empire, 1914–1921."

Lee, D. E., ed., *The Outbreak of the First World War: Who Was Responsible?*§ (1958; rev. ed., 1963). A source book, with excerpts from differing points of view.

Liddell-Hart, B. H., *A History of the World War, 1914–1918* (1930). A survey by a leading British strategist.

May, A. J., *The Passing of the Hapsburg Monarchy 1914–1918*, 2 vols. (1966). Austria-Hungary during World War I.

May, E. R., *The World War and American Isolation, 1914–1917*§ (1959; 1966). The fight to keep the United States out of World War I, and its defeat.

Parsons, I. M., *Men Who March Away* (1965). British war poetry, 1914–1918.

Remarque, Erich Maria, *All Quiet on the Western Front*§ (1929; 1962.). This novel was the first to impress the broad public with the horror of modern warfare.

Renouvin, Pierre, *The Immediate Origins of the War (28th June–4th August 1914)* (1928). A balanced view of the question of origins and responsibility, rather severe on the Central Powers.

Ritter, Gerhard, *The Schlieffen Plan* (1958). A detailed analysis of the emergence of the plan, with documents.

Romains, Jules, *Verdun: The Prelude, the Battle* (1939). A novel, part of a cycle called *Men of Good Will*.

Tuchman, Barbara, *The Guns of August*§ (1962). An account of the opening phase of World War I.

Wegerer, Alfred von, *A Refutation of the Versailles War Guilt Thesis* (1930). A German response to the charge that Germany was the sole aggressor.

CHAPTER 23.   THE RUSSIAN REVOLUTION

Borkenau, Franz, *World Communism*§ (1938; 1962). A survey of the activities of the Third International, by a one-time member.

Carr, E. H., *The Bolshevik Revolution, 1917–1923*, 3 vols.§ (1950–1953). Detailed, topical rather than narrative; sympathetic to the general course of Bolshevik policy.

Chamberlain, W. H., *The Russian Revolution, 1917–1921*, 2 vols.§ (1935; 1954). A general history stressing political and military events.

Daniels, R. V., *The Conscience of the Revolution*, (1960). The story of the opposition to the Bolshevik dictatorship within the party.

Daniels, R. V., *Red October* (1967). A narrative of the events leading to the Bolshevik seizure of power.

Degras, Jane, ed., *The Communist International, 1919–1943*, Vol. I: *1919–1922* (1956). Documents.

Denikin, A. I., *The White Army* (1930). By the commander of the principal anti-Bolshevik force, the Volunteer Army.

Deutscher, Isaac, *The Prophet Armed*§ (1954). The story of Trotsky's rise (1879–1921), by an ardent admirer.

Florinsky, M. T., *The End of the Russian Empire*§ (1931; 1961). Russia during World War I and the role of the war in causing the collapse of the old regime.

Katkov, George, *Russia, 1917* (1967). An investigation of the more obscure forces involved in the fall of the imperial regime, including German sedition.

Kerensky, Alexander, *The Kerensky Memoirs*, (1965). The autobiography of the last Prime Minister of the Provisional Government.

Kerensky, Alexander, and R. P. Browder, *The Russian Provisional Government, 1917*, 3 vols. (1961). A collection of documents bearing on the policies of the Provisional Government.

Nicholas II and Alexandra, *The Letters of the Tsar to the Tsaritsa, 1914–1917* (1929). A collection of private exchanges, miraculously preserved.

Pares, Bernard, *The Fall of the Russian Monarchy*§ (1939). By a British historian who was an eyewitness of the events.

Pipes, Richard, *The Formation of the Soviet Union* (1954; rev. ed. 1964). The history of the disintegration of the Russian Empire and the establishment of the multinational Communist state (1917–1923).

Radkey, O. H., *The Election to the Russian Constituent Assembly of 1917* (1950). An analysis of the voting and its results.

Reed, John, *Ten Days That Shook the World*§ (1919). A literary rendition of the Bolshevik power seizure, by a sympathetic American witness.

Schapiro, L. B., *The Communist Party of the Soviet Union*§ (1960; 1964). In view of the importance of the party, this is in effect a history of the Soviet Union and its government.

Schapiro, L. B., *The Origin of the Communist Autocracy*§ (1955; 1965). The story of the suppression by the Communist regime of internal dissent during Lenin's lifetime.

Sukhanov, N. N., *The Russian Revolution, 1917*, ed. Joel Carmichael§ (1955; 1962). A

condensed translation of the 7-volume Russian work by a hostile socialist who was in the midst of the events.

Trotsky, Leon, *The History of the Russian Revolution*, 3 vols. (1932–1933). Not so much a historical study as a personal account by a leading actor.

Ulam, A. B., *The Bolsheviks* (1965). The rise of Bolshevism in the form of a biography of Lenin.

Wheeler-Bennett, J. W., *Brest-Litovsk*§ (1956; 1963). An account of the Russo-German peace negotiations after the Bolshevik power seizure.

Wolfe, Bertram, *Three Who Made a Revolution*§ (1948; 4th ed. 1964). The lives of Lenin, Trotsky, and Stalin before they became rulers of Russia.

Wrangel, N. E., *From Serfdom to Bolshevism* (1927). Recollections of the last commander of the White forces.

Zeman, Z. A. B., ed., *Germany and the Revolution in Russia, 1915–1918* (1958). Selected documents bearing on German-Bolshevik relations found in captured archives of the German Foreign Ministry.

CHAPTER 24.   MODERN THOUGHT

Allen, G. W., *William James* (1967). A biography.

Ayer, A. J., *Language, Truth and Logic*§ (1936; 2nd rev. ed). An introduction to logical positivism.

Bergson, Henri, *Creative Evolution* (1907; 1944). The main work of the influential late nineteenth-century French philosopher, stressing difference between intelligence and instinct.

Cline, B. L., *The Questioners* (1965). An introduction to the history of the quantum theory.

Einstein, Albert, *Ideas and Opinions*§ (1954; 1960). An anthology of Einstein's pronouncements on men, politics, and scientific questions.

Frank, Philipp, *Einstein: His Life and Times* (1947). An intellectual biography, by a disciple and a leading philosopher of science.

Glover, Edward, *Freud or Jung?*§ (1950; 1963). Jung interpreted by a Freudian, with predictable results.

Heisenberg, Werner, *Philosophic Problems of Nuclear Science* (1952). The intellectual implications of post-quantum physics by a leading modern scientist.

Heisenberg, Werner, *The Physicist's Conception of Nature* (1958). A philosophical essay.

Hughes, H. S., *Consciousness and Society*§ (1958; 1961). Stress on innovations in the conception of man's place in the human environment, 1890–1930.

Infeld, Leopold, *Albert Einstein*§ (1950; 1953). An introduction to Einstein's theory.

Jacobi, Jolande, *The Psychology of C. G. Jung*§ (1942; rev. ed. 1963). By a follower.

James, William, *Essays on Faith and Morals*§ (1897). Representative selections.

Jones, Ernest, *The Life and Work of Sigmund Freud*, 3 vols. (1953–1957;§ abr. Lionel Trilling and Steven Marcus, 1961). The author is the leading exponent of Freudian psychology in England.

Müller-Freienfels, Richard, *The Evolution of Modern Psychology* (1935). General introduction to various modern psychological schools.

Perry, R. B., *Philosophy of the Recent Past* (1926). Bergson, William James, and other thinkers of their time.

Planck, Max, *Scientific Autobiography, and Other Papers* (1949). By the discoverer of quanta; his philosophy of life and science.

Planck, Max, *Where Is Science Going?* (1932). Reflections on science and its place in modern life.

Rieff, Philip, *Freud*§ (1959; 1961). An introduction to Freud and his teachings.

Sartre, Jean-Paul, *Existentialism and Human Emotions*§ (1948; 1965). Popular exposition of existential philosophy by its most popular exponent.

Schrödinger, Erwin, *Science Theory and Man*§ (1957) [*Science and the Human Temperament* (1935)]. By a leading physicist, the author of the "uncertainty principle"; stresses the importance of chance in science and the flaws in common-sense causal thinking.

White, M. G., ed., *The Age of Analysis*§ (1955). An anthology of modern philosophic texts with brief introductions.

CHAPTER 25. MODERN TASTE

Barr, Alfred, ed., *Masters of Modern Art* (1954). An introduction to Modernism in the visual arts.

Bowra, C. M., *The Heritage of Symbolism*§ (1943; 1961). Valery, Rilke, S. George, Blok, Yeats.

Collaer, Paul, *A History of Modern Music*§ (1961). An introduction.

Giedion, Sigfried, *Space, Time and Architecture* (1941; 4th rev. ed. 1962). Shows the interrelationship and purposefulness of modern art.

Haftmann, Werner, *Painting in the Twentieth Century*, 2 vols.§ (1961; new ed. 1965).

Hitchcock, H. R., *Architecture, Nineteenth and Twentieth Centuries* (1958; 2nd ed. 1963).

Humphrey, Robert, *Stream of Consciousness in the Modern Novel*§ (1954; 1962).

Joedicke, Jürgen, *A History of Modern Architecture* (1959).

Leymarie, Jean, *French Painting*, Vol. III: *The Nineteenth Century from David to Seurat* (1962). Classicism, Realism, and Impressionism, all richly illustrated.

Mackail, J. W., *The Life of William Morris*, 2 vols. (1899). A standard biography of the pioneer of modern design.

Madsen, S. T., *Art Nouveau* (1967). A survey of the decorative style popular at the turn of the century.

Pevsner, Nikolaus, *Pioneers of Modern Design*§ (1936; 1964) The origins, from William Morris to World War I, with stress on architecture and the applied arts.

Rewald, John, *The History of Impressionism* (1946; rev. ed. 1962).

Rewald, John, *Post-Impressionism: From Van Gogh to Gauguin*, Vol. I. (1956).

Salazar, Adolfo, *Music in our Time* (1946).

Wilson, Edmund, *Axel's Castle*§ (1931; 1959). A survey of Symbolic and post-Symbolic literature, 1870–1930.

CHAPTER 26. THE TWENTIES

Birdsall, Paul, *Versailles Twenty Years After* (1941). Opposes the view that the Versailles Treaty was responsible for the collapse of peace in the 1930s.

Eyck, Erich, *A History of the Weimar Republic*, trans. H. P. Hanson and R. G. L. Waite, 2 vols. (1962–1963). Vol. I: *From the Collapse of the Empire to Hindenburg's Election*; Vol. II: *From the Locarno Conference to Hitler's Seizure of Power*.

Finer, Herman, *Mussolini's Italy*§ (1935; 1964). A survey of the history and life of Italy during the first decade of fascism.

Halperin, S. W., *Germany Tried Democracy*§ (1946; 1965). The Weimar Republic, a political history.

Link, A. S., *Woodrow Wilson* (1963). A biography.

Macartney, C. A., and A. W. Palmer, *Independent Eastern Europe* (1962). Eastern Europe between the wars.

Mamatey, V. S., *The United States and East Central Europe, 1914–1918* (1957). American diplomacy and the emergence of independent states on the ruins of Austria-Hungary.

Mowat, C. L., *Britain Between the Wars, 1918–1940* (1955). A survey.

Nicolson, Harold, *Peacemaking*§ (1919; 1965).

Reflections on the Paris Conference by a diplomat-historian and a participant.

Rosenberg, Arthur, *A History of the German Republic* (1936; 1965). The Weimar Republic.

Rothschild, Joseph, *Pilsudski's Coup d'État* (1966). A monograph tracing the establishment of dictatorship in Poland (1926).

Walters, F. P., *A History of the League of Nations* 2 vols. (1952). From its foundation to the end of World War II.

Wiskemann, Elizabeth, *Europe of the Dictators, 1919–1945*§ (1966). A brief survey of the destruction of democracy and the rise and fall of authoritarian states on the Continent.

CHAPTER 27. TOTALITARIANISM

Arendt, Hannah, *The Origins of Totalitarianism*§ (1951; 1966). Shows progression from anti-Semitism through imperialism to totalitarianism, concentrating on Soviet Russia and Nazi Germany.

Baumont, Maurice, J. H. E. Fried, and E. Vermeil, eds., *The Third Reich* (1955). The antecedents of nazism, its ascent and its manifestation, by an international group of scholars.

Beck, F., and W. Godin, *Russian Purge and the Extraction of Confession* (1951). An analysis of the Stalinist terror.

Bullock, Alan, *Hitler, A Study in Tyranny*§ (1952; rev. ed. 1964). A biography.

Carr, E. H., *History of Soviet Russia: The Interregnum, 1923–1924* and *Socialism in One Country, 1924–1926*§ 2 vols. (1954; 1961). Devoted to the struggle for succession and Stalin's triumph.

Cohn, N. R. C., *Warrant for Genocide* (1967). "The myth of the Jewish world conspiracy."

Dallin, David, and B. I. Nicolaevsky, *Forced Labor in Soviet Russia* (1947). A history of Soviet concentration camps by two Russian émigré socialists.

Deutscher, Isaac, *The Prophet Unarmed*§ (1959). The Trotsky-Stalin struggle in the form of a Trotsky biography.

Eschenburg, Theodor, *et al.*, *The Path to Dictatorship, 1918–1933*§ (1966). Essays by ten historians on the collapse of the Weimar Republic and the Nazi seizure of power.

Fainsod, Merle, *How Russia is Ruled* (1953; rev. ed. 1963). Soviet political institutions.

Fischer, Ruth, *Stalin and German Communism* (1948). A prominent one-time member describes the history of the German Communist party from its emergence until the late 1920s, when Stalin took over.

Ginzburg, Evgeniia, *The Wayward Path* (1967). Recollections of the Stalinist purges by a Communist, now living in Russia.

Hodson, H. V., *Slump and Recovery, 1929–1937* (1938). An economic analysis of the depression.

Khrushchev, Nikita S., *The Crimes of the Stalin Era* (1956). Khrushchev's "secret speech" at the Twentieth Party Congress, revealing facts about Stalin and his terror.

Milosz, Czeslaw, *The Captive Mind*§ (1953; 1955). A Polish writer who escaped from Stalinist Poland describes what it is like for an intellectual to live under totalitarianism.

Orwell, George, *1984*§ (1949; 1963). An anti-utopian novel depicting life in an imaginary totalitarian state.

Reitlinger, Gerald, *The SS* (1957). Himmler and his apparatus of mass murder.

Robbins, Lionel, *The Great Depression* (1934). An economist's view.

Schoenbaum, David, *Hitler's Social Revolution*§ (1966). The Nazi policy toward various social groups before World War II.

Solzhenitsyn, Alexander, *One Day in the Life of Ivan Denisovich*§ (1963). A semi-fictional account of a Stalinist concentration camp by a Soviet writer speaking from personal experience.

Souvarine, Boris, *Stalin* (1939). A biography, ends in 1937.

Stern, F. R., *The Politics of Cultural Despair*§ (1961; 1963). Three sketches of German prophets of cultural nihilism as background to the rise of nazism.

Talmon, Jacob, *The Origins of Totalitarian Democracy*§ (1952; 2nd ed. 1965). Distinguishes between "liberal" and "totalitarian" democracies, and traces the latter in the thought of eighteenth-century believers in human perfectibility.

Wheeler-Bennett, J. W., *The Nemesis of Power* (1953; 2nd ed.). "The German army in politics, 1918–1945."

Zamiatin, Evgenii I., *We*§ (1924; 1959). An anti-utopian novel by a Russian writer.

CHAPTER 28. THE DISSOLUTION
OF THE MIDDLE CLASS

Brown, A. J., *The Great Inflation, 1939–1951* (1955). A rather technical discussion of what has happened to the value of money during 1939–1951, a period the author regards as "one of the greatest, if not the greatest" inflation in world history.

Burnham, James, *The Managerial Revolution*§ (1941; 1960). Asserts that managers are taking over the modern world.

Camp, W. D., *Marriage and the Family in France Since the Revolution* (1961). A statistical study of marital and familial institutions in France for the purpose of ascertaining the fate of both.

Djilas, Milovan, *The New Class*§ (1957; (1961). A Yugoslav Communist and friend of Tito depicts the emergence in Communist countries of a class of bureaucratic exploiters.

Graves, Robert, and Alan Hodge, *The Long Week-end*§ (1940). An amusing account of British life between the wars.

Hoggart, Richard, *The Uses of Literacy*§ (1957; 1961). The culture of the working class in the first half of the twentieth century as influenced by mass publications.

McGregor, O. R., *Divorce in England* (1957). Divorce legislation and incidence during the century following the easing of divorce procedures.

Marwick, Arthur, *The Deluge* (1966). The effects of World War I on British society, 1914–1920.

Mills, C. W., *White Collar*§ (1951; 1962). A sociological study of the American salaried class and its role in modern life.

Strachey, Lytton, *Eminent Victorians*§ (1918; 1963). A collection of four biographical essays intended to ridicule the Victorians by showing they were human after all.

Taylor, J. C., *Futurism* (1961). The artistic side of the Futurist movement.

Wingfield-Stratford, Esmé, *The Victorian Sunset* (1932). A social and cultural account of England 1870–1900, stressing the gradual erosion of Victorian values.

(*See also* bibliography, General Literature—Economic and Social: Palm; and Chapter 18: Lowndes.)

CHAPTER 29. WORLD WAR II

Bettelheim, Bruno, *The Informed Heart* (1960). A psychologist's reflections on man, based on his experiences in Nazi concentration camps.

Broad, Lewis, *Winston Churchill*, 2 vols. (1958–1959). A biography, the bulk devoted to the years of World War II.

Chuikov, V. I., *The Battle for Stalingrad* (1964). Recollections of a Russian commander.

Churchill, Winston, *War Speeches*, 3 vols. (1951–1952).

Clark, Alan, *Barbarossa*§ (1964). The Russian-German war, 1941–1945.

Collier, J. B., *The Defence of the United Kingdom* (1957). The Battle of Britain and Hitler's invasion plans constitute a major part of this military narrative.

Dallin, Alexander, *German Rule in Russia, 1941–1945* (1957). Nazi occupation of Russia and its effect on the population. *The Dark Side of the Moon* (1946). Polish prisoners and refugees, interned in the Soviet Union, describe life in forced labor camps; with a Preface by T. S. Eliot.

Gehl, Jürgen, *Austria, Germany, and the Anschluss, 1931–1938* (1963). The antecedents of Hitler's annexation of Austria.

Gilbert, Martin, and Richard Gott, *The Appeasers* (1963). "British policy toward Nazi Germany" and its follies.

Greenfield, K. R., ed., *Command Decisions* (1959). An analysis of a number of crucial military decisions by the Allied and Axis powers during World War II.

Kogon, Eugen, *The Theory and Practice of Hell*§ (1950). A description of the Nazi concentration camp world by one who was an inmate for six years.

Langsam, W. C., *Historic Documents of World War II*§ (1958). A selection.

Milward, A. S., *The German Economy at War* (1964). The role of the economy in the German war effort.

Plievier, Theodor, *Stalingrad*§ (1948). A novel of the great battle, written by a German participant.

Poliakov, Leon, *Harvest of Hate* (1954). The Nazi genocide of European Jewry.

Reitlinger, Gerald, *The Final Solution*§ (1953; 1961). The murder of European Jews by the Nazis.

Rossi, Angelo, *The Russo-German Alliance, August 1939–June 1941* (1951). A diplomatic account.

Rothfels, Hans, *The German Opposition to Hitler* (1948; 1962). From the early 1930s through the July, 1944, plot.

Rowse, A. L., *Appeasement*§ (1961). An impassioned condemnation, by a historian who saw the appeasers in action at close range.

Royal Institute of International Affairs, *Documents on International Affairs, 1939–1946* (1958). Vol. I contains documents on the immediate antecedents of World War II; Vol. II is called *Hitler's Europe* and deals with the Nazi "New Order."

Royal Institute of International Affairs, *Survey of International Affairs 1939–1946* (1954). Vol. I, *The Eve of War, 1939*, describes the diplomacy of that year.

Sherwood, R. E., *Roosevelt and Hopkins*§ (1948; rev. ed. 1950; 1960). Offers many insights into U.S. policy during World War II.

Snell, J. L., *Illusion and Necessity*§ (1964). A diplomatic history of World War II.

Snell, J. L., *et al.*, *The Meaning of Yalta*§ (1956; 1966). An attempt to clarify confusion about the controversial conference.

Sontag, R. J., and J. S. Beddie, *Nazi-Soviet Relations, 1939–1941* (1948). Documents, captured after the collapse of Germany, dealing with the origins and destiny of the Hitler-Stalin alliance.

Thomas, Hugh, *The Spanish Civil War*§ (1961; 1965). An account of the conflict in which the Nazis, Fascists, Communists, and Anarchists tried their strength, while the democracies watched paralyzed.

Trevor-Roper, Hugh, ed., *Hitler's War Directives, 1939–1945* (1964). Documents recording Hitler's grand strategy.

Weinberg, G. L., *Germany and the Soviet Union, 1939–1941* (1954). The Nazi-Soviet alliance.

Weiss, Peter, *The Investigation*§ (1966). A documentary play based on records of the trial of the guards who had served at Auschwitz.

Werth, Alexander, *Russia at War, 1941–1945*§ (1964). A historic account by a correspondent who had been an eyewitness.

Wheeler-Bennett, J. W., *Munich*§ (1948; 1966). The story of West's capitulation to the dictators in 1938.

Young, Peter, *World War, 1939–1945* (1966). A history of the major operations and engagements.

CHAPTER 30.   THE COLD WAR

Allulieva, Svetlana, *Twenty Letters to a Friend* (1967). Stalin and his domestic life, observed by his daughter.

Bor-Komorowski, Tadeusz, *The Secret Army* (1951). The story of the uprising of the Polish Home Army in Warsaw (1944) by its commander.

Brzezinski, Z. K., *The Soviet Bloc*§ (1960; rev. ed. 1967). A political history of the independent Communist states and satellites, and their relationship with the Soviet Union.

Davison, W. P., *The Berlin Blockade* (1958). The story of the Airlift to the beleaguered city.

Djilas, Milovan, *Conversations with Stalin*§ (1962). An intimate of Tito describes his experiences with Stalin and the Soviet ruling élite.

Feis, Herbert, *Churchill, Roosevelt, Stalin*§ (1957). A study of wartime diplomacy and the roots of the Cold War, centered on the three Allied leaders.

Fejtö, François, *Behind the Rape of Hungary* (1957). The subjugation of Hungary by the Communists and the 1956 revolt.

Jones, J. M., *The Fifteen Weeks*§ (1955; 1965). The formulation of the Truman Doctrine and Marshall Plan, by a State Department official who participated in the decisions.

Kennan, G. F., *Memoirs, 1928–1950* (1967). The recollections of a leading participant in the formulation of U.S. policy toward Soviet Russia after World War II.

Korbel, Josef, *The Communist Subversion of Czechoslovakia, 1938–1948* (1958). A Czech participant tells the story of the destruction of democracy in his country.

Kulski, W. W., *Peaceful Coexistence* (1959). Post-Stalinist Soviet foreign policy in theoretical and historical perspective.

Laqueur, W. Z., and Leopold Labedz, eds., *Polycentrism* (1962). The breakdown of the Communist monolith after the death of Stalin.

Lasky, M. J., ed., *The Hungarian Revolution* (1957). "The story of the October [1956] uprising as recorded in documents, dispatches, eye-witness accounts, and world-wide reactions."

Librach, Jan, *The Rise of the Soviet Empire*§ (1964; rev. ed. 1966). The expansion of the Soviet Union and the growth of its domain.

Mannoni, D. O., *Prospero and Caliban*§ (1956; 1964). A Freudian view of the effects of colonial rule on master and mastered.

Mehnert, Klaus, *Peking and Moscow*§ (1963; 1964). The historic antecedents of the Sino-Soviet rift.

Mikolajczyk, Stanislaw, *The Rape of Poland* (1948). The head of the Polish Peasant party tells of the Sovietization of Poland.

Price, H. B., *The Marshall Plan and Its Meaning* (1955). The origins, development, and results of the European Economic Recovery Program.

Seton-Watson, Hugh, *Neither War nor Peace*§ (1960). Reflections on the forces involved in the Cold War.

Spanier, J. W., *American Foreign Policy Since World War II*§ (1960; 2nd rev. ed. 1965). A comprehensive survey of the Cold War.

Truman, Harry S., *Memoirs*, 2 vols.§ (1958). Sheds light on the Cold War, its origins and development.

White, Theodore H., *Fire in the Ashes* (1953). A journalist's view of post-1945 Europe and America's role in rekindling the smouldering flame of life.

Zagoria, D. S., *The Sino-Soviet Conflict, 1956–1961*§ (1962; 1964). A Chinese specialist traces the origins of the rift.

Zinner, Paul, ed., *National Communism and Popular Revolt in Eastern Europe*§ (1956). Documents bearing on the 1956 upheavals in Poland and Hungary.

Zinner, Paul, *Revolution in Hungary* (1962). Hungary from the end of World War II to the revolt of 1956, based in part on interviews with refugees.

(*See also* bibliography, General Literature—Russia: Kennan.)

CHAPTER 31.   EUROPE AND THE WORLD

Graubard, S. R., ed., *A New Europe?*§ (1964). A collection of essays on European society and politics of the 1950s, with a look toward the future.

Haas, E. B., *The Uniting of Europe* (1958). The history of integration from 1950 to the Treaty of Rome (1957).

Harrod, R. F., *The Life of John Maynard Keynes*§ (1951; 1963). By an eminent economist.

Henderson, W. O., *The Genesis of the Common Market* (1963). The antecedents of economic cooperation and integration from the eighteenth century to the formation of the European Economic Community.

Hutchison, Keith, *The Decline and Fall of British Capitalism* (1950; 1966). The British economy from 1880 to World War II.

Kitzinger, U. W., *The Politics and Economics of European Integration*§ (1963; 1965). An Englishman views (sympathetically) the emergence of the Common Market.

Shonfield, Andrew, *Modern Capitalism*§ (1965). Argues that the economy of the West is no longer capitalist; stresses the growing importance of the public sector.

Index

Free love, 480, 733
Free trade, 294, 319, 327, 330–333, 427, 439–440, 471; de-colonization and, 823–824
Freemasonry, 189
Freischütz, Der (Weber), 351
French and Indian War, 244
French Congress of the National Federation of Trade Unions, 504
French East India Company, 40
French Empire, in post-World War II period, 826–827; *see also* France
French Revolution, 173, 191–192, 201, 225, 267, 280, 282, 291, 293, 296, 303, 317, 345, 360, 377, 380, 484, 727; anticlericalism in, 251; Committee of Public Safety, 260–262, 264; Directory (*1795–1799*), 262, 265, 269–271; dissolution of monarchy, 258–259; Estates General, and bourgeois revolt, 253–255; internal enemies in, 258–260; and Jacobins, 257, 259–261; legacy of, 262–265; and National Assembly, 255; and people of Paris, 259; Reign of Terror in, 260–264; Revolutionary Tribunal, 259–262; and Roman Catholic Church, 258; September massacres (*1792*), 259; symbols of, in allegory, *illus.*, 265; Thermidorean reaction, 262
French Revolution, The (Wordsworth), 360
French Union, 826
Freud, Sigmund, 169, 652–656; *illus.*, 654
Friedland, Battle of, 279
Friedrich, Caspar David, 352, 370; paintings by, 370–371
From the Other Shore (Herzen), 384
Fugger, Jakob, 103; *illus.*, 103
Fugger family, 102–103
Führer, concept of, 705–706
Fulton, Robert, 325
Functionalism, in art, 669–670
Fuseli, John Henry, painting by, 343
Futurism, 465, 738–739
Futurism (Taylor), 739 n.

G

Galápagos Islands, 411
Galen, 141
Galileo Galilei, 127, 130, 133–137, 144–145, 151, 417, 640; *illus.*, 135; conflict with Church, 151–153, 166; law of falling bodies, 137–138, 143
Gallipoli campaign (*1915*), 594
Galsworthy, John, 679
Galvani, Luigi, 428
Gama, Vasco da, 26–27; *illus.*, 27
Gare Saint-Lazare (Monet), *illus.*, 456
Garibaldi, Giuseppe, 394; *illus.*, 394
Gas chambers, Germany, 763–764
Gaskell, Elizabeth Cleghorn, 334, 422
Gasoline, 429
Gaudí, Antoni, 670, 671; architecture by, 671
Gauguin, Paul, 664; *illus.*, 664; paintings by, 664, 665
Gautier, Théophile, 348
General Confederation of Labor, 504
General German Labor Association, 505
General strike, Europe, 504–505
Geneva, Republic of, 228, 248
Genius of Christianity, The (Chateaubriand), 357

Genoa, Republic of, 227–228, 248, 267–268
Genoese traders, 23, 27, 103
Gentleman on Way to the Hunt (Degas), *illus.*, 568
Gentz, Friedrich von, 296
Geoffrin, Mme., Paris salon of, 208
Geology, 411
Geometry, analytical, 146
George I (England), 239
George II (England), 239; *illus.*, 241
George III (England), 386
George IV (England), 386
George V (England), *illus.*, 538
Gérard, Francois, drawing by, 250
German Democratic Republic, 802
German Empire, 398, 400, 542
German Federal Republic, 802; *see also* West Germany
German History in the Time of the Reformation (Ranke), 356
Germanic Confederation, 301, 305, 327–328, 384, 395
German mark, depreciation of, 696
German National Socialist Labor party (NSDAP), 716–717
German Social Democracy, 506, 508–509
Germany, 242–243, 443, 445, 467, 485, 491, 505, 542, 544; Anglo-German rivalry, 556–559; anti-Comintern pact with Italy, 746; Bismarck and, 395, 397–400; blitzkrieg tactics of, 750–751; communism in, 695–697, 716, 719–720; declares war on U.S. (*1941*), 761; decline of liberalism in, 524–529; extermination camps in, 763; foreign investments, 548; Four-Year Plan, 723–724; industrialization in, 319, 327–328, 427, 431, 437–441; industrial revival under Nazis, 723–724; inflation in, 696, 729–730, *illus.*, 729, 731; Japan pact, 749; in League of Nations, 697; merchant navy surrendered to Allies, 696; "mercy" killings in, 765; middle class, in (post-World War I), 729–730; and Napoleonic empire, 279–280; nationalism in, 282–283, 400, 719–725; National Labor Front, 724; Nazi totalitarianism in, 719–725; occupation of Poland, Norway, and Denmark, 752–753; overseas migration from, 447; post-World War II partition of, 800–801; post-World War II political parties, 834–835; reparations from, 685, 694–696; revolutions of *1848*, 379, 383–384; and Soviet alliance, 694, 749–750, 779; unemployment reduction in, 724; unification of, 280, 395–400, 539, 541, *map,* 396; urbanization of, 334; and Versailles Treaty, 684–685; Weimar Republic, 695–697, 716; working class in post-World War II era, 741; world trade and, 441; in World War I, 587–607; in World War II, 743–765
Germinal (Zola), 334
Gestapo, reign of terror by, 761–762
Gibbon, Edward, 186
Gide, André, 585
Gil de Castro, José, painting by, 305
Gioberti, Vincenzo, 357
Giovinezza, Italy, 701
Girodet, Anne Louis, painting by, 358
Girondists, 259–260
Gisze, Georg (Holbein), *illus.*, 98
Gladstone, William E., 515–516; *illus.*, 517

Glorious Revolution (*1688*), 236
Gneisenau, August, 284
Goa, 28, 37, 40
Gobineau, Joseph de, 419
God, concept of, in Enlightenment, 170–171; materialism and, 416; and Romantic impulse, 370; 17th-century views on nature of, 158
Goebbels, Joseph, 718, 722
Goering, Hermann, 782; *illus.*, 720, 778
Goethe, Johann Wolfgang von, 339, 341, 345, 360, 400; *illus.*, 345
Gogol, Nicolas, 346
Gold, in Africa, 27; in America, 31–32, 67; mercantilism, 113–114
Gold Exchange Standard, 708–709
Goldsmith, Oliver, 218
Gold standard, 435; abandonment of, 709
Gomulka, Wladyslaw, 816
Goncharov, I. A., 423
Góngora y Argote, Luis de, 78; *illus.*, 78
Gotha Congress (*1875*), 505
Gothic Revival, 353; *illus.*, 352
Gottached, Johann Christoph, 208
Government, by consent of governed, 173, 249; controls of, and liberal theorists, 295; forms of, in Enlightenment, 175; minimum of, 174, 240; and society, 227–230
Goya y Lucientes, Francisco de, etching by, 285
Grain, England's trade regulations on, 116
Granada, 64, 74
Grand Alliance, in World War II, 765–767
Gravitation, law of, 139, 165, 172
Gray, Thomas, 345
Great Britain, 262, 270, 272, 277, 443, 467, 483, 485, 489, 491, 505; agricultural collapse in (*1870s*), 442; Anglo-German rivalry, 556–559; and American Revolution, 243–246; birth rate in post-World War I era, 735; and colonialism in Africa, 549–553; Common Market and, 833; and Congress of Vienna (*1814–1815*), 298–300; and Crimean War, 404, 540; de-colonization process and, 823–824; economic liberalism in, 329–333; in 18th century, 236–241; foreign investments, 548; France and, in 18th century, 242–243; general strike (*1926*), 692, *illus.*, 692; gold standard abandoned, 709; impoverishment following World War I, 824; industrialization in, 307, 317–318, 427, 436–437; inflation in, 728–729; labor movement, 691–692; liberalism in, 297, 306–307, 311, 315, 515–516; maritime supremacy of, 278; mid-Victorian, 386–388; mutual defense treaties in World War I, 694; Napoleon and, 270, 277–278, 281; naval blockade, World War I, 685; overseas migration from, 447; politics in interwar period, 692; in post-World War I period, 691–693; saturation bombings by, 767; self-employed in, 740; social unrest and reform, 19th century, 307–311; and trade overseas, 547; union of England and Scotland (*1707*), 319; urbanization of, 334; wartime taxation in, 728; in World War I, 591, 593–595, 600, 604, 607; in World War II, 742–755, 765–771

K

Motion picture, in 20th century, 679
Movement in the Street (Bonnard), *illus.*, 581
Mozart, Wolfgang Amadeus, 673
Mrs. Dalloway (Woolf), 678
Mumford, Lewis, 457
Mun, Thomas, 115
Munch, Edvard, lithograph by, 652
Munich: Nazi party rally in, *illus.*, 705; University of, 358
Munich agreement of *1938*, 746–749
Munich *coup d'état*, Hitler and, 718
Murat, Joachim, 280
Murillo, Bartolomé, 78
Murmansk Run, *illus.*, 766
Music, 348–351, 375, 473; modern, 673–675; programmatic, 351; tonality and atonality in, 673, 675
Mussolini, Benito, 705, 718, 724; attacks Ethiopia, 745; and Bolshevik Revolution, 700; declares war on France and Great Britain, 754; March on Rome (*1922*), 700; rise of, 698–701; on totalitarianism concept, 703; *illus.*, 699, 701
Mussorgsky, Modest, 673
Mutations, 414
Mutual Aid as a Factor in Evolution (Kropotkin), 418
Mysteries of Paris, The (Sue), 486

N

Nabis, painting movement of, 580, 585
Nagasaki, bombing of, 775
Nagy, Imre, 818
Namier, Lewis, 379, 381
Nantes, Edict of (*1598*), 59
Napier, John, 146
Naples, kingdom of, 64, 280, 305, 394
Napoleon I, *see* Napoleon Bonaparte
Napoleon III (France), 314, 388–391, 393, 399, 455, 520, 563, 587; *illus.*, 389, 486
Napoleon Bonaparte, 262, 542, 686–687; *illus.*, 266, 274, 287; ancestors of, 267–268; appraisal of, 291; and Continental System, 281–282; downfall, 289; in Egypt, 270; as emperor, 275; as First Consul, 271–275; government of, 272; and "Hundred Days," 289–290; laws under, 273; mastery of Europe, 275–282; *maps* of campaigns, 278, 279; police system of, 286; policies on religion, 273–274; relatives of, (*see* Bonaparte); rise to power, 268–271; on St. Helena, 290
Napoleonic Ideas (Louis Napoleon), 388
Nasser, Gamal Abdel, 814
"National Apostasy" (Keble), sermon, 358
National Assembly, France, 255; Germany, 384
National Convention, France, 259–262
Nationalism, 251, 264–265, 282–286, 293, 297, 303, 357, 379–380, 383, 388, 392, 397–398, 400, 436, 512, 531–533; in colonial countries, 823–824; of industry and land in Russia, 632
National Liberal party, Germany, 398, 526
National Liberation Fronts, 798
National self-determination, 297, 306, 315, 385, 686, 689–691, 757

National Service Act (*1916*), Germany, 601, 633
National Society, Italy, 394
National System of Political Economy (List), 439
National workshops, France, 382, 495
NATO, *see* North Atlantic Treaty Organization
Natural history, 166
Natural law, 176, 181, 192, 356
Natural philosophy, 169–170, 186
Natural religion, 170–172
Natural rights of man, 173, 188, 203
Natural sciences, 165, 172, 179; philosophy and, 169
Natural selection, 412–414
Nature, 646
Nature, Enlightenment and, 170, 373; man's place in, 158–159; mechanistic concept of, 294; orderliness of, 155; Romantics and, 373; 17th-century scientists and, 156–159; teleological view of, 156
Navigation Act of *1660*, 50
Navigation Acts, 244, 330
Nazarenes, painting movement of, 353
Nazi party and nazism, 463; anti-Semitism of, 723–725; army and, 722–723; extermination of Jews by, 762–765; power seizure by, 716–719; program of, 718–719; rallies of, 724–725, *illus.*, 705, 724; as war criminals, 803
Nelson, Adm. Horatio, 270, 278
Neoconservatism, 512, 523
Neo-Darwinian biology, 414
Neo-liberalism, postwar period, 833–838
Neo-Malthusianism, 445
Neo-mercantilism, 427
Neopaganism, middle class and, 736–739
Neoplatonism, 358
Netherlands, 262, 315; French invasion of (*1792*), 258; kingdom of, 300–301; liberalism in, 518; and Napoleonic empire, 279; revolt in (*1830*), 315; United Provinces of, 227–228; *see also* Dutch; Holland
Neuroses, Freud's theory of, 169, 654
Neuschwanstein Castle, 353
Neutron, 646
New Amsterdam, 41, 43
New City, The (Sant'Elia), 465; *illus.*, 464
Newcomen engine, 322–323; *illus.*, 316, 322
Newcomes, The (Thackeray), 471
New Deal, U.S., 836
New Economic Policy (NEP), 710–711, 713
New France, 59
New Harmony, Ind., 494; Owen's plan for, *illus.*, 495
New Lanark, Scotland, 494
Newman, John Henry, 358
"New Order," Nazi rule of, 761–765, 782
New Principles of Political Economy (Sismondi), 499
New South Wales, 483
New Spain, 31, 53, 71
Newspapers, mass culture and, 461, 487
Newton, Isaac, 127, 138–139, 146, 160–161, 165, 170, 177, 186, 218, 417, 453, 465, 640; *illus.*, 138, 156
New Zealand, 34, 61, 483, 545, 594
Nice, France, 393

Nicholas I (Russia), 286, 306–307, 403–404
Nicholas II (Russia), 505, 532, 611–614, 634, 556; 687; *illus.*, 542
Nicholas, Grand Duke (Russia), *illus.*, 594
Niebuhr, Barthold, 356
Nietzsche, Friedrich, 424–425, 657, 699
Nightingale, Florence, 482
Nihilism, post-World War I, 737–739
Nimitz, Adm. Chester W., 768
Ninth Symphony (Beethoven), 349
Nitrate industry, 433, 434
Nkruma, Kwame, 705
Nobel, Alfred, 431, 458
Nobel prizes, 679
Nobility, Austrian, 303; conservatism of, 297; 18th-century, 227–229; English, 240; and enlightened despots, 204; following *1815*, 251; France, 97, 232–233, 236, 252–254, 274–275; Polish, 230–231; Russian, 197–198
Normandy invasion (*1944*), 771–772, *illus.*, 771
North Africa, campaign in, 768–769
North Atlantic Treaty Organization (NATO), 806, 809, 813, 832
North German Confederation (*1867*), 398–399
Northwest Passage, to Indies, 34
Norway, 483; German occupation of, 753; separation from Sweden, 519
"Nose, The" (Gogol), 347
Notes from the Underground (Dostoevsky), 425
Nouvelle Héloïse, La (Rousseau), 206
Novalis (Baron Friedrich von Hardenberg), 344 n., 357
Nova Scotia, 36
Novel, the, 346–347, 421–425, 479, 677–679
Number, role of, in Scientific Revolution, 145–147
Numerals, Arabic, 146; Roman, 145–146
Nürnberg Laws (*1935*), 530, 723
Nürnberg war crimes trials, 803

O

Oberon (Weber), 351
Oblomov (Goncharov), 423
O'Connor, Feargus, 311
October Manifesto (*1905*), 533
Ode on a Grecian Urn (Keats), 377
"Ode to Joy" (Schiller), 350
Ode to the West Wind (Shelley), 365
Oedipe (Voltaire), 211
Oedipus complex, 654
Oersted, Christian, 428
Okinawa, Battle of, 774
Old Shepherd's Chief Mourner, The (Landseer), *illus.*, 477
Oligarchy, 228–229, 241
Olivares, Gaspar de Guzmán, 81; *illus.*, 78
Oliver Twist (Dickens), 422
On the Civil and Moral Primacy of the Italians (Gioberti), 357
On the Family (Alberti), 472
"On the Jewish Question" (Marx), 496
"On the Limits of Natural Science" (Du Bois-Reymond), 415
On the Revolutions of the Heavenly Bodies (Copernicus), 127, 151

S